T0180078

Lecture Notes in Computer Science   12625

More information about this subseries at http://www.springer.com/series/7412

Hiroshi Ishikawa · Cheng-Lin Liu ·
Tomas Pajdla · Jianbo Shi (Eds.)

Computer Vision – ACCV 2020

15th Asian Conference on Computer Vision
Kyoto, Japan, November 30 – December 4, 2020
Revised Selected Papers, Part IV

 Springer

Editors
Hiroshi Ishikawa
Waseda University
Tokyo, Japan

Cheng-Lin Liu
Institute of Automation of Chinese Academy
of Sciences
Beijing, China

Tomas Pajdla
Czech Technical University in Prague
Prague, Czech Republic

Jianbo Shi
University of Pennsylvania
Philadelphia, PA, USA

ISSN 0302-9743   ISSN 1611-3349   (electronic)
Lecture Notes in Computer Science
ISBN 978-3-030-69537-8   ISBN 978-3-030-69538-5   (eBook)
https://doi.org/10.1007/978-3-030-69538-5

LNCS Sublibrary: SL6 – Image Processing, Computer Vision, Pattern Recognition, and Graphics

This Springer imprint is published by the registered company Springer Nature Switzerland AG
The registered company address is: Gewerbestrasse 11, 6330 Cham, Switzerland

Preface

The Asian Conference on Computer Vision (ACCV) 2020, originally planned to take place in Kyoto, Japan, was held online during November 30 – December 4, 2020. The conference featured novel research contributions from almost all sub-areas of computer vision.

We received 836 main-conference submissions. After removing the desk rejects, 768 valid, complete manuscripts were submitted for review. A pool of 48 area chairs and 738 reviewers was recruited to conduct paper reviews. As in previous editions of ACCV, we adopted a double-blind review process to determine which of these papers to accept. Identities of authors were not visible to reviewers and area chairs; nor were the identities of the assigned reviewers and area chairs known to authors. The program chairs did not submit papers to the conference.

Each paper was reviewed by at least three reviewers. Authors were permitted to respond to the initial reviews during a rebuttal period. After this, the area chairs led discussions among reviewers. Finally, an interactive area chair meeting was held, during which panels of three area chairs deliberated to decide on acceptance decisions for each paper, and then four larger panels were convened to make final decisions. At the end of this process, 254 papers were accepted for publication in the ACCV 2020 conference proceedings.

In addition to the main conference, ACCV 2020 featured four workshops and two tutorials. This is also the first ACCV for which the proceedings are open access at the Computer Vision Foundation website, by courtesy of Springer.

We would like to thank all the organizers, sponsors, area chairs, reviewers, and authors. We acknowledge the support of Microsoft's Conference Management Toolkit (CMT) team for providing the software used to manage the review process.

We greatly appreciate the efforts of all those who contributed to making the conference a success, despite the difficult and fluid situation.

December 2020

Hiroshi Ishikawa
Cheng-Lin Liu
Tomas Pajdla
Jianbo Shi

Organization

General Chairs

Ko Nishino	Kyoto University, Japan
Akihiro Sugimoto	National Institute of Informatics, Japan
Hiromi Tanaka	Ritsumeikan University, Japan

Program Chairs

Hiroshi Ishikawa	Waseda University, Japan
Cheng-Lin Liu	Institute of Automation of Chinese Academy of Sciences, China
Tomas Pajdla	Czech Technical University, Czech Republic
Jianbo Shi	University of Pennsylvania, USA

Publication Chairs

Ichiro Ide	Nagoya University, Japan
Wei-Ta Chu	National Chung Cheng University, Taiwan
Marc A. Kastner	National Institute of Informatics, Japan

Local Arrangements Chairs

Shohei Nobuhara	Kyoto University, Japan
Yasushi Makihara	Osaka University, Japan

Web Chairs

Ikuhisa Mitsugami	Hiroshima City University, Japan
Chika Inoshita	Canon Inc., Japan

AC Meeting Chair

Yusuke Sugano	University of Tokyo, Japan

Area Chairs

Mathieu Aubry	École des Ponts ParisTech, France
Xiang Bai	Huazhong University of Science and Technology, China
Alex Berg	Facebook, USA
Michael S. Brown	York University, Canada

Tat-Jun Chin	University of Adelaide, Australia
Yung-Yu Chuang	National Taiwan University, Taiwan
Yuchao Dai	Northwestern Polytechnical University, China
Yasutaka Furukawa	Simon Fraser University, Canada
Junwei Han	Northwestern Polytechnical University, China
Tatsuya Harada	University of Tokyo/RIKEN, Japan
Gang Hua	Wormpex AI Research, China
C. V. Jawahar	IIIT Hyderabad, India
Frédéric Jurie	Université de Caen Normandie, France
Angjoo Kanazawa	UC Berkeley, USA
Rei Kawakami	Tokyo Institute of Technology, Japan
Tae-Kyun Kim	Imperial College London, UK
Zuzana Kukelova	Czech Technical University in Prague, Czech Republic
Shang-Hong Lai	Microsoft AI R&D Center, Taiwan
Ivan Laptev	Inria Paris, France
Laura Leal-Taixe	TU Munich, Germany
Yong Jae Lee	UC Davis, USA
Vincent Lepetit	Université de Bordeaux, France
Hongdong Li	Australian National University, Australia
Guangcan Liu	NUIST, China
Li Liu	National University of Defense Technology, China
Risheng Liu	Dalian University of Technology, China
Si Liu	Beihang University, China
Yasuyuki Matsushita	Osaka University, Japan
Hajime Nagahara	Osaka University, Japan
Takayuki Okatani	Tohoku University/RIKEN, Japan
Carl Olsson	Lund University, Sweden
Hyun Soo Park	University of Minnesota, USA
Shmuel Peleg	Hebrew University of Jerusalem, Israel
Shin'ichi Satoh	National Institute of Informatics, Japan
Torsten Sattler	Chalmers University of Technology, Sweden
Palaiahnakote Shivakumara	University of Malaya, Malaysia
Hao Su	UC San Diego, USA
Siyu Tang	ETH Zurich, Switzerland
Radu Timofte	ETH Zurich, Switzerland
Yoshitaka Ushiku	OMRON SINIC X, Japan
Gul Varol	University of Oxford, UK
Kota Yamaguchi	Cyberagent, Inc., Japan
Ming-Hsuan Yang	UC Merced, USA
Stella X. Yu	UC Berkeley/ICSI, USA
Zhaoxiang Zhang	Chinese Academy of Sciences, China
Wei-Shi Zheng	Sun Yat-sen University, China
Yinqiang Zheng	National Institute of Informatics, Japan
Xiaowei Zhou	Zhejiang University, China

Additional Reviewers

Sathyanarayanan
  N. Aakur
Mahmoud Afifi
Amit Aides
Noam Aigerman
Kenan Emir Ak
Mohammad
  Sadegh Aliakbarian
Keivan Alizadeh-Vahid
Dario Allegra
Alexander Andreopoulos
Nikita Araslanov
Anil Armagan
Alexey Artemov
Aditya Arun
Yuki M. Asano
Hossein Azizpour
Seung-Hwan Baek
Seungryul Baek
Max Bain
Abhishek Bajpayee
Sandipan Banerjee
Wenbo Bao
Daniel Barath
Chaim Baskin
Anil S. Baslamisli
Ardhendu Behera
Jens Behley
Florian Bernard
Bharat Lal Bhatnagar
Uttaran Bhattacharya
Binod Bhattarai
Ayan Kumar Bhunia
Jia-Wang Bian
Simion-Vlad Bogolin
Amine Bourki
Biagio Brattoli
Anders G. Buch
Evgeny Burnaev
Benjamin Busam
Holger Caesar
Jianrui Cai
Jinzheng Cai

Fanta Camara
Necati Cihan Camgöz
Shaun Canavan
Jiajiong Cao
Jiale Cao
Hakan Çevikalp
Ayan Chakrabarti
Tat-Jen Cham
Lyndon Chan
Hyung Jin Chang
Xiaobin Chang
Rama Chellappa
Chang Chen
Chen Chen
Ding-Jie Chen
Jianhui Chen
Jun-Cheng Chen
Long Chen
Songcan Chen
Tianshui Chen
Weifeng Chen
Weikai Chen
Xiaohan Chen
Xinlei Chen
Yanbei Chen
Yingcong Chen
Yiran Chen
Yi-Ting Chen
Yun Chen
Yun-Chun Chen
Yunlu Chen
Zhixiang Chen
Ziliang Chen
Guangliang Cheng
Li Cheng
Qiang Cheng
Zhongwei Cheng
Anoop Cherian
Ngai-Man Cheung
Wei-Chen Chiu
Shin-Fang Ch'ng
Nam Ik Cho
Junsuk Choe

Chiho Choi
Jaehoon Choi
Jinsoo Choi
Yukyung Choi
Anustup Choudhury
Hang Chu
Peng Chu
Wei-Ta Chu
Sanghyuk Chun
Ronald Clark
Maxwell D. Collins
Ciprian Corneanu
Luca Cosmo
Ioana Croitoru
Steve Cruz
Naresh Cuntoor
Zachary A. Daniels
Mohamed Daoudi
François Darmon
Adrian K. Davison
Rodrigo de Bem
Shalini De Mello
Lucas Deecke
Bailin Deng
Jiankang Deng
Zhongying Deng
Somdip Dey
Ferran Diego
Mingyu Ding
Dzung Anh Doan
Xingping Dong
Xuanyi Dong
Hazel Doughty
Dawei Du
Chi Nhan Duong
Aritra Dutta
Marc C. Eder
Ismail Elezi
Mohamed Elgharib
Sergio Escalera
Deng-Ping Fan
Shaojing Fan
Sean Fanello

Moshiur R. Farazi
Azade Farshad
István Fehérvári
Junyi Feng
Wei Feng
Yang Feng
Zeyu Feng
Robert B. Fisher
Alexander Fix
Corneliu O. Florea
Wolfgang Förstner
Jun Fu
Xueyang Fu
Yanwei Fu
Hiroshi Fukui
Antonino Furnari
Ryo Furukawa
Raghudeep Gadde
Vandit J. Gajjar
Chuang Gan
Bin-Bin Gao
Boyan Gao
Chen Gao
Junbin Gao
Junyu Gao
Lin Gao
Mingfei Gao
Peng Gao
Ruohan Gao
Nuno C. Garcia
Georgios Georgakis
Ke Gong
Jiayuan Gu
Jie Gui
Manuel Günther
Kaiwen Guo
Minghao Guo
Ping Guo
Sheng Guo
Yulan Guo
Saurabh Gupta
Jung-Woo Ha
Emanuela Haller
Cusuh Ham
Kai Han
Liang Han

Tengda Han
Ronny Hänsch
Josh Harguess
Atsushi Hashimoto
Monica Haurilet
Jamie Hayes
Fengxiang He
Pan He
Xiangyu He
Xinwei He
Yang He
Paul Henderson
Chih-Hui Ho
Tuan N.A. Hoang
Sascha A. Hornauer
Yedid Hoshen
Kuang-Jui Hsu
Di Hu
Ping Hu
Ronghang Hu
Tao Hu
Yang Hua
Bingyao Huang
Haibin Huang
Huaibo Huang
Rui Huang
Sheng Huang
Xiaohua Huang
Yifei Huang
Zeng Huang
Zilong Huang
Jing Huo
Junhwa Hur
Wonjun Hwang
José Pedro Iglesias
Atul N. Ingle
Yani A. Ioannou
Go Irie
Daisuke Iwai
Krishna Murthy
    Jatavallabhula
Seong-Gyun Jeong
Koteswar Rao Jerripothula
Jingwei Ji
Haiyang Jiang
Huajie Jiang

Wei Jiang
Xiaoyi Jiang
Jianbo Jiao
Licheng Jiao
Kyong Hwan Jin
Xin Jin
Shantanu Joshi
Frédéric Jurie
Abhishek Kadian
Olaf Kaehler
Meina Kan
Dimosthenis Karatzas
Isay Katsman
Muhammad Haris Khan
Vijeta Khare
Rawal Khirodkar
Hadi Kiapour
Changick Kim
Dong-Jin Kim
Gunhee Kim
Heewon Kim
Hyunwoo J. Kim
Junsik Kim
Junyeong Kim
Yonghyun Kim
Akisato Kimura
A. Sophia Koepke
Dimitrios Kollias
Nikos Kolotouros
Yoshinori Konishi
Adam Kortylewski
Dmitry Kravchenko
Sven Kreiss
Gurunandan Krishnan
Andrey Kuehlkamp
Jason Kuen
Arjan Kuijper
Shiro Kumano
Avinash Kumar
B. V. K. Vijaya Kumar
Ratnesh Kumar
Vijay Kumar
Yusuke Kurose
Alina Kuznetsova
Junseok Kwon
Loic Landrieu

Dong Lao
Viktor Larsson
Yasir Latif
Hei Law
Hieu Le
Hoang-An Le
Huu Minh Le
Gim Hee Lee
Hyungtae Lee
Jae-Han Lee
Jangho Lee
Jungbeom Lee
Kibok Lee
Kuan-Hui Lee
Seokju Lee
Sungho Lee
Sungmin Lee
Bin Li
Jie Li
Ruilong Li
Ruoteng Li
Site Li
Xianzhi Li
Xiaomeng Li
Xiaoming Li
Xin Li
Xiu Li
Xueting Li
Yawei Li
Yijun Li
Yimeng Li
Yin Li
Yong Li
Yu-Jhe Li
Zekun Li
Dongze Lian
Zhouhui Lian
Haoyi Liang
Yue Liao
Jun Hao Liew
Chia-Wen Lin
Guangfeng Lin
Kevin Lin
Xudong Lin
Xue Lin
Chang Liu

Feng Liu
Hao Liu
Hong Liu
Jing Liu
Jingtuo Liu
Jun Liu
Miaomiao Liu
Ming Liu
Ping Liu
Siqi Liu
Wentao Liu
Wu Liu
Xing Liu
Xingyu Liu
Yongcheng Liu
Yu Liu
Yu-Lun Liu
Yun Liu
Zhihua Liu
Zichuan Liu
Chengjiang Long
Manuel López Antequera
Hao Lu
Hongtao Lu
Le Lu
Shijian Lu
Weixin Lu
Yao Lu
Yongxi Lu
Chenxu Luo
Weixin Luo
Wenhan Luo
Diogo C. Luvizon
Jiancheng Lyu
Chao Ma
Long Ma
Shugao Ma
Xiaojian Ma
Yongrui Ma
Ludovic Magerand
Behrooz Mahasseni
Mohammed Mahmoud
Utkarsh Mall
Massimiliano Mancini
Xudong Mao
Alina E. Marcu

Niki Martinel
Jonathan Masci
Tetsu Matsukawa
Bruce A. Maxwell
Amir Mazaheri
Prakhar Mehrotra
Heydi Méndez-Vázquez
Zibo Meng
Kourosh Meshgi
Shun Miao
Zhongqi Miao
Micael Carvalho
Pedro Miraldo
Ashish Mishra
Ikuhisa Mitsugami
Daisuke Miyazaki
Kaichun Mo
Liliane Momeni
Gyeongsik Moon
Alexandre Morgand
Yasuhiro Mukaigawa
Anirban Mukhopadhyay
Erickson R. Nascimento
Lakshmanan Nataraj
K. L. Navaneet
Lukáš Neumann
Shohei Nobuhara
Nicoletta Noceti
Mehdi Noroozi
Michael Oechsle
Ferda Ofli
Seoung Wug Oh
Takeshi Oishi
Takahiro Okabe
Fumio Okura
Kyle B. Olszewski
José Oramas
Tribhuvanesh Orekondy
Martin R. Oswald
Mayu Otani
Umapada Pal
Yingwei Pan
Rameswar Panda
Rohit Pandey
Jiangmiao Pang
João P. Papa

Nanne van Noord
Subeesh Vasu
Javier Vazquez-Corral
Andreas Velten
Constantin Vertan
Rosaura G. VidalMata
Valentin Vielzeuf
Sirion Vittayakorn
Konstantinos Vougioukas
Fang Wan
Guowei Wan
Renjie Wan
Bo Wang
Chien-Yi Wang
Di Wang
Dong Wang
Guangrun Wang
Hao Wang
Hongxing Wang
Hua Wang
Jialiang Wang
Jiayun Wang
Jingbo Wang
Jinjun Wang
Lizhi Wang
Pichao Wang
Qian Wang
Qiaosong Wang
Qilong Wang
Qingzhong Wang
Shangfei Wang
Shengjin Wang
Tiancai Wang
Wenguan Wang
Wenhai Wang
Xiang Wang
Xiao Wang
Xiaoyang Wang
Xinchao Wang
Xinggang Wang
Yang Wang
Yaxing Wang
Yisen Wang
Yu-Chiang Frank Wang
Zheng Wang
Scott Wehrwein

Wei Wei
Xing Wei
Xiu-Shen Wei
Yi Wei
Martin Weinmann
Michael Weinmann
Jun Wen
Xinshuo Weng
Thomas Whelan
Kimberly Wilber
Williem Williem
Kwan-Yee K. Wong
Yongkang Wong
Sanghyun Woo
Michael Wray
Chenyun Wu
Chongruo Wu
Jialian Wu
Xiaohe Wu
Xiaoping Wu
Yihong Wu
Zhenyao Wu
Changqun Xia
Xide Xia
Yin Xia
Lei Xiang
Di Xie
Guo-Sen Xie
Jin Xie
Yifan Xing
Yuwen Xiong
Jingwei Xu
Jun Xu
Ke Xu
Mingze Xu
Yanyu Xu
Yi Xu
Yichao Xu
Yongchao Xu
Yuanlu Xu
Jia Xue
Nan Xue
Yasushi Yagi
Toshihiko Yamasaki
Zhaoyi Yan
Zike Yan

Keiji Yanai
Dong Yang
Fan Yang
Hao Yang
Jiancheng Yang
Linlin Yang
Mingkun Yang
Ren Yang
Sibei Yang
Wenhan Yang
Ze Yang
Zhaohui Yang
Zhengyuan Yang
Anbang Yao
Angela Yao
Rajeev Yasarla
Jinwei Ye
Qi Ye
Xinchen Ye
Zili Yi
Ming Yin
Zhichao Yin
Ryo Yonetani
Ju Hong Yoon
Haichao Yu
Jiahui Yu
Lequan Yu
Lu Yu
Qian Yu
Ruichi Yu
Li Yuan
Sangdoo Yun
Sergey Zakharov
Huayi Zeng
Jiabei Zeng
Yu Zeng
Fangneng Zhan
Kun Zhan
Bowen Zhang
Hongguang Zhang
Jason Y. Zhang
Jiawei Zhang
Jie Zhang
Jing Zhang
Kaihao Zhang
Kaipeng Zhang

Lei Zhang
Mingda Zhang
Pingping Zhang
Qian Zhang
Qilin Zhang
Qing Zhang
Runze Zhang
Shanshan Zhang
Shu Zhang
Wayne Zhang
Xiaolin Zhang
Xiaoyun Zhang
Xucong Zhang
Yan Zhang
Zhao Zhang
Zhishuai Zhang
Feng Zhao
Jian Zhao
Liang Zhao
Qian Zhao
Qibin Zhao

Ruiqi Zhao
Sicheng Zhao
Tianyi Zhao
Xiangyun Zhao
Xin Zhao
Yifan Zhao
Yinan Zhao
Shuai Zheng
Yalin Zheng
Bineng Zhong
Fangwei Zhong
Guangyu Zhong
Yaoyao Zhong
Yiran Zhong
Jun Zhou
Mo Zhou
Pan Zhou
Ruofan Zhou
S. Kevin Zhou
Yao Zhou
Yipin Zhou

Yu Zhou
Yuqian Zhou
Yuyin Zhou
Guangming Zhu
Ligeng Zhu
Linchao Zhu
Rui Zhu
Xinge Zhu
Yizhe Zhu
Zhe Zhu
Zhen Zhu
Zheng Zhu
Bingbing Zhuang
Jiacheng Zhuo
Mohammadreza
   Zolfaghari
Chuhang Zou
Yuliang Zou
Zhengxia Zou

Contents – Part IV

Generative Models for Computer Vision

Deep Learning for Computer Vision

In-sample Contrastive Learning and Consistent Attention for Weakly Supervised Object Localization

Minsong Ki[1], Youngjung Uh[2,3], Wonyoung Lee[3], and Hyeran Byun[1,3(✉)]

[1] Department of Computer Science, Yonsei University, Seoul, Republic of Korea
{kms2014,hrbyun}@yonsei.ac.kr
[2] Department of Applied Information Engineering, Yonsei University,
Seoul, Republic of Korea
[3] Graduate School of Artificial Intelligence, Yonsei University,
Seoul, Republic of Korea
{yj.uh,lwy8555}@yonsei.ac.kr

Abstract. Weakly supervised object localization (WSOL) aims to localize the target object using only the image-level supervision. Recent methods encourage the model to activate feature maps over the entire object by dropping the most discriminative parts. However, they are likely to induce excessive extension to the backgrounds which leads to overestimated localization. In this paper, we consider the background as an important cue that guides the feature activation to cover the sophisticated object region and propose contrastive attention loss. The loss promotes similarity between foreground and its dropped version, and, dissimilarity between the dropped version and background. Furthermore, we propose foreground consistency loss that penalizes earlier layers producing noisy attention regarding the later layer as a reference to provide them with a sense of backgroundness. It guides the early layers to activate on objects rather than locally distinctive backgrounds so that their attentions to be similar to the later layer. For better optimizing the above losses, we use the non-local attention blocks to replace channel-pooled attention leading to enhanced attention maps considering the spatial similarity. Last but not least, we propose to drop background regions in addition to the most discriminative region. Our method achieves state-of-the-art performance on CUB-200-2011 and ImageNet benchmark datasets regarding `top-1 localization accuracy` and `MaxBoxAccV2`, and we provide detailed analysis on our individual components. The code will be publicly available online for reproducibility.

1 Introduction

Fully supervised approaches have demonstrated excellent performance by training convolution neural network (CNN) with human annotations, *e.g.*, bounding

Electronic supplementary material The online version of this chapter (https://doi.org/10.1007/978-3-030-69538-5_1) contains supplementary material, which is available to authorized users.

© Springer Nature Switzerland AG 2021
H. Ishikawa et al. (Eds.): ACCV 2020, LNCS 12625, pp. 3–18, 2021.
https://doi.org/10.1007/978-3-030-69538-5_1

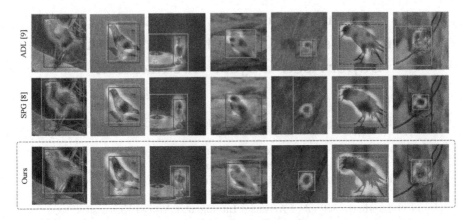

Fig. 1. Comparison of methods for generating activation maps on the CUB [16] dataset. We display the final results obtained by ADL [9] (first row), SPG [8] (second row), and our method (last row). The red boxes are the ground-truth and the green boxes are the predicted ones. Activation maps are illustrated in heatmap color scale. ADL tries to activate more on less discriminative parts but ends in excessive extension to background. SPG tries to suppress background but still over-estimates the object regions. In contrast, our method covers the whole object delicately without extending to background. (Color figure online)

box for object localization, pixel-wise class labels for semantic segmentation [1–5]. However, they cost huge human labor to obtain accurate annotations. Therefore, weakly supervised approaches that use only image-level supervision have received significant attention over the various computer vision tasks [6–12]. Especially, weakly supervised object localization (WSOL) is a challenging task that pursues both classification and the localization of the target object where the training datasets provide only the class labels.

For example, Zhou et al. [6] generate class activation maps (CAM) using the classification model with a global average pooling (GAP). CAM highlights the class-specific discriminative regions in a given image [7–9,13]. The crucial pitfall of the activation maps is that it focuses on discriminative parts (*e.g.*, the head of a bird) rather than including the full extent of the object. To mitigate this limitation, recent methods [9,14,15] propose to erase the most discriminative parts by thresholding to spread out the activations to less discriminative regions. However, they are likely to induce excessive extension to the backgrounds which over-estimates bounding boxes (Fig. 1).

In this paper, we propose four ingredients for more accurate attention over the entire object: contrastive attention loss, foreground consistency loss, non-local attention block and dropped foreground mask. The contrastive attention loss draws the foreground feature and its erased version close together, and pushes the erased foreground feature away from the background feature (Sect. 3.2). It helps the learned representation to reflect only the object region rather than the backgrounds which are usually helpful for classification but harmful to localization. The foreground consistency loss penalizes disagreement of attentions between layers to provide early layers with a sense of backgroundness (Sect. 3.3). While usual low-level features are activated on locally distinctive regions (*e.g.*, edges) regardless of the presence of the objects, adding foreground consistency loss boosts the activations on the object regions while suppressing the activations on the background regions. Furthermore, we apply the non-local attention blocks to produce enhanced attention maps considering the similarity between locations in a feature map (Sect. 3.4). It allows boosting weights on the regions having similar features with the most discriminative parts to pursue correct activation. Last but not least, we propose a dropped foreground mask which drops the background region as well as the most discriminative region. It prohibits the model from excessively spreading attention to backgrounds.

Our method achieves state-of-the-art performance in terms of the conventional `top-1 localization accuracy` and the `MaxBoxAccV2` [17].

In summary, our main contributions are:

- We propose a contrastive attention loss that favors similarity between foreground feature and its dropped version and dissimilarity between the dropped foreground feature and background feature.
- We propose a foreground consistency loss that provides a sense of localization to earlier layers by guiding their features to be consistent with a high-level layer.
- We propose a dropped foreground mask which drops the background region and the most discriminative region.
- Our method achieves state-of-the-art performance on CUB-200-2011 and ImageNet benchmark datasets in terms of `top-1 localization accuracy` and `MaxBoxAccV2`.

2   Related Work

Weakly Supervised Object Localization (WSOL). Given only the class labels with the images, most of the WSOL methods train a classifier and extract CAM [6]. CAM indicates the strength of activation in every location in the feature map to stimulate the corresponding class [7–9,13]. Recent methods [6–10,13] propose erasing the most discriminative region of the feature map to spread out the activations to the regions which are less discriminative but still in the object. Hide-and-Seek (HaS) [13] divides a training image into a grid of evenly-divided patches and selects a random patch to be hidden. Adversarial complementary learning (ACoL) [7] and attention-based dropout layer (ADL) [9] partially drop the most discriminative region by thresholding on the feature map. MEIL [18] runs two branches, one with erasing and one without erasing, and impose both branch with classification task. These approaches guide the models to discover previously neglected object regions. Our method steps further to consider background as a region to drop so that the model does not spread the activation excessively to the background.

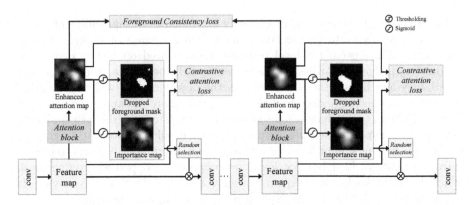

Fig. 2. Overview of the proposed method. The non-local attention block generates the enhanced attention map reflecting the similarity between locations. We create a dropped foreground mask and an importance map using thresholding and sigmoid activation, respectively. The selected map is multiplied with the input feature to feed the next layer. Foreground consistency loss encourages the consistency between the early and last layer. We calculate the contrastive attention loss at each convolution layer where our non-local attention block is inserted.

Several methods have been proposed to suppress the background and localize the whole object. Zhang et al. [8] present self-produced guidance (SPG) that generates three pixel-wise masks (foreground, background, and undefined areas). Each mask is used as auxiliary supervision. However, it requires to find the optimal six hyperparameters for producing the three masks. We also focus on the background but introduce simpler and more effective way.

Yang et al. [10] use a non-local block following every convolution-pooling block. While their non-local blocks are inserted within the main stem of the network, our non-local attention blocks are branch from the main stem and produce attention maps to be multiplied to the main convolutional features at chosen layers.

Contrastive Visual Representation Learning. Contrastive learning [19] tries to distinguish similar and dissimilar pairs of samples by embedding the samples as feature representations. Recent self-supervised learning methods [20,21] learn representations by maximizing agreement between differently augmented views of the same image. They also consider the different images to minimize the agreement for negative pairs.

Inspired by [20,21], we define a contrastive prediction task for WSOL. Instead of building similar and dissimilar pairs of image samples, we regard the foreground region except for the most discriminative part (*i.e.*, the dropped foreground) as an anchor, and build the positive pair with the original foreground and the negative pair with the background. Our contrastive objective does not require a large batch size or large queue because it finds the pairs within an image. Separating the foreground representation and the background representation is suitable for WSOL task.

3   Proposed Method

This section describes elements of the proposed method and how we employ them on the networks.

3.1   Network Overview

As shown in Fig. 2, we augment classification network with the non-local attention blocks (Sect. 3.4) and train it with the contrastive attention loss (Sec. 3.2) and the foreground consistency loss (Sect. 3.3). The non-local attention block receives a feature map $\mathbf{F}$ and provides an enhanced attention map $\mathbf{A}$ which becomes an importance map $\tilde{\mathbf{A}}$ through sigmoid activation and a dropped foreground mask $\mathbf{M}_{\mathrm{dfg}}$ by thresholding (Eq. 1). The dropped foreground mask or the importance map is randomly chosen based on a drop_rate and the chosen one is applied to the input feature by pixel-wise multiplication (element-wise multiplication with broadcasting over the channel dimension). The importance map is not to be dropped but to be applied to the feature map. The dropped foreground mask encourages activation of the input feature on less discriminative parts except background to maximize classification accuracy without losing localization accuracy, while the importance map rewards higher activation on the most discriminative part.

In the attention branch, the enhanced attention map and the dropped foreground mask from a non-local attention block are used to compute the contrastive attention loss. In addition, the enhanced attention maps from multiple non-local attention blocks are used to compute the foreground consistency loss.

The differences with ADL [9] in the forward process are that we use the dropped foreground mask instead of drop mask and the attention map is produced by our non-local attention block instead of vanilla convolutional feature. Figure 3 illustrates the importance map, our dropped foreground mask, and the drop mask in [9]. Our dropped foreground mask $\mathbf{M}_{\mathrm{dfg}}$ is defined by:

$$\mathbf{M}_{\mathrm{dfg}} = \mathbb{1}[\mathbf{A} < \theta_{\mathrm{fg}}] \wedge \mathbb{1}[\mathbf{A} > \theta_{\mathrm{bg}}], \tag{1}$$

where $\mathbb{1}$ denotes a matrix with the same shape with the input having ones according to the logical operation, $\wedge$ denotes logical and operation, and θ's are the pre-defined thresholds. Unlike the drop masks from ACoL [7] and ADL [9], our dropped foreground mask remedies excessive expansion of activation on the backgrounds by further erasing background regions in the mask.

The contrastive attention loss and the foreground consistency loss are computed wherever the attention maps are extracted.

3.2   Contrastive Attention Loss

Contrastive loss [20] is a function whose value is low when a query is similar to its equivalent instance and dissimilar to its different instances. Likewise, we design a contrastive attention loss whose value is low when a dropped foreground feature

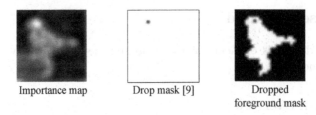

Importance map   Drop mask [9]   Dropped
                                              foreground mask

Fig. 3. Examples of the importance map $\tilde{\mathbf{A}}$, the drop mask from [9], and our dropped foreground mask $\mathbf{M}_{\mathrm{dfg}}$.

z_{dfg} is similar to a foreground feature $\mathbf{z}_{\mathrm{fg}}$ and dissimilar to a background feature $\mathbf{z}_{\mathrm{bg}}$ (Fig. 4). The features $\mathbf{z}_\alpha$ are obtained by masked global average pooling of $\mathbf{F} \odot \mathbf{M}_\alpha$ where

$$\mathbf{M}_{\mathrm{fg}} = \mathbb{1}[\mathbf{A} > \theta_{\mathrm{bg}}],$$
$$\mathbf{M}_{\mathrm{bg}} = \mathbb{1}[\mathbf{A} < \theta_{\mathrm{bg}}],$$
(2)

and the masked global average pooling is spatial average pooling of the pixels whose value on the mask is 1. Then, the contrastive attention loss is given by

$$\mathcal{L}_{\mathrm{ca}} = \mathbb{E}_{\mathbf{x}}[[(d(z_{\mathrm{dfg}}, z_{\mathrm{fg}}) - d(z_{\mathrm{dfg}}, z_{\mathrm{bg}}) + m]_+],$$
(3)

where $[\cdot]_+ = \max(\cdot, 0)$ and $d(\cdot, \cdot)$ denotes L_2 distance in auxiliary 128-dimensional embedding by 1×1 convolution. m denotes the margin.

Our contrastive attention loss guides the attention map to spread until it reaches boundary because including backgrounds in the attention map is penalized by the dissimilarity term. In addition, the similarity term favors homogenous features between the most discriminative part and less discriminative parts in the foreground region. Our contrastive attention loss does not require mining positive and negative samples as in triplet loss [22] nor managing large negative samples [20,21]. Since we regard the masked features $\mathbf{z}_{\mathrm{dfg}}, \mathbf{z}_{\mathrm{fg}}$ and $\mathbf{z}_{\mathrm{bg}}$ from one image as an anchor, a positive sample and a negative sample, respectively.

3.3   Foreground Consistency Loss

Attention maps roughly are the magnitude of activation on every location. Convolutions in early layers activate more on locally distinctive regions such as edges and corners [23], without inspecting the entire extent of objects due to their limited receptive field. To relieve this problem, we propose a foreground consistency loss that encourages attention maps from early layers to resemble later layers (Fig. 2).

Let A_i and A_j are the attention maps from early and later layers, respectively. Then we define the foreground consistency loss as:

$$\mathcal{L}_{fc} = \left\| A_i - A_j \right\|_2^2,$$
(4)

where $\| \cdot \|_2$ denotes L_2 norm of a matrix.

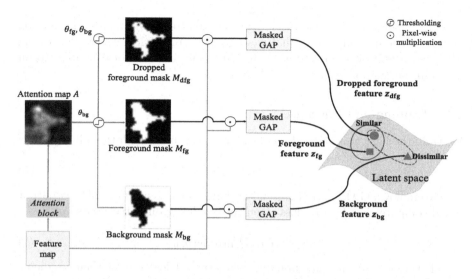

Fig. 4. The details of the contrastive attention loss, where A denotes an enhanced attention map from a non-local attention block. We generate three maps and features to compare the similarity in embedding space. $\odot$ denotes pixel-wise multiplication. The contrastive attention loss is computed on an embedding space.

Gradients from the foreground consistency loss only run through the early layer to achieve the abovementioned goal. It reduces the noisy activations outside the object and boosts activations in the object.

3.4 Non-local Attention Block

In order to provide additional capacity for the network to produce a correct attention map, we employ non-local block [24] instead of average channel pooling of the convolutional features [9,25]. Given a feature map, our non-local attention block embeds it into three different embeddings and outputs spatial summation of the third one weighted by similarity between the first two embeddings. Then the enhanced attention map is defined by its channel-pooled result.

Specifically, the block receives a feature map $x \in R^{C \times H \times W}$ from a convolution layer. For simplicity, we omit the mini-batch dimension. We define $f(x), g(x) \in R^{\tilde{C} \times H \times W}, z(x) \in R^{C \times H \times W}$ that use 1×1 convolution layer for embedding. Then, $f(x), g(x)$ and $z(x)$ are reshaped to $f(x), g(x) \in R^{\tilde{C} \times HW}, z(x) \in R^{C \times HW}$, respectively.

The enhanced attention map A is given by:

$$A = \mathbb{E}_C[\text{Softmax}(f(x)^T g(x)) \odot z(x)], \qquad (5)$$

where $\mathbb{E}_C$ denotes average pooling over the channel dimension.

The non-local attention block produces the enhanced attention map regarding similarities between locations. It unleashes the receptive field of the layer and provides an additional clue for deciding where to attend. Our non-local attention block is different from [10] in that we organize it only when generating several enhanced attention maps. Yang et al. [10] apply the non-local module to all layers in the main branch with residual connection.

3.5   Training and Inference

We train the base network and non-local attention block with the full objective:

$$\mathcal{L}_{total} = \mathcal{L}_{cls} + \mathcal{L}_{ca} + \mathcal{L}_{fc} \tag{6}$$

We employ a GAP layer at the end of the network to produce softmax output $\hat{y}$ and compute classification loss given the one-hot ground truth label y:

$$\mathcal{L}_{cls} = \text{CrossEntropy}(\hat{y}, y) \tag{7}$$

All network weights are updated wherever all losses send their gradients towards the input, while the foreground consistency loss does not convey gradients to its reference layer.

Our non-local attention block is applied only during training and deactivated in the testing phase. The input image goes through only the vanilla model to produce the class assignment. Then we follow [17] to extract the heatmap which leads to the bounding boxes by thresholding and its connected multi-contour.

4   Experiments

4.1   Experimental Setup

Datasets. We evaluate the proposed method on two benchmark datasets: CUB-200-2011 [16] and ILSVRC [26] (ImageNet) for WSOL task, from which only the image-level labels are used in training. Many weak-supervision methods have used full supervision to some extent, directly or indirectly for hyperparameter tuning. Since the amount of full supervision used for hyperparameter tuning is not consistent, it has been ambiguous using the previous evaluation metric for a fair comparison. We follow the recent evaluation metric [17] which fixes the amount of full supervision only for hyperparameter search. Each dataset is divided into three subsets: `train-weaksup`, `train-fullsup` and `test`. The `train-weaksup` includes images only with the class labels for training. The `train-fullsup` contains images with full supervision, which has bounding boxes as well. It is left free for the users to use the `train-fullsup` for hyperparameter search. They collected five images per class (total 1,000 images) from Flickr for CUB experiments, and ten images per class (total 10,000 images) from ImageNetV2 [27] for ImageNet experiments, respectively. The `test` split for the final number is the same as the standard WSOL settings on CUB and ImageNet experiments [7–9,17,28]. In the CUB dataset, there are 5,994 images for training and 5,794 for testing from 200 bird species. ImageNet consists of 1.2M

Table 1. Hyperparameters (drop_rate, γ_{fg}, γ_{bg}) for each backbone.

Backbone	drop_rate	γ_{fg}	γ_{bg}
VGG [29]	0.33	0.72	1.2
InceptionV3 [30]	0.69	0.86	1.2
ResNet50 [31]	0.85	0.95	1.2

training images 10K test images for 1,000 classes. All experimental analyses of the proposed method are conducted on the test split of the two abovementioned datasets.

Evaluation Metrics. We use top-1 classification accuracy and top-1 localization accuracy, and MaxBoxAccV2 [17].

Top-1 classification accuracy is the ratio of correct classification. The conventional top-1 localization accuracy measures ratio of the samples with the right class and the bounding box of IoU greater than 0.5.

MaxBoxAcc measures ratio of the samples with the correct box, while the correctness is defined by an IoU criterion δ at the optimal activation threshold. MaxBoxAccV2 averages MaxBoxAcc at three IoU criterions $\delta \in \{30, 50, 70\}$ to address diverse demands for localization fineness. It is similar to the common GT-known metric but differs in that it evaluates on *three IoUs* by extracting the bounding box with *the optimal score map threshold*. We use % symbol as a *percent point* for mentioning differences on comparisons.

Implementation Details. We build the proposed method upon three CNN backbones: VGG16 [29], InceptionV3 [30], and Resnet50 [31]. We need three hyperparameters: drop_rate for randomly choosing the importance map or the dropped foreground mask, θ_{fg} and θ_{bg} for thresholding. The threshold θ_{fg} is set to the maximum intensity of **A** times pre-defined ratio γ_{fg}. The θ_{bg} is set to average intensity of **A** times pre-defined ratio γ_{bg}. The specific values of the hyperparameters for each backbone are shown in Table 1.

The layers, from which the enhanced attention maps are extracted, are chosen to be the same with the baseline method [9]. We also calculate our contrastive attention loss and foreground consistency loss for all layers where attention maps are produced. We set the batch size to 32, weight decay to 0.0001, margin m to 1. The initial learning rate and the momentum of the SGD optimizer are set to 0.001 and 0.9, respectively. We start from loading weights from the model pre-trained on the ImageNet classification [26] and then fine-tuned the network. Our model is implemented using PyTorch and trained using two NVIDIA GeForce RTX 2080 Ti GPUs for approximately three hours. The input images are randomly cropped to 224 × 224 pixels after being resized to 256 × 256 pixels. During testing phase, we directly resize the input images to 224 × 224.

4.2   Ablation Study

We first show detailed experiments to validate effectiveness of each component. We fix the ResNet50 [31] as a backbone and add or remove each component. The experiments are performed on the CUB `test` split. The difference in performance in % represents percent points.

Ablation of the Proposed Losses. Table 2 shows that both the contrastive attention loss and the foreground consistency loss are the crucial element for the improved performance. Ours without the contrastive attention loss achieves 2% lower performance than the full setting. The loss has positive effect on all three IoU thresholds. The foreground consistency loss also plays an important role of improvement by 0.79%. It especially boosts the accuracy at IoU 0.7. We suggest that the loss helps precisely estimating the location of the object in the early layer by providing the hints from the later layer. Using the both losses leads to balanced improvements over all IoU thresholds. In addition, contrastive attention loss with the normalized temperature-scaled cross-entropy loss *(NT-Xent)* [20,21] also shows improvements to some extent. Its result can be found in the supplementary material.

Effectiveness of the Non-local Attention Block. If we use the vanilla attention map which is the channel-pooled result of the convolutional feature, the performance drops by 0.62% (the fourth row in Table 2). It shows that considering the relationship between pixels in feature map helps localizing where to attend.

Effectiveness of the Dropped Foreground Mask. Here we validate the effectiveness of replacing the drop mask [9] with the dropped foreground mask M_{dfg}. Without the replacement, the model achieves 1.12% lower performance than the full setting (the fifth row in Table 2). Also, only replacing the drop mask with the dropped foreground mask improves the performance of the baseline [9]

Table 2. The ablation study for each element of our method on Resnet50 [31] backbone in terms of `MaxBoxAccV2`. Contrastive: contrastive attention loss. $\mathcal{L}_{fc}$: foreground consistency loss. Non-local: non-local attention block. M_{dfg}: dropped foreground mask. All elements contribute to the performance improvement.

Methods	MaxBoxAccV2@IoU (%)			
	0.3	0.5	0.7	Mean
Baseline [9]	91.82	64.78	18.43	58.34 (-4.86)
Ours w/o contrastive	94.79	70.84	17.98	61.20 (-2.00)
Ours w/o $\mathcal{L}_{fc}$	**96.51**	72.14	18.57	62.41 (-0.79)
Ours w/o non-local	95.80	71.62	20.32	62.58 (-0.62)
Ours w/o M_{dfg}	96.42	72.21	17.62	62.08 (-1.12)
Ours (full)	96.18	**72.79**	**20.64**	**63.20**

Table 3. Performance comparison regarding at which layer to insert our attention block. The contrastive attention loss and the foreground consistency loss are in use for all cases. The `conv_5_3` layer is fixed as the reference layer and its performance is left empty because the foreground consistency loss requires at least two layers. We add the layers from later to earlier and report their performance in a cumulative setting.

Location	Top-1 classification	MaxBoxAccV2
conv_5_3	–	–
+ pool_4	74.23	64.67
+ pool_3	73.35	**66.72**
+ pool_2	66.26	63.25
+ pool_1	62.68	62.18

by 0.87%. We suppose that the dropped foreground mask improves ours more than the baseline because the additional two losses and the non-local attention block provide an extra guide for better importance map.

Location of Our Attention Block. We investigate the influence of where to insert our non-local attention block on VGG16 [29], and report the results in Table 3. The `conv_5_3` layer is fixed as the reference layer for the foreground consistency and its preceding layers are added one by one cumulatively. The setting with top three layers, which is the same as the baseline [9], achieves the best performance in terms of `MaxBoxAccV2`. Adding the attention blocks on `pool_1` and `pool_2` layers decreases the performance. We suppose that the reason is their small receptive field which leads to noisy activations on extremely locally salient regions. Hence, we do not use the attention mechanism on the two earliest layers.

Table 4. `MaxBoxAccV2` [17] comparison with the state-of-the-art methods. The results for each backbone represent the average of the three IoU thresholds 0.3, 0.5, and 0.7. VGG: VGG16 [29]. Inc: InceptionV3 [30]. Res: ResNet50 [31]. The best and the second best entries in a column are marked in boldface and italic, respectively.

Methods	ImageNet				CUB-200-2011			
	VGG	Inc	Res	Mean	VGG	Inc	Res	Mean
CAM [6]	60.0	63.4	63.7	62.4	63.7	56.7	63.0	61.1
HaS [13]	60.6	63.7	63.4	*62.6*	63.7	53.4	64.7	60.6
ACoL [7]	57.4	63.7	62.3	61.2	57.4	56.2	**66.5**	60.0
SPG [8]	59.9	63.3	63.3	62.2	56.3	55.9	60.4	57.5
ADL [9]	59.8	61.4	63.7	61.7	66.3	58.8	58.4	*61.1*
CutMix [28]	59.4	**63.9**	63.3	62.2	62.3	57.5	62.8	60.8
Ours	**61.3**	62.8	**65.1**	**63.1**	66.7	60.3	63.2	**63.4**

Table 5. Detailed `MaxBoxAccV2` [17] comparison with the runner-up methods on each dataset. We compare ours and the second best methods on each dataset and each backbone in terms of `MaxBoxAccV2` including individual measures on the three IoU criterions. Mean indicates that the average value of the three IoU thresholds. VGG: VGG16 [29]. Inc: InceptionV3 [30]. Res: ResNet50 [31]. Bold texts denote the best performance in each column.

| | Method | Backbone | Top-1 | MaxBoxAccV2@IoU (%) | | | |
				0.3	0.5	0.7	Mean
CUB-200-2011	ADL	VGG	54.95	97.72	78.06	23.04	66.28
	Ours	VGG	73.35	96.20 (−1.5)	77.20 (−0.8)	26.75 (+3.7)	**66.72** (+0.5)
	ADL	Inc	41.03	93.77	65.79	16.86	58.81
	Ours	Inc	64.01	95.89 (+2.1)	67.93 (+2.2)	17.20 (+0.4)	**60.34** (+1.2)
	ADL	Res	66.60	91.82	64.76	18.43	58.34
	Ours	Res	80.35	96.18 (+4.3)	72.79 (+8.0)	20.64 (+2.2)	**63.20** (+4.9)
ImageNet	HaS	VGG	68.26	80.72	62.15	38.89	60.59
	Ours	VGG	69.21	81.45 (+0.7)	63.20 (+1.1)	39.35 (+2.2)	**61.33** (+0.8)
	HaS	Inc	69.07	83.95	66.27	40.94	**63.72**
	Ours	Inc	71.31	82.44 (−1.5)	65.21 (−1.0)	40.87 (−0.1)	62.84 (−0.9)
	HaS	Res	75.39	83.71	65.22	41.26	63.40
	Ours	Res	76.54	84.26 (+0.5)	67.62 (+2.4)	43.58 (+2.3)	**65.15** (+1.7)

4.3 Comparison with State-of-the-art Methods

We compare our method with the state-of-the-art WSOL methods in terms of the `MaxBoxAccV2` [17], `top-1 localization` and `top-1 classification accuracy`.

MaxBoxAccV2 [17]**.** Table 4 shows comparison of `MaxBoxAccV2` across all competitors on ImageNet and CUB. Our method outperforms all existing methods in terms of `MaxBoxAccV2` (Mean) and most of backbone choices. Table 5 shows detailed comparison with the runner-up methods of each dataset. Our method boosts performance especially when IoU criterions are 0.5 and 0.7 except when Inception network is the backbone. Our method exhibits the largest improvement when employed on ResNet backbone.

Top-1 Localization Accuracy. `Top-1 localization accuracy` on the ImageNet and CUB datasets is shown in Table 6. Our model outperforms the state-of-the-art methods on most settings. Note that we do not perform hyperparameter tuning using the `train-fullsup` split following the competitors for a fair comparison.

Top-1 Classification Accuracy. Table 7 compares our method with the state-of-the-art methods in terms of `top-1 classification accuracy`. While some other methods compromise classification accuracy for improving localization, our method achieves the best `MaxBoxAccV2` and localization accuracy without damaging the classification accuracy.

Table 6. Conventional Top-1 localization accuracy comparison with the state-of-the-art methods. The values are taken from their respective papers. Bold texts denote the best performance in each backbone network.

Methods	ImageNet			CUB-200-2011		
	VGG	Inc	Res	VGG	Inc	Res
CAM [6]	42.8	46.3	–	37.1	43.7	49.4
HaS [13]	–	–	–	–	–	–
ACoL [7]	45.8	–	–	45.9	–	–
SPG [8]	–	48.6	–	–	46.6	–
ADL [9]	44.9	48.7	–	52.4	53.0	–
CutMix [28]	43.5	–	47.3	–	52.5	54.8
MEIL [18]	46.8	**49.5**	–	57.5	–	–
Ours	**47.2**	49.3	**48.4**	**57.5**	**56.1**	**56.1**

Table 7. Top-1 classification performance of the state-of-the-art methods. Hyperparameters for each method are optimally selected for the localization performances on train-fullsup split. Bold texts denote the best performance. MEIL does not provide code for reproduction and its values are taken from the paper. Other values are reproduction from [17].

Methods	ImageNet				CUB-200-2011			
	VGG	Inc	Res	Mean	VGG	Inc	Res	Mean
CAM [6]	66.48	70.56	75.05	70.70	50.10	70.70	71.50	64.10
HaS [13]	68.26	69.07	75.39	70.91	75.90	64.50	69.70	70.10
ACoL [7]	64.55	71.81	73.09	69.82	71.80	71.50	71.10	71.40
SPG [8]	67.76	71.12	73.26	70.71	72.10	46,20	50.50	56.30
ADL [9]	67.58	61.17	71.99	66.91	55.00	41.00	66.60	54.20
CutMix [28]	66.36	69.16	75.71	70.41	48.40	71.00	73.00	64.10
MEIL [18]	70.27	73.31	-	-	74.77	74.55	-	
Ours	69.21	76.54	71.31	**72.35**	73.40	64.00	80.40	**72.60**

4.4   Qualitative Results

Figure 1 compares activation maps and estimated bounding boxes from ADL [9], SPG [8] and ours. ADL excessively covers backgrounds because it simply encourages the model to use less discriminative parts, and SPG still over-estimates the bounding boxes although it tries to suppress background. In contrast, our method focuses on the entire object more accurately and estimates tighter bounding boxes. Figure 5 illustrates more examples from our model. Our method not only spreads out of the most discriminative parts, but also restrains the activations in the object regions. Note that the water and mirrored image of the pelican does not earn large activation even though they are helpful cue for classification (the second row of the second column).

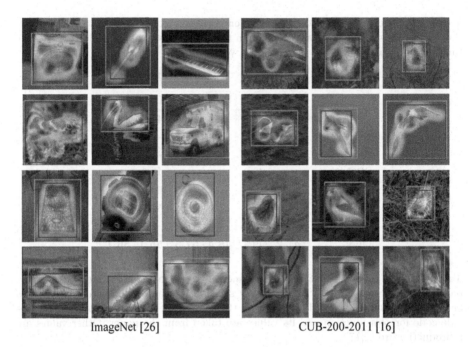

ImageNet [26]   CUB-200-2011 [16]

Fig. 5. Qualitative examples of activation map and localization produced by our model on the ImageNet and CUB test split. The red boxes are the ground-truth and the green boxes are the predicted ones. These maps output with colors ranging from red (higher importance) to blue (lower importance like a background). (Color figure online)

5   Conclusion

In this paper, we consider the background as an important clue for localizing the entire object without excessive coverage and present two novel objective functions. The crucial weakness of the previous methods is that they focus on discriminative parts rather than localizing the whole object, or extend too much on the background. The proposed contrastive attention loss guides the model to spread the attention map within the objects. The foreground consistency loss decreases the activation to backgrounds in the early layers. The generated attention map not only better localizes the target object but also suppresses the background concurrently. In addition, our non-local attention block enhances the attention map with a larger capacity to better optimize the proposed losses. We achieve state-of-the-art performance on ImageNet and CUB-200-2011 datasets and provide detailed analysis on the effects of our individual components.

Acknowledgements. This work was supported by the National Research Foundation of Korea grant funded by Korean government (No. NRF-2019R1A2C2003760) and Artificial Intelligence Graduate School Program (YONSEI UNIVERSITY) under Grant 2020-0-01361. We thank Junsuk choe for his valuable discussion.

References

1. Chen, K., et al.: Towards accurate one-stage object detection with AP-loss. In: Proceedings of the IEEE Conference on Computer Vision and Pattern Recognition, pp. 5119–5127 (2019)
2. Zhu, C., He, Y., Savvides, M.: Feature selective anchor-free module for single-shot object detection. In: Proceedings of the IEEE Conference on Computer Vision and Pattern Recognition, pp. 840–849 (2019)
3. Chen, X., Girshick, R., He, K., Dollár, P.: TensorMask: a foundation for dense object segmentation. In: Proceedings of the IEEE International Conference on Computer Vision, pp. 2061–2069 (2019)
4. Robinson, A., Lawin, F.J., Danelljan, M., Khan, F.S., Felsberg, M.: Learning fast and robust target models for video object segmentation. In: Proceedings of the IEEE/CVF Conference on Computer Vision and Pattern Recognition, pp. 7406–7415 (2020)
5. Li, Z., Zhou, F., Yang, L.: Fast single shot instance segmentation. In: Jawahar, C.V., Li, H., Mori, G., Schindler, K. (eds.) ACCV 2018. LNCS, vol. 11364, pp. 257–272. Springer, Cham (2019). https://doi.org/10.1007/978-3-030-20870-7_16
6. Zhou, B., Khosla, A., Lapedriza, A., Oliva, A., Torralba, A.: Learning deep features for discriminative localization. In: Proceedings of the IEEE Conference on Computer Vision and Pattern Recognition, pp. 2921–2929 (2016)
7. Zhang, X., Wei, Y., Feng, J., Yang, Y., Huang, T.S.: Adversarial complementary learning for weakly supervised object localization. In: Proceedings of the IEEE Conference on Computer Vision and Pattern Recognition, pp. 1325–1334 (2018)
8. Zhang, X., Wei, Y., Kang, G., Yang, Y., Huang, T.: Self-produced guidance for weakly-supervised object localization. In: Ferrari, V., Hebert, M., Sminchisescu, C., Weiss, Y. (eds.) ECCV 2018. LNCS, vol. 11216, pp. 610–625. Springer, Cham (2018). https://doi.org/10.1007/978-3-030-01258-8_37
9. Choe, J., Shim, H.: Attention-based dropout layer for weakly supervised object localization. In: Proceedings of the IEEE Conference on Computer Vision and Pattern Recognition, pp. 2219–2228 (2019)
10. Yang, S., Kim, Y., Kim, Y., Kim, C.: Combinational class activation maps for weakly supervised object localization. In: The IEEE Winter Conference on Applications of Computer Vision, pp. 2941–2949 (2020)
11. Son, J., Kim, D., Lee, S., Kwak, S., Cho, M., Han, B.: Forget and diversify: regularized refinement for weakly supervised object detection. In: Jawahar, C.V., Li, H., Mori, G., Schindler, K. (eds.) ACCV 2018. LNCS, vol. 11364, pp. 632–648. Springer, Cham (2019). https://doi.org/10.1007/978-3-030-20870-7_39
12. Lee, P., Uh, Y., Byun, H.: Background suppression network for weakly-supervised temporal action localization. In: AAAI, pp. 11320–11327 (2020)
13. Kumar Singh, K., Jae Lee, Y.: Hide-and-seek: forcing a network to be meticulous for weakly-supervised object and action localization. In: Proceedings of the IEEE International Conference on Computer Vision, pp. 3524–3533 (2017)
14. Wei, Y., Feng, J., Liang, X., Cheng, M.M., Zhao, Y., Yan, S.: Object region mining with adversarial erasing: a simple classification to semantic segmentation approach. In: Proceedings of the IEEE Conference on Computer Vision and Pattern Recognition, pp. 1568–1576 (2017)
15. Hou, Q., Jiang, P., Wei, Y., Cheng, M.M.: Self-erasing network for integral object attention. In: Advances in Neural Information Processing Systems, pp. 549–559 (2018)

16. Welinder, P., et al.: Caltech-UCSD Birds 200. Technical report CNS-TR-2010-001, California Institute of Technology (2010)
17. Choe, J., Oh, S.J., Lee, S., Chun, S., Akata, Z., Shim, H.: Evaluating weakly supervised object localization methods right. In: Proceedings of the IEEE/CVF Conference on Computer Vision and Pattern Recognition, pp. 3133–3142 (2020)
18. Mai, J., Yang, M., Luo, W.: Erasing integrated learning: a simple yet effective approach for weakly supervised object localization. In: Proceedings of the IEEE/CVF Conference on Computer Vision and Pattern Recognition, pp. 8766–8775 (2020)
19. Hadsell, R., Chopra, S., LeCun, Y.: Dimensionality reduction by learning an invariant mapping. In: 2006 IEEE Computer Society Conference on Computer Vision and Pattern Recognition (CVPR 2006), vol. 2, pp. 1735–1742. IEEE (2006)
20. He, K., Fan, H., Wu, Y., Xie, S., Girshick, R.: Momentum contrast for unsupervised visual representation learning. In: Proceedings of the IEEE/CVF Conference on Computer Vision and Pattern Recognition, pp. 9729–9738 (2020)
21. Chen, T., Kornblith, S., Norouzi, M., Hinton, G.: A simple framework for contrastive learning of visual representations. arXiv preprint arXiv:2002.05709 (2020)
22. Chen, W., Chen, X., Zhang, J., Huang, K.: Beyond triplet loss: a deep quadruplet network for person re-identification. In: Proceedings of the IEEE Conference on Computer Vision and Pattern Recognition, pp. 403–412 (2017)
23. Zeiler, M.D., Fergus, R.: Visualizing and understanding convolutional networks. In: Fleet, D., Pajdla, T., Schiele, B., Tuytelaars, T. (eds.) ECCV 2014. LNCS, vol. 8689, pp. 818–833. Springer, Cham (2014). https://doi.org/10.1007/978-3-319-10590-1_53
24. Wang, X., Girshick, R., Gupta, A., He, K.: Non-local neural networks. In: Proceedings of the IEEE Conference on Computer Vision and Pattern Recognition, pp. 7794–7803 (2018)
25. Baek, K., Lee, M., Shim, H.: PsyNet: self-supervised approach to object localization using point symmetric transformation. In: AAAI, pp. 10451–10459 (2020)
26. Russakovsky, O., et al.: ImageNet large scale visual recognition challenge. Int. J. Comput. Vis. **115**, 211–252 (2015). https://doi.org/10.1007/s11263-015-0816-y
27. Recht, B., Roelofs, R., Schmidt, L., Shankar, V.: Do ImageNet classifiers generalize to imagenet? arXiv preprint arXiv:1902.10811 (2019)
28. Yun, S., Han, D., Oh, S.J., Chun, S., Choe, J., Yoo, Y.: CutMix: regularization strategy to train strong classifiers with localizable features. In: Proceedings of the IEEE International Conference on Computer Vision, pp. 6023–6032 (2019)
29. Simonyan, K., Zisserman, A.: Very deep convolutional networks for large-scale image recognition. arXiv preprint arXiv:1409.1556 (2014)
30. Szegedy, C., Vanhoucke, V., Ioffe, S., Shlens, J., Wojna, Z.: Rethinking the inception architecture for computer vision. In: Proceedings of the IEEE Conference on Computer Vision and Pattern Recognition, pp. 2818–2826 (2016)
31. He, K., Zhang, X., Ren, S., Sun, J.: Deep residual learning for image recognition. In: Proceedings of the IEEE Conference on Computer Vision and Pattern Recognition, pp. 770–778 (2016)

Exploiting Transferable Knowledge for Fairness-Aware Image Classification

Sunhee Hwang, Sungho Park, Pilhyeon Lee, Seogkyu Jeon, Dohyung Kim, and Hyeran Byun[✉]

Department of Computer Science, Yonsei University, Seoul, Republic of Korea
{sunny16,qkrtjdgh18,lph1114,jone9312,dohkim02,hrbyun}@yonsei.ac.kr

Abstract. Recent studies have revealed the importance of fairness in machine learning and computer vision systems, in accordance with the concerns about the unintended social discrimination produced by the systems. In this work, we aim to tackle the fairness-aware image classification problem, whose goal is to classify a target attribute (*e.g.*, attractiveness) in a fair manner regarding protected attributes (*e.g.*, gender, age, race). To this end, existing methods mainly rely on protected attribute labels for training, which are costly and sometimes unavailable for real-world scenarios. To alleviate the restriction and enlarge the scalability of fair models, we introduce a new framework where a fair classification model can be trained on datasets without protected attribute labels (*i.e.*, target datasets) by exploiting knowledge from pre-built benchmarks (*i.e.*, source datasets). Specifically, when training a target attribute encoder, we encourage its representations to be independent of the features from the pre-trained encoder on a source dataset. Moreover, we design a Group-wise Fair loss to minimize the gap in error rates between different protected attribute groups. To the best of our knowledge, this work is the first attempt to train the fairness-aware image classification model on a target dataset without protected attribute annotations. To verify the effectiveness of our approach, we conduct experiments on CelebA and UTK datasets with two settings: the conventional and the transfer settings. In the both settings, our model shows the fairest results when compared to the existing methods.

1 Introduction

Artificial Intelligence (AI) systems have been widely used for decision making such as visual recognition [1], criminal justice [2], or employment [3]. Although AI systems are proved to be effective, they have raised concerns due to their biased results against some human characteristics such as gender, age, or race,

---

S. Hwang, S. Park, P. Lee—Equal contributions.

Electronic supplementary material The online version of this chapter (https://doi.org/10.1007/978-3-030-69538-5_2) contains supplementary material, which is available to authorized users.

© Springer Nature Switzerland AG 2021
H. Ishikawa et al. (Eds.): ACCV 2020, LNCS 12625, pp. 19–35, 2021.
https://doi.org/10.1007/978-3-030-69538-5_2

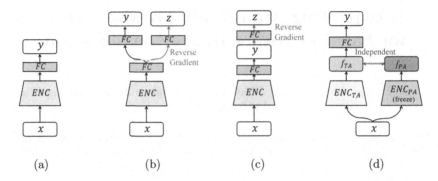

Fig. 1. Illustrations of four different classification models: (a) conventional classification model, (b) Protected Attribute Adversarial Learning (PAAL) [5,15] with domain adversarial training of neural network [16], (c) Adversarial De-biasing (AdvDe) [14], and (d) Ours. x and y denote an input image and its target attribute label respectively, while z represents its protected attribute label. Unlike the previous fairness-aware methods, our model is trained without z by leveraging a pre-trained protected attribute encoder on another dataset.

which are referred to as protected attributes. As pointed out in the literature [4–6], AI models are highly dependent on training datasets, thus they tend to learn unfair thoughts or biases from the datasets and produce discriminatory outputs. For example, image captioning models may generate biased captions against gender, $i.e.$, while captions for images with women are biased towards shopping or cooking, those for images with men are inclined towards driving or shooting [7]. In addition, face recognition systems usually perform well on Caucasians, yet they often fail to identify faces of other races [8,9]. To prevent socially negative impacts, researchers have paid their attention to developing fair AI models that produce unbiased results with regard to protected attributes [10–14].

To build fair models, previous methods mainly focus on excluding information related to protected attributes from the feature representation by utilizing a domain adaptation technique [5,15], adversarial de-biasing [14], or disentangled representation learning [10,17]. Despite their impressive improvements in the perspective of fairness, they still have limitations in that protected attribute labels for new datasets are inevitably required when they are supposed to be deployed in a new circumstance. Acquiring additional annotations of protected attributes is time-consuming and may be even infeasible in real-world situations, which limits the scalability of the fair models.

Therefore, we set two goals in this paper: 1) predicting target attributes ($e.g.$, attractiveness) in a fair way with respect to protected attributes ($e.g.$, gender, age), namely fairness-aware image classification, and 2) transferring knowledge about protected attributes from a pre-built dataset ($i.e.$, source dataset) to another dataset without protected attribute labels ($i.e.$, target dataset).

To this end, we introduce a new framework with two encoders, where one encoder pre-trained on a source dataset provides guidance on protected attributes and the other encoder fairly predicts target attributes according to the guidance. In Fig. 1, we compare our method to the existing approaches with the simple diagram illustrations. Given an input image x, the conventional classification model (Fig. 1a) is trained to predict the target label y without considering protected attributes. Upon the conventional model, the previous fairness-aware approaches (Fig. 1b and Fig. 1c) adopt gradient reversal layers to make their models unable to predict the protected attribute label z. On the other hand, our method (Fig. 1d) does not exploit the label z. Instead, it encourages the feature representation f_{TA} to be independent of the representation f_{PA} from the pretrained protected attribute encoder. By doing so, our model can learn the fair representation with respect to the protected attribute without using z.

Technically, we introduce a Feature Independency Triplet loss to promote the independency of the features from two different encoders. In specific, we first select three samples in a target dataset and encode them with the pretrained protected attribute encoder. Next, we choose one of them as an anchor and calculate the feature distances between the anchor and the other samples. The sample with a larger distance is set to a positive sample and the other to a negative one. Then, in the feature space of the target attribute encoder, we pull the positive sample to the anchor while pushing the negative sample away from the anchor. This encourages the independency between the representations from the target and protected attribute encoders. In addition, we propose a Group-wise Fair loss to minimize the difference in error rates between protected attribute groups. Firstly, we cluster the features from the protected attribute encoder into k groups. Then, we train the target attribute encoder to equalize the error rates of target attribute classification among the groups by minimizing their Wasserstein distance. These two proposed losses work complementarily to each other and enable the target attribute encoder to learn fair representation in terms of the protected attribute without explicit labels.

Our key contributions are summarized as follows:

- We propose a new framework for fairness-aware image classification, where fair representations can be learned without protected attribute labels by exploiting knowledge from external pre-built benchmarks.
- We design a Feature Independency Triplet loss to reduce the dependency between representations of two encoders for protected attributes and target attributes.
- To further improve fairness, we introduce a Group-wise Fair loss to minimize the gap between the error rates of different protected attribute groups.
- We compare our method with existing fairness-aware classification approaches on two most popular benchmarks: CelebA and UTK datasets. The results validate the effectiveness of our model, achieving the fairest results regarding *Equality of Opportunity* in two experimental settings, namely the conventional and the transfer settings. Notably, our method in the transfer setting shows fairer results than the existing methods in the conventional setting, which confirms the efficacy of our transfer learning approach.

2   Related Work

2.1   Fairness-Aware Image Classification

Recently, fairness studies in computer vision mainly attempt to solve the societal bias problems on image classification task [5,13,15,18,19]. There are two mainstreams of fairness-aware approaches for mitigating biases related to protected attributes: pre-processing and in-processing.

Pre-processing methods aim at constructing a new de-biased dataset from an original biased dataset with respect to protected attributes. Quadrianto *et al.* [13] propose a data-to-data translation method that maps a biased dataset into a fair dataset. Meanwhile, Sattigeri *et al.* [19] introduce a method generating a de-biased dataset based on Generative Adversarial Networks (GANs) [20] with two fairness-aware constraints, *Demographic Parity* [21] and *Equality of Opportunity* [12].

In-processing approaches devise new algorithms to eliminate discriminatory factors in models. They mainly focus on learning invariant feature representations against protected attributes (*e.g.*, gender, age, race). For example, inspired by the domain adversarial training of neural network [16], Wang *et al.* [5] train an image classification model to misclassify the protected attribute label with a Gradient Reversal Layer (GRL) [16] but to correctly classify target labels at the same time. Similarly, Kim *et al.* [15] utilize an adversarial strategy [20,22] and the gradient reversal technique [16] to eliminate unwanted biases by minimizing the mutual information between the feature embedding and the protected attribute. Besides, Adversarial De-biasing [14] is introduced to make the prediction for the target label which is not predictive for the protected attribute label.

Overall, prior methods achieve fair results in pre-processing and in-processing ways, but they still suffer from the essentially required cost for obtaining additional protected attribute labels for new datasets. On the contrary, our method leverages information from the pre-built source dataset to perform fair classification on the target dataset without protected attribute labels.

2.2   Transfer Learning in Computer Vision

Transfer learning is an important research topic that focuses on exploiting knowledge from a problem to tackle a different but related problem [23]. Since transfer learning allows utilizing pre-trained models for various tasks with time-saving, it draws much attention from researchers in the computer vision domain. For instance, transfer learning is actively investigated in image captioning [24], classification [25], generation [26], and object detection [27].

However, transfer learning has not been investigated for fairness-aware image classification. Herein, we are the pioneering work to obtain knowledge for protected attributes from the source dataset and transfer it into the target dataset without protected attribute labels to tackle fairness-aware image classification.

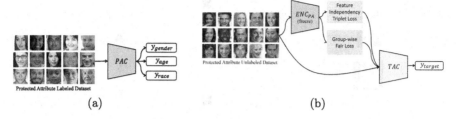

Fig. 2. Overview of the proposed framework for transfer learning. (a) In the first stage, we train the Protected Attribute Classifier (PAC) to predict three protected attributes on the source dataset in a multi-task way. (b) Then, we train the Target Attribute Classifier (TAC) on the target dataset to classify target attributes in a fair way regarding the protected attributes. To make the training without protected attribute labels feasible, we propose to utilize the encoder of the pre-trained PAC with Feature Independency Triplet Loss and Group-wise Fair Loss.

3   Fairness Definition

Fairness of the AI system can be defined as the ability to produce fair decisions with regard to protected attributes such as gender. The most widely used definition is *Equality of Opportunity* [12], which is based on the principal that individuals should be provided equal opportunities for desired results. Formally, all protected attribute groups should have the same true positive rates for the target attribute as follows:

$$\mathcal{P}(\hat{Y} = 1 | p = 0, Y = 1) = \mathcal{P}(\hat{Y} = 1 | p = 1, Y = 1), \tag{1}$$

where p, Y, $\hat{Y} \in \{0, 1\}$ denote the protected attribute, the target attribute, and the prediction respectively. In this work, we focus on improving fairness in terms of *Equality of Opportunity*.

4   Approach

Our main goal is to train a fair classification model on the target dataset without protected attribute labels. To this end, we devise a two-step strategy for transfer learning as illustrated in Fig. 2. In the first step, we train a Protected Attribute Classifier (PAC) using the source dataset with protected attribute labels (Fig. 2a). Then, we leverage the representation from the encoder of the PAC to transfer knowledge about protected attributes to a Target Attribute Classifier (TAC) (Fig. 2b). By utilizing the obtained knowledge in the first stage, the TAC is able to learn fair representations without explicit protected attribute labels. Specifically, to transfer knowledge of the PAC into the TAC, we introduce a Feature Independency Triplet loss and a Group-wise Fair loss, which will be detailed in this section.

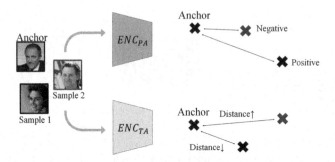

Fig. 3. Schematic visualization of the Feature Independency Triplet loss. In the feature space of the encoder of the protected attribute classifier (ENC_{PA}), we select three samples and choose one of them as an anchor. Then, we set the sample with a larger feature distance from the anchor to be a positive sample and the other to be a negative sample. Afterwards, in the space of the encoder of the target attribute classifier (ENC_{TA}), the Feature Independency Triplet loss minimizes the feature distance between the anchor and the positive sample, while maximizing the distance between the negative pair.

4.1 Protected Attribute Classifier

We first train the Protected Attribute Classifier (PAC) on the source dataset to encode representations with respect to multiple protected attributes. The PAC consists of a feature encoder with several convolutional layers (ENC_{PA}) and fully connected layers. Given a set of training data $X_s = \{x_1, x_2, ..., x_n\}$, gender labels $Y_g = \{g_1, g_2, ..., g_n\}$, age labels $Y_a = \{a_1, a_2, ..., a_n\}$, and race labels $Y_r = \{r_1, r_2, ..., r_n\}$, we optimize the PAC by minimizing three cross-entropy loss functions simultaneously:

$$\mathcal{L}_{PAC} = -\sum_{i=1}^{n} g_i log(\hat{g}_i) - \sum_{i=1}^{n} a_i log(\hat{a}_i) - \sum_{i=1}^{n} r_i log(\hat{r}_i), \tag{2}$$

where $\hat{g}$, $\hat{a}$, $\hat{r}$, and n denote the prediction of three different classifiers and the number of samples in the source dataset respectively.

4.2 Target Attribute Classifier

The Target Attribute Classifier (TAC) is composed of a convolutional feature encoder (ENC_{TA}) and fully connected layers. Given a set of training images $X_t = \{x_1, x_2, ..., x_m\}$ and corresponding labels $Y_t = \{t_1, t_2, ..., t_m\}$, we train the TAC with the following cross-entropy loss function:

$$\mathcal{L}_{target} = -\sum_{i=1}^{m} t_i log(\hat{t}_i), \tag{3}$$

where $\hat{t}_i$ and m denote the prediction of the target attribute classifier and the number of samples in the target dataset respectively.

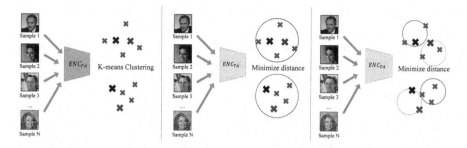

Fig. 4. The process of the Group-wise Fair loss. We group input images by k-means clustering based on their protected attribute features from the ENC_{PA}. Afterwards, during training the target attribute classifier, we aim to minimize the error rate discrepancy between different groups. The same process is performed in the subgroups as well.

4.3 Feature Independency Triplet Loss

We propose a Feature Independency Triplet loss to encourage target attribute features from ENC_{TA} to be independent of the protected attributes. Figure 3 shows the schematic visualization for the Feature Independency Triplet loss. Firstly, we randomly select two samples x_i and x_j for each anchor sample x_a in the mini-batch $X = [x_1, x_2, ..., x_k]$ of the target dataset, where k is the batch size. The anchor and the selected samples are encoded by the pre-trained ENC_{PA} into f_a, f_i, and f_j respectively. Based on the anchor feature f_a, we calculate the euclidean distance $d(f_a, f_i)$ and $d(f_a, f_j)$. We assign the sample which is more distant from x_a to a positive sample x_p and the other to a negative sample x_n. Thereafter, we construct k tuples $[(x_a^1, x_p^1, x_n^1), (x_a^2, x_p^2, x_n^2), ..., (x_a^k, x_p^k, x_n^k)]$, where the negative sample x_n^i is more similar to the anchor sample x_a^i in terms of the protected attributes. The Feature Independency Triplet loss is defined as:

$$\mathcal{L}_{triplet} = \sum_{i=1}^{N} \max(d(h_a^i, h_p^i) - d(h_a^i, h_n^i) + \alpha, 0), \tag{4}$$

where h_a^i, h_p^i, and h_n^i are encoded features of x_a^i, x_p^i, and x_n^i from ENC_{TA} respectively.

4.4 Group-Wise Fair Loss

We introduce a Group-wise Fair loss to further reinforce the fairness of our model with respect to the protected attributes (See Fig. 4). Inspired by the prior work [28], we aim to minimize the discrepancy on misclassification rate between different protected attribute groups as follows:

$$minimize|P(\hat{y} \neq y|G_1) - P(\hat{y} \neq y|G_2)|, \tag{5}$$

where $\hat{y}$ and y denote the prediction and the target label respectively. G_1 and G_2 indicate the different protected attribute groups respectively.

However, since protected attribute labels are unavailable for the target dataset, we exploit the transferred knowledge of protected attributes from ENC_{PA} in order to separate the groups in terms of protected attributes. Specifically, we extract features $F = [f_1, f_2, ..., f_m]$ of input images from the target dataset $X_t = [x_1, x_2, ..., x_m]$ using the pre-trained ENC_{PA}. Then, we cluster X_t into two groups G_1 and G_2 with the k-means clustering algorithm based on F. Subsequently, to satisfy the Eq. (5), we minimize the Wasserstein distance between the two groups G_1 and G_2 in terms of the last fully connected features H_g from ENC_{TA}. The Wasserstein distance between two groups G_1 and G_2 are as follows:

$$\mathcal{W}(H_{G_1}, H_{G_2}) = \inf_{\gamma \in \prod(H_{G_1}, H_{G_2})} \mathbb{E}_{(z_1, z_2) \sim \gamma}[\|z_1 - z_2\|]. \tag{6}$$

where $\prod(H_{G_1}, H_{G_2})$ is the set of all joint distributions $\gamma(z_1, z_2)$ whose marginals are respectively H_{G_1} and H_{G_2}.

Although Group-wise Fair loss improves fairness between the protected attribute groups, the bias in terms of the target attribute still exists. Therefore, we propose a loss to minimize the Wasserstein distance between output features of subgroups as follows:

$$\mathcal{W}(H_{G_1^+}, H_{G_1^-}) = \inf_{\gamma \in \prod(H_{G_1^+}, H_{G_1^-})} \mathbb{E}_{(z_1, z_2) \sim \gamma}[\|z_1 - z_2\|].$$
$$\mathcal{W}(H_{G_2^+}, H_{G_2^-}) = \inf_{\gamma \in \prod(H_{G_2^+}, H_{G_2^-})} \mathbb{E}_{(z_1, z_2) \sim \gamma}[\|z_1 - z_2\|], \tag{7}$$

where G^+ and G^- respectively denote the group of positive samples and negative samples in terms of the target attribute respectively, while G_1 and G_2 are distinguished in terms of the protected attribute.

4.5 Full Objective Function for TAC

The final objective function for training the TAC is defined as:

$$\mathcal{L}_{TAC} = \lambda_1 \mathcal{L}_{target} + \lambda_2 \mathcal{L}_{triplet} + \lambda_3 \mathcal{L}_{group}, \tag{8}$$

where λ_* are the hyper-parameter for balancing the losses.

5   Experiment

We conduct experiments on two classification tasks: (1) attractiveness classification on CelebA dataset [29] and (2) race classification on UTK Face dataset [30]. For the quantitative evaluation in terms of fairness, we measure the *Equality of Opportunity (Eq.Opp.)* [12], which is defined as:

$$Eq.Opp. = |TPR_{p=0} - TPR_{p=1}|, \tag{9}$$

where TPR and p denote True Positive Rate (TPR) and a binary protected attribute label respectively.

Table 1. Dataset bias of the attractiveness attribute towards Male, Young, and Pale Skin attributes on CelebA dataset [29].

		Male			Young			Pale Skin		
		Train	Valid	Test	Train	Valid	Test	Train	Valid	Test
TA = 1	PA = 1	19,014	2,651	1,914	78,239	9,404	9,116	5,021	595	610
	PA = 0	64,589	7,681	7,984	48,549	5,428	5,998	78,582	9,737	9,288
TA = 0	PA = 1	49,247	5,807	5,801	5,364	928	782	1,984	261	230
	PA = 0	29,920	3,728	4,263	30,618	4,107	4,066	77,183	9,274	9,834

5.1 Experimental Settings

- **Attractiveness Classification**: For the attractiveness classification task, we train the PAC on UTK Face dataset with three protected attributes, gender, age, and race. We set 19,708, 2,000, and 2,000 images of UTK dataset for training, validation, and test set, respectively. Then, we train the TAC on CelebA dataset to classify the attractiveness attribute. CelebA dataset is composed of train, validation, and test set with 162,770, 19,867, and 19,962 images respectively. The bias in the CelebA dataset is demonstrated in Table 1. Since age and race attributes do not exist in CelebA dataset, we substitute them with young and pale skin attributes. We pre-process all the images by randomly cropping (178×178) and resizing to 64×64 in CelebA dataset.
- **Race Classification**: For the race attribute classification task (Caucasian or others), we train the PAC on CelebA dataset with only the gender attribute since it does not contain age and race attributes. Then, the TAC is trained to classify the race attribute on UTK Face dataset. In this experiment, we manually compose UTK Face dataset to be biased in terms of the protected attribute as follows: 4,000 Caucasian male, 1,000 other male, 1,000 Caucasian female, and 4,000 other female images for the training set, 1,000 images of each group for the test set, and others for the validation set. We use the cropped images of UTK Face dataset and resize it into 64×64.

5.2 Implementation Details

For the TAC and PAC, we use ResNet-18 [1] as our backbone network. We implement our networks in the Pytorch framework [31] and use the Adam optimizer [32] with $\beta_1 = 0.5$, $\beta_2 = 0.999$, learning rate $= 10^{-4}$, and the batch size of 256. We early-stop training when the network converges in the validation set. All the networks are trained from scratch to prevent the model learning any unwanted biases from the datasets used for pre-training. For all experiments, we set λ_1, λ_2 and λ_3 as 1, 1e$-$3, and 1e$-$3, respectively. In the classification phase, we use the same threshold of 0.5 to fairly compare the methods.

Table 2. Protected attribute classification results on UTK Face and CelebA dataset. Top three rows indicate the result of UTK Face dataset, and last row denotes the result of CelebA dataset.

Dataset	Attribute [Labels]	Validation	Test
UTK Face	Gender [Male, Female]	0.87	0.86
	Race [White, Black, Asian, Indian, Others]	0.75	0.73
	Age [0 9, 10 19, ..., 50+]	0.59	0.57
CelebA	Gender [Male, Female]	0.97	0.96

5.3   Comparative Methods

To validate the effectiveness of our method, we compare it to the following approaches:

- **ResNet-18**: we adopt ResNet-18 [1] as the conventional classification model. The last fully connected layer is replaced with three fully connected layers with batch normalization and ReLU activation following [16].
- **Protected attribute adversarial learning**: we compare our model to a protected attribute adversarial learning approach (PAAL) [5,15]. We adopt ResNet-18 as a backbone network and add two parallel branches on top of that for the domain adversarial training of neural network [16]: a classifier with three fully connected layers for the target label and Gradient Reversal Layers (GRL) composed of three fully connected layers for mitigating bias to the protected attribute.
- **Adversarial de-biasing**: We also compare our model with the Adversarial De-biasing (AdvDe) approach [14]. On top of the ResNet-18, we add one fully connected layer for adversarially training the model not to predict the protected attribute.

5.4   Protected Attribute Classification

Table 2 shows the protected attribute classification accuracies on CelebA and UTK Face datasets. Our model achieves the top-1 classification accuracy of 86%, 73%, and 57% for gender, race, and age attributes on CelebA dataset respectively, and the accuracy of 96% for the gender attribute on UTK Face dataset.

Table 3. Equality of Opportunity (*Eq.Opp.*) for attractiveness classification on CelebA dataset [29] with respect to the two protected attributes: Young (age related) and Male. The lower is better. ResNet-18 is trained without any protected attribute labels. While Adversarial de-biasing and Protected Attribute Adversarial Learning models are trained with protected attribute labels of the target dataset, our method utilizes those of the source dataset.

	True Positive Rate		*Eq.Opp.*	True Positive Rate		*Eq.Opp.*
	Young = 1	Young = 0		Male = 1	Male = 0	
ResNet-18 [1]	86.21	65.60	20.61	63.85	89.55	25.70
AdvDe [14]	83.95	68.41	15.54	67.35	85.10	17.75
PAAL [5,15]	91.87	80.31	11.56	81.35	94.24	12.89
Ours (All)	95.95	90.28	**5.61**	87.25	97.48	**10.23**

Table 4. Equality of Opportunity (*Eq.Opp.*) for attractiveness classification on CelebA dataset [29] regarding the skin color related protected attribute (Pale Skin).

	True Positive Rate		*Eq.Opp.*
	Pale Skin = 1	Pale Skin = 0	
ResNet-18 [1]	92.46	84.07	8.39
AdvDe [14]	91.80	83.93	7.85
PAAL [5,15]	94.26	90.04	4.22
Ours	99.18	95.26	**3.92**

5.5   Attractiveness Classification

We conduct comparison on the attractiveness classification results as shown in Table 3 and Table 4. As described in Sect. 3, the objective of our model is to ensure *Equality of Opportunity* on different protected attributes such as gender, age, and race. In these experiments, the results demonstrate that our model achieves the fairest results on CelebA dataset with respect to the Young (5.61), Male (10.23), and Pale Skin (3.92) attributes.

In addition, we verify the contributions of our proposed loss functions through an ablation study as shown in Table 5. We evaluate the results of models only with the Feature Independency Triplet loss or the Group-wise Fair loss, and the full model. Table 5 shows that our loss function improves fairness step by step.

Furthermore, we validate that the improvement of our model is not caused by an additional usage of the source dataset through the experimental results in two different settings, as shown in Table 6. In the first setting (*i.e.*, conventional setting), we conduct comparison with the comparative models by setting both the source and the target datasets to CelebA dataset (denoted with asterisk (*)). For this setting, we only consider gender as the protected attribute. In the second setting (*i.e.*, transfer setting), we compare fairness of all the models trained with protected attribute labels in UTK Face dataset and target attribute labels in CelebA dataset (denoted with dagger (†)). In both setting, our method shows the fairest results, verifying its effectiveness.

Table 5. Ablation Study on CelebA dataset for attractiveness classification. *Eq.Opp.* denotes Equality of Opportunity.

	True Positive Rate		Eq.Opp.	True positive rate		Eq.Opp.
	Young = 1	Young = 0		Male = 1	Male = 0	
Triplet Loss	93.66	83.63	10.03	80.36	95.87	15.51
Group-wise Fair Loss	93.90	84.27	9.63	82.08	95.79	13.71
All	95.95	90.28	5.61	87.25	97.48	10.23

Table 6. Equality of Opportunity (*Eq.Opp.*) for attractiveness classification on CelebA dataset [29] in terms of gender attribute. ResNet-18 (first row) is trained without any protected attribute. Asterisk (*) (2–5 rows) and dagger (†) (6–8 rows) denote the results of the conventional and the transfer settings, respectively.

	True Positive Rate		Eq.Opp.
	Male = 1	Male = 0	
ResNet-18 [1]	63.85	89.55	25.70
AdvDe* [14]	81.35	94.24	12.89
PAAL* [5,15]	67.35	85.10	17.75
Ours*	88.51	97.77	**9.26**
AdvDe† [14]	68.90	89.58	20.98
PAAL† [5,15]	73.46	94.40	20.94
Ours†	87.25	97.48	**10.23**

5.6   Race Classification

We also compare the race classification results of our model to baseline [1], AdvDe [14], and PAAL [5,15]. For this experiment, we set CelebA dataset as the source dataset and UTK Face dataset as the target dataset. As shown in Table 7, our model achieves the fairest *Eq.Opp.* of 1.7.

Moreover, to see how our model works under varying levels of the bias in the training dataset, we change the composition of training samples among four groups: Caucasian Males, Other Males, Caucasian Females, and Other Females. In Table 8, our method performs better in terms of both accuracy and fairness (*Eq.Opp.*) in less imbalanced setting, as expected. In contrast, the gap of *Eq.Opp.* between the baseline and our model is larger in extremely imbalanced settings. This indicates that our model works well in the challenging situations.

5.7   t-SNE Visualization

To deeply analyze the effectiveness of our model, we visualize the representations from the TAC and other models using t-SNE method [33]. We first train them to fairly classify attractiveness attributes in terms of gender attributes on CelebA dataset and conduct visualization on 1,000 male and 1,000 female images randomly sampled in the test set. The visualization results are shown in Fig. 5, where the dark and light blue color denote female and male samples, respectively. We observe that the representations of female and male samples are separately grouped in other methods, indicating the bias towards the gender attribute. In contrast, the representations of our method are more scattered with respect to the gender attribute. This demonstrates that our model successfully learns fair representations with respect to the protected attribute.

Table 7. Equality of Opportunity (*Eq.Opp.*) for race classification on UTK Face dataset [30], where we set the protected attribute as gender.

	True Positive Rate		Eq.Opp.
	Male = 1	Male = 0	
ResNet-18 [1]	86.4	67.2	19.2
AdvDe [14]	86.6	68.3	18.3
PAAL [5, 15]	76.8	73.8	3.0
Ours	76.1	74.4	**1.7**

Table 8. Equality of Opportunity (*Eq.Opp.*) for race classification on UTK Face dataset [30] under different statistics. We present the ratio of the number of training images in the following four cases: (Male,Caucasian):(Female,Others):(Male,Others): (Female,Caucasian).

Ratio	ResNet-18 [1] (without de-biasing)			Ours		
	True Positive Rate		*Eq.Opp.*	True Positive Rate		*Eq.Opp.*
	Male = 1	Male = 0		Male = 1	Male = 0	
1:1:1:1	86.8	84.8	2.0	86.1	87.5	1.4
1.5:1.5:1:1	79.6	87.0	7.3	84.7	86.5	1.8
4:4:1:1	67.2	86.4	19.2	74.4	76.1	1.7
9:9:1:1	57.3	81.8	24.5	61.0	64.8	3.8

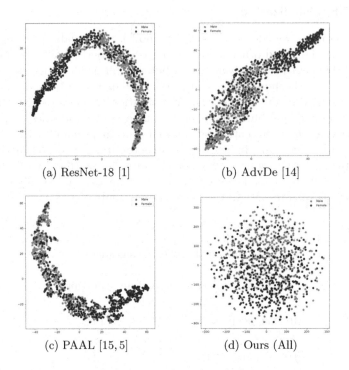

(a) ResNet-18 [1]   (b) AdvDe [14]

(c) PAAL [15, 5]   (d) Ours (All)

Fig. 5. t-SNE Visualization [33] on CelebA dataset [29]. We visualize the representations of the attractiveness classifiers. Each of dark/light blue group denotes randomly selected female and male samples respectively. Less clustered are better.

6   Conclusion

In this paper, we tackled the problem of the biased results of AI systems in terms of sensitive characteristics, such as gender, age, or race. Since various real-world datasets do not have annotations for protected attributes, we proposed a framework for fairness-aware image classification, which can be trained on a dataset without protected attribute labels (*i.e.*, target dataset) by transferring knowledge from another dataset with protected attribute labels (*i.e.*, source dataset).

To leverage the knowledge, we introduced the Feature Independency Triplet loss which encourages the representation for target attributes to be independent of protected attributes. Moreover, we designed the Group-wise Fair loss to minimize the discrepancy on the misclassification rates among protected attribute groups. To validate the effectiveness of our method, we conducted experiments of facial attribute classification on CelebA and UTK Face datasets. Our experiments demonstrate that the proposed method achieved the fairest performance in terms of *Equality of Opportunity*. In addition, through the t-SNE visualization, we showed that our representations are invariant to protected attributes.

To summary, we present a knowledge transfer method which works between two datasets with similar domains (*i.e.*, face images). However, the transfer between different domains is not investigated in this work. Adopting domain adaptation techniques would be interesting for future work.

Acknowledgement. This research was supported by Next-Generation Information Computing Development Program through the National Research Foundation of Korea (NRF) funded by the Ministry of Science and ICT (NRF-2017M3C4A7069370) and Institute for Information & communications Technology Planning & Evaluation (IITP) grant funded by the Korea government (MSIT) (Development of framework for analyzing, detecting, mitigating of bias in AI model and training data) under Grant 2019-0-01396 and (Artificial Intelligence Graduate School Program (YONSEI UNIVERSITY)) under Grant 2020-0-01361.

References

1. He, K., Zhang, X., Ren, S., Sun, J.: Deep Residual Learning for Image Recognition. In: Proceedings of the IEEE Conference on Computer Vision and Pattern Recognition, pp. 770–778 (2016)
2. Barenstein, M.: Propublica's compas data revisited. arXiv preprint arXiv:1906.04711 (2019)
3. Farnadi, G., Babaki, B., Getoor, L.: Fairness in relational domains. In: Proceedings of the 2018 AAAI/ACM Conference on AI, Ethics, and Society. AIES 2018, pp. 108–114. Association for Computing Machinery, New York (2018)
4. Brandao, M.: Age and gender bias in pedestrian detection algorithms. In: The IEEE/CVF Conference on Computer Vision and Pattern Recognition (CVPR) Workshops (2019)
5. Wang, T., Zhao, J., Yatskar, M., Chang, K.W., Ordonez, V.: Balanced datasets are not enough: estimating and mitigating gender bias in deep image representations. In: The IEEE International Conference on Computer Vision (ICCV) (2019)
6. Hwang, S., Byun, H.: Unsupervised image-to-image translation via fair representation of gender bias. In: The IEEE International Conference on Acoustics, Speech and Signal Processing (ICASSP), pp. 1953–1957. IEEE (2020)
7. Zhao, J., Wang, T., Yatskar, M., Ordonez, V., Chang, K.W.: Men also like shopping: reducing gender bias amplification using corpus-level constraints. In: Proceedings of the 2017 Conference on Empirical Methods in Natural Language Processing, Copenhagen, Denmark, pp. 2979–2989. Association for Computational Linguistics (2017)
8. Wang, M., Deng, W., Hu, J., Tao, X., Huang, Y.: Racial faces in the wild: reducing racial bias by information maximization adaptation network. In: Proceedings of the IEEE International Conference on Computer Vision, pp. 692–702 (2019)
9. Garcia, M.: Racist in the machine: the disturbing implications of algorithmic bias. World Policy J. **33**, 111–117 (2016)
10. Park, S., Kim, D., Hwang, S., Byun, H.: Readme: representation learning by fairness-aware disentangling method. arXiv preprint arXiv:2007.03775 (2020)
11. Hutchinson, B., Mitchell, M.: 50 years of test (un)fairness: lessons for machine learning. In: Proceedings of the Conference on Fairness, Accountability, and Transparency. FAT* 2019, pp. 49–58. Association for Computing Machinery, New York (2019)

12. Hardt, M., Price, E., Srebro, N.: Equality of opportunity in supervised learning. In: Proceedings of the 30th International Conference on Neural Information Processing Systems. NIPS 2016, pp. 3323–3331. Curran Associates Inc., Red Hook (2016)
13. Quadrianto, N., Sharmanska, V., Thomas, O.: Discovering fair representations in the data domain. In: The IEEE Conference on Computer Vision and Pattern Recognition (CVPR) (2019)
14. Zhang, B.H., Lemoine, B., Mitchell, M.: Mitigating unwanted biases with adversarial learning. In: Proceedings of the 2018 AAAI/ACM Conference on AI, Ethics, and Society. AIES 2018, pp. 335–340. Association for Computing Machinery, New York (2018)
15. Kim, B., Kim, H., Kim, K., Kim, S., Kim, J.: Learning not to learn: training deep neural networks with biased data. In: The IEEE Conference on Computer Vision and Pattern Recognition (CVPR) (2019)
16. Ajakan, H., Germain, P., Larochelle, H., Laviolette, F., Marchand, M.: Domain-adversarial neural networks. arXiv preprint arXiv:1412.4446 (2014)
17. Creager, E., et al.: Flexibly fair representation learning by disentanglement. In Chaudhuri, K., Salakhutdinov, R. (eds.) Proceedings of the 36th International Conference on Machine Learning. Volume 97 of Proceedings of Machine Learning Research, Long Beach, California, USA, pp. 1436–1445. PMLR (2019)
18. Hendricks, L.A., Burns, K., Saenko, K., Darrell, T., Rohrbach, A.: Women also snowboard: overcoming bias in captioning models. In: Ferrari, V., Hebert, M., Sminchisescu, C., Weiss, Y. (eds.) ECCV 2018. LNCS, vol. 11207, pp. 793–811. Springer, Cham (2018). https://doi.org/10.1007/978-3-030-01219-9_47
19. Sattigeri, P., Hoffman, S.C., Chenthamarakshan, V., Varshney, K.R.: Fairness GAN: generating datasets with fairness properties using a generative adversarial network. IBM J. Res. Dev. **63**(4/5), 3:1–3:9 (2019)
20. Goodfellow, I., et al.: Generative adversarial nets. In: Advances in Neural Information Processing Systems, pp. 2672–2680 (2014)
21. Edwards, H., Storkey, A.: Censoring representations with an adversary. International Conference on Learning Representations (2016)
22. Chen, X., Duan, Y., Houthooft, R., Schulman, J., Sutskever, I., Abbeel, P.: InfoGAN: interpretable representation learning by information maximizing generative adversarial nets. In: Advances in Neural Information Processing Systems, pp. 2172–2180 (2016)
23. West, J., Ventura, D., Warnick, S.: Spring research presentation: a theoretical foundation for inductive transfer. Brigham Young University, College of Physical and Mathematical Sciences 1 (2007)
24. Wang, C., Yang, H., Meinel, C.: Image captioning with deep bidirectional LSTMs and multi-task learning. ACM Trans. Multimedia Comput. Commun. Appl. **14**, 1–20 (2018)
25. Lee, K.H., He, X., Zhang, L., Yang, L.: CleanNet: transfer learning for scalable image classifier training with label noise. In: The IEEE Conference on Computer Vision and Pattern Recognition (CVPR) (2018)
26. Gamrian, S., Goldberg, Y.: Transfer learning for related reinforcement learning tasks via image-to-image translation. In: Chaudhuri, K., Salakhutdinov, R. (eds.) Proceedings of the 36th International Conference on Machine Learning. Volume 97 of Proceedings of Machine Learning Research, Long Beach, California, USA, pp. 2063–2072. PMLR (2019)
27. Ren, S., He, K., Girshick, R., Sun, J.: Faster R-CNN: towards real-time object detection with region proposal networks. In: Advances in Neural Information Processing Systems, pp. 91–99 (2015)

28. Zafar, M.B., Valera, I., Gomez Rodriguez, M., Gummadi, K.P.: Fairness beyond disparate treatment & disparate impact: learning classification without disparate mistreatment. In: Proceedings of the 26th International Conference on World Wide Web, pp. 1171–1180 (2017)
29. Liu, Z., Luo, P., Wang, X., Tang, X.: Deep learning face attributes in the wild. In: Proceedings of International Conference on Computer Vision (ICCV) (2015)
30. Zhang, Z., Song, Y., Qi, H.: Age progression/regression by conditional adversarial autoencoder. In: IEEE Conference on Computer Vision and Pattern Recognition (CVPR). IEEE (2017)
31. Paszke, A., et al.: PyTorch: an imperative style, high-performance deep learning library. In: Wallach, H., Larochelle, H., Beygelzimer, A., d'Alché-Buc, F., Fox, E., Garnett, R. (eds.) Advances in Neural Information Processing Systems 32, pp. 8024–8035. Curran Associates, Inc. (2019)
32. Kingma, D.P., Ba, J.: Adam: a method for stochastic optimization. arXiv preprint arXiv:1412.6980 (2014)
33. van der Maaten, L., Hinton, G.: Visualizing data using t-SNE. J. Mach. Learn. Res. **9**, 2579–2605 (2008)

Introspective Learning by Distilling Knowledge from Online Self-explanation

Jindong Gu[1,2]($\boxtimes$), Zhiliang Wu[1,2], and Volker Tresp[1,2]

[1] University of Munich, Munich, Germany
{jindong.gu,volker.tresp}@siemens.com
[2] Siemens AG, Corporate Technology, Munich, Germany

Abstract. In recent years, many methods have been proposed to explain individual classification predictions of deep neural networks. However, how to leverage the created explanations to improve the learning process has been less explored. The explanations extracted from a model can be used to guide the learning process of the model itself. Another type of information used to guide the training of a model is the knowledge provided by a powerful teacher model. The goal of this work is to leverage the self-explanation to improve the learning process by borrowing ideas from knowledge distillation. We start by investigating the effective components of the knowledge transferred from the teacher network to the student network. Our investigation reveals that both the responses in non-ground-truth classes and the class-similarity information in teacher's outputs contribute to the success of the knowledge distillation. Motivated by the conclusion, we propose an implementation of introspective learning by distilling knowledge from online self-explanations. The models trained with the introspective learning procedure outperform the ones trained with the standard learning procedure, as well as the ones trained with different regularization methods. When compared to the models learned from peer networks or teacher networks, our models also show competitive performance and requires neither peers nor teachers.

1 Introduction

When human subjects imagine visual objects without actual sensory stimuli, there is still significant activity in their visual cortices [1]. This implies that the internal representations in our visual cortex are used to reason about images. Similarly, when explaining classifications of neural networks, the existing model-aware explanation methods create explanations based on internal feature representations of neural networks. The explanation of each prediction identifies the relationship between input features and outputs. For instance, in image classification, saliency maps are proposed to explain how each input pixel is relevant to different classes, [2–6] to name a few.

It has been shown that the performance of human decisions is related to the explanations during introspection in the brain [7,8]. In the deep learning community, there is no clear definition of introspective learning. In this work,

© Springer Nature Switzerland AG 2021
H. Ishikawa et al. (Eds.): ACCV 2020, LNCS 12625, pp. 36–52, 2021.
https://doi.org/10.1007/978-3-030-69538-5_3

we define *introspective learning* as learning with explanations created from the underlying model itself. In recent years, the explanations extracted from the learned models are mainly used to gain trust from users in real-world applications and help machine learning experts understand the predictions. How to leverage the explanations to improve the model itself has not been well explored.

Broadly speaking, learning with explanations falls into the framework of learning using privileged information [9,10]. In classical supervised learning, the training data are $\{(x_1, y_1), \cdots, (x_n, y_n)\}$ where (x_i, y_i) is an input-label pair, y_i is a c-dimensional vector, and c is the number of output classes. In the framework of learning using privileged information, additional information x_i^* about (x_i, y_i) is provided by an intelligent teacher. The training data are therefore formed by a collection of triplets

$$\{(x_1, x_1^*, y_1), \cdots, (x_n, x_n^*, y_n)\}. \tag{1}$$

For instance, x_i^* can be the softened outputs of a teacher model [11]. In this work, we consider the explanation E_i created for the classification of (x_i, y_i) as the privileged information.

When the softened outputs of a powerful teacher model are provided as the privileged information, the learning process is known as knowledge distillation (KD) as defined by Hinton et al. [12], where a student network is trained to match its softened outputs to the teacher's.

In this work, we first investigate the effective components in the knowledge distillation. Our investigation shows that both the responses in non-ground-truth classes and class-similarity information in teacher's outputs contribute to the effectiveness of knowledge distillation. Motivated by the conclusions, we propose a novel training procedure to train networks by leveraging online self-explanations.

In our introspective learning paradigm, for the classification of the i-th sample x_i, we create one saliency map for each output class, i.e., $E_i = (e_i^1, e_i^2, \cdots, e_i^c)$ where c is the total number of output classes. The saliency map (explanation) is a heatmap of the same size as the input. The individual values of the heatmap indicate the relevance of the corresponding input features. The explanation e_i^j is a function of the input x_i, the underlying model M and the target class y_i^j, namely $e_i^j = f_e(x_i, M, y_i^j)$ where y_i^j is the j-th output class index of the i-th example. They contain neither additional human prior knowledge nor knowledge of a powerful teacher model. We leverage the explanations to guide the training process in each training epoch.

It is perhaps not obvious why explanations can be used to improve the model at all. Our hypothesis is that the explanations can be leveraged to help the training process to find a better local minimum in a way similar to KD. [13] observes that small networks often have the same representation capacity as large networks. Compared with large networks, it is more difficult to converge to good local minima. In our work, we leverage explanations to help the training process to find a better local minimum.

The contributions of our work are two-fold. Firstly, we investigate which components of KD contribute to its success. Secondly, inspired by the investigation results, we propose a way to implement introspective learning by distilling knowledge from self-explanations. The rest of the paper is structured as follows: Sect. 2 reviews related work. Section 3 and 4 describe the two contributions. Section 5 conducts experiments to show that our proposed learning procedure can achieve competitive performance even without any teacher. The last section concludes the paper.

2   Related Work

Explanation: The explanation of a classification for the j-th class e_i^j illustrates how relevant the input features are to the prediction of the j-th class. Vanilla Gradient (*Grad*) takes the gradient of an output neuron with respect to the input as an explanation [2]. Guided Backpropagation (*GuidedBP*) differs from the Grad approach in handling ReLU layers, where only positive gradients are propagated through the ReLU layers [3]. [4] multiplies the Grad with the input (*Grad*Input*) to deal with numerical stability. [14] shows that *Grad*Input* is equivalent to LRP [15] and DeepLIFT [4]. Another commonly used approach (*Grad-CAM*) combines the feature maps linearly using the averaged gradients of each feature map [5].

All the approaches introduced above require only a single backpropagation to create an explanation, while SmoothGrad [16] and IntergratedGrad [17] require dozens of passes. Some other approaches require two backpropagations, e.g., Contrastive LRP, although they create visually pleasing and class-discriminative explanations [18,19]. The explanations created by these saliency methods are often applied to diagnose models.

Regularization: We briefly introduce closely related regularization techniques. Label Smoothing [20] replaces the one-hot labels with soft labels where α is specified for the ground-truth class, and $(1-a)$ is evenly distributed to other classes (α is often set as 0.9). [21] proposed to penalize low entropy predictions, called Confidence Penalty. Another commonly used regularization is Dropout [22], which drops each neuron of a layer with a certain probability.

Knowledge Distillation: The knowledge of a teacher model can be used to guide the training of a student model. Many works focus on different forms of the dark knowledge extracted from the teacher, e.g., soft outputs [12,23], Hints (intermediate representations) [24], Activation-based. Gradient-based attention [25], and Flow between layers [26].

Recent research shows that a more powerful teacher and a peer network can help train a student. [27] shows that a poorly-trained teacher with much lower accuracy than the student can still improve the latter significantly, and a student can also enhance the teacher by reversing the KD procedure. [28] distills knowledge from a peer network with a similar capacity. The peer network can even be with the same architecture; it is known as Born-Again Network. The work [29] searches for better student architectures to learn distilled knowledge. Deep Mutual Learning [30] train multiple students with the same architecture and regularize their outputs to be similar, where each student can outperform the one trained alone without mutual learning. In this work, we propose to learn from a student itself by distilling knowledge from its explanations.

Effectiveness of KD: [12] argues that the success of KD can be attributed to the information in the logit distribution that describes the similarity between output categories. [28] investigates gradients of the loss in KD and shows that weighting training examples with the teacher's confidence can also improve the student model's performance. In this work, we conduct further experiments to reveal effective components in KD.

3   Understanding Dark Knowledge

In our introspective learning, the explanations extracted from the learned models are used to improve model performance, while the knowledge provided by another teacher model is used In KD. To borrow ideas from the success of KD, we investigate the dark knowledge that improves the student in KD.

Given a training example (x_i, y_i) and the number of output classes c, the logits and the output probabilities of a network are $a_i = (a_i^1, a_i^2, \cdots, a_i^c)$ and $p_i = \text{softmax}(a_i) = (p_i^1, p_i^2, \cdots, p_i^c)$ respectively. We denote the target outputs as t_i. The target can be the one-hot labels y_i in supervised learning, while it can also be the softened output probabilities of a teacher model q_i in KD.

In both cases, given a mini-batch $\{(x_i, y_i)\}_{i=1}^b$, the gradient of the cross-entropy loss $\mathcal{L} = \frac{1}{b} \sum_{i=1}^b ce(p_i, t_i)$ with respect to the logit a^j is

$$\frac{\partial \mathcal{L}}{\partial a^j} = \frac{1}{b} \sum_{i=1}^b \frac{\partial \mathcal{L}}{\partial a_i^j} = \frac{1}{b} \sum_{i=1}^b (p_i^j - t_i^j). \tag{2}$$

Without loss of generality, the samples in the mini-batch can be divided into two parts: $\{(x_i)\}_{i=1}^s$ with the j-th class as the ground-truth class ($y_i^j = 1$) and $\{(x_i)\}_{i=s+1}^b$ with other classes as ground-truth classes ($y_i^j = 0$). In the case of the standard supervised learning where $t = y$ (denoted as **CE** for cross entropy), the gradient can be formulated as

$$\frac{\partial \mathcal{L}}{\partial a^j} = \frac{1}{b} \left(\sum_{i=1}^s (p_i^j - 1) + \sum_{i=s+1}^b p_i^j \right). \tag{3}$$

In the case of training with KD where $t = q$ (denoted as **KD**[1]), the gradient can be formulated as

$$\frac{\partial \mathcal{L}}{\partial a^j} = \frac{1}{b} \left(\sum_{i=1}^s (p_i^j - q_i^j) + \sum_{i=s+1}^b (p_i^j - q_i^j) \right). \tag{4}$$

[28] argues that the teacher's confidence is the effective component of KD, and KD simply performs importance weighting. With one-hot labels, they propose

---

[1] Similar to [28], the temperature of softmax in KD is hidden to simplify notations.

Table 1. Test Accuracy (%) of CNNs on CIFAR10 dataset: the teacher CNN-10 achieves 90,04% test accuracy, and the performance of students are listed. CWTM-P corresponds to CWTM-Permut, and CWTM-R to CWTM-Random.

	Model	CE	KD	CWTM	CWTM-P	CWTM-R	DKPP
Student1	CNN-8	86,86(±0.30)	88,48(±0.33)	87,03(±0.26)	87,41(±0.32)	87,22(±0.17)	87,73(±0.37)
Student2	CNN-6	85,18(±0.32)	86,55(±0.32)	85,65(±0.38)	85,74(±0.33)	85,25(±0.31)	86,30(±0.42)

to weigh each sample by the teacher's confidence in its maximum value, i.e., Confidence Weighted by Teacher Max (**CWTM**).

$$\frac{\partial \mathcal{L}}{\partial a^j} = \sum_{i=1}^{s} \frac{q_i^{max}}{\sum_{j=1}^{b} q_j^{max}} * (p_i^j - 1) + \sum_{i=s+1}^{b} \frac{q_i^{max}}{\sum_{j=1}^{b} q_j^{max}} * p_i^j \tag{5}$$

where q_i^{max} is the maximum of teacher's outputs $\boldsymbol{q}_i$.

To check the effectiveness of class-similarity information, they randomly permute the teacher's non-argmax outputs of predicted distribution on a sample, i.e., Dark Knowledge with Permuted Predictions (**DKPP**). The q_i^j in the second term of Eq. 4 is replaced by q_i^k, which is one of the permuted non-argmax outputs. By doing this, the information about the similarity between classes is removed.

We design two experiments to verify the effectiveness of teacher's confidence: 1) **CWTM-Permut**: the teacher's confidence (argmax outputs) is randomly permuted inside a batch, namely the weight of the sample $(\boldsymbol{x}_i, \boldsymbol{y}_i)$ in Eq. 5 is set as $\frac{q_k^{max}}{\sum_{j=1}^{n} q_j^{max}}$ where k is one of the permuted sample indexes; 2) **CWTM-Random**: q_i^{max} in Eq. 5 is replaced by a random value selected from $[\beta, 1)$ as the teacher's confidence.

We conduct experiments on CIFAR10 [31] using convolutional neural networks (CNN). The used CNNs consist of convolutional layers followed by max-pooling and ends with a fully connected layer. The teacher we use has ten convolutional layers, called CNN-10, and the two students are CNN-8 and CNN-6, respectively. The standard data augmentation is applied to the training data: 4 pixels are padded on each side, and a 32×32 patch is randomly cropped from the padded images or their horizontal flip. The β in CWTM-Random is 0.5, which ensures that q_i^{max} corresponds to the maximal value. All models are trained with a batch size of 128 for 160 epochs using SGD with a learning rate of 0.01 and moment 0.9. The test performance is shown in Table 1. All the scores reported in this paper are averaged on five trials in forms of mean(±std).

In Table 1, KD outperforms the classical supervised learning CE, which indicates that the targets specified by the teacher do help the training of the students. CWTM outperforms the baseline CE. **The improvement cannot be attributed to the teacher's confidence since both CWTM-Permut and CWTM-Random also outperform CE.** Therefore, the success of KD cannot attributed to the teacher's confidence itself (i.e., the maximal output).

Furthermore, as shown in [28], CWTM does not always outperform CE. We also found that CWTM-Random is very sensitive to the choice of β. The non-uniform sampled importance leads to the possible improvement of CWTM variants. We conjecture that it might improve the model by helping the optimization to escape saddle points. Further exploration is left in future work.

DKPP removes the class-similarity information contained in teacher's outputs by permuting logits of non-ground-truth classes. **DKPP still clearly outperforms CE, which means the responses in non-ground-truth classes contribute to the effectiveness of KD.** Similar to Labels Smoothing, the responses in non-ground-truth classes prevent the student from becoming overconfident. Furthermore, we can also observe that there is a gap between DKPP and KD. Compared to KD, **the student performance does decrease by removing the similarity information in the teacher's outputs. The class-similarity information also contributes to the effectiveness of KD.** These two effective components are further discussed in Sect. 5.4.

The observations above are consistent with [28], but we gain more insights into the KD technique with more experiments. From these observations, we conclude that both non-ground-truth classes' responses and class-similarity information in the teacher's outputs contribute to the success of KD.

4   Introspective Learning with Online Self-explanations

In this section, we focus on improve the model performance with the explanations created on it. Given a training sample $(\boldsymbol{x}_i, \boldsymbol{y}_i)$ and a neural network $f(\cdot)$ to be trained, the outputs of the forward inference are $\boldsymbol{p}_i$. A saliency method is applied on the neural network to generate one explanation for each output class $\boldsymbol{E}_i = (\boldsymbol{e}_i^1, \boldsymbol{e}_i^2, \cdots, \boldsymbol{e}_i^c)$.

One desired property of the explanations $\boldsymbol{E}_i$ is that the explanations are class-discriminative. In terms of a single sample, the similarity between explanations corresponds to the similarity between output classes. For instance, if the similarity between the explanations of two output classes $sim(\boldsymbol{e}_i^1, \boldsymbol{e}_i^2)$ is high, the 1st output class and the 2nd one are similar to each other. The similarity can be measured with different metrics, such as cosine distance, multi-scale mean squared error [32], and Wasserstein distance [33]. In our experiments, we find that the simplest one (i.e., Cosine distance) already captures the similarity between two created explanations.

This section proposes an algorithm to train neural networks with the online self-explanations created during training. As shown in Algorithm 1, our LE (**L**earning with **E**xplanations) consists of two training stages.

In the first training stage, the network is trained with one-hot labels. The goal is to initialize the network to a good starting point for generating meaningful explanations. Without warming up, the created explanations are almost random initially, which will mislead the training process.

In the second training stage, the network is trained with online soft labels extracted from online self-explanations. Given a training sample $(\boldsymbol{x}_i, \boldsymbol{y}_i)$, without

---

Algorithm 1: Introspective Learning with Online Self-explanations

---
Data: training samples $\{(\boldsymbol{x}_i, \boldsymbol{y}_i)\}_{i=1}^n$, a smooth factor α
Result: a well-trained neural network

Stage 1 (Warm-up Training):
    train the network with one-hot labels $\mathcal{L}(\boldsymbol{p}_i, \boldsymbol{y}_i)$;

Stage 2 (Training with Online Self-explanations):
 for *each epoch* **do**
    make forward inference $\boldsymbol{p}_i = f(\boldsymbol{x}_i)$;
    generate explanations $\boldsymbol{E}_i = (\boldsymbol{e}_i^1, \boldsymbol{e}_i^2, \cdots, \boldsymbol{e}_i^c)$;
    generate targets $\boldsymbol{q}_i = (q_i^1, q_i^2, \cdots, q_i^c)$ with $\boldsymbol{E}_i$ and $\boldsymbol{y}_i$;
    train with the loss $\mathcal{L}(\boldsymbol{p}_i, \boldsymbol{q}_i) + \lambda \mathcal{L}(\boldsymbol{p}_i, \boldsymbol{y}_i)$
 end

---

loss of generality, we assume the c-th class is the ground truth $y_i^c = 1$. In each epoch, we first classify the sample $\boldsymbol{p}_i = f(\boldsymbol{x}_i)$ and create explanations $\boldsymbol{E}_i$ for every classification prediction. We then create new targets $\boldsymbol{q}_i = (q_i^1, q_i^2, \cdots, q_i^c)$ to compute the loss instead of using the one-hot labels or soft labels provided by a teacher. The new targets $\boldsymbol{q}_i$ are based on the explanations $\boldsymbol{E}_i$ and the one-hot labels $\boldsymbol{y}_i$. The one corresponds to the ground-truth class is specified with a pre-defined value $q_i^c = \alpha$, and the ones correspond to other classes are computed as

$$q_i^k = (1 - \alpha) * \frac{cos(\boldsymbol{e}_i^k, \boldsymbol{e}_i^c) + 1}{\sum_{m=1}^{c-1}(cos(\boldsymbol{e}_i^m, \boldsymbol{e}_i^c) + 1)} \tag{6}$$

where $k \neq c$. Since $cos(\boldsymbol{e}_i^k, \boldsymbol{e}_i^c) \in [-1, 1]$, 1 is added to the similarity value for numerical stability. The training process is also regularized by a cross-entropy term with one-hot labels and a common weight-decay term.

Rationale Behind the Proposed Learning Procedure: Our proposed learning procedure is motivated by the conclusions drawn in Sect. 3. We propose new targets to guide the training of the network. With the proposed targets, the responses in non-ground-truth classes (wrong responses) prevent the network from becoming over-confident. The wrong responses are not randomly computed but with the information about the explanations. As the similarity between classes corresponds to the similarity between their explanations, the proposed targets contain class-similarity information. Therefore, our learning procedure includes effective components of KD without requiring a powerful teacher model. In other words, our proposed learning procedure can be seen as distilling knowledge directly from online explanations.

Computational Cost of the Proposed Learning Procedure: In our proposed algorithm, an extra cost to compute the explanations is required. For each training sample in a mini-batch, c explanations are required to compute the corresponding targets. Using the implementation trick in [34], all c explanations

Table 2. Test accuracy (%) of CNNs trained with different regularizations on CIFAR10 dataset. Our proposed LE outperforms the standard training procedure CE and others with various regularization methods.

Model	CE	Dropout	LS	CP	LE($Grad\text{-}CAM$)
ResNet14	90,26(± 0.33)	90,33(± 0.15)	90,52(± 0.12)	90,42(± 0.14)	**91,21**(± 0.07)
ResNet8	87,95(± 0.32)	88,02(± 0.02)	88,14(± 0.16)	88,25(± 0.13)	**88,70**(± 0.18)

can be obtained in a single backward pass. Hence, compared to the computationally expensive teacher model in KD, the extra cost brought by our learning procedure is much less.

5   Experiments

Following the previous work [35], we use ResNet [36] in our experiment. On CIFAR10, the standard data augmentation is applied as in Sect. 3. The models are trained with a batch size of 128 for 160 epochs using SGD. We start with a learning rate of 0.1, divide it by 10 at the 80-th and the 120-th epoch. In the proposed algorithm, we set the smoothing factor $\alpha = 0.9$ and the regularization strength $\lambda = 0.1$.

The method we use to create explanations is the commonly used *Grad-CAM*. It requires to specify a layer to create explanations. And we choose the last convolutional layer. The effectiveness of different explanation methods is also analyzed in Sect. 5.4.

We compare the model trained with our proposed algorithm with the ones trained with different regularizations, the ones learned from peer networks, and the ones learned from a strong teacher. We further investigate our proposal with ablation studies in order to validate our hypothesis in the paper.

5.1   Networks Trained with Regularizations

The proposed algorithm can be viewed as a regularization method. It regularizes the networks so that their predictions are consistent with their explanations. In this experiment, we compare our method with other regularization methods, including Dropout, Label Smoothing (LS), and Confidence Penalty (CP).

For Dropout, we drop neurons of the last layer of each block-layer with the drop rate in the range [0,1, 0.25, 0.5, 0.75], where 0.1 corresponds to the best performance. For LS, we vary the smoothing factor over [0.6, 0.7, 0.8, 0.9], where a factor of 0.9 turns out to be the best. For CP, we vary the penalty strength over [0.1, 0.3, 0.5, 1.0, 2.0, 4.0, 8.0], where the value of 0.5 gives the best result. The corresponding performance is listed in Table 2.

All the regularizations outperform the baseline CE by alleviating the overfitting problem. Meanwhile, our method LE is superior to other regularization methods. LS is similar to ours, which is expected, as it also has responses in

Table 3. Test error (%) of MLPs trained with various regularizations on MNIST dataset. In our implementation, our LE achieves the best with tiny variance.

Implementations	CE	Dropout	LS	CP	$LE_{(Grad)}$
[21]	–	$1.28_{(\pm 0.06)}$	$1.23_{(\pm 0.06)}$	$1.17_{(\pm 0.06)}$	–
[38]	1.38	1.34	1.40	1.36	–
Ours	$1.39_{(\pm\,0.05)}$	$1.27_{(\pm 0.02)}$	$1.25_{(\pm 0.02)}$	$1.18_{(\pm 0.06)}$	$\mathbf{1,10}_{(\pm 0.03)}$

non-ground-truth classes in its specified targets. However, in LS, the specified response for each non-ground-truth class is the same. It results in the loss of information in the logits about the similarity between classes [37]. Different from LS, the specified targets in our method LE include the class-similarity information.

Following the research line, we also compare our method with others in the setting of previous work [21,38]. Concretely speaking, an Multilayer Perceptron (MLP) with fully connected layers of the form 784-1024-1024-10 and ReLU activations is trained on the MNIST dataset [39]. All models are trained with a batch size of 16 for 50 epochs using SGD with a learning rate of 0.01 and moment 0.9.

When training MLPs with our proposed algorithm, we applied *Grad* approach to create explanations since *Grad-CAM* is only specific for CNNs. 10 epochs are used for warm-up training in our learning procedure. For other regularizations, we explore their hyper-parameters in the same space as above and show the best of the exploration.

The comparison results in this simple setting are shown in Table 3. The scores of the first two rows are taken from their papers. The third row shows our implementations. In this simple setting with MLP, our method LE also outperforms other regularization methods. We only compare with the popular and state-of-the-art regularization methods and the ones related to our work. The score of VIB regularization proposed in [38] is not listed since the setting is slightly different. Even though they require 12,03% more parameters and 200 epochs to train (test error 1,13%), our score still slight outperform theirs.

We also visualize the created explanations during training in Fig. 1. In each row, the first column shows the original image, and others columns show explanations corresponding to different classes $E_i = (e_i^1, e_i^2, \cdots, e_i^{10})$ (10 classes both in MNIST and in CIFAR10).

From Fig. 1, we find that the generated explanations are consistent with human's prior knowledge. For instance, in the first row of Fig. 1a, the score under the explanation of the last column (the ground-truth class) is $cos(e_i^*, e_i^*) = 1$. In the explanations corresponding to digits of 4 and 7, part of input features supports the corresponding scores. the similarity between the explanation of digit 4 and the explanation of the digit 9 (ground-truth class) is high. Besides, the similarity between the explanation of digit 7 and the explanation of the digit 9 is also high. Also, In the first row of Fig. 1b, the explanation of the ground-truth class focuses on the pixels of the truck, while others focus on irrelevant pixels.

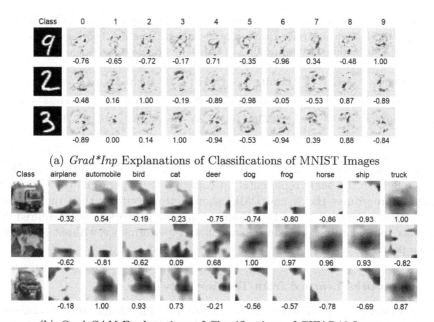

(a) *Grad*Inp* Explanations of Classifications of MNIST Images

(b) *Grad-CAM* Explanations of Classifications of CIFAR10 Images

Fig. 1. The explanations and the similarity scores: For each image, we generate an explanation for each output class. The score under each explanation is the similarity score between the corresponding class and the ground truth class.

The explanation of *automobile* class is more similar to that of the ground-truth class, and the corresponding cosine distance score is higher than that of others.

5.2 Networks Learned from Peer Networks

In our proposed algorithm, we trains a network with knowledge in explanations created on the same network. In this section, we compare the model trained with our learning procedure with the ones learned from peer networks.

We first train a ResNet8 using one-hot labels. Using its outputs as targets, we then train another ResNet8 from scratch. The second network is called Born-Again Network (BAN). We explore the temperature in the range of [1, 2, 5, 10, 20]. The training process can also be regularized by a cross-entropy term computed with one-hot true labels (BAN+L). The regularization strength is $\lambda = 0.1$. Similarly, we conduct experiments on ResNet14.

Another way to learn from peer networks is to train two networks at the same time. The loss of each network consists of two terms: a cross-entropy term computed with one-hot labels and a regularization term corresponding to the KL distance between outputs of the two networks. The regularization strength is $\lambda = 0.1$. With such loss, the two networks learn from each other, which is called Deep Mutual Learning (DML).

Table 4. Test accuracy (%) of CNNs learned from peer networks on CIFAR10. Compared to those students trained with a peer network (i.e., a network with the same structure), our learning procedure LE$_{(Grad\text{-}CAM)}$ shows the best.

Model	CE	DML	BAN	BAN+L	LE$_{(Grad\text{-}CAM)}$
ResNet14	90,26$_{(\pm0.33)}$	90,39$_{(\pm0.15)}$	90,58$_{(\pm0.15)}$	90,83$_{(\pm0.28)}$	**91,21**$_{(\pm0.07)}$
ResNet8	87,95$_{(\pm0.32)}$	88,23$_{(\pm0.27)}$	87,22$_{(\pm0.03)}$	88,03$_{(\pm0.33)}$	**88,70**$_{(\pm0.18)}$

The test accuracy is shown in Table 4. In BAN, although the two ResNet8 networks have the same representation capacity, it outperforms the CE. Both training procedures (BAN and DML) show better accuracy than the baseline CE without requiring a teacher. However, a peer network is still required. In contrast, our learning procedure shows better performance without a teacher and a peer.

5.3 Networks Learned from Teacher Networks

A large number of publications focus on the dark knowledge to be transferred from a teacher to a student, where Hinton et al. first represent the knowledge with soft labels (outputs of the teacher) as KD [12]. In other works, the knowledge is presented by the intermediate representations (Hint) [24], teacher's attention(AT) [25] or Flow of solution procedure (FSP) [26].

The setting in each method is as follows: Hint) we take the representation of the 2nd layer of ResNet26 as the Hint. AT) We use activation-based attentions where activation of feature maps are averaged over the channel dimension and normalized. The attention in all three layers of ResNet26 is captured to guide the training of the student. FSP) The flows between the 1st and the 2nd layers and between the 2nd and the 3rd layers are transferred from the teacher ResNet26 to the student. Following the experimental setup in these papers, we combine AT, FSP with Hinton's KD to achieve better distillation effectiveness.

Another way to learn from the teacher is to learn with the help of an assistant (TAKD) [35]. The learning procedure first distills the knowledge from the teacher to an assistant and then distills knowledge from the assistant to a student. In our experiments, we apply Hinton's distillation method in both distillation stages. I.e., the teachers, the assistants and the students are (ResNet26 → ResNet20 → ResNet14) and (ResNet26 → ResNet14 → ResNet8), respectively.

In all distillation methods, similar to [40], the temperature is set to 4, and $\lambda = 0.1$ for the regularization corresponding to a cross-entropy term with one-hot labels. All other settings follow the original papers.

The test accuracy of each distillation method is shown in Table 5. Our proposed algorithm outperforms most of the distillation methods. Furthermore, without requiring a separate teacher network, LE is also comparable to the best method. We found that the rank of different KD methods is sensitive to the experimental setting. Our learning procedure achieves competitive performance without the cost to search for a suitable teacher model.

Table 5. Test accuracy (%) of CNNs learned from more powerful teacher networks on CIFAR10: The teacher ResNet26 achieves 91,51%. Compared to those students trained with a teacher, Our learning procedure LE$_{(Grad\text{-}CAM)}$ achieves competitive performance requiring no teacher.

Model	KD	Hint	AT_Hinton	FSP_Hinton	TAKD	LE$_{(Grad\text{-}CAM)}$
ResNet14	91,14(±0.19)	91,29(±0.19)	91,31(±0.19)	**91,42**(±0.19)	91,27(±0.19)	91,21 (± 0.07)
ResNet8	88,07(±0.36)	88,52(±0.19)	88,15(±0.19)	88,11(±0.19)	88,09(±0.19)	**88,70**(±0.18)

5.4 Ablation Study

Class-Similarity Information in Explanations. We hypothesis that class-similarity information in explanations contributes to the success of the proposed algorithm is validated through the ablation study. In the second training stage of Algorithm 1, we create new targets $q_i = (q_i^1, q_i^2, \cdots, q_i^c)$ using explanations. The responses in non-ground-truth classes contain class-similarity information. In the experiments, we permute the elements in q_i except for the one corresponding to ground-truth classes (LE-Permut). By doing this, the class-similarity information provided by explanations is removed. The performance is shown in Table 6.

Table 6. Test accuracy (%) of models trained with the proposed learning procedure on MNIST and CIFAR10 datasets.

Datasets	MNIST	CIFAR10	
Models	MLP1024	ResNet14	ResNet8
CE	98,61(±0.05)	90,26(±0.33)	87,95(±0.32)
LE-Permut	98,81(±0.04)	90,91(±0.16)	88,22(±0.05)
LE(*Grad*)	98,90(±0.03)	91,01(±0.12)	88,27(±0.05)
LE(*Grad-CAM*)	–	91.21(±0.07)	88,70(±0.18)

Compared with LE-Permut, both LE(*Grad*) and LE(*Grad-CAM*) show better performance. The observation indicates that class-similarity information is an essential component of the proposed algorithm. Another effective component that contributes to the our algorithm's effectiveness is the responses in the non-ground-truth classes, which is shown by the observation, that LE-Permut outperforms the baseline CE without similarity information.

Interestingly, LE-Permut also outperforms the Label Smoothing (LS) (90,52(± 0.12)% on ResNet14, 88,14(± 0.16)% on ResNet8). LS sets the same response for all the non-ground-truth classes, which leads to the fact that the learned representations of a class have the same distance as those of other classes. The responses in non-ground-truth classes in LS prevents overfitting problem. However, the symmetry property constrains the learning of representations.

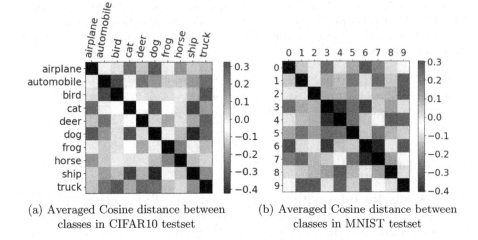

(a) Averaged Cosine distance between classes in CIFAR10 testset

(b) Averaged Cosine distance between classes in MNIST testset

Fig. 2. Visualization of class-similarity information in explanations

By randomly specify the response in the non-ground-truth classes, LE-Permut prevents both overfitting problem and the symmetry problem.

We also visualize the class-similarity information in Fig. 2. Each grid corresponds to the cosine distance between two explanations of two classes. The distance scores are averaged across the images in the test dataset. In Fig. 3a, the two classes in each pair $\{(truck, automobile), (dog, cat)\}$ are similar to each other. In Fig. 3b, we observe that the two classes in each class pair $\{(0,6), (1,7), (3,5), (4,9)\}$ are more similar to each other than other class pairs. The observations are consistent with the human's prior knowledge. It is therefore not surprising that the model can be improved by such knowledge.

Learning with Different Explanation Methods. In most experiments above, we apply *Grad-CAM* (one of the state-of-the-art methods) to create explanations. The method is shown to create class-discriminative explanations, which can better describe the relationship between classes than others. In this Section, we show how the effectiveness of our proposed learning procedure is affected by different saliency (explanation) methods.

In Sect. 2, we introduce four popular and efficient saliency methods to create explanations, *Grad, Grad*Input, GuidedBP* and *Grad-CAM*. The work [41] using Spearman Rank Correlation to evaluates the class-discriminativeness of each saliency method quantitatively. The evaluation results shows that the methods can be ordered by the class-discriminativeness as: *Grad*Input< GuidedBP < Grad < Grad-CAM*.

We apply them in the proposed learning procedure, respectively. The test accuracy of models is shown in Fig. 3. The order by class-discriminativeness is consistent with the order by corresponding test accuracy. When the saliency method is more class-discriminative, the class-similarity information in their explanations is more accurate, the performance of the corresponding model is better.

We claim that the similarity information between classes is an effective component of KD. Our learning procedure integrates the effective component by extracting similarity information from self-explanations. This experiment further confirms our claims.

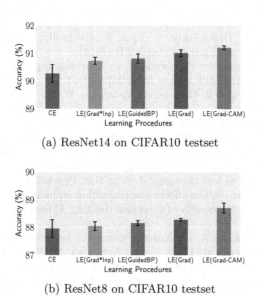

(a) ResNet14 on CIFAR10 testset

(b) ResNet8 on CIFAR10 testset

Fig. 3. Test accuracy (%) of models learned with the proposed learning procedure with different explanation methods: The one trained with the state-of-the-art explanation method (*Grad-CAM*) shows the best performance.

6   Conclusion and Future Work

Knowledge distillation (KD) explores the capacity of neural networks with privileged information provided by a strong teacher network. This work reveals the effective components of KD. Motivated by the findings, we propose an introspective learning algorithm to explore the network capacity by leveraging online self-explanation. The models trained with our proposed algorithm outperform those trained with the standard training procedure and various regularizations. Compared to the ones learned from peer networks or powerful teacher networks, our algorithm still shows competitive performance without peers or teachers.

To the best of our knowledge, this is the first work to leverage online explanations to improve the model training process. Our proposed algorithm illustrates one way to extract knowledge from saliency map explanations. The explanations beyond saliency maps [42–44] can also be applied to implement introspective learning in a different way. We leave other possibilities to learn with explanations in future investigation.

References

1. Kastner, S., Pinsk, M.A., Weerd, P.D., Desimone, R., Ungerleider, L.G.: Increased activity in human visual cortex during directed attention in the absence of visual stimulation. Neuron **22**, 751–761 (1999)
2. Simonyan, K., Vedaldi, A., Zisserman, A.: Deep inside convolutional networks: visualising image classification models and saliency maps. In: ICLR (2013)
3. Springenberg, J.T., Dosovitskiy, A., Brox, T., Riedmiller, M.A.: Striving for simplicity: the all convolutional net. In: ICLR (2014)
4. Shrikumar, A., Greenside, P., Kundaje, A.: Learning important features through propagating activation differences. In: ICML (2017)
5. Selvaraju, R.R., Cogswell, M., Das, A., Vedantam, R., Parikh, D., Batra, D., et al.: Grad-cam: visual explanations from deep networks via gradient-based localization. In: ICCV, pp. 618–626 (2017)
6. Gu, J., Tresp, V.: Contextual prediction difference analysis for explaining individual image classifications. arXiv preprint arXiv:1910.09086 (2019)
7. Wilson, T.D., Schooler, J.W.: Thinking too much: introspection can reduce the quality of preferences and decisions. J. Pers. Soc. Psychol. **60**(2), 181–192 (1991)
8. Leisti, T., Häkkinen, J.: The effect of introspection on judgment and decision making is dependent on the quality of conscious thinking. Conscious. Cogn. **42**, 340–351 (2016)
9. Vapnik, V., Vashist, A.: A new learning paradigm: learning using privileged information. Neural Netw. Off. J. Int. Neural Netw. Soc. **22**(5–6), 544–557 (2009)
10. Vapnik, V., Izmailov, R.: Learning using privileged information: similarity control and knowledge transfer. J. Mach. Learn. Res. **16**, 2023–2049 (2015)
11. Lopez-Paz, D., Bottou, L., Schölkopf, B., Vapnik, V.: Unifying distillation and privileged information. In: ICLR (2015)
12. Hinton, G., Vinyals, O., Dean, J.: Distilling the knowledge in a neural network. stat 1050, 9 2015
13. Ba, J., Caruana, R.: Do deep nets really need to be deep? In: NeurIPS (2013)
14. Ancona, M.B., Ceolini, E., Öztireli, C., Gross, M.: Towards better understanding of gradient-based attribution methods for deep neural networks. In: ICLR (2017)
15. Bach, S., Binder, A., Montavon, G., Klauschen, F., Müller, K.R., Samek, W.: On pixel-wise explanations for non-linear classifier decisions by layer-wise relevance propagation. PLoS One **10**, e0130140 (2015)
16. Smilkov, D., Thorat, N., Kim, B., Viégas, F., Wattenberg, M.: SmoothGrad: removing noise by adding noise. arXiv preprint arXiv:1706.03825 (2017)
17. Sundararajan, M., Taly, A., Yan, Q.: Axiomatic attribution for deep networks. In: ICML (2017)
18. Gu, J., Yang, Y., Tresp, V.: Understanding individual decisions of CNNs via contrastive backpropagation. In: Jawahar, C.V., Li, H., Mori, G., Schindler, K. (eds.) ACCV 2018. LNCS, vol. 11363, pp. 119–134. Springer, Cham (2019). https://doi.org/10.1007/978-3-030-20893-6_8
19. Gu, J., Tresp, V.: Saliency methods for explaining adversarial attacks. arXiv preprint arXiv:1908.08413 (2019)
20. Szegedy, C., et al.: Going deeper with convolutions. In: CVPR (2014)
21. Pereyra, G., Tucker, G., Chorowski, J., Kaiser, L., Hinton, G.: Regularizing neural networks by penalizing confident output distributions. In: ICLR Workshop (2017)
22. Srivastava, N., Hinton, G., Krizhevsky, A., Sutskever, I., Salakhutdinov, R.: Dropout: a simple way to prevent neural networks from overfitting. J. Mach. Learn. Res. **15**, 1929–1958 (2014)

23. Buciluǎ, C., Caruana, R., Niculescu-Mizil, A.: Model compression. In: Proceedings of the 12th ACM SIGKDD International Conference on Knowledge Discovery and Data Mining, pp. 535–541 (2006)
24. Romero, A., Ballas, N., Kahou, S.E., Chassang, A., Gatta, C., Bengio, Y.: FitNets: hints for thin deep nets. In: ICLR (2014)
25. Zagoruyko, S., Komodakis, N.: Paying more attention to attention: improving the performance of convolutional neural networks via attention transfer. In: ICLR (2016)
26. Yim, J., Joo, D., Bae, J., Kim, J.: A gift from knowledge distillation: fast optimization, network minimization and transfer learning. In: CVPR, pp. 4133–4141 (2017)
27. Yuan, L., Tay, F.E., Li, G., Wang, T., Feng, J.: Revisiting knowledge distillation via label smoothing regularization. In: IEEE/CVF Conference on Computer Vision and Pattern Recognition (CVPR) (2020)
28. Furlanello, T., Lipton, Z.C., Tschannen, M., Itti, L., Anandkumar, A.: Born again neural networks. In: ICML (2018)
29. Gu, J., Tresp, V.: Search for better students to learn distilled knowledge. arXiv preprint arXiv:2001.11612 (2020)
30. Zhang, Y., Xiang, T., Hospedales, T.M., Lu, H.: Deep mutual learning. In: CVPR (2018) 4320–4328
31. Krizhevsky, A., et al.: Learning multiple layers of features from tiny images. Technical report, Citeseer (2009)
32. Wang, Z., Simoncelli, E.P., Bovik, A.C.: Multiscale structural similarity for image quality assessment. In: 2003 The Thirty-Seventh Asilomar Conference on Signals, Systems & Computers, vol. 2, pp. 1398–1402. IEEE (2003)
33. Villani, C.: The Wasserstein distances. In: Villani, C. (ed.) Optimal Transport. Grundlehren der mathematischen Wissenschaften (A Series of Comprehensive Studies in Mathematics), vol. 338, pp. 93–111. Springer, Berlin (2009). https://doi.org/10.1007/978-3-540-71050-9_6
34. Goodfellow, I.: Efficient per-example gradient computations. Technical report, Google Inc., Mountain View, CA, (2015)
35. Mirzadeh, S.I., Farajtabar, M., Li, A., Ghasemzadeh, H.: Improved knowledge distillation via teacher assistant: bridging the gap between student and teacher. arXiv preprint arXiv:1902.03393 (2019)
36. He, K., Zhang, X., Ren, S., Sun, J.: Deep residual learning for image recognition. In: 2016 IEEE Conference on Computer Vision and Pattern Recognition (CVPR), pp. 770–778 (2015)
37. Muller, R.J., Kornblith, S., Hinton, G.E.: When does label smoothing help? ArXiv abs/1906.02629 (2019)
38. Alemi, A.A., Fischer, I., Dillon, J.V., Murphy, K.: Deep variational information bottleneck. In: ICLR (2017)
39. LeCun, Y., Bottou, L., Bengio, Y., Haffner, P., et al.: Gradient-based learning applied to document recognition. Proc. IEEE 86, 2278–2324 (1998)
40. Crowley, E.J., Gray, G., Storkey, A.J.: Moonshine: distilling with cheap convolutions. In: Advances in Neural Information Processing Systems, pp. 2888–2898 (2018)
41. Adebayo, J., Gilmer, J., Muelly, M., Goodfellow, I., Hardt, M., Kim, B.: Sanity checks for saliency maps. In: NeurIPS, pp. 9525–9536 (2018)
42. Gu, J., Tresp, V.: Semantics for global and local interpretation of deep neural networks. arXiv preprint arXiv:1910.09085 (2019)

43. Kim, B., Wattenberg, M., Gilmer, J., Cai, C., Wexler, J., Viegas, F., et al.: Interpretability beyond feature attribution: quantitative testing with concept activation vectors (TCAV). In: International Conference on Machine Learning, pp. 2668–2677. PMLR (2018)
44. Gu, J., Tresp, V.: Neural network memorization dissection. arXiv preprint arXiv:1911.09537 (2019)

Hyperparameter-Free Out-of-Distribution Detection Using Cosine Similarity

Engkarat Techapanurak[1]([email]) (iD), Masanori Suganuma[1,2] (iD),
and Takayuki Okatani[1,2] (iD)

[1] Tohoku University, Sendai 980-8579, Japan
{engkarat,suganuma,okatani}@vision.is.tohoku.ac.jp
[2] RIKEN Center for AIP, Saitama, Japan

Abstract. The ability to detect out-of-distribution (OOD) samples is vital to secure the reliability of deep neural networks in real-world applications. Considering the nature of OOD samples, detection methods should not have hyperparameters that need to be tuned depending on incoming OOD samples. However, most recently proposed methods do not meet this requirement, leading to a compromised performance in real-world applications. In this paper, we propose a simple and computationally efficient, hyperparameter-free method that uses cosine similarity. Although recent studies show its effectiveness for metric learning, it remains uncertain if cosine similarity works well also for OOD detection. There are several differences in the design of output layers from the metric learning methods; they are essential to achieve the best performance. We show through experiments that our method outperforms the existing methods on the evaluation test recently proposed by Shafaei et al. which takes the above issue of hyperparameter dependency into account; it achieves at least comparable performance to the state-of-the-art on the conventional test, where other methods but ours are allowed to use explicit OOD samples for determining hyperparameters. Lastly, we provide a brief discussion of why cosine similarity works so well, referring to an explanation by Hsu et al.

1 Introduction

It is widely recognized that deep neural networks tend to show unpredictable behaviors for *out-of-distribution* (OOD) samples, i.e., samples coming from a different distribution from that of the training samples. They often give high confidence (i.e., high softmax value) to OOD samples, not only to *in-distribution* (ID) samples (i.e., test samples from the same distribution as the training samples). Therefore, it has been a major research topic to detect OOD samples in classification performed by deep neural networks; many methods have been proposed so far [1–8].

Electronic supplementary material The online version of this chapter (https://doi.org/10.1007/978-3-030-69538-5_4) contains supplementary material, which is available to authorized users.

H. Ishikawa et al. (Eds.): ACCV 2020, LNCS 12625, pp. 53–69, 2021.
https://doi.org/10.1007/978-3-030-69538-5_4

A problem with the existing methods, especially those currently recognized as the state-of-the-art in the community, is that they have hyperparameters specific to OOD detection. They determine these hyperparameters using a certain amount of OOD samples as 'validation' data; that is, these studies assume the availability of (at least a small amount of) OOD samples. This assumption, however, is unlikely to hold true in practice; considering the definition of OOD, it is more natural to assume its distribution to be unknown. Even when the assumption is indeed wrong, it will be fine if OOD detection performance is insensitive to the choice of the hyperparamters, more rigorously, *if the hyperparameters tuned on the assumed OOD samples generalize well to incoming OOD samples we encounter in practice.* However, a recent study [9] indicates that this is not the case, concluding that none of the existing methods is ready to use, especially for the tasks with high-dimensional data space, e.g., image classification.

In this paper, we propose a novel method that uses cosine similarity for OOD detection, in which class probabilities are modeled using softmax of scaled cosine similarity. It is free of any hyperparameters associated with OOD detection, and thus there is no need to access OOD samples to determine hyperparameters, making the proposed method free from the above issue. We show through experiments that it outperforms the existing methods by a large margin on the recently proposed test [9], which takes the above issue of hyperparameter dependency into account; it also attains at least comparable performance to the state-of-the-art methods on the conventional test, in which the other methods but ours tune hyperparameters using explicit OOD samples.

It should be noted that a concurrent work [10] also shows the effectiveness of softmax of the scaled cosine similarity for OOD detection. Our method is technically mostly the same, but the present paper shows several different results/conclusions from their paper. The paper [10] shows a conjecture that the scaling factor of the cosine similarity approximates the probability of an input being in-distribution, contributing to improved detection performance. In this paper, however, we show empirical evidence that this is not the case. It is also noted that, although recent methods for metric learning [11–16] similarly employ scaled cosine similarity as well, they do not guarantee its effectiveness on OOD detection. There are several differences from them in the output layer's design, which contributes to detection accuracy. Concerning this, we provide a detailed ablation study to clarify the method's differences from common metric learning approaches.

2 Related Works

2.1 Uncertainty of Prediction

It is known that when applied to classification tasks, deep neural networks often exhibit overconfidence for unseen inputs. Many studies have been conducted to find a solution to this issue. A popular approach is to evaluate uncertainty of a prediction and use it as its reliability measure. There are many studies on this approach, most of which are based on the framework of Bayesian neural networks or its approximation [17–20]. It is reported that predicted uncertainty is useful for real-world applications [21–25]. However, it is still an open problem to accurately evaluate uncertainty. There are also studies on calibration of confidence scores [26–28]. Some studies propose to build a meta system overseeing the classifier that can estimate the reliability of its prediction [29,30].

2.2   Out-of-Distribution (OOD) Detection

Detection Methods. A more direct approach to the above issue is OOD detection. A baseline method that thresholds confidence score, i.e., the maximum softmax output, is evaluated in [1]. This study presents a design of experiments for evaluation of OOD detection methods, which has been employed in the subsequent studies. Since then, many studies have been conducted. It should be noted that these methods have hyperparameters for OOD detection, which need to be determined in some way. Some studies assume a portion of OOD samples to be given and regard them as a 'validation' set, by which the hyperparemters are determined.

ODIN [2] applies perturbation with a constant magnitude ϵ to an input x in the direction of increasing the confidence score (i.e., the maximum softmax) and then uses the increased score in the same way as the baseline. An observation behind this procedure is that such perturbation tends to increase confidence score more for ID samples than for OOD samples. Rigorously, x is perturbed to increase a temperature-scaled softmax value. Thus, ODIN has two hyperparameters ϵ and the softmax temperature. In the experiments reported in [2], ϵ as well as the temperature are determined by using a portion of samples from a target OOD dataset; this is done for each pair of ID and OOD datasets.

The current state-of-the-art of OOD detection is achieved by the methods [3,4] employing input perturbation similar to ODIN. It should be noted that there are many studies with different motivations, such as generative models [31,32], a prior distribution [6], robustification by training networks to predict word embedding of class labels [5], pretraining of networks [33,34], and batchwise fine-tuning [7].

In [4], a method that employs an ensemble of networks and similar input perturbation is proposed, achieving the state-of-the-art performance. In the training step of this method, ID classes are split into two sets, one of which is virtually treated as ID classes and the other as OOD classes. A network is then trained so that the entropy for the former samples is minimized while that for the latter samples is maximized. Repeating this for different K splits of classes yields K leave-out classifiers (i.e., networks). At test time, an input x is given to these K networks, whose outputs are summed to calculate ID class scores and an OOD score, where x is perturbed with magnitude ϵ in the direction of minimizing the entropy. In the experiments, ϵ, the temperature, and additional hyperparameters are determined by selecting a particular dataset (i.e., iSUN [35]) as the OOD dataset, and OOD detection performance on different OOD datasets is evaluated.

In [3], another method is proposed, which models layer activation over ID samples with class-wise Gaussian distributions. It uses the induced Mahalanobis distances to class centroids for conducting the classification as well as OOD detection. It employs logistic regression integrating information from multiple layers and input perturbation similar to ODIN, which possesses several hyperparameters. For their determination, it is suggested to use explicit OOD samples, as in ODIN [2]. Another method is additionally suggested to avoid this potentially unrealistic assumption, which is to create adversarial examples for ID samples [36] and use them as OOD samples, determining the hyperparameters. However, even this method is not free of hyperparameters; the creation of adversarial examples needs at least one (i.e., perturbation magnitude). It is not discussed how to choose it in their paper.

Evaluation Methods. Most of the recent studies employ the following evaluation method [1]. Specifying a pair of ID and OOD datasets (e.g.., CIFAR-10 for ID and SVHN for OOD), it measures accuracy of distinguishing the OOD samples and ID samples. As the task is detection, appropriate metrics are used, such as accuracy at true positive rate (TPR) = 95%, area under the ROC curve (AUROC), and under the precision-recall curve (AUPR). As is noted in Sect. 1, most of the existing methods assume the availability of OOD samples and use them to determine their hyperparameters. Note that these OOD samples are selected from the *true* OOD dataset specified in this evaluation method. We will refer to this *one-vs-one* evaluation.

Recently, Shafaei et al. have raised a concern about the dependency of the existing methods on the explicit knowledge of the true OOD dataset, and proposed a novel evaluation method that aims at measuring the practical performance of OOD detection [9]. It assumes an ID dataset and multiple OOD datasets $\mathcal{D} = \{D_1, \ldots\}$ for evaluation. Then, the evaluation starts with choosing one dataset $D_i \in \mathcal{D}$ and use the samples from it to determine the hyperparameters of the method under evaluation; it then evaluates its detection accuracy when regarding each of the other datasets in $\mathcal{D}$ (i.e., $\mathcal{D} \backslash D_i$) as the OOD dataset, reporting the average accuracy over $\mathcal{D} \backslash D_i$. Note that this test returns the accuracy for each dataset in $\mathcal{D}$ (used for the assumed OOD dataset). We will refer to this *less-biased* evaluation.

2.3   Cosine Similarity

The proposed method employs softmax of scaled cosine similarity instead of ordinary softmax of logits. A similar approach has already been employed in recent studies of metric learning, such as L_2-constrained softmax [11], SphereFace [12], NormFace [13], CosFace [14], ArcFace [15], AdaCos [16], etc. Although it may seem straightforward to apply these methods to OOD detection, to the authors' knowledge, there is no study that has tried this before.

These metric learning methods are identical in that they use cosine similarity. They differ in i) if and how the weight w or the feature f of the last layer are normalized; ii) if and how margins are used with the cosine similarity to encourage maximization of inter-class variance and minimization of intra-class variance; and iii) how the scale parameter (i.e., s in (3)) is treated, i.e., as either a hyperparameter, a learnable parameter [13], or other [16]. According to this categorization, our method is the most similar to NormFace [13] and AdaCos [16], in which both w and f are normalized and no margin is utilized. However, our method still differs from these metric learning methods in that it predicts s along with class probabilities at inference time. Ours also differs in that it uses a single fully-connected layer to compute the cosine similarity, whereas these metric learning methods use two fully-connected layers.

3 Proposed Method

3.1 Softmax of Scaled Cosine Similarity

The standard formulation of multi-class classification is to make the network predict class probabilities for an input, and use cross-entropy loss to evaluate the correctness of the prediction. The predicted class probabilities are obtained by applying softmax to the linear transform $Wf + b$ of the activation or feature f of the last layer, and then the loss is calculated assuming 1-of-K coding of the true class c as

$$\mathcal{L} = -\log \frac{e^{w_c^\top f + b_c}}{\sum_{i=1}^{C} e^{w_i^\top f + b_i}}, \tag{1}$$

where $W = [w_1, \ldots, w_C]^\top$ and $b = [b_1, \ldots, b_C]^\top$.

Metric learning attempts to learn feature space suitable for the purpose of open-set classification, e.g., face verification. Unlike earlier methods employing triplet loss [37,38] and contrastive loss [39,40], recent methods [13–15] modify the loss (1) and minimize the cross entropy loss as with the standard multi-class classification. The main idea is to use the cosine of the angle between the weight w_i and the feature f as a class score. Specifically, $\cos \theta_i \equiv w_i^\top f / (\|w_i\| \|f\|)$ is used instead of the logit $w_i^\top f + b_i$ in (1); then a new loss is given as

$$\mathcal{L} = -\log \frac{e^{\cos \theta_c}}{\sum_{i=1}^{C} e^{\cos \theta_i}}. \tag{2}$$

The behavior of softmax, i.e., how soft its maximum operation will be, depends on the distribution of its inputs, which can be controlled by a scaling parameter of the inputs, called temperature T. This parameter is used for several purposes [26,41]. In metric learning methods, it is employed to widen the range $[-1, 1]$ of $\cos \theta_i$'s inputted to softmax; specifically, all the input cosine $\cos \theta_i$'s are scaled by a parameter $s(= 1/T)$, revising the above loss as

$$\mathcal{L} = -\log \frac{e^{s \cos \theta_c}}{\sum_{i=1}^{C} e^{s \cos \theta_i}}. \tag{3}$$

3.2   Predicting the Scaling Parameter

In most of the metric learning methods employing similar loss functions, the scaling parameter s in (3) is treated as either a hyperparameter chosen in a validation step or a parameter automatically determined in the training step [13,16] There is yet another method for determining s, which is to predict it from f together with class probabilities. This makes the method hyperparameter-free. Moreover, we empirically found that this performs the best. Among several ways of computing s from f, the following works the best:

$$s = \exp\{\mathrm{BN}(\boldsymbol{w}_s^\top \boldsymbol{f} + b_s)\}, \qquad (4)$$

where BN is batch normalization [42], and $\boldsymbol{w}_s$ and b_s are the weight and bias of the added branch to predict s.

3.3   Design of the Output Layer

In the aforementioned studies of metric learning, ResNets are employed as a base network and are modified to implement the softmax of cosine similarity. Modern CNNs like ResNets are usually designed to have a single fully-connected (FC) layer between the final pooling layer (i.e., global average pooling) and the network output. As ReLU activation function is applied to the inputs of the pooling layer, if we use the last FC layer for computing cosine similarity (i.e., treating its input as f and its weights as $\boldsymbol{w}_i$'s), then the elements of f take only non-negative values. Thus, the metric learning methods add an extra single FC layer on top of the FC layer and use the output of the first FC layer as f, making f (after normalization) distribute on the whole hypersphere. In short, the metric learning methods employ two FC layers at the final section of the network.

However, we found that for the purpose of OOD detection, having two fully-connected layers does not perform better than simply using the output of the final pooling layer as f. Details will be given in our experimental results. Note that in the case of a single FC layer, as f takes only non-negative values, f resides in the first quadrant of the space, which is very narrow subspace comparative to the entire space.

To train the modified network, we use a standard method. In our experiments, we employ SGD with weight decay as the optimizer, as in the previous studies of OOD detection [2–5]. In several studies of metric learning [14,15,43], weight decay is also employed on all the layers of networks. However, it may have different effects on the last layer of the network employing cosine similarity, where weights are normalized and thus its length does not affect the loss. In our experiments, we found that it works better when we do not apply weight decay to the last layer.

3.4   Detecting OOD Samples

Detecting OOD samples is performed in the following way. Given an input $\boldsymbol{x}$, our network computes $\cos\theta_i$ $(i = 1, \ldots, C)$. Let i_{max} be the index of the maximum of these cosine values. We use $\cos\theta_{i_{max}}$ for distinguishing ID and OOD samples. To be specific, setting a threshold, we declare x is an OOD sample if $\cos\theta_{i_{max}}$ is lower than it. Otherwise, we classify x into the class i_{max} with the predicted probability $e^{s\cos\theta_{i_{max}}}/\sum e^{s\cos\theta_i}$.

4 Experimental Results

4.1 Experimental Settings

We conducted experiments to evaluate the proposed method and compare it with existing methods.

Evaluation Methods. We employ the one-vs-one and less-biased evaluation methods explained in Sect. 2.2. The major difference between the two is in the assumption of prior knowledge about OOD datasets, which affects the determination of the hyperparameters of the OOD detection methods under evaluation. Note therefore that *the difference does not matter for our method*, as it does not need any hyperparameter; it only affects the other compared methods.

One-vs-one Evaluation. This evaluation assumes one ID and one OOD datasets. A network is trained on the ID dataset and each method attempts to distinguish ID and OOD samples using the network. Each method may use a fixed number of samples from the specified OOD datasets for its hyperparameter determination. We followed the experimental configurations commonly employed in the previous studies [2–4].

Less-biased Evaluation. This evaluation uses one ID and many OOD datasets. Each method may access one of the OOD datasets to determine its hyperparameters but its evaluation is conducted on the task of distinguishing the ID samples and samples from each of the other OOD datasets. We followed the study of Shafaei et al. [9] with slight modifications. First, we use AUROC instead of detection accuracy for evaluation metrics (additionally, accuracy at TPR= 95% and AUPR-IN in the supplementary material), as we believe that they are better metrics for detection tasks, and they are employed in the one-vs-one evaluation. Second, we add more OOD datasets to those used in their study to further increase the effectiveness and practicality of the evaluation.

Tasks and Datasets. We use CIFAR-10/100 for the target classification tasks in all the experiments. Using them as ID datasets, we use the following OOD datasets in one-vs-one evaluation: TinyImageNet (cropped and resized) [44], LSUN (cropped and resized) [45], iSUN [35],[1] SVHN [46] and Food-101 [47] For the less-biased evaluation, we additionally use STL-10 [48], MNIST [49], NotMNIST, and Fashion MNIST [50]. As for STL-10 and Food-101, we resize their images to 32×32 pixels.

---

[1] Datasets are available at https://github.com/facebookresearch/odin.

Remark. We found that the cropped images of TinyImageNet and LSUN that are provided by the GitHub repository of [2], which are employed in many recent studies, have a black frame of two-pixel width around them; see the supplementary material for details. Although we are not sure if this is intentional, considering that the frame will make OOD detection easier, we use two versions with/without the black frame in our experiments; the frame-free version is indicated by '*' in what follows. In the main paper, we show mainly results on the frame-free versions. Those on the original versions are shown in the supplementary material, although it does not affect our conclusion.

Networks and Their Training. For networks, we employ the two CNNs commonly used in the previous studies, i.e., *Wide ResNet* [51] and *DenseNet* [52] as the base networks. Following [2], we use WRN-28-10 and DenseNet-100-12 having 100 layers with growth rate 12. The former is trained with batch size $= 128$ for 200 epochs with weight decay $= 0.0005$, and the latter is trained with batch size $= 64$ for 300 epochs with weight decay $= 0.0001$. Dropout is not used in the both networks. We employ a learning rate schedule, where the learning rate starts with 0.1 and decreases by $1/10$ at 50% and 75% of the training steps.

The proposed method modifies the final layer and the loss of the base networks. Table 1 shows comparisons between the base networks and their modified version. The numbers are an average over five runs and their standard deviations are shown in parenthesis. It is seen that the modification tends to lower classification accuracy by a small amount. If this difference does matter, one may use the proposed network only for OOD detection and the standard network for ID classification.

Table 1. Performance of the base networks and their modified versions for the proposed method for the task of classification of ID (in-distribution) samples.

Network	In-Dist	Testing Accuracy	
		Standard	Cosine
Dense-100-12	CIFAR-10	95.11(0.10)	94.92(0.04)
	CIFAR-100	76.97(0.24)	75.65(0.12)
WRN-28-10	CIFAR-10	95.99(0.09)	95.72(0.05)
	CIFAR-100	81.04(0.37)	78.53(0.28)

Compared Methods. The methods we compare are as follows: the baseline method [1], ODIN [2], Mahalanobis detector [3][2], and leave-out ensemble [4]. The last two methods are reported to achieve the highest performance in the case of a single network and multiple networks, respectively. We conduct experiments separately with the first three and the last one due to the difference in settings. We report those with the leave-out ensemble in the supplementary material.

---

[2] We used the publicly available code: https://github.com/pokaxpoka/deep_Maha lanobis_detector.

All these methods (but the baseline) have hyperparameters for OOD detection. For ODIN and the Mahalanobis detector, we follow the authors' methods [2,3] to determine them using a portion of the true OOD dataset. For the leave-out ensemble (comparisons in the supplementary material), we use the values of detection accuracy from its paper [4], in which the authors use a specific OOD dataset (iSUN) for hyperparameter determination.

4.2 Comparison by Less-Biased Evaluation

We first show the performance of the four methods, i.e., the baseline, ODIN, the Mahalanobis detector, and ours, measured by the less-biased evaluation method. Figure 1 shows the results[3]. The details of the experimental settings are as follows. We use either CIFAR-10 or CIFAR-100 for the ID dataset. For the actual OOD dataset, we choose one of the eleven datasets described above and evaluate the OOD detection performance on each of the eleven ID-OOD pairs. For each ID-OOD pair, we use one of the rest (i.e., ten datasets) as a hypothesized OOD dataset, using which the hyperparameters are chosen for ODIN and Mahalanobis detector. We iterate this for the ten datasets. For each method/setting, we evaluate five models trained from different initial values. Finally, we calculate, for each method on each ID-OOD pair, the mean and standard deviation of AUROC (a bar and its error bar in Fig. 1) over the five models and the ten hypothesized datasets (for ODIN and Mahalanobis).

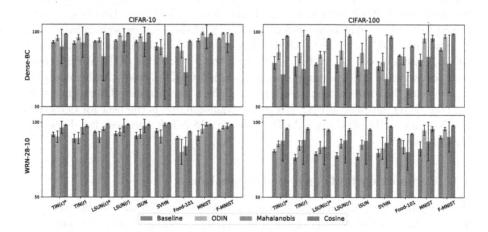

Fig. 1. OOD detection performance (AUROC) measured by the less-biased evaluation [9] for the baseline method [1], ODIN, [2] and the Mahalanobis detector [3], and the proposed one (denoted as 'Cosine'). Other metrics, i.e., accuracy at TPR = 95% and AUPR-IN, are reported in the supplementary material.

---

[3] A complete table including other metrics, i.e., accuracy at TPR = 95% and AUPR-IN, is shown in the supplementary material.

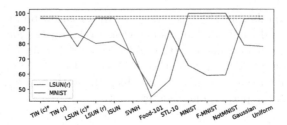

Fig. 2. Dependency of detection performance (AUROC) on the assumed OOD datasets (whose names are given in the horizontal axis) used for determining hyperparameters. Mahalanobis detector (solid lines) [3] and our method (broken lines). CIFAR-100 is used as ID and either LSUN(r) (in red color) or MNIST (in green color) is used as true OOD. DenseNet-100-12 is used for the network. Our method does not have hyperparameters and thus is independent of the assumed OOD dataset. (Color figure online)

It is seen from Fig. 1 that the proposed method consistently achieves better performance than others. It is noted that the Mahalanobis detector, which shows the state-of-the-art performance in the conventional (i.e., one-vs-one) evaluation, shows unstable behaviors; the mean of AUROC tends to vary significantly and the standard deviation is very large depending on the dataset used for hyperparameter determination. The same observation applies to ODIN.

This clearly demonstrates the issue with these methods, that is, their performance is dependent on the choice of the hyperparameters. On the other hand, the proposed method performs consistently for all the cases. This is also confirmed from Fig. 2, which shows a different plot of the same experimental result; it shows AUROC for a *single* OOD dataset instead of the *mean* over multiple OOD datasets shown in Fig. 1. It is seen that the performance of the Mahalanobis detector varies a lot depending on the assumed OOD dataset. Additionally, it can be seen that the dataset yielding the highest performance differs for different true OOD datasets; iSUN, TIN(r), or Gaussian etc. is the best for detecting LSUN(r) as OOD, whereas F-MNIST or NotMNIST is the best for detecting MNIST as OOD.

4.3   Comparison by One-vs-one Evaluation

We then show the comparison of the same four methods in the one-vs-one evaluation, which is employed in the majority of the previous studies. We ran each method five times from the training step, where the network weights are initialized randomly, and report the mean and standard deviation here. Table 2 shows the results. It is observed that the proposed method achieves better or at least competitive performance to the others. When using DenseNet-100-12, the proposed method consistently achieves higher performance than the Mahalanobis detector on almost all the datasets.

Table 2. OOD detection performance of the four methods measured by conventional one-vs-one evaluation.

ID	OOD	AUROC				ID	OOD	AUROC			
		Base [1]	ODIN [2]	Maha [3]	Cosine			Base [1]	ODIN [2]	Maha [3]	Cosine
Dense-100-12 CIFAR-10	TIN (c)	94.90(0.43)	98.79(0.32)	94.48(1.19)	**98.89(0.24)**	WRN-28-10 CIFAR-10	TIN (c)	93.86(0.90)	95.88(1.01)	95.99(1.04)	**98.35(0.32)**
	TIN (c)*	93.26(0.85)	96.67(0.97)	97.36(0.39)	**98.74(0.23)**		TIN (c)*	91.79(1.57)	92.17(2.19)	**98.50(0.11)**	98.17(0.33)
	TIN (r)	92.67(1.23)	97.20(1.17)	**98.91(0.23)**	98.82(0.29)		TIN (r)	89.21(2.65)	90.60(3.21)	**99.15(0.18)**	97.65(0.66)
	LSUN (c)	95.57(0.20)	98.48(0.14)	89.06(3.21)	**99.09(0.12)**		LSUN (c)	95.41(0.26)	97.20(0.15)	92.65(1.33)	**99.19(0.07)**
	LSUN (c)*	93.72(0.39)	96.41(0.52)	93.63(0.69)	**98.83(0.18)**		LSUN (c)*	93.67(0.50)	95.08(0.42)	96.90(0.35)	**98.98(0.07)**
	LSUN (r)	94.28(0.52)	98.43(0.49)	90.00(0.23)	**99.19(0.22)**		LSUN (r)	92.45(1.48)	94.48(1.70)	**99.37(0.13)**	98.59(0.34)
	iSUN	93.62(0.83)	97.92(0.71)	98.95(0.21)	**99.20(0.19)**		iSUN	91.22(2.05)	93.25(2.43)	**99.29(0.10)**	98.48(0.36)
	SVNH	90.28(2.47)	95.11(0.48)	98.89(0.37)	**99.11(0.36)**		SVNH	94.43(1.30)	93.34(3.60)	99.28(0.09)	**99.52(0.24)**
	Food-101	89.87(0.44)	92.06(0.71)	80.38(3.83)	**93.98(0.54)**		Food-101	89.71(0.90)	89.18(2.37)	90.43(1.54)	**93.95(0.41)**
CIFAR-100	TIN (c)	83.70(4.00)	94.48(3.21)	92.97(1.63)	**97.90(0.29)**	CIFAR-100	TIN (c)	84.47(1.24)	91.72(1.10)	92.58(2.60)	**96.76(0.34)**
	TIN (c)*	79.32(4.14)	88.54(4.27)	93.18(0.39)	**97.31(0.45)**		TIN (c)*	80.90(0.90)	87.08(1.29)	**96.45(0.30)**	95.91(0.42)
	TIN (r)	77.07(6.35)	88.14(6.92)	96.81(0.27)	**97.82(0.53)**		TIN (r)	76.67(2.03)	86.28(2.43)	**97.82(0.13)**	95.84(0.67)
	LSUN (c)	82.92(0.59)	94.72(0.59)	91.65(2.96)	**96.73(0.31)**		LSUN (c)	81.91(1.31)	91.75(0.44)	80.48(1.14)	**96.09(0.62)**
	LSUN (c)*	78.46(0.91)	87.89(1.13)	85.44(1.85)	**95.52(0.32)**		LSUN (c)*	79.17(1.25)	88.06(0.46)	91.13(0.52)	**94.92(0.65)**
	LSUN (r)	78.44(5.41)	90.38(4.76)	97.00(0.15)	**97.59(0.75)**		LSUN (r)	78.00(1.95)	87.90(1.83)	**97.80(0.15)**	95.18(0.86)
	iSUN	76.89(6.28)	88.27(6.49)	97.04(0.10)	**97.45(0.73)**		iSUN	77.29(2.15)	87.07(2.00)	**97.66(0.14)**	95.39(0.55)
	SVNH	77.36(2.83)	91.60(0.73)	96.48(0.68)	**96.90(0.79)**		SVNH	79.82(2.49)	93.46(1.05)	**97.96(0.49)**	97.52(0.41)
	Food-101	84.38(0.48)	**90.82(0.60)**	67.14(1.39)	90.79(0.49)		Food-101	89.25(0.40)	90.76(0.35)	91.15(0.66)	**92.53(0.38)**

4.4 Ablation Study

Although the proposed method employs softmax of cosine similarity equivalent to metric learning methods, there are differences in detailed designs, even compared with the most similar NormFace [13]. To be specific, they are the scale prediction (referred to as *Scale* in Table 3), the use of a single FC layer instead of two FC layers (*Single FC*), and non-application of weight decay to the last FC layer (*w/o WD*). To see their impacts on performance, we conducted an ablation study, in which WRN-28-10 is used for the base network and TinyImageNet (resized) is chosen for an OOD dataset.

Table 3 shows the results. Row 1 shows the results of the baseline method [1], which are obtained in our experiments. Row 2 shows the results obtained by incorporating the scale prediction in the standard networks; to be specific, s predicted from f according to (4) is multipled with logits as $s \cdot (\boldsymbol{w}_i \boldsymbol{f} + b_i)$ $(i = 1, \ldots, C)$, which are then normalized by softmax to yield the cross-entropy loss. As is shown in Row 2, this simple modification to the baseline boosts the performance, which is surprising.

Row 3 and below show results when cosine similarity is used for OOD detection. Rows 3 to 6 show the results obtained when a fixed value (i.e., 16, 32, 64, 128) is chosen for s. It is observed from this that the application of scaling affects a lot detection performance, and it tends to be sensitive to their choice. This means that, if s is treated as a fixed parameter, it will become a hyperparameter that needs to be tuned for each dataset. Row 7 shows the result when the scale is predicted from f as in Row 1 but with cosine similarity. It is seen that this provides results comparable to the best case of manually chosen scales.

Row 8 shows the results obtained by further stopping application of weight decay to the last layer, which is the proposed method. It is seen that this achieves the best performance for both CIFAR-10 and CIFAR-100. Rows 9 and 10 show the results obtained by the network having two FC layers in its final part, as in the recent metric learning methods. Following the studies of metric learning, we use 512 units in the intermediate layer. In this architecture, it is better to employ

Table 3. Ablation tests for evaluating the contribution of different components (i.e., 'Cosine', 'Single FC', 'Scale', and 'w/o WD'; see details from the main text) of the proposed method. AUROCs for detection of OOD samples (TinyImageNet (resized)) are shown.

	Cosine	Single FC	Scale	w/o WD	C-10	C-100
(1)	Baseline [1]				89.22	76.59
(2)	✗	✓	Pred	✗	95.74	88.70
(3)	✓	✓	16	✗	94.09	82.76
(4)	✓	✓	32	✗	96.53	89.02
(5)	✓	✓	64	✗	87.06	95.66
(6)	✓	✓	128	✗	62.02	94.82
(7)	✓	✓	Pred	✗	95.16	91.30
(8)	✓	✓	**Pred**	✓	**97.66**	**95.84**
(9)	✓	✗	Pred	✗	94.71	87.55
(10)	✓	✗	Pred	✓	89.90	86.96

weight decay in the last layer as with the metric learning methods (i.e., Rows 9 vs 10). In conclusion, these results confirm that the use of cosine similarity as well as all the three components are indispensable to achieve the best performance.

5   Effectiveness of the Scaling Factor

5.1   Explanation by Hsu et al.

Our method and that of Hsu et al. [10] share the key component, the scaled cosine similarity, $s \cos \theta_i$, in which the angle θ_i with the i-th class centroid as well as the scale s are both *predicted* from the input x. In [10], not s but its inverse (i.e., $1/s$), denoted by $g(x)$, is predicted in a different way. The authors argue that $g(x)$ approximates $p(d_{in}|x)$, the probability of the input x being in-distribution. They then argue that this contributes to better OOD detection performance. However, this explanation contradicts with empirical observation, and therefore it must be wrong. Figure 3 (the upper row) shows the histograms of $g(x)$, which is computed according to the method of [10], for ID and OOD samples. Here, we use CIFAR-100 for the ID dataset and several others for OOD datasets; test samples are used for both. As is clearly seen, $g(x)$ is statistically not larger for ID samples than OOD samples, although its value should be consistently larger for ID than OOD samples if their argument is true. The lower row of Fig. 3 shows the histograms of the cosine similarity that is used for detecting OOD samples, showing its ability to distinguish ID and OOD samples. In short, $g(x)$ cannot be seen as an approximation of $p(d_{in}|x)$ and it alone cannot detect OOD samples with good accuracy. The authors show that using dropout regularization induces different behavior of $g(x)$ between ID and OOD samples, but it is not employed

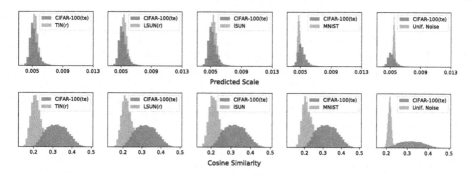

Fig. 3. Upper: Histograms of $g(x)$ of [10] for samples from ID (CIFAR-100) and different OOD datasets, respectively. Lower: Histograms of the cosine similarity for the same ID and OOD samples. The network is WRN-28-10 and dropout is not employed.

in the main experiments evaluating OOD detection performance. Although it is not clear why the use of dropout makes $g(x)$ behave (slightly) differently, it should be concluded that the aforementioned claim on $g(x)$ is not the reason for the good performance of OOD detection.

5.2 Why Is Predicting s Essential?

Then, why is it essential to make the network predict the scale s. We remind the readers that we use $\cos \theta_i$ without s to detect OOD samples, which is the case as well with [10]. Thus, it is obviously associated not with prediction but with learning; that is, it contributes to better learning of feature space for OOD detection. An observation from our experiments is that s tends to be small at the initial training stage and becomes larger as the training goes, as shown in Fig. 4. This is reasonable since small s induces high entropy (i.e., softmax scores being more uniform and flattened) and large s induces low entropy; at the initial stage, there are a lot of misclassifications due to random weight initialization, leading to large cross-entropy loss, which will be compensated by making s small. More importantly, once the network has learned to correctly classify ID samples, or specifically, once it has learned to be able to consistently output max-logits for the correct classes, then s will start to become large; the minimization of the loss will be achieved not by reorganizing the feature space but by making s larger. We conjecture that this mechanism serves as a regularization to avoid overfitting the learned feature space to ID samples, while such overfitting occurs in the training of the standard networks. We believe that this leads to the difference in the OOD detection performance between the proposed cosine networks and standard networks.

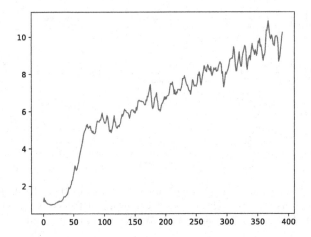

Fig. 4. Evolution of the scale s in first training epoch. The x-axis shows the training step.

6   Summary and Conclusions

In this paper, we have presented a novel method for OOD detection, and experimentally confirmed its superiority to existing approaches. We started our discussion with the observation that existing methods have hyperparameters specific to OOD detection, and their performance can be sensitive to their determination. The proposed method does not have such hyperparameters. It is based on the softmax of scaled cosine similarity and can be used with any networks by replacing their output layer. Training is performed by the standard method, i.e., minimizing a cross-entropy loss on the target classification task. Although a similar approach has already been employed in metric learning methods, the proposed method has several technical differences, which are essential to achieve high OOD detection performance, as was demonstrated in our ablation test. We have shown experimental comparisons between the proposed method and the existing methods using two different evaluation methods, i.e., the less-biased evaluation recently proposed in [9] and the conventional one-vs-one evaluation. In the former evaluation, which takes the above issue with hyperparameter determination into account, the proposed method shows clear superiority to others. Our method also shows at least comparable performance to them in the conventional evaluation. These results support the practicality of the proposed method in real-world applications. Lastly, we have briefly discussed why cosine similarity is effective for OOD detection.

Acknowledgements. This work was partly supported by JSPS KAKENHI Grant Number JP19H01110.

References

1. Hendrycks, D., Gimpel, K.: A baseline for detecting misclassified and out-of-distribution examples in neural networks. In: Proceedings of the International Conference on Learning Representations (2017)
2. Liang, S., Li, Y., Srikant, R.: Enhancing the reliability of out-of-distribution image detection in neural networks. In: Proceedings of the International Conference on Learning Representations (2017)
3. Lee, K., Lee, K., Lee, H., Shin, J.: A simple unified framework for detecting out-of-distribution samples and adversarial attacks. In: Advances in Neural Information Processing Systems (2018)
4. Vyas, A., Jammalamadaka, N., Zhu, X., Das, D., Kaul, B., Willke, T.L.: Out-of-distribution detection using an ensemble of self supervised leave-out classifiers. In: Proceedings of the European Conference on Computer Vision (ECCV), pp. 550–564 (2018)
5. Shalev, G., Adi, Y., Keshet, J.: Out-of-distribution detection using multiple semantic label representations. In: Proceedings of the European Conference on Computer Vision (ECCV), pp. 550–564 (2018)
6. Malinin, A., Gales, M.: Predictive uncertainty estimation via prior networks. In: Advances in Neural Information Processing Systems (2018)
7. Yu, Q., Aizawa, K.: Unsupervised out-of-distribution detection by maximum classifier discrepancy. In: Proceedings of the IEEE/CVF International Conference on Computer Vision, pp. 9518–9526 (2019)
8. Macêdo, D., Ludermir, T.: Neural networks out-of-distribution detection: hyperparameter-free isotropic maximization loss, the principle of maximum entropy, cold training, and branched inferences. arXiv:2006.04005 (2020)
9. Shafaei, A., Schmidt, M., Little, J.J.: A less biased evaluation of out-of-distribution sample detectors. In: Proceedings of the British Machine Vision Conference (2019)
10. Hsu, Y.C., Shen, Y., Jin, H., Kira, Z.: Generalized odin: detecting out-of-distribution image without learning from out-of-distribution data. In: Proceedings of the IEEE/CVF Conference on Computer Vision and Pattern Recognition, pp. 10951–10960 (2020)
11. Ranjan, R., Castillo, C.D., Chellappa, R.: L2-constrained softmax loss for discriminative face verification. arXiv:1703.09507 (2017)
12. Liu, W., Wen, Y., Yu, Z., Li, M., Raj, B., Song, L.: Sphereface: deep hypersphere embedding for face recognition. In: Proceedings of the IEEE Conference on Computer Vision and Pattern Recognition, pp. 212–220 (2017)
13. Wang, F., Xiang, X., Cheng, J., Yuille, A.L.: Normface: L2 hypersphere embedding for face verification. In: Proceedings of the 25th ACM international conference on Multimedia, pp. 1041–1049 (2017)
14. Wang, H., et al.: Cosface: large margin cosine loss for deep face recognition. In: Proceedings of the IEEE Conference on Computer Vision and Pattern Recognition, pp. 5265–5274 (2018)
15. Deng, J., Guo, J., Xue, N., Zafeiriou, S.: Arcface: additive angular margin loss for deep face recognition. In: Proceedings of the IEEE/CVF Conference on Computer Vision and Pattern Recognition, pp. 4690–4699 (2019)
16. Zhang, X., Zhao, R., Qiao, Y., Wang, X., Li, H.: Adacos: adaptively scaling cosine logits for effectively learning deep face representations. In: Proceedings of the IEEE/CVF Conference on Computer Vision and Pattern Recognition, pp. 10823–10832 (2019)

17. Gal, Y., Ghahramani, Z.: Dropout as a bayesian approximation: representing model uncertainty in deep learning. In: Proceedings of the International Conference on Machine Learning, pp. 1050–1059 (2016)
18. Lakshminarayanan, B., Pritzel, A., Blundell, C.: Simple and scalable predictive uncertainty estimation using deep ensembles. In: Advances in Neural Information Processing Systems (2017)
19. Azizpour, H., Teye, M., Smith, K.: Bayesian uncertainty estimation for batch normalized deep networks. In: Proceedings of the International Conference on Machine Learning, pp. 4907–4916 (2018)
20. Gast, J., Roth, S.: Lightweight probabilistic deep networks. In: Proceedings of the Conference on Computer Vision and Pattern Recognition, pp. 3369–3378 (2018)
21. Kendall, A., Gal, Y.: What uncertainties do we need in bayesian deep learning for computer vision? In: Advances in Neural Information Processing Systems (2017)
22. Leibig, C., Allken, V., Ayhan, M.S., Berens, P., Wahl, S.: Leveraging uncertainty information from deep neural networks for disease detection. Sci. Rep. **7**, 17816 (2017)
23. DeVries, T., Taylor, G.W.: Leveraging uncertainty estimates for predicting segmentation quality. arXiv:1807.00502 (2018)
24. Blum, H., Sarlin, P.E., Nieto, J., Siegwart, R., Cadena, C.: Fishyscapes: a benchmark for safe semantic segmentation in autonomous driving. In: Proceedings of the IEEE/CVF International Conference on Computer Vision Workshops (2019)
25. Bevandić, P., Krešo, I., Oršić, M., Šegvić, S.: Simultaneous semantic segmentation and outlier detection in presence of domain shift. In: Fink, G.A., Frintrop, S., Jiang, X. (eds.) DAGM GCPR 2019. LNCS, vol. 11824, pp. 33–47. Springer, Cham (2019). https://doi.org/10.1007/978-3-030-33676-9_3
26. Guo, C., Pleiss, G., Sun, Y., Weinberger, K.Q.: On calibration of modern neural networks. In: Proceedings of the International Conference on Machine Learning, pp. 1321–1330 (2017)
27. Kuleshov, V., Fenner, N., Ermon, S.: Accurate uncertainties for deep learning using calibrated regression. In: Proceedings of the International Conference on Machine Learning, pp. 2796–2804 (2018)
28. Subramanya, A., Srinivas, S., Babu, R.V.: Confidence estimation in deep neural networks via density modelling. In: Proceedings of International Conference on Multimedia and Expo (2017)
29. Scheirer, W.J., Rocha, A., Micheals, R.J., Boult, T.E.: Meta-recognition: the theory and practice of recognition score analysis. IEEE Trans. Pattern Anal. Mach. Intell. **33**, 1689–1695 (2011)
30. Chen, T., Navrátil, J., Iyengar, V., Shanmugam, K.: Confidence scoring using whitebox meta-models with linear classifier probes. In: Proceedings of the International Conference on Artificial Intelligence and Statistics, pp. 1467–1475 (2018)
31. Lee, K., Lee, H., Lee, K., Shin, J.: Training confidence-calibrated classifiers for detecting out-of-distribution samples. In: Proceedings of the International Conference on Learning Representations (2018)
32. Ren, J., et al.: Likelihood ratios for out-of-distribution detection. In: Advances in Neural Information Processing Systems (2019)
33. Hendrycks, D., Mazeika, M., Dietterich, T.G.: Deep anomaly detection with outlier exposure. In: Proceedings of the International Conference on Learning Representations (2019)
34. Hendrycks, D., Lee, K., Mazeika, M.: Using pre-training can improve model robustness and uncertainty. In: Proceedings of the International Conference on Machine Learning, pp. 2712–2721 (2019)

35. Xu, P., Ehinger, K.A., Zhang, Y., Finkelstein, A., Kulkarni, S.R., Xiao, J.: Turk-ergaze: crowdsourcing saliency with webcam based eye tracking. arXiv:1504.06755 (2015)
36. Goodfellow, I.J., Shlens, J., Szegedy, C.: Explaining and harnessing adversarial examples. In: Proceedings of the International Conference on Learning Representations (2015)
37. Wang, J., et al.: Learning fine-grained image similarity with deep ranking. In: Proceedings of the IEEE Conference on Computer Vision and Pattern Recognition, pp. 1386–1393 (2014)
38. Schroff, F., Kalenichenko, D., Philbin, J.: Facenet: a unified embedding for face recognition and clustering. In: Proceedings of the Conference on Computer Vision and Pattern Recognition, pp. 815–823 (2015)
39. Hadsell, R., Chopra, S., LeCun, Y.: Dimensionality reduction by learning an invariant mapping. In: IEEE Computer Society Conference on Computer Vision and Pattern Recognition (CVPR 2006), Vol. 2, pp. 1735–1742. IEEE (2006)
40. Sun, Y., Wang, X., Tang, X.: Sparsifying neural network connections for face recognition. In: Proceedings of the IEEE Conference on Computer Vision and Pattern Recognition, pp. 4856–4864 (2016)
41. Hinton, G., Vinyals, O., Dean, J.: Distilling the knowledge in a neural network. In: Advances in Neural Information Processing Systems (2014)
42. Ioffe, S., Szegedy, C.: Batch normalization: Accelerating deep network training by reducing internal covariate shift. In: Proceedings of the International Conference on Machine Learning, pp. 448–456 (2015)
43. Liu, W., Wen, Y., Yu, Z., Yang, M.: Large-margin softmax loss for convolutional neural networks. In: Proceedings of the International Conference on Machine Learning (2016)
44. Deng, J., Dong, W., Socher, R., Li, L.J., Li, K., Fei-Fei, L.: Imagenet: a large-scale hierarchical image database. In: Proceedings of the Conference on Computer Vision and Pattern Recognition, pp. 248–255. IEEE (2009)
45. Yu, F., Zhang, Y., Song, S., Seff, A., Xiao, J.: Lsun: construction of a large-scale image dataset using deep learning with humans in the loop. arXiv:1506.03365 (2015)
46. Netzer, Y., Wang, T., Coates, A., Bissacco, A., Wu, B., Ng, A.Y.: Reading digits in natural images with unsupervised feature learning. In: Advances in Neural Information Processing Systems Workshop on Deep Learning and Unsupervised Feature Learning (2011)
47. Bossard, L., Guillaumin, M., Van Gool, L.: Food-101 – mining discriminative components with random forests. In: Fleet, D., Pajdla, T., Schiele, B., Tuytelaars, T. (eds.) ECCV 2014. LNCS, vol. 8694, pp. 446–461. Springer, Cham (2014). https://doi.org/10.1007/978-3-319-10599-4_29
48. Coates, A., Lee, H., Ng, A.Y.: An analysis of single layer networks in unsupervised feature learning. In: Proceedings of the International Conference on Artificial Intelligence and Statistics, pp. 215–223 (2011)
49. LeCun, Y., et al.: Gradient-based learning applied to document recognition. Proc. IEEE **86**(11), 2278–2324 (1998)
50. Xiao, H., Rasul, K., Vollgraf, R.: Fashion-mnist: a novel image dataset for benchmarking machine learning algorithms. arXiv:1708.07747 (2017)
51. Zagoruyko, S., Komodakis, N.: Wide residual networks. In: Proceedings of the British Machine Vision Conference (2016)
52. Huang, G., Liu, Z., Van Der Maaten, L., Weinberger, K.Q.: Densely connected convolutional networks. In: Proceedings of the Conference on Computer Vision and Pattern Recognition, pp. 4700–4708 (2017)

Meta-Learning with Context-Agnostic Initialisations

Toby Perrett[(✉)], Alessandro Masullo, Tilo Burghardt, Majid Mirmehdi,
and Dima Damen

Department of Computer Science, University of Bristol, Bristol, UK
Toby.Perrett@bristol.ac.uk

Abstract. Meta-learning approaches have addressed few-shot problems by finding initialisations suited for fine-tuning to target tasks. Often there are additional properties within training data (which we refer to as context), not relevant to the target task, which act as a distractor to meta-learning, particularly when the target task contains examples from a novel context not seen during training.

We address this oversight by incorporating a context-adversarial component into the meta-learning process. This produces an initialisation which is both context-agnostic and task-generalised. We evaluate our approach on three commonly used meta-learning algorithms and four case studies. We demonstrate our context-agnostic meta-learning improves results in each case. First, we report few-shot character classification on the Omniglot dataset, using alphabets as context. An average improvement of 4.3% is observed across methods and tasks when classifying characters from an unseen alphabet. Second, we perform few-shot classification on Mini-ImageNet, obtaining context from the label hierarchy, with an average improvement of 2.8%. Third, we perform few-shot classification on CUB, with annotation metadata as context, and demonstrate an average improvement of 1.9%. Fourth, we evaluate on a dataset for personalised energy expenditure predictions from video, using participant knowledge as context. We demonstrate that context-agnostic meta-learning decreases the average mean square error by 30%.

1 Introduction

Current deep neural networks require significant quantities of data to train for a new task. When only limited labelled data is available, meta-learning approaches train a network initialisation on other *source* tasks, so it is suitable for fine-tuning to new few-shot *target* tasks [1]. Often, training data samples have additional properties, which we collectively refer to as *context*, readily available through metadata. We give as an example the *alphabet* in a few-shot character recognition task (Fig. 1). This is distinct from multi-label problems as we pursue invariance to the context (i.e. alphabet), so as to generalise to unseen contexts in fine-tuning, rather than predicting its label.

In this work, we focus on problems where the target task is not only novel but does not have the same context as tasks seen during training. This is a difficult

© Springer Nature Switzerland AG 2021
H. Ishikawa et al. (Eds.): ACCV 2020, LNCS 12625, pp. 70–86, 2021.
https://doi.org/10.1007/978-3-030-69538-5_5

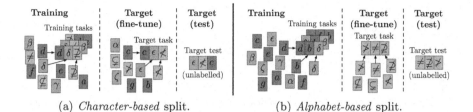

(a) *Character-based* split.   (b) *Alphabet-based* split.

Fig. 1. Visualisation of how context (e.g. alphabets, shown as different colours) can contribute to train/target splits. In commonly-used split (a), a classifier could overfit on context with no ill effects. If there is novel context, as in (b), this will prove problematic. In this paper, we show how context-agnostic meta-learning can benefit performance on few-shot target tasks without shared context.

problem for meta-learners, as they can overfit on context knowledge to generate an initialisation, which affects the suitability for fine-tuning for tasks with novel contexts. Prior works on meta-learning have not sought to exploit context, even when readily available [1–13]. We propose a meta-learning framework to tackle both task-generalisation and context-agnostic objectives, jointly. As with standard meta-learning, we aim for trained weights that are suitable for few-shot fine-tuning to target. Note that concepts of *context* and *domain* might be incorrectly confused. Domains are typically different datasets with a significant gap, whereas context is one or more distractor signals within one dataset (e.g. font or writer for character classification), and can be either discrete or continuous.

Figure 2 presents an overview of the proposed framework, illustrated on the application of character classification. We assume that both task labels (e.g. character classification) and context labels (e.g. alphabet) are available for the training data. At each iteration of meta-learning, we randomly pick a task (Fig. 2(a)), and optimise the model's weights for both task-generalisation (Fig. 2(c)) and context-agnosticism (Fig. 2(d)) objectives. This is achieved through keeping two copies of the model's weights (Fig. 2(b)), one for each objective, and then updating the primary weights with a mixture of both results (Fig. 2(e)). These learnt weights are not only task-generalisable but importantly have been trained in an adversarial manner on context labels.

To demonstrate the generality of our framework, and the opportunities in considering context, we show that it is applicable to three commonly used few-shot meta-learning algorithms [1,4,7], and test our context-agnostic meta-learning framework on four diverse problems, showing clear improvements compared to prior work and baselines. The first problem (Sect. 4) is Omniglot character classification [14]. We show that when using an alphabet-based split, our approach improves over non context-aware meta-learning approaches by 4.3%. The second (Sect. 5) is Mini-ImageNet [10] few-shot classification, where image classification is the task, and broader class group labels are the context. An improvement of 2.8% is observed when utilising our approach. The third (Sect. 6) is few-shot classification CUB [15], where the primary colour of each bird (taken

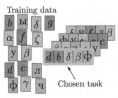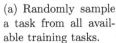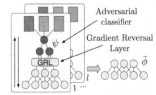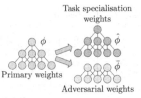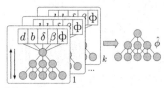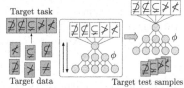

(a) Randomly sample a task from all available training tasks.

(b) Two copies are taken of the primary network weights.

(c) k rounds of optimisation on the chosen task, without context knowledge, to update $\hat{\phi}$.

(d) l rounds of context-adversarial optimisation, passing the gradients though a gradient reversal layer to update $\bar{\phi}$.

(e) Update primary weights from task-specific and context-agnostic optimisations.

(f) After meta-learning, the primary network can be fine-tuned for a new few-shot target task that might not share context with the training set.

Fig. 2. A visualisation of the proposed context-agnostic meta-learning approach through a character classification example (context shown as character colours) using an alphabet-based split (Fig. 1(b)). The method is detailed in Algorithm 1, where (a) to (e) corresponds to one outer loop iteration, which is repeated on random training tasks. (f) shows fine-tuning to target. (Color figure online)

from annotations in metadata) is the context. An improvement of 1.9% is found in this case. The fourth (Sect. 7) is predicting energy expenditure of people performing daily activities from video [16]. For this problem, we consider calorie prediction as the task, and the identities as the context. We show that our approach drops the Mean Square Error (MSE) from 2.0 to 1.4.

2 Related Work

Few-shot Learning: Existing few-shot methods belong to one of three categories: generative approaches [17,18], embedding-based meta-learners [9–11] and adaptation-based meta-learners [1–8,12,13]. Adaptation-based meta-learners produce initial models which can be fine-tuned quickly to unseen tasks, using limited labelled data. One widely-used method is Model Agnostic Meta-Learning (MAML) [1], where repeated specialisation on tasks drawn from the training set encourages the ability to adapt to new tasks with little data. Later variations on this approach include promoting training stability [4] and improving training speed and performance on more realistic problems with deeper architectures [7]. Some works have learned alternative training curricula [3] or modified the task specialisation [2,8]. Others have learned alternative fine-tuning mechanisms [12,13] or pseudo-random labels [6] to help with adaptation to unseen tasks. These adaptation-based meta-learners contrast with embedding-based meta-learners, which find a space where the few-shot task can be embedded. A classifier is then constructed in this space, e.g. by comparing distances of target samples to seen source samples [10].

None of the above works have exploited context available from metadata of the training data. Further, they have been evaluated on datasets where additional context knowledge is not available [18,19], where context is shared between the training and target split [10,14] or combinations of the above [13,20]. We select adaptation-based meta-learning as the most suitable candidate for few-shot tasks with context. This is because there is likely to be insufficient target data for generative approaches, and target samples from a novel context are unlikely to embed well in the space constructed by embedding-based meta-learners.

Domain Adaptation/Generalisation: Different from domains, contexts are additional labels present within the same dataset, can be continuous and one sample could be associated with multiple contexts. However, methods that attempt domain adaptation and generalisation are relevant for achieving context-agnostic learning. Domain adaptation techniques aim to align source and target data. Some works use domain statistics to apply transformations to the feature space [21], minimise alignment errors [22], generate synthetic target data [23,24] or learn from multiple domains concurrently [25–27]. Adversarial domain classifiers have also been used to adapt a single [28–30] and multiple [31] source domains to a target domain. The disadvantage of all these approaches is that sufficient target data is required, making them unsuitable for few-shot learning. Domain generalisation works find representations agnostic to the dataset a sample is from. Approaches include regularisation [32], episodic training [33,34] and adversarial learning [35]. In this paper, we build on adversarial training, as in [28–31,35] for context-agnostic few-shot learning.

3   Proposed Method

We start Sect. 3.1 by formulating the problem, and explaining how it differs from commonly-tackled meta-learning problems. In Sect. 3.2, we detail our proposal to introduce context-agnostic training during meta-learning.

3.1   Problem Formulation

Commonalities to Other Meta-learning Approaches: The input to our method is labelled training data for a number of tasks, as well as limited (i.e. few-shot) labelled data for target tasks. Adaptation-based meta-learning is distinct from other learning approaches in that the trained model is not directly used for inference. Instead, it is optimised for fine-tuning to a target task. These approaches have two stages: (1) the meta-learning stage - generalisable weights across tasks are learnt, suitable for fine-tuning, and (2) the fine-tuning to target stage - initialisation weights from the meta-learning stage are updated given a limited amount of labelled data from the target task. This fine-tuned model is then used for inference on test data on the target task. Throughout this section, we will focus on stage (1), i.e. the meta-learning stage, as this is where our contribution lies.

Our Novelty: We consider problems where the unseen target task does not share context labels with the training data. We assume each training sample has both a task label and a context label. The context labels are purely auxiliary - they are not the prediction target of the main network. We utilise context labels to achieve context-agnostic meta-learning using tasks drawn from the training set and argue that incorporating context-agnosticism provides better generalisation. This is particularly important when the set of context labels in the training data is small, increasing the potential discrepancy between tasks.

3.2   Context-Agnostic Meta-Learning

Our contribution is applicable to adaptation-based meta-learning algorithms which are trained in an episodic manner. This means they use an inner update loop to fine-tune the network weights on a single task, and an outer update loop which incorporates changes made by the inner loop into a set of primary network weights [1,2,4,5,7]. To recap, none of these algorithms exploit context knowledge, and although they differ in the way they specialise to a single task in the inner loop, they all share a common objective:

$$\min_{\phi} \mathbb{E}_\tau \left[L_\tau \left(U_\tau^k (\phi) \right) \right], \tag{1}$$

where ϕ are the network weights, τ is a randomly sampled task and L_τ is the loss for this task. U_τ denotes an update which is applied k times, using data from task τ. Algorithm 1 shows (in black) the core of the method employed by [1,4,7], including the inner and outer loop structure common to this class of meta-learning technique. They differ in the way they calculate and backpropagate ∇L_τ in the inner specialisation loop (where different order gradients are applied, and various other training tricks are used). This step appears in Algorithm 1 L7-10 and Fig. 2(c). However, they can all be modified to become context-agnostic in the same way - this is our main contribution (shown in blue in the algorithm), which we discuss next.

To achieve context-agnostic meta-learning, we propose to train a context-adversarial network alongside the task-specialised network. This provides a second objective to our meta-learning. We update the meta-learning objective from Eq. 1 to include this context-adversarial objective, to become

$$\min_{\phi,\psi} \mathbb{E}_\tau \left[L_\tau \left(U_\tau^k (\phi) \right) + \lambda L_C \left(U_C^l (\psi,\phi) \right) \right], \tag{2}$$

where L_C is a context loss, given by an associated context network with weights ψ, which acts on the output of the network with weights ϕ. $U_C (\psi,\phi)$ is the

1 Initialise primary network with parameters ϕ.
2 Initialise adversarial network with parameters ψ.
3 Link primary and adversarial networks with GRL
4 **for** *Iteration in outer loop* **do**
5 | Select random task τ.
6 | Set $\hat{\phi} = \phi$ and $\bar{\phi} = \phi$.
7 | **for** *Iteration in inner specialisation loop* **do**
8 | | Construct batch with samples from task τ.
9 | | Calculate L_τ.
10 | | Optimise $\hat{\phi}$ w.r.t. L_τ.
11 | **end**
12 | **for** *Iteration in inner adversarial loop* **do**
13 | | Construct batch with samples from training dataset.
14 | | Add context label noise with probability ϵ.
15 | | Calculate L_C.
16 | | Optimise ψ and $\bar{\phi}$ w.r.t. L_C
17 | **end**
18 | Update $\phi \leftarrow \phi + \alpha(\hat{\phi} - \phi + \lambda(\bar{\phi} - \phi))$.
19 **end**

Algorithm 1: Context-agnostic meta-learning framework. Proposed additions which can be encapsulated by existing adaptation-based meta-learning approaches, such as [1,4,7], are in blue.

adversarial update which is performed l times. The relative contribution of L_C is controlled by λ. Because L_C and L_τ both operate on ϕ, they are linked and should be optimised jointly. Equation 2 can thus be decomposed into two optimisations:

$$\phi = \arg\min_{\phi} \left(L_\tau \left(U_\tau^k (\phi) \right) - \lambda L_C \left(U_C^l (\psi, \phi) \right) \right) \tag{3}$$

$$\psi = \arg\min_{\psi} \left(L_C \left(U_C^l (\psi, \phi) \right) \right). \tag{4}$$

We can observe the adversarial nature of L_C in Eqs. 3 and 4, where, while ψ attempts to minimise L_C, ϕ attempts to extract features which are context-agnostic (i.e. maximise L_C). To optimise, we proceed with two steps. The first is to update the context predictor ψ using the gradient $\nabla_\psi L_C(\psi, \phi)$. This is performed l times, which we write as

$$U_C^l \left(\nabla_\psi L_C(\psi, \phi) \right). \tag{5}$$

A higher l means the adversarial network trains quicker, when balanced against k to ensure ψ and ϕ learn together in an efficient manner. The second step is to update the primary network with weights ϕ with the gradient

$$\nabla_\phi L_\tau \left(U_\tau^k(\phi) \right) - \lambda \nabla_\phi L_C \left(U_C^l (\psi, \phi) \right). \tag{6}$$

The first term corresponds to the contribution of the task-specific inner loop. The method in [7] reduces this quantity to $\left(\phi - U_\tau^k(\phi)\right)/\alpha$, where α is the learning rate. λ is a weighting factor for the contribution from the adversarial classifier, which can analogously be reduced to $\lambda\left(\phi - U_C^l(\psi, \phi)\right)/\alpha$. It can be incorporated by backpropagating the loss from ψ through a gradient reversal layer (GRL) to ϕ. As well as performing Eqs. 5 and 6, we also perform each iteration of the l adversarial updates U_C with respect to ψ and ϕ concurrently.

In practice, the process above can be simplified by taking two copies of the primary weights at the start of the process as shown in Algorithm 1, which matches the illustration in Fig. 2. At each outer iteration, we first choose a task (Algorithm 1 L5) and make two copies of the primary weights ϕ (L6): $\hat{\phi}$ (weights used for the task-specialisation inner loop) and $\bar{\phi}$ (weights used for the context-adversarial inner loop). The task specialisation loop is then run on $\hat{\phi}$ (L7-10). Next, the adversarial loop is run on $\bar{\phi}$ and ψ (L12-17). The primary weights ϕ are updated using weighted contributions from task-specialisation ($\hat{\phi}$) and context-generalisation ($\bar{\phi}$) (L18). Note that using two separate copies of the weights ensures that the task-specialisation inner loop is as similar as possible to the one fine-tuned for the target task.

The optimiser state and weights for the adversarial network with weights ψ are persistent between outer loop iterations so ψ can learn context as training progresses. This contrasts with the optimisers acting on the $\hat{\phi}$ and $\bar{\phi}$, which are reset every outer loop iteration for the next randomly selected task to encourage the initialisation to be suitable for fast adaptation to a novel task.

Following standard meta-learning approaches, the weight initialisations ϕ can be fine-tuned to an unseen target task. After fine-tuning on the few-shot labelled data from target tasks, this updated model can be used for inference on unlabelled data from these target tasks (see Fig. 2(f)). No context labels are required for the target, as the model is trained to be context-agnostic. Our method is thus suitable for fine-tuning to the target task when new context is encountered, as well as when contexts overlap.

Next, we explore four problems for evaluation. Recall that our approach assumes both task and context labels are available during training. In all our cases studies, we select datasets where context is available, or can be discovered, from the metadata.

4   Case Study 1: Character Classification

Problem Definition. Our first case study is few-shot image classification benchmark - Omniglot [14]. We consider the task as character classification and the context as which alphabet a character is from. We follow the standard setup introduced in [10], which consists of 1- and 5-shot learning on sets of 5 and 20 characters (5- or 20-way) from 50 alphabets. However, we make one major and important change. Recall, we have suggested that existing meta-learning techniques are not designed to handle context within the training set, or context-discrepancy between training and target. The protocol from [10] uses a *character*-based split, where an alphabet can contribute characters to *both* train and target tasks (Fig. 1(a)). Instead, we eliminate this overlap by ensuring that the characters are from different alphabets, i.e. an *alphabet*-based split (Fig. 1(b)).

Evaluation and Baselines. We evaluate the proposed context-agnostic framework using three meta-learners: MAML++ [4], MAML [1] and REPTILE [7]. Note that other adaptation-based meta-learning methods could also be used by substituting in their specific inner-specialisation loops [2,5]. Unmodified versions are used as baselines, and are compared against versions which are modified with our proposed context agnostic (CA) component. We accordingly refer to our modified algorithms as CA-MAML++, CA-MAML and CA-REPTILE. We report results without transduction, that is batch normalisation statistics are not calculated from the entire target set in advance of individual sample classification. This is more representative of a practical application. As in [10], the metric is top-1 character classification accuracy. We run experiments on the full dataset, and also on a reduced number of alphabets. With 5 alphabets, for example, characters from 4 alphabets are used for training, and a few-shot task is chosen from the 5th alphabet only. As the number of alphabets in training decreases, a larger context gap would be expected between training and target. We report averages over 10 random train/target splits, and keep these splits consistent between experiments on the same number of alphabets.

Implementation Details. The widely-used architecture, optimiser and hyperparameters introduced in [10], are used. We implement the adversarial context predictor in the proposed context-agnostic methods as a single layer which takes the penultimate features layer (256D) as input with a cross-entropy loss applied to the output, predicting the alphabet. Context label randomisation is used in the adversarial classifier, where 20% of the context labels are changed. This stops the context adversarial loss tending to zero too quickly (similar to label smoothing [36]). We use $l = 3$ (Eq. 2) for all Omniglot experiments. The context-agnostic component increases the training time by 20% for all methods.

Results. Table 1 shows the results of the proposed framework applied to [1,4,7] on 5–50 alphabets, using the alphabet-based split shown in Fig. 1(b). We report results per method, to show our proposed context-agnostic component improves on average across all methods, tasks and numbers of alphabets. 85% of individual method/task/alphabet combinations show an improvement, with a further 10% being comparable (within 1% accuracy). Overall, the proposed framework gives an average performance increase of 4.3%. This improvement is most pronounced for smaller numbers of alphabets (e.g. average improvements of $>=6.2\%$, 4.9% and 4.2% for 5 and 10 alphabets for [1,4,7] respectively). This trend is shown in Fig. 3(a), and supports our earlier hypothesis that the inclusion of a context-agnostic component is most beneficial when the context overlap between the train and target data is smaller. Figure 3(b) shows the improvement for each XS YW task, averaged over the number of alphabets. Larger improvements are

Table 1. Character classification accuracy on Omniglot, using an alphabet-based split, with the number of training alphabets varied between 5 and 50. XS YW indicates X-shot fine-tuning at a Y-way classification tasks. Base methods are compared against context-agnostic (CA) versions.

Task	Method	Number of Alphabets					Task	Method	Number of Alphabets				
		5	10	15	20	50			5	10	15	20	50
1S 20W	MAML++ [4]	58.7	57.2	64.7	**85.6**	89.6	5S 20W	MAML++ [4]	81.0	84.1	92.4	93.5	95.8
	CA-MAML++	**72.3**	67.6	**82.4**	84.8	**90.9**		CA-MAML++	**84.8**	**90.8**	**96.0**	**94.5**	**96.3**
	MAML [1]	61.4	78.2	81.5	83.7	87.5		MAML [1]	81.7	83.8	84.0	91.2	**89.0**
	CA-MAML	69.8	**82.8**	82.1	**89.8**	**93.8**		CA-MAML	**86.0**	**91.8**	**92.9**	**93.1**	86.9
	REPTILE [7]	11.9	18.1	37.6	51.6	64.9		REPTILE [7]	58.4	68.1	76.7	**76.0**	78.0
	CA-REPTILE	**20.7**	**21.8**	**39.5**	**55.5**	**66.5**		CA-REPTILE	**61.1**	**73.7**	**78.3**	75.8	**81.6**
1S 5W	MAML++ [4]	97.4	96.2	**94.9**	93.4	93.7	5S 5W	MAML++ [4]	**99.4**	**99.3**	**98.7**	97.0	96.8
	CA-MAML++	**98.1**	**97.1**	90.1	**95.8**	**97.1**		CA-MAML++	99.3	98.6	98.5	**99.4**	**96.9**
	MAML [1]	86.1	87.0	**96.1**	94.4	90.5		MAML [1]	96.6	95.8	97.2	97.9	98.9
	CA-MAML	**94.5**	**91.3**	94.7	**96.0**	**96.2**		CA-MAML	**97.8**	**98.5**	**97.6**	**98.6**	**99.1**
	REPTILE [7]	52.2	68.8	79.4	75.5	77.5		REPTILE [7]	85.2	85.6	**93.2**	88.5	89.4
	CA-REPTILE	**62.2**	**76.9**	**83.4**	**83.2**	**85.5**		CA-REPTILE	**88.3**	**94.4**	92.4	**91.6**	**92.9**

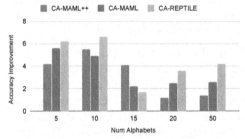

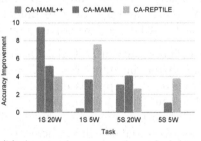

(a) Averaged over the 1- and 5-shot, 5- and 20-way tasks, showing the effect of the number of unique context labels (i.e. alphabets).

(b) Averaged over number of alphabets (5, 10, 15, 20 and 50), showing how each task is affected.

Fig. 3. Accuracy improvements given by our context-agnostic (CA-) versions of [1,4,7] using the alphabet-based split (shown in Fig. 1(b)).

observed for all methods on the 1-shot versions of 5- and 20-way tasks, with [7] improving the most on 1S 5W and [1,4] improving the most on 1S 20W.

For the ablation studies, we use [7] as our base meta-learner as it is the least computationally expensive. Based on preliminary studies, we believe the behaviour is consistent, and the conclusions stand, for the other methods. In the results above, we used $\lambda = 1.0$ for the contribution of our adversarial component λ (Eq. 1). Next, we provide results on how varying λ can affect the model's performance. For this, we use 5S 5W, 10 alphabet task. Figure 4 shows training progress with $\lambda = \{10.0, 2.0, 1.0, 0.5, 0.1\}$. We can see that a high weighting ($\lambda = 10.0$) causes a drop in training accuracy around iteration 40K, as the

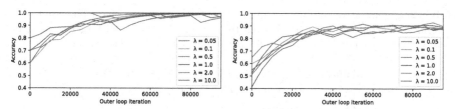

(a) Accuracy on the training set after the inner loops.

(b) Accuracy on the target set after fine-tuning to the target task.

Fig. 4. These plots show how the weighting (λ) of the context-adversarial component affects training and target performance during one run of the 5-shot/5-way 10 alphabet task using an alphabet-based split.

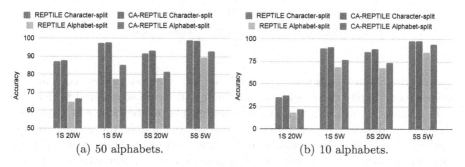

(a) 50 alphabets.

(b) 10 alphabets.

Fig. 5. Comparison of character-based and alphabet-based training/target splits using 50 and 10 alphabets. (Color figure online)

optimisation prioritises becoming context-agnostic over the ability to specialise to a task. However, the figure shows reasonable robustness to the choice of λ.

Next, we investigate the differences between character-based and alphabet-based training/target splits (visualised in Fig. 1). Figure 5 shows the effects of context-agnosticism when evaluating on character-based splits and alphabet-based splits. Figure 5(a) uses 50 alphabets for comparison, and Fig. 5(b) uses 10 alphabets. While both approaches are comparable on character-based splits (blue vs red), we show a clear improvement in using our context-agnostic meta-learning approach when tested on alphabet-based splits (yellow vs green). This is a sterner test due to the training and target sets being made up from data with different contexts. The context-agnostic version is significantly better for all cases and both alphabet sizes.

Finally, as previous approaches only evaluate on the easier character-based split for Omniglot, using all 50 alphabets, we provide comparative results to published works on this setup. We list reported results from [1,4,7] as well as our replications to ensure a direct comparison (the same codebase and splits can be used with and without the context-agnostic component). For this setup, we use the same data augmentation as [1,4,7]. Results are given in Table 2, which

Table 2. Comparative results on Omniglot using the standard character-based split. *: results reported in cited papers. Even though both training and target tasks share context, our CA contribution maintains performance on this standard split.

Method	5S 5W	1S 5W	5S 20W	1S 20W
MAML++ [4]*	99.9	99.4	99.3	97.7
MAML++ [4]	99.9	99.5	98.7	95.4
CA-MAML++	99.8	99.5	98.8	95.6
MAML [1]*	99.8	98.6	98.9	95.8
MAML [1]	99.8	99.3	97.0	92.3
CA-MAML	99.8	99.3	97.2	94.8
REPTILE [7]*	98.9	95.4	96.7	88.1
REPTILE [7]	98.9	97.3	96.4	87.3
CA-REPTILE	98.6	97.6	95.9	87.8

confirms that context-agnostic versions of the base methods achieve comparable performance, despite there being shared context between source and target.

In summary, this section presented experiments on the Omniglot character classification dataset. We show that, on average, our proposed context-agnostic approach gives performance improvements across all methods and tasks, particularly for smaller alphabet sizes, which introduce a bigger context gap between training and target.

5   Case Study 2: General Image Classification

Problem Definition. Our second case study uses the few-shot image classification benchmark - Mini-ImageNet [10]. We use the experimental setup introduced in [10], where the task is a 1- or 5-shot 5-way classification problem. Similar to our previous case study, we aim for context labels, and a context-based split. This dataset has no readily-available context labels, and there is a large overlap between the train and target splits (e.g.. 3 breeds of dog in target, 12 in train). We address this by manually assigning 12 superclass labels, which we use as context. We then ensure that superclasses used for training and testing are distinct.

Evaluation, Baselines and Implementation. Similar to Sect. 4, we evaluate using MAML++ [4] and MAML [1]. Unmodified versions are used as baselines, and are compared against versions which are modified with our proposed CA component. Transduction is not used, and the metric is top-1 image classification accuracy. The same architecture, hyperparameters etc. as in [4] are used. We use $k = 5$ (Eq. 1) and $l = 2$ (Eq. 2). Results are given for the original Mini-ImageNet splits and our superclass-based splits with context labels.

Results. Table 3 shows the results on the original train/target split and the new splits with no shared context. Results show comparable performance for

Table 3. Results on Mini-ImageNet and CUB using the original splits which have shared context between train and target tasks, and the new context-based splits with no shared context between training and target tasks.

Method	Mini-ImageNet				CUB			
	Original split		Context Split		Original split		Context Split	
	1S 5W	5S 5W	1S 5W	5S 5W	1S 5W	5S 5W	1S 5W	5S 5W
MAML++ [4]	**52.0**	**68.1**	40.1	60.1	**38.7**	57.2	42.2	56.7
CA-MAML++	51.8	**68.1**	**44.4**	**61.5**	38.0	**58.4**	**43.3**	**57.9**
MAML [1]	**48.3**	**64.3**	41.1	56.5	42.5	**56.1**	37.7	54.7
CA-MAML	**48.3**	64.2	**43.3**	**59.5**	**42.6**	55.9	**40.3**	**57.5**

the original split, but importantly improved performance in the context-based split. Our context-agnostic component improves over [1,4] by an average 3.3% on the most difficult 1S 5W task. An average 2.2% improvement is also seen on the easier 5S 5W task. Similar to Omniglot, note that few shot classification on Mini-ImageNet is more challenging (by an average of 8.7% across all methods) when there is no shared context between training and target data.

6   Case Study 3: Fine-Grained Bird Classification

Problem Definition. For our third case study, we use the few-shot fine-grained bird classification benchmark CUB [15]. CUB contains a large amount of meta-data from human annotators. For context labels, we have taken each bird's primary colour, but could have chosen a number of others e.g. bill shape. The CUB dataset has 200 classes, with 9 different primary colours. We ensure splits are distinct with respect to this property.

Evaluation, Baselines and Implementation. We use the same setup as for Mini-ImageNet (Sect. 5).

Results. Table 3 shows the results on the original train/target splits and the new splits with no shared context (i.e. no shared primary colour). When there is less shared context between train and target data, our context-agnostic component improves over [1,4] by an average of 1.9% across all tasks, whilst performance is maintained on the original split.

7   Case Study 4: Calorie Estimation from Video

Problem Definition. In this fourth problem, we use the dataset from [37], where the task is to estimate energy expenditure for an input video sequence of an indiviual carrying out a variety of actions. Different from the first three case studies, this is a regression task, rather than a classification one, as calorie readings are continuous. The target task is to estimate the calorimeter reading

Table 4. MSE for all 10 participants on the Calorie dataset, using leave-one-out cross-validation. A lower MSE indicates better results. Methods with only an average reported are results taken from the referenced publications.

Method	P1	P2	P3	P4	P5	P6	P7	P8	P9	P10	Avg
MET Lookup [16]	-	-	-	-	-	-	-	-	-	-	2.25
Tao et al. [37]	-	-	-	-	-	-	-	-	-	-	1.69
Pre-train only	1.21	**0.89**	0.88	1.86	1.24	**2.46**	7.50	**0.89**	1.25	3.11	2.13
Pre-train/fine-tune	0.58	1.64	0.75	0.53	1.13	4.26	5.83	1.29	1.41	3.53	2.10
REPTILE [7]	0.48	1.65	0.52	0.90	2.12	3.28	6.48	1.26	**0.83**	2.58	2.01
CA-REPTILE	**0.39**	1.11	**0.46**	**0.48**	**0.87**	2.68	**3.75**	1.07	0.87	**2.32**	**1.40**

for seen, as well as unseen, actions. Importantly, the individual captured forms the context. Alternative context labels could include, for example, age or Body Mass Index (BMI). Our objective is thus to perform meta-learning to generalise across actions, as well as being individual-agnostic, for calorie prediction of a new individual. We use silhouette footage and calorimeter readings from 10 participants performing a number of daily living tasks as derived from the SPHERE Calorie dataset of [16]. Using a relatively small amount of data to fine-tune to target is appropriate because collecting data from individuals using a calorimeter is expensive and cumbersome.

Evaluation and Baselines. Ten-fold leave-one-person-out cross-validation is used for evaluation. We report results using MSE across all videos for each subject. For fine-tuning to target, we use labelled calorie measurements from the first 32 s (i.e. the first 60 video samples, where each sample is 30 frames subsampled at 1 fps) of the target subject. Evaluation is then performed using the remaining data from the target subject, which is 28 min on average. We compare the following methods, using cross-fold, leave-one-person-out validation:

- Metabolic Equivalent (MET) from [16]. This offers a baseline of calorie estimation through a look-up table of actions and their duration. This has been used as a baseline on this dataset previously.
- Method from Tao et al. [37] that utilises IMU and depth information not used by our method.
- Pre-train - standard training process, trained on 9 subjects and tested on target subject without fine-tuning.
- Pre-train/fine-tune - standard training process on 9 subjects and fine-tuned on the target subject.
- REPTILE - meta-learning from [7] on 9 subjects and fine-tuned on target.
- CA-REPTILE - our proposed context-agnostic meta-learning approach.

Note that we chose to use [7] as the baseline few-shot method because it is less computationally expensive (important when scaling up the few shot-problem to video) than [1,4], as discussed in Sect. 2.

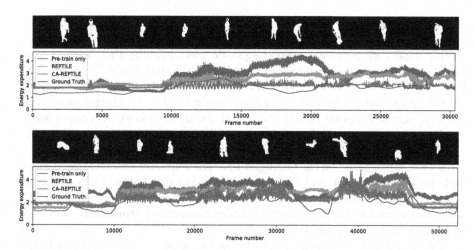

Fig. 6. Example energy expenditure predictions on two sequences from different participants in the Calorie dataset.

Implementation Details. Images are resized to 224 × 224, and fed to a ResNet-18 architecture [38]. No previous works have addressed this individual-agnostic personalisation problem. Following [16], it is believed that a window of 30 s is required as input for energy expenditure prediction. We sample the data at 1 fps and use the ResNet CNN's output from the penultimate layer as input to a Temporal Convolutional Network (TCN) [39] for temporal reasoning. Our model is trained end-to-end using Adam [40] and contains 11.2M parameters. We use $k = 10$ (Eq. 1) and $l = 1$ (Eq. 2) for all Calorie experiments. A lower value of l is required than for Omniglot, as context information is easier for the adversarial network to learn (i.e. people are easier to distinguish than alphabets). MSE is used as the regression loss function. Augmentation during training consists of random crops and random rotations up to 30°. The same architecture is used for all baselines (except MET and [37]), making results directly comparable.

Results. Table 4 compares the various methods. The context-agnostic meta-learning method obtains a 35% reduction in MSE over the pre-training only, a 33% reduction over the pre-train/fine-tune model, and a 30% improvement over the non context-agnostic version. For 3 out of 10 individuals, pre-training outperforms any fine-tuning. We believe this is due to these participants performing actions at the start of the sequence in a different manner to those later. However, our context-agnostic approach offers the best fine-tuned results.

Figure 6 shows qualitative silhouette sequences with calorimeter readings as groundtruth, which are to compared to predictions from our method and baselines. Results demonstrate that the context-agnostic version estimates the ground truth curve better than other methods from participants with low and high energy expenditure variability.

8 Conclusion

In this paper, we proposed context-agnostic meta-learning that learns a network initialisation which can be fine-tuned quickly to new few-shot target problems. An adversarial context network acts on the initialisation in the meta-learning stage, along with task-specialised weights, to learn context-agnostic features capable of adapting to tasks which do not share context with the training set. This overcomes a significant drawback with current few-shot meta-learning approaches, that do not exploit context which is often readily available. The framework is evaluated on the Omniglot few-shot character classification dataset and the Mini-ImageNet and CUB few-shot image recognition tasks, where it demonstrates consistent improvements when exploiting context information. We also evaluate on a few-shot regression problem, for calorie estimation from video, showing significant improvements.

This is the first work to demonstrate the importance and potential of incorporating context into few-shot methods. We hope this would trigger follow-up works on other problems, methods and contexts.

Data Statement: Our work uses publicly available datasets. Proposed context-based splits are available at http://github.com/tobyperrett/context_split.

Acknowledgement. This work was performed under the SPHERE Next Steps Project, funded by EPSRC grant EP/R005273/1.

References

1. Finn, C., Abbeel, P., Levine, S.: Model-agnostic meta-learning for fast adaptation of deep networks. In: International Conference on Machine Learning, pp. 1126–1135 (2017)
2. Rusu, A.A., et al.: Meta-learning with latent embedding optimization. International Conference on Learning Representations (2019)
3. Sun, Q., Chua, Y.L.T.S.: Meta-transfer learning for few-shot learning. In: Proceedings of the IEEE/CVF Conference on Computer Vision and Pattern Recognition, pp. 403–412 (2019)
4. Antoniou, A., Edwards, H., Storkey, A.: How to train your MAML. In: International Conference on Learning Representations (2019)
5. Finn, C., Xu, K., Levine, S.: Probabilistic model-agnostic meta-learning. In: Advances in Nerual Information Processing Systems (2018)
6. Sun, Q., Li, X., Liu, Y., Zheng, S., Chua, T.S., Schiele, B.: Learning to self-train for semi-supervised few-shot classification. In: Advances in Nerual Information Processing Systems (2019)
7. Nichol, A., Achiam, J., Schulman, J.: On first-order meta-learning algorithms. arXiv preprint arXiv:1803.02999 (2018)
8. Bertinetto, L., Henriques, J.F., Torr, P.H.S., Vedaldi, A.: Meta-learning with differentiable closed-form solvers. In: International Conference on Learning Representations (2019)
9. Snell, J., Swersky, K., Zemel, R.: Prototypical networks for few-shot learning. In: Advances in Neural Information Processing Systems (2017)

10. Vinyals, O., Blundell, C., Lillicrap, T., Kavukcuoglu, K., Wierstra, D.: Matching networks for one shot learning. In: Advances in Neural Information Processing Systems (2016)
11. Ren, M., et al.: Meta-learning for semi-supervised few-shot classification. In: International Conference on Learning Representations (2018)
12. Requeima, J., Gordon, J., Bronskill, J., Nowozin, S., Turner, R.E.: Fast and flexible multi-task classification using conditional neural adaptive processes. In: Advances in Nerual Information Processing Systems (2019)
13. Tseng, H.Y., Lee, H.Y., Huang, J.B., Yang, M.H.: Cross-domain few-shot classification via learned feature-wise transformation. In: International Conference on Learning Representations (2020)
14. Lake, B.M., Salakhutdinov, R., Tnenbaum, J.B.: Human-level concept learning through probabilistic program induction. Science **350**, 1332–1338 (2015)
15. Wah, C., Branson, S., Welinder, P., Perona, P., Belongie, S.: The caltech-ucsd birds-200-2011 dataset. Technical report (2011)
16. Tao, L., et al.: Calorie counter: RGB-depth visual estimation of energy expenditure at home. In: Chen, C.-S., Lu, J., Ma, K.-K. (eds.) ACCV 2016. LNCS, vol. 10116, pp. 239–251. Springer, Cham (2017). https://doi.org/10.1007/978-3-319-54407-6_16
17. Zhang, R., Che, T., Bengio, Y., Ghahramani, Z., Song, Y.: Metagan: an adversarial approach to few-shot learning. In: Advances in Neural Information Processing Systems (2018)
18. Dwivedi, S.K., Gupta, V., Mitra, R., Ahmed, S., Jain, A.: Protogan: towards few shot learning for action recognition. In: Proceedings of the IEEE/CVF International Conference on Computer Vision Workshops (2019)
19. Oreshkin, B.N., Rodriguez, P., Lacoste, A.: Tadam: Task dependent adaptive metric for improved few-shot learning. In: Advances in Neural Information Processing Systems (2018)
20. Triantafillou, E., et al.: Meta-dataset: A dataset of datasets for learning to learn from few examples. In: International Conference on Learning Representations (2019)
21. Panareda Busto, P., Gall, J.: Open det domain adaptation. In: International Conference on Computer Vision (2017)
22. Haeusser, P., Frerix, T., Mordvintsev, A., Cremers, D.: Associative domain adaptation. In: International Conference on Computer Vision (2017)
23. Hoffman, J., et al.: Cycada: Cycle-consistent adversarial domain adaptation. In: International Conference on Machine Learning, pp. 1989–1998 (2018)
24. Huang, S.W., Lin, C.T., Chen, S.P., Wu, Y.Y., Hsu, P.H., Lai, S.H.: AugGAN: cross domain adaptation with gan-based data augmentation. In: European Conference on Computer Vision, pp. 718–731 (2018)
25. Rebuffi, S.A., Bilen, H., Vedaldi, A.: Learning multiple visual domains with residual adapters. In: Advances in Neural Information Processing Systems (2017)
26. Perrett, T., Damen, D.: DDLSTM: dual-domain LSTM for cross-dataset action recognition. In: Proceedings of the IEEE/CVF Conference on Computer Vision and Pattern Recognition, pp. 7852–7861 (2019)
27. Li, Y., Vasconcelos, N.: Efficient multi-domain network learning by covariance normalization. In: Computer Vision and Pattern Recognition (2019)
28. Ganin, Y., Lempitsky, V.: Unsupervised domain adaptation by backpropagation. In: International Conference on Machine Learning, pp. 1180–1189 (2015)

29. Zhang, Y., Tang, H., Jia, K., Tan, M.: Domain-symmetric networks for adversarial domain adaptation. In: Proceedings of the IEEE/CVF Conference on Computer Vision and Pattern Recognition, pp. 5031–5040 (2019)
30. Kang, B., Feng, J.: Transferable meta learning across domains. In: Conference on Uncertainty in Artificial Intelligence, pp. 177–187 (2018)
31. Schoenauer-Sebag, A., Heinrich, L., Schoenauer, M., Sebag, M., Wu, L.F., Altschuler, S.J.: Multi-domain adversarial learning. In: International Conference on Learning Representations (2019)
32. Balaji, Y., Sankaranarayanan, S., Chellappa, R.: Metareg: towards domain generalization using meta-regularization. In: Proceedings of the 32nd International Conference on Neural Information Processing Systems, pp. 1006–1016 (2018)
33. Li, D., Zhang, J., Yang, Y., Liu, C., Song, Y.Z., Hospedales, T.: Episodic training for domain generalization. In: Proceedings of the IEEE/CVF International Conference on Computer Vision, pp. 1446–1455 (2019)
34. Dou, Q., Castro, D.C., Kamnitsas, K., Glocker, B.: Domain generalization via model-agnostic learning of semantic features. In: Advances in Nerual Information Processing Systems (2019)
35. Li, H., Pan, S.J., Wang, S., Kot, A.C.: Domain generalization with adversarial feature learning. In: Proceedings of the IEEE Conference on Computer Vision and Pattern Recognition, pp. 5400–5409 (2018)
36. Salimans, T., Goodfellow, I., Zaremba, W., Cheung, V., Radford, A., Chen, X.: Improved techniques for training GANs. In: Advances in Neural Information Processing Systems (2016)
37. Tao, L., et al.: Energy expenditure estimation using visual and inertial sensors. IET Comput. Vis. **12**, 36–47 (2018)
38. He, K., Zhang, X., Ren, S., Sun, J.: Deep residual learning for image recognition. In: Proceedings of the IEEE Conference on Computer Vision and Pattern Recognition, pp. 770–778 (2016)
39. Bai, S., Kolter, J.Z., Koltun, V.: An empirical evaluation of generic convolutional and recurrent networks for sequence modeling. arXiv preprint arXiv:1803.01271 (2018)
40. Kingma, D.P., Ba, J.: Adam: a method for stochastic optimization. In: International Conference on Learning Representations (2015)

Second Order Enhanced Multi-glimpse Attention in Visual Question Answering

Qiang Sun[1], Binghui Xie[2], and Yanwei Fu[2(✉)]

[1] Academy for Engineering and Technology, Fudan University, Shanghai, China
18110860051@fudan.edu.cn
[2] School of Data Science, and MOE Frontiers Center for Brain Science, Shanghai Key Lab of Intelligent Information Processing Fudan University Fudan University, Shanghai, China
{16307130163,yanweifu}@fudan.edu.cn

Abstract. Visual Question Answering (VQA) is formulated as predicting the answer given an image and question pair. A successful VQA model relies on the information from both visual and textual modalities. Previous endeavours of VQA are made on the good attention mechanism, and multi-modal fusion strategies. For example, most models, till date, are proposed to fuse the multi-modal features based on implicit neural network through cross-modal interactions. To better explore and exploit the information of different modalities, the idea of second order interactions of different modalities, which is prevalent in recommendation system, is re-purposed to VQA in efficiently and explicitly modeling the second order interaction on both the visual and textual features, learned in a shared embedding space. To implement this idea, we propose a novel Second Order enhanced Multi-glimpse Attention model (SOMA) where each glimpse denotes an attention map. SOMA adopts multi-glimpse attention to focus on different contents in the image. With projected the multi-glimpse outputs and question feature into a shared embedding space, an explicit second order feature is constructed to model the interaction on both the intra-modality and cross-modality of features. Furthermore, we advocate a semantic deformation method as data augmentation to generate more training examples in Visual Question Answering. Experimental results on VQA v2.0 and VQA-CP v2.0 have demonstrated the effectiveness of our method. Extensive ablation studies are studied to evaluate the components of the proposed model.

Keywords: Visual Question Answering · Multi-glimpse attention · Second order

Y. Fu–This work was supported in part by NSFC Projects (U62076067), Science and Technology Commission of Shanghai Municipality Projects (19511120700, 19ZR1471800).

H. Ishikawa et al. (Eds.): ACCV 2020, LNCS 12625, pp. 87–103, 2021.
https://doi.org/10.1007/978-3-030-69538-5_6

1 Introduction

Visual Question Answering (VQA) has been topical recently, as its solution has relied on the successful models in both computer vision and natural language communities. VQA provides a simple and effective testbed to verify whether AI can truly understand the semantic meaning of vision and language. To this end, numerous efforts have been made towards improving the VQA models by better representations [1], attention [2–5] and fusion strategies.

Despite various fusion mechanisms have been proposed, most of them focus on the fusion features of cross-modality. The early proposed models fuse the cross-modal features with first order interaction such as concatenation [6,7]. Recently the bi-linear based methods [8–10] have been proposed to capture the fine-grained cross-modal features with second order interaction. Multimodal Tucker Fusion (MUTAN) [10] proposes an effective bi-linear fusion for visual and textual features based on low-rank matrix decomposition. Furthermore, it is essential and necessary to extend the first order or bi-linear fusion models to high order fusion ones, in order to better grasp the rich and yet complex information, existed in both visual and textual features. On the other hand, the explicit high order fusion has been widely adopted in many applications, e.g., in recommendation tasks [11,12], and yet to a lesser extent VQA. For example, DeepFM [11] adopts the factorized machine (FM) to construct the explicit second order features of deep features.

However it is nontrivial to apply the explicit high order method to VQA, as most of visual object features, in principle, are orderless with respect to the different semantic attributes. This is quite different from the attribute embeddings (*e.g.,* age, gender) of recommendation, which are arranged in a fixed order. To overcome this problem, the multi-glimpse attention strategy is re-introduced, and re-purposed as the ordered visual representations; and each glimpse is corresponding to one type of attribute. To this end, a novel Second Order enhanced Multi-glimpse Attention (SOMA) model is thus proposed to construct the explicit high order features from the multi-glimpse outputs and the question features. The SOMA calculates, in an embedding space, the interactions of features from both intra-modality (*i.e.* interaction between different glimpse outputs) and cross-modality (*i.e.,* interaction between glimpse output and question feature). To fully utilize the outputs of multi-glimpse attention, we feed each attended features to an independent prediction branch, ensuring that each glimpse has focused on the question-related objects.

Furthermore, despite several large-scale VQA datasets have been contributed to the community, effectively learning a deep VQA network still suffers from the training data scarcity, and *long-tailed* distributed question-answer pairs. Particularly, as in [13], only a limited number of question and answer pairs appeared frequently, whilst most of the other ones have only sparse examples. To alleviate this problem, a novel data augmentation strategy has been proposed in this paper. Typically, data augmentation, e.g., cropping and resizing images, aims at synthesizing new instances by training examples. Most of previous data augmentation strategies are conducted in visual features space, rather than semantic space. Remarkably, as a task requiring the high-level reasoning, the VQA should demand the data augmentation method by integrating the semantic information of each modality. To this end, a data augmentation method – semantic deformation, is proposed in this paper, by randomly removing some visual object and adds some noise visual instance. The images are dynamically augmented by randomly removing some visual objects, to create the more diverse visual inputs. Such a technique is further adopted as a self-supervised mechanism to improve the learning process of attention.

Formally, in this paper, we propose a Second Order enhanced Multi-glimpse Attention (SOMA) to tackle the tasks of visual question answering. As shown in Fig. 1, the model has several key components, including multi-glimpse attention module, second order module and classifier. The multi-glimpse attention module has different attention preference to different semantic aspects of question in each glimpse, which makes the attended feature more robust. The second order module explicitly models the interaction both on intra-modality and cross-modality by embedding the visual and textual features into a shared space. The classifier is strengthened with branch loss, which is able to provide a more direct supervised signal for each glimpse and the second module.

To sum up, we have several contributions as follows. (1) A second order module to construct the explicit second order features from the outputs of multi-glimpse and question feature in a shared embedding space. (2) Branch loss as a prediction signal to make each glimpse have better learning ability and attention performance. (3) A semantic deformation method with semantic objects cropping, noise objects adding and negative sample loss regularization. (4) Extensive experiments and ablation studies have shown the effectiveness of SOMA and semantic deformation.

2   Related Work

Visual Question Answering (VQA). The goal of visual question answering is to predict an answer on the given question and image pair [13,14]. The dominant methods solve this problem as a classification task. A canonical model has three main stages: visual and textual feature extraction [1,15], attention [2,5,16] and fusion strategy. The textual features from questions are mainly extracted from RNN based methods or Transformer. Recently, the object visual features from Faster-RCNN are preferred to the grid visual features by ResNet. Extensive attention models are proposed to identify the question-related information in the image, including question guided attention [1,15], co-attention [5,16,17], self-attention [4,5] and stacked attention [2,18]. The fusion of visual and textual features includes first order [6,7] and high order solution [8,9].

Attention. Attention mechanism is a key component in the canonical VQA model. Visual attention exploits the visual grounding information to identify the salient regions for questions in early works [1,2]. Some co-attention models [4,16] find textual attention is also beneficial to detect the related words in questions along with visual attention. Recently, models with stacked self-attention layers

[4,5,19,20] have achieved state-of-the-art results on VQA task. But the multi-layer architecture makes it require a large computation cost. Studies [8,18] have shown multi-glimpse attention is more robust by generating more than one attention map. However, the relation between different attention results has not been well studied yet.

Fusion. Fusion in VQA aims to combine visual and textual features. The two main factors of fusion are interaction granularity and orders. Coarse-grained first order fusion methods [6,7] combine the aggregated visual feature and question feature by concatenation. The simple first order fusion is limited to model the complex interactions of two modalities. Coarse-grained second order fusion approaches [8–10] advocate the effective bi-linear pooling between aggregated visual and textual features. Fine-grained second order fusion approach BAN [3] applies bi-linear attention between visual objects and question words and uses the sum pooling to obtain the fusion feature. MFH [18] is the most related work to our paper. It first adopts bi-linear attention between grid visual features and question features to generate multi-glimpse output. Then it concatenates the multi-glimpse output into one visual feature for cross-modality bilinear fusion. In contrast, our approach projects the multi-glimpse output and question feature into a shared embedding space to gather the interaction of cross-modality and intra-modality simultaneously. Inspired by the success of explicit high order features in recommendation tasks [11,12], We construct an explicit second order feature in the shared embedding space as fusion. Since our fusion is based on the result of multi-glimpse attention, its granularity is more flexible, which means it is fine-grained if each attention map is near a one-hot vector.

Data Augmentation. Due to the dynamic nature of vision and language combination, the current scale of VQA dataset is insufficient for the deep neural network based model. In image classification, the traditional data augmentation methods include cropping, resizing, flipping, rotation, mixup [21–23] on the input space. The manifold mixup method [23] is proposed to interpolate the training instances in the hidden layer and label space. Counterfactual Sample Synthesizing (CSS [24]) use critical objects masking to generate numerous samples for robust model training. Inspired by manifold mixup, we propose a semantic deformation method in the visual semantic space by instance-level cropping and noise adding.

Self-supervised Learning. The intrinsic structure information in the domain data can be utilized as an extra supervised signal for machine learning. In computation vision, the relative position of image patches [25], colorization [26], inpainting [27] and jigsaw problem [28] are formulated as surrogate tasks. In NLP tasks, the language model skip-gram [29,30] learns the word embedding via context prediction in NLP tasks. Particularly, it adopts negative sampling to distinguish the learned vector from noise distribution. For the semantic deformation examples, we propose a hinge loss on the attention score of noise instance as an extra supervised signal by the assumption that a noise instance in VQA should be ignored with high possibility.

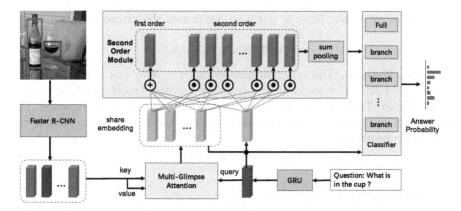

Fig. 1. The framework of SOMA. The main components of SOMA are multi-glimpse attention, second order module and classifier. Extracted visual features and question feature are fed to the multi-glimpse attention module to generate the attended visual features. The attended visual features and question feature are taken as inputs of the second order module. Finally, the attended visual feature, second order feature and the question feature are put into the classifier.

3   Approach

Overview. We formulate the visual question answering task, as a classification problem to calculate the answer a possibility $p(a \mid \mathbf{Q}, \mathbf{I})$ conditioned on the question $\mathbf{Q}$ and image $\mathbf{I}$. In this paper, we propose a novel framework – Second Order enhanced Multi-glimpse Attention (SOMA). SOMA is composed of three components: multi-glimpse attention module, second order module and classifier. The whole pipeline is illustrated in Fig. 1. Multiple attended visual features are generated through the multiple-glimpse attention module with different semantic similarity preferences. The question embedding and attended visual features are fed into the second order module to produce the second order feature. Then the second order feature, attended visual features and question embedding are further passed to the classifier. During training, in addition to the full prediction, a branch prediction is used as an extra supervised signal for each glimpse in the classifier.

3.1   Feature Extraction

Typically, we have the image $\mathbf{I}$, question $\mathbf{Q}$ into the vision feature set $\mathbf{V}$ and the question embedding $\mathbf{q}$. Thus the original task of calculating $p(a|\mathbf{Q},\mathbf{I})$ is translated into obtaining $p(a|\mathbf{q}, \mathbf{V})$.

Visual Features. The visual feature set $\mathbf{V} = \{v_1, \ldots, v_k\}$, $v_i \in \mathbb{R}^{D_v}$ is the output of Faster R-CNN as described in Bottom-up [1]. The Faster R-CNN model is pre-trained on Visual Genome [31] and the object number k is fixed at

36 in our experiments. Thus, in our case, we denote the extracted visual object set as:

$$\mathbf{V} = \mathrm{RCNN}(\mathbf{I}, \theta_{\mathrm{RCNN}}). \tag{1}$$

Question Feature. The question embedding $\mathbf{q} \in \mathbb{R}^{D_t \times 1}$ is obtained from a single layer GRU. The words in the question are first transformed into a vector by GloVe. Then the word vectors are fed into the GRU in sequence. The last hidden state vector is taken as the question embedding. We represent the question embedding as:

$$\mathbf{q} = \mathrm{GRU}(\mathbf{Q}, \theta_{\mathrm{GRU}}). \tag{2}$$

3.2 Multi-glimpse Attention

To answer a question about an image, the attention map in one glimpse is used to identify the visual grounding objects. In multi-glimpse attention mechanism, each glimpse may have different semantic similarity preference, some prefer to attend the question-related colors, some prefer to attend the question-related shapes and so on. We adopt the multi-glimpse attention mechanism to make the attention results more robust and diverse. First, we project the visual feature set $\mathbf{V} \in \mathbb{R}^{k \times d_v}$ and question embedding $\mathbf{q} \in \mathbb{R}^{1 \times d_t}$ into a shared embedding space by $\mathbf{W}_v \in \mathbb{R}^{D_v \times D_h}$ and $\mathbf{W}_t \in \mathbb{R}^{D_t \times D_h}$ respectively. The two latent features are further combined through element products and then to generate the attention weight $A \in \mathbb{R}^{k \times m}$ as:

$$\mathbf{A} = \mathrm{softmax}\left(\left(\mathrm{ReLU}\left(\mathbf{1}\left(\mathbf{q}\mathbf{W}_t\right)\right) \odot \mathrm{ReLU}\left(\mathbf{V}\mathbf{W}_v\right)\right)\mathbf{W}_G\right) \tag{3}$$

where $\mathbf{1} \in \mathbb{R}^{k \times 1}$ is an all-one vector by using k ones to expand the $\mathbf{q}$. $\mathbf{W}_G \in \mathbb{R}^{d_h \times m}$ and m is the number of glimpses. The softmax function is performed on the first dimension to generate weights on the k objects for each glimpse.

It then calculates the question attended visual features $\mathbf{G} \in \mathbb{R}^{m \times d_v}$ as a product of the attention weights and the original visual feature set,

$$\mathbf{G} = \mathbf{A}^T \mathbf{V}. \tag{4}$$

3.3 Second Order Module

We introduce the denotation for the second order module. Particularly, we introduce a score prediction task over a scalar variable set $\{x_1, x_2, \ldots, x_n\}$ as below,

$$\hat{y} = w_0 + \sum_{i=1}^{n} w_i x_i + \sum_{i=1}^{n-1} \sum_{j=i+1}^{n} <v_i, v_j> x_i x_j \tag{5}$$

where $\hat{y}$ is the predicted score, w_0 is the bias, $\sum_{i=1}^{n} w_i x_i$ represents the score from first order interaction and the last term denotes the impact of second order interaction. The inner product $<v_i, v_j>$ represents the coefficient for the interaction of variable x_i and x_j.

We propose a second order interaction module for the question and visual features as shown in Fig. 1. The question feature is first projected into the visual feature space. The concatenation of question feature and the attended visual features are further transformed into a shared embedding space as:

$$\mathbf{E} = \text{ReLU}([\mathbf{G}; \text{ReLU}(\mathbf{q}\mathbf{W}_{qv})]\mathbf{W}_{ve}) \tag{6}$$

where $\mathbf{W}_{qv} \in \mathbb{R}^{d_t \times d_v}$, $\mathbf{W}_{ve} \in \mathbb{R}^{d_v \times d_e}$ and d_e is the dimension of the latent space.

We construct the explicit second-order feature $\mathbf{s}$ over a vector variable set $\mathbf{E} = [\mathbf{e}_1; \mathbf{e}_2, \dots, \mathbf{e}_{m+1}]$ as below:

$$\mathbf{s} = \sum_{i=1}^{m+1} \mathbf{e}_i + \sum_{i=1}^{m} \sum_{j=i+1}^{m+1} \mathbf{e}_i \circ \mathbf{e}_j \tag{7}$$

where $\circ$ denotes Hadamard product. The first term represents the impact of first order features and the second term reflects the importance of second order interactions. For simplicity and efficiency, the coefficients of this vector version FM are all fixed at 1. We argue that a proper embedding space learned by $\mathbf{W}_{ve}$ can alleviate this impact.

3.4 Classifier

The classifier takes the question embedding, multi-glimpse outputs and second order feature as inputs. It contains two subcomponent types: branch prediction module and full prediction module. The branch prediction is used for each glimpse or the second order feature. The full prediction takes all the glimpse outputs and second order features as inputs.

Branch Prediction. To encourage each glimpse and the second order module to gather the information for answering, we feed each of them into an independent branch prediction module. In the branch prediction module the visual feature and question feature are first transformed into a hidden space, then projected by a fully connected layer to the answer space as follows:

$$\mathbf{h}_x = \text{ReLU}\left((\text{ReLU}\left(\mathbf{q}\mathbf{W}_{qh}\right) \circ \text{ReLU}\left(\mathbf{v}_x\mathbf{W}_{xh}\right))\right)$$
$$\hat{\mathbf{a}}_x = \text{sigmoid}\left(\mathbf{h}_x\mathbf{W}_{xa}\right)$$

where $\mathbf{v}_x \in \{\mathbf{g}_1, \mathbf{g}_2, \dots, \mathbf{g}_m, \mathbf{s}\}$, $\mathbf{W}_{qh} \in \mathbb{R}^{d_t \times d_h}$, $\mathbf{W}_{xh} \in \mathbb{R}^{d_v \times d_h}$, $\mathbf{W}_{xa} \in \mathbb{R}^{d_h \times d_a}$.

Full Prediction. To fully utilize all the information in each branch, we concatenate all the hidden features in branches into $\mathbf{h}$, then map it into the answer space by a linear transformation.

$$\mathbf{h} = [\mathbf{h}_1, \mathbf{h}_2, \dots, \mathbf{h}_{m+1}]$$
$$\hat{\mathbf{a}} = \text{sigmoid}\left(\mathbf{h}\mathbf{W}_{ha}\right)$$

where $\mathbf{h} \in \mathbb{R}^{(m+1) \times d_h}$ and $\mathbf{W}_{ha} \in \mathbb{R}^{(m+1)d_h \times d_a}$.

Loss Function. The total loss for prediction is composed of two parts: loss for branch prediction and loss for full prediction. The branch loss is scaled by a factor α_b.

$$L = L_f + \alpha_b L_b \tag{8}$$

Both the full prediction loss and branch prediction loss adopt binary cross-entropy (BCE) as the loss function.

$$L_f = \text{BCE}\,(\hat{a}, a)$$

$$L_b = \sum_{x=1}^{m+1} \text{BCE}\,(\hat{a}_x, a)$$

3.5   Data Augmentation by Semantic Deformation

We observe that, with a high probability, humans are able to answer questions when some objects in the image are occluded, or some un-related 'noise' objects are existing in the image. Inspired by this, we propose an object-level data augmentation method – semantic deformation. Essentially, it contains two key steps, *i.e.*, semantic objects cropping and semantic objects adding.

Semantic Objects Cropping. The size k of visual object set $\mathbf{V}$ from Faster R-CNN is usually very large to make sure that it contains the necessary objects for question answering. If we randomly remove a small number of k_r objects from the original visual object set, the remaining object set will still contain the clues for answering with high probability. We choose the k_r over a uniform distribution over 1 to R_{max}, where the R_{max} is the maximum number of objects that can be removed.

$$k_r = \text{uniform}(1, R_{max})$$
$$\mathbf{V}_{selected} = \text{select}(\mathbf{V}, k - k_r)$$

Semantic Objects Adding. We add k_a semantic noise objects to the visual object set from a randomly picked image. The number k_a of noise objects is a uniform distribution over 1 to A_{max}. The selected visual object set and the added noise object set can be merged into a new semantic image by concatenation.

$$k_a = \text{uniform}(1, A_{max})$$
$$\mathbf{V}_{add} = \text{select}(\mathbf{V}', k_a)$$
$$\mathbf{V}_{new} = \text{concate}(\mathbf{V}_{selected}, \mathbf{V}_{add})$$

Negative Example Loss. Intuitively, the added noise objects are unrelated to the question and visual context with a big chance. The irrelevance can be utilized as a self-supervised signal to guide the model where not to look. We apply a negative example loss to punish the model when the attention score on the added noise object surpasses a threshold.

$$L_{neg} = \sum_{g=1}^{m} \sum_{i=k-k_r+1}^{k-k_r+k_a} \max(0, \mathbf{A}_{i,g} - \tau) \tag{9}$$

where $\mathbf{A}_{i,g}$ is the attention score on the i-th object in the g-th glimpse, τ is the threshold attention value for noise objects. The negative loss is added to the total loss by a factor of α_{neg}.

$$L = L_f + \alpha_b L_b + \alpha_{neg} L_{neg} \tag{10}$$

where α_b is the coefficient.

4 Experiments

4.1 Datasets

We evaluate our model both on VQA v2.0 [32] and VQA-CP v2.0 [33]. VQA v2.0 contains 204k images from MS-COCO dataset [34] and 1.1M human-annotated questions. The dataset is built to alleviate the language bias problem existing in VQA v1.0. VQA v2.0 dataset makes the image matter by building complementary pairs as $<Question_A, Img_A, Ans_A>$ and $<Question_A, Img_B, Ans_B>$, which share the question but with different images and answers. The dataset is divided into 3 folder: 443K for training, 214K for validation and 453K for testing. VQA-CP v2.0 generates the new training and testing splits with changing priors from VQA dataset. The changing priors setting requires the model to learn the ground concept in images rather than memorizing the dataset bias. For each image, question pair, there are 10 human annotated answers. The evaluation metric for the predicted answer is defined as below:

$$\text{Acc}(ans) = \min \left\{ \frac{\#humans \quad that \quad said \quad ans}{3}, 1 \right\} \tag{11}$$

4.2 Implementation Details

Model Setting. The hyper-parameters of the proposed model in the experiments are as follows. The dimension of visual features d_v, question feature d_t, second order feature d_e and hidden feature d_h are set to 2048, 1024, 2048 and 2048 respectively. The number of candidate answers is set to 3129 according to the occurrence frequency. The glimpses number in attention is $m \in \{1, 2, 4, 6, 8\}$. We empirically set the branch loss factor α_b to 0.2.

Training Setting. In training, we choose the Adamax optimizer with learning rate $min(t \times 10^{-3}, 4 \times 10^{-3})$ for the first 10 epochs and then decayed by 1/5 for every 2 epochs. The model is trained by 13 epochs with a clip value of 0.25 and

96   Q. Sun et al.

Table 1. The Results of SOMA and other previous state-of-the-art methods on VQA v2.0 test-dev and test-std splits. The accuracy of each answer type on test-dev split is listed separately.

Method	test-dev				test-std
	Y/N	No.	Other	All	All
VQA team-LSTM+CNN [32]	-	-	-	-	54.22
MCB [8] reported in [32]	-	-	-	-	62.27
Bottom-up [1]	81.82	44.21	56.05	65.32	65.67
MF-SIG-VG [35]	81.29	42.99	55.55	64.73	-
CoR-3 [36]	84.98	47.19	58.64	68.19	68.59
MFH [18]	-	-	-	66.12	-
MuRel [37]	84.77	49.84	57.85	68.03	68.41
DCN [17]	83.51	46.61	57.26	66.87	66.97
Counter [38]	83.14	**51.62**	58.97	68.09	68.41
SOMA(ours)	84.86	47.59	59.06	68.38	68.67
SOMA + Semantic Deformation	**84.87**	47.71	**59.12**	**68.43**	**68.71**

batch size of 256. When tested at VQA v2.0 test-dev and test-std split, we train the model on training, validation and extra genome dataset. The performance on VQA v2.0 validation dataset is evaluated by the model trained on training split. The result on VQA-CP v2.0 test split is evaluated by the model trained on the training split.

Semantic Deformation Setting. We denote the maximum number of objects removed and objects added as R_{max} and A_{max} respectively. They are both set to 4 by default. The negative sample loss factor α_{neg} and threshold τ is set to 1.0 and 0.18 respectively.

4.3 Results and Analysis

Results on VQA v2.0. First, we evaluate SOMA model on VQA v2.0 dataset. The results of our model and other attention based methods are summarized in Table 1. Bottom-up model is the winner of VQA v2.0 Challenge 2017 which utilizes the visual features from Faster R-CNN. Multimodal Compact Bilinear Pooling (MCB) [8] adopts count-sketch projection to calculate the outer product of visual feature and textual feature in a lower dimensional space. Multimodal Factorized High-order Pooling (MFH) [18] cascades multiple low rank matrix factorization based bilinear fusion modules. MuRel [37] adopts bilinear fusion to represent the interactions between question and visual vectors. Dense Co-Attention Network (DCN) is composed of co-attention layers for visual and textual modalities. Counter [38] is specialized to count objects in VQA by utilizing the graph of objects. In contrast to MFH, our model SOMA projects the visual and textual features into a shared embedding space and models the interaction of intra-modality and cross-modality simultaneously in the second order

Table 2. The Results of SOMA and other previous state-of-the-art methods on VQA-CP v2.0 test splits. Models with * have been trained by [39].

Method	test			
	Y/N	Num	Other	All
SAN [2]	38.35	11.14	21.74	24.96
GVQA [33]	57.99	13.68	22.14	31.30
RAMEN [39]	-	-	-	39.21
BAN [3]*	-	-	-	39.31
Bottom-up [1]*	-	-	-	38.01
Bottom-up + AttAlign [40]	42.5	11.4	43.8	38.5
Bottom-up + AdvReg [41]	**65.5**	**15.5**	35.5	**41.2**
SOMA(ours)	43.0	12.9	**47.3**	40.8

module. The results on VQA v2.0 show that SOMA improves the Bottom-up baseline with a margin of 3% overall, which demonstrates the effectiveness of the second order module. Furthermore, we apply the semantic deformation strategy in training and the results show that performance has been boosted on all answer types. Since we train the model with semantic deformation in the same epochs, the improvement is totally a benefit for free.

Results on VQA-CP v2.0. In this experiment, we compare SOMA with other competitors on VQA-CP v2.0 dataset. Ground visual Question Answering model (GVQA) disentangles the recognition of visual concepts from answer identification. Bilinear Attention Network (BAN) [3] develops an effective way to utilize multiple bilinear attention maps in a residual way. Bottom-up + AttAlign aligns

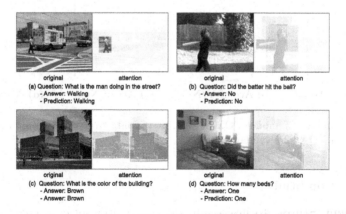

Fig. 2. Qualitative examples of the prediction results on VQA v2.0 dataset for model SOMA. In each example, the left part is the original image and the right part is the illustration of attention. Below the image is the question, ground-truth answer and predicted answer respectively.

the model attention with human attention to increase the robustness. Bottom-up + AdvReg trains a VQA model and a question-only model. It uses the question-only model as an adversary to discourage the VQA model to keep the language bias in its learned question feature. Table 2 shows that SOMA outperforms the bottom-up model with a margin of 2.3% in total. And it is only below to Bottom-up + AdvReg with a minor gap. To be noticed, Bottom-up + AdvReg is specially designed to prevent the model from overfitting the bias. While SOMA achieves this score with no special design and it can perform well on both VQA v2.0 and VQA-CP v2.0 dataset.

Qualitative Results. To better reveal the insight of our model, we give some qualitative results. Particularly, to qualitatively analyze SOMA, we visualize the input image, question and predicted answer in Fig. 2. The examples have shown that SOMA is able to attend to the question related region in the image during answering. This also validates the efficacy of our model.

Table 3. Ablation experiments results on VQA v2.0 validation split. SOMA w/o SO denotes the model without utilizing the second order feature. SOMA w/o BL denotes the model without using branch loss. The comparisons are performed on all the models with the glimpse number of 4.

Model	Y/N	Num	Other	ALL
SOMA w/o SO	82.98	45.00	57.31	65.34
SOMA w/o BL	82.96	44.64	57.04	65.15
SOMA (full)	**83.20**	**45.07**	**57.46**	**65.51**

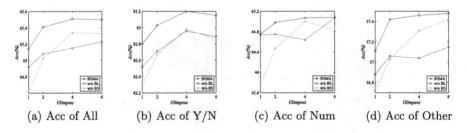

(a) Acc of All   (b) Acc of Y/N   (c) Acc of Num   (d) Acc of Other

Fig. 3. Accuracies of model SOMA and its variants over different glimpses $G \in \{1, 2, 4, 6\}$ on VQA v2.0 validation split.

4.4   Ablation Study

Component Study. To investigate the contribution of each component, we train a full SOMA model with the glimpse number of 4 as a baseline. Then we propose two variants of SOMA. (1) SOMA w/o SO denotes the model does not contain the second order module for the multi-glimpse attention output. (2)

SOMA w/o BL indicates the model does not conclude the branch loss of each glimpse. As shown in Table 3, the overall performance of SOMA w/o SO and SOMA w/o BL drops 0.17% and 0.36% respectively. Figure 3 further shows that the full model outperforms the variants on all glimpse $G \in \{1, 2, 4, 6\}$ in all answer types. We notice that the overall performance of the full model with the glimpse number of 2 is even better than the variants with the glimpse number of 4 or 6.

Table 4. Performance and model size of SOMA over the number of glimpses. Accuracy denotes the prediction accuracy on VQA v2.0 validation split. Params represent the total parameter size of the model. FLOP denotes float point operation cost. Computation cost is evaluated when the number of visual objects is 36 and the question contains 7 words over the glimpse number $G \in \{1, 2, 4, 6\}$.

Glimpse	Accuracy	#Params	#FLOPs
1	65.14	82M	420M
2	65.41	105M	475M
4	65.51	151M	586M
6	65.50	198M	696M

Performance and Cost. It is important to investigate the relationship between performance and cost, especially in real word application. Table 4 quantitatively shows the accuracy, model size and computation cost (FLOPs) trends over the glimpse number. The result shows that SOMA achieves the best performance when the number of glimpse is 4.

4.5 Experiments of Data Augmentation

Table 5. The performance of SOMA with semantic deformation on VQA v2.0 val split. SOMA indicates the baseline with 4 glimpses. SOMA + C indicates cropping on the input visual features of SOMA. SOMA + CA denotes cropping and noise adding. SOMA + CAN represents cropping and noise adding with negative example loss.

Model	SOMA	SOMA+C	SOMA+CA	SOMA+CAN
All	65.51	65.52	65.60	65.61

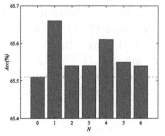
(a) Variant Deformation Number

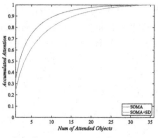
(b) Accumulated Attention

Fig. 4. (a) Performance of Semantic Deformation for different deformation number N, which denotes the maximum object removed and added number. The red dash line denotes the baseline which is the case $N = 0$. (b) Accumulated attention for the most attended M objects. (Color figure online)

Data Augmentation Evaluation. To analyze semantic deformation, we propose serval variants and perform the ablation study on VQA v2.0 validation split. We train a SOMA model with the glimpse number of 4 as the baseline. Three variants are proposed by taking first n steps in semantic objects cropping, semantic objects adding and negative example loss applying gradually. The results in Table 5 show that semantic cropping, noise object adding are all beneficial to improve the performance of the baseline. And negative example loss is effective when the noise object adding strategy is used. When all the three techniques are used, the trained model achieves the best performance of 65.61% on the validation split. Furthermore, we conduct a series of experiments with different maximum numbers for objects removed and added in semantic deformation. Figure 4(a) shows that the model with semantic deformation can beat the baseline with a slighter margin when the maximum number is from 1 to 6. Figure 4(b) indicates that the accumulated attention of SOMA model grows

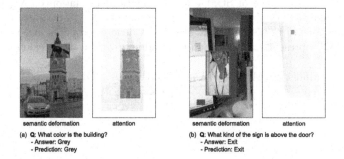

semantic deformation   attention   semantic deformation   attention

(a) **Q:** What color is the building?   (b) **Q:** What kind of the sign is above the door?
   - Answer: Grey   - Answer: Exit
   - Prediction: Grey   - Prediction: Exit

Fig. 5. Qualitative examples of Semantic Deformation. The left image is the training image from semantic deformation. The red box denotes the bounding box of removed semantic objects. And the patch with green frames represents the added noise objects. The right image is the visualization results of attention maps. (Color figure online)

slower when trained with semantic deformation, which means the model gains robustness by attending to more related objects.

Data Augmentation Example. To qualitatively analyze why semantic deformation works, we visualize a randomly generated image from semantic deformation as in Fig. 5. For simplicity, we do not plot all of the 36 bounding boxes. We only show the bounding boxes of removed semantic objects and added semantic objects. Actually, the 36 bounding box has a lot of overlaps which make the visual feature set with high redundancy. Intuitively, we can see that the model is able to answer the question with a high possibility from the necessary grounding visual information.

In this paper, we propose a Second Order enhanced Multi-glimpse Attention (SOMA) model for Visual Question Answering. SOMA adopts a second order module to explicitly model the interaction on both the intra-modality and cross-modality in the shared embedding for multi-glimpse outputs and question feature. The branch loss is added to enhance each glimpse for better feature learning and attention ability. Furthermore, we advocate a novel semantic deformation method as data augmentation for VQA, which can generate the new image in the semantic space by semantic object cropping and semantic object adding. A negative example loss is introduced to provide a self-supervised signal for where not to look. The experiments on VQA v2.0 and VQA-CP v2.0 have shown the effectiveness of SOMA and semantic deformation. In feature works, we would like to design a better strategy for noise objects picking and apply semantic deformation to more multi-modal tasks.

References

1. Anderson, P., et al.: Bottom-up and top-down attention for image captioning and visual question answering. In: CVPR. Volume 3, pp. 6077–6086 (2018)
2. Yang, Z., He, X., Gao, J., Deng, L., Smola, A.: Stacked attention networks for image question answering. In: Proceedings of the IEEE Conference on Computer Vision and Pattern Recognition, pp. 21–29 (2016)
3. Kim, J.H., Jun, J., Zhang, B.T.: Bilinear attention networks. In: Advances in Neural Information Processing Systems, pp. 1564–1574 (2018)
4. Gao, P., et al.: Dynamic fusion with intra-and inter-modality attention flow for visual question answering. In: Proceedings of the IEEE Conference on Computer Vision and Pattern Recognition, pp. 6639–6648 (2019)
5. Yu, Z., Yu, J., Cui, Y., Tao, D., Tian, Q.: Deep modular co-attention networks for visual question answering. In: Proceedings of the IEEE Conference on Computer Vision and Pattern Recognition, pp. 6281–6290 (2019)
6. Shih, K.J., Singh, S., Hoiem, D.: Where to look: focus regions for visual question answering. In: Proceedings of the IEEE Conference on Computer Vision and Pattern Recognition, pp. 4613–4621 (2016)
7. Zhou, B., Tian, Y., Sukhbaatar, S., Szlam, A., Fergus, R.: Simple baseline for visual question answering. arXiv preprint arXiv:1512.02167 (2015)
8. Fukui, A., Park, D.H., Yang, D., Rohrbach, A., Darrell, T., Rohrbach, M.: Multimodal compact bilinear pooling for visual question answering and visual grounding. arXiv preprint arXiv:1606.01847 (2016)

9. Kim, J.H., On, K.W., Lim, W., Kim, J., Ha, J.W., Zhang, B.T.: Hadamard product for low-rank bilinear pooling. arXiv preprint arXiv:1610.04325 (2016)

10. Ben-Younes, H., Cadene, R., Cord, M., Thome, N.: Mutan: multimodal tucker fusion for visual question answering. In: Proceedings of the IEEE International Conference on Computer Vision, pp. 2612–2620 (2017)

11. Guo, H., Tang, R., Ye, Y., Li, Z., He, X.: Deepfm: a factorization-machine based neural network for ctr prediction. arXiv preprint arXiv:1703.04247 (2017)

12. Lian, J., Zhou, X., Zhang, F., Chen, Z., Xie, X., Sun, G.: xdeepfm: combining explicit and implicit feature interactions for recommender systems. In: Proceedings of the 24th ACM SIGKDD International Conference on Knowledge Discovery & Data Mining, pp. 1754–1763 (2018)

13. Antol, S., et al.: VQA: visual question answering. In: Proceedings of the IEEE International Conference on Computer Vision, pp. 2425–2433 (2015)

14. Malinowski, M., Fritz, M.: A multi-world approach to question answering about real-world scenes based on uncertain input. In: Advances in Neural Information Processing Systems, pp. 1682–1690 (2014)

15. Kazemi, V., Elqursh, A.: Show, ask, attend, and answer: A strong baseline for visual question answering. arXiv preprint arXiv:1704.03162 (2017)

16. Lu, J., Yang, J., Batra, D., Parikh, D.: Hierarchical question-image co-attention for visual question answering. In: Advances In Neural Information Processing Systems, pp. 289–297 (2016)

17. Nguyen, D.K., Okatani, T.: Improved fusion of visual and language representations by dense symmetric co-attention for visual question answering. In: Proceedings of the IEEE Conference on Computer Vision and Pattern Recognition, pp. 6087–6096 (2018)

18. Yu, Z., Yu, J., Xiang, C., Fan, J., Tao, D.: Beyond bilinear: generalized multimodal factorized high-order pooling for visual question answering. IEEE Trans. Neural Netw. Learn. Syst. **29**, 5947–5959 (2018)

19. Li, L.H., Yatskar, M., Yin, D., Hsieh, C.J., Chang, K.W.: Visualbert: a simple and performant baseline for vision and language. arXiv preprint arXiv:1908.03557 (2019)

20. Lu, J., Batra, D., Parikh, D., Lee, S.: Vilbert: pretraining task-agnostic visiolin-guistic representations for vision-and-language tasks. In: Advances in Neural Information Processing Systems, pp. 13–23 (2019)

21. Simonyan, K., Zisserman, A.: Very deep convolutional networks for large-scale image recognition. arXiv preprint arXiv:1409.1556 (2014)

22. Zhang, H., Cisse, M., Dauphin, Y.N., Lopez-Paz, D.: mixup: beyond empirical risk minimization. arXiv preprint arXiv:1710.09412 (2017)

23. Verma, V., et al.: Manifold mixup: better representations by interpolating hidden states. arXiv preprint arXiv:1806.05236 (2018)

24. Chen, L., Yan, X., Xiao, J., Zhang, H., Pu, S., Zhuang, Y.: Counterfactual samples synthesizing for robust visual question answering. In: Proceedings of the IEEE/CVF Conference on Computer Vision and Pattern Recognition, pp. 10800–10809 (2020)

25. Doersch, C., Gupta, A., Efros, A.A.: Unsupervised visual representation learning by context prediction. In: Proceedings of the IEEE International Conference on Computer Vision, pp. 1422–1430 (2015)

26. Zhang, R., Isola, P., Efros, A.A.: Colorful image colorization. In: Leibe, B., Matas, J., Sebe, N., Welling, M. (eds.) ECCV 2016. LNCS, vol. 9907, pp. 649–666. Springer, Cham (2016). https://doi.org/10.1007/978-3-319-46487-9_40

27. Pathak, D., Krahenbuhl, P., Donahue, J., Darrell, T., Efros, A.A.: Context encoders: feature learning by inpainting. In: Proceedings of the IEEE Conference on Computer Vision and Pattern Recognition, pp. 2536–2544 (2016)
28. Noroozi, M., Favaro, P.: Unsupervised learning of visual representations by solving jigsaw puzzles. In: Leibe, B., Matas, J., Sebe, N., Welling, M. (eds.) ECCV 2016. LNCS, vol. 9910, pp. 69–84. Springer, Cham (2016). https://doi.org/10.1007/978-3-319-46466-4_5
29. Mikolov, T., Chen, K., Corrado, G., Dean, J.: Efficient estimation of word representations in vector space. arXiv preprint arXiv:1301.3781 (2013)
30. Mikolov, T., Sutskever, I., Chen, K., Corrado, G.S., Dean, J.: Distributed representations of words and phrases and their compositionality. In: Advances in Neural Information Processing Systems, pp. 3111–3119 (2013)
31. Krishna, R., et al.: Visual genome: connecting language and vision using crowdsourced dense image annotations. Int. J. Comput. Vis. **123**, 32–73 (2017)
32. Goyal, Y., Khot, T., Summers-Stay, D., Batra, D., Parikh, D.: Making the v in vqa matter: elevating the role of image understanding in visual question answering. In: CVPR. Volume 1, pp. 6904–6913 (2017)
33. Agrawal, A., Batra, D., Parikh, D., Kembhavi, A.: Don't just assume; look and answer: overcoming priors for visual question answering. In: Proceedings of the IEEE Conference on Computer Vision and Pattern Recognition, pp. 4971–4980 (2018)
34. Lin, T.-Y., et al.: Microsoft COCO: common objects in context. In: Fleet, D., Pajdla, T., Schiele, B., Tuytelaars, T. (eds.) ECCV 2014. LNCS, vol. 8693, pp. 740–755. Springer, Cham (2014). https://doi.org/10.1007/978-3-319-10602-1_48
35. Zhu, C., Zhao, Y., Huang, S., Tu, K., Ma, Y.: Structured attentions for visual question answering. In: Proceedings of the IEEE International Conference on Computer Vision, pp. 1291–1300 (2017)
36. Wu, C., Liu, J., Wang, X., Dong, X.: Chain of reasoning for visual question answering. In: Advances in Neural Information Processing Systems, pp. 273–283 (2018)
37. Cadene, R., Ben-Younes, H., Cord, M., Thome, N.: Murel: multimodal relational reasoning for visual question answering. arXiv preprint arXiv:1902.09487 (2019)
38. Zhang, Y., Hare, J., Prügel-Bennett, A.: Learning to count objects in natural images for visual question answering. arXiv preprint arXiv:1802.05766 (2018)
39. Shrestha, R., Kafle, K., Kanan, C.: Answer them all! toward universal visual question answering models. In: Proceedings of the IEEE Conference on Computer Vision and Pattern Recognition, pp. 10472–10481 (2019)
40. Selvaraju, R.R., et al.: Taking a hint: leveraging explanations to make vision and language models more grounded. In: Proceedings of the IEEE International Conference on Computer Vision, pp. 2591–2600 (2019)
41. Ramakrishnan, S., Agrawal, A., Lee, S.: Overcoming language priors in visual question answering with adversarial regularization. In: Advances in Neural Information Processing Systems, pp. 1541–1551 (2018)

Localize to Classify and Classify to Localize: Mutual Guidance in Object Detection

Heng Zhang[1,3]([⊠]) [iD], Elisa Fromont[1,4] [iD], Sébastien Lefevre[2] [iD],
and Bruno Avignon[3]

[1] Univ Rennes, IRISA, Rennes, France
{heng.zhang,elisa.fromont}@irisa.fr
[2] Univ Bretagne Sud, IRISA, Lorient, France
sebastien.lefevre@irisa.fr
[3] ATERMES Company, Salbris, France
bavignon@atermes.fr
[4] IUF, Inria, Paris, France

Abstract. Most deep learning object detectors are based on the anchor mechanism and resort to the Intersection over Union (IoU) between predefined anchor boxes and ground truth boxes to evaluate the matching quality between anchors and objects. In this paper, we question this use of IoU and propose a new anchor matching criterion guided, during the training phase, by the optimization of both the localization and the classification tasks: the predictions related to one task are used to dynamically assign sample anchors and improve the model on the other task, and vice versa. Despite the simplicity of the proposed method, our experiments with different state-of-the-art deep learning architectures on PASCAL VOC and MS COCO datasets demonstrate the effectiveness and generality of our Mutual Guidance strategy.

1 Introduction

Supervised object detection is a popular task in computer vision that aims at localizing objects through bounding boxes and assigning each of them to a predefined class. Deep learning-based methods largely dominate this research field and most recent methods are based on the anchor mechanism [1–12]. Anchors are predefined reference boxes of different sizes and aspect ratios uniformly stacked over the whole image. They help the network to handle object scale and shape variations by converting the object detection problem into an anchor-wise bounding box regression and classification problem. Most state-of-the-art anchor-based object detectors resort to the Intersection over Union (IoU) between the predefined anchor boxes and the ground truth boxes (called IoU_{anchor} in the following)

Electronic supplementary material The online version of this chapter (https://doi.org/10.1007/978-3-030-69538-5_7) contains supplementary material, which is available to authorized users.

H. Ishikawa et al. (Eds.): ACCV 2020, LNCS 12625, pp. 104–118, 2021.
https://doi.org/10.1007/978-3-030-69538-5_7

Fig. 1. Anchors A and anchors B have the same IoU with ground truth box but different visual semantic information. The ground truth in each image is marked as dotted-line box. Better viewed in colour. (Color figure online)

to assign the sample anchors to an object (positive anchors) or a background (negative anchors) category. These assigned anchors are then used to minimize the bounding box regression and classification losses during training.

This IoU_{anchor}-based anchor matching criterion is reasonable under the assumption that anchor boxes with high IoU_{anchor} are appropriate for localization and classification. However, in reality, the IoU_{anchor} is insensitive to object's content/context, thus not "optimal" to be used, as such, for anchor matching. In Fig. 1, we show several examples where IoU_{anchor} does not well reflect the matching quality between anchors and objects: anchors A and anchors B have exactly the same IoU_{anchor} but possess very different matching qualities. For example, on the first line of Fig. 1, anchors A covers a more representative and informative part of the object than anchors B; On the second line, anchors B contains parts of a nearby object which hinders the prediction on the jockey/left person.

Deep learning-based object detection involves two sub-tasks: instance localization and classification. Predictions for these two tasks tell us "where" and "what" objects are on the image respectively. During the training phase, both tasks are jointly optimized by gradient descent, but the static anchor matching strategy does not explicitly benefit from the joint resolution of the two tasks, which may then yield to a task-misalignment problem, i.e., during the evaluation phase, the model might generate predictions with correct classification but imprecisely localized bounding boxes as well as predictions with precise localization but wrong classification. Both predictions significantly reduce the overall detection quality.

To address these two limitations of the existing IoU_{anchor}-based strategy, we propose a new, adaptive anchor matching criterion guided by the localization and by the classification tasks mutually, i.e., resorting to the bounding box regression prediction, we dynamically assign training anchor samples for optimizing classification and vice versa. In particular, we constrain anchors that are well-localized to also be well-classified (*Localize to Classify*), and those well-classified to also be well-localized (*Classify to Localize*). These strategies lead to a content/context-sensitive anchor matching and avoid the task-misalignment problem. Despite the simplicity of the proposed strategy, *Mutual Guidance* brings consistent Average Precision (AP) gains over the traditional static strategy with different deep learning architectures on PASCAL VOC [13] and MS COCO [14] datasets, especially on strict metrics such as AP75. Our method is expected to be more efficient on applications that require a precise instance localization, e.g., autonomous driving, robotics, outdoor video surveillance, etc.

The rest of this paper is organized as follows: in Sect. 2, we discuss some representative related work in object detection. Section 3 provides implementation details of the proposed *Mutual Guidance*. Section 4 compares our dynamic anchor matching criterion to the traditional static criterion with different deep learning architectures on different public object detection datasets, and discusses reasons for the precision improvements. Section 5 brings concluding remarks.

2   Related Work

Modern CNN-based object detection methods can be divided into two major categories: two-stage detectors and single-stage ones. Both categories give similar performance with a small edge in accuracy for the former and in efficiency for the latter. Besides, both categories of detectors are massively based on the anchor mechanism which usually resorts to IoU_{anchor} for evaluating the matching quality between anchors and objects when assigning training labels and computing the bounding box regression and classification losses for a training example. Our method aims to improve this anchor matching criterion.

2.1   Anchor-Based Object Detection

Two-stage Object Detectors. Faster RCNN [1] defines the generic paradigm for two-stage object detectors: it first generates a sparse set of Regions of Interest (RoIs) with a Region Proposal Network (RPN), then classifies these regions and refines their bounding boxes. The RoIs are generated by the anchor mechanism. Multiple improvements have been proposed based on this framework: R-FCN [2] suggests position-sensitive score maps to share almost all computations on the entire image; FPN [3] uses a top-down architecture and lateral connections to build high-level semantic feature maps at all scales; PANet [4] enhances the multi-scale feature fusion by adding bottom-up path augmentation to introduce accurate localization signals in lower layers; Libra RCNN [5] proposes the Balanced Feature Pyramid to further integrate multi-scale information into FPN; TridentNet [15] constructs a parallel multi-branch architecture and adopts a scale-aware training scheme for training object scale specialized detection branches. Cascade RCNN [6] further extends the two-stage paradigm into a multi-stage paradigm, where a sequence of detectors are trained stage by stage.

Single-stage Object Detectors. SSD [7] and YOLO [16] are the fundamental methods for single-stage object detection. From this basis, many other works have been

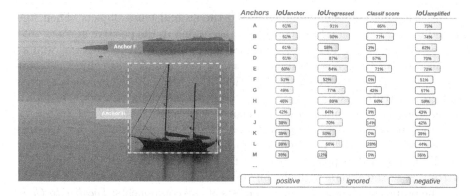

Fig. 2. Illustration of different anchor matching strategies for the boat image resorting to IoU_{anchor} (static), $IoU_{regressed}$ (*Localize to Classify*) and $IoU_{amplified}$ (*Classify to Localize*). Anchors A-M are predefined anchor boxes around the boat in the picture (only F and H are visualized as examples). Better viewed in colour. (Color figure online)

proposed: FSSD [10] aggregates contextual information into the detector by concatenating features of different scales; RetinaNet [9] proposes the Focal Loss to tackle the imbalanced classification problem that arises when trying to separate the actual object to detect from the massive background; RFBNet [11] proposes Receptive Field Block, which takes the relationship between the size and the eccentricity of the reception fields into account; RefineDet [17] introduces an additional stage of refinement for anchor boxes; M2Det [12] stacks multiple thinned U-shape modules to tackle the so-called appearance-complexity variations. While these methods introduce novel architectures to improve results for the object detection task, they all rely on the standard IoU_{anchor}-based matching. We identify this component as a possible limitation and propose a novel matching criterion, that could be adapted to any existing deep architecture for object detection.

2.2   Anchor-Free Object Detection

The idea of anchor-free object detection consists in detecting objects not from predefined anchors boxes, but directly from particular key-points [18–21] or object centres [22–25]. However, these methods do not lead to a substantial accuracy advantage compared to anchor-based methods. The main idea of our *Mutual Guidance* could also be applied to this class of object detectors, and the experimental results with anchor-free detectors are included in the supplementary material.

3   Approach

As already sketc.hed in the introduction, in order to train an anchor-based object detector, the predefined anchors should be assigned as *positive* ("it is a true object") or *negative* ("it is a part of the background") according to an evaluation of the matching between the anchors and the ground truth objects. Then, the bounding box regression loss is optimized according to the positive anchors, and the instance classification loss is optimized according to the positive as well as the negative anchors. When training an anchor-based single-stage object detector with a static anchor matching strategy, the IoU between predefined anchor boxes and ground truth boxes (IoU_{anchor}) is the usual matching criterion. As shown in the IoU_{anchor} column of Fig. 2, anchors with more than 50% of IoU_{anchor} are labelled as "positive", those with less than 40% of IoU_{anchor} are labelled as "negative", the rest are "ignored anchors". Note that at least one anchor should be assigned as positive, hence if there is no anchor with more than 50% of IoU_{anchor}, the anchor with the highest IoU_{anchor} is considered.

The proposed *Mutual Guidance* consists of two components: *Localize to Classify* and *Classify to Localize*.

3.1   Localize to Classify

If an anchor is capable to precisely localize an object, this anchor must cover a good part of the semantically important area of this object and thus could be considered as an appropriate positive sample for classification. Drawing on this, we propose to leverage the IoU between regressed bounding boxes (i.e., the network's localization predictions) and ground truth boxes (noted $IoU_{regressed}$) to better assign the anchor labels for classification. Inspired by the usual IoU_{anchor}, we compare $IoU_{regressed}$ to some given thresholds (discussed in the next paragraph) and then define anchors with $IoU_{regressed}$ greater than a high threshold as positive samples, and those with $IoU_{regressed}$ lower than a low threshold as negative samples (see $IoU_{regressed}$ column of Fig. 2).

We now discuss a dynamic solution to set the thresholds. A fixed threshold (e.g., 50% or 40%) does not seem optimal since the network's localization ability gradually improves during the training procedure and so does the $IoU_{regressed}$ for each anchor, leading to the assignment of more and more positive anchors which destabilizes the training. To address this issue, we propose a dynamic thresholding strategy. Even though the IoU_{anchor} is not the best choice to accurately indicate the matching quality between anchors and objects, the number of assigned *positive* and *ignored* anchors does reflect the global matching conditions (brought by the size and the aspect ratio of the objects to detect), thus these numbers could be considered as reference values for our dynamic criterion. As illustrated in Fig. 2, while applying the IoU_{anchor}-based anchor matching strategy with the thresholds being 50% and 40%, the number of positive anchors (N_p) and ignored anchors (N_i) are noted ($N_p = 6$ and $N_i = 3$ for the boat). We then use these numbers to label the N_p highest $IoU_{regressed}$ anchors as positive, and the following N_i anchors as ignored. More formally, we exploit the N_p-th largest $IoU_{regressed}$ as our positive anchor threshold, and the (N_p+N_i)-th largest $IoU_{regressed}$ as our ignored anchor threshold. Using this, our *Localize to Classify* anchor matching strategy evolves with the network's localization capacity and maintains a consistent number of anchor samples assigned to both categories (positive/negative) during the whole training procedure.

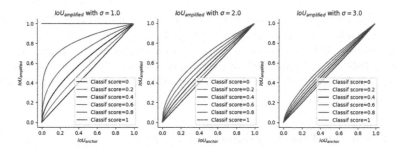

Fig. 3. Illustration of $IoU_{amplified}$ with different σ values (1, 2 or 3). $IoU_{amplified} = IoU_{anchor}$ when $Classif\ score = 0$.

3.2   Classify to Localize

As with the *Localize to Classify* process, the positive anchor samples in *Classify to Localize* are assigned according to the network's classification predictions (noted *Classif score*). Specifically, *Classif score* is the predicted classification score for the object category, e.g., the *Classif score* of Fig. 2 indicates the classification score for the *boat* category.

Nevertheless, this *Classif score* is not effective enough to be used directly for assigning good positive anchors for the bounding box regression optimization. It is especially true at the beginning of the training process, when the network's weights are almost random values and all predicted classification scores are close to zero. The $IoU_{regressed}$ is optimized on the basis of the IoU_{anchor}, therefore we have $IoU_{regressed} \geq IoU_{anchor}$ in most cases (even at the beginning of the training), and this property helps to avoid such cold start problem and ensures training stability. Symmetrically to the *Localize to Classify* strategy, we now propose a *Classify to Localize* strategy based on an $IoU_{amplified}$ defined as:

$$IoU_{amplified} = (IoU_{anchor})^{\frac{\sigma-p}{\sigma}} \qquad (1)$$

where σ is a hyper-parameter aiming at adjusting the degree of amplification, p represents the mentioned *Classif score*. Inspired by the "focal loss" [9], we chose Eq. 1 as the simplest one able to amplify the IoU of anchors according to the correct classification predictions p. Its behavior is shown in Fig. 3. The $IoU_{amplified}$ is always higher than the IoU_{anchor}, and the amplification is proportional to the predicted *Classif score*. In particular, the amplification is stronger for smaller σ (note that σ should be larger than 1), and disappears when σ becomes large.

Similarly to the *Localize to Classify* strategy, we apply a dynamic thresholding strategy to keep the number of assigned positive samples for the localization task and for the classification task consistent, e.g., we assign in Fig. 2, the top 6 anchors with the highest $IoU_{amplified}$ as positive samples. Note that there is no need for selecting ignored or negative anchors for the localization task since the background does not have an associated ground truth box.

As discussed in Sect. 1, IoU_{anchor} is not sensitive to the content or the context of an object. Our proposed *Localize to Classify* and *Classify to Localize*, however, attempt to adaptively label the anchor samples according to their visual content and context information. Considering anchor F and anchor H in Fig. 2, one can tell that anchor H is better than anchor F for recognizing this boat, even with a smaller IoU_{anchor}. Using both our strategies, anchor H has been promoted to positive thanks to its excellent prediction quality on both tasks whereas anchor F has been labelled as negative even though it has a large IoU_{anchor}.

3.3   About the Task-Misalignment Problem

Since *Localize to Classify* and *Classify to Localize* are independent strategies, they could possibly assign contradictory positive/negative labels (e.g., the anchor C in Fig. 2 is labelled negative for the classification task but positive for the bounding box regression task). This happens when one anchor entails a good prediction on one task and a poor prediction on the other (i.e. they are misaligned predictions). Dealing with such contradictory labels, as we do with *Mutual Guidance*, does not harm the training process. On the contrary, our method tackles the task-misalignment problem since the labels for one task are assigned according to the prediction quality on the other task, and vice versa. This mechanism forces the network to generate aligned predictions: if the classification prediction from one anchor is good while its localization prediction is bad, the *Mutual Guidance* will give a positive label on the localization task to this anchor, to constrain it to be better at localizing as well while giving a negative label (i.e. background) on the classification task to avoid misaligned predictions. In fact, the predicted classification score of this mislocalized anchor should be low enough for the anchor to be suppressed by the NMS procedure in the inference phase. The same reasoning holds for a good localization prediction with a bad classification one.

On the contrary, if a network always assigns similar positive/negative labels (as done in standard IoU_{anchor}-based methods) to both tasks during training, one cannot guarantee that there will be no misalignment of the localization and the classification predictions at inference time. Keeping anchors (after NMS) with misaligned predictions is harmful for strict evaluation metrics such as AP75.

4   Experiments

4.1   Experimental Setting

Network Architecture and Parameters. In order to test the generalization performance of the proposed method, we implement our method on the single-stage object detectors FSSD [10], RetinaNet [9] and RFBNet [11] using both ResNet-18 [26] or VGG-16 [27] as backbone networks in our experiments. Note that RFBNet is not implemented with ResNet-18 as backbone since the two architectures are not compatible. The backbone networks are pre-trained on ImageNet-1k classification dataset [28]. We adopt the Focal Loss [9] and Balanced L1 Loss [5] as our instance classification and bounding box regression loss functions respectively for all experiments. The input image resolution is fixed to 320×320 pixels for all experiments (single scale training and evaluation). Unless specified, all other implementation details are the same as in [11]. Following the results of Fig. 3, we decided to fix our only new hyper-parameter σ to 2 for all experiments. σ is used to set the degree of amplification when computing $IoU_{amplified}$ in Eq. (1). It needs to be greater than 1 for the exponent to be positive and lower than 3 since this does not bring any amplification as shown in Fig. 3.

Datasets and Evaluation Metrics. Extensive experiments are performed on two benchmark datasets: PASCAL VOC [13] and MS COCO [14]. PASCAL VOC dataset has 20 object categories. Similarly to previous works, we utilize the combination of VOC2007 and VOC2012 trainval sets for training, and rely on the VOC2007 test for evaluation. MS COCO dataset contains 80 classes. Our experiments on this dataset are conducted on the train2017 and val2017 set for training and evaluation respectively. For all datasets, we use the evaluation metrics introduced in the MS COCO benchmark: the Average Precision (AP) averaged over 10 IoU thresholds from 0.5 to 0.95, but also AP50, AP75, AP_s, AP_m, AP_l. AP50 and AP75 measure the average precision for a given IoU threshold (50% and 75%, respectively). The last three aim at focusing on small ($area < 32^2$), medium ($32^2 < area < 96^2$) and large ($area > 96^2$) objects respectively. Since the size of the objects greatly varies between MS COCO and PASCAL VOC, these size-dependent measures are ignored when experimenting with PASCAL VOC dataset.

4.2 Results

Experiments on PASCAL VOC. We evaluate the effectiveness of both components (*Localize to Classify* and *Classify to Localize*) of our proposed approach w.r.t. the usual IoU_{anchor}-based matching strategy when applied on the same deep learning architectures. The results obtained on the PASCAL VOC dataset are given in Table 1. Both proposed anchor matching strategies consistently boost the performance of the "vanilla" networks and their combination (*Mutual Guidance*) leads to the best AP and all other evaluation metrics.

In particular, we observe that the improvements are small on AP50 (around 0.5%) but significant on AP75 (around 3%), which means that we obtain *more precise detections*. As analysed in Sect. 3.3, this comes from the task-misalignment problem faced with the usual static anchor matching methods. This issue leads to retain well-classified but poorly-localized predictions and suppress well-localized but poorly-classified predictions, which in turns results in a significant drop of the AP score at strict IoU thresholds, e.g., AP75. In *Mutual Guidance*, however, training labels for one task are dynamically assigned according to the prediction quality on the other task and vice versa. This connection makes the classification and localization tasks consistent along all training phases and as such avoids this task-misalignment problem.

Table 1. Comparison of different anchor matching strategies (the usual IoU_{anchor}-based, proposed *Localize to Classify*, *Classify to Localize* and *Mutual Guidance*) for object detection. Experiments are conducted on the PASCAL VOC dataset. The best score for each architecture is in bold.

Model	Matching strategy	AP	AP50	AP75
FSSD with ResNet-18 backbone	IoU_{anchor}-based	50.3%	75.5%	53.7%
	Localize to Classify	51.8%	76.1%	55.9%
	Classify to Localize	51.0%	76.1%	54.3%
	Mutual Guidance	**52.1%**	**76.2%**	**55.9%**
FSSD with VGG-16 backbone	IoU_{anchor}-based	54.1%	80.1%	58.3%
	Localize to Classify	56.0%	80.3%	60.6%
	Classify to Localize	54.4%	79.9%	58.5%
	Mutual Guidance	**56.2%**	**80.4%**	**61.4%**
RetinaNet with ResNet-18 backbone	IoU_{anchor}-based	51.1%	75.8%	54.8%
	Localize to Classify	53.4%	76.5%	57.2%
	Classify to Localize	51.9%	75.9%	55.8%
	Mutual Guidance	**53.5%**	**76.9%**	**57.4%**
RetinaNet with VGG-16 backbone	IoU_{anchor}-based	55.2%	80.2%	59.6%
	Localize to Classify	57.4%	81.1%	62.6%
	Classify to Localize	56.2%	80.1%	61.7%
	Mutual Guidance	**57.7%**	**81.1%**	**62.9%**
RFBNet with VGG-16 backbone	IoU_{anchor}-based	55.6%	80.9%	59.6%
	Localize to Classify	57.2%	80.9%	61.6%
	Classify to Localize	55.9%	80.8%	60.2%
	Mutual Guidance	**57.9%**	**81.5%**	**62.6%**

We also notice that *Localize to Classify* alone brings, for all five architectures, a higher improvement than *Classify to Localize* alone. We hypothesize two possible reasons for this: 1) most object detection errors come from wrong classification instead of imprecise localization, so the classification task is more difficult than the localization task and thus, there is more room for the improvement on this task; 2) the amplification proposed in Eq. (1) may not be the most appropriate one to take advantage of the classification task for optimizing the bounding box regression task.

Experiments on MS COCO. We then conduct experiments on the more difficult MS COCO [14] dataset and report our results in Table 2. Note that according to the scale range defined by MS COCO, APs of small, medium and large objects are listed. In this dataset also, our *Mutual Guidance* strategy consistently brings some performance gains compared to the IoU_{anchor}-based baselines. We notice that our AP gains on large objects is significant (around 2%). This is because larger objects generally have more matched positive anchors, which offers more

Table 2. AP performance of different architectures for object detection on MS COCO dataset using 2 different anchor matching strategies: the usual IoU_{anchor}-based one and our complete approach marked as *Mutual Guidance*. The best score for each architecture is in bold.

Model	Matching strategy	AP	$AP50$	$AP75$	AP_s	AP_m	AP_l
FSSD with ResNet-18 backbone	IoU_{anchor}-based	26.1%	42.8%	26.7%	8.6%	29.1%	41.0%
	Mutual Guidance	**27.0%**	**42.9%**	**28.2%**	**9.5%**	**29.7%**	**43.0%**
FSSD with VGG-16 backbone	IoU_{anchor}-based	31.1%	48.9%	32.7%	13.3%	37.2%	44.7%
	Mutual Guidance	**32.0%**	**49.3%**	**33.9%**	**13.7%**	**37.8%**	**46.4%**
RetinaNet with ResNet-18 backbone	IoU_{anchor}-based	27.8%	44.5%	28.6%	10.4%	31.6%	42.6%
	Mutual Guidance	**28.7%**	**44.9%**	**29.9%**	**11.0%**	**32.2%**	**44.8%**
RetinaNet with VGG-16 backbone	IoU_{anchor}-based	32.3%	50.3%	34.0%	14.3%	37.9%	46.7%
	Mutual Guidance	**33.6%**	**50.8%**	**35.7%**	**15.4%**	**38.9%**	**48.8%**
RFBNet with VGG-16 backbone	IoU_{anchor}-based	33.4%	51.6%	35.1%	14.2%	38.3%	49.1%
	Mutual Guidance	**34.6%**	**52.0%**	**36.8%**	**15.8%**	**39.0%**	**51.1%**

room for improvements to our method. Since the *Mutual guidance* strategy only involves the training phase, and since there is no difference between IoU_{anchor}-based and our method during the evaluation phase, these improvements can be considered cost-free.

4.3   Qualitative Analysis

Label Assignment Visualization. Here, we would like to explore the reasons for the performance improvements by visualizing the difference in the label assignment between the IoU_{anchor}-based strategy and the *Mutual Guidance* strategy during training. Some examples are shown in Fig. 4. White dotted-line boxes represent ground truth boxes; Red anchor boxes are assigned as positive by IoU_{anchor}-based strategy, while considered as negative or ignored by *Localize to Classify* (the top two lines in Fig. 4) or *Classify to Localize* (the bottom two lines in Fig. 4); Green anchor boxes are assigned as positive by *Localize to Classify* but negative or ignored by IoU_{anchor}-based; Yellow anchor boxes are assigned as positive by *Classify to Localize* but negative or ignored by IoU_{anchor}-based. From these examples, we can conclude that the IoU_{anchor}-based strategy only assigns the "positive" label to anchors with sufficient IoU with the ground truth box, regardless of their content/context, whereas our proposed *Localize to Classify* and *Localize to Classify* strategies dynamically assign "positive" labels to anchors covering semantic discriminant parts of the object (e.g., upper body of a person, main body of animals), and assign "negative" labels to anchors with complex background, occluded parts, or anchors containing nearby objects. We believe that our proposed instance-adaptive strategies make the label assignment more reasonable, which is the main reason for performance increase.

Fig. 4. Visualization of the difference in the label assignment during training phase (images are resized to 320 × 320 pixels). Red, yellow and green anchor boxes are positive anchors assigned by IoU_{anchor}-based, *Localize to Classify* and *Classify to Localize* respectively. Zoom in to see details. (Color figure online)

Detection Results Visualization. Figure 5 illustrates on a few images from the PASCAL VOC dataset the different behaviours shown by our *Mutual Guidance* method and the baseline anchor matching strategy. As analysed in Sect. 3.3, we can find misaligned predictions (good at classification but poor at localization) from IoU_{anchor}-based anchor matching strategy. As shown in the figure, our method gives better results when different objects are close to each other in the image, e.g. "man riding a horse" or "man riding a bike". With the usual IoU_{anchor}-based anchor matching strategy, the instance localization and classification tasks are optimized independently of each other. Hence, it is possible that, during the evaluation phase, the classification prediction relies on one object whereas the bounding box regression targets the other object. However, such a problem is rarer with the *Mutual Guidance* strategy. Apparently, our anchor matching strategies introduce interactions between both tasks and makes the predictions of localization and classification aligned, which substantially eliminated such false positive predictions.

Fig. 5. Examples of detection results using an IoU_{anchor}-based anchor matching strategy (odd lines) and our proposed *Mutual Guidance* one (even lines). The results are given for all images after applying a Non-Maximum Suppression process with a IoU threshold of 50%. Zoom in to see details.

5   Conclusion

In this paper, we question the use of the IoU between predefined anchor boxes and ground truth boxes as a good criterion for anchor matching in object detection and study the interdependence of the two sub-tasks (i.e. localization and classification) involved in the detection process. We propose a *Mutual Guidance* mechanism, which provides an adaptive matching between anchors and objects by assigning anchor labels for one task according to the prediction quality on the other task and vice versa. We assess our method on different architectures and different public datasets and compare it with the traditional static anchor matching strategy. Reported results show the effectiveness and generality of this *Mutual Guidance* mechanism in object detection.

References

1. Ren, S., He, K., Girshick, R.B., Sun, J.: Faster R-CNN: towards real-time object detection with region proposal networks. In: Cortes, C., Lawrence, N.D., Lee, D.D., Sugiyama, M., Garnett, R. (eds.) Advances in Neural Information Processing Systems 28: Annual Conference on Neural Information Processing Systems 2015, Montreal, Quebec, Canada, 7–12 December 2015, pp. 91–99 (2015)
2. Dai, J., Li, Y., He, K., Sun, J.: R-FCN: object detection via region-based fully convolutional networks. In: Lee, D.D., Sugiyama, M., von Luxburg, U., Guyon, I., Garnett, R. (eds.) Advances in Neural Information Processing Systems 29: Annual Conference on Neural Information Processing Systems 2016, Barcelona, Spain, 5–10 December 2016, pp. 379–387 (2016)
3. Lin, T., Dollár, P., Girshick, R.B., He, K., Hariharan, B., Belongie, S.J.: Feature pyramid networks for object detection. In: 2017 IEEE Conference on Computer Vision and Pattern Recognition, CVPR 2017, Honolulu, HI, USA, 21–26 July 2017, pp. 936–944. IEEE Computer Society (2017)
4. Liu, S., Qi, L., Qin, H., Shi, J., Jia, J.: Path aggregation network for instance segmentation. In: 2018 IEEE Conference on Computer Vision and Pattern Recognition, CVPR 2018, Salt Lake City, UT, USA, 18–22 June 2018, pp. 8759–8768. IEEE Computer Society (2018)
5. Pang, J., Chen, K., Shi, J., Feng, H., Ouyang, W., Lin, D.: Libra R-CNN: towards balanced learning for object detection. In: IEEE Conference on Computer Vision and Pattern Recognition, CVPR 2019, Long Beach, CA, USA, 16–20 June 2019, pp. 821–830. Computer Vision Foundation / IEEE (2019)
6. Cai, Z., Vasconcelos, N.: Cascade R-CNN: delving into high quality object detection. In: 2018 IEEE Conference on Computer Vision and Pattern Recognition, CVPR 2018, Salt Lake City, UT, USA, 18–22 June 2018, pp. 6154–6162. IEEE Computer Society (2018)
7. Liu, W., et al.: SSD: single shot multiBox detector. In: Leibe, B., Matas, J., Sebe, N., Welling, M. (eds.) ECCV 2016. LNCS, vol. 9905, pp. 21–37. Springer, Cham (2016). https://doi.org/10.1007/978-3-319-46448-0_2
8. Redmon, J., Farhadi, A.: Yolov3: an incremental improvement. CoRR abs/1804.02767 (2018)
9. Lin, T., Goyal, P., Girshick, R.B., He, K., Dollár, P.: Focal loss for dense object detection. In: IEEE International Conference on Computer Vision, ICCV 2017, Venice, Italy, 22–29 October 2017, pp. 2999–3007. IEEE Computer Society (2017)
10. Li, Z., Zhou, F.: FSSD: feature fusion single shot multibox detector. CoRR abs/1712.00960 (2017)
11. Liu, S., Huang, D., Wang, Y.: Receptive field block net for accurate and fast object detection. In: Ferrari, V., Hebert, M., Sminchisescu, C., Weiss, Y. (eds.) ECCV 2018. LNCS, vol. 11215, pp. 404–419. Springer, Cham (2018). https://doi.org/10.1007/978-3-030-01252-6_24

12. Zhao, Q., et al.: M2det: a single-shot object detector based on multi-level feature pyramid network. In: The Thirty-Third AAAI Conference on Artificial Intelligence, AAAI 2019, The Thirty-First Innovative Applications of Artificial Intelligence Conference, IAAI 2019, The Ninth AAAI Symposium on Educational Advances in Artificial Intelligence, EAAI 2019, Honolulu, Hawaii, USA, 27 January - 1 February 2019, pp. 9259–9266. AAAI Press (2019)

13. Everingham, M., Gool, L.V., Williams, C.K.I., Winn, J.M., Zisserman, A.: The pascal visual object classes (VOC) challenge. Int. J. Comput. Vis. **88**, 303–338 (2010)

14. Lin, T.-T., et al.: Microsoft COCO: common objects in context. In: Fleet, D., Pajdla, T., Schiele, B., Tuytelaars, T. (eds.) ECCV 2014. LNCS, vol. 8693, pp. 740–755. Springer, Cham (2014). https://doi.org/10.1007/978-3-319-10602-1_48

15. Li, Y., Chen, Y., Wang, N., Zhang, Z.: Scale-aware trident networks for object detection. In: 2019 IEEE/CVF International Conference on Computer Vision, ICCV 2019, Seoul, Korea (South), 27 October - 2 November 2019, pp. 6053–6062. IEEE (2019)

16. Redmon, J., Divvala, S.K., Girshick, R.B., Farhadi, A.: You only look once: unified, real-time object detection. In: 2016 IEEE Conference on Computer Vision and Pattern Recognition, CVPR 2016, Las Vegas, NV, USA, 27–30 June 2016, pp. 779–788. IEEE Computer Society (2016)

17. Zhang, S., Wen, L., Bian, X., Lei, Z., Li, S.Z.: Single-shot refinement neural network for object detection. In: 2018 IEEE Conference on Computer Vision and Pattern Recognition, CVPR 2018, Salt Lake City, UT, USA, 18–22 June 2018, pp. 4203–4212. IEEE Computer Society (2018)

18. Law, H., Deng, J.: CornerNet: detecting objects as paired keypoints. In: Ferrari, V., Hebert, M., Sminchisescu, C., Weiss, Y. (eds.) Computer Vision – ECCV 2018. LNCS, vol. 11218, pp. 765–781. Springer, Cham (2018). https://doi.org/10.1007/978-3-030-01264-9_45

19. Law, H., Teng, Y., Russakovsky, O., Deng, J.: Cornernet-lite: Efficient keypoint based object detection. CoRR abs/1904.08900 (2019)

20. Zhou, X., Zhuo, J., Krähenbühl, P.: Bottom-up object detection by grouping extreme and center points. In: IEEE Conference on Computer Vision and Pattern Recognition, CVPR 2019, Long Beach, CA, USA, 16–20 June 2019, pp. 850–859. Computer Vision Foundation / IEEE (2019)

21. Duan, K., Bai, S., Xie, L., Qi, H., Huang, Q., Tian, Q.: Centernet: keypoint triplets for object detection. In: 2019 IEEE/CVF International Conference on Computer Vision, ICCV 2019, Seoul, Korea (South), 27 October - 2 November 2019, pp. 6568–6577. IEEE (2019)

22. Zhou, X., Wang, D., Krähenbühl, P.: Objects as points. CoRR abs/1904.07850 (2019)

23. Zhu, C., He, Y., Savvides, M.: Feature selective anchor-free module for single-shot object detection. In: IEEE Conference on Computer Vision and Pattern Recognition, CVPR 2019, Long Beach, CA, USA, 16–20 June 2019, pp. 840–849. Computer Vision Foundation / IEEE (2019)

24. Tian, Z., Shen, C., Chen, H., He, T.: FCOS: fully convolutional one-stage object detection. In: 2019 IEEE/CVF International Conference on Computer Vision, ICCV 2019, Seoul, Korea (South), 27 October - 2 November 2019, pp. 9626–9635. IEEE (2019)

25. Kong, T., Sun, F., Liu, H., Jiang, Y., Shi, J.: Foveabox: beyond anchor-based object detector. CoRR abs/1904.03797 (2019)

26. He, K., Zhang, X., Ren, S., Sun, J.: Deep residual learning for image recognition. In: 2016 IEEE Conference on Computer Vision and Pattern Recognition, CVPR 2016, Las Vegas, NV, USA, 27–30 June 2016, pp. 770–778. IEEE Computer Society (2016)
27. Simonyan, K., Zisserman, A.: Very deep convolutional networks for large-scale image recognition. In: Bengio, Y., LeCun, Y. (eds.) 3rd International Conference on Learning Representations, ICLR 2015, San Diego, CA, USA, 7–9 May 2015, Conference Track Proceedings (2015)
28. Deng, J., Dong, W., Socher, R., Li, L., Li, K., Li, F.: Imagenet: a large-scale hierarchical image database. In: 2009 IEEE Computer Society Conference on Computer Vision and Pattern Recognition (CVPR 2009), Miami, Florida, USA, 20–25 June 2009, pp. 248–255. IEEE Computer Society (2009)

Unified Density-Aware Image Dehazing and Object Detection in Real-World Hazy Scenes

Zhengxi Zhang, Liang Zhao, Yunan Liu, Shanshan Zhang$^{(\boxtimes)}$, and Jian Yang

PCA Lab, Key Lab of Intelligent Perception and Systems for High -Dimensional Information of Ministry of Education, Jiangsu Key Lab of Image and Video Understanding for Social Security, School of Computer Science and Engineering, Nanjing University of Science and Technology, Nanjing, China
{zxzhang,liangzhao,liuyunan,shanshan.zhang,csjyang}@njust.edu.cn

Abstract. It is an important yet challenging task to detect objects on hazy images in real-world applications. The major challenge comes from low visual quality and large haze density variations. In this work, we aim to jointly solve the image dehazing and the object detection tasks in real hazy scenarios by using haze density as prior knowledge. Our proposed **U**nified **D**ehazing a**n**d **D**etection (UDnD) framework consists of three parts: a residual-aware haze density classifier, a density-aware dehazing network, and a density-aware object detector. First, the classifier exploits the residuals of hazy images to accurately predict density levels, which provide rich domain knowledge for the subsequent two tasks. Then, we design respectively a **H**igh-**R**esolution **D**ehazing **N**etwork (HRDN) and a Faster R-CNN-based multi-domain object detector to leverage the extracted density information and tackle hazy object detection. Experiments demonstrate that UDnD performs favorably against other methods for object detection in real-world hazy scenes. Also, HRDN achieves better results than state-of-the-art dehazing methods in terms of PSNR and SSIM. Hence, HRDN can conduct haze removal effectively, based on which UDnD is able to provide high-quality detection results.

1 Introduction

Object detection in hazy scenes is important for outdoor vision systems, *e.g.* video surveillance and autonomous driving; yet it is an extremely challenging task. The challenges mainly come from two aspects. On the one hand, hazy images are usually of poor visual quality that caused by low contrast, color distortion and blur *etc.* [1], making it more difficult to discriminate interesting objects from background clutters. On the other hand, haze density varies tremendously in real-world applications, leading to variations w.r.t. visual quality; these non-negligible intra-domain gaps make object detectors hard to converge.

Z. Zhang and L. Zhao—Equal contribution.

© Springer Nature Switzerland AG 2021
H. Ishikawa et al. (Eds.): ACCV 2020, LNCS 12625, pp. 119–135, 2021.
https://doi.org/10.1007/978-3-030-69538-5_8

A straightforward solution to hazy object detection is to first apply image dehazing and then perform object detection on dehazed images. Most previous work follow this strategy, isolating dehazing and detection [2,3]. Since dehazing methods are not able to fully recover latent clear images, it is not guaranteed that the dehazed images are optimal for object detection [2,4]. From this perspective, it is favorable to jointly solve the two tasks, so as to obtain detection-friendly dehazed images and more accurate detection results. In [5], a unified pipeline is first proposed for hazy object detection. However, in their method, each model is designed to process one fixed density level, without handling density variations.

Another line of work uses domain adaptation techniques to tackle the task. They take clear images as the source domain and hazy images as the target domain; and then they try to lift the target domain performance to the source domain level by closing the domain gap via feature alignment [6,7]. However, in practice the domain gap is too large to handle, and it becomes especially more complex when there even exist significant intra-domain gaps in the hazy domain.

In this paper, we deal with the above mentioned two challenges in one coherent framework by taking advantage of both lines of work. We perform image dehazing to reduce the clear-hazy domain gap and then use the simplest domain adaptation method of fine-tuning to adapt a detector based on the clear domain to the dehazed domain. In the whole procedure, we take into account the intra-domain differences of hazy images by separating feature extraction for different haze density levels. Specifically, we propose a Unified density-aware Dehazing and Detection (UDnD) framework for solving image dehazing and object detection in a joint way. First, a modified VGG-Net [8] is introduced to predict haze density using hazy residuals. Then, we design a density switch module to multiplex different haze levels. For dehazing, we make modifications to HRNetV2 [9] by up-sampling with transposed convolution [10] and summing up features from different scales. The object detector then takes the dehazed image as input and switches to the branch dictated by the density level.

The contributions of this work are as follows:

- We propose a UDnD framework to jointly solve dehazing and detection. It for the first time deals with the inter-domain and intra-domain gaps in both image dehazing and hazy object detection, making them mutually benefit.
- We build a residual-aware classifier that predicts haze density levels to assist image dehazing and object detection. To the best of our knowledge, we are the first to explicitly predict haze density as prior knowledge for Convolutional Neural Networks (CNNs).
- A novel dehazing method HRDN is introduced, which sums multi-resolution representations to recover finer details. Guided by haze levels, HRDN is able to integrate density-specific knowledge into the network so as to divide and conquer single image dehazing.
- Experiments are conducted on two real-world hazy datasets, where the proposed UDnD outperforms the vanilla detector and the density-unaware counterparts. We also evaluate our dehazing method on two synthetic datasets, showing better performance than previous state-of-the-art methods. These

results demonstrate that our unified framework can handle the two types of domain gaps and give more accurate detection results in real hazy conditions.

2   Related Work

Since we address the problem of hazy object detection by unifying single image dehazing and multi-domain learning, we will review related work in the above three aspects, respectively.

2.1   Hazy Object Detection

The performance of object detection has been boosted by deep learning. Many CNN-based detectors have been proposed during the past few years, including Faster R-CNN (FRCNN) [11], FPN [12], YOLO [13] and SSD [14]. Albeit obtaining satisfactory performance under clear-weather conditions, none of these models could work seamlessly in hazy scenes without some kind of adaptation.

An intuitive idea for solving hazy object detection is to adopt a two-stage approach, *i.e.* performing dehazing and detection separately. Following this, Li *et al.* [2] study the effect of dehazing on various detectors. They find that applying image dehazing as pre-processing is not very helpful and sometimes even harms the performance. In [3] and [4], similar conclusions are drawn for semantic segmentation and image classification. The main reason is that existing dehazing methods are not good enough to reconstruct high-quality clear images for subsequent high-level vision tasks [4]. To address this issue, Li *et al.* [5] jointly optimize dehazing and detection, achieving better results than traditional two-stage approaches on synthetic images. Though our method is also trained on synthetic images, we demonstrate end-to-end performance on real-world data, and our haze-density-specific gating function improves on their results.

On the other side, some methods adapt a detector from the clear domain to the hazy domain for hazy object detection. They typically find a way to measure the distance between feature distributions of both domains and then train a feature extractor to minimize that distance. Inspired by [15], recent work measure the distance by learning a domain classifier in an adversarial manner [6,7,16–19]. Chen *et al.* [6] present a Domain Adaptive Faster R-CNN (DA-FRCNN) to tackle image-level and instance-level domain shifts. [7] proposes to align the features from regions with objects. However, they do not consider intra-domain gaps in the target hazy domain, which are induced by density variations.

Our unified density-aware framework integrates ideas from both sides. The dehazing and the detection sub-networks are jointly optimized. Particularly, we alleviate the intra-domain gaps by utilizing density levels. In accordance with previous methods, we use FRCNN as the baseline detector for experiments. But in principle, our method can be applied to any arbitrary CNN-based detector.

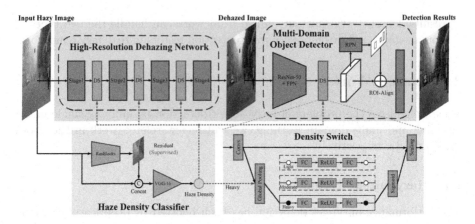

Fig. 1. An overview of the proposed unified density-aware image dehazing and object detection framework. It takes a real-world hazy image as input and first predicts its haze density level via a residual-aware classifier. The predicted density is then fed into a density switch module, which is used for multi-domain learning in the subsequent tasks. The whole network is optimized end-to-end.

2.2 Single Image Dehazing

Early dehazing methods stick to the standard optical model [20] and rely on hand-crafted priors [21–26]. Instead of manually designing features, CNN-based methods learn mappings directly from synthetic data. They usually estimate the transmission map and the atmospheric light, separately or jointly, as intermediate results, and then apply the reverse of the optical model [5,27–35]. However, estimating transmission in hazy scenes is an ill-posed problem, and it gets even worse when the colors of objects are similar to those of atmospheric lights [36]. Therefore, some methods [36–38] try to recover haze-free images directly via end-to-end frameworks, without reliance on the optical model.

The intra-domain gaps, *i.e.* haze density variations, cannot be ignored [3]. Some efforts have been made to incorporate haze density analysis into dark channel prior [39,40]. Dai *et al.* [41] train an AlexNet [42] to regress the attenuation coefficient. Recently, [30] uses multiple network stages to progressively estimate the transmission map and fuses the outputs from different stages, each of which is supervised by synthetic transmission of a fixed density level.

Instead, we handle the intra-domain gaps by explicitly predicting the haze density level and using it as prior knowledge for our end-to-end dehazing network.

2.3 Multi-Domain Learning

Multi-domain learning refers to learning effective representations for data from distinct domains [43]. It can be achieved by setting shared and domain-specific parameters, which resembles domain adaptation [44,45]. Previous work build domain-specific Batch Normalization (BN) layers [46] on otherwise shared networks [47–49]. Inspired by Squeeze-and-Excitation (SE) networks [50,51] introduces a data-driven SE adapter to adjust network activations.

In this work, we consider different haze levels as distinct domains and propose a density switch module to recalibrate features based on the haze density.

3   Proposed Method

In this section, we will first provide an overview of our proposed method and then explain each component in more detail.

3.1   Overview

We propose a coherent framework UDnD to jointly optimize image dehazing and object detection. Our method consists of three parts: a haze density classifier f, a dehazing module DH and a detection module DT. The classifier assigns each hazy image x^h a density level $\hat{d} = f(x^h)$. The dehazing module maps x^h to the latent clear image $\hat{x}^c = DH(x^h, \hat{d}; \theta_{DH})$, with $\hat{d}$ as domain knowledge. The detector takes $\hat{x}^c$ and $\hat{d}$ as input and outputs a structured prediction $\hat{y} = DT(\hat{x}^c, \hat{d}; \theta_{DT})$. Overall, our pipeline can be formulated as

$$\hat{y} = DT(DH(x^h, f(x^h); \theta_{DH}), f(x^h); \theta_{DT}), \tag{1}$$

where x^h is the hazy image and $\hat{y}$ is the detection result. We only presume DH and DT to be differentiable and assume nothing about f beyond providing discrete labels. The entire architecture is illustrated in Fig. 1.

Let x^h be a hazy image from the training set, with clear ground truth x^c and object detection annotations y. The overall loss function for our UDnD is

$$\begin{aligned}\mathcal{L}(x^h, x^c, y; \theta_{DH}, \theta_{DT}) &= \lambda\mathcal{L}_{dehazing}(x^c, DH(x^h, f(x^h); \theta_{DH})) \\ &\quad + \mu\mathcal{L}_{detection}(y, DT(\hat{x}^c, f(x^h); \theta_{DT})),\end{aligned} \tag{2}$$

where $\hat{x}^c = DH(x^h, f(x^h); \theta_{DH})$ is the dehazed result of x^h. We use two weights λ and μ to balance the reconstruction term ($\mathcal{L}_{dehazing}$) and the task-driven term ($\mathcal{L}_{detection}$), which are described in Sect. 3.3 and Sect. 3.4 respectively. Note that the term $\hat{x}^c$ guarantees that the dehazing sub-network is supervised by the detection loss as long as μ is non-zero, while the dehazing loss does not directly affect the detection sub-network. The haze density classifier is used for extracting prior knowledge in our settings, thereby not updated in Eq. 2; which means our framework is compatible to prior-based density estimation methods [52] as well.

3.2   Residual-Aware Haze Density Classifier

The standard optical model [20] formulates the hazing process as

$$x^h(i) = x^c(i)t(i) + L(1 - t(i)), \tag{3}$$

where $x^h(i)$ is the observed hazy image at pixel location i, $x^c(i)$ is the clear scene radiance, and L is the atmospheric light. The transmission map $t(i)$ is obtained using the distance $\ell(i)$ from the scene to the camera lens by $t(i) = \exp(-\beta\ell(i))$. Larger attenuation coefficient β indicates denser haze. For homogeneous haze, the Meteorological Optical Range (MOR) [53], *i.e.* visibility in meters, depends on β through $MOR = \frac{2.996}{\beta}$. It follows that $\beta \geq 2.996 \times 10^{-3}\,\mathrm{m}^{-1}$, where the equality holds for the lightest haze by definition.

We formulate haze density estimation as a classification problem. The predicted density should satisfy $\hat{d} \in \{1, \ldots, C\}$, where C is the total number of predefined density levels. Following [41], we set three levels: light, moderate and heavy; but our method can be extended to finer granularity given proper datasets. The haze density serves as domain label, guiding the update of domain-specific parameters in the subsequent dehazing and detection networks.

Inspired by [54], we observe that the residual of a hazy image, *i.e.* difference from its clear counterpart, is informative because the hazy image is a weighted sum of the clear image and the atmospheric light according to Eq. 3. Therefore, we propose a residual-aware haze density classifier that exploits the hazy residual. The details are depicted in Fig. 1. We stack 3 residual blocks [55] to estimate the residual, which is concatenated with the original hazy image to yield the 6-channel input for a modified VGG-16 [8].

Loss Function. The density classifier is optimized through a joint loss function:

$$\mathcal{L}_{classification} = \alpha\mathcal{L}_{res} + \mathcal{L}_{cls}, \tag{4}$$

where $\mathcal{L}_{res}$ is the L_1 loss for residual regression and $\mathcal{L}_{cls}$ is the cross-entropy loss for density classification. Additionally, α is used to balance the two tasks and is set to 0.2 in our experiments.

3.3   Density-Aware High-Resolution Dehazing Network

As is illustrated in Fig. 1, we propose a density-aware **H**igh-**R**esolution **D**ehazing **N**etwork (HRDN). The backbone is based on HRNetV2 [9], which maintains high-resolution representations and conducts repeated fusion to encourage interaction between multi-scale features. Different from HRNetV2, we only use 4 basic residual blocks in each network stage to prevent overfitting. The downsampling operations in the stem are removed because dehazing is a pixel-level dense regression task. Moreover, we replace all the bilinear up-sampling units with transposed convolutions [10] to recover more details. To enforce a coarse-to-fine reconstruction process, we fuse the up-sampled features by summing them up instead of performing channel-wise concatenation like HRNetV2, which also reduces the computation cost as a side effect.

Density Switch. With the predicted haze density level from Sect. 3.2 as prior knowledge, we expect to handle density variations via multi-domain learning. Inspired by [51], we design a density switch module with multiple SE adapters, each corresponding to one type of density. From Fig. 1 we can see, the estimated haze level controls density switches by specifying which branch to take and what parameters to update, thus separating the feature extraction for different

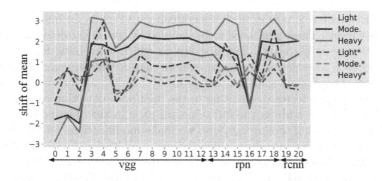

Fig. 2. Shift of mean values over convolutional activations of a vanilla FRCNN on various haze density levels. The vertical axis shows the difference between hazy (dehazed) and clear images. The horizontal axis gives the layer index. "*" indicates the dehazed images produced by our HRDN. The detector is trained on clear images. After dehazing, the activations become more similar to those of clear images, but certain intra-domain gaps remain.

densities. We add density switches before the 2nd, 3rd and 4th stages of HRDN, enabling the network to divide and conquer the intra-domain gaps.

Loss Function. Existing dehazing methods utilize various loss functions, such as L_1 loss [37], MSE loss [5], smooth L_1 loss [31], perceptual loss [35], and adversarial loss [38]. Their weighted combinations are widely adopted. Despite improvements in performance, complicated loss functions increase the burden of hyper-parameter tuning and make the model hard to converge. Inspired by [56], we empirically find that a single SSIM loss works well:

$$\mathcal{L}_{dehazing}(x^c, \hat{x^c}) = 1 - SSIM(x^c, \hat{x^c}), \tag{5}$$

where x^c denotes the ground truth clear image and $\hat{x^c}$ denotes the dehazed image. The constant 1 here is added to ensure the loss value is non-negative.

3.4 Density-Aware Multi-Domain Object Detector

Although the hazy images have been processed by our dehazing network to reduce the inter-domain gaps, there still exist non-negligible intra-domain gaps among the dehazed images, which are caused by haze density variations. We provide some evidence via observing the convolutional activations of a vanilla FRCNN detector on the validation set of Foggy Cityscapes-DBF [41]. We collect the mean activations [51] for images of different densities, compute their differences from those of clear images before and after dehazing, and take these differences as domain gap measurements. A comparison is shown in Fig. 2. We have the following observations: (1) Prior to dehazing, the inter-domain gaps increase monotonically with haze density. (2) The inter-domain gaps are significantly reduced by dehazing, and thus dehazing serves as an effective pre-processing step. (3) Even after dehazing, the intra-domain gaps remain for images of different density levels. These gaps need to be handled by the object detector. (4) The differences vary across layers. The first layers, which learn basic feature detection filters such as edges and corners, exhibit considerable amount of shifts. In other words, the domain gaps are not properly handled at the very beginning and they propagate forward, resulting in the final poor detection results.

In this work, we address the intra-domain gaps in the dehazed domain via multi-domain learning. Following [5,6], we make modifications on FRCNN. As is shown in Fig. 1, we introduce a density-aware multi-domain object detector by appending a density switch module to the ResNet-50 [55] and FPN [12]. By using the density switch, the detector will route images of different densities to desired branches, where different channel weights are computed to adjust the features. The weighted features are then fed into the Region Proposal Network (RPN) with density-specific information encoded.

Loss Function. We employ ROI-Alignment [57] to obtain the corresponding feature vector for each proposal from RPN. Finally, the category label is predicted via an ROI-wise classifier. The loss function for our multi-domain detector is inherited from the vanilla FRCNN [11] for simplicity:

$$\mathcal{L}_{detection} = \mathcal{L}_{rpn} + \mathcal{L}_{roi}. \tag{6}$$

Both the RPN loss ($\mathcal{L}_{rpn}$) and the ROI loss ($\mathcal{L}_{roi}$) consist of classification and localization terms, which are cross-entropy loss and smooth L_1 loss, respectively.

4   Experiments

In this section, we first briefly introduce the datasets and the evaluation metrics used for our experiments, followed by the implementation details. After that, we will provide a comparison against other methods on hazy object detection to demonstrate the effectiveness of our UDnD framework. We will also show the performance of the proposed HRDN compared with state-of-the-art dehazing methods. Finally, we will do some ablation study in terms of domain adaptation techniques, loss functions, and unified training strategies.

4.1   Datasets

The object detectors are trained on synthetic hazy images generated using Eq. 3, but are evaluated on real hazy images. Whereas the dehazing methods are evaluated on synthetic data, only for which the ground truth are available.

Synthetic Datasets
OTS and SOTS-outdoor. RESIDE [2] contains both indoor and outdoor hazy scenes. We adopt the Outdoor Training Set (OTS) and the outdoor subset of Synthetic Objective Testing Set (SOTS-outdoor), and ensure the ground truth

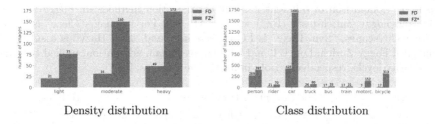

Density distribution   Class distribution

Fig. 3. Haze density distributions and class distributions of Foggy Driving (FD) and Foggy Zurich-test* (FZ*). Both datasets are composed of real-world hazy images. The density levels in (a) are predicted by our residual-aware haze density classifier. In (b), the relatively low number of instances in classes except car and person is not a surprise because hazy weather discourages road traffic.

clear images in OTS do not overlap with those in SOTS-outdoor through data cleaning [31]. The cleaned OTS has 296,695 hazy images with the atmospheric light $L \in [0.8, 1.0]$ and the attenuation coefficient $\beta \in [0.04, 0.2]$, generated out of 8,477 clear images. SOTS-outdoor has 500 hazy images.

Foggy Cityscapes-DBF. Foggy Cityscapes-DBF (FC-DBF) [41] derives from Cityscapes [58] and consists of a large and diverse set of urban street hazy scenes. There are a total of 8,925 images for training and 1,500 images for validation, both equally divided into three density levels ($\beta \in \{0.005, 0.01, 0.02\}$). We follow the screening criteria in [3] and use the selected 1,650 (550×3) high-quality synthetic hazy images to fine-tune the object detectors. This dataset is denoted as FC-DBF-refine. The bounding box annotations of these hazy images are automatically inherited from their clear-weather counterparts.

Real-World Datasets

Foggy Driving. Foggy Driving (FD) [3] is a collection of 101 hazy images of driving scenes, among which 51 images are captured at various areas of Zurich by a cell phone camera and others are selected from the Web.

Foggy Zurich. Foggy Zurich [41] is comprised of 3,808 images that are video frames depicting hazy road scenes in Zurich and its suburbs. Different from FD, these images are collected with a GoPro Hero 5 camera. We manually select 400 images of diverse scenes and haze densities, and annotate them carefully to create a new test set, namely Foggy Zurich-test* (FZ*). The statistics of FD and FZ* are shown in Fig. 3. We can see they both include various haze density levels. In particular, FZ* has significantly more annotated objects than FD, and thus can be served as a more convincing test set.

4.2 Evaluation Metrics

For hazy object detection, we adopt Average Precision (AP) and mean Average Precision (mAP) that is the average of APs over all classes. Additionally, the

Table 1. Comparison of different hazy object detection methods on Foggy Driving (FD) and Foggy Zurich-test* (FZ*) w.r.t. mAP (%). For training, "Clear" is clear-weather Cityscapes, "Syn. Hazy" is FC-DBF-refine , and "Real Hazy" is a subset of unlabelled Foggy Zurich. DA, UT and DL denote domain adaptation, unified training and density levels, respectively. Bold indicates the best results.

Methods	Components			Training sets			Test sets	
	DA	UT	DL	Clear	Syn. Hazy	Real Hazy	FD	FZ*
Vanilla FRCNN [11]				✓			18.26	17.31
DA-FRCNN [6]	✓			✓	✓		19.13	17.80
				✓		✓	19.58	18.52
				✓	✓	✓	22.68	19.27
JAOD-FRCNN [5]	✓	✓		✓	✓		22.17	19.14
Our UDnD	✓	✓	✓	✓	✓		**24.90**	**22.89**

mean of AP scores over the most frequent classes (car and person) is reported as mAP* for evaluating the detectors from a more practical perspective.

For dehazing, Peak Signal-to-Noise Ratio (PSNR) and Structural Similarity Index (SSIM) [59] are used as standard quality measures. In particular, we investigate the effect of dehazing on detection with mAP.

4.3 Implementation Details

We take the FRCNN model pre-trained on Cityscapes by MMDetection [60,61] as baseline and initialization. The dehazing sub-network is pre-trained on OTS. First, we implement an improved version of two-stage approaches by freezing the dehazing part of our UDnD framework. We name this pipeline Dehazing and Detection (DnD) and fine-tune it on FC-DBF-refine for 9 epochs. SGD algorithm [62] is employed with a mini-batch size of 1 and an initial learning rate of 0.001, which decays polynomially. For UDnD, the input images are randomly cropped and resized to 512×512. The dehazing and the detection sub-networks are jointly optimized based on the DnD model with the same strategy. We set $\lambda = 1$ and $\mu = 1$ in Eq. 2 via cross-validation.

For dehazing, the models are trained from scratch with 256×256 image patches. Adam [63] is used for optimization with a mini-batch size of 4. The initial learning rate is 0.0001. We train the models up to 100 epochs on FC-DBF and adopt the cosine annealing schedule [64]. In consistent with [31], we train the networks on OTS with a patch size of 240×240 for 10 epochs and decay the learning rate by half after every 2 epochs. **Our code and trained models are available at** https://github.com/xiqi98/UDnD.

4.4 Comparison on Object Detection in Real-World Hazy Scenes

We choose three methods for comparison: vanilla FRCNN [11], a baseline trained on clear images only; DA-FRCNN [6], a state-of-the-art method using domain

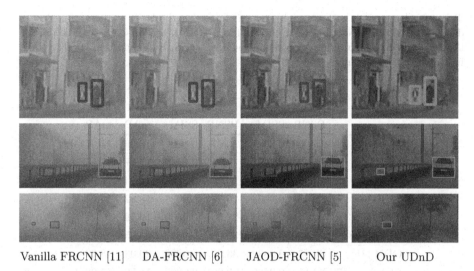

Vanilla FRCNN [11]   DA-FRCNN [6]   JAOD-FRCNN [5]   Our UDnD

Fig. 4. Examples of object detection results in real-world hazy scenes. Green boxes are true positives and red ones are missing recalls. In addition to detection, JAOD-FRCNN and the proposed UDnD provide dehazed images as well. JAOD-FRCNN tends to over-dehaze and produce artifacts that affect detection, while the vanilla FRCNN and DA-FRCNN miss some difficult objects. Our UDnD achieves a higher recall for hazy object detection.

adaptation; and JAOD-FRCNN [5], the only previous method jointly solving image dehazing and object detection.

We conduct evaluations on FD and FZ*, and report the results in Table 1, from which we have the following observations: (1) The vanilla FRCNN obtains the lowest mAP on both test sets, as it is trained on clear images only, without access to hazy images at all. It indicates that involving hazy images for training helps. (2) It boosts the performance by adapting the detector from clear to hazy images. For DA-FRCNN, the result on FD improves by more than 4 points over the baseline, when both synthetic and real-world data are used for training. Please note that for domain adaptation methods, real hazy images are needed to reach high performance. (3) JAOD-FRCNN achieves comparable performance to DA-FRCNN, showing that dehazing also serves as an effective way to reduce the inter-domain gaps. (4) Our method UDnD, which incorporates haze density information, obtains the best results. Specifically, it outperforms the vanilla FRCNN by ∼6 and ∼5 points on FD and FZ*, respectively; and it also improves on the results of DA-FRCNN, showing the benefits of a unified pipeline. Compared to JAOD-FRCNN, the obtained ∼3 points gain on FZ* demonstrates that the density switch module is helpful for dealing with the intra-domain differences, and thus leads to better detection performance.

Table 2. Comparison with state-of-the-art dehazing methods. To evaluate the effect of dehazing on object detection, we use a vanilla FRCNN based on Cityscapes to process the dehazed images produced by each model on OTS, and report mAP (%). Bold indicates the best results.

Methods	Dehazing				Detection	
	SOTS-outdoor		FC-DBF		FD	FZ*
	PSNR	SSIM	PSNR	SSIM	mAP	mAP
-/-	15.92	0.8029	16.07	0.8792	18.26	17.31
DCP [23]	16.32	0.8007	17.91	0.8749	17.07	17.50
NLD [21]	18.07	0.8016	16.53	0.8595	14.24	12.56
AOD-Net [5]	23.49	0.9063	20.79	0.9028	18.32	16.44
DCPDN [35]	26.74	0.9393	27.05	0.9630	19.79	17.71
EPDN [38]	29.61	0.9582	32.00	0.9812	19.25	18.62
GDN [31]	30.87	0.9832	33.07	0.9880	20.03	18.69
FFA-Net [37]	32.15	0.9806	30.99	0.9803	18.79	17.08
Our HRDN	**33.27**	**0.9877**	**35.08**	**0.9899**	**20.56**	**19.03**

Table 3. Effect of different domain adaptation techniques w.r.t. mAP and mAP* (%) that is the mean of APs over car and person. These experiments are conducted using our DnD pipeline. Bold indicates the best results.

Domain adaptation techniques			FD		FZ*	
Dehazing	Fine-tuning	Density switch	mAP	mAP*	mAP	mAP*
–	–	–	18.26	28.40	17.31	30.94
✓	–	–	19.84	29.29	18.26	32.45
✓	✓	–	22.70	29.68	19.57	34.85
✓	✓	✓	**23.15**	**30.42**	**20.49**	**35.33**

The qualitative comparison is illustrated in Fig. 4. We can see UDnD is better at handling small objects, occluded objects and dense haze, which demonstrates its effectiveness in real-world hazy object detection.

4.5   Comparison with State-of-the-Art Dehazing Methods

Our residual-aware haze density classifier achieves 97.60% accuracy on the validation set of FC-DBF, improving upon [41] by 3.33 points.

The proposed HRDN is evaluated against state-of-the-art dehazing methods [5,21,23,31,35,37,38] in terms of dehazing and detection performance. The results are shown in Table 2. We can observe that HRDN achieves the best performance on the two dehazing datasets, with margins of +1.12dB and +2.01dB in PSNR compared to the second best methods on SOTS-outdoor and the validation set of FC-DBF, respectively.

Table 4. Comparison of loss functions on the validation set of FC-DBF. The density switch modules in HRDN are disabled. Bold indicates the best results.

Loss functions	PSNR	SSIM
L_1	32.94	0.9831
Smooth L_1	31.58	0.9772
SSIM	31.11	0.9868
$L_1 + SSIM$	**33.11**	**0.9872**

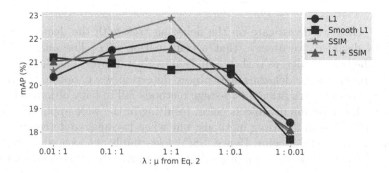

Fig. 5. Effect of different dehazing loss functions and $\lambda : \mu$ ratios on the detection performance of UDnD. We report mAP (%) on Foggy Zurich-test*.

Meanwhile, we use mAP as an additional task-driven metric. Hazy images from FD and FZ* are pre-processed by each dehazing model trained on OTS before fed into the vanilla FRCNN. From the last two columns of Table 2, we can see our HRDN obtains the best results w.r.t. mAP on both test sets. Some methods, *e.g.* FFA-Net, tend to overfit the synthetic training data, and thus obtain relatively low mAP on the two real-world datasets; other methods like DCPDN fall short on image dehazing.

To summarize, our dehazing method HRDN not only outperforms previous methods in terms of PSNR and SSIM, but is also more helpful for high-level vision tasks, such as object detection.

4.6 Ablation Study

Domain Adaptation. We study three techniques for tackling domain gaps, namely dehazing, fine-tuning and density switch, based on our DnD pipeline. Table 3 shows the effect of the three sequentially. Dehazing and fine-tuning are used to deal with the clear-hazy gaps, and the density switch module is used to handle haze density variations. They all bring performance gains of 1–2 points each, justifying that UDnD can handle both types of domain gaps.

Loss Function. In Fig. 5, we study the effect of different dehazing loss functions on the final detection performance, and find that a single SSIM loss works well.

Table 5. Effect of updating different sub-networks of UDnD. We report mAP and APs (%) over all classes of Foggy Zurich-test*. Bold indicates the best results.

Sub-Networks		pers.	rider	car	truck	bus	train	moto.	bicy.	mAP
Dehazing	Detection									
–	✓	25.34	21.63	45.32	3.26	14.46	30.07	13.37	10.48	20.49
✓	–	25.98	18.13	45.26	3.22	**16.93**	32.73	14.94	11.23	21.05
✓	✓	**26.03**	**24.41**	**48.66**	**5.74**	6.02	**37.00**	**21.46**	**13.78**	**22.89**

However, when we investigate on the dehazing task with the density switches in HRDN disabled, we observe that a combination of L_1 loss and SSIM loss achieves the best results, as is shown in Table 4. It indicates that there is a mismatch between image dehazing and object detection w.r.t. optimization goal, which explains why traditional two-stage methods fail in hazy object detection. We argue that haze mainly affects color, resulting in the wide application of L_1 loss and MSE loss in dehazing methods; but when it comes to detection, structure matters more than color. Hence, SSIM loss stands out as a good objective function for both tasks because of its emphasis on the structural information.

Unified Training. We evaluate our unified training strategy by freezing the weights of different pre-trained sub-networks while keeping the same loss. The results in Table 5 show that disabling joint optimization of the dehazing and the detection sub-networks leads to a performance drop of ∼2 points w.r.t. mAP, manifesting the importance of a unified framework.

5   Conclusion

We have presented a **U**nified density-aware **D**ehazing and **D**etection (UDnD) framework for image reconstruction and object detection in hazy conditions, motivated by the ideas to jointly optimize the two tasks and to exploit haze density as prior knowledge. We propose a residual-aware classifier to estimate haze density, a density-aware **H**igh-**R**esolution **D**ehazing **N**etwork (HRDN) to divide and conquer various hazy scenarios, and a density-aware multi-domain object detector to tackle the final detection task. These collectively constitute a unified pipeline for hazy object detection. Experiments demonstrate the effectiveness of each module and the entire framework in real-world hazy scenes.

Acknowledgement. This work was supported by the National Science Fund of China (Grant Nos. 61702262, U1713208), Funds for International Cooperation and Exchange of the National Natural Science Foundation of China (Grant No. 61861136011), Natural Science Foundation of Jiangsu Province, China (Grant No. BK20181299), Young Elite Scientists Sponsorship Program by CAST (2018QNRC001), the Fundamental Research Funds for the Central Universities" (Grant No.30920032201), and Science and Technology on Parallel and Distributed Processing Laboratory (PDL) Open Fund (WDZC20195500106).

References

1. Li, Y., You, S., Brown, M.S., Tan, R.T.: Haze visibility enhancement: a survey and quantitative benchmarking. CVIU **165**, 1–16 (2017)
2. Li, B., et al.: Benchmarking single-image dehazing and beyond. IEEE Trans. Image Process. **28**, 492–505 (2019)
3. Sakaridis, C., Dai, D., Van Gool, L.: Semantic foggy scene understanding with synthetic data. IJCV **126**, 973–992 (2018)
4. Pei, Y., Huang, Y., Zou, Q., Lu, Y., Wang, S.: Does haze removal help CNN-based image classification? In: ECCV, pp. 682–697 (2018)
5. Li, B., Peng, X., Wang, Z., Xu, J., Feng, D.: Aod-net: all-in-one dehazing network. In: ICCV, pp. 4770–4778 (2017)
6. Chen, Y., Li, W., Sakaridis, C., Dai, D., Van Gool, L.: Domain adaptive faster R-CNN for object detection in the wild. In: CVPR, pp. 3339–3348 (2018)
7. Zhu, X., Pang, J., Yang, C., Shi, J., Lin, D.: Adapting object detectors via selective cross-domain alignment. In: CVPR, pp. 687–696 (2019)
8. Simonyan, K., Zisserman, A.: Very deep convolutional networks for large-scale image recognition. In: ICLR (2015)
9. Wang, J., et al.: Deep high-resolution representation learning for visual recognition. IEEE Trans. Pattern Anal. Mach. Intell. (2019)
10. Dumoulin, V., Visin, F.: A guide to convolution arithmetic for deep learning. arXiv preprint arXiv:1603.07285 (2016)
11. Ren, S., He, K., Girshick, R., Sun, J.: Faster r-cnn: towards real-time object detection with region proposal networks. TPAMI **39**, 1137–1149 (2017)
12. Lin, T.Y., Dollar, P., Girshick, R., He, K., Hariharan, B., Belongie, S.: Feature pyramid networks for object detection. In: CVPR, pp. 2117–2125 (2017)
13. Redmon, J., Divvala, S., Girshick, R., Farhadi, A.: You only look once: unified, real-time object detection. In: CVPR, pp. 779–788 (2016)
14. Liu, W., Anguelov, D., Erhan, D., Szegedy, C., Reed, S., Fu, C.Y., Berg, A.C.: SSD: single shot multibox detector. In: ECCV, pp. 21–37 (2016)
15. Ben-David, S., Blitzer, J., Crammer, K., Kulesza, A., Pereira, F., Vaughan, J.W.: A theory of learning from different domains. Mach. Learn. **79**, 151–175 (2010)
16. He, Z., Zhang, L.: Multi-adversarial faster-RCNN for unrestricted object detection. In: ICCV, pp. 6668–6677 (2019)
17. Saito, K., Ushiku, Y., Harada, T., Saenko, K.: Strong-weak distribution alignment for adaptive object detection. In: CVPR, pp. 6956–6965 (2019)
18. Saito, K., Watanabe, K., Ushiku, Y., Harada, T.: Maximum classifier discrepancy for unsupervised domain adaptation. In: CVPR, pp. 3723–3732 (2018)
19. Zheng, Y., Huang, D., Liu, S., Wang, Y.: Cross-domain object detection through coarse-to-fine feature adaptation. arXiv preprint arXiv:2003.10275 (2020)
20. Koschmieder, H.: Theorie der horizontalen sichtweite. Beitrage zur Physik der freien Atmosphare, pp. 33–53 (1924)
21. Berman, D., treibitz, T., Avidan, S.: Non-local image dehazing. In: CVPR, pp. 1674–1682 (2016)
22. Fattal, R.: Dehazing using color-lines. TOG **34**, 1–14 (2014)
23. He, K., Sun, J., Tang, X.: Single image haze removal using dark channel prior. TPAMI **33**, 2341–2353 (2011)
24. Meng, G., Wang, Y., Duan, J., Xiang, S., Pan, C.: Efficient image dehazing with boundary constraint and contextual regularization. In: ICCV, pp. 617–624 (2013)
25. Tan, R.T.: Visibility in bad weather from a single image. In: CVPR, pp. 1–8 (2008)

26. Zhu, Q., Mai, J., Shao, L.: A fast single image haze removal algorithm using color attenuation prior. TIP **24**, 3522–3533 (2015)
27. Cai, B., Xu, X., Jia, K., Qing, C., Tao, D.: Dehazenet: an end-to-end system for single image haze removal. TIP **25**, 5187–5198 (2016)
28. Deng, Z., et al.: Deep multi-model fusion for single-image dehazing. In: ICCV, pp. 2453–2462 (2019)
29. Li, R., Pan, J., Li, Z., Tang, J.: Single image dehazing via conditional generative adversarial network. In: CVPR, pp. 8202–8211 (2018)
30. Li, Y., et al.: Lap-net: level-aware progressive network for image dehazing. In: ICCV, pp. 3276–3285 (2019)
31. Liu, X., Ma, Y., Shi, Z., Chen, J.: Griddehazenet: attention-based multi-scale network for image dehazing. In: ICCV, pp. 7314–7323 (2019)
32. Liu, Y., Pan, J., Ren, J., Su, Z.: Learning deep priors for image dehazing. In: ICCV, pp. 2492–2500 (2019)
33. Ren, W., Liu, S., Zhang, H., Pan, J., Cao, X., Yang, M.H.: Single image dehazing via multi-scale convolutional neural networks. In: ECCV, pp. 154–169 (2016)
34. Yang, D., Sun, J.: Proximal dehaze-net: a prior learning-based deep network for single image dehazing. In: ECCV, pp. 702–717 (2018)
35. Zhang, H., Patel, V.M.: Densely connected pyramid dehazing network. In: CVPR, pp. 3194–3203 (2018)
36. Ren, W., et al.: Gated fusion network for single image dehazing. In: CVPR, pp. 3253–3261 (2018)
37. Qin, X., Wang, Z., Bai, Y., Xie, X., Jia, H.: Ffa-net: feature fusion attention network for single image dehazing. In: AAAI, pp. 11908–11915 (2020)
38. Qu, Y., Chen, Y., Huang, J., Xie, Y.: Enhanced pix2pix dehazing network. In: CVPR, pp. 8160–8168 (2019)
39. Li, R., Kintak, U.: Haze density estimation and dark channel prior based image defogging. In: ICWAPR, pp. 29–35 (2018)
40. Yeh, C.H., Kang, L.W., Lin, C.Y., Lin, C.Y.: Efficient image/video dehazing through haze density analysis based on pixel-based dark channel prior. In: ISIC, pp. 238–241 (2012)
41. Dai, D., Sakaridis, C., Hecker, S., Van Gool, L.: Curriculum model adaptation with synthetic and real data for semantic foggy scene understanding. IJCV **128**, 1182–1204 (2019)
42. Krizhevsky, A., Sutskever, I., Hinton, G.E.: Imagenet classification with deep convolutional neural networks. In: NeurIPS, pp. 1097–1105 (2012)
43. Nam, H., Han, B.: Learning multi-domain convolutional neural networks for visual tracking. In: CVPR, pp. 4293–4302 (2016)
44. Long, M., Cao, Y., Wang, J., Jordan, M.I.: Learning transferable features with deep adaptation networks. arXiv preprint arXiv:1502.02791 (2015)
45. Mallya, A., Davis, D., Lazebnik, S.: Piggyback: adapting a single network to multiple tasks by learning to mask weights. In: ECCV, pp. 67–82 (2018)
46. Ioffe, S., Szegedy, C.: Batch normalization: Accelerating deep network training by reducing internal covariate shift. In: ICML, pp. 448–456 (2015)
47. Bilen, H., Vedaldi, A.: Universal representations: The missing link between faces, text, planktons, and cat breeds. arXiv preprint arXiv:1701.07275 (2017)
48. Rebuffi, S.A., Bilen, H., Vedaldi, A.: Learning multiple visual domains with residual adapters. In: NeurIPS, pp. 506–516 (2017)
49. Rebuffi, S.A., Bilen, H., Vedaldi, A.: Efficient parametrization of multi-domain deep neural networks. In: CVPR, pp. 8119–8127 (2018)

50. Hu, J., Shen, L., Sun, G.: Squeeze-and-excitation networks. In: CVPR, pp. 7132–7141 (2018)
51. Wang, X., Cai, Z., Gao, D., Vasconcelos, N.: Towards universal object detection by domain attention. In: CVPR, pp. 7289–7298 (2019)
52. Choi, L.K., You, J., Bovik, A.C.: Referenceless prediction of perceptual fog density and perceptual image defogging. TIP **24**, 3888–3901 (2015)
53. NOAA: Federal meteorological handbook no. 1: Surface weather observations and reports (2005)
54. Zhang, H., Patel, V.M.: Density-aware single image de-raining using a multi-stream dense network. In: CVPR, pp. 695–704 (2018)
55. He, K., Zhang, X., Ren, S., Sun, J.: Deep residual learning for image recognition. In: CVPR, pp. 770–778 (2016)
56. Ren, D., Zuo, W., Hu, Q., Zhu, P., Meng, D.: Progressive image deraining networks: a better and simpler baseline. In: CVPR, pp. 3937–3946 (2019)
57. He, K., Gkioxari, G., Dollar, P., Girshick, R.: Mask R-CNN. In: ICCV, pp. 2961–2969 (2017)
58. Cordts, M., et al.: The cityscapes dataset for semantic urban scene understanding. In: CVPR, pp. 3213–3223 (2016)
59. Wang, Z., Bovik, A.C., Sheikh, H.R., Simoncelli, E.P.: Image quality assessment: from error visibility to structural similarity. TIP **13**, 600–612 (2004)
60. Chen, K., et al.: Mmdetection: open mmlab detection toolbox and benchmark. arXiv preprint arXiv:1906.07155 (2019)
61. Paszke, A., et al.: Pytorch: an imperative style, high-performance deep learning library. In: NeurIPS, pp. 8024–8035 (2019)
62. Ruder, S.: An overview of gradient descent optimization algorithms. arXiv preprint arXiv:1609.04747 (2016)
63. Kingma, D.P., Ba, J.: Adam: a method for stochastic optimization. arXiv preprint arXiv:1412.6980 (2014)
64. Loshchilov, I., Hutter, F.: SGDR: stochastic gradient descent with warm restarts. arXiv preprint arXiv:1608.03983 (2016)

Part-Aware Attention Network
for Person Re-identification

Wangmeng Xiang[1] , Jianqiang Huang[2] , Xian-Sheng Hua[2] ,
and Lei Zhang[1,2]($\boxtimes$)

[1] Department of Computing, The Hong Kong Polytechnic University,
Kowloon, Hong Kong
{cswxiang,cslzhang}@comp.polyu.edu.hk
[2] Artificial Intelligence Center, Alibaba DAMO Academy, Hangzhou, China
{jianqiang.hjq,xiansheng.hxs}@alibaba-inc.com

Abstract. Multi-level feature aggregation and part feature extraction
are widely used to boost the performance of person re-identification (Re-
ID). Most multi-level feature aggregation methods treat feature maps on
different levels equally and use simple local operations for feature fusion,
which neglects the long-distance connection among feature maps. On the
other hand, the popular horizon pooling part based feature extraction
methods may lead to feature misalignment. In this paper, we propose
a novel Part-aware Attention Network (PAN) to connect part feature
maps and middle-level features. Given a part feature map and a source
feature map, PAN uses part features as queries to perform second-order
information propagation from the source feature map. The attention is
computed based on the compatibility of the source feature map with the
part feature map. Specifically, PAN uses high-level part features of different human body parts to aggregate information from mid-level feature
maps. As a part-aware feature aggregation method, PAN operates on all
spatial positions of feature maps so that it can discover long-distance
relations. Extensive experiments show that PAN achieves leading performance on Re-ID benchmarks Market1501, DukeMTMC, and CUHK03.

1 Introduction

Person re-identification (Re-ID) aims to recognize a person of interest from the
gallery by using a query image or video clip. The state-of-the-art person Re-ID
methods [1–6] usually employ a convolutional neural network (CNN) to extract
the feature vector of a person, and use metric learning or classification loss to
enforce the learned feature representations to be discriminative. How to design
an efficient and effective network structure for feature extraction is critical for
high-performance person Re-ID.

Recent CNN-based person Re-ID methods mainly fall into two territories.
1) The first is creating more effective metrics to fully explore the relations
between features [7–12]. For example, Cheng *et al.* [13] designed a multi-channel
part-based CNN model under the triplet framework. Chen *et al.* [12] applied a

© Springer Nature Switzerland AG 2021
H. Ishikawa et al. (Eds.): ACCV 2020, LNCS 12625, pp. 136–152, 2021.
https://doi.org/10.1007/978-3-030-69538-5_9

quadruplet loss with a margin based online hard negative mining. 2) The second is designing efficient and effective architecture for feature extraction [1,14–18], where off-the-shelf feature extractors and prior knowledge about the human body are employed. For instance, PCB [5] utilizes ResNet50 backbone and applies horizon strip pooling and refined part pooling to extract discriminative and mutual distinctive human part features. MGN [19] employs a multi-branch network and applies horizon strip pooling on each branch.

One popular direction for effective architecture design is fusing features from different layers of a network. Existing multi-scale and multi-level Re-ID methods [16,20–23] typically use multi-branch or directly apply convolutional layers on mid-level features to generate multi-level feature maps, and fuse the feature maps by element-wise operation. However, combining different levels of features in this way has several problems. First, the spatial resolution of high-level features is reduced largely, and fine details may be lost during the down-sampling process, making the feature fusion less effective. Second, both residual and concatenation connections are local operations, neglecting the long-range relationships between different layers of feature maps. Last but not least, due to the lack of guidance, background, noise, and distractors will also be fused to the target feature maps and result in inferior performance.

In this paper, we present a Part-aware Attention Network (PAN) by using a Part-aware Attention Module (PAM) to bridge different layers' feature maps in a CNN. A part feature map $\mathbf{P}$ is first generated. Then given feature maps $\mathbf{X}$, PAM takes a feature vector in $\mathbf{P}$ as a query vector and compute its compatibility with features in $\mathbf{X}$, resulting in a comparability map $\mathbf{M}$. The feature warping is then computed by the weighted sum of $\mathbf{X}$ over $\mathbf{M}$. PAN has several advantages over previous works. First, PAM operates on every position of the original source feature map in a top-down manner so that the fine details of middle-level features can be kept to reveal the long-range relations between different parts of an object or human. Second, PAM can be applied to multi-granularity to propagate the information from low-level or mid-level features to high-level part features. The compatibility maps show that PAN can focus on distinctive regions while neglecting the background.

The contributions of this paper are two folds. First, a novel module, namely PAM, is proposed, which uses the distinctively learned part features to aggregate information from the source features under the CNN framework. Second, the proposed PAN can propagate useful information from low-level or mid-level features to high-level part features, suppressing background, and distractors while keeping fine-grained details. Our proposed PAN is simple and demonstrates exceptional performance. Our experiments show that PAN significantly boosts the performance of the baseline and achieves leading performance on person ReID.

2   Related Works

Multi-level Feature Aggregation. It has been found that fusing the feature maps from multiple layers in CNN can result in better feature discrimination ability because features from different layers deliver different levels of semantic information. Generally, features from shallower layers encode image local structures and more fine-grained information, however, they lack global semantic information and often contain noises. Features of deeper layers are believed to contain high-level global semantics but lose spatial and detailed information. Therefore, multi-level feature aggregation has been widely used in many computer vision tasks [21, 24–27].

Multi-level networks can be implemented by using multiple branches on different scales and regions. Li et al. [22] proposed a network with multiple branches to fuse local and global features for human feature representation. Qian et al. [23] proposed a multi-scale stream layer, which is inspired by GoogLeNet [28] to learn features on different scales. FPN [27] combines feature maps of different scales with element-wise operations. Some methods try to use layers with various scales in a bottom-up manner. For example, SKNet [29] uses multiple branches with different kernel sizes. ACNet [30] adaptively determines connections among feature nodes, which is a general form of connections in CNNs, MLP, or NLN [31].

Attention Mechanism for Person Re-identification. Attention mechanism has been used in many computer vision tasks to regularize the network to focus on essential signals without being interfered with much by outliers. Zhao et al. [14] used convolutional layers to learn spatial attention masks for different human parts, which are applied to the feature maps to select the region of interests. In addition to spatial attention, channel attention has also been studied in [22], where the spatial dimension is squeezed and the channel scaling is learned by fully connected layers.

Our work is related to the self-attention [32] and non-local neural networks [31]. Self-attention [32] allows the model to identify multiple locations of the encoded features for machine translation. In [31], a non-local layer is proposed as a basic building block, and a non-local operation is employed to capture spatial and temporal long-range correlations within a feature map. However, the non-local operation has a high time and space complexity when applied to spatially large feature maps. Besides, when the non-local operation is applied to high-level feature maps, the performance gain is marginal because the spatial resolution of high-level feature maps is relatively small. Our work differs from [31,32] in that we consider the relations between two feature maps on different layers of a CNN.

A top-down attention module is proposed in [33], which takes the final feature representation as a query vector to extract information from the mid-level feature maps. However, the spatial structure of the final feature map is also valuable for fine-grained feature learning. For example, the human body prior is important for person ReID. Simply applying max/avg pooling on the final feature map to aggregate information from mid-level features without considering the spatial structure of the final feature map will limit the model performance. Besides, we use attention modules to learn part features automatically, which utilize the part feature prior to relieve the misalignment issue. Our experiments show that

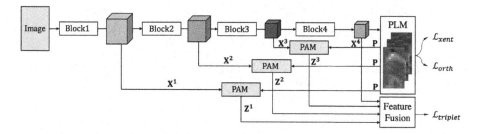

Fig. 1. Illustration of our proposed PAN.

PAN can aggregate the information while retaining the spatial structure of the feature map. Different spatial parts of the final feature map would extract useful information from different parts of the objects.

3   Part-aware Attention Network

The motivation of the proposed Part-aware Attention Network (PAN) is to enhance the attentiveness of feature extraction with learned part features. As illustrated in Fig. 1, it contains two modules: part-aware attention module and part feature learning module. The part-aware attention module uses part features as attentiveness guidance and provides strong supervision information for the network at the middle layers. Part feature learning module generates part features by applying both spatial and channel attention to the output of the feature extraction backbone. The output features of PAM are then fused to generate final feature representation. We introduce these modules in the sections below.

3.1   Part-aware Attention

The Part-aware Attention Module (PAM) takes part features as guidance for feature learning at the middle layers of the network. We use $\mathbf{P}$ to represent the part feature map, which is the combination of part feature vectors. The details of the part feature learning module would be introduced in the next section. The part-aware attention calculation between a part feature vector $\mathbf{P}_i$ and the middle-level feature map $\mathbf{X}$ can be represented as follows:

$$\mathbf{Z}_i = \frac{\theta(\mathbf{P}_i, \mathbf{X}) f(\mathbf{X})}{N}. \tag{1}$$

where N is the number of total positions in $\mathbf{X}$. PAM takes a target part feature vector $\mathbf{P}_i$ as query and computes its compatibility score with $\mathbf{X}$ using function θ. After computing the compatibility score for each pair of $\mathbf{P}_i$ and $\mathbf{X}$, the feature mapping is computed as a weighted sum over feature map $f(\mathbf{X})$. This process generates a mapping feature $\mathbf{Z}_i$ for every $\mathbf{P}_i$. Function f transforms feature

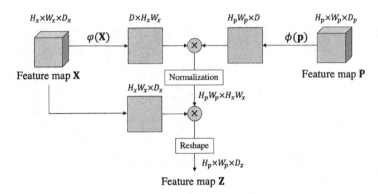

Fig. 2. Our proposed part-aware attention module, which can be applied between part features and middle-level features of a CNN.

map **X** for mapping. The feature map is then normalized with constant N. For implementation of θ, we apply dot-product due to its simplicity and efficiency:

$$\theta(\mathbf{P}_i, \mathbf{X}) = \phi(\mathbf{P}_i)^T \psi(\mathbf{X}), \tag{2}$$

where the function ϕ and ψ transform the features to the same embedding space D. The dimension of D is a hyper parameter, and we would discuss it in the ablation study section. It is worth mentioning that when dot-product is applied, the compatibility score computation can be viewed as applying a 1×1 convolution on the feature map **X** with kernel $\mathbf{P}_i$.

Combining Eqs. 1–2, we can reformulate the part-aware feature attention module as below:

$$\mathbf{Z} = \phi(\mathbf{P})\psi(\mathbf{X})^T f(\mathbf{X}), \tag{3}$$

where ϕ, ψ and f are convolutional layers, which learn to transform features. The computation process is illustrated in Fig. 2. The input feature maps **X** and **P** are transformed and reshaped so that the computation of compatibility score and feature mapping can be represented as matrix multiplication. The aggregated feature could then be added or concatenated to generate the final feature.

For middle-level feature extraction of PAN, we apply PAM between part features with outputs of the middle blocks of networks. For instance, as shown in Fig. 1, when resnet50 is used as the backbone network, the first three block outputs $\mathbf{X}^l, l \in \{1, 2, 3\}$ and part feature **P** are used for PAM. PAN can efficiently take the high-level feature map as the query and gather the feedback information from low-level or mid-level feature maps. The features from mid-level layers of a neural network could provide more part details of the human body in person Re-ID. It is an efficient way for multi-level feature learning, where features from different layers of the network are all mapped to the final feature map. This is more computationally efficient than multi-branch networks for multi-scale feature learning, and is more powerful than vanilla addition or concatenation connection for feature fusion, as it operates on all spatial positions.

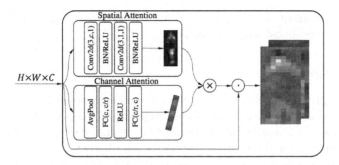

Fig. 3. The proposed part-feature learning module. It contains spatial and channel attention to learn part feature maps.

3.2 Multi-granularity Part Feature Learning

The typical part feature generation process uses priors in humans to model different parts of the human body. For example, human part masks and horizon strips are two popular pooling strategies for learning discriminative human body part representations [5,14]. Horizon strip [5] is a popular strategy for human part feature generation, due to its simplicity and effectiveness. It divides the final feature map evenly into multiple regions in the height direction. For the feature map of each region, average pooling is applied and the feature is passed into an embedding learning layer. However, this can cause misalignment of the human body due to the differences in the human body in scale, and a person may not be well located at the center of the image. Although, the refined part pooling can be used to reduce the influences of outliers, however, the initial part feature generation can still be affected by the misalignment.

We propose a part-feature learning module (PLM) to learn the part representation automatically. As shown in Fig. 3, the module consists of both channel and spatial attention layers. The spatial attention module consists of a convolutional layer, BN layer, and ReLU activation. The design of the channel attention layer follows [34], where average pooling, fully connected layers, and ReLU activation are used to obtain channel scale vector. To obtain multiple granularities of part features, we propose a multi-granularity part learning strategy. For granularity at scale-i, several i parts are learned automatically by PLM. Here, we use $\mathbf{s}_j^i \in \mathbb{R}^{h \times w}$ to represent the spatial attention mask, where $h \times w$ represents the spatial position in a feature map, (i, j) represents mask for scale i and part $j \in \{1, \ldots, i\}$. Denote by $\mathbf{c}^i \in \mathbb{R}^c$ the channel attention vector. The total attention mask is $\mathbf{m}_j^i = \mathbf{c}^i \otimes \mathbf{s}_j^i \in \mathbb{R}^{c \times h \times w}$. For example, $\mathbf{m}^1$ is the proposed body part at scale 1 ; two distinct part region $\mathbf{m}_1^2, \mathbf{m}_2^2$ are learned at scale 2 to divide the feature map into two parts. As shown in Fig. 1, given the $\mathbf{X}^4 \in \mathbb{R}^{c \times h \times w}$, which is generated by the backbone feature extractor, the part feature vector can be computed as $\text{AvgPool}(\mathbf{m}_j^i \odot \mathbf{X}^4)$. The final part feature map $\mathbf{P}$ is the combination of all part feature vectors. All the part features are trained with cross-entropy loss, and we use orthogonal regularization to learn distinct part-feature maps.

This multi-granularity part feature learning strategy can learn different granular part features and boost learning efficiency.

3.3 Loss Functions

In addition to the classical cross-entropy loss [35], denoted by L_{xent}, we also employ the triplet loss and an orthogonal regularization loss to train our models. For triplet loss, we adopt the online hard triplet mining strategy proposed in [36], which considers the hardest triplets within a mini-batch.

To enforce the learned part regions to be distinctive, we add an orthogonal regular term to reduce the overlap of different part masks:

$$\mathcal{L}_{orth} = \frac{1}{L} \sum_{l \in \{1, \dots L\}} \|\mathbf{M}^l \mathbf{M}^{l^T} - \mathbf{I}\|_{\mathbf{F}}, \tag{4}$$

where $\mathbf{M}^l$ is the part region masks at scale-l and each row of it represents a part region. L is the total number of scales. $\mathbf{I}$ is an identity matrix.

We apply cross-entropy loss L_{xent} on every part features generated by part feature learning module. The triplet loss $L_{triplet}$ is applied to the final feature representation (i.e., the concatenation of all part features). The final loss function is:

$$\mathcal{L} = \mathcal{L}_{xent} + \lambda_1 \mathcal{L}_{triplet} + \lambda_2 \mathcal{L}_{orth}, \tag{5}$$

where $\mathcal{L}_{xent}$ is the sum of all the part cross-entropy loss functions, $\mathcal{L}_{triplet}$ is the triplet loss for the final feature and λ_1 and λ_2 are trade-off parameters.

3.4 Discussion

Multi-level Feature Fusion. Most current multi-level feature fusion methods use element-wise operations such as addition or concatenation to fuse feature maps from different layers. Since the channel and spatial dimensions of the feature maps are different, usually a function f is first applied to downsample and reshape the source feature map, and then a function g is applied to fuse the source and target feature maps. Both f and g are usually implemented by convolutional layers. Though simple to implement, the downsides of this process are two folds. First, the downsampling function f would reduce the spatial dimensions of the feature map and lose fine-scale information contained in the feature maps. Second, the fusing function g neglects the long-range relations between two feature maps, as convolution only operates within a local area. The proposed PAN overcomes these problems by considering fine-grained pair-wise relations between feature maps.

Comparison with Other Attention Based Methods. Some previous works on Re-ID have also utilized attention modules in feature extraction. For example, HAN [22] utilizes spatial and channel attention in the middle layers of the

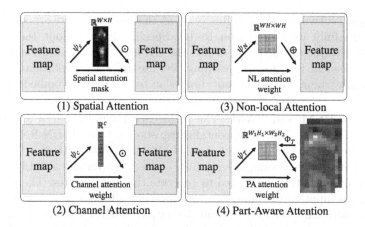

Fig. 4. Comparison of part-aware attention with other attention methods. (1) *Spatial attention* applies convolution and softmax functions to produce a spatial mask. (2) *Channel attention* uses fully connected layer to generate a scale vector. (3) *Non-local attention* uses self-similarity to generate a self attention matrix. (4) Our *part-aware attention* generates part-aware attention map for different human parts.

network. Both SCAN [37] and IANet [38] use self-attention module in the network design, which is similar to non-local (NL) [31] module. Spatial attention, channel attention, and self-attention can all be viewed as bottom-up attention methods, while our proposed PAM is a top-down attention module. Figure 4 compares PAM with other attention methods. We can see that PAM uses both source feature map and target feature map to compute the attention maps of different parts, while other methods only use source feature map for attention computation.

PAM is related to NL modules but they have significant differences. NL modules capture long-range relations within a feature map, while PAM operates across different feature maps. To map the low-level or mid-level features to high-level part features, PAM takes the part features learned from deeper layers (often have more high-level semantic information) as a query to explore the discriminative information from shallower layers of a network. Besides, due to the reduced spatial resolution along with the feed-forward process in CNN, the computational cost of PAM is significantly less than the vanilla self-attention methods or NL methods.

4   Experiments on Person ReID

4.1   Implementation Details

Data Preprocessing. We use the same data pre-processing methods on all datasets. In the training stage, common data augmentation methods are applied to images, including random flipping, shifting, zooming, cropping, random erasing [39]. The images are then resized to 384×128.

Backbone Network. We use ResNet50 as the backbone network since it has been successfully used in person Re-ID. Specifically, we adopt the modified ResNet50 architecture in [5], in which the stride of last convolutional layer is set to 1 to benefit final feature learning. We use a 1×1 convolutional layer for embedding learning and set output dimension to 256 for each embedding layer.

Settings of PLM and PAM. The PLM contains both spatial and channel attention. The spatial attention contains two stacked Conv2D-BN-ReLU blocks, as shown in Fig. 3. The design of channel attention follows SE-Net [34], which consists of an average pooling layer, a fully connected layer and a ReLU. The two attention maps are then combined to generate the part features. The PAM aim to transform input feature maps to the same embedding space. We first use a 1×1 convolutional layer to transform the output dimension of the feature maps according to the fusion method. For addition and concatenation based feature fusion, we set the output dimension of feature map $\mathbf{Z}$ in Eq. 3 equals to the dimension of $\mathbf{P}$ and $\mathbf{X}$, respectively.

Optimization. Our model is trained by randomly selecting 8 identities with 4 samples each identity as a batch. The SGD optimizer is employed. The learning rate is set to 1×10^{-1} for the parameters of PAN, embedding layer and softmax classification layer, and the rate is set to 1×10^{-2} for the pre-trained parameters of the network. The learning rate is divided by 10 after 5000 and 7500 iterations, and the training is stopped after 10,000 iterations.

4.2   Ablation Study

The Number of Granularity in PLM. In this section, we study how the number of granularity affects the performance of our multi-granularity PLM method and compare it with the horizon strip pooling method [5]. Each pooled part feature is followed by an embedding learning layer and a softmax cross-entropy loss function. We test 3, 6, and 8 parts of horizon stripe, as well as four different granularity. All the features are then passed to an individual embedding layer and softmax loss function. The final person feature representation is the concatenation of all part features. For the simplicity of experiments, we set $\lambda_1 = 1$, $\lambda_2 = 10^{-3}$ throughout the experiments.

The experimental results are listed in Table 1. Part feature learning module (PLM) performs better than horizon strip pooling when they have the same total part number. For instance, three granularity scales PLM (combined with scale 1, 2 and 3) and 6-part horizon pooling have the same part number and final feature dimension, while three scales PLM outperforms 6-part horizon strip pooling by 0.8% on mAP. Using more than three scales will not further improve the performance of PAM. As we use orthogonal regularization term to force the learned attention maps to be distinct, using too many granularity scales may divide the human body into too many parts, and deteriorate the performance. We empirically found that using three granularity scales leads to the best results. For simplicity, we use PLM with three scales by default in the following experiments.

Table 1. Results of different part feature extraction strategies on Market1501.

Method		Top1	Top5	Top10	mAP
Global pooling		86.0	94.3	96.2	68.9
Horizonstrips	3 parts	91.7	96.8	97.9	78.1
	6 parts	92.5	96.8	98.1	79.5
	8 parts	92.4	97.0	98.0	79.2
Multi-granularity	$\{1\}$	90.0	96.4	97.4	75.4
	$\{1,2\}$	91.8	96.4	97.5	78.9
	$\{1,2,3\}$	**92.9**	**97.4**	**98.4**	**80.4**
	$\{1,2,3,4\}$	92.8	96.9	98.1	79.9

Table 2. The effectiveness of PAN on Market1501. *Baseline* stands for the model trained without the multi-layer connection.

Model	D	Top1	mAP	Param	Memory	Time
Baseline	–	93.0	81.1	27.8M	17.79G	72 s
Baseline_w	–	93.4	81.8	29.2M	17.80G	74 s
Conv_a	–	93.5	82.0	35.2M	17.83G	76 s
Conv_c	–	93.7	82.5	32.3M	17.81G	75 s
PAN_a	128,128,128	93.5	83.0	32.5M	17.81G	75 s
	256,256,256	93.8	83.5	33.5M	17.82G	77 s
	256,512,1024	93.9	83.6	36.6M	17.84G	79 s
PAN_c	128,128,128	93.8	83.7	33.0M	17.82G	76 s
	256,256,256	94.3	84.2	33.9M	17.83G	76 s
	256,512,1024	94.3	84.1	37.0M	17.85G	78 s
NL	128,256,512	93.9	83.9	30.5M	21.63G	79 s
PAN_c + NL	128,256,512/256	94.8	85.3	36.7M	21.66G	84 s

Feature Fusion in PAN. We investigate how to fuse the transformed features in the proposed PAN. The baseline is a plain ResNet50 network with PLM and trained with triplet loss and softmax loss. PAN_a and PAN_c stand for applying PAN and fusing features with addition or concatenation. We use *Conv* connection blocks Conv_a and Conv_c for better comparison, which contains convolution $(kernel = 1, stride = 2)$, batch normalization and ReLU. For convolution, the channel dimension is gradually increased to 2048 for addition connection $(256 \to 512, 512 \to 1024, 1024 \to 2048)$, and retain the same for concatenation.

In Table 2, the models trained with feature mapping (PAN_a and PAN_c) improve the performance over baseline network by 1.9% and 2.6% on mAP when the inter-channel number D is 128. Increasing the number of inter-channels D can further increase the performance. We choose inter-channel to be 256 for all the three blocks by considering the trade-off between parameter number and

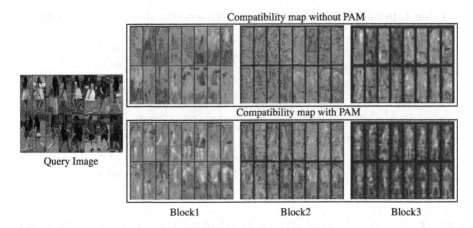

Fig. 5. Compatibility maps of PAM for different blocks of ResNet50. The compatibility map is computed by using the first scale part feature vector of PLM against block1-3 (ref to Eq. 2). The strength of yellow color indicates the degree of compatibility. The top right panel shows the compatibility maps without PAM, which are vague and unclear. The bottom right panel shows the compatibility maps with PAM. PAM learns to focus on discriminative parts and can capture long-distance relations. (Color figure online)

performance. The performance gain by both connections (PAN_a and PAN_c) over $Conv_a$ and $Conv_c$ provides evidence that PAN leverage extra information, and it is not simply due to the increase of number of parameters, as PAN_a and PAN_c have less parameters than $Conv_a$ and $Conv_c$ and faster at inference. We use feature maps of the third stage as the local feature and last stage as global feature to construct the Baseline$_w$, it performs better than using global feature alone but lower than our proposed method. The test time is measured by using 1 Quadro GV100 GPU. The results show that PAN has small extra computational cost and it is efficient in practice.

Benefit of Orthogonal Regularization Term. We conducted experiments to investigate the role of orthogonal regularization. The parameter is $\{0, 10^{-1}, 10^{-2}, 10^{-3}, 10^{-4}\}$. The mAP are 80.36%, 80.21%, 80.87%, 81.14%, 80.46%, respectively. We thus choose $10-3$ in our experiment. One can see that the benefit over no orthogonal regularization is 0.78%.

Visualization of PAM. Figure 5 shows the compatibility map (computed using Eq. 2) of the first scale part feature vector from PLM against feature maps of first three blocks. The yellow color indicates the strength of the compatibility. To better illustrate the advantages brought by proposed method, in the top right panel of Fig. 5 we show the compatibility maps without using PAM, which are vague and unclear. The bottom right panel shows the compatibility maps with PAM. We can see that PAM learns to capture the correlations between outputs of

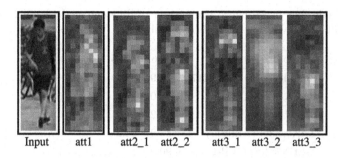

Input   att1   att2_1   att2_2   att3_1   att3_2   att3_3

Fig. 6. A closer look of the compatibility maps of PAM.

different blocks, and propagate information from mid-level and low-level feature maps to high-level features to enhance the discriminative parts of human body. The compatibility maps of first two stages focus on color and texture. While for the third stage, the compatibility maps represent different human parts and their combinations. This observation indicates PAN learns distinct semantics mapping from different stages of networks.

In Fig. 6, we provide a closer look of PAM at different granularity of the third stage. For the first granularity scale, the attention map focus on the whole body. In the second granularity scale, the body is roughly divided into two parts. While in the third granularity scale, the network learns to divide the body into three parts. As we can see, all the parts are quite different at each granularity scale, which indicates PLM's ability to learn distinct body part feature.

Non-local Module and PAN. As we mentioned in the related work section, the non-local (NL) module used in the previous work [31] is different from our proposed PAN. NL module captures long-range relations within a feature map, while our proposed PAN operates across different feature maps. NL module can be complementary to our PAN module according to their different functionalities.

We conduct experiments to add NL modules after block1-3. Dot product is used the compatibility computation and the inter-channel is set to half of the original channels. We also downsample the feature map by default. The training memory consumption is tested with batch size 128. The result is in Table 2. Since the output resolution of block4 is much smaller than earlier blocks (4 times to 16 times smaller in ResNet50), PAN is much faster and costs less memory than NL for compatibility computation. NL module can improve the performance over *baseline* but with a higher computation and memory cost. Combining NL with PAN can further improve the performance by 0.9%/1.4% on Top1/mAP.

4.3 Comparison with State-of-the-Arts

In this section we compare our PAN_c, denoted by PAN for simplicity in the following parts, with state-of-the-art methods on the three benchmark person

Table 3. Single-shot performance comparison of different methods on Market1501. Methods with * are attention methods and with # are fusion methods.

Method	Top1	Top5	Top10	mAP
Spindle# [16] (CVPR17)	76.9	91.5	94.6	–
DLPA [14] (ICCV17)	81.0	92.0	94.7	63.4
SSM [40] (CVPR17)	82.2	–	–	68.8
TriNet [36] (Arxiv17)	84.9	94.2	–	69.1
MLFN# [3] (CVPR18)	90.0	–	–	74.3
HA-CNN* [22] (CVPR18)	91.2	–	–	75.7
DuATM* [4] (CVPR18)	91.4	97.1	–	76.6
PCB [5] (ECCV18)	93.8	97.5	98.5	81.6
MGN# [19] (MM18)	95.7	–	–	86.9
Local CNN* [41] (MM18)	95.9	–	–	87.4
IANet* [38] (CVPR19)	94.4	–	–	83.1
Pyramid# [42] (CVPR19)	95.7	98.4	99.0	88.2
MHN* [43] (ICCV19)	95.1	98.1	98.9	85.0
ABD-Net* [44] (ICCV19)	95.6	–	–	88.3
SONA* [45] (ICCV19)	95.6	98.5	99.2	88.8
ST-ReID [46] (AAAI19)	97.2	99.3	99.5	86.7
PAN*	96.0	98.6	99.3	89.0

Re-ID datasets. We adopt BNNeck in [47] to further boost the performance of our model. All the reported results are single-query without re-ranking.

Market1501. Market1501 is one of the largest benchmark datasets for Person Re-ID, and many methods have been reported on this dataset. We compare the proposed method with most of the state-of-the-arts. The experimental results are shown in Table 3. With ResNet50 as the pre-trained network, the proposed PAN approach achieves 89% mAP and 96.0% CMC top1. PAN outperforms PCB [5] by 2.2% on CMC top1 and 7.4% on mAP, which applies horizon part pooling and refine part pooling on the final feature map, on Market1501. Comparing to multi-branch methods such as Spindle [16], MLFN [3], HA-CNN [22] and MGN [19], PAN is a single branch ResNet50 with target aware mid-level feature connections and much less parameters. It surpasses the MGN [19] on all three datasets. PAN outperforms Local CNN [41], which fuses local and global features in the mid-level of CNN with Local CNN module. It also outperforms state-of-the-art local-global fusion method Pyramid [42] and self-attention method IANet [38]. Comparing with recent bottom-up attention methods SONA [45], ABD-Net [44] and MHN [43], our method considers both bottom-up and top-down attention and achieves slightly better performance. This indicates the effectiveness of PAN, which use the part feature as guidance to fully utilize the mid-level features of network.

CUHK03. On CUHK03, we follow the new protocol proposed in [48] and conduct experiments using labeled datasets. The results are shown in Table 4. PAN achieves 82.5% CMC top1 and 80.4% mAP on CUHK03 labeled dataset, respectively, which are leading results on the CUHK03 dataset. PAN exceeds DaRE [49], which applies deep supervision to the mid-level features without considering the spatial structure of feature maps. It also outperforms multi-branch attention method CAMA [50] with much less parameters.

DukeMTMC-ReID. On this dataset, we compare our method with all the state-of-the-art methods in the literature. As shown in Table 5, our model achieves much better performance than other methods. The proposed PAN obtains 89.5% Top1 accuracy and 79.2% mAP, respectively. PAN beats several attention and multi-scale based methods, including HA-CNN [22] (harmonious attention and local features of every building block are extracted and processed), IANet [38] (self-attention embedded in the middle of the networks), Pyramid [42] (multi-loss and pyramidal model to incorporate local and global information), SONA [45] (Second-order attention with dropblock), ABD-Net [44] (Channel and Position attention) and MHN [43] (mixed high-order attention). PAN efficiently suppresses the background noise and utilize the useful middle-level features. The strong performance shows that PAN is a promising direction to utilize attention for feature fusion.

Table 4. Single-shot performance comparison on CUHK03 dataset.

Method	Top1	mAP
SVDNet [1] (ICCV17)	41.5	37.3
HA-CNN* [22] (CVPR18)	44.4	41.0
MLFN# [3] (CVPR18)	54.7	49.2
DaRE [49] (CVPR18)	58.1	53.7
Local CNN* [41] (MM18)	58.7	53.8
MGN* [19] (MM18)	68.0	67.4
CAMA [50] (CVPR19)	70.1	66.5
MHN* [43] (ICCV19)	77.2	72.4
SONA* [45] (ICCV19)	81.4	79.2
PAN*	82.5	80.4

Table 5. Single-shot performance comparison on DukeMTMC-ReID.

Method	Top1	mAP
HA-CNN* [22] (CVPR18)	80.5	63.8
Local CNN* [41] (MM18)	82.2	66.0
PCB [5] (ECCV18)	83.3	69.2
MGN# [19] (MM18)	88.7	78.4
IANet* [38] (CVPR19)	87.1	73.4
MHN* [43] (ICCV19)	89.1	77.2
SONA* [45] (ICCV19)	89.4	78.3
ABD-Net* [44] (ICCV19)	89.0	78.6
ST-ReID [46] (AAAI19)	94.0	82.8
PAN*	89.5	79.2

5 Conclusions

We proposed a simple yet effective part-aware attention network to leverage and strength multi-layer features in convolutional neural networks. The so-called part-aware attention network (PAN) connects source features to the target features and learns to leverage their pair-wise correspondence for feature enhancement. It considers not only the local spatial relations of multi-layer feature maps but also the long-range relations among them. In person Re-ID, PAN provides an effective way to facilitate the interaction between low-level/middle-level features and high-level features to strength the discrimination of human body. Detailed analysis and extensive experiments were conducted on three widely used datasets to validate the effectiveness of our PAN approach for person Re-ID.

Acknowledgements. This research is supported by the China NSFC grant (no. 61672446).

References

1. Sun, Y., Zheng, L., Deng, W., Wang, S.: SVDNet for pedestrian retrieval. In: ICCV (2017)
2. Chen, Y., Zhu, X., Gong, S.: Person re-identification by deep learning multi-scale representations. In: CVPR (2017)
3. Chang, X., Hospedales, T.M., Xiang, T.: Multi-level factorisation net for person re-identification. In: CVPR, vol. 1, p. 2 (2018)
4. Si, J., et al.: Dual attention matching network for context-aware feature sequence based person re-identification. In: CVPR (2018)
5. Sun, Y., Zheng, L., Yang, Y., Tian, Q., Wang, S.: Beyond part models: person retrieval with refined part pooling (and a strong convolutional baseline). In: Ferrari, V., Hebert, M., Sminchisescu, C., Weiss, Y. (eds.) ECCV 2018. LNCS, vol. 11208, pp. 501–518. Springer, Cham (2018). https://doi.org/10.1007/978-3-030-01225-0_30
6. Suh, Y., Wang, J., Tang, S., Mei, T., Lee, K.M.: Part-aligned bilinear representations for person re-identification. In: Ferrari, V., Hebert, M., Sminchisescu, C., Weiss, Y. (eds.) Computer Vision – ECCV 2018. LNCS, vol. 11218, pp. 418–437. Springer, Cham (2018). https://doi.org/10.1007/978-3-030-01264-9_25
7. Shi, H., et al.: Embedding deep metric for person re-identification: a study against large variations. In: Leibe, B., Matas, J., Sebe, N., Welling, M. (eds.) ECCV 2016. LNCS, vol. 9905, pp. 732–748. Springer, Cham (2016). https://doi.org/10.1007/978-3-319-46448-0_44
8. Liao, S., Hu, Y., Zhu, X., Li, S.Z.: Person re-identification by local maximal occurrence representation and metric learning. In: CVPR (2015)
9. Jose, C., Fleuret, F.: Scalable metric learning via weighted approximate rank component analysis. In: Leibe, B., Matas, J., Sebe, N., Welling, M. (eds.) ECCV 2016. LNCS, vol. 9909, pp. 875–890. Springer, Cham (2016). https://doi.org/10.1007/978-3-319-46454-1_53
10. Song, H.O., Xiang, Y., Jegelka, S., Savarese, S.: Deep metric learning via lifted structured feature embedding. In: CVPR (2016)

11. Liao, S., Li, S.Z.: Efficient PSD constrained asymmetric metric learning for person re-identification. In: ICCV (2015)
12. Chen, W., Chen, X., Zhang, J., Huang, K.: Beyond triplet loss: a deep quadruplet network for person re-identification. In: CVPR (2017)
13. Cheng, D., Gong, Y., Zhou, S., Wang, J., Zheng, N.: Person re-identification by multi-channel parts-based CNN with improved triplet loss function. In: CVPR (2016)
14. Zhao, L., Li, X., Wang, J., Zhuang, Y.: Deeply-learned part-aligned representations for person re-identification. In: ICCV (2017)
15. Li, D., Chen, X., Zhang, Z., Huang, K.: Learning deep context-aware features over body and latent parts for person re-identification. In: CVPR (2017)
16. Zhao, H., et al.: Spindle Net: person re-identification with human body region guided feature decomposition and fusion. In: CVPR (2017)
17. Zheng, Z., Zheng, L., Yang, Y.: Pedestrian alignment network for large-scale person re-identification. In: CVPR (2017)
18. Zhang, Y., Li, X., Zhao, L., Zhang, Z.: Semantics-aware deep correspondence structure learning for robust person re-identification. In: IJCAI (2016)
19. Wang, G., Yuan, Y., Chen, X., Li, J., Zhou, X.: Learning discriminative features with multiple granularities for person re-identification. arXiv e-prints (2018)
20. Liu, X., et al.: HydraPlus-Net: attentive deep features for pedestrian analysis. In: Proceedings of the IEEE International Conference on Computer Vision, pp. 1–9 (2017)
21. Chen, Y., Zhu, X., Gong, S.: Person re-identification by deep learning multi-scale representations. In: The IEEE International Conference on Computer Vision (ICCV) Workshops (2017)
22. Li, W., Zhu, X., Gong, S.: Harmonious attention network for person re-identification. In: CVPR, vol. 1, p. 2 (2018)
23. Qian, X., Fu, Y., Jiang, Y., Xiang, T., Xue, X.: Multi-scale deep learning architectures for person re-identification. CoRR abs/1709.05165 (2017)
24. Long, J., Shelhamer, E., Darrell, T.: Fully convolutional networks for semantic segmentation. In: Proceedings of the IEEE Conference on Computer Vision and Pattern Recognition, pp. 3431–3440 (2015)
25. Yair, N., Michaeli, T.: Multi-scale weighted nuclear norm image restoration. In: IEEE Conference on Computer Vision and Pattern Recognition (2018)
26. Branson, S., Beijbom, O., Belongie, S.: Efficient large-scale structured learning. In: Proceedings of the IEEE Conference on Computer Vision and Pattern Recognition, pp. 1806–1813 (2013)
27. Kirillov, A., Girshick, R., He, K., Dollar, P.: Panoptic feature pyramid networks. In: Proceedings of the IEEE/CVF Conference on Computer Vision and Pattern Recognition (CVPR) (2019)
28. Szegedy, C., et al.: Going deeper with convolutions. In: CVPR (2015)
29. Li, X., Wang, W., Hu, X., Yang, J.: Selective kernel networks (2019)
30. Ding, X., Guo, Y., Ding, G., Han, J.: ACNet: strengthening the kernel skeletons for powerful CNN via asymmetric convolution blocks. In: The IEEE International Conference on Computer Vision (ICCV) (2019)
31. Wang, X., Girshick, R., Gupta, A., He, K.: Non-local neural networks. In: CVPR (2018)
32. Vaswani, A., et al.: Attention is all you need. In: Guyon, I., et al. (eds.) Advances in Neural Information Processing Systems 30, pp. 5998–6008. Curran Associates, Inc. (2017)

33. Jetley, S., Lord, N.A., Lee, N., Torr, P.H.S.: Learn to pay attention. In: ICLR (2018)
34. Hu, J., Shen, L., Sun, G.: Squeeze-and-excitation networks (2018)
35. Bishop, C.M.: Pattern Recognition and Machine Learning. Information Science and Statistics, 1st edn. Springer, New York (2006)
36. Hermans, A., Beyer, L., Leibe, B.: In defense of the triplet loss for person re-identification. arXiv preprint arXiv:1703.07737 (2017)
37. Zhang, R., et al.: SCAN: self-and-collaborative attention network for video person re-identification. CoRR abs/1807.05688 (2018)
38. Hou, R., Ma, B., Chang, H., Gu, X., Shan, S., Chen, X.: Interaction-and-aggregation network for person re-identification. In: Proceedings of the IEEE Conference on Computer Vision and Pattern Recognition, pp. 9317–9326 (2019)
39. Zhong, Z., Zheng, L., Kang, G., Li, S., Yang, Y.: Random erasing data augmentation. arXiv preprint arXiv:1708.04896 (2017)
40. Bai, S., Bai, X., Tian, Q.: Scalable person re-identification on supervised smoothed manifold (2017)
41. Yang, J., Shen, X., Tian, X., Li, H., Huang, J., Hua, X.S.: Local convolutional neural networks for person re-identification. In: 2018 ACM Multimedia Conference on Multimedia Conference, pp. 1074–1082. ACM (2018)
42. Zheng, F., et al.: Pyramidal person re-identification via multi-loss dynamic training. In: Proceedings of the IEEE Conference on Computer Vision and Pattern Recognition, pp. 8514–8522 (2019)
43. Chen, B., Deng, W., Hu, J.: Mixed high-order attention network for person re-identification. In: Proceedings of the IEEE International Conference on Computer Vision, pp. 371–381 (2019)
44. Chen, T., et al.: ABD-Net: attentive but diverse person re-identification. In: Proceedings of the IEEE International Conference on Computer Vision, pp. 8351–8361 (2019)
45. Xia, B.N., Gong, Y., Zhang, Y., Poellabauer, C.: Second-order non-local attention networks for person re-identification. In: Proceedings of the IEEE International Conference on Computer Vision, pp. 3760–3769 (2019)
46. Wang, G., Lai, J., Huang, P., Xie, X.: Spatial-temporal person re-identification, pp. 8933–8940 (2019)
47. Luo, H., et al.: A strong baseline and batch normalization neck for deep person re-identification. IEEE Trans. Multimedia **22**, 2597–2609 (2019)
48. Zhong, Z., Zheng, L., Cao, D., Li, S.: Re-ranking person re-identification with k-reciprocal encoding (2017)
49. Wang, Y., et al.: Resource aware person re-identification across multiple resolutions. In: Proceedings of the IEEE Conference on Computer Vision and Pattern Recognition, pp. 8042–8051 (2018)
50. Yang, W., Huang, H., Zhang, Z., Chen, X., Huang, K., Zhang, S.: Towards rich feature discovery with class activation maps augmentation for person re-identification. In: Proceedings of the IEEE Conference on Computer Vision and Pattern Recognition, pp. 1389–1398 (2019)

Image Captioning Through Image Transformer

Sen He[1], Wentong Liao[2(✉)], Hamed R. Tavakoli[3], Michael Yang[4],
Bodo Rosenhahn[2], and Nicolas Pugeault[5]

[1] CVSSP, University of Surrey, Guildford, UK
senhe752@gmail.com
[2] Leibniz University of Hanover, Hanover, Germany
liao@tnt.uni-hannover.de
[3] Nokia Technologies, Espoo, Finland
[4] University of Twente, Enschede, The Netherlands
[5] School of Computing Science, University of Glasgow, Glasgow, Scotland

Abstract. Automatic captioning of images is a task that combines the
challenges of image analysis and text generation. One important aspect
of captioning is the notion of attention: how to decide what to describe
and in which order. Inspired by the successes in text analysis and translation, previous works have proposed the *transformer* architecture for
image captioning. However, the structure between the *semantic units* in
images (usually the detected regions from object detection model) and
sentences (each single word) is different. Limited work has been done to
adapt the transformer's internal architecture to images. In this work, we
introduce the ***image transformer***, which consists of a modified encoding transformer and an implicit decoding transformer, motivated by the
relative spatial relationship between image regions. Our design widens
the original transformer layer's inner architecture to adapt to the structure of images. With only regions feature as inputs, our model achieves
new state-of-the-art performance on both MSCOCO offline and online
testing benchmarks. The code is available at https://github.com/wtliao/
ImageTransformer.

1 Introduction

Image captioning is the task of describing the content of an image in words.
The problem of automatic image captioning by AI systems has received a lot
of attention in the recent years, due to the success of deep learning models for
both language and image processing. Most image captioning approaches in the
literature are based on a *translational* approach, with a visual encoder and a
linguistic decoder. One challenge in automatic translation is that it cannot be
done word by word, but that other words influence then meaning, and therefore the translation, of a word; this is even more true when translating across

---

S. He, W. Liao—Equal contribution.

© Springer Nature Switzerland AG 2021
H. Ishikawa et al. (Eds.): ACCV 2020, LNCS 12625, pp. 153–169, 2021.
https://doi.org/10.1007/978-3-030-69538-5_10

modalities, from images to text, where the system must decide *what* must be described in the image. A common solution to this challenge relies on attention mechanisms. For example, previous image captioning models try to solve *where* to look in the image [1–4] (now partly solved by the Faster-RCNN object detection model [5]) in the encoding stage and use a recurrent neural network with attention mechanism in the decoding stage to generate the caption. But more than just to decide what to describe in the image, recent image captioning models propose to use attention to learn how regions of the image relate to each other, effectively encoding their *context* in the image. Graph convolutional neural networks [6] were first introduced to relate regions in the image; however, those approaches [7–10] usually require auxiliary models (e.g. visual relationship detection and/or attribute detection models) to build the visual scene graph in the image in the first place. In contrast, in the natural language processing field, the transformer architecture [11] was developed to relate embedded words in sentences, and can be trained end to end without auxiliary models explicitly detecting such relations. Recent image captioning models [12–14] adopted the transformer architectures to implicitly relate informative regions in the image through dot-product attention achieving state-of-the-art performance.

However, the transformer architecture was designed for machine translation of text. In a text, a word is either to the left or to the right of another word, with different distances. In contrast, images are two-dimensional (indeed, represent three-dimensional scenes), so that a region may not only be on the left or right of another region, it may also contain or be contained in another region. The relative spatial relationship between the semantic units in images has a larger degree of freedom than that in sentences. Furthermore, in the decoding stage of machine translation, a word is usually translated into another word in other languages (one to one decoding), whereas for an image region, we may describe its context, its attribute and/or its relationship with other regions (one to more decoding). One limitation of previous transformer-based image captioning models [12–14] is that they adopt the transformer's internal architecture designed for the machine translation, where each transformer layer contains a single (multi-head) dot-product attention module. In this paper, we introduce the *image transformer* for image captioning, where each transformer layer implements multiple sub-transformers, to encode spatial relationships between image regions and decode the diverse information in image regions.

The difference between our method and previous transformer based models [12–14] is that our method focuses on the *inner architectures* of the transformer layer, in which we widen the transformer module. Yao *et al.* [10] used a hierarchical concept in the encoding part of their model, our model focuses on the local spatial relationships for each query region whereas their method is a global tree hierarchy. Furthermore, our model does not require auxiliary models (*i.e.*, for visual relation detection and instance segmentation) to build the visual scene graph. Our encoding method can be viewed as the combination of a visual semantic graph and a spatial graph which use a transformer layer to implicitly combine them without auxiliary relationship and attribute detectors (Fig. 1).

Fig. 1. Image captioning vs machine translation.

The contributions of this paper can be summarised as follows:

- We propose a novel internal architecture for the transformer layer adapted to the image captioning task, with a modified attention module suited to the complex natural structure of image regions.
- We report thorough experiments and ablation study were done in the work to validate our proposed architecture, state-of-the-art performance was achieved on the MSCOCO image captioning offline and online testing dataset with only region features as input.

The rest of the paper is organized as follows: Sect. 2 reviews the related attention-based image captioning models; Sect. 3 introduces the standard transformer model and our proposed image transformer; followed by the experiment results and analysis in Sect. 4; finally, we will conclude this paper in Sect. 5.

2 Related Work

We characterize current attention-based image captioning models into single-stage attention models, two-stages attention models, visual scene graph based models, and transformer-based models. We will review them one by one in this section.

2.1 Single-Stage Attention Based Image Captioning

Single-stage attention-based image captioning models are the models where attention is applied at the decoding stage, where the decoder attends to the most informative region [15] in the image when generating a corresponding word.

The availability of large-scale annotated datasets [16,17] enabled the training of deep models for image captioning. Vinyals *et al.* [18] proposed the first deep model for image captioning. Their model uses a CNN pre-trained on ImageNet [16] to encode the image, then a LSTM [19] based language model is used to decode the image features into a sequence of words. Xu *et al.* [1] introduced an attention mechanism into image captioning during the generation of each word, based on the hidden state of their language model and the previous generated word. Their attention module generates a matrix to weight each receptive field in the encoded feature map, and then feed the weighted feature map and the previous generated word to the language model to generate the next word. Instead of only attending to the receptive field in the encoded feature map, Chen *et al.* [2] added a feature channel attention module, their channel attention module re-weight each feature channel during the generation of each word. Not all the words in the sentence have a correspondence in the image, so Lu *et al.* [20] proposed an adaptive attention approach, where their model has a visual sentinel which adaptively decides when and where to rely on the visual information.

The single-stage attention model is computational efficient, but lacks accurate positioning of informative regions in the original image.

2.2   Two-Stages Attention Based Image Captioning

Two stage attention models consists of *bottom-up* attention and *top-down* attention, where bottom-up attention first uses object detection models to detect multiple informative regions in the image, then top-down attention attends to the most relevant detected regions when generating a word.

Instead of relying on the coarse receptive fields as informative regions in the image, as single-stage attention models do, Anderson *et al.* [3] train the detection models on the *Visual Genome* dataset [21]. The trained detection models can detect 10–100 informative regions in the image. They then use a two-layers LSTM network as decoder, where the first layer generates a state vector based on the embedded word vector and the mean feature of the detected regions and the second layer uses the state vector from the previous layer to generate a weight for each detected region. The weighted sum of detected regions feature is used as a context vector for predicting the next word. Lu *et al.* [4] developed a similar network, but with a detection model trained on *MSCOCO* [22], which is a smaller dataset than *Visual Genome*, and therefore less informative regions are detected.

The performance of two-stage attention based image captioning models is improved a lot against single-stage attention based models. However, each detected region is isolated from others, lacking the relationship with other regions.

2.3   Visual Scene Graph Based Image Captioning

Visual scene graph based image captioning models extend two-stage attention models by injecting a graph convolutional neural network to relate detected informative regions, and therefore refine their features before feeding into the decoder.

Yao *et al.* [7] developed a model which consists of a semantic scene graph and a spatial scene graph. In the semantic scene graph, each region is connected with other semantically related regions, those relationships are usually determined by a visual relationship detector among a union box. In the spatial scene graph, the relationship between two regions is defined by their relative positions. Then the feature of each node in the scene graph is refined with their related nodes through graph neural networks [6]. Yang *et al.* [8] use an auto-encoder, where they first encode the graph structure in the sentence based on the SPICE [23] evaluation metric to learn a dictionary, then the semantic scene graph is encoded using the learnt dictionary. The previous two works treat the semantic relationships as edges in the scene graph, while Guo *et al.* [9] treat them as nodes in the scene graph. Also, their decoder focuses on different aspects of a region. Yao *et al.* [10] further introduces the tree hierarchy and instance level feature into the scene graph.

Introducing the graph neural network to relate informative regions yields a sizeable performance improvement for image captioning models, compared to two-stage attention models. However, it requires auxiliary models to detect and build the scene graph at first. Also those models usually have two parallel streams, one responsible for the semantic scene graph and another for spatial scene graph, which is computationally inefficient.

2.4 Transformer Based Image Captioning

Transformer based image captioning models use the dot-product attention mechanism to relate informative regions implicitly.

Since the introduction of original transformer model [11], more advanced architectures were proposed for machine translation based on the structure or the natural characteristic of sentences [24–26]. In image captioning, AoANet [12] uses the original internal transformer layer architecture, with the addition of a *gated linear layer* [27] on top of the multi-head attention. The object relation network [14] injects the relative spatial attention into the dot-product attention. Another interesting result described by Herdade *et al.* [14] is that the simple position encoding (as proposed in the original transformer) did not improve image captioning performance. The entangled transformer model [13] features a dual parallel transformer to encode and refine visual and semantic information in the image, which is fused through gated bilateral controller.

Compared to scene graph based image captioning models, transformer based models do not require auxiliary models to detect and build the scene graph at first, which is more computational efficient. However current transformer based models still use the inner architecture of the original transformer, designed for text, where each transformer layer has a single multi-head dot-product attention refining module. This structure does not allow to model the full complexity of relations between image regions, therefore we propose to change the inner architecture of the transformer layer to adapt it to image data. We widen the transformer layer, such that each transformer layer has multiple refining modules for different aspects of regions both in the encoding and decoding stages.

3 Image Transformer

In this section, we first review the original transformer layer [11], we then elaborate the encoding and decoding part for the proposed *image transformer* architecture.

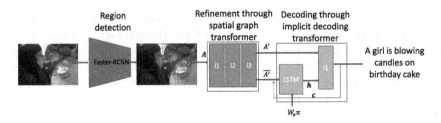

Fig. 2. The overall architecture of our model, the refinement part consists of 3 stacks of spatial graph transformer layer, and the decoding part has a LSTM layer with a implicit decoding transformer layer.

3.1   Transformer Layer

A transformer consists of a stack of multi-head dot-product attention based transformer refining layer.

In each layer, for a given input $A \in \mathbb{R}^{N \times D}$, consisting of N entries of D dimensions. In natural language processing, the input entry can be the embedded feature of a word in a sentence, and in computer vision or image captioning, the input entry can be the feature describing a region in an image. The key function of transformer is to refine each entry with other entries through multi-head dot-product attention. Each layer of a transformer first transforms the input into queries ($Q = AW_Q$, $W_Q \in \mathbb{R}^{D \times D_k}$), keys ($K = AW_K$, $W_K \in \mathbb{R}^{D \times D_k}$) and values ($V = AW_V$, $W_A \in \mathbb{R}^{D \times D_v}$) though linear transformations, then the scaled dot-product attention is defined by:

$$\text{Attention}(Q, K, V) = \text{Softmax}\left(\frac{QK^T}{\sqrt{D_k}}\right) V, \tag{1}$$

where D_k is the dimension of the key vector and D_v the dimension of the value vector ($D = D_k = D_v$ in the implementation). To improve the performance of the attention layer, multi-head attention is applied:

$$\text{MultiHead}(Q, K, V) = \text{Concat}(\text{head}_1, \ldots, \text{head}_h)W_O,$$
$$\text{head}_i = \text{Attention}(AW_{Q_i}, AW_{K_i}, AW_{V_i}). \tag{2}$$

The output from the multi-head attention is then added with the input and normalised:

$$A_m = \text{Norm}(A + \text{MultiHead}(Q, K, V)), \tag{3}$$

where $\text{Norm}(\cdot)$ denote layer normalisation.

The transformer implements residual connections in each module, such that the final output of a transformer layer is:

$$A^{'} = \text{Norm}(A_m + \phi(A_m W_f)), \tag{4}$$

where ϕ is a feed-forward network with non-linearity.

Each refining layer takes the output of its previous layer as input (the first layer takes the original input). The decoding part is also a stack of transformer refining layers, which take the output of encoding part as well as the embedded features of previous predicted word.

3.2 Spatial Graph Encoding Transformer Layer

(a)   (b)

Fig. 3. (a) Image with detected regions; (b) An example of query region in the image (man in the red bounding box), and its neighbor regions (regions in blue bounding boxes, bull, umbrella, etc.), child regions (regions in the yellow bounding boxes, hair, cloth). (Color figure online)

In contrast to the original transformer, which only considers spatial relationships between query and key pairs as **neighborhood**, we propose to use a spatial graph transformer in the encoding part, where we consider three common categories of spatial relationship for each query region in a graph structure: *parent, neighbor*, and *child* (an example shown in Fig. 3). Thus we widen each transformer layer by adding three sub-transformer layers in parallel in each layer, each sub-transformer responsible for a category of spatial relationship, all sharing the same query. In the encoding stage, we define the relative spatial relationship between two regions based on their overlap. We first compute the graph adjacent matrices $\Omega_p \in \mathbb{R}^{N \times N}$ (parent node adjacent matrix), $\Omega_n \in \mathbb{R}^{\in N \times N}$ (neighbor node adjacent matrix), and $\Omega_c \in \mathbb{R}^{\in N \times N}$ (child node adjacent matrix) for all regions in the image:

$$\Omega_p[l,m] = \begin{cases} 1, \text{ if } \dfrac{\text{Area}(l \cap m)}{\text{Area}(l)} \geqslant \epsilon \text{ and } \dfrac{\text{Area}(l \cap m)}{\text{Area}(l)} > \dfrac{\text{Area}(l \cap m)}{\text{Area}(m)} \\ 0, \text{ otherwise.} \end{cases}$$

$$\Omega_c[l,m] = \Omega_p[m,l]$$

$$\text{with } \sum_{i \in \{p,n,c\}} \Omega_i[l,m] = 1$$

(5)

where $\epsilon = 0.9$ in our experiment. The spatial graph adjacent matrices are used as the spatial hard attention embedded into each sub-transformer to combine

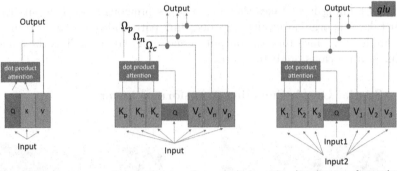

Fig. 4. The difference between the original transformer layer and the proposed encoding and decoding transformer layers.

the output of each sub-transformer in the encoder. More specifically, the original encoding transformer defined in Eqs. (1) and (2) are reformulated as:

$$\text{Attention}(Q, K_i, V_i) = \Omega_i \circ \text{Softmax}\left(\frac{QK_i^T}{\sqrt{d}}\right)V_i, \tag{6}$$

$\circ$ is the Hadamard product, and

$$A_m = \text{Norm}\left(A + \sum_{i\in\{p,n,c\}} \text{MultiHead}(Q, K_i, V_i)\right). \tag{7}$$

As we widen the transformer, we halve the number of stacks in the encoder to achieve similar complexity as the original one (3 stacks, while the original transformer features 6 stacks). With our formulation, we combined the spatial graph and semantic graph (the scene graph based methods [7,9] require two branches to encode them) into a transformer layer. Note that the original transformer architecture is a special case of the proposed architecture, when no region in the image either contains or is contained by another.

3.3   Implicit Decoding Transformer Layer

Our decoder consists of a LSTM [28] layer and an implicit transformer decoding layer, which we proposed to decode the diverse information in a region in the image. The LSTM layer is a common memory module and the transformer layer infers the most relevant region in the image through dot product attention.

At first, the LSTM layer receives the mean of the output ($\overline{A} = \frac{1}{N}\sum_{i=1}^{N} A_i'$) from the encoding transformer, a context vector (c_{t-1}) at last time step and the embedded feature vector of current word in the ground truth sentence:

$$\begin{aligned} x_t &= [W_e\pi_t, \overline{A} + c_{t-1}] \\ h_t, m_t &= \text{LSTM}(x_t, h_{t-1}, m_{t-1}) \end{aligned} \tag{8}$$

where, W_e is the word embedding matrix, π_t is the tth word in the ground truth. The output state h_t is then transformed linearly and treated as the query for the input of the implicit decoding transformer layer. The difference between the original transformer layer and our implicit decoding transformer layer is that we also widen the decoding transformer layer by adding several sub-transformers in parallel in one layer, such that each sub-transformer can implicitly decode different aspects of a region. It is formalised as follows:

$$A_{t,i}^D = \text{MultiHead}(W_{DQ}h_t, W_{DKi}A', W_{DVi}A') \tag{9}$$

Then, the mean of the sub-transformers' output is passed through a gated linear layer (GLU) [27] to extract the new context vector (c_t) at the current step by channel:

$$c_t = \text{GLU}\left(h_t, \frac{1}{M}\sum_{i=1}^{M} A_{t,i}^D\right) \tag{10}$$

The context vector is then used to predict the probability of word at time step t:

$$p(y_t|y_{1:t-1}) = \text{Softmax}(w_p c_t + b_p) \tag{11}$$

The overall architecture of our model is illustrated in Fig. 2, and the difference between the original transformer layer and our proposed encoding and decoding transformer layer is showed in Fig. 4.

3.4 Training Objectives

Given a target ground truth as a sequence of words $y_{1:T}^*$, for training the model parameters θ, we follow the previous method, such that we first train the model with cross-entropy loss:

$$L_{XE}(\theta) = -\sum_{t=1}^{T} \log(p_\theta(y_t^*|y_{1:t-1}^*)) \tag{12}$$

then followed by self-critical reinforced training [29] optimizing the CIDEr score [30]:

$$L_R(\theta) = -E_{(y_{1:T}\sim p_\theta)}[r(y_{1:T})] \tag{13}$$

where r is the score function and the gradient is approximated by:

$$\nabla_\theta \approx -(r(y_{1:T}^s) - (\hat{y}_{1:T})) \nabla_\theta \log p_\theta(y_{1:T}^s) \tag{14}$$

4   Experiment

4.1   Datasets and Evaluation Metrics

Our model is trained on the MSCOCO image captioning dataset [17]. We follow Karpathy's splits [32], with 11,3287 images in the training set, 5,000 images in

Table 1. Comparison on MSCOCO Karpathy offline test split. * means fusion of two models. † means SENet [31] as feature extraction backbone

Model	Bleu1	Bleu4	METEOR	ROUGE-L	CIDEr	SPICE
Single-stage model						
Att2all [29]	–	34.2	26.7	55.7	114.0	–
Two-stages model						
n-babytalk [4]	75.5	34.7	27.1	–	107.2	20.1
up-down [3]	79.8	36.3	27.7	56.9	120.1	21.4
Scene graph based model						
GCN-LSTM* [7]	80.9	38.3	28.6	58.5	128.7	22.1
AUTO-ENC [8]	80.8	38.4	28.4	58.6	127.8	22.1
ALV* [9]	–	38.4	28.5	58.4	128.6	22.0
GCN-LSTM-HIP*† [10]	–	39.1	28.9	**59.2**	130.6	22.3
Transformer based model						
Entangle-T* [13]	**81.5**	**39.9**	28.9	59.0	127.6	22.6
AoA [12]	80.2	38.9	**29.2**	58.8	129.8	22.4
VORN [14]	80.5	38.6	28.7	58.4	128.3	22.6
Ours	80.8	39.5	29.1	59.0	**130.8**	**22.8**

the validation set and 5,000 images in the test set. Each image has 5 captions as ground truth. We discard the words which occur less than 4 times, and the final vocabulary size is 10,369. We test our model on both Karpathy's offline test set (5,000 images) and MSCOCO online testing datasets (40,775 images). We use Bleu [33], METEOR [34], ROUGE-L [35], CIDEr [30], and SPICE [23] as evaluation metrics.

4.2   Implementation Details

Following previous work, we first train Faster R-CNN on Visual Genome [21], use resnet-101 [36] as backbone, pretrained on ImageNet [16]. For each image, we can detect 10–100 informative regions, the boundaries of each are first normalised and then used to compute the spatial graph matrices. We then train our proposed model for image captioning using the computed spatial graph matrices and extracted features for each image region. We first train our model with *cross-entropy* loss for 25 epochs, the initial learning rate is set to 2×10^{-3}, and we decay the learning rate by 0.8 every 3 epochs. Our model is optimized through Adam [37] with a batch size of 10. We then further optimize our model by reinforced learning for another 35 epochs. The size of the decoder's LSTM layer is set to 1024, and beam search of size 3 is used in the inference stage.

4.3 Experiment Results

We compare our model's performance with published image captioning models. The compared models include the top performing single-stage attention model, Att2all [29]; two-stages attention based models, n-babytalk [4] and up-down [3]; visual scene graph based models, GCN-LSTM [7], AUTO-ENC [8], ALV [9], GCN-LSTM-HIP [10]; and transformer based models Entangle-T [13], AoA [12], VORN [14]. The comparison on the MSCOCO Karpathy offline test set is illustrated in Table 1. Our model achieves new state-of-the-art on the CIDEr and SPICE score, while other evaluation scores are comparable to the previous top performing models. Note that because most visual scene graph based models fused semantic and spatial scene graph, and require the auxiliary models to build the scene graph at first, our model is more computationally efficient. VORN [14] also integrated spatial attention in their model, and our model performs better than them among all kinds of evaluation metrics, which shows the superiority of our spatial graph transformer layer. The MSCOCO online testing results are listed in Table 2, our model outperforms previous transformer based model on several evaluation metrics.

Table 2. Leaderboard of recent published models on the MSCOCO online testing server. * means fusion of two models. † means SENet [31] as feature extraction backbone

Model	B1		B4		M		R		C	
	c5	c40	c5	c40	c5	c40	c5	c40	c5	c40
Scene graph based model										
GCN-LSTM* [7]	80.8	95.9	38.7	69.7	28.5	37.6	58.5	73.4	125.3	126.5
AUTO-ENC* [8]	–	–	38.5	69.7	28.2	37.2	58.6	73.6	123.8	126.5
ALV* [9]	79.9	94.7	37.4	68.3	28.2	37.1	57.9	72.8	123.1	125.5
GCN-LSTM-HIP*† [10]	81.6	95.9	39.3	71.0	28.8	38.1	59.0	74.1	127.9	130.2
Transformer based model										
Entangle-T* [13]	81.2	95.0	38.9	70.2	28.6	38.0	58.6	73.9	122.1	124.4
AoA [12]	81.0	95.0	39.4	71.2	29.1	38.5	58.9	74.5	126.9	129.6
Ours	81.2	95.4	39.6	71.5	29.1	38.4	59.2	74.5	127.4	129.6

4.4 Ablation Study and Analysis

In the ablation study, we use AoA [12] as a strong baseline[1] (with a single multi-head dot-product attention module per layer), which add the gated linear layer [27] on top of the multi-head attention. In the encoder part, we study the spatial relationship's effect in the encoder, where we ablate the spatial relationship by simply taking the mean output of three sub-transformers in each layer by

---

[1] Our experiments are based on the code released at: https://github.com/husthuaan/ AoANet.

reformulating Eqs. 6 and 7 as: $\text{Attention}(Q, K_i, V_i) = \text{Softmax}\left(\frac{QK_i^T}{\sqrt{d}}\right)V_i, A_m = \text{Norm}\left(A + \frac{1}{3}\sum_{i \in \{p,n,c\}} \text{MultiHead}(Q, K_i, V_i)\right)$. We also study where to use our proposed spatial graph encoding transformer layer in the encoding part: in the first layer, second layer, third layer or three of them? In the decoding part, we study the effect of the number of sub-transformers (M in Eq. 10) in the implicit decoding transformer layer.

Table 3. Ablation study, results reported without RL training. baseline+layer1 means only the first layer of encoding transformer uses our proposed spatial transformer layer, other layers use the original one. M is the number of sub-transformers in the decoding transformer layer.

Model	Bleu1	Bleu4	METEOR	ROUGE-L	CIDEr	SPICE
baseline (AoA)	77.0	36.5	28.1	57.1	116.6	21.3
Positions to embed our spatial graph encoding transformer layer						
baseline+layer1	77.8	36.8	28.3	57.3	118.1	21.3
baseline+layer2	77.2	36.8	28.3	57.3	118.2	21.3
baseline+layer3	77.0	37.0	28.2	57.1	117.3	21.2
baseline+layer1, 2, 3	77.5	37.0	28.3	57.2	118.2	21.4
Effect of spatial relationships in the encoder						
baseline+layer1, 2, 3 w/o spatial rela	77.5	36.8	28.2	57.1	117.8	21.4
Number of sub-transformers in the implicit decoding transformer layer						
baseline+layer1, 2, 3 ($M=2$)	77.5	37.6	28.4	57.4	118.8	21.3
baseline+layer1, 2, 3 ($M=3$)	78.0	37.4	28.4	57.6	119.1	21.6
baseline+layer1, 2, 3 ($M=4$)	77.5	37.8	28.4	57.5	118.6	21.4

As we can see from Table 3, by widening the encoding transformer layer, there is a significant improvement on the model's performance. While not every layers in the encoding transformer are equal, when we use our proposed transformer layer at the top layer of the encoding part, the improvement was reduced. This may be because spatial relationships at the top layer of the transformer are not as informative, we use our spatial transformer layer at all layers in the encoding part. When we reduce the spatial relationship in our proposed wider transformer layer, there is also some performance reduction, which shows the importance of the spatial relationship in our design. After widening the decoding transformer, the improvement was further increased (the CIDEr score increased from 118.2 to 119.1 after widening the decoding transformer layer with 3 sub-transformers), while not more wider gives better result, with 4 sub-transformers in the decoding transformer layer, there is some performance decrease, therefore the final design of our decoding transformer layer has 3 sub-transformers in parallel. The qualitative example of our models results is illustrated in Fig. 5. As we can see, the baseline model without spatial relationships wrongly described the police officers on a red bus (top right), and people on a train (bottom left).

GT:
- A traffic light over a street surrounded by tall buildings.
- A black and white shot of a city with a tall skyscraper in the .
- Some buildings a traffic light and a cloudy sky.
- A black and white photograph of a stop light from the street.
- A traffic light and street sign surrounded by buildings.

Baseline: A couple of traffic lights on a city street.
Ours: A traffic light on a street with a building.

GT:
- A group of police officers standing in front of a red bus.
- Three bikers by a red bus in the street.
- A big red bus by some people on motorcycles.
- Some men on bikes are passing a red bus.
- Parking officials are riding beside a red bus.

Baseline: A group of police officers on a red bus.
Ours: A group of police officers on motorcycles in front of a red bus.

GT:
- An image of a train that is going down the tracks.
- Some people are standing on rocks with a railroad.
- A train moving along a track on a hill during the day.
- A single train car passing tracks on a hill.

Baseline: A group of people on a train on the tracks.
Ours: A train is traveling down the tracks on a mountain.

GT:
- A man is holding a cell phone in front of a mountain.
- An older man standing on top of a snow covered slops.
- A man looking at a vast mountain landscape.
- A man takes a picture of snowy mountains with his cell phone.

Baseline: A man is taking a picture of a mountain range.
Ours: A man taking a picture of a mountain with a cell phone.

Fig. 5. Qualitative examples from our method on the MSCOCO image captioning dataset [17], compared against the ground truth annotation and a strong baseline method (AoA [12]). (Color figure online)

Encoding Implicit Graph Visualisation: The transformer layer can be seen as an implicit graph, which relates the informative regions through dot-product attention. Here we visualise how our proposed spatial graph transformer layer learn to connect the informative regions through attention in Fig. 6. In the top example, the original transformer layer strongly relates the train with the people on the mountain, yields wrong description, while our proposed transformer layer relates the train with the tracks and mountain; in the bottom example, the original transformer relates the bear with its reflection in water and treats them as 'two bears', while our transformer can distinguish the bear from its reflection and relate it to the snow area.

Decoding Feature Space Visualisation: We also visualised the output of our decoding transformer layer (Fig. 7). Compared to the original decoding transformer layer, which only has one sub-transformer inside it. The output of our proposed implicit decoding transformer layer covers a larger area in the reduced feature space than the original one, which means that our decoding transformer layer decoding more information in the image regions. In the original feature space (1,024 dimensions) from the output of decoding transformer layer, we compute the trace of the feature maps' co-variance matrix from 1,000 examples, the trace for original transformer layer is 30.40 compared to 454.57 for our wider decoding transformer layer, which indicates that our design enables the decoder's output to cover a larger area in the feature space. However, it looks like individual sub-transformers in the decoding transformer layer still do not learn to disentangle different factors in the feature space (as there is no distinct cluster from the output of each sub-transformer), we speculate this is because we have no direct supervision to their output, which may not able to learn the disentangled feature automatically [38].

Baseline

Ours

A group of people on the train on the tracks   A train is traveling down the tracks on a mountain

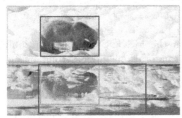

Two polar bears are playing in the water   A polar bear walking in the snow

Fig. 6. A visualization of how the query region relates to its other key regions through attention, the region in the red bounding box is the query region and other regions are key regions. The transparency of each key region shows its dot-product attention weight with the query region. Higher transparency means larger dot-product attention weight, vice versa. (Color figure online)

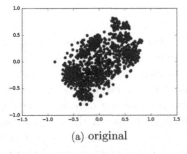
(a) original

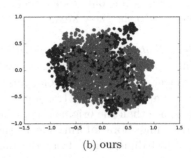
(b) ours

Fig. 7. t-SNE [39] visualisation of the output from decoding transformer layer (1,000 examples), different color represent the output from different sub-transformers in the decoder in our model. (Color figure online)

5   Discussion and Conclusion

In this work, we introduced the *image transformer* architecture. The core idea behind the proposed architecture is to widen the original transformer layer, designed for machine translation, to adapt it to the structure of images. In the encoder, we widen the transformer layer by exploiting the spatial relationships between image regions, and in the decoder, the wider transformer layer can decode more information in the image regions. Extensive experiments were done to show the superiority of the proposed model, the qualitative and quantitative analyses were illustrated in the experiments to validate the proposed encoding and decoding transformer layer. Compared to the previous top models in image captioning, our model achieves a new state-of-the-art SPICE score, while in the other evaluation metrics, our model is either comparable or outperforms the previous best models, with a better computational efficiency.

We hope our work can inspire the community to develop more advanced transformer based architectures that can not only benefit image captioning but also other computer vision tasks which need relational attention inside it. Our code will be shared with the community to support future research.

References

1. Xu, K., et al.: Show, attend and tell: neural image caption generation with visual attention. In: International Conference on Machine Learning, pp. 2048–2057 (2015)
2. Chen, L., et al.: SCA-CNN: spatial and channel-wise attention in convolutional networks for image captioning. In: Proceedings of the IEEE Conference on Computer Vision and Pattern Recognition, pp. 5659–5667 (2017)
3. Anderson, P., et al.: Bottom-up and top-down attention for image captioning and visual question answering. In: Proceedings of the IEEE Conference on Computer Vision and Pattern Recognition, pp. 6077–6086 (2018)
4. Lu, J., Yang, J., Batra, D., Parikh, D.: Neural baby talk. In: Proceedings of the IEEE Conference on Computer Vision and Pattern Recognition, pp. 7219–7228 (2018)
5. Ren, S., He, K., Girshick, R., Sun, J.: Faster R-CNN: towards real-time object detection with region proposal networks. In: Advances in Neural Information Processing Systems, pp. 91–99 (2015)
6. Kipf, T.N., Welling, M.: Semi-supervised classification with graph convolutional networks. arXiv preprint arXiv:1609.02907 (2016)
7. Yao, T., Pan, Y., Li, Y., Mei, T.: Exploring visual relationship for image captioning. In: Ferrari, V., Hebert, M., Sminchisescu, C., Weiss, Y. (eds.) Computer Vision – ECCV 2018. LNCS, vol. 11218, pp. 711–727. Springer, Cham (2018). https://doi.org/10.1007/978-3-030-01264-9_42
8. Yang, X., Tang, K., Zhang, H., Cai, J.: Auto-encoding scene graphs for image captioning. In: Proceedings of the IEEE Conference on Computer Vision and Pattern Recognition, pp. 10685–10694 (2019)
9. Guo, L., Liu, J., Tang, J., Li, J., Luo, W., Lu, H.: Aligning linguistic words and visual semantic units for image captioning. In: Proceedings of the 27th ACM International Conference on Multimedia, pp. 765–773 (2019)

10. Yao, T., Pan, Y., Li, Y., Mei, T.: Hierarchy parsing for image captioning. In: Proceedings of the IEEE International Conference on Computer Vision, pp. 2621–2629 (2019)
11. Vaswani, A., et al.: Attention is all you need. In: Advances in Neural Information Processing Systems, pp. 5998–6008 (2017)
12. Huang, L., Wang, W., Chen, J., Wei, X.Y.: Attention on attention for image captioning. In: Proceedings of the IEEE International Conference on Computer Vision, pp. 4634–4643 (2019)
13. Li, G., Zhu, L., Liu, P., Yang, Y.: Entangled transformer for image captioning. In: Proceedings of the IEEE International Conference on Computer Vision, pp. 8928–8937 (2019)
14. Herdade, S., Kappeler, A., Boakye, K., Soares, J.: Image captioning: transforming objects into words. In: Advances in Neural Information Processing Systems, pp. 11135–11145 (2019)
15. Luo, W., Li, Y., Urtasun, R., Zemel, R.: Understanding the effective receptive field in deep convolutional neural networks. In: Advances in Neural Information Processing Systems, pp. 4898–4906 (2016)
16. Deng, J., Dong, W., Socher, R., Li, L.J., Li, K., Fei-Fei, L.: ImageNet: a large-scale hierarchical image database. In: IEEE Conference on Computer Vision and Pattern Recognition, pp. 248–255. IEEE (2009)
17. Chen, X., et al.: Microsoft COCO captions: data collection and evaluation server. arXiv preprint arXiv:1504.00325 (2015)
18. Vinyals, O., Toshev, A., Bengio, S., Erhan, D.: Show and tell: a neural image caption generator. In: Proceedings of the IEEE Conference on Computer Vision and Pattern Recognition, pp. 3156–3164 (2015)
19. Gers, F.A., Schmidhuber, J., Cummins, F.: Learning to forget: continual prediction with LSTM. Neural Comput. **12**, 2451–2471 (2000)
20. Lu, J., Xiong, C., Parikh, D., Socher, R.: Knowing when to look: adaptive attention via a visual sentinel for image captioning. In: Proceedings of the IEEE Conference on Computer Vision and Pattern Recognition, pp. 375–383 (2017)
21. Krishna, R., et al.: Visual genome: connecting language and vision using crowd-sourced dense image annotations. Int. J. Comput. Vis. **123**(1), 32–73 (2017). https://doi.org/10.1007/s11263-016-0981-7
22. Lin, T.-Y., et al.: Microsoft COCO: common objects in context. In: Fleet, D., Pajdla, T., Schiele, B., Tuytelaars, T. (eds.) ECCV 2014. LNCS, vol. 8693, pp. 740–755. Springer, Cham (2014). https://doi.org/10.1007/978-3-319-10602-1_48
23. Anderson, P., Fernando, B., Johnson, M., Gould, S.: SPICE: semantic propositional image caption evaluation. In: Leibe, B., Matas, J., Sebe, N., Welling, M. (eds.) ECCV 2016. LNCS, vol. 9909, pp. 382–398. Springer, Cham (2016). https://doi.org/10.1007/978-3-319-46454-1_24
24. Hao, J., Wang, X., Shi, S., Zhang, J., Tu, Z.: Multi-granularity self-attention for neural machine translation. arXiv preprint arXiv:1909.02222 (2019)
25. Wang, X., Tu, Z., Wang, L., Shi, S.: Self-attention with structural position representations. arXiv preprint arXiv:1909.00383 (2019)
26. Wang, Y.S., Lee, H.Y., Chen, Y.N.: Tree transformer: integrating tree structures into self-attention. arXiv preprint arXiv:1909.06639 (2019)
27. Dauphin, Y.N., Fan, A., Auli, M., Grangier, D.: Language modeling with gated convolutional networks. In: Proceedings of the 34th International Conference on Machine Learning-Volume 70, pp. 933–941. JMLR (2017)
28. Hochreiter, S., Schmidhuber, J.: Long short-term memory. Neural Comput. **9**, 1735–1780 (1997)

29. Rennie, S.J., Marcheret, E., Mroueh, Y., Ross, J., Goel, V.: Self-critical sequence training for image captioning. In: Proceedings of the IEEE Conference on Computer Vision and Pattern Recognition, pp. 7008–7024 (2017)
30. Vedantam, R., Lawrence Zitnick, C., Parikh, D.: CIDEr: consensus-based image description evaluation. In: Proceedings of the IEEE Conference on Computer Vision and Pattern Recognition, pp. 4566–4575 (2015)
31. Hu, J., Shen, L., Sun, G.: Squeeze-and-excitation networks. In: Proceedings of the IEEE Conference on Computer Vision and Pattern Recognition, pp. 7132–7141 (2018)
32. Karpathy, A., Fei-Fei, L.: Deep visual-semantic alignments for generating image descriptions. In: Proceedings of the IEEE Conference on Computer Vision and Pattern Recognition, pp. 3128–3137 (2015)
33. Papineni, K., Roukos, S., Ward, T., Zhu, W.J.: BLEU: a method for automatic evaluation of machine translation. In: Proceedings of the 40th Annual Meeting on Association for Computational Linguistics, pp. 311–318. Association for Computational Linguistics (2002)
34. Banerjee, S., Lavie, A.: METEOR: an automatic metric for MT evaluation with improved correlation with human judgments. In: Proceedings of the ACL Workshop on Intrinsic and Extrinsic Evaluation Measures for Machine Translation and/or Summarization, pp. 65–72 (2005)
35. Lin, C.Y.: ROUGE: a package for automatic evaluation of summaries. In: Proceedings of the ACL Workshop on Text Summarization Branches Out, p. 10 (2004)
36. He, K., Zhang, X., Ren, S., Sun, J.: Deep residual learning for image recognition. In: Proceedings of the IEEE Conference on Computer Vision and Pattern Recognition, pp. 770–778 (2016)
37. Kingma, D.P., Ba, J.: Adam: a method for stochastic optimization. arXiv preprint arXiv:1412.6980 (2014)
38. Locatello, F., et al.: Challenging common assumptions in the unsupervised learning of disentangled representations. In: Proceedings of the 36th International Conference on Machine Learning-Volume 97, pp. 4114–4124. JMLR (2019)
39. Maaten, L.v.d., Hinton, G.: Visualizing data using T-SNE. J. Mach. Learn. Res. 9, 2579–2605 (2008)

Feature Variance Ratio-Guided Channel Pruning for Deep Convolutional Network Acceleration

Junjie He, Bohua Chen, Yinzhang Ding, and Dongxiao Li[✉]

Zhejiang University, Hangzhou 310027, China
{he_junjie,chenbohua,dingyzh,lidx}@zju.edu.cn

Abstract. Most existing channel pruning approaches utilize the magnitude of network parameters to guide the pruning process. However, these methods suffer from some limitations in modern networks, where the magnitude of parameters can vary independently of the importance of corresponding channels. To recognize redundancies more accurately and therefore, accelerate networks better, we propose a novel channel pruning criterion based on the Pearson correlation coefficient. The criterion preserves the features that are essentially informative to the given task and avoids the influence of useless parameter scales. Based on this criterion, we further establish our channel pruning framework named Feature Variance Ratio-guided Channel Pruning (FVRCP). FVRCP prunes channels globally with little human intervention. Moreover, it can automatically find important layers in the network. Extensive numerical experiments on CIFAR-10 and ImageNet with widely varying architectures present state-of-the-art performance of our method.

1 Introduction

Deep convolutional neural networks (CNNs) have achieved state-of-the-art performance in various computer vision tasks [1–4]. One essential foundation of such great success lies in the deep and wide architectures, which are always accompanied by the expensive computational costs. As a result, deploying these models on resource-constrained devices (e.g., smartphones and IoT systems) becomes extremely difficult. To address this issue, various model acceleration methods [5–9] have been proposed to improve the computational efficiency of CNNs. Among them, channel pruning [10–15] becomes a prevalent one due to its hardware-friendly implementation and surprising ability to reduce a large amount of computation overhead without compromising model performance.

Channel pruning aims to remove redundant channels in the convolutional layers. Existing practices in this field for identifying unimportant channels mainly resort to the magnitude of parameters, e.g., the norm of channel weights [16,17],

Electronic supplementary material The online version of this chapter (https://doi.org/10.1007/978-3-030-69538-5_11) contains supplementary material, which is available to authorized users.

© Springer Nature Switzerland AG 2021
H. Ishikawa et al. (Eds.): ACCV 2020, LNCS 12625, pp. 170–186, 2021.
https://doi.org/10.1007/978-3-030-69538-5_11

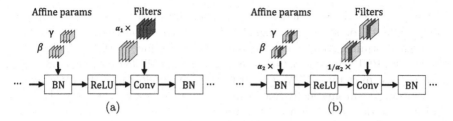

Fig. 1. Illustration of two equivalent transformations for a typical network: (a) scale a filter by α_1 ($\alpha_1 > 0$); (b) scale a pair of affine parameters of BN by α_2 ($\alpha_2 > 0$) and inversely scale the corresponding channel weights in the next convolutional layer. γ and β are scaling and shifting factors, respectively. These transformations change the magnitude of parameters but do not change the function of *any* channels.

the norm of filters [10,13], and the absolute value of scaling factors of batch normalization (BN) layers [12,14]. These methods hypothesize that the channels with small magnitude parameters contribute little to the network and then are less important. However, it can be shown that the parameter magnitude cannot faithfully characterize the channel importance in modern networks. For the typically used convolutional network with BN and rectified linear unit (ReLU)[1] as shown in Fig. 1, there are two equivalent transformations [19,20] by which we can change the magnitudes of network parameters arbitrarily without changing the information flow (and therefore the importance of each channel) in the network: 1) scale the filters in an intermediate layer by a positive factor, since BN normalizes convolutional output and the scaling effect of filters is canceled; 2) scale the affine parameters of BN by a positive factor and simultaneously inversely scale the corresponding channel weights in the next layer, as ReLU is positively homogeneous which satisfies $\text{ReLU}(\alpha x) = \alpha \text{ReLU}(x)$ for all $\alpha > 0$. A robust channel importance metric should be invariant to these transformations while the conventional magnitude-based ones do not. This suggests that despite good acceleration ratios achieved, existing pruning methods are still suboptimal. The magnitudes of parameters are less relevant to the identification of channel importance. Useful features may be falsely discarded with the approaches based on them, which severely impair model performance.

In this paper, with the goal of recognizing redundancies more accurately and therefore, accelerating networks better, we propose a novel channel pruning criterion based on the Pearson correlation coefficient. Specifically, we exploit the Pearson correlation coefficient to assess the information loss of convolutional output feature maps resulted from pruning. The feature variance ratio is then constructed as an importance metric to guide the pruning process. Different from the conventional magnitude-based metrics, the new metric *avoids* the influence of the scale of the convolutional filters and the scale of the affine parameters of BN layers. It is interpretable from the feature-correlation perspective and easy to calculate. With proposed metric, we can directly prune channels for a

---

[1] ReLU can be replaced with other positively homogeneous functions like PReLU [18].

pre-trained network in a single-shot (i.e., globally prune once) with little fine-tuning while still preserving its high performance. After that, we further establish our channel pruning framework, named Feature Variance Ratio-guided Channel Pruning (FVRCP). In contrast to prior works [11,21,22] that require handcrafted layer-wise pruning ratios, FVRCP prunes channels globally with little human intervention. It automatically finds the important layers for the network, which inspires us to design better architectures.

The numerical experiments on CIFAR-10 and ImageNet with widely varying architectures present state-of-the-art performance of FVRCP. For example, on the large-scale ImageNet dataset, when pruning 40% FLOPs of PreResNet-50, FVRCP improves the original PreResNet model by 0.05% in top-1 accuracy; when pruning 43% FLOPs of MobileNets, FVRCP causes zero accuracy drop, exceeding the uniform baseline [23] by 2.2%.

The major contributions of this paper are summarized as follows: First, we propose a novel interpretable channel importance metric based on the Pearson correlation coefficient. The new metric avoids the influence of parameter scales and identifies the channels that are essentially informative to the given task. Second, we propose FVRCP framework to prune channels for CNNs globally with little human intervention. FVRCP automatically finds compact structures in the network and reduces the overwhelming computational burden.

2   Related Work

Weight Pruning. Convolutional neural network acceleration has been extensively studied in recent years. Weight pruning [9, 24–28] tries to find and remove unimportant connections in the network. Early work [29] in the 1990s uses the Hessian of loss function to determine the importance of connections. Recently, Han et al. [9,25] propose an iterative method that prunes connections with small weights. Dong et al. [28] prune the parameters of each layer based on a layer-wise error function. Though these methods achieve high compression ratios, they result in irregular networks, of which the speedup can only be achieved in specialized software or hardware that supports sparse matrix operation.

Channel Pruning. To be free of customized platforms and extra operations, many approaches [10–14,16,21,30–32] directly prune regular channels for the network. Li et al. [13] prune channels based on the ℓ_1-norm of filters. He et al. [10] select unimportant channels with an ℓ_2-norm criterion. Liu et al. [12] leverage the scaling factors in batch normalization layer to remove insignificant channels. Liu and Sun [31] employ an evolutionary algorithm with a meta network to search for the best channel pruning strategies. In these works, the magnitudes of network parameters are always utilized to establish their pruning frameworks [10,12–14,21]. However, as shown in Fig. 1, the information transmitted by the magnitude of parameters about the importance of network channels can be extremely limited. Besides, most approaches [10,11,13,15,21,22] require human experts to design layer-wise pruning ratios. Determining these layer-wise

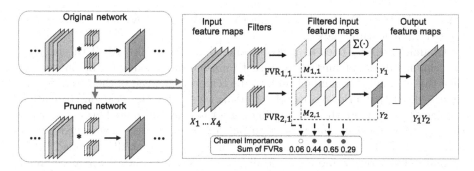

Fig. 2. Feature variance ratio-guided channel pruning. The channel with small sum of FVRs (*red dotted elements in the right side*) will be pruned.

pruning ratios not only requires specialized knowledge but also greatly reduces the search space of pruning under which we cannot achieve the optimal compression ratio.

Other Methods. Apart from pruning, there are many other excellent works for CNN accelerations, such as knowledge distillation [8,33], quantization [7,34–36], and low-rank decomposition [5,6]. All these approaches are orthogonal to our work, and one can combine them to accelerate networks further.

3   Methodology

We first introduce some notations that will be used throughout this paper. Let $X \in \mathbb{R}^{C \times H_{in} \times W_{in}}$ and $Y \in \mathbb{R}^{N \times H_{out} \times W_{out}}$ be a standard convolutional input and output feature maps, respectively. C and N denote the number of input and output channels. Moreover, let X_i be the i-th feature map in X, Y_j be the j-th feature map in Y, and $K_{j,i}$ be the $D_h \times D_w$ kernel corresponding to X_i and Y_j.

Batch normalization [19] enables faster training and better generalization of deep CNNs and now is becoming a standard component in deep learning. We focus on the batch normalized networks in this paper, but it should be noted that our method can be extended to the general networks (see supplementary). Recall that BN is normally inserted immediately after convolution, which normalizes convolutional outputs by subtracting the mean and dividing the standard deviation, and then rescale and re-shift them.

3.1   Construction of Feature Variance Ratio

To facilitate the investigation of the importance of each channel, we first consider the convolution with a single filter $K_{j,:}$. The corresponding output is:

$$Y_j = \sum_{i=1}^{C} M_{j,i} = \sum_{i=1}^{C} K_{j,i} * X_i, \tag{1}$$

where $*$ denotes 2D convolution operation and $M_{j,i} = K_{j,i} * X_i$ denotes the filtered input feature map.

Channel pruning tries to pick up some channels to discard. If the pruning of a channel does not hurt the inherent information encoded in the output Y_j, then this channel is redundant and can be removed. Instead of the Mean Square Error (MSE) that prior works [11,22] used, we employ the Pearson correlation coefficient to measure the information loss caused by pruning. This comes from the fact that the scale and bias of output feature maps are normalized by the following BN. The inherent information of Y_j is substantially encoded in its normalized version, or more specifically, the direction of the vector represented by the normalized version in high-dimensional feature space. Pearson correlation coefficient, which characterizes the linear correlation between two variables or equivalently the geometrical angle between two zero-mean vectors, is more precise to describe this loss.

Suppose that we prune the i_0-th channel from the input tensor X. Then the output feature map becomes:

$$Y'_j = \sum_{i=1, i \neq i_0}^{C} M_{j,i}. \tag{2}$$

The Pearson correlation coefficient between Y_j and Y'_j is defined as:

$$r_{j,i_0} = \frac{\sum_{p,q} \left(y'_{j,p,q} - \bar{y}'_j\right)\left(y_{j,p,q} - \bar{y}_j\right)}{\sqrt{\sum_{p,q}\left(y'_{j,p,q} - \bar{y}'_j\right)^2}\sqrt{\sum_{p,q}\left(y_{j,p,q} - \bar{y}_j\right)^2}}, \tag{3}$$

where $y_{j,p,q}$, $y'_{j,p,q}$ represent the (p,q)-th elements of Y_j and Y'_j respectively, and $\bar{y}_j$, $\bar{y}'_j$ are their corresponding average values. Larger absolute value of the Pearson correlation coefficient indicates more linear association between Y_j and Y'_j and thus less information loss caused by the pruning of i_0-th channel. When the Pearson correlation coefficient has the value $r_{j,i_0} = \pm 1$, there is no information loss. In other words, the distance between 1 and r^2_{j,i_0} can be exploited to determine the information richness of i_0-th input channel (and thus its importance).

However, the most widely recognized disadvantage of the Pearson correlation coefficient is that it is computationally intensive. Especially here we should compute it for the thousands of channels in the network. We hope to have a metric that not only reflects the channel importance effectively but also is computationally efficient. To this end, we propose the Feature Variance Ratio (FVR) indicator. Specifically, it is the variance ratio of the filtered feature map of X_{i_0}, i.e., M_{j,i_0}, to the output feature map Y_j, and can be calculated as:

$$\mathrm{FVR}_{j,i_0} = \frac{\sigma^2_{Mj,i_0}}{\sigma^2_{Y_j}} = \frac{\frac{1}{H_{out}W_{out}}\sum_{p,q}(m_{j,i_0,p,q} - \bar{m}_{j,i_0})^2}{\frac{1}{H_{out}W_{out}}\sum_{p,q}(y_{j,p,q} - \bar{y}_j)^2}, \tag{4}$$

where $m_{j,i_0,p,q}$ represents the (p,q)-th element of M_{j,i_0} and $\bar{m}_{j,i_0}$ is the average value. Intuitively, FVR_{j,i_0} implies the strength of X_{i_0} to Y_j. When FVR_{j,i_0} is small, X_{i_0} becomes an offset component of Y_j, and pruning it will not destroy the inherent feature structure of output feature map. More importantly, it can be shown that FVR is highly correlated with Pearson correlation coefficient.

Proposition 1. *Let x, y be two n-dimensional data vectors with elements $\{x_i\}$ and $\{y_i\}$, respectively. Assume their Pearson correlation coefficient is r_{xy}, i.e.,*

$$r_{xy} = \frac{\sum_i (x_i - \bar{x})(y_i - \bar{y})}{\sqrt{\sum_i (x_i - \bar{x})^2}\sqrt{\sum_i (y_i - \bar{y})^2}}, \tag{5}$$

where $\bar{x} = \sum_i x_i/n, \bar{y} = \sum_i y_i/n$. Let $\varepsilon_i = y_i - x_i, i = 1, 2, ..., n$, be the residuals of data elements, forming a vector ε. Suppose that the variances of ε and y are σ_ε^2, σ_y^2 respectively, and $\sigma_y^2 > 0$, $\sigma_\varepsilon^2 \neq \sigma_y^2$. Then we have:

$$0 \leq 1 - r_{xy}^2 \leq \frac{\sigma_\varepsilon^2/\sigma_y^2}{(1 - \sigma_\varepsilon/\sigma_y)^2}. \tag{6}$$

We provide the proof in the supplementary material. By Proposition 1 and the fact that $Y_j = Y_j' + M_{j,i_0}$, we obtain:

$$0 \leq 1 - r_{j,i_0}^2 \leq \frac{\mathrm{FVR}_{j,i_0}}{(1 - \sqrt{\mathrm{FVR}_{j,i_0}})^2}. \tag{7}$$

Equation 7 reveals the relationship between FVR_{j,i_0} and r_{j,i_0}^2. The right side of this equation is monotonically increasing with increasing FVR_{j,i_0} in $[0, 1]$, and tends to zero as $\mathrm{FVR}_{j,i_0} \to 0$. This implies that smaller FVR_{j,i_0} corresponds to the smaller $1 - r_{j,i_0}^2$, and in the limit case we have:

$$\lim_{\mathrm{FVR}_{j,i_0} \to 0} 1 - r_{j,i_0}^2 = 0. \tag{8}$$

From the above, we conclude that FVR_{j,i_0} is an effective alternative metric for measuring importance of X_{i_0} to Y_j. The smaller FVR_{j,i_0} is, the less information loss caused by pruning X_{i_0}, and thus the less important the i_0-th channel is.

3.2 Channel Importance Based on FVR

The importance metric FVR mentioned in Sect. 3.1 is constructed on a single output feature map. In fact, there is more than one filter in a convolutional layer. An input feature map engages in the formation of multiple output feature maps. To completely measure the importance of a channel in the network, we take the sum of its corresponding FVRs across all output feature maps, as Fig. 2 illustrated:

$$\mathrm{SFVR}_{i_0} = \sum_{j=1}^{N} \mathrm{FVR}_{j,i_0} = \sum_{j=1}^{N} \frac{\sigma_{M_{j,i_0}}^2}{\sigma_{Y_j}^2}. \tag{9}$$

We define SFVR (omit i_0 for clarity) as the channel importance and prune the channels that have small ones. Indeed, the essence of this pruning philosophy is similar to that of Principal Component Analysis (PCA) for dimensionality reduction. PCA discards the principal components that have small variances in the original data to reduce dimensions, since these components possess little energy and disposing of them will not lead to great loss. Here we also discard the components (input channels) that have small variances because they are less informative to the given task. Dividing by the variances of output feature maps can be regarded as a normalization technique for output dimensions.

Despite the different numbers of output channels, which affects the summation, the channel importance defined in Eq. 9 is comparable across all layers. Consider a situation where the filtered input feature maps $M_{j,i}, i = 1, \ldots, C$, are orthogonal each other with the same variance $\sigma^2_{M_j}$, and the number of input channels is equal to that of output channels, i.e., $C = N$. Then we have $\text{SFVR}_{i_0} = \sum_{j=1}^{N} \sigma^2_{M_j} / \sigma^2_{Y_j} = \sum_{j=1}^{N} 1/C = 1$, which is a constant independent of layers. It illustrates that if the channels of all layers are utilized fully and equally, the pruning criterion will not prefer to prune any layers, which is consistent with our intuition. Moreover, if the filtered input feature maps $M_{j,i}, i = 1, \ldots, C$, are identical to each other with the variance $\sigma^2_{M_j}$, then $\text{SFVR}_{i_0} = \sum_{j=1}^{N} \sigma^2_{M_j} / \sigma^2_{Y_j} = \sum_{j=1}^{N} 1/C^2 = 1/C$, which implies that the layer with more channels will be pruned first. It is also natural since in this case the layers that have more channels are more redundant. All these suggest that SFVR can be compared across different layers, and it will automatically find important layers in the network. More details can be seen in Sect. 4.4.

Linear Transformation Invariance. A key mathematical property of SFVR is that it is invariant under separate changes in bias and scale in output feature maps. That is, for any scalar a_j $(a_j \neq 0)$ and b_j, $\hat{Y}_j = a_j Y_j + b_j$, we have:

$$\sum_{j=1}^{N} \frac{\sigma^2_{\widehat{M}_{j,i_0}}}{\sigma^2_{\hat{Y}_j}} = \sum_{j=1}^{N} \frac{a_j^2 \sigma^2_{M_{j,i_0}}}{a_j^2 \sigma^2_{Y_j}} = \sum_{j=1}^{N} \frac{\sigma^2_{M_{j,i_0}}}{\sigma^2_{Y_j}}, \tag{10}$$

where $\widehat{M}_{j,i_0} = a_j M_{j,i_0} + d_{j,i_0}$ $(\sum_{i=1}^{C} d_{j,i} = b_j)$ is the transformed feature map of M_{j,i_0}. The property implies that SFVR is insensitive to the scale and bias of output feature maps, which is not surprising since we have considered that the influence of scale and bias of convolutional output feature maps will be canceled by the following BN transform and they do not encode any information.

Network Equivalent Transformation Invariance. As mentioned earlier, due to the positively homogenous property of ReLU and normalization process of BN, there exist two equivalent transformations by which we can change the magnitude of network parameters without altering the function of corresponding channels. A robust channel importance metric should be invariant to these changes while the conventional magnitude-based ones do not. In contrast, it can be easily verified that our proposed SFVR is not affected by these transforms (detailed in the supplementary). It is more effective in identifying redundant channels in modern networks.

3.3   Implementation via Moving Average Statistics

The proposed channel importance metric SFVR is composed of two parts, namely, $\sigma^2_{Y_j}$ and $\sigma^2_{M_{j,i_0}}$. To apply in practice, we need to estimate them.

Algorithm 1. Algorithm Description of FVRCP

1: **Initialize:** planned pruning ratio $r = 0$
2:                    gradual pruning schedule $\mathcal{T}_{\mathcal{N},\mathcal{R}}(\cdot)$
3: **for** *epoch* = 1 to $\mathcal{N}$ **do**
4:        Update parameters and moving average statistics
5:        Compute SFVR for each channel as Eq. 12
6:        Let $r \leftarrow \mathcal{T}_{\mathcal{N},\mathcal{R}}(epoch)$
7:        **while** (pruned FLOPs ratio $< r$) **do**
8:            Remove the channel with smallest SFVR
9:        **end while**
10: **end for**
11: Fine-tune the pruned model until it converges

Given the fact that BN normalizes convolutional outputs, we can directly leverage the statistical information provided by BN to estimate $\sigma^2_{Y_j}$ without any additional computation. Instead of batch sample statistics, we employ moving average statistics of BN for the stability and reliability of estimate. However, since the mainstream implementation of convolution is *im2col*, which transforms whole convolution into matrix multiplication [37,38], we cannot directly compute $\sigma^2_{M_{j,i_0}}$. Although we can decompose the regular convolution into several fine-grained operations such as depthwise convolution with summation, it will greatly affect the speed of forward computation of the model on modern computing devices like GPUs. To address this issue, we consider the following relaxation:

$$
\sigma^2_{M_{j,i_0}} = \frac{1}{H_{out}W_{out}} \sum_{p,q} (m_{j,i_0,p,q} - \bar{m}_{j,i_0})^2
$$

$$
= \frac{1}{H_{out}W_{out}} \sum_{p,q} \left| (R_{i_0,p,q} - \bar{R}_{i_0}) * K_{j,i_0} \right|^2 \tag{11}
$$

$$
\leq \|K_{j,i_0}\|^2_F \frac{1}{H_{out}W_{out}} \sum_{p,q} \|R_{i_0,p,q} - \bar{R}_{i_0}\|^2_F ,
$$

where $\|\cdot\|_F$ denotes the Frobenius norm, $R_{i_0,p,q}$ denotes the receptive field of $m_{j,i_0,p,q}$ on X_{i_0}, and $\bar{R}_{i_0} = \sum_{p,q} R_{i_0,p,q}/(H_{out}W_{out})$. The right side of Eq. 11 is an upper bound for $\sigma^2_{M_{j,i_0}}$. It contains only two terms. One is the Frobenius norm of kernel weights, and the other is the statistic of input feature map X_{i_0}. Both of them can be conveniently computed without any modification to the network architecture. We use this bound to approximate $\sigma^2_{M_{j,i_0}}$. Same with $\sigma^2_{Y_j}$, to stabilize the estimation, we retain the moving average statistics of input feature maps in each training iteration and employ them when pruning.

By the approximation of $\sigma^2_{M_{j,i_0}}$, the channel importance then we calculate for the i_0-th input channel becomes:

$$\text{SFVR}^*_{i_0} = \frac{1}{H_{out}W_{out}} \sum_{p,q} \left\| R_{i_0,p,q} - \bar{R}_{i_0} \right\|^2_F \sum_{j=1}^{N} \frac{\|K_{j,i_0}\|^2_F}{\sigma^2_{Y_j}}. \tag{12}$$

From Eq. 11, we see that SFVR* puts more emphasis on the channels that are filtered by the larger kernels, which is acceptable since larger kernels have stronger learning abilities.

Table 1. Comparison of pruning results on CIFAR-10. "Global" indicates whether the method is a global channel pruning algorithm.

Model	Method	Global	Baseline Acc.	Pruned Acc.	Acc. ↓	FLOPs	FLOPs ↓ (%)
ResNet-56	Li *et al.* [13]	No	93.04	93.06	−0.02	90.9M	27.6
	NISP [30]	Yes	–	–	0.03	–	43.6
	CP [11]	No	92.8	91.8	1.0	–	50.0
	FVRCP-50	Yes	**93.41**	**93.64**	**−0.23**	**62.6M**	**50.1**
ResNet-110	Li *et al.* [13]	No	93.53	93.30	0.23	155M	38.6
	NISP [30]	Yes	–	–	0.18	–	43.8
	GAL [40]	Yes	93.50	92.74	0.76	130.2M	48.5
	FVRCP-70	Yes	**94.06**	**93.86**	**0.20**	**75.8M**	**70.0**
DenseNet-40	Liu *et al.* [12]	Yes	93.89	94.35	−0.46	120M	57.6
	C-SGD [32]	No	93.81	94.56	−0.75	113.0M	60.1
	GAL [40]	Yes	94.81	93.23	1.58	80.9M	71.4
	FVRCP-60	Yes	**94.83**	**94.60**	**0.23**	**113.0M**	**60.1**
	FVRCP-75	Yes	**94.83**	**93.91**	**0.92**	**70.6M**	**75.0**

3.4   Channel Pruning Framework

With a well-trained convolutional network, our proposed Feature Variance Ratio-guided Channel Pruning (FVRCP) procedures are illustrated in Algorithm 1.

We employ the gradual pruning technique in [39]. During pruning, the FLOPs pruning ratio is increased quadratically from zero to the preset target ratio ($\mathcal{R}$ in Algorithm 1), and at the end of each epoch, we globally select the channels that have small importance to remove until achieving the planned pruning ratio at that epoch. The gradual pruning technique helps smooth the pruning process and prevents the algorithm from degradation. The final fine-tuning is also an important technique to recover pruned accuracy.

4   Experiments

In this section, we evaluate our channel importance metric and channel pruning framework on CIFAR-10 [41] and ImageNet [42] with several popular architectures. All the experiments are implemented using TensorFlow [43] on NVIDIA TITAN V GPUs.

4.1   Experimental Settings

On CIFAR-10, we conduct gradual pruning for 40 epochs with a mini-batch size of 128 and a fixed learning rate of 0.01. The standard data augmentation is adopted including padding and random cropping. After that, we fine-tune the model for 40 epochs with a learning rate of 0.001. On ImageNet, we conduct gradual pruning for 20 epochs. The mini-batch size is 256. The learning rate

Table 2. Comparison of pruning results on ImageNet.

Model	Method	Global	Baseline Top1	Baseline Top5	Pruned Top1	Pruned Top5	FLOPs	FLOPs ↓ (%)
ResNet-18	SFP [10]	No	70.28	89.63	67.10	87.78	1.06B	41.8
	FPGM [21]	No	70.28	89.63	68.34	88.53	1.06B	41.8
	FVRCP-42	Yes	**70.23**	**89.36**	**68.88**	**88.39**	1.05B	42.0
ResNet-50	ThiNet [22]	No	72.88	91.14	72.04	90.67	2.59B	36.8
	C-SGD [32]	No	75.33	92.56	75.27	92.46	2.59B	36.8
	SFP [10]	No	76.15	92.87	74.61	92.06	2.38B	41.8
	HRank [44]	No	76.15	92.87	74.98	92.33	2.30B	43.8
	CP [11]	No	–	92.2	–	90.8	–	50.0
	FPGM [21]	No	76.15	92.87	74.83	92.32	1.90B	53.5
	Hinge [45]	Yes	–	–	74.70	–	1.90B	53.5
	FVRCP-40	Yes	**76.09**	**92.90**	**76.04**	**92.92**	2.45B	40.0
	FVRCP-50	Yes	**76.09**	**92.90**	75.42	92.52	2.04B	50.0
PreResNet-50	FVRCP-40	Yes	**76.01**	**92.86**	76.06	92.82	2.45B	40.0
	FVRCP-50	Yes	**76.01**	**92.86**	75.49	92.47	2.04B	50.0
	FVRCP-60	Yes	**76.01**	**92.86**	74.93	92.33	1.63B	60.0

Table 3. Comparison of pruned MobileNet V1 on ImageNet. The latency is tested on TITAN V GPU and Intel Xeon E3-1230 CPU with a batch size of 32.

Model	FLOPs	Top1 Acc.	Latency GPU	CPU
Baseline [23]	569M	70.6%	1.23 ms	17.27 ms
0.75× MobileNet V1 [23]	325M	68.4%	0.95 ms	12.23 ms
FVRCP-43	**324M**	**70.6%**	**0.91 ms**	**11.18 ms**
NetAdapt [46]	284M	69.1%	–	–
FVRCP-50	**284M**	**69.8%**	**0.88 ms**	**10.28 ms**
0.5× MobileNet V1 [23]	149M	63.7%	0.71 ms	7.48 ms
FVRCP-74	**149M**	**65.5%**	**0.69 ms**	**6.35 ms**

during pruning is 0.01. The fine-tuning is for 20 epochs with an initial learning rate of 0.001 and decayed by 0.1 at 10 epochs. All networks are trained using stochastic gradient descent (SGD) with Nesterov momentum 0.9.

4.2 Comparison with State-of-the-Art Methods

Table 1 shows our channel pruning results on CIFAR-10 dataset. As we see, FVRCP method achieves state-of-the-art performance. With 50.0% FLOPs reduction for ResNet-56, CP [11] causes 1.0% loss in accuracy while FVRCP improves 0.23%. With almost zero performance loss on ResNet-110, FVRCP achieves a 70.0% FLOPs reduction, much higher than the 38.6% reduction by Li *et al.* [13] who use ℓ_1-norm of filters to guide the pruning process.

We further evaluate FVRCP on the large-scale ImageNet dataset, as shown in Table 2. Again, FVRCP presents outstanding performance. On ResNet-18, FVRCP achieves the same theoretical speedup with FPGM [21] and SFP [10], but its top-1 accuracy surpasses FPGM by more than 0.5% and significantly exceeds 67.1% obtained by SFP which is heuristically based on the ℓ_2-norm of filters. For ResNet-50, FVRCP reduces 50% FLOPs with only 0.38% top-5 accuracy drop, outperforming CP [11] by 1.02%. Moreover, note that almost all compared methods cannot prune channels globally for the network. These approaches require human experts to carefully design layer-wise pruning ratios (e.g., sensitive analysis [13]), which is laborious in practice.

MobileNets use the depthwise separable convolution instead of common convolution, which has greatly reduced the redundancy, but our method can further compress it. As demonstrated in Table 3, with 43% FLOPs reduction, the pruning of FVRCP causes zero performance degradation, exceeding the $0.75\times$ uniform baseline [23] by 2.2%. Under the same FLOPs constraints, FVRCP significantly outperforms the AutoML method NetAdapt [46] by 0.7% but uses much less memory and computational resources.

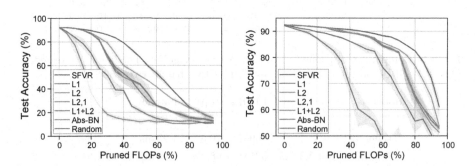

Fig. 3. Single-shot pruning without fine-tuning (*left*) and with 10 fine-tuning epochs (*right*) on pre-activation ResNet-20 on CIFAR-10. All experiments are repeated 5 times with different random seeds. ± standard derivation is reported with shaded region.

4.3   Effect of Channel Importance Metric

To demonstrate the effectiveness of the proposed channel importance metric, which avoids the influence of redundant parameter scales, we perform the pruning experiments with it as well as some parameter magnitude-based ones. For the fair comparison, we conduct pruning at single-shot without any fine-tuning. The compared metrics include commonly used absolute value of BN scales [12,14], ℓ_1, ℓ_2-norm of channel weights [16,17] and their variants ($(\ell_1 + \ell_2)/2$-norm and $\ell_{2,1}$-norm $\|K_{:,i}\|_{2,1} = \sum_{j=1}^{N} \|K_{j,i}\|_F$ (group Lasso regularizer [17]). The statistics of input feature maps for SFVR have been calculated on the training set during model training.

The left graph of Fig. 3 shows the comparison results. The pruned accuracies of pre-activation ResNet-20 of SFVR are significantly better than that of parameter magnitude-based ones. It is not surprising since the magnitude of parameters contains redundant information (recall that ResNets employ BN and ReLU activation), and the metrics that are directly based on it cannot assess channel importance accurately. The curve of SFVR which drops slowly at first and then rapidly also illustrates that SFVR can better characterize channel importance (prunes unimportant channels first). The right graph of Fig. 3 compares the single-shot pruning with few fine-tuning epochs with a fixed learning rate of 0.001. As shown, the networks pruned by our metric recover from the pruning more quickly. Even with few fine-tuning epochs, our pruned network can achieve high performance. For more comparisons, please refer to the supplementary.

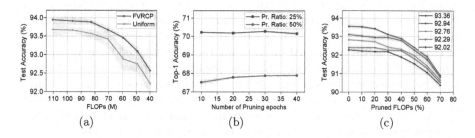

(a)   (b)   (c)

Fig. 4. (a) Comparison of uniformly scaled ResNet-56 and FVRCP-pruned ones on CIFAR-10. The accuracy and FLOPs of pruning baseline are 93.65% and 125.5M, respectively. (b) ImageNet top-1 accuracies of FVRCP-pruned ResNet-18 with different numbers of pruning epochs. (c) FVRCP pruning results of ResNet-32 with five different baseline accuracies (*shown in the legend*) on CIFAR-10. Each trial is repeated 5 times.

4.4   Comparison with Uniform Channel Reduction

Uniform channel reduction (uniformly reducing filters in each layer) is commonly used in practice to reduce model size. However, such strategy is based on empirical analysis, failing to achieve the optimal compression ratios. Figure 4(a)

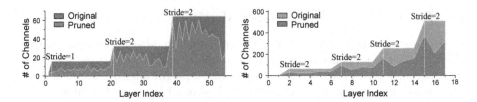

Fig. 5. Pruned architectures of ResNet-56 (*left*) and ResNet-18 (*Right*) with 50% FLOPs reduction.

compares the accuracy of uniformly scaled ResNet-56 with FVRCP automatically pruned ones. To ensure the convergence, we train each uniformly scaled ResNet-56 for 600 epochs, much longer than the usually adopted benchmark (160 [1]). The results show that the pruned ResNet-56 model outperforms the uniformly scaled one regardless of FLOPs constraints, resulting in a more efficient architecture.

Neural Architecture Search. In network design, people are curious about what is the best channel allocation policies. Lots of human experts are dedicated to manually designing the channel size of each layer. A recent study [47] argues that the global channel pruning can be viewed as an architecture search method and automatically finds good layer-wise channel numbers. We visualize the pruned architecture by FVRCP, trying to find some design heuristic. Figure 5 illustrates the pruned architectures of ResNet-56 and ResNet-18 with 50% FLOPs reduction. Interestingly, we find that the channels in the downsampling layers are more retained. It is natural since when there is downsampling, the resolution of feature maps decreases, and thus there should be more channels to prevent the information loss. The same phenomenon has also been observed in [31] in pruned MobileNets, but with ResNets we see more interesting things. We note that the channels in the second layer of the residual block are also more kept. We argue that this mainly results from the shortcut connections by which the input feature maps in the first layer of residual block can be losslessly transferred into later layers while the input feature maps in the second layer cannot (and therefore becomes more important). Moreover, we observe that the higher layers in the last two stages of ResNet-56 are pruned more aggressively. We suspect it is because CIFAR-10 classification is a simple task (only 10 classes) and ResNet-56 is such a deep network that higher layers are underutilized. In contrast to this, for the shallow network ResNet-18 on large-scale ImageNet dataset, we do not observe a similar phenomenon. These facts inspire us to allocate channel numbers in a better way, on which we would do further study in the future.

4.5 Sensitivity Analysis

Number of Pruning Epochs. We change the number of pruning epochs from 10 to 40 on ImageNet on ResNet-18 to explore its influence. As shown in Fig. 4(b), with small FLOPs pruning ratio (25%), increasing pruning epochs does not improve pruned accuracy while with the large one (50%), it does. We attribute this to the smoothness of pruning process. For the large pruning ratio, too few pruning epochs leads to the sharp pruning at the end of each epoch, which may result in irreversible damage to the network. When the pruning epochs increases, pruning process becomes smooth, and the pruned accuracy is then improved.

Pre-trained Model Performance. Figure 4(c) illustrates FVRCP pruning results of ResNet-32 with five different baseline accuracies. The higher the baseline is, the better the pruned ones are. It is not surprising since FVRCP preserves the principal features in the network and the network that has higher baselines extracts more general and representative features. Also, we note that FVRCP maintains the model performance over a wide range of pruning ratios regardless of original accuracies. It implies that there are indeed a lot of redundancies in commonly trained networks and with FVRCP we can discover and remove them.

4.6 Visualization of Feature Maps

Figure 6 visualizes the randomly selected five output feature maps in the original and pruned *Block1-Conv2* layer of ResNet-18. The average Pearson correlation coefficient of each layer after pruning is also reported. Consistent with theoretical analysis, the output feature maps before and after pruning by our metric are highly correlated, outperforming Li *et al.* [13] and Liu *et al.* [12] significantly. Li

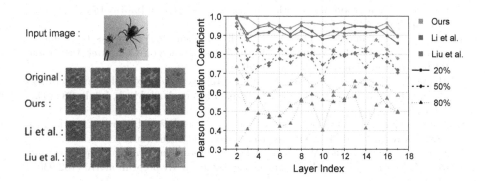

Fig. 6. Visualization of randomly selected five output feature maps in *Block1-Conv2* layer of ResNet-18 as well as those after pruning 50% channels of that layer (*left*). The average Pearson coefficient of each layer between original output feature maps and those after pruning 20%, 50%, and 80% channels of that layer is also reported (*right*).

et al. employ the ℓ_1-norm of filters to guide the pruning. However, the norms of filters are normalized by the following BN transform. Their values are less helpful in recognizing redundant channels. Liu *et al.* leverage the scaling factors of BN layer to conduct pruning, but the inadequate magnitude of scaling factors can be completely compensated by the following convolution. Useful features will be falsely discarded in these two methods, which severely impair model performance. In contrast, our metric preserves essentially informative channels. It discovers the compact structure embedded in the original convolutions, which improves the representation of feature maps as well as the efficiency of networks.

5   Conclusions

In this paper, we presented a novel channel importance metric based on the Pearson correlation coefficient. The new metric identifies essentially informative channels. Compared with conventional parameter magnitude-based ones, it avoids the influence of redundant parameter scales resulted from the properties of batch normalization and activation layers. Further, we established a channel pruning framework named FVRCP. FVRCP prunes channels globally with little human intervention. It automatically finds important layers in the network. On several benchmarks, FVRCP achieves state-of-the-art results.

References

1. He, K., Zhang, X., Ren, S., Sun, J.: Deep residual learning for image recognition. In: Proceedings of the IEEE Conference on Computer Vision and Pattern Recognition, pp. 770–778 (2016)
2. Krizhevsky, A., Sutskever, I., Hinton, G.E.: Imagenet classification with deep convolutional neural networks. In: Advances in Neural Information Processing Systems, pp. 1097–1105 (2012)
3. Ren, S., He, K., Girshick, R., Sun, J.: Faster r-cnn: towards real-time object detection with region proposal networks. In: Advances in Neural Information Processing Systems, pp. 91–99 (2015)
4. Long, J., Shelhamer, E., Darrell, T.: Fully convolutional networks for semantic segmentation. In: Proceedings of the IEEE Conference on Computer Vision and Pattern Recognition, pp. 3431–3440 (2015)
5. Zhang, X., Zou, J., He, K., Sun, J.: Accelerating very deep convolutional networks for classification and detection. IEEE Trans. Pattern Anal. Mach. Intell. **38**, 1943–1955 (2015)
6. Tai, C., Xiao, T., Zhang, Y., Wang, X., et al.: Convolutional neural networks with low-rank regularization. arXiv preprint arXiv:1511.06067 (2015)
7. Zhou, A., Yao, A., Guo, Y., Xu, L., Chen, Y.: Incremental network quantization: towards lossless CNNs with low-precision weights. arXiv preprint arXiv:1702.03044 (2017)
8. Hinton, G., Vinyals, O., Dean, J.: Distilling the knowledge in a neural network. In: NIPS Deep Learning and Representation Learning Workshop (2015)
9. Han, S., Mao, H., Dally, W.J.: Deep compression: Compressing deep neural networks with pruning, trained quantization and huffman coding. arXiv preprint arXiv:1510.00149 (2015)

10. He, Y., Kang, G., Dong, X., Fu, Y., Yang, Y.: Soft filter pruning for accelerating deep convolutional neural networks. In: Proceedings of the Twenty-Seventh International Joint Conference on Artificial Intelligence, IJCAI-18, International Joint Conferences on Artificial Intelligence Organization, pp. 2234–2240 (2018)
11. He, Y., Zhang, X., Sun, J.: Channel pruning for accelerating very deep neural networks. In: Proceedings of the IEEE International Conference on Computer Vision, pp. 1389–1397 (2017)
12. Liu, Z., Li, J., Shen, Z., Huang, G., Yan, S., Zhang, C.: Learning efficient convolutional networks through network slimming. In: Proceedings of the IEEE International Conference on Computer Vision, 2736–2744 (2017)
13. Li, H., Kadav, A., Durdanovic, I., Samet, H., Graf, H.P.: Pruning filters for efficient convnets. arXiv preprint arXiv:1608.08710 (2016)
14. Ye, J., Lu, X., Lin, Z., Wang, J.Z.: Rethinking the smaller-norm-less-informative assumption in channel pruning of convolution layers. In: International Conference on Learning Representations (2018)
15. Zhuang, Z., et al.: Discrimination-aware channel pruning for deep neural networks. In: Advances in Neural Information Processing Systems, pp. 875–886 (2018)
16. Li, Y., et al.: Exploiting kernel sparsity and entropy for interpretable CNN compression. In: Proceedings of the IEEE Conference on Computer Vision and Pattern Recognition, pp. 2800–2809 (2019)
17. Wen, W., Wu, C., Wang, Y., Chen, Y., Li, H.: Learning structured sparsity in deep neural networks. In: Advances in Neural Information Processing Systems, pp. 2074–2082 (2016)
18. He, K., Zhang, X., Ren, S., Sun, J.: Delving deep into rectifiers: surpassing human-level performance on imagenet classification. In: Proceedings of the IEEE International Conference on Computer Vision, pp. 1026–1034 (2015)
19. Ioffe, S., Szegedy, C.: Batch normalization: accelerating deep network training by reducing internal covariate shift. In: Bach, F., Blei, D. (eds.) Proceedings of the 32nd International Conference on Machine Learning, Proceedings of Machine Learning Research, Lille, France, vol. 37,pp. 448–456. PMLR (2015)
20. Dinh, L., Pascanu, R., Bengio, S., Bengio, Y.: Sharp minima can generalize for deep nets. In: Proceedings of the 34th International Conference on Machine Learning, vol. 70, pp. 1019–1028. JMLR. org (2017)
21. He, Y., Liu, P., Wang, Z., Hu, Z., Yang, Y.: Filter pruning via geometric median for deep convolutional neural networks acceleration. In: Proceedings of the IEEE Conference on Computer Vision and Pattern Recognition, pp. 4340–4349 (2019)
22. Luo, J.H., Wu, J., Lin, W.: Thinet: A filter level pruning method for deep neural network compression. In: Proceedings of the IEEE International Conference on Computer Vision, pp. 5058–5066 (2017)
23. Howard, A.G., et al.: Mobilenets: efficient convolutional neural networks for mobile vision applications. arXiv preprint arXiv:1704.04861 (2017)
24. Guo, Y., Yao, A., Chen, Y.: Dynamic network surgery for efficient DNNs. In: Advances In Neural Information Processing Systems, pp. 1379–1387 (2016)
25. Han, S., Pool, J., Tran, J., Dally, W.: Learning both weights and connections for efficient neural network. In: Advances in Neural Information Processing Systems, pp. 1135–1143 (2015)
26. Tung, F., Mori, G.: Clip-q: deep network compression learning by in-parallel pruning-quantization. In: Proceedings of the IEEE Conference on Computer Vision and Pattern Recognition, pp. 7873–7882 (2018)
27. Zhang, T., et al.: A systematic dnn weight pruning framework using alternating direction method of multipliers. In: Proceedings of the European Conference on Computer Vision (ECCV), pp. 184–199 (2018)

28. Dong, X., Chen, S., Pan, S.: Learning to prune deep neural networks via layer-wise optimal brain surgeon. In: Advances in Neural Information Processing Systems, pp. 4857–4867 (2017)
29. LeCun, Y., Denker, J.S., Solla, S.A.: Optimal brain damage. In: Advances in Neural Information Processing Systems, pp. 598–605 (1990)
30. Yu, R., et al.: Nisp: pruning networks using neuron importance score propagation. In: Proceedings of the IEEE Conference on Computer Vision and Pattern Recognition, pp. 9194–9203 (2018)
31. Liu, Z., et al.: Metapruning: meta learning for automatic neural network channel pruning. In: Proceedings of the IEEE International Conference on Computer Vision, pp. 3296–3305 (2019)
32. Ding, X., Ding, G., Guo, Y., Han, J.: Centripetal SGD for pruning very deep convolutional networks with complicated structure. In: Proceedings of the IEEE Conference on Computer Vision and Pattern Recognition, pp. 4943–4953 (2019)
33. Kim, J., Park, S., Kwak, N.: Paraphrasing complex network: network compression via factor transfer. In: Advances in Neural Information Processing Systems, pp. 2760–2769 (2018)
34. Wang, K., Liu, Z., Lin, Y., Lin, J., Han, S.: Haq: hardware-aware automated quantization with mixed precision. In: Proceedings of the IEEE Conference on Computer Vision and Pattern Recognition, pp. 8612–8620 (2019)
35. Zhu, C., Han, S., Mao, H., Dally, W.J.: Trained ternary quantization. arXiv preprint arXiv:1612.01064 (2016)
36. Son, S., Nah, S., Mu Lee, K.: Clustering convolutional kernels to compress deep neural networks. In: Proceedings of the European Conference on Computer Vision (ECCV), pp. 216–232 (2018)
37. Chellapilla, K., Puri, S., Simard, P.: High performance convolutional neural networks for document processing. In: International Workshop on Frontiers in Handwriting Recognition (2006)
38. Chetlur, S., et al.: cudnn: Efficient primitives for deep learning. arXiv preprint arXiv:1410.0759 (2014)
39. Zhu, M., Gupta, S.: To prune, or not to prune: exploring the efficacy of pruning for model compression. arXiv preprint arXiv:1710.01878 (2017)
40. Lin, S., et al.: Towards optimal structured cnn pruning via generative adversarial learning. In: Proceedings of the IEEE Conference on Computer Vision and Pattern Recognition, pp. 2790–2799 (2019)
41. Krizhevsky, A., Hinton, G., et al.: Learning multiple layers of features from tiny images. Technical report, Citeseer (2009)
42. Russakovsky, O., et al.: Imagenet large scale visual recognition challenge. Int. J. Comput. Vis. **115**, 211–252 (2015)
43. Abadi, M., et al.: Tensorflow: Large-scale machine learning on heterogeneous distributed systems. arXiv preprint arXiv:1603.04467 (2016)
44. Lin, M., et al.: Hrank: Filter pruning using high-rank feature map. In: CVPR 2020: Computer Vision and Pattern Recognition, pp. 1529–1538 (2020)
45. Li, Y., Gu, S., Mayer, C., Gool, L.V., Timofte, R.: Group sparsity: the hinge between filter pruning and decomposition for network compression. In: CVPR 2020: Computer Vision and Pattern Recognition, pp. 8018–8027 (2020)
46. Yang, T.J., et al.: Netadapt: platform-aware neural network adaptation for mobile applications. In: Proceedings of the European Conference on Computer Vision (ECCV), pp. 285–300 (2018)
47. Liu, Z., Sun, M., Zhou, T., Huang, G., Darrell, T.: Rethinking the value of network pruning. arXiv preprint arXiv:1810.05270 (2018)

Learn More, Forget Less:
Cues from Human Brain

Arijit Patra and Tapabrata Chakraborti[✉]

Department of Engineering Science, University of Oxford, Oxford, UK
{arijit.patra,tapabrata.chakraborty}@eng.ox.ac.uk

Abstract. Humans learn new information incrementally while consolidating old information at every stage in a lifelong learning process. While this appears perfectly natural for humans, the same task has proven to be challenging for learning machines. Deep neural networks are still prone to catastrophic forgetting of previously learnt information when presented with information from a sufficiently new distribution. To address this problem, we present NeoNet, a simple yet effective method that is motivated by recent findings in computational neuroscience on the process of long-term memory consolidation in humans. The network relies on a pseudorehearsal strategy to model the working of relevant sections of the brain that are associated with long-term memory consolidation processes. Experiments on benchmark classification tasks achieve state-of-the-art results that demonstrate the potential of the proposed method, with improvements in additions of novel information attained without requiring to store exemplars of past classes.

Keywords: Pseudorehearsal · Continual learning · Catastrophic forgetting

1 Introduction

Humans learn continually throughout life in small steps: we acquire and consolidate new knowledge through abstract representations in the context of existing knowledge. The idea of 'lifelong learning' [1], though natural to humans, has proven difficult to replicate in connectionist architectures like deep networks, where there is a tendency of losing the representation of a learned distribution when presented with data from a different distribution. This issue of 'catastrophic forgetting' is not only encountered when learning a new task, but even with the same task under conditions such as addition of new classes of data [2].

Multiple studies [1,3] have established the stability-plasticity dilemma to be a central tenet of the forgetting problem in both biological and artificial neural networks. The trade-off between stable memories from past learnt information or acquired experiences tend to be in conflict with the desired plasticity towards absorption of new knowledge in neural pathways [4]. Recent experiments

A. Patra and T. Chakraborti—Both authors are equally contributed.

H. Ishikawa et al. (Eds.): ACCV 2020, LNCS 12625, pp. 187–202, 2021.
https://doi.org/10.1007/978-3-030-69538-5_12

in computational neuroscience were able to shed light on this phenomenon, and established that the formation of stable memories in the brain happens without significant conflict with acquisition of new short-term memories by a process called long-term consolidation [5]. In this hypothesis, memory consolidation happens over varying time horizons. It links primarily three regions in the brain - the hippocampus, which deals with the processing of immediate information, which then associates learnt features to a region called prefrontal cortex that consolidates very recent memories ('working memory'), and a third region called the neocortex assembles memories from the prefrontal cortex to form stable long-term reservoirs of learnt knowledge, with the hippocampus being able to independently access the neocortex for matching tasks between novel arrivals of sensory inputs to old stable memories, completing a three-stage closed loop [6].

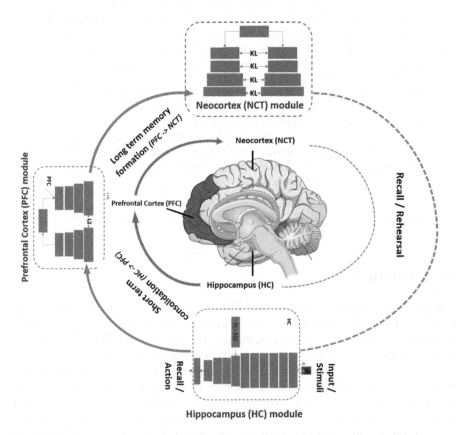

Fig. 1. Schematic diagram of proposed NeoNet and correspondences with brain regions. Structures of the mammalian brain relevant to the study are labelled in orange and the corresponding neural network modules in green. Memory formation pathways are bold arrows (orange for brain pathways, green for the brain-inspired modules); recall pathways are dotted. Detailed diagrams of modules are included in later sections. (Color figure online)

While neural networks used in vision are not exact replica of actual neural pathways by a long shot, there have been analogous design choices over the years. The stability-plasticity balance in artificial neural networks has often been described as analogous to that hypothesized for mammalian brains [7] as discovered experimentally for the latter in memory modelling experiments [4,8]. Can models based on discoveries in neuroscience regarding memory functions of the human brain help to design neural networks better and mitigate the problem of forgetting during continual learning? This is not a new problem in machine vision, but still an open problem. Can the theories of complimentary learning in the neocortex and the pre-frontal cortex help achieve this goal? The present work explores this possibility by modelling multi-stage recall mechanisms along with the learning tasks, similar to the three-stage model for long term consolidation [6]. For the first stage where new information is obtained and decisions are made on sensory inputs, the hippocampus is primarily responsible in the brain, with information on past knowledge through memory recall from the prefrontal cortex and the neocortex. We model the hippocampus with a classifier that has access to the incoming inputs, and is responsible for the classification task. The memory modules are modelled as autoencoders that can be trained to generate prior representations to serve as 'snapshots' of previously seen information. This analogous design is summarized in Fig. 1.

1.1   Related Work

In neuroscience studies, the dual-memory theory looks at the hippocampus and the cortex as key units towards knowledge absorption from the environment. This has been studied in memory retention evaluations in patients of anterograde and retrograde amnesia [9]. Studies on long-term recall from the cortex [10,11] propose a REM sleep driven consolidation mechanism [12], with learnt knowledge being subsequently overwritten from the hippocampus. Advances in neuroscience regarding the functioning of the human memory in context of information acquisition, consolidation, storage and retrieval, has influenced the design of recent bio-inspired neural network solutions to forgetting. GeppNet [13] and FearNet [14] are two such examples.

GeppNet introduced by Gepperth and Karaoguz in 2016 [13], it is a bio-inspired network that reorganizes the input onto a two-dimensional lattice via a self-organising map (SOM) to form a "long term memory", which is then used by a linear classifier. GeppNet performs rehearsal on all previous training data, plus if sufficiently new data is presented at any stage, the SOM is updated accordingly, otherwise left as is, thus avoiding forgetting older data easily. GeppNet+STM is a variant that employs a memory buffer to store new samples, such that the oldest sample is removed when presented with a new sample. The main difference between the two models is that GeppNet+STM only re-trains in specific time intervals, and in between those intervals any new labeled incoming data is stored in the buffer. Thus GeppNet+STM is better at storing old data, since the original GeppNet is updated whenever new labeled data come in.

FearNet, introduced by Kemker and Kanan in 2017 [14] and published in 2018, draws inspiration from fear conditioning in mice [8] and presents a pseudorehearsal scheme to approximate the recall of memories from the median prefrontal cortex (mPFC). They design a module inspired by the hippocampus to perform novelty detection on incoming data [15], and encode learnt representations into the mPFC inspired autoencoder during 'sleep' stages. FearNet considers only feature representations and thus all models are fully-connected and use feature representations in the form of ResNet-50 embeddings directly.

1.2   Research Gap and Solution Approach

Limitation of Existing Models. The main constraint of FearNet (2018) is that the entire memory consolidation occurs in the PFC module modelled on pre-frontal cortex of the brain. However, recent studies on memory consolidation of the brain suggest that it occurs in multiple-stages: first, there is a plastic storage of short term memory at the pre-frontal cortex, but there is a further consolidation of long term memory in the neocortex. The latter part is not modelled in FearNet, thus not taking the advantage of plasticity-stability balance in the two sections of the brain, which if suitably exploited, can be expected to yield higher robustness against forgetting during incremental learning. GeppNet (2016) also suffers from similar drawbacks. The use of a single module inspired by the pre-frontal cortex causes the stability-plasticity balance to be governed with a single module. Thus, the representations learnt during initial learning sessions are substituted over time. In the absence of a more stable retention module, the quality of rehearsal representations declines over successive iterations, causing diminishing performance over longer horizons of incremental class addition. We find that inclusion of a separate module for stable long-term knowledge retention, inspired by the stable memory consolidation in the Neocortex (NCT), addresses the issue of diminishing retention performance over longer incremental task sets.

Contributions of Proposed Model. The proposed NeoNet adds the model of the neocortex along with associated changes in the training protocol to enforce a division of primary responsibility towards plasticity and stability between the two generative components (unlike in prior art related to pseudorehearsal and generative approaches) through two main contributions as follows:

1. A *Neocortex (NCT) Module* is added to take into account that human memory consolidation occurs in stages in different parts of the brain: short term memory in pre-frontal cortex and long term memory in neocortex. We hypothesize that in incremental learning scenarios where new class data can arrive over extended time in a large number of increments, knowledge retention and a consequent generation of suitable rehearsal exemplars will become progressively challenging. Thus, we need stable memory components that are relatively unaffected when adapting to more recent information.

2. A *Multi-stage Pseudo-Rehearsal* process is proposed to improve the training regime. This helps to strike a balance between accommodating new knowledge while maintaining previous knowledge: plasticity in the pre-frontal cortex and stability in the neocortex.

2 Methodology

In this section, we explain first the main new functionalities of the proposed network and the benefits thereof. Then we go on to describe the technical details of the main modules that constitute the network architecture.

2.1 Main Functionalities of the Proposed Model

1) Short-long term memory balance

Model components are motivated by the process of memory consolidation from short-term working memory to long-term memory and subsequent reconsolidation processes. In mammals, such systems-level consolidation has been observed to occur in a circuit beginning with immediate processing in the hippocampus, followed by transfer of information to the pre-frontal cortex which acts as the primary reservoir of working memory. Finally, long-term consolidation occurs over extended time by transferring memories to the synaptically stable neocortex from the plastic prefrontal cortex [5]. This biological process serves as an analogy for the proposed machine learning method.

We consider the hippocampal processing to represent the detection of novel classes in input data streams (Step 1, Fig. 2). The storage of temporary working memory (which occurs to a lesser degree in the hippocampus as well, but is confined to the PFC in our task for simplicity) is implemented in an autoencoder module inspired by the pre-frontal cortex. The encoding of seen classes happens immediately after the HC training for the session is completed as class exemplar representations are extracted in the form of first fully-connected logits and treated as inputs and target outputs for the PFC autoencoder (Step 2, Fig. 2). Over the next sessions, when the HC module is being adapted to data from new classes, the PFC decoder utilizes the stored class mean and the diagonalized covariance matrices to generate class feature representations which are used to encode stable long term memories into the encoder-decoder architecture representative of the neocortex (NCT) (Step 3, Fig. 2). This second encoding process is carried out in parallel with the HC training stages beyond the first session.

2) Stability-plasticity balance through multi-stage pseudo-rehearsal

The intuition behind having two stages of pseudo-rehearsal is that the transfer and consolidation of information over several stages from plastic to stable memories [5]. Computationally, such a pipeline enables us to implement a distributed stability-plasticity balance. The neocortex (NCT) module imposes a relatively strict regularisation on its parameters in terms of the encoding-decoding processes and thus represents stability in memory storage. The pre-frontal cortex

(PFC) module allows for a more flexible encoding of exemplar features over multiple sessions with relatively weak guarantees of parameter preservation resulting in a comparatively relaxed regime, thus representing plasticity in memory storage.

Sequential learning is performed as a sequence of training sessions over which the architecture needs to demonstrate competitive accuracy while retaining past knowledge. There are N sessions considered, each with K classes consisting of a variable number of instances. Feature representations from each class in a session are used to compute class means and covariance matrices that are utilised for pseudo generative replay in later stages.

1. *HC module:* In a training session M ($1 < M \leq N$), the HC module learns a classification task on available classes. Note that a secondary input branch is used after the convolutional layers of the HC network during incremental training to enable the introduction of generated embeddings for previously seen classes. In subsequent incremental learning stages, these embeddings are generated through the dual pseudo-rehearsal scheme.
2. *PFC module:* The learning in the HC stage is followed by extraction of representations over validation set instances per class considered. These exemplar feature representations are then used to train the autoencoder based PFC module where a reconstruction error is coupled with the classification loss to learn reproducible class reconstructions
3. *NCT module:* For long-term stable memory storage, the representations so generated are encoded on to the NCT module inspired by the neocortex. The long-term storage interval is approximated within L successive training sessions, and thus, when the HC network is trained on the Mth session, the encodings from the PFC are written on to the NCT, which thus far would have been exposed to representations up to the $(M - L)^{th}$ session only.

2.2   Design of Components

1) Hippocampus (HC) Module. This is designed for immediate knowledge absorption upon arrival of labeled data by means of a convolutional model enforcing a Bergman distance based classification scheme, inspired by the probabilistic framework of [15] with the minimization objective formulated as:

$$P(c|x) = \frac{z_c}{\sum_{c_1} z_{c_1}} \tag{1}$$

Where,

$$z_c = 1/\delta + \min_j |x - w_{c,j}|^2 \tag{2}$$

δ is a small correction factor to ensure boundedness, $W_{c,j}$ is the jth stored example for class c, and x is the incoming sample. The architecture is schematically represented in Fig. 1, and implements a sequence of convolutional operations, followed by fully-connected layers. The network is so implemented as to be

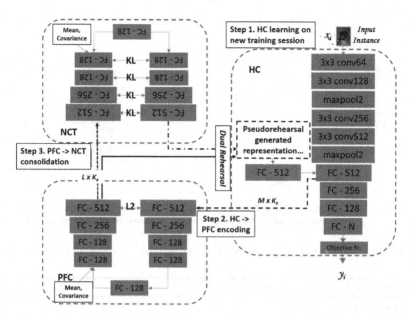

Fig. 2. Three modules of the architecture, HC (for immediate processing), PFC (for short-term storage), NCT (long-term stable storage of learnt representations) shown with encoding and rehearsal pathways.

able to take dual input: the auxiliary input layer is appended directly to the fully connected set, allowing 1-D feature representations. This allows generated exemplars of a past task to be a feature representation from the autoencoder modules instead of stored past exemplars. This is analogous to the mammalian ability to encode salient information about surroundings with very few exemplars and the ability to form associations with prior knowledge.

2) Pre-frontal Cortex (PFC) Module. Mimicking the function of its namesake in the human brain, the PFC module encodes memories of the current task while the data is still available after the HC training, with the decoder arm learning to reconstruct these exemplars with a high degree of fidelity. The encoder and decoder branches are constructed as fully-connected autoencoder layers being downsampled and upsampled respectively. To allow adaptation to novel data and allow for encoding steps to occur with a sufficient plasticity (modeling short term memory handling in human brain), the reconstruction error is used only between the finally generated representations and the input without intermediate regularization. Class mean features and class specific covariance matrices are retained in the memory and used to sample representations to be used as input to the PFC to generate pseudo-exemplars through the decoder. Such attempts at pseudo-rehearsal, proposed by [16] and revived by [14] allow generating past representations without requiring actual storage of exemplars.

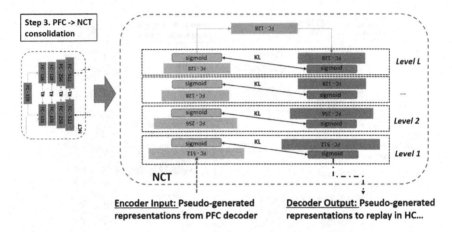

Encoder Input: Pseudo-generated   Decoder Output: Pseudo-generated
representations from PFC decoder   representations to replay in HC...

Fig. 3. Long term memory consolidation in the proposed Neocortex (NCT) module

---

Algorithm 1: NeoNet Training Protocol

---

1 **Define** parameters

  – K = no. of classes, p = no. of classes per incremental learning step.
  – S = max no. of increments = $K/2/p + 1$.
  – L = no. of increments between HC to PFC and between PFC to NCT.

Perform base class training

  – K = Base train HC with $K/2$ classes.
  – S = Fine-tune HC $\rightarrow$ PFC, PFC $\rightarrow$ NCT.
  – L = Retain base μ, σ for incremental learning.

Perform incremental learning
Initialise counters $M = 0; M' = 0$;
while $M < S$ **do**

$\quad$ $M = M + 1$;
$\quad$ **while** $M' < M$ **do**
$\quad\quad$ $M' = M' + 1$;
$\quad\quad$ Short consolidation: fine-tune HC $\rightarrow$ PFC;
$\quad\quad$ Long consolidation: **if** $M' < M - L$ **then** fine-tune PFC $\rightarrow$ NCT;
$\quad$ **end**
$\quad$ **Update** μ, σ;
$\quad$ **Rehearsal:** Feeback NCT representation into HC;
$\quad$ **Adaptation:** Adapt HC on incremental classes;
end

---

3) Neocortex (NCT) Module. In the human brain, the long term potentiation of memories (synaptic consolidation) occurs over extended time, and manifests as a transfer of relevant working memories from the pre-frontal cortex into the neocortex. The neocortex inspired NCT module is treated as a standard autoencoder deriving reconstructed class exemplars from the PFC module to create more stable encodings. The schematic details of the NCT module along with the long term memory consolidation process therein is presented in Fig. 3 and also represented in Algorithm 1. The design considerations are as follows:

- Contrary to the relaxed regularization requirements in the PFC reconstruction to ensure plasticity, the NCT module attempts to facilitate stability in the learnt representation memories, and hence requires more specific regularization. For the choice of the intermediate regularization, we focus on the possibility to include a formulation that inherently prioritizes the preservation of the most salient learnt knowledge and ensure minimal disruption to the task specific parameter importance. Such a formulation should ideally be expressible as an information content measure.
- Because of the possible interpretation of intermediate representations as normalized values for feature salience probabilities, the corresponding stages of the encoder and decoder are mutually regularized with a KL divergence measure. This allows implicit consolidation of parameters most pertinent to such encoding generation as the KL divergence is used between the decoder arm optimized for an immediate previous set of classes and the encoder arm being exposed to the new arriving representations.
- The usage of a KL divergence approach enables an implicit measure of parameter importance because of the correspondence with the Fisher information matrix. The second derivative of the KL divergence that yields a Fisher metric in a product form with parameter perturbation squared [17].
- As the objective function minimized in this module is essentially a summation over the KL divergences computed across corresponding normalized encoder and decoder layers, the gradient descent algorithm optimizes the derivative of this summation of KL divergences.

3 Experiments and Results

3.1 Experimental Setup

Model Setup: The model architectures are shown in Fig. 2 and Fig. 3. All layers in all the modules are initialized with a Xavier scheme [18]. The number of fully-connected units at the encoder input/decoder output is kept the same for the PFC and NCT modules and equal to the first fully-connected layer in the HC to ensure compatibility of feature representations. The specific dimensions of the features were established through a grid search on the number of units, checking for suitability from 128 to 1024 units. The suitable number of layers used in the encoders and decoders and in the HC module were found for each dataset and the finally chosen configurations were the ones that performed the best on average across datasets with 50% of classes considered. The training, validation and test split was maintained at 60:20:20 in all cases.

Training: Initial training of the HC is carried for 500 epochs, followed by PFC consolidation over 200 epochs. The learning rate in the encoder is kept the same as the HC model and that of the decoder is initially kept at 1/10th of the HC learning rate and is decreased by a factor of 10 every 50 epochs. This is to ensure that the decoder arm efficiently learns to regenerate prior representations. In the NCT module, the learning rate regime is kept similar to the PFC but training is carried out for 250 epochs to ensure a stable consolidation of representations. Replay settings involve representations generated from both the PFC and NCT modules supplied together to the auxiliary input of the HC.

Baselines: Considering the class-incremental focus here, we consider the multi-class adaptation of learning without forgetting (LwF.MC), iCaRL [19], LwM [20] and incremental rebalancing classifier (ICR) [21]. Also, due to our neuroscience motivations, we also compare with FearNet [14] and GeppNet+STM (Gepp-STM) [13]. Since our test performances are evaluated using the HC module (with pseudorehearsal inputs), we modify architectures of iCaRL, LwM, ICR and LWF.MC to have the same sequence of convolutional and fully-connected layers while implementing their methods for exemplar storage and replay (details in Appendix) for a fair comparison. A cosine distance based distillation loss is implemented for the ICR baseline in line with the setting in the original paper.

Datasets: Incremental learning tasks are performed on the CIFAR 100 dataset [22], CalTech 256 [23] and CUB-200 [24] datasets. CIFAR-100, consisting of 100 classes of images of 32×32 pixels. CUB-200 has 200 classes of images of birds, curated for a fine-grained classification task. We use the 2011 version of CUB-200. CalTech-256 provides 256 categories of at least 80 images per category, including images with clutter and an overall increased difficulty compared to CIFAR-100. The datasets are chosen to evaluate the model on progressively difficult image classification tasks.

Evaluation Metrics: We adapt metrics of evaluation proposed by Kemker et al. [25] to our incremental learning performance in terms of prior task accuracy retention, and the present task accuracy. *Normalized accuracy of learning new tasks* is the average validation performance on the test data of all classes in the current session and indicates generalization ability over new data distributions. Mathematically it may be formulated as $E_{new} = \frac{1}{N-1} \sum_{2}^{N} \frac{A_{new}}{A_{all}}$, where A_{new} is the validation accuracy on the new classes seen in the most current session. *Normalized accuracy of retaining old knowledge* is the accuracy on the initial set of classes after all classes have been trained. Mathematically this may be formulated as $E_{init} = \frac{1}{N-1} \sum_{2}^{N} \frac{A_{init}}{A_{all}}$, where A_{init} is the accuracy for the classes considered on the initial training session after all sessions are completed and A_{all} is the accuracy on the validation data of all classes in the dataset. The past performance at current session is an average over all the prior sessions with respect to class-wise mean validation performances.

3.2   Results and Analysis

Quantitative Results: In the first session, a proportion of the classes are used to train the models (initially half of available classes are trained for in the first session, with subsequent ablations of 25% and 75%), followed by increments of 2, 5 and 10 classes in successive sessions. Results for the method in these settings with baselines are shown in Table 1. On the ability to preserve knowledge, the model is seen to resist losing out salient information over prior tasks, post the overall completion. In order to capture the overall dynamics of information retention, the final overall performance obtained by testing the finally obtained HC configuration on validation data across all classes has been used to normalize the metrics (A_{all} in E_{init} and E_{new} expressions). Thus, higher the values of E_{new}, better is the generalization on new tasks, and higher values of E_{init} imply superior knowledge retention. So, higher values for both imply the agent is better both in mitigating forgetting and improving generalization.

Table 1. Performance on CIFAR 100, Caltech 256, CUB 200

Model	CIFAR 100						CALTECH 256					
	2 classes		5 classes		10 classes		2 classes		5 classes		10 classes	
	E_{init}	E_{new}	E_{init}	E_{new}	E_{init}	E_{new}	E_{init}	E_{new}	E_{init}	E_{new}	E_{init}	E_{new}
iCaRL	0.912	0.807	0.903	0.795	0.822	0.821	0.830	0.582	0.837	0.608	0.813	0.612
LwF.MC	0.796	0.752	0.813	0.764	0.817	0.832	0.653	0.547	0.681	0.566	0.692	0.580
LwM	0.857	0.705	0.783	0.805	0.876	0.813	0.847	0.661	0.853	0.655	0.825	0.657
FEL	0.801	0.814	0.797	0.820	0.809	0.836	0.773	0.672	0.784	0.658	0.861	0.603
FearNet	0.929	0.820	0.937	0.802	0.941	0.829	0.873	0.673	0.871	0.658	0.896	0.670
ICR	0.861	0.697	0.795	0.812	0.837	0.786	0.851	0.684	0.858	0.634	0.837	0.621
NeoNet	0.935	0.885	0.945	0.874	0.952	0.893	0.922	0.731	0.907	0.756	0.918	0.768

Model	CUB 200					
	2 classes		5 classes		10 classes	
	E_{init}	E_{new}	E_{init}	E_{new}	E_{init}	E_{new}
iCaRL	0.874	0.573	0.792	0.610	0.881	0.601
LwF.MC	0.638	0.471	0.743	0.541	0.675	0.572
LwM	0.858	0.612	0.853	0.632	0.840	0.629
FEL	0.703	0.784	0.710	0.682	0.673	0.791
FearNet	0.879	0.637	0.883	0.677	0.902	0.683
ICR	0.825	0.570	0.794	0.630	0.805	0.675
NeoNet	0.913	0.721	0.923	0.668	0.954	0.775

One of the objectives of proposing a separation between primarily plastic and primary stable generative modules was to ensure that long-term consolidation of the learnt representations can be effectively accomplished. This is necessary for adequate retention when adding a new classes over a large number of incremental

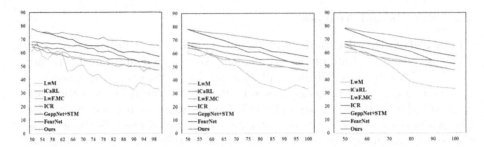

Fig. 4. Mean test accuracy on already learnt classes for the CIFAR 100 experiments, upon new increments of 2 classes (left), 5 classes (middle) and 10 classes (right). Number of base classes is 50. The X-axis shows the number of classes the model has been exposed to at that point, and the Y-axis shows the mean accuracy on all these classes.

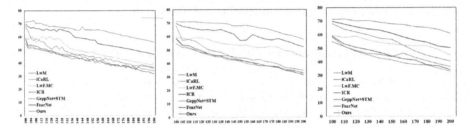

Fig. 5. Mean test accuracy on already learnt classes for the CUB 200 dataset, upon new increments of 2 classes (left), 5 classes (middle) and 10 classes (right). Number of base classes is 100. X-axis shows the number of classes the model has been exposed to at that point, Y-axis shows mean accuracy on all these classes. The decline in mean accuracy is much slower for the NeoNet in the 2-class and 5-class long-range incremental additions, due to the separation of stable and plastic generative components.

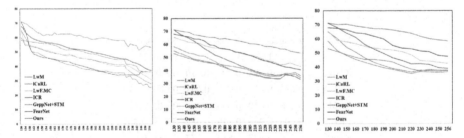

Fig. 6. Mean test accuracy on already learnt classes for Caltech 256 dataset, upon new increments of 2 classes (left), 5 classes (middle) and 10 classes (right). Number of base classes is 112. The decline in mean accuracy is much slower for the NeoNet in the 2-class and 5-class long-range incremental additions, due to the separation of the stable and plastic generative components.

sessions, such as the cases where 2 classes per stage are added beyond the base class training (leading to 25 incremental stages for the CIFAR 100, 50 for CUB-200, 64 for Caltech 256 when starting with base model pre-trained on 50% of classes). In such long incremental horizons, we find our model to have a much better retention of knowledge as seen by the mean class accuracies over these incremental stages (Fig. 4, 5 and 6) even with relatively difficult datasets such as CUB-200 and CalTech 256. Compared to other brain-inspired architectures that explicitly relied on a memory consolidation module, our incorporation of an NCT module to mimic long term memory formation leads to a more gradual decline in overall performance. Thus, a more robust pseudorehearsal strategy is formed by utilising concepts from long-term memory consolidation research.

Table 2. Effect of variation in PFC to NCT consolidation volumes

	CIFAR 100		CUB 200		CALTECH 256	
	E_{init}	E_{new}	E_{init}	E_{new}	E_{init}	E_{new}
L = 0.25M	0.922	0.823	0.902	0.653	0.899	0.677
L = 0.50M	0.947	0.828	0.910	0.649	0.907	0.672
L = 0.75M	0.949	0.826	0.917	0.649	0.910	0.671

Table 3. Effect of variation in NCT regularization extent

	CIFAR 100		CUB 200		CALTECH 256	
	E_{init}	E_{new}	E_{init}	E_{new}	E_{init}	E_{new}
KL (1+2+3+4)	0.947	0.828	0.910	0.649	0.907	0.672
KL (1+2+3)	0.902	0.813	0.869	0.637	0.871	0.671
KL (1+2)	0.887	0.814	0.843	0.629	0.835	0.672
KL (2)	0.801	0.809	0.782	0.626	0.779	0.668

Table 4. Effect of variation in initial session base class volume

	CIFAR 100		CUB 200		CALTECH 256	
	E_{init}	E_{new}	E_{init}	E_{new}	E_{init}	E_{new}
Base = 25%	0.912	0.819	0.892	0.636	0.903	0.668
Base = 50%	0.946	0.825	0.910	0.643	0.902	0.672
Base = 75%	0.948	0.837	0.913	0.648	0.908	0.689

Ablation Studies:

- *Table 2:* We evaluate the balance in plasticity and stability between the PFC and NCT modules by varying the number of classes L to be written in a session from the PFC to the NCT between 1 to M, which is the total number of classes available in a session. In the 10-stage class increment experiment with half of classes available at the initial training, we consider L to be 25%,50% and 75% of M ($M = 10$ here) and report the results in Table 2. The differential consolidation implemented by varying L impacts the overall knowledge retention of the model as seen by the decline in E_{init} being inversely proportional to the percentage of classes per session that is directly transferred from PFC to NCT. Over multiple sessions new classes arrive and the PFC being relatively plastic preferentially adapts parameters to new distributions. So its decoder is relatively impaired in its ability to generate representations of previous classes as compared to those generated right after the original encoding session. This causes the efficiency of rehearsal to diminish over multiple sessions. New class accuracies are practically unaffected by this change as the HC module is directly validated on the data without reliance on external exemplars.
- *Table 3:* In the NCT module, varying the extent of KL divergence measure, can affect the quality of the generated representations and the ability of the model to retain important weights close to optimal values. This affects the overall ability to preserve prior information and is evident in the alterations in performance on recall of past tasks. For this experiment, we consider the setting of 50% classes being available at initial training and L set at 50% on 10-class increment stages. There are four levels of the KL regularization corresponding to the four sets of encoder decoder layers. It is observed in Table 3 that the post completion base knowledge accuracy shows a steady decline with the removal of KL divergence regularization stages in NCT, as evident from the steadily declining E_{init} values. Adaptations to new data remain relatively unaffected as the rehearsal only sporadically impacts new representation learning except in cases where the joint training with past exemplars leads to particularly optimal initializations allowing for improvements in learning on new data.
- *Table 4:* We show the overall effects of changing the proportion of classes trained for in the initial training session. Unlike in Table 2, where the assumption was that 50% of the classes in a dataset are trained for in the first session itself, here we consider initial availability of 25% and 75% with the remaining subjected to 10-class incremental stages. The last stage accounts for the remaining classes, which may be less than 10, thus the discrepancy in the 10-class stage metrics for the otherwise similar experimental state in Table 2. The inclusion of more classes in the initial session is seen to improve the final knowledge retention. The learning regime is seen to prioritize initial sessions more than subsequent replays and a more voluminous base knowledge translates into higher final accuracies.

4   Conclusion

We show that incorporating recent understanding of multi-stage short-long term human memory consolidation into deep incremental/continual learning helps in limiting forgetting previously learnt information, especially when presented with incrementally arriving significant numbers of new class sessions. We do this by designing modules of a deep architecture based on three sections of the brain: Hippocampus for initial processing of incoming data and working memory, Prefrontal cortex for short term memory with plasticity and Neocortex for long term memory with stability. These modules work in tandem and improved results are obtained in standard incremental learning experiments against benchmark methods on public datasets.

References

1. Parisi, G.I., Kemker, R., Part, J.L., Kanan, C., Wermter, S.: Continual lifelong learning with neural networks: a review. Neural Netw. 113, 54–71 (2019)
2. Goodfellow, I.J., Mirza, M., Xiao, D., Courville, A., Bengio, Y.: An empirical investigation of catastrophic forgetting in gradient-based neural networks. arXiv:1312.6211 (2013)
3. Zhang, L., et al.: A simplified computational memory model from information processing. Sci. Rep. 6, 37470 (2016)
4. French, R.M.: Catastrophic forgetting in connectionist networks. Trends Cogn. Sci. 3, 4 (1999)
5. Fiebig, F., Lansner, A.: Memory consolidation from seconds to weeks: a three-stage neural network model with autonomous reinstatement dynamics. Front. Comput. Neurosci. 8, 64 (2014)
6. Manohar, S.G., Zokaei, N., Fallon, S.J., Vogels, T., Husain, M.: Neural mechanisms of attending to items in working memory. Neurosci. Biobehav. Rev. 101, 1–12 (2019)
7. Mermillod, M., Bugaiska, A., Bonin, P.: The stability-plasticity dilemma: investigating the continuum from catastrophic forgetting to age-limited learning effects. Front. Psychol. 4, 504 (2013)
8. Kitamura, T., et al.: Engrams and circuits crucial for systems consolidation of a memory. Science 356, 6333 (2017)
9. Marslen-Wilson, W.D., Teuber, H.L.: Memory for remote events in anterograde amnesia: recognition of public figures from newsphotographs. Neuropsychologia 13, 353–364 (1975)
10. Tomita, H., Ohbayashi, M., Nakahara, K., Hasegawa, I., Miyashita, Y.: Top-down signal from prefrontal cortex in executive control of memory retrieval. Nature 401, 699 (1999)
11. Maddock, R.J., Garrett, A.S., Buonocore, M.H.: Remembering familiar people: the posterior cingulate cortex and autobiographical memory retrieval. Neuroscience 104, 667–676 (2001)
12. Siegel, J.M.: The rem sleep-memory consolidation hypothesis. Science 294, 1058–1063 (2001)
13. Gepperth, A., Karaoguz, C.: A bio-inspired incremental learning architecture for applied perceptual problems. Cogn. Comput. 8, 5 (2016)

14. Kemker, R., Kanan, C.: FearNet: brain-inspired model for incremental learning. arXiv:1711.10563 (2017)
15. Specht, D.F.: Probabilistic neural networks. Neural Netw. **3**, 109–118 (1990)
16. Robins, A.: Catastrophic forgetting, rehearsal and pseudorehearsal. Connection Sci. **7**, 123–146 (1995)
17. Dabak, A.G., Johnson, D.H.: Relations between Kullback-Leibler distance and Fisher information. Technical report (2002)
18. Glorot, X., Bengio, Y.: Understanding the difficulty of training deep feedforward neural networks. In: Proceedings of the Thirteenth International Conference on Artificial Intelligence and Statistics, pp. 249–256 (2010)
19. Rebuffi, S.A., Kolesnikov, A., Sperl, G., Lampert, C.H.: iCaRL: incremental classifier and representation learning. In: Proceedings of the IEEE Conference on Computer Vision and Pattern Recognition, pp. 2001–2010 (2017)
20. Dhar, P., Singh, R.V., Peng, K.C., Wu, Z., Chellappa, R.: Learning without memorizing. In: Proceedings of the IEEE Conference on Computer Vision and Pattern Recognition, pp. 5138–5146 (2019)
21. Hou, S., Pan, X., Loy, C.C., Wang, Z., Lin, D.: Learning a unified classifier incrementally via rebalancing. In: Proceedings of the IEEE Conference on Computer Vision and Pattern Recognition, pp. 831–839 (2019)
22. Krizhevsky, A., Hinton, G.: Learning multiple layers of features from tiny images. Technical report, University of Toronto (2009)
23. Griffin, G., Holub, A., Perona, P.: Caltech-256 Object Category Dataset. California Institute of Technology (2007)
24. Welinder, P., et al.: Caltech-UCSD birds 200, California institute of technology. CNS-TR- 2010-001 (2010)
25. Kemker, R., McClure, M., Abitino, A., Hayes, T., Kanan, C.: Measuring catastrophic forgetting in neural networks. In: AAAI Conference on Artificial Intelligence (2018)

Knowledge Transfer Graph for Deep Collaborative Learning

Soma Minami[1]([✉]), Tsubasa Hirakawa[2], Takayoshi Yamashita[1],
and Hironobu Fujiyoshi[3]

[1] Department of Computer Science, Chubu University, Kasugai-shi 487-0027, Japan
`minami@mprg.cs.chubu.ac.jp, takayoshi@isc.chubu.ac.jp`
[2] Chubu Institute for Advanced Studies, Chubu University,
Kasugai-shi 487-0027, Japan
`hirakawa@mprg.cs.chubu.ac.jp`
[3] Department of Robotics, Chubu University, Kasugai-shi 487-0027, Japan
`fujiyoshi@isc.chubu.ac.jp`

Abstract. Knowledge transfer among multiple networks using their outputs or intermediate activations have evolved through manual design from a simple teacher-student approach to a bidirectional cohort one. The major components of such knowledge transfer framework involve the network size, the number of networks, the transfer direction, and the design of the loss function. However, because these factors are enormous when combined and become intricately entangled, the methods of conventional knowledge transfer have explored only limited combinations. In this paper, we propose a novel graph representation called knowledge transfer graph that provides a unified view of the knowledge transfer and has the potential to represent diverse knowledge transfer patterns. We also propose four gate functions that control the gradient and can deliver diverse combinations of knowledge transfer. Searching the graph structure enables us to discover more effective knowledge transfer methods than a manually designed one. Experimental results show that the proposed method achieved performance improvements.

1 Introduction

Deep neural networks have accomplished significant progress by designing their internal structure (e.g., a network's module [1–4] and architecture search [5–8]). The performance of existing networks can be further improved by knowledge transfer among multiple networks, such as knowledge distillation (KD) [9] and deep mutual learning (DML) [10], in extensive tasks without any additional dataset. These methods, which we call "collaborative learning," transfer knowledge between multiple networks using their outputs and/or intermediate activations.

Collaborative learning has been manually designed in extensive studies [9–16], including the simple teacher-student approach [9], self-distillation [12],

© Springer Nature Switzerland AG 2021
H. Ishikawa et al. (Eds.): ACCV 2020, LNCS 12625, pp. 203–217, 2021.
https://doi.org/10.1007/978-3-030-69538-5_13

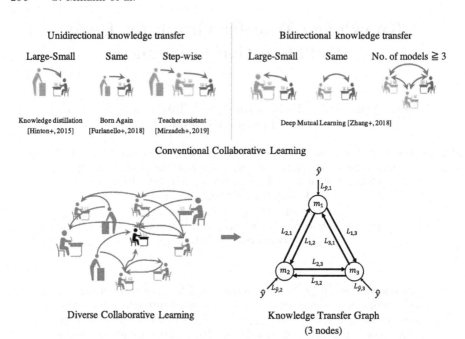

Fig. 1. Concept of the proposed method. From left to right, unidirectional and bidirectional knowledge transfer proposed by previous studies, the goals of our study, and the knowledge transfer graph representation we propose. In the graph, each node represents a network, each edge represents the direction of knowledge transfer, and $L_{s,t}$ represents the loss function used for training node t. The graph can represent diverse collaborative learning, including conventional methods.

an intermediation by teacher assistant [13], and the bidirectional cohort approach [10]. The major components of such collaborative learning are the network size, the number of networks, the transfer direction, and the design of the loss function. In general, increasing the number of networks tends to improve the performance of the target network [10,13–15]. Cho *et al.* [17] also pointed out that larger models do not often make better teachers. The methods of conventional knowledge transfer have only explored limited combinations because the combination of the key factors is enormous and has become intricately entangled. Therefore, it is necessary to extensively explore diverse patterns of collaborative learning to achieve more effective knowledge transfer.

In this research, we explore more diverse knowledge transfer patterns in the above key factors for collaborative learning. Figure 1 shows the concept of our research. We propose a novel graph representation called *knowledge transfer graph* that can represent both conventional and new collaborative learning. A knowledge transfer graph provides a unified view of knowledge transfer and has the potential to represent diverse knowledge transfer patterns. In the graph, each node represents a network, and each edge represents a direction of knowledge transfer. On each edge, we define a loss function that is used for transferring knowledge between the two nodes linked by the edge. Combinations of these loss functions can represent any collaborative learning with pair-wise knowledge transfer. In this paper, we propose four types of gate functions (through gate, cutoff gate, linear gate, correct gate) that are introduced into loss functions. These gate functions control the loss value, thereby delivering different effects of knowledge transfer. By arranging the loss functions at each edge, the graphs enable the representation of diverse collaborative learning patterns. Knowledge transfer graphs are searched for the network model on each node and the gate function on each edge, which enables us to discover a more effective knowledge transfer method than a manually designed one.

Our contributions are as follows.

- We propose a knowledge transfer graph that represents conventional and new collaborative learning.
- We propose four types of gates function (through gate, cutoff gate, linear gate, correct gate) to control backpropagation while training the networks. The knowledge transfer graph optimizes the gates by means of a hyperparameter search, which can achieve diverse collaborative learning.
- We found that our optimized graphs outperformed conventional methods.

2   Related Work

2.1   Unidirectional Knowledge Transfer

In unidirectional knowledge transfer, the outputs of a pre-trained network are used as pseudo labels in addition to supervised labels for learning a target network effectively. Hinton et al. [9] proposed knowledge distillation, which trains a student network by using teacher network's outputs. They succeeded in effectively transferring the teacher's internal representation to the student by introducing a temperature parameter into the softmax function. Furlanello et al. [12] demonstrated that KD can also train effectively in cases where the teacher network's architecture is the same as that of the student network. Mirzadeh et al. [13] proposed a method that adds a middle network, called a teacher assistant, between a teacher and student. When there is a large performance gap between the teacher and the student, students can be effectively trained by separating them with a middle network. Various approaches that transfer from intermediate layers have been also proposed [11,18–20], e.g. hint [11], flow of activations between layers [18], and attention map [19]. [21–23] transfer mutual relations of data samples in a mini-batch. Distillation has been applied to object detection [24], domain adaptation [25], text-to-speech [26], etc.

2.2   Bidirectional Knowledge Transfer

In the bidirectional method, which was first proposed by Zhang et al. [10], there is no pre-trained teacher; randomly initialized students teach each other by transferring their knowledge. Even when using networks with identical structures, the

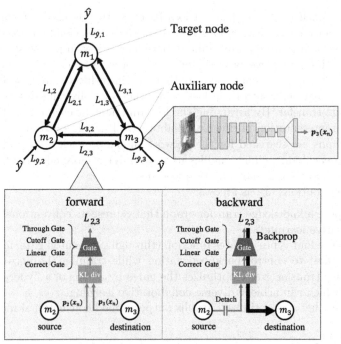

Fig. 2. Knowledge transfer graph (for 3-node case). Each node represents a model, and a loss function $L_{s,t}$ is defined for each edge. $\hat{y}$ is a label. $L_{s,t}$ calculates the KL divergence from the outputs of two nodes and then passes it through a gate function. The calculated loss gradient information is only propagated in the direction of the arrow. We can also represent unidirectional knowledge transfer by cutting off edges with a cutoff gate.

accuracy is improved. Zhang *et al.* pointed out that DML is connected to entropy regularization [27,28]. In this method, all loss functions used in each network are identical. There could be more potential variants in collaborative learning if a combination of different loss functions was used. Further improvements in accuracy can be achieved by using the ensemble outputs of collaboratively trained networks as teachers [14,15], and by sharing the intermediate layers of these networks [14,15,29]. DML has been applied to large scale distributed training [30] and re-identification [31]. Dual student [16] is a method of bidirectional knowledge transfer in semi-supervised learning.

3 Proposed Method

We explore graph structures representing diverse knowledge transfer by combining loss functions with four types of gate. We describe how to represent knowledge transfer graphs in Sect. 3.1, loss function of our proposed method in

Sect. 3.2, four types of gate function in Sect. 3.3, optimization method of each model in Sect. 3.4, and graph optimization method in Sect. 3.5.

3.1 Knowledge Transfer Graph Representation

Figure 2 shows the knowledge transfer graph representation with three nodes. In the proposed method, the direction of knowledge transfer between networks is represented by a directed graph, and a different loss function is defined for each edge. By defining different loss functions, it is possible to express various knowledge transfer methods.

We define a directed graph where node m_i represents the ith model used for training. Each edge represents the directions in which gradient information is transferred. In this paper, we refer to a node that transfers its knowledge to another as a source node, and a node to which the source node transfers its knowledge as a destination node. The losses calculated from the outputs of the two models are back-propagated towards the destination node. Losses are not back-propagated to the source node.

3.2 Loss Function

The mini-batch comprising the image of the nth sample $\boldsymbol{x}_n$ and the label $\hat{y}_n$ is represented as $\mathcal{B} = \{\boldsymbol{x}_n, \hat{y}_n\}_{n=1}^N$, and the batch size of mini-batch $\mathcal{B}$ is represented as $|\mathcal{B}|$. The label $\hat{y}_n$ represents class id. The number of models used for learning is M, and the source and destination nodes are m_s and m_t, respectively.

When obtaining the difference in output probabilities between nodes, we use the Kullback-Leibler (KL) divergence $KL(\boldsymbol{p}_s(\boldsymbol{x}_n)\|\boldsymbol{p}_t(\boldsymbol{x}_n))$. Here, $\boldsymbol{p}_s$ and $\boldsymbol{p}_t$ are the outputs of the source and destination nodes, respectively, and consist of probability distributions normalized by the softmax function.

If the one-hot vector representation of the label $\hat{y}_n$ is $\boldsymbol{p}_{\hat{y}_n}$, the loss between $\boldsymbol{p}_{\hat{y}_n}$ and the output $\boldsymbol{p}_t(\boldsymbol{x}_n)$ of destination node t is calculated using the cross-entropy function $H(\boldsymbol{p}_{\hat{y}_n}, \boldsymbol{p}_t(\boldsymbol{x}_n))$. $H(\boldsymbol{p}_{\hat{y}_n}, \boldsymbol{p}_t(\boldsymbol{x}_n))$ can be decomposed into the sum of KL divergence and entropy as follows:

$$
\begin{aligned}
H(\boldsymbol{p}_{\hat{y}_n}, \boldsymbol{p}_t(\boldsymbol{x}_n)) &= KL(\boldsymbol{p}_{\hat{y}_n}\|\boldsymbol{p}_t(\boldsymbol{x}_n)) + H(\boldsymbol{p}_{\hat{y}_n}, \boldsymbol{p}_{\hat{y}_n}) \\
&= KL(\boldsymbol{p}_{\hat{y}_n}\|\boldsymbol{p}_t(\boldsymbol{x}_n)).
\end{aligned}
\tag{1}
$$

Here, since $\boldsymbol{p}_{\hat{y}_n}$ is a one-hot vector, its entropy $H(\boldsymbol{p}_{\hat{y}_n}, \boldsymbol{p}_{\hat{y}_n})$ is zero. Therefore, the loss between the label and the output can also be represented by the KL divergence in the same way as the loss between the node outputs. In the following, $\boldsymbol{p}_{\hat{y}_n}$ is denoted by $\boldsymbol{p}_0(\boldsymbol{x}_n)$.

$L_{s,t}$ represents the loss function used when knowledge is propagated from the source node m_s to the destination node m_t, which is defined by

$$
L_{s,t} = \sum_n^{|\mathcal{B}|} G_{s,t}(KL(\boldsymbol{p}_s(\boldsymbol{x}_n)\|\boldsymbol{p}_t(\boldsymbol{x}_n))),
\tag{2}
$$

where $G_{s,t}(\cdot)$ is a gate function.

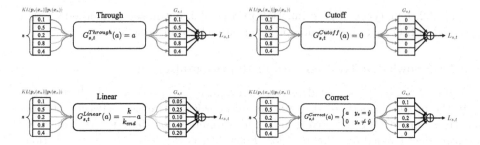

Fig. 3. Illustration of four types of gates.

Finally, the loss function of the destination node m_t is expressed as the sum of losses for all nodes as follows:

$$L_t = \sum_{s=0,s\neq t}^{M} L_{s,t}.$$ (3)

3.3 Gates

If all information is transferred to the destination node from the source node throughout the entire training phase, the learning of the destination node is liable to be disrupted. We introduce a gate that controls the gradient to a destination node by weighting losses for each training sample. We define four types of gate: through gate, cutoff gate, linear gate, and correct gate, and are illustrated in Fig. 3. A through gate simply passes through the losses of each training sample without any changes.

$$G_{s,t}^{Through}(a) = a$$ (4)

A cutoff gate is a gate that performs no loss calculation. It can be used to cut off any edge in a knowledge transfer graph. This function is required in methods such as KD, where knowledge transfer is only performed in one direction.

$$G_{s,t}^{Cutoff}(a) = 0$$ (5)

A linear gate changes its loss weighting linearly with time during training. It has a small weighting at the initial epoch, and its weighting becomes larger as training progresses.

$$G_{s,t}^{Linear}(a) = \frac{k}{k_{end}} a$$ (6)

Here, k is the number of the current iteration, and k_{end} is the total number of iteration at the end of the training.

A correct gate is a gate that only passes the losses of samples whose source node is correct. If the top-1 class number of a source node m_s is y_s, a correct gate can be expressed as

$$G_{s,t}^{Correct}(a) = \begin{cases} a & y_s = \hat{y} \\ 0 & y_s \neq \hat{y}. \end{cases}$$ (7)

Algorithm 1. Network parameter update

Input: Number of nodes M, number of epochs E
Initialize: Initialize all network weights, or read in the weights of a pre-trained network

    for _ = 1 to E **do**
        Input the same image x_n to each network.
        Obtain the output $p_1(x_n), p_2(x_n), \cdots, p_M(x_n)$.
        Obtain the loss L_n according to Eq. (3).
        Obtain the update quantity of m_n from the gradient L_n.
        Update the weights of all networks.
    end for

When the source node is not a pre-trained model, the propagation of false information can be suppressed at the initial epoch. While a linear gate weights the overall loss, a correct gate selects the samples from which the loss is calculated.

3.4 Proposed Algorithm

Algorithm 1 shows how to update the network parameters of each node during training. First, all the model weights are randomly initialized unless all the gates $G_{i,t}$ corresponding to nodes m_i are cutoff gates, in which case m_i is initialized with the weights of the pre-trained model. The pre-trained model is trained only with the labels, using the same dataset as the one used for the following hyperparameter search (the details are described in Sect. 3.5). Here, m_i is frozen during training and its weights are not updated. This node performs a role being equivalent to that of the teacher network used in KD.

The losses are obtained by inputting the same samples to all nodes. Gradients are obtained from the resulting losses, and all nodes are updated simultaneously. The gradient of loss L_t obtained from Eq. (3) is back-propagated only to node m_t, and has no effect on the other nodes. In DML, after updating the weights of the first node, the training samples are input again to the updated nodes to obtain an output. The losses between every node are then recalculated from this outputs, and gradient descent is performed for the second node. These steps are repeated until every node has been updated. The drawback of DML is that this updating method causes a significant increase in computational cost as the number of nodes increases. In our proposed method, since the weights of every node are updated during a single forward calculation, it is possible to reduce the computational cost during training.

3.5 Graph Optimization

We refer to an optimized node by hyperparameter search as a target node m_1, and nodes that supports training of the target node as auxiliary nodes. A target node to be optimized is specified, and the knowledge transfer graph is optimized to maximize the accuracy of this node. The hyperparameters to be optimized are the model type of the auxiliary nodes and the gate type on each edge. The size of the search space for this optimization is $M^{(n-1)} \cdot G^{N^2}$, where N is the number of nodes, M is the number of model types, and G is the number of gate types. For example, if $N = 3$, $M = 3$, and $G = 4$, there are over one million patterns.

We used the Asynchronous Successive Halving Algorithm (ASHA) [32] as the hyperparameter optimization method. First, using D GPU servers, we randomly create a knowledge transfer graph with D servers and perform distributed asynchronous learning. In each knowledge transfer graph, the accuracy of the target node is evaluated using validation set at epochs $1, 2, 4, \cdots, 2^k$. If this accuracy is in the lower 50% of all the accuracy values evaluated in the past, the graph is abandoned and training is performed again after generating a new graph. This process is repeated until the total number of trials reaches T. ASHA can achieve improvements in terms of both temporal efficiency and accuracy by performing a random search with active early termination in a parallel distributed environment. We performed optimization with $D = 30$ and $T = 1500$.

4   Experiments

We performed experiments to determine the efficacy of knowledge transfer graphs searched by ASHA. We describe the graphs visualization in Sect. 4.2, comparison to conventional methods in Sect. 4.3, investigation of the performance of a target node when the graph lacks diversity in Sect. 4.4 and evaluation of graph transferability between different datasets in Sect. 4.5.

4.1   Experimental Setting

Datasets. We used the CIFAR-10, CIFAR-100 [33], and Tiny-ImageNet [34], which are typically used for general object recognition. CIFAR-10 and CIFAR-100 consist of 50,000 images for training and 10,000 images for testing. Both datasets consist of images with dimensions of 32×32 pixels and include labels for 10 and 100 classes, respectively. Data augmentation was performed by processing the training images with 4-pixel padding (reflection), random cropping, and random flipping. Data augmentation was not applied to the test images. For optimizing graphs, we randomly split the training samples into 10,000 samples as the validation set and 40,000 samples as the training set. The Tiny-ImageNet consists of 100,000 training images and 10,000 test images sampled from the ImageNet [35]. This dataset consists of images with dimensions of 64×64 pixels and labels for 200 classes. The data augmentation settings were the same as those for the CIFAR datasets. For optimizing graphs, we randomly split the training samples into 10,000 samples as the validation set and 90,000 samples as the training set.

Models. We used three networks: ResNet32, ResNet110 [36], and Wide ResNet 28-2 [37]. Table 1 shows the accuracy achieved when each model was trained with supervised labels only. However, when training with Tiny-ImageNet, since the images are larger in size, the stride of the initial convolution layer was set to 1.

Implementation Details. For the optimization algorithm, we used SGD and Nesterov momentum in all experiments. The initial learning rate was 0.1, the momentum was 0.9, and the batch size was 64. When training on CIFAR, the learning rate was reduced to one tenth every 60 epochs, for a total of 200 epochs. When training on the Tiny-ImageNet, the learning rate was reduced to one tenth at the 40th, 60th, and 70th epochs, for a total of 80 epochs. The reported accuracy values with test set are averaged over five trials with a fixed graph structure implemented after obtaining the optimized graph. The standard deviation over each set of five trials is also shown. Our experiments were implemented using the Pytorch framework [38] for deep learning and the Optuna framework [39] for hyperparameter searching. The computations were performed using 90 Quadro P5000 servers. Our implementation is available at https://github.com/somaminami/DCL.

4.2 Visualization of Graphs

Figure 4 shows the visualization of the knowledge transfer graphs with two to seven nodes optimized on CIFAR-100. For all numbers of nodes, the target node had much better accuracy than that in individual learning (see Table 1). The accuracy of nodes other than the target node was also improved. We found that ResNet32 and ResNet110 were selected as the nodes of top-1 graphs as well as the highest performance Wide ResNet 28-2, and the performance of the target node tended to improve when the number of nodes was increased. Our quantitative evaluation is discussed in Sect. 4.4.

4.3 Comparison with Conventional Methods

Table 2 compares the performance of the proposed and conventional methods on CIFAR-100. "Ours" shows the results of the proposed method for optimized graphs with two, three, or four nodes. "KD [9]" uses a pre-trained Wide ResNet 28-2 network as a teacher, and sets the temperature parameter to $T = 2$. In "DML [10]" using over three nodes, all student networks have the same

Table 1. Accuracy of vanilla models. Mean and standard deviation of single network accuracies on test set.

Model	CIFAR-10	CIFAR-100	TinyImageNet
ResNet32	92.99 ± 0.28	70.71 ± 0.39	52.89 ± 0.18
ResNet110	94.01 ± 0.28	72.59 ± 0.54	55.49 ± 0.55
Wide ResNet 28-2	94.40 ± 0.07	74.60 ± 0.38	58.60 ± 0.25

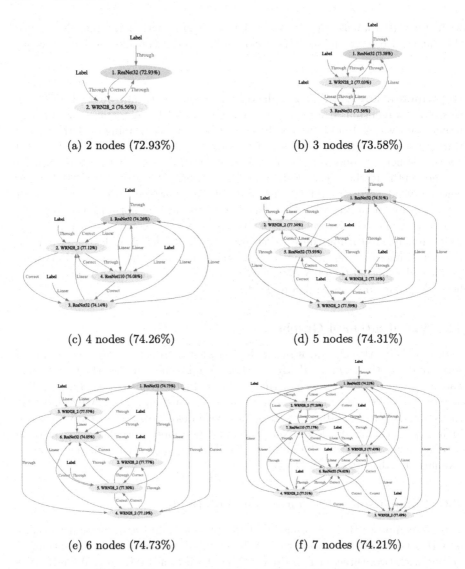

(a) 2 nodes (72.93%)

(b) 3 nodes (73.58%)

(c) 4 nodes (74.26%)

(d) 5 nodes (74.31%)

(e) 6 nodes (74.73%)

(f) 7 nodes (74.21%)

Fig. 4. Knowledge transfer graph optimized on CIFAR-100. Red node is the target node, and "Label" represents supervised labels. At each edge, the selected gate is shown, exclusive of cutoff gate. Numbers in parentheses show the accuracy achieved in one out of five trials. (Color figure online)

architecture. Since the proposed method chooses which model to use as a hyper parameter, it is possible to select the optimal combination of models. In "Song *et al.* [14]" and "ONE [15]", the intermediate layers of multiple networks are shared during training. Then, only layers that are close to the output layer are branched, and the ensemble output of the branched output layers is used as a teacher.

Table 2. Comparison with conventional methods on CIFAR-100. "*" denotes a pre-trained model. T is a temperature parameter. "**" denotes a value cited from the paper.

Method	Accuracy (Node 1)	Node 1	Node 2	Node 3	Node 4
Vanilla	70.71 ± 0.39	ResNet32	–	–	–
DML [10]	72.00 ± 0.44	ResNet32	ResNet32	–	–
KD ($T = 2$) [9]	71.88 ± 0.78	ResNet32	WRN28-2*	–	–
DML [10]	72.71 ± 0.18	ResNet32	WRN28-2	–	–
Ours	**72.88** ± 0.41	ResNet32	WRN28-2	–	–
DML [10]	72.09 ± 0.43	ResNet32	ResNet32	ResNet32	–
DML [10]	72.89 ± 0.21	ResNet32	WRN28-2	ResNet32	–
Ours	**73.46** ± 0.28	ResNet32	WRN28-2	ResNet32	–
DML [10]	72.76 ± 0.35	ResNet32	ResNet32	ResNet32	ResNet32
Song [14]	73.68** ± 0.26	(4 × ResNet32 with shared intermediate layers)			
ONE [15]	73.42** ± N/A	(4 × ResNet32 with shared intermediate layers)			
DML [10]	72.87 ± 0.49	ResNet32	WRN28-2	ResNet32	ResNet110
Ours	**74.06** ± 0.34	ResNet32	WRN28-2	ResNet32	ResNet110

Compared with the results of DML having the same nodes with the proposed method, the proposed method outperforms the accuracy. The result of Song et al. [14] is close to the proposed method in the case of four nodes. Because their method shares the intermediate layers as described above, their method could acquire parameters to extract more representative features. The proposed method achieved the best result, although it does not share the intermediate layers updates parameters using only the gradients computed from the loss of auxiliary nodes and teacher label. Therefore, transferring knowledge from an intermediate layer could improve the performance of the target node, which is one of our future works.

4.4 Comparison with Graphs Lacking Diversity

Figure 5 shows the accuracy of target nodes in graphs searched on CIFAR-10, CIFAR-100, and Tiny-ImageNet. The comparison is a non-diverse graph, where each edge has only a through gate and each node is the same model as that of the graph, which is similar to the conventional unidirectional method [10].

The proposed method achieved higher accuracy than the comparative method in every condition, thus demonstrating the importance of using gates to control the gradient. Moreover, the optimized graphs tended to improve the accuracy when the number of nodes was increased in CIFAR-100. The fixed gates method has the same loss function on all the edges, making it difficult to generate diversity even when the number of nodes is increased.

In our experiments, due to the limitation of computational resources, we ran only 1,000 trials for searching the knowledge transfer graphs. This may not be sufficient because the search space exponentially increases with the number of nodes. Moreover, if we searched on a larger number of trials, it might be possible to acquire a better knowledge transfer graph than we discovered. We will explore this possibility in future work.

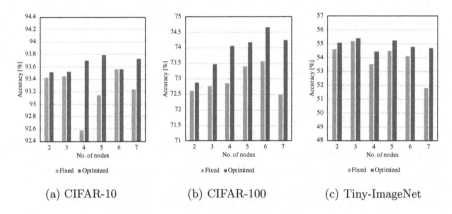

(a) CIFAR-10   (b) CIFAR-100   (c) Tiny-ImageNet

Fig. 5. Results of optimization on various datasets. ResNet32 was used as the target node. "Fixed" indicates all gates are through gates. "Optimized" indicates they have been optimized.

Table 3. Accuracy of reused graphs optimized on another dataset. Graphs are trained on CIFAR-100, where graphs are searched on CIFAR-10 or CIFAR-100. Target node is ResNet32. Bold/Italic indicate best and second best results.

No. of nodes	Fixed to through gate	Searched on different dataset (CIFAR-10)	Searched on same dataset (CIFAR-100)
2	72.62 ± 0.33	*72.50* ± 0.33	**72.88** ± 0.41
3	72.77 ± 0.26	**73.63** ± 0.18	*73.46* ± 0.28
4	72.86 ± 0.44	*73.76* ± 0.25	**74.06** ± 0.34
5	73.40 ± 0.15	**74.62** ± 0.24	*74.18* ± 0.21

4.5 Graph Transferability

We investigated the generalization ability of graphs on different datasets. Table 3 shows accuracies of the networks trained on CIFAR-100, where the graphs are searched on CIFAR-10 or CIFAR-100. CIFAR-10, which is a 10-class dataset consisting of images of vehicles and animals, has a different distribution from CIFAR-100, which is a 100-class dataset featuring plants, insects, furniture, etc.

The graphs searched on CIFAR-10 achieved the comparable performance as those searched on CIFAR-100. The results indicate that the knowledge transfer graph can be reused to different dataset. As such, the reused graphs can greatly reduce the computational cost, since the searching process can be omitted.

5 Conclusion and Future Work

In this paper, we propose a new learning method for more flexible and diverse combinations of knowledge transfer using a novel graph representation called knowledge transfer graph. The graph provides a unified view of the knowledge transfer and has the potential to represent diverse knowledge transfer patterns. We also propose four gate functions that can deliver diverse combinations of knowledge transfer. Searching the graph structure, we discovered remarkable graphs that achieved significant performance improvements. We searched graphs over 1,000 trials, but the actual search space is much larger. A more exhaustive search will be the focus of future work.

Since our proposed method defines nodes as individual networks, it only transfers knowledge from the output layers of these networks. Future work will include knowledge transfer from an intermediate layer. It should also be possible to perform knowledge transfer using the ensemble inference of multiple networks. Other interesting possibilities include the introduction of an encoder/decoder model, and the use of multitasking.

Acknowledgement. This paper is based on results obtained from a project, JPNP18002, commissioned by the New Energy and Industrial Technology Development Organization (NEDO).

References

1. Huang, G., Liu, Z., Van Der Maaten, L., Weinberger, K.Q.: Densely connected convolutional networks. In: IEEE Conference on Computer Vision and Pattern Recognition, pp. 4700–4708 (2017)
2. Han, D., Kim, J., Kim, J.: Deep pyramidal residual networks. In: IEEE Conference on Computer Vision and Pattern Recognition (2017)
3. Xie, S., Girshick, R., Dollár, P., Tu, Z., He, K.: Aggregated residual transformations for deep neural networks. In: IEEE Conference on Computer Vision and Pattern Recognition (2017)
4. Hu, J., Shen, L., Sun, G.: Squeeze-and-excitation networks. In: IEEE Conference on Computer Vision and Pattern Recognition (2018)
5. Zoph, B., Le, Q.V.: Neural architecture search with reinforcement learning. In: International Conference on Learning Representations (2017)
6. Liu, C., et al.: Progressive neural architecture search. In: Ferrari, V., Hebert, M., Sminchisescu, C., Weiss, Y. (eds.) ECCV 2018. LNCS, vol. 11205, pp. 19–35. Springer, Cham (2018). https://doi.org/10.1007/978-3-030-01246-5_2
7. Pham, H., Guan, M., Zoph, B., Le, Q., Dean, J.: Efficient neural architecture search via parameters sharing. In: International Conference on Machine Learning, pp. 4095–4104 (2018)
8. Liu, H., Simonyan, K., Yang, Y.: DARTS: differentiable architecture search. In: International Conference on Learning Representations (2019)
9. Hinton, G., Vinyals, O., Dean, J.: Distilling the knowledge in a neural network. In: NIPS Deep Learning and Representation Learning Workshop (2015)
10. Zhang, Y., Xiang, T., Hospedales, T.M., Lu, H.: Deep mutual learning. In: IEEE Conference on Computer Vision and Pattern Recognition (2018)

11. Romero, A., Ballas, N., Kahou, S.E., Chassang, A., Gatta, C., Bengio, Y.: FitNets: hints for thin deep nets. In: International Conference on Learning Representations (2015)
12. Furlanello, T., Lipton, Z., Tschannen, M., Itti, L., Anandkumar, A.: Born again neural networks. In: International Conference on Machine Learning, Volume 80 of Proceedings of Machine Learning Research, Stockholmsmässan, Stockholm Sweden, pp. 1607–1616. PMLR (2018)
13. Mirzadeh, S.I., Farajtabar, M., Li, A., Ghasemzadeh, H.: Improved knowledge distillation via teacher assistant: bridging the gap between student and teacher. arXiv preprint arXiv:1902.03393 (2019)
14. Song, G., Chai, W.: Collaborative learning for deep neural networks. In: Advances in Neural Information Processing Systems, pp. 1837–1846 (2018)
15. Lan, X., Zhu, X., Gong, S.: Knowledge distillation by on-the-fly native ensemble. In: Advances in Neural Information Processing Systems, pp. 7527–7537 (2018)
16. Ke, Z., Wang, D., Yan, Q., Ren, J., Lau, R.W.: Dual student: breaking the limits of the teacher in semi-supervised learning. In: Proceedings of the IEEE International Conference on Computer Vision (2019)
17. Cho, J.H., Hariharan, B.: On the efficacy of knowledge distillation. In: International Conference on Computer Vision (2019)
18. Yim, J., Joo, D., Bae, J., Kim, J.: A gift from knowledge distillation: fast optimization, network minimization and transfer learning. In: IEEE Conference on Computer Vision and Pattern Recognition, pp. 4133–4141 (2017)
19. Zagoruyko, S., Komodakis, N.: Paying more attention to attention: improving the performance of convolutional neural networks via attention transfer. In: International Conference on Learning Representations (2017)
20. Heo, B., Kim, J., Yun, S., Park, H., Kwak, N., Choi, J.Y.: A comprehensive overhaul of feature distillation. In: International Conference on Computer Vision (2019)
21. Park, W., Kim, D., Lu, Y., Cho, M.: Relational knowledge distillation. In: IEEE Conference on Computer Vision and Pattern Recognition (2019)
22. Yu, L., Yazici, V.O., Liu, X., Weijer, J.v.d., Cheng, Y., Ramisa, A.: Learning metrics from teachers: compact networks for image embedding. In: IEEE Conference on Computer Vision and Pattern Recognition (2019)
23. Liu, Y., et al.: Knowledge distillation via instance relationship graph. In: IEEE Conference on Computer Vision and Pattern Recognition (2019)
24. Chen, G., Choi, W., Yu, X., Han, T., Chandraker, M.: Learning efficient object detection models with knowledge distillation. In: Advances in Neural Information Processing Systems, pp. 742–751 (2017)
25. Chen, Y., Li, W., Van Gool, L.: ROAD: reality oriented adaptation for semantic segmentation of urban scenes. In: IEEE Conference on Computer Vision and Pattern Recognition, pp. 7892–7901 (2018)
26. Oord, A.v.d., et al.: Parallel WaveNet: fast high-fidelity speech synthesis. arXiv preprint arXiv:1711.10433 (2017)
27. Chaudhari, P., et al.: Entropy-SGD: biasing gradient descent into wide valleys. In: International Conference on Learning Representations (2017)
28. Pereyra, G., Tucker, G., Chorowski, J., Kaiser, L., Hinton, G.: Regularizing neural networks by penalizing confident output distributions. In: International Conference on Learning Representations (2017)
29. Sun, D., Yao, A., Zhou, A., Zhao, H.: Deeply-supervised knowledge synergy. In: IEEE Conference on Computer Vision and Pattern Recognition (2019)

30. Anil, R., Pereyra, G., Passos, A., Ormandi, R., Dahl, G.E., Hinton, G.E.: Large scale distributed neural network training through online distillation. arXiv preprint arXiv:1804.03235 (2018)
31. Zhang, X., et al.: AlignedReID: surpassing human-level performance in person re-identification. arXiv preprint arXiv:1711.08184 (2017)
32. Li, L., et al.: Massively parallel hyperparameter tuning. arXiv preprint arXiv:1810.05934 (2018)
33. Krizhevsky, A., Hinton, G.: Learning multiple layers of features from tiny images. Technical report, Citeseer (2009)
34. Tiny imagenet visual recognition challenge (2015). https://tiny-imagenet. herokuapp.com/
35. Russakovsky, O., et al.: ImageNet large scale visual recognition challenge. Int. J. Comput. Vis. **115**, 211–252 (2015)
36. He, K., Zhang, X., Ren, S., Sun, J.: Deep residual learning for image recognition. In: IEEE Conference on Computer Vision and Pattern Recognition, pp. 770–778 (2016)
37. Zagoruyko, S., Komodakis, N.: Wide residual networks. In: British Machine Vision Conference, pp. 87.1–87.12. BMVA Press (2016)
38. Paszke, A., et al.: PyTorch: an imperative style, high-performance deep learning library. In: Advances in Neural Information Processing Systems, pp. 8026–8037 (2019)
39. Akiba, T., Sano, S., Yanase, T., Ohta, T., Koyama, M.: Optuna: a next-generation hyperparameter optimization framework. In: Proceedings of the 25th ACM SIGKDD International Conference on Knowledge Discovery & Data Mining, pp. 2623–2631 (2019)

Regularizing Meta-learning
via Gradient Dropout

Hung-Yu Tseng[1]([✉]), Yi-Wen Chen[1], Yi-Hsuan Tsai[2], Sifei Liu[3], Yen-Yu Lin[4], and Ming-Hsuan Yang[1,5]

[1] University of California, Merced, Merced, USA
{htseng6,ychen319}@ucmerced.edu
[2] NEC Laboratories America, Princeton, USA
[3] Nvidia Research, Santa Clara, USA
[4] National Chiao Tung University, Hsinchu, Taiwan
[5] Google Research, Cambridge, USA

Abstract. With the growing attention on learning-to-learn new tasks using only a few examples, meta-learning has been widely used in numerous problems such as few-shot classification, reinforcement learning, and domain generalization. However, meta-learning models are prone to overfitting when there are no sufficient training tasks for the meta-learners to generalize. Although existing approaches such as Dropout are widely used to address the overfitting problem, these methods are typically designed for regularizing models of a single task in supervised training. In this paper, we introduce a simple yet effective method to alleviate the risk of overfitting for gradient-based meta-learning. Specifically, during the gradient-based adaptation stage, we randomly drop the gradient in the inner-loop optimization of each parameter in deep neural networks, such that the augmented gradients improve generalization to new tasks. We present a general form of the proposed gradient dropout regularization and show that this term can be sampled from either the Bernoulli or Gaussian distribution. To validate the proposed method, we conduct extensive experiments and analysis on numerous computer vision tasks, demonstrating that the gradient dropout regularization mitigates the overfitting problem and improves the performance upon various gradient-based meta-learning frameworks.

1 Introduction

In recent years, significant progress has been made in meta-learning, which is also known as *learning to learn*. One common setting is that, given only a few training examples, meta-learning aims to learn new *tasks* rapidly by leveraging

---

H.-Y. Tseng and Y.-W. Chen—Equal contribution.

Electronic supplementary material The online version of this chapter (https://doi.org/10.1007/978-3-030-69538-5_14) contains supplementary material, which is available to authorized users.

the past experience acquired from the known tasks. It is a vital machine learning problem due to the potential for reducing the amount of data and time for adapting an existing system. Numerous recent methods successfully demonstrate how to adopt meta-learning algorithms to solve various learning problems, such as few-shot classification [1–3], reinforcement learning [4,5], and domain generalization [6,7].

Despite the demonstrated success, meta-learning frameworks are prone to overfitting [8] when there do not exist sufficient training tasks for the meta-learners to generalize. For instance, the mini-ImageNet [9] few-shot classification dataset contains only 64 training categories. Since the training tasks can be only sampled from this small set of classes, meta-learning models may overfit and fail to generalize to new testing tasks.

Significant efforts have been made to address the overfitting issue in the supervised learning framework, where the model is developed to learn a *single* task (*e.g.*, recognizing the same set of categories in both training and testing phases). The Dropout [10] method randomly drops (zeros) intermediate activations in deep neural networks during the training stage. Relaxing the limitation of binary dropout, the Gaussian dropout [11] scheme augments activations with noise sampled from a Gaussian distribution. Numerous methods [12–16] further improve the Dropout method by injecting structural noise or scheduling the dropout process to facilitate the training procedure. Nevertheless, these methods are developed to regularize the models to learn a single task, which may not be effective for meta-learning frameworks.

In this paper, we address the overfitting issue [8] in gradient-based meta-learning. As shown in Fig. 1(a), given a new task, the meta-learning framework aims to adapt model parameters θ to be θ' via the gradients computed according to the few examples (support data $\mathcal{X}^s$). This gradient-based adaptation process is also known as the *inner-loop* optimization. To alleviate the overfitting issue, one straightforward approach is to apply the existing dropout method to the model weights directly. However, there are two sets of model parameters θ and θ' in the inner-loop optimization. As such, during the meta-training stage, applying normal dropout would cause inconsistent randomness, *i.e.*, dropped neurons, between these two sets of model parameters. To tackle this issue, we propose a dropout method on the gradients in the inner-loop optimization, denoted as *DropGrad*, to regularize the training procedure. This approach naturally bridges θ and θ', and thereby involves only one randomness for the dropout regularization. We also note that our method is model-agnostic and generalized to various gradient-based meta-learning frameworks such as [1,17,18]. In addition, we demonstrate that the proposed dropout term can be formulated in a general form, where either the binary or Gaussian distribution can be utilized to sample the noise, as demonstrated in Fig. 1(b).

To evaluate the proposed DropGrad method, we conduct experiments on numerous computer vision tasks, including few-shot classification on the mini-ImageNet [9], online object tracking [19], and few-shot viewpoint estimation [20], showing that the DropGrad scheme can be applied to and improve different tasks. In addition, we present comprehensive analysis by using various meta-learning frameworks, adopting different dropout probabilities, and explaining which layers to apply gradient dropout. To further demonstrate the generalization ability of DropGrad, we perform a challenging cross-domain few-shot classification task, in which the meta-training and meta-testing sets are from two different distributions, *i.e.*, the mini-ImageNet and CUB [21] datasets. We show that with the proposed method, the performance is significantly improved under the cross-domain setting. Our source code is available at https://github.com/hytseng0509/DropGrad.

In this paper, we make the following contributions:

- We propose a simple yet effective gradient dropout approach to improve the generalization ability of gradient-based meta-learning frameworks.
- We present a general form for gradient dropout and show that both binary and Gaussian sampling schemes mitigate the overfitting issue.
- We demonstrate the effectiveness and generalizability of the proposed method via extensive experiments on numerous computer vision tasks.

2   Related Work

Meta-Learning. Meta-learning aims to adapt the past knowledge learned from previous tasks to new tasks with few training instances. Most meta-learning algorithms can be categorized into three groups: 1) Memory-based approaches [2,22] utilize recurrent networks to process few training examples of new tasks sequentially; 2) Metric-based frameworks [3,9,23,24] make predictions by referring to the features encoded from the input data and training instances in a generic metric space; 3) Gradient-based methods [1,8,17,18,25–27] learn to optimize the model via gradient descent with few examples, which is the focus of this work. In the third group, the MAML [1] approach learns model initialization (*i.e.*, initial parameters) that is amenable to fast fine-tuning with few instances. In addition to model initialization, the MetaSGD [18] method learns a set of learning rates for different model parameters. Furthermore, the MAML++ [17] algorithm makes several improvements based on the MAML method to facilitate the training process with additional performance gain. However, these methods are still prone to overfitting as the dataset for the training tasks is insufficient for the model to adapt well. Recently, Kim *et al.* [8] and Rusu *et al.* [26] address this issue via the Bayesian approach and latent embeddings. Nevertheless, these methods employ additional parameters or networks which entail significant computational overhead and may not be applicable to arbitrary frameworks. In contrast, the proposed gradient dropout regularization does not impose any overhead and thus can be readily integrated into the gradient-based models mentioned above.

Dropout Regularization. Built upon the Dropout [10] method, various schemes [12–15,28] have been proposed to regularize the training process of deep neural networks for supervised learning. The core idea is to inject noise into intermediate activations when training deep neural networks. Several recent studies improve the regularization on convolutional neural networks by making the injected structural noise. For instance, the SpatialDropout [14] method drops the entire channel from an activation map, the DropPath [13,16] scheme chooses to discard an entire layer, and the DropBlock [12] algorithm zeros multiple continuous regions in an activation map. Nevertheless, these approaches are designed for deep neural networks that aim to learn a *single* task, *e.g.*, learning to recognize a fixed set of categories. In contrast, our algorithm aims to regularize the gradient-based meta-learning frameworks that suffer from the overfitting issue on the *task*-level, *e.g.*, introducing new tasks.

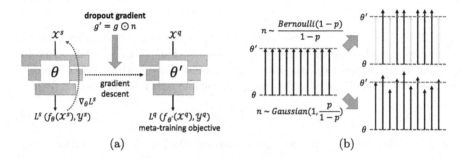

Fig. 1. Illustration of the proposed method. (a) The proposed DropGrad method imposes a noise term n to augment the gradient in the inner-loop optimization during the meta-training stage. (b) The DropGrad method samples the noise term n from either the Bernoulli or Gaussian distribution, in which the Gaussian distribution provides a better way to account for uncertainty.

3   Gradient Dropout Regularization

Before introducing details of our proposed dropout regularization on gradients, we first review the gradient-based meta-learning framework.

3.1   Preliminaries for Meta-learning

In meta-learning, multiple tasks $\mathcal{T} = \{T_1, T_2, ..., T_n\}$ are divided into meta-training $\mathcal{T}^{\text{train}}$, meta-validation $\mathcal{T}^{\text{val}}$, and meta-testing $\mathcal{T}^{\text{test}}$ sets. Each task T_i consists of a support set $D^s = (\mathcal{X}^s, \mathcal{Y}^s)$ and a query set $D^q = (\mathcal{X}^q, \mathcal{Y}^q)$, where $\mathcal{X}$ and $\mathcal{Y}$ are a set of input data and the corresponding ground-truth. The support set D^s represents the set of few labeled data for learning, while the query set D^q indicates the set of data to be predicted.

Given a novel task and a parametric model f_θ, the objective of a gradient-based approach during the meta-training stage is to minimize the prediction loss L^q on the query set D^q according to the signals provided from the support set D^s, and thus the model f_θ can be adapted. Figure 1(a) shows an overview of the MAML [1] method, which offers a general formulation of gradient-based frameworks. For each iteration of the meta-training phase, we first randomly sample a task $T = \{D^s, D^q\}$ from the meta-training set T^{train}. We then adapt the initial parameters θ to be task-specific parameters θ' via gradient descent:

$$\theta' = \theta - \alpha \odot g, \tag{1}$$

where α is the learning rate for gradient-based adaptation and $\odot$ is the operation of element-wise product, $i.e.$, Hadamard product. The term g in (1) is the set of gradients computed according to the objectives of model f_θ on the support set $D^s = (\mathcal{X}^s, \mathcal{Y}^s)$:

$$g = \nabla_\theta L^s(f_\theta(\mathcal{X}^s), \mathcal{Y}^s). \tag{2}$$

We call the step of (1) as the inner-loop optimization and typically, we can do multiple gradient steps for (1), $e.g.$, smaller than 10 in general. After the gradient-based adaptation, the initial parameters θ are optimized according to the loss functions of the adapted model $f_{\theta'}$ on the query set $D^q = (\mathcal{X}^q, \mathcal{Y}^q)$:

$$\theta = \theta - \eta \nabla_\theta L^q(f_{\theta'}(\mathcal{X}^q), \mathcal{Y}^q), \tag{3}$$

where η is the learning rate for meta-training. During the meta-testing stage, the model f_θ is adapted according to the support set D^s and the prediction on query data $\mathcal{X}^q$ is made without accessing the ground-truth $\mathcal{Y}^q$ in the query set. We note that several methods are built upon the above formulation introduced in the MAML method. For example, the learning rate α for gradient-adaptation is viewed as the optimization objective [17,18], and the initial parameters θ are not generic but conditional on the support set D^s [26].

3.2   Gradient Dropout

The main idea is to impose uncertainty to the core objective during the meta-training step, $i.e.$, the gradient g in the inner-loop optimization, such that θ' receives gradients with noise to improve the generalization of gradient-based models. As described in Sect. 3.1, adapting the model θ to θ' involves the gradient update in the inner-loop optimization formulated in (2). Based on this observation, we propose to randomly drop the gradient in (2), $i.e.$, g, during the inner-loop optimization, as illustrated in Fig. 1. Specifically, we augment the gradient g as follows:

$$g' = g \odot n, \tag{4}$$

where n is a noise regularization term sampled from a pre-defined distribution. With the formulation of (4), in the following we introduce two noise regularization strategies via sampling from different distributions, $i.e.$, the Bernoulli and Gaussian distributions.

Binary DropGrad. We randomly zero the gradient with the probability p, in which the process can be formulated as:

$$g' = g \odot n_b, \quad n_b \sim \frac{Bernoulli(1-p)}{1-p}, \tag{5}$$

where the denominator $1-p$ is the normalization factor. Note that, different from the Dropout [10] method which randomly drops the intermediate activations in a supervised learning network under a single task setting, we perform the dropout on the gradient level.

Gaussian DropGrad. One limitation of the Binary DropGrad scheme is that the noise term n_b is only applied in a binary form, which is either 0 or $1-p$. To address this disadvantage and provide a better regularization with uncertainty, we extend the Bernoulli distribution to the Gaussian formulation. Since the expectation and variance of the noise term n_b in the Binary DropGrad method are respectively $E(n_b) = 1$ and $\sigma^2(n_b) = \frac{p}{1-p}$, we can augment the gradient g with noise sampled from the Gaussian distribution:

$$g' = g \odot n_g, \quad n_g \sim Gaussian(1, \frac{p}{1-p}). \tag{6}$$

Algorithm 1: Applying DropGrad on MAML [1]

---

1 **Require:** a set of training tasks $\mathcal{T}^{\text{train}}$, adaptation learning rate α, meta-learning rate η
2 randomly initialize θ
3 **while** *training* **do**
4   randomly sample a task $T = \{D^s(\mathcal{X}^s, \mathcal{Y}^s), D^q(\mathcal{X}^q, \mathcal{Y}^q)\}$ from $\mathcal{T}^{\text{train}}$
5      $g = \nabla_\theta L^s(f_\theta(\mathcal{X}^s), \mathcal{Y}^s)$
6   compute g' according to (5) or (6)   // Apply DropGrad
7      $\theta' = \theta - \alpha \times g'$
8      $\theta = \theta - \eta \nabla_\theta L^q(f_{\theta'}(\mathcal{X}^q), \mathcal{Y}^q)$
9 **end**

As a result, two noise terms n_b and n_g are statistically comparable with the same dropout probability p. In Fig. 1(b), we illustrate the difference between the Binary DropGrad and Gaussian DropGrad approaches. We also show the process of applying the proposed regularization using the MAML [1] method in Algorithm 1, while similar procedures can be applied to other gradient-based meta-learning frameworks, such as MetaSGD [18] and MAML++ [17].

4 Experimental Results

In this section, we evaluate the effectiveness of the proposed DropGrad method by conducting extensive experiments on three learning problems: few-shot classification, online object tracking, and few-shot viewpoint estimation. In addition, for the few-shot classification experiments, we analyze the effect of using binary and Gaussian noise, which layers to apply DropGrad, and performance in the cross-domain setting.

4.1   Few-Shot Classification

Few-shot classification aims to recognize a set of new categories, *e.g.,* five categories (5-way classification), with few, *e.g.,* one (1-shot) or five (5-shot), example images from each category. In this setting, the support set D^s contains the few images $\mathcal{X}^s$ of the new categories and the corresponding categorical annotation $\mathcal{Y}^s$. We conduct experiments on the mini-ImageNet [9] dataset, which is widely used for evaluating few-shot classification approaches. As a subset of the ImageNet [29], the mini-ImageNet dataset contains 100 categories and 600 images for each category. We use the 5-way evaluation protocol in [30] and split the dataset into 64 training, 16 validating, and 20 testing categories.

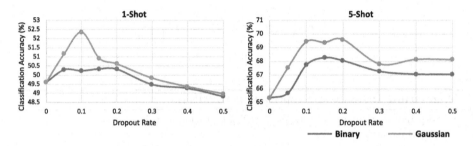

Fig. 2. Comparison between the proposed Binary and Gaussian DropGrad methods. We compare the 1-shot (*left*) and 5-shot (*right*) performance of MAML [1] trained with two different forms of DropGrad under various dropout rates on mini-ImageNet. The proposed DropGrad method is particularly effective with the dropout rate in $[0.1, 0.2]$. Moreover, the Gaussian DropGrad method consistently obtains better results compared to the Binary DropGrad scheme. Therefore, we apply the Gaussian DropGrad method with the dropout rate of 0.1 or 0.2 in all of our experiments.

Implementation Details. We apply the proposed DropGrad regularization method to train the following gradient-based meta-learning frameworks: MAML [1], MetaSGD [18], and MAML++ [17]. We use the implementation from Chen *et al.* [31] for MAML and use our own implementation for MetaSGD.[1] We use the ResNet-18 [32] model as the backbone network for both MAML and MetaSGD. As for MAML++, we use the original source code.[2] Similar to recent studies [26], we also pre-train the feature extractor of ResNet-18 by minimizing the classification loss on the 64 training categories from the mini-ImageNet dataset for the MetaSGD method, which is denoted by MetaSGD*.

For all the experiments, we use the *default hyper-parameter settings* provided by the original implementation. Moreover, we select the model according to the validation performance for evaluation (*i.e., early stopping strategy*).

Comparison between Binary and Gaussian DropGrad. We first evaluate how the proposed Binary and Gaussian DropGrad methods perform on the

---

[1] https://github.com/wyharveychen/CloserLookFewShot.
[2] https://github.com/AntreasAntoniou/HowToTrainYourMAMLPytorch.

MAML framework with different values of the dropout probability p. Figure 2 shows that both methods are effective especially when the dropout rate is in the range of $[0.1, 0.2]$, while setting the dropout rate to 0 is to turn the proposed DropGrad method off. Since the problem of learning from only one instance (1-shot) is more complicated, the overfitting effect is less severe compared to the 5-shot setting. As a result, applying the DropGrad method with a dropout rate larger than 0.3 degrades the performance. Moreover, the Gaussian Drop-Grad method consistently outperforms the binary case on both 1-shot and 5-shot tasks, due to a better regularization term n_g with uncertainty. We then apply the Gaussian DropGrad method with the dropout rate of 0.1 or 0.2 in the following experiments.

Table 1. Few-shot classification results on mini-ImageNet. The Gaussian Drop-Grad method improves the performance of gradient-based models on 1-shot and 5-shot classification tasks.

Model	1-shot	5-shot
MAML [1]	$49.61 \pm 0.92\%$	$65.72 \pm 0.77\%$
MAML w/ Gaussian DropGrad	$\mathbf{52.35 \pm 0.86\%}$	$\mathbf{69.42 \pm 0.73\%}$
MetaSGD [18]	$51.51 \pm 0.87\%$	$69.67 \pm 0.75\%$
MetaSGD w/ Gaussian DropGrad	$\mathbf{53.38 \pm 0.93\%}$	$\mathbf{71.14 \pm 0.72\%}$
MetaSGD*	$60.44 \pm 0.87\%$	$72.55 \pm 0.54\%$
MetaSGD* w/ Gaussian DropGrad	$\mathbf{61.69 \pm 0.84\%}$	$\mathbf{73.33 \pm 0.57\%}$
MAML++ [17]	$50.21 \pm 0.50\%$	$68.66 \pm 0.46\%$
MAML++ w/ Gaussian DropGrad	$\mathbf{51.13 \pm 0.50\%}$	$\mathbf{69.80 \pm 0.46\%}$

Table 2. Performance of applying DropGrad to different layers. We conduct experiments on the 5-shot classification task using MAML on mini-ImageNet. It is more helpful in improving the performance by dropping the gradients closer to the output layers (*e.g.*, FC and Block4 + FC).

Origin	FC	Block4 + FC	Full	Block1 + Conv	Conv
$65.72 \pm 0.77\%$	$68.93 \pm 0.55\%$	$69.02 \pm 0.57\%$	$69.42 \pm 0.73\%$	$64.96 \pm 0.80\%$	$65.53 \pm 0.75\%$

Comparison with Existing Dropout Methods. To show that the proposed DropGrad method is effective for gradient-based meta-learning frameworks, we compare it with two existing dropout schemes applied on the network activations in both f_θ and f'_θ. We choose the Dropout [10] and SpatialDropout [14] methods, since the former is a commonly-used approach while the latter is shown to be effective for applying to 2D convolutional maps. The performance of MAML on 5-shot classification on the mini-ImageNet dataset is: *DropGrad* $69.42 \pm 0.73\%$, *SpatialDropout* $68.09 \pm 0.56\%$, and *Vanilla Dropout* $67.44 \pm 0.57\%$. This demonstrates the benefit of using the proposed DropGrad method, which effectively tackles the issue of inconsistent randomness between two different models f_θ and f'_θ in the inner-loop optimization of gradient-based meta-learning frameworks.

Overall Performance on the Mini-ImageNet Dataset. Table 1 shows the results of applying the proposed Gaussian DropGrad method to different frameworks. The results validate that the proposed regularization scheme consistently improves the performance of various gradient-based meta-learning approaches. In addition, we present the curve of validation loss over training episodes from MAML and MetaSGD on the 5-shot classification task in Fig. 3. We observe that the overfitting problem is more severe in training the MetaSGD method since it consists of more parameters to be optimized. The DropGrad regularization method mitigates the overfitting issue and facilitates the training procedure.

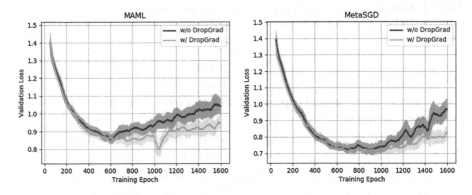

Fig. 3. Validation loss over training epochs. We show the validation curves of the MAML (*left*) and MetaSGD (*right*) frameworks trained on the 5-shot mini-ImageNet dataset. The curves and shaded regions represent the mean and standard deviation of validation loss over 50 epochs. The curves validate that the proposed DropGrad method alleviates the overfitting problem.

Table 3. 5-shot classification results of MAML under various hyper-parameter settings. We study the learning rate α and number of iterations n_{inner} in the inner-loop optimization of MAML using mini-ImageNet dataset.

α, n_{inner}	0.01, 5 (original)	0.1, 5	0.001, 5	0.01, 3	0.01, 7
MAML [1]	$65.72 \pm 0.77\%$	$65.98 \pm 0.79\%$	$58.55 \pm 0.80\%$	$64.84 \pm 0.80\%$	$68.11 \pm 0.74\%$
MAML w/ DropGrad	$\mathbf{69.42 \pm 0.73\%}$	$\mathbf{67.78 \pm 0.73\%}$	$\mathbf{64.05 \pm 0.79\%}$	$\mathbf{65.42 \pm 0.80\%}$	$\mathbf{69.65 \pm 0.70\%}$

Layers to Apply DropGrad. We study which layers in the network to apply the DropGrad regularization in this experiment. The backbone ResNet-18 model contains a convolutional layer (Conv) followed by 4 residual blocks (Block1, Block2, Block3, Block4) and a fully-connected layer (FC) as the classifier. We perform the Gaussian DropGrad method on different parts of the ResNet-18 model for MAML on the 5-shot classification task. The results are presented in

Table 2. We find that it is more critical to drop the gradients closer to the output layers (*e.g.,* FC and Block4 + FC). Applying the DropGrad method to the input side (*e.g.,* Block1 + Conv and Conv), however, may even negatively affect the training and degrade the performance. This can be explained by the fact that features closer to the output side are more abstract and thus tend to overfit. As using the DropGrad regularization term only increases a negligible overhead, we use the *Full* model, where our method is applied to all layers in the experiments unless otherwise mentioned.

Hyper-Parameter Analysis. In all experiments shown in Sect. 4, we use the default hyper-parameter values from the original implementation of the adopted methods. In this experiment, we explore the hyper-parameter choices for MAML [1]. Specifically, we conduct an ablation study on the learning rate α and the number of inner-loop optimizations n_{inner} in MAML. As shown in Table 3, the proposed DropGrad method improves the performance consistently under different sets of hyper-parameters.

Table 4. Cross-Domain performance for few-shot classification. We use the mini-ImageNet and CUB datasets for the meta-training and meta-testing steps, respectively. The improvement of applying the proposed DropGrad method is more significant in the cross-domain cases than the intra-domain ones.

Model	1-Shot	5-Shot
MAML [1]	$31.52 \pm 0.52\%$	$45.56 \pm 0.51\%$
MAML w/ Dropout [10]	$31.84 \pm 0.49\%$	$46.48 \pm 0.50\%$
MAML w/ DropGrad	$\mathbf{33.20 \pm 0.67\%}$	$\mathbf{51.05 \pm 0.56\%}$
MetaSGD [18]	$34.52 \pm 0.63\%$	$49.22 \pm 0.58\%$
MetaSGD w/ Dropout [10]	$35.01 \pm 0.54\%$	$52.35 \pm 0.58\%$
MetaSGD w/ DropGrad	$\mathbf{36.77 \pm 0.72\%}$	$\mathbf{55.13 \pm 0.72\%}$
MetaSGD*	$43.98 \pm 0.77\%$	$57.95 \pm 0.81\%$
MetaSGD* w/ DropGrad	$\mathbf{45.33 \pm 0.81\%}$	$\mathbf{59.94 \pm 0.82\%}$
MAML++ [17]	$40.73 \pm 0.49\%$	$60.57 \pm 0.49\%$
MAML++ w/ Dropout [10]	$41.75 \pm 0.49\%$	$61.48 \pm 0.49\%$
MAML++ w/ DropGrad	$\mathbf{44.27 \pm 0.50\%}$	$\mathbf{63.79 \pm 0.48\%}$

4.2 Cross-domain Few-Shot Classification

To further evaluate how the proposed DropGrad method improves the generalization ability of gradient-based meta-learning models, we conduct a cross-domain experiment, in which the meta-testing set is from an *unseen* domain. We use the cross-domain scenario introduced by Chen *et al.* [31], where the meta-training step is performed on the mini-ImageNet [9] dataset while the meta-testing evaluation is conducted on the CUB [33] dataset. Note that, different

228   H.-Y. Tseng et al.

from Chen *et al.* [31] who select the model according to the validation performance on the CUB dataset, we pick the model via the validation performance on the mini-ImageNet dataset for evaluation. The reason is that we target at

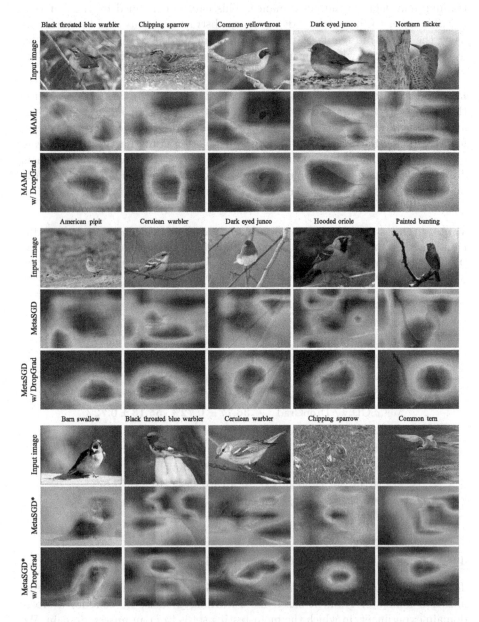

Fig. 4. Class activation maps (CAMs) for cross-domain 5-shot classification. The mini-ImageNet and CUB datasets are used for the meta-training and meta-testing steps, respectively. Models trained with the proposed DropGrad (the third row for each example) focus more on the objects than the original models (the second row for each example).

analyzing the generalization ability to the unseen domain, and thus we do not utilize any information provided from the CUB dataset.

Table 4 shows the results using the Gaussian DropGrad method. Since the domain shift in the cross-domain scenario is larger than that in the intra-domain case (*i.e.*, both training and testing tasks are sampled from the mini-ImageNet dataset), the performance gains of applying the proposed DropGrad method reported in Table 4 are more significant than those in Table 1. The results demonstrate that the DropGrad scheme is able to effectively regularize the gradients and transfer them for learning new tasks in an unseen domain.

Table 5. Precision and success rate on the OTB2015 dataset. The DropGrad method can be applied to visual tracking and improve the tracking performance.

Model	Precision	Success rate
MetaCREST [19]	0.7994	0.6029
MetaCREST w/ DropGrad	**0.8172**	**0.6145**
MetaSDNet [19]	0.8673	0.6434
MetaSDNet w/ DropGrad	**0.8746**	**0.6520**

To further understand the improvement by the proposed method under the cross-domain setting, we visualize the class activation maps (CAMs) [34] of the images in the unseen domain (CUB). More specifically, during the testing time, we adapt the learner model f_θ with the support set D^s. We then compute the class activation maps of the data in the query set D^q from the last convolutional layer of the updated learner model f'_θ. Figure 4 demonstrates the results of the MAML, MetaSGD, and MetaSGD* approaches. The models trained with the proposed regularization method show the activation on more discriminative regions. This suggests that the proposed regularization improves the generalization ability of gradient-based schemes, and thus enables these methods to adapt to the novel tasks sampled from the unseen domain.

Comparison with the Existing Dropout Approach. We also compare the proposed DropGrad approach with existing Dropout [10] method under the cross-domain setting. We apply the existing Dropout scheme on the network activations in both f_θ and f'_θ. As suggested by Ghiasi *et al.* [12], we use the dropout rate of 0.3 for the Dropout method. As the results shown in Table 4, the proposed DropGrad method performs favorably against the Dropout approach. The larger performance gain from the DropGrad approach validates effectiveness of imposing uncertainty on the inner-loop gradient for the gradient-based meta-learning framework. On the other hand, since applying the conventional Dropout causes the inconsistent randomnesses between two different sets of parameters f_θ and f'_θ, which is less effective compared to the proposed scheme.

230   H.-Y. Tseng et al.

4.3   Online Object Tracking

Visual object tracking targets at localizing one particular object in a video sequence given the bounding box annotation in the first frame. To adapt the model to the subsequent frames, one approach is to apply online adaptation during tracking. The Meta-Tracker [19] method uses meta-learning to improve two state-of-the-art online trackers, including the correlation-based CREST [35] and the detection-based MDNet [36], which are denoted as MetaCREST and MetaSDNet. Based on the error signals from future frames, the Meta-Tracker updates the model during offline meta-training, and obtains a robust initial network that generalizes well over future frames. We apply the proposed DropGrad method to train the MetaCREST and MetaSDNet models with evaluation on the OTB2015 [37] dataset.

Fig. 5. Qualitative results of object online tracking on the OTB2015 dataset. Red boxes are the ground-truth, yellow boxes represent the original results, and green boxes stand for the results where the DropGrad method is applied. Models trained with the proposed DropGrad scheme are able to track objects more accurately. (Color figure online)

Implementation Details. We train the models using the original source code.[3] For meta-training, we use a subset of a large-scale video detection dataset [38], and the 58 sequences from the VOT2013 [39], VOT2014 [40] and VOT2015 [41] datasets, excluding the sequences in the OTB2015 database, based on the same settings in the Meta-Tracker [19]. We apply the Gaussian DropGrad method

---

[3] https://github.com/silverbottlep/meta_trackers.

with the dropout rate of 0.2. We use the default hyper-parameter settings and evaluate the performance with the models at the last training iteration.

Object Tracking Results. The results of online object tracking on the OTB2015 dataset are presented in Table 5. The one-pass evaluation (OPE) protocol without restarts at failures is used in the experiments. We measure the precision and success rate based on the center location error and the bounding-box overlap ratio, respectively. The precision is calculated with a threshold 20, and the success rate is the averaged value with the threshold ranging from 0 to 1 with a step of 0.05. We show that applying the proposed DropGrad method consistently improves the performance in precision and success rate on both MetaCREST and MetaSDNet trackers. We present sample results of object online tracking in Fig. 5. We apply the proposed DropGrad method on the MetaCREST and MetaSDNet methods and evaluate these models on the OTB2015 dataset. Compared with the original MetaCREST and MetaSDNet, models trained with the DropGrad method track objects more accurately.

Table 6. Viewpoint estimation results. The DropGrad method can be applied to few-shot viewpoint estimation frameworks to mitigate the overfitting problem.

Model	Acc30 ($\uparrow$)	MedErr ($\downarrow$)
MetaView [20]	$45.00 \pm 0.45\%$	$33.60 \pm 0.94°$
MetaView w/ DropGrad	$\mathbf{46.16 \pm 0.55\%}$	$\mathbf{33.10 \pm 0.82°}$

4.4 Few-Shot Viewpoint Estimation

Viewpoint estimation aims to estimate the viewpoint (*i.e.*, 3D rotation), denoted as $R \in SO(3)$, between the camera and the object of a specific category in the image. Given a few examples (*i.e.*, 10 images in this work) of a novel category with viewpoint annotations, few-shot viewpoint estimation attempts to predict the viewpoint of arbitrary objects of the same category. In this problem, the support set D^s contains few images $\mathbf{x}^s$ of a new class and the corresponding viewpoint annotations $\mathbf{y}^s$. We conduct experiments on the ObjectNet3D [42] dataset, a viewpoint estimation benchmark dataset which contains 100 categories. Using the same evaluation protocol in [20], we extract 76 and 17 categories for training and testing, respectively.

Implementation Details. We apply the regularization on the MetaView [20] method, which is a meta-Siamese viewpoint estimator that applies gradient-based adaptation for novel categories. We obtain the source code from the authors, and keep all the default setting for training. We apply the Gaussian DropGrad scheme with the dropout rate of 0.1. Since there is no validation set available, we pick the model trained in the last epoch for evaluation.

Viewpoint Estimation Results. We show the viewpoint estimation results in Table 6. The evaluation metrics include Acc30 and MedErr, which represent the percentage of viewpoints with rotation error under 30° and the median rotation error, respectively. The overall performance is improved by applying the proposed DropGrad method to the MetaView model during training.

5   Conclusions

In this work, we propose a simple yet effective gradient dropout approach for regularizing the training of gradient-based meta-learning frameworks. The core idea is to impose uncertainty by augmenting the gradient in the adaptation step during meta-training. We propose two forms of noise regularization terms, including the Bernoulli and Gaussian distributions, and demonstrate that the proposed DropGrad improves the model performance in three learning tasks. In addition, extensive analysis and studies are provided to further understand the benefit of our method. One study on cross-domain few-shot classification is also conducted to show that the DropGrad method is able to mitigate the overfitting issue under a larger domain gap.

References

1. Finn, C., Abbeel, P., Levine, S.: Model-agnostic meta-learning for fast adaptation of deep networks. In: ICML (2017)
2. Santoro, A., Bartunov, S., Botvinick, M., Wierstra, D., Lillicrap, T.: Meta-learning with memory-augmented neural networks. In: ICML (2016)
3. Snell, J., Swersky, K., Zemel, R.: Prototypical networks for few-shot learning. In: NIPS (2017)
4. Gupta, A., Mendonca, R., Liu, Y., Abbeel, P., Levine, S.: Meta-reinforcement learning of structured exploration strategies. In: NeurIPS (2018)
5. Rakelly, K., Zhou, A., Quillen, D., Finn, C., Levine, S.: Efficient off-policy meta-reinforcement learning via probabilistic context variables. In: ICML (2019)
6. Balaji, Y., Sankaranarayanan, S., Chellappa, R.: Metareg: Towards domain generalization using meta-regularization. In: NeurIPS (2018)
7. Li, D., Yang, Y., Song, Y.Z., Hospedales, T.M.: Learning to generalize: Meta-learning for domain generalization. In: AAAI (2018)
8. Kim, T., Yoon, J., Dia, O., Kim, S., Bengio, Y., Ahn, S.: Bayesian model-agnostic meta-learning. In: NeurIPS (2018)
9. Vinyals, O., Blundell, C., Lillicrap, T., Wierstra, D., et al.: Matching networks for one shot learning. In: NIPS (2016)
10. Srivastava, N., Hinton, G., Krizhevsky, A., Sutskever, I., Salakhutdinov, R.: Dropout: a simple way to prevent neural networks from overfitting. JMLR **15**, 1929–1958 (2014)
11. Wang, S., Manning, C.: Fast dropout training. In: ICML (2013)
12. Ghiasi, G., Lin, T.Y., Le, Q.V.: Dropblock: a regularization method for convolutional networks. In: NeurIPS (2018)
13. Larsson, G., Maire, M., Shakhnarovich, G.: Fractalnet: ultra-deep neural networks without residuals. In: ICLR (2017)
14. Tompson, J., Goroshin, R., Jain, A., LeCun, Y., Bregler, C.: Efficient object localization using convolutional networks. In: CVPR (2015)

15. Wan, L., Zeiler, M., Zhang, S., Le Cun, Y., Fergus, R.: Regularization of neural networks using dropconnect. In: ICML (2013)
16. Zoph, B., Vasudevan, V., Shlens, J., Le, Q.V.: Learning transferable architectures for scalable image recognition. In: CVPR (2018)
17. Antoniou, A., Edwards, H., Storkey, A.: How to train your maml. In: ICLR (2019)
18. Li, Z., Zhou, F., Chen, F., Li, H.: Meta-sgd: Learning to learn quickly for few shot learning. arXiv preprint arXiv:1707.09835 (2017)
19. Park, E., Berg, A.C.: Meta-tracker: fast and robust online adaptation for visual object trackers. In: Ferrari, V., Hebert, M., Sminchisescu, C., Weiss, Y. (eds.) ECCV 2018. LNCS, vol. 11207, pp. 587–604. Springer, Cham (2018). https://doi.org/10.1007/978-3-030-01219-9_35
20. Tseng, H.Y., et al.: Few-shot viewpoint estimation. In: BMVC (2019)
21. Welinder, P., et al.: Caltech-ucsd birds 200. Technical report CNS-TR-2010-001, California Institute of Technology (2010)
22. Rezende, D.J., Mohamed, S., Danihelka, I., Gregor, K., Wierstra, D.: One-shot generalization in deep generative models. JMLR **48**, (2016)
23. Oreshkin, B., López, P.R., Lacoste, A.: Tadam: task dependent adaptive metric for improved few-shot learning. In: NeurIPS (2018)
24. Sung, F., Yang, Y., Zhang, L., Xiang, T., Torr, P.H., Hospedales, T.M.: Learning to compare: relation network for few-shot learning. In: CVPR (2018)
25. Finn, C., Xu, K., Levine, S.: Probabilistic model-agnostic meta-learning. In: NeurIPS (2018)
26. Rusu, A.A., et al.: Meta-learning with latent embedding optimization. In: ICLR (2019)
27. Ravi, S., Beatson, A.: Amortized bayesian meta-learning. In: ICLR (2019)
28. Goodfellow, I.J., Warde-Farley, D., Mirza, M., Courville, A., Bengio, Y.: Maxout networks. In: ICML (2013)
29. Deng, J., Dong, W., Socher, R., Li, L.J., Li, K., Fei-Fei, L.: ImageNet: a large-scale hierarchical image database. In: CVPR (2009)
30. Ravi, S., Larochelle, H.: Optimization as a model for few-shot learning. In: ICLR (2017)
31. Chen, W.Y., Liu, Y.C., Kira, Z., Wang, Y.C., Huang, J.B.: A closer look at few-shot classification. In: ICLR (2019)
32. He, K., Zhang, X., Ren, S., Sun, J.: Deep residual learning for image recognition. In: CVPR (2016)
33. Hilliard, N., Phillips, L., Howland, S., Yankov, A., Corley, C.D., Hodas, N.O.: Few-shot learning with metric-agnostic conditional embeddings. arXiv preprint arXiv:1802.04376 (2018)
34. Zhou, B., Khosla, A., Lapedriza, A., Oliva, A., Torralba, A.: Learning deep features for discriminative localization. In: CVPR (2016)
35. Song, Y., Ma, C., Gong, L., Zhang, J., Lau, R.W.H., Yang, M.H.: Crest: convolutional residual learning for visual tracking. In: ICCV (2017)
36. Nam, H., Han, B.: Learning multi-domain convolutional neural networks for visual tracking. In: CVPR (2016)
37. Wu, Y., Lim, J., Yang, M.H.: Object tracking benchmark. TPAMI (2015)
38. Russakovsky, O., et al.: Imagenet large scale visual recognition challenge. IJCV (2015)
39. Kristan, M., et al.: T.V.: The visual object tracking vot2013 challenge results. In: ICCV Workshop (2013)
40. Kristan, M., et al., A.L.: The visual object tracking vot2014 challenge results. In: ECCV Workshop (2014)

41. Kristan, M., et al., G.N.: The visual object tracking vot2015 challenge results. In: ICCV Workshop (2015)
42. Xiang, Yu., et al.: ObjectNet3D: a large scale database for 3D object recognition. In: Leibe, B., Matas, J., Sebe, N., Welling, M. (eds.) ECCV 2016. LNCS, vol. 9912, pp. 160–176. Springer, Cham (2016). https://doi.org/10.1007/978-3-319-46484-8_10

Vax-a-Net: Training-Time Defence Against Adversarial Patch Attacks

T. Gittings[1]([✉]), S. Schneider[2], and J. Collomosse[1]

[1] Centre for Vision Speech and Signal Processing (CVSSP), University of Surrey,
Guildford, UK
{t.gittings,s.schneider,j.collomosse}@surrey.ac.uk
[2] Surrey Centre for Cyber Security (SCCS), University of Surrey, Guildford, UK

Abstract. We present Vax-a-Net; a technique for immunizing convolutional neural networks (CNNs) against adversarial patch attacks (APAs). APAs insert visually overt, local regions (patches) into an image to induce misclassification. We introduce a conditional Generative Adversarial Network (GAN) architecture that simultaneously learns to synthesise patches for use in APAs, whilst exploiting those attacks to adapt a pre-trained target CNN to reduce its susceptibility to them. This approach enables resilience against APAs to be conferred to pre-trained models, which would be impractical with conventional adversarial training due to the slow convergence of APA methods. We demonstrate transferability of this protection to defend against existing APAs, and show its efficacy across several contemporary CNN architectures.

1 Introduction

Convolutional neural networks (CNNs) are known to be vulnerable to adversarial examples: minor changes made to an image that significantly affect the classification outcome [10,31]. Adversarial examples may be generated by pixel-level perturbation of the image, introducing covert yet fragile changes that induce misclassification [4,8,10,19]. More recently, adversarial patches or 'stickers' have been proposed [3,7,8], creating overt changes within local image regions that exhibit robustness to affine transformation, and even to printing. Despite the increasing viability of such 'adversarial patch attacks' (APAs) to confound CNNs in the wild, there has been little work exploring defences against them (Fig. 1).

The core contribution of this paper is a new method to defend CNNs against image misclassification due to APAs. Existing defences typically seek to detect and remove patches in a pre-processing step prior to inference; *e.g.* exploiting the high visual salience of such patches. Yet the manipulation or removal of salient content often degrades model performance (Table 1). To avoid these problems we propose adapting the method of adversarial training to the realm of APAs. We

Electronic supplementary material The online version of this chapter (https://doi.org/10.1007/978-3-030-69538-5_15) contains supplementary material, which is available to authorized users.

H. Ishikawa et al. (Eds.): ACCV 2020, LNCS 12625, pp. 235–251, 2021.
https://doi.org/10.1007/978-3-030-69538-5_15

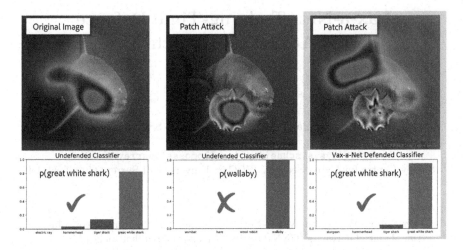

Fig. 1. Vax-a-Net vaccinates pre-trained CNNs against adversarial patch attacks (APAs); small image regions crafted to induce image misclassification. A shark is correctly classified by a VGG CNN (left), but fooled by an APA [3] (middle). Vax-a-Net applies defensive training to improve the CNN's resilience to the APA (right). Visualizations show CNN attention (via Grad-CAM [25]).

leverage the idea of generative adversarial networks (GANs) [9] to simultaneously synthesise effective adversarial patches to attack a target CNN model, whilst fine-tuning that target model to enhance its resilience against such attacks. Existing APA methods synthesise a patch via optimizations that take several minutes to converge [3,8]. In order to incorporate patch synthesis into the training loop, patch generation is run via inference pass on the Generator which takes less than one second. Furthermore, patch generation is also class-conditional; a single trained generator can create patches of many classes. Moreover, we demonstrate that the protection afforded to the model transfers to also defend against existing APA techniques [3,8].

We show for the first time that adversarial training may be leveraged to adapt a pre-trained CNN model's weights to afford it protection against state of the art APAs. We demonstrate this for both untargeted attacks (seeking misclassification) and targeted attacks (seeking misclassification to a specific class) over several contemporary CNN architectures. We demonstrate that a CNN may be 'vaccinated' against two state of the art APA techniques [3,8] despite neither being invoked in that process. Immunising a CNN model against APA via further training, contrasts with existing APA defences that filter images to mitigate patches at inference time. We show our method better preserves classification accuracy, and has a higher defence success rate than inference-time defences [11,20].

The adoption of CNNs within safety-critical autonomous systems opens a new facet of cyber-security, aimed on one hand to train networks resilient to adversarial attacks, and on the other to evaluate resilience by developing new attacks. This paper makes explicit that connection through adversarial training to immunise CNNs against this emerging attack vector.

2   Related Work

Szegedy *et al.* introduced adversarial attacks through minor perturbations of pixels [31] to induce CNN image misclassification. Goodfellow *et al.* later introduced the fast gradient sign method (FGSM, [10]) to induce such perturbations quickly in a single step, exploiting linearity of this effect in input space. These methods require access to the target model in order to backpropagate gradients to update pixels, inducing high frequency noise that is fragile to resampling. Later work improved robustness to affine transformation [19], whilst minimising perceptibility of the perturbations [4]. Gittings *et al.* [8] improved robustness using Deep Image Prior [34] to regularise perturbations to the manifold of natural images. Nevertheless current attacks remain susceptible to minor scaling or rotation. Other work made use of generative architectures to produce more effective attacks [1, 2, 28, 35].

Adversarial Patch Attacks. Brown *et al.* demonstrated that adversarial patches could be used to fool classifiers; they restricted the perturbation to a small region of the image and explicitly optimised for robustness to affine transformations [3]. Both Brown *et al.*, and later Gittings *et al.* [8] backpropagate through the target model to generate 'stickers' that can be placed anywhere within the image to create a successful attack. This optimization process can take several minutes for one single patch. Karmon *et al.* showed in LaVAN that the patches can be much smaller if robustness to affine transformation is not required [14] but require pixel-perfect positioning of the patch which is impractical for real APAs. In the complementary area of object detection (rather than image classification, addressed in this paper) Liu *et al.* disabled an object detector using a small patch in one corner of the frame [16]. Eykholt *et al.* applied adversarial patches to traffic signs, explicitly optimising for printability [7]. Chen *et al.* performed a similar attack on an object detector with Stop signs [5]. Thys *et al.* attacked a person detector using a printable patch [33].

Defences at Training Time. Whilst introducing adversarial examples, Szegedy *et al.* also proposed *adversarial training* to defend against them [31]. Adversarial training is a form of data augmentation that introduces adversarial examples during the training process in order to promote robustness. This method was impractical when first proposed due to the slow speed of producing adversarial examples making it infeasible to do so during training, but this was resolved by Goodfellow *et al.*'s FGSM [10], and later others with more general fast gradient methods [17, 26]. Kurakin *et al.* applied adversarial training to the ImageNet dataset for the first time [15]. Jang *et al.* make use of a recursive attack generator for more effective adversarial training on MNIST and CIFAR-10 [13]. Papernot *et al.* applied the idea of distilling the knowledge of one neural network onto another in a way that masks the gradients at test time and prevents an

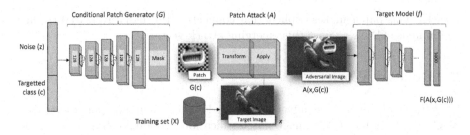

Fig. 2. Proposed architecture for using adversarial training to robustify a model f against adversarial patch attacks. The conditional patch generator G can synthesise adversarial patches for f attacking multiple classes. We alternately train G and f to promote the resilience of the model against APAs [3,8].

attacker from being able to use backpropagation [21]. All the above only train or fine-tune models to defend against adversarial image examples, rather than defending against localised patch attacks i.e. APAs as in our work.

Defences at Inference Time. Meng and Chen observed that by approximating the manifold of natural images it is possible to remove perturbations within an adversarial image as a pre-process at inference time. By projecting the full image onto this manifold [18]; they approximated the input image using an autoencoder. Samangouei et al., and separately Jalal et al., use a GAN in place of an autoencoder [12,24] to similarly remove adversarial perturbations.

Naseer et al. [20] have created one of the few defences against localised perturbations i.e. APAs. They observe that adversarial patches are regions of the image with especially high gradient (this is likely how they draw attention over other areas of the image). By applying local gradient smoothing (LGS) – conceptually the opposite of a bilateral/edge-preserving blur – patches are neutralised but at the cost of lowering the classification accuracy on clean images, since classifiers rely upon structural edge detail as a recognition cue. Hayes [11] created a different method to defend against localised adversarial attacks. The defence is split into two stages: detection and removal. To detect the patch they create a saliency map using guided backpropagation and assume that a collection of localised salient features implies that there is a patch. To remove the patch, an image in-painting algorithm [32] is applied to the masked region cleaned up via some morphological filtering.

Rather than attempt to detect and erase adversarial patches, Vax-a-net takes a generative adversarial approach to simultaneously create attack patches and fine-tune the model to 'vaccinate' it against APAs.

3   Method

Consider a CNN classifier $f : \mathbb{R}^m \to \mathbb{R}^k$ pre-trained to map a source image x to vector of probabilities $f(x)$, encoding the chance of the image containing each of a set of classes $c \in \mathcal{Y}$. Adversarial image attacks introduce a perturbation

Epoch	500	1000	1500	2000	2500

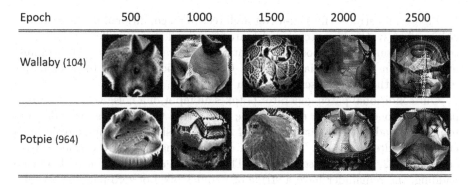

| Wallaby (104) |
| Potpie (964) |

Fig. 3. Representative patches sampled from our generator at training epochs 500–2500 for two attack classes. Patches were generated to defend a VGG-19 model trained on ImageNet.

$r \in \mathbb{R}^m$ to that source image such that $\arg\max_i(f_i(x + r)) \neq \arg\max_i(f_i(x))$. We say such attacks are *untargeted*; seeking only to induce misclassification. If our aim is to introduce a perturbation r such that $\arg\max_i(f_i(x + r)) = c$ we say the attack is *targeted* to a specific class (i).

Most adversarial images $x + r$ are covert attacks; typically a barely perceptable r, distributed across the whole image, is sought. By contrast, adversarial patch attacks (APAs) have been introduced as overt attacks, in which an adversarial patch ('sticker') is synthesised and composited into a region of an image in order to induce misclassification. We define a region of interest (ROI) via binary mask $M \in [0,1]$. In this case we seek perturbation r, which can be large, to create a composite image

$$\hat{x} = M \odot r + (1 - M) \odot x \tag{1}$$

where $\odot$ is element-wise multiplication. A single adversarial patch capable of attacking multiple images can be created by sampling x in mini-batches from a set of training images (versus learning r over a single image, as is typical for whole image case), as we now explain.

3.1 Conditional Patch Generation

Our aim is to defend a pre-trained CNN classifier model against adversarial patch attacks exclusively through modifications in the training process. Although this has been achieved with good success for adversarial image examples, the process of adversarial training used in that case does not apply straightforwardly to the case of adversarial patches. Existing methods of adversarial training require patches to be synthesised at each step of the training process, which is impractical as existing APA methods can take several minutes to synthesise patches. To mitigate this, we adapt the idea of a conditional Deep Convolutional Generative Adversarial Network (DC-GAN) [23], to synthesise effective adversarial patches while simultaneously training the model to defend against those patches.

Figure 2 illustrates the Vax-a-Net architecture; a conditional patch generator G is used to synthesise patches which are then applied via a differentiable affine transformation and compositing operation to a training image. The training image is then classified via the target CNN f which we wish to defend; this model plays the role of discriminator in the GAN.

Our conditional patch generator G takes an input of a noise vector z, accompanied by a one-hot vector encoding the class c that the attack is targeting, and produces an adversarial patch of size 64×64. It consists of five up-convolutional layers with filter size 4×4. The number of output channels for the hidden layers are 1024, 512, 256, 128 respectively. The first layer has a stride of 1 and no padding, the remainder have a stride of 2 and 1 pixel of zero-padding. We use batch normalisation after each layer, and leaky-ReLu activation. Our proposed loss function for the generator is

$$L_G = \mathbb{E}_{c,z,x,t,l} J(f(A(G(z,c),x,l,t)),c), \tag{2}$$

where A is the patch application operator, which we will define and explain further in Sect. 3.2, and J is the cross-entropy loss between the output of f and the target class.

Fig. 4. Patches sampled from our conditional generator G to attack an undefended VGG-19 model. (Color figure online)

In our work we explore G capable of producing effective patches for 1–50 different ImageNet classes (Sect. 4.4). Figure 4 shows the patches that a conditional generator for 10 classes can produce after 500 epochs of training without training the discriminator, i.e. these are patches effective at attacking the undefended network. Figure 3 shows how patch content evolves as training proceeds beyond the initial training, taking into account the discriminator. The patches resemble abstract versions of the object they are attacking, but with striking colour to attract attention away from other objects.

3.2   Patch Application and Target Model

The output of our generator $G(z,c)$ is an image of size 64×64, which we must turn into a patch and apply to the image. First we apply a circular mask to create a round patch (after [3,8]). Next we apply the patch p to the image x at location l and with an affine transformation t. We denote the output of this operation as $A(p,x,l,t)$. We use an expectation over transformation to ensure the patch works in any location and with any affine transformation applied. In our training, we enable random rotation of up to $\pi/4$, scaling to between 1% and 25% of the image, and translation to any location on the image.

The training process consists of two stages. Initially the discriminator (classifier) is frozen, and we train our generator to produce effective adversarial patches. We then alternate between training the generator and discriminator for each batch, in the usual manner for training a GAN.

The loss function for G was defined in Eq. 2. Our loss function for f is

$$L_f = \mathbb{E}_{c,z,x,w,t,l}(J(f(A(G(z,c),x,l,t)),y) + J(f(x),y) + \lambda J(f(w),c)), \quad (3)$$

where w are images of class c. Recall that $J(f(x),y)$ is the cross-entropy loss between the output of CNN f applied to classify the image x and the ground truth class y. In practice to approximate the expectation we sample x in minibatches from a set of training images, and for each image we randomly pick $c \neq y$ from our set of attack classes (Sect. 4), l, t from fixed distributions $\mathcal{L}$, $\mathcal{T}$, and z from a standard normal distribution. The first term of the loss ensures that the model correctly classifies images with patches, the second ensures that the model continues to correctly classify images without patches, and the third is to ensure that it continues to correctly classify images of class c. We empirically selected the weight λ of the third term to have a value of 2.

3.3   Training Methodology

The architecture of our generator is close to standard for a GAN, and in place of the discriminator we have a CNN classifier which we intend to robustify. Instead of using the discriminator as a tool to enable the generator to learn how to sample from some underlying distribution from which the training data are drawn (e.g. the distribution of natural images), we are using a similar architecture to perform a different task. The main difference stems from our final goal; to end up with a discriminator that is not fooled by any patches (hence a generator with a low success rate), which is the opposite of a regular GAN. Another difference is that our discriminator is a classifier for many (here, 1000 ImageNet classes) not a binary classifier for real/fake, again meaning that the generator will never be able to achieve its goal since the goalposts constantly move $i.e.$ there is no underlying static distribution that it will approximate.

We pre-train the generator for 500 epochs before alternating the training of both for each batch. For the generator we use an Adam optimiser with learning rate 0.001 and for the discriminator, Adam with learning rate of 2×10^{-7}.

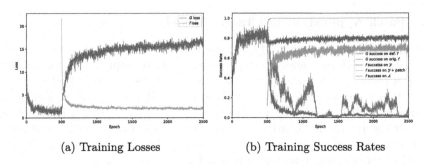

(a) Training Losses   (b) Training Success Rates

Fig. 5. Training losses and success rates for our VaN defence. (a) shows the losses for G and f. Recall that for the first 500 epochs f is not trained, hence why its line is missing. (b) shows the training success rates of patches from G applied to the current f (blue), as well as the original f (green). It also shows the success of f at classifying images from $\mathcal{Y}$, with (orange) and without (red) patches, and also $\mathcal{A}$ (purple) see Sect. 4 (Color figure online)

Figure 5 shows both the losses and the success rates on the training data for both G and f. We observe that during the 500 epoch pre-training phase for G its loss L_G becomes close to zero and its attack success rate climbs to ~80%, showing that we can produce effective adversarial patches with our conditional generator. Once the discriminator is updated, it quickly learns not to be fooled by the patches, so the success rates for f increase while those for G decrease. The success rate of patches produced by G when applied to the original model is quite erratic, but declines over time. This confirms that f is diverging from its original state, and that the set of patches effective at fooling it diverges from those that originally fooled the undefended model.

Table 1. Control: Accuracy of models over the set of test images without attacks $\hat{\mathcal{I}}$, reported for all ImageNet classes ($\mathcal{Y}$) and the subset of these classes used to form patches for APA ($\mathcal{A}$). Reported as top-1 accuracy for the undefended model, and the model defended by our method (D-VaN) or baselines.

Method	All classes $\mathcal{Y}$			Attack classes $\mathcal{A}$ [8]		
	VGG	Inception	IRN-v2	VGG	Inception	IRN-v2
Undefended	0.692	0.770	0.788	0.616	0.704	0.772
D-VaN/Ours	**0.725**	**0.772**	**0.803**	**0.908**	**0.868**	**0.884**
D-WM	0.492	–	0.523	0.396	–	0.476
D-LGS	0.476	0.688	0.708	0.492	0.660	0.692

Table 2. Success rate of defences against adversarial patch attacks covering 10% or 25% of the image. We report figures for our Vax-a-Net defence (D-VaN) as well as baseline defences and undefended models. The defence success rate is the proportion of images classified correctly despite the application of APA (higher is better).

Architecture	Defence	A-ADS [3]		A-DIP [8]	
		10%	25%	10%	25%
VGG	Undefended	0.041	0.006	0.016	0.001
	D-VaN(D)	0.410	0.147	0.422	0.154
	D-Van(U)	**0.642**	**0.495**	**0.643**	**0.483**
	D-WM	0.232	0.136	0.212	0.101
	D-LGS	0.120	0.020	0.115	0.008
Inception	Undefended	0.068	0.014	0.082	0.028
	D-VaN(D)	0.513	0.235	0.537	0.303
	D-VaN(U)	**0.684**	**0.541**	**0.689**	**0.542**
	D-LGS	0.237	0.069	0.201	0.066
IRN-v2	Undefended	0.093	0.023	0.087	0.035
	D-VaN(D)	0.607	0.350	0.546	0.299
	D-VaN(U)	**0.750**	**0.642**	**0.746**	**0.628**
	D-WM	0.455	0.365	0.438	0.347
	D-LGS	0.252	0.072	0.218	0.060

4   Experiments and Discussion

We evaluate our proposed Vax-a-Net (VaN) method for defending against adversarial patch attacks (APAs) on image classification models trained using three popular network architectures; VGG-19 [27], Inception-v3 [30], and Inception-ResNet-v2 (IRN-v2) [29].

Baselines. We compare the efficacy of our Vax-a-Net defence (**D-VaN**) against 2 baseline APA defences: the local gradient smoothing (**D-LGS**) method of Naseer *et al.* [20] and the watermark removal method (**D-WM**) of Hayes [11]. We test the effectiveness of our defence and the baseline defences against 2 baseline patch attacks; the adversarial stickers (**A-ADS**) method of Brown *et al.* [3], and the deep image prior based (**A-DIP**) method of Gittings *et al.* [8]. For all attacks we used public open source implementations, but for defences due to absence of author code we use our own implementations in the open-source PyTorch library [22]. Due to the architecture of the pre-trained network available in PyTorch and the nature of the defence we were unable to implement D-WM on the Inception-v3 model, and results for this model were not originally reported.

Datasets. We evaluate over the ImageNet [6] dataset containing 1k object classes $\mathcal{Y}$, using the published training (1.2M images) and test (50k images; 50 per class) partitions. For each of the architectures tested we use a model

Table 3. Success rate of attacks against our models defended by Vax-a-Net, as well as models defended with the baselines, and undefended models. The attack success rate is the proportion of images classified as the adversarial target class when APA is applied (lower is better).

Architecture	Defence	A-ADS [3]		A-DIP [8]	
		10%	25 %	10%	25%
VGG	Undefended	0.910	0.990	0.962	0.999
	D-VaN(D)	0.053	0.385	0.075	0.353
	D-VaN(U)	**0.012**	**0.031**	**0.010**	**0.035**
	D-WM	0.516	0.544	0.553	0.661
	D-LGS	0.553	0.903	0.577	0.952
Inception	Undefended	0.880	0.979	0.871	0.953
	D-VaN(D)	0.047	0.332	0.027	0.214
	D-VaN(U)	**0.016**	**0.046**	**0.008**	**0.017**
	D-LGS	0.557	0.765	0.645	0.833
IRN-v2	Undefended	0.884	0.949	0.881	0.923
	D-VaN(D)	**0.004**	0.180	0.018	0.238
	D-VaN(U)	0.005	**0.016**	**0.005**	**0.020**
	D-WM	0.304	0.284	0.314	0.267
	D-LGS	0.587	0.825	0.679	0.875

pre-trained on ImageNet, distributed with PyTorch. We refer to these as **undefended models**. Our proposed defence (D-VaN) involves further training of undefended models using the same training set. The test set comprises 50k images upon which attacks are mounted, each by inserting one adversarial patch. Let this unaltered test set be $\hat{\mathcal{I}}$. The patch is crafted to encourage an image containing object of ground truth class $y \in \mathcal{Y}$ to be misclassified a single target class $c \in \mathcal{A}$; we use the subset of 10 attack classes $\mathcal{A} \subset \mathcal{Y}$ proposed by Gittings *et al.* [8]. We evenly distribute these attack classes across the test set; let this **set of attack images** be $\mathcal{I}$.

Metrics. We measure the **attack success rate** as the proportion of $\mathcal{I}$, containing patches crafted to indicate misclassification as $c \in \mathcal{A}$ result in those image being misclassified as a; *i.e.* the success rate of a *targeted attack*. We measure the **defence success rate** as the proportion of $\mathcal{I}$ that are correctly classified as their true class y (despite the APA). Thus the inverse of the defence success rate, is the *untargeted* attack success rate *i.e.* where any misclassification occurs due to the APA. All success rates are expressed as the percentage of the 50k attack image set $\mathcal{I}$ constructed with the APA analysed in that experiment. All experiments were run for 1000 iterations training and 5 restarts.

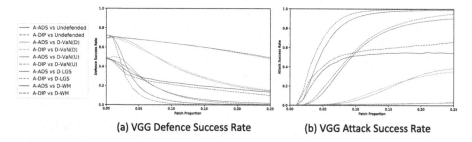

Fig. 6. Success rates of defended VGG-19 networks against APAs for patches covering up to 25% of the image.

4.1   D-VaN vs Baseline Defences

We first evaluate the performance of our defence (D-VaN) at reducing the effectiveness of adversarial patches synthesised by existing APA attack methods A-ADS [3] and A-DIP [8]. Both of these methods are white-box attacks, that run backpropagation through the model in order to generate patches to attack it.

We mount such attacks against our defence, the two baseline defences, and an undefended model as a control. In the case of the baseline methods we use patches that are trained on the undefended network, and then apply them to the defended network, since the defence layers are not usually differentiable. In the case of our model we attack it using patches generated on both the defended and undefended networks; D-VaN(D)/D-VaN(U). This measures transferability of the learned protection against attack from our generator G to the A-ADS and A-DIP attacks. We report both D-VaN(D) and D-VaN(U) because they can each highlight different flaws in a network's defences, and both make sense as real-world attack vectors.

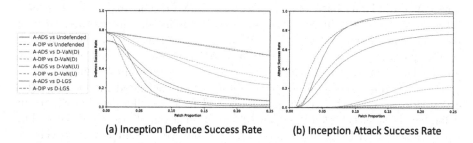

Fig. 7. Success rates of defended Inception-v3 networks against APAs for patches covering up to 25% of the image. We do not include a line for D-WM since the implementation of the defence was incompatible with Inception-v3.

We consider patches of a variety of sizes up to 25% of the total image area. Patches are placed randomly, anywhere in the image, and with a random rotation of up to $\pi/8$ for all experiments.

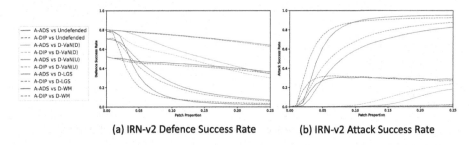

(a) IRN-v2 Defence Success Rate   (b) IRN-v2 Attack Success Rate

Fig. 8. Success rates of defended InceptionResNet-v2 networks against APAs for patches covering up to 25% of the image.

In Table 1 we report the accuracy of our model and all the baseline models on images with no adversarial attack, for $\mathcal{Y}$ and $\mathcal{A}$. The two baseline defences substantially reduce the accuracy of the model on the unattacked images, which is very significant for most applications since adversarial examples are relatively rare, *i.e.* clean images represent the overwhelming majority of samples that will be encountered in the real world. Our defended network maintains the accuracy of the undefended classifier on this set for all 3 classifiers we tested. We also note that no defence method significantly reduces model sensitivity for $\mathcal{A}$ given clean images, which could cheat the trial by failing to ever identify images as these adversarial test classes.

4.2   Network Architecture and Patch Size

Table 2 reports the improved resilience of models under our defence, showing significantly higher defence success rates for VGG, Inception and IRN-v2 architectures at 41.0%, 51.3%, and 60.7% and 14.7%, 23.5%, and 35.0% respectively for smaller and larger patches in the case of D-VaN(D). For smaller patches these rates are at least 30% higher than the closest baseline defence method, and for larger patches they are comparable. If we consider instead D-VaN(U), then for smaller patches the accuracy is reduced by only at most 25% from the original, and for larger patches it is still greater than 60% of its original value.

Table 3 shows the reduced vulnerability of our defended models, for all 3 architectures. Again the reduction is most evident for smaller patches, where our defended classifier is fooled less than 10% as often as our closest competitor. The performance at for larger patch sizes is closer, but we still outperform baselines. In the case of D-VaN(U), our attack success rate is reduced to less than 5% for all networks, even for the largest patches.

Figures 6, 7 and 8 show the dependence of attack and defence success rates on size, for our defence method as well as the baseline methods. Our method is an effective defence for all three architectures we are testing, and at all scales of patch. The performance of our method degrades as the size of the patch increases, which is expected since the patch covers up to 25% of the image, possibly occluding some salient object detail.

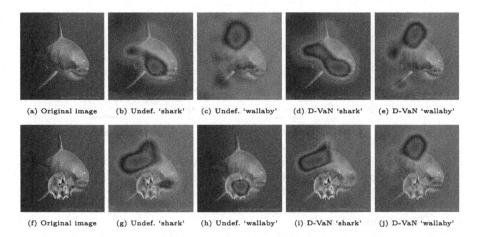

(a) Original image   (b) Undef. 'shark'   (c) Undef. 'wallaby'   (d) D-VaN 'shark'   (e) D-VaN 'wallaby'

(f) Original image   (g) Undef. 'shark'   (h) Undef. 'wallaby'   (i) D-VaN 'shark'   (j) D-VaN 'wallaby'

Fig. 9. Grad-CAM [25] visualisations for our VaN defended VGG network vs the undefended model. The original image (a) is classified (correctly) as a great white shark by both the undefended and defended (D-VaN) models, whereas the patch image is misclassified as a shark by the undefended model, but classified correctly by the defended (D-VaN) model. (Color figure online)

4.3 Attention Under Attack

Figure 9 uses Grad-CAM [25] to localise CNN attention for a particular class, for both our D-VaN defended model and the undefended model. Here the model is being attacked via A-ADS with target class of 'wallaby' whereas the true class of the image is 'great white shark'. Note that all plots are normalised; blue/purple relatively high attention, green/blue relative low. For images flooded with green/blue, there was low response for that class (c, e, g, j).

On the original image (a) with no patch, our model (d) and the undefended model (b) perform similarly. Both decide on the most likely class as shark, and both identify the region containing the shark as being of high importance. For this unattacked image, the response for the counterfactual class 'wallaby' is naturally low and both (c, e) pick a somewhat arbitrary area in the image that was of low importance to the correct decision (shark).

When the adversarial patch A-ADS targeting the counterfactual class is introduced (lower row), the undefended model identifies that patch region as very high salience for the wallaby class (h) and decides on wallaby, whereas our D-VaN defended model does not change its decision from shark, and does not attend to the patch (i). Forcing Grad-CAM to explain shark for the undefended model (which was not the decision outcome, so produces low attention) the original model picks out the area of the shark unoccluded by the patch (g) as does our defended model (i). In our case the model can correctly identify the shark, but in the original case it cannot since its attention was attracted by the wallaby patch. For completeness we show the defended model does not localise wallaby even when forced to explain wallaby in the attacked image (j).

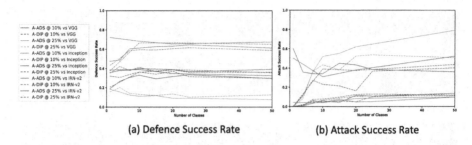

(a) Defence Success Rate   (b) Attack Success Rate

Fig. 10. Success rate of defended networks as we vary the number of classes of APA that our conditional generator produces.

4.4 Class Generalization

In Fig. 10 we examine the effect of changing the number of classes which our conditional generator produces. We train each of the three network architectures to defend against between 1 and 50 classes of adversarial patch, and we evaluate their performance against both A-ADS and A-DIP attacks with patches taking up 10% or 25% of the image. We find that the defence success rate is consistent as the number of classes changes for each network and for each patch size, showing that our method does not break down as the number of classes is increased. For the attack success rate we note that for the most part it increases slightly as the number of classes increases. The exception is large A-ADS patches on Inception-v3 and InceptionResNet-v2 architectures, for which our model loses performance when targeting a very small number of classes. This suggests value in the attack class diversity availabile during training due to our conditional patch generator G.

4.5 Timing Information

Table 4 compares the time taken for inference using our method and baselines. An inference pass on the defended model takes the same time as on the undefended model; the architecture is unchanged. However our defence does take 2–3 h of training to 'vaccinate' the model. This process only needs to be run once, as does training the model *a priori*. The baseline APA defences run as a pre-process at inference time, and so take longer (and also degrade accuracy; Table 1). All runs used an NVIDIA GeForce GTX 1080 Ti GPU.

4.6 Physical Experiment

To test the effectiveness of our defence against attacks in the physical world, where the appearance of the patch could differ from its digital form, we generated a patch to attack a VGG network targeting ImageNet class 964 "potpie" using A-ADS. We placed this patch on or around objects of 47 different ImageNet classes found in the physical world, for a total of 126 photographs of a patch. The photos

Table 4. Inference time (seconds) for an undefended VGG model trained on ImageNet, and that model with our defence or baseline defences applied.

Method	VGG	Inception	IRN-v2
Undefended	**0.10**	**0.08**	**0.16**
D-VaN/Ours	**0.10**	**0.08**	**0.16**
D-WM	1.35	-	1.08
D-LGS	0.32	0.40	0.45

were taken on a Google Pixel 2 smartphone. The undefended classifier returned adversarial vs. correct class 84 vs 9 times (attack success rate 90.3%), whereas the Vax-A-Net defended classifier returned similarly 5 vs 71 (attack success rate 6.6%).

5 Conclusion

We proposed Vax-a-Net; a method to 'immunise' (defend) CNN classifiers against adversarial patch attacks without degrading the performance of the model on clean data and without slowing down the inference time. In the process of achieving this we produced a conditional generator for adversarial patches, and then we used an adversarial training methodology to update the generator during training rather than having to synthesise patches from scratch at each iteration. We showed experimentally that our method performs better than the baseline defences in both a targeted and untargeted sense, and across three different popular network architectures. Furthermore we showed that our network is resilient to patches produced by two different attacks, and to patches that are produced either on our defended network or on the original undefended network, which demonstrates that our defence taught the network real robustness to these patches, and not simply to hide its gradient or to ignore a group of specific patches. Future work could look into extending these methodologies to defend networks for different tasks, such as patch attacks on object detectors.

Acknowledgment. The first author was supported by an EPSRC Industrial Case Award with Thales, United Kingdom.

References

1. Bai, T., Zhao, J., Zhu, J., Han, S., Chen, J., Li, B.: Ai-gan: attack-inspired generation of adversarial examples. arXiv preprint arXiv:2002.02196 (2020)
2. Baluja, S., Fischer, I.: Learning to attack: adversarial transformation networks. In: Proceedings of the AAAI (2018)
3. Brown, T.B., Mané, D., Roy, A., Abadi, M., Gilmer, J.: Adversarial patch. arXiv preprint arXiv:1712.09665 (2017)

4. Carlini, N., Wagner, D.: Towards evaluating the robustness of neural networks. In: Proceedings of the IEEE Symposium on Security and Privacy (2017)
5. Chen, S.T., Cornelius, C., Martin, J., Chau, D.H.: Shapeshifter: robust physical adversarial attack on faster R-CNN object detector. In: Proceedings of the Joint European Conference on Machine Learning and Knowledge Discovery in Databases (2018)
6. Deng, J., Dong, W., Socher, R., Li, L.J., Li, K., Fei-Fei, L.: ImageNet: a large-scale hierarchical image database. In: Proceedings of the CVPR (2009)
7. Eykholt, K., et al.: Robust physical-world attacks on deep learning visual classification. In: Proceedings of the CVPR (2018)
8. Gittings, T., Schneider, S., Collomosse, J.: Robust synthesis of adversarial visual examples using a deep image prior. In: Proceedings of the BMVC (2019)
9. Goodfellow, I., et al.: Generative adversarial nets. In: Proceedings of the NIPS (2014)
10. Goodfellow, I.J., Shlens, J., Szegedy, C.: Explaining and harnessing adversarial examples. arXiv preprint arXiv:1412.6572 (2014)
11. Hayes, J.: On visible adversarial perturbations & digital watermarking. In: Proceedings of the CVPR Workshops (2018)
12. Ilyas, A., Jalal, A., Asteri, E., Daskalakis, C., Dimakis, A.G.: The robust manifold defense: Adversarial training using generative models. arXiv preprint arXiv:1712.09196 (2017)
13. Jang, Y., Zhao, T., Hong, S., Lee, H.: Adversarial defense via learning to generate diverse attacks. In: Proceedings of the ICCV (2019)
14. Karmon, D., Zoran, D., Goldberg, Y.: LaVAN: Localized and visible adversarial noise. In: Proceedings of the ICML (2018)
15. Kurakin, A., Goodfellow, I., Bengio, S.: Adversarial machine learning at scale. arXiv preprint arXiv:1611.01236 (2016)
16. Liu, X., Yang, H., Liu, Z., Song, L., Li, H., Chen, Y.: Dpatch: an adversarial patch attack on object detectors. arXiv preprint arXiv:1806.02299 (2018)
17. Lyu, C., Huang, K., Liang, H.N.: A unified gradient regularization family for adversarial examples. In: Proceedings of the International Conference on Data Mining (2015)
18. Meng, D., Chen, H.: MagNet. In: Proceedings of the Conference on Computer and Communications Security (2017)
19. Moosavi-Dezfooli, S.M., Fawzi, A., Frossard, P.: Deepfool: a simple and accurate method to fool deep neural networks. In: Proceedings of the CVPR (2016)
20. Naseer, M., Khan, S., Porikli, F.: Local gradients smoothing: Defense against localized adversarial attacks. In: Proceedings of the WACV (2019)
21. Papernot, N., McDaniel, P., Wu, X., Jha, S., Swami, A.: Distillation as a defense to adversarial perturbations against deep neural networks. In: Proceedings of the IEEE Symposium on Security and Privacy (2016)
22. Paszke, A., et al.: Pytorch: an imperative style, high-performance deep learning library. In: Proceedings of the NIPS (2019)
23. Radford, A., Metz, L., Chintala, S.: Unsupervised representation learning with deep convolutional generative adversarial networks. arXiv preprint arXiv:1511.06434 (2015)
24. Samangouei, P., Kabkab, M., Chellappa, R.: Defense-GAN: protecting classifiers against adversarial attacks using generative models. In: Proceedings of the ICLR (2018)

25. Selvaraju, R.R., Cogswell, M., Das, A., Vedantam, R., Parikh, D., Batra, D.: GRAD-CAM: visual explanations from deep networks via gradient-based localization. In: Proceedings of the ICCV (2017)
26. Shaham, U., Yamada, Y., Negahban, S.: Understanding adversarial training: Increasing local stability of supervised models through robust optimization. Neurocomputing **307**, 195–204 (2018)
27. Simonyan, K., Zisserman, A.: Very deep convolutional networks for large-scale image recognition. arXiv preprint arXiv:1409.1556 (2014)
28. Song, Y., Shu, R., Kushman, N., Ermon, S.: Constructing unrestricted adversarial examples with generative models. In: Proceedings of the NIPS (2018)
29. Szegedy, C., Ioffe, S., Vanhoucke, V., Alemi, A.A.: Inception-v4, inception-resnet and the impact of residual connections on learning. In: Proceedings of the AAAI (2017)
30. Szegedy, C., Vanhoucke, V., Ioffe, S., Shlens, J., Wojna, Z.: Rethinking the inception architecture for computer vision. In: Proceedings of the CVPR (2016)
31. Szegedy, C., Zaremba, W., Sutskever, I., Bruna, J., Erhan, D., Goodfellow, I., Fergus, R.: Intriguing properties of neural networks. arXiv preprint arXiv:1312.6199 (2013)
32. Telea, A.: An image inpainting technique based on the fast marching method. J. Graph. Tools **9**(1), 23–34 (2004)
33. Thys, S., Van Ranst, W., Goedemé, T.: Fooling automated surveillance cameras: adversarial patches to attack person detection. In: Proceedings of the CVPR Workshops (2019)
34. Ulyanov, D., Vedaldi, A., Lempitsky, V.: Deep image prior. In: Proceedings of the CVPR (2018)
35. Xiao, C., Li, B., Zhu, J.Y., He, W., Liu, M., Song, D.: Generating adversarial examples with adversarial networks. arXiv preprint arXiv:1801.02610 (2018)

Towards Optimal Filter Pruning
with Balanced Performance
and Pruning Speed

Dong Li[1,2]([✉]), Sitong Chen[2], Xudong Liu[2], Yunda Sun[2], and Li Zhang[1,2]

[1] Tsinghua University, Beijing 100084, China
[2] Nuctech AI R&D Center, Beijing 100084, China
{li.dong,chensitong,liuxudong,sunyunda,zhangli}@nuctech.com

Abstract. Filter pruning has drawn more attention since resource constrained platform requires more compact model for deployment. However, current pruning methods suffer either from the inferior performance of one-shot methods, or the expensive time cost of iterative training methods. In this paper, we propose a balanced filter pruning method for both performance and pruning speed. Based on the filter importance criteria, our method is able to prune a layer with approximate layer-wise optimal pruning rate at preset loss variation. The network is pruned in the layer-wise way without the time consuming prune-retrain iteration. If a pre-defined pruning rate for the entire network is given, we also introduce a method to find the corresponding loss variation threshold with fast converging speed. Moreover, we propose the layer group pruning and channel selection mechanism for channel alignment in network with short connections. The proposed pruning method is widely applicable to common architectures and does not involve any additional training except the final fine-tuning. Comprehensive experiments show that our method outperforms many state-of-the-art approaches.

1   Introduction

Despite the fact that neural network based approaches have achieved significant performance improvement in many computer vision tasks, the deployment of these over-parameterized model often requires high computing power and large memory footprint, which are not available on resource constrained platform such as mobile phone. To tackle this problem, researchers propose different methods for network compression and inference acceleration, including lightweight architecture designing [1,2], network pruning [3–5], weight quantization [6,7], matrix factorization [8], knowledge distillation [9], etc.

D. Li, S. Chen—Contributed equally to this work.

Electronic supplementary material The online version of this chapter (https://doi.org/10.1007/978-3-030-69538-5_16) contains supplementary material, which is available to authorized users.

© Springer Nature Switzerland AG 2021
H. Ishikawa et al. (Eds.): ACCV 2020, LNCS 12625, pp. 252–267, 2021.
https://doi.org/10.1007/978-3-030-69538-5_16

Among these methods, network pruning has drawn much attention since it is able to reduce the number of model parameters and operations simultaneously. It can be categorized as structure pruning and non-structure pruning. Non-structure pruning sets unimportant weights to zero to achieve high sparsity [10,11], while sparse operation requires specialized hardware [12] or software [13] libraries to speed up the inference process, which limits the usage of the pruned network. Structure pruning is also recognized as filter pruning or channel pruning since it is implemented by removing filters in the original network. This coarse-grained filter-level pruning can be treated as modification to the network architecture, so it does not damage the usability of the model. In this paper, we propose a filter pruning method to shrink network size and accelerate its inference at the same time.

The key issue of filter pruning is selecting the unimportant filters to be pruned at a given compression ratio. To solve this combinatorial optimization problem, most methods evaluate the importance of filters then either prune them in a one-shot manner, or iteratively prune-retrain the model. On the one hand, one-shot approaches often prune filters in each layer based on some pre-defined prune rate and particular properties of the trained model [5,14–18], which are more prone to over-pruning or under-pruning at certain layers. On the other hand, iterative pruning based on greedy criteria increases the time cost and computation burden [17,19,20]. Also, some of these methods jointly optimize original objective function with compression, thus the loss function becomes more complex and difficult to converge due to the hyper-parameters introduced. Filter pruning is by far an unsolved problem, since the optimal prune rate of each layer is hard to obtain.

Our approach is a balanced method which is able to approximate the layer-wise optimal pruning rate with limited time and computing resource. Given a trained convolutional network, we observe that removing a convolution kernel in certain layer leads to different changes of loss function and accuracy, while the accuracy drop has a highly positive correlation with the absolute value of loss function change, which we denote it as the loss variation. Based on the criteria of gradient and magnitude of filters, the contribution to loss variation of different filters can be accurately estimated. As these gradients are able to compute by back propagation, we select batches of data to evaluate the importance of each filter per layer by inferences within single epoch. We propose an algorithm to obtain the maximum pruning rate in each layer, constrained by a threshold of loss variation. We use binary search to find the combination of filters which are sorted by importance, so the maximized number of filters can be pruned in one-shot. After all layers are done, the pruned model is fine-tuned only once. To verify the effectiveness of our method, we conduct a series of filter pruning experiments using CIFAR-10 [21] and ImageNet [22] dataset. Our result outperforms the state-of-the-art algorithms with many major network architectures, including VGG [23], GoogLeNet [24], ResNet [25], DenseNet [26], etc.

In summary, our main contribution is the proposed filter pruning method to approximately obtain layer-wise optimal pruning rate, which is able to prune a layer with maximum pruning rate at given loss variation without the time consuming prune-retrain iteration. For pre-defined pruning rate of entire network, our method is able to converge to the particular pruning rate without additional fine-tuning. We introduce binary search to help the layer-wise pruning and the global pruning rate converging, so that our method balances the performance of pruned network and pruning speed. The proposed method is widely applicable to common architectures of convolutional networks. Comprehensive experiments show that our method is able to achieve higher compression ratio with lower accuracy drop compared with the state-of-the-art approaches.

2   Related Work

Network pruning obtains a more compact model by removing redundant connections from the original network, thereby reducing the number of parameters and operations. Early researches on this topic are mainly addressed by removing weight-level connections for sparse pruning. Since the applicability of sparse network is limited, recent works are more focused on structure pruning methods, which can be further categorized as one-shot filter pruning and iterative filter pruning.

Sparse Pruning. Inspired by neurobiology, the optimal brain damage [3] and the optimal brain surgeon [4] removed unimportant connections according to the analysis of Hessian matrix of the loss function. Han et al. [10] determined the importance of weights in the network through the weight value, and reduce the redundancy by deleting smaller weights. Srinivas [11] proposed a data-free method to remove the redundant parameters of the fully-connected layer. Because of the sparsity of the weight tensor, these unstructured pruned model only accelerate the inference process on specialized platforms.

One-Shot Filter Pruning refers to all redundant filters in a network are pruned before fine-tuning. Some methods estimated the importance of filters based on the characteristics of the filter itself, including L1 norms [5], geometric median [17], etc. Others evaluated the filter redundancy by analyzing the information of the feature map. Hu et al. [14] used the sparsity of the output of each layer to choose the redundant filter. He et al. [16] used the least square to reconstruct the error and LASSO regression to remove filters layer by layer. Luo et al. [15] pruned filters based on the statistical information of next layer. Yu et al. [27] proposed a method based on importance score propagation, which back-propagates the score of the final response layer to each filter to determine whether the filter is redundant. However, these methods usually depend on a heuristic metric to set the pruning rate of each layer in advance. Although one-shot pruning algorithm is capable to reduce time cost, it is prone to suffer from inferior compression ratio and accuracy.

Iterative Filter Pruning selectively prune one or more filters followed by training to recover the model performance in each iteration. Liu et al. [28] performs sparse training on the scale factor of BN, and removes the filter with a smaller scale factor according to the pruning rate corresponding to each layer. Molchanov et al. [29] proposed a criterion based on Taylor expansion to evaluate the importance of filters, then applied with greedy pruning strategy. Reinforcement learning was introduced in AMC [19] for pruning, it set rewards by constraining FLOPs, accuracy and specific compression ratios in continuous space. You et al. [30] proposed the Gate Batch Normalization module, and added the FLOPs hyper-parameters to the training objective to compress the model. Huang et al. [20] proposed a data-driven method to learn the architecture of the network, introduced a new scaling factor and corresponding sparse regularization, and defined pruning as a joint sparse regularization optimization problem. Lin et al. [31] added a mask to each filter and obtained the final model by generative adversarial learning. The dynamic pruning scheme [32] globally pruned unimportant filters and adjusted the network dynamically, with a mechanism to restore the filters that were mis-pruned. Instead of pruning negligible filters, recent work [33] proposed an optimization objective to generate multiple identical filters then remove them to achieve pruning goals. A major drawback for iterative pruning is the extensive computational burden. Additionally, the pruning strategies based on training iterations often change the optimization function, and even introduce a large number of hyper-parameters, which will make the training more difficult to converge.

3 Our Method

3.1 Filter Importance Evaluation

Given a trained network, we randomly select a group of filters and set their weights to zero, then we use the pruned network to forward all the samples to calculate loss variation and accuracy drop. It is observed that the accuracy drop is almost directly proportional to loss variation. Figure 1 has shown the correlation between loss variation and accuracy drop for VGG16 trained on CIFAR-10.

For computer vision application, the majority of trained models are convolutional neural networks. We denote the dataset $\mathcal{D} = \{\mathcal{X}, \mathcal{Y}\}$ consists of N samples, $\mathcal{X} = \{\mathbf{x}_0, \mathbf{x}_1, \cdots, \mathbf{x}_N\}, \mathcal{Y} = \{y_0, y_1, \cdots, y_N\}$, where $\mathbf{x}_i$ and y_i are image and label of i-th sample, respectively. In a trained network with L layers, the filters can be parameterized as $\mathcal{W} = \{\mathbf{w}_1^{(1)}, \mathbf{w}_1^{(2)}, \cdots, \mathbf{w}_L^{(C_L)}\}$, i.e. for k-th filter in l-th layer, the weights are $\mathbf{w}_l^{(k)} \in \mathbb{R}^{C_{l-1} \times p \times p}$ with $l \in [1, 2, \cdots, L]$ and $k \in [1, 2, \cdots, C_l]$, where C_l represents the number of channels in l-th layer. We denote the pruned network as $\mathcal{W}'$ which sets a subset of filters of $\mathcal{W}$ to zero, i.e. $\mathbf{w}_l^{(k)} = \mathbf{0}$ represents the k-th filter of l-th layer is pruned. Since the accuracy drop is directly related to the loss variation, the filter pruning can be defined as the optimization problem:

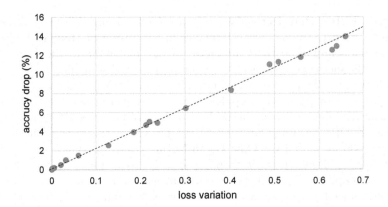

Fig. 1. Correlation between loss variation and accuracy drop. Samples are collected from pruning results of VGG16 trained on CIFAR-10.

$$\min_{\mathcal{W}'} |\mathcal{L}(\mathcal{D}; \mathcal{W}') - \mathcal{L}(\mathcal{D}; \mathcal{W})|$$
$$\text{s.t.} \quad \|\mathcal{W}'\|_0 \leqslant \beta \|\mathcal{W}\|_0 \tag{1}$$

where $\mathcal{L}(\cdot)$ is the loss function and $\gamma = 1 - \beta$ is the specific pruning rate. Solving combinatorial optimization problem (1) is impractical for modern networks, so we evaluate the importance of filters by certain criterion, then use it as the prior knowledge for pruning. The saliency of single filter can be evaluated by calculating the loss variation on the dataset after pruning:

$$\Delta\mathcal{L}(\mathcal{D}; \mathcal{W}, \mathbf{w}_l^{(k)} = \mathbf{0}) = \left| \mathcal{L}(\mathcal{D}; \mathcal{W}, \mathbf{w}_l^{(k)} = \mathbf{0}) - \mathcal{L}(\mathcal{D}; \mathcal{W}) \right| \tag{2}$$

we have first-order approximation by Taylor expansion:

$$\left| \mathcal{L}(\mathcal{D}; \mathcal{W}, \mathbf{w}_l^{(k)} = \mathbf{0}) - \mathcal{L}(\mathcal{D}; \mathcal{W}) \right| \approx \left| \frac{\partial \mathcal{L}(\mathcal{D}; \mathcal{W})}{\partial \mathbf{w}_l^{(k)}} \mathbf{w}_l^{(k)} \right| = \boldsymbol{G}_l^{(k)} \tag{3}$$

In this paper, $\boldsymbol{G}_l^{(k)}$ is used as the criterion to evaluate the importance of k-th filter in l-th layer. To prune a single filter from a network, the least value of (3) of all the filters is selected. It is consistent with the intuition that the filter with smaller gradient and magnitude should be pruned first.

3.2   Layer-Wise Optimal Pruning Rate Searching

The value of $\boldsymbol{G}_l^{(k)}$ is calculated once by forwarding and backwarding all samples from the dataset. In greedy-based methods, the filters are sorted by importance and the unimportant filters are pruned together by their ranks. We propose a layer-wise pruning method to improve the sub-optimal solution caused by cross-layer greedy strategies.

Algorithm 1. Optimal pruning rate searching in l-th layer

1: **Input:** original network weights $\mathcal{W}$, $\{score_k\}$ with $k \in [1, 2, \cdots, C_l]$, threshold θ, original network loss φ
2: **Output:** new weights $\mathcal{W}'$ with l-th layer pruned
3: $rank \leftarrow C_l/2$
4: $step \leftarrow rank$
5: $\{index_k\} \leftarrow \text{sort}(\{score_k\})$ ▷ in ascending order, $score_{index_1}$ is the smallest
6: $prune_{id} \leftarrow \{\}$
7: **while** True **do**
8:     **if** $step < 1$ **then**
9:         **break**
10:    **end if**
11:    Pruning: $\mathbf{w}_l^{(i)} \leftarrow \mathbf{0}$ with $i \in [index_1, index_2, \cdots, index_{rank}]$
12:    Forward all samples to compute the loss φ' with l-th layer pruned
13:    $step \leftarrow step/2$
14:    **if** $|\varphi' - \varphi| > \theta$ **then**
15:        $rank \leftarrow rank - step$
16:    **else**
17:        $prune_{id} \leftarrow \{index_k\}$ with $k \in [1, 2, \cdots, rank]$
18:        $rank \leftarrow rank + step$
19:    **end if**
20: **end while**
21: Pruning: $\mathbf{w}_l^{(k)} \leftarrow \mathbf{0}$ for $k \in prune_{id}$
22: **Return** $\mathcal{W}'$

Suppose there are $N = M \times P$ samples in the dataset $\mathcal{D}$, where M is the batch size and P is the number of batches. In l-th layer, we have $score_k$ to represent the importance of k-th filter evaluated on the dataset.

$$score_k = \sum_{i=1}^{P} \frac{z_{ik}}{C_l} \tag{4}$$

In (4), C_l is the number of filters in l-th layer, z_{ik} is the index of k-th filter in ascending order after i-th batch running and sorting for $G_l^{(k)}$. As Sect. 3.1 mentioned, the decrease of model accuracy is consistent with the loss variation, so we can use the loss variation as a hyper-parameter for the layer-wise pruning. We treat it as a search problem, aiming to find maximum number of filters to be pruned per layer to achieve high compression ratio within the loss variation range. We define the original trained network loss as $\varphi = \mathcal{L}(\mathcal{D}; \mathcal{W})$ and introduce a parameter θ that represents the threshold of the loss variation. To accelerate the pruning, we use binary search to avoid the re-evaluation of filter pruning one by one. The algorithm that searches for the optimal pruning rate in one layer is described in Algorithm 1. The ablation study for Algorithm 1 indicates that the binary search speeds up the pruning process by 5–10×.

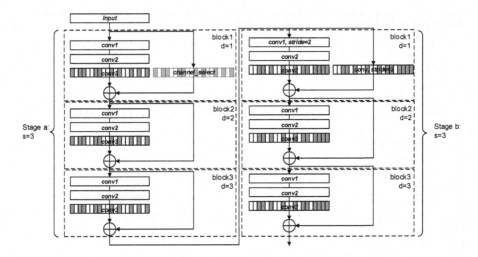

Fig. 2. Group pruning method for shortcut connections in ResNet-like networks. For one stage, the last layers of each block are pruned together in a group such that they have the same retained filters. Gray color indicates the corresponding filter is pruned. Since stage a has 3 blocks and the shortcut in each block is an identity connection, a channel_select layer (in red) is introduced to mask out the pruned channels of input; while stage b has 3 blocks with first shortcut connected by convolutional downsampling, so it can be pruned in a group. (Color figure online)

For network architectures with shortcut connections, such as ResNet, the output channels of the last convolutional layers of each block must be the same, as shown in Fig. 2. It is because that the shortcut connections require the output channels of these layers are aligned. Therefore, we put the last layers of each block in one stage together as a group for pruning. We define d as the depth of each block in one stage, s denotes the maximum value of d. Empirically, we find that the lower-level convolution kernels tend to have weaker representative capability than the high-level ones, so the scoring weight of the lower-level convolution kernels are reduced. The weighted sum for group pruning is conducted by Eq. 5:

$$score_k = \sum_{i=1}^{K} \frac{d_i}{s} \cdot score_{k,d_i} \qquad (5)$$

where d_i represents depth of i-th block in one stage, with $i \in [1, 2, \cdots, K]$ and K is the number of blocks. During pruning, the filters with the same index in the group will be pruned together according to $score_k$ ranking. For some stages, the input channels are directly short connected to blocks, hence we introduce a non-parametric layer for channel selection, whose output channel layout is copied from the group pruning result. After the layer-wise optimal pruning rate searching, the layer-wise results are connected for the pruned network, then it is fine-tuned on the training dataset to obtain the final model.

Algorithm 2. Filter pruning with global pruning rate γ

1: **Input:** original network weights $\mathcal{W}$, γ, initial value of threshold θ_{init}, pruning rate tolerance ε
2: **Output:** pruned network weights $\mathcal{W}'$ with global pruning rate γ', s.t. $|\gamma' - \gamma| \leqslant \varepsilon$
3: $\theta_{upper} \leftarrow \theta_{init}$
4: $\theta_{lower} \leftarrow 0$
5: $\gamma' \leftarrow 0$
6: Forward/backward network $\mathcal{W}$ on $\mathcal{D}$ once, compute original loss φ and $\{score_k\}_l$
    for $l \in [1, 2, \cdots, L]$ and $k \in [1, 2, \cdots, C_l]$ ▷ Eq. 3 and 4.
7: **while** $|\gamma' - \gamma| > \varepsilon$ **do**
8:      $\mathcal{W}' \leftarrow \mathcal{W}$
9:      **for all** l in L layers **do**
10:          run pruning Alg. 1 with $(\mathcal{W}, \{score_k\}_l, \theta_{upper}, \varphi)$
11:          update $\mathcal{W}'$ with pruned l-th layer
12:      **end for**
13:      $\gamma' \leftarrow 1 - \|\mathcal{W}'\|_0 / \|\mathcal{W}\|_0$
14:      $step \leftarrow \theta_{upper} - \theta_{lower}$
15:      **if** $\gamma' > \gamma$ **then**
16:          $\theta_{upper} \leftarrow (\theta_{upper} + \theta_{lower})/2$
17:      **else**
18:          $\theta_{lower} \leftarrow \theta_{upper}$
19:          $\theta_{upper} \leftarrow \theta_{upper} + 2 \times step$
20:      **end if**
21: **end while**
22: Finetune the pruned network $\mathcal{L}(\mathcal{D}; \mathcal{W}')$ once.
23: **Return** $\mathcal{W}'$, γ', θ_{upper}

3.3 Pruning with Global Constraints

In many cases, there are constraints for the whole network, such as global pruning rate γ defined in (1), performance loss, etc. Here we take pre-defined pruning rate γ as the global constraint. We find that there is a positive correlation between the loss variation and the layer-wise pruning rate, it implies that the loss variation also positively correlated to the global pruning rate. More details of the statistics are listed our supplementary material. We propose a similar binary search method for the loss variation threshold θ, thereby approximate the global pruning constraint γ. The algorithm is described in Algorithm 2.

Compared to iterative training based pruning methods, our approach only needs fine-tuning the entire network for once. Although pruning with global constraint requires binary search of the loss variation threshold, it only involves multiple times of forwarding, which runs much faster than multiple times of re-training. As the following experiments indicate, our method is able to achieve the balance between performance and pruning speed.

4   Experiments

We evaluate our algorithm on two commonly used datasets (CIFAR-10 and ImageNet) with popular networks implemented by PyTorch [34]. The pruning results and performance are compared with several state-of-the-art algorithms in recent years.

4.1   Experiments Settings

Experiments Setup for CIFAR-10. CIFAR-10 is a 10-class image classification dataset containing 50,000 training images and 10,000 test images. In our experiments, we apply VGG16_BN with a plain structure [23], GoogLeNet with Inception module [24], ResNet-56/110 with residual module [25] and DenseNet-40 with dense connections [26] to verify the effectiveness of our algorithm. For the ResNet-56/110 network on CIFAR-10, the first shortcut of each stage (excluding the first stage) is a downsample and data-filling layer. In order to ensure the channels are aligned, the channel selection layer is added as shown in Fig. 2. In the fine-tuning phase, we use a NVIDIA Tesla V100 GPU to train the pruned model. We solve the optimization problem by SGD with a Nesterov momentum of 0.9 and weight decay of 1e-4. The network is trained for 400 epochs. The initial learning rate is 0.01, it is decayed by a factor of 10 every 100 epochs. The batch size is 128.

Experiments Setup for ImageNet. ImageNet [22] is a large image dataset with 1000 classes, containing 1,281,167 training images and 50,000 validation images. In the experiments, we use ResNet-50 to demonstrate our pruning performance on two NVIDIA Tesla V100 GPUs. In the fine-tuning phase, the optimizer parameters are set to be the same as the parameters in CIFAR-10 experiments. The pruned network is fine-tuned for 120 epochs with batch size 256. The initial learning rate is 0.001 and divided by 10 every 30 epochs.

4.2   Results on CIFAR-10

VGG16_BN. The performance of different compression algorithms are shown in Table 1. PR denotes the pruning rate and FLOPs denotes floating point operations. Ours-0.12 indicates that the threshold of loss variation is 0.12. Compared with L1, SSS, GAL-0.1, and HRank-A, Ours-0.12 has clear advantages for both FLOPs and parameters. Ours-0.12 reduces FLOPs by 70.29% and deletes 87.72% of the parameters, while its Top-1 accuracy keeps almost the same as the baseline. For Ours-0.2, although the reductions of FLOPs and parameters are almost the same as those of HRank-B, the Top-1 accuracy is 2.36% higher than that of HRank-B.

Table 1. The pruning results on CIFAR-10. L1*, SSS* and ApoZ* are the results in GAL.

Model	Method	Top-1 (%)	FLOPs (PR)	Parameters (PR)
VGG16_BN	Baseline	93.96	313.73M (0.00%)	14.98M (0.00%)
	L1* [5]	93.40	206.00M (34.34%)	5.40M (63.95%)
	SSS* [20]	93.02	183.13M (41.63%)	3.93M (73.76%)
	GAL-0.1 [31]	93.42	171.89M (45.21%)	2.67M (82.17%)
	HRank-A [35]	93.43	145.61M (53.59%)	2.51M (83.24%)
	Ours-0.12	**93.95**	**93.22M (70.29%)**	**1.84M (87.72%)**
	HRank-B [35]	91.23	73.70M (76.51%)	1.78M (88.12%)
	Ours-0.2	**93.59**	**73.81M (76.47%)**	**1.45M (90.32%)**
GoogLeNet	Baseline	95.05	1.52B (0.00%)	6.15M (0.00%)
	L1* [5]	94.54	1.02B (32.89%)	3.51M (42.93%)
	Random	94.54	0.96B (36.84%)	3.58M (41.79%)
	GAL-0.05 [31]	94.56	0.94B (38.16%)	3.12M (49.27%)
	ApoZ* [14]	92.11	0.76B (50.00%)	2.85M (53.66%)
	HRank-A [35]	94.53	0.69B (54.60%)	2.74M (55.45%)
	Ours-0.0045	**95.19**	**0.57B (62.50%)**	**1.76M (71.38%)**
	HRank-B [35]	94.07	0.45B (70.39%)	1.86M (69.76%)
	Ours-0.01	**94.77**	**0.40B (73.68%)**	**1.14M (81.46%)**
DenseNet-40	Baseline	94.81	282.92M (0.00%)	1.04M (0.00%)
	Liu et al.-40% [28]	94.81	190.00M (32.84%)	0.66M (36.54%)
	GAL-0.01 [31]	94.61	182.92M (35.34%)	0.67M (35.58%)
	HRank-A [35]	94.24	167.41M (40.82%)	0.66M (36.54%)
	Zhao et al. [36]	93.16	156.00M (44.86%)	0.42M (59.62%)
	Ours-0.02	**94.61**	**154.34M (45.45%)**	**0.59M (43.27%)**
	HRank-B [35]	93.68	110.15M (61.07%)	0.48M (53.85%)
	Ours-0.04	**93.49**	**95.69M (66.18%)**	**0.37M (64.42%)**
ResNet-56	Baseline	93.26	125.49M (0.00%)	0.85M (0.00%)
	L1* [5]	93.06	90.90M (27.56%)	0.73M (14.12%)
	NISP [27]	93.01	81.00M (35.45%)	0.49M (42.35%)
	HRank-A [35]	93.17	62.72M (50.02%)	0.49M (42.35%)
	He et al. [16]	90.80	62.00M (50.59%)	-
	Ours-0.019	**93.64**	**59.84M (52.31%)**	**0.52M (38.82%)**
	GAL-0.8 [31]	91.58	49.99M (60.16%)	0.29M (65.88%)
	HRank-B [35]	90.72	32.52M (74.08%)	0.27M (68.24%)
	Ours-0.055	**91.54**	**25.72M (79.50%)**	**0.25M (70.59%)**
ResNet-110	Baseline	93.50	252.89M (0.00%)	1.72M (0.00%)
	L1* [5]	93.30	155.00M (38.71%)	1.16M (32.56%)
	GAL-0.5 [31]	92.55	130.20M (48.52%)	0.95M (44.77%)
	HRank [35]	93.36	105.70M (58.20%)	0.70M (59.30%)
	Ours-0.007	**93.73**	**98.04M (61.23%)**	**0.89M (48.26%)**

ResNet56/110. The results for ResNet56/110 are shown in Table 1. Firstly, we look into the result of ResNet56. Compared with L1, Ours-0.019 obtains more FLOPs and parameters reductions with higher Top-1 accuracy, and even its accuracy is 0.38% higher than the baseline. Although Ours-0.019 has a slightly lower pruning rate than NISP and HRank-A, it achieves larger reductions in FLOPs (52.31% vs. 35.45% by NISP and 52.31% vs. 50.02% by HRank-A) and better Top-1 accuracy (93.64% vs. 93.01% by NISP and 93.47% vs. 93.17% by HRank-A). Therefore, it can be verified that our method is able to greatly reduce the amount of calculation and memory footprint while achieves better model performance. From the result, Ours-0.055 can obtain a network with higher compression ratio, its FLOPs is reduced by 79.50%, parameters are pruned by 70.59%, at the cost of Top-1 accuracy drop by only 1.72%. Compared with GAL-0.8, Ours-0.055 achieves much higher pruning rate of FLOPs and parameters though their accuracies are almost the same. Meanwhile, it outperforms HRank-B in all three aspects.

Next, we analyze the result of ResNet110. Ours-0.007 leads to an improvement in Top-1 accuracy over the baseline model (93.73% vs. 93.50%) with 61.23% FLOPs and 48.26% parameters reductions. Its performance is significantly better than L1 and GAL-0.5. Compared with HRank, Ours-0.007 achieves higher reduection rate of FLOPs (61.23% by Ours-0.007 vs. 58.20% by HRank) and better accuracy (93.73% by Ours-0.007 vs. 93.36% by HRank), although the parameter pruning rate is lower.

DenseNet-40. Table 1 summarizes the result of DenseNet-40. Although Liu et al. [28] retains the same accuracy as the baseline, the compression ratio is relatively low, reducing FLOPs by only 32.84%. For Ours-0.02, 45.45% of FLOPs and 43.27% of the parameters are reduced, and the decrease of accuracy is only 0.20%. Ours-0.02 achieves a better performance compared with HRank-A and Zhao et al. [36]. Compared with GAL-0.01, Ours-0.02 has a big gain on both FLOPs and parameters pruning rate with the same Top-1 accuracy. For Ours-0.04, the Top-1 accuracy is 0.19% lower than that of HRank-B, but our method obtains more reductions of FLOPs and parameters.

GoogleNet. The results of GoogleNet are shown in Table 1. Ours-0.0045 obtains 95.19% Top-1 accuracy, which is even 0.14% higher than the baseline, and 64.47% of FLOPs and 73.17% of parameters are removed. It outperforms L1, Random, GAL-0.05, APoZ and HRank-A. Furthermore, we set the threshold to 0.01 to increase the pruning rate of the network. Ours-0.01 achieves a better performance than HRank-B (94.77% acc vs. 94.07% by HRank-B, 73.68% reduction of FLOPs vs. 70.39% by HRank-B, 81.46% reduction of parameters vs. 69.76% by HRank-B).

4.3   Results on ImageNet

Experiments are also conducted on the ImageNet dataset using ResNet50, and the results are shown in Table 2. As indicated by the results, our method has achieved a significant gain on both performance and compression ratios compared with several state-of-the-art methods. Specifically, we set the thresholds to 0.05, 0.09, 0.2 and 0.35 respectively to obtain different pruning rates. Ours-0.05 outperforms GAL-0.5, SSS-26 and HRank-A. It removes 43.03% FLOPs from baseline, while still yields 75.79% Top-1 accuracy and 92.82% Top-5 accuracy, improves the result of SSS-32 [20] and He et al. [16] by a large margin. In addition, Ours-0.09 achieves 75.04% Top-1 accuracy and 92.29% Top-5 accuracy with

53.30% and 40.16% reductions of FLOPs and parameters, respectively. Moreover, compared to GDP-0.6, GAL-0.5-joint, GAL-1, GDP-0.5 and HRank-B, Ours-0.2 has apparent advantages in all aspects, including Top-1/Top-5 accuracy as well as FLOPs and parameters reductions. For Ours-0.35, 75.80% FLOPs and 68.55% parameters are removed, its 70.58% Top-1 accuracy and 90.00% Top-5 accuracy are significantly better than those of GAL-1-joint and ThiNet-50. Compared with HRank-C, Ours-0.35 achieves higher Top-1 and Top-5 accuracy with the similar FLOPs and parameters reductions. Therefore, the ImageNet experiments indicate that our method also works well on large and complex datasets.

Table 2. Pruning results of Resnet-50 on ImageNet.

Method	Top-1 (%)	Top-5 (%)	FLOPs (PR)	Parameters (PR)
Baseline	76.15	92.87	4.09B (0.00%)	25.50M (0.00%)
SSS-32 [20]	74.18	91.91	2.82B (31.05%)	18.60M (27.06%)
He et al. [16]	72.30	90.80	2.73B (33.25%)	–
Ours-0.05	**75.79**	**92.82**	**2.33B (43.03%)**	**17.93M (29.69%)**
GAL-0.5 [31]	71.95	90.94	2.33B (43.03%)	21.20M (16.86%))
SSS-26 [20]	71.82	90.79	2.33B (43.03%)	15.60M (38.82%)
HRank-A [35]	74.98	92.33	2.30B (43.76%)	16.15M (36.67%)
Ours-0.09	**75.04**	**92.29**	**1.91B (53.30%)**	**15.26M (40.16%)**
GDP-0.6 [32]	71.19	90.71	1.88B (54.03%)	–
GAL-0.5-joint [31]	71.80	90.82	1.84B (55.01%)	19.31M (24.27%)
GAL-1 [31]	69.88	89.75	1.58B (61.37%)	14.67M (42.47%)
GDP-0.5 [32]	69.58	90.14	1.57B (61.61%)	–
HRank-B [35]	71.98	91.01	1.55B (62.10%)	13.77M (46.01%)
Ours-0.2	**73.06**	**91.30**	**1.31B (67.97%)**	**10.84M (57.49%)**
GAL-1-joint [31]	69.31	89.12	1.11B (72.86%)	10.21M (59.96%)
ThiNet-50 [15]	68.42	88.30	1.10B (73.11%)	8.66M (66.04%)
HRank-C [35]	69.10	89.58	0.98B (76.04%)	8.27M (67.59%)
Ours-0.35	**70.58**	**90.00**	**0.99B (75.80%)**	**8.02M (68.55%)**

4.4 Results on Object Detection Task

The proposed method is also applicable to other major computer vision tasks such as object detection. We take the SSD [37] (PyTorch version) as an example, its backbone network is similar to VGG16 and we prune it with VOC0712 dataset. Table 3 shows that our method is effective for object detection task, for example, it removes 30.92% FLOPs and 34,80% Parameters from baseline with improvement of 0.1% mAP. In fact, it is widely applicable to any network with common CNN structures.

Table 3. Pruning results of SSD on VOC0712.

Method	mAP (%)	FLOPs (PR)	Parameters (PR)
Baseline	77.68	31.40B (0.00%)	26.29M (0.00%)
Ours-0.05	77.78	21.69B (30.92%)	17.14M (34.80%)
Ours-0.1	77.14	18.27B (41.82%)	14.17M (46.10%)
Ours-0.3	76.45	12.22B (61.08%)	9.29M (64.66%)
Ours-0.5	75.83	9.69B (30.92%)	6.87M (16.67%)

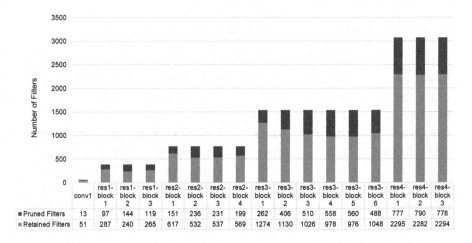

Fig. 3. Statistics of pruned (orange) and retained (blue) filters of ResNet50 on ImageNet with Ours-0.2 method. Shortcuts with convolutional layers are not included. (Color figure online)

4.5 Filter Pruning Analysis

As shown in Fig. 3, we reveal the pruning details about Ours-0.2 result on ImageNet dataset. We count the number of pruned/retained filters in all the layers except the shortcut connections with convolutional filters of ResNet50. For simplicity, the filter numbers of layers in the same block have been added together, the full result of each layer can be found in our supplementary material.

In ResNet50, there are 16 residual-blocks and one convolutional layer. Figure 3 shows that the pruned filters mainly distribute in the high-level blocks. The filters of the high-level blocks contain more semantic information in detail, some of which are redundant. Empirically, removing these filters has less impact on the performance of the network. Meanwhile, the pruning rate of each block is different as illustrated in Fig. 3, which also proves that our method attempts to search for the optimal pruning rate in each layer.

5   Conclusions

In this paper, we propose a method to search the optimal pruning rate in a layer-wise manner and only needs fine-tuning for once. Based on the filter importance criterion derived from loss variation and first-order approximation, convolutional networks can be pruned efficiently. The group pruning and channel selection mechanism are also introduced to adapt with shortcut connections in networks. For practical usage, binary search the threshold accelerates pruning at a given global pruning rate for the entire network without extra fine-tuning. Experiments demonstrate that our method outperforms previous state-of-the-art pruning methods on different datasets and networks. The code is available at https://github.com/Nuctech-AI/LBS_pruning.

References

1. Howard, A.G., et al.: Mobilenets: efficient convolutional neural networks for mobile vision applications. arXiv preprint arXiv:1704.04861 (2017)
2. Zhang, X., Zhou, X., Lin, M., Sun, J.: Shufflenet: an extremely efficient convolutional neural network for mobile devices. In: Proceedings of the IEEE Conference on Computer Vision and Pattern Recognition, pp. 6848–6856 (2018)
3. LeCun, Y., Denker, J.S., Solla, S.A.: Optimal brain damage. In: Advances in Neural Information Processing Systems, pp. 598–605 (1990)
4. Hassibi, B., Stork, D.G.: Second order derivatives for network pruning: optimal brain surgeon. In: Advances in Neural Information Processing Systems, pp. 164–171 (1993)
5. Li, H., Kadav, A., Durdanovic, I., Samet, H., Graf, H.P.: Pruning filters for efficient convnets. arXiv preprint arXiv:1608.08710 (2016)
6. Courbariaux, M., Bengio, Y., David, J.P.: Binaryconnect: training deep neural networks with binary weights during propagations. In: Advances in Neural Information Processing Systems, pp. 3123–3131 (2015)
7. Hubara, I., Courbariaux, M., Soudry, D., El-Yaniv, R., Bengio, Y.: Quantized neural networks: Training neural networks with low precision weights and activations. The Journal of Machine Learning Research **18**, 6869–6898 (2017)
8. Denton, E.L., Zaremba, W., Bruna, J., LeCun, Y., Fergus, R.: Exploiting linear structure within convolutional networks for efficient evaluation. In: Advances in neural information processing systems. (2014) 1269–1277
9. Hinton, G., Vinyals, O., Dean, J.: Distilling the knowledge in a neural network. arXiv preprint arXiv:1503.02531 (2015)
10. Han, S., Pool, J., Tran, J., Dally, W.: Learning both weights and connections for efficient neural network. In: Advances in Neural Information Processing Systems, pp. 1135–1143 (2015)
11. Srinivas, S., Babu, R.V.: Data-free parameter pruning for deep neural networks. arXiv preprint arXiv:1507.06149 (2015)
12. Han, S., et al.: EIE: efficient inference engine on compressed deep neural network. ACM SIGARCH Computer Architecture News **44**, 243–254 (2016)
13. Park, J., et al.: Faster CNNs with direct sparse convolutions and guided pruning. arXiv preprint arXiv:1608.01409 (2016)

14. Hu, H., Peng, R., Tai, Y., Tang, C., Trimming, N.: A data-driven neuron pruning approach towards efficient deep architectures. arXiv preprint arXiv:1607.03250 (2016)
15. Luo, J.H., Wu, J., Lin, W.: Thinet: a filter level pruning method for deep neural network compression. In: Proceedings of the IEEE International Conference on Computer Vision, pp. 5058–5066 (2017)
16. He, Y., Zhang, X., Sun, J.: Channel pruning for accelerating very deep neural networks. In: Proceedings of the IEEE International Conference on Computer Vision, pp. 1389–1397 (2017)
17. He, Y., Liu, P., Wang, Z., Hu, Z., Yang, Y.: Filter pruning via geometric median for deep convolutional neural networks acceleration. In: Proceedings of the IEEE Conference on Computer Vision and Pattern Recognition, pp. 4340–4349 (2019)
18. Molchanov, P., Mallya, A., Tyree, S., Frosio, I., Kautz, J.: Importance estimation for neural network pruning. In: Proceedings of the IEEE Conference on Computer Vision and Pattern Recognition, pp. 11264–11272 (2019)
19. He, Y., Lin, J., Liu, Z., Wang, H., Li, L.J., Han, S.: AMC: automl for model compression and acceleration on mobile devices. In: Proceedings of the European Conference on Computer Vision (ECCV). (2018) 784–800
20. Huang, Z., Wang, N.: Data-driven sparse structure selection for deep neural networks. In: Ferrari, V., Hebert, M., Sminchisescu, C., Weiss, Y. (eds.) ECCV 2018. LNCS, vol. 11220, pp. 317–334. Springer, Cham (2018). https://doi.org/10.1007/978-3-030-01270-0_19
21. Krizhevsky, A., Hinton, G., et al.: Learning multiple layers of features from tiny images (2009)
22. Russakovsky, O., et al.: Imagenet large scale visual recognition challenge. Int. J. Comput. Vision 115, 211–252 (2015)
23. Simonyan, K., Zisserman, A.: Very deep convolutional networks for large-scale image recognition. arXiv preprint arXiv:1409.1556 (2014)
24. Szegedy, C., et al.: Going deeper with convolutions. In: Proceedings of the IEEE Conference on Computer Vision and Pattern Recognition, pp. 1–9 (2015)
25. He, K., Zhang, X., Ren, S., Sun, J.: Deep residual learning for image recognition. In: Proceedings of the IEEE Conference on Computer Vision and Pattern Recognition, pp. 770–778 (2016)
26. Huang, G., Liu, Z., Van Der Maaten, L., Weinberger, K.Q.: Densely connected convolutional networks. In: Proceedings of the IEEE Conference on Computer Vision and Pattern Recognition, pp. 4700–4708 (2017)
27. Yu, R., et al.: NISP: pruning networks using neuron importance score propagation. In: Proceedings of the IEEE Conference on Computer Vision and Pattern Recognition, pp. 9194–9203 (2018)
28. Liu, Z., Li, J., Shen, Z., Huang, G., Yan, S., Zhang, C.: Learning efficient convolutional networks through network slimming. In: Proceedings of the IEEE International Conference on Computer Vision, pp. 2736–2744 (2017)
29. Molchanov, P., Tyree, S., Karras, T., Aila, T., Kautz, J.: Pruning convolutional neural networks for resource efficient inference. arXiv preprint arXiv:1611.06440 (2016)
30. You, Z., Yan, K., Ye, J., Ma, M., Wang, P.: Gate decorator: global filter pruning method for accelerating deep convolutional neural networks. In: Advances in Neural Information Processing Systems, pp. 2133–2144 (2019)
31. Lin, S., et al.: Towards optimal structured CNN pruning via generative adversarial learning. In: Proceedings of the IEEE Conference on Computer Vision and Pattern Recognition, pp. 2790–2799 (2019)

32. Lin, S., Ji, R., Li, Y., Wu, Y., Huang, F., Zhang, B.: Accelerating convolutional networks via global & dynamic filter pruning. IJCA **I**, 2425–2432 (2018)
33. Ding, X., Ding, G., Guo, Y., Han, J.: Centripetal SGD for pruning very deep convolutional networks with complicated structure. In: Proceedings of the IEEE Conference on Computer Vision and Pattern Recognition, pp. 4943–4953 (2019)
34. Paszke, A., et al.: Automatic differentiation in pytorch (2017)
35. Lin, M., et al.: Hrank: filter pruning using high-rank feature map. In: Proceedings of the IEEE/CVF Conference on Computer Vision and Pattern Recognition, pp. 1529–1538 (2020)
36. Zhao, C., et al.: Variational convolutional neural network pruning. In: Proceedings of the IEEE Conference on Computer Vision and Pattern Recognition, pp. 2780–2789 (2019)
37. Liu, W., et al.: SSD: single shot MultiBox detector. In: Leibe, B., Matas, J., Sebe, N., Welling, M. (eds.) ECCV 2016. LNCS, vol. 9905, pp. 21–37. Springer, Cham (2016). https://doi.org/10.1007/978-3-319-46448-0_2

Contrastively Smoothed Class Alignment
for Unsupervised Domain Adaptation

Shuyang Dai[1]([✉]), Yu Cheng[2], Yizhe Zhang[3], Zhe Gan[2], Jingjing Liu[2],
and Lawrence Carin[1]

[1] Duke University, Durham, USA
{shuyang.dai,lcarin}@duke.edu
[2] Microsoft Dynamics 365 AI Research, Redmond, USA
{yu.cheng,zhe.gan,jingjl}@microsoft.com
[3] Microsoft Research, Redmond, USA
yizhe.zhang@microsoft.com

Abstract. Recent unsupervised approaches to domain adaptation primarily focus on minimizing the gap between the source and the target domains through refining the feature generator, in order to learn a better alignment between the two domains. This minimization can be achieved via a domain classifier to detect target-domain features that are divergent from source-domain features. However, when optimizing via such domain-classification discrepancy, ambiguous target samples that are not smoothly distributed on the low-dimensional data manifold are often missed. To solve this issue, we propose a novel Contrastively Smoothed Class Alignment (CoSCA) model, that explicitly incorporates both intra- and inter-class domain discrepancy to better align ambiguous target samples with the source domain. CoSCA estimates the underlying label hypothesis of target samples, and simultaneously adapts their feature representations by optimizing a proposed contrastive loss. In addition, Maximum Mean Discrepancy (MMD) is utilized to directly match features between source and target samples for better global alignment. Experiments on several benchmark datasets demonstrate that CoSCAoutperforms state-of-the-art approaches for unsupervised domain adaptation by producing more discriminative features.

1 Introduction

Deep neural networks (DNNs) have significantly improved the state of the art on many supervised tasks [1–4]. However, without sufficient training data, DNNs often generalize poorly to new tasks or new environments [5]. This is known as dataset bias or a domain-shift problem [6]. Unsupervised domain adaptation (UDA) [7,8] aims to generalize a model learned from a source domain with rich annotated data to a new target domain without any labeled data. Recently, many approaches have been proposed to learn transferable representations, by simultaneously matching feature distributions across different domains [9,10].

Motivated by [11–13] introduced a min-max game: a domain discriminator is learned by minimizing the error of distinguishing data samples from the source and

Electronic supplementary material The online version of this chapter (https://doi.org/10.1007/978-3-030-69538-5_17) contains supplementary material, which is available to authorized users.

© Springer Nature Switzerland AG 2021
H. Ishikawa et al. (Eds.): ACCV 2020, LNCS 12625, pp. 268–283, 2021.
https://doi.org/10.1007/978-3-030-69538-5_17

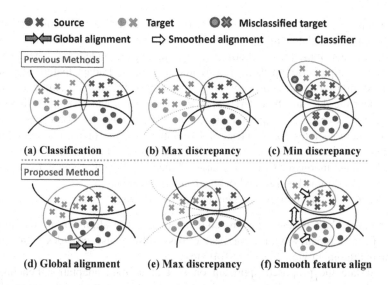

Fig. 1. Comparison between previous classifier-discrepancy-based methods and our proposed CoSCA in the *feature* space. **Top:** The region of vacancy created by maximum discrepancy reduces the smoothness of alignment between ambiguous target samples and source samples, leading to sub-optimal solutions. This problem becomes more severe when global domain alignment is not considered. **Bottom:** Demonstration of global alignment and class-conditional adaptation by using the proposed CoSCA. After classifier discrepancy is maximized, the proposed contrastive loss moves ambiguous target samples near the decision boundary towards their neighbors and separates them from non-neighbors.

the target domains, while a feature generator learns transferable features that are indistinguishable by the domain discriminator. This imposes that the learned features are domain-invariant. Additionally, a feature classifier ensures that the learned features are discriminative in the source domain. Despite promising results, these adversarial methods suffer from inherent algorithmic weaknesses [14]. Specifically, the generator may manifest ambiguous features near class boundaries [15]: while the generator manages to fool the discriminator, some target-domain features may still be misclassified. In other words, the model merely aligns the global marginal distribution of the two domains and ignores the class-conditional decision boundaries.

To overcome this issue, recent UDA models further align class-level distributions by taking the decision boundary into consideration. These methods either rely on iteratively refining the decision boundary with empirical data [14, 16], or utilizing multi-view information [17]. Alternatively, the maximum classifier discrepancy (MCD) [15] model conducts a min-max game between a feature generator and two classifiers. Ambiguous target samples that are far from source-domain samples can be detected when the discrepancy between the two classifiers is maximized, as shown in Fig. 1(b). Meanwhile, as the generator fools the classifiers, the generated target features may fall into the source feature regions. However, the target samples may not be smooth on the low-dimensional manifold [18, 19], meaning that neighboring samples may not belong to the same class. As a result, some generated target features could be miscategorized as shown in Fig. 1(c).

In this paper, we propose the **C**ontrastively **S**moothed **C**lass **A**lignment (CoSCA) model to improve the latent alignment of class-conditional feature distributions between source and target domains, by alternatively estimating the underlying label hypothesis of target samples to map them into tighter clusters, and adapt feature representations based on a proposed contrastive loss. Specifically, by aligning ambiguous target samples near the decision boundaries with their neighbors and distancing them from non-neighbors, CoSCA enhances the alignment of each class in a contrastive manner. Figure 1(f) demonstrates an enhanced and smoothed version of the class-conditional alignment. Moreover, as shown in Fig. 1(d), Maximum Mean Discrepancy (MMD) is included to better merge the source and target domain feature representations. The overall framework is trained end-to-end in an adversarial manner.

Our principal contributions are summarized as follows:

- We propose CoSCA, a novel approach that smooths class alignment for maximizing classifier discrepancy with a contrastive loss. CoSCA also provides better global domain alignment via the use of MMD loss.
- We validate the proposed approach on several domain adaptation benchmarks. Extensive experiments demonstrate that CoSCA achieves state-of-the-art results on several benchmarks.

2   Related Work

Unsupervised Domain Adaptation. A practical solution for domain adaptation is to learn domain-invariant features whose distribution is similar across the source and the target domains. For example, Sener *et al.* [20] proposed using clustering techniques and pseudo-labels to obtain discriminative features. Long *et al.* proposed DAN [21] and JAN [22] to minimize the MMD or variations of MMD between two domains. Adversarial domain adaptation integrates adversarial learning and domain adaptation in a two-player game [10,12,13]. Following this idea, most existing adversarial learning methods reduce feature differences by fooling a domain discriminator [8,23]. However, these methods fail to consider the relationship between target samples and the class-conditional decision boundaries when aligning features [15], while only merging the source and the target domains.

Class-Conditional Alignment. To address the aforementioned issue, recent work enforces class-level alignment while aligning global marginal distributions. Associative domain adaptation (ADA) [9] reinforces associations across domains directly in the embedding space, to extract features that are statistically domain-invariant and class-discriminative. Adversarial Dropout Regularization (ADR) [16] and Maximum Classifier Discrepancy (MCD) [15] were proposed to train a neural network in an adversarial manner, avoiding generating non-discriminative features lying in the region near the decision boundary. In [22,24] the authors considered class information when measuring domain discrepancy. Co-regularized Domain Adaptation (Co-DA) [17] utilized multi-view information to match the marginal feature distributions corresponding to the class-conditional distributions. Compared with previous work that executed the alignment by optimizing "hard" metrics [15,17], we propose to smooth the alignment iteratively, with explicitly defined loss (Fig. 2).

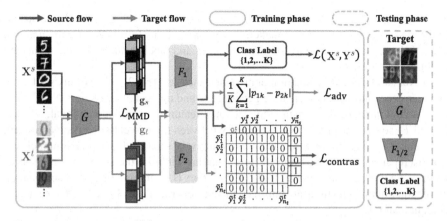

Fig. 2. Framework of the proposed CoSCA. The inputs are $\mathbf{X}^s$ with label $\mathbf{Y}^s$ from the source domain and unlabeled $\mathbf{X}^t$ from the target domain. The model contains a shared feature generator G and two feature classifiers F_1 and F_2. $\mathcal{L}_{\text{MMD}}$ is calculated using the generated feature mean of the source and target, *i.e.*, g_s and g_t respectively. $\mathcal{L}_{\text{adv}}$ is the classifier discrepancy calculated based on the probability outputs p_1 and p_2 of $F_1(G(\mathbf{X}^t))$ and $F_2(G(\mathbf{X}^t))$, respectively. $\mathcal{L}_{\text{contras}}$ is the contrastive loss calculated for both source-and-target and target-and-target samples.

Contrastive Learning. The intuition for contrastive learning is to let the model under-stand the difference between one set (*e.g.*, data points) and another, instead of only characterizing a single set [25]. This idea has been explored in previous works that model intra-class compactness and inter-class separability (*e.g.*, distinctiveness loss [26], contrastive loss [27], triplet loss [28]) and tangent distance [29]. It has also been extended to consider several assumptions in semi-supervised and unsupervised learn-ing [19,30], such as the low-density region (or cluster) assumption [19,29] that the decision boundary should lie in the low-density region, rather than crossing the high-density region. Recently, contrastive learning was applied in UDA [31], in which the intra/inter-class domain discrepancy were modeled. In comparison, our work is based on the MCD framework, utilizing the low-density assumption and focusing on sepa-rating the ambiguous target data points by optimizing the contrastive objective, allow-ing the decision boundary to sit in the low-density region, *i.e.*, region of vacancy, and smoothness assumption.

3 Approach

Unsupervised domain adaptation seeks to generalize a learned model from a source domain to a target domain, the latter following a different (but related) data distribu-tion from the former. Specifically, the source- and target-domain samples are denoted $\mathcal{S} = \{(\mathbf{x}_1^s, y_1^s), ..., (\mathbf{x}_i^s, y_i^s), ..., (\mathbf{x}_{N_s}^s, y_{N_s}^s)\}$, and $\mathcal{T} = \{\mathbf{x}_1^t, ..., \mathbf{x}_i^t, ..., \mathbf{x}_{N_t}^t\}$, respec-tively, where $\mathbf{x}_i^s$ and $\mathbf{x}_i^t$ are the input, and $y_i^s \in \{1, 2, ..., K\}$ represents the data labels of K classes in the source domain. The target domain shares the same label types as the source domain, but we possess no labeled examples from the target domain. We are interested in learning a deep network G that reduces domain shift in the data distribution across S and T, in order to make accurate predictions for y_i^t. We use the notation $(\mathbf{X}^s, \mathbf{Y}^s)$ to describe the source-domain samples and labels, and $\mathbf{X}^t$ for the unlabeled target-domain samples.

Adversarial domain adaptation approaches such as [15,32] achieve this goal via a two-step procedure: i) train a feature generator G and the feature classifiers F_1, F_2 with the source-domain data, to ensure the generated features are class-conditional; ii) train F_1 and F_2 so that the prediction discrepancy between the two classifiers is maximized, and train G to generate features that are distinctively separated. The maximum classifier discrepancy detects the target features that are far from the support of the source domain. As the generator tries to fool the classifiers (i.e., minimizing the discrepancy), these target-domain features are enforced to be categorized and aligned with the source-domain features.

However, only measuring divergence between F_1 and F_2 can be considered first-order moment matching, which may be insufficient for adversarial training. Previous work also observed similar issues [33,34]. We address this challenge by adding the Maximum Mean Discrepancy (MMD) loss, that matches the difference via higher-order moments. Also, the class alignment in existing UDA methods takes into account the intra-class domain discrepancy only, which makes it difficult to separate samples within the same class that are close to the decision boundary. Thus, in addition to the discrepancy loss, we also measure both intra- and inter-class discrepancy across domains. Specifically, we propose to minimize the distance among target-domain features that fall into the same class based on decision boundaries, and separate those features from different categories. During this process, ambiguous target features are simultaneously kept away from the decision boundaries and mapped into the high-density region, achieving better class alignment.

3.1 Global Alignment with MMD

Following [15], we first train a feature generator $G(\cdot)$ and two classifiers $F_1(G(\cdot))$ and $F_2(G(\cdot))$ to minimize the softmax cross-entropy loss using the data from the labeled source domain S, defined as:

$$\mathcal{L}(\mathbf{X}^s, \mathbf{Y}^s) = -\mathbb{E}_{(\mathbf{x}^s, y^s) \sim (\mathbf{X}^s, \mathbf{Y}^s)} \left[\sum_{k=1}^{K} \mathbb{1}_{[k=y^s]} \log p_1(\mathbf{y}|\mathbf{x}^s) \right.$$
$$\left. + \sum_{k=1}^{K} \mathbb{1}_{[k=y^s]} \log p_2(\mathbf{y}|\mathbf{x}^s) \right] \tag{1}$$

where $p_1(\mathbf{y}|\mathbf{x})$ and $p_2(\mathbf{y}|\mathbf{x})$ are the probabilistic output of the two classifiers $F_1(G(\mathbf{x}))$ and $F_2(G(\mathbf{x}))$, respectively.

In addition to (1), we explicitly minimize the distance between the source and target feature distributions with MMD. The main idea of MMD is to estimate the distance between two distributions as the distance between sample means of the projected embeddings in a Hilbert space. Minimizing MMD is equivalent to minimizing all orders of moments [35]. In practice, the squared value of MMD is estimated with empirical kernel mean embeddings:

$$\mathcal{L}_{\text{MMD}}(\mathbf{X}^s, \mathbf{X}^t) = \sum_{i=1}^{n_s} \sum_{j=1}^{n_t} k(\phi(\frac{\mathbf{g}_s}{||\mathbf{g}_s||}), \phi(\frac{\mathbf{g}_t}{||\mathbf{g}_t||}))$$

$$\mathbf{g}_s = \frac{1}{n_s} \sum_{i=1}^{n_s} G(\mathbf{x}_i^s), \quad \mathbf{g}_t = \frac{1}{n_t} \sum_{i=1}^{n_t} G(\mathbf{x}_i^t)$$

(2)

where $\phi(\cdot)$ is the kernel mapping, $\mathbf{g}_s \in \mathcal{R}^n$, $\mathbf{g}_t \in \mathcal{R}^n$, with n_t and n_s denoting the size of a training mini-batch of the data from the source domain $\mathcal{S}$ and the target domain $\mathcal{T}$, respectively; $|| \cdot ||$ denotes the ℓ_2-norm. With the MMD loss $\mathcal{L}_{\text{MMD}}$, the normalized features in the two domains are encouraged to be distributed identically, leading to better global domain alignment.

3.2 Contrastively Smoothed Class Alignment

Discrepancy Loss. The discrepancy loss represents the level of disagreement between the two feature classifiers in prediction for target-domain samples. Specifically, the discrepancy loss between F_1 and F_2 is defined as:

$$d(p_1(\mathbf{y}|\mathbf{x}), p_2(\mathbf{y}|\mathbf{x})) = \frac{1}{K} \sum_{k=1}^{K} \left| p_{1_k}(\mathbf{y}|\mathbf{x}) - p_{2_k}(\mathbf{y}|\mathbf{x}) \right|$$

(3)

where $| \cdot |$ denotes the ℓ_1-norm, and $p_{1_k}(\cdot)$ and $p_{2_k}(\cdot)$ are the probability output of p_1 and p_2 for the k-th class, respectively. Accordingly, we can define the discrepancy loss over the target domain $\mathcal{T}$:

$$\mathcal{L}_{\text{adv}}(\mathbf{X}^t) = \mathbb{E}_{\mathbf{x}^t \sim \mathbf{X}^t} \left[d(p_1(\mathbf{y}|\mathbf{x}^t), p_2(\mathbf{y}|\mathbf{x}^t)) \right]$$

(4)

Adversarial training is conducted in the MCD [15] setup:

$$\min_{F_1, F_2} \mathcal{L}(\mathbf{X}^s, \mathbf{Y}^s) - \lambda \mathcal{L}_{\text{adv}}(\mathbf{X}^t)$$

$$\min_G \mathcal{L}_{\text{adv}}(\mathbf{X}^t)$$

(5)

where λ is a hyper-parameter. Minimizing the discrepancy between the two classifiers F_1 and F_2 induces smoothness for the clearly classified target-domain features, while the region in the vacancy among the ambiguous ones remains non-smooth. Moreover, MCD only utilizes the unlabeled target-domain samples, while ignoring the labeled source-domain data when estimating the discrepancy.

Contrastive Loss. To further optimize G to estimate the underlying label hypothesis of target-domain samples, we propose to measure the intra- and inter-class discrepancy across domains, conditional on class information. By using an indicator defined as $c(y, y') = \begin{cases} 1, & y = y' \\ 0, & y \neq y' \end{cases}$, we define the contrastive loss between $\mathcal{S}$ and $\mathcal{T}$ as:

$$\mathcal{L}_{\text{contras}}^{\mathcal{S} \leftrightarrow \mathcal{T}} = \sum_{\mathbf{x}_i^s \in \mathcal{S}, \mathbf{x}_j^t \in \mathcal{T}} L_{\text{dis}}(G(\mathbf{x}_i^s), G(\mathbf{x}_j^t), c(y_i^s, \widetilde{y}_j^t))$$

(6)

where L_{dis} is a distance measure (defined below), and $\tilde{y}_j^t$ is the predicted target label for $\mathbf{x}_j^t$. Specifically, (6) covers two types of class-aware domain discrepancies: i) intra-class domain discrepancy ($y_i^s = \tilde{y}_j^t$); and ii) inter-class domain discrepancy ($y_i^s \neq \tilde{y}_j^t$). Note that y_i^s is known, providing some supervision for parameter learning. Similarly, we can define the constrastive loss between $\mathcal{T}$ and $\mathcal{T}$ as:

$$\mathcal{L}_{\text{contras}}^{\mathcal{T} \leftrightarrow \mathcal{T}} = \sum_{\mathbf{x}_i^t, \mathbf{x}_j^t \in \mathcal{T}} L_{\text{dis}}(G(\mathbf{x}_i^t), G(\mathbf{x}_j^t), c(\tilde{y}_i^t, \tilde{y}_j^t)) \tag{7}$$

To obtain the indicator $c(y, y')$, estimated target label $\tilde{y}_i^t$ is required. Specifically, for each data sample $\mathbf{x}_j^t$, a pseudo label is predicted based on the maximum posterior probability of the two classifiers:

$$\tilde{y}_j^t = \underset{k \in \{1,2,...,K\}}{\arg\max} \Big\{ p(F_1(G(\mathbf{x}_j^t)) = k|\mathbf{x}) \\ + p(F_2(G(\mathbf{x}_j^t)) = k|\mathbf{x}) \Big\} \tag{8}$$

Ideally, based on the indicator, L_{dis} should ensure the gathering of features that fall in the same class, while separating those in different categories. Following [19], we utilize contrastive Siamese networks [36], which can learn an invariant mapping to a smooth and coherent feature space and perform well in practice:

$$L_{\text{dis}} = \begin{cases} ||G(\mathbf{x}_i) - G(\mathbf{x}_j)||^2 & c_{ij} = 1 \\ \max(0, m - ||G(\mathbf{x}_i) - G(\mathbf{x}_j)||)^2 & c_{ij} = 0 \end{cases} \tag{9}$$

where $c_{ij} = c(y_i, y_j)$ and m is a pre-defined margin. The margin loss constrains the neighboring features to be consistent. Based on the above definitions of source-and-target and target-and-target contrastive losses, the overall objective is:

$$\mathcal{L}_{\text{contras}}(\mathbf{X}^s, \mathbf{Y}^s, \mathbf{X}^t) = \mathcal{L}_{\text{contras}}^{\mathcal{S} \leftrightarrow \mathcal{T}} + \mathcal{L}_{\text{contras}}^{\mathcal{T} \leftrightarrow \mathcal{T}} \tag{10}$$

Minimizing the contrastive loss $\mathcal{L}_{\text{contras}}$ encourages features in the same class to aggregate together while pushing unrelated pairs away from each other. In other words, the semantic feature approximation is enhanced to induce smoothness between data in the feature space.

3.3 Training Procedure

We optimize G, F_1 and F_2 by combining all of the aforementioned losses, performed in an adversarial training manner. Specifically, we first train the classifiers F_1 and F_2 and the generator G to minimize the objective:

$$\min_{F_1, F_2, G} \mathcal{L}(\mathbf{X}^s, \mathbf{Y}^s) + \lambda_1 \mathcal{L}_{\text{MMD}}(\mathbf{X}^s, \mathbf{X}^t) \tag{11}$$

We then train the classifiers F_1 and F_2 while keeping the generator G fixed. The objective is:

$$\min_{F_1, F_2} \mathcal{L}(\mathbf{X}^s, \mathbf{Y}^s) - \lambda_2 \mathcal{L}_{\text{adv}}(\mathbf{X}^t) \tag{12}$$

Algorithm 1. Training procedure of CoSCA.

1: **Input:** Source domain samples $\{\mathbf{x}_i^s, y_i^s\}$, and target domain samples $\{\mathbf{x}_j^t\}$. Hyper-parameters $\lambda_1, \lambda_2, \lambda_3$, and inner-loop iteration τ and δ.
2: **Output:** Classifiers F_1 and F_2, and generator G.

3: **for** *iter* from 1 to *max_iter* **do**
4:    Sample a mini-batch of source samples $[\mathbf{x}_i^s, y_i^s]$ and target samples $[\mathbf{x}_j^t]$.

5:    *# Update both the generator and the classifiers*
6:    Compute $\mathcal{L}(\mathbf{X}^s, \mathbf{Y}^s)$ on $[\mathbf{x}_i^s, y_i^s]$.
7:    Compute $\mathcal{L}_{\text{MMD}}(\mathbf{X}^s, \mathbf{X}^t)$ on $[\mathbf{x}_i^s, \mathbf{x}_j^t]$.
8:    Update G, F_1 and F_2 using (11).

9:    *# Update the classifiers*
10:    **for** *inner_loop_iter₁* from 1 to τ **do**
11:        Compute $\mathcal{L}(\mathbf{X}^s, \mathbf{Y}^s)$ on $[\mathbf{x}_i^s, y_i^s]$.
12:        Compute $\mathcal{L}_{\text{adv}}(\mathbf{X}^t)$ on $\mathbf{x}_j^t$.
13:        Fix G, update F_1 and F_2 using (12).
14:    **end for**

15:    *# Update the feature generator*
16:    **for** *inner_loop_iter₂* from 1 to δ **do**
17:        Compute $\mathcal{L}_{\text{adv}}(\mathbf{X}^t)$ on $\mathbf{x}_j^t$.
18:        Compute $\mathcal{L}_{\text{contras}}(\mathbf{X}^s, \mathbf{Y}^s, \mathbf{X}^t)$ on $[\mathbf{x}_i^s, y_i^s, \mathbf{x}_j^t]$.
19:        Fix F_1 and F_2, update G using (13).
20:    **end for**
21: **end for**

Lastly, we train the generator G with the following objective, while keeping both F_1 and F_2 fixed:

$$\min_G \ \lambda_2 \mathcal{L}_{\text{adv}}(\mathbf{X}^t) + \lambda_3 \mathcal{L}_{\text{contras}}(\mathbf{X}^s, \mathbf{Y}^s, \mathbf{X}^t) \tag{13}$$

where λ_1, λ_2 and λ_3 are hyper-parameters that balance the different objectives. These steps are repeated, with the full approach summarized in Algorithm 1. In our experiments, the inner-loop iteration numbers τ and δ are both set to 2.

Class-Aware Sampling. When training with the contrastive loss, it is important to sample a mini-batch of data with all the classes, to allow (10) to be fully trained. Following [31], we use a class-aware sampling strategy. Specifically, we randomly select a subset of each class, from which a mini-batch is sampled. Consequently, in each mini-batch, we are able to estimate the intra/inter-class discrepancy.

Dynamic Parameterization of λ_3. In our implementation, we adapt a dynamic $\omega(t)$ to parameterize λ_3. We set $\omega(t) = \exp[-\theta(1 - \frac{t}{\text{max-epochs}})]\lambda_3$, which is a Gaussian curve ranging from 0 to λ_3; this is employed to prevent unlabeled target features gathering in the early stage of training, as the pseudo labels might be unreliable.

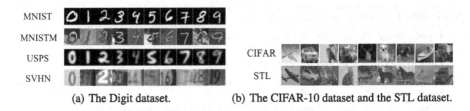

(a) The Digit dataset.   (b) The CIFAR-10 dataset and the STL dataset.

Fig. 3. Sample images from the Digit, CIFAR-10 and STL datasets. Images from each column belong to the same class, while each row corresponds to a domain.

4   Experiments

We evaluate the proposed model primarily on image datasets. To compare with MCD [15] as well as the state-of-the-art results in [14,17], we evaluate on the same datasets used in those studies: the digit datasets (*i.e.*, MNIST, MNISTM, Street View House Numbers (SVHN), and USPS), CIFAR-10, and STL-10. We also conduct experiments on the VisDA dataset, *i.e.*, large-scale images. Our model can also be applied to non-visual domain adaptation tasks. Specifically, to show the flexibility of our model, we also evaluate it on the Amazon Reviews dataset.

For visual domain adaptation tasks, the proposed model is implemented based on VADA [14] and Co-DA [17] to avoid any incidental difference caused by network architecture. However, different from these methods, our model does not require a discriminator, and only adopts the architecture for the feature generator G and the classifier F. Specifically, G has 9 convolutional layers with several dropout, max-pool, Gaussian noise and global pool layers (details can be found in the Supplementary Material). Both F_1 and F_2 are one-layer MLPs. We also include instance normalization [14,37], achieving superior results on several benchmarks. For the VisDA dataset, we implemented our model based on Self-ensembling Domain Adaptation (SEDA) [38]. To compare with MCD and Contrastive Adaptation Network (CAN) [31] (codebase not available) in both experiments, we re-implemented them using the exact architecture as our model.

In addition to the aforementioned baseline models, we also include results from recently proposed unsupervised domain adaptation models. Note that standard domain adaptation methods (such as Transfer Component Analysis (TCA) [39] and Subspace Alignment (SA) [40]) are not included; these models only work on pre-extracted features, and are often not scalable to large datasets. Instead, we mainly compare our model with methods based on adversarial neural networks.

For the non-visual task, we adopt a one-layer CNN structure from previous work [41]. The feature generator G consists of three components, including a 300-dimensional word embedding layer using GloVe [42], a one-layer CNN with ReLU, and a max-over-time pooling through which the final sentence representation is obtained. The classifiers F_1 and F_2 can be decomposed into one dropout layer and one fully connected output layer.

Table 1. Results on visual domain adaptation tasks. Source-Only corresponds to training a classifier in the source domain and applying it directly to the target domain, without any adaptation. Models with instance-normalized input are implemented using the same network architecture. Results with † are reported in [15].

Source domain	MNIST	SVHN	MNIST	MNIST	CIFAR	STL
Target domain	SVHN	MNIST	MNISTM	USPS	STL	CIFAR
MMD [21]	–	71.1	76.9	81.1	–	–
DANN [8]	35.7	71.1	81.5	77.1	–	–
DSN [44]	40.1	82.7	83.2	91.3	–	–
ATT [45]	52.8	86.2	94.2	–	–	–
With instance-normalized input:						
Souce-only	40.9	82.4	59.9	76.7	77.0	62.6
VADA [14]	73.3	94.5	95.7	–	78.3	71.4
Co-DA [17]	**81.3**	98.6	97.3	–	80.3	74.5
MCD [15]	68.7	96.2†	96.7	94.2†	78.1	69.2
SEDA [38]	37.5	**99.2**	–	98.2	80.1	74.2
CAN [31]	67.1	94.8	96.2	97.5	77.3	70.4
CoSCA	80.7	98.7	**98.9**	**99.3**	**81.7**	**75.2**

4.1 Digit Datasets

There are four types of digit images (*i.e.*, four domains). MNIST and USPS are both hand-written gray-scale images, with relatively small domain difference. MNISTM [8] is a dataset built upon MNIST by adding randomly colored image patches from BSD500 dataset [43]. SVHN includes colored images of street numbers. All images are rescaled to $32 \times 32 \times 3$. Sample images of all four digit datasets are presented in Fig. 3(a).

MNIST→SVHN. While both MNIST and SVHN include images of digits, there exists a large domain gap between these two datasets. As gray-scale handwritten digits, MNIST has much lower dimensionality than SVHN, which contains cropped street-view images of house numbers. Specifically, each image from SVHN has a colored background, which sometimes contains multiple digits, and might be blurry. This makes MNIST→SVHN a much harder adaptation task than other digit datasets. It is shown recently in [14] that instance normalization allows the classifier to be invariant to channel-wide scaling and shifting of the input pixel intensities, greatly improving the adaptation performance on MNIST→SVHN (73.3%). With instance normalization, our proposed CoSCA achieves test accuracy of 80.7%, as shown in Table 1, competitive with state-of-the-art results from [17].

Notice that MCD does not provide adequate performance. Figure 4(a) plots the t-SNE embedding of the features learned by MCD. Domains are indicated by different colors, and classes are indicated by different digit numbers. MCD fails to align the features of the two domains globally due to the large domain gap. In other words, the maximized discrepancy provides too many ambiguous target-domain samples. As a result,

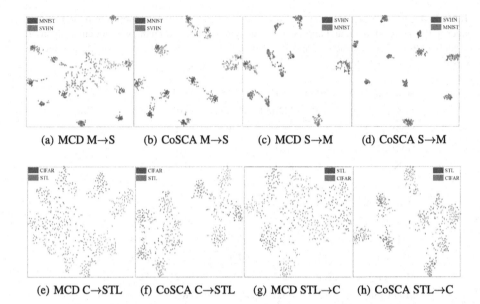

(a) MCD M→S   (b) CoSCA M→S   (c) MCD S→M   (d) CoSCA S→M

(e) MCD C→STL   (f) CoSCA C→STL   (g) MCD STL→C   (h) CoSCA STL→C

Fig. 4. t-SNE embedding of the features $G(x)$ for MNIST (M) → SVHN (S) and STL → CIFAR (C). Color indicates domain, and the digit number is the label. The ideal situation is to mix the two colors with the same label, representing domain-invariant features. The t-SNE plots for the other datasets are provided in the Supplementary Material.

the feature generator may not be able to properly align them with the source-domain samples. In comparison, as shown in Fig. 4(b), CoSCA utilizes the MMD between the source and the target domain features, thus maintaining a better global domain alignment. With further smoothed class-conditional adaptation, it outperforms MCD.

SVHN→MNIST. Classification with the MNIST dataset is easier than others. As shown in Table 1, source-only achieves 82.4% on SVHN→MNIST with instance normalization. Therefore, even with the same amount of domain difference, performance on SVHN→MNIST is much better than MNIST→SVHN across all compared models. The test accuracy of our model achieves 98.7%.

MNIST→MNISTM. Since MNISTM is a colored version of MNIST, there exists a one-to-one matching between the two datasets, *i.e.*, a domain adaptation model would perform well as long as domain-invariant features are properly extracted. CoSCA provides better results than Co-DA, yielding a test accuracy of 98.9%.

MNIST→USPS. Evaluation on MNIST and USPS datasets is also conducted to compare our model with other baselines. The proposed method achieves an excellent result of 99.3%.

4.2 CIFAR-10 and STL-10 Datasets

CIFAR-10 and STL-10 are both 10-class datasets, with each image containing an animal or a type of transportation. Images from each class are much more diverse than the digit datasets, with higher intrinsic dimensionality, which makes it a harder domain adaptation task. There are 9 overlapping classes between these two datasets. Figure 3(b)

Table 2. Test accuracy of ResNet101 model fine-tuned on the VisDA dataset. Results with † are reported in [15], while the others are implemented using the same network architecture.

Model	Plane	Bcycl	Bus	Car	Horse	Knife	Mcycl	Person	Plant	Sktbrd	Train	Truck	Mean
Source Only	55.1	53.3	61.9	59.1	80.6	17.9	79.7	31.2	81.0	26.5	73.5	8.5	52.4†
MMD [21]	87.1	63.0	76.5	42.0	90.3	42.9	85.9	53.1	49.7	36.3	85.8	20.7	61.1†
DANN [8]	81.9	77.7	82.8	44.3	81.2	29.5	65.1	28.6	51.9	54.6	82.8	7.8	57.4†
MCD [15]	89.1	80.8	82.9	70.9	91.6	56.5	89.5	79.3	90.9	76.1	88.3	29.3	77.1
CAN [31]	91.4	78.9	79.1	72.8	93.2	63.4	82.4	68.6	93.2	88.3	84.1	**39.2**	77.9
SEDA [38]	95.3	87.1	84.2	58.3	94.4	**89.6**	87.9	79.1	92.8	**91.3**	**89.6**	37.4	82.2
CoSCA	**95.7**	**87.4**	**85.7**	**73.5**	**95.3**	72.8	**91.5**	**84.8**	**94.6**	87.9	87.9	36.8	**82.9**

shows some sample images from each class. CIFAR provides images of size 32×32 and a large training set of 50,000 image samples, while STL contains higher quality images of size 96×96, but with a much smaller training set of 5,000 samples. Following [14, 17, 38], we remove non-overlapping classes from these two datasets and resize the images from STL to 32×32.

STL→CIFAR is more difficult than CIFAR→STL, due to the small training set in STL. For the latter, the source-only model with no adaptation involved achieves an accuracy of 77.0%. With adaptation, the margin-of-improvement is relatively small, while CoSCA provides the best improvement of 4.7% among all the models (Table 1). For STL→CIFAR, our model yields a 12.6% margin-of-improvement and an accuracy of 75.2%. Figures 4(e), 4(f), 4(g), and 4(h) provide t-SNE plots for MCD and our model, respectively, which shows our model achieves much better alignment for each class.

4.3 VisDA Dataset

The VisDA dataset is a large-scale image dataset that evaluates the adaptation from synthetic-object to real-object images. Images from the source domain are synthetic renderings of 3D models from different angles and lighting conditions. There are 152,397 image samples in the source domain, and 55,388 image samples in the target domain. The image size, after rescaling as in [15], is $224 \times 224 \times 3$. A model architecture with ResNet101 [4] pre-trained on Imagenet is required. There are 12 different object categories in VisDA, shared by the source and the target domains.

Table 2 shows the test accuracy of different models in all object classes. The class-aware methods, namely MCD [15], SEDA [38] and our proposed CoSCA, outperform the source only model in all categories. In comparison, the methods that are mainly based on distribution matching do not perform well in some of the categories. CoSCA outperforms MCD, showing the effectiveness of contrastive loss and MMD global alignment. In addition, it performs better than SEDA in most categories, demonstrating its robustness in handling large scale images.

Table 3. Results on the Amazon reviews dataset. Results with † are reported by [46,47].

	Source-only	DANN [8]	PBLM [46]	MCD [15]	DAS [47]	CoSCA
Accuracy	79.13	80.29†	80.40†	81.35	81.96†	**83.17**

Table 4. Ablation study on CoSCA with different variations of MCD on MNIST→SVHN, STL→CIFAR, and Amazon Reviews.

Model	MNIST SVHN	STL CIFAR	Amazon Reviews
MCD [15]	68.7	69.2	81.35
MCD+MMD	72.1	70.2	81.73
MCD+Contras	75.9	73.4	82.56
CoSCA	**80.7**	**75.2**	**83.17**

4.4 Amazon Reviews Dataset

We also evaluate CoSCA on the Amazon Reviews dataset collected by Blitzer *et al.* [48]. It contains reviews from several different domains, with 1000 positive and 1000 negative reviews in each domain.

Table 3 shows the average classification accuracy of different methods, including DANN [8] DAS [47] and PBLM [46]. We use the same model architecture and parameter setting for MCD and the source-only model. Results show that the proposed CoSCA outperforms all other methods. Specifically, it improves the performance from test accuracy of 81.96% to 83.17%, when compared to the state-of-the-art method DAS. MCD achieves 81.35%, which is also outperformed by CoSCA.

4.5 Ablation Study

To further demonstrate the improvement of CoSCA over MCD [15], we conduct an ablation study. Specifically, with the same network architecture and setup, we compare model performance among 1) MCD, 2) MCD with smooth alignment (MCD+Contras), 3) MCD with global alighnment (MCD+MMD), and 4) CoSCA, to validate the effectiveness of adding contrastive loss $\mathcal{L}_{contras}$ and MMD loss $\mathcal{L}_{MMD}$ to MCD. As MCD has already achieved superior performance on some of the benchmark datasets, we mainly choose those tasks on which MCD does not perform very well, in order to better analyze the margin of improvement. Therefore, MNIST→SVHN, STL→CIFAR and Amazon Reviews are selected for this experiment (Table 4).

Effect of Contrastive Alignment. We compare CoSCA with MCD as well as its few variations, to validate the effectiveness of the proposed contrastive alignment. Table 4 provides the test accuracy for every model across the selected benchmark datasets. For MNIST→SVHN, MCD+Contrastive outperforms MCD by 7.2%. For STL→CIFAR and Amazon Reviews, the margin of improvement is 4.2% and 1.21%, respectively (less significant than MNIST→SVHN, possibly due to the smaller domain difference).

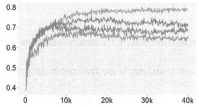

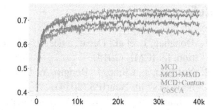

(a) Validation accuracy vs number of iterations for MNIST→SVHN.

(b) Validation accuracy vs number of iterations for STL→CIFAR.

Fig. 5. Ablation study on CoSCA and different variations of MCD.

Note that the results of MCD+Contras are still worse than CoSCA, demonstrating the effectiveness of the global domain alignment and the framework design of our model.

Effect of MMD. We further investigate how the MMD loss can impact the performance of our proposed CoSCA. Specifically, for MNIST→SVHN, MCD+MMD achieves a test accuracy of 72.1%, only lifting the original result of MCD by 3.4%. For STL→CIFAR and Amazon Reviews, the margin-of-improvement is 1.0% and 0.38%, respectively. While this validates the effectiveness of having global alignment in the MCD framework, the improvement is small. Without a smoothed class-conditional alignment, MCD still encounters misclassified target features during training, leading to a sub-optimal solution. Notice that when comparing CoSCA with MCD+Contras, the improvement for MNIST→SVHN is significant (as shown in Fig. 5(a)), with validation accuracy and training stability enhanced. This demonstrates the importance of global alignment when there exists a large domain difference.

5   Conclusions

We have proposed Contrastively Smoothed Class Alignment (CoSCA) for the UDA problem, by explicitly combining intra-class and inter-class domain discrepancy and optimizing class alignment through end-to-end mini-batch training. Experiments on several benchmarks demonstrate that our model can outperform state-of-the-art baselines. Our experimental analysis shows that CoSCA learns more discriminative target domain features, and the introduced MMD feature matching improves the global domain alignment. For future work, we will extend our model to other domain-adaptation tasks. Another direction to explore concerns development of a theoretical interpretation of contrastive learning for domain adaptation, particularly characterizing its effects on the alignment of source and target domain feature distributions.

Acknowledgements. The authors would like to thank the anonymous reviewers for their insightful comments. The research at Duke University was supported in part by DARPA, DOE, NIH, NSF and ONR.

References

1. Donahue, J., et al.: Decaf: a deep convolutional activation feature for generic visual recognition. In: ICML (2014)
2. Yosinski, J., Clune, J., Bengio, Y., Lipson, H.: How transferable are features in deep neural networks? In: NeurIPS (2014)
3. Simonyan, K., Zisserman, A.: Very deep convolutional networks for large-scale image recognition. In: ICLR (2015)
4. He, K., Zhang, X., Ren, S., Sun, J.: Deep residual learning for image recognition. In: CVPR (2016)
5. Torralba, A., Efros, A.A.: Unbiased look at dataset bias. In: CVPR (2011)
6. Gretton, A., Smola, A.J., Huang, J., Schmittfull, M., Borgwardt, K.M., Schölkopf, B.: Covariate shift by kernel mean matching. In: MIT press (2009)
7. Pan, S.J., Yang, Q., et al.: A survey on transfer learning. IEEE Trans. Knowl. Data Eng. 22(6), 770–783 (2010)
8. Ganin, Y., et al.: Domain-adversarial training of neural networks. In: JMLR (2016)
9. Haeusser, P., Frerix, T., Mordvintsev, A., Cremers, D.: Associative domain adaptation. In: ICCV (2017)
10. Tzeng, E., Hoffman, J., Darrell, T., Saenko, K.: Simultaneous deep transfer across domains and tasks. In: ICCV (2015)
11. Goodfellow, I., et al.: Generative adversarial nets. In: NeurIPS (2014)
12. Tzeng, E., Hoffman, J., Saenko, K., Darrell, T.: Adversarial discriminative domain adaptation. In: CVPR (2017)
13. Ganin, Y., Lempitsky, V.: Unsupervised domain adaptation by backpropagation. arXiv preprint arXiv:1409.7495 (2014)
14. Shu, R., Bui, H.H., Narui, H., Ermon, S.: A dirt-t approach to unsupervised domain adaptation. In: ICLR (2018)
15. Saito, K., Watanabe, K., Ushiku, Y., Harada, T.: Maximum classifier discrepancy for unsupervised domain adaptation. In: CVPR (2018)
16. Saito, K., Ushiku, Y., Harada, T., Saenko, K.: Adversarial dropout regularization. arXiv preprint arXiv:1711.01575 (2017)
17. Kumar, A., et al.: Co-regularized alignment for unsupervised domain adaptation. In: NeurIPS (2018)
18. Chapelle, O., Scholkopf, B., Zien, A.: Semi-supervised learning. IEEE Trans. Neural Networks 20(3), 542–542 (2009)
19. Luo, Y., Zhu, J., Li, M., Ren, Y., Zhang, B.: Smooth neighbors on teacher graphs for semi-supervised learning. In: CVPR (2017)
20. Sener, O., Song, H.O., Saxena, A., Savarese, S.: Learning transferrable representations for unsupervised domain adaptation. In: NeurIPS (2016)
21. Long, M., Cao, Y., Wang, J., Jordan, M.: Learning transferable features with deep adaptation networks. In: ICML (2015)
22. Long, M., Zhu, H., Wang, J., Jordan, M.I.: Unsupervised domain adaptation with residual transfer networks. In: NeurIPS (2016)
23. Long, M., CAO, Z., Wang, J., Jordan, M.I.: Conditional adversarial domain adaptation. In: NeurIPS (2018)
24. Pei, Z., Cao, Z., Long, M., Wang, J.: Multi-adversarial domain adaptation. In: AAAI (2018)
25. Zou, J.Y., Hsu, D.J., Parkes, D.C., Adams, R.P.: Contrastive learning using spectral methods. In: NeurIPS (2013)
26. Dai, B., Lin, D.: Contrastive learning for image captioning. In: NeurIPS (2017)

27. Hadsell, R., Chopra, S., LeCun, Y.: Dimensionality reduction by learning an invariant mapping. In: CVPR (2006)
28. Wang, J., et al.: Learning fine-grained image similarity with deep ranking. In: CVPR (2014)
29. Rifai, S., Dauphin, Y.N., Vincent, P., Bengio, Y., Muller, X.: The manifold tangent classifier. In: NeurIPS (2011)
30. Li, C., Xu, K., Zhu, J., Zhang, B.: Triple generative adversarial nets. In: NeurIPS (2017)
31. Kang, G., Jiang, L., Yang, Y., Hauptmann, A.G.: Contrastive adaptation network for unsupervised domain adaptation. In: CVPR (2019)
32. Kim, M., Sahu, P., Gholami, B., Pavlovic, V.: Unsupervised visual domain adaptation: A deep max-margin gaussian process approach. arXiv preprint arXiv:1902.08727 (2019)
33. Arora, S., Ge, R., Liang, Y., Ma, T., Zhang, Y.: Generalization and equilibrium in generative adversarial nets (GANs). In: ICML (2017)
34. Tsai, Y.H., Hung, W.C., Schulter, S., Sohn, K., Yang, M.H., Chandraker, M.: Learning to adapt structured output space for semantic segmentation. In: CVPR (2018)
35. Gretton, A., Borgwardt, K.M., Rasch, M.J., Schölkopf, B., Smola, A.: A kernel two-sample test. In: JMLR (2012)
36. Bromley, J., Guyon, I., LeCun, Y., Säckinger, E., Shah, R.: Signature verification using a "siamese" time delay neural network. In: NeurIPS (1994)
37. Ulyanov, D., Vedaldi, A., Lempitsky, V.: Instance normalization: The missing ingredient for fast stylization. arXiv preprint arXiv:1607.08022 (2016)
38. French, G., Mackiewicz, M., Fisher, M.: Self-ensembling for domain adaptation. In: ICLR (2018)
39. Pan, S.J., Tsang, I.W., Kwok, J.T., Yang, Q.: Domain adaptation via transfer component analysis. IEEE Trans. Neural Networks (2011)
40. Fernando, B., Habrard, A., Sebban, M., Tuytelaars, T.: Unsupervised visual domain adaptation using subspace alignment. In: ICCV (2013)
41. Kim, Y.: Convolutional neural networks for sentence classification. In: EMNLP (2014)
42. Pennington, J., Socher, R., Manning, C.: Glove: Global vectors for word representation. In: EMNLP (2014)
43. Arbelaez, P., Maire, M., Fowlkes, C., Malik, J.: Contour detection and hierarchical image segmentation. In: PAMI (2011)
44. Bousmalis, K., Trigeorgis, G., Silberman, N., Krishnan, D., Erhan, D.: Domain separation networks. In: NeurIPS (2016)
45. Saito, K., Ushiku, Y., Harada, T.: Asymmetric tri-training for unsupervised domain adaptation. In: ICML (2017)
46. Ziser, Y., Reichart, R.: Pivot based language modeling for improved neural domain adaptation. In: ACL (2018)
47. He, R., Lee, W.S., Ng, H.T., Dahlmeier, D.: Adaptive semi-supervised learning for cross-domain sentiment classification. In: ACL (2018)
48. Blitzer, J., Dredze, M., Pereira, F.: Domain adaptation for sentiment classification. In: ACL (2007)

Double Targeted Universal Adversarial Perturbations

Philipp Benz[✉], Chaoning Zhang, Tooba Imtiaz, and In So Kweon

Korea Advanced Institute of Science and Technology (KAIST), Daejeon, South Korea
pbenz@kaist.ac.kr, chaoningzhang1990@gmail.com

Abstract. Despite their impressive performance, deep neural networks (DNNs) are widely known to be vulnerable to adversarial attacks, which makes it challenging for them to be deployed in security-sensitive applications, such as autonomous driving. Image-dependent perturbations can fool a network for one specific image, while universal adversarial perturbations are capable of fooling a network for samples from all classes without selection. We introduce a double targeted universal adversarial perturbations (DT-UAPs) to bridge the gap between the instance-discriminative image-dependent perturbations and the generic universal perturbations. This universal perturbation attacks one targeted source class to sink class, while having a limited adversarial effect on other non-targeted source classes, for avoiding raising suspicions. Targeting the source and sink class simultaneously, we term it double targeted attack (DTA). This provides an attacker with the freedom to perform precise attacks on a DNN model while raising little suspicion. We show the effectiveness of the proposed DTA algorithm on a wide range of datasets and also demonstrate its potential as a physical attack (Code: https://github. com/phibenz/double-targeted-uap.pytorch).

1 Introduction

Despite the recent success of deep learning [1–5], deep neural networks (DNNs) remain vulnerable to adversarial attacks [6–11]. This poses a threat for deploying DNNs in security-sensitive applications, such as autonomous driving and robotics. Various attack methods [12] have been proposed in the past few years, which can be roughly divided into two main categories: image-dependent attacks [6,7,13–15] and universal attacks [16–20]. Image-dependent attacks construct perturbations tailored for a specific input image to be misclassified by the network; while universal attack methods aim to generate one single universal adversarial perturbation (UAP) that can fool the network for most samples of all classes.

Bridging the gap between the discriminative nature of image-dependent perturbations and the non-discriminative universal perturbation, we propose to attack a certain source class while limiting the influence of the attack on other,

---

P. Benz and C. Zhang—Equal contribution.

© Springer Nature Switzerland AG 2021
H. Ishikawa et al. (Eds.): ACCV 2020, LNCS 12625, pp. 284–300, 2021.
https://doi.org/10.1007/978-3-030-69538-5_18

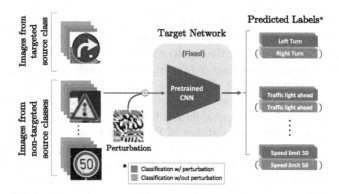

Fig. 1. Overview of the Double Targeted Attack (DTA). In this example, the perturbation causes the network to classify images of the targeted source class **right turn** as the sink class **left turn**. Image classifications from the non-targeted source classes remain unaltered. The DT-UAP is added to all image samples.

non-targeted classes. More specifically, we aim to fool the network with a single perturbation that can systematically shift a certain source class to a different sink class of choice. Since the proposed attack targets both the source and the sink class, we name it double targeted attack (DTA). To avoid confusion, while other works [15,20] use the term "target class", we adopt "sink class" instead, since the proposed DTA also has target class(es) on the source side.

In this work, we focus on the exploration of universal perturbations due to their merit of being image-agnostic. This property eases the attack procedure for real-time applications such as autonomous driving or robotics, as the perturbation can be constructed in advance, and applying the prepared perturbation only requires one summation [16]. UAPs attack all classes, making it obvious to an observer that a system is under attack. For achieving a more covert universal attack, class-discriminative universal adversarial perturbation (CD-UAP) has been introduced in [8] to attack chosen class(es) on the source side. It would be more challenging yet meaningful to not only being class-discrimiantve on the source side, but also targets on the sink side. Compared with existing UAP attacks, DTA can be more dangerous in practice, since it allows precise attacks with flexible control over the targeted source class and the sink class. Applying double targeted universal adversarial perturbations (DT-UAP) can have fatal implications in practice. For instance, in the context of autonomous driving, an attacker can intentionally craft a perturbation to fool a network to misclassify traffic signs from "turn left" to "turn right" as shown in Fig. 1.

Technically, the proposed DTA does not strictly fall into the group of universal attacks, since it does not attack all classes. However, the DTA crafts one single perturbation that can be applied to the entire data distribution, which is similar to the existing UAPs [16]. It is a non-trivial task to craft the DT-UAP because there is an inherent conflict between two objectives. For the samples from the targeted source class, the goal of the crafted perturbation is to shift their classification output to the sink class. This will inevitably have a similar influence on the non-targeted source classes, which conflicts with the goal of the attack being discriminative between the targeted source class and other non-targeted source classes. Inspired by [8], we have designed an algorithm that explicitly deals with the trade-off between them.

To demonstrate its effectiveness, we evaluate the proposed DTA on five classification datasets from different domains for various DNN architectures.

Our results establish the existence of DT-UAPs to attack data samples discriminatively. Though the designed DTA algorithm is mainly for perturbing samples to be misclassified from one targeted source class into one sink class, it can also be extended for shifting multiple targeted source classes to one sink class. We validate this specific attack scenario on the ImageNet dataset. Overall, our proposed algorithm has been validated to be effective to achieve discriminative targeted attacks with extensive experiments on different datasets and scenarios. Finally, we also demonstrate the potential of DTA being applied as a physical attack.

2 Related Work

2.1 Image-Dependent Attacks

Adversarial attacks, which craft one perturbation specifically for one input image to fool a network are called image-dependent attacks. Szegedy et al. optimized such perturbations by using box-constrained L-BFGS [6]. Goodfellow et al. then introduced the Fast Gradient Sign Method (FGSM), an efficient one-step attack to generate adversarial examples [7]. The iterative variant of FGSM (I-FGSM) updates the perturbation by only a fraction of the allowed upper bound in each iteration [13]. Integrating the momentum term into the iterative process of I-FGSM (MI-FGSM) further improved the success rate of adversarial attacks [21]. DeepFool [14] is also an iterative attack, manipulating the models' decision boundaries in the perturbation crafting process. Incorporating the minimization of the perturbation magnitude into the optimization function, Carlini and Wagner (C&W) introduced another three variants of image-dependent attacks [15]. Another effective multi-step attack variant was introduced by Madry et al. using projected gradient descent (PGD) to craft adversaries [22]. The proposed DTA differentiates itself by attacking an entire class instead of only a single image.

2.2 Universal Attacks

A universal adversarial perturbation (UAP) is a single perturbation, which enables fooling a network for most input samples. Accumulating image-dependent perturbations by iteratively applying DeepFool [14], Moosavi et al. crafted the first UAPs [16]. In another variant, UAPs are crafted by leveraging the Jacobian matrices of the networks' hidden layers [17]. Assuming no access to the original training data, Fast Feature Fool proposed to generate data-free

UAPs by optimizing the feature change caused by the applied UAP [18]. Generative Adversarial Perturbations (GAP) were proposed by Poursaeed *et al.* [20], using generative models to craft image-dependent and universal perturbations. Data-free targeted UAP has been introduced in [9], showing UAP have dominant features ovre images. The almost absent computational overhead (single summation) in the deployment of UAPs, makes them a favorable choice for the attack of real-world applications. Despite being universal, our proposed DTA differentiates itself from the existing universal attacks in its class-discriminative nature, i.e. by having a different influence on a sample depending on whether or not it belongs to the targeted source class. CD-UAP has been introduced in [8], our DT-UAP also targets on the sink side and thus constitutes a more challenging task. Moreover, we show that our DTA can also been used in physical attack [23, 24].

2.3   Attack on Autonomous Driving and Robotics

Deep learning has achieved the maturity to be deployed in safety and security-critical applications, such as autonomous driving [25] and robotics [26]. The threat of adversarial attacks in these applications has also been widely explored. For example, Melis *et al.* [27] demonstrated the vulnerability of robots to the adversarially manipulated input images with the techniques in [6], and argue that secure robotics need to adopt strategies to enforce DNNs to learn more robust representations. Attack on the learning policy of robotics has been explored in [28]. Considering adversarial attacks in the context of autonomous driving, [29] generates UAPs to attack road sign classifiers. Another work [30] performs an attack in autonomous driving with traffic signs. Besides the classical classification dataset to evaluate the adversarial attack method, we also evaluate the proposed method on a traffic sign dataset and another robotics-related dataset.

3   Double Targeted Attack

3.1   Problem Formulation

The purpose of the proposed attack is to craft a single perturbation to shift one targeted source class to a different sink class. The source class to be attacked as well as the sink class are determined by the attacker to realize a flexible and precise attack. We term it double targeted attack (DTA).

Let $x \sim X$ denote a single sample from a distribution in $\mathbb{R}^d$, and $\hat{F}(x) = p$ being a classification function, mapping input $x \in \mathbb{R}^d$ to a predicted class $p \in [1, C]$ for a classification problem of C classes. Here the classification function is represented through a DNN parameterized by the weights θ. For most samples from the targeted source class $x_t \sim X_t$, we seek a perturbation δ that satisfies the constraint

$$\hat{F}(x_t + \delta) = y_{\text{sink}} \quad \text{subject to} \quad ||\delta||_p \leq \epsilon, \tag{1}$$

where the sink class satisfies $y_{\text{sink}} \neq F(x_t)$, and ϵ indicates the magnitude limit for the l_p norm of the crafted perturbation δ. Note that limiting X_t in Eq. 1

to a single image results in an image-dependent targeted attack. Meanwhile, it is equivalent to a non-discriminative targeted universal attack if the targeted samples X_t comprise the entire dataset X.

Empirically, we find that a perturbation crafted under the constraint of Eq. 1 also shifts samples from the non-targeted source classes into the sink class with a high targeted fooling ratio. To incorporate covertness within the proposed attack, this effect of non-targeted samples $x_{nt} \sim X_{nt}$ shifting to the sink class should be minimized. The crafted perturbation should ideally shift instances from the chosen source class to a different sink class while having limited influence on the samples from the non-targeted source classes. More specifically, the proposed DTA has two objectives: (1) to increase the targeted fooling ratio for the samples from the chosen source class to the chosen sink class; (2) to decrease the targeted fooling ratio for samples from the non-targeted source class(es) into the sink class, where the targeted fooling ratio is defined as the ratio of samples fooled into the sink class. These two objectives contradict each other, leading to an inevitable trade-off. In the following subsection, we state the loss function for DTA and design the algorithm for explicitly handling this trade-off between the two objectives.

3.2 DTA Loss Design

To achieve selectivity among the targeted source class and non-targeted source classes, we explicitly design different loss functions for the two. For the targeted class and the non-targeted classes, the loss is indicated by $\mathcal{L}_t$ and $\mathcal{L}_{nt}$, respectively. The final loss $\mathcal{L}$ can then be calculated as:

$$\mathcal{L} = \mathcal{L}_t + \alpha \mathcal{L}_{nt}, \tag{2}$$

where α is a hyper-parameter for weighting the trade-off between $\mathcal{L}_t$ and $\mathcal{L}_{nt}$. In practice, this hyper-parameter can be fine-tuned by the attacker for a specific task. For simplicity, we set α to 1 in all of our experiments. We empirically found that this setting works well when the same number of samples are sampled from X_t and X_{nt} in every iteration update.

For the targeted class, the loss $\mathcal{L}_t$ should shape the perturbation to fool the network by shifting the prediction from the source class into the sink class. This can be realized through (1) decreasing the logit value for the originally predicted class $\hat{L}_p$ with $p = \arg\max(\hat{L}(x_t))$ to not being the highest logit anymore, while (2) increasing the logit for the sink class $\hat{L}_{\text{sink}}$, to be the dominant logit, where $\hat{L}(\cdot)$ indicates the function mapping to the logit values and $\hat{L}_i$ is the specific logit value of class i. Thus, $\mathcal{L}_t$ can be decomposed into two parts as follows:

$$\mathcal{L}_t = \mathcal{L}_{t1} + \mathcal{L}_{t2}, \text{ with} \tag{3}$$

$$\mathcal{L}_{t1} = \max(\hat{L}_p(x_t + \delta) - \max_{i \neq p}(\hat{L}_i(x_t + \delta)), 0) \tag{4}$$

$$\mathcal{L}_{t2} = \max(\max_{i \neq y_{\text{sink}}} (\hat{L}_i(x_t + \delta) - \hat{L}_{\text{sink}}(x_t + \delta)), -D) \tag{5}$$

Algorithm 1: Double Targeted Attack Algorithm

Input: Data distribution X, Classifier $\hat{F}$, Loss function $\mathcal{L}$, Mini-batch size m,
　　　Number of iterations I, Perturbation magnitude ϵ
Output: Perturbation vector δ

$X_t \subseteq X$ 　　　　　　　　　　　　　　　　　▷ Subset
$X_{nt} \subseteq X$ 　　　　　　　　　　　　　　　　▷ Subset
$\delta \leftarrow 0$ 　　　　　　　　　　　　　　　　　▷ Initialize
for $iteration = 1, \ldots, I$ **do**
　　$B_t \sim X_t \colon |B_t| = \frac{m}{2}$ 　　　　　　　　▷ Randomly sample
　　$B_{nt} \sim X_{nt} \colon |B_{nt}| = \frac{m}{2}$ 　　　　　▷ Randomly sample
　　$B \leftarrow B_t \bigcup B_{nt}$ 　　　　　　　　　　　▷ Concatenate
　　$g_\delta \leftarrow \underset{B}{\mathbb{E}}[\nabla_\delta \mathcal{L}]$ 　　　　　　　　　　　▷ Calculate gradient
　　$\delta \leftarrow \mathtt{Optim}(g_\delta)$ 　　　　　　　　　　▷ Update perturbation
　　$\delta \leftarrow \frac{\delta}{||\delta||_p}\epsilon$ 　　　　　　　　　　　　　▷ Projection
end

---

where the hyper-parameter D constitutes an intensity value of the dominance of the targeted logit value. A higher D implies a higher chance that the sample will be classified as the sink class. For the non-targeted source classes, we adopt the widely used cross-entropy function as:

$$\mathcal{L}_{nt} = \mathcal{X}(\hat{L}(x_{nt} + \delta), \mathbb{1}(\hat{F}(x_{nt}))) \tag{6}$$

with $\mathbb{1}(\cdot)$ indicating a one-hot encoded vector of C classes. In practice, an attacker can change the hyper-parameters according to the requirements. For instance, the attacker can increase the parameter α in Eq. 2 to increase the covertness of the proposed attack accompanied by a relatively low targeted fooling ratio for the targeted class, or increase the parameter D in order to achieve stronger classifications into the sink class.

To balance the two contradicting objectives, clamping of the logit values was adopted in $\mathcal{L}_t$. Without this clamping operation, the loss part of the targeted classes $\mathcal{L}_t$ can prevail by shifting the samples from the targeted source class to the sink class, while disregarding the other objective of limiting the influence on samples from the non-targeted classes. Since this loss clamping is applied to every targeted source class sample in the batch, it can also facilitate avoiding any sample dominating over other samples for contributing to the gradient of the universal perturbation. A similar clamping technique has been applied in [15] but with the objective to achieve a minimum-magnitude (image-dependent) perturbation that can attack a specific sample.

3.3 DTA Algorithm

With the loss functions defined above, the procedure to craft DT-UAPs with DTA is shown in Algorithm 1. For each perturbation update iteration, we include samples from both the targeted source class and the non-targeted source classes.

More specifically, we randomly select the same number (half of the mini-batch size) of samples from the targeted source class and the non-targeted source classes to form B_t and B_{nt}, which can be concatenated to one batch B. We then calculate the loss parts $\mathcal{L}_t$ and $\mathcal{L}_{nt}$ referring to Eq. 3 and Eq. 6, respectively. The total loss $\mathcal{L}$ can then be calculated referring to Eq. 2. This procedure illustrates how the loss $\mathcal{L}$ in Algorithm 1 is calculated. The perturbation can then be updated with the loss gradient calculated with respect to the perturbation. Note that the gradient thus computed is the expected gradient, i.e. the average of the gradients in this mini-batch. For the update of the perturbation, we can adopt any existing optimizer, but we empirically found that the ADAM [31] optimizer converges the fastest for our method. In the final step, the perturbation is projected to the l_p-ball with radius ϵ in order to satisfy the magnitude constraint. This process is repeated for I iterations. Mini-batch training and balancing the sample amount from the two data distributions result in a simple yet effective algorithm. Our algorithm is mainly inspired by [8,9]. Their algorithm has been shown to outperform UAP [16] and GAP [20] by a large margin, achieving SOTA performance for universal attack. Here, we tailor it to suite our purpose of being double targeted.

4   Results and Analysis

4.1   Experimental Setup

We apply the proposed DTA to various deep convolutional neural network architectures and construct perturbations on various datasets: CIFAR-10 [32], GTSRB [33], EuroSAT [34], YCB [35] and large-scale ImageNet [36]. CIFAR-10 and ImageNet are two commonly used benchmark datasets for image classification tasks. The GTSRB dataset consists of 43 classes of different German traffic signs and is a commonly used dataset for autonomous driving applications. The EuroSAT dataset is used for land cover classification tasks via satellite images categorized into 10 classes. The YCB dataset is a benchmark dataset for robotic manipulation and consists of a total of 98 classes of daily life objects.

For the different datasets, we evaluate DTA with at least two different networks. Overall, we explore various DNN architectures, including VGG-16 [37], ResNet-20/50 [38], Inception-V3 [39] and MobileNet-V2 [40]. To evaluate our approach, we use the metric of the targeted fooling ratio κ, which is defined as the ratio of samples fooled into the sink class. We apply the targeted fooling ratio to the targeted source class and non-targeted source classes, indicated by κ_t and κ_{nt}, respectively. Consequently, the higher (lower) κ_t (κ_{nt}), the better. For the following experiments, we set the number of iterations to $I = 500$, adopt the l_∞ norm and cap the perturbation magnitude at $\epsilon = 15$ for images in the range $[0, 255]$. All our experiments are performed using the PyTorch (v.0.4.1) [41] framework on a single GPU TITAN X (Pascal). Note that for crafting the perturbation, we only use the correctly classified images from the training dataset and report the results on all samples from the validation dataset.

Table 1. Experimental results for the Double Targeted Attack (DTA) for the datasets CIFAR-10, GTSRB, EuroSAT, YCB and ImageNet under 10 scenarios S_0 to S_9. For each scenario, the targeted fooling ratios for the targeted source samples (κ_t) and the non-targeted source samples (κ_{nt}) are reported. All numbers are reported in %.

Dataset	Model	S_0		S_1		S_2		S_3		S_4		S_5		S_6		S_7		S_8		S_9		Avg	
		κ_t	κ_{nt}	κ_t	κ_{nt}	κ_t	κ_{nt}	κ_t	κ_{nt}	κ_t	κ_{nt}	κ_t	κ_{nt}	κ_t	κ_{nt}	κ_t	κ_{nt}	κ_t	κ_{nt}	κ_t	κ_{nt}	κ_t	κ_{nt}
CIFAR-10	VGG-16	77.5	20.5	83.5	22.0	78.2	14.7	81.4	21.5	73.0	18.6	79.1	14.2	75.1	15.1	76.7	24.6	75.0	20.3	86.2	16.6	78.6	18.8
	ResNet-20	78.8	26.1	84.6	28.0	84.0	24.3	84.2	26.9	77.1	22.0	82.1	21.3	83.8	14.7	72.9	33.2	80.0	27.8	89.8	22.3	81.7	24.7
GTSRB	VGG-16	89.0	0.2	100	1.1	87.1	1.2	72.2	0.6	91.0	1.3	83.6	2.4	88.3	1.1	80.0	0.7	95.0	1.9	81.1	1.7	86.7	1.2
	ResNet-20	84.3	0.5	100	1.6	53.1	0.2	77.8	1.8	87.6	2.9	77.1	4.4	70.0	2.7	88.3	1.2	80.0	0.3	64.4	0.7	78.3	1.6
EuroSAT	ResNet-50	96.2	33.0	98.8	18.0	95.2	31.1	96.6	22.1	99.2	28.7	95.0	24.0	94.4	44.3	96.3	17.6	96.3	24.5	91.2	22.7	95.9	26.6
	Inception-V3	94.3	28.7	95.2	18.9	93.8	41.4	99.2	56.3	93.0	29.4	93.0	24.2	91.6	34.6	96.0	21.8	96.8	31.6	89.2	18.8	94.2	30.6
YCB	ResNet-50	100	14.5	100	24.2	100	32.4	96.7	38.0	100	33.5	99.2	38.3	100	44.4	99.2	41.7	100	19.0	100	33.1	99.5	31.9
	Inception-V3	100	16.6	100	30.0	100	38.7	99.2	31.2	100	12.9	98.3	20.0	100	32.2	100	36.6	100	17.3	100	39.2	99.8	27.5
ImageNet	VGG-16	72.0	10.3	96.0	19.5	90.0	19.5	82.0	28.3	74.0	15.9	82.0	13.0	66.0	8.9	64.0	12.9	66.0	21.5	70.0	26.1	76.2	17.6
	ResNet-50	74.0	13.9	94.0	21.4	82.0	15.2	72.0	20.9	62.0	13.6	84.0	15.5	72.0	9.8	66.0	21.4	66.0	17.3	62.0	18.1	73.4	16.7
	Inception-V3	78.0	10.0	86.0	15.7	86.0	12.2	78.0	15.6	58.0	9.5	76.0	12.9	70.0	8.9	72.0	15.7	62.0	18.9	66.0	17.8	73.2	13.7
	MobileNet-V2	74.0	11.3	94.0	17.0	88.0	20.4	70.0	15.3	72.0	16.0	84.0	15.0	74.0	14.5	74.0	21.7	72.0	18.8	70.0	21.9	77.2	17.2

Table 2. Targeted source class to sink class mapping for the datasets CIFAR-10, GTSRB, YCB, EuroSAT, and ImageNet.

S	CIFAR-10	GTSRB	YCB	EuroSAT	ImageNet
S_0	bird → airplane	turn right ahead → turn left ahead	large clamp → strawberry	Herb. Vegetation → Annual Crop	wig → lab coat
S_1	deer → frog	end prev. limitation → end no passing	flat screwdriver → mini soccer ball	Industrial → Permanent Crop	photocopier → castle
S_2	frog → cat	no passing → no Lkw permitted	cups type f → larger marker	Permanent Crop → Highway	flagpole → sewing machine
S_3	ship → cat	wild animals possible → bicycle lane	hammer → lego duplo type i	River → Highway	jersey → rain barrel
S_4	truck → horse	no vehicles permitted → speed limit 70	cups type c → toy airplane part i	Sea Lake → Residential	theater curtain → brass
S_5	airplane → deer	no passing → speed limit 60	tuna fish can → plastic nut	Residential → Pasture	drilling platf. → pomegranate
S_6	horse → dog	slippery road → uneven surfaces	tomato soup can → cups type g	Permanent Crop → River	fireboat → aircraft carrier
S_7	dog → frog	pedestrian crossing → double curves	cups type h → chain	Pasture → Permanent Crop	torch → golfcart
S_8	dog → deer	speed limit 20 → Speed Limit 120	marbles type 3 → key	Pasture → Industrial	candle → howler monkey
S_9	airplane → automobile	road narrows right → children crossing	cups type j → toy airplane part k	Annual Crop → Forest	ruddy turnstone → kuvasz

4.2 Quantitative Results

We evaluate the effectiveness of the proposed DTA by randomly selecting 10 source-to-sink shift scenarios indicated by S_0 to S_9 for each dataset. The results are summarized in Table 1, where we report the targeted fooling ratio for both the targeted class κ_t and the non-targeted classes κ_{nt} for each scenario. The exact mapping of the targeted source class to the sink class can be found in Table 2.

Overall, the results in Table 1 indicate that DTA achieves reasonable performance for different mapping scenarios on a wide range of datasets. This conclusion stems from two major observations. First, the targeted fooling ratio for the targeted classes (κ_t) is quite high. Second, there is a significant gap between κ_t and κ_{nt}, which indicates that the crafted perturbation is discriminative between targeted class and non-targeted classes. We further analyze the performance of each dataset.

CIFAR-10. With an average κ_t of around 80%, DTA performs reasonably well on CIFAR-10, fooling most of the targeted source class into the sink class. The gap between κ_t and κ_{nt} is about 58%, indicating sufficient selectivity.

GTSRB. For the task of road sign classification, our proposed DTA can even achieve a 100% targeted fooling ratio for scenario S_1 while maintaining a very low targeted fooling ratio of 1.1% and 1.6% for VGG-16 and ResNet-20, respectively, on the non-targeted source samples. Overall, DTA exhibits high κ_t values, while maintaining the lowest κ_{nt} values among all examined datasets. Therefore, DTA achieves the highest gap between κ_t and κ_{nt} for the GTSRB dataset. The low κ_{nt} indicates that the perturbations for attacking GTSRB are especially covert. We speculate that the reason behind the high performance on the GTSRB dataset is that the in-class variation is very small, making the discriminative attack a relatively easy task.

EuroSAT and YCB. The results of DTA on the EuroSAT and YCB datasets exhibit similar behavior, with very high values for κ_t, above 94%, while having κ_{nt} values of around 30%. With a gap of more than 60%, DTA poses a strong, covert threat for applications deploying satellite images and classification tasks for robotic manipulation.

ImageNet. The results show that DTA is able to fool a network for a single class out of the 1000 into a sink class for all 4 investigated DNNs, namely VGG-16, ResNet-50, Inception-V3, and MobileNet-V2. For specific scenarios such as S_3 or S_4, there can be a relatively large performance gap among different DNN architectures. Overall, with an average κ_t of around 75% and an average κ_{nt} of 16%, different DNNs have comparable performance.

4.3   Qualitative Results

In this subsection, we illustrate perturbations and perturbed samples generated by the proposed DTA. Figure 2 shows the original targeted source image, along with the amplified universal perturbation and the resulting adversarial image.

It can be observed that the DTA produces patterns with different characteristics for each dataset. The adversarial image is still identifiable as a source class instance to a human observer, however, the DNN classifies the manipulated image (from the targeted source class) with high confidence into the sink class.

4.4 Universal Multi2One Targeted Perturbation

Finally, we extend the DT-UAPs to a more challenging scenario to demonstrate an extension of the DTA. To this end, we alter the objective from one targeted source class to instead support multiple source classes (MS) while still leading the samples from these classes to one sink class. Due to this property of classifying multiple source classes to one sink class, we term the resulting perturbation a universal Multi2One targeted perturbation. Crafting such perturbations is more challenging since multiple source classes add complexity which has to be compensated by the universal perturbation. We evaluate this attack for 4 scenarios, which are detailed in Table 4 under the same settings as before. The results in Table 3 show that our proposed DTA also achieves reasonable performance in the case of shifting multiple targeted source classes into the sink class.

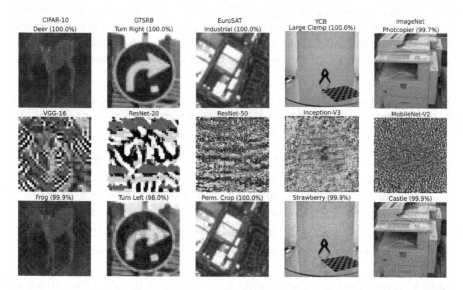

Fig. 2. Examples of adversarial perturbations for various datasets and networks. The figure shows the original images (top), an amplified version of the corresponding perturbations (middle) and the resulting adversarial examples (bottom). The confidence values of the network and the predicted labels are stated above the images. The target network is indicated above the amplified perturbation.

4.5   Ablation Analysis

In the following, we perform ablation studies for the proposed DTA algorithm. All ablation experiments are performed on ResNet-20 for CIFAR-10 and ResNet-50 for the ImageNet dataset.

Loss Function. We perform an ablation study for the loss function design. In Table 5 the performance of DTA for different loss function configurations is shown. We observe that our chosen loss design $\mathcal{L}_t + \mathcal{L}_{nt}$ achieves the best performance. In particular, we observe that excluding the non-targeted loss part $\mathcal{L}_{nt}$ results in a very high κ_t close to 100% for both, the CIFAR-10 and ImageNet dataset. However, the κ_{nt} also increases drastically compared to the result obtained using $\mathcal{L}_t + \mathcal{L}_{nt}$. The average κ_{nt} for ImageNet is 74.5%, and that for CIFAR-10 is even higher with a value of 98.7%. This clearly shows that under the absence of $\mathcal{L}_{nt}$, DTA fails to achieve the objective of being discriminative between samples from the targeted source class and non-targeted source classes. With the existence of $\mathcal{L}_{nt}$, the absence of either $\mathcal{L}_{t1}$ or $\mathcal{L}_{t2}$ also leads to inferior performance. Moreover, with the existence of $\mathcal{L}_{nt}$, we further explore another variant of $\mathcal{L}_t$ adopting the cross-entropy (CE) loss indicated as $\mathcal{L}_t^{CE}$. Similar to $\mathcal{L}_t$, $\mathcal{L}_t^{CE}$ is decomposed into two parts $\mathcal{L}_{t1}^{CE}$ and $\mathcal{L}_{t2}^{CE}$. $\mathcal{L}_{t1}^{CE}$ aims to reduce the logit value of the source class logit by calculating the negative cross-entropy between the network output and the one hot encoded source class label and $\mathcal{L}_{t2}^{CE}$ aims to increase the sink class logit by calculating the cross-entropy between the network

Table 3. Experimental results for the universal Multi2One targeted perturbation on ImageNet under 4 scenarios MS_0 to MS_3. For each scenario, κ_t κ_{nt} are reported. All numbers are reported in %.

Model	MS_0		MS_1		MS_2		MS_3		Avg	
	κ_t	κ_{nt}	κ_t	κ_{nt}	κ_t	κ_{nt}	κ_t	κ_{nt}	κ_t	κ_{nt}
VGG16	63.3	24.9	69.3	33.7	76.0	25.8	69.3	26.8	69.5	27.8
ResNet-50	64.0	30.1	63.3	32.3	78.7	29.2	62.7	23.2	67.2	28.7
Inception-V3	58.0	19.4	56.7	23.8	66.7	19.0	66.7	20.8	62.0	20.8
MobileNet-V2	68.0	27.2	66.0	28.0	74.0	25.6	66.0	24.4	68.5	26.3

Table 4. Targeted source classes to sink class mapping for the Multi2One attack on ImageNet.

MS	ImageNet
MS_0	affenpinscher, black grouse, alp $\rightarrow$ mosque
MS_1	necklace, four-poster, jersey $\rightarrow$ llama
MS_2	wig, photocopier, flagpole $\rightarrow$ castle
MS_3	granny smith, dragonfly, drilling platform $\rightarrow$ brass

output and the one hot encoded sink class label. We observe that this setup also achieves inferior performance compared to $\mathcal{L}_t + \mathcal{L}_{nt}$. The reason for this inferior performance can be attributed to the nature of the CE loss manipulating all logits, and not clamping the loss values.

Dominance Value D. Further, we investigate the influence of the dominance value D for clamping the loss part $\mathcal{L}_{t2}$. Figure 3 (left) shows the targeted fooling rates κ_t and κ_{nt} plotted over various dominance values. We observe that the value of D has a significant influence on the behavior of the proposed DTA. Increasing D increases both κ_t and κ_{nt}. More specifically, κ_t increases and saturates with further increasing D, while κ_{nt} increases almost linearly with the increase of D. The results show that it is beneficial to choose an appropriate D for achieving high κ_t with relatively low κ_{nt}. However, here we only aim to show the influence of the hyper-parameter D on the behavior of the proposed DTA and do not intend to find the optimal value which is dependent on the choice of models and dataset.

Perturbation Magnitude ϵ. One constraint of adversarial perturbations is to be bound to a certain magnitude range. Here we investigate the influence of the perturbation magnitude ϵ and report the results in Fig. 3 (right). A sharp increase of κ_t can be observed for ϵ values between 2.5 and 10 saturating around a targeted fooling ratio of 90% for further increased ϵ values, while κ_{nt} increases more steadily with increasing ϵ values.

Table 5. Analysis of the influence of different loss function configurations. For each scenario of the 4 different scenarios, κ_t and κ_{nt} are reported. All numbers are reported in %.

$\mathcal{L}$	Dataset	S_0		S_1		S_2		S_3		Avg	
		κ_t	κ_{nt}	κ_t	κ_{nt}	κ_t	κ_{nt}	κ_t	κ_{nt}	κ_t	κ_{nt}
$\mathcal{L}_t + \mathcal{L}_{nt}$	CIFAR-10	78.8	26.1	84.6	28.0	84.0	24.3	84.2	26.9	82.9	26.3
	ImageNet	74.0	13.9	94.0	21.4	82.0	15.2	72.0	20.9	80.5	17.9
$\mathcal{L}_t^{CE} + \mathcal{L}_{nt}$	CIFAR-10	77.4	46.1	89.4	49.6	88.8	44.6	88.1	57.0	85.9	49.3
	ImageNet	66.0	10.4	98.0	29.5	92.0	29.2	78.0	27.0	83.5	24.0
$\mathcal{L}_t$	CIFAR-10	99.2	97.9	99.6	98.4	99.7	99.3	100	99.3	99.6	98.7
	ImageNet	100	68.5	100	76.7	94.0	67.3	98.0	85.4	98.0	74.5
$\mathcal{L}_{t1} + \mathcal{L}_{nt}$	CIFAR-10	18.1	3.4	17.1	2.7	23.0	5.8	2.8	4.9	15.3	4.2
	ImageNet	0.0	0.0	0.0	0.1	0.0	0.0	0.0	0.1	0.0	0.1
$\mathcal{L}_{t2} + \mathcal{L}_{nt}$	CIFAR-10	81.9	32.4	88.9	38.9	89.4	34.4	90.0	35.3	87.6	35.3
	ImageNet	78.0	23.7	96.0	31.4	90.0	22.7	76.0	30.1	85.0	27.0

Table 6. Influence of α in Eq. 2 on the targeted fooling ratios κ_t and κ_{nt}.

Dataset	0.1		0.5		1		2		10	
	κ_t	κ_{nt}	κ_t	κ_{nt}	κ_t	κ_{nt}	κ_t	κ_{nt}	κ_t	κ_{nt}
CIFAR-10	98.0	68.4	90.1	37.8	84.6	28.0	70.8	15.3	29.4	5.1
ImageNet	98.0	60.6	94.0	31.5	94.0	21.4	90.0	9.0	0.0	0.1

Weighting Factor α. One way an attacker can control the behavior of DTA is by manipulating the weighting factor α in Eq. 2. In Table 6 we evaluate the influence of α on κ_t and κ_{nt}. Higher values of α lead to lower values of κ_{nt}, since α weights the contribution of $\mathcal{L}_{nt}$ to the final loss value. Even though this behavior is desired, κ_t decreases simultaneously. For an effective attack, an attacker might consider a large gap between κ_t and κ_{nt}, where neither a too large nor too small α is beneficial.

Number of Available Training Samples. Finally, we investigate the influence of the available number of training samples on the attack behavior. In Table 7 we report the influence of the number of available training samples per class on the attack performance. With the same number of training iterations, we find that a smaller number of training samples per class lead to lower κ_t and κ_{nt} and the gap between κ_t and κ_{nt} decreases accordingly. However, with as small as 50 samples per class, the algorithm still works reasonably well. For example, for ImageNet κ_t is 50% while κ_{nt} is as low as 2.9%.

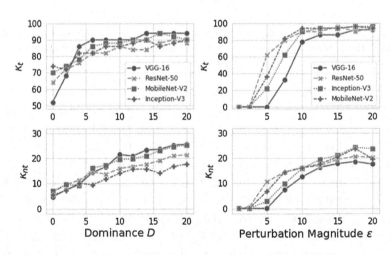

Fig. 3. Analysis of the influence of the dominance value D (left) and perturbation magnitude ϵ (right) on the targeted fooling ratios κ_t (top) and κ_{nt} (bottom) for the ImageNet dataset.

Table 7. Influence of number of training samples per class on the targeted fooling ratios κ_t and κ_{nt}.

Dataset	50		100		250		500		1000	
	κ_t	κ_{nt}	κ_t	κ_{nt}	κ_t	κ_{nt}	κ_t	κ_{nt}	κ_t	κ_{nt}
CIFAR-10	46.7	18.4	60.2	20.3	73.9	22.7	80.9	27.6	83.2	27.8
ImageNet	50.0	2.9	64.0	4.3	86.0	12.5	94.0	19.0	96.0	17.7

Table 8. Quantitative results for the generated DT-Patch on ImageNet

Hammer → Hummingbird		Screwdriver → Go-Kart		Coffee Mug → Chocolate Sauce	
κ_t	κ_{nt}	κ_t	κ_{nt}	κ_t	κ_{nt}
80.0	42.7	92.0	44.9	96.0	41.6

5 Double Targeted Patch

We extend DT-UAP to a physical-world attack [23, 24] by generating a physical patch. We apply the concept of the DTA to attack one source class to a sink class. We choose VGG-16 trained on ImageNet as the target network. For generating a physical patch, we restrict the perturbation to a circular area, as well as its magnitude to lie in image range, i.e. $x + \delta \in [0, 1]$. We show three cases by choosing the source-sink class pairs as indicated in Table 8. Despite being a more challenging scenario than the original adversarial patch, we observe from

Fig. 4. Real-world examples of the DT-Patch for three different scenarios (see Table 8).

Table 8 that κ_t is larger than κ_{nt} by a non-trivial margin. This indicates that the patch fulfills the objective. The qualitative results in Fig. 4 show the applied patch fooling the source into the sink class, while having no influence on a sample from a non-targeted class.

6   Conclusion and Future Work

We proposed DTA to extend the exisiting UAP and CD-UAP for a more flexible attack control. The generated DT-UAP shifts one predefined source class into one predefined sink class, simultaneously attempts to minimize the targeted fooling ratio for samples from the non-targeted source classes. The effectiveness of DTA is demonstrated with extensive experiments on multiple datasets for different network architectures. We further presented an extension of DTA to the Multi2One scenario, driving multiple source classes into one sink class. With some preliminary results we found it also worked for a very challenging Multi2Multi scenario with limited success, and leave further explorations for future work.

References

1. Sutskever, I., Hinton, G.E., Krizhevsky, A.: Imagenet classification with deep convolutional neural networks. In: Advances in Neural Information Processing Systems, pp. 1097–1105 (2012)
2. Hinton, G., et al.: Deep neural networks for acoustic modeling in speech recognition. IEEE Signal Process. Mag. **29**, 82–97 (2012)
3. Collobert, R., Weston, J.: A unified architecture for natural language processing: Deep neural networks with multitask learning. In: Proceedings of the 25th International Conference on Machine Learning, pp. 160–167. ACM (2008)
4. Zhang, C., Rameau, F., Kim, J., Argaw, D.M., Bazin, J.C., Kweon, I.S.: Deepptz: deep self-calibration for PTZ cameras. In: Winter Conference on Applications of Computer Vision (WACV) (2020)
5. Zhang, C., et al.: Revisiting residual networks with nonlinear shortcuts. In: British Machine Vision Conference (BMVC) (2019)
6. Szegedy, C., et al.: Intriguing properties of neural networks. arXiv preprint arXiv:1312.6199 (2013)
7. Goodfellow, I.J., Shlens, J., Szegedy, C.: Explaining and harnessing adversarial examples. arXiv preprint arXiv:1412.6572 (2014)
8. Zhang, C., Benz, P., Imtiaz, T., Kweon, I.S.: CD-UAP: class discriminative universal adversarial perturbation. In: AAAI Conference on Artificial Intelligence (AAAI) (2020)
9. Zhang, C., Benz, P., Imtiaz, T., Kweon, I.S.: Understanding adversarial examples from the mutual influence of images and perturbations. In: Conference on Computer Vision and Pattern Recognition (CVPR) (2020)
10. Liu, H., et al.: Universal adversarial perturbation via prior driven uncertainty approximation. In: Proceedings of the IEEE International Conference on Computer Vision, pp. 2941–2949 (2019)

11. Benz, P., Zhang, C., Imtiaz, T., Kweon, I.S.: Data from model: extracting data from non-robust and robust models. In: CVPR Workshop on Adversarial Machine Learning in Computer Vision (2020)
12. Akhtar, N., Mian, A.: Threat of adversarial attacks on deep learning in computer vision: a survey. IEEE Access **6**, 14410–14430 (2018)
13. Kurakin, A., Goodfellow, I., Bengio, S.: Adversarial machine learning at scale. arXiv preprint arXiv:1611.01236 (2016)
14. Moosavi-Dezfooli, S.M., Fawzi, A., Frossard, P.: Deepfool: a simple and accurate method to fool deep neural networks. In: Proceedings of the IEEE Conference on Computer Vision and Pattern Recognition, pp. 2574–2582 (2016)
15. Carlini, N., Wagner, D.: Towards evaluating the robustness of neural networks. In: IEEE Symposium on Security and Privacy (SP). IEEE 2017, pp. 39–57 (2017)
16. Moosavi-Dezfooli, S.M., Fawzi, A., Fawzi, O., Frossard, P.: Universal adversarial perturbations. In: Proceedings of the IEEE Conference on Computer Vision and Pattern Recognition, pp. 1765–1773 (2017)
17. Khrulkov, V., Oseledets, I.: Art of singular vectors and universal adversarial perturbations. In: Proceedings of the IEEE Conference on Computer Vision and Pattern Recognition, pp. 8562–8570 (2018)
18. Mopuri, K.R., Garg, U., Babu, R.V.: Fast feature fool: A data independent approach to universal adversarial perturbations. In: 2017 British Conference on Machine Vision (BMVC), IEEE (2017)
19. Metzen, J.H., Kumar, M.C., Brox, T., Fischer, V.: Universal adversarial perturbations against semantic image segmentation. In: 2017 IEEE International Conference on Computer Vision (ICCV), pp. 2774–2783. IEEE (2017)
20. Poursaeed, O., Katsman, I., Gao, B., Belongie, S.: Generative adversarial perturbations. In: Proceedings of the IEEE Conference on Computer Vision and Pattern Recognition, pp. 4422–4431 (2018)
21. Dong, Y., et al.: Boosting adversarial attacks with momentum. In: Proceedings of the IEEE Conference on Computer Vision and Pattern Recognition (2018)
22. Madry, A., Makelov, A., Schmidt, L., Tsipras, D., Vladu, A.: Towards deep learning models resistant to adversarial attacks. arXiv preprint arXiv:1706.06083 (2017)
23. Brown, T.B., Mané, D., Roy, A., Abadi, M., Gilmer, J.: Adversarial patch (2017)
24. Liu, A., Wang, J., Liu, X., Cao, B., Zhang, C., Yu, H.: Bias-based universal adversarial patch attack for automatic check-out (2020)
25. Sallab, A.E., Abdou, M., Perot, E., Yogamani, S.: Deep reinforcement learning framework for autonomous driving. Electron. Imaging **2017**, 70–76 (2017)
26. Sünderhauf, N., et al.: The limits and potentials of deep learning for robotics. Int. J. Robot. Res. **37**, 405–420 (2018)
27. Melis, M., Demontis, A., Biggio, B., Brown, G., Fumera, G., Roli, F.: Is deep learning safe for robot vision. Adversarial examples against the iCub humanoid. CoRR, abs/1708.06939 (2017)
28. Clark, G., Doran, M., Glisson, W.: A malicious attack on the machine learning policy of a robotic system. In: 17th IEEE International Conference on Trust, Security And Privacy In Computing and Communications/12th IEEE International Conference on Big Data Science And Engineering (TrustCom/BigDataSE). IEEE 2018, pp. 516–521 (2018)
29. Eykholt, K., et al.: Robust physical-world attacks on deep learning visual classification. In: Proceedings of the IEEE Conference on Computer Vision and Pattern Recognition, pp. 1625–1634 (2018)
30. Morgulis, N., Kreines, A., Mendelowitz, S., Weisglass, Y.: Fooling a real car with adversarial traffic signs. arXiv preprint arXiv:1907.00374 (2019)

31. Kingma, D.P., Ba, J.: Adam: A method for stochastic optimization (2014)
32. Krizhevsky, A.: Learning multiple layers of features from tiny images. Technical report (2009)
33. Stallkamp, J., Schlipsing, M., Salmen, J., Igel, C.: Man vs. computer: benchmarking machine learning algorithms for traffic sign recognition. Neural Networks **32**, 323–332 (2012)
34. Helber, P., Bischke, B., Dengel, A., Borth, D.: Eurosat: A novel dataset and deep learning benchmark for land use and land cover classification. IEEE Journal of Selected Topics in Applied Earth Observations and Remote Sensing (2019)
35. Calli, B., Singh, A., Walsman, A., Srinivasa, S., Abbeel, P., Dollar, A.M.: The YCB object and model set: Towards common benchmarks for manipulation research. In: International Conference on Advanced Robotics (ICAR). IEEE 2015, pp. 510–517 (2015)
36. Deng, J., Dong, W., Socher, R., Li, L.J., Li, K., Fei-Fei, L.: Imagenet: a large-scale hierarchical image database. In: IEEE Conference on Computer Vision and Pattern Recognition. IEEE 2009, pp. 248–255 (2009)
37. Simonyan, K., Zisserman, A.: Very deep convolutional networks for large-scale image recognition. arXiv preprint arXiv:1409.1556 (2014)
38. He, K., Zhang, X., Ren, S., Sun, J.: Identity mappings in deep residual networks. In: Leibe, B., Matas, J., Sebe, N., Welling, M. (eds.) ECCV 2016. LNCS, vol. 9908, pp. 630–645. Springer, Cham (2016). https://doi.org/10.1007/978-3-319-46493-0_38
39. Szegedy, C., Vanhoucke, V., Ioffe, S., Shlens, J., Wojna, Z.: Rethinking the inception architecture for computer vision. In: Proceedings of the IEEE Conference on Computer Vision and Pattern Recognition, pp. 2818–2826 (2016)
40. Sandler, M., Howard, A., Zhu, M., Zhmoginov, A., Chen, L.C.: Mobilenetv 2: Inverted residuals and linear bottlenecks. In: Proceedings of the IEEE Conference on Computer Vision and Pattern Recognition, pp. 4510–4520 (2018)
41. Paszke, A., et al.: Pytorch: An imperative style, high-performance deep learning library. In: Advances in Neural Information Processing Systems, pp. 8024–8035 (2019)

Adversarially Robust Deep Image Super-Resolution Using Entropy Regularization

Jun-Ho Choi[1], Huan Zhang[2], Jun-Hyuk Kim[1], Cho-Jui Hsieh[2],
and Jong-Seok Lee[1(✉)]

[1] School of Integrated Technology, Yonsei University, Seoul, Korea
{ideariobosome,junhyuk.kim,jong-seok.lee}@yonsei.ac.kr
[2] Department of Computer Science, University of California, Los Angeles, CA, USA
huanzhang@ucla.edu, chohsieh@cs.ucla.edu

Abstract. Image super-resolution has been widely employed in various applications with boosted performance thanks to the deep learning techniques. However, many deep learning-based models are highly vulnerable to adversarial attacks, which is also applied to super-resolution models in recent studies. In this paper, we propose a defense method that is formulated as an entropy regularization loss for model training, which can be augmented to the original training loss of super-resolution models. We show that various state-of-the-art super-resolution models trained with our defense method are more robust against adversarial attacks than their original versions. To the best of our knowledge, this is the first attempt of adversarial defense for deep super-resolution models.

1 Introduction

Image super-resolution, which is a task to obtain an image having higher spatial resolution than the given image, is one of the most actively researched image enhancement techniques in recent days. Notably, development of the deep learning technology brings significant improvement in the performance of super-resolution over conventional image upsampling methods such as bicubic and bilinear upscaling. Consequently, deep learning-based super-resolution has been successfully applied to the real-world applications, including medical imaging, remote sensing, biometric identification, and visual surveillance [1].

While the deep learning shows promising results in various research fields, concerns about the vulnerability of deep learning-based algorithms against malicious attacks have arisen. Many studies have shown that the adversarial attacks, which add unnoticeable small perturbations to the given image, can fool the target classification model to produce wrong results [2,3]. Recently, such

---

Electronic supplementary material The online version of this chapter (https://doi.org/10.1007/978-3-030-69538-5_19) contains supplementary material, which is available to authorized users.

© Springer Nature Switzerland AG 2021
H. Ishikawa et al. (Eds.): ACCV 2020, LNCS 12625, pp. 301–317, 2021.
https://doi.org/10.1007/978-3-030-69538-5_19

vulnerability has also been observed beyond classification problems. In the deep super-resolution models, the state-of-the-art deep models produce largely deteriorated outputs [4] or lead erroneous results when they are used as pre-processing steps for other computer vision tasks [5]. Defense methods have been proposed for deep classification models to ensure robustness against adversarial attacks [2,6–9], but not for super-resolution models.

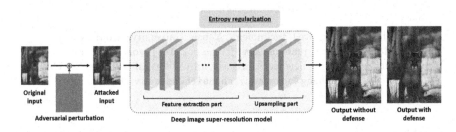

Fig. 1. Illustration of the proposed defense method against adversarial attacks on deep image super-resolution models.

In this paper, we propose a novel defense method, which can be applied to various deep image super-resolution models. Our method aims to reduce the sensitivity of the target super-resolution model to adversarial perturbations by adjusting the activation patterns of an intermediate layer. For this, our method employs a probability density estimator, which is used to obtain the probabilities of the intermediate feature values. Our method then tries to reduce the entropy of the estimated probability distribution by minimizing an entropy regularization loss during model training. As a result, the intermediate features do not change much when an adversarial perturbation is introduced in the input image, and thus undesirable degradation of the super-resolved output image can be prevented effectively. We conduct thorough experimental investigations and ablation studies in order to evaluate the proposed method. In addition, we examine the feasibility of utilizing our method together with the adversarial training strategy. To the best of our knowledge, this is the first approach to defend super-resolution models against adversarial attacks. The idea of our method is illustrated in Fig. 1.

2   Related Work

2.1   Image Super-Resolution

Recently, many deep learning-based image super-resolution methods have been proposed. One of the earliest approaches is the super-resolution convolutional neural network (SRCNN) model [10], which consists of two convolutional layers. After that, much deeper and more complex models are introduced to achieve better performance. For example, Lim et al. [11] propose the enhanced deep super-resolution (EDSR) model, which employs more than 30 convolutional layers. In addition, EDSR contains residual blocks that have skip connections for better training procedures. Zhang et al. [12] propose the residual channel attention network (RCAN) model, which adds a channel attention mechanism to the residual blocks to handle the intermediate features efficiently. Li et al. [13] develop the multi-scale residual network (MSRN) model that employs convolutional layers having various kernel sizes to utilize image features in a multi-scale manner.

While many approaches including the aforementioned ones aim to achieve high quantitative performance with large networks in terms of peak signal-to-noise ratio (PSNR), some proposals focus on different objectives. For instance, Ledig et al. [14] build a model named SRGAN, which employs a discriminator network of the generative adversarial network (GAN) [15] for their super-resolution method named SRResNet to improve the perceptual quality of the super-resolved outputs. Ahn et al. [16] propose the cascading residual network (CARN) model, which employs cascading residual blocks to reduce the model size without performance degradation. Some other recent approaches employ quantitative score prediction [17], wavelet transform [18], and so on.

2.2 Adversarial Attacks

Many researchers reveal the vulnerability of deep image classifications models against various adversarial attacks such as optimization-based [19] and gradient sign-based [2] methods. While most of the studies focus on attacking classification models, the vulnerability of deep models for other tasks has been noted recently. For example, Ganeshan et al. [20] propose the feature disruptive attack (FDA) method, which attempts to perturb the intermediate features of the given deep model. Choi et al. [4] develop an attack method for super-resolution models, which extends the iterative fast gradient sign method (I-FGSM) developed for the classification task. They also extend the attack-agnostic vulnerability measure for classification, named cross Lipschitz extreme value for network robustness (CLEVER) [21], to the super-resolution task.

2.3 Defense Against Adversarial Attacks

Defense methods against adversarial attacks have been proposed for the classification models. One of the well-known effective solutions is adversarial training, which uses adversarial examples as training data [2,7,8]. Another approach is to pre-process the input images to reduce the amount of perturbations, such as JPEG compression [6] and random resizing [9]. Since super-resolution is one of the image enhancement techniques, it is sometimes used as a defense method for classification models [22]. However, no method has been proposed to defend the super-resolution models themselves against adversarial attacks.

3   Proposed Method

Our defense method for a deep super-resolution model basically aims to make the intermediate activations of the model be insensitive against adversarial perturbations. For this, we build our method with the following two components. First, we train the model in such a way that the entropy of the probability distribution for the intermediate activation values is minimized, so that the distribution of activations remains similar across different input images. Second, random noise is added to the intermediate activations during training so that the insensitivity is further enhanced.

Consider a super-resolution model denoted by $S(\cdot)$, which outputs a super-resolved high-resolution image $\mathbf{X}_{SR}$ from a low-resolution input image $\mathbf{X}_{LR}$, i.e., $\mathbf{X}_{SR} = S(\mathbf{X}_{LR})$. The main objective of the super-resolution task is to minimize the reconstruction loss function $\mathcal{L}_r$, which calculates the quantitative difference between the output image $\mathbf{X}_{SR}$ and its corresponding ground-truth image $\mathbf{X}_{HR}$. For this, pixel-wise L_1 [11,12,16] or L_2 [14] losses are typically used. Other losses can also be appended as part of the reconstruction loss, e.g., adversarial loss [14] and perceptual loss [17]. Our method defines an additional loss function, the entropy regularization loss function $\mathcal{L}_e$, and uses it together with the original reconstruction loss function for model training.

Let $\mathbf{\Phi} \in \mathbb{R}^{W \times H \times D}$ denote the features extracted from a selected intermediate layer of $S(\cdot)$, where W, H, and D are the width, height, and channel dimensions, respectively. Our defense method aims to regulate $\mathbf{\Phi}$ by minimizing the entropy value for each channel. This can be summarized as

$$\mathcal{L}_e = -\frac{1}{WHD} \sum_{d \in D} \sum_{w \in W} \sum_{h \in H} \log_2 p_d(\mathbf{\Phi}_{w,h,d}) \tag{1}$$

where $p_d(\cdot)$ is the probability density function for the d-th channel and $\mathbf{\Phi}_{w,h,d}$ is the value of $\mathbf{\Phi}$ at (w, h, d)[1]. We add this loss function to the original loss function, i.e.,

$$\mathcal{L} = \mathcal{L}_r + \lambda \mathcal{L}_e \tag{2}$$

where λ is a hyperparameter that controls the amount of the contribution of the entropy regularization.

To calculate $\mathcal{L}_e$, it is necessary to estimate the probability density function of the features. Recently, methods to estimate cumulative distribution using neural networks have been proposed [23–25]. Once the cumulative distribution function $c_d(\cdot)$ is obtained, the corresponding probability density function $p_d(\cdot)$ can be derived as $p_d(x) = \frac{\partial}{\partial x} c_d(x)$. Adopting the recent method in [23], we design a neural network-based cumulative distribution estimation method to enable end-to-end optimization of super-resolution models for minimizing the objective function in (2). Suppose that $c_d(\cdot)$ is obtained by a cascade of K functions, i.e.,

$$c_d(\cdot) = f_{d,K}\left(f_{d,K-1}\left(f_{d,K-2}(\ldots)\right)\right) \tag{3}$$

---

[1] Note that the entropy is expressed by the sum over the feature elements, not by the sum over the feature values.

where $f_{d,i}$ takes an $m_{d,i}$-dimensional vector as input and outputs an $m_{d,i+1}$-dimensional vector (i.e., $\mathbb{R}^{m_{d,i}} \to \mathbb{R}^{m_{d,i+1}}$). Note that $m_{d,1} = 1$ (feature values) and $m_{d,K+1} = 1$ (probability values). Then,

$$p_d(\cdot) = f'_{d,K} \cdot f'_{d,K-1} \cdots f'_{d,1} \tag{4}$$

where $f'_{d,i}$ is the derivative of $f_{d,i}$. Since $p_d(\cdot)$ outputs a probability value, both $c_d(\cdot)$ and $p_d(\cdot)$ must be within $[0,1]$. In addition, $c_d(\cdot)$ must be monotonically increasing. To meet these constraints, we design the functions $f_{d,i}$ as

$$f_{d,i}(\mathbf{x}) = \begin{cases} \sigma(\mathbf{M}_{d,i}\mathbf{x} + \mathbf{b}_{d,i}) & \text{if } i = K \\ g_{d,i}(\mathbf{M}_{d,i}\mathbf{x} + \mathbf{b}_{d,i}) & \text{otherwise} \end{cases} \tag{5}$$

$$g_{d,i}(\mathbf{x}) = \mathbf{x} + \mathbf{a}_{d,i} \circ \tanh(\mathbf{x}) \tag{6}$$

where $\mathbf{M}_{d,i}$ is a matrix, $\mathbf{a}_{d,i}$ and $\mathbf{b}_{d,i}$ are vectors, $\sigma(\cdot)$ is the sigmoid function, $\tanh(\cdot)$ is the hyperbolic tangent function, and $\circ$ denotes the element-wise multiplication. The sigmoid function in $f_{d,K}(\cdot)$ forces the range of $c_d(x)$ to be within $[0,1]$. Then, the derivatives of the functions are given as

$$f'_{d,i}(\mathbf{x}) = \begin{cases} \sigma'(\mathbf{M}_{d,i}\mathbf{x} + \mathbf{b}_{d,i}) \cdot \mathbf{M}_{d,i} & \text{if } i = K \\ \text{diag}\left(g'_{d,i}(\mathbf{M}_{d,i}\mathbf{x} + \mathbf{b}_{d,i})\right) \cdot \mathbf{M}_{d,i} & \text{otherwise} \end{cases} \tag{7}$$

$$g'_{d,i}(\mathbf{x}) = 1 + \mathbf{a}_{d,i} \circ \tanh'(\mathbf{x}). \tag{8}$$

To make the range of $p_d(x)$ be within $[0,1]$, we replace $\mathbf{M}_{d,i}$ and $\mathbf{a}_{d,i}$ with

$$\mathbf{M}_{d,i} = \text{softplus}(\hat{\mathbf{M}}_{d,i}) \tag{9}$$

$$\mathbf{a}_{d,i} = \tanh(\hat{\mathbf{a}}_{d,i}). \tag{10}$$

This also ensures the monotonicity of $c_d(\cdot)$. To summarize, K and $m_{d,i}$ are the hyperparameters and $\hat{\mathbf{M}}_{d,i}$, $\hat{\mathbf{a}}_{d,i}$, and $\mathbf{b}_{d,i}$ are the parameters to be trained.

From the cumulative distribution $c_d(\cdot)$ obtained by our neural network-based estimator, we estimate the probability $p_d(\cdot)$ by considering feature values within $\mathbf{\Phi}_{w,h,d} - (\delta/2)$ and $\mathbf{\Phi}_{w,h,d} + (\delta/2)$ to be similar to $\mathbf{\Phi}_{w,h,d}$, i.e.,

$$p_d(\mathbf{\Phi}_{w,h,d}) = c_d\left(\mathbf{\Phi}_{w,h,d} + \frac{\delta}{2}\right) - c_d\left(\mathbf{\Phi}_{w,h,d} - \frac{\delta}{2}\right) \tag{11}$$

where δ determines the range of the similarity.

In addition, to further enhance the insensitivity of the feature values to perturbations by the attack, we apply random uniform noise to $\mathbf{\Phi}$ i.e.,

$$\mathbf{\Phi} \leftarrow \mathbf{\Phi} + \mathbf{\Gamma} \tag{12}$$

where $\mathbf{\Gamma}$ is the uniform noise in a range of $[-\delta/2, \delta/2]$. Because $\mathbf{\Gamma}$ changes at every training iteration, the super-resolution model is trained to consider similar feature values as the same in order to generate outputs consistently. Note that the random uniform noise is applied only during training.

4   Experiments

We conduct experiments with state-of-the-art deep super-resolution models to evaluate the proposed method. This section provides the experimental settings, including target models, evaluation methods, and evaluation conditions.

4.1   Super-Resolution Models

Our method can be applied to various deep super-resolution models. We select six representative models for our experiments, including EDSR [11], SRResNet [14], SRGAN [14], RCAN [12], MSRN [13], and CARN [16]. All these models have similar structures, i.e., the input low-resolution image is processed through convolutional layers, and upsampling is performed at the final stage, as illustrated in Fig. 1. EDSR consists of several residual blocks, whose structure is widely used in many other state-of-the-art super-resolution models. In this paper, we employ the baseline version of EDSR. SRResNet employs batch normalization and parametric ReLU [26]. SRGAN is an extended version of SRResNet, which employs a discriminator network to improve the perceptual quality of the upscaled images. RCAN employs the so-called "residual in residual" structure and a channel attention mechanism to utilize channel-wise features more thoroughly. MSRN consists of convolutional layers having different kernel sizes from 1×1 to 5×5. CARN is a lightweight super-resolution model in terms of the model size, and it is reported that CARN is one of the most robust super-resolution models against adversarial attacks due to its small model size [4].

According to the training procedures specified in the original papers, we train EDSR, RCAN, MSRN, and CARN on the DIV2K dataset [27], and SRResNet and SRGAN on a 350k subset of the ImageNet dataset [28]. The L_1 loss function with the pixel value range of $[0, 255]$ is used for training the EDSR, RCAN, MSRN, and CARN models. The L_2 loss function with the pixel value range of $[-1, 1]$ is used for training the SRResNet and SRGAN models. We consider super-resolution at a scaling factor of 4 in all experiments.

4.2   Attack Methods

We employ two types of attack methods that are applicable to super-resolution: feature-based attack and gradient-based attack.

For the feature-based attack, we employ the feature disruptive attack (FDA) [20], which aims to reduce the variance of the activation at intermediate layers of the target model. For a given intermediate feature Φ, the objective is to maximize the following function:

$$\log \left(\left|\left| \{\Phi_{whd} | \Phi_{whd} < C(w,h)\} \right|\right|_2 \right) - \log \left(\left|\left| \{\Phi_{whd} | \Phi_{whd} > C(w,h)\} \right|\right|_2 \right) \quad (13)$$

where $C(w, h)$ is the mean values across the channel dimension. Since it does not depend on the final output, this attack method can be applied to various deep models in addition to classification models. The perturbations in the input image are found iteratively while the L_∞ norm of the perturbations is kept smaller than a constant ϵ. We conduct our experiment with various values of ϵ. The number of iterations (nb_{iter} in [20]) is set to 50. The amount of the perturbations at each iteration (ϵ_{iter} in [20]) is set to ϵ/nb_{iter}.

For the gradient-based attack, we employ the iterative fast gradient sign method (I-FGSM), which is first introduced for the classification task [8] and recently extended for the super-resolution task [4]. It iteratively finds the attacked input $\widetilde{\mathbf{X}}_{LR}$ by

$$\widetilde{\mathbf{X}}_{LR}^{(t+1)} = \widetilde{\mathbf{X}}_{LR}^{(t)} + \frac{\alpha}{T} \cdot \mathrm{sgn}\left(\nabla \left|\left| S(\widetilde{\mathbf{X}}_{LR}^{(t)}) - S(\mathbf{X}_{LR}) \right|\right|_2\right) \tag{14}$$

where α and T are the hyperparameters that controls the amount of the perturbations and $\mathrm{sgn}(\cdot)$ is the sign function. We set $T = 50$ and use various values of α to evaluate our proposed method.

We also employ other gradient-based methods (see the supplementary material), which show similar results as I-FGSM.

4.3   Evaluation Conditions

Our probability density estimator is attached to the last layer right before the upsampling part for each super-resolution model as shown in Fig. 1. For probability estimation, we set $K = 4$ and $m_{d,2} = m_{d,3} = m_{d,4} = 3$. We set $\lambda = 1$ for the EDSR, RCAN, MSRN, and CARN models and $\lambda = 0.1$ for the SRResNet and SRGAN models[2]. The effect of the value of λ is also examined (Sect. 5.3). We set $\delta = 1$, and the effect of changing this value is also examined (Sect. 5.5). For the attacks, we employ $\{\epsilon, \alpha\} \in [1/255, 2/255, 4/255, 8/255, 16/255, 32/255]$ for FDA and I-FGSM.

We evaluate the effectiveness of our defense method against the adversarial attack methods primarily in terms of PSNR[3]. PSNR is one of the most widely used metrics for evaluating quality of the super-resolved images. To conduct comprehensive analysis of our proposed method, we measure the PSNR values in two-fold: for low-resolution images and super-resolved images. The PSNR for low-resolution images is measured between the original input $\mathbf{X}_{LR}$ and the attacked one $\widetilde{\mathbf{X}}_{LR}$, which quantifies the amount of the added perturbations. The PSNR for super-resolved images is measured between the original output $\mathbf{X}_{SR}$ and the output obtained from the attacked input $\widetilde{\mathbf{X}}_{SR}$. If a super-resolution model is more robust than another model, the attack method would have difficulty to successfully attack the model, and thus attempt to add a larger amount of perturbations. Therefore, the PSNR values of the low-resolution and high-resolution images would become smaller and larger, respectively, than those for the less robust model.

---

[2] We use a smaller λ value for these models because of the different loss function and range of the pixel values, as explained in Sect. 4.1.

[3] We observed that the results in terms of structural similarity (SSIM) also show similar tendency to those in terms of PSNR.

In addition, we also employ CLEVER [21], which is an attack-independent vulnerability measure originally developed for classification models. It is also extended for super-resolution [4]. It draws N_s random perturbations having values within $[-\alpha_c, \alpha_c]$ and calculates

$$\max_j \left\| \nabla \left\| S(\mathbf{X}_{LR} + \mathbf{\Delta}^{(j)}) - S(\mathbf{X}_{LR}) \right\|_2 \right\|_1 \tag{15}$$

where $\mathbf{\Delta}^{(j)}$ is the j-th random perturbation. A larger value of the CLEVER index means higher vulnerability. We set $N_s = 1024$ and $\alpha_c = 1/255$ as in [4].

We employ three popular image datasets, which are Set5 [29], Set14 [30], and BSD100 [31]. The results for BSD100 are reported in this paper. The results for the other datasets are reported in the supplementary material.

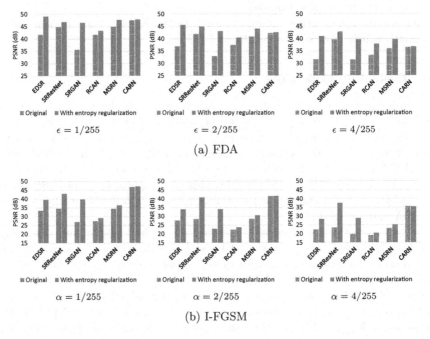

Fig. 2. PSNR values of the super-resolved images for different models trained only with the original reconstruction loss (gray colors) and with both the reconstruction and entropy regularization losses (blue colors). A larger PSNR indicates better robustness. (Color figure online)

5   Results

5.1   Model Comparison

We first compare the performance of the super-resolution methods in terms of PSNR for the FDA and I-FGSM attacks. Figure 2 shows the PSNR values of the super-resolved images for different amounts of perturbations. Overall, the performance decreases when the amount of perturbations (i.e., ϵ and α) increases since there is more room to conceal malicious perturbations in the input images. Among the six super-resolution models trained without our defense method, CARN shows the highest robustness, which can be observed as the highest PSNR values except for the case of FDA with $\epsilon = 4/255$. It is also observed that I-FGSM is stronger than FDA, lowering the PSNR values more significantly.

The results in Fig. 2 show that our defense method is effective for various deep super-resolution models and attack methods. For example, for FDA with $\epsilon = 4/255$, our method enhances the quality of the output images of EDSR from 31.65 dB to 41.03 dB. All of the models trained with our entropy regularization achieve higher PSNR values than those trained without entropy regularization, except for the case of CARN attacked by I-FGSM with $\alpha = 4/255$.

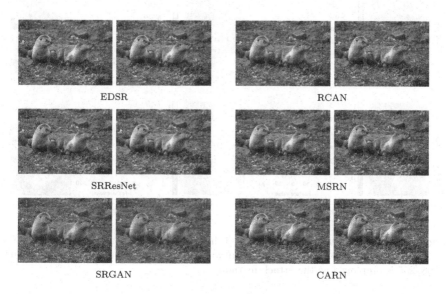

EDSR

RCAN

SRResNet

MSRN

SRGAN

CARN

Fig. 3. Images obtained from the super-resolution models trained without (left panels) and with (right panels) entropy regularization. FDA ($\epsilon = 8/255$) is employed as the attack method.

Figure 3 depicts example super-resolved images under the FDA attack. The left-side and right-side images represent outputs obtained from the models trained without and with our entropy regularization method, respectively. Without defense, the models tend to output super-resolved images having undesirable textures, which come from the perturbations included in the input images. In contrast, our defense method reduces the quality degradation significantly.

We investigate the effect of our method on the intermediate features of the super-resolution models. Figure 4 shows the features (averaged along the channel dimension) and their distribution at the intermediate layer of the EDSR model where the entropy regularization is applied (i.e., the layer before the upsampling part). When the proposed defense method is not employed, the intermediate layer tends to output the features that are emphasized on the edges, which usually contain high-frequency information. In addition, the distribution of the features is more dispersed than that obtained from the model trained with the entropy regularization, which can be observed in the histograms. When the perturbations, which contain high-frequency components, are introduced in the low-resolution input image by the attack, both the edge regions and the perturbations are amplified, producing corrupted features. Accordingly, the distribution of the feature values is also affected; it is more dispersed than that for the unattacked input.

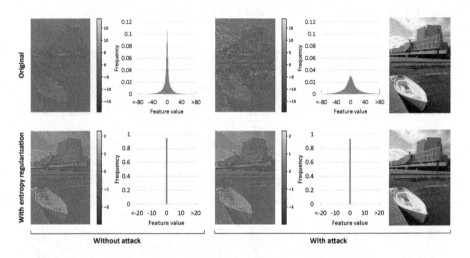

Fig. 4. Intermediate features, histograms of the intermediate feature values, and output images of the EDSR models trained without and with entropy regularization. FDA with $\epsilon = 8/255$ is employed as the attack method.

On the other hand, the model trained with our defense method shows a different mechanism of finding information useful for upsampling from the given input, which results in a different pattern of the intermediate features. Since the activation of the intermediate layer is not heavily concentrated on the edge regions, unlike the model trained without entropy regularization, the perturbations are not significantly amplified. In addition, the distribution of the feature values for the attacked input remains similar to that for the original input. Thanks to the reduced sensitivity against adversarial attacks, a relatively small difference between the features obtained from the original and attacked images is observed in the defended model. Because of these effects, the model trained with the entropy regularization is much more robust against the adversarial attack, as shown in the rightmost images in the figure.

5.2 Ablation Study

Our method consists of two components, i.e., probability estimation of intermediate features for entropy regularization and random noise injection to the features. We examine the effects of these two. Figure 5 compares the performance
of the EDSR models trained with only one of the two components or both. In
Figs. 5(a) and 5(b), a lower low-resolution (LR) PSNR value means that the
adversarial attack adds a larger amount of perturbations to the given input, and
a higher super-resolved (SR) PSNR value means that the output image is more
similar to the original output. Thus, a model with its graph closer to the upper
left corner can be considered to have higher robustness. In Fig. 5(c), we plot the
CLEVER index with the SR PSNR value for each image attacked by I-FGSM
with $\alpha = 1/255$. In this graph, a model having data points closer to the lower
right corner is considered to be more robust.

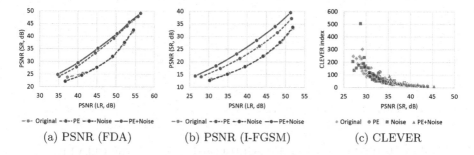

(a) PSNR (FDA)   (b) PSNR (I-FGSM)   (c) CLEVER

Fig. 5. Performance comparison in terms of PSNR and CLEVER index values for
the EDSR models trained without any defense (Original), with probability estimation
(PE), with random noise (Noise), and both (PE+Noise). Six data points of each case
in (a) and (b) correspond to six different values of ϵ and α, respectively. Different data
points of each case in (c) correspond to different input images.

Overall, the models employing the probability estimation show better performance in terms of both the PSNR values and CLEVER indices. Employing
the random uniform noise along with the probability estimation provides even
more improved performance than employing only the probability estimation.
However, employing only the random uniform noise does not improve robustness. In this case, we observed that the range of the intermediate feature values
increases. This indicates that the model is trained to produce feature values that
have sufficiently large differences so that the differences exceed the magnitude
of the noise. These results support that estimating and reducing the entropy of
the intermediate features is beneficial to defend against adversarial attacks. In
addition, adding random noise does not directly improve the robustness but can
boost the effectiveness of the probability estimation.

5.3   Adjusting λ

As explained in Sect. 3, the hyperparameter λ in (2) adjusts the relative contributions of the reconstruction loss and the entropy regularization loss. Hence, we can expect that a larger λ value will improve the robustness against adversarial attacks but possibly at the cost of reconstruction quality reduction. To examine this, we train the EDSR models with different values of λ.

Figure 6 shows the results. As expected, the models trained with larger λ values show better performance. The PSNR values for the original low-resolution images (without attack) are measured as 27.54, 27.53, 27.28, and 26.41 dB for $\lambda = 0$, 0.1, 1, and 10, respectively. Therefore, the tradeoff relationship exists between the reconstruction loss and the entropy regularization loss, but the amount of performance degradation for unattacked input images is marginal. This indicates that our method efficiently improves the robustness against adversarial attacks with preserving the original performance.

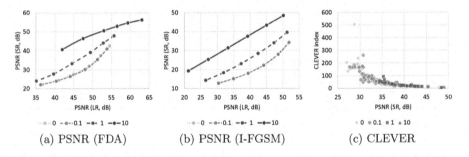

(a) PSNR (FDA)   (b) PSNR (I-FGSM)   (c) CLEVER

Fig. 6. Performance comparison in terms of PSNR and CLEVER index values for the EDSR models trained with different values of λ.

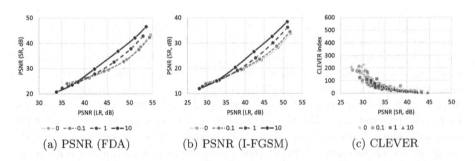

(a) PSNR (FDA)   (b) PSNR (I-FGSM)   (c) CLEVER

Fig. 7. Performance comparison in terms of PSNR and CLEVER index values for the EDSR models trained with different values of λ, where the entropy regularization loss is applied to the first convolutional layer.

5.4 Target Layer for Entropy Regularization

While we use the entropy regularizer for the last layer of the feature extraction part, the same mechanism can also be applied to any other intermediate layers. We test the case where the regularization is performed at the first layer. The results are shown in Fig. 7 for comparison with Fig. 6.

It is observed that although the defense is slightly successful for small amounts of perturbations (i.e., the region with large PSNR values for low-resolution images), the entropy regularization is much less effective for improving robustness in comparison to the results in Fig. 6. There could be two reasons. First, the functional complexity of only one convolutional layer is not sufficiently high to adjust the features for entropy minimization, whereas several layers can co-operate to adjust the features at the last layer. Second, even though the first layer reduces the effect of the attack, small perturbations that still exist in the features can be undesirably amplified through the subsequent layers. Therefore, employing our defense method in the latter part of a model is more effective than using it in the former part.

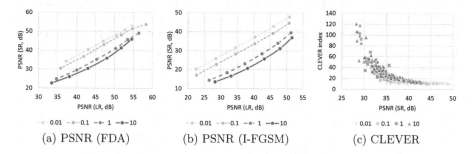

(a) PSNR (FDA)   (b) PSNR (I-FGSM)   (c) CLEVER

Fig. 8. Performance comparison in terms of PSNR and CLEVER index values for the EDSR models trained with different values of δ.

5.5 Adjusting δ

To examine the effect of δ, we train EDSR with different values of δ, where λ is set to 1. Figure 8 shows the results. It is observed that as δ gets smaller, the robustness against the attacks is improved. Meanwhile, the PSNR values for the original (unattacked) low-resolution images are 26.89, 27.13, 27.28, and 27.34 dB for $\delta = 0.01, 0.1, 1$, and 10, respectively. As explained in Sect. 3, the hyperparameter δ adjusts the similarity range in calculating the probabilities of the features. A smaller value of δ improves the robustness against the attacks by forcing the feature values to be more similar through entropy minimization, but slightly reduces the reconstruction quality, similarly to a larger value of λ.

5.6   Combining with Adversarial Training

There is no prior work on defending super-resolution models against adversarial attacks, and it is not straightforward to adopt most defense methods developed particularly for classification tasks due to the different characteristics between the two tasks. As explained in Sect. 2.3, there are two popular defense approaches in classification: pre-processing of input images and adversarial training. Unlike classification, however, pre-processing degrades the original performance of the super-resolution methods because it inevitably introduces quality degradation of the input low-resolution image. For example, when the random resizing method [9] is applied to the input image, PSNR of the super-resolved output image by EDSR is significantly reduced from 27.54 dB to 26.32 dB.

On the other hand, the adversarial training approach is applicable to the super-resolution tasks by generating adversarial examples from the attack methods for super-resolution, e.g., FDA or I-FGSM. Therefore, we develop a simple adversarial training method and investigate whether our entropy regularization method can collaborate with it to further improve the robustness of super-resolution models. To generate adversarial training examples, we choose I-FGSM in (14) as an attack method, where α and T are set to 8/255 and 1, respectively. For each training iteration, an adversarial perturbation for each input low-resolution image is calculated. Then, both the original low-resolution images and the attacked low-resolution images serve as inputs, where the corresponding ground-truth high-resolution images remain the same.

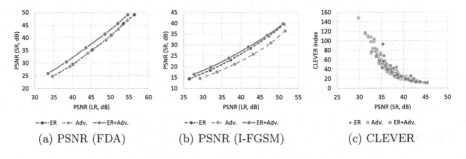

(a) PSNR (FDA)   (b) PSNR (I-FGSM)   (c) CLEVER

Fig. 9. Performance comparison in terms of PSNR and CLEVER index values for the EDSR models trained with entropy regularization (ER), adversarial training (Adv.) and both (ER+Adv.).

We train the EDSR models with our entropy regularization method, the aforementioned adversarial training, and both. Figure 9 compares the performance of the models. The entropy regularization and adversarial training show similar performance against the FDA method. However, for the I-FGSM attack, the entropy regularization shows better performance than the adversarial training. Interestingly, the model trained with both defense methods achieves the best performance for both attack methods. This proves that 1) our proposed method itself is effective in defending the super-resolution models, and 2) our method can collaborate with the adversarial training method to further improve the robustness against adversarial attacks.

6 Conclusion

We proposed a defense method designed for deep super-resolution models to defend against adversarial examples. Our method manipulates the intermediate features of the given model by estimating their probability density and regularizing their entropy value, where the random noise is also utilized to boost effectiveness of the regularization. The experimental results showed that the proposed method can significantly improve the robustness of the state-of-the-art deep super-resolution models without significant degradation of the original performance. We also showed the synergy when our method is combined with adversarial training.

Acknowledgement. This work was supported by the NRF grant funded by the Korea government (MSIT) (NRF-2020R1F1A1070631), and the Artificial Intelligence Graduate School Program (Yonsei University, 2020-0-01361).

References

1. Yue, L., Shen, H., Li, J., Yuan, Q., Zhang, H., Zhang, L.: Image super-resolution: the techniques, applications, and future. Signal Process. **128**, 389–408 (2016)
2. Goodfellow, I.J., Shlens, J., Szegedy, C.: Explaining and harnessing adversarial examples. In: Proceedings of the International Conference on Learning Representations (2015)
3. Su, D., Zhang, H., Chen, H., Yi, J., Chen, P.-Y., Gao, Y.: Is robustness the cost of accuracy? – a comprehensive study on the robustness of 18 deep image classification models. In: Ferrari, V., Hebert, M., Sminchisescu, C., Weiss, Y. (eds.) ECCV 2018, Part XII. LNCS, vol. 11216, pp. 644–661. Springer, Cham (2018). https://doi.org/10.1007/978-3-030-01258-8_39
4. Choi, J.H., Zhang, H., Kim, J.H., Hsieh, C.J., Lee, J.S.: Evaluating robustness of deep image super-resolution against adversarial attacks. In: Proceedings of the IEEE International Conference on Computer Vision, pp. 303–311 (2019)
5. Yin, M., Zhang, Y., Li, X., Wang, S.: When deep fool meets deep prior: adversarial attack on super-resolution network. In: Proceedings of the ACM International Conference on Multimedia, pp. 1930–1938 (2018)
6. Das, N., et al.: SHIELD: fast, practical defense and vaccination for deep learning using JPEG compression. In: Proceedings of the ACM International Conference on Knowledge Discovery & Data Mining, pp. 196–204 (2018)
7. Huang, R., Xu, B., Schuurmans, D., Szepesvári, C.: Learning with a strong adversary. In: Proceedings of the International Conference on Learning Representations (2016)
8. Kurakin, A., Goodfellow, I., Bengio, S.: Adversarial machine learning at scale. In: Proceedings of the International Conference on Learning Representations (2017)

9. Xie, C., Wang, J., Zhang, Z., Ren, Z., Yuille, A.: Mitigating adversarial effects through randomization. In: Proceedings of the International Conference on Learning Representations (2018)
10. Dong, C., Loy, C.C., He, K., Tang, X.: Learning a deep convolutional network for image super-resolution. In: Fleet, D., Pajdla, T., Schiele, B., Tuytelaars, T. (eds.) ECCV 2014, Part IV. LNCS, vol. 8692, pp. 184–199. Springer, Cham (2014). https://doi.org/10.1007/978-3-319-10593-2_13
11. Lim, B., Son, S., Kim, H., Nah, S., Lee, K.M.: Enhanced deep residual networks for single image super-resolution. In: Proceedings of the IEEE Conference on Computer Vision and Pattern Recognition Workshops, pp. 136–144 (2017)
12. Zhang, Y., Li, K., Li, K., Wang, L., Zhong, B., Fu, Y.: Image super-resolution using very deep residual channel attention networks. In: Ferrari, V., Hebert, M., Sminchisescu, C., Weiss, Y. (eds.) ECCV 2018, Part VII. LNCS, vol. 11211, pp. 294–310. Springer, Cham (2018). https://doi.org/10.1007/978-3-030-01234-2_18
13. Li, J., Fang, F., Mei, K., Zhang, G.: Multi-scale residual network for image super-resolution. In: Ferrari, V., Hebert, M., Sminchisescu, C., Weiss, Y. (eds.) ECCV 2018, Part VIII. LNCS, vol. 11212, pp. 527–542. Springer, Cham (2018). https://doi.org/10.1007/978-3-030-01237-3_32
14. Ledig, C., et al.: Photo-realistic single image super-resolution using a generative adversarial network. In: Proceedings of the IEEE Conference on Computer Vision and Pattern Recognition, pp. 4681–4690 (2017)
15. Goodfellow, I., et al.: Generative adversarial nets. In: Proceedings of the Advances in Neural Information Processing Systems, pp. 2672–2680 (2014)
16. Ahn, N., Kang, B., Sohn, K.-A.: Fast, accurate, and lightweight super-resolution with cascading residual network. In: Ferrari, V., Hebert, M., Sminchisescu, C., Weiss, Y. (eds.) ECCV 2018, Part X. LNCS, vol. 11214, pp. 256–272. Springer, Cham (2018). https://doi.org/10.1007/978-3-030-01249-6_16
17. Choi, J.H., Kim, J.H., Cheon, M., Lee, J.S.: Deep learning-based image super-resolution considering quantitative and perceptual quality. Neurocomputing 398, 347–359 (2020)
18. Deng, X., Yang, R., Xu, M., Dragotti, P.L.: Wavelet domain style transfer for an effective perception-distortion tradeoff in single image super-resolution. In: Proceedings of the IEEE International Conference on Computer Vision, pp. 3076–3085 (2019)
19. Szegedy, C., et al: Intriguing properties of neural networks. In: Proceedings of the International Conference on Learning Representations (2014)
20. Ganeshan, A., Babu, R.V.: FDA: feature disruptive attack. In: Proceedings of the IEEE International Conference on Computer Vision, pp. 8069–8079 (2019)
21. Weng, T.W., et al.: Evaluating the robustness of neural networks: an extreme value theory approach. In: Proceedings of the International Conference on Learning Representations (2018)
22. Mustafa, A., Khan, S.H., Hayat, M., Shen, J., Shao, L.: Image super-resolution as a defense against adversarial attacks. IEEE Trans. Image Process. 29, 1711–1724 (2019)
23. Ballé, J., Minnen, D., Singh, S., Hwang, S.J., Johnston, N.: Variational image compression with a scale hyperprior. In: Proceedings of the International Conference on Learning Representations (2018)
24. Magdon-Ismail, M., Atiya, A.: Density estimation and random variate generation using multilayer networks. IEEE Trans. Neural Netw. 13, 497–520 (2002)

25. Magdon-Ismail, M., Atiya, A.F.: Neural networks for density estimation. In: Proceedings of the Advances in Neural Information Processing Systems, pp. 522–528 (1999)
26. He, K., Zhang, X., Ren, S., Sun, J.: Delving deep into rectifiers: surpassing human-level performance on ImageNet classification. In: Proceedings of the IEEE International Conference on Computer Vision, pp. 1026–1034 (2015)
27. Agustsson, E., Timofte, R.: NTIRE 2017 challenge on single image super-resolution: dataset and study. In: Proceedings of the IEEE Conference on Computer Vision and Pattern Recognition Workshops, pp. 126–135 (2017)
28. Russakovsky, O., et al.: ImageNet large scale visual recognition challenge. Int. J. Comput. Vision **115**, 211–252 (2015)
29. Bevilacqua, M., Roumy, A., Guillemot, C., Alberi-Morel, M.L.: Low-complexity single-image super-resolution based on nonnegative neighbor embedding. In: Proceedings of the British Machine Vision Conference, pp. 1–10 (2012)
30. Zeyde, R., Elad, M., Protter, M.: On single image scale-up using sparse-representations. In: Boissonnat, J.-D., et al. (eds.) Curves and Surfaces 2010. LNCS, vol. 6920, pp. 711–730. Springer, Heidelberg (2012). https://doi.org/10.1007/978-3-642-27413-8_47
31. Martin, D., Fowlkes, C., Tal, D., Malik, J.: A database of human segmented natural images and its application to evaluating segmentation algorithms and measuring ecological statistics. In: Proceedings of the IEEE International Conference on Computer Vision, pp. 416–423 (2001)

Online Knowledge Distillation
via Multi-branch Diversity Enhancement

Zheng Li[1,2], Ying Huang[1,3], Defang Chen[4], Tianren Luo[1], Ning Cai[1],
and Zhigeng Pan[1(✉)]

[1] Virtual Reality and Intelligent Systems Research Institute, Hangzhou Normal
University, Hangzhou, China
{lizheng1,luotianren,caining}@stu.hznu.edu.cn, {yw52,zgpan}@hznu.edu.cn
[2] School of Information Science and Engineering, Hangzhou Normal University,
Hangzhou, China
[3] Alibaba Business School, Hangzhou Normal University, Hangzhou, China
[4] College of Computer Science, Zhejiang University, Hangzhou, China
defchern@zju.edu.cn

Abstract. Knowledge distillation is an effective method to transfer the
knowledge from the cumbersome teacher model to the lightweight student model. Online knowledge distillation uses the ensemble prediction
results of multiple student models as soft targets to train each student
model. However, the homogenization problem will lead to difficulty in further improving model performance. In this work, we propose a new distillation method to enhance the diversity among multiple student models. We introduce **F**eature **F**usion **M**odule (**FFM**), which improves the
performance of the attention mechanism in the network by integrating
rich semantic information contained in the last block of multiple student models. Furthermore, we use the **C**lassifier **D**iversification (**CD**)
loss function to strengthen the differences between the student models
and deliver a better ensemble result. Extensive experiments proved that
our method significantly enhances the diversity among student models
and brings better distillation performance. We evaluate our method on
three image classification datasets: CIFAR-10/100 and CINIC-10. The
results show that our method achieves state-of-the-art performance on
these datasets.

1 Introduction

Knowledge distillation [1], as one of the key methods in model compression, the
distillation process usually starts by training a high-capacity teacher model. A
student model will actively learn the soft label or feature representation [11]
generated by teacher model. The purpose of distillation is to train a more compact and accurate student model through the knowledge transferred from the
teacher network. In recent years, the convolutional neural network has made very
impressive achievements in many vision tasks [2–6]. But it requires high cost of
computation and memory in inference, making the deployment of CNN difficult

© Springer Nature Switzerland AG 2021
H. Ishikawa et al. (Eds.): ACCV 2020, LNCS 12625, pp. 318–333, 2021.
https://doi.org/10.1007/978-3-030-69538-5_20

in resource-limited mobile devices. Knowledge distillation was proposed to solve these problems. In the meantime, other types of model compression techniques such as network pruning [7–9] and network quantization [10–12] have also been proposed.

Traditional knowledge distillation [13–15] is a two-stage process. We should first train a teacher model, then get a student model by distilling the teacher model. Although this approach can obtain a higher quality student model by aligning the predictions of the teacher model, it is still a complex approach that requires more computational resources. Online knowledge distillation [16] successfully simplifies the training process by reducing the need for pretrained teacher model. Existing online knowledge distillation methods [17–19] learns not only from the ground truth labels but also from the ensemble results of multiple branches. We refer to each branch as a separate student model. This method can improve the performance of models with arbitrary capacity and obtain better generalization ability.

Averaging the predictions of each branch is a very simple way to get the ensemble results. This approach tend to cause branches to quickly homogenize, hurting the distillation performance [20,21]. However, [17,19] found that the accuracy of the final result improves if different weights were applied to each peer. In OKDDip [19], this paper introduces the concept of two-level distillation method, builds diverse peers by applying a self-attention mechanism [22]. Self-attention in OKDDip needs two fully connected layers separately as transformation matrices to obtain importance scores, which increases the complexity of time and space. In ONE [17], the gate module uses features from the second block of its backbone network as input to generate the importance score of the corresponding branch. However, this feature contains little semantic information which leads to limited improvement in image classification tasks.

In this work, we propose a new distillation strategy to enhance the diversity among branches which can significantly improve the effectiveness of online knowledge distillation. By introducing Feature Fusion Module(FFM) to fuse the features of the last layer of multiple branches, we make full use of the diversity of semantic information contained in multiple branches to improve the attention performance [23]. Since a large diversity of branches can help ensemble-based online KD methods achieve better results, inspired by [24], we propose the CD loss to prevent homogeneity between branches by explicitly forcing their features to be learned orthogonally. This loss function serves as a regularization term to prevent group performance degradation caused by homogenization. Unlike other methods in which all branches converge into similar one. By using our method, each branch keeps their uniqueness. Based on [19], a two-level knowledge distillation framework is adopted. We build a network with m branches, including $m-1$ auxiliary branches and a group leader. The knowledge generated by these diverse peers will be distilled into the group leader, and the remaining peers will be discarded. In order to reduce the consumption of computing resources, we only keep the group leader as the final deployment model.

Our contributions of this work can be summarized as follows:

- We propose Feature Fusion Module (FFM) which can better fuse diverse semantic information from multiple branches and improves the performance of the attention mechanism.
- We introduce the Classifier Diversification (CD) loss function. As a regularization term, it effectively reduces the homogenization among branches, improves the accuracy of ensemble results and leads to a better student model.
- The extensive experiments and analysis verify that our proposed method can effectively enhance branch diversity and train better student models on different image classification datasets: CIFAR-10/100 [25] and CINIC-10 [26].

2   Related Work

2.1   Knowledge Distillation

Knowledge distillation [1] has been widely used in many scenarios involving deep learning algorithms, such as virtual experiments in VR, autonomous driving and so on. It provides an useful method that allows the complex teacher model to be compressed to a more lightweight student model by aligning the student model with the teacher model. When training the target model, this method takes advantage of the extra supervisory signal provided by the soft output of the teacher model. There are also many works [13–15,27] made explorations based on this idea. In FitNets [13], the student model attempts to mimic the intermediate representation directly from the teacher network. Attention Transfer [14] transfers an attention map of a teacher model into a student and [28] proposes a similar method using mean weights. In flow-based knowledge distillation [15], the student is encouraged to mimic the teacher's flow matrices, which are derived from the inner product between feature maps in two layers. [29] saves the computation by using singular value decomposition to compress feature maps.

There are also innovative works exploring alternatives to the usual student-teacher training paradigm. Generative Adversarial Learning [30] is proposed to generate realistic-looking images from random noise using neural networks. The ideas in the adversarial network are applied to knowledge distillation [31–33]. In MEAL [31], the generators were employed to synthesize student features and the discriminator was used to discriminate between teacher and student outputs for the same image. In [33], this work adopts adversarial method to discover adversarial samples supporting decision boundary. With the supervision of discriminator, student can better mimic the behavior of teacher model. In addition, many works [34–37] have also explored the relationship between the samples. [34] propose that similar input pairs in the teacher network tends to produce similar activations in the student network. A few recent papers [37–39] have shown that models of the same architecture can also be distilled. Snapshot distillation [39] uses the cyclic learning rate policy, in which the last snapshot of each cycle is used as the teacher for all iterations in the next cycle, and the teacher is used to provide supervision signal.

2.2   Online Knowledge Distillation

Traditional knowledge distillation methods have two stages that require a pre-trained teacher model to provide soft output for distillation. Different from above complex training methods, several works adopts collaboratively training strategy. Simultaneously training a group of student models based on each other's predictions is an effective single-stage distillation method, which can be a good substitute for pretrained teacher models. Some methods [16,18] solve this problem. The online knowledge distillation was completed through mutual instruction between two peers [16]. However, the lack of a high-capacity teacher model will decrease the distillation efficiency. In [17,40], each student model learns from the average of the predictions generated by a group of students and obtains a better teacher model effect. ONE found that simply averaging the results would reduce the diversity among students, affecting the training of branch-based models. ONE generates the importance score corresponding to each student through the gate module. By assigning different importance score to each branch, a high-capacity teacher model is constructed, which can leverage knowledge from training data more effectively. OKDDip [19] proposed the concept of two-level distillation. The ensemble results of auxiliary peer networks were distilled into the group leader. The diversified peer network plays a key role in improving distillation performance.

3   Online Knowledge Distillation via Multi-branch Diversity Enhancement

The architecture of our proposed method is illustrated in Fig. 1. Our method is based on a two-level distillation procedure. The network has $m - 1$ auxiliary branches and one group leader. In the first level distillation, each branch learns not only from the ground truth label but also from the weighted ensemble targets obtained through Feature Fusion Module. These results play the role of a teacher model to teach each branch. In the second level distillation, the knowledge learned by the group is further distilled into the group leader. To save computing resources, we use the group leader for the final deployment.

3.1   Formulation

In knowledge distillation, the student uses the output of the teacher as an additional supervisory signal for network training. Given a dataset of N training samples $D = \{(x_i, y_i)\}_i^N$, where $y_i \in \{1, 2, ..., C\}$. Here, x_i is the ith training sample, y_i is the corresponding ground truth label and C is the total number of image classes. Take the training sample as the input of the teacher network, we will get the output logits $t_i = (t_i^1, ..., t_i^c)$. The logits vector after softmax will get the ith probability value q_i^j,

$$q_i^j = \frac{exp(t_i/T)}{\sum_{j=1}^{C} exp(t_i^j/T)} \tag{1}$$

First-Level Distillation

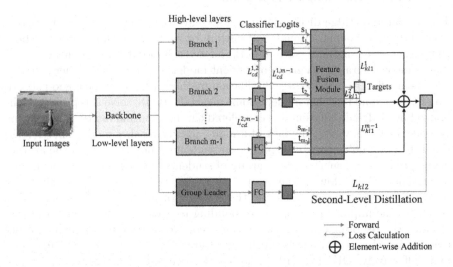

Fig. 1. The overall framework of our proposed method. Each branch and shared low-level layers constitute an individual student model. This is a two-level distillation process. For the first-level distillation, each auxiliary branch learns from their ensemble targets. The second-level distillation transfers the knowledge learned by the group to the group leader. L_{cd} denotes the proposed classifier diversification loss. L_{kl} denotes the KL divergence loss. We omit the cross entropy loss L_{ce} for simplicity. We will introduce these loss functions in detail in the third section. Best viewed in color.

where T is the temperature parameter. An increase in the parameter T will make the probability distribution smoother. When training teachers, T is set to 1. When distilling knowledge from the teacher model to the student model, T is usually set to 3.

In order to train a multi-class image classification model, our goal is to minimize the cross entropy between the predicted class probabilities q_i and the corresponding ground truth label distribution y_i,

$$L_{ce} = H(y_i, q_i) \tag{2}$$

where $H(p, q) = -\sum_i p_i log q_i$.

Knowledge transfer is achieved by aligning the probability distribution q generated by the student with the target distribution t. The temperature parameter T should be the same for teacher and student networks. Specifically, we use KL (Kullback-Leibler) Divergence as the loss function:

$$L_{kl} = KL(t, q) = \sum_{i,j} t_{ij} log \frac{t_{ij}}{q_{ij}} \tag{3}$$

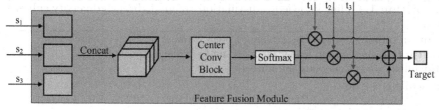

Fig. 2. We take the case of three auxiliary branches as an example. Feature maps s_i from each branch will be concatenated together, and then fed into the center convolution block. The center block is made of several convolutional layers, batch normalization and ReLU activation function. The last layer of this block is fully connected layer. This block is designed to fuse the semantic representation from multiple branches. Compared with other methods, more semantic information can effectively improve the performance of the module. The final target is obtained by the weighted sum of logits t_i of all auxiliary branches.

3.2 Feature Fusion Module

An overview of the Feature Fusion Module is described in Fig. 2. Features from a single layer contain less information than features from multiple layers. Many approaches [41–44] try to take advantage of more diversed features to get better model performance. We take the features of the last block from multiple branches as the input of the Feature Fusion Module. Since deeper layers in the network lead to richer semantic information, this approach can enrich features with high-level semantic information. Our experiment proves that the weights generated from this method can achieve better results.

$$t_e = \sum_{i=0}^{m-1} f_i(s_1, s_2, ..., s_{m-1}) \cdot t_i \qquad (4)$$

where $f(\cdot)$ denotes the function of center block in the FFM. This function will output the corresponding importance score for each branch and also satisfy $\sum_{i=1}^{m} f_i(s_1, s_2, ..., s_{m-1}) = 1$. s_k denotes the feature map of the last block from the $(m-1)^{th}$ branch. t_k denotes the logits from the mth branch. t_e denotes the weighted ensemble target.

3.3 Classifier Diversification Loss

The diversity has an important influence on the accuracy of the final ensemble results. For better results, we expect peer classifiers to classify samples based on different viewpoints. So we restrict the weight of classifiers, force them to be diversed. We use

$$L_{cd} = \sum_{i=0}^{m-1} \sum_{j=i+1}^{m} L_{cd}^{i,j} = \sum_{i=0}^{m-1} \sum_{j=i+1}^{m} |W_i^T W_j| \qquad (5)$$

Algorithm 1. Online knowledge distillation via multi-branch diversity enhancement

---

Input: Training dataset D ; Training Epoch Number ϵ ; Branch Number β
Output: Trained group leader model θ^0 and auxiliary models $\{\theta^i\}_{i=1}^m$
Initialize: e=1; Randomly initialize $\{\theta^i\}_{i=0}^m$

1: **while** e $\leq \epsilon$ **do**
2:      Compute the predictions of all auxiliary branches $\{\theta^i\}_{i=1}^m$ with Eq. (1);
3:      Get each branch's weight through FFM;
4:      Compute the target logits with Eq. (4);
5:      Compute the CD loss L_{cd} with Eq. (5);
6:      Compute the distillation loss L_{kl1} and L_{kl2} with Eq. (3);
7:      Compute the total loss function with Eq. (8);
8:      Update the model parameters $\{\theta^i\}_{i=0}^m$
9:      e=e+1
10: **end while**
Model eployment: Use group leader θ^0;

---

where W_i is the fully connected layers' weights of peer classifiers. If the weights of fully connected layers between peers get similar, it means there are more homogenization among them. This loss function acts as a regularization term to prevent homogenization. This will force each classifier to learn different features under this limit. Experiments show that this loss function improves the diversity of peer classifiers and improves the distillation efficiency. We will explain in detail in the ablation study.

3.4   Loss Function and Algorithm

To get a better understanding of our method, we describe the process in Algorithm 1. Our distillation method is a two-level procedure. For the first level distillation, each auxiliary branch learns the knowledge distilled from the soft targets t_e generated by FFM. The distillation loss of all auxiliary branches is

$$L_{kl1} = \sum_{i=1}^{m-1} KL(t_e, q_i) \qquad (6)$$

In the second-level distillation, the knowledge learned by the group will be distilled to the group leader. Same as OKDDip, we average the predictions of all branches to get t_{avg}. The distillation of the group leader is

$$L_{kl2} = KL(t_{avg}, q_{gl}) \qquad (7)$$

To sum up, the loss function of the whole neural network is:

$$L = \sum_{i=1}^{m} L_{ce}^i + \alpha T^2 L_{kl1} + \beta T^2 L_{kl2} + \gamma L_{cd} \qquad (8)$$

where α, β and γ are the balance parameter to balance the loss term. The first term is the sum of all branches' cross entropy loss.

4 Experiment

In this section, we evaluate our method on five popular neural networks (ResNet-50, ResNet-110 [4], ResNext-50(32 × 4d) [45], Xception [46], ShuffleNet V2-1.0 [47]) and three image classification benchmark dataset: CIFAR-10/100 [25] and CINIC-10 [26]. We also compare our method with closely related works, including ONE and OKDDip. In addition to the classification ability, we also conduct several ablation studies on the feature fusion module and classifier diversification loss, of which the result indicates that the proposed method has better generalization performance compared with other methods. All the reported results are averaged based on three runs.

4.1 Datasets and Settings

Datasets. There are three datasets in our experiments. CIFAR-10 and CIFAR-100 [25] both contains 50,000 training images and 10,000 test images, which come from 10/100 classes. CINIC-10 consists of images from both CIFAR and ImageNet [48]. It has 270,000 images and 10 classes. The size in CINIC-10 is the same as in CIFAR. It contains 90,000 training images and 90,000 test images, all at a resolution of 32 × 32. The top-1 classification error rate are reported.

Settings. We implement all the networks and training procedures in Pytorch [49]. We conduct all experiments on an NVIDIA GeFore RTX 2080Ti GPU. For all datasets, we follow the experimental setting of [19]. For data augmentation, we apply standard random crop and horizontal flip to all images. We use SGD [50] as the optimizer with Nesterov momentum 0.9 and weight decay $5e - 4$ during training. We set mini-batch size to 128. We use the standard learning schedule. The learning rate starts from 0.1 and divided by 10 at 150 and 225 iterations, for a total of 300 iterations. We set $m = 4$, means that there are three auxiliary branches and a group leader. We separate the last two blocks of each backbone network for CIFAR-10/100 and CINIC-10. We empirically set $T = 3$ to generate soft predictions. We set $\alpha = 1$, $\beta = 2$ and $\gamma = 5e - 8$ to balance the loss term in Eq. 6.

We compare our method with several online knowledge distillation methods. In OKDDip, it has two network settings: branch-based and network-based. The branch-based approach refers to student models sharing multiple convolutional layers, separated from each other after a specified layer. The network-based method means that all student models do not share any convolutional layers, and each student is an independent model. The principles of these two approaches are close, so the branch-based method can well validate the effectiveness of our method. In all the experiments, we use branch-based setting for comparison. Baseline means the original model trained on the dataset without any modification.

Table 1. Error rate (top-1, %) on CIFAR-10.

Models	Baseline	Our method	Gain
ResNet-32	6.38 ± 0.10	**5.45 ± 0.07**	0.93
ResNet-110	5.46 ± 0.02	**4.47 ± 0.02**	0.99
ResNext-50(32 × 4d)	5.05 ± 0.12	**4.66 ± 0.05**	0.39
Xception	5.70 ± 0.08	**5.19 ± 0.05**	0.51
ShuffleNetV2-1.0	9.21 ± 0.04	**8.36 ± 0.03**	0.85

Table 2. Error rate (top-1, %) on CIFAR-100.

Models	Baseline	ONE	OKDDip	Our method
ResNet-32	28.39 ± 0.04	25.76 ± 0.04	25.45 ± 0.10	**24.84 ± 0.06**
ResNet-110	23.85 ± 0.17	21.94 ± 0.13	21.01 ± 0.16	**20.52 ± 0.13**
ResNext-50(32 × 4d)	20.43 ± 0.19	18.24 ± 0.03	17.90 ± 0.06	**17.55 ± 0.06**
Xception	21.71 ± 0.06	19.69 ± 0.06	19.66 ± 0.07	**19.55 ± 0.11**
ShuffleNetV2-1.0	28.76 ± 0.12	25.23 ± 0.11	25.28 ± 0.18	**25.17 ± 0.10**

4.2 Results on CIFAR-10/100

Table 1 and Table 2 compares the top-1 classification error rate on CIFAR-10 and CIFAR-100 based on five different backbone networks. The result generated by ONE is the averaged accuracy of all branches. The results of OKDDip and ours are the accuracy of the group leader. From these two tables, it clearly shows that our method achieves a lower error rate on the same backbone network. Specifically, our method improves the accuracy of various baseline network by 3% to 4% on CIFAR-100. The network with higher capacity generally benefits more from our method. Our methods improves the state-of-the-art methods by 0.61%, 0.49% and 0.35% with ResNet-32, ResNet-110 and ResNext-50, respectively. These results showing that our method is more effective than existing methods. When the baseline model has lower capacity, our method can also slightly improve the accuracy compared with other methods.

In Table 3, we compare our method with another two-level distillation method OKDDip on three backbone networks. The results of compared methods are the averaged ensemble results of three branches on three backbone networks in the second-level distillation. Since the ensemble results act as a teacher to teach the group leader, a more accurate result can train a better group leader. It is also seen that our method improves the OKDDip method by 0.59%, 0.57% and 0.34% with ResNet-32, ResNet-110 and ResNext-50. Generally, our method successfully enhanced the diversity among different branches and brings improvement to distillation performance.

Table 3. Error rate (top-1, %) of ensemble results on CIFAR-100.

Models	OKDDip	Our method	Gain
ResNet-32	23.22	**22.63**	0.59
ResNet-110	19.42	**18.85**	0.57
ResNext-50(32 × 4d)	17.02	**16.68**	0.34

Diversity Measurement. We use the interrater agreement in [21] as the metric to measure the branch diversity. This method is defined as:

$$s = 1 - \frac{\frac{1}{T}\sum_{k=1}^{m} \rho(x_k)(T - \rho(x_k))}{m(T-1)\bar{p}(1-\bar{p})} \qquad (9)$$

where T is the total number of classifiers, $\rho(x_k)$ is the number of classifiers that classify x correctly, $\bar{p}$ is the average accuracy of individual classifiers and m is the total number of test samples. OKDDip and our method obtained 0.633 and 0.549 respectively (CIFAR-100 & ResNet-32). The smaller the s measurement, the larger the diversity. From this results, we can see that our method actually increase the branch diversity.

4.3   Results on CINIC-10

CINIC-10 dataset is larger and more challenging than CIFAR-10 but not as difficult as ImageNet. We adopt the same data preprocessing as those of CIFAR-10/100 experiments.

Table 4. Error rates (top-1, %) on CINIC-10.

Models	Baseline	ONE	OKDDip	Our method
ResNet-32	15.96 ± 0.13	14.60 ± 0.09	14.41 ± 0.10	**14.28 ± 0.12**
ResNet-110	13.99 ± 0.06	12.29 ± 0.09	12.21 ± 0.11	**11.86 ± 0.08**
ResNext-50(32 × 4d)	13.65 ± 0.12	12.19 ± 0.04	12.20 ± 0.06	**12.02 ± 0.07**

Table 4 compares the top-1 classification error rates based on three backbone networks trained by different methods. From this table, we observed that our method outperforms baseline by 1.68%, 2.13% and 1.63% on ResNet-32, ResNet-110 and ResNext-50 respectively. Our method also improves the state-of-the-art method by 0.13%, 0.35% and 0.18% on three backbone networks. We can find that the improvement in generalization performance is very limited on this dataset. High-capacity networks tend to perform better. But the accuracy of ResNext-50 is slightly lower than ResNet-110 although its baseline performance is better.

Table 5. Error rates (top-1, %) of ensemble results on CINIC-10.

Models	OKDDip	Our method	Gain
ResNet-32	13.55	**13.44**	0.11
ResNet-110	11.35	**10.98**	0.37
ResNext-50(32 × 4d)	11.77	**11.54**	0.23

In Table 5, we compare our method with OKDDip. We can find that our method outperforms OKDDip by 0.11%, 0.37% and 0.23% on ResNet-32, ResNet-110 and ResNext-50. While it can be observed that all the methods seem not to increase as much as that in CIFAR-100 experiments. We guess it is because the homogenization problem becomes serious when we conduct experiments on easier datasets. We still need to explore solutions to solve the homogenization problem in the future.

4.4   Ablation Study

Table 6. Ablation study: error rates (top-1, %) for ResNet-32 on CIFAR-100.

Gate	SA	FFM	CD	Top-1 error	Top-5 error
		✓		25.40	6.19
	✓			25.45	6.33
✓				25.76	6.39
		✓	✓	**24.84**	**6.08**
	✓		✓	25.18	6.10
✓			✓	25.31	6.11

In this section, we conduct various ablation studies to validate the effectiveness of our proposed FFM and CD loss. We use ResNet-32 on the CIFAR-100 dataset to show the benefit of our components. We also compare our FFM with other knowledge distillation methods, including gate module in ONE and self-attention (SA) mechanism in OKDDip.

In Table 6, we report the top-1 and top-5 error rates of different methods. The remaining experimental settings are consistent with previous experiment. We carefully conducted six experiments on the network components. We compared the performance of three attention modules in the same experimental settings. When FFM is used only, the performance of our method has slightly exceeded other methods. This shows that FFM makes the student network learns more knowledge during the distillation. Compared with gate module in ONE, our method improves the top-1 error rates by 0.36% and top-5 error rates by 0.2%.

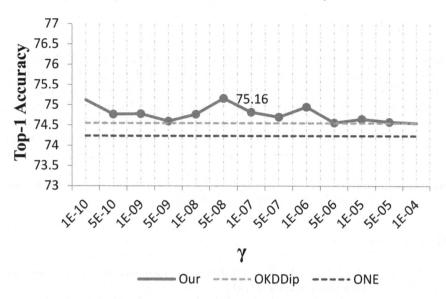

Fig. 3. Sensitivity to γ on CIFAR-100 for ResNet-32.

This result proves that our method effectively utilizes the rich semantic information of multiple branches. When we combine different attention mechanism with classifier diversification loss, our results clearly show that our method surpasses other methods. The combination of FFM and CD loss has more obvious improvement. Compared with the independent FFM, the combination improves the top-1 error rates by 0.56% and the top-5 error rates by 0.08%. Our method clearly enhances the diversity among branches and improves the generalization ability of the student model. From this table, we observe that CD loss really plays the most important role in the overall improvements.

Figure 3 demonstrates how the performance of our method is affected by the choice of hyperparameter γ of the CD loss. We plot the top-1 accuracy on the CIFAR-100 for ResNet-32 group leader trained with γ ranging from $1e - 10$ to $1e - 4$. In this figure, the dash line indicates the mean accuracy of other methods. We can find that our method still has robust performance against varying γ values. The green dot indicates the parameter we are using. We should note that the choice of parameters will affect the optimization process. If the parameter is too large, this will lead to too much diversity among the branches, and eventually will not converge. If the parameter is too small, the CD loss function will be difficult to play the role of regularization. In that case, the value of this loss function will be very small, making the loss function ineffective. This figure shows that CD loss has a significant effect on distillation performance within a proper range.

5   Conclusion

In online knowledge distillation, diversity is always an important and challenging issue. In this work, we proposed the Feature Fusion Module and Classifier Diversification loss, which effectively enhances the diversity among multiple branches. By increasing branch diversity and using more diversed semantic information, we have significantly improved the performance of online knowledge distillation. Experiments show that our method achieves the state-of-the-art performance among several popular datasets without additional training and inference costs.

Acknowledgement. This work is supported by National Key Research and Development Project of China (Grant No. 2018YFB1004901).

References

1. Hinton, G., Vinyals, O., Dean, J.: Distilling the knowledge in a neural network. arXiv preprint arXiv:1503.02531 (2015)
2. Krizhevsky, A., Sutskever, I., Hinton, G.E.: ImageNet classification with deep convolutional neural networks. In: Advances in Neural Information Processing Systems, pp. 1097–1105 (2012)
3. Simonyan, K., Zisserman, A.: Very deep convolutional networks for large-scale image recognition. arXiv preprint arXiv:1409.1556 (2014)
4. He, K., Zhang, X., Ren, S., Sun, J.: Deep residual learning for image recognition. In: Proceedings of the IEEE Conference on Computer Vision and Pattern Recognition, pp. 770–778 (2016)
5. Long, J., Shelhamer, E., Darrell, T.: Fully convolutional networks for semantic segmentation. In: Proceedings of the IEEE Conference on Computer Vision and Pattern Recognition, pp. 3431–3440 (2015)
6. Redmon, J., Divvala, S., Girshick, R., Farhadi, A.: You only look once: unified, real-time object detection. In: Proceedings of the IEEE Conference on Computer Vision and Pattern Recognition, pp. 779–788 (2016)
7. Han, S., Mao, H., Dally, W.J.: Deep compression: compressing deep neural networks with pruning, trained quantization and Huffman coding. arXiv preprint arXiv:1510.00149 (2015)
8. Lebedev, V., Lempitsky, V.: Fast convnets using group-wise brain damage. In: Proceedings of the IEEE Conference on Computer Vision and Pattern Recognition, pp. 2554–2564 (2016)
9. Molchanov, P., Tyree, S., Karras, T., Aila, T., Kautz, J.: Pruning convolutional neural networks for resource efficient inference. arXiv preprint arXiv:1611.06440 (2016)
10. Rastegari, M., Ordonez, V., Redmon, J., Farhadi, A.: XNOR-Net: ImageNet classification using binary convolutional neural networks. In: Leibe, B., Matas, J., Sebe, N., Welling, M. (eds.) ECCV 2016. LNCS, vol. 9908, pp. 525–542. Springer, Cham (2016). https://doi.org/10.1007/978-3-319-46493-0_32
11. Wu, J., Leng, C., Wang, Y., Hu, Q., Cheng, J.: Quantized convolutional neural networks for mobile devices. In: Proceedings of the IEEE Conference on Computer Vision and Pattern Recognition, pp. 4820–4828 (2016)

12. Wang, K., Liu, Z., Lin, Y., Lin, J., Han, S.: HAQ: hardware-aware automated quantization with mixed precision. In: Proceedings of the IEEE Conference on Computer Vision and Pattern Recognition, pp. 8612–8620 (2019)
13. Romero, A., Ballas, N., Kahou, S.E., Chassang, A., Gatta, C., Bengio, Y.: FitNets: hints for thin deep nets. arXiv preprint arXiv:1412.6550 (2014)
14. Zagoruyko, S., Komodakis, N.: Paying more attention to attention: improving the performance of convolutional neural networks via attention transfer. arXiv preprint arXiv:1612.03928 (2016)
15. Yim, J., Joo, D., Bae, J., Kim, J.: A gift from knowledge distillation: fast optimization, network minimization and transfer learning. In: Proceedings of the IEEE Conference on Computer Vision and Pattern Recognition, pp. 4133–4141 (2017)
16. Zhang, Y., Xiang, T., Hospedales, T.M., Lu, H.: Deep mutual learning. In: Proceedings of the IEEE Conference on Computer Vision and Pattern Recognition, pp. 4320–4328 (2018)
17. Zhu, X., Gong, S., et al.: Knowledge distillation by on-the-fly native ensemble. In: Advances in Neural Information Processing Systems, pp. 7517–7527 (2018)
18. Anil, R., Pereyra, G., Passos, A., Ormandi, R., Dahl, G.E., Hinton, G.E.: Large scale distributed neural network training through online distillation. arXiv preprint arXiv:1804.03235 (2018)
19. Chen, D., Mei, J.P., Wang, C., Feng, Y., Chen, C.: Online knowledge distillation with diverse peers. In: Proceedings of the AAAI Conference on Artificial Intelligence, pp. 3430–3437 (2020)
20. Kuncheva, L.I., Whitaker, C.J.: Measures of diversity in classifier ensembles and their relationship with the ensemble accuracy. Mach. Learn. **51**, 181–207 (2003)
21. Zhou, Z.H.: Ensemble Methods: Foundations and Algorithms. CRC Press, Boca Raton (2012)
22. Zhang, H., Goodfellow, I., Metaxas, D., Odena, A.: Self-attention generative adversarial networks. In: International Conference on Machine Learning, pp. 7354–7363 (2019)
23. Vaswani, A., et al.: Attention is all you need. In: Advances in Neural Information Processing Systems, pp. 5998–6008 (2017)
24. Saito, K., Ushiku, Y., Harada, T.: Asymmetric tri-training for unsupervised domain adaptation. In: International Conference on Machine Learning, vol. 70, pp. 2988–2997 (2017)
25. Krizhevsky, A., Hinton, G.: Learning multiple layers of features from tiny images. Technical report (2009)
26. Darlow, L.N., Crowley, E.J., Antoniou, A., Storkey, A.J.: CINIC-10 is not ImageNet or CIFAR-10. arXiv preprint arXiv:1810.03505 (2018)
27. Ba, J., Caruana, R.: Do deep nets really need to be deep? In: Advances in Neural Information Processing Systems, pp. 2654–2662 (2014)
28. Yun, S., Park, J., Lee, K., Shin, J.: Regularizing class-wise predictions via self-knowledge distillation. In: Proceedings of the IEEE Conference on Computer Vision and Pattern Recognition, pp. 13876–13885 (2020)
29. Lee, S.H., Kim, D.H., Song, B.C.: Self-supervised knowledge distillation using singular value decomposition. In: Ferrari, V., Hebert, M., Sminchisescu, C., Weiss, Y. (eds.) ECCV 2018. LNCS, vol. 11210, pp. 339–354. Springer, Cham (2018). https://doi.org/10.1007/978-3-030-01231-1_21
30. Goodfellow, I., et al.: Generative adversarial nets. In: Advances in Neural Information Processing Systems, pp. 2672–2680 (2014)

31. Shen, Z., He, Z., Xue, X.: MEAL: multi-model ensemble via adversarial learning. In: Proceedings of the AAAI Conference on Artificial Intelligence, vol. 33, pp. 4886–4893 (2019)

32. Xu, Z., Hsu, Y.C., Huang, J.: Training shallow and thin networks for acceleration via knowledge distillation with conditional adversarial networks. arXiv preprint arXiv:1709.00513 (2017)

33. Heo, B., Lee, M., Yun, S., Choi, J.Y.: Knowledge distillation with adversarial samples supporting decision boundary. In: Proceedings of the AAAI Conference on Artificial Intelligence, vol. 33, pp. 3771–3778 (2019)

34. Park, W., Kim, D., Lu, Y., Cho, M.: Relational knowledge distillation. In: Proceedings of the IEEE Conference on Computer Vision and Pattern Recognition, pp. 3967–3976 (2019)

35. Peng, B., et al.: Correlation congruence for knowledge distillation. In: Proceedings of the IEEE International Conference on Computer Vision, pp. 5007–5016 (2019)

36. Tarvainen, A., Valpola, H.: Mean teachers are better role models: weight-averaged consistency targets improve semi-supervised deep learning results. In: Advances in Neural Information Processing Systems, pp. 1195–1204 (2017)

37. Xie, Q., Luong, M.T., Hovy, E., Le, Q.V.: Self-training with noisy student improves ImageNet classification. In: Proceedings of the IEEE Conference on Computer Vision and Pattern Recognition, pp. 10687–10698 (2020)

38. Furlanello, T., Lipton, Z.C., Tschannen, M., Itti, L., Anandkumar, A.: Born again neural networks. arXiv preprint arXiv:1805.04770 (2018)

39. Yang, C., Xie, L., Su, C., Yuille, A.L.: Snapshot distillation: teacher-student optimization in one generation. In: Proceedings of the IEEE Conference on Computer Vision and Pattern Recognition, pp. 2859–2868 (2019)

40. Song, G., Chai, W.: Collaborative learning for deep neural networks. In: Advances in Neural Information Processing Systems, pp. 1832–1841 (2018)

41. Huang, G., Liu, Z., Van Der Maaten, L., Weinberger, K.Q.: Densely connected convolutional networks. In: Proceedings of the IEEE Conference on Computer Vision and Pattern Recognition, pp. 4700–4708 (2017)

42. Ronneberger, O., Fischer, P., Brox, T.: U-Net: convolutional networks for biomedical image segmentation. In: Navab, N., Hornegger, J., Wells, W.M., Frangi, A.F. (eds.) MICCAI 2015. LNCS, vol. 9351, pp. 234–241. Springer, Cham (2015). https://doi.org/10.1007/978-3-319-24574-4_28

43. Li, H., Xiong, P., Fan, H., Sun, J.: DFANet: deep feature aggregation for real-time semantic segmentation. In: Proceedings of the IEEE Conference on Computer Vision and Pattern Recognition, pp. 9522–9531 (2019)

44. Sun, D., Yao, A., Zhou, A., Zhao, H.: Deeply-supervised knowledge synergy. In: Proceedings of the IEEE Conference on Computer Vision and Pattern Recognition, pp. 6997–7006 (2019)

45. Xie, S., Girshick, R., Dollár, P., Tu, Z., He, K.: Aggregated residual transformations for deep neural networks. In: Proceedings of the IEEE Conference on Computer Vision and Pattern Recognition, pp. 1492–1500 (2017)

46. Chollet, F.: Xception: deep learning with depthwise separable convolutions. In: Proceedings of the IEEE Conference on Computer Vision and Pattern Recognition, pp. 1251–1258 (2017)

47. Ma, N., Zhang, X., Zheng, H.-T., Sun, J.: ShuffleNet V2: practical guidelines for efficient CNN architecture design. In: Ferrari, V., Hebert, M., Sminchisescu, C., Weiss, Y. (eds.) Computer Vision – ECCV 2018. LNCS, vol. 11218, pp. 122–138. Springer, Cham (2018). https://doi.org/10.1007/978-3-030-01264-9_8

48. Deng, J., Dong, W., Socher, R., Li, L.J., Li, K., Fei-Fei, L.: ImageNet: a large-scale hierarchical image database. In: Proceeding of the IEEE Conference on Computer Vision and Pattern Recognition, pp. 248–255. IEEE (2009)
49. Paszke, A., et al.: PyTorch: an imperative style, high-performance deep learning library. In: Advances in Neural Information Processing Systems, pp. 8026–8037 (2019)
50. Ruder, S.: An overview of gradient descent optimization algorithms. arXiv preprint arXiv:1609.04747 (2016)

Rotation Equivariant Orientation Estimation for Omnidirectional Localization

Chao Zhang[1(✉)], Ignas Budvytis[1,2], Stephan Liwicki[1], and Roberto Cipolla[1,2]

[1] Cambridge Research Lab, Toshiba Europe Ltd, Cambridge, UK
{chao.zhang,stephan.liwicki}@crl.toshiba.co.uk
[2] Department of Engineering, University of Cambridge, Cambridge, UK
{ib255,rc10001}@cam.ac.uk

Abstract. Deep learning based 6-degree-of-freedom (6-DoF) direct camera pose estimation is highly efficient at test time and can achieve accurate results in challenging, weakly textured environments. Typically, however, it requires large amounts of training images, spanning many orientations and positions of the environment making it impractical for medium size or large environments. In this work we present a direct 6-DoF camera pose estimation method which alleviates the need for orientation augmentation at train time while still supporting any SO(3) rotation at test time. This property is achieved by the following three step procedure. Firstly, omni-directional training images are rotated to a common orientation. Secondly, a fully rotation equivariant DNN encoder is applied and its output is used to obtain: (i) a rotation invariant prediction of the camera position and (ii) a rotation equivariant prediction of the probability distribution over camera orientations. Finally, at test time, the camera position is predicted robustly due to an in-built rotation invariance, while the camera orientation is recovered from the relative shift of the peak in the probability distribution of camera orientations. We demonstrate our approach on synthetic and real-image datasets, where we significantly outperform standard DNN-based pose regression (i) in terms of accuracy when a single training orientation is used, and (ii) in training efficiency when orientation augmentation is employed. To the best of our knowledge, our proposed rotation equivariant DNN for localization is the first direct pose estimation method able to predict orientation without explicit rotation augmentation at train time.

1 Introduction

Visual localization aims at finding the position and orientation of the input camera sensor with respect to a known environment, using image alone. Its significance in many practical applications, including autonomous driving [1],

Electronic supplementary material The online version of this chapter (https://doi.org/10.1007/978-3-030-69538-5_21) contains supplementary material, which is available to authorized users.

© Springer Nature Switzerland AG 2021
H. Ishikawa et al. (Eds.): ACCV 2020, LNCS 12625, pp. 334–350, 2021.
https://doi.org/10.1007/978-3-030-69538-5_21

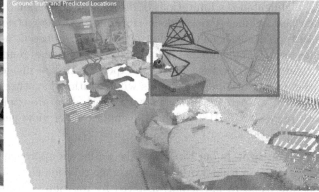

Fig. 1. Given equirectangular input of arbitrary orientation (left images), our method predicts 6-DoF camera poses (green - ground truth, red - predictions). Note that our method does not require any rotation augmentation at train time and hence significantly increases convergence speed. Left column, shows query images from Stanford 2D3DS [25] dataset under arbitrary orientations and corresponding camera pose predictions are highlighted on the right. Our method is capable of rotation invariant position prediction and efficient orientation estimation. (Color figure online)

robotics [2] and augmented reality [3,4], inspires numerous publications over the years [5–19]. Nevertheless, robust localization in complex environments remains a challenge to-date [20–23].

Classical localization using feature correspondences dates back decades ago [5–7], and some of these methods remain competitive today especially in mid- and large-scale environments [21,24]. Nevertheless, recent advances in deep learning particularly improve upon localization with challenging lighting, appearance changes and in run-time performance [10,14,19]. In our work, we target deep localization with a particular focus on generalization for invariance to camera orientation.

Localization with deep neural networks (DNNs) has been tackled using image retrieval [8], relative pose regression [9–11], scene coordinate regression [12–15] and direct camera pose estimation [16–19] approaches. Image retrieval approaches formulate localization as a problem of finding the image most similar to the query image. Relative pose regression methods use image feature correspondences between query and retrieved image to further refine the pose. Scene coordinate regression methods perform an efficient image to point cloud feature matching to find camera pose, while direct pose estimation approaches typically regress the position and orientation of the camera directly, in an end-to-end setup. We deal with the former type as we present a new approach to pose regression under challenging rotations at test time, but our method is applicable to other frameworks.

PoseNet [16] presents an early approach to direct pose estimation using DNNs, and it has been a popular framework since [17,19]. Recently, however,

[23] highlighted the limitations of direct pose regression methods, and compared their performance to networks performing the image retrieval task. In particular, both type of methods struggle to generalise to unseen, novel viewpoints, hence collection of large amounts of images (or utilisation of rendered views) is required if good test performance is to be expected. In [26] image retrieval is improved by enhancing original viewpoints with additional synthetically generated views. Similarly, warped RGB images with depth data are exploited to improve deep pose regression in [18], while [19] applies novel view generation for DNNs by leveraging the sparsity of SIFT features [27].

Contribution. In our work, we take a different approach to improving the deep pose regression framework, as we leverage rotation equivariance to improve view generalization. In particular, inspired by rotation equivariant deep learning on spheres [28–30], we formulate localization for spherical, omni-directional input (see Fig. 1). We estimate camera position via regression from the feature response of the rotation invariant decoder, while camera orientation is extracted from the relative orientation in rotation equivariant feature response. Our contributions are as follows:

1. We present the first rotation invariant, deep camera position regression network.
2. We introduce rotation equivariant decoder and a sample efficient classification loss to generate camera rotation estimation in full SO(3) from only **one** rotation observation in training data, without rotation augmentation.
3. We evaluate our method on synthetic and real datasets.

The rest of this work is divided as follows. Section 2 discusses relevant work in localisation. Section 3 provides details of our proposed localization method. Sections 4 and 5 describe the experiment setup and corresponding results.

2   Related Work

In this section, we discuss relevant works on deep learning based localization, and, in particular, direct pose regression methods. We also review equivariant feature learning in the context of pose estimation and spherical deep learning. The interested readers are referred to [20–23] for a more detailed review of localization approaches.

2.1   Localization Using Deep Neural Networks

Localization methods which use deep learning have received much interest in recent years [8–19]. Typical approaches tackle the task *via* place recognition, relative pose regression, scene coordinate regression or direct camera pose estimation.

Place Recognition methods formulate the localization task as image retrieval problem where 6-DoF camera pose estimation is not required. Examples include

NetVLAD [8] which generates an image descriptor that is aggregated from local descriptors taken from convolutional responses at pixel level. PlaNet [31] formulates the place recognition task as a classification problem using quantized camera coordinates.

Relative Pose Regression methods use image retrieval followed by relative pose estimation between query and retrieved images to refine the pose prediction. In [9], a Siamese network is employed to find the pose transformation between two images. Additionally, end-to-end implementations for the retrieval and refinement are presented in [10] and [11].

Scene Coordinate Regression approaches predict 2D-to-3D point correspondences *via* per pixel regression of scene coordinates. They obtain a 6-DoF camera pose prediction by absolute pose estimation. Differentiable RANSAC optimization is presented in [12] where a DNN is employed for hypothesis scoring. In [13] an angle-based re-projection loss is optimized, while [14] produces a differentiable score from RANSAC inlier counts. A scene coordinate regression with semantic labels is presented in [15].

Direct Pose Estimation provides pose predictions directly using convolutional DNNs. PoseNet [16] regresses to camera pose from image signals alone using a simple deep learning framework. However, absolute pose regression has poor generalization to unseen viewpoints and thus requires well sampled training data [23] if good test performance is expected. An LSTM module is employed by [17] to reduce overfitting in the final fully connected layers as structured feature correlation is introduced. In [18] and [19] original dataset views for training are enhanced with novel view generation, for RGB-D and RGB input respectively.

In our work we consider direct pose estimation due to its train and test time speed and simplicity. We overcome the problem of overfitting by training from densely sampled locations using artificially rendered images of the scene of interest. Our method does not require different samples of orientations and demonstrates orders of magnitude faster convergence at training, and significant improved performance at test time.

2.2 Omni-Directional Localization and Equivariant Features

Omni-directional sensor input increases the field of view for the localization task and more importantly rotations are easily handled by simply moving the pixels on the image sphere. Distortions due to camera pose, otherwise introduced by the planar image projection are reduced [32]. Therefore, spherical images present a very attractive input to camera pose estimation. Early works introduce rotation invariant omni-directional localization using color histograms [33–35] or Eigenspace models [36,37]. Later, SIFT features [27] were adapted to spherical input for wide angle localization tasks [38].

In recent years, many classical feature matching tasks have been revisited with deep learning. For example, SIFT [27] is reformulated using spacial transformer networks [39] to introduce scale and rotation equivariance in DNNs

[40,41], all be it only approximately. In [42], DNNs exploiting harmonic filters are used for guaranteed rotation equivariant features. Neither, however, are trivially applicable to spherical input.

Research on spherical CNN computations include [43] which projects convolutional filters onto the tangent plane of the sphere, [44–47] who apply convolutions on an unfolded icosahedron mesh, and [48] who employ kernels on a HEALPix spheres. Most do not support rotation invariance, while non-trivial equivariance is not supported by any. Rotation invariance is also only approximate due to required mesh alignments. Fundamental rotation equivariance for spherical CNNs is first presented in [28] and [29]. We base our method on [29] which leverages convolutions in a spherical fourier representation to ensure equivariance. In [30], a simplification is introduce to [29] using the Clebsch-Gordan decomposition.

We apply omni-directional localization since it allows for (i) rotation invariant camera position estimation, and based on the convolutions presented by [29] (ii) efficient, rotation equivariant orientation estimation from feature responses. We emphasize, to the best of our knowledge, we propose the first approach which exploits rotation equivariance for the localization task.

3   Leveraging Rotation Equivariance for Localization

Our method, illustrated in Fig. 2, consists of three modules: (i) the rotation equivariant spherical encoder (ii) the rotation invariant decoder for camera position regression, and (iii) the rotationally equivariant orientation classifier which shifts its prediction according to the camera rotation. Below, we describe each part in detail.

3.1   Equivariant Spherical Encoder

The first module consists of a rotation equivariant feature encoder inspired by the spherical convolutions introduced in [29] and the general architecture of ResNet-18 [49]. Specifically, we adapt the work of [29] to perform rotationally equivariant feature extraction for the localization task. Our intention is two-fold. Firstly, theoretically sound rotation equivariant feature response can be integrated [29] to provide rotation invariant feature response which is a useful property for robustly predicting camera positions while being agnostic to orientation. Secondly, rotation equivariance allows us to formulate a framework in which only a single orientation needs to be observed during training.

We build our encoder in the following way. First, we apply S^2Conv [29] on the spherical input images to create an output feature map that is indexed by rotations in SO(3). After that, we replicate the typical ResNet-18 architecture [49] using three SO(3)Conv [29] based ResNet blocks (see Fig. 2). Here, the S^2Conv convolution corresponds to a convolution of a 2D pattern with a 2D surface on the spherical manifold, where the spherical manifold is shifted using

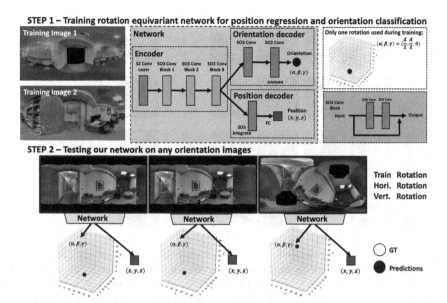

Fig. 2. Training and testing frameworks are shown. For training, we use artificially rendered images of fixed orientation in the global mesh. Our feature encoder is a spherical CNN inspired by the ResNet-18 architecture [49], consisting of a $S2$Conv layer and multiple ResBlocks composed of SO(3)Conv layers. By design feature maps are fully rotation equivariant (also see Fig. 3). The output features are fed into a rotation invariant decoder for position regression, while orientation prediction leverages further equivariant SO(3)Conv layers ending with a single channel SO(3) cube feature response. In training we classify a particular cell of this cube for the fixed training orientation. At test time we support arbitrary orientations, as the classification peak rotates accordingly within the SO(3) cube response.

SO(3) rotations, analogous to filter translations in standard convolution operations on planar images. Since the output shifts with input orientation changes, rotation equivariance is achieved, similar to translation equivariance in standard CNN. Note, the output is now indexed by SO(3). The SO(3)Conv operates on feature maps in SO(3), and, similarly to S^2Conv convolutions, it applies a 2D filter on the spherical manifold under rotations in SO(3) (also see [29] for more detail). We emphasize, each output is fully rotation equivariant, as it changes according to input orientation changes. The final layer's output is represented by a 3D cube, where feature responses are indexed using the XYZ Euler angles representation of rotations.

In our implementation, each ResBlock is made of SO(3)Conv-BN-ReLU-SO(3)Conv-BN. At the end of each block, the input is added to the result before ReLU. In comparison to 2D feature maps, a 3D feature map representation requires significantly larger GPU memory resources. To reduce memory requirements, we resize input images to $64 \times 64px$ in our experiments. Following [29], bandwidths relating to the spatial dimension are $32, 16, 8, 8, 8$, and the num-

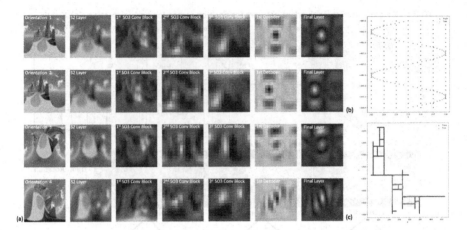

Fig. 3. Analysis of equivariance. (a) Random channels of feature map responses at initial layer, after ResBlocks, and orientation decoder for varying input orientations are shown (we average the output of the features indexed by the roll rotation of the XYZ Euler angles for visualization). Note, feature map responses change following the input image camera orientation. In the final layer for orientation, a strong single peak is formed. We show train locations (blue) and test locations (red) of the SceneCity Grid (b) and SceneCity Small (c) dataset from our experiments in Sect. 4. (Color figure online)

ber of features are $3, 32, 64, 128, 128$. The final output feature map is of size $128 \times 16 \times 16 \times 16$. The resulting 3D feature map encoder forms the input to our position and orientation decoder heads. Figure 3 shows example filter responses.

3.2   Invariant Position Regressor

Our pose decoder includes two output heads. The position head is used to regress the 3D camera position $(x, y, z) \in \mathbb{R}^3$. To achieve this, we leverage the rotation-equivariance of our encoder, as we integrate over SO(3) space to produce a rotation-invariant position prediction. The final fully connected layer is used to regress the position vector in $\mathbb{R}^3$. Note, this is similar to standard PoseNet [16] where spatial aggregation is followed by one or more fully connected layers to perform pose regression. In contrast to the special aggregation in PoseNet, our aggregation results in a theoretically fully rotationally invariant feature vector and thus reduces the learning requirements for our network significantly.

Mean squared loss is used for training the position regression. Note that, instead of predicting the position directly, we use PCA whitening to normalize the GT coordinates. We find this helps the general position task, as input values are consistent across training sets even if training coordinates vary largely in scales for different datasets.

3.3   Equivariant Orientation Classifier

To the best of our knowledge, the orientation decoder represents the first rotation equivariant CNN for orientation prediction. In particular, we formulate the orientation prediction as an equivariant classification task. This is motivated by the fact that S^2Conv and $SO(3)$Conv convolutions preserve orientation information throughout layers, and hence the 3D feature response in the XYZ Euler angle-based cube feature map represents the change in the orientation of inputs. We capitalize on this by forcing train time images to have the same orientation throughout the dataset, without loss of generalization[1], and provide the classification to have a single channel SO(3)Conv layer with softmax and cross entropy loss. We can then recover the orientation of images at test time by finding the relative shift of the softmax layer output in the SO(3) cube of XYZ Euler angles. Examples of feature responses obtained at different layers are visualized in Fig. 3. Notice, as we rotate the image along azimuth and elevation, the feature response moves accordingly. The orientation decoder is implemented as SO(3)Conv-SO(3)Conv-Softmax. Note that, in our implementation, the XYZ Euler angles relate to azimuth ($\alpha \in [-\pi, \pi)$), elevation ($\beta \in [-\frac{\pi}{2}, \frac{\pi}{2}]$) and roll ($\gamma \in [-\pi, \pi)$). Since our output is quantized by the classification task, the number of possible rotations is controlled by the output resolution of the cube. Therefore, there is a trade-off between rotational accuracy and efficiency. In our experiments, we show 64^3 to be a promising choice.

4   Experimental Setup

This section provides a brief description of datasets used, network training details and evaluation protocol.

4.1   Datasets

Two datasets with known camera location and orientation are used to evaluate and compare our method with two direct 6-DoF pose regression methods, PoseNet [16] and SphereNet [43].

SceneCity [50]. This dataset contains equirectangular images rendered from two artificial cities, one big and one small. The small city, used in our experiments is first applied to localization in [51]. The environment contains 102 buildings and 156 road segments. Additionally to images, the dataset provides a 3D textured mesh which can be used to render additional images with desired camera locations and orientations. In our evaluations, we use the dataset in two ways: (i) We take a small street segment of the map (about 6 m × 20 m) and render 147 training images and 100 test images. This dataset is denoted SceneCity Grid, shown in Fig. 3(b). Training images are densely sampled with equal spacing. And the test

---

[1] Since input is omni-directional image, camera orientation can be adjusted with minimal loss.

images are sampled along a sin curve. (ii) We use the original Small SceneCity locations from [51] for training and testing. The training set consists of 1146 locations, while the test set has 300 locations as shown in Fig. 3(c).

Stanford 2D3DS [25]. This dataset consists of 1413 equirectangular images captured in an indoor environment. The dataset covers 6 areas of approximately 6000 m^2. It has been widely used in spherical semantic segmentation and depth estimation tasks [44,47,52]. The dataset is accompanied by 3D point clouds with textures and ground truth camera poses of provided images. In this work we present the effectiveness of our approach on two scenarios. In both cases, we train the model on synthetically rendered images. They differ in the testing stage. The first is to test on synthetic images, while the latter involves testing on images captured in real scenes. Note, the second task is especially challenging due to the simulation to real gap [53]. In summary, we use all 1413 real images as well as their rendered counterparts as test data. For training data, we render images with random origins within a radius of 30 cm around the test locations. In total, 7065 synthetic training images are generated. Following the protocol in [53], we use aggressive non-geometric augmentation (Gaussian blur, additive Gaussian noise, contrast change, image-wise and channel-wise brightness change) of Blender rendered images in order to increase localization performance on real images (see supplementary material for details).

4.2   Training Setup and Evaluation Protocol

Our localization network in Sect. 3 is implemented in PyTorch [54]. Equirectangular images are resized to 64×64 px as input to the network in all experiments unless stated otherwise. We use an Adam optimizer with polynomial learning rate scheduler with initial learning rate set to 10^{-4}. We train the network with batch size 20 and up to 3k epochs. We use an ℓ2-norm for position regression loss and a cross entropy loss for orientation. We weight the position loss at $\times 100$, as we find the rotation task converges faster. Our network is trained from scratch, as no pretraining is performed.

We evaluate our method based on average (avg) and median (med) Euclidean distance on position and angular divergence. Our method is compared with standard implementations of direct pose regression using planar and spherical convolutions. Full omnidirectional images are provided as input. In particular, PoseNet [16] is implemented with a ResNet-18 [49] backbone followed by two fully connected layers for pose regression. The ResNet-18 features are pretrained on ImageNet [55]. We employ the convolutions in SphereNet [43] to implement a version of PoseNet for spherical input. Here, unlike PoseNet, the convolutions are designed to work on spherical data by applying distortion corrected grid kernels on equirectangular images. In essence, this method applies 2D convolutions on the tangent planes of the sphere. A pretrained spherical VGG-16 [56] backbone is used as the encoder of SphereNet since filters are easily applied to the spherical convolutions. Following [16], the position regression loss is based on ℓ2-norm while orientation loss is based on ℓ2-norm using quaternion.

Table 1. Ablation study on SceneCity Grid. Our method is compared to PoseNet and SphereNet under varying rotation augmentation on training data, and tested on different positions and (i) original training rotations (ii) random y-axis rotations, and (iii) random SO(3) rotations. The average (avg) and median (med) position and orientation errors are reported. The most challenging experiments include random orientations in testing (**bold**). We highlight the version of PoseNet, SphereNet and our method used in remaining experiments. Additionally, we show results for varying orientation decoder resolution (shown in parentheses), and PoseNet and our method trained without PCA whitening (denoted by PoseNet* and Ours*(64^3) respectively).

Method	Aug. Type	Epochs	Original Rot.				Rand. y-axis Rot.				Random SO(3)			
			Pos.(m)		Rot.(°)		Pos.(m)		Rot.(°)		Pos.(m)		Rot.(°)	
			Avg	Med	Avg	Med	Avg	Med	Avg	Med	Avg	Med	Avg	Med
PoseNet	None	30k	0.20	0.20	0.00	0.00	4.85	4.66	90.0	90.0	**5.78**	5.43	**128**	128
	y-axis	30k	0.29	0.29	1.22	0.99	0.31	0.30	1.81	1.62	**5.73**	5.19	**120**	118
	SO(3)	30k	0.36	0.34	3.94	3.52	0.39	0.39	5.48	5.37	**0.35**	0.35	**5.62**	5.30
SphereNet	None	30k	0.19	0.17	0.00	0.00	5.33	5.31	90.0	90.0	**7.48**	6.47	**128**	128
	y-axis	30k	0.41	0.33	4.41	4.05	6.05	3.56	44.3	44.9	**8.84**	6.48	**122**	120
	SO(3)	30k	0.35	0.32	5.25	4.89	0.42	0.39	7.18	5.86	**0.38**	0.36	**6.98**	6.68
Ours(64^3)	none	3k	0.11	0.09	4.20	4.20	0.12	0.10	4.20	4.20	**0.17**	0.16	**5.05**	5.05
	SO(3)	3k	0.22	0.17	2.54	2.51	0.19	0.17	4.21	4.20	**0.19**	0.16	**2.54**	2.32
Ours(32^3)	None	3k	0.12	0.11	8.34	8.34	0.15	0.14	13.4	14.0	**0.18**	0.17	**13.2**	13.6
Ours(128^3)	None	3k	0.15	0.15	2.10	2.10	0.22	0.21	3.12	3.18	**0.31**	0.28	**2.78**	3.02
PoseNet*	SO(3)	30k	0.63	0.55	3.44	3.26	0.51	0.56	4.51	3.53	**0.72**	0.67	**7.88**	7.57
Ours*(64^3)	None	3k	0.16	0.17	4.20	4.20	0.36	0.31	4.69	4.90	**0.37**	0.31	**4.73**	5.14

5   Results

In this section we present the following results: (i) an ablation study on augmentation, orientation decoder resolution and PCA whitening (ii) experiments on larger synthetic datasets and (iii) experiments on real data.

5.1   Ablation Studies on SceneCity Grid

Our ablation uses the SceneCity Grid dataset, which consists of densely sampled training and testing locations to provide optimal data for pose regression networks, and will not suffer from interpolation or extrapolation issues [23]. Results are shown in Table 1.

Rotation Augmentation: It is known that PoseNet [16] and its variants are prone to overfitting to training data [23]. In this section we investigate how geometric training augmentation based on rotations affects the performance. In particular, we investigate testing on images from new positions but with original training rotations, horizontally rotated (rotations around y-axis), and randomly rotated by any SO(3) rotation. Unsurprisingly, both SphereNet and PoseNet demonstrate relatively good performance for the matching pairs of train and test data rotations, achieving better than 0.5 m accuracy for position. Nevertheless, they overfit to training data and poorly generalize to unseen orientations, decreasing performance to above 5 m position errors. Note, only with full rotational augmentation, localization with arbitrary camera orientations is successful. We also emphasize, more training epochs (30k versus 3k in our method) are required to make this kind of methods competitive. In contrast, our method demonstrates good position and orientation predictions in all scenarios archiving below 0.2 m position error with about 5° error on orientations. Such results are even reached for the most challenging case with one rotation during training and any orientation at testing. Thus, our method successfully generalizes one training orientation to arbitrary test orientations.

Orientation Decoder Resolution: Our decoder for orientation prediction is parameterized by the size of the output feature cube. Hence, its predictions are inherently quantized. In a second ablation study we evaluate our method with output cube of size 32^3, 64^3 and 128^3. Here, higher resolution improves the orientation accuracy at the expense of slightly reduced position accuracy: 13.2° error with 0.18 m error for 32^3, 5.05° error with 0.17 m error for 64^3 and 2.78° error with 0.31 m error for 128^3. This is due to the fact that the difficulty of the classification task is increased, and thus reduces capacity for improved position loss. Finally, we note that the usage of full rotational augmentation reduces the effect of quantization (from 5.05° to 2.54° error at 64^3), but at the cost of training efficiency. Hence we conclude that a resolution of 64^3 without rotation augmentation is most suitable for our method.

PCA Whitening: Finally we investigate the effect of PCA whitening to conclude our ablation. PCA whitening of position coordinates improves the position prediction for both, PoseNet and our method, by about twice the accuracy (to 0.72 m and 0.37 m respectively). It normalizes the position coordinates to a common range which makes training easier.

5.2   Testing on Larger Synthetic Environments

In this section, we evaluate our method on two larger environments: SceneCity Small and Stanford-2D3DS, as described in Sect. 4.1.

SceneCity Small: Similarly to SceneCity Grid, SceneCity Small is adjusted to have fixed camera orientations for all training poses. During test time, random orientations are used. For PoseNet and SphereNet, full SO(3) rotation augmentation is applied, while our method only sees a single training rotation. Figure 4 shows the performance curve over the evaluated epoch. Our method performs best, and converges much quicker than PoseNet and SphereNet. We emphasize, our decoder for rotation with cross entropy loss converges especially fast. Overall, our method achieves 2.22 m error for position, while PoseNet and SphereNet have 4.39 m and 6.07 m error respectively. Our rotation error is competitive with 9.41° error. Finally we note, PoseNet with only horizontal orientation augmentation fails.

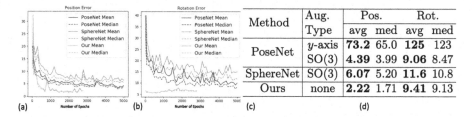

Method	Aug. Type	Pos. avg	med	Rot. avg	med
PoseNet	y-axis	**73.2**	65.0	**125**	123
PoseNet	SO(3)	**4.39**	3.99	**9.06**	8.47
SphereNet	SO(3)	**6.07**	5.20	**11.6**	10.8
Ours	none	**2.22**	1.71	**9.41**	9.13

(a)   (b)   (c)   (d)

Fig. 4. Evaluation on SceneCity Small for our method compared to PoseNet and SphereNet. (a) Position and (b) orientation errors are shown over epochs. Note, our method achieves high performance ($<2\,$m) within 2k epochs, while rotation error of $<10°$ is reached after less than 600 epochs (close to theoretical limit due to quantization which is about $5°$). In the table we compare the methods quantitatively on the test set of SceneCity Small with random orientations. Additionally, PoseNet with y-axis augmentation is presented.

Table 2. Quantitative results on Standford 2D3DS, comparing our method to PoseNet and SphereNet. A set of columns on the left side of the table, contain testing results on synthetic images, while the columns on the right side contain equivalent results on real images. Our network significantly outperforms competing methods on the random orientation test data for both synthetic and real images.

Method	Aug Type	Synthetic Images								Real Images							
		Orig. Rotation				Rand. Rotation				Orig.				Rand. Rotation			
		Pos.		Rot.		Pos.		Rot.		Pos.		Rot.		Pos.		Rot.	
		Avg	Med	Avg	Med	Avg	Med	Avg	Med	Avg	Med	Avg	Med	Avg	Med	Avg	Med
PoseNet	y-axis	1.76	1.58	9.70	5.70	**20.3**	18.4	**121**	117	2.75	1.95	15.4	7.45	**20.2**	18.5	**123**	119
	SO(3)	1.92	1.59	25.6	21.3	**2.10**	1.75	**27.7**	23.2	4.59	2.41	40.6	28.0	**6.25**	3.40	**51.3**	36.5
SphereNet	SO(3)	1.89	1.53	24.7	20.0	**2.35**	1.78	**32.7**	26.5	3.86	2.29	38.5	26.7	**4.81**	2.92	**50.5**	38.3
Ours	none	0.98	0.84	10.9	8.47	**1.79**	1.54	**13.3**	12.6	3.07	1.64	18.2	9.15	**3.57**	2.45	**25.6**	13.1

Stanford 2D3DS: Synthetic results of our method in comparison with PoseNet and SphereNet are shown on the left set of columns of Table 2. For random test rotations, our method with single training orientation outperforms PoseNet and SphereNet on rotation estimation, achieving $13.3°$. Notice also, we improve upon position error since our aggregation in the rotation invariant position head simplifies the learning task for the fully connected layer of the regression – here PoseNet and SphereNet perform with 2.10 m and 2.35 m respectively while our method produces only 1.79 m error. Finally, we emphasize, our method is limited by the classification quantization in the orientation decoder as we use a 64^3 output resolution. Qualitative results are shown in Fig. 6.

5.3 Results on a Real Image Testing Set

We use the real images for evaluation on Stanford 2D3DS. Note, training data is synthetically rendered using Blender as described in Sect. 4.1. Again, we compare our method with no rotation augmentation with PoseNet and SphereNet with

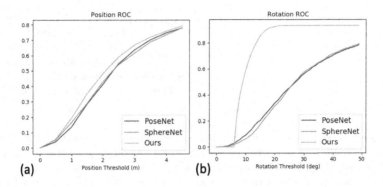

Fig. 5. ROC curve of position and rotation errors. We plot the percentage of data points with predictions below a given threshold for either position (a) or orientation (b) for our method, PoseNet and SphereNet, trained on synthetic images and tested on real images from Stanford 2D3DS. While our method is comparable for position prediction, we significantly improve upon orientation prediction. Here more than 50% of the data points are predicted within 10° error. Competing methods only achieve such an accuracy for predictions within 30°.

full SO(3) rotation augmentation in training. We test on two versions of test data: one with original orientations and one with random orientations.

The final columns of Table 2 show the results. The performance of PoseNet is slightly improved with horizontal augmentation since the dataset is biased towards horizontally consistent data. Here, PoseNet achieves 2.75 m while we reach 3.07 m accuracy. Nevertheless, this version of PoseNet overfits and does not generalize to random rotations. Overall, our method performs best, at 3.57 m position error and 25.6° orientation error. Qualitative results are shown in Fig. 6.

We draw the receiver operating characteristic (ROC) curve in Fig. 5, which calculates the percentage of test images within a specific position error or rotation error threshold. The results are generated by testing on real images with original camera location and rotation. Comparing position accuracy, our method obtains competitive results to other methods that need full augmentation. In terms of orientation, our method outperforms other methods with a large margin, having 80% orientations predicted within 15°. This demonstrates our gain of formulating orientation estimation as a classification problem with rotation equivariant response.

Finally we note, in general the performance on real images drops compared to synthetic images in Sect. 5.2. For example, the performance of our method reduces from 1.79 m to 3.57 m and 13.3° to 25.6° when moving from synthetic to real data. Similar performance drops are observed by all methods. Although intensive data augmentations is used (Sect. 4.1), there is a significant performance gap between synthetic and real data. We attribute this issue to direct pose regression being sensitive to the difference of training and testing data. A possible remedy for reducing such a domain gap is to apply image domain

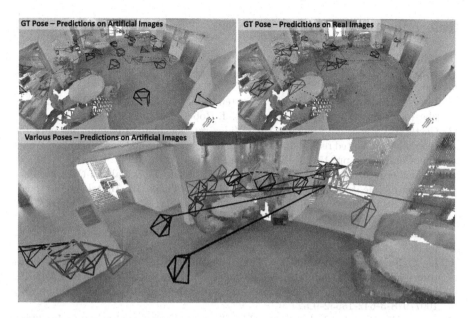

Fig. 6. Qualitative predictions of our method (red), PoseNet (blue) and SphereNet (black) on Stanford-2D3DS, quantitative results of which are reported in Table 2. Green camera poses correspond to the ground truth. Pose prediction results on synthetic images at original camera locations is shown top-left, while evaluation on real images is shown top-right. Results of synthetic tests with random orientations are shown at the bottom. Overall, our method predicts poses closer to ground truth. For real images, pose prediction suffers, but our method still provides good camera orientations. (Color figure online)

translation [57] during the test stage before feeding input to the network. Another approach could be to consider auxiliary tasks such as scene coordinate regression or depth estimation to improve the generalization ability. We leave such investigation to future work.

6 Conclusion

In this work we proposed a novel network for rotation equivariant camera pose estimation. This work is motivated by spherical equivariant convolutions, and the need of scalable 6-DoF camera pose estimation networks which can be efficiently trained. Our method learns arbitrary camera orientations from only a single orientation in training, significantly improving training efficiency in terms of epochs needed. In our evaluation, we demonstrate our approach on synthetic and real image input, where we significantly outperform standard DNN-based pose regression. Finally, we emphasize, to the best of our knowledge, our proposed rotation equivariant DNN for omnidirectional localization is the first direct pose estimation method able to predict orientation without explicit rotation augmentation at train time.

References

1. Häne, C., et al.: 3D visual perception for self-driving cars using a multi-camera system: calibration, mapping, localization, and obstacle detection. Image Vis. Comput. **68**, 14–27 (2017)
2. Lim, H., Sinha, S.N., Cohen, M.F., Uyttendaele, M., Kim, H.J.: Real-time monocular image-based 6-dof localization. Int. J. Robot. Res. **34**, 476–492 (2015)
3. Castle, R., Klein, G., Murray, D.W.: Video-rate localization in multiple maps for wearable augmented reality. In: 2008 12th IEEE International Symposium on Wearable Computers, pp. 15–22. IEEE (2008)
4. Middelberg, S., Sattler, T., Untzelmann, O., Kobbelt, L.: Scalable 6-DOF localization on mobile devices. In: Fleet, D., Pajdla, T., Schiele, B., Tuytelaars, T. (eds.) ECCV 2014. LNCS, vol. 8690, pp. 268–283. Springer, Cham (2014). https://doi.org/10.1007/978-3-319-10605-2_18
5. Schindler, G., Brown, M., Szeliski, R.: City-scale location recognition. In: CVPR, pp. 1–7. IEEE (2007)
6. Li, Y., Snavely, N., Huttenlocher, D.P.: Location recognition using prioritized feature matching. In: Daniilidis, K., Maragos, P., Paragios, N. (eds.) ECCV 2010. LNCS, vol. 6312, pp. 791–804. Springer, Heidelberg (2010). https://doi.org/10.1007/978-3-642-15552-9_57
7. Zhang, W., Kosecka, J.: Image based localization in urban environments. In: Third International Symposium on 3D Data Processing, Visualization, and Transmission (3DPVT'06), pp. 33–40. IEEE (2006)
8. Arandjelovic, R., Gronat, P., Torii, A., Pajdla, T., Sivic, J.: Netvlad: CNN architecture for weakly supervised place recognition. In: CVPR, pp. 5297–5307 (2016)
9. Melekhov, I., Ylioinas, J., Kannala, J., Rahtu, E.: Relative camera pose estimation using convolutional neural networks. In: Blanc-Talon, J., Penne, R., Philips, W., Popescu, D., Scheunders, P. (eds.) ACIVS 2017. LNCS, vol. 10617, pp. 675–687. Springer, Cham (2017). https://doi.org/10.1007/978-3-319-70353-4_57
10. Balntas, V., Li, S., Prisacariu, V.: Relocnet: continuous metric learning relocalisation using neural nets. In: ECCV, pp. 751–767 (2018)
11. Nakashima, R., Seki, A.: Sir-net: scene-independent end-to-end trainable visual relocalizer. In: 3DV, pp. 472–481. IEEE (2019)
12. Brachmann, E., et al.: Dsac-differentiable ransac for camera localization. In: CVPR, pp. 6684–6692 (2017)
13. Li, X., Ylioinas, J., Verbeek, J., Kannala, J.: Scene coordinate regression with angle-based reprojection loss for camera relocalization. In: ECCV, pp. 0–0 (2018)
14. Brachmann, E., Rother, C.: Learning less is more-6d camera localization via 3d surface regression. In: CVPR, pp. 4654–4662 (2018)
15. Budvytis, I., Teichmann, M., Vojir, T., Cipolla, R.: Large scale joint semantic re-localisation and scene understanding via globally unique instance coordinate regression. In: BMVC (2019)
16. Kendall, A., Grimes, M., Cipolla, R.: Posenet: a convolutional network for real-time 6-dof camera relocalization. In: ICCV, pp. 2938–2946 (2015)
17. Walch, F., Hazirbas, C., Leal-Taixe, L., Sattler, T., Hilsenbeck, S., Cremers, D.: Image-based localization using lstms for structured feature correlation. In: ICCV, pp. 627–637 (2017)
18. Handa, A., Patraucean, V., Badrinarayanan, V., Stent, S., Cipolla, R.: Understanding real world indoor scenes with synthetic data. In: CVPR, pp. 4077–4085 (2016)

19. Purkait, P., Zhao, C., Zach, C.: Synthetic view generation for absolute pose regression and image synthesis. In: BMVC, p. 69 (2018)
20. Piasco, N., Sidibé, D., Demonceaux, C., Gouet-Brunet, V.: A survey on visual-based localization: on the benefit of heterogeneous data. Pattern Recogn. **74**, 90–109 (2018)
21. Sattler, T., et al.: Benchmarking 6dof outdoor visual localization in changing conditions. In: CVPR, pp. 8601–8610 (2018)
22. Garcia-Fidalgo, E., Ortiz, A.: Vision-based topological mapping and localization methods: a survey. Robot. Auton. Syst. **64**, 1–20 (2015)
23. Sattler, T., Zhou, Q., Pollefeys, M., Leal-Taixe, L.: Understanding the limitations of cnn-based absolute camera pose regression. In: CVPR, pp. 3302–3312 (2019)
24. Sattler, T., et al.: Are large-scale 3d models really necessary for accurate visual localization? In: CVPR, pp. 1637–1646 (2017)
25. Armeni, I., Sax, S., Zamir, A.R., Savarese, S.: Joint 2d–3d-semantic data for indoor scene understanding. arXiv preprint arXiv:1702.01105 (2017)
26. Irschara, A., Zach, C., Frahm, J.M., Bischof, H.: From structure-from-motion point clouds to fast location recognition. In: CVPR, pp. 2599–2606. IEEE (2009)
27. Lowe, D.G.: Distinctive image features from scale-invariant keypoints. IJCV **60**, 91–110 (2004)
28. Esteves, C., Allen-Blanchette, C., Makadia, A., Daniilidis, K.: Learning so (3) equivariant representations with spherical cnns. In: ECCV, pp. 52–68 (2018)
29. Cohen, T.S., Geiger, M., Köhler, J., Welling, M.: Spherical cnns. In: ICLR (2018)
30. Kondor, R., Lin, Z., Trivedi, S.: Clebsch-gordan nets: a fully fourier space spherical convolutional neural network. In: NeurIPS, pp. 10117–10126 (2018)
31. Weyand, T., Kostrikov, I., Philbin, J.: PlaNet - photo geolocation with convolutional neural networks. In: Leibe, B., Matas, J., Sebe, N., Welling, M. (eds.) ECCV 2016. LNCS, vol. 9912, pp. 37–55. Springer, Cham (2016). https://doi.org/10.1007/978-3-319-46484-8_3
32. Zhang, C., He, S., Liwicki, S.: A spherical approach to planar semantic segmentation. In: BMVC (2020)
33. Ulrich, I., Nourbakhsh, I.: Appearance-based place recognition for topological localization. In: ICRA, vol. 2, pp. 1023–1029. IEEE (2000)
34. Blaer, P., Allen, P.: Topological mobile robot localization using fast vision techniques. In: ICRA, vol. 1, pp. 1031–1036. IEEE (2002)
35. Gonzalez-Barbosa, J.J., Lacroix, S.: Rover localization in natural environments by indexing panoramic images. In: ICRA, vol. 2, pp. 1365–1370. IEEE (2002)
36. Kröse, B.J., Vlassis, N., Bunschoten, R., Motomura, Y.: A probabilistic model for appearance-based robot localization. Image Vis. Comput. **19**, 381–391 (2001)
37. Winters, N., Gaspar, J., Lacey, G., Santos-Victor, J.: Omni-directional vision for robot navigation. In: Proceedings IEEE Workshop on Omnidirectional Vision, pp. 21–28. IEEE (2000)
38. Hansen, P., Corke, P., Boles, W., Daniilidis, K.: Scale invariant feature matching with wide angle images. In: IEEE International Conference on Intelligent Robots and Systems, pp. 1689–1694. IEEE (2007)
39. Jaderberg, M., Simonyan, K., Zisserman, A., et al.: Spatial transformer networks. In: NeurIPS, pp. 2017–2025 (2015)
40. Yi, K.M., Trulls, E., Lepetit, V., Fua, P.: LIFT: learned invariant feature transform. In: Leibe, B., Matas, J., Sebe, N., Welling, M. (eds.) ECCV 2016. LNCS, vol. 9910, pp. 467–483. Springer, Cham (2016). https://doi.org/10.1007/978-3-319-46466-4_28

41. Zhang, X., Yu, F.X., Karaman, S., Chang, S.F.: Learning discriminative and transformation covariant local feature detectors. In: CVPR, pp. 6818–6826 (2017)
42. Worrall, D.E., Garbin, S.J., Turmukhambetov, D., Brostow, G.J.: Harmonic networks: deep translation and rotation equivariance. In: CVPR, pp. 5028–5037 (2017)
43. Coors, B., Condurache, A.P., Geiger, A.: Spherenet: learning spherical representations for detection and classification in omnidirectional images. In: ECCV, pp. 518–533 (2018)
44. Jiang, C., Huang, J., Kashinath, K., Marcus, P., Niessner, M., et al.: Spherical cnns on unstructured grids. In: ICLR (2019)
45. Lee, Y., Jeong, J., Yun, J., Cho, W., Yoon, K.J.: Spherephd: applying cnns on a spherical polyhedron representation of 360deg images. In: CVPR, pp. 9181–9189 (2019)
46. Cohen, T., Weiler, M., Kicanaoglu, B., Welling, M.: Gauge equivariant convolutional networks and the icosahedral CNN. In: ICML, pp. 1321–1330 (2019)
47. Zhang, C., Liwicki, S., Smith, W., Cipolla, R.: Orientation-aware semantic segmentation on icosahedron spheres. In: ICCV, pp. 3533–3541 (2019)
48. Krachmalnicoff, N., Tomasi, M.: Convolutional neural networks on the healpix sphere: a pixel-based algorithm and its application to cmb data analysis. Astron. Astrophys. **628**, A129 (2019)
49. He, K., Zhang, X., Ren, S., Sun, J.: Deep residual learning for image recognition. In: CVPR, pp. 770–778 (2016)
50. Zhang, Z., Rebecq, H., Forster, C., Scaramuzza, D.: Benefit of large field-of-view cameras for visual odometry. In: ICRA, pp. 801–808. IEEE (2016)
51. Budvytis, I., Sauer, P., Cipolla, R.: Semantic localisation via globally unique instance segmentation. In: BMVC (2018)
52. Zioulis, N., Karakottas, A., Zarpalas, D., Daras, P.: Omnidepth: dense depth estimation for indoors spherical panoramas. In: ECCV, pp. 448–465 (2018)
53. Li, J., Budvytis, I., Cipolla, R.: Indoor re-localisation using synthetic data. Department of Engineering, University of Cambridge, Technical report: ENG-TR.003, ISSN 2633–68369 (2020)
54. Paszke, A., et al.: Pytorch: an imperative style, high-performance deep learning library. In: Advances in Neural Information Processing Systems, pp. 8026–8037 (2019)
55. Deng, J., Dong, W., Socher, R., Li, L.J., Li, K., Fei-Fei, L.: Imagenet: a large-scale hierarchical image database. In: CVPR (2009)
56. Simonyan, K., Zisserman, A.: Very deep convolutional networks for large-scale image recognition. arXiv preprint arXiv:1409.1556 (2014)
57. Murez, Z., Kolouri, S., Kriegman, D., Ramamoorthi, R., Kim, K.: Image to image translation for domain adaptation. In: CVPR, pp. 4500–4509 (2018)

Contextual Semantic Interpretability

Diego Marcos[1(✉)], Ruth Fong[2], Sylvain Lobry[1], Rémi Flamary[3],
Nicolas Courty[4], and Devis Tuia[1,5]

[1] Wageningen University, Wageningen, The Netherlands
diego.marcos@wur.nl
[2] Oxford University, Oxford, UK
[3] CMAP, École Polytechnique, Palaiseau, France
[4] IRISA, University Bretagne Sud, CNRS, Rennes, France
[5] EPFL, Sion, Switzerland

Abstract. Convolutional neural networks (CNN) are known to learn
an image representation that captures concepts relevant to the task, but
do so in an implicit way that hampers model interpretability. However,
one could argue that such a representation is hidden in the neurons and
can be made explicit by teaching the model to recognize semantically
interpretable attributes that are present in the scene. We call such an
intermediate layer a *semantic bottleneck*. Once the attributes are learned,
they can be re-combined to reach the final decision and provide both an
accurate prediction and an explicit reasoning behind the CNN decision.
In this paper, we look into semantic bottlenecks that capture *context*: we
want attributes to be in groups of a few meaningful elements and partici-
pate jointly to the final decision. We use a two-layer semantic bottleneck
that gathers attributes into interpretable, sparse groups, allowing them
contribute differently to the final output depending on the context. We
test our contextual semantic interpretable bottleneck (CSIB) on the task
of landscape scenicness estimation and train the semantic interpretable
bottleneck using an auxiliary database (SUN Attributes). Our model
yields in predictions as accurate as a non-interpretable baseline when
applied to a real-world test set of Flickr images, all while providing clear
and interpretable explanations for each prediction.

Keywords: Interpretability · Explainable AI · Sparsity

1 Introduction

Deep learning, in particular convolutional neural networks (CNNs), is increasingly being applied to important yet sensitive domains, such as autonomous driving, facial recognition, and medical applications. One significant driver behind

R. Flamary—Partially funded through the project OATMIL ANR-17-CE23-0012 and
3IA Cote d'Azur Investments ANR-19-P3IA-0002 of the French National Research
Agency.

Electronic supplementary material The online version of this chapter (https://
doi.org/10.1007/978-3-030-69538-5_22) contains supplementary material, which is
available to authorized users.

© Springer Nature Switzerland AG 2021
H. Ishikawa et al. (Eds.): ACCV 2020, LNCS 12625, pp. 351–368, 2021.
https://doi.org/10.1007/978-3-030-69538-5_22

Fig. 1. We learn contextual groupings (colored coded) of semantic attributes (middle icons) in order to make predictions (right) (e.g., the meaning of "road" depends on the presence of other attributes). (Color figure online)

the success of CNNs is their capacity to learn to approximate complex functions from large amount of data by automatically tuning millions of parameters. However, this power comes at the expense of interpretability: because of the complexity of CNNs, their internal reasoning can not be easily assessed by humans. This has implications on scientific and societal levels (Fig. 1).

The highly parameterized nature of CNNs enables them to solve a given task in a variety of ways. Some of these solutions might rely on spurious cues that would harm generalization [1]. This is well illustrated by numerous works on adversarial examples [2,3], in which small perturbations, imperceptible to the human eye, are added to an image and subsequently cause a model to fail. Furthermore, one can easily find thousands of natural images on which CNNs fail (*e.g.*, real-world adversarial examples) [4]. Together, these findings cast doubt on the decision functions learned by CNNs and motivate the need for models that are more transparent in their decision-making process.

As deep learning (and its promise of efficient automation) increasingly affects various aspects of human life, the impenetrable complexity of this class of models also becomes a pressing societal issue. For instance, some governmental entities introduced bills for the regulation of decisions based on algorithms (*e.g.* Equal Credit Opportunity Act in the USA, General Data Protection Regulation in the EU). While research focused on understanding deep learning predictions is on the rise (see Sect. 2), [5] highlights that there still is a gap between the understanding of explanability of the machine learning community and that of lawmakers. Explanations are one way to achieve a degree of interpretability, which can generally be defined as follows: "systems are interpretable if their operations can be understood by a human" [6]. Moreover, the majority of methods that aim to elucidate CNN decisions generate an explanation *a posteriori*; this might induce the risk of a false sense of transparency and trustworthiness [7].

In this paper, we make three main contributions. First, we introduce a novel, explicitly interpretable architecture and training paradigm. Our model first learns to predict an intermediate, semantically explicit task (e.g., predicting attributes). These intermediate attributes are then used to make the final prediction on a downstream task. In particular, we do this by learning a new, sparse, and easily interpretable grouping layer that allows attributes to interact with each other. We call our proposed layer a Contextual Semantic Interpretable Bottleneck (CSIB). Second, we demonstrate the interpretability of our model via a novel combination of visualizations. Using Sankey plots, we visualize both task-specific groups of attributes learned by our model as well as instance-specific explanations that quantify how each attribute (and group) contributed to a model's final prediction. We also highlight the image regions each group captures. Together with details on how much each group contributes to the final score, we are able to visualize with clarity, fidelity, and depth the model's decision-making process. Third, we perform a thorough, empirical analysis of our method applied to the task of scenicness estimation. Here, we demonstrate that our model performs comparably to a baseline CNN when evaluating a real-world set of Flickr images (there is a performance gap when evaluating on a held-out set from the training distribution). Lastly, we show our paradigm uniquely allows us to identify and explain systematic errors our model makes.

2 Related Work

Post-hoc Interpretability. Most interpretability research introduces post-hoc methods that aim to explain any black-box model (see [8] for an interpretability survey). Much attention has been focused on the problem of attribution, *i.e.* the identification of image regions (via heatmaps) that are responsible for a model's output [9–19]. Although attribution methods can be applied to any model, the produced heatmaps lack richness, as they only highlight which image regions are decision relevant, but are unable to characterize a specific semantic reasoning or how those image regions interact. Depending on their formulation, they can also be misleading, as [20] highlights.

Another line of research focuses on understanding the global properties of CNNs. One approach to this problem is to study CNNs in a scientific manner, *i.e.* by generating and testing hypotheses about CNN properties (e.g., sparse vs. distributed encoding [21–24], invariance vs. sensitivity to geometric transformations [15,25]), or visualizing stimuli preferred by a network [9,15,26–31]. Another direction is to summarize a complex model with a simpler, more interpretable model (e.g., a sparse linear classifier or shallow decision tree) [32–36]. Our work is most related to an approach introduced by several recent works [24,37,38] that identify how semantic concepts are represented in a network by training linear probes on intermediate features to perform concept classification. While these techniques focus on learning post-hoc how concepts are encoded, our method explicitly learns intermediate features that correspond to concepts.

Interpretability by Design. In contrast to post-hoc approaches, "interpretable-by-design" paradigms focus on designing models that are explicitly interpretable. A number of works have proposed models that generate explanations alongside predictions. A few papers utilize multiple modalities in their model to produce explanations [39–41]. Another approach is to include an attention mechanism that constrains information flow [42,43]. Then, the attended features can be used as an explanation. These are not explicitly designed to be human-interpretable, although [44] constrains attended features to match desired explanations.

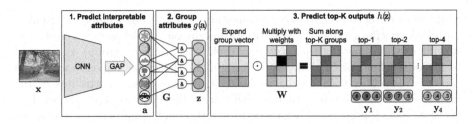

Fig. 2. Model overview. Our CSIB model learns to 1., predict human-interpretable attributes, 2., form sparse groups of attributes that describe broader, task-relevant concepts, and 3., output predictions using the top-K groups.

A shortcoming of models optimized to produce explanations is that there is often a tradeoff between their explanatory and predictive components (e.g., a generated explanation may not be both faithful to the model and easily interpretable).

Another direction focuses on encouraging a model to have interpretable intermediate features. Several works have introduced interpretable variational autoencoders [45,46] by encouraging the latent space to be disentangled (i.e., independent factors of variation). Regarding image classifiers, [47] constrains features to be sparse, discriminative "parts" detectors, while [48] introduces Bag-Nets, interpretable classifiers that sum up evidence from small input patches.

Our work is most similar to [49] and [50]. [49] introduce "semantic bottleneck networks," which encourage the features of the bottleneck between an encoder and decoder to align with semantic concepts. Their design incurs a negligible loss in accuracy on the final segmentation task. However, the relationship between the semantic bottleneck and output prediction is a highly non-linear decoder, making it difficult to study. To improve the interpretability of the semantic bottleneck, [50] use an semantic bottleneck based on attribute prediction and a linear layer to map onto the final task. The linear mapping makes the relation between the concepts in the bottleneck and the final task easily interpretable; however, this forces each concept to contribute independently and linearly, with no regard for the presence of other concepts.

Context. Visually similar attributes might be understood differently depending on what other elements are present, making contextualization important both for human and machine visual tasks [51,52]. [53] learns the causal relationship between pairs of object instances (e.g., cars and wheels) as well as the relationships between objects and background context, while [54] leverages a bayesian causal model to explore the impact of counterfactuals using concepts learned from self-supervision. In order to leverage context, ScenarioNet [55] proposes to find "scenarios," groups of commonly co-occurring concepts, by learning a sparse dictionary on the co-occurrence matrix of concepts in the training set. These scenarios are then treated as classes and predicted jointly with the final task, allowing to see which scenarios are present in the image. However, this does not necessarily mean that the final decision is conditioned on the detected scenarios. We propose to connect the semantic bottleneck with the final output by using non-linear, simple, and sparse relations, so that the mapping is transparent and easy to study, while being powerful enough to solve the visual task.

3   Contextual Semantically Interpretable Bottleneck (CSIB)

Our proposed approach is illustrated in Fig. 2 and relies on two steps. First, we train a predictor of binary attributes using a standard CNN. The attributes are then computed by $\mathbf{a} = \text{CNN}(\mathbf{x})$ and all carry the semantics encoded by the attribute dataset. They can be object or more complex concepts contained in the images and multiple attributes can be present in a given image $\mathbf{x}$. Second, we train and interpretable function f that uses the attributes to obtain a final prediction $\mathbf{y} = f(\mathbf{a}) = f(\text{CNN}(\mathbf{x}))$. The function f should be simple enough so that a human observer can easily understand how each attribute contributes to the result. A common choice for a simple and interpretable function is a linear mapping $\mathbf{y} = \mathbf{W}\mathbf{a}$ [50]. However, such a function is unable to capture an important process for image understanding: *contextualization*. This is because the contribution of an attribute to the output in the linear case is independent on the presence of other attributes.

Our solution consists of learning the groups of interaction by using a composition of two simple, but non-linear, functions: $\mathbf{z} = g(\mathbf{a}; \mathbf{G})$, parametrized by the sparse matrix $\mathbf{G}$, which extracts relevant groups of attributes, and $\mathbf{y} = h(\mathbf{z}; \mathbf{W})$, parametrized by $\mathbf{W}$, which captures the relations between the groups and the output. In the following we detail the three elements that compose our model: the CNN that extracts attributes, and the functions g and h.

3.1   Attribute Prediction

We train a standard CNN to predict the presence probability vector $\mathbf{a} \in [0,1]^A$ of A attributes by minimizing the multi-label classification loss based on binary cross entropy, $\mathcal{L}_{\text{attr}}$, on an attribute dataset. Training the model predicting the attributes typically needs labels not available for the dataset used for the final task $\mathbf{y}$. Therefore, to minimize $\mathcal{L}_{\text{attr}}$, we resort to an auxiliary dataset providing the attributes labels via image/attributes. Note that these two datasets can be disjoint and there is no need for images with both types of annotations. By choosing the appropriate set of attributes we are able to obtain a model that makes use of the desired visual cues while being invariant to undesired attributes.

3.2   Attribute Grouping Function $g(\cdot)$

Given the attributes $\mathbf{a}$ predicted in the images, we now want to group them into semantically meaningful groups. To do so, we use a grouping function $\mathbf{z} = f(\mathbf{a})$ that groups attributes together into a vector of group presence probabilities $\mathbf{z} \in [0,1]^Z$, with Z the number of groups. This function is parametrized by the sparse non-negative matrix $\mathbf{G} \in [0,1]^{Z \times A}$. Each row $\mathbf{G}_{i,:}$ represents one group and is constrained on the probability simplex $(G_{i,j} \geq 0, \sum_j G_{i,j} = 1, \forall i)$ by orthogonal projection after each SGD step [56]. The output for group z_i is computed as:

$$z_i = \prod_{j=1...A} a_i^{\mathbf{G}_{i,j}}. \tag{1}$$

This corresponds to a weighted geometric mean and acts as a soft-AND logical function, which means that a group i will only be fully active $(z_i = 1)$ if, for every attribute j required by the group $(G_{i,j} > 0)$, the attribute is fully present $(a_j = 1)$. Also, it suffices that one of these attributes is absent $(a_j = 0)$ to result in $z_i = 0$. Since all the attributes for which $G_{i,j} > 0$ must be present for the group to become active, $\mathbf{G}$ tends to become sparse during the learning process. This is a direct consequence of the projection onto the simplex which is naturally sparse. To increase numerical stability, the operation is implemented as a standard linear mapping over the log probabilities of the attributes:

$$\mathbf{z} = e^{\mathbf{G} \log(\mathbf{a})}, \tag{2}$$

which allows us to use a numerically stable implementation of log-sum-exp.

Unsupervised Group Pretraining. The soft-AND function in Eq. (1) will output values close to zero if one or more of the attributes that correspond to a high weight $G_{i,j}$ are not present. Therefore, initializing $\mathbf{G}$ with random weights, encoding for random groups that are thus not very likely to exist, results in mostly inactive groups and a very low learning signal. To make sure that $\mathbf{G}$ is initialized with groups that are present in the dataset, we first minimize the following loss on $\mathbf{Z} \in [0,1]^{B \times Z}$ corresponding to the concatenation for a batch of images with batch size B:

$$\mathcal{L}_{\text{groups}}(\mathbf{Z}) = \mathcal{L}_{\text{on}}(\mathbf{Z}) + \mathcal{L}_{\text{off}}(\mathbf{Z}) + \mathcal{L}_H(\mathbf{Z}). \tag{3}$$

The first two terms are designed to encourage the groups to become diverse. For a group to be of any use, it needs to be active in at least a few images. In addition, we want to make sure that at least one group is active per image. For this reason, we encourage the highest values along each row and each column of $\mathbf{Z}$ to be close to one, the highest possible value:

$$\mathcal{L}_{\text{on}}(\mathbf{Z}) = -\sum_{i=1}^{Z} \max_u (Z_{ui}) - \sum_{u=1}^{B} \max_i (Z_{ui}). \tag{4}$$

At the same time, we want to make sure that no particular group is active in all the samples of the batch, because such group would not be a discriminative one. We therefore minimize the maximum of the lowest per-group values:

$$\mathcal{L}_{\text{off}}(\mathbf{Z}) = \max_u (\min_i (Z_{u,i})). \tag{5}$$

However, this is not enough to guarantee the diversity in the groups. Ideally, we would want the batch-wise vector of group activations $\mathbf{Z}_{:,i}$ and $\mathbf{Z}_{:,j}$ of any two groups to be as different as possible. Simultaneously, we would like the groups to help discriminate between images, and thus the sample-wise vectors of group activations $\mathbf{Z}_{u,:}$ and $\mathbf{Z}_{v,:}$ of any pair of images should also be as different as possible. We encourage this by maximizing the cross-entropy $H(\mathbf{u}, \mathbf{v}) = -\sum_i u_i \log(v_i)$ between all pairs of per-group activation vectors and all pairs of per-sample activation vectors:

$$\mathcal{L}_H(\mathbf{Z}) = -\sum_{i,j \neq i} H\left(\frac{\mathbf{Z}_{:,i}}{\sum_k Z_{k,i}}, \frac{\mathbf{Z}_{:,j}}{\sum_k Z_{k,j}}\right) - \sum_{i,j \neq i} H\left(\frac{\mathbf{Z}_{i,:}}{\sum_k Z_{i,k}}, \frac{\mathbf{Z}_{j,:}}{\sum_k Z_{j,k}}\right) \quad (6)$$

Note that the regularization term above will have the effect of promoting the activations across groups and images to the maximally independent, tending towards source separation. Minimizing $\mathcal{L}_{\text{groups}}$ provides $\mathbf{G}$ with a set of initial groups that do occur in some images ($\mathcal{L}_{\text{on}}$) but not in all ($\mathcal{L}_{\text{off}}$) and that are discriminative and different from each other ($\mathcal{L}_H$).

3.3   Output Contribution Function $h(\cdot)$

Given the group activations $\mathbf{z}$, we want a function $\mathbf{y} = h(\mathbf{z})$ that produces the desired final output $\mathbf{y} \in \mathbb{R}^Y$. Function h is parametrized by matrix $\mathbf{W} \in \mathbb{R}^{Y \times Z}$.

We want as few groups as possible to contribute to the output $\mathbf{y}$. This can be enforced by taking only the top-K most contributing groups to compute $\mathbf{y}$, as proposed in [57]. The following steps have to be taken:

- A matrix element-wise multiplication $\mathbf{Y} = \mathbf{W} \circ \mathbf{z}$, where $\mathbf{z}$ is broadcasted to the shape of $\mathbf{W} \in \mathbb{R}^{Y \times Z}$.
- A sparsification of $\mathbf{Y}$ by keeping only the top-K values in each row and setting the rest to zero.
- Row-wise sum to obtain $\mathbf{y}$.

In order to avoid choosing a value of K a priori, we compute $\mathbf{y}$ using multiple K values and apply a loss to each output. The specific loss used at this stage is problem-dependent (e.g. MSE for regression, cross entropy for classification, etc.). The average of such losses is the final output loss, $\mathcal{L}_y$.

3.4   CSIB Training Strategy

The training procedure to minimize the described losses consists of three steps:

1. Train the CNN to predict the concepts in the semantic bottleneck by minimizing $\mathcal{L}_{\text{attr}}$. Note that this provides no learning signal to $\mathbf{G}$ nor $\mathbf{W}$.
2. Keeping the weights of the CNN frozen, minimize $\mathcal{L}_{\text{groups}}$ to initialize $\mathbf{G}$ with relevant and discriminative groups.
3. Finetune the whole model end-to-end on the final task by minimizing $\mathcal{L}_{\text{attr}} + \lambda \mathcal{L}_y$, with $\lambda << 1$ to ensure that the performance on attribute prediction is not degraded.

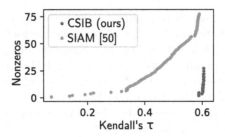

Fig. 3. Average number of attributes with a nonzero contribution to the final output against the resulting Kendall's τ score. The number of nonzeros was varied by increasingly pruning the smaller contributions. Our model allows for much more concise explanations.

4 Experiments in Landscape Scenicness Prediction

4.1 Experimental Set-Up

In the experiments below, we aim at predicting the scenicness (*i.e.* landscape beauty) score of a collection of images. The training images come from the ScenicOrNot [58] dataset, collected across Great Britain, and where each image has an average scenicness score (between 1 and 10), obtained by crowdsourcing. Out of the 212,104 available images, we used the first 180,000, ordered by image ID, for training, the following 5,000 for validation and the rest we held out for testing. Given the subjectivity of the final task, we want to make the reasoning of the model explicit by using a semantic bottleneck that detects attributes occurring in the image as an intermediate task: therefore, the semantic bottleneck is trained to predict the presence of the 102 classes of the SUN Attributes [59] dataset. We use the same train-test splits as in [59]. Previous works have already established that there is a correlation between some of these attributes and scenicness [60,61], and with SCIB we aim at constraining this further and explain scenicness using exclusively this pre-defined set of attributes.

For attribute prediction, we finetune a ResNet-50 [62], pre-trained on ImageNet [63]. We remove the last layer of the pre-trained model and add a 1×1 convolutional layer to map down the 2048 activation maps to the 102 SUN attributes, followed by a global average pooling. The model is trained using Stochastic Gradient Descent (SGD) with 0.9 momentum for 20,000 iterations with a batch size of 10. The learning rate is initially 0.002 and is decayed by a factor of 4 after 10,000 and 15,000 iterations. In the second step (group initialization), we initialize the sparse grouping matrix $\mathbf{G}$ with 150 groups in an unsupervised way by minimizing $\mathcal{L}_{\text{groups}}$. The learning rate was fixed at 0.002 for 4,000 iterations with a batch size of 100. Note that, as mentioned in Sect. 3.4 above, the ResNet-50 base model was left frozen, allowing for a larger batch size, which is important to capture the diversity between groups in $\mathcal{L}_{\text{groups}}$. As a last step (finetuning), $\lambda\mathcal{L}_y$ is minimized along with $\mathcal{L}_{\text{attr}}$ for 50,000 iterations and $\lambda = 0.1$. This time the whole model is trained end-to-end and two batches

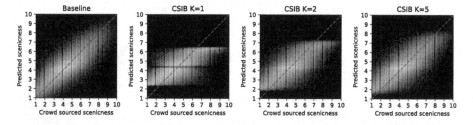

Fig. 4. Scatter plots showing our CSIB model's predictions for different K, which controls the number of groups used to make the final prediction (see Fig. 5 for groups).

of size 10 are used in every iteration, one from SenicOrNot and one from SUN Attributes. The learning rate is initially 0.002 and is decayed by a factor of 4 after 10,000 and 20,000 and 30,000 iterations. We train simultaneously with nine levels of top-K sparsity: $K = 1, 2, ..., 8, 150$. Since $\mathbf{W}$ is initialized will all zeros, the dense branch is important to make sure that all groups receive a learning signal. The bias of the last layer ($\mathbf{W}$) is fixed to the average scenicness value on the training set, a score of 4.43, and is kept constant.

4.2 Numerical Comparisons Within ScenicOrNot

On the ScenicOrNot test set, both CSIB and the baseline are able to generalize well, with CSIB showing a small drop in performance in terms of Kendall's τ [64] and root mean square error (RMSE), comparable to the one observed in [50] (see Table 1). However, [50] requires many more attributes to contribute to the result compared to CSIB, as shown in Fig. 3, making the explanations provided by CSIB more desirable in terms of the number of required *cognitive chunks* [65]. This highlights the effectiveness in terms of sparsification of the proposed constrained optimization. In addition, we observe only a minor degradation in the performance on the task of attribute prediction with respect to a baseline trained exclusively on that task. CSIB enables us to choose at test time the number of groups that can contribute to the final result by setting the K parameter in the top-K activation layer. Figure 4 depicts the results for $K \in \{1, 2, 5\}$ in the form

Table 1. Task performance. ScenicOrNot (SoN) results are reported using Kendall's τ ranking metric and root mean square error (RMSE); average precision (AP) is reported for SUN (higher is better for τ and AP; lower is better for RMSE). Performance plateaus at $K = 5$ for our CSIB model; our model underperforms the baseline.

		CSIB			
	Baseline	$K = 1$	$K = 2$	$K = 5$	$K = 7$
SoN Kendall's τ	0.645	0.580	0.603	0.609	0.609
SoN RMSE	0.940	1.111	1.037	1.018	1.019
SUN AP	0.610	0.601			

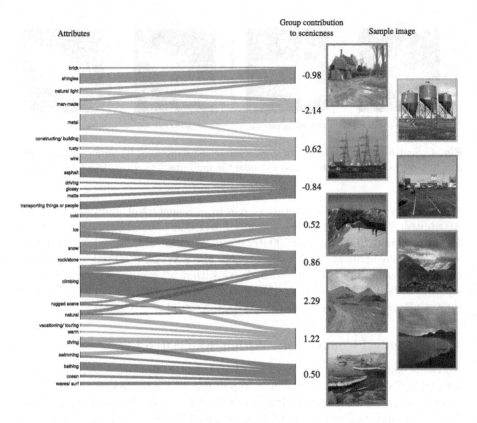

Fig. 5. Learned groups for scenicness estimation. Line thickness denotes the contribution of a SUN Attribute (left) to a group. For each group, we show its scenicness score (middle) and an example image (right). The groups and their scores appear coherent and consistent with the task. They are also sparse and interpretable: only 27 of 102 attributes are chosen and only 9 groups (out of a possible 150) become relevant. (Color figure online)

of scatter plots. When using $K = 1$, CSIB is not able to predict very high or very low values, since the maximum deviation from the average it can predict is $[-2.14, 2.29]$, which corresponds to the contribution of the most contributing groups (see red and yellow groups in Fig. 5). At the same time, values close to the average are also missed, since the top-1 layer is required to choose the single most contributing group among the groups present, forcing the output away from the average. This undesirable behaviour is already corrected by setting $K = 2$. The accuracy saturates when using $K = 5$, where the model is capable of predicting more extreme values of scenicness in a comparable way to the baseline, although it maintains a bias towards the average in the extreme cases. Such a small value of K, together with the sparsity of $\mathbf{G}$, allows to easily understand the relations encoded in CSIB (see Sect. 4.3). We observed that finetuning the whole model

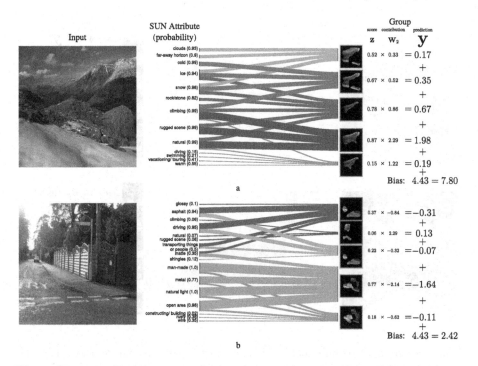

Fig. 6. Diagram of attribute contribution for a scenic image (top: GT = 9.43, baseline = 8.39) and an unscenic one (bottom: GT = 1.6, baseline = 2.18). These explanations point to a sensible decision-making process.

end-to-end (step 3 in Sect. 3.4) was important to obtain the mentioned results, with a Kendall's τ of 0.468 before finetuning.

4.3   Visualization of the Model

Entire Model. The semantics captured by SCIB, together with the high sparsity, allow us to comprehend the reasoning used to compute the output from the attributes in the semantic bottleneck. Figure 5 depicts the model by showing the contribution of each attribute to the groups (the weights in $\mathbf{G}$) that contribute more than 0.5 score points towards the scenicness values. This already provides a good understanding of the relations learned and encoded in the model. For instance, the last two groups (orange and brown) show that "diving" and "swimming" are assigned higher scores if they co-occur with "climbing" and "natural." We also see that it typically assigns high scores to wilderness-related attributes and low scores for those related to man-made elements. In the same figure, we also provide an image that scores strongly for that group.

Individual Results. Individual decisions for specific images are also easily interpretable. Using the activations in CSIB, we can now visualize which paths are

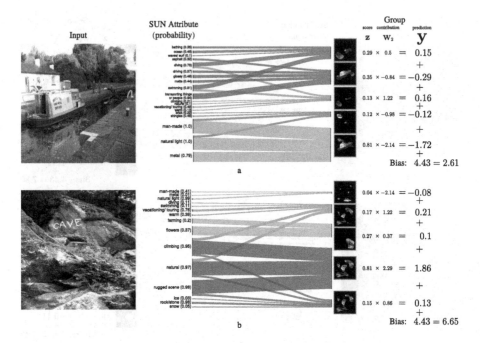

Fig. 7. Diagram of attribute contribution for an underpredicted image (top: GT = 7.17, baseline = 3.66) and an overpredicted one (bottom: GT = 2.11, baseline = 6.65). Our CSIB model allows us to understand why it disagrees with ground truth annotations.

followed to reach the final decision. Figure 6 shows two examples with $K = 5$. In this figure, the thickness of the lines is proportional to the contribution of the attribute to the group, which depends on the presence of the other attributes required by the group due to the multiplicative nature of Eq. (1). The part of the images contributing the most to the groups is depicted using thresholded activation maps. In these two cases, we can see how the explanations suit the images and our preconceptions of landscape beauty, with the first one rated with a 7.8/10 due to the rugged snowy mountain scene and the second one a mere 2.4/10 because of its man-made nature. On the other hand, Fig. 7 depicts the same visualization for two images in which there is a strong disagreement with the crowdsourced value. In the first case, the man-made look of the image and the transport-related aspect of the boat trigger the model to predict a low score, while in the second case the ruggedness and climbing-related aspects dominate, while the graffiti and the narrow view of the image are ignored, since these cannot be captured by the attributes used.

4.4 Validation of the Group Predictions by Geographical Distribution

Being the attributes learned from a dataset that is disjoint from the one used for the final task (*i.e.* we have no test set of the 102 SUN attributes on the

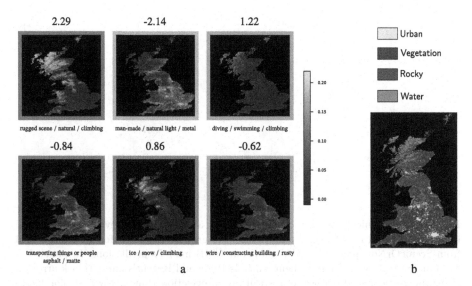

Fig. 8. a. Geographical distribution of group activations. For each image, the number on top is the group's scenicness score, and the three most contributing attributes for the group are shown below. Group colors are taken from Fig. 5. **b. Land-cover of Great Britain.** Data from [66]. (Color figure online)

ScenicOrNot images), we evaluate the performance of the attribute prediction on the SoN images qualitatively, by mapping the geographical distribution of the average activation of the groups (Fig. 8a) and comparing them to the 2012 CORINE land-cover map [66] of Great Britain (Fig. 8b). The learned groups with mountain-related attributes show a good overlap with the bare soil and rock surfaces in the landcover map, and the group that also includes snow and ice is more present in mountainous regions of Scotland. The groups with man-made attributes overlap with urban areas, and the ones with water activities are most active along the coast and in the lake filled northwest. These results suggest a good performance of the attribute detector on the SoN image dataset.

4.5 Generalization: Numerical Results on 1.7M Flickr Images

In order to test its generalization capabilities, we applied both CSIB and the baseline over a large set of 1.7 million geo-located outdoor images obtained from Flickr. Although no scenicness ground truth is available for these images, we can create a map of scenicness based on the values predicted on the Flickr dataset (depicted in Fig. 9b, c, e and f), and compare it to the map obtained using the ScenicOrNot ground truth (Fig. 9a and d). In Table 2 we show the results of comparing these values averaged over grids of different size (5000 × 5000, 500 × 500 and 50 × 50 bins across the region), and we consistently see that the results of the baseline and CSIB are numerically equivalent, with the CSIB being slightly better in terms of RMSE and behind in terms Kendall's τ.

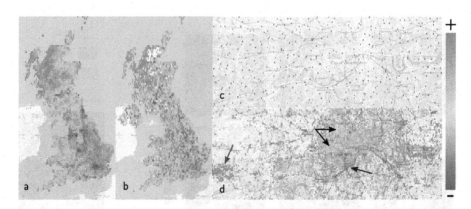

Fig. 9. Geographical distribution of scenicness at the national level (a and b) and in London (c and d). Panels a and c show the ground truth scenicness interpolated from ScenicOrNot; panels b and d show our CSIB model's predictions. In panel d, a few London regions are quite salient, such as Hyde and Regent's parks (black arrows), Heathrow airport (red arrow) and a railway intersection (blue arrow). (Color figure online)

Table 2. Performance on Flickr images. We evaluate models on 1.7M Flickr images in Great Britain and bin the predictions spatially at different scales; we then compare the spatial predictions against ScenicOrNot ground truth averages. Our CSIB model performs comparably to the baseline (higher is better for τ; lower is better for RMSE).

	5000 bins		500 bins		50 bins	
	Baseline	CSIB	Baseline	CSIB	Baseline	CSIB
Kendall's τ	0.399	0.391	0.384	0.382	0.624	0.621
RMSE	1.528	1.497	1.213	1.166	0.749	0.679

This suggests that the better performance of the baseline on ScenicOrNot might be partially attributable to over-fitting to the dataset, and that restricting the model to be inherently interpretable with CSIB reduces its capacity to overfit, but not the capability to generalize. Figure 9 shows maps of scenicness at two different scales (100 and 5000 bins) using the ScenicOrNot ground truth and CSIB results on the Flickr images. Figure 9a/b at the country level, showcases the agreement of both maps. Figure 9c/d show the maps for London. At this scale the sparsity of ScenicOrNot becomes apparent. On the map produced by CSIB, scenicness seems to be predicted highest in green areas (such as the Hyde and Regent's parks) and lowest in areas of transport infrastructure, such as railroads and airport (see Fig. 9d). These conclusions regarding the notion of scenicness validate the relations captured by CSIB from the dataset and that are clearly visible and interpretable from the model itself (as seen in Fig. 5).

5   Conclusion

We presented a paradigm to make the decision making process of a CNN inherently interpretable, which we call a Contextual Semantic Interpretable Bottleneck (CSIB). A standard CNN is trained to detect human-interpretable attributes. These attributes are then used to determine the final decision in a contextual and sparse manner (*i.e.* the meaning an attribute takes on is dependent on what other attributes are present, and only a select subset of attributes are used to form a small number of groups). This makes it possible to understand what relationships the model has learned by simply inspecting its weights as well as which of these relationships have been used for an individual image. Note that CSIB requires an auxiliary dataset containing attributes relevant to the final task. Nevertheless, the same attribute predictor can be reused for multiple downstream tasks; this would also enable model comparisons *across* tasks and reveal what attribute groupings are relevant to which tasks.

We demonstrate the validity of our method on a scenicness estimation task; we use the ScenicOrNot dataset and also evaluate on a large set (1.7M images) of real-world images from Flickr. CSIB is able to generate a map of scenicness to the same level of accuracy as that of a non-interpretable baseline. Lastly, we show how visualization techniques can be combined in order to explain what (and how) visual information has been leveraged in our model's decision making process. This allows us to understand the instances in which our model disagrees with the labelled annotation, among other things. In conclusion, we introduce a novel architecture that is both inherently interpretable and powerful enough so as to not sacrifice in real-world performance. This suggests that the assumed tradeoff between interpretability and performance may not always be necessary.

References

1. Lapuschkin, S., Wäldchen, S., Binder, A., Montavon, G., Samek, W., Müller, K.R.: Unmasking Clever Hans predictors and assessing what machines really learn. Nat. Commun. **10**, 1096 (2019)
2. Szegedy, C., et al.: Intriguing properties of neural networks. arXiv preprint arXiv:1312.6199 (2013)
3. Kurakin, A., Goodfellow, I., Bengio, S.: Adversarial examples in the physical world. arXiv preprint arXiv:1607.02533 (2016)
4. Hendrycks, D., Zhao, K., Basart, S., Steinhardt, J., Song, D.: Natural adversarial examples. arXiv preprint arXiv:1907.07174 (2019)
5. Edwards, L., Veale, M.: Slave to the algorithm: why a right to an explanation is probably not the remedy you are looking for. Duke L. & Tech. Rev. **16**, 18 (2017)
6. Biran, O., Cotton, C.: Explanation and justification in machine learning: a survey. In: IJCAI-17 Workshop on Explainable AI (XAI), vol. 8, no. 1 (2017)
7. Rudin, C.: Stop explaining black box machine learning models for high stakes decisions and use interpretable models instead. Nat. Mach. Intell. **1**, 206–215 (2019)
8. Gilpin, L.H., Bau, D., Yuan, B.Z., Bajwa, A., Specter, M., Kagal, L.: Explaining explanations: an overview of interpretability of machine learning. In: 2018 IEEE 5th International Conference on Data Science and Advanced Analytics (DSAA), pp. 80–89. IEEE (2018)

9. Simonyan, K., Vedaldi, A., Zisserman, A.: Deep inside convolutional networks: visualising image classification models and saliency maps. In: Proceedings of ICLR Workshop (2014)
10. Springenberg, J.T., Dosovitskiy, A., Brox, T., Riedmiller, M.: Striving for simplicity: The all convolutional net (2015)
11. Zhou, B., Khosla, A., Lapedriza, A., Oliva, A., Torralba, A.: Learning deep features for discriminative localization. In: Proceedings of CVPR (2016)
12. Selvaraju, R.R., Cogswell, M., Das, A., Vedantam, R., Parikh, D., Batra, D.: Grad-CAM: visual explanations from deep networks via gradient-based localization. In: Proceedings of ICCV (2017)
13. Zhang, J., Bargal, S.A., Lin, Z., Brandt, J., Shen, X., Sclaroff, S.: Top-down neural attention by excitation backprop. IJCV **126**, 1084–1102 (2018)
14. Bach, S., Binder, A., Montavon, G., Klauschen, F., Müller, K.R., Samek, W.: On pixel-wise explanations for non-linear classifier decisions by layer-wise relevance propagation. PLoS One **10**, e0130140 (2015)
15. Zeiler, M.D., Fergus, R.: Visualizing and understanding convolutional networks. In: Fleet, D., Pajdla, T., Schiele, B., Tuytelaars, T. (eds.) ECCV 2014, Part I. LNCS, vol. 8689, pp. 818–833. Springer, Cham (2014). https://doi.org/10.1007/978-3-319-10590-1_53
16. Ribeiro, M.T., Singh, S., Guestrin, C.: "Why should i trust you?" explaining the predictions of any classifier. In: SIGKDD (2016)
17. Fong, R., Vedaldi, A.: Interpretable explanations of black boxes by meaningful perturbation. In: Proceedings of ICCV (2017)
18. Petsiuk, V., Das, A., Saenko, K.: RISE: Randomized input sampling for explanation of black-box models. In: Proceedings of BMVC (2018)
19. Fong, R., Patrick, M., Vedaldi, A.: Understanding deep networks via extremal perturbations and smooth masks. In: Proceedings of ICCV (2019)
20. Adebayo, J., Gilmer, J., Goodfellow, I., Hardt, M., Kim, B.: Sanity checks for saliency maps. In: Proceedings of NeurIPS (2018)
21. Morcos, A.S., Barrett, D.G., Rabinowitz, N.C., Botvinick, M.: On the importance of single directions for generalization. arXiv preprint arXiv:1803.06959 (2018)
22. Zhou, B., Sun, Y., Bau, D., Torralba, A.: Revisiting the importance of individual units in CNNs via ablation. arXiv preprint arXiv:1806.02891 (2018)
23. Bau, D., Zhou, B., Khosla, A., Oliva, A., Torralba, A.: Network dissection: quantifying interpretability of deep visual representations. In: Proceedings of CVPR (2017)
24. Fong, R., Vedaldi, A.: Net2Vec: quantifying and explaining how concepts are encoded by filters in deep neural networks. In: Proceedings of CVPR (2018)
25. Lenc, K., Vedaldi, A.: Understanding image representations by measuring their equivariance and equivalence. Int. J. Comput. Vision **127**(5), 456–476 (2018). https://doi.org/10.1007/s11263-018-1098-y
26. Mahendran, A., Vedaldi, A.: Understanding deep image representations by inverting them. In: Proceedings of CVPR (2015)
27. Nguyen, A., Dosovitskiy, A., Yosinski, J., Brox, T., Clune, J.: Synthesizing the preferred inputs for neurons in neural networks via deep generator networks. In: Proceedings of NeurIPS (2016)
28. Bau, D., Zhou, B., Khosla, A., Oliva, A., Torralba, A.: Network dissection: quantifying interpretability of deep visual representations. In: Proceedings of the IEEE Conference on Computer Vision and Pattern Recognition, pp. 6541–6549 (2017)
29. Olah, C., Mordvintsev, A., Schubert, L.: Feature visualization. Distill **2**, e7 (2017)

30. Ulyanov, D., Vedaldi, A., Lempitsky, V.: Deep image prior. In: Proceedings of CVPR (2018)
31. Mordvintsev, A., Pezzotti, N., Schubert, L., Olah, C.: Differentiable image parameterizations. Distill **3**, e12 (2018)
32. Bastani, O., Kim, C., Bastani, H.: Interpretability via model extraction. arXiv (2017)
33. Lakkaraju, H., Kamar, E., Caruana, R., Leskovec, J.: Interpretable & explorable approximations of black box models. arXiv (2017)
34. Tan, S., Caruana, R., Hooker, G., Koch, P., Gordo, A.: Learning global additive explanations for neural nets using model distillation. In: Proceedings of NeurIPS Workshop (2018)
35. Zhang, Q., Cao, R., Shi, F., Wu, Y.N., Zhu, S.C.: Interpreting CNN knowledge via an explanatory graph. In: Proceedings of AAAI (2018)
36. Zhang, Q., Yang, Y., Ma, H., Wu, Y.N.: Interpreting CNNs via decision trees. In: Proceedings of CVPR (2019)
37. Zhou, B., Sun, Y., Bau, D., Torralba, A.: Interpretable basis decomposition for visual explanation. In: Ferrari, V., Hebert, M., Sminchisescu, C., Weiss, Y. (eds.) ECCV 2018, Part VIII. LNCS, vol. 11212, pp. 122–138. Springer, Cham (2018). https://doi.org/10.1007/978-3-030-01237-3_8
38. Kim, B., Wattenberg, M., Gilmer, J., Cai, C., Wexler, J., Viegas, F., et al.: Interpretability beyond feature attribution: Quantitative testing with concept activation vectors. In: Proceedings of ICML (2018)
39. Hendricks, L.A., Akata, Z., Rohrbach, M., Donahue, J., Schiele, B., Darrell, T.: Generating visual explanations. In: Leibe, B., Matas, J., Sebe, N., Welling, M. (eds.) ECCV 2016, Part IV. LNCS, vol. 9908, pp. 3–19. Springer, Cham (2016). https://doi.org/10.1007/978-3-319-46493-0_1
40. Zhang, Z., Xie, Y., Xing, F., McGough, M., Yang, L.: MDNet: a semantically and visually interpretable medical image diagnosis network. In: Proceedings of CVPR (2017)
41. Huk Park, D., et al.: Multimodal explanations: justifying decisions and pointing to the evidence. In: Proceedings of CVPR (2018)
42. Xiao, T., Xu, Y., Yang, K., Zhang, J., Peng, Y., Zhang, Z.: The application of two-level attention models in deep convolutional neural network for fine-grained image classification. In: Proceedings of CVPR (2015)
43. Lu, J., Yang, J., Batra, D., Parikh, D.: Hierarchical question-image co-attention for visual question answering. In: Proceedings of NIPS (2016)
44. Ross, A.S., Hughes, M.C., Doshi-Velez, F.: Right for the right reasons: Training differentiable models by constraining their explanations. arXiv preprint arXiv:1703.03717 (2017)
45. Chen, X., Duan, Y., Houthooft, R., Schulman, J., Sutskever, I., Abbeel, P.: InfoGAN: interpretable representation learning by information maximizing generative adversarial nets. In: Proceedings of NIPS (2016)
46. Higgins, I., et al.: beta-VAE: learning basic visual concepts with a constrained variational framework. In: Proceedings of ICLR (2017)
47. Zhang, Q., Nian Wu, Y., Zhu, S.C.: Interpretable convolutional neural networks. In: Proceedings of CVPR (2018)
48. Brendel, W., Bethge, M.: Approximating CNNs with bag-of-local-features models works surprisingly well on ImageNet. In: Proceedings of ICLR (2019)
49. Losch, M., Fritz, M., Schiele, B.: Interpretability beyond classification output: Semantic bottleneck networks. arXiv preprint arXiv:1907.10882 (2019)

50. Marcos, D., Lobry, S., Tuia, D.: Semantically interpretable activation maps: what-where-how explanations within CNNs. arXiv preprint arXiv:1909.08442 (2019)
51. Oliva, A., Torralba, A.: The role of context in object recognition. Trends Cogn. Sci. **11**, 520–527 (2007)
52. Barenholtz, E.: Quantifying the role of context in visual object recognition. Vis. Cogn. **22**, 30–56 (2014)
53. Lopez-Paz, D., Nishihara, R., Chintala, S., Scholkopf, B., Bottou, L.: Discovering causal signals in images. In: Proceedings of CVPR (2017)
54. Harradon, M., Druce, J., Ruttenberg, B.: Causal learning and explanation of deep neural networks via autoencoded activations. arXiv (2018)
55. Daniels, Z.A., Metaxas, D.: ScenarioNet: an interpretable data-driven model for scene understanding. In: IJCAI Workshop on XAI, vol. 33 (2018)
56. Shalev-Shwartz, S., Singer, Y.: Efficient learning of label ranking by soft projections onto polyhedra. J. Mach. Learn. Res. **7**, 1567–1599 (2006)
57. Sun, Y., Ravi, S., Singh, V.: Adaptive activation thresholding: dynamic routing type behavior for interpretability in convolutional neural networks. In: Proceedings of ICCV (2019)
58. ScenicOrNot (2020). http://scenicornot.datasciencelab.co.uk. Accessed 03 Mar 2020
59. Patterson, G., Xu, C., Su, H., Hays, J.: The SUN attribute database: beyond categories for deeper scene understanding. Int. J. Comput. Vision **108**(1), 59–81 (2014). https://doi.org/10.1007/s11263-013-0695-z
60. Seresinhe, C.I., Preis, T., Moat, H.S.: Using deep learning to quantify the beauty of outdoor places. R. Soc. Open Sci. **4**, 170170 (2017)
61. Workman, S., Souvenir, R., Jacobs, N.: Understanding and mapping natural beauty. In: Proceedings of ICCV, pp. 5589–5598 (2017)
62. He, K., Zhang, X., Ren, S., Sun, J.: Deep residual learning for image recognition. In: Proceedings of CVPR (2016)
63. Russakovsky, O., et al.: ImageNet large scale visual recognition challenge. Int. J. Comput. Vision **115**(3), 211–252 (2015). https://doi.org/10.1007/s11263-015-0816-y
64. Kendall, M.G.: A new measure of rank correlation. Biometrika **30**, 81–93 (1938)
65. Doshi-Velez, F., Kim, B.: Towards a rigorous science of interpretable machine learning. arXiv preprint arXiv:1702.08608 (2017)
66. CORINE Land Cover - Copernicus Land Monitoring Service (2020). https://land.copernicus.eu/pan-european/corine-land-cover. Accessed 03 Mar 2020

Few-Shot Object Detection
by Second-Order Pooling

Shan Zhang[1], Dawei Luo[2], Lei Wang[3], and Piotr Koniusz[1,4(✉)]

[1] Australian National University, Canberra, Australia
Piotr.Koniusz@anu.edu.au
[2] Beijing University of Posts and Telecommunications, Beijing, China
[3] University of Wollongong, Wollongong, Australia
[4] Data61/CSIRO, Clayton South, Australia

Abstract. In this paper, we tackle a challenging problem of Few-shot Object Detection rather than recognition. We propose Power Normalizing Second-order Detector consisting of the Encoding Network (EN), the Multi-scale Feature Fusion (MFF), Second-order Pooling (SOP) with Power Normalization (PN), the Hyper Attention Region Proposal Network (HARPN) and Similarity Network (SN). EN takes support image crops and a query image per episode to produce covolutional feature maps across several layers while MFF combines them into multi-scale feature maps. SOP aggregates them per support image while PN detects the presence of visual feature instead of counting its frequency of occurrence. HARPN cross-correlates the PN pooled support features against the query feature map to match regions and produce query region proposals that are then aggregated with SOP/PN. Finally, support and query second-order descriptors are passed to SN.

Our approach performs well because: (i) HARPN leverages SOP/PN for cross-correlation of detected rather than counted support features with query features which improves region proposals, (ii) SOP/PN capture second-order statistics per region proposal and factor out spatial locations, and (iii) PN limits the complexity of the space of functions over which HARPN and SN learn. These properties lead to the state of the art on the PASCAL VOC 2007/12, MS COCO and the FSOD datasets.

1 Introduction

Over the past years, several deep learning object detectors have achieved remarkable performance [1–6]. However, these models usually rely on a large number of fully-annotated bounding boxes for training and they cannot be easily extended to unseen classes not provided during training. Thus, in a practical scenario, the fully-annotated training is insufficient for a given target detection task with novel classes, which limits the applicability of the model.

Electronic supplementary material The online version of this chapter (https://doi.org/10.1007/978-3-030-69538-5_23) contains supplementary material, which is available to authorized users.

H. Ishikawa et al. (Eds.): ACCV 2020, LNCS 12625, pp. 369–387, 2021.
https://doi.org/10.1007/978-3-030-69538-5_23

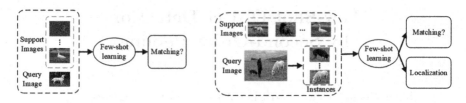

Fig. 1. The difference between few-shot (left) image- and (right) instance-level recognition. In contrast to classification problems, query images for few-shot object detection contain multiple objects to be localized and recognized.

In contrast, humans learn to recognize new objects even with a little supervision which highlights the superiority of biological vision over artificial CNNs. This inspires us to develop a Few-shot Object Detection (FSOD) network which is trained on just a few of training samples. In recent years, researchers have explored few-shot learning [7–13]. However, such off-the-shelf few-shot classifiers cannot be directly applied to the FSOD problem which requires simultaneous classification (novel classes) and localization of objects. Taking Prototypical Networks [7] and SoSN [14] as examples, it is unclear how to utilize the framework for matching and localization as irrelevant objects within the query image distract the few-shot detector. In short, few-shot classification is an image-level task where the few-shot learner relies on images of a single object to classify. In contrast, few-shot object detector represents an instance classification problem for which a query image includes multiple objects. Thus, the instance-level task needs to predict bounding boxes not just classify objects, as shown in Fig. 1.

The idea of few-shot object detection has recently been explored [15–19]. However, different from these approaches, we focus on utilizing robust second-order statistics for FSOD. Furthermore, in contrast to two-stage pipeline [15,18,19] where proposals of various sizes produce descriptors of varying sizes, our second-order representation describes regions as SPD matrices which capture multivariate Normal distributions. Such SPD matrices have constant size independent of the spatial dimensions of feature maps. Thus, we disregard the Region of Interest (ROI) pooling which suffers from subsampling and the order of features by their spatial locations (high discriminativity but poor repeatability of exact feature combinations across locations harms similarity learning).

Second-order statistics of data features have advanced the state of art in object recognition [20–22]. Second-order Pooling (SOP) has been extended to CNNs as a trainable layer for few-shot image classification [14,23–25]. Inspired by these models, we design a Few-shot Object Detection by leveraging SOP. As second-order statistics contain an expected value of co-occurrences of visual features, this often introduces a nuisance variability related to the frequency of certain co-occurrences that vary from object to object of the same class [24]. Thus, SOP requires Power Normalization (PN) which reduces this nuisance variability as demonstrated later in the text. We conjecture that such nuisance variability, relative to limited variations if PN is used, is approximately quadratic w.r.t. the input filter size of Hyper Attention Region Proposal Network (HARPN) as well as the shot number Z. Thus, PN is particularly well-suited for FSOD.

As different convolutional layers capture visual details at different scales of observation *e.g.*, fine-to-coarse or simplistic-to-composite, approaches [6,26,27] have shown that multi-layer feature combinations yield better proposals and detection results than features of a single layer. Particularly, the combination of larger number of fine-to-coarse CNN features is more beneficial compared to using features of neighboring layers which are strongly correlated [6]. Thus, we use coarse-to-fine features to leverage strong semantics from the deep convolutional layers as well as highly localized features from early layers of the network.

Finally, we investigate how to robustly generate bounding boxes via HARPN. In particular, we propose a channel-wise cross-correlation between support features detected via SOP/PN from the support representation (spatial locations are factored out) to highlight matching features across all spatial locations of the query feature map which is fed to RPN for generation of region proposals.

In this paper, we address the challenge of few-shot object detection. At the test time, through a few of support images of novel target object, FSOD strives to detect all objects in the query set that belong to the target object category. To devise the proposed framework termed Power Normalizing Second-order Detector (PNSD), we make four contributions:

i. We make the first attempt to embed SOP and PN into the FSOD.
ii. In our framework, the HARPN remodels the query feature maps via channel-wise cross-correlation to obtain robust ROI proposals whose statistical content is captured by PN-normalized SOP descriptors rather than ROI pooling.
iii. Our SOP descriptors are obtained from coarse-to-fine feature maps which improves the proposal generation and detection.
iv. In our Supplementary Material, we demonstrate statistically the benefit of Power Normalization for HARPN and similarity learning with SN. We show that PN limits the space of functions involved in learning by HARPN and SN which prevents overfitting and benefits FSOD more than classification.

Extensive experimental evaluations in the few-shot setting on three widely used object detection benchmarks, that is PASCAL VOC 2007/12, MS COCO and FSOD, show the effectiveness of our PNSD. The rest of the paper is organized as follows. In Sect. 2, we summarize the work most related to this paper. Our PNSD approach is described in detail in Sect. 4 before Preliminaries in Sect. 3. Experimental results are reported and analyzed in Sect. 5. Finally, we conclude the paper in Sect. 6.

2   Related Work

In what follows, we describe popular general object detection and few-shot learning algorithms followed by a short discussion on Second-order Pooling.

Object Detection is a classical problem in computer vision. In early years, object detection was usually formulated as a sliding window classification problem using handcrafted features [28–30]. With the rise of deep learning [31], CNN-based detectors have become dominant approaches which can be further divided into two categories: proposal-free detectors and proposal-based detectors.

The first line of work follows a one-stage training strategy and does not explicitly generate proposal boxes [1,2,32,33]. The second line, pioneered by R-CNN, first extracts class-agnostic region proposals of the potential objects from a given image. These boxes are then further refined and classified into different categories by a dedicated module [3–6]. An advantage of this strategy is that it can filter out many negative locations by the Region Proposal Network (RPN) module which facilitates recognition. RPN-based methods usually perform better than proposal-free methods with state-of-the-art results [34] for the detection task. The methods mentioned above, however, work in an intensive supervision manner and are hard to extend to novel classes with only few examples.

Few-shot learning is mainly inspired by the human ability to learn new concepts from a limited number of samples. Recently, many few-shot classification approaches have been developed with the aim to classify images of novel classes given very few labeled examples. These approaches can be divided into metric learning, meta-learning and 'optimization for fast adaptation' approaches. The aim of metric-learning [13,35,36] based few-shot classification is to derive a similarity metric that can be directly applied to the inference of unseen classes supported by a set of labeled examples (*ie.*, support set). Koch [35] presents the first principled approach that employs Siamese networks for one-shot image classification. Prototypical Networks [7] learns a model that computes distances between a datapoint and prototype representations of each class. The approach of [7,11,37] parametrizes the optimization algorithm to predict the parameters of a few-shot detector via a meta-learner. Ravi and Larochelle [8] propose an LSTM meta-learner that is trained to attain a quick convergence of few-shot learner. Recent methods address subspace-based learning [38], gradient modulation [39] and few-shot action recognition [40]. However, most existing methods focus on image classification but rarely on more practical tasks such as semantic segmentation [41–43], human motion prediction [44] or object detection [15,19].

Due to numerous bounding-boxes, object detection is more time-consuming than image-level classification. Thus, such work would be practically impactful if the novel classes and object bounding boxes could be predicted by a few-shot learner. Approach [15] transfers knowledge from a larger to a smaller dataset by minimizing the gap between source and target domains but it requires to be fine-tuned for novel categories. To solve this issue, approach [19] proposed a general few-shot object detection network that learns the matching metric between image pairs based on the Faster R-CNN framework, termed Few-shot Object Detection (FSOD). Different from [19] leveraging the first-order representation, we focus on second-order representations to capture co-occurrences of features and we investigate Power Normalization whose goal is to reduce the harmful variability of features. In place of the ROI pooing, SOP/PN are used.

Second-order statistics have been studied in the context of texture recognition [45,46] through so-called Region Covariance Descriptors (RCD), and further applied to object category recognition [20]. Co-occurrence patterns can also be used in the CNN setting *ie.*, approach [47] extracts feature vectors at two separate locations in feature maps followed by an outer product to form a CNN co-occurrence layer. Approach [22,24] performs spectral second-order pooling for fine-grained image classification. SoSN [14,22] leverages second-order pooling and Power Normalization for end-to-end training of one- and few-shot image classification pipeline (single object per image). In contrast, we develop a few-shot detector that tackle multi-object localisation and classification.

Power Normalization deals with the so-called burstiness of first- and second-order statistics which is 'the property that a given visual element appears more times in an image than a statistically independent model would predict'. Power Normalization [48] suppresses this burstiness by performing likelihood-inspired feature detection rather than feature counting [20,24,48]. The specific variant of PN, namely MaxExp feature pooling [22,48] can be interpreted as a detector of 'at least one particular visual word being present in an image' which is further extended to so-called SigmE pooling [22,24] for auto-correlation matrices that contain both positive and negative values. Furthermore, Spectral MaxExp pooling [22,24] performs decorrelation of features which boosts discriminativness. Papers [24,49] point that many PN functions are closely related, however, they do not analyze why PN is well-suited to few-shot learning. In our Supplementary Material, we analyze PN in the context of few-shot object detection.

3   Preliminaries

Below we review our notations and demonstrate how to calculate second-order statistics and Power Normalization.

Notations. Let $x \in \mathbb{R}^d$ be a d-dimensional feature vector. I_N stands for the index set $\{1, 2, \cdots, N\}$. Moreover, for a matrix $\mathbf{X}$, we denote $\mathbf{X}\mathbf{X}^T = \uparrow \otimes_2 \mathbf{X}$. We also define $\mathbf{1} = [1, ..., 1]^T$ ('all ones' vector). Typically, capitalised boldface symbols such as $\mathbf{\Phi}$ denote matrices, lowercase boldface symbols such as ϕ denote vectors and regular case such as $\Phi_{i,j}$, ϕ_i, n or Z denote scalars e.g., $\Phi_{i,j}$ is the (i, j)-th coefficient of ϕ.

Second-order Pooling and Power Normalization. Let a set $\mathcal{N}$ point to indices of feature vectors stacked as column vectors so that $\mathbf{\Phi} = [\phi_n]_{n \in \mathcal{N}}$. To perform SOP, one can simply form an auto-correlation matrix $\mathbf{M} = \frac{1}{N}\mathbf{\Phi}\mathbf{\Phi}^T$ where $N = |\mathcal{N}|$. As alluded to in the introduction, we desire to perform detection of feature co-occurrences rather than counting. Additionally, we have to deal with the evidence of correlation and anti-correlation in the auto-correlation matrix (positive and negative coefficients). Thus, we employ a so-called SigmE PN function [24] which is designed just for this purpose, and it is defined as:

$$\mathcal{G}_{\text{SigmE}}(\mathbf{M}; \eta) = \frac{2}{1 + e^{-\eta \mathbf{M}/(\text{Tr}(\mathbf{M}) + \lambda)}} - 1, \qquad (1)$$

where $1 \leq \eta \approx N$ interpolates between counting and detection, $\lambda \approx 1e^{-6}$ is a regularization constant and the trace $\text{Tr}(\cdot)$ stops diagonal from exceeding one.

To decorrelate features from a support image and match them against query in Hyper Attention RPN introduced below, among other variants, we use a

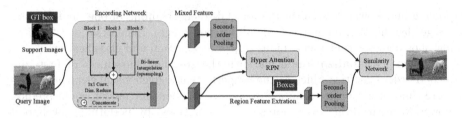

Fig. 2. Our PNSD. The query image and support crops are processed by the Encoding Network to form coarse-to-fine features via the Multi-scale Feature Fusion. The Hyper Attention RPN module (Fig. 3) detects support features via SOP/PN and cross-correlates them against query regions. Support features per crop and query features per region are passed via SOP/PN to form query-support descriptors passed to the Similarity Network for localization and classification.

variant of Spectral Power Normalization, known as Spectral MaxExp [22, 24]:

$$\widehat{\mathcal{G}}_{\mathrm{MaxExp}}(\mathbf{M}; \eta) = \mathbb{I} - (\mathbb{I} - \mathbf{M}/(\mathrm{Tr}(\mathbf{M}) + \lambda))^{\eta}. \tag{2}$$

4   Proposed Approach

Below we present our Power Normalizing Second-order Detector network followed by a description of its individual components.

Overview. The algorithm operates on so-called L-way Z-shot episodes which are formed by sampling a query image containing multiple objects, and Z support crops per each of L sampled classes. The training protocol ensures that query classes corresponding to objects in the query image have some matches in the support set. At the test time, given annotated support crops of novel classes, one can localize and classify objects in the query image.

Inspired by a recent FSOD architecture [19], our Power Normalizing Second-order Detector for FSOD, denoted PNSD for short, consists of (i) the Encoding Network (EN), (ii) the Multi-scale Feature Fusion (MFF), (iii) Second-order Pooling (SOP) with Power Normalization (PN), (iv) the Hyper Attention Region Proposal Network (HARPN) and (v) the Similarity Network (SN). Figure 2 shows our architecture for one support image as an example.

The role of EN is to generate image-level convolutional feature vectors (descriptors) whose fine-to-coarse nature is represented by MFF. The task of HARPN is to generate region proposals on the query image. SOP and PN are applied in two manners: (i) as a module of HARPN to improve the region proposals and (ii) as descriptors of the support crops and descriptors of region proposals which results in constant size representations independent of sizes of crops and region proposals. Finally, SN takes such formed query-support pairs and learns localization and similarity with a combination of two objectives.

Encoding Network. We use ResNet-50 with $f : (\mathbb{R}^{W \times H}; \mathbb{R}^{|\mathcal{F}|}) \rightarrow \mathbb{R}^{K \times N}$ realizing EN and MFF, where W and H are the width and height of an input, $N = N_W \cdot N_H$ and K are the total number of spatial locations and numbers of features (channel-wise) in the feature map after concatenation of outputs of *Block1*, *Block3* and *Block5* (up-sampled to match the large spatial size) of ResNet-50 and reducing their dimensionality channel-wise by 1×1 conv. implemented in MFF. Furthermore, we denote the final support and query maps by $\boldsymbol{\Phi} \in \mathbb{R}^{K \times N}$ and $\boldsymbol{\Phi}^* \in \mathbb{R}^{K \times N^*}$, where $\boldsymbol{\Phi} = f(\boldsymbol{X}; \mathcal{F})$ and $\boldsymbol{\Phi}^* = f(\boldsymbol{X}^*; \mathcal{F})$, the support crop $\boldsymbol{X} \in \mathbb{R}^{W \times H}$ and query image $\boldsymbol{X} \in \mathbb{R}^{W^* \times H^*}$. The parameters $\mathcal{F}$ of EN are shared between support and query passes. EN is shown in Fig. 2.

Hyper Attention RPN. The role of the Region Proposal Network (RPN) is to produce candidate regions from the query feature map containing objects. However, traditional RPN generates many candidate regions which become a burden for the detector. In contrast, few-shot detection requires generation of object candidates from the query image that match support regions from a given episode to reduce the number of proposals and improve the quality of recognition. To this end, we introduce the Hyper attention RPN module (Fig. 3) which modulates the query feature map to produce proposals relevant to support crops. In contrast to approach [19] which applies average pooling to support features to cross-correlate the feature expectation against the query feature maps, we conjecture that using Power Normalization *e.g.*, SigmE [24] or Spectral Max-Exp [22] function, is required to obtain a good matching between support-query pairs. Specifically, the query feature map contains multiple regions which may match objects from the support set. In contrast, support maps each describe a single object. Thus, matching the expectation of features of support set (average pooling) against spatial locations in the query makes such an attention modulator heavily variant w.r.t. the number of activations of a given support feature. These activations depend on the size of support object, pose, repeatable visual stimuli, *etc.*. To filter this variability, we propose to use SigmE function which acts as a detector of features rather than counter (average pooling) [24] or Spectral MaxExp which partially decorrelates features (stat. independence) [22]. We propose three variants generating the attention modulator $\boldsymbol{a} \in \mathbb{R}^K$:

$$\text{First-order (FO)+PN:} \quad \boldsymbol{a}_{\text{FO+PN}} = \mathcal{G}_{\text{SigmE}}(\boldsymbol{\Phi} \cdot \mathbf{1}/N; \eta) \tag{3}$$

$$\text{Sec.-order Spec. Diag. Corr. (SOSD)+PN:} \quad \boldsymbol{a}_{\text{SOSD+PN}} = \text{Diag}\left(\widehat{\mathcal{G}}_{\text{MaxExp}}(\mathbf{M}; \eta)\right) \tag{4}$$

$$\text{Second-order Self Corr. (SOSC)+PN:} \quad \boldsymbol{a}_{\text{SOSC+PN}} = \mathcal{G}_{\text{SigmE}}(\mathbf{M} \cdot \mathbf{1}/K; \eta) \tag{5}$$

To summarize, the above operators fulfil the following roles:

i. First-order+PN (FO+PN) detects if on average the majority of features per channel in the support feature matrix $\boldsymbol{\Phi}$ are positive or negative.
ii. Second-order Spectral Diagonal Correlation+PN (SOSD+PN) captures if there is at least one feature detected per channel across support features given the auto-correlation support matrix $\mathbf{M}$ is partially decorrelated.

S. Zhang et al.

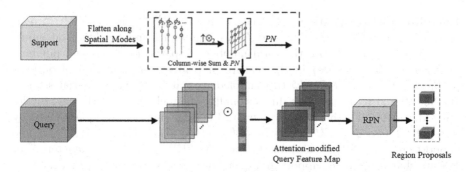

Fig. 3. Hyper Attention RPN. The support features are passed by SOP to produce a $K \times K$ matrix to form attention modulator $\boldsymbol{a} \in \mathbb{R}^K$ according to Sect. 4. Then the attention-modulated query feature map is obtained and fed to RPN for generation of proposals. Figure 4 is a close-up on the center of HARPN.

iii. Second-order Self Correlation+PN (SOSC+PN) detects an evidence of at least one feature per channel across support features and takes into account feature spread to other channels, which is related to compact pooling [50].

In what follows, we evaluate the above three attention modulators by performing cross-correlation with the query feature map by applying $\boldsymbol{\Phi}' = \boldsymbol{a} \odot \boldsymbol{\Phi}^*$, where $\odot$ is the channel-wise multiplication of a chosen attention modulator $\boldsymbol{a}$ with $\boldsymbol{\Phi}^*$ across all spatial locations and $\boldsymbol{\Phi}'$ is the attention-modulated query feature map. Finally, network $h(\boldsymbol{\Phi}'; \mathcal{H})$ produces proposals and $\mathcal{H}$ are the parameters-to-learn of the Hyper Attention RPN. Following approach [3], this module is trained jointly with EN via loss L_{rpn}.

Similarity Network. The similarity network, denoted by $s : (\mathbb{R}^{K \times K}; \mathbb{R}^{|S|}) \to \mathbb{R}^5$ (sim. score, x_t, y_t, x_b, y_b), is tasked with learning to distinguish similar/dissimilar support-query pairs represented by support-query PN-normalized SOP matrices. Typically, we denote $s(\mathbf{M}, \mathbf{M}^*; \mathcal{S})$, where $\mathbf{M}, \mathbf{M}^* \in \mathbb{R}^{K \times K}$ are support and query matrices, and $\mathcal{S}$ are the parameters-to-learn of the similarity network.

For the L-way Z-shot problem with D proposals from HARPN, we have $L \times Z \times D$ support image regions $\{\mathbf{X}_n\}_{n \in \mathcal{U}}$ from set $\mathcal{U}$ and their corresponding descriptors $\{\boldsymbol{\Phi}_n\}_{n \in \mathcal{U}}$ obtained from EN. We average $\boldsymbol{\Phi}$ of the support crops sampled for a given proposal and belonging to the same category, and we compute $L \times D$ PN-normalized SOP matrices $\mathbf{M}$ each representing one of L classes. We assume one query image $\mathbf{X}^*$ with its query feature maps $\{\boldsymbol{\Phi}^*\}_{n \in \mathcal{W}}$ from set $\mathcal{W}$ of D candidate regions from HARPN. The matrices $\mathbf{M}$ and $\mathbf{M}^*$ belong to one of L classes in the subset $C^{\ddagger} \equiv \{c_1, ..., c_L\} \subset \mathcal{I}_C \equiv \mathcal{C}$. The L-way Z-shot learning step is defined as alternating between learning (i) feature maps via EN and proposals via HARPN and learning (ii) feature maps via EN, bounding box regression (query) and the query-support similarity by minimizing

$$\sum_{d \in \mathcal{I}_D} \sum_{l \in \mathcal{I}_L} L_{sim}\left(s(\mathbf{M}_{dl}, \mathbf{M}_d^*, \mathcal{S})\right) + L_{box}\left(s(\mathbf{M}_{dl}, \mathbf{M}_d^*, \mathcal{S})\right) \qquad (6)$$

with respect to $\mathcal{F}$ and $\mathcal{S}$ parameters of EN and SN. During training, we use the multi-task loss $L = L_{rpn} + L_{sim} + L_{box}$ but we alternate between miniminzing w.r.t.(i) $\mathcal{F}$ and $\mathcal{H}$ and (ii) $\mathcal{F}$ and $\mathcal{S}$. The loss L_{box} for the bounding-box regression is defined as in [3] and the similarity loss is the binary cross-entropy.

SN Architecture is shown in Fig. 5. Firstly, support/query matrices ($64 \times 64 \times 1$) are passed to a small CNN to produce $6 \times 6 \times C$ feature maps passed to so-called relation heads. Scores from all heads are averaged for final matching scores. *Global-Relation Head* concatenates support/query maps into a $6 \times 6 \times 2C$ map and pools it into a $1 \times 1 \times 2C$ map passed to 2 FC layers (+ReLU). *Local-Relation Head* applies $1 \times 1 \times C$ conv. to maps ($6 \times 6 \times 2C$). We slide support features as a filter against query features to get local similarity passed to FC. *Patch-Relation Head* uses conv. layers (+ReLU) and pooling (zero padding) on $6 \times 6 \times 2C$ map. Two FCs generate matching scores and bounding box predictions, respectively.

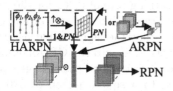

Fig. 4. Architecture of HARPN.

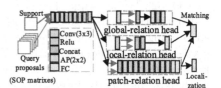

Fig. 5. Architecture of SN.

5   Experimental Result

Below we verify the effectiveness of the proposed PNSD approach by comparing it with the state of the art on challenging benchmarks such as PASCAL VOC 2007/12 [51], MS COCO [52] and FSOD [19]. We also perform ablation studies of each component of PNSD on PASCAL VOC 2007 and KITTI [53].

5.1   Datasets

For the PASCAL VOC 2007/12 dataset, we adopt the 15/5 base/novel category split settings as in [16]. As recommended, we use the training and validation sets from PASCAL VOC 2007 and 2012 as training data and the testing set from PASCAL VOC 2007 for evaluation. For the MS COCO dataset, we follow the work of [18] to adopt the 20 categories that overlap with PASCAL VOC as the novel categories for evaluation, and we use the remaining 60 categories of MS COCO as the training categories. For the FSOD dataset, we split its 1000 categories into 800/200 for training and testing, respectively.

Table 1. Comparison with SOTA on the PASCAL VOC 2007 testing set (5-shot protocol). The mAP metric is used.

Method	Novel					
	bird	bus	cow	mbike	sofa	mean
FRCN[3]	31.3	36.9	**54.1**	26.5	36.2	36.9
LSTD[15]	22.8	52.5	31.3	45.6	40.3	38.5
FR[16]	30.0	**62.7**	43.2	**60.6**	39.6	47.2
Meta[18]	52.5	55.9	52.7	54.6	41.6	51.5
PNSD	**53.6**	60.2	51.3	55.6	**42.5**	**52.6**

Method	Base															
	aero	bike	boat	bottle	car	cat	chair	table	dog	horse	person	plant	sheep	train	tv	mean
FRCN[3]	68.4	**75.2**	59.2	**54.8**	74.1	80.8	42.8	56.0	68.9	77/8	75.5	34.7	66.1	71.2	66.2	64.8
LSTD[15]	70.9	71.3	59.8	41.1	**77.1**	81.9	45.1	**67.2**	78.0	78.9	70.7	**41.6**	63.8	**79.7**	66.8	66.3
FR[16]	65.3	73.5	54.7	39.5	75.7	81.1	35.1	62.5	72.8	78.8	68.6	41.5	59.2	76.2	69.2	63.6
Meta[18]	68.1	73.9	59.8	54.2	80.1	82.9	48.8	62.8	80.1	81.4	77.2	37.2	65.7	75.8	70.6	67.9
PNSD	**69.3**	74.8	**61.5**	53.4	80.2	**82.3**	**49.6**	61.8	**80.8**	**82.6**	**77.9**	35.8	**68.6**	78.2	**70.9**	**68.5**

5.2   Implementation Details

Our model is based on the ResNet-50 pre-trained on ImageNet [54] and MS COCO [52]. We fine-tune the network with a learning rate of 0.002 for the first 56000 iterations and 0.0002 for another 4000 iterations. Unless stated otherwise, all training and testing images are resized such that the shorter side has 600 pixels and the longer side is capped at 1000 pixels to fit into the GPU memory. Each support image in the few-shot object detection is cropped based on ground-truth box, bi-linearly interpolated and padded to a square region of 320 × 320 pixels. In the following experiments, we report the commonly used metrics for FSOD such as mAP, AP, AP_{50} and AP_{75}. All codes are implemented in PyTorch.

5.3   Comparison with the State-of-the-art

PASCAL VOC 2007/12. The proposed PNSD is compared with Feature Reweighting (FR) [16], LSTD [15] and FRCN [3] in Table 1. FSOD [19] does not provide results on PASCAL VOC and its authors indicated the code cannot be easily adapted to it. According to Table 1, we achieve the overall best performance for both novel and base classes (5-shot setting). A significant performance gain without any fine-tuning (approximately 5.4% and 2.2% on mAP) is attained against the second best method retrained on novel categories. Table 1 also reveals the generalization fragility of FRCN [3] under the few-shot setting: without adequate training images, it detects poorly objects from novel classes. In contrast, our PNSD the Hyper Attention PRN (HARPN) and the SOP/PN pooling demonstrates superior performance on novel-class object detection.

MS COCO. Table 2 compares our PNSD with FR [16], Meta R-CNN [18] and FSOD [19] on MS COCO minival set for 20 novel categories for a 10-shot detection protocol. As shown, PNSD works best among all the methods in comparison. It outperforms FSOD (the second best) by 4.2%, 1.3% and 1.9% on AP, AP_{50} and AP_{75}, respectively. Although the gains are lesser than those obtained on PASCAL VOC, they are consistent and also significant considering that MS COCO is more challenging in terms of complexity and the dataset size.

FSOD. Below we use the FSOD testing set with 200 novel categories on the 5-shot detection protocol. We compare our PNSD with FSOD [19], LSTD [15] and LSTD (FRCN [3]) where we re-implement BD and TK (modules of LSTD) based on Faster-RCNN for fair comparison[1]. Table 3 shows that our PNSD produces the highest AP_{50} and AP_{75} values (*ie.*, 29.8% and 22.6%) among the four methods. Note that LSTD has to transfer knowledge from the source to target domain by retraining on novel categories while our PNSD and [19] are directly applied to detect novel categories.

Table 2. Comparison with SOTA on the MS COCO minival set.

Shot	Method	AP	AP_{50}	AP_{75}
10	LSTD [15]	3.2	8.1	2.1
	FR [16]	5.6	12.3	4.6
	Meta [18]	8.7	19.18	6.6
	FSOD [19]	11.1	20.4	10.6
	PNSD	**15.3**	**21.7**	**12.5**

Table 3. Comparison with SOTA on the FSOD testing set.

Shot	Method	AP_{50}	AP_{75}
5	LSTD (FRCN) [15]	23.0	12.9
	LSTD [15]	24.2	13.5
	FSOD [19]	27.5	19.4
	PNSD	**29.8**	**22.6**

5.4 Ablation Study

Below we analyze the effectiveness of each component of the proposed PNSD approach. To this end, we compare PNSD with four variations proposed by us in Table 4. We report the mAP with a threshold of 0.5 for evaluation in the real-world application scenarios *e.g.*, urban scene datasets for driving applications (KITTI), and we use the PASCAL VOC setup. The following ablation studies are based on 5/10-shot object detection setting.

Multi-scale Feature Fusion. To show the advantage of using fine-to-coarse feature representations, we modify variant V1 from Table 4 to use only features from *Block5*. Figure 6 indicates the superiority of MFF with a performance gain of 1.53% (PNSD's 70.73% *vs.* V1's 69.20%) on KITTI dataset. Also, with the PASCAL VOC setup, Table 7 shows that MFF boosts PNSD performance both in novel classes (52.6% *vs.* 52.3% in 5-shot; 61.9% *vs.* 60.1% in 10-shot) and in base classes (68.5% *vs.* 66.8% in 5-shot; 70.3% *vs.* 68.9% in 10-shot).

---

[1] FSOD is a new dataset released in 2020. Its format differs from datasets such as VOC and COCO. Only few approaches (listed in Table 3) experimented on FSOD.

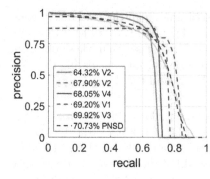

Table 4. Four variants of PNSD.

Variant	Operation	Validation
V1	HARPN + SOP + PN	MFF
V2	MFF + (FO + PN) + SOP + PN	HARPN
V2-	MFF + RPN + SOP + PN	HARPN
V3	MMF + HARPN + PN	SOP
V4	MFF + HARPN + SOP	PN

Fig. 6. mAP for *car* on four variants of PNSD (KITTI, 10-shot).

Hyper Attention RPN. We also analyze the improvement brought by the HARPN which considers an improved feature detection strategy on support representation. As shown in Fig. 6, our PNSD outperforms the variant V2 from Table 4 (70.73% *vs.* 67.90%) which leverages the regular attention RPN [19]. For the PASCAL VOC setup, Table 7 shows that our PNSD wins on novel classes (52.6% *vs.* 43.1% in 5-shot; 61.9% *vs.* 55.6% in 10-shot) and base classes (68.5% *vs.* 57.5% in 5-shot; 70.3% *vs.* 66.4% in 10-shot) due to the HAPRN.

Second-Order Pooling, Power Normalization and HARPN. Firstly, we note that HARPN has better recall than the regular RPN [19] (96.81% *vs.* 93.57%), as shown in Table 5. Figure 7 evaluates HARPN variants from Sect. 4 and it shows that SOSD+PN and SOSC+PN outperform standard first-order ARPN [19] by nearly 20% mAP. First-order pooling over support feature maps paired with SigmE function (FO+PN) also shows a large gain. Second-order Self Correlation with SigmE (SOSC+PN) brings visible gain however Second-order Spectral Diagonal Correlation with MaxExp (SOSD+PN) performs the best. We conjecture that SOSC and SOSD take into account the channel- and spectrum-wise correlations between features of the support representation which improves their attentive expressiveness. Finally, PN benefits the attention modulator by detecting features and discarding their counts (nuisance variability). We discuss this theoretical standpoint in the Supplementary Material where we show that using PN reduces the family of functions during learning which reduces the learning complexity.

Second-Order Pooling Regions. As features are pooled over arbitrarily sized ROIs to attain a fixed size representation, typical ROI pooling is highly discriminative but also non-repetitive as features correspond to spatial locations. Thus, we take variant V3 in Table 4 which uses the traditional ROI pooling instead of our SOP, that is the features are bi-linearly interpolated along the spatial modes of feature maps to 7×7 size. Figure 6 shows that PNSD (with SOP/PN)

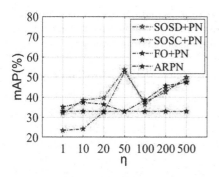

Fig. 7. mAP as a function of η for four variants of HARPN (VOC2007 dataset, novel classes, 5-shot).

Table 5. Proposal Recall under different variants of PSND. The region proposal number is 100 for evaluation (IoU = 0.5).

Method	Proposal recall
$PNSD_{Block5}$	88.04
$PNSD_{Block1,3,5}$	90.43
$PNSD_{Block1,3,5} + ARPN$	93.57
$PNSD_{Block1,3,5} + HARPN$	**96.81**

performs better than V3 (70.73% *vs.* 69.92%) with PN. For the PASCAL VOC setup, Table 7 confirms the superiority of our PNSD (with SOP/PN) over ROI pooling with PN in V3. PSND achieves 1.9%/1.6% improvement (52.6% *vs.* 50.7% in 5-shot; 61.9% *vs.* 60.3% in 10-shot) on novel classes. SOP is a good choice for describing ROIs as it captures second-order statistical moments while factoring out spatial modes. In our Supplementary Material we show how to efficiently compute SOP on a large number of region proposals with Integral Histograms.

Power Normalization in SOP Descriptors. As indicated previously, PN discards the nuisance variability related to the frequency of certain visual features whose quantity is affected by the scale, pose, and texture areas of objects *etc.*. Thus, we compare PNSD with its variant V4 from Table 4 whose SOP descriptors do not use PN. Figure 6 shows that our SOP descriptors with PN yield a notable performance gain of 2.68% over V4 on KITTI dataset (*ie.*, 70.73% *vs.* 68.05%). For the PASCAL VOC, Table 7 shows that our PNSD significantly outperforms the variant V4 on both base classes (68.5% *vs.* 65.3% in 5-shot ; 70.3% *vs.* 68.7% in 10-shot) and novel classes (52.6% *vs.* 47.5% in 5-shot; 61.9% *vs.* 59.4% in 10-shot). In our Supplementary Material we show that PN on SOP reduces the family of functions during relational learning (SN takes two SOP descriptors to compare them) which reduces the learning complexity.

Aggregating Z-Support Descriptors. Operator ($\otimes$) first averages over Z-support conv. feat. maps per class followed by the outer-product on the mean support (spatial modes are factored here). Operator ($\otimes$+L) performs the outer-product on Z-support feature vectors per class separately prior to the computation of average. Table 6 shows that operator ($\otimes$+L) outperforms operator ($\otimes$).

Table 6. Ablation studies of SOP descriptors (mAP on VOC2007, testing on novel and base classes, 5-shot).

Method	Novel	Base
SOSD + PN($\otimes$)	52.1	68.0
SOSD + PN($\otimes$+L)	**52.6**	**68.5**
SOSC + PN($\otimes$+L)	51.9	67.8
SOSC + PN($\otimes$)	52.4	68.1

Table 7. Ablation studies on four variants (mAP on VOC2007 testing set for novel classes and base classes).

Shot	Method	Novel	Base
5	V1	52.3	66.8
	V2	43.1	57.5
	V2-	41.9	53.8
	V3	50.7	66.3
	V4	47.5	65.3
	PNSD	**52.6**	**68.5**
10	V1	60.1	68.9
	V2	55.6	66.4
	V2-	54.7	64.3
	V3	60.3	69.0
	V4	59.4	68.7
	PNSD	**61.9**	**70.3**

5.5 Visualization of Detection Results

To better illustrate the proposed PNSD framework, the detection results of several variants are visualized in Fig. 8 to show how they improve upon FSOD. The four columns illustrate PNSD-V1, PNSD-V2, PNSD-V4 and PNSD, respectively. The ground-truth label of object is provided in red, with the green boxes delineating the detected objects.

Comparing the results of PNSD-V1 and PNSD, we can see a performance improvement thanks to its informative features. The differences between PNSD-V2 and PNSD demonstrate that HARPN helps RPN reject irrelevant proposals so as to improve detections. In this case, our PNSD detector can potentially avoid duplication. Finally, comparing the results of PNSD-V4 and PNSD, one can clearly see the significant help of Power Normalization because which discards nuisance variability in the same class. SOP with the SigmE function (which performs Power Normalization) benefits the subsequent similarity learning by SN. Finally, it is worth noting that our PNSD framework consistently outperforms better than all four variants constructed for the purpose of ablation studies.

Fig. 8. The visualization of novel-class objects detected by different PNSD variants: PNSD-V1, PNSD-V2, PNSD-V4, and PNSD (from left to right). Some bounding boxes in the first column are missed. The second column shows duplicates and inaccurate localization. The class label is wrongly recognized in the third column. Ground-truth annotated labels are marked with red colour and detection results with green rectangles. (Color figure online)

6   Conclusions

In this paper, we propose a Power Normalizing Second-order Detector for Few-Shot Object Detection (PNSD) to address few-shot object detection. Our model extends the R-CNN family through embedding second-order statistics and Power Normalization into HARPN and ROI descriptors. HARPN improve the proposal quality while MFF provide fine-to-coarse features. In order to demonstrate the effectiveness of PNSD, we have conducted extensive quantitative and qualitative experiments on several datasets. Our Supplementary Material demonstrates theoretically why Power Normalization is so valuable for HARPN and similarity learning with SN.

References

1. Redmon, J., Farhadi, A.: YOLO9000: better, faster, stronger. In: 2017 IEEE Conference on Computer Vision and Pattern Recognition, CVPR 2017, Honolulu, HI, USA, 21–26 July 2017, pp. 6517–6525. IEEE Computer Society (2017)
2. Redmon, J., Farhadi, A.: Yolov3: an incremental improvement. CoRR abs/1804.02767 (2018)
3. Ren, S., He, K., Girshick, R.B., Sun, J.: Faster R-CNN: towards real-time object detection with region proposal networks. In: Cortes, C., Lawrence, N.D., Lee, D.D., Sugiyama, M., Garnett, R. (eds.) Advances in Neural Information Processing Systems 28: Annual Conference on Neural Information Processing Systems 2015, Montreal, Quebec, Canada, 7–12 December 2015,pp. 91–99 (2015)

4. Girshick, R.B.: Fast R-CNN. In: 2015 IEEE International Conference on Computer Vision, ICCV 2015, Santiago, Chile, 7–13 December 2015, pp. 1440-1448. IEEE Computer Society (2015)
5. Lin, T., Dollár, P., Girshick, R.B., He, K., Hariharan, B., Belongie, S.J.: Feature pyramid networks for object detection. In: 2017 IEEE Conference on Computer Vision and Pattern Recognition, CVPR 2017, Honolulu, HI, USA, 21–26 July 2017, pp. 936–944. IEEE Computer Society (2017)
6. Kong, T., Yao, A., Chen, Y., Sun, F.: HyperNet: towards accurate region proposal generation and joint object detection. In: 2016 IEEE Conference on Computer Vision and Pattern Recognition, CVPR 2016, Las Vegas, NV, USA, 27–30 June 2016, pp. 845–853. IEEE Computer Society (2016)
7. Snell, J., Swersky, K., Zemel, R.S.: Prototypical networks for few-shot learning. In: Guyon, I., et al. (eds.) Advances in Neural Information Processing Systems 30: Annual Conference on Neural Information Processing Systems 2017, Long Beach, CA, USA, 4–9 December 2017, pp. 4077–4087 (2017)
8. Ravi, S., Larochelle, H.: Optimization as a model for few-shot learning. In: 5th International Conference on Learning Representations, ICLR 2017, Toulon, France, 24–26 April 2017. Conference Track Proceedings, OpenReview.net (2017)
9. Santoro, A., Bartunov, S., Botvinick, M., Wierstra, D., Lillicrap, T.P.: Meta-learning with memory-augmented neural networks. In: Balcan, M., Weinberger, K.Q. (eds.) Proceedings of the 33nd International Conference on Machine Learning, ICML 2016, JMLR Workshop and Conference Proceedings, New York City, NY, USA, 19–24 June 2016, vol. 48, pp. 1842–1850. JMLR.org (2016)
10. Vinyals, O., Blundell, C., Lillicrap, T., Kavukcuoglu, K., Wierstra, D.: Matching networks for one shot learning. In: Lee, D.D., Sugiyama, M., von Luxburg, U., Guyon, I., Garnett, R. (eds.) Advances in Neural Information Processing Systems 29: Annual Conference on Neural Information Processing Systems 2016, Barcelona, Spain, 5–10 December 2016, pp. 3630–3638 (2016)
11. Finn, C., Abbeel, P., Levine, S.: Model-agnostic meta-learning for fast adaptation of deep networks. In: Precup, D., Teh, Y.W. (eds.) Proceedings of the 34th International Conference on Machine Learning, ICML 2017, Proceedings of Machine Learning Research, Sydney, NSW, Australia, 6–11 August 2017, vol. 70, pp. 1126–1135. PMLR (2017)
12. Cai, Q., Pan, Y., Yao, T., Yan, C., Mei, T.: Memory matching networks for one-shot image recognition. In: 2018 IEEE Conference on Computer Vision and Pattern Recognition, CVPR 2018, Salt Lake City, UT, USA, 18–22 June 2018, pp. 4080–4088. IEEE Computer Society (2018)
13. Sung, F., Yang, Y., Zhang, L., Xiang, T., Torr, P.H.S., Hospedales, T.M.: Learning to compare: Relation network for few-shot learning. In: 2018 IEEE Conference on Computer Vision and Pattern Recognition, CVPR 2018, Salt Lake City, UT, USA, 18–22 June 2018, pp. 1199–1208. IEEE Computer Society (2018)
14. Zhang, H., Koniusz, P.: Power normalizing second-order similarity network for few-shot learning. In: IEEE Winter Conference on Applications of Computer Vision, WACV 2019, Waikoloa Village, HI, USA, 7–11 January 2019, pp. 1185–1193. IEEE (2019)
15. Chen, H., Wang, Y., Wang, G., Qiao, Y.: LSTD: a low-shot transfer detector for object detection. In: McIlraith, S.A., Weinberger, K.Q. (eds.) Proceedings of the Thirty-Second AAAI Conference on Artificial Intelligence, (AAAI-18), the 30th innovative Applications of Artificial Intelligence (IAAI-18), and the 8th AAAI Symposium on Educational Advances in Artificial Intelligence (EAAI-18), New Orleans, Louisiana, USA, 2–7 February 2018, pp. 2836–2843. AAAI Press (2018)

16. Kang, B., Liu, Z., Wang, X., Yu, F., Feng, J., Darrell, T.: Few-shot object detection via feature reweighting. In: 2019 IEEE/CVF International Conference on Computer Vision, ICCV 2019, Seoul, Korea (South), 27 October–2 November 2019, pp. 8419–8428. IEEE (2019)

17. Karlinsky, L., et al.: RepMet: representative-based metric learning for classification and few-shot object detection. In: IEEE Conference on Computer Vision and Pattern Recognition, CVPR 2019, Long Beach, CA, USA, 16–20 June 2019, pp. 5197–5206. Computer Vision Foundation/IEEE (2019)

18. Yan, X., Chen, Z., Xu, A., Wang, X., Liang, X., Lin, L.: Meta R-CNN: towards general solver for instance-level low-shot learning. In: 2019 IEEE/CVF International Conference on Computer Vision, ICCV 2019, Seoul, Korea (South), 27 October–2 November 2019, pp. 9576–9585. IEEE (2019)

19. Fan, Q., Zhuo, W., Tai, Y.: Few-shot object detection with attention-rpn and multi-relation detector. CoRR abs/1908.01998 (2019)

20. Koniusz, P., Yan, F., Gosselin, P., Mikolajczyk, K.: Higher-order occurrence pooling for bags-of-words: visual concept detection. IEEE Trans. Pattern Anal. Mach. Intell. **39**, 313–326 (2017)

21. Koniusz, P., Wang, L., Cherian, A.: Tensor representations for action recognition. IEEE Trans. Pattern Anal. Mach. Intell. (2020)

22. Koniusz, P., Zhang, H.: Power normalizations in fine-grained image, few-shot image and graph classification. IEEE Trans. Pattern Anal. Mach. Intell. (2020)

23. Koniusz, P., Tas, Y., Porikli, F.: Domain adaptation by mixture of alignments of second-or higher-order scatter tensors. In: 2017 IEEE Conference on Computer Vision and Pattern Recognition, CVPR 2017, Honolulu, HI, USA, 21–26 July 2017, pp. 7139–7148. IEEE Computer Society (2017)

24. Koniusz, P., Zhang, H., Porikli, F.: A deeper look at power normalizations. In: 2018 IEEE Conference on Computer Vision and Pattern Recognition, CVPR 2018, Salt Lake City, UT, USA, 18–22 June 2018, pp. 5774–5783. IEEE Computer Society (2018)

25. Zhang, H., Zhang, J., Koniusz, P.: Few-shot learning via saliency-guided hallucination of samples. In: IEEE Conference on Computer Vision and Pattern Recognition, CVPR 2019, Long Beach, CA, USA, 16–20 June 2019, pp. 2770–2779. Computer Vision Foundation/IEEE (2019)

26. Liu, L., Shen, C., van den Hengel, A.: Cross-convolutional-layer pooling for image recognition. IEEE Trans. Pattern Anal. Mach. Intell. **39**, 2305–2313 (2017)

27. Huang, G., Liu, Z., Weinberger, K.Q.: Densely connected convolutional networks. CoRR abs/1608.06993 (2016)

28. Dalal, N., Triggs, B.: Histograms of oriented gradients for human detection. In: 2005 IEEE Computer Society Conference on Computer Vision and Pattern Recognition (CVPR 2005), San Diego, CA, USA, 20–26 June 2005, pp. 886–893. IEEE Computer Society (2005)

29. Forsyth, D.A.: Object detection with discriminatively trained part-based models. IEEE Comput. **47**, 6–7 (2014)

30. Viola, P.A., Jones, M.J.: Rapid object detection using a boosted cascade of simple features. In: 2001 IEEE Computer Society Conference on Computer Vision and Pattern Recognition (CVPR 2001), with CD-ROM, Kauai, HI, USA, 8–14 December 2001, pp. 511–518. IEEE Computer Society (2001)

31. Krizhevsky, A., Sutskever, I., Hinton, G.E.: Imagenet classification with deep convolutional neural networks. In: Bartlett, P.L., Pereira, F.C.N., Burges, C.J.C., Bottou, L., Weinberger, K.Q. (eds.) Advances in Neural Information Processing Systems 25: 26th Annual Conference on Neural Information Processing Systems 2012, Proceedings of a meeting, Lake Tahoe, Nevada, United States, 3–6 December 2012, pp. 1106–1114 (2012)
32. Lin, T., Goyal, P., Girshick, R.B., He, K., Dollár, P.: Focal loss for dense object detection. In: IEEE International Conference on Computer Vision, ICCV 2017, Venice, Italy, 22–29 October 2017, pp. 2999–3007. IEEE Computer Society (2017)
33. Liu, S., Huang, D., Wang, Y.: Receptive field block net for accurate and fast object detection. In: Ferrari, V., Hebert, M., Sminchisescu, C., Weiss, Y. (eds.) ECCV 2018. LNCS, vol. 11215, pp. 404–419. Springer, Cham (2018). https://doi.org/10.1007/978-3-030-01252-6_24
34. Singh, B., Najibi, M., Davis, L.S.: SNIPER: efficient multi-scale training. In: Bengio, S., Wallach, H.M., Larochelle, H., Grauman, K., Cesa-Bianchi, N., Garnett, R. (eds.) Advances in Neural Information Processing Systems 31: Annual Conference on Neural Information Processing Systems 2018, NeurIPS 2018, Montréal, Canada, 3–8 December 2018, pp. 9333–9343 (2018)
35. Koch, G., Zemel, R., Salakhutdinov, R.: Siamese neural networks for one-shot image recognition. In: ICML Deep Learning Workshop, Lille, vol. 2 (2015)
36. Shyam, P., Gupta, S., Dukkipati, A.: Attentive recurrent comparators. In Precup, D., Teh, Y.W., (eds.) Proceedings of the 34th International Conference on Machine Learning, ICML 2017, Proceedings of Machine Learning Research, Sydney, NSW, Australia, 6–11 August 2017, vol. 70, pp. 3173–3181. PMLR (2017)
37. Gidaris, S., Komodakis, N.: Dynamic few-shot visual learning without forgetting. In: 2018 IEEE Conference on Computer Vision and Pattern Recognition, CVPR 2018, Salt Lake City, UT, USA, 18–22 June 2018, pp. 4367–4375. IEEE Computer Society (2018)
38. Simon, C., Koniusz, P., Nock, R., Harandi, M.: Adaptive subspaces for few-shot learning. In: 2009 IEEE Computer Society Conference on Computer Vision and Pattern Recognition, CVPR 2020 (2020)
39. Simon, C., Koniusz, P., Nock, R., Harandi, M.: On modulating the gradient for meta-learning. In: Vedaldi, A., Bischof, H., Brox, T., Frahm, J.-M. (eds.) ECCV 2020. LNCS, vol. 12353, pp. 556–572. Springer, Cham (2020). https://doi.org/10.1007/978-3-030-58598-3_33
40. Zhang, H., Zhang, L., Qi, X., Li, H., Torr, P.H.S., Koniusz, P.: Few-shot action recognition with permutation-invariant attention. In: Vedaldi, A., Bischof, H., Brox, T., Frahm, J.-M. (eds.) ECCV 2020. LNCS, vol. 12350, pp. 525–542. Springer, Cham (2020). https://doi.org/10.1007/978-3-030-58558-7_31
41. Dong, N., Xing, E.P.: Few-shot semantic segmentation with prototype learning. In: British Machine Vision Conference 2018, BMVC 2018, Newcastle, UK, 3–6 September 2018, p. 79. BMVA Press (2018)
42. Michaelis, C., Bethge, M., Ecker, A.S.: One-shot segmentation in clutter. In: Dy, J.G., Krause, A. (eds.) Proceedings of the 35th International Conference on Machine Learning, ICML 2018, Proceedings of Machine Learning Research, Stockholmsmässan, Stockholm, Sweden, 10–15 July 2018, vol. 80, pp. 3546–3555. PMLR (2018)

43. Hu, T., Yang, P., Zhang, C., Yu, G., Mu, Y., Snoek, C.G.M.: Attention-based multi-context guiding for few-shot semantic segmentation. In: The Thirty-Third AAAI Conference on Artificial Intelligence, AAAI 2019, The Thirty-First Innovative Applications of Artificial Intelligence Conference, IAAI 2019, The Ninth AAAI Symposium on Educational Advances in Artificial Intelligence, EAAI 2019, Honolulu, Hawaii, USA, 27 January–1 February 2019, pp. 8441–8448. AAAI Press (2019)

44. Gui, L.-Y., Wang, Y.-X., Ramanan, D., Moura, J.M.F.: Few-shot human motion prediction via meta-learning. In: Ferrari, V., Hebert, M., Sminchisescu, C., Weiss, Y. (eds.) ECCV 2018. LNCS, vol. 11212, pp. 441–459. Springer, Cham (2018). https://doi.org/10.1007/978-3-030-01237-3_27

45. y Terán, A.R.M., Gouiffès, M., Lacassagne, L.: Enhanced local binary covariance matrices (ELBCM) for texture analysis and object tracking. In: Eisert, P., Gagalowicz, A. (eds.) 6th International Conference on Computer Vision/Computer Graphics Collaboration Techniques and Applications, MIRAGE 2013, Berlin, Germany, 06–07 June 2013, pp. 10:1–10:8. ACM (2013)

46. Tuzel, O., Porikli, F., Meer, P.: Region covariance: a fast descriptor for detection and classification. In: Leonardis, A., Bischof, H., Pinz, A. (eds.) ECCV 2006. LNCS, vol. 3952, pp. 589–600. Springer, Heidelberg (2006). https://doi.org/10.1007/11744047_45

47. Shih, Y., Yeh, Y., Lin, Y., Weng, M., Lu, Y., Chuang, Y.: Deep co-occurrence feature learning for visual object recognition. In: 2017 IEEE Conference on Computer Vision and Pattern Recognition, CVPR 2017, Honolulu, HI, USA, 21–26 July 2017, pp. 7302–7311. IEEE Computer Society (2017)

48. Koniusz, P., Yan, F., Gosselin, P.H., Mikolajczyk, K.: Higher-order occurrence pooling on mid-and low-level features: visual concept detection (2013)

49. Koniusz, P., Yan, F., Mikolajczyk, K.: Comparison of mid-level feature coding approaches and pooling strategies in visual concept detection. Comput. Vis. Image Underst. **117**, 479–492 (2013)

50. Zhu, H., Koniusz, P.: Generalized factorized bilinear graph convolutional networks for text classification. ArXiV (2020)

51. Everingham, M., Gool, L.V., Williams, C.K.I., Winn, J.M., Zisserman, A.: The pascal visual object classes (VOC) challenge. Int. J. Comput. Vis. **88**, 303–338 (2010)

52. Lin, T.Y., et al.: Microsoft COCO: common objects in context. In: Fleet, D., Pajdla, T., Schiele, B., Tuytelaars, T. (eds.) ECCV 2014. LNCS, vol. 8693, pp. 740–755. Springer, Cham (2014). https://doi.org/10.1007/978-3-319-10602-1_48

53. Geiger, A., Lenz, P., Stiller, C., Urtasun, R.: Vision meets robotics: the KITTI dataset. Int. J. Rob. Res. **32**, 1231–1237 (2013)

54. Deng, J., Dong, W., Socher, R., Li, L., Li, K., Li, F.: ImageNet: a large-scale hierarchical image database. In: 2009 IEEE Computer Society Conference on Computer Vision and Pattern Recognition (CVPR 2009), Miami, Florida, USA, 20–25 June 2009, pp. 248–255. IEEE Computer Society (2009)

Depth-Adapted CNN for RGB-D Cameras

Zongwei Wu[1]($\boxtimes$) ⓘ, Guillaume Allibert[2], Christophe Stolz[1],
and Cédric Demonceaux[1] ⓘ

[1] VIBOT ERL CNRS 6000, ImViA, Université Bourgogne Franche-Comté,
Le Creusot, France
zongwei_wu@etu.u-bourgogne.fr,
{christophe.stolz,cedric.demonceaux}@u-bourgogne.fr
[2] Université Côte d'Azur, CNRS, I3S, Nice, France
allibert@i3s.unice.fr

Abstract. Conventional 2D Convolutional Neural Networks (CNN) extract features from an input image by applying linear filters. These filters compute the spatial coherence by weighting the photometric information on a fixed neighborhood without taking into account the geometric information. We tackle the problem of improving the classical RGB CNN methods by using the depth information provided by the RGB-D cameras. State-of-the-art approaches use depth as an additional channel or image (HHA) or pass from 2D CNN to 3D CNN. This paper proposes a novel and generic procedure to articulate both photometric and geometric information in CNN architecture. The depth data is represented as a 2D offset to adapt spatial sampling locations. The new model presented is invariant to scale and rotation around the X and the Y axis of the camera coordinate system. Moreover, when depth data is constant, our model is equivalent to a regular CNN. Experiments of benchmarks validate the effectiveness of our model.

1 Introduction

Recent researches [1,2] prove that CNN has achieved significant progress in applications like classification, object detection, scene understanding, etc. However, the performance of 2D CNN is limited by its regular receptive field (RF) and focuses more on photometric information rather than geometry which is not directly available on RGB images. To overcome this issue, approaches such as [3,4] modify the size of the convolution grid to contain all possible variations. Region-based CNN [5–7] and their successors manage to find the Region of Interests of the object (RoI) and realize CNN on each RoI.

Recently, sensor technologies have achieved great progress in scene representation. Sensors such as Kinect, high-resolution radar, or Lidar can provide the depth map as supplementary information to RGB image. This provides the possibility to reconstruct the 3D scene with the help of both complementary modalities, which is seen as a possible improvement in CNN [8–12]. In the past

© Springer Nature Switzerland AG 2021
H. Ishikawa et al. (Eds.): ACCV 2020, LNCS 12625, pp. 388–404, 2021.
https://doi.org/10.1007/978-3-030-69538-5_24

few years, a common approach is to take the depth map as an extra channel or extra images (HHA). While these works have proved better performance with additional depth information, variance to scale and rotation remains unsolved. In the left of Fig. 1, we can see that for two parallel rails forming the vanishing effect, the receptive fields have the same size and shape. To extract this feature in conventional CNN, either a dataset containing all variations is required, or the model should be complex enough to learn this feature.

(a) Conventional convolution   (b) Convolution adapted to the depth

Fig. 1. Illustration of Depth-Adapted Convolution Network. The receptive field (RF) of conventional 2D CNN has a regular shape and fixed size, as shown in the left image. While with the RGB-D image, the additional cognition on depth provides the possibility to better understand RGB image. As shown in the right figure, with the depth information on the rail, we can easily link the vanishing effect with the RGB image. Inspired by this observation, we try to find a 3D planar RF whose projection on image includes more spatial information than fixed RF. In such a way, the modified 2D RF can enable progress in existing 2D CNN.

To overcome this issue, in this paper, we propose an end-to-end network named Depth-adapted CNN (Z-ACN). Z-ACN remains as an image convolution (2D). Instead of using a fixed receptive field, we enable an additional 2D offset to transform the shape. The new shape should be adapted to the geometry. We assume that pixels on the same 3D plane tend to share the same class. This 3D plane and depth variance have a high correlation. As illustrated in Fig. 1, we display the projection of the 3D plane of the rail on the image plane as the adapted 2D RF. It describes better the vanishing effect than a fixed RF on the left. Note that the offset is computed from the depth image with traditional computer vision algorithms that do not require gradient during back-propagation. This helps us to improve the performance of 2D CNN without complicating the model.

The main contributions of Z-ACN are summarized as follow :

– We propose a generic convolutional model that adapts the 2D grid to the geometry which breaks the fixed form. This enables our model to be invariant to scale and rotation.

- The grid transformation is produced by traditional computer vision algorithms (without learning), which can be easily computed with minimal cost.
- Z-ACN can be easily integrated into any conventional CNN.

2   Related Work

A classic image convolution is formulated as:

$$\mathbf{y}(p) = \sum_{p_n \in \mathbf{R}(\mathbf{p})} \mathbf{w}(p_n) \cdot \mathbf{x}(p + p_n). \tag{1}$$

where $\mathbf{w}$ is the weight matrix. $\mathbf{R}(\mathbf{p})$ is the grid for point p. Physically it represents a local neighborhood on input feature map. $\mathbf{R}(\mathbf{p})$ defines the size, scale and shape of RF. For a standard 3×3 filter (e.g. standard regular shape with dilation Δd), the $\mathbf{R}(\mathbf{p})$ is given by:

$$\mathbf{R}(\mathbf{p}) = a\vec{u} + b\vec{v} \tag{2}$$

where $(\vec{u}, \vec{v})$ is the pixel coordinate system of input feature map and $(a, b) \in (\Delta d \cdot \{-1, 0, 1\})^2$. With the same input variables, different CNNs have different types of the weight matrix, grid (size, scale, shape) or pooling method.

2.1   Scale in 2D RGB Image Convolution

Due to the fixed size of RF, conventional image convolution has difficulties to adapt to objects on different scales. To deal with this problem, one popular approach is to use dilated convolution [13,14]. By maintaining the kernel size but enlarging the RF, dilated convolution proves its performance on large-scale problems. Another direction is to use different scales in the network. Multi-scale approach [4,15,16] and pyramid approach [17–19] enable progress with CNN by considering different RF scales. But the size of these RFs is in general predefined. Moreover, as the RF shape is always regular, these methods are not eligible to deal with a non-standard object like rotated, cropped, or distorted.

2.2   2D Deformable Model

To learn maximum geometry information in a 2D image, researches start to insert additional transformation parameters in networks. [20] proposes a spatial transformer to align feature map. Deformable-CNN (DeformCNN) [21] learns a dense spatial transformation to augment spatial sampling location, which breaks the regular shape of RF. [22] adapts the DeformCNN to learn the unevenly distributed context features to improve the RoI location. Applications on videos like [23,24] take consecutive frames and use DeformCNN to align the input frames to restore the video. Nevertheless, all these methods train the offset as extra parameters during back-propagation. The objective of the deformable model is to adapt the sampling locations of CNN. This means that if the geometry properties of the camera are known in advance, it should be possible to determine the sampling position without training. One successful application is the spherical CNNs [25–27]. These methods take advantage of the prior knowledge of image distortion to inject it explicitly into the model. In this paper, we will present how we extend this idea to another geometry property, the depth.

2.3 CNN for 3D Representation

Rich information on geometry provides various methods to realize 3D convolution. The volumetric representation [28–30] feeds voxel data into 3D CNN. It seems to be a trivial method to deal with 3D data. However, as data is often sparse on the 3D scene, it may waste huge memory consumption for less useful information. Different from the voxel representation, [31,32] propose to use directly the point cloud representation. Different 3D CNN methods are trying to adapt to the irregularity of point cloud. [33] integrates a x-transformation to leverage the spatially-local correlation of point cloud [34] introduces a spatially deformable convolution based on kernel points to study the local geometry. [35] learns the mapping from geometry relations to high-level relations between points to get a shape awareness. [36] defines convolution as an SLP (Single-Layer Perceptron) with a nonlinear activator.

Some reaches also try to reduce the model complexity. [37] adapts CRF (Conditional Random Fields) to reduce the model parameters. Multi-view method [38–41] reforms 3D CNN to become the combination of 2D CNNs. [38] profits from Lidar to get bird-view and front-view information in addition to a traditional RGB image. [39] uses depth image to generate the 3D volumetric representation after which projections on x,y,z planes are learned respectively by 2D CNN. 3D CNN achieves better results than RGB CNN but requires further development on problems such as memory cost, data resolution, and computing time.

2.4 RGB-D Representation

Different from voxel and point cloud, RGB-D can profit from its image-like form and contain both photometric and geometry information. Early CNNs on RGB-D images commonly follow 2 directions. One direction is to use a depth map to create 3D point clouds where the spatial information is learned [42,43]. This shares the same disadvantages on memory and computation cost. Another direction is to realize two separate convolutions on both RGB image and depth map and then apply a fusion in the network [10,12]. Some works [2,8,9,11] encode depth map to HHA image which have the same dimension of RGB image. This doubles the number of parameters and does not solve the problem of fixed size and shape of RF.

Recent works begin to adapt depth information in the convolution of the RGB image. Frustum methods [44,45] compute 2D RoI on RGB image and back-project them to 3D with the help of depth, which avoids the problem of regular shape. However, a huge part of computation has been done with the point cloud, which joins the disadvantages of 3D CNN. [46] analyzes the depth similarity to adjust the weight for a conventional RF. [47] projects 3D convolution on the 2D image which can adjust the size of RF to the depth. But for both methods, the RF shape remains regular.

In this paper, we present a different vision to integrate depth information. Inspired by the idea of deformable convolution [21], our method introduces an offset into the basic operations of CNN that breaks the limitation of the fixed structure. Different from state-of-the-art methods that train the offset as a variable in the network, our offset is computed directly from depth with traditional computer vision algorithms. Thus, our model does not add extra parameters needing to be learned. It can be easily integrated into any existing model by replacing simply convolution by guided deformable convolution. The final convolutional network remains 2D but with further geometric information.

3   Depth-Adapted Convolution Network

A 2D convolutional grid adapted to the depth information is the prospective topic in computer vision. Different from the conventional convolution Eq. 2, the Z-ACN is presented as:

$$\mathbf{y}(p) = \sum_{p_n \in \mathbf{R}(p)} \mathbf{w}(p_n) \cdot \mathbf{x}(p + p_n + \Delta p_n). \tag{3}$$

The convolution may be operated on the irregular positions $p_n + \Delta p_n$ as the offset Δp_n may be fractional. To address the issue, we use the bilinear interpolation which is the same as that proposed in [21].

The model requires 2 inputs: input feature map and depth map. The feature map is denoted as $\mathbf{x} \in \mathbf{R}^{c_i \times h \times w}$, where c_i is the number of input feature channel, h and w are the height and weight of the input feature map. The depth map is denoted as $\mathbf{D} \in \mathbf{R}^{h \times w}$. $\mathbf{D}$ is used to adapt the spatial sampling locations by computing the offset, denoted as $\Delta p \in \mathbf{R}^{c_{off} \times h_1 \times w_1}$, where h_1 and w_1 are the height and weight of the output feature map and $c_{off} = 2 \times N \times N$ for a $N \times N$ filter. Different from DCNN, our offset does not require gradient during back-propagation. The output feature map is denoted as $\mathbf{y} \in \mathbf{R}^{c_o \times h_1 \times w_1}$, where c_o is the number of output feature channels.

In the following parts, we will explain how the Z-ACN works to compute the 2D offset from depth.

3.1   Back-Projection on 3D Space

Without loss of generality, we suppose that the camera fits the pinhole model. With RGB-D image, it is possible to back-project a 2D point $p(u_0, v_0)$ to 3D point, denoted as $P_0(X_0, Y_0, Z_0)$. In $p(u_0, v_0)$, instead of a fixed RF $\mathbf{R}(p)$, we would like to propose a deformable RF by taking into account the geometric information (Fig. 2).

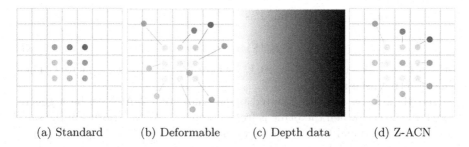

(a) Standard   (b) Deformable   (c) Depth data   (d) Z-ACN

Fig. 2. Effect of offset on a 3 × 3 kernel. a) shows a standard 2D convolution with dilation equals to 1. b) shows the offset computed from deformable convolution [21]. c) is the available depth data. The represented figure shows a linear change in depth value. From left to right, the scene becomes deeper. d) illustrates offset computed by Z-ACN which is adapted to depth.

Let us note $P_i = (X_i, Y_i, Z_i)$ the 3D points back-projected from $\mathbf{R(p)}$. i takes value from 0 to $N \times N$ where $N \times N$ is the size of kernel. We extract the plane π which passes through P_0 and fits the best to all P_i :

$$\vec{n} = \arg \min_{(n_1, n_2, n_3)} \sum_i ||n_1(X_i - X_0) + n_2(Y_i - Y_0) + n_3(Z_i - Z_0)||^2 \quad (4)$$

where $\vec{n} = (n_1, n_2, n_3)$ is an approximation of the normal of the plane π computed by singular value decomposition.

3.2 3D Planar Grid

For a 2D point $p(u_0, v_0)$, we may consider a conventional 2D convolution on image plane as realizing a planar convolution on a fronto-parallel plane on its back-projection $P_0(X_0, Y_0, Z_0)$ in 3D scene. By introducing the importance of depth, Z-ACN replaces the fronto-parallel plane by the new-defined plane π that is adapted to the depth. In other words, Z-ACN computes a new planar and regular grid, denoted as $R_{3D}(P_0)$. $R_{3D}(P_0)$ is centered on P_0 and its regular shape is defined by an orthonormal basis $(\vec{x'}, \vec{y'})$ on π. We fix $\vec{x'}$ horizontal $(\vec{x'} = (\alpha, 0, \beta))$. As $\vec{x'}$ is on the plane π defined by its normal $\vec{n} = (n_1, n_2, n_3)$, we have :

$$\vec{x'} \cdot \vec{n} = 0, \quad ||\vec{x'}||^2 = 1, \quad ||\vec{n}||^2 = 1 \quad (5)$$

Analytically, we can compute the value for $\vec{x}$ and $\vec{y} = \vec{n} \times \vec{x'}$, such that:

$$\vec{x'} = \begin{bmatrix} \dfrac{n_3}{\sqrt{1-n_2^2}} \\ 0 \\ -\dfrac{n_1}{\sqrt{1-n_2^2}} \end{bmatrix}, \quad \vec{y'} = \begin{bmatrix} -\dfrac{n_1 n_2}{\sqrt{1-n_2^2}} \\ \sqrt{1-n_2^2} \\ -\dfrac{n_2 n_3}{\sqrt{1-n_2^2}} \end{bmatrix} \quad (6)$$

To conclude, $R_{3D}(P_0)$ is defined as :

$$R_{3D}(P_0) = a\vec{x'} + b\vec{y'} \tag{7}$$

with $(a, b) \in (-k_u, 0, k_u) \times (-k_v, 0, k_v)$ where (k_u, k_v) are scale factors. Their values will be discussed in Sect. 3.4.

The 3D grid on a depth-adapted plane guarantees Z-ACN to be a generic model. In the case when the plane is front-parallel, Z-ACN performs in the same way as a conventional CNN. Indeed, we have $\vec{n} = (n_1, n_2, n_3) = (0, 0, 1)$. From Eq. 6, we have $\vec{x'} = (1, 0, 0)$ and $\vec{y'} = (0, 1, 0)$, which represent the regular shape for 3D grid. Thus, the projection on the image plane performs the same as a conventional or dilated convolution. Otherwise, being generic enables Z-ACN to be invariant to scale and rotation.

3.3   Z-ACN

We denote $\mathbf{R'(p)}$ the projection of $R_{3D}(P_0)$ on the image plane, which forms the Z-ACN :

$$\begin{aligned} \mathbf{y}(p) &= \sum_{p_n \in \mathbf{R'(p)}} \mathbf{w}(p) \cdot \mathbf{x}(p + p_n). \\ &= \sum_{p_n \in \mathbf{R(p)}} \mathbf{w}(p) \cdot \mathbf{x}(p + p_n + \Delta p_n) \end{aligned} \tag{8}$$

Different from the conventional grid $\mathbf{R(p)}$, the newly computed $\mathbf{R'(p)}$ breaks the regular size and shape with the additional offset which contains more geometry information.

3.4   Scale Factor

The scale factors (k_u, k_v) are designed to be constant to guarantee the equal surface of 3D RF. In such a way, with the variance of depth, due to the perspective effect, the projected 2D RF on image plane will have different sizes.

The value of scale factors can be chosen in function of user's needs. In our application, we want Z-ACN performs the same as a conventional 2D convolution on a particular point $p(u_0, v_0)$ whose associated plane in Eq. 4 is fronto-parallel $\{Z | Z = Z_p\}$. In other words :

$$\sum_{p_n \in \mathbf{R'(p)}} \mathbf{w}(p_n) \cdot \mathbf{x}(p + p_n) = \sum_{p_n \in \mathbf{R(p)}} \mathbf{w}(p_n) \cdot \mathbf{x}(p + p_n) \tag{9}$$

By taking into account the dilation Δd and the camera intrinsic parameters (f_u, f_v) and by combing Eq. 2 and Eq. 7, we have:

$$\begin{aligned} k_u &= \Delta d \times \frac{Z_p}{f_u} \\ k_v &= \Delta d \times \frac{Z_p}{f_v} \end{aligned} \tag{10}$$

For any point with a deeper depth value than Z_p, the associated RF will be smaller. Otherwise, the associated RF will be equal or larger, which approves the fact of being adapted to scale.

3.5 Understand Z-ACN

Recent researches prove the performance of 2D CNN to understand the 3D scene. However, due to the regular grid, 2D CNN is more suitable for rigid objects where the deformation is minimal. To break this limit, there are 2 possibles ways. The first one is to augment the size of the dataset to contain all possible variations [48,49] while the second is to augment the complexity, thus the ability, of network [1,50,51].

The latest advances in 3D sensors provide rich information about the geometry of 3D objects. 3D data can have different representations such as voxel, point cloud, and multi-view image. Studies [29,38,52] show the impact of different representation on the performance. However, these approaches based on 3D data suffer from high computation complexity.

RGB-D images seem to be the most accessible and light data that articulates both 2D and 3D advantages. Z-ACN takes this particularity to include the depth into the convolution by adjusting the 2D convolutional grid. This pattern is integrated into Eq. 3. To get a better understanding of Z-ACN, Fig. 3 shows the depth-adapted 2D grid of a given input neuron (the center). In the case of conventional CNN, the shape of the grid is fixed as regular, which has difficulties to deal with 3D information. With the Z-ACN, the grid is adjusted to geometry. As shown in Fig. 3, the receptive field for a nearer point is larger than that of a farther point. Receptive fields on the same plane also have different shapes that are adapted to the camera-projection effect. These patterns increase 2D CNN's performance to adapt to potential transformation without complicating the network nor augmenting the size of the dataset.

4 Experiment Work

As a generic model, Z-ACN can apply to all applications such as classification, segmentation, object detection, etc. In this paper, we evaluate our model on the problem of semantic segmentation. For any given CNN, we follow the same configuration on loss function and optimizer and replace only the convolution by Z-ACN operation. The whole work is realized under the Pytorch framework. We use the official deformable convolution from the torchvision package. The scale factor in Eq. 10 is computed with the mean of the input depth map. We repeat all experiments three times on an Nvidia 2080 Ti GPU and report the average model performance.

Experiments are realized with the NYUv2 dataset [49]. We take 1,449 RGB-D images with pixel-wise labels. We split them into 795 training images and 654 testing images. For labels, we follow respectively the 13-class settings and the 37-class settings. Note that Z-ACN works with RGB-D images, but the input

Fig. 3. The left figure shows the depth map. Instead of conventional 2D regular RF, Z-ACN is a generic model that takes into account the geometry. Red points on the right hand represent our RF for a 3 × 3 kernel. As shown in the image, our model enables a modification on the convolution grid that describes better the geometry in a 2D image, which helps to be invariant to rotation. With the variation of depth, the surface convolution grid changes as well, which helps to be invariant to scale. (Color figure online)

of CNN models remains RGB. The depth information is only introduced in the guided deformable convolution. In other words, adapted CNN models only extract features from the RGB image, which is the same as the initial CNN model. Only the sample position is guided by the depth. To make difference from classical RGB input and classical RGB-D or RGB + HHA input, we denote RGB(D) as the input of Z-ACN.

4.1   Integrating Depth in RGB Convolution

As the Z-ACN is invariant to scale and rotation, in this section, we want to show that Z-ACN should achieve better results than conventional convolution in existing architecture. We choose U-Net [53] as our baseline. We train U-Net with respectively RGB input, RGB-D input, and RGB(D) input. All models are trained from scratch with the NYUv2 dataset following 13-class settings. We use conventional cross-entropy as loss function, SGD optimizer with initial learning rate 0.0001, momentum 0.99, and batch size 1.

We evaluate the performance by regarding common metrics: overall accuracy, mean accuracy, mean intersection over union, and frequent weighted intersection over union. Overall Accuracy (Acc) stands for the proportion of correctly predicted pixels in the whole image. Mean Accuracy (mAcc) further analyzes the accuracy averaged over all the classes. Intersection over Union (IoU) studies the proportion of overlap area between the predicted segmentation and the ground truth divided by the area union and averaged over all the classes. Frequency Weighted Intersection over Union (fwIoU) further analyzes the IoU weighted by the total pixel ratio of each class.

Mathematically, suppose that we have s_i the number of pixels with the ground truth class i. We can compute the total number of all pixels: $s = \sum_i s_i$. n_{ij} denotes the number of pixels with ground truth class i and predicted as class j, n_c denotes the number of total classes. The model is evaluated by:

- Overall Acc: $Acc = \sum_i \frac{n_{ii}}{s}$
- Mean ACC: $mAcc = \frac{1}{n_c} \sum_i \frac{n_{ii}}{s}$
- mean Intersection over Union: $mIoU = \frac{1}{n_c} \sum_i \frac{n_{ii}}{s_i + \sum_j n_{ji} - n_{ii}}$
- Frequency Weighted Intersection over Union: $fwIoU = \frac{1}{s} \sum_i s_i \frac{n_{ii}}{s_i + \sum_j n_{ji} - n_{ii}}$

The results of our experiments are summarised in Table 1. We can observe that the network with additional depth information achieves a better result than the network with RGB only images. But the result with RGB(D) input outperforms that with RGB-D input. Compared to RGB and RGB-D input, the improvement with Z-ACN was +3.2% and +2.8% for the pixel-wise accuracy; +3.9% and +5.1% for class accuracy; +4.6% and +3.2% for mean Intersection of Union; and +2.8% and +2.1% for Frequent Weighted Intersection of Union. Note that the number of parameters is the same to extract features from the RGB image, which is also the case of Z-ACN. But for the network with RGB-D input, it requires a slightly higher number of parameters due to the input size. Nevertheless, it is still outperformed by our model. This result proves that Z-ACN integrates depth information more effectively in the RGB CNN.

Table 1. Comparison with different inputs on U-Net on NYUv2 test set following 13-class setting. Networks are trained from scratch. We test respectively U-Net with RGB input, with RGB-D input and with RGB(D) inputs. All evaluations perform at 640×480 resolution. We show that Z-ACN attends better result than other inputs.

NYUv2 13 class		RGB	RGB-D	RGB(D)
U-Net [53]	Acc (%)	52.4	52.8	**55.6**
	mAcc (%)	40.4	39.2	**44.3**
	mIoU (%)	27.2	28.6	**31.8**
	fwIoU (%)	36.9	37.6	**39.7**

4.2 Comparison with the State-of-the-art

As the Z-ACN is invariant to scale and rotation around the X and the Y axis from the camera coordinate system, we want to show that Z-ACN should achieve similar results with less learning parameters. In other words, our model should enable a CNN model with fewer feature channels to have similar performance. To the best of our knowledge, [47] is the latest research working in the same direction with RGB-D images.

To prove this idea, we adopt a modified ResNet-18 [50] as our backbone. We replace the conventional convolution by Z-ACN. We change the size of all convolutional kernels to be 3×3. We reduce the number of feature channels by 2^4. The input of our network is classical the RGB(D) image. We use the skip-connected fully convolutional architecture [2]. This network is trained from scratch. We train the new model with the NYUv2 dataset following 37-class settings for a complex scene analyzing. We randomly sample 20% rooms from the training set as the validation set. The model is trained with the logarithm loss function.

We compare Z-ACN with 3D representation such as PointNet [31], Conv3D [37,43] and 2D representation such as DeformCNN [21] and SurfConv [47]. Conv3D and PointNet use the hole-filled dense depth map provided by the dataset to create voxel input. For PointNet, the source code is used to uses RGB plus gravity-aligned point cloud. The recommended configuration [31] is used to randomly sample points. The sample number is set to be 25k. For Conv3D, the SSCNet architecture [37] is used and is trained with flipped - TSDF and RGB. The resolution is reduced to be $240 \times 144 \times 240$ voxel grid. For Deform-CNN, RGB images and HHA images are chosen as input for a fair comparison. For SurfConv, we compare with both the 1-level model and the recommended 4-level model [47] (the 4-level model requires a resampling on the input image to be adapted to the different levels of depth). For all the above-mentioned models, we follow the same configuration and learning settings as discussed in [47]. Thus we compare directly with the presented results.

Table 2. Comparison with different models with NYUv2 test set following 37-class settings. All results except ours are extracted from [47]. Our model is trained from scratch with the same settings.

NYUv2 37 class	Input	# of param	mIoU (%)	Acc (%)
PointNet [31]	voxel + RGB	1675k	6.9	47.4
Conv3D [37,43]	voxel + RGB	241k	13.2	49.9
DeformCNN [21]	HHA + RGB	101k	12.8	55.1
SurfConv1 [47]	HHA + RGB	65k	12.3	53.7
SurfConv4 [47]	HHA + RGB	65k	13.1	53.5
Z-ACN (ours)	RGB(D)	65k	**13.5**	**57.2**

As shown in Table 2, Z-ACN achieves better results compared to all other methods:

- Compared to PointNet, Z-ACN uses only 4% of its number of parameters but achieves +7% on mIoU and + 10% on Acc.
- Compared to Conv3D, Z-ACN uses less than 30% of its number of parameters to achieves close but better results on mIoU and +7% on Acc.

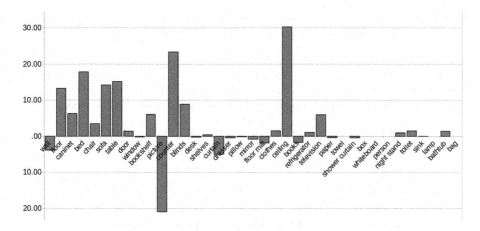

Fig. 4. Illustration of average improved percentage of per-class IoU. We compare Z-ACN with SurfConv single-level, with the exact same CNN model. Models are trained from scratch. On NYUv2, we improve 25/37 classes with 6.1% mean IoU increment.

- Compared to DeformCNN which also adds offset to the convolution, Z-ACN uses only 65% of its parameters as the offset in Z-ACN does not require gradient during back-propagation. Z-ACN still achieves close but better results on mIoU and +2% on Acc.
- Compared to SurfConv, with 1-level configuration (the same size of input data) and the same model (FCN + ResNet-18), Z-ACN achieves +1% on mIoU and +4% on Acc. Compared to 4-level which resamples input data, Z-ACN remains to be better in both mIoU and Acc.

Figure 4 illustrates the average improvement of per-class IoU between Z-ACN and SurfConv1. As our model adapts convolution to a local plane, it should be sensitive to depth differences. We can observe that Z-ACN achieves significantly better results on objects with large sizes such as floor, bed, sofa, table, counter, and ceiling. Recognizably, large-size objects can be easily distinguished from other objects because commonly they don't share the same 3D plane. This result meets our expectations. Wall is also a large-size object, but as shown in Fig. 3, there might be other objects such as pictures on the same plane which adds ambiguities to our model.

Different from 3D representation, the Z-ACN remains a light-weight 2D CNN which consumes significantly less memory. Z-ACN performs also better than other state-of-the-art models with RGB-only input. The result validates the effectiveness of integrating depth information in convolution by adapting the sampling position.

4.3 Adapting to Existing Model

Previous results show that the memory requirement of our network is low but it can still achieve better results compared to memory-consuming approaches. As

Z-ACN does not add extra learning parameters to the existing model, we can take advantage of heavier models to further improve its performance.

Table 3. Comparison between Deeplab with VGG-16 as encoder and Z-ACN on NYUv2 test set following 13-class setting and 37-class setting. Networks are trained from scratch. We show that our model attends better result than initial model.

NYUv2 13 class	Acc (%)	mAcc (%)	mIoU (%)	fwIoU (%)
Baseline	63.9	49.0	36.7	48.6
Z-ACN	**69.4**	**56.5**	**43.8**	**55.1**
NYUv2 37 class	Acc (%)	mAcc (%)	mIoU (%)	fwIoU (%)
Baseline	70.0	34.3	25.7	54.9
Z-ACN	**73.5**	**36.8**	**28.4**	**58.8**

We choose VGG-16 [51] as our CNN network which is widely used in the NYUv2 dataset. We use Deeplab [1] with VGG-16 as the baseline. This model requires 20520k parameters. A quantitative comparison between the initial model and Z-ACN is summarized in Table 3. We use common metrics and configurations presented in Sect. 4.1. Both models are trained from scratch with the NYUv2 dataset following respectively 13-class settings and 37-class settings.

Table 3 illustrates that with more parameters, CNN can achieve better results. It also shows that our model Z-ACN can improve the performance of a memory-consuming model as well, without adding extra parameters.

5   Conclusions

Z-ACN is a novel and generic model to include geometry data provided by RGB-D images in 2D CNN. When the depth is unknown, e.g. RGB images, or when the scene is planar and the image plane is parallel to this scene, Z-ACN performs in the same way as dilated or conventional convolution which helps to be invariant to scale. In other cases, it provides a novel method to adapt the receptive field to the geometry, which is invariant to scale and rotation around the X and the Y axis from the camera coordinate system. This design helps to improve the performance of existing CNN to attend the same result by reducing the computation cost, or to achieve better results without complicating the network architecture nor adding extra training parameters.

We demonstrated the effectiveness of Z-ACN on semantic segmentation task. Results are trained from scratch. In future works, we will figure out how to adapt Z-ACN to existing pre-trained models and how to adapt the geometry in the pooling layer. We will also try to extend the application to other popular tasks like normal or depth estimation, instance segmentation, or even pass from RGB-D image to 3D dataset.

Acknowledgements. We gratefully acknowledge Zhuyun Zhou for her support and proofread. We also thank Clara Fernandez-Labrador, Marc Blanchon, and Zhihao Chen for the discussion. This research is supported by the French National Research Agency through ANR CLARA (ANR-18-CE33-0004) and financed by the French Conseil Régional de Bourgogne-Franche-Comté.

References

1. Chen, L.C., Papandreou, G., Kokkinos, I., Murphy, K., Yuille, A.L.: Deeplab: semantic image segmentation with deep convolutional nets, atrous convolution, and fully connected crfs. IEEE Trans. Pattern Anal. Mach. Intell. **40**, 834–848 (2017)
2. Long, J., Shelhamer, E., Darrell, T.: Fully convolutional networks for semantic segmentation. In: Proceedings of the IEEE Conference on Computer Vision and Pattern Recognition, pp. 3431–3440 (2015)
3. Chen, L.C., Papandreou, G., Schroff, F., Adam, H.: Rethinking atrous convolution for semantic image segmentation. arXiv preprint arXiv:1706.05587 (2017)
4. Eigen, D., Fergus, R.: Predicting depth, surface normals and semantic labels with a common multi-scale convolutional architecture. In: Proceedings of the IEEE International Conference on Computer Vision, pp. 2650–2658 (2015)
5. Girshick, R.: Fast r-cnn. In: Proceedings of the IEEE International Conference on Computer Vision, pp. 1440–1448 (2015)
6. Girshick, R., Donahue, J., Darrell, T., Malik, J.: Rich feature hierarchies for accurate object detection and semantic segmentation. In: Proceedings of the IEEE Conference on Computer Vision and Pattern Recognition, pp. 580–587 (2014)
7. He, K., Gkioxari, G., Dollár, P., Girshick, R.: Mask r-cnn. In: Proceedings of the IEEE International Conference on Computer Vision, pp. 2961–2969 (2017)
8. Hazirbas, C., Ma, L., Domokos, C., Cremers, D.: FuseNet: incorporating depth into semantic segmentation via fusion-based CNN architecture. In: Lai, S.-H., Lepetit, V., Nishino, K., Sato, Y. (eds.) ACCV 2016. LNCS, vol. 10111, pp. 213–228. Springer, Cham (2017). https://doi.org/10.1007/978-3-319-54181-5_14
9. Hu, X., Yang, K., Fei, L., Wang, K.: Acnet: attention based network to exploit complementary features for RGBD semantic segmentation. In: 2019 IEEE International Conference on Image Processing (ICIP), pp. 440–1444. IEEE (2019)
10. Lin, D., Chen, G., Cohen-Or, D., Heng, P.A., Huang, H.: Cascaded feature network for semantic segmentation of RGB-D images. In: Proceedings of the IEEE International Conference on Computer Vision, pp. 1311–1319 (2017)
11. Park, S.J., Hong, K.S., Lee, S.: Rdfnet: RGB-D multi-level residual feature fusion for indoor semantic segmentation. In: Proceedings of the IEEE International Conference on Computer Vision, PP. 4980–4989 (2017)
12. Wang, J., Wang, Z., Tao, D., See, S., Wang, G.: Learning common and specific features for RGB-D semantic segmentation with deconvolutional networks. In: Leibe, B., Matas, J., Sebe, N., Welling, M. (eds.) ECCV 2016. LNCS, vol. 9909, pp. 664–679. Springer, Cham (2016). https://doi.org/10.1007/978-3-319-46454-1_40
13. Chen, L.C., Zhu, Y., Papandreou, G., Schroff, F., Adam, H.: Encoder-decoder with atrous separable convolution for semantic image segmentation. In: Proceedings of the European Conference on Computer Vision (ECCV), pp. 801–818 (2018)
14. Yu, F., Koltun, V.: Multi-scale context aggregation by dilated convolutions. arXiv preprint arXiv:1511.07122 (2015)

15. Chen, L.C., Yang, Y., Wang, J., Xu, W., Yuille, A.L.: Attention to scale: scale-aware semantic image segmentation. In: Proceedings of the IEEE Conference on Computer Vision and Pattern Recognition, pp. 3640–3649 (2016)
16. Xia, F., Wang, P., Chen, L.-C., Yuille, A.L.: Zoom better to see clearer: human and object parsing with hierarchical auto-zoom net. In: Leibe, B., Matas, J., Sebe, N., Welling, M. (eds.) ECCV 2016. LNCS, vol. 9909, pp. 648–663. Springer, Cham (2016). https://doi.org/10.1007/978-3-319-46454-1_39
17. Li, Y., Chen, Y., Wang, N., Zhang, Z.: Scale-aware trident networks for object detection. In: Proceedings of the IEEE International Conference on Computer Vision, pp. 6054–6063 (2019)
18. Lin, T.Y., Dollár, P., Girshick, R., He, K., Hariharan, B., Belongie, S.: Feature pyramid networks for object detection. In: Proceedings of the IEEE Conference on Computer Vision and Pattern Recognition, pp. 2117–2125 (2017)
19. Zhao, H., Shi, J., Qi, X., Wang, X., Jia, J.: Pyramid scene parsing network. In: Proceedings of the IEEE Conference on Computer Vision and Pattern Recognition, pp. 2881–2890 (2017)
20. Jaderberg, M., Simonyan, K., Zisserman, A., et al.: Spatial transformer networks. In: Advances in Neural Information Processing Systems, pp. 2017–2025 (2015)
21. Dai, J., et al.: Deformable convolutional networks. In: Proceedings of the IEEE International Conference on Computer Vision, pp. 764–773 (2017)
22. Zhang, C., Kim, J.: Object detection with location-aware deformable convolution and backward attention filtering. In: Proceedings of the IEEE Conference on Computer Vision and Pattern Recognition, pp. 9452–9461 (2019)
23. Tian, Y., Zhang, Y., Fu, Y., Xu, C.: TDAN: temporally-deformable alignment network for video super-resolution. In: Proceedings of the IEEE/CVF Conference on Computer Vision and Pattern Recognition, pp. 3360–3369 (2020)
24. Wang, X., Chan, K.C., Yu, K., Dong, C., Change Loy, C.: EDVR: video restoration with enhanced deformable convolutional networks. In: Proceedings of the IEEE Conference on Computer Vision and Pattern Recognition Workshops (2019)
25. Eder, M., Price, T., Vu, T., Bapat, A., Frahm, J.M.: Mapped convolutions. arXiv preprint arXiv:1906.11096 (2019)
26. Tateno, K., Navab, N., Tombari, F.: Distortion-aware convolutional filters for dense prediction in panoramic images. In: Proceedings of the European Conference on Computer Vision (ECCV), pp. 707–722 (2018)
27. Coors, B., Paul Condurache, A., Geiger, A.: Spherenet: learning spherical representations for detection and classification in omnidirectional images. In: Proceedings of the European Conference on Computer Vision (ECCV), pp. 518–533 (2018)
28. Maturana, D., Scherer, S.: 3D convolutional neural networks for landing zone detection from lidar. In: 2015 IEEE International Conference on Robotics and Automation (ICRA), pp. 3471–3478. IEEE (2015)
29. Maturana, D., Scherer, S.: Voxnet: a 3D convolutional neural network for real-time object recognition. In: 2015 IEEE/RSJ International Conference on Intelligent Robots and Systems (IROS), pp. 922–928. IEEE (2015)
30. Wu, Z., et al.: 3D shapenets: a deep representation for volumetric shapes. In: Proceedings of the IEEE Conference on Computer Vision and Pattern Recognition, pp. 1912–1920 (2015)
31. Qi, C.R., Su, H., Mo, K., Guibas, L.J.: Pointnet: deep learning on point sets for 3D classification and segmentation. In: Proceedings of the IEEE Conference on Computer Vision and Pattern Recognition, pp. 652–660 (2017)

32. Qi, C.R., Yi, L., Su, H., Guibas, L.J.: Pointnet++: deep hierarchical feature learning on point sets in a metric space. In: Advances in Neural Information Processing Systems, pp. 5099–5108 (2017)
33. Li, Y., Bu, R., Sun, M., Wu, W., Di, X., Chen, B.: Pointcnn: convolution on x-transformed points. In: Advances in Neural Information Processing Systems, pp. 820–830 (2018)
34. Thomas, H., Qi, C.R., Deschaud, J.E., Marcotegui, B., Goulette, F., Guibas, L.J.: KPCONV: flexible and deformable convolution for point clouds. In: Proceedings of the IEEE International Conference on Computer Vision, pp. 6411–6420 (2019)
35. Liu, Y., Fan, B., Xiang, S., Pan, C.: Relation-shape convolutional neural network for point cloud analysis. In: Proceedings of the IEEE Conference on Computer Vision and Pattern Recognition, pp. 8895–8904 (2019)
36. Liu, Y., Fan, B., Meng, G., Lu, J., Xiang, S., Pan, C.: Densepoint: learning densely contextual representation for efficient point cloud processing. In: Proceedings of the IEEE International Conference on Computer Vision, pp. 5239–5248 (2019)
37. Tchapmi, L., Choy, C., Armeni, I., Gwak, J., Savarese, S.: Segcloud: semantic segmentation of 3D point clouds. In: 2017 International Conference on 3D Vision (3DV), pp. 537–547. IEEE (2017)
38. Chen, X., Ma, H., Wan, J., Li, B., Xia, T.: Multi-view 3D object detection network for autonomous driving. In: Proceedings of the IEEE Conference on Computer Vision and Pattern Recognition, pp. 1907–1915 (2017)
39. Ge, L., Liang, H., Yuan, J., Thalmann, D.: 3D convolutional neural networks for efficient and robust hand pose estimation from single depth images. In: Proceedings of the IEEE Conference on Computer Vision and Pattern Recognition, pp. 1991–2000 (2017)
40. Li, B., Zhang, T., Xia, T.: Vehicle detection from 3D lidar using fully convolutional network. arXiv preprint arXiv:1608.07916 (2016)
41. Qi, C.R., Su, H., Nießner, M., Dai, A., Yan, M., Guibas, L.J.: Volumetric and multi-view cnns for object classification on 3D data. In: Proceedings of the IEEE Conference on Computer Vision and Pattern Recognition, pp. 5648–5656 (2016)
42. Song, S., Xiao, J.: Deep sliding shapes for a modal 3D object detection in RGB-D images. In: Proceedings of the IEEE Conference on Computer Vision and Pattern Recognition, pp. 808–816 (2016)
43. Song, S., Yu, F., Zeng, A., Chang, A.X., Savva, M., Funkhouser, T.: Semantic scene completion from a single depth image. In: Proceedings of the IEEE Conference on Computer Vision and Pattern Recognition, pp. 1746–1754 (2017)
44. Qi, C.R., Liu, W., Wu, C., Su, H., Guibas, L.J.: Frustum pointnets for 3D object detection from RGB-D data. In: Proceedings of the IEEE Conference on Computer Vision and Pattern Recognition, pp. 918–927 (2018)
45. Tang, Y.S., Lee, G.H.: Transferable semi-supervised 3D object detection from RGB-D data. In: Proceedings of the IEEE International Conference on Computer Vision, pp. 1931–1940 (2019)
46. Wang, W., Neumann, U.: Depth-aware CNN for RGB-D segmentation. In: Proceedings of the European Conference on Computer Vision (ECCV), pp. 135–150 (2018)
47. Chu, H., Ma, W.C., Kundu, K., Urtasun, R., Fidler, S.: Surfconv: Bridging 3D and 2D convolution for RGB-D images. In: Proceedings of the IEEE Conference on Computer Vision and Pattern Recognition, pp. 3002–3011 (2018)
48. Deng, J., Dong, W., Socher, R., Li, L.J., Li, K., Fei-Fei, L.: Imagenet: a large-scale hierarchical image database. In: 2009 IEEE Conference on Computer Vision and Pattern Recognition, pp. 248–255. IEEE (2009)

49. Silberman, N., Hoiem, D., Kohli, P., Fergus, R.: Indoor segmentation and support inference from RGBD images. In: Fitzgibbon, A., Lazebnik, S., Perona, P., Sato, Y., Schmid, C. (eds.) ECCV 2012. LNCS, vol. 7576, pp. 746–760. Springer, Heidelberg (2012). https://doi.org/10.1007/978-3-642-33715-4_54
50. He, K., Zhang, X., Ren, S., Sun, J.: Deep residual learning for image recognition. In: Proceedings of the IEEE Conference on Computer Vision and Pattern Recognition, pp. 770–778 (2016)
51. Simonyan, K., Zisserman, A.: Very deep convolutional networks for large-scale image recognition. arXiv preprint arXiv:1409.1556 (2014)
52. Huang, J., You, S.: Point cloud labeling using 3D convolutional neural network. In: 2016 23rd International Conference on Pattern Recognition (ICPR), pp. 2670–2675. IEEE (2016)
53. Ronneberger, O., Fischer, P., Brox, T.: U-Net: convolutional networks for biomedical image segmentation. In: Navab, N., Hornegger, J., Wells, W.M., Frangi, A.F. (eds.) MICCAI 2015. LNCS, vol. 9351, pp. 234–241. Springer, Cham (2015). https://doi.org/10.1007/978-3-319-24574-4_28

Generative Models for Computer Vision

Over-Exposure Correction via Exposure and Scene Information Disentanglement

Yuhui Cao[1,2], Yurui Ren[1,2], Thomas H. Li[1,3], and Ge Li[1,2(✉)]

[1] School of Electronics and Computer Engineering, Peking University, Shenzhen,
China
{yuhuicao,yrren}@pku.edu.cn, geli@ece.pku.edu.cn
[2] Peng Cheng Laboratory, Shenzhen, China
[3] Advanced Institute of Information Technology, Peking University, Hangzhou, China
tli@aiit.org.cn

Abstract. Over-exposure correction is an important problem of great
consequence to social media industries. In this paper, we propose a novel
model to tackle this task. Considering that reasonable enhanced results
can still vary in terms of exposure, we do not strictly enforce the model
to generate identical results with ground-truth images. On the contrary,
we train the network to recover the lost scene information according
to the existing information of the over-exposure images and generate
naturalness-preserved images. Experiments compared with several state-
of-the-art methods show the superior performance of the proposed network. Besides, we also verify our hypothesis with ablation studies. Our
source code is available at https://github.com/0x437968/overexposure-
correction-dise.

1 Introduction

In photography, exposure is one of the most important parameters that determine the subjective quality of the captured images. Unreasonable exposure can
lead to significant quality degradation. Over-exposure is one of the typical quality
degradation phenomenons. Due to the limited dynamic range of digital cameras,
relatively bright areas of the scene will be saturated. Therefore, it is important
to reasonably recover the saturated information and enhance the quality of overexposed images. In general, overexposure correction aims to generate alternative
contents for saturated regions according to the existing image information while
maintaining the global contrast (Fig. 1).

Image inpainting also requires generating plausible pixels for corrupted holes
according to uncorrupted contents. Along with the rapid progress in deep learning in recent years, inpainting methods [5–9] achieve excellent development.
Many methods can generate realistic alternative results. However, it is unreasonable to employ inpainting methods on the over-exposure correction task.
There are some important differences between these two tasks. Firstly the
missing regions of the images in inpainting are random masks but the overexposed regions in over-exposure correction are correlated. Secondly, to generate

H. Ishikawa et al. (Eds.): ACCV 2020, LNCS 12625, pp. 407–422, 2021.
https://doi.org/10.1007/978-3-030-69538-5_25

(a) Input   (b) Zhang *et al.*[1]   (c) DRHT[2]   (d) Hdrcnn[3]

(e) Lu *et al.*[4]   (f) Yu *et al.*[5]   (g) Ours   (h) Ground-truth

Fig. 1. Over-exposure correction results of several image correction methods. As shown in (b)–(f), existing methods have the limitation in recovering the saturated details of the overexposed region. In comparison, as shown in (h), we recover the saturated details and generate a naturalness-preserved result.

reasonable results, the existing contents of the overexposed image are required to be adjusted in the over-exposure correction task.

High Dynamic Range (HDR) images can convey much richer contrasts than conventional Low Dynamic Range (LDR) images. Inverse tone mapping aims to transform the LDR contents into HDR contents, the saturated region in the LDR image has to be recovered in this process. Previous methods of inverse tone mapping employ individual heuristics or optionally use manual intervention to enhance LDR images. Considering the excellent inference ability of convolution neural network, recent works DrTMo [10], Hdrcnn [3], DRHT [2] utilize deep convolutional neural networks to infer HDR results, then they can correct the images exposure by tone mapping, conventional methods or deep learning [11]. Unfortunately, existing inverse tone mapping methods pay more attention to the projection of existing contents but not the recovery of missing contents. The goal of the over-exposure task emphasizes the recovery of the missing contents more than adjusting the existing contents.

In this paper, we find that the reasonable correction result of an overexposed image is not unique, *i.e.* they may vary in terms of exposure. Therefore, it is unreasonable to force the network to predict identical results with ground-truth images. The network can not focus on missing information reconstruction. It struggles to predict identical results with ground-truth images. Hence, the over-exposure correction method should merely recover that information which is unrelated to camera exposure. To achieve this goal, we propose a novel method for over-exposure correction via global exposure and scene information disen-tanglement. We first train a disentanglement network to split the exposure and scene information of images. Then we utilize the pre-trained disentanglement network to constrain the recovery network. We train this network to generate results with the same scene information with ground-truth images. Meanwhile, we use GAN [12] to constrain the results to have the same distribution with ground-truth images. Experiments compared with the state-of-the-art methods show the superior performance of our proposed methods. Ablation studies also prove our hypothesis.

Our main contributions are as follows:

1) We tackle the over-exposure correction problem by disentangling global exposure and scene information.
2) We show that the performance of the network can be largely improved by reconstructing the scene information which is unrelated to the image exposure.
3) Our methods achieve remarkable results compared with state-of-the-art methods.

2 Related Work

We discuss the works that are relevant to the over-exposure correction task in this section, including over-exposure correction in Sect. 2.1, inverse tone mapping in Sect. 2.2, image inpainting in Sect. 2.3.

2.1 Over-Exposure Correction

Although overexposed image correction is an important task for many kinds of researches, there is not much previous work directly addressing this problem. Some early works assume that the ratios between different color channels are invariant [13] or gradual [14] in local image regions. However, both methods can only handle pixels which have one or two channels overexposed and all overexposed pixels are left untouched. To deal with this problem. Guo et al. [15] separate the input images into lightness and color. Then different smooth operators are performed to these components to correct the inputs. Although this algorithm can generate some color information in overexposed regions, it cannot recover the complicated texture. Considering the excellent performance of the Retinex theory in the under-exposure correction task, SICE [16] proposes a network to respectively recover the reflectance and illumination maps by using the Retinex theory. Then they reconstruct the results by combining these two components. Zhang et al. [1] propose a dual illumination estimation to simultaneously process under-exposure and over-exposure images. But the method can not recover vivid textures while dealing with the images which are overexposed in all RGB channels.

2.2 Inverse Tone Mapping

Inverse tone mapping is used to describe the methods that expand Low Dynamic Range (LDR) images for the generation of High Dynamic Range (HDR) images

[17]. HDR images contain a broader range of physical information of scenes than LDR images. Therefore, generating HDR images from captured LDR images is an ill-posed problem. It requires the algorithms to recover the lost dynamic information from the over/under-exposed regions in LDR images. Previous methods of inverse tone mapping employ individual heuristics or optionally use manual intervention to enhance LDR images. Rapid progress in deep learning inspired recent learning-based methods. DrTMo [10] and Hdrcnn [3] introduce the learning-based approach by training the LDR and HDR image pairs and infer a reasonable HDR image from an LDR input. DRHT [2] further uses an auto-encoder network to map the generated HDR images back to LDR images. However, existing inverse tone mapping methods always pay more attention to the projection of existing contents but not the recovery of missing information.

2.3   Image Inpainting

Existing inpainting methods can be mainly divided into two groups: conventional methods that use diffusion-based or patch-based methods and learning-based methods that employ convolutional neural networks to infer pixels for the missing regions. The conventional methods such as [18–20]. The synthesize pixels by propagating the neighborhood region's appearance to the target holes searching and copying similar image patches from the uncorrupt region. However, the diffusion-based methods can only deal with small holes in background inpainting tasks. The patch-based methods can not generate reasonable results for images with unique structures.

Recently, many learning-based methods [5,6,8,9,21,22] are proposed by formulating inpainting as a conditional image generation problem. A significant advantage of the deep-learning-based methods is that they can infer results by extracting meaningful semantic information. Context Encoder [6] propose an auto-encoder network for image inpainting. However, this method often generates results with visual artifacts. To solve this problem, Iizuka et al. [7] use both local and global discriminators to improve the quality of the generated images. In order to make better predictions, Yu et al. [5] propose contextual attention to building a remote connection when generated contents are distant with existing information. Liu et al. [21] believe the pixels in the masked holes of the inputs introduce artifacts to the results. Therefore, they propose partial convolution to force the network to use uncorrupted pixels only.

3   Proposed Method

Given an overexposed image, our goal is to generate a naturalness-preserved result with complete scene information. In order to encourage the network to learn the scene information unrelated to image exposure, we first train a disentanglement network to separate the image exposure and scene information. Then we utilize the pre-trained disentanglement network to generate the scene information. Our proposed model consists of two parts: 1) Disentanglement network.

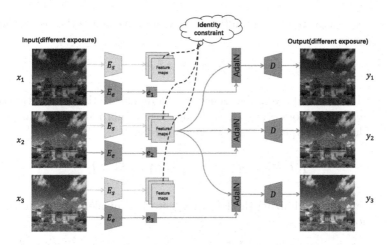

Fig. 2. Overview of the disentanglement network, the network includes scene information encoder E_s, exposure informaiton encoder E_e and decoder D. We set $N = 3$.

2) Recovery network. In the following subsections, we particularly introduce our model.

3.1 Disentanglement Network

Our disentanglement network can separate the scene information and the exposure information of images. As shown in Fig. 2, scene encoder E_s extracts the scene information of the inputs and the exposure encoder E_e extracts the images exposure information. In order to guarantee that the encoders can extract meaningful features. We use decoder D to reconstruct the inputs.

This encoder E_s should extract the scene information that is unrelated to image exposure. To achieve this goal, we use N multi-exposure images $x_1, x_2, ..., x_N$ which are captured with different exposure as the network inputs. Let $s_1, s_2, ..., s_N$ represent the feature maps which are extracted by E_s and $e_1, e_2, ..., e_N$ represent the exposure information vectors of E_s. The scene information in the same scene should be identical, therefore we define the scene loss as follows:

$$\mathcal{L}_{Ds} = \sum_{i=1}^{N} \|s_i - \bar{s}\|_1 \tag{1}$$

where $\bar{s}$ represents the mean of s. This loss ensures that the image exposure will not influence the scene feature maps.

In order to guarantee complete scene information in s_i, we further reconstruct the inputs by decoder D. During the training, we randomly select a feature from $s_1, s_2, ..., s_N$ as the input of decoder D. Meanwhile, we inject the N exposure feature vectors into the picked scene feature via AdaIN [23]. Then we get N

results $y_1, y_2, ..., y_N$ that are in different exposure. We define the reconstruction loss as follows:

$$\mathcal{L}_{Dr} = \sum_{i=1}^{N} \|y_i - x_i\|_1 \tag{2}$$

Meanwhile, we add a KL divergence loss to regularize the distribution of the exposure feature vectors $e_1, e_2, ..., e_N$ to be close to normal distribution $p(z) \sim N(0,1)$. The KL divergence loss is defined as follows:

$$KL(q(e_i)\|p(z)) = -\int q(e_i) \log \frac{p(z)}{q(e_i)} dz \tag{3}$$

As shown in [24], minimizing the KL divergence is equivalent to minimizing the following loss:

$$\mathcal{L}_{KL} = \frac{1}{2} \sum_{i=1}^{N} (\mu_i^2 + \sigma_i^2 - \log(\sigma_i^2) - 1) \tag{4}$$

where μ is the mean of e, and σ is the standard of e. e is sampled as $e = \mu + z \circ \sigma$, where $p(z) \sim N(0,1)$, and $\circ$ represents element-wise multiplication.

Besides, to help the recovery of more vivid textures. We add the style loss of the perceptual loss [25] between the outputs and ground-truth images:

$$\mathcal{L}_{Dstyle}(x,y) = \left\|G^\phi(x) - G^\phi(y)\right\|_F^2 \tag{5}$$

where G^ϕ represents the output features' Gram matrices of VGG-19 network [26] which is pre-trained on ImageNet [27].

The full objective function of the disentanglement network is a weighted sum of all the losses from (1) to (5):

$$\mathcal{L}_D = \lambda_s \mathcal{L}_{Ds} + \lambda_r \mathcal{L}_{Dr} + \lambda_{KL} \mathcal{L}_{KL} + \lambda_{style} \mathcal{L}_{Dstyle} \tag{6}$$

3.2   Recovery Network

In this section, we introduce the recovery network. As shown in Fig. 3, we set the overexposed image x as the input of generator G. Then we train the generator G to recovery the scene information. We compute the *Manhattan distance* of the scene feature maps by using pre-trained E_s. Therefore, our scene information reconstruction loss is defined as follows:

$$\mathcal{L}_{Rsr} = \|E_s(\widehat{y}) - E_s(y)\|_1 \tag{7}$$

Meanwhile, we add the adversarial loss to mimic the distribution of true images:

$$\mathcal{L}_{adv} = \mathbb{E}_{y \sim p(y)}[\log D_e(y)] + \mathbb{E}_{x \sim p(x)}[\log(1 - D_e(G(x)))] \tag{8}$$

where D_e tries to maximize the objective function to distinguish between our recovered results and ground-truth images. On the contrary, G aims to minimize

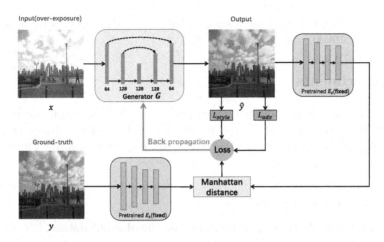

Fig. 3. Overview of the recovery network. We utilize the pre-trained scene information encoder E_s to constrain the recovery network.

the loss to make our recovered results look similar to real samples in ground-truth images.

We also add the style loss of [25] to recover more vivid textures:

$$\mathcal{L}_{Rstyle}(\widehat{y}, y) = \left\| G^{\phi}(\widehat{y}) - G^{\phi}(y) \right\|_F^2 \tag{9}$$

The full loss of the recovery network is defined as follows:

$$\mathcal{L}_R = \gamma_{sr}\mathcal{L}_{Rsr} + \gamma_{adv}\mathcal{L}_{adv} + \gamma_{style}\mathcal{L}_{Rstyle} \tag{10}$$

3.3   Implement Details

Disentanglement Network. For the architecture of the disentanglement network, we follow similar structures as the one used [4]. We employ the convolutional layer and the residual block [28] as the basic components of the network. In order to generate multi-exposure images, we use the method [29] proposed by Ying *et al.* to adjust the exposure of the image and guarantee that the exposure changed images won't overexposed. During the training, we use Adam solver to update our encoders and decoder. The learning rate is fixed in 0.0001. In all the experiments, we use 256×256 images with a batch size of 4 for training. For the hyper-parameters, we set $\lambda_s = 1000$, $\lambda_r = 50$, $\lambda_{KL} = 0.01$, $\lambda_{style} = 1000$ and $N = 3$.

Recovery Network. For the recovery network, we employ the auto-encoder architecture on the generator G. We use Adam solver to update our generator and discriminator. The learning rate of the generator is fixed in 0.0001 and the learning rate of the discriminator is fixed in 0.00001. In all the experiments, we use 256×256 images with a batch size of 4 for training. For the hyper-parameters, we set $\gamma_{sr} = 10000$, $\gamma_{adv} = 2$, $\gamma_{style} = 2000$.

4   Experiments

In this section, we first discuss the experiments deploys. Then, we compare our method against several state-of-the-art methods including Zhang et al. [1], DRHT [2], Hdrcnn [3], Lu et al. [4], Yu et al. [5]. Finally, we analyze the ablation study.

4.1   Experiments Deploys

Datasets. We implement our experiments on the place365 dataset [30]. Considering that the images containing sky, human face are very easily overexposed in photography. We elaborately pick 5000 outdoor images and 2400 images of the human portrait as our ground-truth images in the place365 dataset [30] and all of the images are in the normal exposure. Then we use the method [29] proposed by Ying et al. to adjust the exposure of images and obtain overexposed images from the ground-truth images. For each image, the ratio of exposure between the overexposed image and the ground-truth image is randomly selected in [1.8,2.4]. All images are resized to 256×256. For the outdoor dataset, we use 4000 images for training and 1000 images for testing. In the portrait dataset, we use 2000 images for training and 400 images for testing.

Evaluation Metrics. For the evaluation of experiments, considering that the reasonable correction results of an overexposed image are not unique in the over-exposure correction task, it is unreasonable to use metric which is sensitive about image exposure such as PSNR. We first use *Fréchet Inception Distance*(FID) [31] and *Kernel Inception Distance*(KID) [32] to measure the performance. Considering the outperformance of deep features compared with classic metrics, we also use LPIPS [33] to evaluate the performance. Besides, considering that the output of the scene encoder E_s can represent the scene information of the inputs. We formulate Scene Information Identity(SII) as the scene information evaluation metric:

$$SII(y, \widehat{y}) = \|E_s(y) - E_s(\widehat{y})\|_1 \tag{11}$$

4.2   Comparisons

We compare the proposed method with Hdrcnn [3], DRHT [2], Zhang et al. [1], Yu et al. [5] and Lu et al. [4]. Both Hdrcnn [3] and DRHT [2] are the inverse tone mapping methods that use an auto-encoder network to infer the HDR image from an LDR input. Zhang et al. [1] is a Retinex-based conventional method which can process both over-exposure and under-exposure by inverting the inputs. Yu et al. [5] is an excellent inpainting method and Lu et al. [4] is a deblurring method.

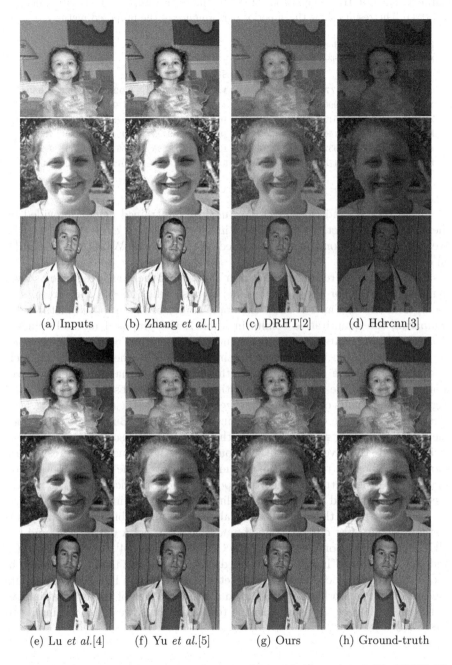

Fig. 4. Visual portrait comparisons of our method with Zhang *et al.* [1], DRHT [2], Hdrcnn [3], Lu *et al.* [4] and Yu *et al.* [5]. The size of images on the bottom row is 512 × 512 and the others are 256 × 256.

Table 1. Quantitative comparisons of our method with other methods. SII is defined in Eq. 11. The results show the superior performance of the proposed method.

Datasets	Outdoor				Portrait			
Methods	Metrics							
	FID	KID	LPIPS	SII	FID	KID	LPIPS	SII
Ours	**4.1477**	**−6.1942**	**0.0210**	**1.1110**	**19.2002**	**−8.9204**	**0.0252**	**0.6594**
Yu et al. [5]	10.8996	−5.6884	0.0398	3.5771	28.3579	-8.4790	0.0321	0.7399
Zhang et al. [1]	13.1616	−5.6805	0.1407	16.2549	41.3969	−7.8780	0.1252	4.3884
DRHT [2]	15.7146	−5.1977	0.1001	16.3488	47.3493	−7.4641	0.1430	7.2226
Hdrcnn [3]	14.9932	−5.3118	0.1737	13.7195	59.1835	−6.5646	0.2350	7.9029
Lu et al. [4]	17.8173	−5.1606	0.0826	5.1949	41.0575	−7.9727	0.0732	3.0559

For DRHT [2] and Hdrcnn [3]. We use the pre-trained model[1] provided by the authors to predict the overexposed images. For Zhang et al. [1], we test the overexposed images on the code provided by the authors. We retrain [5] and [4] on our datasets.

The quantitative results are shown in Table 1 and the visual results are shown Fig. 4 and Fig. 5. For the visual results, we also add 512×512 size results in the bottom row of Fig. 4 to show the applicability of the proposed method. By comparing the quantitative results in Table 1, the proposed method achieves the remarkable results in the experiments. As shown in Fig. 5(b), Zhang et al. [1] has the limitation in recovering missing information when all RGB channels are overexposed. We can realize that the inverse tone mapping methods pay more attention to the projection of existing contents via observing Fig. 4(c) and Fig. 4(d). The results of Yu et al. [5] are relatively well in the mid-row of Fig. 5(f). That may is because of the coarse-to-fine architectures. But as shown in both the mid and bottom rows of Fig. 4(f), the results of [5] also exist unreasonable artifacts and still have a big gap with our results. Some meaningful results are shown in the bottom row of Fig. 5. Our method recovers the missing contents on the road and the textures of the overexposed cloud. Specifically, we also recover the details at the end of double amber lines (i.e., red box in Fig. 5(h)).

To further prove the generalization ability and applicability of the proposed method, we also test our pre-trained model on the CelebA dataset [34] and the SICE dataset [16]. Some results on the CelebA dataset [34] are shown in Fig. 6 and the overexposed inputs are obtained in the same way that is mentioned in Sect. 4.1. The results on the SICE dataset [16] are shown in Fig. 7 and the inputs are from the real world. Considering that the large size of the original images in the SICE dataset [16] can make the testing difficult, we resize the inputs to 768×512.

---

[1] HDR images are required in DRHT [2] and Hdrcnn [3], therefore we can not retrain these two methods.

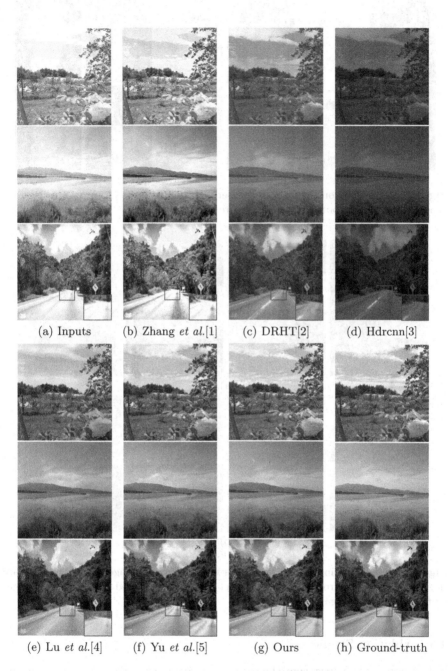

(a) Inputs   (b) Zhang *et al.*[1]   (c) DRHT[2]   (d) Hdrcnn[3]

(e) Lu *et al.*[4]   (f) Yu *et al.*[5]   (g) Ours   (h) Ground-truth

Fig. 5. Visual outdoor comparisons of our method with Zhang *et al.* [1], DRHT [2], Hdrcnn [3], Lu *et al.* [4] and Yu *et al.* [5]. (Color figure online)

Fig. 6. Visual results on the CelebA dataset [34]. Images on the top row are the over-exposed inputs. The bottom row images are our results.

Fig. 7. Visual results in the real world. For each subfigure, images on the top row are the inputs which are from the SICE dataset [16] and are resized to 768 × 512. Images on the bottom row are our results.

4.3   Ablation Studies

In this paper, we believe that the reasonable correction result of an overexposed image is not unique. Therefore it is unreasonable to force the network to generate identical results with ground-truth images. In the ablation studies, we first relace the scene information reconstruction loss with L_1 distance between the generated results and the ground-truth images and maintain the others unchanged to retrain the recovery network. Then we remove one of the Style, GAN, Scene loss and maintain the others unchanged to retrain the recovery network in turn for determining the role of each loss. Qualitative results are shown in Fig. 8. We can see that figures in Fig. 8(e) and 8(b) which are trained without the scene loss exists severe artifacts, but the results in Fig. 8(c), 8(d), 8(f) which are trained with the scene loss are under a good condition. Besides, the comparisons between Fig. 8(c), 8(d), 8(f) also denote that Scene loss has a major contribution to the proposed method. Quantitative results are shown in Table 2. It also could be seen that the comparisons between the results trained with scene loss and the results trained without scene loss denote that the scene loss can largely improve the performance of the recovery network.

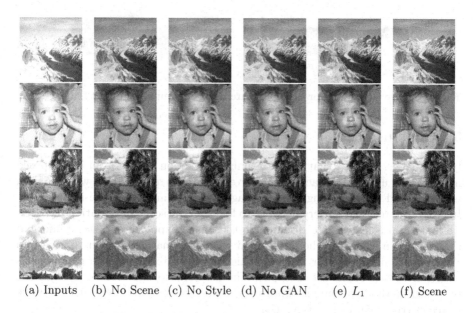

(a) Inputs   (b) No Scene   (c) No Style   (d) No GAN   (e) L_1 (f) Scene

Fig. 8. Visual results of the ablation studies. Figures in (b)-(d) respectively are the ablation results without corresponding loss(*e.g.* results in (b) are trained with GAN and Style loss). Figures in (e) are the results trained with GAN, Style, L_1 loss and results in (f) are trained with Style, GAN, Scene loss. The comparisons between the different ablation results show the significant impacts of the scene loss.

4.4   Failure Cases

Despite the aforementioned success, our method contains limitations in recovering the details of a large continuously overexposed region. Figure 9 shows two examples. Although our method can recover the most textures of the overexposed region, there are limitations in recovering the center of the overexposed region. This is because limited information is given in the input images.

Table 2. Quantitative results of the ablation studies. SII is defined in Eq. 11. The results verify the significant impacts of Scene loss.

Datasets	Outdoor				Portrait			
Loss	Metrics							
	FID	KID	LPIPS	SII	FID	KID	LPIPS	SII
Style, GAN, Scene	**4.1477**	**−6.1942**	**0.0210**	1.1110	19.2002	−8.9204	0.0252	0.6594
Style, GAN,L_1	8.8833	−5.8798	0.0719	1.8312	20.5921	−8.8673	0.0270	0.7792
Style, GAN	9.1331	−5.8819	0.0767	1.6240	19.8518	−8.8826	0.0262	0.7630
GAN, Scene	5.4939	−6.1175	0.0249	**1.0205**	18.2920	−8.9328	**0.0222**	**0.6107**
Style, Scene	4.6370	−6.1759	0.0250	1.6615	**17.9326**	**−8.9596**	0.0235	0.6914

(a)   (b)

Fig. 9. Failure examples. For each subfigure, left is the input and right is the result.

5   Conclusion

In this paper, we find that the reasonable correction result of an overexposed image is not unique. To tackle the over-exposure correction task, we propose a novel method via disentangling the image exposure and the scene information. In order to force the recovery network to focus on the scene information recovery, we first train a network to disentangle the image exposure and scene information, and then we utilize the pre-trained scene information encoder to constrain the recovery network. Our method achieves remarkable results in comparisons with other state-of-the-art methods. The ablation studies also verify that the proposed method can largely improve the performance by forcing the network to reconstruct the scene information.

Acknowledgements. This work was supported by Key-Area Research and Development Program of Guangdong Province (No.2019B121204008), National Natural Science Foundation of China and Guangdong Province Scientific Research on Big Data (No. U1611461). In addition, we thank the anonymous reviewers for their time and valuable comments.

References

1. Zhang, Q., Nie, Y., Zheng, W.S.: Dual illumination estimation for robust exposure correction. Comput. Graph. Forum **38**, 243–252 (2019)
2. Yang, X., Xu, K., Song, Y., Zhang, Q., Wei, X., Lau, R.W.: Image correction via deep reciprocating HDR transformation. In: The IEEE Conference on Computer Vision and Pattern Recognition (CVPR) (2018)

3. Eilertsen, G., Kronander, J., Denes, G., Mantiuk, R.K., Unger, J.: HDR image reconstruction from a single exposure using deep CNNs. ACM Trans. Graph. **36**, 1–15 (2017)
4. Lu, B., Chen, J.C., Chellappa, R.: Unsupervised domain-specific deblurring via disentangled representations. In: Proceedings of the IEEE Computer Society Conference on Computer Vision and Pattern Recognition 2019-June, pp. 10217–10226 (2019)
5. Yu, J., Lin, Z., Yang, J., Shen, X., Lu, X., Huang, T.S.: Generative image inpainting with contextual attention. In: Proceedings of the IEEE Computer Society Conference on Computer Vision and Pattern Recognition, pp. 5505–5514 (2018)
6. Pathak, D., Krahenbuhl, P., Donahue, J., Darrell, T., Efros, A.A.: Context encoders: feature learning by inpainting. In: Proceedings of the IEEE Computer Society Conference on Computer Vision and Pattern Recognition 2016-December, pp. 2536–2544 (2016)
7. Iizuka, S., Simo-Serra, E., Ishikawa, H.: Globally and locally consistent image completion. ACM Trans. Graph. **36**, 1–14 (2017)
8. Ren, Y., Yu, X., Zhang, R., Li, T.H., Liu, S., Li, G.: Structureflow: image inpainting via structure-aware appearance flow. In: The IEEE International Conference on Computer Vision (ICCV) (2019)
9. Zhang, R., Ren, Y., Qiu, J., Li, G.: Base-detail image inpainting. In: BMVC (2019)
10. Endo, Y., Kanamori, Y., Mitani, J.: Deep reverse tone mapping. ACM Trans. Graph. **36**, 1–177 (2017)
11. Gharbi, M., Chen, J., Barron, J.T., Hasinoff, S.W., Durand, F.: Deep bilateral learning for real-time image enhancement. CoRR abs/1707.02880 (2017)
12. Goodfellow, I., et al.: Generative adversarial nets. In: Ghahramani, Z., Welling, M., Cortes, C., Lawrence, N.D., Weinberger, K.Q., (eds.): Advances in Neural Information Processing Systems 27. Curran Associates, Inc. pp. 2672–2680 (2014)
13. Zhang, X., Brainard, D.H.: Estimation of saturated pixel values in digital color imaging. J. Opt. Soc. Am. A **21**, 2301–2310 (2004)
14. Masood, S., Zhu, J., Tappen, M.: Automatic correction of saturated regions in photographs using cross-channel correlation. Comput. Graph. Forum **28**, 1861–1869 (2009)
15. Guo, D., Cheng, Y., Zhuo, S., Sim, T.: Correcting over-exposure in photographs. In: 2010 IEEE Computer Society Conference on Computer Vision and Pattern Recognition, pp. 515–521 (2010)
16. Cai, J., Gu, S., Zhang, L.: Learning a deep single image contrast enhancer from multi-exposure images. IEEE Trans. Image Process. **27**, 2049–2062 (2018)
17. Banterle, F., Ledda, P., Debattista, K., Chalmers, A.: Inverse tone mapping, pp. 349–356 (2006)
18. Takahashi, T.: Image inpainting. Kyokai Joho Imeji Zasshi/Journal of the Institute of Image Information and Television Engineers **71**, 503–504 (2017)
19. Barnes, C., Shechtman, E., Finkelstein, A., Goldman, D.B.: PatchMatch: a randomized correspondence algorithm for structural image editing. ACM Trans. Graph. (Proc. SIGGRAPH) **28**(3), 24 (2009)
20. Hays, J., Efros, A.A.: Scene completion using millions of photographs. ACM Trans. Graph. **26**, 1–7 (2007)
21. Liu, G., Reda, F.A., Shih, K.J., Wang, T., Tao, A., Catanzaro, B.: Image inpainting for irregular holes using partial convolutions. CoRR abs/1804.07723 (2018)
22. Li, J., Wang, N., Zhang, L., Du, B., Tao, D.: Recurrent feature reasoning for image inpainting. In: The IEEE/CVF Conference on Computer Vision and Pattern Recognition (CVPR) (2020)

23. Huang, X., Belongie, S.: Arbitrary style transfer in real-time with adaptive instance normalization. In: Proceedings of the IEEE International Conference on Computer Vision 2017-October, pp. 1510–1519 (2017)
24. Kingma, D.P., Welling, M.: Auto-encoding variational bayes. In: 2nd International Conference on Learning Representations, ICLR 2014 - Conference Track Proceedings, pp. 1–14 (2014)
25. Johnson, J., Alahi, A., Fei-Fei, L.: Perceptual losses for real-time style transfer and super-resolution. In: Leibe, B., Matas, J., Sebe, N., Welling, M. (eds.) ECCV 2016. LNCS, vol. 9906, pp. 694–711. Springer, Cham (2016). https://doi.org/10.1007/978-3-319-46475-6_43
26. Simonyan, K., Zisserman, A.: Very deep convolutional networks for large-scale image recognition. In: International Conference on Learning Representations (2015)
27. Deng, J., Dong, W., Socher, R., Li, L., Li, K., Fei-Fei, L.: Imagenet: a large-scale hierarchical image database. In: 2009 IEEE Conference on Computer Vision and Pattern Recognition, pp. 248–255 (2009)
28. He, K., Zhang, X., Ren, S., Sun, J.: Deep residual learning for image recognition. CoRR abs/1512.03385 (2015)
29. Ying, Z., Li, G., Ren, Y., Wang, R., Wang, W.: A new low-light image enhancement algorithm using camera response model. In: Proceedings - 2017 IEEE International Conference on Computer Vision Workshops, ICCVW 2017 2018-January, pp. 3015–3022 (2017)
30. Zhou, B., Lapedriza, A., Khosla, A., Oliva, A., Torralba, A.: Places: a 10 million image database for scene recognition. IEEE Trans. Pattern Anal. Mach. Intell. **40**(6), 1452–1464 (2017)
31. Heusel, M., Ramsauer, H., Unterthiner, T., Nessler, B., Hochreiter, S.: GANs trained by a two time-scale update rule converge to a local Nash equilibrium. In: Advances in Neural Information Processing Systems 2017-December, pp. 6627–6638 (2017)
32. Binkowski, M., Sutherland, D., Arbel, M., Gretton, A.: Demystifying mmd gans. ArXiv abs/1801.01401 (2018)
33. Zhang, R., Isola, P., Efros, A.A., Shechtman, E., Wang, O.: The unreasonable effectiveness of deep features as a perceptual metric. In: Proceedings of the IEEE Computer Society Conference on Computer Vision and Pattern Recognition, pp. 586–595 (2018)
34. Liu, Z., Luo, P., Wang, X., Tang, X.: Deep learning face attributes in the wild. In: Proceedings of International Conference on Computer Vision (ICCV) (2015)

Novel-View Human Action Synthesis

Mohamed Ilyes Lakhal[1]([✉]), Davide Boscaini[2], Fabio Poiesi[2], Oswald Lanz[2], and Andrea Cavallaro[1]

[1] Centre for Intelligent Sensing, Queen Mary University of London, London, UK
{m.i.lakhal,a.cavallaro}@qmul.ac.uk
[2] Technologies of Vision, Fondazione Bruno Kessler, Povo, Italy
{dboscaini,poiesi,lanz}@fbk.eu

Abstract. Novel-View Human Action Synthesis aims to synthesize the movement of a body from a virtual viewpoint, given a video from a real viewpoint. We present a novel 3D reasoning to synthesize the target viewpoint. We first estimate the 3D mesh of the target body and transfer the rough textures from the 2D images to the mesh. As this transfer may generate sparse textures on the mesh due to frame resolution or occlusions. We produce a semi-dense textured mesh by propagating the transferred textures both locally, within local geodesic neighborhoods, and globally, across symmetric semantic parts. Next, we introduce a context-based generator to learn how to correct and complete the residual appearance information. This allows the network to independently focus on learning the foreground and background synthesis tasks. We validate the proposed solution on the public NTU RGB+D dataset. The code and resources are available at https://bit.ly/36u3h4K.

1 Introduction

Novel-view human action synthesis is the problem of reproducing a person performing an action from a virtual viewpoint [1]. The ability to synthesize of one or more novel viewpoints of an action is attractive for extended reality [2], action recognition [3] and free-viewpoint video [4].

Recent works [5–8] have shown the ability to synthesize high-quality images, but with limiting assumptions on the input data. SiCloPe [5] takes a frontal input image and uses canonical views to reconstruct the 3D mesh through supervision. However, using a ground-truth mesh from real images is not a realistic assumption. Similarly, PIFu [6] predicts a dense 3D occupancy field using multiple input views. This method expects high-resolution ground-truth mesh and a neutral background which hinder generalization to real-world scenarios when backgrounds are cluttered. The method proposed in [9] creates an animated version of an image containing a person in the center. An initial mesh is first

---

Electronic supplementary material The online version of this chapter (https://doi.org/10.1007/978-3-030-69538-5_26) contains supplementary material, which is available to authorized users.

© Springer Nature Switzerland AG 2021
H. Ishikawa et al. (Eds.): ACCV 2020, LNCS 12625, pp. 423–441, 2021.
https://doi.org/10.1007/978-3-030-69538-5_26

estimated and then corrected. However, the mesh construction part is computationally costly and incompatible with the extension of the model to videos. Furthermore, the texture filling is based on heuristics or requires human intervention. If multiple real views of the same scene are available, the rendering of an arbitrary virtual view can be successfully addressed [10,11]. For example, the method proposed in Bansal *et al.* [11] combines the information available from multiple camera views to reconstruct the geometry of a static scene. Then, a neural network based model is used to compose the dynamics on top of the static scene. However, with only a single video (view) as input the problem becomes much more challenging and largely unexplored. To the best of our knowledge, VDNet [1] is the only previous work addressing it.

Thanks to the rapid development on human mesh recovery [12–16], we can obtain 3D representations from images or videos. Our approach consists of a two-stage pipeline. In the first stage we exploit a novel 3D reasoning to produce a sparse initialization for the virtual view. In the second stage we introduce Geometric texture Transfer Network (GTNet), a context-based generator that aims to correct and complete such initial guess by learning the residual appearance information. For each frame captured from the real view we estimate the 3D mesh of the human actor using [14] where the parameters of the Skinned Multi-Person Linear (SMPL) model [17] are learned to morph a canonical 3D model of the human body to fit the 2D projection of the human actor pose and shape. Given such 3D model, we transfer the appearance information from the 2D video to the 3D mesh. This results in a sparse texture on the 3D mesh because of occlusions. We propose to compute the missing information by exploiting the knowledge of the 3D model both at a local and global scale. Locally, missing values within a geodesic neighborhood are computed by interpolating the input sparse texture. More globally, if a part of the 3D model (e.g. an arm or a leg) lacks texture information but its symmetric counterpart contains it, we propagate it. The texture on the mesh (in 3D) obtained in this way is then projected (rendered) on the novel view (in 2D). The estimated 3D model thus acts as a proxy to transfer appearance information from the input (real) view to the target (virtual) view. The design of our approach is inspired by pixel warping methods [18,19] that create realistic human images from existing frames (or views). Differently from VDNet [1], we exploit the geometric properties of the input prior to facilitate the transfer to the target view. Unlike motion-transfer methods (*e.g.* [20]), we learn the geometry and the appearance of a novel (virtual) view.

2   Related Work

Methods for novel-view synthesis that focus on humans can be based on computer graphics, learning, or combining 3D mesh representations and learning. These methods are discussed in this section jointly with a discussion on the importance of the modality used to synthesize the novel-view.

Novel-View Image Synthesis. Graphics based methods [6,21,22] rely on the abundance of ground-truth data to achieve high quality synthesis. For example [22–24] use image or sequence of frames to learn the displacement of clothing on top of the SMPL [17] model. Differently, the methods in [5,6] use high quality human mesh representations from the Renderpeople dataset[1]. These representations enable the model to achieve high quality results, but fail to generalize in uncontrolled setups and need a few viewpoints, which may be hard to obtain, to perform the synthesis.

Learning (or data-driven) approaches [1,3,25,26] use spatial cues about the human subject to synthesize the target view. A drawback of such approaches is the poor generalization to unseen views and the difficulty to handle occlusions.

A new direction of work considers the use of a 3D model estimated directly from raw images [27–29]. Liu et al. [28] enforce feature warping of the input view in the network structure to synthesize the novel view.

Video Synthesis. We categorise the methods solving this problem into two classes: unconstrained or constrained synthesis. The first category tries to learn the distribution of the data during training. The video is therefore a sample from the learned distribution [30–32]. Since the datasets available are most often a sparse representation of the distribution of the true data, the generated videos generally are limited to few applications. The constrained video synthesis [20,33, 34] relies on context (e.g. image sequence [20]) or spatial cues (e.g. keypoints [33, 34]). Applications include action imitation [20] and video prediction [35].

Novel-View Video Synthesis. Recently, Lakhal et al. [1] introduced the task of *novel-view video synthesis* which shares the challenges of both the novel view synthesis (i.e dealing with occlusion) and video synthesis (i.e maintaining temporal consistency across frames). The assumptions are the availability of only one input view and the modalities about the target view which can be either given or computed. Furthermore, the problem is different from the pose-guided human image synthesis [25] where the background synthesis is not taken into account, the pose is not constrained to the view (i.e. cannot model the 3D structure of the scene), and these methods fail to maintain temporal consistency. In this paper, we show that by estimating the texture we can approximate the target feature with a simple mapping. Using the proposed context-based architecture, the network can focus on the background synthesis. We exploit the 3D mesh information and use the input-target view association as guidance in the novel-view synthesis process. Also, we explicitly handle the temporal consistency of the synthesized frames. Furthermore, we handle self occlusions using visible information and transfer it to neighboring occluded parts.

Prior Modalities. Deep learning based methods made progress on estimating accurate modalities (e.g. depth and 2D/3D keypoints) from object priors

---

[1] https://renderpeople.com/, accessed September 2020.

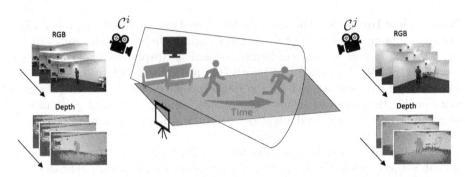

Fig. 1. Given a video of a person performing an action recorded from an input view $\mathcal{C}^i$, we synthesize how it would appear from a target (or virtual) view $\mathcal{C}^j$. Each view can be captured with a set of modalities (e.g. RGB, depth, skeleton).

(*e.g.* human). This includes human pose estimation [36], human part segmentation [37], or human mesh recovery [12,14]. The performance of a neural network-based generator for novel-view synthesis relies heavily on the modalities derived from the prior used about the target view (we only consider human priors). Early works rely on 2D keypoints of the human body joints [25,38–44].

The skeleton indicates the spatial location of the person on the target view. The network then has to learn how to extract and transfer appearance information from the input view to generate the target image. A segmentation map could be considered as another modality [45,46]. DensePose [47] maps the pixels of an RGB image of human to a 3D surface and is used in [46,48]. Li *et al.* [29] proposed to represent the pose as a rendered 3D body mesh.

3   Method

3.1   Problem Definition

Let $\mathcal{C} = \{\mathcal{C}^i\}_{i=1}^V$ be V static cameras (views) placed at different positions in a scene. Each view $i \in \{1, \ldots, V\}$ is represented as a sequence of RGB images $x_t^i \in \mathbb{R}^{w \times h \times 3}$ of width w and height h pixels and indexed by the timestep $t = 1, \ldots, T$. The sequence $x^i = \{x_t^i\}_{t=1}^T$ is an instance of the scene captured from the input view camera $\mathcal{C}^i$. Each view contains M different modalities $p^i = \{p_1^i, \ldots, p_M^i\}$ *e.g.* depth and skeleton (see Fig. 1). Each modality has to at least spatially localise the person in the scene (*i.e.*, foreground). The modalities of the virtual view are computed by transforming p^i with the information in both $\mathcal{C}^i$ and $\mathcal{C}^j$.

The aim of novel-view video synthesis is to reconstruct the RGB sequence x^j of a scene from an input view to a target view. Given a parametric function $G_{i \to j}$ called *generator* we have: $x^j = G_{i \to j}(x^i, p^j)$.

3.2   3D Human Body Prior

We model the foreground using a 3D mesh assuming that the video stream contains only humans. We use the estimated 3D mesh as a proxy to transfer the

x^i $x^j + \mathcal{M}^j$ $\mathcal{S}^j$ $\mathcal{O}^j_{t+1 \to t}$ $\mathcal{T}_{i \to j}$

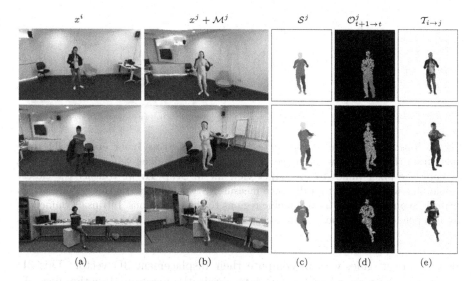

(a)   (b)   (c)   (d)   (e)

Fig. 2. Target view modalities obtained with the 3D human body prior extracted from NTU-RGB+D dataset [49]: (a) input view; (b) target view with the rendered mesh; (c) segmentation map; (d) foreground motion; (e) texture transfer.

appearance information from the input view to the novel view. In this section, we show that we can compute other modalities of the target view by fully exploiting the one-to-one correspondence between vertices of the 3D mesh (Fig. 2).

Foreground Prior. We model the foreground (*i.e.* the target subject) using a geometric approach that exploits one-to-one correspondences between the vertices of the 3D meshes from the real and virtual views. As in [14], we model the human body using the SMPL model [17]. A set of three connected vertices defines a face on the 3D mesh. The SMPL model is composed of $N_f = 13776$ faces that are uniquely identified by a face map $\mathcal{F}$. Given the camera $\mathcal{C}^i \in \mathcal{C}$ and a projection function (*e.g.* a renderer [50]) the mesh in rendered on the camera $\mathcal{C}^i$ producing a data structure $F^i \in \mathbb{R}^{w \times h}$ (*i.e.* projecting the faces onto the image plane of the camera $\mathcal{C}^i$) and the rendering of the 3D body mesh $\mathcal{M}^i$ (Fig. 2(b)).

Human Part Segmentation. Let us decompose the human body representation into B parts (*e.g.* head and arms). Since for the SMPL the map $\mathcal{F}$ has a fix set of faces, we cluster it into parts[2] such that: $\mathcal{F} = \{\mathcal{F}_b\}_{b=1}^B$. Therefore, each face $f \in F^i$ can belong to any of the B classes or to the background.

Foreground Motion. We exploit the data-structure $\{F^i_t\}_{t=1}^T$ to extract the foreground motion information. Specifically, because mesh vertices are uniquely

---

[2] In practice, we manually annotate each of the N_f face into a unique body-part label.

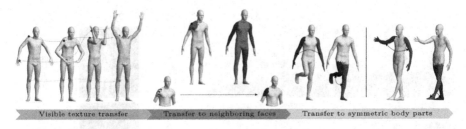

Fig. 3. Illustration of the proposed texture transfer. **Step I:** for every visible face index from the input view mesh, we accumulate its RGB pixel value over time. Then, we copy the pixel values to the target view mesh. **Step II:** we transfer the closest visible face with respect to a distance measure. **Step III:** we transfer texture across intrinsic symmetries, *i.e.* from the blue regions to the red regions. Intrinsic symmetries are independent on the pose of the subject. (Color figure online)

identified over time, we can compute their displacement 3D vector. This 3D vector can be projected on the image to obtain the foreground motion flow. As in [35] we use a backward motion flow to warp the frame for each time step to help the foreground synthesis. Given a face $f \in F_{t+1}^i$ (resp. F_t^i) at pixel location (u_x, u_y) (resp. (u_x', u_y')), let $\mathcal{O}_{t+1 \to t}^i$ be the motion vector at (u_x, u_y), which is computed as $(u_x - u_x', u_y - u_y')$.

Texture Transfer. The structure $F_t^i \in \mathbb{R}^{w \times h}$ is the projection of the 3D human mesh of the person in x_t^i at time step t onto the image plane of camera $\mathcal{C}^i$. A key observation to make is that we can exploit the association between F_t^i and x_t^i in order to estimate a rough foreground on the image plane of the camera $\mathcal{C}^j$. The proposed Symmetric Texture Transfer extends this idea to improve the target foreground appearance through three steps (Fig. 3). The first step consists of tracking each visible face in F_t^i over time. If a face $f \in F_t^i$ is at position (u_x, u_y) we copy the pixel value of x_t^i. The face-pixel association is then stored in a hashmap where the keys are the face number and the values are the pixels. If at time $t+k$ the face f is detected we add it and at time step T we keep the median of the detected pixels. The second step transfers pixels from the hashmap to an image indexed by F^j. Specifically, given a face $f \in \mathcal{F}$, we rank the neighboring faces as a function of the distance $\textbf{dist} : \mathcal{F} \times \mathcal{F} \to \mathbb{R}$ defined on the surface manifold of a template mesh. Because the Euclidean distance is not a suitable metric to measure distances of vertices on a deformable surface, we use the geodesic distance [51] that is invariant to intrinsic deformation of the mesh. The computation of the geodesic distances produces the matrix $\mathbf{F} \in \mathbb{R}^{M \times M}$, where the element in the uth row and v^{th} column is $\mathbf{F}_{uv} = \{\textbf{dist}(f, f') | f, f' \in \mathcal{F}\}$. Using $\mathbf{F}$ we transfer the texture of the n-nearest neighbor face to the image. The final step uses symmetry between body part in order to transfer occluded pixels (see Supplementary Material).

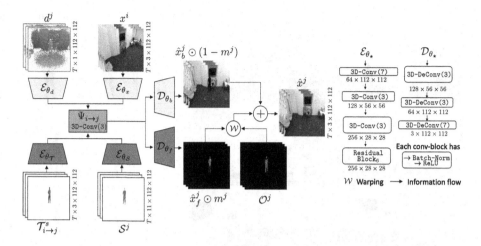

Fig. 4. Architecture of the proposed GTNet model. We encode each modality using a separate encoder to approximate the feature point of the target view with $\Psi_{i\rightarrow j}$. We decode the background and the foreground separately. Note that we also enforce explicit temporal modeling using the estimated foreground motion.

We use a template gender neutral 3D mesh with a canonical pose to compute the pairwise distance map $\mathbf{F} \in \mathbb{R}^{N_f \times N_f}$ (see Fig. 3(a)). The reason is that for Euclidean distance it is computationally not possible to compute it for each frame of the dataset. Furthermore, computing a geodesic distance is much more computationally expensive than an Euclidean distance. The texture transfer $\mathcal{T}_{i\rightarrow j}^s$ approximates the foreground of the novel-view and is not used as a final prediction.

3.3 Geometric Texture Transfer Network (GTNet)

The burden over the network to synthesize the novel view can be mitigated if we exploit the 3D mesh. The texture-transfer $\mathcal{T}_{i\rightarrow j}^s$ provides a good estimate of the foreground of target view x^j. Therefore we consider that $\mathcal{T}_{i\rightarrow j}^s$ is an informative input to the network and we only need to learn the residual to correct elements like mis-transferred textures or lighting. Since the texture $\mathcal{T}_{i\rightarrow j}^s$ is a good approximation of the foreground, we chose a context-based network structure.

Architecture. GTNet jointly learns to synthesize the foreground and background (see Fig. 4). The network takes the input view video x^i (resp. depth modality d^j) and encodes it with feature mapping $\mathcal{E}_{\theta_x}$ (resp. $\mathcal{E}_{\theta_d}$). These features constitute the background information. Similarly, we encode the texture transfer $\mathcal{T}_{i\rightarrow j}^s$ (resp. segmentation map $\mathcal{S}^s$) to represent the foreground information in the latent space. Now to approximate the target feature ϵ^j using the operator $\Psi_{i\rightarrow j}$ we rely on a 3D Convolutional Neural Network layer, this will

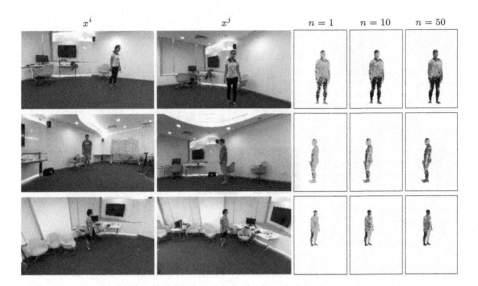

Fig. 5. Comparison of the traditional texture transfer methods (e.g. [28]) and the proposed transfer method with $n \in \{10, 50\}$ nearest neighbor transfer.

enforce the temporal consistency on the bottleneck layer. We therefore have the following (Fig. 5):

$$\hat{\epsilon}^j \approx \Psi_{i \rightarrow j}(\oplus_{k \in \mathcal{I}} \mathcal{E}_{\theta_k}(k)); \mathcal{I} = \{x^i, d^j, \mathcal{S}^j, \mathcal{T}^s_{i \rightarrow j}\}, \tag{1}$$

where $\oplus$ is the concatenation operation. As motivated earlier, we separate the synthesis of the foreground and the background using dedicated decoders $\mathcal{E}_{\theta_f}$ and $\mathcal{E}_{\theta_b}$, respectively. The synthesized foreground (resp. background) is obtained as: $\hat{x}^j_f = \mathcal{D}_{\theta_f}(\hat{\epsilon}^j)$ (resp. $\hat{x}^j_b = \mathcal{D}_{\theta_b}(\hat{\epsilon}^j)$). The synthesized video $\hat{x}^j$ is therefore:

$$\hat{x}^j = \hat{x}^j_f \odot m^j + \hat{x}^j_b \odot (1 - m^j), \tag{2}$$

where $\odot$ is the Hadamard product and m^j is the foreground mask obtained by the binarization of F^j.

In order to enforce temporal constraints, we propose to use the foreground motion from the mesh displacement vectors in the synthesized frame to add motion information. The frame synthesis of view j at time step t is defined as:

$$\hat{x}^j_{f,t} = \begin{cases} \hat{x}^j_{f,t} & \text{if } t = 1 \\ \tilde{x}^j_{f,t} + \zeta.\mathcal{W}(\hat{x}^j_{f,t-1}, O^j_{t+1 \rightarrow t}) & \text{if } t \in [2..T], \end{cases} \tag{3}$$

where $\mathcal{W}$ is a residual warping function, $\hat{x}^j_{f,t}$ (resp. $O^j_{t+1 \rightarrow t}$) is the foreground prediction (resp. foreground motion) of the view j. $\tilde{x}^j_{f,t}$ is the initial synthesized frame of the generator and ζ is a controlling factor defined empirically (Table 3). We force the model to focus on the residue with respect to the previous time step

$t-1$. Note that when training a generator, $\mathcal{W}(\hat{x}^j_{f,t-1}, O^j_{t+1\to t})$ is computed by a forward pass (and freezing the weights). Thus when applying the reconstruction pixel-wise loss, the network would only learn the residual over $\tilde{x}^j_{f,t}$.

Training Losses. Instead of the traditional L_1 used in the literature, we employ a Huber loss [52] to penalize the video synthesis produced by the generator. Differently from the L_2, the Huber loss is more robust to outliers and, differently from the L_1 loss, the Huber loss considers the directions of the error magnitude. The reconstruction loss L_r between the generated videos (both foreground and background branch) $\hat{x}^j$ and the ground-truth x^j at t is

$$
L_r = \begin{cases} 0.5(\hat{x}^j_t, -x^j_t)^2, & \text{if } |\hat{x}^j_t, -x^j_t| < 1 \\ |\hat{x}^j_t, -x^j_t| - 0.5, & \text{otherwise} \end{cases} \tag{4}
$$

To enforce the perceptual quality over the generated videos we use the temporal perceptual loss [1]. This loss extends the so-called perceptual loss [53] by penalising the generated videos on a spatio-temporal feature space using a 3D CNN network ϕ (called perceptual network). The temporal perceptual loss is defined as:

$$
L_p = \sum_{k=1}^{L} \frac{1}{T_k w_k h_k c_k} \left\| \phi_k(\hat{x}^j) - \phi_k(x^j) \right\|_2, \tag{5}
$$

where T_k, w_k, h_k, c_k are the temporal dimension (*i.e. timesteps*), width, height and the number of channel of at the k-th layer of the perceptual network ϕ, respectively. Furthermore, we use adversarial loss [54] in order to add high frequency details in the synthesized frames. Given our generator $G_{i\to j}$ and a discriminator D, the conditional adversarial loss is given as:

$$
L_a = \mathbb{E}_{x^i,x^j}\left[\log(D(x^i, x^j))\right] + \mathbb{E}_{x^i}\left[\log(1 - D(x^i, \hat{x}^j))\right]. \tag{6}
$$

The total training loss is given by $L = L_r + \lambda_p L_p + \lambda_a L_a$, with $\lambda_p = \lambda_a = 0.01$.

4   Experiments

This section evaluates the proposed GTNet. Section 4.1 describes the training protocol. Section 4.2 provides the ablation of each component of the proposed pipeline. Section 4.2 compares our method with the state-of-the art VDNet [1].

4.1   Experimental Setup

Dataset. We use NTU RGB+D [49], the only large-scale synchronized multiview action recognition dataset (see Fig. 6), which consists of of videos captured using three synchronized cameras with two front views and one side view. The dataset contains 80 views with 40 distinct subjects and 60 actions. Following [1], we use the cross-subject split.

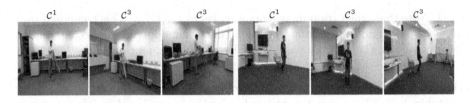

Fig. 6. Sample frames from the NTU RGB+D dataset. The 3 views are captured with cameras placed with horizontal angle of: $-45°, 0°, +45°$.

Evaluation Metrics. We assess the performance using two criteria: (i) the generated video visual quality; (ii) the accuracy of the pose of the individual. For the visual quality, we use Structural Similarity (SSIM), Peak Signal-to-Noise-Ratio (PSNR) [55] (we also report their masked version [25]) and Fréchet Video Distance (FVD) [56]. We use Percentage of Correct Keypoints (PCK) [57] for the pose evalutation.

Implementation Details. To obtain a temporally consistent 3D mesh we combine OpenPose [36] with [14]. We used an NVIDIA Tesla V100 16GB RAM GPU to train our model. We use Adam optimizer [58] with $(\alpha_1, \alpha_2) = (0.5, 0.999)$ and a learning rate of $2\cdot 10^{-5}$ (Fig. 8 and Table 4).

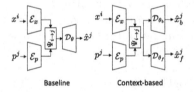

Fig. 7. Model ablation.

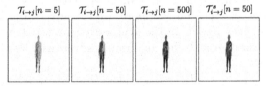

Fig. 8. Texture transfer vs. Symmetric texture transfer (occluded region: orange pixel).(Color figure online)

Table 1. Quality of the foreground estimation. Key. M: mask; S.: SSIM; P. PSNR; Euc: Euclidean; []: nearest neighbour value n.

Step.	Notation.	M-S.	M-P.
II (Euc.)	$\mathcal{T}_{i\to j}[500]$	.952	26.85
II	$\mathcal{T}_{i\to j}[500]$	.952	26.86
II, III	$\mathcal{T}^s_{i\to j}[50]$	.953	26.92
I, II, III	$\mathcal{T}^s_{i\to j}[50]$	.954	27.16

Table 2. Baseline ablation. Key. M: mask; S.: SSIM; P. PSNR; Mod. modality; BL: baseline; Hb: Huber.

Model	Mod.	S.	M-S.	P.	M-P.	FVD
BL ($\Psi^{lin}_{i\to j}$)	$\mathcal{M}^j_{2D}$	.534	.957	17.62	26.13	10.81
	$\mathcal{M}^j_{2D}$	.628	.964	18.39	27.73	7.51
BL ($\Psi^{conv}_{i\to j}$)	$\mathcal{T}_{i\to j}$	.680	.969	19.83	29.13	6.79
	$\mathcal{T}^s_{i\to j}$	.688	.970	19.85	29.12	6.57
GTNet (L_1)	$\mathcal{T}_{i\to j}$	.693	.977	20.26	31.81	6.81
GTNet (Hb)	$\mathcal{T}_{i\to j}$	.709	.976	20.63	31.70	6.44

Table 3. Sensitivity analysis of the warping factor with $T = 24$.

ζ	0	.1	.01	.001
SSIM	.624	**.635**	.623	.612
PSNR	18.35	**18.41**	18.17	18.19

Table 4. Synthesis performance using different model weight using $T = 8$.

	VDNet [1]			GTNet	
#layers	6 (3D)	6	18	6	6 (3D)
#params	112.74M	34.70M	77.20M	12.35M	99.20M
SSIM	.821	.698	.711	.709	**.823**
M-SSIM	.972	N/A	N/A	.976	**.981**

4.2 Ablation Studies

We provide a detailed evaluation of each component of the proposed pipeline. Unless otherwise stated, we use a 2D-ResNet$_6$ [59] for the ablation.

Texture Transfer. We show the result of the contribution of each step in the texture transfer:

- **Step II (Euclidean): F** computed with Euclidean pairwise distance.
- **Step II: F** computed with geodesic pairwise distance.
- **Step II + III:** Symmetric texture transfer.
- **Step I + II + III:** Symmetric texture transfer with temporal context.

Results from Table 1 show that the symmetric texture transfer helps to better estimate the foreground with only a kernel size of $n = 50$ instead of 500 without the symmetry. Adding the temporal context for the hashmap construction improves further. Figure 7 shows a challenging case of texture transfer between views with and without the body symmetry transfer.

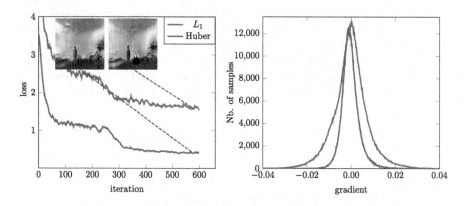

Fig. 9. Training curves analysis of GTNet.

Baseline Models. GTNet has a separate decoder for the foreground and the background. Therefore, we chose a generator with a single decoder as the baseline (see Fig. 6). GTNet is key to refine the texture transfer. To verify this we consider three variants of the input to the network: $\mathcal{M}_{2D}^j$, $\mathcal{T}_{i \to j}$, and $\mathcal{T}_{i \to j}^s$.

We propose two variants of $\Psi_{i \to j}$ to assess the feature approximation:

- **Linear:** $\Psi_{i \to j}^{\mathrm{lin}}(\epsilon^i, \pi^j) = \mathbf{W}_{ij}.\epsilon^i + \mathbf{W}_{jj}.\pi^j + b_j$ s.t $\mathbf{W}_{ij}, \mathbf{W}_{jj} \in \mathbb{R}^{m \times m}, b_j \in \mathbb{R}^m$.
- **Convolution:** $\Psi_{i \to j}^{\mathrm{conv}}(\epsilon^i, \pi^j) = \mathrm{conv}_{3 \times 3}(\epsilon^i \oplus \pi^j)$.

The operator $\Psi_{i \to j}$ estimates the feature vector of the target view. The linear version assumes a linearity between the input-view feature and the target-view modalities, whereas, the convolution applies a concatenation operation followed by a convolution operation which refers to a complex mapping (*i.e.* non-linear) between the inputs. Results from Table 2 suggest that better feature approximation leads to better view synthesis. A linear mapping cannot approximate well the target feature ϵ^j. The convolution is the default feature approximation for GTNet.

$\mathcal{M}_{2D}^j$ is the straightforward modality to use for the synthesis using 3D mesh. Table 2 shows that Baseline($\mathcal{M}_{2D}^j$) underperforms compared to Baseline($\mathcal{T}_{i \to j}$). This suggests that the texture transfer helps the network to refine the foreground. Having a better estimate (*i.e.* $\mathcal{T}_{i \to j}^s$) improves further. With the Baseline the network has to focus on both synthesizing the foreground and background. Using the context based approach in GTNet helps the model to focus on the background synthesis and to refine only the foreground. The other conclusion is the texture $\mathcal{T}_{i \to j}^s$ approximates better the foreground.

Hyperparameters. We analyse the model performance while validating the effect of the loss, warping factor and model weights.

Using a Huber reconstruction loss in GTNet(Huber) improves the quality of the synthesized videos (see Table 2). We investigate this further by plotting the training loss and the histogram of the gradient at the last convolutional kernel of the decoder of GTNet (see Fig. 9). For the gradient we noticed a significantly smaller variance, which we deem to be due to the non-smoothness of the L_1 loss around the origin. By analysing the output of the generator trained with these two losses, we observe that the generator trained with L_1 loss outputs black artifacts during the first epochs which may cause mode collapse [60].

Table 5. Models performance using a pose estimator [36].

Model	$\mathbf{L}_2$	PCK [57]		
		0.20	0.05	0.01
VDNet [1]	4.37	99.3	92.4	51.2
Baseline	4.06	99.4	**93.6**	55.3
GTNet	**3.95**	**99.5**	93.0	**57.6**

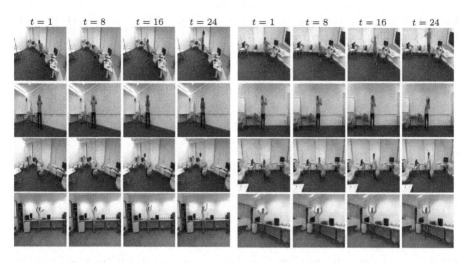

Fig. 10. Sample frames on novel-view synthesis. (left): input view video sequence x^i; (right): synthesized target view $\hat{x}^j$ using the proposed GTNet.

From Table 3 we note the improvement using the warping introduced in Eq. 3. This in fact helps the generator to only learn the residual from previous frame $\hat{x}^j_{t-1}$. We therefore keep $\zeta = .1$ as the default value for the warping function.

We report a good foreground synthesis even with a 2D-ResNet compared to VDNet. However, the network could not synthesize well the background. This is because without the temporal context the network will synthesize the background independently for each time step. With the 3D-ResNet we obtain better video synthesis compared to VDNet with many fewer trainable weights.

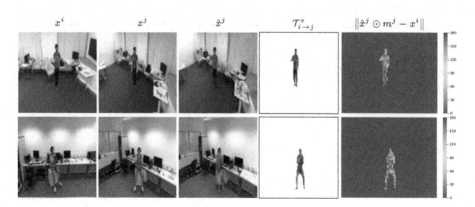

Fig. 11. Visualisation of the learned residual of $\mathcal{T}^s_{i \to j}$ using GTNet.

Table 6. Comparison between the proposed GTNet and VDNet [1] on NTU RGB+D. Key. ζ controlling factor (see Sect. 3.3).

Model	Modality	↑ SSIM	↑ M-SSIM	↑ PSNR	↑ M-PSNR	↓ FVD
VDNet [1]	s^j	.749	.964	20.78	28.27	7.35
	d^j	.794	.970	22.47	29.46	6.60
	$d^j + s^j$	.821	.972	23.18	29.70	5.78
GTNet($\zeta = 0$)	$\mathcal{M}_{2D}^j$	.703	.976	20.16	30.95	6.34
GTNet($\zeta = 0$)	$\mathcal{T}_{i \to j}$	.767	.979	22.03	31.98	5.62
GTNet($\zeta = 0$)	$\mathcal{T}_{i \to j} + \mathcal{S}^j$	.714	.978	20.44	31.90	6.42
GTNet($\zeta = 0$)	$\mathcal{T}_{i \to j} + d^j$	.778	.980	22.96	32.04	**4.32**
GTNet($\zeta = .1$)	$\mathcal{T}_{i \to j} + \mathcal{S}^j + d^j$	.787	.980	22.98	32.25	5.06
GTNet($\zeta = .1$)	$\mathcal{T}_{i \to j}^s + \mathcal{S}^j + d^j$	**.823**	**.981**	**23.81**	**32.50**	4.96

Comparison. Results from Table 6 are reported with 3D-ResNet$_6$. Overall, GTNet significantly improves over all the metrics compared to VDNet [1]. GTNet benefits from the depth d^j along with $\mathcal{T}_{i \to j}$. The model GTNet($\mathcal{T}_{i \to j}^s + \mathcal{S}^j + d^j$; $\zeta = .1$) produces superior quality results compared to VDNet.

$\mathcal{T}_{i \to j}$ is derived from the skeleton s^j. It is worth noting that GTNet($\mathcal{T}_{i \to j}$) is superior to VDNet(s^j) (see Table 6). The proposed GTNet produces temporally consistent videos (FVD scores). Table 5 reports the PCK scores of GTNet with the baseline and VDNet. The pose estimator estimates keypoints that are close to the ground-truth with GTNet.

Figure 11 shows the ability of GTNet in refining the textures. Figure 10 shows four examples of typical synthesis results using GTNet. The synthesized novel-view videos are sharper and we can clearly distinguish the movement of the subject. Figure 12 compares three examples of GTNet and VDNet. We can note that indeed the motion is clearly distinct with our model. Note also that thanks to $\mathcal{T}_{i \to j}^j$ the body texture is preserved across the views. In the example of the third row, we can see that GTNet is able to keep the movement of the hand with the object interaction (hat). Figure 13 shows a qualitative example of the pose estimation. The pose estimator is able to extract keypoints similar to the ones extracted from the ground-truth. This is because GTNet has better foreground synthesis (.981 M-SSIM, 32.50 M-PSNR) compared to VDNet (.972 M-SSIM, 29.70 M-PSNR).

x^j VDNet   GTNet

$t = 8$ $t = 16$ $t = 8$ $t = 16$ $t = 8$ $t = 16$

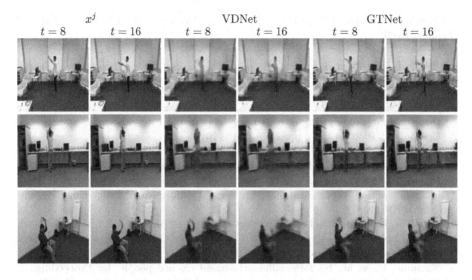

Fig. 12. Sample frames comparing VDNet and GTNet.

x^j GTNet   Baseline   VDNet

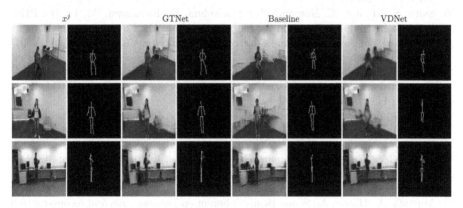

Fig. 13. Comparison of the estimated skeleton.

5 Conclusions

We presented a novel approach to synthesize actions as if they were recorded from a novel view by exploiting geometric and appearance information extracted from the real view. Our geometric approach transfers the textures of the visible parts of the human (foreground) from images to a 3D mesh and re-projects them onto the novel, 2D view. Then, we designed a new encoder-decoder network architecture that learns how to synthesize the occluded parts of the foreground and that tackles the foreground and background tasks separately to achieve high synthesis fidelity. We obtain state-of-the-art synthesis results on the NTU RGB+D dataset.

Acknowledgements. This project acknowledges the use of the ESPRC funded Tier 2 facility, JADE.

References

1. Lakhal, M.I., Lanz, O., Cavallaro, A.: View-LSTM: novel-view video synthesis through view decomposition. In: Proceedings of the International Conference on Computer Vision (ICCV), pp. 7576–7586 (2019)
2. Bertel, T., Campbell, N.D.F., Richardt, C.: MegaParallax: casual 360° panoramas with motion parallax. IEEE Trans. Vis. Comput. Graph. **25**, 1828–1835 (2019)
3. Li, J., Wong, Y., Zhao, Q., Kankanhalli, M.: Unsupervised learning of view-invariant action representations. In: Neural Information Processing Systems (NeurIPS) (2018)
4. Rematas, K., Kemelmacher-Shlizerman, I., Curless, B., Seitz, S.: Soccer on your tabletop. In: Proceedings of the IEEE Conference on Computer Vision and Pattern Recognition (CVPR), pp. 4738–4747 (2018)
5. Natsume, R., et al.: SiCloPe: silhouette-based clothed people. In: Proceedings of the IEEE Conference on Computer Vision and Pattern Recognition (CVPR), pp. 4475–4485 (2019)
6. Saito, S., Huang, Z., Natsume, R., Morishima, S., Kanazawa, A., Li, H.: PIFu: Pixel-aligned implicit function for high-resolution clothed human digitization. In: Proceedings of the International Conference on Computer Vision (ICCV), pp. 2304–2314 (2019)
7. Lombardi, S., Simon, T., Saragih, J., Schwartz, G., Lehrmann, A., Sheikh, Y.: Neural volumes: learning dynamic renderable volumes from images. ACM Trans. Graph. (TOG) **38**, (2019)
8. Thies, J., Zollhöfer, M., Theobalt, C., Stamminger, M., Nießner, M.: Image-guided neural object rendering. In: Proceedings of the International Conference on Learning Representations (ICLR) (2020)
9. Weng, C.Y., Curless, B., Kemelmacher-Shlizerman, I.: Photo Wake-Up: 3D character animation from a single photo. In: Proceedings of the IEEE Conference on Computer Vision and Pattern Recognition (CVPR), pp. 5901–5910 (2019)
10. Mustafa, A., Hilton, A.: Semantically coherent co-segmentation and reconstruction of dynamic scenes. In: Proceedings of the IEEE Conference on Computer Vision and Pattern Recognition (CVPR), pp. 5583–5592 (2017)
11. Bansal, A., Vo, M., Sheikh, Y., Ramanan, D., Narasimhan, S.: 4D visualization of dynamic events from unconstrained multi-view videos. In: Proceedings of the IEEE Conference on Computer Vision and Pattern Recognition (CVPR), pp. 5365–5374 (2020)
12. Bogo, F., Kanazawa, A., Lassner, C., Gehler, P., Romero, J., Black, M.J.: Keep It SMPL: automatic estimation of 3D human pose and shape from a single image. In: Proceedings of the European Conference on Computer Vision (ECCV), pp. 561–578 (2016)
13. Kanazawa, A., Black, M.J., Jacobs, D.W., Malik, J.: End-to-end recovery of human shape and pose. In: Proceedings of the IEEE Conference on Computer Vision and Pattern Recognition (CVPR), pp. 7122–7131 (2018)
14. Kanazawa, A., Zhang, J.Y., Felsen, P., Malik, J.: Learning 3D human dynamics from video. In: Proceedings of the IEEE Conference on Computer Vision and Pattern Recognition (CVPR), pp. 5607–5616 (2019)

15. Kolotouros, N., Pavlakos, G., Black, M.J., Daniilidis, K.: Learning to reconstruct 3D human pose and shape via model-fitting in the loop. In: Proceedings of the International Conference on Computer Vision (ICCV), pp. 2252–2261 (2019)
16. Pavlakos, G., Kolotouros, N., Daniilidis, K.: TexturePose: supervising human mesh estimation with texture consistency. In: Proceedings of the International Conference on Computer Vision (ICCV), pp. 803–812 (2019)
17. Loper, M., Mahmood, N., Romero, J., Pons-Moll, G., Black, M.J.: SMPL: a skinned multi-person linear model. ACM Trans. Graph. (TOG) **34**, 248:1–248:16 (2015)
18. Pishchulin, L., Jain, A., Wojek, C., Andriluka, M., Thormählen, T., Schiele, B.: Learning people detection models from few training samples. In: Proceedings of the IEEE Conference on Computer Vision and Pattern Recognition (CVPR), pp. 1473–1480 (2011)
19. Xu, F., et al.: Video-based characters: creating new human performances from a multi-view video database. ACM Trans. Graph. (TOG) **30**, 32:1–32:10 (2011)
20. Siarohin, A., Lathuillère, S., Tulyakov, S., Ricci, E., Sebe, N.: first order motion model for image animation. In: Neural Information Processing Systems (NeurIPS) (2019)
21. Chen, X., Song, J., Hilliges, O.: Monocular neural image based rendering with continuous view control. In: Proceedings of the International Conference on Computer Vision (ICCV), pp. 4089–4099 (2019)
22. Bhatnagar, B.L., Tiwari, G., Theobalt, C., Pons-Moll, G.: Multi-garment net: learning to dress 3D people from images. In: Proceedings of the International Conference on Computer Vision (ICCV), pp. 5419–5429 (2019)
23. Alldieck, T., Magnor, M., Bhatnagar, B.L., Theobalt, C., Pons-Moll, G.: Learning to reconstruct people in clothing from a single RGB camera. In: Proceedings of the IEEE Conference on Computer Vision and Pattern Recognition (CVPR), pp. 1175–1186 (2019)
24. Alldieck, T., Magnor, M., Xu, W., Theobalt, C., Pons-Moll, G.: Video based reconstruction of 3D people models. In: Proceedings of the IEEE Conference on Computer Vision and Pattern Recognition (CVPR), pp. 8387–8397 (2018)
25. Ma, L., Jia, X., Sun, Q., Schiele, B., Tuytelaars, T., Van Gool, L.: Pose guided person image generation. In: Neural Information Processing Systems (NeurIPS) (2017)
26. Zhao, B., Wu, X., Cheng, Z.Q., Liu, H., Jie, Z., Feng, J.: Multi-view image generation from a single-view. In: Proceedings of the ACM International Conference on Multimedia (ACM-MM), pp. 383–391 (2018)
27. Zanfir, M., Oneata, E., Popa, A.I., Zanfir, A., Sminchisescu, C.: Human synthesis and scene compositing. In: Proceedings of the National Conference on Artificial Intelligence (AAAI), pp. 12749–12756 (2020)
28. Liu, W., Piao, Z., Jie, M., Luo, W., Ma, L., Gao, S.: Liquid warping GAN: a unified framework for human motion imitation, appearance transfer and novel view synthesis. In: Proceedings of the International Conference on Computer Vision (ICCV), pp. 5903–5912 (2019)
29. Li, Y., Huang, C., Loy, C.C.: Dense intrinsic appearance flow for human pose transfer. In: Proceedings of the IEEE Conference on Computer Vision and Pattern Recognition (CVPR), pp. 3688–3697 (2019)
30. Saito, M., Matsumoto, E., Saito, S.: Temporal generative adversarial nets with singular value clipping. In: Proceedings of the International Conference on Computer Vision (ICCV) (2017)

31. Tulyakov, S., Liu, M.Y., Yang, X., Kautz, J.: MoCoGAN: decomposing motion and content for video generation. In: Proceedings of the IEEE Conference on Computer Vision and Pattern Recognition (CVPR), pp. 1526–1535 (2018)

32. Vondrick, C., Pirsiavash, H., Torralba, A.: Generating videos with scene dynamics. In: Neural Information Processing Systems (NeurIPS) (2016)

33. Yang, C., Wang, Z., Zhu, X., Huang, C., Shi, J., Lin, D.: Pose guided human video generation. In: Proceedings of the European Conference on Computer Vision (ECCV), pp. 204–219 (2018)

34. Wang, T.C., Liu, M.Y., Tao, A., Liu, G., Kautz, J., Catanzaro, B.: Few-shot video-to-video synthesis. In: Neural Information Processing Systems (NeurIPS) (2019)

35. Li, Y., Fang, C., Yang, J., Wang, Z., Lu, X., Yang, M.H.: Flow-grounded spatial-temporal video prediction from still images. In: Proceedings of the European Conference on Computer Vision (ECCV), pp. 609–625 (2018)

36. Raaj, Y., Idrees, H., Hidalgo, G., Sheikh, Y.: Efficient online multi-person 2D pose tracking with recurrent spatio-temporal affinity fields. In: Proceedings of the IEEE Conference on Computer Vision and Pattern Recognition (CVPR), pp. 4615–4623 (2019)

37. Yang, L., Song, Q., Wang, Z., Jiang, M.: Parsing r-cnn for instance-level human analysis. In: Proceedings of the IEEE Conference on Computer Vision and Pattern Recognition (CVPR), pp. 364–373 (2019)

38. Siarohin, A., Sangineto, E., Lathuilière, S., Sebe, N.: Deformable GANs for pose-based human image generation. In: Proceedings of the IEEE Conference on Computer Vision and Pattern Recognition (CVPR), pp. 3408–3416 (2018)

39. Pumarola, A., Agudo, A., Sanfeliu, A., Moreno-Noguer, F.: Unsupervised person image synthesis in arbitrary poses. In: Proceedings of the IEEE Conference on Computer Vision and Pattern Recognition (CVPR), pp. 8620–8628 (2018)

40. Liqian, M., Qianru, S., Stamatios, G., Luc, V.G., Bernt, S., Mario, F.: Disentangled Person Image Generation. In: Proceedings of the IEEE Conference on Computer Vision and Pattern Recognition (CVPR), pp. 99–108 (2018)

41. Chan, C., Ginosar, S., Zhou, T., Efros, A.A.: Everybody dance now. In: Proceedings of the International Conference on Computer Vision (ICCV), pp. 5932–5941 (2019)

42. Esser, P., Sutter, E., Ommer, B.: A variational u-net for conditional appearance and shape generation. In: Proceedings of the IEEE Conference on Computer Vision and Pattern Recognition (CVPR), pp. 8857–8866 (2018)

43. Balakrishnan, G., Zhao, A., Dalca, A.V., Durand, F., Guttag, J.: Synthesizing images of humans in unseen poses. In: Proceedings of the IEEE Conference on Computer Vision and Pattern Recognition (CVPR), pp. 8340–8348 (2018)

44. Qian, X., et al.: Pose-normalized image generation for person re-identification. In: Proceedings of the European Conference on Computer Vision (ECCV), pp. 661–678 (2018)

45. Raj, A., Sangkloy, P., Chang, H., Hays, J., Ceylan, D., Lu, J.: SwapNet: image based garment transfer. In: Proceedings of the European Conference on Computer Vision (ECCV), pp. 679–695 (2018)

46. Dong, H., Liang, X., Gong, K., Lai, H., Zhu, J., Yin, J.: Soft-gated warping-GAN for pose-guided person image synthesis. In: Neural Information Processing Systems (NeurIPS) (2018)

47. Alp Güler, R., Neverova, N., Kokkinos, I.: DensePose: dense human pose estimation in the wild. In: Proceedings of the IEEE Conference on Computer Vision and Pattern Recognition (CVPR), pp. 7297–7306 (2018)

48. Neverova, N., Alp Guler, R., Kokkinos, I.: Dense pose transfer. In: Proceedings of the European Conference on Computer Vision (ECCV), pp. 128–143 (2018)

49. Shahroudy, A., Liu, J., Ng, T.T., Wang, G.: NTU RGB+D: a large scale dataset for 3d human activity analysis. In: Proceedings of the IEEE Conference on Computer Vision and Pattern Recognition (CVPR), pp. 1010–1019 (2016)
50. Kato, H., Ushiku, Y., Harada, T.: Neural 3D mesh renderer. In: Proceedings of the IEEE Conference on Computer Vision and Pattern Recognition (CVPR), pp. 3907–3916 (2018)
51. Surazhsky, V., Surazhsky, T., Kirsanov, D., Gortler, S.J., Hoppe, H.: Fast exact and approximate geodesics on meshes. ACM Trans. Graph. (TOG) 24, 553–560 (2005)
52. Huber, P.J.: Robust estimation of a location parameter. Ann. Math. Stat. **35**, 73–101 (1964)
53. Johnson, J., Alahi, A., Fei-Fei, L.: Perceptual losses for real-time style transfer and super-resolution. In: Proceedings of the European Conference on Computer Vision (ECCV), pp. 694–711 (2016)
54. Goodfellow, I., et al.: Generative adversarial nets. In: Neural Information Processing Systems (NeurIPS), pp. 2672–2680 (2014)
55. Wang, Z., Bovik, A.C., Sheikh, H.R., Simoncelli, E.P.: Image quality assessment: from error visibility to structural similarity. IEEE Trans. Image Process. **13**, 600–612 (2004)
56. Unterthiner, T., van Steenkiste, S., Kurach, K., Marinier, R., Michalski, M., Gelly, S.: FVD: a new metric for video generation. In: Proceedings of the International Conference on Learning Representations (ICLR) Workshops (2019)
57. Yang, Y., Ramanan, D.: Articulated human detection with flexible mixtures of parts. IEEE Trans. Pattern Anal. Mach. Intell. (PAMI) **35**, 2878–2890 (2013)
58. Kingma, D.P., Ba, J.: Adam: a method for stochastic optimization. In: Proceedings of the International Conference on Learning Representations (ICLR) (2015)
59. Zhu, J.Y., Park, T., Isola, P., Efros, A.A.: Unpaired image-to-image translation using cycle-consistent adversarial networks. In: Proceedings of the International Conference on Computer Vision (ICCV), pp. 2242–2251 (2017)
60. Che, T., Li, Y., Jacob, A.P., Bengio, Y., Li, W.: Mode regularized generative adversarial networks. In: Proceedings of the International Conference on Learning Representations (ICLR) (2017)

Augmentation Network for Generalised Zero-Shot Learning

Rafael Felix[1,2,3](✉) ⓘ, Michele Sasdelli[1,2,3] ⓘ, Ian Reid[1,2,3] ⓘ,
and Gustavo Carneiro[1,2,3] ⓘ

[1] The University of Adelaide, Adelaide, Australia
{rafael.felixalves,michele.sasdelli,ian.reid,
gustavo.carneiro}@adelaide.edu.au
[2] Australian Institute for Machine Learning (AIML), Adelaide, Australia
[3] Australian Centre for Robotic Vision (ACRV), Brisbane, Australia

Abstract. Generalised zero-shot learning (GZSL) is defined by a training process containing a set of visual samples from seen classes and a set of semantic samples from seen and unseen classes, while the testing process consists of the classification of visual samples from the seen and the unseen classes. Current approaches are based on inference processes that rely on the result of a single modality classifier (visual, semantic, or latent joint space) that balances the classification between the seen and unseen classes using gating mechanisms. There are a couple of problems with such approaches: 1) multi-modal classifiers are known to generally be more accurate than single modality classifiers, and 2) gating mechanisms rely on a complex one-class training of an external domain classifier that modulates the seen and unseen classifiers. In this paper, we mitigate these issues by proposing a novel GZSL method – augmentation network that tackles multi-modal and multi-domain inference for generalised zero-shot learning (AN-GZSL). The multi-modal inference combines visual and semantic classification and automatically balances the seen and unseen classification using temperature calibration, without requiring any gating mechanisms or external domain classifiers. Experiments show that our method produces the new state-of-the-art GZSL results for fine-grained benchmark data sets CUB and FLO and for the large-scale data set ImageNet. We also obtain competitive results for coarse-grained data sets SUN and AWA. We show an ablation study that justifies each stage of the proposed AN-GZSL.

Keywords: Generalised zero-shot learning · Multi-modal inference · Multi-domain inference

---

Electronic supplementary material The online version of this chapter (https://doi.org/10.1007/978-3-030-69538-5_27) contains supplementary material, which is available to authorized users.

H. Ishikawa et al. (Eds.): ACCV 2020, LNCS 12625, pp. 442–458, 2021.
https://doi.org/10.1007/978-3-030-69538-5_27

1   Introduction

As computer vision systems start to be deployed in unstructured environments, they must have the ability to recognise not only the visual classes used during the training process (i.e., the seen classes) but also classes that are not available during training (i.e., unseen classes). The importance of such ability lies in the impracticality of collecting visual samples from all possible classes that will be shown to the system. In this context, approaches categorised as Generalised Zero-Shot Learning (GZSL) [1–3] play an important role due to their ability to classify visual samples from seen and unseen classes. In general, the training of GZSL methods involves the use of visual samples from seen classes and semantic samples (e.g., textual definition) from seen and unseen classes. The rationale behind the use of semantic samples is that they are readily available from various sources, such as Wikipedia, English dictionary [4], or manually annotated attributes [5]. Such training setup can potentially mitigate the issue of collecting visual samples from all possible unseen classes, and the success of GZSL lies in the effective transferring of knowledge between the semantic and visual modalities.

In recent years, we note three different approaches for solving GZSL. One type focuses on training a mapping function from the visual to the semantic space [6], and then inference relies on classification in the semantic space. Another type is based on training a conditional generative model for visual samples. The generated visual samples of unseen classes complement visual samples from the seen classes for a visual classifier [2, 7–14]. Another type relies on an external domain classifier (seen vs unseen) trained with the visual samples from the seen classes via a one-class learning problem. The domain classification is combined with the classification models in each domain [15–19].

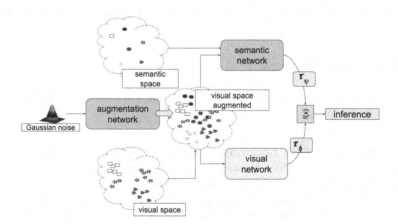

Fig. 1. Our proposed model Augmentation Network for multi-modal and multi-domain Generalised Zero-Shot Learning (AN-GZSL). AN-GZSL is composed of the augmentation network to generates visual samples, the visual and the semantic networks, a classification calibration (represented by τ_ψ and τ_ϕ in (2)) that enables multi-domain classification, and the multi-modal classification that combines the visual and semantic modules.

The GZSL methods above have a couple of issues: 1) even though the training process involves some sort of interaction between the visual and semantic modalities, the inference usually does not rely on a truly multi-modal classification (i.e., where both modalities are jointly used in the process) [2,7,13,15] , which can be considered a weakness given the strong evidence that multi-modal inference can improve classification accuracy [15,19,20]; and 2) the one-class training of external domain classifiers that modulate the seen and unseen classification [15–19] is not a trivial process given the similarity between the seen and unseen class domains. In fact, it can be argued that samples from these domains are drawn from the same distribution, making it challenging to distinguish between them.

In this paper, we introduce the Augmentation Network for multi-modal and multi-domain Generalised Zero-Shot Learning (AN-GZSL) depicted in Fig. 1. The approach introduces a novel loss function that combines the training of three networks: augmentation network, visual network, and semantic network. **The proposed AN-GZSL represents the first method to perform inference with multiple modalities without the use of external domain classifiers for modulating the inference between seen and unseen classes.** The augmentation network is a generative model for visual samples conditioned on the semantic data, the generated visual samples are then used by the visual network (a visual classifier) and by the semantic network (a semantic classifier). The visual and semantic classifiers are then temperature calibrated to enable a modulation-free classification, which alleviates the burden of an external domain classifier. Then, the two calibrated classifiers are combined in a multi-modal classification. We show that the proposed approach produces state-of-the-art GZSL results on the fine-grained benchmark data sets CUB [3,21] and FLO [22] and on the large-scale data set ImageNet [23,24]. We also achieve competitive results for the coarse-grained data sets SUN [3] and AWA [5]. We finally show an ablation study that tests the importance of each component of the proposed model.

2   Literature Review

In this section we describe relevant literature that contextualises and motivates the proposed approach.

Generalised Zero-Shot Learning (GZSL). In recent years, we have observed a growing interest in GZSL. A catalyst for such interest was the paper by Xian et al. [3] that formalises the GZSL problem. Their work introduces a solid experimental setup and a robust evaluation metric based on the harmonic mean between the classification accuracy results of the seen and the unseen visual classes. Recently proposed GZSL methods can be roughly divided into three categories: **semantic attribute prediction, visual data augmentation,** and **domain balancing. Semantic attribute prediction** methods [5,25,26] tackle GZSL by training a regressor that maps visual samples from seen classes to their respective semantic samples. Hence, given a test visual sample (from a seen or unseen class), the regressor maps it into the semantic space, which is then used in a nearest neighbour semantic classification process. The main assumption of this approach is that the mapping from visual to semantic spaces learned from the seen class domain can be transferred to the unseen class domain. Unfortunately, such assumption is unwarranted, and a typical issue of this approach is that test visual samples from seen classes are classified correctly and samples from unseen classes are often incorrectly classified into one of the seen classes – this is referred to as a bias toward the seen classes [3]. Recent research exploring matching functions between visual and semantic samples can address the issue mentioned above, but they still show biased classification toward the seen classes [25].

Visual data augmentation relies on a generative model trained to produce visual samples from the corresponding semantic samples [2,7–10]. Such model allows the generation of visual samples for the unseen classes, which are then used in the modelling of a visual classifier that is trained with real visual samples from seen classes and generated visual samples from unseen classes. Methods based on this approach are effective because they solve, to a certain extent, the bias toward the seen classes [11–14]. Recently, the training process of this approach has been extended, forcing generated visual samples to regress to the corresponding semantic samples, in a multi-modal cycle consistent training [2, 14]. This extension represents the first attempt at a multi-modal training, which allowed further improvements in GZSL results. However, none of the methods above relies on a multi-modal inference process. It is interesting to note that the inference process of **semantic attribute prediction** focuses exclusively on the semantic space, while **visual data augmentation** works solely on the visual space. A multi-modal inference process that effectively merges the two spaces has yet to be proposed.

Domain balancing methods solve the bias toward the seen classes issue with a gating mechanism that modulates the classification of seen and unseen classes [15–19]. In particular, these methods consist of a (generally visual) classifier trained for the seen classes, a (usually semantic) classifier trained for the unseen classes, and a domain classifier for the modulation process [15,17,19].

Even though domain balancing approaches hold outstanding results [15,19], they have the following challenges: 1) the training of multiple domain-specific classifiers, and 2) the non-trivial training of a gating mechanism that needs to classify between seen and unseen classes using a one-class classification process, which is a hard task considering that these classes arguably come from the same data distribution. In this paper, we also rely on visual data augmentation and domain balancing, but differently from the approaches above, our multi-modal classification relies on visual and semantic classifiers trained on all seen and unseen classes (i.e., they are not domain-specific). Furthermore, the balancing between seen and unseen domains is achieved with a classification calibration approach that does not need any gating mechanism.

3   Method

In the next sub-sections, we first formulate the GZSL problem. Then, we introduce our proposed augmentation network for multi-modal and multi-domain generalised zero-shot learning (AN-GZSL), with the explanation of the inference, architecture and training processes.

3.1   Problem Formulation

To formulate the GZSL problem [1,3], we first define the visual data set $\mathcal{D} = \{(\mathbf{x}_i, y_i)\}_{i=1}^{N}$, where $\mathbf{x} \in \mathcal{X} \subseteq \mathbb{R}^K$ denotes a visual sample (acquired from the second to last layer of a pre-trained deep residual nets [27]), and $y \in \mathcal{Y} = \{1, ..., C\}$ denotes the visual class, which can also be described with a one-hot vector $\mathbf{h} \in \{0, 1\}^C$, where the y-th position in $\mathbf{h}$ is assigned to 1, and all the others 0. The visual data set has N samples, denoting the number of images. We also need to define the semantic data set $\mathcal{R} = \{\mathbf{a}_y\}_{y \in \mathcal{Y}}$, which associates visual classes with semantic samples, where $\mathbf{a}_y \in \mathcal{A} \subseteq \mathbb{R}^L$ represents a semantic feature (e.g., *word2vec* features [3]). The semantic data set has as many elements as the number of classes. The set $\mathcal{Y}$ is split into the seen subset $\mathcal{Y}^S = \{1, ..., S\}$, and the unseen subset $\mathcal{Y}^U = \{(S+1), ..., (S+U)\}$. Therefore, $C = S + U$, with $\mathcal{Y} = \mathcal{Y}^S \cup \mathcal{Y}^U$, $\mathcal{Y}^S \cap \mathcal{Y}^U = \emptyset$. Furthermore, $\mathcal{D}$ is also divided into mutually exclusive training and testing visual subsets $\mathcal{D}^{Tr}$ and $\mathcal{D}^{Te}$, respectively, where $\mathcal{D}^{Tr}$ contains a subset of the visual samples belonging to the seen classes, and $\mathcal{D}^{Te}$ has the visual samples from the seen classes held out from training and all samples from the unseen classes. The training data set comprises the semantic data set $\mathcal{R}$ and the training visual subset $\mathcal{D}^{Tr}$, while the testing data set consists of the testing visual subset $\mathcal{D}^{Te}$ and the same semantic data set $\mathcal{R}$.

3.2   AN-GZSL Calibrated Inference

The inference procedure consists of estimating the class label of a test visual sample $\mathbf{x}$ that optimises

$$f(y|\mathbf{x}, \mathcal{R}) = \sigma(\phi(y|\mathbf{x}), \tau_\phi) + \sigma(\psi(y|\mathbf{x}, \mathcal{R}), \tau_\psi), \tag{1}$$

where $f(.)$ denotes the classification function, $\phi(.)$ and $\psi(.)$ represent the visual network (defined in Sect. 3.5) and the semantic network (Sect. 3.4) that return a logit, and $\sigma(.)$ represents the softmax activation function with temperature calibration [28], defined by

$$\sigma(l_y, \tau) = \frac{e^{(l_y/\tau)}}{\sum_{c=1}^{C} e^{(l_c/\tau)}}, \tag{2}$$

where the logit $l_y \in \mathbb{R}$ represents the yth output of a network (i.e., the visual or the semantic), and the temperature scaling τ represents a calibrating factor.

The multi-modal inference in (1) consists of a sum of the results from the visual and semantic classifiers, where the final classification is achieved by

$$y^* = \operatorname*{argmax}_{y \in \mathcal{Y}} f(y|\mathbf{x}, \mathcal{R}). \tag{3}$$

The GZSL inference in (3) balances the seen and unseen classes with a confidence calibrated by the temperature scaling, which is a much simpler strategy than to previously used gating mechanisms [15,18,19] that have to deal with complicated one-class domain classification problems. Furthermore, (3) creates a simple multi-modal inference without any hyper-parameter tuning to combine the classifiers.

3.3 Augmentation Network

The augmentation network relies on a generative model [13] trained to produce visual samples conditioned on their semantic samples. This model allows to generate visual samples for the unseen classes that together with real visual samples from the seen classes are used to train a classifier [2,7–14]. This approach has been recently extended with a cycle consistency loss that regularises the training process [2]. The augmentation network is optimised with a Wasserstein generative adversarial network (WGAN) [29] loss and cycle-consistent loss [2], defined by

$$\ell_{AN} = \ell_{WGAN} + \ell_{CYC}, \tag{4}$$

where ℓ_{WGAN} represents the WGAN loss [29] that optimises a conditional generator network $g(.)$ and discriminator network $d(.)$. The loss ℓ_{WGAN} is defined by

$$\ell_{WGAN} = \mathbb{E}_{(\mathbf{x},\mathbf{a}) \sim \mathbb{P}_s^{x,a}}[d(\mathbf{x}, \mathbf{a}; \theta_d)] - \mathbb{E}_{(\tilde{\mathbf{x}},\mathbf{a}) \sim \mathbb{P}_g^{x,a}}[d(\tilde{\mathbf{x}}, \mathbf{a}; \theta_d)]$$
$$- \kappa \mathbb{E}_{(\hat{\mathbf{x}},\mathbf{a}) \sim \mathbb{P}_\alpha^{x,a}}[(\|\nabla_{\hat{\mathbf{x}}} d(\hat{\mathbf{x}}, \mathbf{a}; \theta_d)\|_2 - 1)^2], \tag{5}$$

where $\mathbb{E}[.]$ represents the expected value operator. The joint distribution of visual and semantic samples from the seen classes is given by $\mathbb{P}_s^{x,a}$, and $\mathbb{P}_g^{x,a}$ represents the joint distribution of semantic and visual samples produced by the augmented network using the generator network, as follows: $\tilde{\mathbf{x}} \sim g(\mathbf{a}, \mathbf{z}; \theta_g)$, where $\mathbf{z} \sim \mathcal{N}(0, \mathbf{I})$. The coefficient κ in (5) weights the contribution of the third term of the loss, and the joint distribution of the semantic and visual samples produced by $\hat{\mathbf{x}} \sim \alpha \mathbf{x} + (1-\alpha)\tilde{\mathbf{x}}$ with $\alpha \sim \mathcal{U}(0,1)$ (i.e., uniform distribution) is given by $\mathbb{P}_\alpha^{x,a}$. In this network, the generator receives a semantic sample $\mathbf{a}$ and a noise vector $\mathbf{z} \sim \mathcal{N}(0, \mathbf{I})$ to generate visual samples, $\nabla_{\hat{\mathbf{x}}}$ represents the gradient penalty [29]. Then, the discriminator network aims to differentiate the generated from the real visual samples [2]. The loss ℓ_{CYC} provides a cycle-consistent training regularisation which guarantees that generated visual samples can reconstruct the corresponding semantic samples. The loss ℓ_{CYC} is defined by

$$\ell_{CYC} = \mathbb{E}_{\mathbf{a} \sim \mathbb{P}_s^a, \mathbf{z} \sim \mathcal{N}(0,\mathbf{I})} \left[\|\mathbf{a} - r(g(\mathbf{a}, \mathbf{z}; \theta_g); \theta_r)\|_2^2 \right]$$
$$+ \mathbb{E}_{\mathbf{a} \sim \mathbb{P}_u^a, \mathbf{z} \sim \mathcal{N}(0,\mathbf{I})} \left[\|\mathbf{a} - r(g(\mathbf{a}, \mathbf{z}; \theta_g); \theta_r)\|_2^2 \right], \tag{6}$$

where the function $r(.)$ represents a regressor network parameterised by θ_r that estimates the original semantic samples from the visual samples generated by $g(.)$, the latent variable $\mathbf{z}$ represents Gaussian noise, and the distributions of the semantic samples of seen and unseen domains are represented by $\mathbb{P}_s^a$ and $\mathbb{P}_u^a$. In contrast to previous approaches [2, 7–14], our proposed augmentation network feeds the visual *and* semantic networks with generated visual samples from both domains – this allows the visual and semantic classifiers to jointly learn an effective discriminating space for *all seen and unseen classes*.

3.4 Semantic Network

The semantic network consists of a bilinear neural network, novel in this application, which extends the ranking loss proposed by Akata et al. [25]. We define the semantic network as $\psi(y|\mathbf{x}, \mathcal{R}) = \mathbf{x}^T \theta_\psi \mathbf{a}_y$, represented by a bi-linear model parameterised by $\theta_\psi \in \mathbb{R}^{K \times L}$, with $\mathbf{a}_y \in \mathcal{R}$ and $\mathbf{x}$ being either a real sample from a seen class or a generated sample from an unseen class. *This approach is the first to use data augmentation to train a semantic classifier, when compared to the one in [25]*. For training we optimise the semantic loss loss, defined by

$$\ell_{SN} = \sum_{i=1}^{M} \sum_{c=1}^{C} \lambda(\mathbf{x}_i, \theta_\psi, \mathbf{a}_{y_i}, \mathbf{h}_i) \Big[h_{i,c} + \mathbf{x}_i^T \theta_\psi \mathbf{a}_{y_i} - \mathbf{x}_i^T \theta_\psi \mathbf{a}_c \Big]_+, \tag{7}$$

where $[.]_+$ represents the hinge loss, $\mathbf{a}_{y_i}$ denotes the semantic vector associated with the class y_i of the ith training sample, $h_{i,c}$ represents the cth position of the one-hot vector for the ith training sample $\mathbf{h}_i$, and M is the size of the training set (including the generated visual features), and $\mathbf{a}_c$ is a semantic vector associated with a class. In (7), the term inside of the hinge loss consists of a compatibility bi-linear loss,

$$\beta(\mathbf{x}_i, \theta_\psi, \mathbf{a}_c, \mathbf{a}_{y_i}, h_{i,c}) = h_{i,c} + \mathbf{x}_i^T \theta_\psi \mathbf{a}_{y_i} - \mathbf{x}_i^T \theta_\psi \mathbf{a}_c, \tag{8}$$

and $\lambda(.)$ represents a ranking regularization, defined by

$$\lambda(\mathbf{x}_i, \theta_\psi, \mathbf{a}_{y_i}, \mathbf{h}_i) = \left(\sum_{c=1}^{C} \mathbb{1}\Big(\beta(\mathbf{x}_i, \theta_\psi, \mathbf{a}_c, \mathbf{a}_{y_i}, h_{i,c}) \Big) \right)^{-1}, \tag{9}$$

where $\mathbb{1}(.)$ represents a Heaviside step function, with the divisor computing the ranking of the transformation according to the semantic data set.

The optimisation of (7) forces $\psi(y|\mathbf{x}, \mathcal{R})$ to be higher when $\mathbf{x}$ and $\mathbf{a}_y$ match correctly. This result is then calibrated by (2) to enable an effective multi-domain classification.

3.5 Visual Network

The visual network is a fully connected neural network represented by $\phi(y|\mathbf{x})$, parameterised by θ_ϕ, where $\mathbf{x}$ can be a real sample from a seen class or a generated sample from an unseen class. The network is trained with the usual cross-entropy loss defined by ℓ_{VN}. Similarly to the semantic classifier, this visual classifier is also calibrated with (2) for the multi-domain classification.

3.6   AN-GZSL Training

The loss function for our proposed AN-GZSL model is defined by

$$\ell_{AN-GZSL} = \ell_{AN} + \ell_{VN} + \ell_{SN}, \tag{10}$$

which is minimised to estimate the parameters $\theta_g, \theta_d, \theta_r, \theta_\phi, \theta_\psi$. For training, we use the visual samples produced by the augmentation network as input to the proposed visual and semantic networks. This approach not only augments the number of samples from the seen classes, but it also generates samples from the unseen classes. In practice, we perform an alternating training where we first optimise θ_g, θ_d and θ_r, then we optimise θ_ψ and θ_ϕ. Empirically, we have observed that the augmentation network tends to generate random samples at early stages of training [30]. Hence, the alternating strategy provides stronger gradients signal for the optimisation of θ_ψ and θ_ϕ, at late stages. After all the optimisation of (10) are completed, the temperatures (τ_ϕ and τ_ψ in Eq. 1) are quickly estimated by grid-search using the logits of a validation set held out from training [28].

4   Experiments

In this section, we describe the benchmark data sets, evaluation criteria and the setup adopted for the experiments. Then, we present a set of ablation studies and the results of the proposed method, which are compared with the state of the art (SOTA).

4.1   Data Sets

We assess the proposed method on publicly available benchmark GZSL data sets. More specifically, we perform experiments on CUB-200-2011 [3,21], FLO [22], SUN [3], and AWA [3,5] with the GZSL experimental setup described by Xian et al. [3]. We also perform GZSL experiments on ImageNet [23,24]. The data sets CUB and FLO are generally regarded as fine-grained, while AWA and SUN are coarse-grained, and ImageNet is large-scale[1].

For the semantic features, we use the 1024-dimensional vector produced by CNN-RNN [31] for CUB-200-2011 [3] and FLO [22]. These semantic features are extracted from a set of textual description of 10 sentences per image. To define a unique semantic sample per-class, the semantic features of all images belonging to each class are averaged [3]. For the SUN and AWA data sets, we use manually annotated semantic features (attributes) containing 102 and 85 dimensions, respectively [3]. For the visual samples, we follow the protocol by Xian et al. [3], where the features are represented by the activation of the 2048-dimensional top pooling layer of ResNet-101 [27], obtained for the image. To guarantee reproducible and consistent results, we follow the data set split proposed by Xian et al. [3], which prevents the model to violate the zero-shot conditions.

---

[1] See supplementary material for more information on data sets.

For the ImageNet experiment [23], there can be several testing splits for GZSL (e.g., 2-hop, 3-hop), which rely on the training set of 1K classes and testing set on 22K classes. However, recent studies reported that such splits show overlap between seen and unseen classes for GZSL [2]. To demonstrate the robustness of the proposed approach to large data sets, we experiment with ImageNet [23] for a split containing 100 classes for testing [24] and the standard 1K classes for training [24], without any overlap between seen and unseen classes. For ImageNet, we used 500-dimensional semantic samples [24] and 2048-dimensional ResNet-features, where images are resized to 256×256 pixels, cropped to 224×224 pixels, normalised with means $(0.485, 0.456, 0.406)$ and standard deviations $(0.229, 0.224, 0.225)$ per RGB channel [3].

4.2   Evaluation Protocol

The evaluation protocol is based on computing the average per-class top-1 accuracy measured independently for each class before dividing their cumulative sum by the number of classes [3]. For GZSL, after computing the average per-class top-1 accuracy on seen classes $\mathcal{Y}^S$ and unseen classes $\mathcal{Y}^U$, we compute the harmonic mean of the seen and the unseen classification accuracy [3]. We also show results using the receiver operating characteristics (ROC) curve that measures the seen and the unseen classification accuracy over many operating points of the classifier [1].

4.3   Implementation Details

In this section, we describe the implementation details for the augmentation network, visual network and semantic networks that compose the model AN-GZSL, in terms of the model architecture and hyper-parameters (e.g. *number of epochs, batch size, number of layers, learning rate, weight decay, and learning rate decay*). Firstly, the augmentation network (composed of a generator (θ_g), a discriminator (θ_d), and a regressor (θ_r)) is defined in terms of a generative adversarial network (GAN) with cycle-consistency loss [2]. The generator consists of a single hidden layer with 4096 nodes and LeakyReLU activation [32] with an output layer of 2048 nodes (same dimension as ResNet [27] feature layer). The discriminator consists of a single hidden layer with 4096 nodes with a LeakyReLU activation function, the output layer has no activation. Secondly, the visual network (θ_ϕ) consists of a model parameterised with one fully connected layer from the 2048-dimensional visual space into label space $\mathcal{Y}$. Thirdly, the semantic network (θ_ψ) is defined as a bi-linear model [25] that matches the 2048-dimensional visual space with the semantic space. We introduce a dropout layer (rate equal to 0.2) for the visual and the semantic networks for regularisation during training. On all the benchmark data sets [13] we generate 300 visual samples per class for the training of the visual and the semantic networks. Temperature calibration (2) is done after the training finding the parameters τ_ψ and τ_ϕ with grid search minimization of the losses for the visual and semantic networks, using the validation set [3] (this procedure does not require re-training of the whole model). Finally, we perform a Bayesian inference using Monte-Carlo dropout [33] because recent results suggest that such Bayesian inference can improve classification calibration and accuracy [34]. All hyper-parameters of the proposed AN-GZSL model are estimated with standard model selection methods on the validation sets proposed by Xian et al. [3].

4.4 Ablation Study

In Table 1, we report the ablation study for the proposed method AN-GZSL. First, we report the results for inference computed by the visual network ($AN-GZSL^\phi$). Second, $AN-GZSL^\psi$ reports the results for our semantic network. Then, $AN-GZSL^{\tau=1}$ shows the combination of the visual and semantic network without the temperature calibration. $AN-GZSL^{T=1}$ shows the results without MC dropout inference, and the last row shows the results with MC dropout using the calibrated (i.e., multi-domain) multi-modal networks.

Table 1. GZSL results using per-class average top-1 accuracy on the test sets of unseen classes $\mathcal{Y}^U$, seen classes $\mathcal{Y}^S$, and H-mean result H – all results shown in percentage. The highlighted values represent the best ones for each column. The rows represents the results for the visual classifier $\phi(.)$, semantic classifier $\psi(.)$, AN-GZSL without temperature calibration ($\tau = 1$), AN-GZSL without Bayesian inference ($T = 1$), and AN-GZSL, respectively. All the components are required to obtain the best H-mean.

Classifier	CUB			FLO			SUN			AWA		
	$\mathcal{Y}^U$	$\mathcal{Y}^S$	H	$\mathcal{Y}^U$	$\mathcal{Y}^S$	H	$\mathcal{Y}^U$	$\mathcal{Y}^S$	H	$\mathcal{Y}^U$	$\mathcal{Y}^S$	H
$AN-GZSL^\phi$	46.2	**61.5**	52.8	60.0	70.8	65.0	48.7	33.1	39.4	55.4	64.8	59.7
$AN-GZSL^\psi$	**77.7**	41.8	54.4	**84.9**	36.6	51.2	47.2	21.6	29.6	46.4	**67.3**	54.9
$AN-GZSL^{\tau=1}$	46.2	**61.5**	52.8	60.1	70.9	65.1	**53.3**	32.8	40.6	55.6	65.0	60.0
$AN-GZSL^{T=1}$	62.3	54.7	58.2	66.5	**84.4**	74.4	48.8	33.1	39.5	55.2	69.4	61.5
$AN-GZSL$	60.5	56.6	**58.5**	80.7	69.3	**74.5**	41.7	**37.1**	**41.7**	**58.2**	66.1	**61.9**

4.5 Results

In Table 2, we compare the GZSL results on CUB, FLO, SUN and AWA, produced by the proposed model AN-GZSL and several other methods previously proposed in the field. These methods are split into three groups: semantic approach, generative approach and domain balancing. We report the following metrics in Table 2: the accuracy for the unseen domain ($\mathcal{Y}^U$), the seen domain ($\mathcal{Y}^S$) and the harmonic-mean (H) between the two. Table 3 shows the top-1 accuracy on ImageNet for the proposed AN-GZSL and the results reported by previous methods on the same experimental setup.

In Fig. 2, we show the ROC results of the proposed method AN-GZSL, and the cycle-WGAN [2], which has code available online and represents the SOTA for the measure, to the best of our knowledge. Furthermore, Fig. 2 shows seen and unseen classification results for previously published GZSL methods (please

Table 2. GZSL results using per-class average top-1 accuracy on the test sets of unseen classes ($\mathcal{Y}^U$), seen classes ($\mathcal{Y}^S$), and H-mean result (H); – all results shown in percentage. The highlighted values represent the best for each column.

Classifier	CUB			FLO			SUN			AWA		
	$\mathcal{Y}^U$	$\mathcal{Y}^S$	H	$\mathcal{Y}^U$	$\mathcal{Y}^S$	H	$\mathcal{Y}^U$	$\mathcal{Y}^S$	H	$\mathcal{Y}^U$	$\mathcal{Y}^S$	H
Semantic approach												
DAP [5]	4.2	25.1	7.2	–	–	–	1.7	67.9	3.3	0.0	**88.7**	0.0
IAP [5]	1.0	37.8	1.8	–	–	–	0.2	72.8	0.4	2.1	78.2	4.1
DEVISE [35]	23.8	53.0	32.8	9.9	44.2	16.2	16.9	27.4	20.9	13.4	68.7	22.4
SJE [36]	23.5	59.2	33.6	13.9	47.6	21.5	14.7	30.5	19.8	11.3	74.6	19.6
LATEM [37]	15.2	57.3	24.0	6.6	47.6	11.5	14.7	28.8	19.5	7.3	71.7	13.3
ESZSL [38]	12.6	63.8	21.0	11.4	56.8	19.0	11.0	27.9	15.8	6.6	75.6	12.1
ALE [25]	23.7	62.8	34.4	13.3	61.6	21.9	21.8	33.1	26.3	16.8	76.1	27.5
PQZSL [39]	43.2	51.4	46.9	–	–	–	35.1	35.3	35.2	31.7	70.9	43.8
AREN [40]	38.9	78.7	52.1	–	–	–	19.0	38.8	25.5	–	–	–
MLSE [41]	22.3	71.6	34.0	–	–	–	20.7	36.4	26.4	–	–	–
Generative approach												
SAE [42]	8.8	18.0	11.8	–	–	–	7.8	54.0	13.6	1.8	77.1	3.5
f-CLSWGAN [43]	43.8	60.6	50.8	58.8	70.0	63.9	47.9	32.4	38.7	56.0	62.8	59.2
cycle-WGAN [2]	46.0	60.3	52.2	59.1	71.1	64.5	48.3	33.1	39.2	56.4	63.5	59.7
CADA-VAE [12]	51.6	53.5	52.4	–	–	–	47.2	35.7	40.6	57.3	72.8	64.1
GDAN [8]	39.3	66.7	49.5	–	–	–	38.1	**89.9**	**53.4**	–	–	–
GMN [11]	56.1	54.3	55.2	–	–	–	**53.2**	33.0	40.7	61.1	71.3	**65.8**
Zhu et al. [44]	33.4	**87.5**	48.4	–	–	–	–	–	–	–	–	–
LisGAN [9]	46.5	57.9	51.6	57.7	**83.8**	68.3	42.9	37.8	40.2	52.6	76.3	62.3
External Domain Classifier												
CMT [18]	7.2	49.8	12.6	–	–	–	8.1	21.8	11.8	0.9	87.6	1.8
DAZSL [15]	41.0	60.5	48.9	59.6	81.4	68.8	35.3	40.2	37.6	**64.8**	51.7	57.5
Ours												
$AN - GZSL$	**60.5**	56.6	**58.5**	**80.7**	69.3	**74.5**	41.7	37.1	41.7	58.2	66.1	61.9

Table 3. GZSL ImageNet results – all results shown in percentage. Please see caption of Table 2 for details on each measure. The highlighted values represent the best ones.

Classifier	$\mathcal{Y}^U$	$\mathcal{Y}^S$	H
f-CLSWGAN [13]	0.7	–	–
cycle-WGAN [2]	1.5	**66.5**	2.8
$AN - GZSL$	**2.5**	47.4	**4.8**

refer to Table 2 for the original references). We represent previous methods [13] by single (diamond-shaped) points denoting the results for seen and unseen classification accuracies – this is because previous methods only report a single operating point for the classification of seen and unseen classes).

Using the graph in Fig. 2, we compute the AUSUC on each data set for AN-GZSL – results are shown in the supplementary material. Moreover, we

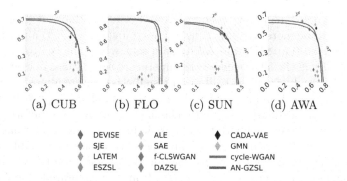

(a) CUB   (b) FLO   (c) SUN   (d) AWA

◆ DEVISE	◆ ALE	◆ CADA-VAE
◆ SJE	◆ SAE	◆ GMN
◆ LATEM	◆ f-CLSWGAN	━━ cycle-WGAN
◆ ESZSL	◆ DAZSL	━━ AN-GZSL

Fig. 2. ROC curves for the proposed method AN-GZSL, and several baseline and state-of-the-art methods (please see text and Table 2 for details about the methods). Note that these graphs are used to compute the AUSUC. (best seen on the digital format with colors). (Color figure online)

added the results reported by the previous methods EZSL [38], fCLSWGAN [13], cycle-WGAN [2] and DAZSL [15]. We were able to compute the AUSUC results for AN-GZSL and cycle-WGAN, but the other AUSUC results were extracted from [15].

5 Discussions

Ablation Study. Table 1 shows the importance of each component of AN-GZSL, where the H-mean tends to be higher for the multi-modal approach, compared to each individual modality. The multi-domain multi-modal method that relies on Bayesian inference (last row) shows the highest H-mean on all data sets. The similarity between the results of the un-calibrated ($AN - GZSL^{\tau=1}$) and the visual network $AN - GZSL^{\phi}$ suggests that un-calibrated multi-modal classifiers rely entirely on the visual classifiers. This is explained by the fact that the classification results produced by the un-calibrated semantic classifier show classification probabilities close to a uniform distribution, in contrast to the un-calibrated visual classifier that shows more non-uniform distributions. However, when calibration is applied, the classification probabilities produced by both classifiers are pushed further away from the uniform distribution, which means that the sum of calibrated classifiers can produce results that are different from the original visual and semantic classifiers. In fact, Table 1 shows that the AN-GZSL classification accuracy is always higher than single-modality classification results. This multi-modal calibrated classifier also produces the most balanced classification results between the seen and unseen domains for all data sets. These results suggest that our proposed method provides a way to correct some of the mistakes made using an individual modality. For example, this can happen when the classification probabilities of the correct class are relatively high for both modalities, but not the highest in any modality, and when summed, the correct class receives the highest confidence.

Another important point to notice from Table 1 is that our proposed AN-GZSL seems to be more advantageous in fine-grained (i.e., CUB and FLO) than in coarse-grained (i.e., SUN and AWA) data sets, where the key to explain such discrepancy lies in the effectiveness of temperature calibration. In coarse-grained data sets, the results from the calibrated visual classifier are almost binary, with the highest classification probability close to one and all other probability values close to zero. The calibrated semantic classifier shows a more uniform distribution, which when combined with the almost binary results of the visual classifier is less effective (than in fine-grained problems) to change a possibly incorrect visual classifier result for the multi-domain multi-modal model. On the other hand, in fine-grained data sets, the results from the calibrated visual classifier are farther from binary, which when combined with the results from the semantic classifier can be more effective to change an incorrect visual classifier result for the multi-domain multi-modal model. We speculate that this different performance between visual classifiers can be explained by the cluttered or the scattered nature of visual class distributions in fine-grained or coarse-grained data sets – that is, more cluttered distributions provide more space for improvement with an effective temperature calibration.

A final point from Table 1 is the apparent more accurate classification results for the unseen classes than for the seen classes for most of the data sets. We studied this issue by running an unpaired t-test to check the significance of these results, and for CUB, FLO and AWA the p-values are larger than 0.05, implying that we cannot reject the null hypothesis (i.e., the hypothesis that there is no significant difference between seen and unseen classification accuracies). For SUN, the p-value is smaller than 0.05, which we believe is due to the large size of the data set. It is important to note that previous methods have also reported similar classification results for SUN [2,13]. Nevertheless, it is worth mentioning that the seen and unseen classification results represent the performance of a particular adjustable operating point of the methods, as shown in Fig. 2. Hence, measures that summarise the seen vs unseen classification, like H-mean or AUSUC, can characterise better the method performance, but the dependence of H-mean on an operating point makes it less reliable than AUSUC, so we advocate the use of AUSUC as a more general measure for GZSL approaches.

Comparison with SOTA. In Table 2, we notice a clear trend of the proposed AN-GZSL to perform substantially better than the SOTA in terms of H-mean and classification accuracy on unseen classes for fine-grained (CUB and FLO) data sets, and competitively for coarse-grained data sets (SUN and AWA). This result shows that the more challenging classification problem offered by the fine-grained data sets represents an ideal situation for exploring multi-modal and multi-domain classification. We discuss in the ablation study above, the reasons behind the superior performance in fine-grained data sets of our proposed AN-GZSL method.

Another interesting point to observe from Table 2 is that none of the competing methods stand out as a clear SOTA approach for all data sets since one method can be better in one data set, but worse in others. In fact, out of the four data sets studied, AN-GZSL is better in two, GDAN is better in one and GMN is better in another. It is also worth comparing the performance of previous semantic approaches in Table 3, and our proposed semantic network, represented by $AN - GZSL^{\psi}$ in Table 1. This comparison is important because our proposed semantic network introduces one significant novelty, which is the use of visual data augmentation for training the semantic classifier. Our proposed $AN - GZSL^{\psi}$ produces substantially better results in terms of H-mean and classification accuracy on unseen classes for CUB, FLO and AWA.

In terms of the large-scale data set ImageNet, we show in Table 3 that the proposed method establishes a new SOTA in terms of the H-mean result. More specifically, the proposed method achieves around 80% of relative H-mean improvement. We speculate that these results can be explained by the similar challenges present in fine-grained and large-scale data sets. Also, the proposed approach scales as well as f-CLSWGAN [13] and cycle-WGAN [2] with respect to the number of classes and samples.

Seen and Unseen Classification Graphs. Figure 2 shows the trade-off between the classification of seen and unseen classes for GZSL methods. In particular, it is interesting to notice a fact that is prevalent in GZSL methods, which is the classification imbalance that usually favours the seen classes – the figure illustrates that the majority of the previous methods (represented by diamonds) lie at the bottom-right part of the graphs, indicating the preference for seen classes. In terms of seen and unseen curves, the more balanced methods (see Table 2) usually lies close to the elbow of the curve, located at the top-right part of the graph.

AUSUC. Figure 2 shows that the proposed approach, AN-GZSL, outperforms previous methods on data sets CUB, SUN and FLO. For AWA, we achieve competitive performance, where the proposed method is the second best. It is worth emphasising that the AUSUC measure provides a more complete assessment of GZSL methods, where it is no longer necessary to commit to a particular operating point of the classification of seen and unseen classes.

6 Conclusions and Future Work

In this paper, we introduce a new approach to perform GZSL using a multi-modal multi-domain augmentation network. The proposed approach is the first to explore visual data augmentation for training visual *and* semantic classifiers, enabling a truly and novel multi-modal training and inference for GZSL. In addition, we show that the calibration of those visual and semantic classifiers provide an effective multi-domain classification, where the classification of seen and unseen classes are accurate and well balanced. The experimental results show that the proposed approach has established new state-of-the-art GZSL harmonic mean results for three benchmark data sets (CUB, FLO, and Imagenet).

In particular, we report results that are substantially better than the previous methods on CUB and FLO, which are fine-grained data sets, and competitive on SUN and AWA, which are coarse-grained data sets. Moreover, the results of the proposed approach outperform previous methods on Imagenet data set by a large margin. Also, our proposed AN-GZSL achieves the best performance in terms of AUSUC for three benchmark data sets.

In the future, we intend to study more thoroughly the reason behind the performance difference observed between fine-grained and coarse-grained data sets. We will also investigate why it is challenging to obtain high classification accuracy on the unseen classes of the large scale ImageNet data set.[2]

References

1. Chao, W.-L., Changpinyo, S., Gong, B., Sha, F.: An empirical study and analysis of generalized zero-shot learning for object recognition in the wild. In: Leibe, B., Matas, J., Sebe, N., Welling, M. (eds.) ECCV 2016. LNCS, vol. 9906, pp. 52–68. Springer, Cham (2016). https://doi.org/10.1007/978-3-319-46475-6_4
2. Felix, R., Vijay Kumar, B.G., Reid, I., Carneiro, G.: Multi-modal cycle-consistent generalized zero-shot learning. In: Ferrari, V., Hebert, M., Sminchisescu, C., Weiss, Y. (eds.) ECCV 2018. LNCS, vol. 11210, pp. 21–37. Springer, Cham (2018). https://doi.org/10.1007/978-3-030-01231-1_2
3. Xian, Y., Lampert, C.H., Schiele, B., Akata, Z.: Zero-shot learning - a comprehensive evaluation of the good, the bad and the ugly. CoRR abs/1707.00600 (2017)
4. Mikolov, T., Sutskever, I., Chen, K., Corrado, G.S., Dean, J.: Distributed representations of words and phrases and their compositionality. In: Advances in Neural Information Processing Systems, pp. 3111–3119 (2013)
5. Lampert, C.H., Nickisch, H., Harmeling, S.: Learning to detect unseen object classes by between-class attribute transfer. In: 2009 IEEE Conference on Computer Vision and Pattern Recognition, pp. 951–958 (2009)
6. Lampert, C.H., Nickisch, H., Harmeling, S.: Attribute-based classification for zero-shot visual object categorization. IEEE Trans. Pattern Anal. Mach. Intell. **36**, 453–465 (2014)
7. Bucher, M., Herbin, S., Jurie, F.: Generating visual representations for zero-shot classification. In: Proceedings of the IEEE International Conference on Computer Vision, pp. 2666–2673 (2017)
8. Huang, H., Wang, C., Yu, P.S., Wang, C.D.: Generative dual adversarial network for generalized zero-shot learning. In: Proceedings of the IEEE Conference on Computer Vision and Pattern Recognition, pp. 801–810 (2019)
9. Li, J., Jin, M., Lu, K., Ding, Z., Zhu, L., Huang, Z.: Leveraging the invariant side of generative zero-shot learning. arXiv preprint arXiv:1904.04092 (2019)
10. Paul, A., Krishnan, N.C., Munjal, P.: Semantically aligned bias reducing zero shot learning. In: Proceedings of the IEEE Conference on Computer Vision and Pattern Recognition, pp. 7056–7065 (2019)
11. Sariyildiz, M.B., Cinbis, R.G.: Gradient matching generative networks for zero-shot learning. In: Proceedings of the IEEE Conference on Computer Vision and Pattern Recognition, pp. 2168–2178 (2019)

---

[2] This work was partially supported by Australian Research Council grants (FT190100525 and CE140100016).

12. Schonfeld, E., Ebrahimi, S., Sinha, S., Darrell, T., Akata, Z.: Generalized zero-and few-shot learning via aligned variational autoencoders. In: Proceedings of the IEEE Conference on Computer Vision and Pattern Recognition, pp. 8247–8255 (2019)
13. Xian, Y., Lorenz, T., Schiele, B., Akata, Z.: Feature generating networks for zero-shot learning. arXiv (2017)
14. Verma, V.K., Arora, G., Mishra, A., Rai, P.: Generalized zero-shot learning via synthesized examples. In: The IEEE Conference on Computer Vision and Pattern Recognition (CVPR) (2018)
15. Atzmon, Y., Chechik, G.: Adaptive confidence smoothing for generalized zero-shot learning. In: Proceedings of the IEEE Conference on Computer Vision and Pattern Recognition, pp. 11671–11680 (2019)
16. Bhattacharjee, S., Mandal, D., Biswas, S.: Autoencoder based novelty detection for generalized zero shot learning. In: 2019 IEEE International Conference on Image Processing (ICIP), pp. 3646–3650. IEEE (2019)
17. Felix, R., Harwood, B., Sasdelli, M., Carneiro, G.: Generalised zero-shot learning with domain classification in a joint semantic and visual space. In: 2019 Digital Image Computing: Techniques and Applications (DICTA). IEEE (2019)
18. Socher, R., Ganjoo, M., Manning, C.D., Ng, A.: Zero-shot learning through cross-modal transfer. In: Advances in Neural Information Processing Systems, pp. 935–943 (2013)
19. Zhang, H., Koniusz, P.: Model selection for generalized zero-shot learning. In: Proceedings of the European Conference on Computer Vision (ECCV), pp. 0–0 (2018)
20. Zhou, Z.H.: Ensemble Methods: Foundations and Algorithms. Chapman and Hall/CRC, Boca Raton (2012)
21. Welinder, P., et al.: Caltech-ucsd birds **200** (2010)
22. Nilsback, M.E., Zisserman, A.: Automated flower classification over a large number of classes. In: 2008 Sixth Indian Conference on Computer Vision, Graphics & Image Processing. ICVGIP'08, pp. 722–729. IEEE (2008)
23. Deng, J., Dong, W., Socher, R., Li, L.J., Li, K., Fei-Fei, L.: Imagenet: a large-scale hierarchical image database. In: 2009 IEEE Conference on Computer Vision and Pattern Recognition CVPR 2009, pp. 248–255. IEEE (2009)
24. Wang, P., Liu, L., Shen, C., Huang, Z., van den Hengel, A., Shen, H.T.: Multi-attention network for one shot learning. In: IEEE Conference on Computer Vision and Pattern Recognition (CVPR), pp. 22–25 (2017)
25. Akata, Z., Perronnin, F., Harchaoui, Z., Schmid, C.: Label-embedding for image classification. IEEE Trans. Pattern Anal. Mach. Intell. **38**, 1425–1438 (2016)
26. He, K., Zhang, X., Ren, S., Sun, J.: Delving deep into rectifiers: surpassing human-level performance on imagenet classification. In: The IEEE International Conference on Computer Vision (ICCV) (2015)
27. He, K., Zhang, X., Ren, S., Sun, J.: Deep residual learning for image recognition. In: Proceedings of the IEEE Conference on Computer Vision and Pattern Recognition, pp. 770–778 (2016)
28. Guo, C., Pleiss, G., Sun, Y., Weinberger, K.Q.: On calibration of modern neural networks. In: Proceedings of the 34th International Conference on Machine Learning-Volume 70, JMLR. org, pp. 1321–1330 (2017)
29. Arjovsky, M., Chintala, S., Bottou, L.: Wasserstein gan. arXiv (2017)
30. Goodfellow, I., et al.: Generative adversarial nets. In: Advances in Neural Information Processing Systems, pp. 2672–2680 (2014)
31. Reed, S., Akata, Z., Lee, H., Schiele, B.: Learning deep representations of fine-grained visual descriptions. In: Proceedings of the IEEE Conference on Computer Vision and Pattern Recognition, pp. 49–58 (2016)

32. Maas, A.L., Hannun, A.Y., Ng, A.Y.: Rectifier nonlinearities improve neural network acoustic models. In: Proceedings of the ICML vol. 30, p. 3 (2013)
33. Gal, Y., Ghahramani, Z.: Dropout as a bayesian approximation: insights and applications. In: Deep Learning Workshop ICML (2015)
34. Gal, Y., Hron, J., Kendall, A.: Concrete dropout. In: Advances in Neural Information Processing Systems, pp. 3581–3590 (2017)
35. Frome, A., Corrado, G.S., Shlens, J., Bengio, S., Dean, J., Mikolov, T., et al.: Devise: a deep visual-semantic embedding model. In: Advances in Neural Information Processing Systems, pp. 2121–2129 (2013)
36. Akata, Z., Reed, S., Walter, D., Lee, H., Schiele, B.: Evaluation of output embeddings for fine-grained image classification. In: Proceedings of the IEEE Conference on Computer Vision and Pattern Recognition, pp. 2927–2936 (2015)
37. Xian, Y., Akata, Z., Sharma, G., Nguyen, Q., Hein, M., Schiele, B.: Latent embeddings for zero-shot classification. In: Proceedings of the IEEE Conference on Computer Vision and Pattern Recognition, pp. 69–77 (2016)
38. Romera-Paredes, B., Torr, P.: An embarrassingly simple approach to zero-shot learning. In: International Conference on Machine Learning, pp. 2152–2161 (2015)
39. Li, J., Lan, X., Liu, Y., Wang, L., Zheng, N.: Compressing unknown images with product quantizer for efficient zero-shot classification. In: Proceedings of the IEEE Conference on Computer Vision and Pattern Recognition, pp. 5463–5472 (2019)
40. Xie, G.S., et al.: Attentive region embedding network for zero-shot learning. In: Proceedings of the IEEE Conference on Computer Vision and Pattern Recognition, pp. 9384–9393 (2019)
41. Ding, Z., Liu, H.: Marginalized latent semantic encoder for zero-shot learning. In: Proceedings of the IEEE Conference on Computer Vision and Pattern Recognition, pp. 6191–6199 (2019)
42. Kodirov, E., Xiang, T., Gong, S.: Semantic autoencoder for zero-shot learning. In: Proceedings of the IEEE Conference on Computer Vision and Pattern Recognition, pp. 3174–3183 (2017)
43. Xian, Y., Lorenz, T., Schiele, B., Akata, Z.: Feature generating networks for zero-shot learning. In: 31st IEEE Conference on Computer Vision and Pattern Recognition (CVPR 2018), Salt Lake City, UT, USA (2018)
44. Zhu, P., Wang, H., Saligrama, V.: Generalized zero-shot recognition based on visually semantic embedding. In: Proceedings of the IEEE Conference on Computer Vision and Pattern Recognition, pp. 2995–3003 (2019)

Local Facial Makeup Transfer
via Disentangled Representation

Zhaoyang Sun[1], Feng Liu[1], Wen Liu[2], Shengwu Xiong[1]([✉]), and Wenxuan Liu[1]

[1] School of Computer Science and Technology, Wuhan University of Technology,
Wuhan, China
`xiongsw@whut.edu.cn`
[2] School of Navigation, Wuhan University of Technology, Wuhan, China

Abstract. Facial makeup transfer aims to render a non-makeup face image in an arbitrary given makeup one while preserving face identity. The most advanced method separates makeup style information from face images to realize makeup transfer. However, makeup style includes several semantic clear local styles which are still entangled together. In this paper, we propose a novel unified adversarial disentangling network to further decompose face images into four independent components, i.e., personal identity, lips makeup style, eyes makeup style and face makeup style. Owing to the disentangled makeup representation, our method can not only flexible control the degree of local makeup styles, but also can transfer local makeup styles from different images into the final result, which any other approaches fail to handle. For makeup removal, different from other methods which regard makeup removal as the reverse process of makeup transfer, we integrate the makeup transfer with the makeup removal into one uniform framework and obtain multiple makeup removal results. Extensive experiments have demonstrated that our approach can produce visually pleasant and accurate makeup transfer results compared to the state-of-the-art methods.

1 Introduction

In daily life, it has always been of special interest to humans to improve looks. Consider this scenario: when people see a favorite makeup style, they may always involuntarily envision what effects will be if they wear this makeup. Some applications now offer this virtual makeup function, such as TAAZ, MEITU XIUXIU and DailyMakever.[1] However, these tools only provide a limited number of defined makeup styles and sometimes require specific interaction. Makeup transfer is a way to handle the transfer of arbitrary makeup styles without specific interaction. Due to the diversity and complexity of makeup styles, accurate makeup transfer has always been a very challenging task in both academia and industry.

---

[1] taaz.com, xiuxiu.web.meitu.com, dailymakeover.com.

ⓒ Springer Nature Switzerland AG 2021
H. Ishikawa et al. (Eds.): ACCV 2020, LNCS 12625, pp. 459–473, 2021.
https://doi.org/10.1007/978-3-030-69538-5_28

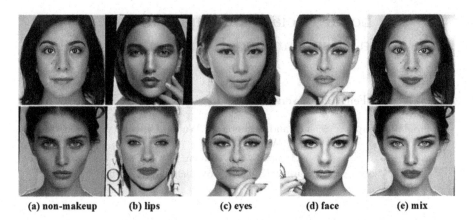

| (a) non-makeup | (b) lips | (c) eyes | (d) face | (e) mix |

Fig. 1. Our results of the mix local makeup transfer. The last column (*e*) are the mix local makeup results, which have the identity information from (*a*), the lips style from (*b*), the eyes style in (*c*) and face style from (*d*).

In practical applications, users strongly hope that the combinations of different makeup styles can be freely achieved. It means that makeup transfer can be performed like trying on clothes, and can transfer local makeup styles from different images into the final result, shown in Fig. 1. Existing approaches [1–6] based on deep learning to makeup transfer have yielded visually pleasant results. For example, Li *et al.* [1] adopted the structure of dualGAN [7] and histogram matching as the makeup loss to achieve pleasant results. Chang *et al.* [2] proposed a style discriminator to promote the makeup transfer in the asymmetric network. The above methods do not separate the makeup style information, the makeup transfer process is thus completed in a black-box network. Recently, the method [5] successfully extracts makeup information from face images, which not only achieves exciting results, but also can control the degree of makeup style. However, the extracted makeup information includes several semantic clear local makeup styles, such as lipstick, eye shadow and foundation, which are still tangled in the makeup information. Therefore, this method still fail to meet the higher requirements of practical applications.

This paper introduces an autoencoder architecture to solve this problem. In particular, our generator contains four encoders to extract the information of personal identity, lips makeup style, eyes makeup style, and face makeup style, respectively. After training, we feed the identity latent variable from the non-makeup image and the local makeup style variables from different makeup images into the decoder to obtain the result of local makeup style combination. The proposed framework is called the mix local makeup transfer in this work. Inspired by recent advances in disentangled representation [8–12], the local makeup loss function we designed forces the disentangling of information, instead of dividing the face image into different regions according to the semantic information and feeding them to the corresponding encoders.

For the case of makeup removal, unlike the existing methods [1,2,5], we consider a face without makeup to be a special case of the makeup face.

Our approach could thus treat the makeup removal and makeup transfer as the same problem. We generate makeup removal results by feeding the identity latent variable from makeup image and the makeup style variables from non-makeup image into the decoder, illustrated in Fig. 2. The makeup removal process could generate multiple results as the input non-makeup image changes. The main contributions of this work are summarized as follows:

- The local makeup loss function we designed forces the disentangling of information, our method decompose face images into four independent components, personal identity, lips makeup style, eyes makeup style and face makeup style.
- With the further disentangling of makeup style, our method can not only flexibly control the degree of every local makeup styles, but also transfer local makeup styles from different images into the final result.
- We integrate the makeup transfer with the makeup removal into one uniform framework and obtain multiple makeup removal results.

2   Related Work

Makeup Transfer: The input of makeup transfer is a non-makeup source image and an arbitrary makeup reference image, the output result receives the makeup style from the reference image while preserving face identity from the source image. To address this issue, Tong et al. [13] mapped the cosmetic contributions of color in the reference image to the non-makeup source image. [14,15] decomposed face images into several layers and transferred each layer by warping the reference makeup image to the non-makeup one. Inspired by recent successful style transfer [16], Liu et al. [17] applied the style transfer technique on facial local components and achieved the makeup transfer. Li et al. [1] tackled the makeup transfer problem by incorporating a instance-level makeup loss into the dualGAN [7] and generated visually pleasant makeup transfer results. Chang et al. [2] extended the CycleGAN [18] to asymmetric networks to enable transferring specific style and removing makeup style together. But the processing of the above methods is completed within a black-box network and can't control the makeup degree. Recently, the method proposed by Gu et al. [5] achieved disentanglement of makeup latent variable from non-makeup features and exchange the makeup information of two pictures to realize the makeup transfer. However, the separated makeup variable contains several semantic clear local makeup styles which are still tangled. So this method still can't transfer local makeup styles from different makeup images into the final result. Our method further decomposes the makeup component into lips makeup style, eyes makeup style and face makeup style by the local makeup loss. As our knowledge, we are the first to achieve the disentanglement of local makeup styles from face images.

Disentangled Representation: Disentangled representation means learning several independent representations from the input data. In unsupervised image-to-image translation tasks, Huang et al. [8] and Lee et al. [9] decomposed image

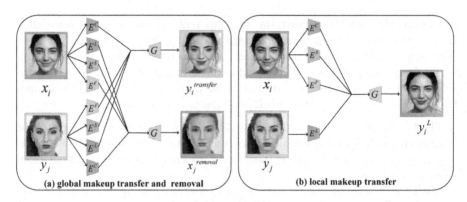

Fig. 2. Our generator contains four encoders $\{E^C, E^L, E^S, E^F\}$ to extract the information of personal identity, lips makeup style, eyes makeup style and face makeup style respectively. We exchange all the makeup latent variables for global makeup transfer and makeup removal in (a). The corresponding local makeup latent variables are recombined for local makeup transfer in (b).

representation into a domain-invariant content variable and a domain-specific style variable to generate multi-modal outputs. Ma *et al.* [10] disentangled a person's image into three main factors, namely foreground, background and pose, then manipulated the factors to generate a new image. Lorenz *et al.* [11] introduced an approach for disentangling appearance and shape by learning parts consistently over all instances of a category. Esser *et al.* [12] enforced disentanglement of the information by an additional classifier that estimates the minimal amount of regularization required. Inspired by these advances in disentangled representation, we disentangle an arbitrary face image into four independent components, including one personal identity and three local makeup styles, then realize makeup transfer and makeup removal by exchanging the corresponding makeup style components, see Fig. 2.

3   Method

3.1   Problem Formulation

Let image sets of non-makeup faces and makeup faces be $X \subset \mathbb{R}^{H \times W \times 3}$ and $Y \subset \mathbb{R}^{H \times W \times 3}$, respectively. $\{x_i\}_{i=1,\cdots,M}$, $x_i \in X$ and $\{y_j\}_{j=1,\cdots,N}$, $y_j \in Y$ represent non-makeup examples and makeup examples, respectively. Here, M, N denote the numbers of non-makeup images and makeup images.

For makeup transfer, the goal is learning mapping functions $\Phi : x_i, y_j \rightarrow y_i^{transfer}$ where $y_i^{transfer}$ has the same makeup style with y_j while preserving the identity from x_i. The local makeup transfer problem can be defined as $\Phi_k : x_i, y_j \xrightarrow{k} y_i^k$, where k represents different semantic regions and $k \in \{lips, eyes, face\}$ in this paper, y_i^k receives the local makeup style of k from y_j

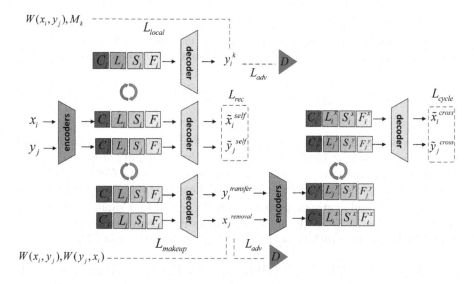

Fig. 3. The architecture of our whole network. The input x_i and y_j through the encoders to get four independent latent variables. First, feed the variables directly to the decoder to get $\tilde{x}_i^{self}$ and $\tilde{y}_j^{self}$. After that, the variables that extracted the local makeup information are exchanged and fed into the decoder to generate $y_i^{transfer}$ and $x_j^{removal}$. Finally, feed the outputs $y_i^{transfer}$ and $x_j^{removal}$ as inputs to the network again to obtain $\tilde{x}_i^{cross}$ and $\tilde{y}_j^{cross}$. For local makeup transfer, the corresponding local makeup latent variables are recombined and fed into the decoder.

while other regions should be identical to x_i. Note that k is not limited to this assignment and the face region defined here does not include lips and eyes.

For makeup removal, since the makeup process may conceal the original appearance, the original face behind cosmetics may have multiple possible results. We assume that a face without makeup to be a special case of the makeup face. Under this assumption, our approach treats makeup removal and makeup transfer as the same problem, makeup removal aims to transfer the makeup style from a non-makeup face image to a makeup face. It sounds strange, because we regard the original appearance of the skin as a makeup style. The makeup removal problem can be similarly defined as $\Phi : y_j, x_i \rightarrow x_j^{removal}$, an unsupervised image translation problem with conditioning, where $x_j^{removal}$ receives the identity from y_j and the makeup style from x_i.

3.2 Makeup Transfer and Removed

As illustrated in Fig. 2, our generator architecture consists of a identity encoder $\{E^C\}$, a lip style encoder $\{E^L\}$, a eye style encoder $\{E^S\}$, a face style encoder $\{E^F\}$ and a decoder $\{G\}$. First of all, we extract the personal identity, lips makeup style, eyes makeup style and face makeup style from a non-makeup image and a makeup image, denote as $C_i = E^C(x_i)$, $L_i = E^L(x_i)$, $S_i = E^S(x_i)$,

$F_i = E^F(x_i)$ and $C_j = E^C(y_j)$, $L_j = E^L(y_j)$, $S_j = E^S(y_j)$, $F_j = E^F(y_j)$, which are then fed into the decoder G to generate the makeup transfer result $y_i^{transfer}$ and makeup removal result $x_j^{removal}$. The formula is described as follows:

$$y_i^{trasnfer} = G(C_i, L_j, S_j, F_j) \tag{1}$$

$$x_j^{removal} = G(C_j, L_i, S_i, F_i) \tag{2}$$

A difficult question lies ahead of us: how to evaluate the makeup similarity of a pair of facial images? We firstly generate synthetic ground truth $W(x_i, y_j)$ by warping y_j onto x_i according to the facial landmarks, then use Colour Profile loss proposed in [4] as the makeup loss to evaluate the makeup similarity of generated image $y_i^{transfer}$ and synthetic ground truth $W(x_i, y_j)$. In a similar way, we use Colour Profile loss to evaluate the makeup similarity of generated image $x_j^{removal}$ and synthetic ground truth $W(y_j, x_i)$. Makeup loss function is as follows:

$$L_{makeup} = -(CP(y_i^{trasnfer}, W(x_i, y_j)) + CP(x_j^{removal}, W(y_j, x_i))) \tag{3}$$

3.3   Local Makeup Transfer

For the local makeup transfer, we only exchange the local disentangled makeup latent variable.

$$y_i^L = G(C_i, L_j, S_i, F_i), y_i^S = G(C_i, L_i, S_j, F_i), y_i^F = G(C_i, L_i, S_i, F_j) \tag{4}$$

where the y_i^L, y_i^S, y_i^F represent the results of the local makeup transfer of the lips, eyes and face regions respectively.

The target of local makeup transfer has two points. 1) The generated result has the same makeup style with the reference makeup image in the specified semantic region. 2) The other semantic regions of the generated result should be identical to the non-makeup image. We use the L1 loss to encourage such local invariant and the local makeup loss function is as follows:

$$L_{local} = \sum_{i=k}^{k \in \{L, S, F\}} \{-\lambda_k CP(y_i^k \circ M_k, W(x_i, y_j) \circ M_k) + \mu_k \|y_i^k \circ \overline{M_k} - x_i \circ \overline{M_k}\|_1\} \tag{5}$$

where λ_k, μ_k are the weights, $\circ$ denotes element-wise multiplication, M_k denotes the mask of corresponding face semantic region and $\overline{M_k}$ stands for reverse. Note that this local makeup loss function drives the disentangling of latent variables instead of feeding the corresponding encoders with the images which segmented by semantics. Face parsing is only used for network training to calculate loss functions, but not for testing.

3.4   Other Loss Functions

Reconstruction Loss: As illustrated in Fig. 3, the reconstruction loss function consists of two parts, one is the self reconstruction, the other is the cross-cycle reconstruction [18]. We feed C_i, L_i, S_i, F_i into G to generate $\tilde{x}_i^{self}$, feed C_j, L_j, S_j, F_j into G to obtain $\tilde{y}_j^{self}$, which should be identical to x_i, y_j respectively. After obtaining the makeup transfer result $y_i^{trasnfer}$ and makeup removal result $x_j^{removal}$, we feed them as input to the network again and generate $\tilde{x}_i^{cross}, \tilde{y}_j^{cross}$, which should be also identical to x_i, y_j respectively. We define the reconstruction loss as:

$$L_{rec} = (\|\tilde{x}_i^{self} - x_i\|_1 + \|\tilde{y}_j^{self} - y_j\|_1) + \lambda_{scale}(\|\tilde{x}_i^{cross} - x_i\|_1 + \|\tilde{y}_j^{cross} - y_j\|_1) \quad (6)$$

Adversarial Loss: We employ adversarial loss to improve the quality of generated images. The discriminator D distinguishes all the fake results from real samples in set X and set Y and the generator G tries to fool the discriminator D. We replace the negative log likelihood objective by a least square loss [19] in adversarial loss:

$$\begin{aligned} L_{adv} = &\mathbb{E}_{x_i}[(D(x_i) - 1)^2] + \mathbb{E}_{y_j}[(D(y_j) - 1)^2] \\ &+ \mathbb{E}_{x_j^{removal}}[(D(x_j^{removal}))^2] + \mathbb{E}_{y_i^{trasnfer}}[(D(y_i^{trasnfer}))^2] \\ &+ \sum_{i=k}^{k \in \{L,S,F\}} \mathbb{E}_{y_i^k}[(D(y_i^k))^2] \end{aligned} \quad (7)$$

Total Loss: To sum up, our total loss is

$$L_{total} = \lambda_{makeup}L_{makeup} + \lambda_{local}L_{local} + \lambda_{rec}L_{rec} + \lambda_{adv}L_{adv} \quad (8)$$

where $\lambda_{makeup}, \lambda_{local}, \lambda_{rec}, \lambda_{adv}$ are weights that control the importance of different objectives.

4   Experiments

4.1   Data Set and Training Details

We use the makeup transfer data set released by Li et al. [5] to conduct all the experiments, which contains 333 non-makeup and 302 makeup high-quality face images.

During training, the input images are resized to 286×286, randomly cropped to 256×256 and horizontally flipped with a probability of 0.5 for data augmentation. We set $\lambda_{makeup} = 4, \lambda_{local} = 1, \lambda_{rec} = 5, \lambda_{adv} = 1$ to balance different objectives. In L_{local}, we gives more attention to the lips and eyes makeup, because these two semantic regions are smaller than the face region. We set $\lambda_L = 50, \lambda_S = 10, \lambda_F = 1$ and set $\mu_L = 1, \mu_S = 1, \mu_F = 4$ for the same reason. In L_{rec}, the λ_{scale} is set 8. We employ the Adam [20] optimizer to train our network for 1000 epochs in all, where the learning rate is fixed as 0.0002. The batch size is set as 1. For capturing more identity details, we add skip connections [21] between the encoder $\{E^C\}$ and the decoder $\{G\}$. The latent variables are

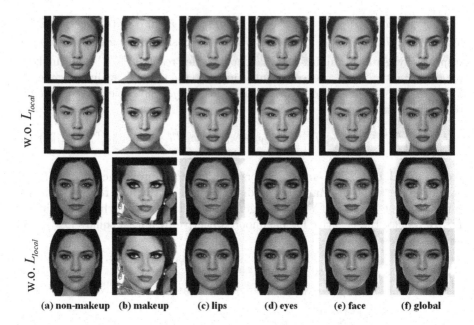

(a) non-makeup   (b) makeup   (c) lips   (d) eyes   (e) face   (f) global

Fig. 4. Ablation study on the local makeup loss. The images from (a) to (f) are the non-makeup source image, makeup reference image, lips makeup transfer result, eyes makeup transfer result, face makeup transfer result and global makeup transfer result respectively. The first and third rows are the results with local makeup loss and the second and fourth rows are the results without local makeup loss.

concatenated along the channel at the bottleneck. The specific structure of the content encoder, attribute encoders and decoder we refer to [5]. The only difference is that the number of output channels of the attribute encoder is reduced by half. For discriminators, we leverage the PatchGANs [22], which distinguishes local image patches to be real or fake.

4.2   Does the Local Makeup Loss Work?

In the network training process, the input to each makeup encoder is the same entire unpreprocessed makeup reference image. The local makeup loss function we designed forces different encoders to learn different information and the disentangling of information. To evaluate the effect of the local makeup loss, the ablation of the local makeup loss function is studied. As shown in Fig. 4, the results with local makeup loss achieved the local makeup transfer target, which have the same makeup style with the reference makeup image in the specified semantic region and the other semantic regions should be identical to the non-makeup image. When we remove this loss function, the effect of local makeup transfer disappears. The ablation experiment further illustrates that the local makeup loss function forces different encoders to learn different makeup information and promotes the decoupling of local makeup information.

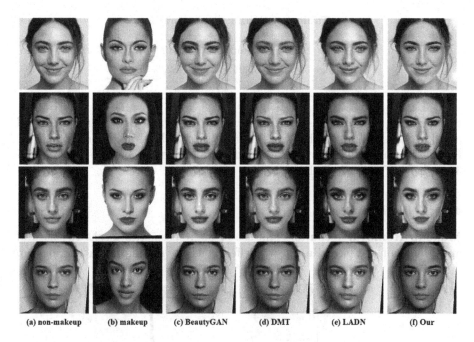

(a) non-makeup   (b) makeup   (c) BeautyGAN   (d) DMT   (e) LADN   (f) Our

Fig. 5. Qualitative comparisons between our results and others. The columns from left to right are non-makeup images, referenced makeup images, the results of BeautyGAN, DMT, LADN and our method.

4.3 Compare with Other Methods

Qualitative Comparison. As demonstrated in Fig. 5, we compare our results with three previous methods, BeautyGAN [1], DMT [6], LADN [5], from qualitative perspectives. The results of other methods are derived from official code or trained models. BeautyGAN and DMT could generate visually realistic transferring results with the histogram match loss. But for the eye area, the style of eye shadows have not been correctly transferred as well. For example, the eye shadow is not reflected in the generated results in row 1, row 4. LADN achieves facial makeup transfer by incorporating multiple local style discriminators. We observed that LADN could handle most eye shadow styles well, but the results are not satisfactory in the last row. Meanwhile, the resulting foundation color is different from the reference image. This phenomenon is evident in the results of row 3, row 4. By contrast, no matter what kind of makeup styles, our methods have yielded satisfactory results. And our outputs are highly consistent with the makeup style of reference images, no matter in lipstick, eye shadow or foundation. Our method can even transfer the shadow on both sides of the cheek to the results, see row 1.

Quantitative Comparison. We randomly selected 5 non-makeup source images and 10 makeup reference images, and generated 50 results of makeup

Table 1. Quantitative comparison

Methods	Our	BeautyGAN	DMT	LADN
Percentage	48.35%	30.94%	12.23%	8.47%

transfer using four methods respectively. Then 17 volunteers were recruited and asked to choose the result they were most satisfied with. As shown in the Table 1, Our method has a higher selection rate 48.35% than other methods beautyGAN 30.94%, DMT 12.23%, LADN 8.47%.

4.4 Other Results

Makeup Removal Results. The use of many cosmetics masks the natural appearance of the face. Restore the effect without makeup from the makeup

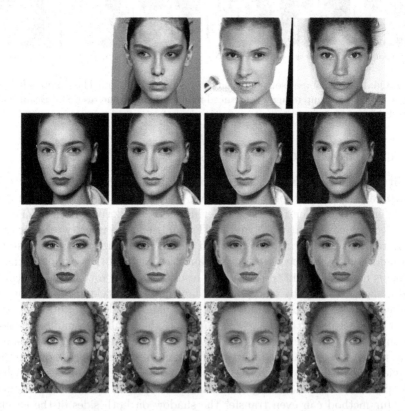

Fig. 6. The makeup removal results. Our approach treats makeup removal and makeup transfer as the same problem. The difference is that the roles of the non-makeup images and the makeup pictures are changed. The first row is the non-makeup reference images and the first column is the makeup source images. The corresponding makeup removal results receive the identity from the makeup source images and the makeup style from the non-makeup reference images.

image, there may be a variety of the results. Other methods [2,5] regard makeup removal as a problem without conditioning. This assumption is more realistic, but yields only a single result. Under our assumption, makeup removal is treated as an unsupervised image translation problem with conditioning. We can get multiple realistic cosmetic removal results by feeding the makeup components from different non-makeup images into the decoder, as demonstrated in Fig. 6. Extensive experimental results further verify the validity of our assumption.

Local Makeup Transfer Results. The methods [2,17] train multiple networks to perform local makeup transfer and can't control the degree of makeup style. By contrast, our approach decomposes the latent variables of makeup style into lips style, eyes style and face style in a network. Our method can not only the local makeup transfer, but also flexibly control the degree of local makeup style which will be shown in the next section. The local makeup transfer results are shown in Fig. 7, our results effectively transfer the local makeup style while keeping the rest regions of the face image unchanged.

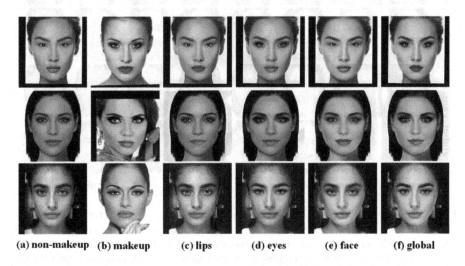

| (a) non-makeup | (b) makeup | (c) lips | (d) eyes | (e) face | (f) global |

Fig. 7. The local makeup transfer results. The first and second columns are non-makeup images and makeup images respectively. The remaining columns from left to right are the results of lips style, eyes style, face style and global style transfer.

Interpolated Makeup Transfer Results. Because of separating several makeup style latent variables from non-makeup features, we can control the degree of local makeup styles. The formula is described as follows:

$$y_i^{inter} = G(C_i, \alpha_L L_i + (1 - \alpha_L)L_j, \alpha_S S_i + (1 - \alpha_S)S_j, \alpha_F F_i + (1 - \alpha_F)F_j) \quad (9)$$

where $\alpha_L, \alpha_S, \alpha_F \in [0, 1]$ are the weights to control the degree of makeup style. We set $\alpha_L, \alpha_S, \alpha_F$ to be the same value and generate the global interpolated

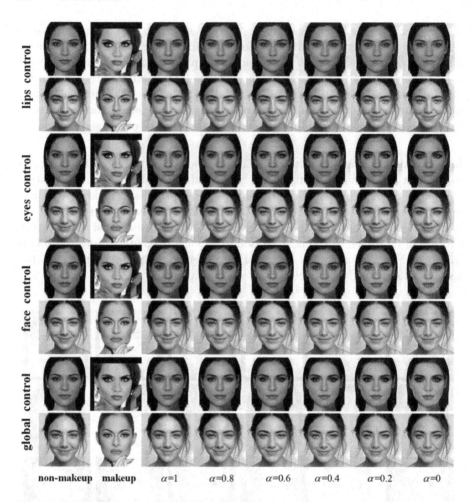

Fig. 8. The interpolated results. The first and second rows are the interpolated results of lips makeup style, we fix $\alpha_S = 1, \alpha_F = 1$, and gradually change α_L from 1 to 0. The third and fourth rows are the interpolated results of eyes makeup style, we fix $\alpha_L = 1, \alpha_F = 1$, and gradually change α_S from 1 to 0. The fifth and sixth rows are the interpolated results of face makeup style, we fix $\alpha_L = 1, \alpha_S = 1$, and gradually change α_F from 1 to 0. In last two rows, we gradually change $\alpha_L, \alpha_S, \alpha_F$ from 1 to 0.

results. Then we fix two of them to 0 or 1 and gradually change the other. As shown in Fig. 8, we have observed that no matter which kind of interpolation transfer, the generator can produce smooth, realistic results.

Mix Local Makeup Transfer Results. At the end of this article, we will further try a very challenging task mentioned at the beginning, mix local makeup transfer we called. We would extract the lips style, eyes style, and face style from three different makeup images and then mix them into one non-makeup image while preserving face identity. This puts forward higher requirements on the disentangling degree of information and the effect of generator. The formula is described as follows:

$$y_i^{mix} = G(C_i, L_p, S_q, F_r), \tag{10}$$

where L_p, S_q and F_r, respectively, denote the lips, eyes and face latent variables from three different makeup images. The result show in Fig. 9. Our results are as consistent as possible with the local makeup styles without losing the sense of authenticity.

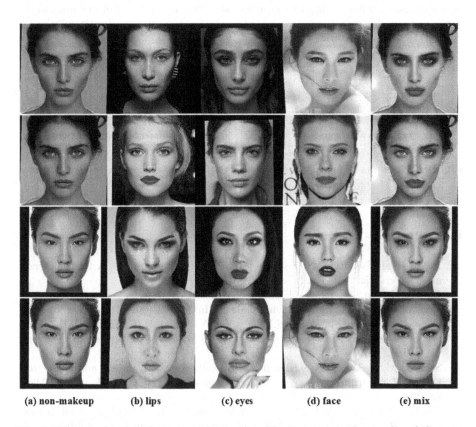

(a) non-makeup   (b) lips   (c) eyes   (d) face   (e) mix

Fig. 9. The mix local makeup transfer results. The last row is the results of the mix local makeup transfer, which receive personal identity from the first row, the lips style from the second row, the eyes style from the third row and the face style from the fourth row.

5   Conclusion

In conclusion, our method decomposes face images into four independent components, including personal identity, lips makeup style, eyes makeup style and face makeup style. Benefit by the disentangling of information, our method can not only flexible control the degree of local makeup styles, but also can transfer local makeup styles from different images into the result. For makeup removal, we integrate the makeup transfer with the makeup removal into one uniform framework and obtain multiple makeup removal results. Extensive experiments have verified the effectiveness of our method compared with other methods. In addition, we tested the generalization capability of our method in complex scenarios, see Fig. 10. For faces with large-poses, our method can still obtain relatively satisfactory results. But a few failure cases of our method were caused by significantly different lighting conditions, which is the focus of our next work.

(a) faces with large-poses   (b) different lighting conditions

Fig. 10. The results of our approach under large-poses and different lighting conditions.

References

1. Li, T., et al.: BeautyGAN: instance-level facial makeup transfer with deep generative adversarial network. In: ACM MM (2018)
2. Chang, H., Lu, J., Yu, F., Finkelstein, A.: PairedCycleGAN: asymmetric style transfer for applying and removing makeup. In: CVPR (2018)
3. Chen, H.J., Hui, K.M., Wang, S.Y., Tsao, L.W., Shuai, H.H., Cheng, W.H.: BeautyGlow: on-demand makeup transfer framework with reversible generative network. In: CVPR (2019)
4. Sarfraz, M.S., Seibold, C., Khalid, H., Stiefelhagen, R.: Content and colour distillation for learning image translations with the spatial profile loss. In: BMVC (2019)
5. Gu, Q., Wang, G., Chiu, M.T., Tai, Y.W., Tang, C.K.: LADN: local adversarial disentangling network for facial makeup and de-makeup. In: ICCV (2019)
6. Zhang, H., Chen, W., He, H., Jin, Y.: Disentangled makeup transfer with generative adversarial network. arXiv preprint arXiv:1907.01144 (2019)
7. Yi, Z., Zhang, H., Tan, P., Gong, M.: DualGAN: unsupervised dual learning for image-to-image translation. In: ICCV (2017)
8. Huang, X., Liu, M.Y., Belongie, S.J., Kautz, J.: Multimodal unsupervised image-to-image translation. In: ECCV (2018)
9. Lee, H.Y., Tseng, H.Y., Huang, J.B., Singh, M., Yang, M.H.: Diverse image-to-image translation via disentangled representations. In: ECCV (2018)
10. Ma, L., Sun, Q., Georgoulis, S., Gool, L.V., Schiele, B., Fritz, M.: Disentangled person image generation. In: CVPR (2018)

11. Lorenz, D., Bereska, L., Milbich, T., Ommer, B.: Unsupervised part-based disentangling of object shape and appearance. In: CVPR (2019)
12. Esser, P., Haux, J., Ommer, B.: Unsupervised robust disentangling of latent characteristics for image synthesis. In: ICCV (2019)
13. Tong, W.S., Tang, C.K., Brown, M.S., Xu, Y.Q.: Example-based cosmetic transfer. In: Proceedings of the Pacific Conference on Computer Graphics and Applications, Pacific Graphics 2007 (2007)
14. Guo, D., Sim, T.: Digital face makeup by example. In: CVPR (2009)
15. Li, C., Zhou, K., Lin, S.: Simulating makeup through physics-based manipulation of intrinsic image layers. In: CVPR (2015)
16. Gatys, L.A., Ecker, A.S., Bethge, M.: Image style transfer using convolutional neural networks. In: CVPR (2016)
17. Liu, S., Ou, X., Qian, R., Wang, W., Cao, X.: Makeup like a superstar: deep localized makeup transfer network. In: IJCAI (2016)
18. Zhu, J.Y., Park, T., Isola, P., Efros, A.A.: Unpaired image-to-image translation using cycle-consistent adversarial networks. In: ICCV (2017)
19. Mao, X., Li, Q., Xie, H., Lau, R.Y.K., Wang, Z.: Multi-class generative adversarial networks with the L2 loss function. arXiv preprint arXiv:1611.04076 (2016)
20. Kingma, D.P., Ba, J.: Adam: a method for stochastic optimization. In: ICLR (2015)
21. Ronneberger, O., Fischer, P., Brox, T.: U-Net: convolutional networks for biomedical image segmentation. In: Navab, N., Hornegger, J., Wells, W.M., Frangi, A.F. (eds.) MICCAI 2015. LNCS, vol. 9351, pp. 234–241. Springer, Cham (2015). https://doi.org/10.1007/978-3-319-24574-4_28
22. Li, C., Wand, M.: Precomputed real-time texture synthesis with Markovian generative adversarial networks. In: ECCV (2016)

OpenGAN: Open Set Generative Adversarial Networks

Luke Ditria, Benjamin J. Meyer[(✉)], and Tom Drummond

ARC Centre of Excellence for Robotic Vision, Monash University, Clayton, Australia
{luke.ditria,benjamin.meyer,tom.drummond}@monash.edu

Abstract. Many existing conditional Generative Adversarial Networks (cGANs) are limited to conditioning on pre-defined and fixed class-level semantic labels or attributes. We propose an open set GAN architecture (OpenGAN) that is conditioned per-input sample with a feature embedding drawn from a metric space. Using a state-of-the-art metric learning model that encodes both class-level and fine-grained semantic information, we are able to generate samples that are semantically similar to a given source image. The semantic information extracted by the metric learning model transfers to out-of-distribution novel classes, allowing the generative model to produce samples that are outside of the training distribution. We show that our proposed method is able to generate 256×256 resolution images from novel classes that are of similar visual quality to those from the training classes. In lieu of a source image, we demonstrate that random sampling of the metric space also results in high-quality samples. We show that interpolation in the feature space and latent space results in semantically and visually plausible transformations in the image space. Finally, the usefulness of the generated samples to the downstream task of data augmentation is demonstrated. We show that classifier performance can be significantly improved by augmenting the training data with OpenGAN samples on classes that are outside of the GAN training distribution.

1 Introduction

Generating new data that matches a target distribution is a challenging problem with applications including image-to-image translation [1–4], data augmentation [5,6] and video prediction [7,8]. A popular approach to this problem is Generative Adversarial Networks (GANs) [9], which train a generator and discriminator network in an adversarial manner. However, such networks have issues with training instability, especially for complicated and multi-modal data, and often

---

L. Ditria and B.J. Meyer—Contributed equally.
Code available: https://github.com/LukeDitria/OpenGAN.

Electronic supplementary material The online version of this chapter (https://doi.org/10.1007/978-3-030-69538-5_29) contains supplementary material, which is available to authorized users.

H. Ishikawa et al. (Eds.): ACCV 2020, LNCS 12625, pp. 474–492, 2021.
https://doi.org/10.1007/978-3-030-69538-5_29

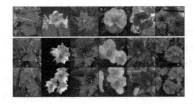

Fig. 1. Given novel class source images (top row of each section), our approach is able to generate 256×256 samples (bottom two rows of each section) that closely match the features of the source. OpenGAN was not trained on the classes shown.

result in a lack of diversity in the generated samples, particularly when training data is limited [10]. Conditional GANs (cGANs) [11] achieve greater control over the generated samples by conditioning the model on information including class labels [12–15], attributes [16–18], textual attributes [19–24] or object pose [25–27]. However, class conditional GANs are unable to generate novel class samples, attribute conditional GANs are limited to a fixed set of pre-defined attributes and pose conditional GANs require hand-labelled and pre-defined pose codes or object landmarks. While some existing methods condition on image-level features using an encoder-decoder architecture [25, 28, 29], these approaches train the encoder concurrently with the generator, enforcing no restrictions on the information encoded in the features. This can undesirably result in significant variation of the discriminative semantic information in samples generated from the same source image, as demonstrated in Sect. 5.6.

In this work, we propose an open set GAN (OpenGAN) that conditions the model on per-image features drawn from a metric space. Deep metric learning approaches have been shown to learn metric spaces that encode both class-level and fine-grained semantic information, and also have the ability to transfer to novel, out-of-distribution classes [30, 30–36]. By conditioning on per-image metric features, our proposed model is not limited to closed-set problems, but can also generate samples from novel classes in the open-set domain (see Fig. 1). Further, this conditioning method results in high intra-class diversity, where that is desirable. Unlike many existing methods, our approach is not conditioned on class-level information alone or pre-defined attributes and poses, but rather on the semantic information extracted by a state-of-the-art deep metric learning model. Additionally, the proposed approach differs from existing feature matching GANs [37], as it does not attempt to match feature moments over the entire dataset, but conditions the model on a per-feature basis. During testing, data can be generated by conditioning on specific source images, or by randomly sampling the metric feature space.

Given a metric feature extracted from a real source image, our model generates images that visually and semantically match the source, as shown in Fig. 1. The generator should not simply reconstruct the source image, but produce images with features that are similar to the source, when passed through the metric learning model. Conditioning the generator on semantically rich features not only allows for the generation of both in-distribution and novel class images, but also for transfer between source domains (Sect. 5.8). Further, OpenGAN can be utilised for data augmentation in classification problems (Sect. 5.9).

The use of a metric learning model is an important design decision. Metric features describe only discriminative semantic information, ignoring all contextual and structural information, such as pose, the quantity and arrangement of objects and other non-discriminative intra-class and inter-class variations. As a result, the generator relies on a latent space noise vector to map this information (and only this information), meaning that the structural and contextual information can be modified without any variation occurring between the semantic content of the source image and generated image. This is unlike in encoder-decoder GAN architectures that learn to extract image features concurrently with the GAN [25,28,29]. For our approach, the content information is cleanly split into two distinct spaces, without the need for the pre-defined, hand-labelled pose and landmark information that is required in previous work [25–27].

2 Related Work

Conditional Generative Models. The two most commonly used generative models in recent times are Generative Adversarial Networks [9] and Variational Auto-Encoders (VAEs) [38]. In this work, we focus on deep convolutional GANs [39]. Several methods have been proposed to achieve greater control over the generated images. Mirza and Osindero [11] condition on class-level labels by supplying one-hot class vectors to both the generator and discriminator. Such an approach can improve both generated image quality and inter-class diversity in the generator distribution. Incorporating class-level information by treating the discriminator as a multi-label classifier has also been shown to improve the quality of generated samples [37,40]. Odena et al. [12] extend this by tasking the discriminator with estimating both the probability distribution over class labels and over the source distribution (i.e. real or fake). Conditional information can also be incorporated by conditional normalisation layers [13,14,41–44], including AdaIN [45] and SPADE [46], which learn the batch normalisation [47] or instance normalisation [48] scale and bias terms as a function of some input.

Beyond class-level conditional information, data generation can also guided by conditioning the model on pre-defined attributes [16–18], such as hair colour and style for face generation. Similarly, generative models can be conditioned on attributes in a textual form by text-to-image synthesis methods [19–24]. GANs can be conditioned on structural information, allowing direct control over the object pose in the generated image. Such methods require hand-labelled and pre-defined pose codes or object landmarks [25–27].

Methods including DAGAN [28], MetaGAN [29] and DR-GAN [25] use an encoder-decoder structure, allowing the generator to be conditioned on image-level features. As such, these approaches are not limited to in-distribution classes by their design, unlike class conditional GANs. However, the encoder and generator are trained simultaneously with no constraints on the information that is represented in the encoder features. Unlike these methods, our approach leverages metric features extracted from a deep metric learning model that is trained prior to the GAN. Metric learning models have a demonstrated efficacy for open set problems [49], as such, our approach is explicitly designed for the open set domain. Further unlike the encoder-decoder GANs, our method results in no semantic variation when changing only the latent vector. This is because all discriminative semantic information is encoded in the metric features and the generator is constrained to produce images with features that match those of the source image. Consequently, the latent vector can only encode the non-discriminative information, such as the object pose, the image background and the number of objects in the image. These feature constraints do not exist in the encoder-decoder GANs.

Nguyen *et al.* [50,51] condition the generator using an auxiliary classifier network by finding the latent vector that results in generated data that strongly activates neurons in the auxiliary network. These so called Plug and Play Generative Networks can generate data that is outside of the generator's training distribution, but is inside the auxiliary network's training distribution. For our approach, the generator and feature extractor training distributions are the same, and the generator can be conditioned on data that is outside of that distribution.

Matching Networks. Training stability of GANs can be improved by performing feature matching [37]. The generator is trained such that the expected value of features extracted from generated data by a given layer of the discriminator matches that of the real data. Similar to feature matching networks are moment matching networks [52–54], which generally try to match all moments of the distributions using maximum mean discrepancy [55,56]. Unlike feature matching networks, our approach attempts to match per-sample source features individually, rather than the expected value. Our generator is also directly conditioned on per-sample features, such that the generated samples match the semantic content of the source features. Further, we use an auxiliary metric learning model to extract features, rather than the discriminator. Our feature matching is also related to perceptual loss functions [57], which use a pre-trained classifier network to match the low and high level features of input and target images for problems such as style transfer.

Metric Learning. Many deep metric learning methods are based on Siamese [58–60] and triplet networks [61], which perform distance comparisons in the feature space. Research often focuses on the generalisation of triplet loss [30, 31] and triplet mining techniques [32,33]. Song *et al.* [34] directly minimise a clustering measure, while Rippel *et al.* propose Magnet loss [35], which explicitly models class distributions in the feature space and penalises class overlap. Other approaches minimise Neighbourhood Component Analysis (NCA) loss over the set of training features [36] or per-class proxy features [62]. Metric learning has been combined with GANs to improve the stability of GAN training [63,64],

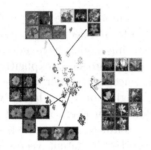

Fig. 2. Visualisation of the metric feature space for 20 novel classes, represented by colour. The feature extractor is not trained on any of the shown flower species, yet examples are co-located based on class. Example images are selected to show similar classes being located nearby. Best viewed zoomed-in. (Color figure online)

as well as to improve the training of a metric learning model [65]. Unlike these methods, we use a metric learning model to condition a GAN on image features.

3   Background

3.1   Generative Adversarial Networks

Let G be a *generator* network that attempts to learn a mapping from a latent space to a target data space. Specifically, an image is generated as $\bar{\mathbf{x}} = G(\mathbf{z})$, where $\mathbf{z}$ is a latent vector sampled from the distribution $p_z = \mathcal{N}(0, 1)$. Further, let D be a *discriminator* network that takes as input an image and attempts to distinguish between the generator distribution and the real data distribution p_d. The two networks are trained in an adversarial fashion, with improvement in one network driving improvement in the other. Greater control over the generated image can be achieved by conditioning both networks on a label $y \in p_d$.

3.2   Deep Metric Learning

OpenGAN is agnostic in terms of the metric learning feature extractor. Although the choice of metric learning model will have some impact, improvement between state-of-the-art models is incremental and unlikely to significantly affect Open-GAN performance. A good metric learning model for this task should have the ability to encode both class-level and fine-grained intra/inter-class variations, and the ability to transfer to novel classes. We use the metric learning method proposed by Meyer *et al.* [36] in our experiments. This method possesses the required characteristics, as shown in the t-SNE visualisation [66] of novel class examples in Fig. 2. Although from outside of the training distribution, examples are clustered by class, with semantically similar classes located nearby.

For a given input image, the network F extracts a d-dimensional feature $\mathbf{f} = [f^{(i)}, ..., f^{(d)}]$. For training, a set of n Gaussian kernel centres are defined in

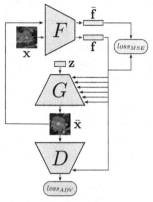

Overview of method.

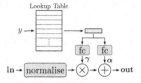

Class conditional normalisation.

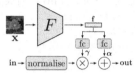

Feature embedding conditional normalisation.

Fig. 3. (a) Overview of our approach. During training, features are extracted from training images and used to condition the GAN via conditional normalisation layers. During testing, features may be extracted from source images or randomly sampled from the metric space. (b) Class conditional normalisation compared to the feature conditional normalisation (c) used in our model.

the feature space as $\mathcal{C} = \{\mathbf{c}_1, ..., \mathbf{c}_n\}$, where $\mathbf{c}_i = [c_i^{(1)}, ..., c_i^{(d)}]$ is the i-th kernel centre. The centres are defined to be the locations of the n training set features, with the weights of F updated during training by minimising the NCA loss [67]. To make training feasible, a cached version of the kernel centres $\hat{\mathcal{C}}$ is stored and updated periodically during training, avoiding the need to do so at every training iteration. The loss minimised during training is shown in Eq. 1, where σ is a hyperparameter and ℓ_i is the class label of the i-th training example. If necessary, approximate nearest neighbour search can be leveraged to make the approach scalable both in terms of the number of classes and training examples.

$$loss_F = -\sum_{\mathbf{c}_i \in \mathcal{C}} \ln \left(\frac{\sum_{\hat{\mathbf{c}}_j \in \hat{\mathcal{C}}, i \neq j, \ell_i = \ell_j} \exp\left(\frac{-\|\mathbf{c}_i - \hat{\mathbf{c}}_j\|^2}{2\sigma^2}\right)}{\sum_{\hat{\mathbf{c}}_k \in \hat{\mathcal{C}}, i \neq k} \exp\left(\frac{-\|\mathbf{c}_i - \hat{\mathbf{c}}_k\|^2}{2\sigma^2}\right)} \right) \tag{1}$$

4 Feature Embedding Conditional GANs

4.1 Overview

Our proposed method consists of three convolutional neural networks: a generator G, a discriminator D and a metric feature extractor F. Network F extracts a feature $\mathbf{f}$ for a sampled training image, which is fed into networks G and D. The generator attempts to produce an image that both fools the discriminator and results in a feature $\bar{\mathbf{f}}$ that closely matches the real feature, when the fake image is passed through network F. The former is achieved via an adversarial (ADV)

480   L. Ditria et al.

Algorithm 1. Training algorithm for OpenGAN.

Require:
    Models F, G, D with parameters $\boldsymbol{\theta}_F$,
    $\boldsymbol{\theta}_G, \boldsymbol{\theta}_D$
    Scale term for feature loss λ
1: Pre-train $\boldsymbol{\theta}_F$ (Sect. 3.2)
2: **while** $\boldsymbol{\theta}_G$ is not converged **do**
3:    Sample $\mathbf{x} \sim p_d$
4:    $\mathbf{f} \leftarrow F(\mathbf{x})$
5:    Sample $\mathbf{z} \sim \mathcal{N}(0,1)$

6:    $\mathcal{L}_D \leftarrow \min(0, 1 - D(\mathbf{x}, \mathbf{f}))$
            $+ \min(0, 1 + D(G(\mathbf{z}, \mathbf{f}), \mathbf{f}))$
7:    $\boldsymbol{\theta}_D \leftarrow \boldsymbol{\theta}_D - \text{Adam}(\nabla \mathcal{L}_D)$
8:    Sample $\mathbf{z} \sim \mathcal{N}(0,1)$
9:    $\bar{\mathbf{x}} \leftarrow G(\mathbf{z}, \mathbf{f})$
10:   $\mathcal{L}_G \leftarrow -D(\bar{\mathbf{x}}, \mathbf{f}) + \lambda \, \|F(\bar{\mathbf{x}}) - \mathbf{f}\|^2$
11:   $\boldsymbol{\theta}_G \leftarrow \boldsymbol{\theta}_G - \text{Adam}(\nabla \mathcal{L}_G)$
12: **end while**

---

loss, while the latter is achieved by a mean squared error (MSE) loss term in the metric feature space (Fig. 3a). During testing, examples can be generated by conditioning on features from specific images or by sampling the feature space.

Features are incorporated into the generator and discriminator by way of feature conditional normalisation layers, described in detail in Sect. 4.3. The normalisation scale and bias terms are learned as a continuous function of the conditioning features, as opposed to a discreet function of class labels in class conditional normalisation. This continuity means that during testing, meaningful interpolation between features can occur. Further, out-of-distribution images can be generated by sampling a desired point in the metric feature space or by conditioning on the feature extracted from a specific novel image.

In a conventional GAN or class conditional GAN framework, generating an image that visually and semantically matches a given source image can be challenging. Additionally, there is no mechanism in the generator training that encourages the ability to transfer to data outside of the training distribution. Conversely, the training of our generator is guided by a feature extractor that transfers to novel classes (see Sect. 3.2) and the ability to condition the generator on a specific source image is built-in to the framework.

We adopt a definition of "open set" that is commonly used in the open set recognition literature [49,68–70], whereby it is assumed that known and novel classes share some common properties, and are drawn from the same subspace of the infinitely large open set space.

4.2 Training Procedure

Network optimisation is outlined in Algorithm 1. The feature extractor is pre-trained, with the weights subsequently frozen. The loss functions minimised by the discriminator and the generator, respectively, are:

$$loss_D = \mathbb{E}_{\mathbf{x} \sim p_d} \left[\min(0, 1 - D(\mathbf{x}, \mathbf{f})) \right] + \mathbb{E}_{\mathbf{x} \sim p_d, \mathbf{z} \sim p_z} \left[\min(0, 1 + D(G(\mathbf{z}, \mathbf{f}), \mathbf{f})) \right], \tag{2}$$

$$loss_G = \mathbb{E}_{\mathbf{x} \sim p_d, \mathbf{z} \sim p_z} \left[-D(G(\mathbf{z}, \mathbf{f}), \mathbf{f}) + \lambda \, \|F(G(\mathbf{z}, \mathbf{f})) - \mathbf{f}\|^2 \right], \tag{3}$$

Table 1. Sample quality comparison (lower scores indicate better quality).

	FID	Intra FID
U-SAGAN [14]	161.74	-
C-SAGAN [14]	66.12	179.67
Ours: T-SM	22.05	103.18
Ours: N-SM	39.51	110.04
Ours: N-RF	31.89	104.90

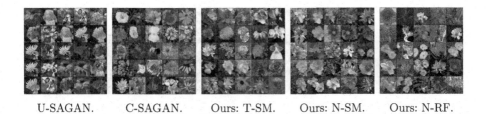

U-SAGAN.   C-SAGAN.   Ours: T-SM.   Ours: N-SM.   Ours: N-RF.

Fig. 4. Uncurated and randomly selected images on the Flowers102 dataset.

where λ is a scaling term for the feature loss component and $\mathbf{f} = F(\mathbf{x})$. Hinge loss [71,72] is used for the adversarial component, while mean squared error is used for the feature loss. Parameters are updated via Adam optimisation [73].

4.3   Feature Conditional Normalisation

Intermediate neural network layer activations can be forced to have similar distributions by including layers that normalise over the entire batch [47] or over each instance individually [48]. Normalisation of activations can lead to faster and more stable training, as well as better overall model performance. Such layers perform the following normalisation on an activation:

$$\hat{m}_i = \gamma \frac{m_i - \mu}{\sqrt{v + \epsilon}} + \alpha \qquad (4)$$

where m_i is the input, $\hat{m}_i$ is the normalised output, μ is the mean, v is the variance and ϵ is a small constant. In conventional normalisation layers, the scale γ and bias α terms are learned model parameters, while for conditional normalisation layers, they are learned as a function of some input. Class conditional normalisation (Fig. 3b) learns a feature per-class that is often input to two fully connected (FC) layers to produce the scale and bias. This limits the GAN to produce only images from (or interpolations between) the training classes.

We propose metric feature embedding conditional normalisation (Fig. 3c), which learns the scale and bias as a function of a feature embedding drawn from a metric space. This allows conditioning on specific images or features.

Ours: T-SM.   Ours: N-SM.   Ours: N-RF.

Fig. 5. Uncurated and randomly selected images on the CelebA dataset.

Fig. 6. Novel class real source images (top row) and resultant generated images (bottom two rows). Although the identities are not present during training, the fake images match the features of the real source images.

5   Experiments

5.1   Implementation Details

The datasets used for evaluation are Oxford Flowers102 [74] and CelebA Faces [75]. Each dataset is split into training and novel classes. The first 82 classes from Flowers102 are used for training, resulting in 6433 training images. For CelebA, identities are used as class labels with the 3300 identities containing the most samples used for training, resulting in 97262 training images. CelebA pose/attribute labels are used for interpolation experiments, but not for training.

The generator and discriminator follow a similar architecture to Self-Attention GAN (SAGAN) [14], but we replace the projection layer in the discriminator with a single feature embedding conditional normalisation layer and a fully connected layer. We also generate images twice the resolution of SAGAN at 256×256 pixels and use a channel width multiplier of 32. Six residual blocks [76] are used in each network, along with spectral normalisation [77] and a single self-attention block [14]. Feature conditional normalisation is used in all residual blocks in the generator but only in the final discriminator block. We find batch normalisation on Flowers102 and instance normalisation on CelebA performs best in practice. A latent space dimension of 128 is used for the generator. For training, a base learning rate of 10^{-4}, batch size of 48 and Adam optimiser [73] with $\beta_1 = 0$ and $\beta_2 = 0.999$ are used. The value of λ is set to 0.01. The GAN is trained for up to 60000 iterations on four Nvidia 1080 Ti GPUs, taking approximately 15 h.

(a)   **(b)**

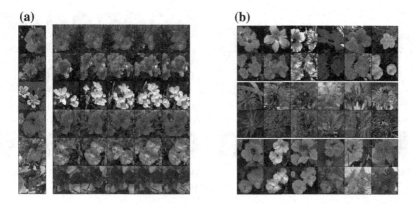

Fig. 7. (a) Fake samples (right) are generated from a fixed feature, extracted from the novel class real samples (left). (b) Examples from three novel classes with a fixed latent vector for each class. Source images (top rows of each section) are used to condition the GAN to produce the fake images (bottom rows).

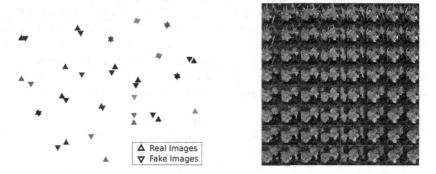

Fig. 8. Novel per-class mean feature embeddings for real and fake images. Colour represents class. (Color figure online)

Fig. 9. Interpolation between two latent vectors (horizontal) and two feature embeddings (vertical).

A ResNet18 architecture [76] with the fully connected layer removed is used for the feature extractor. The model is trained with a base learning rate of 10^{-5}, Gaussian σ of 10 and an Adam optimiser [73] with $\beta_1 = 0.9$ and $\beta_2 = 0.999$. The stored Gaussian centres are updated every 5 epochs.

5.2   Comparison to Baselines

As the proposed method can use any suitable network architecture, the aim of this work is not to improve on state-of-the-art methods in terms of sample quality. Here, we aim to show that our method results in samples of at least comparable quality to appropriate baselines. We compare to two baselines: Unconditional SAGAN (*U-SAGAN*) and Class Conditional SAGAN (*C-SAGAN*) [14]. For fair comparison, these baselines have the same structure as our model, differing only

Pose interpolation in latent space.

Attribute (age, bangs, gender) interpolation in feature space.

Pose interpolation in feature space.

Attribute (age) interpolation in latent space.

Fig. 10. Pose and attribute interpolation.

in terms of the normalisation layers. U-SAGAN uses non-conditional normalisation, while C-SAGAN uses a single conditioning feature per-class (Fig. 3b).

Uncurated qualitative results on the Flowers102 dataset can be seen in Fig. 4 and a quantitative comparison, in terms of the FID and intra-class FID scores [78], is shown in Table 1. For our approach, we investigate sampling features from both the training and novel distributions, as well as two methods of feature sampling: random sampling from normal distributions centred on the class means, and extracting features from sampled real images. Our methods are:

- *Ours: T-SM*: Training distribution, sample means.
- *Ours: N-SM*: Novel distribution, sample means.
- *Ours: N-RF*: Novel distribution, real image features.

Both qualitatively and quantitatively, there is little difference in quality between sampling training and novel distributions, or between the two feature sampling methods. This is also observed on CelebA in Fig. 5. Compared to the baselines, our approach results in both higher quality images and better sample diversity.

5.3   One-Shot Image Generation

In this section, we show that our method is able to generate samples that match the semantic features of source images sampled from the novel distribution. We name this problem "one-shot image generation", however, it is important to note that no updates are made to the network weights using the novel source images; the source images are simply used to condition the generator. Figure 1 demonstrates this ability on both datasets, while further CelebA samples are shown in Fig. 6. Additional Flowers102 samples are shown in Figs. 7a and 7b, with discussion in Sect. 5.4.

Figure 8 shows a t-SNE visualisation [66] of the novel per-class mean features of the real and fake samples when passed through network F. In the majority of cases, the fake mean feature is co-located with the real mean feature.

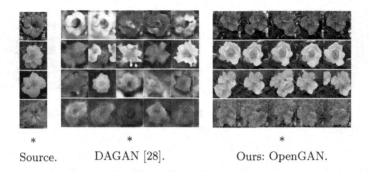

Source.   DAGAN [28].   Ours: OpenGAN.

Fig. 11. Fixed source image per row with random latent vectors. DAGAN samples show significant semantic variation, while OpenGAN samples do not.

5.4 Single Source and Intra-Class Diversity

Our method is able to generate a range of samples from a single source image by randomly sampling the latent vector. This single source diversity is demonstrated in Fig. 7a. The generated samples match the semantic features of the source image, but varying the latent vector results in structural changes, such as the pose and number of flowers present. Intra-class diversity is demonstrated in Fig. 7b by fixing the latent vector and sampling various features from the same class. Due to the fixed latent vector, the structural information is consistent, while the sampling of different features results in fine-grained intra-class differences, such as colour. Again, all source images are from novel classes.

5.5 Latent and Feature Space Interpolation

A two-dimensional interpolation between two latent vectors (horizontal direction) and two feature embeddings (vertical direction) is shown in Fig. 9. The generated samples are required to contain the semantic information encoded in the given feature embedding. As such, interpolation in latent space with a fixed feature results in plausible transformations in the image space, without changes in the fine-grained semantic content. This is unlike latent space interpolation in conventional cGANs, which by design results in intra-class semantic variations.

By training a classifier to predict the binary pose and attribute labels of CelebA, we are able to compute pose/attribute mean latent and feature vectors. If a given attribute is encoded, traversing the line that connects the mean positive and negative vectors will vary that attribute in the image space. As seen in Fig. 10, pose information is encoded only in the latent space, with no pose change seen when interpolating between the mean feature vectors. Conversely, attributes such as age, gender and hair style are encoded only in feature space.

5.6 Split of Information in Latent and Feature Spaces

As seen in Figs. 7 and 10, all discriminative semantic information is encoded in the feature space and only non-discriminative structural information is encoded

Fig. 12. Random sampling of the feature space.   **Fig. 13.** Generating from out-of-domain source images.

in the latent space. In Fig. 11, we show that this clean split does not exist in encoder-decoder style image-conditional GANs, such as DAGAN [28]. We train a DAGAN model using the official implementation on Flowers102. It can be seen that for a fixed source image, DAGAN samples undesirably show significant semantic variation (e.g. the colour of the flower) when varying only the latent space, while OpenGAN samples show no discriminative semantic variation.

5.7   Random Feature Space Sampling

Conventional GANs are able to generate data by randomly sampling the latent space without any external inputs. Our generator is trained not only with latent space sampling, but also feature space sampling. Figure 12 shows that new data can be generated by randomly selecting both the latent and feature vectors. The generated samples are diverse, as well as visually and semantically plausible.

5.8   Out-of-Domain Source Images

We investigate the use of out-of-domain source images, such as paintings and digital art, that have similar semantic content to the training images. As seen in Fig. 13, the fake samples match the semantic features of the source images. This shows that the metric learning model is able to extract relevant information, despite the domain shift.

5.9   OpenGAN for Data Augmentation

In this section, we demonstrate the usefulness of samples generated by OpenGAN to the downstream application of data augmentation for classification. As a baseline, we train a Resnet18 [76] classifier on 500 novel (i.e. outside of the OpenGAN training distribution) CelebA classes, using 1, 2, 5 and 10 training examples per class. The same test set is used for all experiments. To train the classifier with data augmentation, we first sample a batch of real images from the training data set and perform an optimisation step on the classifier. Using the metric features extracted from the sampled real images, a batch of fake images is generated, which is used to perform another optimisation step on the classifier. The randomised generation of fake images and classifier optimisation step is repeated using the same batch of real features until the desired ratio of

Table 2. CelebA data augmentation using OpenGAN samples.

	Real per class	Fake per real	η	Test acc. (%)
Baseline	1	0	-	2.71
With data aug.	1	5	2	**12.13**
Baseline	2	0	-	7.47
With data aug.	2	4	1.5	**22.70**
Baseline	5	0	-	25.98
With data aug.	5	3	1.5	**51.81**
Baseline	10	0	-	52.69
With data aug.	10	2	1.5	**71.98**

fake-to-real data is achieved. A new batch of real images is then sampled and the process repeats. We find that adding small random perturbations to the real conditioning features can be beneficial. The perturbations are Gaussian noise with a zero mean and standard deviation of $\eta\,\sigma_F$, where η is a scaling term and σ_F is the standard deviation of the real features across all dimensions.

For each number of real samples per class, we experiment with fake-to-real data ratios of 1 through 5 and η values of 0, 1.5 and 2. The best performing experiments for each number of real samples per class are shown in Table 2. Data augmentation results in a significant improvement in classification performance, despite the classes being from outside of the OpenGAN training distribution.

6   Conclusion

By conditioning on image features drawn from a metric space, OpenGAN is able to generate samples that are semantically similar to a given source image, including those that are from classes outside of the training distribution. Interpolation in the feature and latent spaces results in semantically plausible samples, with the feature space encoding fine-grained semantic information and the latent space encoding structural information. Finally, generated samples can be used to significantly improve classification performance through data augmentation.

Acknowledgements. This research was supported by the Australian Research Council Centre of Excellence for Robotic Vision (project number CE140100016).

References

1. Isola, P., Zhu, J.Y., Zhou, T., Efros, A.A.: Image-to-image translation with conditional adversarial networks. In: Proceedings of the IEEE Conference on Computer Vision and Pattern Recognition (CVPR), pp. 1125–1134. IEEE (2017)

2. Zhu, J.Y., Park, T., Isola, P., Efros, A.A.: Unpaired image-to-image translation using cycle-consistent adversarial networks. In: Proceedings of the IEEE Conference on Computer Vision and Pattern Recognition (CVPR), pp. 2223–2232. IEEE (2017)

3. Choi, Y., Choi, M., Kim, M., Ha, J.W., Kim, S., Choo, J.: StarGAN: unified generative adversarial networks for multi-domain image-to-image translation. In: Proceedings of the IEEE Conference on Computer Vision and Pattern Recognition. IEEE (2018)

4. Choi, Y., Uh, Y., Yoo, J., Ha, J.W.: StarGAN v2: diverse image synthesis for multiple domains. In: Proceedings of the IEEE Conference on Computer Vision and Pattern Recognition. IEEE (2020)

5. Frid-Adar, M., Diamant, I., Klang, E., Amitai, M., Goldberger, J., Greenspan, H.: Gan-based synthetic medical image augmentation for increased CNN performance in liver lesion classification. Neurocomputing **321**, 321–331 (2018)

6. Xing, Y., et al.: Adversarial pulmonary pathology translation for pairwise chest X-ray data augmentation. In: Shen, D., et al. (eds.) MICCAI 2019, Part VI. LNCS, vol. 11769, pp. 757–765. Springer, Cham (2019). https://doi.org/10.1007/978-3-030-32226-7_84

7. Liang, X., Lee, L., Dai, W., Xing, E.P.: Dual motion GAN for future-flow embedded video prediction. In: Proceedings of the IEEE Conference on Computer Vision and Pattern Recognition (CVPR), pp. 1744–1752. IEEE (2017)

8. Kwon, Y.H., Park, M.G.: Predicting future frames using retrospective cycle GAN. In: Proceedings of the IEEE Conference on Computer Vision and Pattern Recognition (CVPR), pp. 1811–1820. IEEE (2019)

9. Goodfellow, I., et al.: Generative adversarial nets. In: Advances in Neural Information Processing Systems (NeurIPS), pp. 2672–2680 (2014)

10. Gurumurthy, S., Kiran Sarvadevabhatla, R., Venkatesh Babu, R.: DeliGAN: generative adversarial networks for diverse and limited data. In: Proceedings of the IEEE Conference on Computer Vision and Pattern Recognition (CVPR). IEEE (2017)

11. Mirza, M., Osindero, S.: Conditional generative adversarial nets. arXiv preprint arXiv:1411.1784 (2014)

12. Odena, A., Olah, C., Shlens, J.: Conditional image synthesis with auxiliary classifier GANs. In: International Conference on Machine Learning (ICML), pp. 2642–2651 (2017)

13. Miyato, T., Koyama, M.: cGANs with projection discriminator. In: International Conference on Learning Representations (ICLR) (2018)

14. Zhang, H., Goodfellow, I., Metaxas, D., Odena, A.: Self-attention generative adversarial networks. In: International Conference on Machine Learning (ICML) (2019)

15. Brock, A., Donahue, J., Simonyan, K.: Large scale GAN training for high fidelity natural image synthesis. In: International Conference on Learning Representations (ICLR) (2019)

16. Gauthier, J.: Conditional generative adversarial nets for convolutional face generation. Class Project for Stanford CS231N: Convolutional Neural Networks for Visual Recognition, Winter semester, p. 2 (2014)

17. Kaneko, T., Hiramatsu, K., Kashino, K.: Generative attribute controller with conditional filtered generative adversarial networks. In: Proceedings of the IEEE Conference on Computer Vision and Pattern Recognition (CVPR), pp. 7006–7015. IEEE (2017)

18. Lu, Y., Tai, Y.-W., Tang, C.-K.: Attribute-guided face generation using conditional CycleGAN. In: Ferrari, V., Hebert, M., Sminchisescu, C., Weiss, Y. (eds.) ECCV 2018, Part XII. LNCS, vol. 11216, pp. 293–308. Springer, Cham (2018). https://doi.org/10.1007/978-3-030-01258-8_18

19. Reed, S., Akata, Z., Yan, X., Logeswaran, L., Schiele, B., Lee, H.: Generative adversarial text to image synthesis. In: International Conference on Machine Learning (ICML), pp. 1060–1069 (2016)

20. Reed, S.E., Akata, Z., Mohan, S., Tenka, S., Schiele, B., Lee, H.: Learning what and where to draw. In: Advances in Neural Information Processing Systems (NeurIPS), pp. 217–225 (2016)

21. Mansimov, E., Parisotto, E., Ba, J.L., Salakhutdinov, R.: Generating images from captions with attention. In: International Conference on Learning Representations (ICLR) (2016)

22. Zhang, H., et al.: StackGAN++: realistic image synthesis with stacked generative adversarial networks. IEEE Trans. Pattern Anal. Mach. Intell. (TPAMI) **41**, 1947–1962 (2018)

23. Dong, H., Yu, S., Wu, C., Guo, Y.: Semantic image synthesis via adversarial learning. In: IEEE International Conference on Computer Vision (ICCV), pp. 5706–5714. IEEE (2017)

24. Park, H., Yoo, Y., Kwak, N.: MC-GAN: multi-conditional generative adversarial network for image synthesis. In: British Machine Vision Conference (BMVC), BMVA (2018)

25. Tran, L., Yin, X., Liu, X.: Disentangled representation learning GAN for pose-invariant face recognition. In: Proceedings of the IEEE Conference on Computer Vision and Pattern Recognition (CVPR), pp. 1415–1424. IEEE (2017)

26. Ge, Y., Li, Z., Zhao, H., Yin, G., Yi, S., Wang, X., et al.: FD-GAN: pose-guided feature distilling GAN for robust person re-identification. In: Advances in Neural Information Processing Systems (NeurIPS), pp. 1222–1233 (2018)

27. Zakharov, E., Shysheya, A., Burkov, E., Lempitsky, V.: Few-shot adversarial learning of realistic neural talking head models. In: IEEE International Conference on Computer Vision (ICCV). IEEE (2019)

28. Antoniou, A., Storkey, A., Edwards, H.: Data augmentation generative adversarial networks. In: International Conference on Learning Representations Workshops (ICLRw) (2017)

29. Zhang, R., Che, T., Ghahramani, Z., Bengio, Y., Song, Y.: MetaGAN: an adversarial approach to few-shot learning. In: Advances in Neural Information Processing Systems (NeurIPS), pp. 2365–2374 (2018)

30. Song, H.O., Xiang, Y., Jegelka, S., Savarese, S.: Deep metric learning via lifted structured feature embedding. In: Proceedings of the IEEE Conference on Computer Vision and Pattern Recognition (CVPR), pp. 4004–4012. IEEE (2016)

31. Sohn, K.: Improved deep metric learning with multi-class N-pair loss objective. In: Advances in Neural Information Processing Systems (NeurIPS), pp. 1857–1865 (2016)

32. Schroff, F., Kalenichenko, D., Philbin, J.: FaceNet: a unified embedding for face recognition and clustering. In: Proceedings of the IEEE Conference on Computer Vision and Pattern Recognition (CVPR), pp. 815–823. IEEE (2015)

33. Harwood, B., Kumar, B., Carneiro, G., Reid, I., Drummond, T., et al.: Smart mining for deep metric learning. In: IEEE International Conference on Computer Vision (ICCV), pp. 2821–2829. IEEE (2017)

34. Song, H.O., Jegelka, S., Rathod, V., Murphy, K.: Deep metric learning via facility location. In: Proceedings of the IEEE Conference on Computer Vision and Pattern Recognition (CVPR), pp. 2206–2214. IEEE (2017)
35. Rippel, O., Paluri, M., Dollar, P., Bourdev, L.: Metric learning with adaptive density discrimination. In: International Conference on Learning Representations (ICLR) (2016)
36. Meyer, B.J., Harwood, B., Drummond, T.: Deep metric learning and image classification with nearest neighbour Gaussian kernels. In: IEEE International Conference on Image Processing (ICIP), pp. 151–155. IEEE (2018)
37. Salimans, T., et al.: Improved techniques for training GANs. In: Advances in Neural Information Processing Systems (NeurIPS), pp. 2234–2242 (2016)
38. Kingma, D.P., Welling, M.: Auto-encoding variational bayes. arXiv preprint arXiv:1312.6114 (2013)
39. Radford, A., Metz, L., Chintala, S.: Unsupervised representation learning with deep convolutional generative adversarial networks. In: International Conference on Learning Representations (ICLR) (2016)
40. Odena, A.: Semi-supervised learning with generative adversarial networks. arXiv preprint arXiv:1606.01583 (2016)
41. Dumoulin, V., Shlens, J., Kudlur, M.: A learned representation for artistic style. In: International Conference on Learning Representations (ICLR) (2017)
42. De Vries, H., Strub, F., Mary, J., Larochelle, H., Pietquin, O., Courville, A.C.: Modulating early visual processing by language. In: Advances in Neural Information Processing Systems (NeurIPS), pp. 6594–6604 (2017)
43. Karras, T., Laine, S., Aila, T.: A style-based generator architecture for generative adversarial networks. In: Proceedings of the IEEE Conference on Computer Vision and Pattern Recognition (CVPR), pp. 4401–4410. IEEE (2019)
44. Karras, T., Laine, S., Aittala, M., Hellsten, J., Lehtinen, J., Aila, T.: Analyzing and improving the image quality of StyleGAN. In: Proceedings of the IEEE Conference on Computer Vision and Pattern Recognition (CVPR), pp. 8110–8119. IEEE (2020)
45. Huang, X., Belongie, S.: Arbitrary style transfer in real-time with adaptive instance normalization. In: IEEE International Conference on Computer Vision (ICCV), pp. 1510–1519. IEEE (2017)
46. Park, T., Liu, M.Y., Wang, T.C., Zhu, J.Y.: Semantic image synthesis with spatially-adaptive normalization. In: Proceedings of the IEEE Conference on Computer Vision and Pattern Recognition (CVPR), pp. 2337–2346. IEEE (2019)
47. Ioffe, S., Szegedy, C.: Batch normalization: Accelerating deep network training by reducing internal covariate shift. In: International Conference on Machine Learning (ICML), pp. 448–456 (2015)
48. Ulyanov, D., Vedaldi, A., Lempitsky, V.: Instance normalization: The missing ingredient for fast stylization. arXiv preprint arXiv:1607.08022 (2016)
49. Meyer, B.J., Drummond, T.: The importance of metric learning for robotic vision: open set recognition and active learning. In: International Conference on Robotics and Automation (ICRA), pp. 2924–2931. IEEE (2019)
50. Nguyen, A., Dosovitskiy, A., Yosinski, J., Brox, T., Clune, J.: Synthesizing the preferred inputs for neurons in neural networks via deep generator networks. In: Advances in Neural Information Processing Systems (NeurIPS), pp. 3395–3403 (2016)

51. Nguyen, A., Clune, J., Bengio, Y., Dosovitskiy, A., Yosinski, J.: Plug & play generative networks: conditional iterative generation of images in latent space. In: Proceedings of the IEEE Conference on Computer Vision and Pattern Recognition (CVPR). IEEE (2017)
52. Li, Y., Swersky, K., Zemel, R.: Generative moment matching networks. In: International Conference on Machine Learning (ICML), pp. 1718–1727 (2015)
53. Dziugaite, G.K., Roy, D.M., Ghahramani, Z.: Training generative neural networks via maximum mean discrepancy optimization. In: Proceedings of the Thirty-First Conference on Uncertainty in Artificial Intelligence, pp. 258–267 (2015)
54. Li, C.L., Chang, W.C., Cheng, Y., Yang, Y., Póczos, B.: MMD GAN: towards deeper understanding of moment matching network. In: Advances in Neural Information Processing Systems (NeurIPS), pp. 2203–2213 (2017)
55. Gretton, A., Borgwardt, K., Rasch, M., Schölkopf, B., Smola, A.J.: A kernel method for the two-sample-problem. In: Advances in Neural Information Processing Systems (NeurIPS), pp. 513–520 (2007)
56. Gretton, A., Borgwardt, K.M., Rasch, M.J., Schölkopf, B., Smola, A.: A kernel two-sample test. J. Mach. Learn. Res. **13**, 723–773 (2012)
57. Johnson, J., Alahi, A., Fei-Fei, L.: Perceptual losses for real-time style transfer and super-resolution. In: Leibe, B., Matas, J., Sebe, N., Welling, M. (eds.) ECCV 2016, Part II. LNCS, vol. 9906, pp. 694–711. Springer, Cham (2016). https://doi.org/10.1007/978-3-319-46475-6_43
58. Bromley, J., Guyon, I., Lecun, Y., Sackinger, E., Shah, R.: Signature verification using a Siamese time delay neural network. In: Advances in Neural Information Processing Systems (NeurIPS) (1993)
59. Chopra, S., Hadsell, R., LeCun, Y.: Learning a similarity metric discriminatively, with application to face verification. In: Proceedings of the IEEE Conference on Computer Vision and Pattern Recognition (CVPR), vol. 1, pp. 539–546. IEEE (2005)
60. Hadsell, R., Chopra, S., LeCun, Y.: Dimensionality reduction by learning an invariant mapping. In: Proceedings of the IEEE Conference on Computer Vision and Pattern Recognition (CVPR), vol. 2, pp. 1735–1742. IEEE (2006)
61. Hoffer, E., Ailon, N.: Deep metric learning using triplet network. In: Feragen, A., Pelillo, M., Loog, M. (eds.) SIMBAD 2015. LNCS, vol. 9370, pp. 84–92. Springer, Cham (2015). https://doi.org/10.1007/978-3-319-24261-3_7
62. Movshovitz-Attias, Y., Toshev, A., Leung, T.K., Ioffe, S., Singh, S.: No fuss distance metric learning using proxies. In: IEEE International Conference on Computer Vision (ICCV), pp. 360–368. IEEE (2017)
63. Dou, Z.Y.: Metric learning-based generative adversarial network. arXiv preprint arXiv:1711.02792 (2017)
64. Dai, G., Xie, J., Fang, Y.: Metric-based generative adversarial network. In: Proceedings of the 25th ACM International Conference on Multimedia, pp. 672–680. ACM (2017)
65. Zieba, M., Wang, L.: Training triplet networks with GAN. arXiv preprint arXiv:1704.02227 (2017)
66. van der Maaten, L., Hinton, G.: Visualizing data using t-SNE. J. Mach. Learn. Res. **9**, 2579–2605 (2008)
67. Goldberger, J., Hinton, G.E., Roweis, S.T., Salakhutdinov, R.R.: Neighbourhood components analysis. In: Advances in Neural Information Processing Systems (NeurIPS), pp. 513–520 (2005)

68. Bendale, A., Boult, T.: Towards open world recognition. In: Proceedings of the IEEE Conference on Computer Vision and Pattern Recognition (CVPR). IEEE (2015)
69. Bendale, A., Boult, T.E.: Towards open set deep networks. In: Proceedings of the IEEE Conference on Computer Vision and Pattern Recognition (CVPR). IEEE (2016)
70. Ge, Z., Demyanov, S., Chen, Z., Garnavi, R.: Generative OpenMax for multi-class open set classification. In: British Machine Vision Conference (BMVC). BMVA (2017)
71. Lim, J.H., Ye, J.C.: Geometric GAN. arXiv preprint arXiv:1705.02894 (2017)
72. Tran, D., Ranganath, R., Blei, D.: Hierarchical implicit models and likelihood-free variational inference. In: Advances in Neural Information Processing Systems (NeurIPS), pp. 5523–5533 (2017)
73. Kingma, D.P., Ba, J.: Adam: a method for stochastic optimization. In: International Conference on Learning Representations (ICLR) (2015)
74. Nilsback, M.E., Zisserman, A.: Automated flower classification over a large number of classes. In: Indian Conference on Computer Vision, Graphics and Image Processing (2008)
75. Liu, Z., Luo, P., Wang, X., Tang, X.: Deep learning face attributes in the wild. In: IEEE International Conference on Computer Vision (ICCV). IEEE (2015)
76. He, K., Zhang, X., Ren, S., Sun, J.: Deep residual learning for image recognition. In: Proceedings of the IEEE Conference on Computer Vision and Pattern Recognition (CVPR), pp. 770–778. IEEE (2016)
77. Miyato, T., Kataoka, T., Koyama, M., Yoshida, Y.: Spectral normalization for generative adversarial networks. In: International Conference on Learning Representations (ICLR) (2018)
78. Heusel, M., Ramsauer, H., Unterthiner, T., Nessler, B., Hochreiter, S.: GANs trained by a two time-scale update rule converge to a local nash equilibrium. In: Advances in Neural Information Processing Systems (NeurIPS), pp. 6629–6640 (2017)

CPTNet: Cascade Pose Transform Network for Single Image Talking Head Animation

Jiale Zhang[1], Ke Xian[1], Chengxin Liu[1(✉)], Yinpeng Chen[1], Zhiguo Cao[1],
and Weicai Zhong[2]

[1] Key Laboratory of Image Processing and Intelligent Control,
Ministry of Education, School of Artificial Intelligence and Automation,
Huazhong University of Science and Technology, Wuhan 430074, China
{jiale_zhang,cx_liu,zgcao}@hust.edu.cn
[2] Huawei CBG Consumer Cloud Service Search Product and Big Data
Platform Department, Xi'an, China

Abstract. We study the problem of talking head animation from a single image. Most of the existing methods focus on generating talking heads for human. However, little attention has been paid to the creation of talking head anime. In this paper, our goal is to synthesize vivid talking heads from a single anime image. To this end, we propose cascade pose transform network, termed CPTNet, that consists of a face pose transform network and a head pose transform network. Specifically, we introduce a mask generator to animate facial expression (*e.g.*, close eyes and open mouth) and a grid generator for head movement animation, followed by a fusion module to generate talking heads. In order to handle large motion and obtain more accurate results, we design a pose vector decomposition and cascaded refinement strategy. In addition, we create an anime talking head dataset, that includes various anime characters and poses, to train our model. Extensive experiments on our dataset demonstrate that our model outperforms other methods, generating more accurate and vivid talking heads from a single anime image.

1 Introduction

Talking head animation, as the name suggests, refers to the change of facial expression and head movement of anime characters. It is a very interesting task which has broad application scenarios, including game production, filmmaking, and virtual avatars. Recently, great progress has been made in human talking head generation with the introduction of Generative Adversarial Networks (GANs) [1]. For instance, some methods [2–4] are able to synthesize different expressions as well as change attributes of human face, such as hair color, skin and age. However, there is a big difference between human faces and anime faces: patterns of human faces are highly structured, while anime faces are rather diverse. Also, different anime style leads to significant different face patterns, such as small mouth, no nose, and large eyes. Therefore, such methods trained

© Springer Nature Switzerland AG 2021
H. Ishikawa et al. (Eds.): ACCV 2020, LNCS 12625, pp. 493–508, 2021.
https://doi.org/10.1007/978-3-030-69538-5_30

on human datasets (*e.g.*, RaFD [5] and CelebA [6]) cannot be directly used for anime talking head generation.

In this paper, we aim at designing a model for generating anime talking heads, including the change of anime facial expression (*e.g.*, close eyes and open mouth) and the movement of anime head. Since there is no open source anime dataset available on the Internet, we create an anime talking head dataset consisting of 1842 anime IDs. Each anime ID has 150 face poses and 973 head poses with corresponding pose vectors.

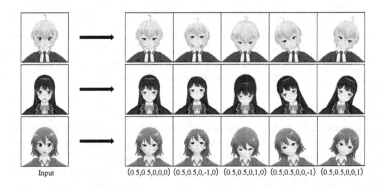

Input   (0.5,0.5,0,0,0) (0.5,0.5,0,-1,0) (0.5,0.5,0,1,0) (0.5,0.5,0,0,-1) (0.5,0.5,0,0,1)

Fig. 1. Some qualitative results on our anime dataset. Given a single anime image (first column) and a target pose vector (last row), our method is able to generate vivid talking heads (from the second column to the sixth column). Specifically, we encode the change of facial expression and head movement into a pose vector (*i.e.*, left eye, right eye, mouth, top-down head, left-right head). Note that the values of eyes and mouth vary from 0 to 1, while head ranges from −1 to 1.

To generate vivid talking heads from a single anime image, we disentangle the problem into two stages: the change of anime facial expression and the movement of anime head. In particular, we propose a two-stage CPTNet, that includes a generator for facial expression, a generator for head movement, and a light-weight combiner, for single image talking head animation. The two generators require a straight anime image and a target pose vector as input, then generate the change of anime facial expression and the movement of anime head, respectively. The generator for facial expression change shares the same architecture and weights with the mask branch of head generator. The head generator has two branches: the mask branch [7] and the grid branch [8]. The mask branch is able to preserve static area via the mask and generate new pixels, but is prone to be blurred at uncertain area. The grid branch can generate clear predictions by bilinear sampling, but it can only copy pixels from the input image and cannot generate new pixels. In order to combine the advantages and make up for the disadvantages of these two branches, we utilize the light-weight combiner to fuse the results of these two branches together. To handle large-scale pose transformations, we further propose a pose vector decomposition and cascaded refinement strategy for the mask branch. As shown in Fig. 1, given a single anime image and a target pose vector, our method is able to generate high-quality anime talking heads from a single image. Note that, by giving different target pose vectors, different poses of talking heads can be generated.

It is worth mentioning that our approach is inspired by Pramook [9] that builds a two-step system for talking head animation. However, our approach is different from his work in three main aspects. First, our approach has no constraints on input image format and anime characters, while Pramook requires an RGBA input and restricts anime head in the center of 128×128 regions of the input image. Second, we can handle larger-scale pose transformations via the pose vector decomposition and cascaded refinement strategy. Finally, weights sharing and light-weight fusion module ensure the efficiency of our model, which only takes up $40M$, while Pramook's model exceeds $300M$.

The contributions of this work can be summarized as follows:

- We present CPTNet, a novel two-stage pose transform network for talking head animation from a single anime image.
- We design a pose vector decomposition and cascaded refinement strategy to handle large-scale pose transformations.
- Extensive experiments on our anime dataset demonstrate the effectiveness of our approach, which outperforms other state-of-the-art methods.

2   Related Work

Generative Adversarial Networks. In recent years, GANs [1] have developed rapidly and have shown surprising results in computer vision, such as image translation [10–14], pose transform [15,16], image generation [17], super-resolution imaging [18], and face expression editing [3,4,19]. A GAN-based architecture contains a generator and a discriminator, while the generator aims at generating realistic fake samples, the discriminator needs to be able to distinguish between the real samples and the fake samples generated by the generator. In training, this idea is completed by an adversarial loss.

Conditional GANs. Conditional GANs have also attracted the attention of researchers. For example, multi-domain transfer [14], human pose transform [15,16], and facial expression editing [3,4,20]. Prior studies have tried to add some conditions to the basic GANs, such as class information [21] and text description [22], to generate images highly relevant to these conditions.

Image-to-Image Translation. Recent studies have shown surprising results in image-to-image translation [10–12,23], e.g., pix2pix [10] can complete image-to-image translation well with paired data. However, sometimes we are unable to obtain paired data in practice. As a result, some unsupervised methods are proposed [11,12,23,24]. For instance, CycleGAN [24], using the strategy of cycle consistent loss to maintain the necessary attributes in input images, is able to complete high-quality image translation with unpaired data. CartoonGAN [12] converts input images to cartoon style, and Art2Real [13] converts art images and real images to each other. Our task is more related to those works that use paired data due to our paired data.

Appearance and Pose Transform. Appearance and pose transform has attracted great attention in recent years. Most works [4,15,16] focus on human appearance and pose transform, such as changing color of hair, gender aging, and generating human talking head. GANimation [7], for instance, can change the appearance and expression of human. It requires a source human image and a target vector as input and then generates the changed image corresponding to the target vector. A few-shot learning method [15] has been proposed to generate human talking head. This method takes a few source human images and a target landmark as input, and generates the target human pose according to the target landmark. However, these works are all designed for human appearance and pose transform, they cannot handle anime characters well. Recently, Pramook [9] proposed a method that can perform anime pose transform through a single anime image and a target vector, which is most related to us. But his model is cumbersome and cannot handle large scale motion. In contrast, our method is efficient and is capable of handling large scale motion.

3   Method

Given an input straight image of anime character and a target pose vector, our goal is to design a network to transform the anime character to arbitrary target pose. Specifically, we disentangle this problem into two subtasks, including face pose transform (*e.g.*, close eyes and open mouth) and head pose transform. To address these two subtasks, we propose a cascade pose transform network. As shown in Fig. 2, our model consists of two stages: face pose transform stage and head pose transform stage. First, a mask generator is applied to transform the anime character to a target face pose (*e.g.*, close eyes and open mouth), then mask and grid branches generate two complementary head pose results according to the target head pose vector. Finally, a light-weight combiner is used to fuse these two results into our final result. Note that the mask generator in face pose transform stage has the same architecture and weights as the mask branch in head pose transform stage. More details will be introduced in the following sections.

3.1   Data Generation

Since there is no related anime dataset on the Internet, we create an anime pose dataset ourselves with a 3D software MikuMikuDance (MMD). Our dataset contains two parts, which are the face pose dataset of anime characters and the head pose dataset of anime characters. Below we will introduce them separately.

There are 1842 model IDs in our anime face pose dataset, and each model ID has 150 poses and corresponding pose vectors. The format of the face pose vector is: (left eye, right eye, mouth), and the value ranges of the three elements

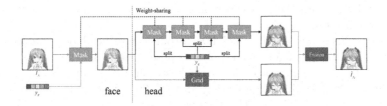

Fig. 2. Overview of our network architecture. Our model consists of two stages: face pose transform stage (*e.g.*, close eyes and open mouth); and head pose transform stage. In face pose transform stage, the mask generator transforms an anime character to a target face pose. In head pose transform stage, mask generator and grid generator are utilized to generate two complementary talking heads. Finally, the fusion module fuses these two results to generate the final result.

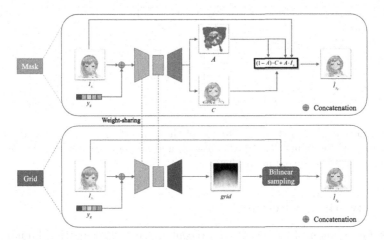

Fig. 3. Mask generator and Grid generator. Given a single anime image and a target pose vector, on one hand, the mask generator generates a single channel mask A and an RGB content image C. Then mask A linearly combines the source image and the content C to obtain the output. On the other hand, the grid generator generates a grid to get the output via bilinear sampling.

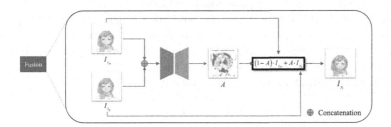

Fig. 4. Fusion. The output I_{y_m} of mask generator and the output I_{y_g} of grid generator are made a concatenation as the input of fusion. The output of fusion is an attention mask A, which guides two source images to fuse to obtain the final result.

are all [0, 1], 0 means the eyes and mouth are fully closed, and 1 means the eyes and mouth are fully open.

Besides, there are 1868 model IDs in our anime head pose dataset, each model ID has 972 poses and corresponding pose vectors. The format of the head pose vector is: (top-down head, left-right head), and the value ranges of the two elements are all [–1,1], corresponding angel [−20°, 20°]. Note that our image resolution is 256 × 256 and the testing set for our task contains 260 anime models. Some examples are shown in Fig. 5.

When we train and test the model, the format of a pose vector that we use is (left eye, right eye, mouth, top-down head, left-right head), which means the combination of face pose vector and head pose vector.

face   head

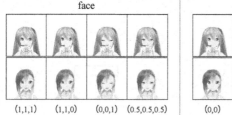 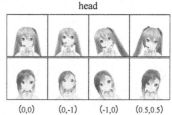

(1,1,1)   (1,1,0)   (0,0,1)   (0.5,0.5,0.5)   (0,0)   (0,-1)   (-1,0)   (0.5,0.5)

Fig. 5. Dataset. The left is an example of the anime face pose dataset, the right is an example of the anime head pose dataset, and the bottom row is the pose vector corresponding to each column of images.

3.2   Network Architecture

Mask Generator. Inspired by the recent success of generating human facial expression [7], we propose to use mask-guided generator to handle pose transform. Figure 3 illustrates the details of mask generator. Given a single image I_{y_s} and a target pose vector y_g, we first make a channel wise concatenation (I_{y_s}, y_g) as input of mask generator. Then the mask generator generates a single channel mask A and an RGB content C, where mask A is designed to guide the network to focus on the transforming pose-related regions.

For instance, in the face stage, the only areas where the input image needs to be changed are the eyes and mouth, while the other areas are kept still, so the network only needs to generate the changed dynamic areas, the remaining static areas can be obtained directly from the input.

Finally, the output image can be obtained as:

$$\hat{I}_{y_g} = (1 - A) \cdot C + A \cdot I_{y_s}, \tag{1}$$

where · denotes element-wise multiplication. This strategy makes the learning process easier as the network only needs to focus on the dynamic areas, the static areas can be obtained from the input directly. However, mask generator is prone to be blurred, and it cannot maintain the color of input image well if given a large-scale pose vector.

Grid Generator. Since mask generator may produce blurry results, we adopt grid generator as a complementary component to synthesize new pose. The details of grid generator are shown in Fig. 3. For the input image and target pose vector, we use the same way as the mask generator. The main difference is that the output of grid generator is a two-channel grid vector, not mask and content. We use the grid vector to synthesize target image by bilinear sampling from the input image, which is similar to appearance flow [8].

The motivation of the grid generator is that bilinear sampling can make full use of the pixel information of the input image. The network only needs to generate a two-channel grid vectors to guide the sampling process from input image, rather than generating a complete RGB image, which significantly reduces the difficulty of learning process. In addition, since bilinear sampling directly copies pixels from the input image to the final image, the color identification of the input image will be well preserved, and the resulting image will not produce obvious blur.

However, the inherent limitation of this method is that it cannot generate new pixels. Therefore, some areas that do not contain relevant pixel information in the input image will not be generated well. Note that grid generator and mask generator share the same weights in encoder and residual blocks [25].

Fusion. The fusion architecture is shown in Fig. 4. After the mask generator and grid generator output the results I_{y_m} and I_{y_g}, we make a channel wise concatenation (I_{y_m}, I_{y_g}) as the input of fusion. Similar to the mask generator, the fusion outputs an attention mask A to guide the two source images to fuse. Finally, the final image can be obtained as:

$$\hat{I}_{y_t} = (1 - A) \cdot I_{y_m} + A \cdot I_{y_g}, \tag{2}$$

The motivation of applying fusion module is straightforward, the mask generator can synthesize new pixels and regions that are not included in the input image, but it may produce a certain degree of blur and the quality of the generated image is not stable, while the images generated by the grid generator are clearer and more stable, but it cannot generate new pixels. Therefore, a fusion module is adopted to combine the advantages of these two generators. It is noticeable that the size of our fusion model is only 5 MB.

3.3 Pose Vector Decomposition

In head pose transform stage, we observe that for large-scale pose vectors, the image generated by the mask branch is very blurry. We infer the reason is that the large-scale transform leads to few static regions, which significantly increases the difficulty of generating dynamic regions for mask generator. To solve this problem, we introduce the pose vector decomposition and cascaded refinement strategy as shown in Fig. 3. Specifically, we decompose large-scale pose vector of head movement into k small-scale pose vectors and pass them through k cascaded mask generators that share weights parameters. For instance, suppose the original large-scale pose vector is $(0, 0, 0, 0, 1)$, we first transform the anime character to a target pose $(0, 0, 0, 0, 1/k)$, then the pose $(0, 0, 0, 0, 2/k)$ is generated based on the result of $(0, 0, 0, 0, 1/k)$. This process repeats until $(0, 0, 0, 0, 1)$ is reached. In practice, we observed that $k = 4$ is sufficient to handle large-scale pose transforms. In this way, the mask generator can repeatedly perform small-scale transform to complete large-scale transform, which improves the final result.

3.4   Learning the Model

At the training stage, our loss function mainly consists of three terms: 1) the adversarial loss for improving the photo-realism of generated pose transformation images. 2) the content loss to improve consistency of generated images with ground truth 3) the perceptual loss to improve the clarity and details of the output.

Adversarial Loss. To make the generated images indistinguishable from real images, we adopt an adversarial loss as

$$L_{adv} = E_{\hat{I}_{y_g} \sim P_s} \left[D \left(\hat{I}_{y_g} \right) \right] - E_{I_{y_g} \sim P_{data}} \left[D \left(I_{y_g} \right) \right] \tag{3}$$

where $\hat{I}_{y_g}$ is the final generated image and I_{y_g} is the corresponding ground truth, P_s stands for the data distribution of synthesized images, P_{data} the distribution of real images. The generator needs to generate real fake images so it tries to maximize this objective, while the discriminator D needs to distinguish between real and fake images so it tries to minimize this objective.

Content Loss. Since our dataset contains pairs of samples, we use L1Loss to measure the distance between the generated image and the ground truth and then update the generator. The content loss is defined as

$$L_{pair} = E_{I_{y_g} \sim P_{data}} \left[\left\| I_{y_g} - \hat{I}_{y_g} \right\|_1 \right] \tag{4}$$

Perceptual Loss. Only a L1Loss constraint on the generated image and ground truth may cause the image to be blurred. So we adopt the perceptual loss [26] as another constraint. We let the generated image and its corresponding ground truth pass through the pre-trained VGG19 network [27], and extract the features of conv1_1, conv2_1, conv3_1, and conv4_2 layers for L1Loss, and finally weighted summation. So the perceptual loss can be obtained as

$$L_p = \sum_j E_{I_{y_g} \sim P_{data}} \left[\left\| \phi_j \left(I_{y_g} \right) - \phi_j \left(\hat{I}_{y_g} \right) \right\|_1 \right] \tag{5}$$

where $\phi_j(\cdot)$ represents the features of jth layer in VGG19, the j here specifically refers to the layers of conv1_1, conv2_1, conv3_1, and conv4_2. We find that this loss function can make the result smoother and clearer.

Full Loss. To generate the target image, we build a loss function L by linearly combining all previous partial losses:

$$L = L_{adv} + \lambda_1 L_{pair} + \lambda_2 L_p \tag{6}$$

where λ_1, λ_2 are the hyper-parameters that control the relative importance of every loss term.

4   Experiments

In this section, we evaluate our model on our own anime pose dataset. First we give the details about our experimental setting. Then we show the results of the face pose transform stage, head pose transform stage, and the final mixed pose separately to analyze the role of each module. Finally, we compare our model with some recent methods on our dataset.

4.1   Experimental Setting

Our generators and discriminator networks are build upon StarGAN [2], as it proved to achieve impressive results for image-to-image transform. For the mask generator, we made slight modification by adding a branch on the last convolutional layer so as to generate a single-channel mask A and an RGB content image C. For the grid generator, we change the last convolutional layer to output a two-channel grid to perform bilinear sampling on input image. As the discriminator, we remove the classification layer. Our fusion module contains only two downsampling layers and two upsampling layers, and output a single-channel mask.

The model is trained on our anime pose dataset mentioned above. We use Adam [28] with learning rate of 0.0001, $\beta_1 = 0.5$, $\beta_2 = 0.999$ and batch size 8. We train for 600000 iterations and linearly decay the learning rate to zero over the last 100000 iterations. We perform one generator update after five discriminator updates. We set $\lambda_1 = 1000$, $\lambda_2 = 200$. It takes about three days to train the model with a single GeForce RTX 2080 Ti GPU.

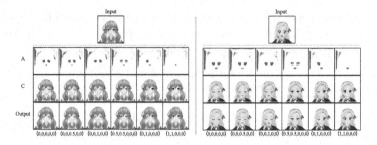

Fig. 6. Face stage. The results of face stage. A represents mask, while C represents content. The last row means the target pose vectors, and every column is the generated mask A, content C, and output corresponding to the target pose vector.

4.2   Ablation Study

In this section, we performed an ablation study to evaluate the role of each of our modules: face stage only, head stage only, and the whole two-stage network. In head stage, we first evaluate the effectiveness of the mask generator, the grid generator and fusion module. Then we perform analysis on our pose vector decomposition and cascaded refinement strategy. We perform a qualitative and quantitative comparison for each of them in Fig. 6 and Table 1.

Face Stage. The face stage is trained to transform the input anime image to a target facial expression (*e.g.*, close eyes and open mouth) according to the target pose vector. Figure 6 shows the mask A, the content C and the final generated result I_{y_g}. Note that the mask generator has learned to focus on the dynamic areas (darker areas) according to the target pose vector. Mask A can well locate the eyes and mouth in the input image, and cover them with gray pixels, which means that these areas need to be obtained from content C, and other white areas mean that they need to be obtained from the input image. In the content C, only the pixels related to the dynamic regions of the eyes and mouth will be carefully generated, the rest are only noise.

Head Stage. The task of the head stage is to complete the movement of the anime character head, including swinging up and down, swinging left and right. Compared with the change of face pose during the face stage, it is obviously more difficult to realize the change of head pose, because most of the regions in the input image are still for the change of face pose, only the eyes and mouth need to be changed, while the head movement requires large areas of change, especially for large-scale target pose vectors. Below we will evaluate the role of each module in the head stage. Some visual results are shown in Fig. 7. "Mask" means we only use the single-stage mask generator, "Mask + MS" means we use the mask generator and pose vector decomposition strategy, "Grid" means we use the grid generator only, "Mask + MS + Grid" means the complete model of head stage.

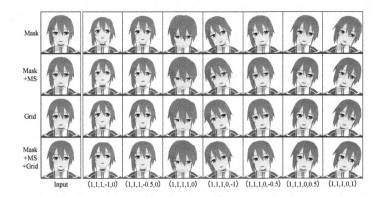

Fig. 7. Head stage. The ablation study of head stage. The first column is the input, while the rest columns are generated images corresponding to the pose vectors on the bottom row. Each row corresponds to a variant of our model. "Mask" means we only use the single-stage mask generator, "Mask + MS" means we use the mask generator and pose vector decomposition strategy, "Grid" means we use the grid generator only, "Mask + MS + Grid" means the complete model of head stage.

The results of "Mask" show the limitation of the single-stage mask generator. It can only handle small-scale head movements , for large-scale head movements, the generation results become very blurry, especially in the hair part. The reason is that large-scale head movement will cause the generated image cannot use the mask to obtain pixels from the corresponding position of the input image, the entire head can only rely on the generator to generate the corresponding content, so the advantage of the mask is basically useless here.

As the results of "Mask + MS" show, when we adopt pose vector decomposition and cascaded refinement strategy for the mask generator, significant improvement can be achieved. Due to the decomposition of the pose vector, the mask generator only needs to perform a small-scale transformation at a time, so that the mask can be used to obtain and copy pixels from the same position in the input image, reducing the blur and improving the quality of the generated image. Also, small-scale transformations reduce the difficulty of learning process. But it still cannot preserve the color identification of the input image.

From the results of "Grid", we can observe that it can perform well in the head movement of anime characters. The final output image is obtained by performing bilinear sampling on input image, so the generated image has several advantages: 1) It eases the blur caused by the direct output image of the deep convolution network [29]. 2) It can preserve the color identification of the input image. However, it can only copy pixels from the relevant areas in the input image, so for some areas that have no relevant information in the input image, such as the neck, messy pixels will appear.

The complete model "Mask + MS + Grid" means we adopt pose vector decomposition and cascaded refinement strategy, and fuse the results of mask generator and grid generator. The visualization demonstrate that the fusion results can not only retain the advantages of each branch, but also alleviate the problems to a certain extent, which leads to more fine-grained results.

4.3   Qualitative Experimental Results

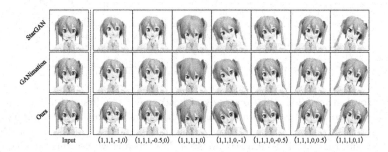

Fig. 8. Qualitative comparison with state-of-the-art. The results of StarGAN, GANimation, and ours. Each column represents a pose corresponding to the pose vector on the bottom row. Our method can generate much clearer results.

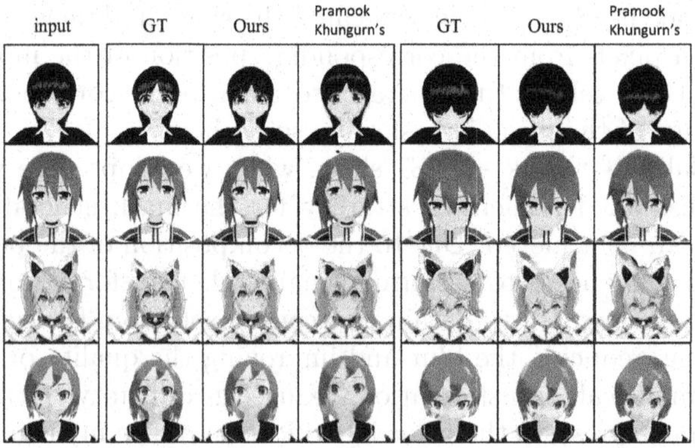

Fig. 9. Qualitative comparison with Pramook's. The results of ours and Pramook's. Each anime input corresponds to two generated poses. Our method can get better results.

Figure 8 shows qualitative experimental results. The first column is the input image, while each remaining column corresponds to a target pose vector. We compare our method with the state-of-the-art facial expression editing methods: StarGAN [2] and GANimation [7].

As shown in Fig. 8, StarGAN and GANimation are prone to generate blurs and artifacts, especially for the large-scale target pose vectors. Instead, our method generates more realistic images with much less blurs and artifacts. Even for the large-scale target pose vectors, our method can still perform well. This is contribute to the pose vector decomposition and cascaded refinement strategy, which is designed to performs anime-like progressive pose transformation rather than a single-step one.

Figure 9 shows the comparison of our and Pramook's method [9]. Due to our pose vector decomposition and cascaded refinement strategy, we can get better results for the large-scale transform.

Table 1. Pose transformation comparison with other methods and our variants.

Method	L1 ↓	RMSE ↓	SSIM ↑
StarGAN [2]	0.0670	0.1974	0.7680
GANimation [7]	0.0611	0.1921	0.7878
Ours (mask)	0.0600	0.1885	0.7899
Ours (grid)	0.0545	0.1867	0.8069
Ours (mask + grid)	0.0541	0.1855	0.8072
Ours (mask + grid + ms)	**0.0525**	**0.1800**	**0.8101**

Table 2. Pose transformation comparison with Pramook's and our method.

Method	L1 ↓	RMSE ↓	SSIM ↑
Pramook's [9]	0.0664	0.2481	0.8022
Ours	**0.0401**	**0.1434**	**0.8417**

4.4   Quantitative Experimental Results

We use L1 norm, RMSE, and SSIM similarity [30] for quantitative evaluations. For the L1 norm and RMSE, the lower the score, the smaller the distance between the generated image and ground truth, in contrast, for SSIM, the higher the score, the greater the similarity between the generated image and ground truth.

As shown in Table 1, "Ours (mask)" means we only use the single stage mask generator, "Ours (grid)" means we use the grid generator only, "Ours (mask + grid)" means we use fusion to fuse the results of mask generator and grid generator, "Ours (mask + grid + ms)" means the complete model, including the pose vector decomposition and cascaded refinement strategy. Compared to other two methods, our method obtains higher SSIM score and lower L1, RMSE scores.

It is worth mention that Pramook's method requires RGBA format images, while images in our dataset are RGB format. So we chose about 100 models from our testing set and manually made them into RGBA format, then we use his open source weights and test code to obtain quantitative results on our dataset. As shown in Table 2, the calculated L1 and RMSE results are much higher than our method. For possible reasons, first we cannot refine the RGBA images to be consistent with his training dataset, because he has his own set of processing code and is not open released, while we can only make them manually. Besides, his method needs the character's head in the 128×128 position in the center of the image, while our dataset and method does not have this constraint. In addition, our method can handle larger motion of head than his.

4.5 Generalization and Yaw Rotation Results

Fig. 10. Generality and Yaw Rotation. The upper part is the generalization results of our model, where input anime images in the first column are downloaded from the Internet. The bottom is the yaw rotation results, our model can handle it as well.

The upper part of Fig. 10 demonstrates the generality of our model, where the input images are downloaded from the Internet, our model shows good generality. For yaw rotation, it is essentially the same as pitch and roll, our model can handle it as well, two examples are shown in the bottom of Fig. 10.

5   Conclusion

In this work, we present a novel cascade pose transform network for talking head animation. Different from previous methods, our approach is capable of generating vivid anime talking heads from a single anime image. Extensive experiments on our anime dataset validate the effectiveness of our approach. In the future, we plan to improve the generalization ability of the model and increase the resolution of the generated image.

Acknowledgments. This work was funded by the DigiX Joint Innovation Center of Huawei-HUST.

References

1. Goodfellow, I., et al.: Generative adversarial nets. In: Proceedings of the Advances in neural information processing systems, pp. 2672–2680 (2014)
2. Choi, Y., Choi, M., Kim, M., Ha, J.W., Kim, S., Choo, J.: Stargan: unified generative adversarial networks for multi-domain image-to-image translation. In: Proceedings of the IEEE Conference on Computer Vision and Pattern Recognition, pp. 8789–8797 (2018)
3. Liu, M., et al.: Stgan: a unified selective transfer network for arbitrary image attribute editing. In: Proceedings of the IEEE Conference on Computer Vision and Pattern Recognition, pp. 3673–3682 (2019)
4. He, Z., Zuo, W., Kan, M., Shan, S., Chen, X.: Attgan: facial attribute editing by only changing what you want. IEEE Trans. Image Process. **28**, 5464–5478 (2019)
5. Langner, O., Dotsch, R., Bijlstra, G., Wigboldus, D.H., Hawk, S.T., Van Knippenberg, A.: Presentation and validation of the Radboud faces database. Cogn. Emot. **24**, 1377–1388 (2010)
6. Liu, Z., Luo, P., Wang, X., Tang, X.: Deep learning face attributes in the wild. In: Proceedings of the IEEE international conference on computer vision, pp. 3730–3738 (2015)
7. Pumarola, A., Agudo, A., Martinez, A.M., Sanfeliu, A., Moreno-Noguer, F.: Ganimation: anatomically-aware facial animation from a single image. In: Proceedings of the European Conference on Computer Vision, pp. 818–833 (2018)
8. Zhou, T., Tulsiani, S., Sun, W., Malik, J., Efros, A.A.: View synthesis by appearance flow. In: Leibe, B., Matas, J., Sebe, N., Welling, M. (eds.) ECCV 2016. LNCS, vol. 9908, pp. 286–301. Springer, Cham (2016). https://doi.org/10.1007/978-3-319-46493-0_18
9. Khungurn, P.: Talking head anime from a single image. https://pkhungurn.github.io/talking-head-anime/ (2019)
10. Isola, P., Zhu, J.Y., Zhou, T., Efros, A.A.: Image-to-image translation with conditional adversarial networks. In: Proceedings of the IEEE Conference on Computer Vision and Pattern Recognition, pp. 1125–1134 (2017)
11. Zhao, Y., Wu, R., Dong, H.: Unpaired image-to-image translation using adversarial consistency loss. arXiv preprint arXiv:2003.04858 (2020)
12. Chen, Y., Lai, Y.K., Liu, Y.J.: Cartoongan: Generative adversarial networks for photo cartoonization. In: Proceedings of the IEEE Conference on Computer Vision and Pattern Recognition, pp. 9465–9474 (2018)
13. Tomei, M., Cornia, M., Baraldi, L., Cucchiara, R.: Art2real: unfolding the reality of artworks via semantically-aware image-to-image translation. In: Proceedings of the IEEE Conference on Computer Vision and Pattern Recognition, pp. 5849–5859 (2019)
14. Shen, F., Yan, S., Zeng, G.: Neural style transfer via meta networks. In: Proceedings of the IEEE Conference on Computer Vision and Pattern Recognition, pp. 8061–8069 (2018)
15. Zakharov, E., Shysheya, A., Burkov, E., Lempitsky, V.: Few-shot adversarial learning of realistic neural talking head models. In: Proceedings of the IEEE International Conference on Computer Vision, pp. 9459–9468 (2019)
16. Liu, W., Piao, Z., Min, J., Luo, W., Ma, L., Gao, S.: Liquid warping gan: a unified framework for human motion imitation, appearance transfer and novel view synthesis. In: Proceedings of the IEEE International Conference on Computer Vision, pp. 5904–5913 (2019)

17. Karras, T., Laine, S., Aila, T.: A style-based generator architecture for generative adversarial networks. In: Proceedings of the IEEE Conference on Computer Vision and Pattern Recognition, pp. 4401–4410 (2019)
18. Ledig, C., et al.: Photo-realistic single image super-resolution using a generative adversarial network. In: Proceedings of the IEEE Conference on Computer Vision and Pattern Recognition, pp. 4681–4690 (2017)
19. Athar, S., Shu, Z., Samaras, D.: Self-supervised deformation modeling for facial expression editing. arXiv preprint arXiv:1911.00735 (2019)
20. Wu, R., Zhang, G., Lu, S., Chen, T.: Cascade ef-gan: Progressive facial expression editing with local focuses. In: Proceedings of the IEEE Conference on Computer Vision and Pattern Recognition, pp. 5021–5030 (2020)
21. Odena, A., Olah, C., Shlens, J.: Conditional image synthesis with auxiliary classifier gans. In: Proceedings of the 34th International Conference on Machine Learning, vol. 70, pp. 2642–2651 (2017) JMLR. org
22. Reed, S., Akata, Z., Yan, X., Logeswaran, L., Schiele, B., Lee, H.: Generative adversarial text to image synthesis. arXiv preprint arXiv:1605.05396 (2016)
23. Wu, R., Gu, X., Tao, X., Shen, X., Tai, Y.W., Jia, J.: Landmark assisted cyclegan for cartoon face generation. arXiv preprint arXiv:1907.01424 (2019)
24. Zhu, J.Y., Park, T., Isola, P., Efros, A.A.: Unpaired image-to-image translation using cycle-consistent adversarial networks. In: Proceedings of the IEEE International Conference on Computer Vision, pp. 2223–2232 (2017)
25. He, K., Zhang, X., Ren, S., Sun, J.: Deep residual learning for image recognition. In: Proceedings of the IEEE Conference on Computer Vision and Pattern Recognition, pp. 770–778 (2016)
26. Johnson, J., Alahi, A., Fei-Fei, L.: Perceptual losses for real-time style transfer and super-resolution. In: Leibe, B., Matas, J., Sebe, N., Welling, M. (eds.) ECCV 2016. LNCS, vol. 9906, pp. 694–711. Springer, Cham (2016). https://doi.org/10.1007/978-3-319-46475-6_43
27. Simonyan, K., Zisserman, A.: Very deep convolutional networks for large-scale image recognition. arXiv preprint arXiv:1409.1556 (2014)
28. Kingma, D.P., Ba, J.: Adam: a method for stochastic optimization. arXiv preprint arXiv:1412.6980 (2014)
29. Radford, A., Metz, L., Chintala, S.: Unsupervised representation learning with deep convolutional generative adversarial networks. arXiv preprint arXiv:1511.06434 (2015)
30. Wang, Z., Bovik, A.C., Sheikh, H.R., Simoncelli, E.P.: Image quality assessment: from error visibility to structural similarity. IEEE Trans. Image Process. **13**, 600–612 (2004)

TinyGAN: Distilling BigGAN for Conditional Image Generation

Ting-Yun Chang$^{(\boxtimes)}$ and Chi-Jen Lu$^{(\boxtimes)}$

Institute of Information Science, Academia Sinica, Taipei, Taiwan
r06922168@ntu.edu.tw, cjlu@iis.sinica.edu.tw
https://www.iis.sinica.edu.tw/en/index.html

Abstract. Generative Adversarial Networks (GANs) have become a powerful approach for generative image modeling. However, GANs are notorious for their training instability, especially on large-scale, complex datasets. While the recent work of BigGAN has significantly improved the quality of image generation on ImageNet, it requires a huge model, making it hard to deploy on resource-constrained devices. To reduce the model size, we propose a black-box knowledge distillation framework for compressing GANs, which highlights a stable and efficient training process. Given BigGAN as the teacher network, we manage to train a much smaller student network to mimic its functionality, achieving competitive performance on Inception and FID scores with the generator having 16× fewer parameters. (The source code and the trained model are publicly available at https://github.com/terarachang/ACCV_TinyGAN).

1 Introduction

Generative Adversarial Networks (GANs) [1] have achieved considerable success in recent years. The framework consists of a generator, which aims to produce a distribution similar to a target one, as well as a discriminator, which aims to distinguish these two distributions. The generator and the discriminator are trained in an alternative way, with the discriminator acting as an increasingly scrupulous critic of the current generator. Conditional GANs (cGANs) [2] are a type of GANs for generating samples based on some given conditional information. Different from unconditional GANs, the discriminator of cGANs is now asked to distinguish the two distributions given the conditional information.

Despite their success, GANs are also known to be hard to train, especially on large-scale, complex datasets such as ImageNet. The recent work of BigGAN [3], a kind of cGANs, demonstrates the benefit of scaling. More precisely, by scaling up both the model size and batch size, some of the training problems can be mitigated, and high-quality images can be generated. However, this also leads to high computational cost and memory footprint, even for inference in test time.

Electronic supplementary material The online version of this chapter (https://doi.org/10.1007/978-3-030-69538-5_31) contains supplementary material, which is available to authorized users.

H. Ishikawa et al. (Eds.): ACCV 2020, LNCS 12625, pp. 509–525, 2021.
https://doi.org/10.1007/978-3-030-69538-5_31

Fig. 1. A comparison between images generated by BigGAN and the proposed Tiny-GAN. Pictures in odd rows are produced by BigGAN, while those in even rows are by TinyGAN given the same input.

One may wonder if it is possible to compress such a large model into a much smaller one. For classification tasks, several techniques have been developed for compressing classifiers, including *knowledge distillation* [4], *network pruning* [5], and *quantization* [6]. For compressing GANs, we find that the concept of knowledge distillation (KD) becomes especially appealing. Based on a *teacher-student framework*, it aims to impart knowledge encoded in a large, well-trained teacher network to a small student network. For GANs, we find it appropriate to consider the input-output relationship of the teacher generator as the knowledge to be distilled. Note that the difficulties of training GANs from scratch may be attributed mostly to the lack of supervision from paired training data. Not sure about what the ideal functionality it should have, the generator turns to chase a moving target provided by an evolving discriminator. On the other hand, having a well-trained generator such as BigGAN as a teacher, we can use it simply as a black box to generate its input-output pairs as training data, and train a student network in a supervised way. Such a supervised learning is typically much easier, with a much more stable and efficient training process. In contrast, training classifiers are usually done in a supervised way already, and hence KD on classifiers usually takes a white-box approach, requiring access to the internal of the teacher networks.

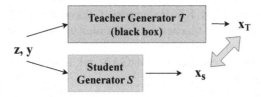

Fig. 2. Illustration of the problem formulation. z is the noise vector, and y is the class label. Our goal is to mimic the functionality of the teacher generator via black-box knowledge distillation.

Although KD has been successfully applied to classification tasks [4,7], it is less studied for image generation. In our work, we leverage BigGAN trained on ImageNet as our teacher network and design a compact, lightweight student network to mimic the functionality of BigGAN. Given a noise vector and a class label as input, we would like the student network to generate a similar, high-quality image like that produced by BigGAN. In this paper, we focus on *black-box KD*, defined as having access to only the input-output functionality of the teacher network, instead of any internal knowledge such as its intermediate features as needed in works such as [4,8]. We claim that this is a meaningful setting for several aspects. First, it allows one to utilize a model without needing the authority to access its model parameters, by simply collecting its input/output pairs. Next, it allows us to discard the teacher network (both generator and discriminator) in the training phase to save memory after collecting such pairs in the preprocessing step. Furthermore, it allows us to adopt a different architecture for the student network, which enables us to substantially reduce the model size from that of BigGAN. Figure 2 is an illustration of our problem formulation, and Fig. 1 shows some sampled results.

We propose several training objectives for distilling BigGAN, including *pixel-level distillation, adversarial distillation*, and *feature-level distillation*. Given the same input, let x_T and x_S be the images generated by the teacher and the student networks respectively. The objective of *pixel-level distillation* is to minimize the distance between x_T and x_S, and here we use the pixel-wise L1 distance. We further utilize a small discriminator to help align our generated distribution to BigGAN's, with the *adversarial distillation* having a similar objective as in standard GAN training, but now taking BigGAN's output distribution as the target one. Finally, as pixel-level distance often leads to blurry images, we apply *feature-level distillation* to mitigate this problem. We achieve this without needing additional parameters, by taking the intermediate features in the discriminator and encouraging those derived from x_S to match those from x_T. In addition to the distillation objectives, we also include the standard cGANs loss, to push our generated distribution towards that of ImageNet as well. Our main contributions are summarized as follows.

- We identify a unique and advantageous property of compressing GANs via knowledge distillation, and initiate the study on the diverse ImageNet.

- We propose a black-box KD framework tailored for GANs, which requires little permission for the teacher networks and highlights an efficient training process.
- Our strategy greatly compresses BigGAN, while our model maintains competitive performance.

We see our contributions as more conceptual than technical. While the task of compressing classifiers has received much attention, to our knowledge, we are the first to explore black-box KD for compressing GANs. Moreover, we identify a unique property of KD on GANs, which enables us to apply rather simple techniques to achieve a substantial compression ratio, and we believe that it is possible to combine our approach with other compression techniques to further reduce the model size. Let us remark that the emphasis of our work is the realization of a simple and efficient strategy to obtain a generator with both good quality and a compact size. Whereas we do not rule out the possibility of training a small-sized, well-performed, and stable GANs from scratch, it is likely to be challenging except for very skilled and experienced experts. In fact, in our attempt to directly train a smaller GAN from scratch, we have encountered those notorious training problems as expected, while we have never experienced any issues of instability when taking our KD approach. Therefore, our work suggests a possibly more reliable way to obtain a lightweight, high-quality generator: instead of directly training one from scratch, one could first train a large generator and then distill from it a small one.

2   Related Work

Generative Adversarial Networks. GANs have excelled in a variety of image generation tasks [9–11]. Still, they are well known for problems such as training instability and sensitivity to hyperparameter choices, requiring great efforts in model tuning. Several works [12–16] have aimed to tackle such problems. Notably, the recent work of [17,18] proposed to constrain the Lipschitz constant of the discriminator function by limiting the spectral norm of its weights, which makes possible high quality class-conditional image generation over large-scale, complex distributions.

BigGAN. BigGAN [3] further scales up GANs by training with considerable model size and batch size on complex datasets. It basically follows previous SOTA architectures [17–19], and proposes two variants, BigGAN and BigGAN-deep, to incorporate the input noises and class labels. Utilizing the truncation trick, i.e., training a model with $z \sim N(0, I)$ but sampling z from a truncated normal (with values falling outside two standard deviations being re-sampled) in test time, BigGAN is able to trade off variety and fidelity. BigGAN demonstrates that GANs benefit dramatically from scaling.

Knowledge Distillation on GANs. Perhaps the work most related to ours is [20], which to our knowledge is the first to apply knowledge distillation on GANs. However, their experiments are conducted on MNIST, CIFAR-10, and CelebA, which are relatively simple with much less image diversity compared to ImageNet. Besides, there are several differences in the settings. First, they do not experiment on conditional generation. Second, they explore teacher-student generators only on the DCGAN architectures, which might be less general and seems easier for the student to mimic a teacher with a similar architecture. Finally, accessing to and updating the teacher discriminator are allowed in their work, while we focus on black-box knowledge distillation, which is more memory efficient during training as we do not need to keep the large teacher network. (Once we synthesized the dataset from BigGAN's generator during the preprocessing phase, we do not need it anymore). To sum up, in this work, we study knowledge distillation on GANs in a more general framework and a harder setting.

Fig. 3. Examples generated by TinyGAN trained with pixel-level distillation loss (Eq. 1) alone, shown in the second row. The first row shows corresponding images produced by BigGAN given the same input.

3 Tiny Generative Adversarial Networks

We first describe how our proposed framework, TinyGAN, distills knowledge from BigGAN. Then, we discuss how TinyGAN incorporates real images from the ImageNet dataset, which further improves the performance.

3.1 BigGAN Distillation

We propose a black-box KD method specifically designed for GANs, which does not need to access the parameters of the teacher network or share a similar network structure. We use BigGAN as the teacher network and train our student network, TinyGAN, with much fewer parameters to mimic its input-output behavior. We will elaborate on several proposed objectives for knowledge distillation in this subsection.

Pixel-Level Distillation Loss. To mimic the functionality of BigGAN, a naive method is to minimize the pixel-level distance between the images generated by BigGAN and TinyGAN given the same input. Formally, let

$$L_{\text{KD\_pix}} = \mathbb{E}_{z \sim p(z), y \sim q(y)}[\|T(z, y) - S(z, y)\|_1], \tag{1}$$

where T is the frozen teacher network (BigGAN's generator), S is our student network, $z \in \mathbb{R}^{128}$ is a latent variable drawn from the truncated normal distribution $p(z)$, and y is the class label sampled from some categorical distribution $q(y)$. However, we found that using such a pixel-level distance alone is not sufficient for modeling complex datasets such as ImageNet, resulting in blurry images as shown in Fig. 3. Thus, we propose the following additional objectives to mitigate this problem.

Adversarial Distillation Loss. To sharpen the generated images, we incorporate a discriminator to help make the images generated by TinyGAN indistinguishable from those by BigGAN. We adopt an adversarial loss

$$L_{\text{KD\_S}} = -\mathbb{E}_{z,y}[D(S(z, y), y)] \tag{2}$$

for the generator, and the loss

$$L_{\text{KD\_D}} = \mathbb{E}_{z,y}[\max(0, 1 - D(T(z, y), y)) + \max(0, 1 + D(S(z, y), y))] \tag{3}$$

for the discriminator, where z is the noise vector, y is the class label, $T(z, y)$ is the image generated by BigGAN, while S and D are respectively the generator and discriminator of our TinyGAN, which are alternatively trained as in usual GAN training. We trained our small-sized discriminator D from scratch, and have experimentally found that projection discriminator with *hinge* adversarial loss proposed by [17] works the best.

Feature-Level Distillation Loss. To further mitigate the problem of generating blurry images using pixel-level distance, we propose a feature-level distillation loss, which does not require any additional parameter. We believe that as the discriminator needs to distinguish the source of images, it must learn some useful features. Hence, we take the features computed at each convolutional layer in the discriminator, and ask TinyGAN to generate images with similar features as those from BigGAN. Formally, let

$$L_{\text{KD\_feat}} = \mathbb{E}_{z,y}[\Sigma_i \alpha_i \|D_i(T(z, y), y) - D_i(S(z, y), y)\|_1], \tag{4}$$

where D_i is the feature vector extracted from the ith-layer of our discriminator, and α_i is the corresponding weight. We put more emphasis on higher-level features and assign larger weights to them.

This objective is similar to the feature matching loss proposed by [21], which encourages the generator to generate images containing intermediate representations similar to those from the real images in order to fool the discriminator. We have also tried to incorporate different kinds of feature-level loss, such as perceptual loss from VGG network [22], but got worse results. Figure 4 illustrates all the proposed distillation objectives.

Preprocessing

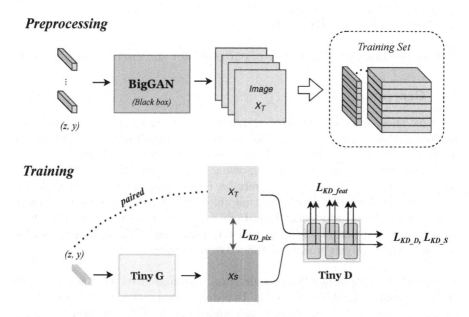

Fig. 4. Illustration of the proposed pipeline and the distillation objectives.

3.2 Learning from Real Distribution

We also allow our model to learn from real images in ImageNet dataset, attempting to ameliorate the mode dropping problem of BigGAN we observed in some classes. Specifically, we use the *hinge* version of the adversarial loss [23]

$$L_{\text{GAN\_D}} = \mathbb{E}_{x,y}[\max(0, 1 - D(x,y))] + \mathbb{E}_{z,y}[\max(0, 1 + D(S(z,y),y))], \quad (5)$$

where x is now the real image sampled from ImageNet. The generator loss $L_{\text{GAN\_S}}$ is the same as $L_{\text{KD\_S}}$ in Eq. (2).

3.3 Full Objective

Finally, the objective to optimize our student generator and discriminator, S and D, are written respectively as

$$L_{\text{S}} = L_{\text{KD\_feat}} + \lambda_1 L_{\text{KD\_pix}} + \lambda_2 L_{\text{KD\_S}} + \lambda_3 L_{\text{GAN\_S}}, \text{ and} \quad (6)$$

$$L_{\text{D}} = L_{\text{KD\_D}} + \lambda_4 L_{\text{GAN\_D}}. \quad (7)$$

Empirically, we gradually decay the weight of the pixel-level distillation loss λ_1 to zero, relying on the discriminator to provide useful guidance. Note that pixel-level distillation loss is still an important term, since it provides stable supervision in the early training phase while discriminator might still be quite naive at that time.

4   Network Architecture

Now we describe the architectures of our generator and discriminator in detail.

4.1   Generator

We have tried different generator architectures and experimentally found that ResNet [24] based generator with class-conditional BatchNorm [25, 26] works better. To keep a tight computation budget, our student generator does not adopt attention-based [19] or progressive-growing mechanisms [27]. To substantially reduce the model size, we mainly rely on using fewer channels and replacing standard convolution by depthwise separable convolution. In addition, we adopt a simpler way to introduce class conditions which also helps the reduction. Overall, our generator has 16× fewer parameters than BigGAN's, while still capable of generating satisfying images of 128 × 128 resolution.

Shared Class Embedding. We provide class information to the generator with class-conditional BatchNorm [25, 26]. To reduce computation and memory costs, similar to BigGAN, we use shared class embedding for different layers, which is linearly transformed to produce the BatchNorm affine parameters [28]. Different from BigGAN, we design a simpler architecture to incorporate the class label. Specifically, we only input the noise vector z to the first layer, and then for each conditional BatchNorm layer, we linearly transform the class embedding $E(y)$ to the gains and biases. Figure 5 is the illustration of our generator architecture.

Depthwise Separable Convolution. To further reduce the model size, we replace all the 3 × 3 standard convolutional layers in our generator with depthwise separable convolution [29], which factorizes a standard convolution into a depthwise convolution and a pointwise convolution, by first applying a single filter to each input channel (depthwise), and then utilizing a 1 × 1 convolution to combine the outputs (pointwise). Depthwise separable convolution uses $\frac{1}{O} + \frac{1}{k \times k}$ fewer parameters than the standard one, where O is the number of output channels and k is the kernel size. We denote TinyGAN using standard conv. layers as TinyGAN-std, and the variant with depth-wise conv. layer as TinyGAN-dw.[1]

4.2   Discriminator

With the supervision from BigGAN, the difficulties of training is greatly reduced and we found that a simple discriminator architecture already works well. Following [17, 18], we use spectral normalized discriminator and introduce the class condition via projection. But instead of utilizing complicated residual blocks, we found that simply stacking multiple convolutional layers with stride as DCGAN [30] works well enough, which greatly reduces the number of parameters. In fact, our discriminator is 10× smaller than that of BigGAN's.

---

[1] Note that all the figures in this paper are generated by the TinyGAN-dw variant.

5 Experiments

5.1 Datasets

ImageNet. The ImageNet ILSVRC 2012 dataset [31] consists of 1,000 image classes, each having approximately 1,300 images. We compressed each image to 128×128 pixels, using the source code released by [17].

Images Generated by BigGAN. We view BigGAN, our teacher network, as a black-box model and collect its input-output pairs to train our student network. For each class, we randomly sample 3,000[2] noise vectors from the truncated normal distribution and collect the corresponding output generated by BigGAN using the official API.[3]

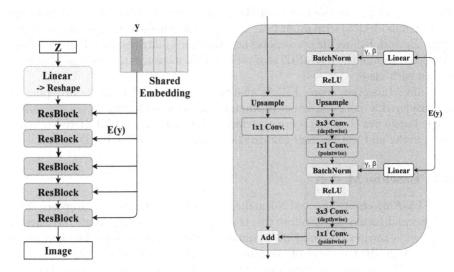

Fig. 5. Student generator S **Fig. 6.** A residual block in S

As we found TinyGAN unable to model some complicated objects well enough, we only report in Table 1 the IS/FID/intra-FID scores measured on *all* animal classes (398 classes in total). It shows that our approach can work well for a large set of homogeneous classes, and we focus on animals as they may have more downstream applications than other classes. Further discussion about experiments on all 1000 classes can be found in the supplementary material.

---

[2] We also tried 1000 instances per class, which already achieves good results; however, no significant improvement was observed when we increased to 4000.

[3] https://tfhub.dev/deepmind/biggan-deep-128/1.

5.2   Evaluation Metrics

Inception Score (IS). IS [32] measures the KL-divergence between the conditional class distribution $p(y|x)$ and the marginal class distribution $p(y)$. Formally,

$$IS = \exp\left(\mathbb{E}_x[KL(p(y|x)\|p(y))]\right). \tag{8}$$

A higher Inception score suggests a better performance. Despite the limitations of IS [33], we still adopt it as it is widely used in prior works.

Fréchet Inception Distance (FID). FID score [34] computes the 2-Wasserstein distance between the two distributions r and g, and is given by

$$FID(r, g) = \|\mu_r - \mu_g\|_2 + \text{Tr}(\Sigma_r + \Sigma_g - 2(\Sigma_r\Sigma_g)^{1/2}). \tag{9}$$

Here, μ_r and μ_g are the means of the final feature vectors extracted from the inception model [35] with input from the real and generated samples respectively, while Σ_r and Σ_g are the corresponding covariance matrices, and Tr is the trace. We also compute the intra-FID score [17], which measures the average FID score within each class.

Unlike Inception score, FID is able to detect intra-class mode dropping. It is considered a more consistent estimator [33], as a model that generates only a single image per class can score a perfect IS but not a good FID. Here we follow prior works and use `TensorFlow toolkit` to calculate IS and FID scores.

5.3   Baseline Models

SNGAN-Projection. Spectral Normalization GAN (SNGAN) [18] proposes spectral normalization to stabilize the training of the discriminator. [17] further proposes a projection-based discriminator, which incorporates the class labels via inner product instead of concatenation. The combined model, denoted as SNGAN-Projection, has shown significant improvements on ImageNet Dataset, and we consider it as a strong baseline model. Statistics in Table 1 are reported using the source code and the pretrained generator released by the authors.[4]

SAGAN. Self-Attention GAN (SAGAN) [19] is built atop SNGAN-projection, and introduces a self-attention mechanism [36,37] into convolutional GANs, in order to model long-range dependencies across image regions. As the authors do not provide a pretrained model and we are unable to train it from scratch due to limits of computation, its scores are left blank in Table 1, and we only compare its model size and computation cost to our TinyGAN. For reference, the IS/FID/intra-FID scores reported in the original paper, evaluated on all 1000 classes, are **52.52/18.7/83.7** respectively.

---

[4] https://github.com/pfnet-research/sngan_projection.

TinyGAN Trained from Scratch. To justify the effectiveness of knowledge distillation on GANs, we also experimented on training TinyGAN from scratch, without the guidance of a teacher network. That is, we use an identical architecture of TinyGAN, but trained it using only the adversarial loss L_{GAN} (Eq. 5).

5.4 Training

The proposed TinyGAN are trained using Adam [38] with $\beta_1 = 0.0$ and $\beta_2 = 0.9$. The learning rates of generator and discriminator are both set to 0.0002 with linear decay. We perform one generator update after 10 discriminator updates. With the stable guidance from the teacher network, no special tricks for training GANs are needed. While BigGAN notes that using a large batch size boosts the

Table 1. Inception Score (IS, higher is better) and Fréchet Inception Distance (FID, lower is better). Ch. is the channel multiplier representing the number of units in each layer. #Par. is total number of parameters. We highlight the generator's parameters G Par. since the discriminator is not required for inference. M denotes million and B is billion.

Model	Ch.	#Par.	G Par.	FLOPs	IS ↑	FID ↓	intra-FID ↓
SNGAN-proj	64	72.0 M	42.0 M	9.10 B	31.4 ± 0.7	29.0	84.1
SAGAN	64	81.5 M	42.0 M	9.18 B	–	–	–
BigGAN-deep	128	85.0 M	50.4 M	8.32 B	**146.1 ± 1.7**	**19.8**	**55.6**
TinyGAN-std	32	12.6 M	9.3 M	2.29 B	94.0 ± 1.2	21.6	70.6
TinyGAN-std	16	6.2 M	2.9 M	0.58 B	68.25 ± 1.0	27.4	88.1
TinyGAN-dw	32	6.4 M	3.1 M	0.44 B	79.19 ± 1.6	24.2	79.1

Fig. 7. A comparison between randomly sampled images generated by TinyGAN-dw (left) and SNGAN-projection (right).

performance, in our TinyGAN, we found that a smaller batch size (32 or 16) works as well. Training takes about 3 days on a single NVIDIA 2080Ti GPU.

5.5   Results

We evaluate TinyGAN on all the 398 animal classes in the ImageNet dataset, and the results are shown in Table 1. We compare the computation cost of TinyGAN with the teacher network (BigGAN-deep) and two strong baseline models discussed before.

Note that our proposed model uses much fewer parameters and floating-point operations than all the other frameworks. We also study the trade-off between model size and performance of different variants of TinyGAN in the last three rows in Table 1. Experiments show that TinyGAN with standard conv. layers (TinyGAN-std) achieves the best performance but uses more parameters. To reduce the model size, we can either reduce the channel multiplier or adopting depth-wise separable conv. layers (TinyGAN-dw). The result shows that aggressively reducing channels leads to a noticeable drop in performance. On the other hand, it is much less significant in TinyGAN-dw, making it a suitable choice under a tight computation budget. Specifically, our generator of TinyGAN-std/TinyGAN-dw has $\sim 18\%/6\%$ parameters and $\sim 28\%/5\%$ FLOPs when compared with the teacher network, and we also have similar reductions from the other two baseline models.

Although there is a performance gap between our TinyGAN-dw and the teacher network, we claim that it is tolerable considering its compact model size, and its better performance over SNGAN-projection in all the metrics. We further compare the image quality of TinyGAN-dw and SNGAN-projection in Fig. 7, where all images are randomly sampled within animal classes. We found that while SNGAN-projection is able to produce sharper images with clear details, perhaps due to its larger model complexity, our TinyGAN focuses on the intended class itself and generates more realistic images with less distortion.[5]

Table 2. Ablation study

Model	FID ↓	intra-FID ↓
TinyGAN-dw	24.2	79.1
$-L_{\text{KD\_feat}}$	54.4	149.2
$-L_{\text{GAN}}$	28.8	89.9
$-L_{\text{KD\_S}}, L_{\text{KD\_D}}$	60.5	157.0
$L_{\text{KD\_pix}}$	107.9	216.0

---

[5] More randomly sampled images for comparisons between TinyGAN and SNGAN-projection can be found in the supplementary material.

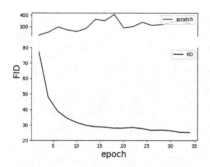
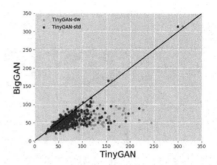

Fig. 8. FID scores during the training phase of TinyGAN-dw (trained from scratch vs. trained with KD losses).

Fig. 9. Comparing intra-FID scores of TinyGAN and BigGAN. Each dot corresponds to a class.

Finally, let us stress that the main point of our work is not to claim how small our network is, but to propose an easy way to train such one. Figure 8 shows the learning curve of TinyGAN-dw, demonstrating a smooth, stable and efficient training process it has. In fact, with our knowledge distillation losses, we have never experienced any training collapse, and most of our effort has been spent on finding the right balance between model size and image quality. On the other hand, we have also experimented on training TinyGAN from scratch, and the blue line in Fig. 8 shows a typical training failure we often encountered. Although we do not rule out the possibility of training a small-size GAN from scratch, based on the network architecture of either TinyGAN, BigGAN, or other baselines, a successful training is likely to be hard without considerable efforts for overcoming those well-known training problems.

5.6 Analysis

Ablation Study. We conduct ablation study to validate those objectives proposed in Sect. 3.1. Table 2 shows the results of omitting L_{KD_feat} (Eq. 4), L_{GAN} (Eq. 5), and L_{KD_S}, L_{KD_D} (Eq. 2,3) respectively, as well as that of using L_{KD_pix} (Eq. 1) alone without the discriminator.

The fifth row in Table 2 shows that adding a discriminator, which only costs a few parameters, is very crucial for the performance. Because the discriminator is trained to discern real from fake images, it guides the generator to produce sharper and more realistic images. Similarly, feature-level distillation loss L_{KD_feat} significantly improves the performance as the generator learns to match the informative features extracted from the discriminator. In addition, omitting adversarial distillation loss L_{KD_S}, L_{KD_D} and keeping the others is equivalent to training a standard cGANs (with the real distribution from ImageNet) while incorporating supervision from the teacher via pixel-wise and feature-wise losses. The notable drop in performance in the fourth row indicates the importance of

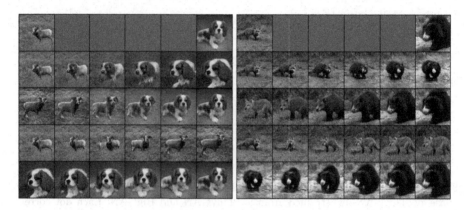

Fig. 10. Interpolations between z, y pairs. The second and third rows interpolate between y with z fixed, while the last two rows interpolate between z with y fixed. Observe that semantics are maintained between two endpoints.

leveraging the discriminator to push the student's output distribution to the teacher's.

In addition to the distillation objectives which provide stable supervision from the teacher, including the standard adversarial loss L_{GAN} further improves the image quality. The ablation study demonstrates that all the proposed objectives in Sect. 3 are useful for training our TinyGAN.

Interpolation. To understand the generalization ability of our TinyGAN-dw, we perform linear interpolations between random noise vectors z_1, z_2 and class labels y_1, y_2.

We first interpolate between the class embedding $E(y_1)$ and $E(y_2)$ with the noise vectors fixed. In Fig. 10, the second and third rows demonstrate that Tiny-GAN can successfully perform category morphing. We then interpolate between the noise vectors z_1 and z_2 with fixed class labels. The last two rows in Fig. 10 show that TinyGAN can also smoothly manipulate some coarse features such as poses and sizes of the animals.

Quality Analysis. Finally, to better understand the weakness of our TinyGAN, we investigate on classes with high intra-FID scores. We first show the positive correlation (Pearson's correlation coefficient $= 0.54, 0.64$) between teacher and student networks (-dw, -std) in Fig. 9, which reveals that TinyGAN's failure in a few classes can be attributed to the teacher network. We then focus on the 10 worst classes with the highest FID scores, which are chambered nautilus, Indian cobra, sea snake, triceratops, tick, ringneck snake, walking stick, trilobite, crayfish, and American lobster. As the samples in Fig. 11 show, most of them have complicated or delicate appearances and bear little resemblance to most of the others, making them hard to model with others by a small network.

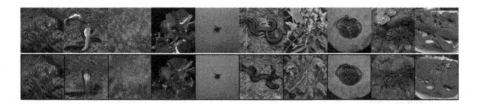

Fig. 11. Samples of the 10 worst classes. The first row is generated by BigGAN and the second row is by TinyGAN-dw.

6   Conclusion

Training GANs from scratch has well-known problems, especially for complex datasets such as ImageNet, and the recent work of BigGAN shows that scaling up GANs can mitigate some of the problems and produce high-quality images. However, it requires huge computational resources not only for training but also for testing, which may prevent its use in resource-limited devices. We propose a novel black-box knowledge distillation method for GANs, which allows us to learn a much smaller generator with competitive performance in an efficient and stable way when given a well-trained large generator such as BigGAN.

Acknowledgement. We would like to thank NTU MiuLab for their support, and all anonymous reviewers for insightful comments.

References

1. Goodfellow, I., et al.: Generative adversarial nets. In: Advances in Neural Information Processing Systems, pp. 2672–2680 (2014)
2. Mirza, M., Osindero, S.: Conditional generative adversarial nets. arXiv preprint arXiv:1411.1784 (2014)
3. Brock, A., Donahue, J., Simonyan, K.: Large scale GAN training for high fidelity natural image synthesis. In: ICLR (2019)
4. Romero, A., Ballas, N., Kahou, S.E., Chassang, A., Gatta, C., Bengio, Y.: FitNets: hints for thin deep nets. arXiv preprint arXiv:1412.6550 (2014)
5. Han, S., Mao, H., Dally, W.J.: Deep compression: compressing deep neural networks with pruning, trained quantization and Huffman coding. In: ICLR (2016)
6. Gong, Y., Liu, L., Yang, M., Bourdev, L.: Compressing deep convolutional networks using vector quantization. In: ICLR (2015)
7. Hinton, G., Vinyals, O., Dean, J.: Distilling the knowledge in a neural network. arXiv preprint arXiv:1503.02531 (2015)
8. Zagoruyko, S., Komodakis, N.: Paying more attention to attention: improving the performance of convolutional neural networks via attention transfer. In: ICLR (2017)
9. Isola, P., Zhu, J.Y., Zhou, T., Efros, A.A.: Image-to-image translation with conditional adversarial networks. In: CVPR (2017)
10. Reed, S., Akata, Z., Yan, X., Logeswaran, L., Schiele, B., Lee, H.: Generative adversarial text to image synthesis. In: ICML (2016)

11. Ledig, C., et al.: Photo-realistic single image super-resolution using a generative adversarial network. In: Proceedings of the IEEE Conference on Computer Vision and Pattern Recognition, pp. 4681–4690 (2017)
12. Che, T., Li, Y., Jacob, A.P., Bengio, Y., Li, W.: Mode regularized generative adversarial networks. In: ICLR (2017)
13. Zhao, J., Mathieu, M., LeCun, Y.: Energy-based generative adversarial network. In: ICLR (2017)
14. Arjovsky, M., Chintala, S., Bottou, L.: Wasserstein GAN. In: ICML (2017)
15. Gulrajani, I., Ahmed, F., Arjovsky, M., Dumoulin, V., Courville, A.C.: Improved training of Wasserstein GANs. In: Advances in Neural Information Processing Systems, pp. 5767–5777 (2017)
16. Salimans, T., Zhang, H., Radford, A., Metaxas, D.: Improving GANs using optimal transport. In: ICLR (2018)
17. Miyato, T., Koyama, M.: cGANs with projection discriminator. In: ICLR (2018)
18. Miyato, T., Kataoka, T., Koyama, M., Yoshida, Y.: Spectral normalization for generative adversarial networks. In: ICLR (2018)
19. Zhang, H., Goodfellow, I., Metaxas, D., Odena, A.: Self-attention generative adversarial networks. arXiv preprint arXiv:1805.08318 (2018)
20. Aguinaldo, A., Chiang, P.Y., Gain, A., Patil, A., Pearson, K., Feizi, S.: Compressing GANs using knowledge distillation. arXiv preprint arXiv:1902.00159 (2019)
21. Wang, T.C., Liu, M.Y., Zhu, J.Y., Tao, A., Kautz, J., Catanzaro, B.: High-resolution image synthesis and semantic manipulation with conditional GANs. In: Proceedings of the IEEE Conference on Computer Vision and Pattern Recognition (2018)
22. Simonyan, K., Zisserman, A.: Very deep convolutional networks for large-scale image recognition. arXiv preprint arXiv:1409.1556 (2014)
23. Lim, J.H., Ye, J.C.: Geometric GAN. arXiv preprint arXiv:1705.02894 (2017)
24. He, K., Zhang, X., Ren, S., Sun, J.: Identity mappings in deep residual networks. In: Leibe, B., Matas, J., Sebe, N., Welling, M. (eds.) ECCV 2016. LNCS, vol. 9908, pp. 630–645. Springer, Cham (2016). https://doi.org/10.1007/978-3-319-46493-0_38
25. Dumoulin, V., Shlens, J., Kudlur, M.: A learned representation for artistic style. In: ICLR (2017)
26. De Vries, H., Strub, F., Mary, J., Larochelle, H., Pietquin, O., Courville, A.C.: Modulating early visual processing by language. In: Advances in Neural Information Processing Systems, pp. 6594–6604 (2017)
27. Karras, T., Aila, T., Laine, S., Lehtinen, J.: Progressive growing of GANs for improved quality, stability, and variation. In: ICLR (2018)
28. Perez, E., Strub, F., De Vries, H., Dumoulin, V., Courville, A.: Film: visual reasoning with a general conditioning layer. In: Thirty-Second AAAI Conference on Artificial Intelligence (2018)
29. Howard, A.G., et al.: MobileNets: efficient convolutional neural networks for mobile vision applications. arXiv preprint arXiv:1704.04861 (2017)
30. Radford, A., Metz, L., Chintala, S.: Unsupervised representation learning with deep convolutional generative adversarial networks. In: ICLR (2016)
31. Russakovsky, O., et al.: ImageNet large scale visual recognition challenge. Int. J. Comput. Vis. **115**, 211–252 (2015)
32. Salimans, T., Goodfellow, I., Zaremba, W., Cheung, V., Radford, A., Chen, X.: Improved techniques for training GANs. In: Advances in Neural Information Processing Systems, pp. 2234–2242 (2016)

33. Lucic, M., Kurach, K., Michalski, M., Gelly, S., Bousquet, O.: Are GANs created equal? A large-scale study. In: Advances in Neural Information Processing Systems, pp. 700–709 (2018)
34. Heusel, M., Ramsauer, H., Unterthiner, T., Nessler, B., Hochreiter, S.: GANs trained by a two time-scale update rule converge to a local nash equilibrium. In: Advances in Neural Information Processing Systems, pp. 6626–6637 (2017)
35. Szegedy, C., et al.: Going deeper with convolutions. In: Proceedings of the IEEE Conference on Computer Vision and Pattern Recognition, pp. 1–9 (2015)
36. Parikh, A.P., Täckström, O., Das, D., Uszkoreit, J.: A decomposable attention model for natural language inference. In: EMNLP (2016)
37. Vaswani, A., et al.: Attention is all you need. In: Advances in Neural Information Processing Systems, pp. 5998–6008 (2017)
38. Kingma, D.P., Ba, J.: Adam: a method for stochastic optimization. In: ICLR (2015)

A Cost-Effective Method for Improving and Re-purposing Large, Pre-trained GANs by Fine-Tuning Their Class-Embeddings

Qi Li[1]($^{(\boxtimes)}$), Long Mai[2], Michael A. Alcorn[1], and Anh Nguyen[1]

[1] Department of Computer Science and Software Engineering, Auburn University,
Auburn, AL 36849, USA
{qzl0019,alcorma}@auburn.edu, anh.ng8@gmail.com
[2] Adobe Inc., San Jose, CA 95110, USA
malong@adobe.com

Abstract. Large, pre-trained generative models have been increasingly popular and useful to both the research and wider communities. Specifically, BigGANs—a class-conditional Generative Adversarial Networks trained on ImageNet—achieved excellent, state-of-the-art capability in generating realistic photos. However, fine-tuning or training BigGANs from scratch is *practically impossible* for most researchers and engineers because (1) GAN training is often unstable and suffering from mode-collapse; and (2) the training requires a significant amount of computation, 256 Google TPUs for 2 days or 8 × V100 GPUs for 15 days. Importantly, many pre-trained generative models both in NLP and image domains were found to contain biases that are harmful to the society. Thus, we need computationally-feasible methods for modifying and re-purposing these huge, pre-trained models for downstream tasks. In this paper, we propose a cost-effective optimization method for improving and re-purposing BigGANs by fine-tuning only the class-embedding layer. We show the effectiveness of our model-editing approach in three tasks: (1) significantly improving the realism and diversity of samples of complete mode-collapse classes; (2) re-purposing ImageNet BigGANs for generating images for Places365; and (3) de-biasing or improving the sample diversity for selected ImageNet classes.

1 Introduction

From GPT-2 [1] to BigGAN [2], large, pre-trained generative models have been increasingly popular and useful to both the research and wider communities. Interestingly, these pre-trained models have remarkably high utility but near-zero re-trainability. That is, GPT-2 or BigGANs were all trained on extremely

Electronic supplementary material The online version of this chapter (https://doi.org/10.1007/978-3-030-69538-5_32) contains supplementary material, which is available to authorized users.

H. Ishikawa et al. (Eds.): ACCV 2020, LNCS 12625, pp. 526–541, 2021.
https://doi.org/10.1007/978-3-030-69538-5_32

large-scale computational infrastructure, which is not available to the rest of the community. In practice, training or fine-tuning such models is impossible to most researchers and engineers. Importantly, pre-trained generative models in both text and image domains were found to capture undesired, hidden biases that may be harmful to the society [3,4]. Therefore, the community needs techniques for fine-tuning and re-purposing pre-trained generative models.

The class-conditional BigGAN [2] has reached an unprecedented state-of-the-art image quality and diversity on ImageNet by using large networks and batch sizes. However, fine-tuning or training BigGANs from scratch is impractical for most researchers and engineers due to two main reasons. First, Generative Adversarial Networks (GANs) training is notoriously unstable and subject to mode-collapse [2,5] i.e. the generated distribution does not capture all modes of the true distribution [5]. Consistent with [6], we observed that BigGAN samples from a set of ~50 classes exhibit substantially lower diversity than samples from other classes do. For example, BigGAN samples from the window screen class are rubbish examples i.e. noisy patterns that are not recognizable to humans (Fig. 1a). Similarly, nematode samples are heavily biased towards green worms

(A) ImageNet   (B) BigGAN [2]   (C) AM (ours)

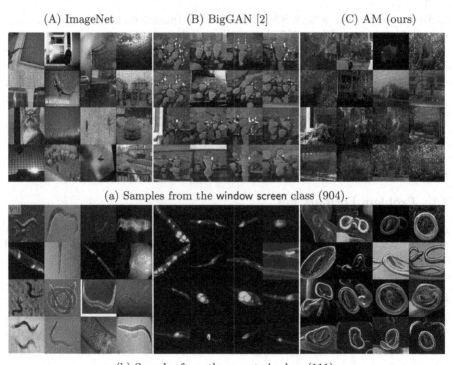

(a) Samples from the window screen class (904).

(b) Samples from the nematode class (111).

Fig. 1. For some classes, 256×256 BigGAN samples (B) have poor realism and diversity (i.e. samples are biased towards one type of data) while the real ImageNet images (A) are diverse. AM samples (C) are of higher diversity than the original BigGAN samples (B). (Color figure online)

on black, but the training data includes worms of a variety of colors and backgrounds (Fig. 1b).

Second, re-training BigGANs requires significantly expensive computation—the original 256×256 model took 48 h of training on 256 Google Cloud TPUs. On more modest hardware of $8 \times$ V100 GPUs, the training is estimated to take more than 2 weeks [7] but has not been found to match the published results in [2]. Importantly, re-training or finetuning BigGANs were found to still cause a set of classes to collapse as observed in a BigGAN-deep model [6] (in addition to BigGAN models) released by [2].

In this paper, we propose a cost-effective method for improving sample diversity of BigGANs and re-purposing it for generating images of unseen classes. Leveraging the intuition that the BigGAN generator is already able to synthesize photo-realistic images for many ImageNet classes [2], we propose to modify *only the class embeddings* while keeping the generator unchanged (Fig. 2). We demonstrate our simple yet effective approach on three different use cases:[1]

1. Changing only the embeddings is surprisingly sufficient to "recover" diverse and plausible samples for complete mode-collapse classes e.g. window screen (Fig. 1a).
2. We can re-purpose a BigGAN, pre-trained on ImageNet, for generating images matching unseen Places365 classes (Sect. 3.2).
3. On ImageNet, our method improves the sample diversity by $\sim 50\%$ for the pre-trained BigGANs released by the authors—at 256×256 and 128×128 resolutions by finding multiple class embeddings for each class (Sect. 3.7). A human study confirmed that our method produced more diverse and similarly realistic images compared to BigGAN samples (Sect. 3.6).

2   Methods

2.1   Problem Formulation

Let G be a class-conditional generator, here a BigGAN pre-trained by [2], that takes a class embedding $c \in \mathbb{R}^{128}$ and a latent vector $z \in \mathbb{R}^{140}$ as inputs and outputs an image $G(c, z) \in \mathbb{R}^{256 \times 256 \times 3}$. We test improving BigGAN's sample diversity by only updating the embeddings (pre-trained during GAN training).

Increasing Diversity.   Intuitively, we search for an input class embedding c of the generator G such that the set of output images $\{G(c, z^i)\}$ is diverse with random latent vectors $z^i \sim \mathcal{N}(0, I)$. Specifically, we encourage a small change in the latent variable to yield a large change in the output image [8] by maximizing:

$$\max_{c} L_D(c) = \mathbb{E}_{z^i, z^j \sim \mathcal{N}(0, I)} \frac{\|\phi(G(c, z^i)) - \phi(G(c, z^j))\|}{\|z^i - z^j\|} \tag{1}$$

---

[1] Code for reproducibility is available at https://github.com/qilimk/biggan-am.

(A) BigGAN [2]   (B) Modifying class embeddings   (C) AM (ours)

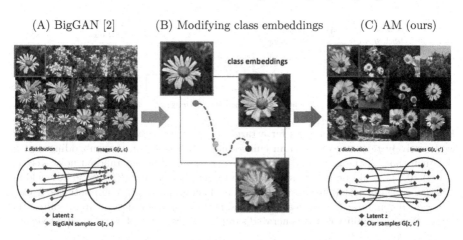

Fig. 2. With BigGAN embeddings (A), the latent z vectors are mapped to nearby points (green ◆) i.e. similarly-looking images. Our embedding optimization moves the original embedding to a new vector where the generated samples (red ◆) are more diverse. Here, the updated class embedding c changes the background of a daisy from green grass (▢) to brown soil (▢). Note that the pose of the flower (controlled by z) remain the same. Effectively, with only a change in the embedding, the latent vectors are re-mapped to more spread-out points or more diverse set of samples (C). (Color figure online)

where $\phi(.)$ is a feature extractor. In [8], $\phi(.)$ is an identity function to encourage pixel-wise diversity. We also tested with $\phi(.)$ being outputs of the conv5 layer and the output softmax layer of AlexNet.

Via hyperparameter tuning, we found that maximizing the above objective via 10 unique pairs of (z^i, z^j) selected from $\mathcal{Z}$ to be effective (full hyperparameter details are in Sect. 2.4).

Activation Maximization. When a class embedding changes, it is critical to keep the generated samples to be still realistic and in the target class. To achieve that, we also move the class embedding c of the generator G such that the output image $G(c, z)$ for any random $z \sim \mathcal{N}(0, I)$ would cause some classifier P to output a high probability for a target class y (Fig. 3). Here, we let P be a pre-trained ImageNet classifier [9] that maps an image $x \in \mathbb{R}^{256 \times 256 \times 3}$ onto a softmax probability distribution over 1,000 output classes. Formally, we maximize the following objective given a pre-defined class y_c:

$$\max_{c} L_{AM}(c) = \mathbb{E}_{z \sim \mathcal{N}(0,I)} \log P(y = y_c \mid G(c, z)) \qquad (2)$$

The above objective is basically a common term in the classification objectives for class-conditional GAN discriminators [2,10,11] and also called the Activation Maximization (AM) in image synthesis using pre-trained classifiers [12–16]. We try to solve the above AM objective via mini-batch gradient descent. That is, we iteratively backpropagate through both the classifier P and the

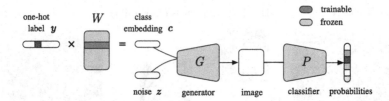

one-hot W class   trainable
label y embedding c frozen

$\times$ =

noise z generator   image   classifier   probabilities

Fig. 3. To improve the samples for a target class represented by a one-hot vector y, we iteratively take steps to find an embedding c (i.e. a row in the embedding matrix W) such that all the generated images $\{G(c, z^i)\}$, for different random noise vectors $z^i \sim \mathcal{N}(0, I)$, would be (1) classified as the target class y; and (2) diverse i.e. yielding different softmax probability distributions. We backpropagate through both the frozen, pre-trained generator G and classifier P and perform gradient descent to maximize the target-class probability of the generated samples over a batch of random latent vectors $\{z^i\}$.

generator G and change the embedding c to maximize the expectation of the log probabilities over a set $\mathcal{Z}$ of random latent vectors.

In sum, we encouraged the samples to be diverse but still remain in a target class y via the full objective function below (where λ is a hyperparameter):

$$\max_{c} \; L_{\text{AM-D}}(c) = L_{\text{AM}} + \lambda L_{\text{D}} \qquad (3)$$

2.2   Datasets and Networks

Datasets. While the generators and classifiers were pre-trained on the full 1000-class ImageNet 2012 dataset, we evaluated our methods on a subset of 50 classes (hereafter, ImageNet-50) where we qualitatively found BigGAN samples exhibit the lowest diversity. The selection of 50 classes were informed by two diversity metrics (see below) but decided by humans before the study.

Generators. We used two pre-trained ImageNet BigGAN generators [2], a 256×256 and a 128×128 model, released by the authors in PyTorch [7]. For the purpose of studying diversity, all generated images in this paper were sampled from the full, non-truncated prior distribution [2].

2.3   Evaluation Metrics

Because there is currently no single metric that is able to capture the multi-dimensional characteristics of an image set [17], we chose a broad range of common metrics to measure sample diversity and sample realism separately.

Diversity. We measured intra-class diversity by randomly sampling 200 image pairs from an image set and computing the MS-SSIM [10] and LPIPS [18] scores for each pair. For each method, we computed a mean score across the 50 classes $\times$ 200 image pairs.

Realism. To measure sample realism, we used three standard metrics: Inception Score (IS) with 10 splits [19], Fréchet Inception Distance (FID) [20], and Inception Accuracy (IA) [10]. These three metrics were computed for every set of 50,000 images = 50 classes × 1000 images. To evaluate the set of mixed samples from both BigGAN and AM embeddings, we randomly select 500 images from each and create a new set contains 1000 images per ImageNet class.

2.4   Implementation Details

We found two effective strategies for implementing the AM method (described in Sect. 2.1) to improve BigGAN samples: (1) searching within a small region around the original embeddings (AM-S); (2) searching within a large region around the mean embedding (AM-L).

Hyperparameters. For AM-S, we randomly initialized the embedding within a Gaussian ball of radius 0.1 around the original embedding. We used a learning rate of 0.01. For AM-L, we randomly initialized the embedding around the mean of all 1000 embeddings and used a larger learning rate of 0.1. For both settings, we maximized Eq. 2 using the Adam optimizer and its default hyperparameters for 200 steps. We re-sampled a set $\mathcal{Z} = \{z^i\}_{20}$ every 20 steps. Every step, we kept the embeddings within $[-0.59, 0.61]$ by clipping. To evaluate each trial, we used the embedding from the last step and sampled 1000 images per class. We ran 5 trials per class with different random initializations. We used 2 to 4 × V100 GPUs for each optimization trial.

Classifiers. In the preliminary experiments, we tested four 1000-class-ImageNet classifiers: AlexNet [9], Inception-v3 [21], ResNet-50 [22], and a ResNet-50 [23] that is robust to pixel-wise noise. By default, we resized the BigGAN output images to the appropriate input resolution of each classifier.

With Inception-v3, we achieved an FID score that is (a) substantially better than those for the other three classifiers (Table S2; 30.24 vs. 48.74), and (b) similar to that of the original BigGAN (30.24 vs. 31.36). The same trends were observed with the Inception Accuracy metrics (Table S2). However, we did not find any substantial qualitative differences among the samples of the four treatments. Therefore, we chose AlexNet because of its fastest run time.

3   Experiments and Results

3.1   Repairing Complete Mode-Collapse Classes of BigGANs

Consistent with [6], we found that BigGAN samples for some classes, e.g. window screen, contain similar, human-unrecognizable patterns (see Fig. 1a). However, re-training BigGANs is impractical to most researchers given its significance computation requirement.

Here, we apply AM-L (see Sect. 2.4) to "repair" the mode-collapse window screen embedding to generate more realistic and diverse images. Intuitively, AM-L enables us to make a larger jump out of the local optimum than AM-S.

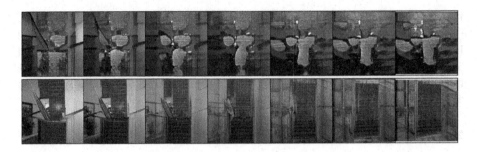

Fig. 4. Interpolation between a z pair in the window screen class using the original Big-GAN embedding (top) yields similar and unrealistic samples. The same interpolation with the embedding found by AM (bottom) produced realistic intermediate samples between two window screen images.

Results. Interesting, by simply changing the embedding, AM-L was able to turn the original rubbish images into a diverse set of recognizable images of window screens (see Fig. 1a). Quantitatively, the AM embedding improved BigGAN window screen samples in all metrics: LPIPS ($0.62 \rightarrow 0.77$), IS ($2.76 \rightarrow 2.91$), and IA ($0.56 \rightarrow 0.7$).

While the embeddings found by our AM methods changed the generated samples entirely, we observed that interpolating in the latent or embedding spaces still yields realistic intermediate samples (Fig. 4).

Significantly Faster Computation. According to a PyTorch BigGAN re-implementation by authors [2], BigGAN training can take at least 15 days on 8 V100 GPUs. This is significantly more time-consuming and costly than our AM approach which takes at most 1 h for generating 5 embeddings (from which users could choose to use one or more) on a single V100 GPU (see Table 1). The original DeepMind's training [2] requires even more expensive and unique hardware of 256 Google Cloud TPU, which is not available to most of the community and so is not compared here.

Table 1. BigGAN training is not only 360× more time-consuming but also almost 3,000× more costly. The AWS on-demand price-per-hour is \$ 24.48 for 8×V100 and \$ 3.06 for 1×V100 [24].

Method	Time (hours)	Number of GPUs (Tesla V100)	AWS price (USD)
1. BigGAN training [7]	24 × 15 days=360	8	8812.8
2. AM optimization	1	1	3.1

Note that our method is essentially finding a new sampler for the same Big-GAN model. After a new embedding is found via optimization, the samples are generated fast via standard GAN sampling procedure [25].

3.2 Synthesizing Places365 Images Using Pre-trained ImageNet BigGAN

While original BigGAN is not able to synthesize realistic images for all 1000 ImageNet classes (see Fig. 1), it does so for a few hundred of classes.

Therefore, here, we test whether it is possible to re-use the same ImageNet BigGAN generator for synthesizing images for unseen categories in the target Places365 dataset [26], which contains 365 classes of scene images. For evaluation, we randomly chose 50 out of 365 classes in Places365 (hereafter, Places-50).

Mean Initialization. As we want to generate images for unseen classes, the Places365-optimal embeddings are intuitively far from the original ImageNet embeddings. Therefore, we chose AM-L (instead of AM-S) for making larges jumps. We ran the AM-L algorithm for 5 trials per class with the same hyper-parameters as in Sect. 3.1 but with a ResNet-18 classifier [22] pre-trained on Places365.

Top-5 Initialization. Besides initializing from mean embeddings, we also tested initializing from the top-5 embeddings whose 10 random generated samples were given the highest average accuracy scores by the Places365 classifier. For example, to synthesize the hotel room images for Places365, the top-1 embedding in the ImageNet dataset is for class quilt (Fig. 6). We reproduced 5 AM-L trials but each was initialized with a unique embedding among the top-5.

Baseline. We used the original BigGAN samples for the top-1 ImageNet classes found from the top-5 initialization procedure above as a baseline.

Qualitative Results. AM-L found many class embeddings that produced plausible images for Places365 scene classes using the same ImageNet BigGAN generator. For example, to match the hotel room class, which does not exist in ImageNet, AM-L synthesized bedroom scenes with lights and windows whereas the top-1 class (quilt) samples mostly shows beds with blankets (Fig. 5). See Fig. 6 for some qualitative differences between the generated images with original vs. AM embeddings for the same set of random latent vectors.

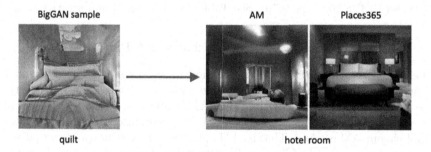

Fig. 5. The closest ImageNet class that the BigGAN was pre-trained to generate is quilt, which contains mostly blankets and pillows. Surprisingly, with AM embeddings, the same BigGAN can generate remarkable images for unseen category of hotel room. The rightmost is an example Places365 image for reference.

(A) Places365 images   (B) Top-1 baseline (BigGAN)   (C) AM-L (ours)

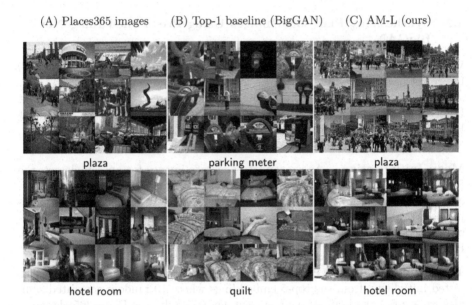

Fig. 6. AM-L generated plausible images for two Places365 classes, plaza (top) and hotel room (bottom), which do *not* exist in the ImageNet training set of the BigGAN generator. For example, AM-L synthesizes images of squares with buildings and people in the background for the plaza class (C) while the samples from the top-1 ImageNet class, here, parking meter, shows parking meters on the street (B). Similarly, AM-L samples for the hotel room class has the unique touches of lighting, lamps, and windows (C) that do not exist in the BigGAN samples for the quilt class (B). The latent vectors are held constant for corresponding images in (B) and (C). See Figs. S21, S22, S23, and S24 for more side-by-side image comparisons.

Quantitative Results. Compared to the baseline, AM-L samples have substantially higher realism in FID (41.25 vs. 53.15) and in ResNet-18 Accuracy scores (0.49 vs. 0.17). In terms of diversity, AM-L and the baseline performed similarly and both were slightly worse than the real images in MS-SSIM (0.42 vs. 0.43) and LPIPS (0.65 vs. 0.70). See Table S3 for detailed quantitative results.

3.3   Improving Sample Diversity of 256 × 256 BigGAN

To evaluate the effectiveness of our method in improving sample diversity for many classes, here, we ran both AM-S and AM-L on 50 classes in ImageNet-50. The goal is to compare the original BigGAN samples vs. a mixed set of samples generated from both the original BigGAN embeddings and AM embeddings found via our AM method. That is, AM optimization is so inexpensive that users can generate many embeddings and use multiple of them to sample images.

BigGAN vs. AM.   Across 50 classes × 5 AM trials, we found that both AM-S and AM-L produced samples of higher diversity than the original BigGAN

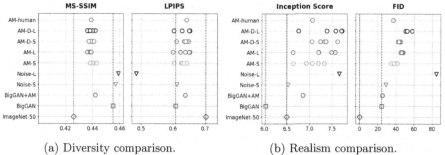

(a) Diversity comparison.   (b) Realism comparison.

Fig. 7. Each point in the four plots is a mean score across 50 classes from one AM optimization trial or one BigGAN model. The ultimate goal here is to close the gap between the BigGAN samples (- - - -) and the ImageNet-50 distribution (- - - -) in all four metrics. Naively adding noise degraded the embeddings in both diversity (MS-SSIM and LPIPS) and quality (IS and FID) scores i.e. the black and gray ▽ actually moved away from the red lines. Our optimization trials, on average, closed the *diversity* gap by ∼50% i.e. the AM circles are half way in between the green and red dash lines (a). By mixing AM samples with the original BigGAN samples, the BigGAN+AM image-set (○) has substantially higher diversity (MS-SSIM and LPIPS) and similar quality (IS and FID) to BigGAN (▢). That is, that multi-embeddings improved the sample diversity of BigGAN without compromising the quality. (Color figure online)

samples. For both MS-SSIM and LPIPS, on average, our AM methods reduced the gap between the original BigGAN and the real data by ∼50% (Fig. 7a; AM-S and AM-L vs. BigGAN).

For all 50 classes, we always found at least 1 out of 10 trials (i.e. both AM-S and AM-L combined) that yielded samples that match the real data in MS-SSIM or LPIPS scores. The statistics also align with our qualitative observations that AM samples often contain a more diverse set of object poses, shapes and backgrounds than the BigGAN samples (see Figs. S9–S11).

BigGAN vs. BigGAN+AM. Most importantly, the set of images generated by both BigGAN and two AM embeddings obtained higher diversity in MS-SSIM and LPIPS while obtaining similar realism FID scores (Fig. 7; BigGAN vs. BigGAN+AM). We constructed each BigGAN+AM set per class using one BigGAN and one AM embedding (selected by humans out of 5 embeddings).

3.4 Adding Noise to or Finetuning the Class Embeddings Did Not Improve Diversity

Adding Noise. A naive attempt to improve sample diversity is adding small random noise to the embedding vector of a low-diversity class. Across 50 classes, we found that adding small noise $\sim \mathcal{N}(0, 0.1)$ almost did not quantitatively change the image quality and diversity (Fig. 7; Noise-S) while adding larger noise $\sim \mathcal{N}(0, 0.3)$ degraded the samples on both criteria (Fig. 7; Noise-L).

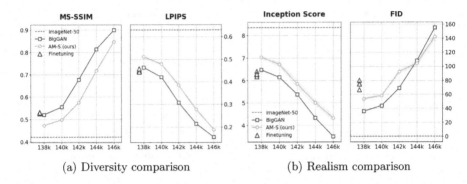

(a) Diversity comparison   (b) Realism comparison

Fig. 8. Each point in the four plots is a mean score across 50 classes and five AM-S trials or one 128 × 128 BigGAN model. Finetuning the 138k snapshot neither improved the sample diversity nor realism (purple Δ vs. green $\square$). Optimizing the embeddings via AM-S consistently improved the diversity in both MS-SSIM and LPIPS (a). IS and FID metrics disagree on whether AM-S (cyan ○) sample quality is better or worse than that of the BigGAN samples. See Fig. 9 for a side-by-side comparison of the samples from these five snapshots. (Color figure online)

For example, daisy samples gradually turned into human-unrecognizable rubbish images as we increased the noise (Fig. S4).

Finetuning. Another strategy to improve sample diversity is to finetune Big-GANs. However, how to finetune a BigGAN to improve its sample diversity is an open question. The BigGAN pre-trained model would start to degrade if we kept training it using the original hyperparameters as reported in [2].

To minimize the GAN training instability and compare with other approaches in this paper, we only finetuned one embedding at a time, keeping the other embeddings and all parameters in the generator and discriminator frozen. Because [2] only released the discriminator for their 128 × 128 generator but not for the 256 × 256 model, we only finetuned the 128 × 128 model. For each class, we added a small amount of noise $\sim \mathcal{N}(0, 0.1)$ to the associated embedding vector and finetuned it using the original BigGAN training objective for 10 iterations until the training collapsed. Across 50 classes × 5 trials, quantitatively, finetuning did not improve the sample diversity but lowered the realism (Fig. 8; purple Δ vs. green $\square$).

3.5 Explicitly Encouraging Diversity Yielded Worse Sample Realism

Inspired by [8], here, we used the sample diversity further by incorporating a diversity term into the previous two AM-S and AM-L methods (Sect. 2.1) to produce two new variants AM-D-S and AM-D-L. We tested encouraging diversity in the (1) image space; (2) conv5 feature space; and (3) softmax outputs of AlexNet and found they can qualitatively bias the optimization towards different interesting spaces of diversity.

However, the addition of the diversity term quantitatively improved the diversity but at a large cost of lower sample quality (Fig. 7b AM-S vs. AM-D-S and AM-L vs. AM-D-L). Similarly, the IA scores of the AM-D methods were consistently lower than those of the original AM methods (Table S1). See Sect. S1 for more details.

We hypothesize that the intrinsic noise from mini-batch SGD [27] also contributes to the increased sample diversity caused by AM embeddings.

3.6   Humans Rated AM Samples More Diverse and Similarly Realistic

Because quantitative image evaluation metrics are imperfect [17], we ran a human study to compare the AM vs. original BigGAN samples. For each class, across all 20 embeddings from 5 trials × 4 methods (AM-S, AM-L, AM-D-S, and AM-D-L), we manually chose one embedding that qualitatively is a balance between diversity and realism to sample images to represent our AM method in the study. As a reference, this set of AM images were more diverse and less realistic than BigGAN samples according to the quantitative metrics (Fig. 7; AM-human vs. BigGAN).

Experiments.   We created two separate online surveys for diversity and realism, respectively. For each class, the diversity survey showed a panel of 8 × 8 AM images side-by-side a panel of 8 × 8 BigGAN samples and asked participants to rate which panel is more diverse on the scale of 1–5. That is, 1 or 5 denotes the left or right panel is clearly more diverse, while 3 indicates both sets are similarly diverse. For each class, the AM and BigGAN panels were randomly positioned left or right. The realism survey was a duplicate of the diversity except that each panel only showed 3 × 3 images so that participants could focus more on the details.

Results.   For both tests, we had 52 participants who are mostly university students and do not work with Machine Learning or GANs. On average, AM samples were rated to be more diverse and similarly realistic compared to Big-GAN samples. That is, AM images were given better than the neutral score of 3, i.e. 2.24 ± 0.85 in diversity and 2.94 ± 1.15 in realism.

Also, AM samples were rated to be more diverse in 42/50 classes and more realistic in 22/50 classes. See Figs. S9–S11 for your own comparisons.

3.7   Generalization to a 128 × 128 BigGAN

To test whether our method generalizes to a different GAN at a lower resolution, we applied our AM-S method (see Sect. 3.1) to a pre-trained 128 × 128 BigGAN released by [7]. As in previous experiments, we ran 50 classes × 5 trials in total. To evaluate each trial, we used the last-step embedding to sample 1000 images per class.

Consistent with the result on the 256 × 256 resolution, here, AM-S improved the diversity over the pre-trained model on both MS-SSIM and LPIPS (Fig. 8a;

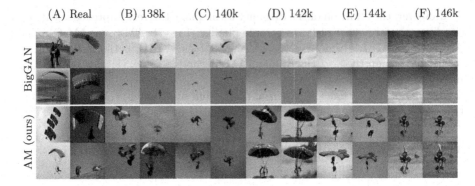

Fig. 9. For the parachute class, the original 128×128 BigGAN samples (top panel) mostly contained tiny parachutes in the sky (B) and gradually degraded into blue sky images only (C–F). AM (bottom panel) instead exhibited a more diverse set of close-up and far-away parachutes (B) and managed to paint the parachutes for nearly-collapsed models (E–F). The samples in this figure correspond to the five snapshots (138k—146k) reported in the quantitative comparison in Fig. 8. See Figs. S6, S7, S8 for more qualitative comparisons. (Color figure online)

138k). In terms of quality, FID and IS showed a mixed result of whether AM-S sample realism is lower or higher. See Fig. S17 for side-by-side comparisons.

3.8 Generalization to Different Training Snapshots of 128×128 BigGAN

We have shown that BigGAN sample diversity can be improved substantially by changing only the embeddings (Sect. 3.1) which revealed that the generator was actually capable of synthesizing those diverse images. Here, we test how much sample diversity and quality can be improved by AM as the BigGAN training gradually collapses, which might impair not only the embeddings but also the generator's parameters.

Experiments. We took the pre-trained 128×128 BigGAN model (saved at the 138k-th iteration) and continued training it for 9000 more iterations with the same hyperparameters as in [7]. We applied the AM-S method with the same hyperparameters as in Sect. 3.7 to four BigGAN snapshots captured at the 140k, 142, 144k, and 146k iteration, respectively.

Results. AM-S consistently improved the sample diversity of all snapshots. For some classes, AM qualitatively improved both sample diversity and quality (Figs. 9 and S6–S8). However, the diversity and realism of both AM-S and the original BigGAN samples gradually dropped together (Fig. 8; AM-S vs. Big-GAN). The result suggests that, as the GAN training gradually collapsed, the synthesis capability is so degraded that changing the class embeddings alone is not sufficient to significantly improve the samples.

4   Related Work

Latent Space Traversal. Searching in the latent space of a GAN generator network to synthesize images has been shown effective for many tasks including (1) in-painting [28]; (2) image editing [29]; (3) creating natural adversarial examples [30]; or (4) feature visualization [14]. While all prior work in this line of research optimized the latent variable z, we instead optimize the class embeddings c of a class-conditional generator over a set of random z vectors.

Our method might be the most related to Plug & Play Generative Networks (PPGN) [13] in that both methods sample from the distribution $p_G(x, y)$ jointly defined by a generator and a pre-trained classifier. While [13] trained an unconditional generator that inverts the features of an ImageNet classifier, our method is generally applicable to any pre-trained class-conditional generator. Importantly, our goal is novel—to improve the sample diversity of any pre-trained class-conditional generator (here, BigGANs) by changing its class embeddings.

Improving Sample Quality. Two methods, MH-GAN [31] and DRS [32], have recently been proposed to improve the samples of a pre-trained GAN by harnessing the discriminator to reject low-probability generated samples. However, these methods are able to only improve sample *quality* but not diversity. In addition, they assume that the discriminator is (a) available, which may not always be the case e.g. in the official BigGAN releases [2]; and (b) optimally trained for their samplers to recover exactly the true distribution. Similar to MH-GAN and PPGN, our method is similar to a Markov chain Monte Carlo (MCMC) sampler that has no rejection steps. A major difference is that we only perform the iterative optimization *once* to update the embedding matrix. After a desired embedding is found, our subsequent samplings of images are fast following standard GANs. In contrast, MH-GAN, DRS, and PPGN samplers often require many rejection or update steps to produce a single image.

Generalization. Understanding the image synthesis capability of a trained GAN generator is an active research area. Recent findings showed that GANs trained on a dataset of scene images contain neurons that can paint common objects such as "trees" or "doors" [33]. [34] found that BigGAN is able to perform some general image transforms such as zoom, rotate or brightness adjustment up to a certain limit. However, these methods optimize only the latent variable [34] or both the latent and the generator parameters [33], but not the class embeddings as ours.

5   Conclusion

We showed that the low sample diversity of pre-trained GAN generators can be improved by simply changing the class embeddings, not the generator. Note that one could "recover" the missing modes using our AM methods and improve the sample quality further by sampling from a truncated prior distribution [2]. Our method is also a promising method for de-biasing GAN models. Compared to finetuning or re-training BigGANs from scratch, our method is more tractable even considering that one has to run five 200-step optimization trials to find a desired class embedding.

References

1. Radford, A., Wu, J., Child, R., Luan, D., Amodei, D., Sutskever, I.: Language models are unsupervised multitask learners. OpenAI Blog 1, 9 (2019)
2. Brock, A., Donahue, J., Simonyan, K.: Large scale GAN training for high fidelity natural image synthesis. In: International Conference on Learning Representations (2019)
3. Johnson, K.: AI weekly: a deep learning Pioneer's teachable moment on AI bias — venturebeat. https://venturebeat.com/2020/06/26/ai-weekly-a-deep-learning-pioneers-teachable-moment-on-ai-bias/. Accessed 07 Aug 2020
4. Sheng, E., Chang, K.W., Natarajan, P., Peng, N.: The woman worked as a babysitter: on biases in language generation. arXiv preprint arXiv:1909.01326 (2019)
5. Arjovsky, M., Bottou, L.: Towards principled methods for training generative adversarial networks. In: 5th International Conference on Learning Representations, ICLR 2017, 24–26 April 2017, Toulon, France, Conference Track Proceedings (2017)
6. Ravuri, S., Vinyals, O.: Seeing is not necessarily believing: limitations of BigGANs for data augmentation (2019)
7. Brock, A.: ajbrock/BigGAN-PyTorch: the author's officially unofficial PyTorch BigGAN implementation. https://github.com/ajbrock/BigGAN-PyTorch. Accessed 25 July 2019
8. Yang, D., Hong, S., Jang, Y., Zhao, T., Lee, H.: Diversity-sensitive conditional generative adversarial networks. In: International Conference on Learning Representations (2019)
9. Krizhevsky, A., Sutskever, I., Hinton, G.E.: ImageNet classification with deep convolutional neural networks. In: Advances in Neural Information Processing Systems, pp. 1097–1105 (2012)
10. Odena, A., Olah, C., Shlens, J.: Conditional image synthesis with auxiliary classifier GANs. In: Proceedings of the 34th International Conference on Machine Learning, JMLR. org, vol. 70, pp. 2642–2651 (2017)
11. Mirza, M., Osindero, S.: Conditional generative adversarial nets. arXiv preprint arXiv:1411.1784 (2014)
12. Nguyen, A., Dosovitskiy, A., Yosinski, J., Brox, T., Clune, J.: Synthesizing the preferred inputs for neurons in neural networks via deep generator networks. In: Advances in Neural Information Processing Systems, pp. 3387–3395 (2016)
13. Nguyen, A., Clune, J., Bengio, Y., Dosovitskiy, A., Yosinski, J.: Plug & play generative networks: Conditional iterative generation of images in latent space. In: Proceedings of the IEEE Conference on Computer Vision and Pattern Recognition, pp. 4467–4477 (2017)
14. Nguyen, A., Yosinski, J., Clune, J.: Understanding neural networks via feature visualization: a survey. arXiv preprint arXiv:1904.08939 (2019)
15. Erhan, D., Bengio, Y., Courville, A., Vincent, P.: Visualizing higher-layer features of a deep network. Univ. Montreal 1341, 1 (2009)
16. Simonyan, K., Vedaldi, A., Zisserman, A.: Deep inside convolutional networks: visualising image classification models and saliency maps. arXiv preprint arXiv:1312.6034 (2013)

17. Borji, A.: Pros and cons of GAN evaluation measures. Comput. Vis. Image Underst. **179**, 41–65 (2019)
18. Zhang, R., Isola, P., Efros, A.A., Shechtman, E., Wang, O.: The unreasonable effectiveness of deep features as a perceptual metric. In: Proceedings of the IEEE Conference on Computer Vision and Pattern Recognition, pp. 586–595 (2018)
19. Salimans, T., Goodfellow, I., Zaremba, W., Cheung, V., Radford, A., Chen, X.: Improved techniques for training GANs. In: Advances in Neural Information Processing Systems, pp. 2234–2242 (2016)
20. Heusel, M., Ramsauer, H., Unterthiner, T., Nessler, B., Hochreiter, S.: GANs trained by a two time-scale update rule converge to a local nash equilibrium. In: Advances in Neural Information Processing Systems, pp. 6626–6637 (2017)
21. Szegedy, C., Vanhoucke, V., Ioffe, S., Shlens, J., Wojna, Z.: Rethinking the inception architecture for computer vision. In: Proceedings of the IEEE Conference on Computer Vision and Pattern Recognition, pp. 2818–2826 (2016)
22. He, K., Zhang, X., Ren, S., Sun, J.: Deep residual learning for image recognition. In: Proceedings of the IEEE Conference on Computer Vision and Pattern Recognition, pp. 770–778 (2016)
23. Engstrom, L., Ilyas, A., Santurkar, S., Tsipras, D., Tran, B., Madry, A.: Learning perceptually-aligned representations via adversarial robustness. arXiv preprint arXiv:1906.00945 (2019)
24. Amazon: Amazon EC2 P3 instance product details. https://aws.amazon.com/ec2/instance-types/p3/. Accessed 7 July 2020
25. Goodfellow, I., et al.: Generative adversarial nets. In: NIPS (2014)
26. Zhou, B., Lapedriza, A., Khosla, A., Oliva, A., Torralba, A.: Places: a 10 million image database for scene recognition. IEEE Trans. Pattern Anal. Mach. Intell. **40**, 1452–1464 (2017)
27. Wu, J., Hu, W., Xiong, H., Huan, J., Braverman, V., Zhu, Z.: On the noisy gradient descent that generalizes as SGD. arXiv preprint arXiv:1906.07405 (2019)
28. Yeh, R.A., Chen, C., Lim, T.Y., Schwing, A.G., Hasegawa-Johnson, M., Do, M.N.: Semantic image inpainting with deep generative models. In: Proceedings of the IEEE Conference on Computer Vision and Pattern Recognition, pp. 5485–5493 (2017)
29. Zhu, J.-Y., Krähenbühl, P., Shechtman, E., Efros, A.A.: Generative visual manipulation on the natural image manifold. In: Leibe, B., Matas, J., Sebe, N., Welling, M. (eds.) ECCV 2016. LNCS, vol. 9909, pp. 597–613. Springer, Cham (2016). https://doi.org/10.1007/978-3-319-46454-1_36
30. Zhao, Z., Dua, D., Singh, S.: Generating natural adversarial examples. In: International Conference on Learning Representations (2018)
31. Turner, R., Hung, J., Frank, E., Saatchi, Y., Yosinski, J.: Metropolis-Hastings generative adversarial networks. In: Chaudhuri, K., Salakhutdinov, R. (eds.) Proceedings of the 36th International Conference on Machine Learning. Proceedings of Machine Learning Research, Long Beach, California, USA, PMLR, vol. 97, pp. 6345–6353 (2019)
32. Azadi, S., Olsson, C., Darrell, T., Goodfellow, I., Odena, A.: Discriminator rejection sampling. In: International Conference on Learning Representations (2019)
33. Bau, D., et al.: Visualizing and understanding generative adversarial networks. In: International Conference on Learning Representations (2019)
34. Jahanian, A., Chai, L., Isola, P.: On the "steerability" of generative adversarial networks. arXiv preprint arXiv:1907.07171 (2019)

RF-GAN: A Light and Reconfigurable Network for Unpaired Image-to-Image Translation

Ali Köksal[1,2] and Shijian Lu[2(✉)]

[1] Institute for Infocomm Research, A*Star, Singapore, Singapore
ali013@e.ntu.edu.sg
[2] Nanyang Technological University, Singapore, Singapore
shijian.lu@ntu.edu.sg

Abstract. Generative adversarial networks (GANs) have been widely studied for unpaired image-to-image translation in recent years. On the other hand, state-of-the-art translation GANs are often constrained by large model sizes and inflexibility in translating across various domains. Inspired by the observation that the mappings between two domains are often approximately invertible, we design an innovative reconfigurable GAN (RF-GAN) that has a small size but is versatile in high-fidelity image translation either across two domains or among multiple domains. One unique feature of RF-GAN lies with its single generator which is reconfigurable and can perform bidirectional image translations by swapping its parameters. In addition, a multi-domain discriminator is designed which allows joint discrimination of original and translated samples in multiple domains. Experiments over eight unpaired image translation datasets (on various tasks such as object transfiguration, season transfer, and painters' style transfer, etc.) show that RF-GAN reduces the model size by up to 75% as compared with state-of-the-art translation GANs but produces superior image translation performance with lower Fréchet Inception Distance consistently.

1 Introduction

Image-to-image translation aims to translate images from a source domain to a target domain so that the translated images have similar appearance, styles, etc. as the images in the target domain. With the fast development of generative adversarial networks (GANs), quite a number of GANs have been reported in recent years which are capable of generating very realistic image-to-image translations in terms of object appearance [1–6], painting styles [7–12], seasonal styles [13,14], etc.

Image-to-image translation GANs can be broadly classified into two categories according to their scalability. The first category performs image translation across two domains only which typically involve two translators (each consists of a generator and a discriminator) such as CycleGAN [14], DiscoGAN [3],

© Springer Nature Switzerland AG 2021
H. Ishikawa et al. (Eds.): ACCV 2020, LNCS 12625, pp. 542–559, 2021.
https://doi.org/10.1007/978-3-030-69538-5_33

Input Images	Translated Images	Input Images	Translated Images	Input Images	Translated Images

horse → zebra   summer → winter   photo → painting

zebra → horse   winter → summer   painting → photo

Fig. 1. The proposed RF-GAN learns a single generator for image translations in oppo-site directions. For translation on object transfiguration, season transfer, and painter style transfer from left to right, RF-GAN can translate images with a reconfigurable G as shown in the top row. By simply reconfiguring G to a new generator G_r via parameter swapping, RF-GAN can translate images back in the opposite direction as shown in the bottom row. RF-GAN reduces the model size by up to 75% as compared with state-of-the-art GANs such as CycleGAN and StarGAN but obtains overall lower Fréchet inception distance (FID) over eight unpaired image translation datasets.

and UNIT [13]. The second category performs image translation across multi-ple domains which typically employs a single generator, a single discriminator as well as additional classifiers (for handling multi-domain translation) such as Star-GAN [15] and DosGAN [16]. These translation GANs have a common constraint that they usually involve a large number of network parameters either due to the double-generator-double-discriminator architecture in cross-domain translation GANs or the additional classifiers in multi-domain translation GANs. As a result, they often face various limitations in many resource-constrained scenarios such as edge computing. Additionally, they also require a large amount of images for training high-fidelity translation models due to the large amount of parameters involved. Another common constraint is about the limited flexibility. Specifically, cross-domain translation GANs cannot scale to handle multi-domain translation tasks without an increase in model size. Multi-domain translation GANs can handle cross-domain translation but their performance often drops a lot as their classifiers encourage generator for multi-domain translation and are susceptible to the noise added by generators.

This paper presents an innovative reconfigurable GAN (RF-GAN) that is small with just a single translator but capable of performing high-fidelity image translation across two domains or among multiple domains. RF-GAN is designed based on the observation that bidirectional mappings between domains are often approximately invertible. It learns a single translator for bidirectional image translations, where the forwards and backwards translations are achieved by swapping the parameters of the same generator as illustrated in Figs. 1 and 2. In addition, a multi-domain discriminator is designed which can discriminate images in opposite translation directions without either multiple domain-specific discriminators or additional classifier as required by most existing translation GANs. Further, RF-GAN can be trained with less training images, or better trained with the same amount of training images as state-of-the-art translation GANs. This is partially due to the much fewer network parameters in RF-GAN (up to 75% less than state-of-the-art GANs as the reconfigurable generators G and G_r share the same set of parameters) that require less images to train. Additionally, RF-GAN employs a single discriminator only which achieve similar effect of doubling training data as compared with state-of-the-art GANs that employ two discriminators or extra classifiers.

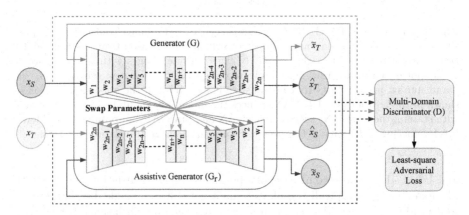

Fig. 2. The architecture of the proposed RF-GAN: RF-GAN consists of a reconfigurable generator G and a multi-domain discriminator D. In each training iteration, G first learns to translate images x_S in domain S to images $\hat{x}_T$ in domain T. G is then reconfigured to an assistive generator G_r by swapping its parameters which learns to translate $\hat{x}_T$ to $\tilde{x}_S$ as well as x_T to $\hat{x}_S$. After that, G_r is reconfigured back to G which further learns to translate from x_S to $\hat{x}_T$ as well as $\hat{x}_S$ to $\tilde{x}_T$ ($\tilde{x}_S$ and $\tilde{x}_T$ for computing reconstruction loss). The multi-domain discriminator D is trained continuously after each translation with x_S, $\hat{x}_T$, x_T, and $\hat{x}_S$ to compute least-square adversarial loss.

The contributions of this work can be summarized in three aspects. First, it designs an innovative RF-GAN that is capable of performing high-fidelity image translation across two domains or among multiple domains. Second, it designs a reconfigurable generator G and a multi-domain discriminator D where G can achieve bidirectional image translation by swapping its parameters and D can perform multi-domain translation without requiring multiple domain-specific discriminators or additional classifiers. As a result, RF-GAN reduces the model size by up to 75% as compared with state-of-the-art GANs, and it can be better trained with the same amount of training images. Third, extensive experiments show that RF-GAN outperforms state-of-the-art GANs such as cross-domain CycleGAN and multi-domain StarGAN consistently across eight public datasets.

2   Related Work

2.1   Generative Adversarial Networks (GANs)

The idea of the original Generative Adversarial Networks (GANs) [17] is to train a generator and a discriminator in an adversarial manner. Specifically, the generator is trained to generate images as realistic as possible for fooling the discriminator, the discriminator is instead trained to distinguish the generated images from real ones as accurate as possible. GANs trained by such adversarial learning can often generate very impressive and realistic images.

With the great success of the adversarial learning, GANs have been studied extensively in recent years [18–21] with applications in various tasks such as image inpainting [22], image synthesis [20,23–27], video generation [28], and 3D modelling [29]. They have also been widely studied for image-to-image translation, more details to be described in the next subsection.

2.2   Image-to-image Translation

Image-to-image translation aims to transform images from one domain to another where images often have different characteristics such as colors, styles, etc. Quite a number of GANs have been designed for the task of image-to-image translation in recent years [2,9,15,30–38], starting from earlier methods that require paired training images from different domains to the recent that can be trained with unpaired images.

For GANs requiring paired training images, [2] presents Pix2pix, a general-purpose translation network that adopts conditional GAN (cGAN) [25] to learn mappings between two sets of paired images. Similarly, [39] employs cGAN to learn the mapping from sketches to photos and AL-GAN [40] uses cGAN to generate scene images conditioning on scene attributes and layout. In addition, [41] presents a △-GAN that uses semi-supervised learning for cross-domain joint distribution matching. To address the lack of diversity of the aforementioned methods, BicycleGAN [42] is designed to generate continuous and multimodal distribution. Paired images provide useful supervision information but collecting paired images from different domains is often time-consuming.

For GANs that can work with unpaired training images, DTN [6] introduces a network with one generator and one discriminator for general purpose translation. Co-GAN [4] proposes a two-generator-two-discriminator network that learns joint distribution of multi-domain images by sharing a latent space. Similarly, UNIT [13] uses a shared latent space but involves a complex framework with two encoders, two generators, and two discriminators. CycleGAN [14] employs two generators to learn bidirectional mappings between two domains and it also employs two discriminators for each of the two domains. Similar to CycleGAN, DiscoGAN [3] uses two generators and two discriminators and employs cycle consistency and reconstruction losses to measure how well source domain images are translated back after translating to the target domain. Similar to BicycleGAN, MUNIT [43], and DRIT [44] aims to generate multiple outputs from one input by decomposing images as content and style.

To address the lack of generalization, many existing cross-domain translation GANs can be adapted to multi-domain translation tasks. In the straightforward adaptation, one model can be used for each binary combination of domains and trained separately. For example, ComboGAN [30] extends cross-domain translation to multi-domain by training less model than straightforward adaptation. In addition, some efforts aim for multi-domain image translation with a small model. For example, StarGAN [15] proposes a model that contains a single conditioned generator, a single discriminator and an auxiliary classifier on top of the discriminator. DosGAN [16] similarly employs a single generator, a single discriminator, and a single pre-trained classifier. SingleGAN [37] instead employs a single generator but multiple discriminators.

Cross-domain translation GANs such as DiscoGAN and CycleGAN have two generators and two discriminators that introduce a large number of network parameters which require a large amount of training images to train. Multi-domain translation GANs such as StarGAN and DosGAN employ a single generator and a single discriminator, but its discriminator is a large network. Our proposed RF-GAN has a single generator and a single discriminator without additional classifier which reduces up to 75% network parameters by comparing the translation GANs. This expands the RF-GAN's applicability in resource-constrained devices and also helps reduce the required training images greatly. On the other hand, it achieves superior translation fidelity consistently as compared with most state-of-the-art translation GANs, largely due to the reconfigurable generator and the multi-domain discriminator to be described in the following Section.

3   The Proposed Method

The proposed RF-GAN learns a single generator for image mapping in opposite directions between domains. It also learns a multi-domain discriminator for bidirectional image discrimination without requiring domain-specific discriminators or extra classifier. A novel training strategy is designed to train the proposed RF-GAN effectively, more details to be presented in the following subsections.

3.1   Reconfigurable Generator

Learning a mapping function to map images in opposite directions takes an iterative learning process in the proposed RF-GAN. Figure 2 shows one learning iteration, where the generator G and G_r (derived by swapping $G's$ parameters) both have an encoder and a decoder. Given images x_S from a source domain S, G first learns to map them to $\hat{x}_T$ in a target domain T conditioned to the category of the target domain. Once G is learned, it is reconfigured to an assistive generator G_r automatically by swapping $G's$ parameters. G_r then learns the mapping from x_T to $\hat{x}_S$ as well as from $\hat{x}_T$ to $\tilde{x}_S$. After that, G_r is reconfigured back to G by swapping its parameters which will further learn the mapping from x_S to x_T and from $\hat{x}_S$ to $\hat{x}_T$. The iterative learning will finally lead to a single reconfigurable generator G. Given new images from domains S and T, G can map images from S to T, and it can simply be reconfigured to G_r (by swapping its parameters) for inverse mapping from T to S. Details of the parameter swapping and generator training will be described in the following three subsections.

Parameter Swapping. The target of the proposed parameter swapping is to learn one generator for image translations in opposite directions. Given images in domains S and T, a mapping function G will be confused and fail to learn well if we directly train it for mappings in the directions $S \rightarrow T$ and $T \rightarrow S$ concurrently. The reason is that for the mapping $S \rightarrow T$, G's encoder parameters will mainly deal with images in domain S and G's decoder parameters will mainly deal with images in domain T. If we concurrently train G for the mapping $T \rightarrow S$, G's encoder parameters will have to deal with images in domain T and its decoder parameters will have to deal with images in domain S. This will confuse G and lead to an undesired mapping function.

We introduce an assistive generator G_r to learn the mapping $T \rightarrow S$. To ensure that we will finally learn a single generator, we design G and G_r in a way that G_r can be simply derived from G by swapping G's parameters. In this way, the proposed RF-GAN first learns G for the mapping $S \rightarrow T$ and then derives G_r (automatically by swapping G's parameters) for learning the mapping $T \rightarrow S$. The iterative learning leads to a reconfigurable G that can handle image translations in opposite directions. For a $2n-$layer network, the mappings for G and G_r can be formulated as follows:

$$
\begin{aligned}
\mathbb{E}_{x_S \sim X_S} G(x_S, y_T) &= \hat{x}_T, \text{ where} \\
G(x_S, y_T) &= x_S \odot W_1 \odot W_2 \odot \ldots \odot W_n \odot W_{n+1} \odot \ldots \odot W_{2n}
\end{aligned}
\tag{1}
$$

$$
\begin{aligned}
\mathbb{E}_{x_T \sim X_T} G_r(x_T, y_S) &= \hat{x}_S, \text{ where} \\
G_r(x_T, y_S) &= x_T \odot W_{2n} \odot W_{2n-1} \odot \ldots \odot W_{n+1} \odot W_n \odot \ldots \odot W_1
\end{aligned}
\tag{2}
$$

where $\odot$ denotes convolution operations, y_S and y_T are the category of domains source S and target T, respectively, and $W_1, ..., W_{2n}$ denote the convolutional layers as shown in Fig. 2.

Generator Architecture. Leveraging on the CycleGAN generator [14], we design a reconfigurable generator for mapping images in opposite directions. Our generator replaces all convolution layers with fractional-strided convolution layers in the second half of the architecture of CycleGAN generator. For a detailed comparison. As fractional-strided convolution is widely used for deconvolution, the use of convolution layers in the first half and fractional-strided convolution layers in the second makes the reconfigurable generator invertible and more suitable for learning bidirectional mapping. Due to the symmetric structure of the

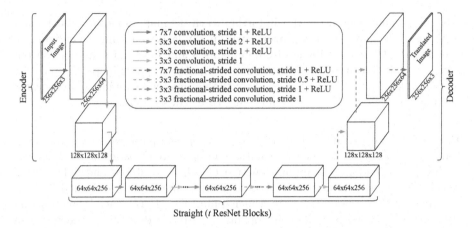

Fig. 3. The proposed reconfigurable generator G has perfect symmetric structures and so symmetric input dimensions which ensure that the parameter swapping in G can be carried out without discrepancy.

reconfigurable generator, convolution layers and fractional-strided convolution layers have the same number of parameters. In another word, W_{1+i} and W_{2n-i}, $i \in [0, n)$ have exactly the same size. This symmetric structure also ensures that the input of each layer (activation size in each layer) has the same symmetric relation as shown in Fig. 3. Note the parameters of CycleGAN generator can also be swapped with certain adaptations such as parameter transposition, but the performance of the new generator is much lower than ours that has a more invertible structure.

As shown in Fig. 3, the architecture consists of three major components including an encoder that progressively down-samples by two convolution with stride 2, a decoder that progressively up-samples by two fractional-strided convolution with stride 0.5, and a straight component with t ResNet blocks [45] (default at 9) in the middle. Similar to the CycleGAN generator, the first half of the straight component in our generator is convolution layers with stride 1. However, the second half changes to fractional-strided convolution layers with stride 1 for parameter swapping. In addition, our generator uses a fractional-strided convolution layer with the same stride as the last convolution layer. Further, both CycleGAN generator and our generator use reflection padding in the first half of the straight component and down-sampling layers, but our generator uses inverse padding (which crops activations from the edges of activations symmetrically) in the second half of the straight and up-sampling layers. Note normalization layers are omitted for the sake of the visual simplicity in Fig. 3.

Generator Training. The generators G and G_r learn alternatively while training the RF-GAN iteratively. In each training iteration, G first translates image x_S in source domain S to images $\hat{x}_T$ in target domain T. After that, G is reconfigured to G_r by automatic swapping G's parameters and G_r then learns to translate $\hat{x}_T$ to $\tilde{x}_S$. Intuitively, x_S and $\tilde{x}_S$ should be the same, but they are never perfectly the same as G_r is not a perfect inverse of G. A reconstruction loss [3,14] between x_S and $\tilde{x}_S$ should therefore be computed to train G and G_r to learn the mappings in the two opposite directions and force them to be approximately inverse of each other:

$$\mathcal{L}^{REC}(G, X_S, X_T) = \mathbb{E}_{(x_S,y_S)\sim(X_S,Y_S)} \|G_r(G(x_S, y_T), y_S) - x_S\|_2$$
$$+ \mathbb{E}_{(x_T,y_T)\sim(X_T,Y_T)} \|G(G_r(x_T, y_S), y_T) - x_T\|_2 \quad (3)$$

In addition, a least-square adversarial loss [46] should be computed with translated images as follows:

$$\mathcal{L}_G^{GAN}(G, D, X_S, X_T) = \mathbb{E}_{(x_S,y_S)\sim(X_S,Y_S)}(D(G(x_S, y_T)) - y_T)^2$$
$$+ \mathbb{E}_{(x_T,y_T)\sim(X_T,Y_T)}(D(G_r(x_T, y_S)) - y_S)^2, \quad (4)$$

where y_S is the label of images in S (x_S) and y_T is the label of images in T (x_T).

The training of G should minimize both reconstruction loss and adversarial loss as formulated as follows:

$$\mathcal{L}_G(G, D, X_S, X_T) = \mathcal{L}_G^{GAN}(G, D, X_S, X_T) + \lambda \mathcal{L}^{REC}(G, X_S, X_T), \quad (5)$$

where λ controls the relative effect between adversarial and reconstruction losses.

Fig. 4. For images x_S in domain S, our reconfigurable generator G can translate them to $\hat{x}_T$ in domain T which can be translated back to $\tilde{x}_S$ in domain S by generator G_r that can be simply reconfigured from G.

Figure 4 illustrates the image mapping with our proposed reconfigurable generator G. As Fig. 4 shows, the reconfigurable generator G is capable of translating images x_S in domain S to images $\hat{x}_T$ in domain T as shown in columns 1 & 4 and columns 2 & 5. At the same time, the reconfigured G_r (from G) is capable of translating ($\hat{x}_T$) back to ($\tilde{x}_S$) in domain S as shown in columns 3 & 6. This clearly shows the effectiveness of our proposed RF-GAN that can learn one mapping function for image mapping in two opposite directions.

3.2 Multi-domain Discriminator

Discriminator in GANs is basically a domain-specific binary classifier which aims to distinguish real and translated images in one specific domain. Therefore, translation GANs such as DiscoGAN [3] and CycleGAN [14] employ two domain-specific discriminators for discriminating images translated in two opposite directions. In the more recent multi-domain translation GANs such as Star-GAN [15], a single discriminator is used for multi-domain discrimination but an auxiliary classifier is employed on top of the discriminator for classifying samples according to their domains. This also applies to DosGAN [16] which also uses a pre-trained classifier together with a discriminator for differentiating samples from more than one domain.

We design a multi-domain discriminator D that can perform image discrimination in opposite directions without requiring either more than one domain-specific discriminators or additional classification. Specifically, our multi-domain discriminator learns to discriminate real images in domain T and the translated images from domain S to domain T (by G), as well as the real images in domain S and the translated images from domain T to domain S (by G_r). The training aims to minimize the following adversarial loss:

$$\mathcal{L}_D(G, D, X_S, X_T) = \mathcal{L}_D^{GAN}(G, D, X_S, X_T) + \mathcal{L}_D^{GAN}(G_r, D, X_T, X_S) \qquad (6)$$

where the two least-square adversarial loss components [46] can be computed in a similar way. One of them can be computed by:

$$\begin{aligned}\mathcal{L}_D^{GAN}(G, D, X_S, X_T) =& \mathbb{E}_{(x_T, y_T) \sim (X_T, Y_T)}(D(x_T) - y_T)^2 \\ &+ \mathbb{E}_{(x_S) \sim (X_S)}(D(G(x_S, y_T)) - y_T^*)^2 \end{aligned} \qquad (7)$$

where y_S, y_T, y_S^*, and y_T^* refer to the label of images in domains S (x_S) and T (x_T), as well as the translated images in domains S ($\hat{x}_S$) and T ($\hat{x}_T$), respectively.

Our multi-domain discriminator is a PatchGAN [47] adapted from [14]. It consists of five 4x4 convolution layers three of which are with stride 2 and the other two are with stride 1. Leaky ReLU is used as the activation function.

Algorithm 1. RF-GAN Training

Input: Generator G, discriminator D, batch of training sets $(x_S, y_S) \in (X_S, Y_S)$ and $(x_T, y_T) \in (X_T, Y_T)$
Output: Updated generator G and discriminator D

1: $\hat{x}_T \leftarrow G(x_S, y_T)$
2: **update** D by $\mathcal{L}_D^{GAN}$ based on x_T and $\hat{x}_T$ with Equation 7
3: $G_r \leftarrow$ reconfigure G
4: $\tilde{x}_S \leftarrow G_r(\hat{x}_T, y_S)$ and $\hat{x}_S \leftarrow G_r(x_T, y_S)$
5: **update** D by $\mathcal{L}_D^{GAN}$ based on x_S and $\hat{x}_S$ with Equation 7
6: $G \leftarrow$ reconfigure G_r
7: $\tilde{x}_T \leftarrow G(\hat{x}_S, y_T)$
8: **update** G by L_G^{GAN} with Equation 4 and L^{REC} with Equation 3

3.3   RF-GAN Training

The RF-GAN employs an assistive generator G_r during its iterative training as illustrated in Fig. 2. Each training iteration consists of two cycles: 1) images x_S in domain S are first translated to $\hat{x}_T$ in domain T by G and then translated back to $\tilde{x}_S$ by G_r (reconfigured from G); 2) images x_T in domain T are translated to $\hat{x}_S$ in domain S by G_r and then translated back to $\tilde{x}_T$ by G (reconfigured from G_r). During this iterative training process, it is critical to keep the association between image domains and the generator G/G_r consistently. Specifically, while G is translating images from domain S to domain T, G_r must translate images from domain T to domain S. Without this association, the cycle consistency will be broken and the generators will be confused easily. We design a sequential training strategy to guarantee this association.

As shown in Algorithm 1 which illustrates single training iteration, generators G and G_r swap their parameters twice to keep their association with image domains. In addition, the update of G is postponed to the end of the training as the loss computation requires the reconstructed images $\tilde{x}_S$ and $\tilde{x}_T$. Different from G, the multi-domain discriminator D is updated twice instead. The first update happens after D learns to discriminate images in domain T x_T and the translated images to domain T $\hat{x}_T$, and the second happens after D learns to discriminate images in domain S x_S and the translated images to domain S $\hat{x}_S$.

During the iterative training of RF-GAN, λ in Eq. 5 weights the reconstruction loss and adversarial loss which is experimentally set at 10. In all evaluations, networks are trained from scratch by applying Adam problem solver [48] with learning rate of 0.0002 and betas 0.5 and 0.999.

4   Experiments

4.1   Datasets and Evaluation Metrics

Datasets: We evaluated RF-GAN over eight public datasets on unpaired image translation. Each dataset consists of a training set and a test set and the eight datasets can be grouped into three categories on object transfiguration, season transfer, and painters' style transfer. The *object transfiguration* category has two datasets including apple↔orange and horse↔zebra. The *season transfer* also contains two datasets including summer↔winter photos of Yosemite and different (four) seasons of the Alps. The *painters' style transfer* has four datasets where each consists of natural photographs in one domain and paintings of one of four artists (Cezanne, Monet, Ukiyo-e, and Van Gogh) in another domain.

Evaluation Metrics: Quantitative evaluation of GAN-synthesized images is still a challenging task [49,50]. We performed quantitative evaluations by using Fréchet Inception Distance (FID) [51] which is one of the most widely used metrics in evaluating GAN-synthesized images. FID measures the similarity between two sets of samples with the range of $[0, \infty)$. It uses inception model [52] and measures the distance between multivariate Gaussian distribution of features

Table 1. Comparison of RF-GAN with DiscoGAN [3], CycleGAN [14], and Star-GAN [15] in the number of generators and discriminators as well as parameter numbers.

Methods	DiscoGAN [3]	CycleGAN [14]	StarGAN [15]	RF-GAN
# generator/s	2	2	1	1
# discriminator/s	2	2	1	1
# parameters (M)	16.560	28.286	53.208	14.143

extracted from an intermediate layer of inception net. While compared with natural images, a lower FID means high fidelity of the synthesized images.

We compare RF-GAN with three state-of-the-art translation GANs including DiscoGAN, CycleGAN, and StarGAN. Table 1 provides their comparison in terms of the number of generator/s, discriminator/s, and size of network parameters with having default number of ResNet block in generators. As Table 1 shows, RF-GAN is 50% smaller than CycleGAN. It is also smaller than DiscoGAN which uses an encoder and decoder with no straight components. Although StarGAN uses a single generator and discriminator, it has many more parameters than RF-GAN because of its auxiliary classifier.

4.2   Experimental Results

In the evaluations, CycleGAN uses a pre-trained model whereas DiscoGAN and StarGAN are trained from scratch. In all evaluations, RF-GAN is trained in the same manner as CycleGAN for 200 epochs from scratch for fair comparisons. Once trained, each sample image in the test set is translated from the source domain to the target domain. FID is then computed between the full test set of the target domain and the generated samples to measure their similarity. Table 2 shows the experimental results where the last column shows the FID between the training and the test sets. Since the training and test sets of photo→Van Gogh contain the same sample images, its FID is zero.

RF-GAN(G) and RF-GAN(G_r) in Table 2 refer to the RF-GANs whose generators are initially trained in the same and opposite directions as listed in Translations column. We can observe that RF-GAN initially trained in either direction achieves similar translation performance, demonstrating the effectiveness of our proposed reconfigurable generator. Note the first four tasks in the RF-GAN column are replicated two times (including RF-GAN training and evaluation) and then compute FID average and variation, just to show the stability of RF-GAN in image translation. The last row shows overall FID scores each of which is computed by the average of normalized FIDs across the ten translation tasks (normalization is computed by Real's FID/GAN's FID). Since the FID of translated images is almost always higher than the FID of real images, the normalized FID usually lies [0, 1] (the bigger the better).

As Table 2 shows, RF-GAN outperforms DiscoGAN consistently by large margins across the ten studied translation tasks. DiscoGAN's much higher FIDs

Table 2. Comparison of RF-GAN with state-of-the-art GANs (in FID): RF-GAN(G)/RF-GAN(G_r) denotes our RF-GAN whose generator is initially trained in the same/opposite direction as listed in the column Translations. For object transfiguration and season transfer in the first three tasks, the translations are bidirectional. For the four painters' style transfer tasks, the translations are from photographs to paintings as translating natural photographs to paintings is more meaningful. FID in the last column is computed between real paintings in the training and test sets (* denotes that training and test samples of photo→Van Gogh are the same so FID zero). The last row 'Overall Score' is the average of normalized FID across the nine translation tasks (photo→Van Gogh not included), where the normalized FID for each task is computed by Real's FID/GAN's FID. Note the first four tasks in the RF-GAN column are replicated two times (for RF-GAN training and evaluation) and then compute FID average and variation, just to show the stability of RF-GAN in image translation.

Translations	Methods					Real
	DiscoGAN [3]	CycleGAN [14]	StarGAN [15]	RF-GAN (G)	RF-GAN (G_r)	*Training vs test*
apple→orange	377.58	181.34	222.71	**173.13±1.34**	178.58	55.31
orange→apple	345.54	164.46	167.68	**136.64±0.07**	143.95	48.36
horse→zebra	414.28	81.25	150.39	38.23±0.29	**37.66**	29.62
zebra→horse	333.23	**143.03**	206.15	143.77±1.84	144.05	89.99
summer→winter	296.75	**82.30**	131.11	99.86	101.79	64.64
winter→summer	296.99	**80.11**	120.65	98.70	91.97	44.87
photo→Cezanne	360.41	216.76	280.43	**212.70**	216.14	180.51
photo→Monet	279.41	133.08	172.02	**128.20**	128.82	108.09
photo→Ukiyo-e	316.84	180.33	212.31	166.38	**150.27**	126.09
photo→Van Gogh	322.99	109.77	211.44	**108.69**	109.61	0*
Overall score	0.25	0.59	0.43	**0.63**	0.63	1

Table 3. Comparison of RF-GAN with StarGAN (in FID) over different seasons of the Alps dataset (multiple domains). Translated images are generated from test samples of the other seasons. 'Overall Score' is calculated similarly as in Table 2.

Translations	Methods		Real
	StarGAN [15]	RF-GAN (G)	*Training vs test*
(summer+autumn+winter)→spring	106.86	**104.45**	94.95
(spring+autumn+winter)→summer	105.88	**90.92**	73.56
(spring+summer+winter)→autumn	108.66	**96.08**	76.48
(spring+summer+autumn)→winter	101.831	**87.68**	78.16
Overall score	0.76	**0.85**	1

could be due to its very simple network structures, though it is still bigger than RF-GAN due to its two-generator-two-discriminator design. In addition, RF-GAN outperforms CycleGAN for object transfiguration and painters' style transfer tasks consistently, though its size is just 50% of the CycleGAN. Further, Tables 2 and 3 show that RF-GAN translates better than StarGAN for either cross-domain or multi-domain translations. Although both have a single

Fig. 5. Illustration of input and translated images by RF-GAN for apple↔orange, horse↔zebra, summer↔winter, photo→Cezanne, photo→Monet, photo→Ukiyo-e, and photo→Van Gogh.

generator and discriminator, the parameter number of StarGAN is up to 3.5 times more than RF-GAN. As a result, StarGAN requires more training samples for training a good translator. Besides, translated images by StarGAN tend to be similar to the input images due to the conflict between its generator and auxiliary classifier as discussed in [37]. All these quantitative results demonstrate the superior performance of our proposed RF-GAN.

4.3 Qualitative Experimental Results

Figures 5 and 6 show qualitative evaluation of RF-GAN where two sample images are translated for each of the seven studied datasets. For the multi-domain translation dataset, one sample is selected for each season and translated to the other seasons. We can see that RF-GAN produces good-quality translations for both cross-domain and multi-domain translation consistently across all translation tasks.

4.4 Ablation Study

An ablation study is performed over two object transfiguration datasets apple ↔ orange and horse↔zebra to show the effectiveness of the reconfigurable generator and multi-domain discriminator in RF-GAN. Two new ablation models Abl. 1 and Abl. 2 are trained as shown in Table 4 where Abl. 1 replaces

Fig. 6. Input images and translated images by RF-GAN for different seasons of the Alps. Input images highlighted by red boxes are translated to other seasons. (Color figure online)

Table 4. Ablation studies: Abl. 1 replaces two CycleGAN discriminators with our multi-domain discriminator. Abl. 2 replaces two CycleGAN generators with our reconfigurable generator. The results show that our reconfigurable generator and multi-domain discriminator outperform the CycleGAN generators and discriminators clearly.

# gen./dis./params. (M)	CycleGAN	Abl. 1	Abl. 2	RF-GAN
	2/2/28.286	2/1/25.521	1/2/16.908	1/1/14.143
apple→orange	181.34	177.03	175.79	173.13
orange→apple	164.46	140.05	139.96	136.64
horse→zebra	81.25	66.97	65.68	38.23
zebra→horse	143.03	151.07	149.24	143.77

CycleGAN's two discriminators with our multi-domain discriminator and Abl. 2 replaces CycleGAN's two generators with our reconfigurable generator. As Table 4 shows, our reconfigurable generator and multi-domain discriminator both outperform CycleGAN's generators and discriminators clearly. While combined, the complete RF-GAN produces the best FID.

5   Conclusion

This paper presents a reconfigurable GAN (RF-GAN) that is small yet capable of translating images realistically. Different from state-of-the-art translation GANs that usually have large model size and network parameters, RF-GAN learns a single reconfigurable generator that can perform bidirectional translations by swapping its parameters. In addition, RF-GAN has a multi-domain discriminator that allows bidirectional discrimination without requiring domain-specific discriminators or additional classifiers. RF-GAN reduces the model size by up to 75% as compared with state-of-the-art translation GANs, and extensive experiments over eight datasets demonstrate its superior performance in FID. We expect that reconfigurable generative networks will inspire new insights and attract more interest in translating high-fidelity images in the near future.

References

1. Chen, X., Xu, C., Yang, X., Tao, D.: Attention-GAN for object transfiguration in wild images. In: Proceedings of the European Conference on Computer Vision (ECCV), pp. 164–180 (2018)
2. Isola, P., Zhu, J.Y., Zhou, T., Efros, A.A.: Image-to-image translation with conditional adversarial networks. CVPR (2017)
3. Kim, T., Cha, M., Kim, H., Lee, J.K., Kim, J.: Learning to discover cross-domain relations with generative adversarial networks. In: Proceedings of the 34th International Conference on Machine Learning, ICML 2017, vol. 70, pp. 1857–1865 (2017) JMLR.org
4. Liu, M.Y., Tuzel, O.:Coupled generative adversarial networks. In: Lee, D.D., Sugiyama, M., Luxburg, U.V., Guyon, I., Garnett, R.,eds.: Advances in Neural Information Processing Systems 29, Curran Associates, Inc. pp. 469–477 (2016)
5. Mejjati, Y.A., Richardt, C., Tompkin, J., Cosker, D., Kim, K.I.: Unsupervised attention-guided image-to-image translation. In: Advances in Neural Information Processing Systems, pp. 3693–3703 (2018)
6. Taigman, Y., Polyak, A., Wolf, L.: Unsupervised cross-domain image generation. ArXiv abs/1611.02200 (2016)
7. Gatys, L.A., Bethge, M., Hertzmann, A., Shechtman, E.: Preserving color in neural artistic style transfer. arXiv preprint arXiv:1606.05897 (2016)
8. Gatys, L.A., Ecker, A.S., Bethge, M.: Image style transfer using convolutional neural networks. In: 2016 IEEE Conference on Computer Vision and Pattern Recognition (CVPR), pp. 2414–2423 (2016)
9. Johnson, J., Alahi, A., Fei-Fei, L.: Perceptual losses for real-time style transfer and super-resolution. In: European Conference on Computer Vision (2016)
10. Liu, H., Navarrete Michelini, P., Zhu, D.: Artsy-GAN: a style transfer system with improved quality, diversity and performance, pp. 79–84 (2018)
11. Tomei, M., Cornia, M., Baraldi, L., Cucchiara, R.: Art2real: unfolding the reality of artworks via semantically-aware image-to-image translation. In: Proceedings of the IEEE Conference on Computer Vision and Pattern Recognition, pp. 5849–5859 (2019)
12. Ulyanov, D., Lebedev, V., Vedaldi, A., Lempitsky, V.: Texture networks: Feedforward synthesis of textures and stylized images. In: Proceedings of the 33rd International Conference on International Conference on Machine Learning, ICML 2016, vol. 48, pp. 1349–1357 (2016). JMLR.org
13. Liu, M.Y., Breuel, T., Kautz, J.: Unsupervised image-to-image translation networks. In: Proceedings of the 31st International Conference on Neural Information Processing Systems, NIPS 2017, USA, Curran Associates Inc. pp. 700–708 (2017)
14. Zhu, J.Y., Park, T., Isola, P., Efros, A.A.: Unpaired image-to-image translation using cycle-consistent adversarial networks. In: IEEE International Conference on Computer Vision (ICCV) (2017)
15. Choi, Y., Choi, M., Kim, M., Ha, J.W., Kim, S., Choo, J.: Stargan: unified generative adversarial networks for multi-domain image-to-image translation. In: Proceedings of the IEEE Conference on Computer Vision and Pattern Recognition, pp. 8789–8797 (2018)
16. Lin, J., Chen, Z., Xia, Y., Liu, S., Qin, T., Luo, J.:Exploring explicit domain supervision for latent space disentanglement in unpaired image-to-image translation. In: IEEE Transactions on Pattern Analysis and Machine Intelligence (2019)

17. Goodfellow, I.J., et al.: Generative adversarial nets. In: Proceedings of the 27th International Conference on Neural Information Processing Systems, NIPS 2014, vol. 2, Cambridge, MA, USA, MIT Press, pp. 2672–2680 (2014)

18. Arjovsky, M., Chintala, S., Bottou, L.: Wasserstein generative adversarial networks. In: Precup, D., Teh, Y.W., (eds.): Proceedings of the 34th International Conference on Machine Learning. vol. 70 of Proceedings of Machine Learning Research., International Convention Centre, Sydney, Australia, PMLR, pp. 214–223 (2017)

19. Denton, E., Chintala, S., Szlam, A., Fergus, R.: Deep generative image models using a laplacian pyramid of adversarial networks. In: Proceedings of the 28th International Conference on Neural Information Processing Systems, NIPS 2015, vol. 1, Cambridge, MA, USA, MIT Press, pp. 1486–1494 (2015)

20. Radford, A., Metz, L., Chintala, S.: Unsupervised representation learning with deep convolutional generative adversarial networks. arXiv preprint arXiv:1511.06434 (2015)

21. Salimans, T., Goodfellow, I., Zaremba, W., Cheung, V., Radford, A., Chen, X.: Improved techniques for training GANs. In: Proceedings of the 30th International Conference on Neural Information Processing Systems, NIPS 2016, USA, Curran Associates Inc. pp. 2234–2242 (2016)

22. Pathak, D., Krähenbühl, P., Donahue, J., Darrell, T., Efros, A.: Context encoders: Feature learning by inpainting (2016)

23. Brock, A., Donahue, J., Simonyan, K.: Large scale GAN training for high fidelity natural image synthesis. ArXiv abs/1809.11096 (2018)

24. Dumoulin, V., et al.: Adversarially learned inference (2016)

25. Mirza, M., Osindero, S.: Conditional generative adversarial nets. ArXiv abs/1411.1784 (2014)

26. Zhan, F., Zhu, H., Lu, S.: Spatial fusion GAN for image synthesis. In: 2019 IEEE Conference on Computer Vision and Pattern Recognition (CVPR), pp. 3653–3662 (2019)

27. Zhan, F., Xue, C., Lu, S.: GA-DAN: geometry-aware domain adaptation network for scene text detection and recognition. In: Proceedings of the IEEE International Conference on Computer Vision, pp. 9105–9115 (2019)

28. Vondrick, C., Pirsiavash, H., Torralba, A.: Generating videos with scene dynamics. In: Proceedings of the 30th International Conference on Neural Information Processing Systems, NIPS 2016, USA, Curran Associates Inc. pp. 613–621 (2016)

29. Wu, J., Zhang, C., Xue, T., Freeman, W.T., Tenenbaum, J.B.: Learning a probabilistic latent space of object shapes via 3d generative-adversarial modeling. In: Proceedings of the 30th International Conference on Neural Information Processing Systems, NIPS 2016, USA, Curran Associates Inc. pp. 82–90 (2016)

30. Anoosheh, A., Agustsson, E., Timofte, R., Van Gool, L.: ComboGAN: unrestrained scalability for image domain translation. In: Proceedings of the IEEE Conference on Computer Vision and Pattern Recognition Workshops. (2018) 783–790

31. Eigen, D., Fergus, R.: Predicting depth, surface normals and semantic labels with a common multi-scale convolutional architecture. In: Proceedings of the 2015 IEEE International Conference on Computer Vision (ICCV), ICCV 2015, Washington, DC, USA, IEEE Computer Society, pp. 2650–2658 (2015)

32. Laffont, P.Y., Ren, Z., Tao, X., Qian, C., Hays, J.: Transient attributes for high-level understanding and editing of outdoor scenes. ACM Trans. Graph. **33** 149:1–149:11 (2014)

33. Lee, H.Y., et al.: DRIT++: diverse image-to-image translation via disentangled representations. arXiv preprint arXiv:1905.01270 (2019)

34. Shih, Y., Paris, S., Durand, F., Freeman, W.T.: Data-driven hallucination of different times of day from a single outdoor photo. ACM Trans. Graph. **32** 200:1–200:11 (2013)

35. Wang, X., Gupta, A.: Generative image modeling using style and structure adversarial networks. ArXiv abs/1603.05631 (2016)

36. Yi, Z., Zhang, H., Tan, P., Gong, M.: DualGAN: unsupervised dual learning for image-to-image translation. In: Proceedings of the IEEE International Conference on Computer Vision, pp. 2849–2857 (2017)

37. Yu, X., Cai, X., Ying, Z., Li, T., Li, G.: SingleGAN: image-to-image translation by a single-generator network using multiple generative adversarial learning. In: Asian Conference on Computer Vision (2018)

38. Zhang, R., Isola, P., Efros, A.A.: Colorful image colorization. In: Leibe, B., Matas, J., Sebe, N., Welling, M. (eds.) ECCV 2016. LNCS, vol. 9907, pp. 649–666. Springer, Cham (2016). https://doi.org/10.1007/978-3-319-46487-9_40

39. Sangkloy, P., Lu, J., Fang, C., Yu, F., Hays, J.: Scribbler: controlling deep image synthesis with sketch and color. In: 2017 IEEE Conference on Computer Vision and Pattern Recognition (CVPR), pp. 6836–6845 (2016)

40. Karacan, L., Akata, Z., Erdem, A., Erdem, E.: Learning to generate images of outdoor scenes from attributes and semantic layouts. CoRR abs/1612.00215 (2016)

41. Gan, Z., et al.: Triangle generative adversarial networks. In: Proceedings of the 31st International Conference on Neural Information Processing Systems, NIPS 2017, USA, Curran Associates Inc. pp. 5253–5262 (2017)

42. Zhu, J.Y., et al.: Toward multimodal image-to-image translation. In: Advances in Neural Information Processing Systems (2017)

43. Huang, X., Liu, M.Y., Belongie, S., Kautz, J.: Multimodal unsupervised image-to-image translation. In: ECCV (2018)

44. Lee, H.Y., Tseng, H.Y., Huang, J.B., Singh, M.K., Yang, M.H.: Diverse image-to-image translation via disentangled representations. In: European Conference on Computer Vision (2018)

45. He, K., Zhang, X., Ren, S., Sun, J.: Deep residual learning for image recognition. In: Proceedings of the IEEE Conference on Computer Vision and Pattern Recognition, pp. 770–778 (2016)

46. Mao, X., Li, Q., Xie, H., Lau, R.Y., Wang, Z., Paul Smolley, S.: Least squares generative adversarial networks. In: Proceedings of the IEEE International Conference on Computer Vision, pp. 2794–2802 (2017)

47. Li, C., Wand, M.: Precomputed real-time texture synthesis with markovian generative adversarial networks. In: Leibe, B., Matas, J., Sebe, N., Welling, M. (eds.) ECCV 2016. LNCS, vol. 9907, pp. 702–716. Springer, Cham (2016). https://doi.org/10.1007/978-3-319-46487-9_43

48. Kingma, D.P., Ba, J.: Adam: a method for stochastic optimization. CoRR abs/1412.6980 (2014)

49. Borji, A.: Pros and cons of GAN evaluation measures. Comput. Vis. Image Underst. **179**, 41–65 (2018)

50. Lucic, M., Kurach, K., Michalski, M., Gelly, S., Bousquet, O.: Are GANs created equal? a large-scale study. In: Bengio, S., Wallach, H., Larochelle, H., Grauman, K., Cesa-Bianchi, N., Garnett, R., (eds.): Advances in Neural Information Processing Systems 31, Curran Associates, Inc. pp. 700–709 (2018)

51. Heusel, M., Ramsauer, H., Unterthiner, T., Nessler, B., Hochreiter, S.: GANs trained by a two time-scale update rule converge to a local nash equilibrium. In: Proceedings of the 31st International Conference on Neural Information Processing Systems, NIPS 2017, USA, Curran Associates Inc. pp. 6629–6640 (2017)
52. Szegedy, C., Vanhoucke, V., Ioffe, S., Shlens, J., Wojna, Z.: Rethinking the inception architecture for computer vision. In: Proceedings of the IEEE Conference on Computer Vision and Pattern Recognition, pp. 2818–2826 (2016)

GAN-Based Noise Model for Denoising Real Images

Linh Duy Tran, Son Minh Nguyen[✉], and Masayuki Arai[✉]

Graduate School of Science and Engineering, Teikyo University,
Utsunomiya, Tochigi 320-8551, Japan
duylinh161287@gmail.com, nguyenminhson1110@gmail.com,
arai@ics.teikyo-u.ac.jp

Abstract. In the present paper, we propose a new approach for realistic image noise modeling based on a generative adversarial network (GAN). The model aims to boost performance of a deep network denoiser for real-world denoising. Although deep network denoisers, such as a denoising convolutional neural network, can achieve state-of-the-art denoised results on synthetic noise, they perform poorly on real-world noisy images. To address this, we propose a two-step model. First, the images are converted to raw image data before adding noise. We then trained a GAN to estimate the noise distribution over a large collection of images (1 million). The estimated noise was used to train a deep neural network denoiser. Extensive experiments demonstrated that our new noise model achieves state-of-the-art performance on real raw images from the Smartphone Image Denoising Dataset benchmark.

Keywords: Deep learning · Denoiser · Generative network · Real-world noisy images

1 Introduction

Noise reduction is a fundamental task in computer vision, and it is used as pre-processing step in many subsequence image processing tasks. Traditional denoising methods include block matching and 3D filtering (BM3D) [1], k-means singular-value decomposition (KSVD) [2], principal component analysis with local pixel grouping (LPGPCA) [3], and weighted nuclear norm minimization (WNNM) [4]; they are designed to remove noise based on the properties of images and noise. In contrast, learning-based methods, such as a denoising convolutional neural network (DnCNN) [5], often use paired-image datasets for mapping from noisy images to clean images. Because the performance of learning-based methods depends on a large training dataset, these methods require a sufficient amount of data. As a result, noisy images are artificially created from clean images with a known type of

Electronic supplementary material The online version of this chapter (https://doi.org/10.1007/978-3-030-69538-5_34) contains supplementary material, which is available to authorized users.

© Springer Nature Switzerland AG 2021
H. Ishikawa et al. (Eds.): ACCV 2020, LNCS 12625, pp. 560–572, 2021.
https://doi.org/10.1007/978-3-030-69538-5_34

noise (e.g., additive white Gaussian, salt and pepper, and Poisson). Learning-based methods outperform most of the traditional methods in synthetic denoising.

However, because synthetic noisy images are generally different from real-world noisy images, the learning-based methods work best on the same type of synthetic noise that they were trained on. They often output poor results when denoising real-world noisy images. Recent studies [6,7] show that the traditional denoising methods outperform learning-based methods when evaluated with real images. In this study, we aimed to improve the performance of learning-based methods for denoising real images.

To resolve this problem, the first approach is collecting a large amount of data for training the models [6–8]. The nearly noise-free images are estimated by an expensive and time-consuming procedure. Extensive analyses have proved need of a dataset with high-quality image pairs for improving real-world denoising performance. For example, the Smartphone Image Denoising Dataset (SIDD) [6] has collected 30,000 image pairs for training and testing. Although the number of images is relatively large, the number of different scenes (10) is limited. Thus, the dataset may not be sufficient to train a large network.

However, creating synthetic data by adding artificial noise to images has a clear advantage: an unlimited amount of training data can be created. However, the learning-based methods that are trained on synthetic noisy data (e.g., Gaussian noise or Poisson noise) perform poorly on real data because the training noise is unrealistic. Thus, another approach is to focus on building a better noise model. Methods such as convolutional blind denoising network (CBDNet) [9] and unprocessing images (UPI) [10] are intended to build a realistic noise model. In particular, according to the UPI method [10], a combination of Gaussian noise and Poisson noise was added to the raw image by means of an inverting process. For data augmentation, GAN-CNN based blind denoiser (GCBD) [11] used a generative adversarial network (GAN) to learn noise rather than noisy images, and the method was tested with zero mean noise. Despite having some limitations, the GCBD method showed the potential of a learning-based method (GAN) to generate natural noise if the expectation of the unknown noise is available. Moreover, the advantages of applying the denoising algorithm before processing in a non-linear camera processing pipeline have been proven [7,12].

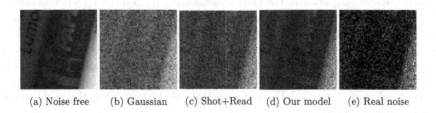

(a) Noise free   (b) Gaussian   (c) Shot+Read   (d) Our model   (e) Real noise

Fig. 1. Different noise model outputs displayed in linear raw space (red channel only).

In light of the above analysis, we adopted a learning-based technique (GAN) to generate noise in raw image data in a large dataset. The proposed model allows us to learn not only synthetic noise but also real noise by using a more realistic dataset for training. Some noisy images generated by noise models are shown in Fig. 1.

The main contributions of the present paper include the following:

- We propose a GAN-based model that can be trained with both synthetic and real noise in raw image data. The generated noise is used to create a paired-image dataset for training a denoising deep neural network (DNN).
- Extensive experiments demonstrated that our method can improve the performance of available denoising DNNs when they denoise real images.

2   Related Work

2.1   Deep Learning-Based Denoisers

The CNN-based methods dominate image denoising, and they have obtained good performance for removing artificial noise, such as additive white Gaussian noise (AWGN). Among them, DnCNN [5] is the first CNN-based blind denoiser. The DnCNN method shows that the residual learning and batch normalization help boost the denoising performance and training speed as well. Many other denoising methods [9,13,14] use the same strategy by using deep neural networks for mapping from noisy images to denoised images. The FFDNet [15] model proposed non-blind denoising by using a noise level map as an additional input. In general, the learning-based methods require abundant paired-image datasets; thus, AWGN is chosen to create the training dataset. These methods can be applied for denoising real-world noisy images; however, due to a lack of real data, their performance on denoising real images is still limited.

Consequently, as another approach to improving real-world image denoising, some recent work has focused on collecting real paired-image datasets. In the studies that created the Darmstadt Noise Dataset (DND) [7] and SIDD [6], the authors proposed extensive procedures to obtain noise-free ground truth images. These procedures require a large number of images to produce a ground truth dataset. Moreover, [6] showed that a deep learning denoiser trained with a high-quality dataset outperforms the classic methods (e.g., BM3D [1]) when denoising real images. Despite this, the number of training images is still relatively small compared with other computer vision tasks (such as image classification). Moreover, it is difficult to apply their process to produce paired images for moving objects. If we can create realistic paired training data, this approach would be promising. We focus on this data augmentation approach because it is generally understood that training data play a critical role in improving the performance of CNN-based methods.

Image denoising can be applied to raw image data as demonstrated in the work of [10]. This method employed a process called "unprocessing" to invert the image processing pipeline. The signal-dependent noise then is added to the clean image to produce a noisy version.

2.2 GAN-Based Denoisers

Generative adversarial networks [16] have been actively studied over the past few years. GAN models can minimize a loss function that classifies output images as real or fake. Given a training dataset, the GAN tries to generate new data with the same statistics as the training data. Recent GAN applications can produce impressive results [17,18], indicating the ability of GANs to learn complex distributions. The idea of applying a GAN to image denoising was first introduced in the work of GCBD [11]. In this work, the generative network was trained to produce noise to create paired-image data. The paired-image data were then used to train a denoising network, such as DnCNN. We adopted this idea for two reasons: first, the GAN can be trained to learn sophisticated real noise. This realistic noise model helps the CNN learn real-world noisy images, thus further boosting the performance of a CNN-based denoiser. Second, the realistic noise model solves the problem of poor denoising performance due to a lack of data.

We improved on prior work [11] not only with some architectural choices but also with the noise formation process. Instead of training the GAN to learn noise in the standard red green blue (sRGB) color space, we trained the GAN model with raw image data obtained by the clean image inverting process described in [10]. We investigated the noise modeling with raw image data and demonstrated the advantages of a GAN for improving the denoising performance for real images.

3 Proposed Method

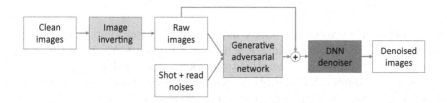

Fig. 2. Overview of proposed model. The "clean" images are converted to raw images through unprocessing. After adding noise, the resulting images are used to train a GAN to produce a noise model. A deep network denoiser uses the GAN output (noise) and clean images to learn how to map (create) clean images from noisy images.

Figure 2 shows the proposed architecture. The proposed method consists of three steps: First, we follow the process that is shown in [10] to invert clean images from sRGB space to raw image data. The inverted images are assumed to be noise-free images. Second, we obtain a noisy version by adding shot and read noise, and we then train the GAN model to learn the noise distribution from the generated data. During this step, the GAN model is also fine-tuned with a real noise dataset (SIDD) to learn the real noise distribution. Finally, the generative network output (noise) and the clean image are used to produce a paired-image dataset, which is fed to a DNN.

3.1   GAN Noise Generator

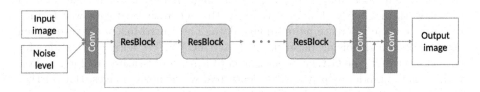

Fig. 3. GAN generator architecture. The model consists of five residual blocks (Res-Blocks, see Fig. 4). Input to the network consists of concatenations of clean images and noise levels, and the generator network outputs estimated noise.

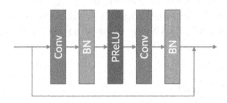

Fig. 4. Residual block (ResBlock)

Architecture: Conventional GAN models [11,19] often map from a random noise vector z to an output image y. In our proposed GAN model, the noise is added to the input of generative network as described in Fig. 3. We pass the additional input "Noise level" to the generator network, in particular, we estimate the shot and read noise parameters of input image and compute a per-pixel of the standard deviation of that noise. Inspired by the super-resolution GAN (SRGAN) model [18], we adopted that paper's model and removed the up-sampling blocks.

Discriminator: We followed a design similar to that of SRGAN. The discriminator network is depicted in Fig. 5.

Training Objective: As described in a previous paper on GANs [16], the aim is to solve a min-max problem between discriminator D and generator G.

$$\min_{G} \max_{D} \mathbb{E}_{x \sim \mathbb{P}_r}[\log(D(x))] + \mathbb{E}_{\tilde{x} \sim \mathbb{P}_g}[\log(1 - D(\tilde{x}))], \qquad (1)$$

Fig. 5. Discriminator architecture. The convolutional units are shown with their corresponding kernel size, number of outputs, and stride. All leaky rectified linear unit (LReLU) layers are set with a negative slope value of 0.2

where $\mathbb{P}_g$ is the synthetic data distribution and $\mathbb{P}_r$ is the real data distribution. Because the output of the generative network is noise, we found that the SRGAN training loss function leads to unstable model training. Arjovsky et al. [20] proposed an alternative objective function, called the Wasserstein distance, which measures the difference between two distributions. Moreover, the Wasserstein GAN with gradient penalty (WGAN-GP) [21] improves the stability of GAN training by introducing a gradient penalty.

$$Loss = \mathbb{E}_{\tilde{x} \sim \mathbb{P}_g}[D(\tilde{x})] - \mathbb{E}_{x \sim \mathbb{P}_r}[D(x)] + \lambda \mathbb{E}_{\hat{x} \sim \mathbb{P}_{\hat{x}}}[\|\nabla_{\hat{x}} D(\hat{x})\|_2 - 1)^2]. \quad (2)$$

In our experiments, we used the Adam optimizer [22] and kept the hyperparameter values from the original WGAN-GP paper ($\alpha = .0002, \beta_1 = 0.5, \beta_2 = 0.9, and\ \lambda = 10$).

Training Steps: For learning real-world noise, we used the following two-step training approach:

- The GAN is pre-trained with a large dataset (MIR dataset) with realistic synthetic noise.
- The pre-trained GAN is then re-trained with another dataset that has real noise (e.g., the SIDD benchmark) but fewer data.

With this training strategy, we can train the GAN to generate more realistic noise while avoiding overfitting of synthetic noise.

3.2 Denoising Neural Network

We produced paired-image data after training the GAN model. The inverted raw image is used as a clean ground truth. In particular, for image denoising networks, we adopt two architectures: DnCNN [5] and UNet-based [23] denoisers.

DnCNN: The DnCNN consists of 17 units with 3 types; more network details can be found in the DnCNN paper [5]. Batch normalization also has been used to speed up the training process and boost the denoising performance. The model predicts the residual image. For the training objective, we used mean squared error (MSE) loss, as suggested in the original paper.

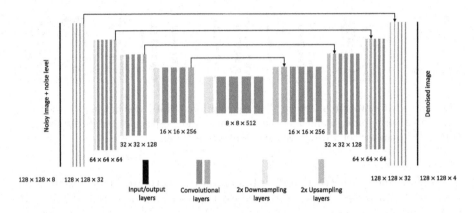

Fig. 6. UNet denoising architecture. Skip connections were added between same-scale encoder and decoder blocks. A 4-channel raw noisy image and noise level are input, and the output is a 4-channel denoised raw image.

UNet: The UNet architecture is depicted in Fig. 6. The model uses skip connections between same-scale encoder and decoder blocks. The input for the UNet denoiser is different from that for the aforementioned DnCNN denoiser. To make the model more robust, we added random noise (shot and read noise) as additional input for the denoising network. The network was trained to predict clean images directly. During the experiment, we found that the MSE loss did not work well as a training objective; thus, we replaced it with the sum of absolute differences loss.

4   Experiment

We performed our experiment on a single machine with an Intel i7-6800 CPU running at 3.40 GHz with 32 GB of RAM and a GeForce GTX 1080 Ti double GPU. The proposed model was implemented in the PyTorch framework [24].

4.1   GAN Training

To train the GAN in a manner similar to that in [10], we used the MIR Flickr extended dataset [25], which contains 1 million high-quality photographic images. The dataset is considered to contain "clean" images. We then randomly cropped each image to the size of 256×256. We randomly flipped the images horizontally and vertically (with probability of 0.5) for data augmentation. Because we did not resize the original image, some small images were not included in the training and validation datasets. We reserved 5% of the data for evaluation. The model learning rate was 10^{-3}, the batch size was 32, and we trained the generative and the discriminative networks for 250,000 iterations.

To train the GAN on a real-world noisy distribution, we then fine-tuned it with a real image dataset (SIDD). The batch size was unchanged, a smaller learning rate (10^{-4}) was used, and the number of training iterations was about 100,000.

4.2 Denoiser Training

The noise produced from the generator network is used to prepare a paired-image dataset for training DNN denoisers. We applied the synthetic data to two denoiser architectures, as described in Subsect. 3.2:

- DnCNN: We kept the batch size of 32, learning rate of 10^{-3}, and training epochs of 10.
- UNet: The model used a batch size of 64, learning rate of 10^{-4}, and 6 training epochs.

4.3 Test Datasets

SIDD: The SIDD benchmark consists of 30,000 image pairs comprising both raw images and images in the sRGB color space. The evaluation set contained 256 × 256 size image patches at 32 random non-overlapping regions for each image. A total of 40 images were used for evaluation (total of 1,280 image patches). The dataset was captured under different settings (cameras, camera settings, and light conditions), resulting in 200 scene instances, of which 160 were for training and 40 were for evaluation purposes. The dataset also provided the estimated noise level for each image, which is used as input in many denoising algorithms. To evaluate denoising method, the SIDD dataset provides an online submission system[1].

DND: The DND consists of 50 pairs of images with real noise and corresponding clean images. The (nearly) noise-free image is obtained by averaging a number of noisy images of the same scene. The dataset contains the images taken from four consumer cameras with wide range of different film speeds. An online submission system determined the denoising performance in terms of peak signal-to-noise ratio (PSNR) and structural similarity (SSIM)[2].

4.4 Results

Real-World Denoising Performance: Table 1 shows the denoising results for the SIDD evaluation dataset. We applied our model to denoise raw image, the metrics are evaluated in both raw image data and after converting to s-RGB space. The proposed model outperforms previous denoising models in both metrics (PSNR and SSIM). In particular, the DnCNN with GAN-based modeling surpassed the original DnCNN by 2.25 dB. In the second test, we see that the proposed noised model improved the performance of UNet by 3.09 dB.

---

[1] https://www.eecs.yorku.ca/~kamel/sidd/benchmark.php.
[2] https://noise.visinf.tu-darmstadt.de/benchmark/.

Table 1. Performance comparison of denoising methods on SIDD benchmark.

Method	Raw		sRGB	
	PSNR	SSIM	PSNR	SSIM
BM3D	45.52	0.980	30.95	0.863
DnCNN	43.30	0.965	28.24	0.829
UNet	45.69	0.976	32.93	0.854
GAN + DnCNN (ours)	45.55	0.980	32.05	0.809
GAN + UNet (ours)	**48.78**	**0.986**	**35.78**	**0.919**

Table 2. Performance comparison of denoising methods on DND benchmark.

Method	Raw		sRGB	
	PSNR	SSIM	PSNR	SSIM
WNNM	46.3	0.9707	37.56	0.9313
EPLL	46.31	0.9679	37.16	0.9291
BM3D	46.64	0.9724	37.78	0.9308
BM3D + VST	47.15	0.9737	37.86	0.9296
DnCNN	47.37	0.9760	38.08	0.9357
N3Net	47.56	0.9767	38.32	0.9384
UPI	48.89	0.9824	40.17	**0.9623**
GAN + DnCNN (Ours)	47.46	0.9769	38.34	0.9418
GAN + UNet (Ours)	**49.04**	**0.9827**	**40.21**	0.9600

Table 2 shows the quantitative results for the DND benchmark [7]. The proposed model performs better than classic methods (e.g., BM3D, WNNM, and EPLL [26]). Compared with other deep learning-based method that using same baseline (DnCNN [5]), our model consistently yields higher PSNR and SSIM values on both raw data and after conversion to s-RGB space. Notably, the proposed model outperforms state-of-the-art method UPI [10] which used the same baseline (UNet) by 0.15 dB in denoising raw image.

Qualitative Results: Figure 7 and Fig. 8 show the output of our model and some state-of-the-art denoisers with the SIDD and DND benchmarks.

Ablation Studies: Table 3 shows ablation studies for various configurations of our model. In the table, "Gaussian, blind" indicates the training data were generated with AWGN and applied to a blind denoiser; "Non-GAN" indicates that instead of using the GAN to produce noisy images, we added noise to the input images using the procedure given in [10]; and "GAN, blind" indicates that we used the GAN noise model but did not add the noise level to the network input. Using the noise level information improves the denoising performance by

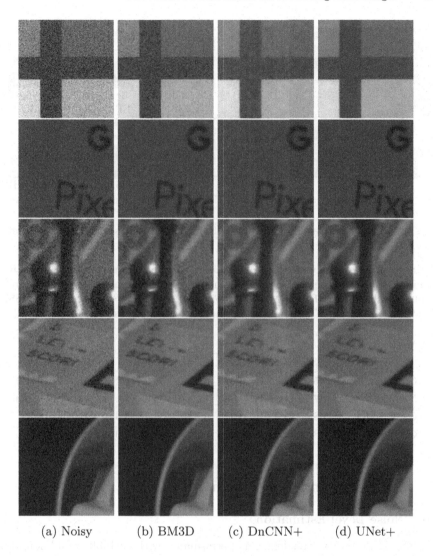

(a) Noisy   (b) BM3D   (c) DnCNN+   (d) UNet+

Fig. 7. Qualitative comparison of denoising methods. First column: noisy images; second column: images denoised using BM3D ($\sigma = 50$); third column: images denoised using DnCNN and GAN-based noise model; fourth column: images denoised using UNet and GAN-based noise model. Zoom in for a better view.

3.7% (PSNR) and 6.7% (SSIM) compared with blind denoising. The GAN noise model increases the performance by 11.1% (PSNR) and 17.6% (SSIM), showing the usefulness of our proposed noise model.

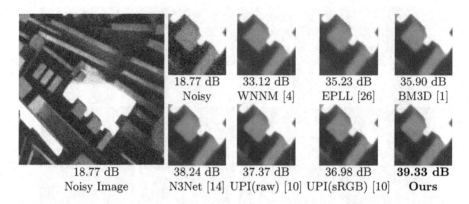

Fig. 8. The results of denoising raw image from DND [7] dataset. Zoom in for a better view.

Table 3. Ablation study on SIDD benchmark. The number in parenthesis is the relative improvement to the our best performing model. To compute the relative improvements, we change PSNR to RMSE ($RMSE = \sqrt{10^{-PSNR/10}}$) and SSIM to DSSIM ($DSSIM = (1 - SSIM)/2$) and then calculate the relative reduction in error.

Method	Raw		sRGB	
	PSNR	SSIM	PSNR	SSIM
Gaussian, blind	45.69 (29.9%)	0.976 (41.7%)	32.93 (28%)	0.854 (44.5%)
Non-GAN	47.76 (11.1%)	0.983 (17.6%)	34.39 (14.8%)	0.897 (21.4%)
GAN, blind	48.45 (3.7%)	0.985 (6.7%)	35.37 (4.6%)	0.913 (6.9%)
GAN, non-blind	48.78 (0.0%)	0.986 (0.0%)	35.78 (0.0%)	0.919 (0.0%)

5   Discussion and Conclusion

5.1   Noise Level Estimation

In Sect. 4.4 we present the denoising performance with both blind and non-blind denoisers. It is noted in [27] that incorporating information about the precise noise level may boost the performance of a denoiser. In the UNet denoiser, we added the random noise level as an additional network input. During the testing phase, the noise level was provided in the metadata. However, in real-world applications, the noise level is generally not available. We think that using a noise level estimation algorithm can further improve our results, and we will investigate this in future work.

5.2   Conclusion

In the present paper, we introduce a GAN-based model for real noise estimation in raw image data. The model consists of an "unprocessing" process to convert images from the sRGB space to raw image data. By using generated noise, we can generate a large amount of data for training a deep DNN. Although our approach contains some limitations, such as relying on prior statistics stored in the metadata and approximations of the noise level, the experimental results show the effectiveness of our data augmentation approach for real-world image denoising.

References

1. Dabov, K., Foi, A., Katkovnik, V., Egiazarian, K.: Image denoising by sparse 3-D transform-domain collaborative filtering. IEEE Trans. Image Process. **16**, 2080–2095 (2007)
2. Aharon, M., Elad, M., Bruckstein, A.: K-SVD: an algorithm for designing over-complete dictionaries for sparse representation. IEEE Trans. Signal Process. **54**, 4311–4322 (2006)
3. Zhang, L., Dong, W., Zhang, D., Shi, G.: Two-stage image denoising by principal component analysis with local pixel grouping. Pattern Recogn. **43**, 1531–1549 (2010)
4. Gu, S., Zhang, L., Zuo, W., Feng, X.: Weighted nuclear norm minimization with application to image denoising. In: Proceedings of the IEEE Conference on Computer Vision and Pattern Recognition, 2862–2869 (2014)
5. Zhang, K., Zuo, W., Chen, Y., Meng, D., Zhang, L.: Beyond a Gaussian denoiser: residual learning of deep CNN for image denoising. IEEE Trans. Image Process. **26**, 3142–3155 (2017)
6. Abdelhamed, A., Lin, S., Brown, M.S.: A high-quality denoising dataset for smartphone cameras. In: Proceedings of the IEEE Conference on Computer Vision and Pattern Recognition, pp. 1692–1700 (2018)
7. Plotz, T., Roth, S.: Benchmarking denoising algorithms with real photographs. In: Proceedings of the IEEE Conference on Computer Vision and Pattern Recognition, pp. 1586–1595 (2017)
8. Anaya, J., Barbu, A.: RENOIR-a benchmark dataset for real noise reduction evaluation. J. Vis. Commun. Image Represent. **51**, 144–154 (2018)
9. Guo, S., Yan, Z., Zhang, K., Zuo, W., Zhang, L.: Toward convolutional blind denoising of real photographs. In: Proceedings of the IEEE Conference on Computer Vision and Pattern Recognition, pp. 1712–1722 (2019)
10. Brooks, T., Mildenhall, B., Xue, T., Chen, J., Sharlet, D., Barron, J.T.: Unprocessing images for learned raw denoising. In: Proceedings of the IEEE Conference on Computer Vision and Pattern Recognition, pp. 11036–11045 (2019)
11. Chen, J., Chen, J., Chao, H., Yang, M.: Image blind denoising with generative adversarial network based noise modeling. In: Proceedings of the IEEE Conference on Computer Vision and Pattern Recognition, pp. 3155–3164 (2018)
12. Park, S.H., Kim, H.S., Lansel, S., Parmar, M., Wandell, B.A.: A case for denoising before demosaicking color filter array data. In: 2009 Conference Record of the Forty-Third Asilomar Conference on Signals, Systems and Computers, pp. 860–864. IEEE (2009)
13. Gharbi, M., Chaurasia, G., Paris, S., Durand, F.: Deep joint demosaicking and denoising. ACM Trans. Graph. (TOG) **35**, 1–12 (2016)
14. Plötz, T., Roth, S.: Neural nearest neighbors networks. Adv. Neural Inf. Process. Syst. **31**, 1087–1098 (2018)

15. Zhang, K., Zuo, W., Zhang, L.: FFDNet: toward a fast and flexible solution for CNN-based image denoising. IEEE Trans. Image Process. **27**, 4608–4622 (2018)
16. Goodfellow, I., et al.: Generative adversarial nets. In: Advances in Neural Information Processing Systems, pp. 2672–2680 (2014)
17. Isola, P., Zhu, J.Y., Zhou, T., Efros, A.A.: Image-to-image translation with conditional adversarial networks. In: Proceedings of the IEEE Conference on Computer Vision and Pattern Recognition, pp. 1125–1134 (2017)
18. Ledig, C., et al.: Photo-realistic single image super-resolution using a generative adversarial network. In: Proceedings of the IEEE Conference on Computer Vision and Pattern Recognition, pp. 4681–4690 (2017)
19. Zhu, F., Chen, G., Heng, P.A.: From noise modeling to blind image denoising. In: Proceedings of the IEEE Conference on Computer Vision and Pattern Recognition, pp. 420–429 (2016)
20. Arjovsky, M., Chintala, S., Bottou, L.: Wasserstein GAN. arXiv preprint arXiv:1701.07875 (2017)
21. Gulrajani, I., Ahmed, F., Arjovsky, M., Dumoulin, V., Courville, A.C.: Improved training of wasserstein GANs. In: Advances in Neural Information Processing Systems, pp. 5767–5777 (2017)
22. Kingma, D.P., Ba, J.: Adam: A method for stochastic optimization. arXiv preprint arXiv:1412.6980 (2014)
23. Ronneberger, O., Fischer, P., Brox, T.: U-Net: convolutional networks for biomedical image segmentation. In: Navab, N., Hornegger, J., Wells, W.M., Frangi, A.F. (eds.) MICCAI 2015, Part III. LNCS, vol. 9351, pp. 234–241. Springer, Cham (2015). https://doi.org/10.1007/978-3-319-24574-4_28
24. Paszke, A., et al.: Automatic differentiation in PyTorch (2017)
25. Huiskes, M.J., Thomee, B., Lew, M.S.: New trends and ideas in visual concept detection: the MIR flickr retrieval evaluation initiative. In: Proceedings of the International Conference on Multimedia Information Retrieval, pp. 527–536 (2010)
26. Zoran, D., Weiss, Y.: From learning models of natural image patches to whole image restoration. In: 2011 International Conference on Computer Vision, pp. 479–486. IEEE (2011)
27. Liu, X., Tanaka, M., Okutomi, M.: Single-image noise level estimation for blind denoising. IEEE Trans. Image Process. **22**, 5226–5237 (2013)

Emotional Landscape Image Generation Using Generative Adversarial Networks

Chanjong Park🆔 and In-Kwon Lee$^{(\boxtimes)}$🆔

Department of Computer Science, Yonsei University, Seoul, Republic of Korea
{cjprist,iklee}@yonsei.ac.kr

Abstract. We design a deep learning framework that generates landscape images that match a given emotion. We are working on a more challenging approach to generate landscape scenes that do not have main objects making it easier to recognize the emotion. To solve this problem, deep networks based on generative adversarial networks are proposed. A new residual unit called emotional residual unit (ERU) is proposed to better reflect the emotion on training. An affective feature matching loss (AFM-loss) optimized for the emotional image generation is also proposed. This approach produced better images according to the given emotions. To demonstrate performance of the proposed model, a set of experiments including user studies was conducted. The results reveal a higher preference in the new model than the previous ones, demonstrating the production of images suitable for the given emotions. Ablation studies demonstrate that the ERU and AFM-loss enhanced the performance of the model.

1 Introduction

Computer vision and graphics applications, such as image classification [1–10], object detection [11–16], and image transformation [17–21], are effectively using deep learning techniques. Also, there have been ongoing studies on image generation using deep learning in recent years [22–29]. These are studies that produce images that match a given condition, for example, images that match the content of a given sentence or word [30–32]. On a higher level, recent studies have shown that machine learning effectively recognizes the emotions expressed in images [33–37]. However, studies that create images from scratch that reveal input emotions are rare due to the inherent ambiguity and abstraction of emotion.

Research on emotion-based image creation has mainly focused on image creation, including objects that express some specific emotions. In particular, studies related to the transformation or generation of human facial expressions based on given input emotions have been successful [38–42]. However, if objects such as people are not clearly present in the image, we must recognize emotions in the feeling and landscape of the whole image. For example, when the scenery in the image is night time, we can feel calm. Daytime images can have energy

© Springer Nature Switzerland AG 2021
H. Ishikawa et al. (Eds.): ACCV 2020, LNCS 12625, pp. 573–590, 2021.
https://doi.org/10.1007/978-3-030-69538-5_35

and excitement. However, the perception of the emotions felt in the image varies from viewer to viewer. As a result, the process of understanding the emotions of an image without an explicit object is complicated and confusing for both people and computers.

Thus, generating landscape images have the advantage of being able to express emotion with the entire image itself, unlike creating an image that includes a specific object. Even if the specified object exists in front of the background, we can change the feeling of the image by replacing the landscape behind the object. Besides, landscape images representing emotions can be used for behavioral therapy and can be used for psychological research, such as investigating how well people perceive emotions or analyzing brain waves from the landscape images [43–48]. So, we will deal with the creation of landscape images that represent emotions. Although there have been studies on how to create a landscape image [49–51], this work will be the first to create a landscape image from emotions.

There are several ways to represent emotions. One way is by categorizing them into classes such as happy, sad, angry, and relaxed, which is the most widely used method and has the advantage of expressing emotion through intuition. The drawback of this method, however, is that the emotions are classified into several other categories that cannot define various emotions in detail, and the criterion for judging a particular emotion is ambiguous. Osgood *et al.* [52] proposed a dimensional representation called the VA model for representing emotions with two variables, V (valence) and A (arousal). Valence represents the level of pleasure. The lower value of valence indicates a negative emotion, and the higher value indicates a positive emotion. Arousal is a level of excitement. The smaller the arousal value, the calmer the emotion. The larger the value, the more active the sensation. We are using this dimensional representation in describing the emotions that are the input conditions in this study.

In this paper, we propose a deep learning-based model using generative adversarial networks (GAN) [53] for generating landscape images from a given emotion. We design the model in a gradually increasing form according to the training process based on Karras *et al.* [54]. The proposed model also contains new residual units and a new loss function to understand the emotional concepts and generate the image based on that emotion. The former is an Emotional Residual Unit (ERU), and the latter is Affective Feature Matching loss (AFM-loss). The ERU and AFM-loss gradually change features in networks in the training process so that generated images are close to the target emotions.

We conducted various experiments to ensure that the output image sufficiently reflects the given emotions. These experiments compare different results when varying the structure of the network and the arrangement of units of ERU. The experiment also includes user surveys and emotional measurements using the trained emotional prediction model to measure the proposed model's performance.

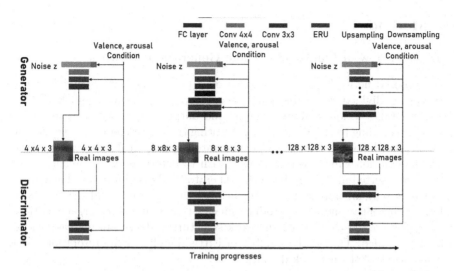

Fig. 1. The overall structure of emotional landscape image generation network. Based on the progressive structure, it shows the process of gradually training from low resolution to high resolution. Incrementally increases from 4×4 structures to 128×128 images. Emotional residual unit (ERU) is inserted into generator and discriminator, which is responsible for accepting emotional conditions and training according to emotion.

The contributions of the paper can be summarized as follows:

- We propose a novel deep learning-based approach that can generate landscape images fitting to target given emotions.
- We propose a new residual unit that can train a deep neural network to adjust emotions.
- We propose a GAN based generation approach to expressing the emotions.
- We propose an affective feature matching loss to express emotions on the generated landscape images effectively.

In this paper, we focus on creating an image representing a particular emotion from scratch, rather than transforming an image that already exists to fit a specific emotion. When we feel an emotion, it is natural to close our eyes and recall an image of that emotion. For human nature, this process of thinking of an image representing the emotions we feel can be more natural than transforming an existing image to match the emotions we feel. Likewise, if artificial intelligence is drawing art, it will be more valuable to create a new image that does not exist by taking emotion into account. Therefore, our work can be used for artificial intelligence that can express emotions. Our work will be a more critical step in that artificial intelligence fundamentally understands emotions than image transformation.

2   Methods

2.1   Overview of Landscape Image Generation Network

The proposed network (Fig. 1) is based on a progressive structure. The whole structure is divided into three parts: generator, discriminator, and ERU. The generator takes a noise vector as input and outputs an image with the target emotion according to the VA value representing the target emotion. The discriminator takes the output image of the generator and the real image as the input with the emotion values so that it can learn to determine if the image is real. ERUs are inserted in the middle of the generator and discriminator. The embedded ERUs play an important role in helping the generator and discriminator, allowing the entire model to produce images that match the target emotions. It should be noted that, as the network structure and size are increased, more ERUs are added. That is the number of ERUs doubles as the resolution of the output image of the network doubles.

2.2   Emotional Residual Unit (ERU)

Long short-term memory (LSTM) [55] and Gated recurrent unit (GRU) [56] continue to transfer features of the previous state to the next state through the cell state structure. Then, the cell state adds or removes features using gate elements with a refined structure. These gates are devices that allow the selected features of the previous state to flow into the next state. When they pass through the gate, features judged significant are retained, and those judged meaningless are discarded.

We apply the gate structure of LSTM and GRU to our model and propose a new unit. The ERU, the new unit, is designed for emotion-based landscape image generation whose structure is shown in Fig. 2. Let $[\cdot, \cdot]$ denote concatenation, $Conv(x)$ denote convolution on x, $\otimes$ denote element-wise multiplication, $\oplus$ denote element-wise addition, and $f(x)$ be a activation function. X is a feature map given as input to ERU, which is fed from the generator or discriminator these are from the layer before entering ERU.

Single-channel valence and arousal maps, V and A, are generated, whose width and height are equal to input X. The two maps are fed with valence and arousal values representing the current target emotion. Then, V and A are concatenated with X channel-wise, respectively. After passing through the convolution layer and sigmoid activation function in turn, the two feature maps can be represented as v and a, respectively. At this time, the sum of each channel of v and a is set to 1.0 like the soft attention method experimentally, as follows:

$$v = f(Conv([V, X])) \text{ and } a = f(Conv([A, X])). \tag{1}$$

For instance, let us assume that the valence and arousal values of the current target emotion are 3.6 and 6.7, respectively, and the size of X given as input is $4 \times 4 \times 32$. Then we create the maps of valence and arousal with dimensions

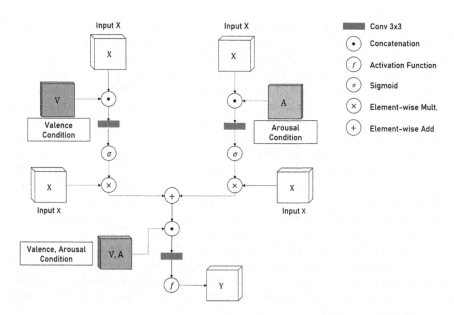

Fig. 2. Structure of the emotional residual unit (ERU). After concatenation of the VA emotional maps to the input feature X of the ERU, respectively, 3×3 convolution and sigmoid function are performed, followed by the element-wise multiplication with input X. After adding the results element-wise, we concatenate the VA map again to the result, and finally, get the output Y after the convolution and activation functions.

of $4 \times 4 \times 1$ and fill the maps with 3.6 and 6.7, respectively. And then we concatenate X with the maps of valence and arousal respectively to generate the two feature maps v and a of size $4 \times 4 \times 33$ (see Eq. (1)). After the two feature maps pass through the convolution and activation layers, respectively, their sizes become equal to the input feature map X.

Now, v and a are element-wise multiplied with input X, respectively, and the results are combined using element-wise addition as follows:

$$m = (v \otimes X) \oplus (a \otimes X). \qquad (2)$$

The combined feature map m in Eq. (2) is concatenated with $[V, A]$, the concatenation of the emotional maps of valence and arousal, and then passed through the convolution layer followed by tanh activation function in turn. Finally, we get Y, the output of ERU, as follows:

$$Y = f(Conv([m, [V, A]])). \qquad (3)$$

2.3 ERU in Landscape Image Generation Network

Our model, which is modeled using the progressive structure as the underlying infrastructure, has features that allow the generator and discriminator to gradually evolve. Because of the image resolution of the data set, the training process is repeated after iterating up to 128×128 resolution. Since GAN tends to capture only the subset of variation found in the training data, we use the minibatch discrimination technique proposed by Salimans *et al.* [57], which adds a minibatch layer to the end of the discriminator. Additionally, to disallow the scenario where the magnitudes of the generator and the discriminator spiral out of control as a result of competition, we use the pixel-wise feature normalization, instead of the batch normalization commonly used to normalize the generator.

In Fig. 1, we can see that ERUs exist as the intermediate unit in the generator and discriminator. In the case of the generator, there is one ERU in the 4×4 resolution training process, and as the resolution increases, the number of ERUs also increases. In other words, there are $k - 1$ ERUs in the generator trained using images with resolution $2^k \times 2^k$, $(2 \leq k \leq 7)$. At the same time, the dimensions of the input and output feature maps of ERUs also depend on the image resolution currently being processed. Note that because the discriminator has the inverted structure of the generator, the arrangement of ERUs in the discriminator also follows a reverse order. Since the proposed model grows gradually, it has the advantage of the progressive structure, which reflects both global and local features.

In our dataset, valence and arousal values are on a scale of 1 to 9, respectively. When the values are assigned to the ERU, the values are normalized to between 0 and 1. Each time an image is trained, the valence and arousal values of the image are given. At this point, the generator's ERU lets the generator learn in the direction of generating an image that expresses a given emotion. Similarly, the ERU in the discriminator is trained to determine if the generated image matches the conditions of the given emotion.

2.4   Affective Feature Matching Loss

Wang *et al.* [20] suggested the feature-matching loss that minimizes the statistical difference between the generated image and the ground truth image by minimizing the difference between the corresponding convolution maps (i.e., feature maps) of discriminator when the generated image and the ground truth image pass through the discriminator. In this work, we propose a new feature-matching loss function called affective feature-matching loss (AFM-loss) by enhancing the existing method to emphasize the reflection of emotional features in the landscape image generation process.

Suppose a generated image and a ground truth image in the dataset have the same target emotion value. The AFM-loss computes the element-wise difference between the feature values (v, a) (i.e., the results of the sigmoid function in Fig. 2) of ERU obtained by Eq. (1) of the generator's output image and the image in the dataset, where the two images are both passing through the convolution layer inside the discriminator's ERU block. The proposed method compares only the features of the convolution layer, where the information of V and A are concatenated. In other words, it does not just make the resulting image similar to the ground truth image but makes the emotion-affected features in the resulting image as similar to the corresponding features in the ground truth image as possible. As a result, the resulting image can be gradually transformed into an image having an emotion close to the target emotion.

Let x be a ground truth image, c_v and c_a be constant valence and arousal values, respectively, and z be an input noise vector. $G(z, c_v, c_a)$ represents the image generated from the generator module. The affective feature matching losses L_v and L_a for valence and arousal are respectively defined by:

$$\mathcal{L}_v = \frac{1}{k} \sum_{i=1}^{k} |D_c(G(z, c_v, c_a), c_v) - D_c(x, c_v)|_i, \tag{4}$$

$$\mathcal{L}_a = \frac{1}{k} \sum_{i=1}^{k} |D_c(G(z, c_v, c_a), c_a) - D_c(x, c_a)|_i, \tag{5}$$

where D_c is the feature of the layer to be compared in the ERU block of the discriminator. The average of all differences between the features in k ERUs becomes the respective feature matching loss for V and A. We take the average experimentally instead of the minimum and maximum.

2.5   Objective Function

The total objective function of the proposed model is defined by:

$$\mathcal{L}_{WGAN}(D) = \mathbb{E}_{x \sim P_{image}}[D(x, c_v, c_a)]$$
$$- \mathbb{E}_{z \sim P_z}[D(G(z, c_v, c_a))]$$
$$+ \lambda(L_v + L_a), \tag{6}$$
$$\mathcal{L}_{WGAN}(G) = \mathbb{E}_{z \sim P_z}[D(G(z, c_v, c_a))]. \tag{7}$$

In Eq. (6) and (7), we use the Wasserstein GAN [58] loss to stabilize the training. x and z refer to image and noise as in Eq. (4) and (5), respectively. Note that the c_v, c_a values in the loss functions are given as the emotional maps in the ERU. λ is a hyper parameter that balances the AFM-loss and GAN loss. For this experiment, we use $\lambda = 100$.

3   Experiments

3.1   Experimental Data

The CGnA10766 is an emotional image dataset built by Kim et al. [37], where 10,766 images are labeled with emotion values, V and A, through the user study. The original CGnA10766 dataset has many images containing objects such as people, animals, and cars. We selected only natural landscape images from the original CGnA10766 dataset, excluding images that contain objects that can have a significant impact on our emotions. Images containing objects that did not significantly affect emotions, such as small boats or bicycles, were classified

Fig. 3. Sample images of natural outdoor scenes without objects such as people, animals, or cars selected from the CGnA10766 dataset.

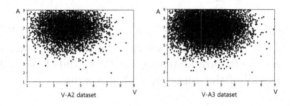

Fig. 4. The valence-arousal distribution of V-A2 dataset (left) and V-A3 dataset (right). The horizontal and vertical axes represent the valence and arousal values, respectively.

as valid natural landscape scenes. We obtained a total of 1,453 images (we call this reduced dataset V-A2) through this classification of the original CGnA10766 dataset (see Fig. 3). We collected more images because there were not enough images in the V-A2 data set, and obtained their VA values using the emotion predictor trained by Kim et al. [37]. We collected 1,204 images from [59], 1,523 images from [60], and 5,039 images from [61], resulting in 10,453 images. We call this final dataset V-A3. The valence-arousal distributions of the V-A2 and V-A3 dataset are shown in Fig. 4. In the figure, the images in our dataset have a slightly lower valence, and slightly higher arousal value than the center, which is clearly shown by the V-A2 dataset's distribution based only on user studies. We guess that the distribution of the dark colors in the landscape images is probably causing a negative and active feeling rather than positive and calm. Fortunately, both datasets have relatively even distributions of emotion values between the minimum and maximum values, which is one of the conditions that a dataset for machine learning must-have.

3.2   Experimental Settings

We trained our model using both the V-A2 and the V-A3 dataset with 100,000 iterations for the first 4×4 resolution and 200,000 iterations for other resolutions. We set the batch size to 16. After the input noise vector of size 126 was

Low Valence

High Valence

Low Arousal

High Arousal

Fig. 5. Example results of proposed model with V-A3 dataset. Valence is small on the left and large on the right. Arousal is small on the top and large on the bottom.

generated, the valence and arousal values were concatenated with the noise vector, and eventually, the input size was 128. In the final stage of generating images of size 128×128, the batch size was set to 8, to prevent memory out. The learning rate was set to 0.001, and leaky ReLU [62] was used as the activation function of the generator. When concatenating the input feature map X and the emotional map in the ERU, the former is concatenated behind the valence or arousal map. Additionally, in the second concatenation in the ERU, a combined valence and arousal map is concatenated forward. In ERU, we used soft attention instead of hard attention because when compared with the Frechet inception distance of the training results with the V-A3 dataset, the soft attention method was as good as compared to the hard attention method. We performed the training with one Nvidia GTX 1080 Ti for a total of (approximately) 10 days.

3.3 Results

Figure 5 shows the example results of the images generated by the trained model. We aligned the resulting images in order of successive valence and arousal values. The results with lower valence have broader sea areas with darker brightness than those with higher valence. On the contrary, high valence results are relatively bright. The results with average valences have both low and high valence

Table 1. Ablation study in terms of FID scores: Non-ERU and Non-AFM loss represent the model without both of ERU and AFM-loss, and AFM-loss, in the proposed model, respectively. E-FID is an averaged FID score computed only from images with similar emotion values.

Dataset	Method	FID	E-FID
V-A2	Non-ERU	4.07	3.53
	Non-AFM loss	3.02	2.45
	Proposed method	**2.78**	**2.11**
V-A3	Non-ERU	3.82	3.30
	Non-AFM loss	2.82	2.30
	Proposed method	**2.51**	**1.87**

characteristics. The resulting images with higher arousal have darker colors and are more versatile than with lower arousal, consistent with the emotions expressed by the high arousal representing more active emotions. In Fig. 5, the resulting images on the 4th rows are considered to represent a red sky, which means that an image containing the ruddy glow in the sky usually has high arousal. Additionally, images with low arousal include the blue sea, which is thought to be due to the calmness of the blue sea. Although the results have some artifacts, the proposed model is demonstrably well-controlled according to the conditions of arousal and valence.

To evaluate the results, we measured the FID score [63]. Also, we conducted an ablation study to verify the ERU and AFM-loss performance of the proposed model (see Table 1). In both the V-A2 and V-A3 datasets, the proposed model with both ERU and AFM-loss shows the lowest FID score (see FID column in the table) based on the total data, which means that the output of the proposed model (with both ERU and AFM-loss) is most statistically similar to the original dataset. Let us consider a 2D space with the mean of valence and arousal values in the dataset as origin and valence and arousal as two axes. The E-FID column in Table 1 shows the average value of the four FID scores computed using only the images in the dataset and output images belonging to each quadrant of the 2D space. In other words, it can be said that the proposed model produces outputs with a feature distribution statistically similar to images in a dataset with target emotions.

3.4 User Study

To evaluate the results objectively, a series of user studies were conducted on the Amazon Mturk platform [64]. In these experiments, images were given to the subjects, and then they were instructed to select the valence and arousal values they considered appropriate. Figure 6 shows how the valence and arousal were selected in the user experiments. The valence and arousal values were divided into five ranges, from low to high, respectively, and the subject had to choose

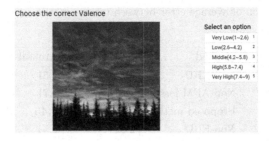

Fig. 6. Example of a scene during a user study

one. Selecting the interval was easier, more intuitive than numbering valence and arousal, for the subjects who did not have a good understanding of the VA model. We use the results of our model that was trained with both V-A2 dataset and V-A3 dataset in the user study.

Before the evaluation phase, the user first learned about the VA representation through the training phase. We presented a randomly selected image from the dataset, and the subject was instructed to select VA values of the image. Users who answered outliers that were very different from the average answer were excluded from the next evaluation phase. In the evaluation phase, 200 resulting images were used respectively for the V-A2 and the V-A3 dataset, including 60 results from the model with neither ERU nor AFM-loss, 60 results with ERU only, and 80 results from the complete proposed model. Approximately 10,000 evaluations were performed on 400 images by nearly 1000 subjects. In other words, an image was rated by an average of 25 users. The evaluations were performed for VA values in one of five intervals, each with $[1, 2.6), [2.6, 4.2), [4.2, 5.8), [5.8, 7.4)$, and $[7.4, 9]$. The average of user answers was then calculated using the median of the selected intervals. The error is the difference between the average of evaluated emotion value and the target emotion. Outlier answers were removed using the method of inter-quartile range (IQR). Table 2 shows average of error margins with the target emotion. The complete proposed method was measured to show the least error with the target emotion for both datasets. Considering that the size of one interval is 1.6, the figure is quite low. Besides, the valence error of most images was within 2, as was with the case of arousal. This result demonstrates that our model generates appropriate images for the condition of the target emotion.

Additionally, we conducted an ablation study to verify the ERU and AFM-loss performance of the proposed model. As shown in Table 2, the objects to be compared are the results of the proposed model, the non-ERU model, and the non-AFM model. The non-ERU model eliminates the ERU from the model, and the non-AFM model eliminates AFM-loss in the loss function. In the case of non-ERU models, AFM-loss cannot be applied because there is no ERU. As a result of the statistical analysis of the average error difference between the non-ERU model and the complete model with the independent samples' z-test, a significant difference was found in the 95% confidence interval. The average

Table 2. Comparison of average error between target emotion and results of the user study.

Dataset	Method	Valence-error	Arousal-error
	Non-ERU	2.73	2.51
V-A2	Non-AFM loss	1.92	1.71
	Proposed method	**1.67**	**1.45**
	Non-ERU	2.62	2.54
V-A3	Non-AFM loss	1.81	1.68
	Proposed method	**1.56**	**1.38**

Table 3. Performance comparison of the three models

Method	The emotional GAN	MHingeGAN	Our method
Valence-error	2.58	1.81	**1.56**
Arousal-error	2.56	1.77	**1.38**
Preference	15.7	34.5	**49.8**
FID	4.85	2.53	**2.51**
E-FID	4.14	1.88	**1.87**

error difference between the non-AFM loss model and the complete model was not statistically significant under the same conditions but showed numerically noticeable differences.

3.5   Comparison with Other Model

We trained the V-A3 dataset that produced better results than the V-A2 dataset to produce results for comparison with the Emotional GAN [65], which is the baseline for comparing the proposed method. The V-A3 dataset has a continuous emotional condition, however, the Emotional GAN receives this condition as a categorized discrete value. Therefore, only the images in the VA plane with emotion values within 0.5 of the difference in both the valence and arousal values, representing anger, anxiety, disgust, etc., were used. For instance, according to Kuperman *et al.* [66], anger has values of 2.5 and 5.65 in the VA plane. Thus, we classified images with valence between [2.0, 3.0] and arousal between [5.15, 6.15] as anger. We also compared the results of our model with Kavalerov *et al.* (MHingeGAN) [67] model having the best performance among the conditional GANs. Because our model was not a method of transforming an existing image, but a method of creating a new image with a target emotion from noise, our method was compared only with other works that create an image from noise.

The comparison results between the different methods are shown in Table 3. The average of user preference and VA value errors were collected through user

Table 4. The averages of predicted VA errors using the machine learning model of Kim *et al.* [37]

Dataset	Method	Valence-error	Arousal-error
V-A2 dataset	Non-ERU	2.74	3.05
	Non-AFM loss	1.94	1.68
	Proposed method	**1.74**	**1.59**
V-A3 dataset	Non-ERU	2.5	2.8
	Non-AFM loss	1.87	1.75
	The emotional GAN	2.35	2.68
	MHingeGAN	1.85	1.79
	Proposed method	**1.69**	**1.51**

studies. In particular, the average of errors was investigated in the same way as in Sect. 3.4. The meaning of FID and E-FID is as in Table 1. In the case of FID and E-FID scores, the proposed model showed similar performance to MHingeGAN. However, there were significant differences in the error for the target emotion VA values, and our model recorded nearly 1.5 times more preference values.

3.6 Comparison Using Machine Learning Model

To conduct a quantitative method of the ablation study rather than a qualitative one, we measured the emotion in the resulting images of both models trained from V-A2 and V-A3 dataset using the emotion predicting deep learning model of Kim *et al.* [37]. In the case of using V-A3 dataset, we additionally measured the emotion in resulting images of the Emotional GAN and MHingeGAN. For each method, 100 result images were used. Table 4 lists the valence and arousal error values for each method. The proposed method showed the lowest errors which imply that our method of using ERU and AFM-loss is the most appropriate also about the perspective of the machine learning model.

4   Conclusions

In this work, we designed a machine learning framework with a novel structure and generated emotion-based landscape scene images. To create an image that fits well with a given target emotion, we proposed a new structure called ERU that includes a unique concatenation structure. This structure had a significant and positive effect on emotional conditioning. We also presented a new feature matching loss that could highlight emotion-related features. We demonstrated that this model could generate landscape images that have target emotions. The suggested model had the limitation of generating images that contained artifacts or did not match the target emotion when valence and arousal were so small or so large (see Fig. 7(a)). When people watch natural landscape scenes, they usually

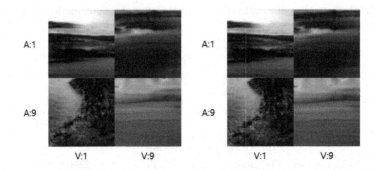

Fig. 7. The limitations of our model. The target emotion was given very large or very small Valence and Arousal values. The arousal changes vertically, with 1 on top and 9 on the bottom. The valence changes horizontally, with 1 on the left and 9 on the right (a) semantic location failure case (b)

do not feel extremely small or large arousal or valence. As a result, there are not enough natural landscape scene images in the data set that incorporates these extreme emotions. Another limitation is the case that the semantic position of the object in the resulting image is wrong, as in the left part of the figure (see the left image in Fig. 7(b)). In the figure, dark seas and gloomy skies were included in the results to represent depressed emotions with low valence and arousal values, with the positions of the sea and sky swapped up and down. In some cases, colors that are not typically seen in natural landscapes appear in the resulting image (see the right image in Fig. 7(b)). These cases appear because the model focuses only on expressing specific emotions and fails to set the correct semantic position or misses natural colors. It is not easy to strike a balance between expressing the target emotion and creating a realistic image.

We studied only natural scenes without objects in this work. In future works, we will be able to study how to create emotion-based images with scenes in which objects and backgrounds perfectly synchronize in terms of the given emotion. In addition to images, we can also apply the method in this work to video domains.

Acknowledgement. This research was supported by the MSIT(Ministry of Science and ICT), Korea, under the ITRC (Information Technology Research Center) support program (IITP-2020-2018-0-01419) supervised by the IITP (Institute for Information and Communications Technology Planning and Evaluation) and the National Research Foundation of Korea (NRF) grant funded by the Korea government (MSIT) (No. NRF-2020R1A2C2014622).

References

1. Yang, J., She, D., Sun, M.: Joint image emotion classification and distribution learning via deep convolutional neural network. IJCA I, 3266–3272 (2017)

2. Shi, C., Pun, C.: Multiscale superpixel-based hyperspectral image classification using recurrent neural networks with stacked autoencoders. IEEE Trans. Multimed. **22**, 487–501 (2019)
3. Lyu, F., Wu, Q., Hu, F., Wu, Q., Tan, M.: Attend and imagine: multi-label image classification with visual attention and recurrent neural networks. IEEE Trans. Multimed. **21**, 1971–1981 (2019)
4. Dong, L., et al.: CUNet: a compact unsupervised network for image classification. IEEE Trans. Multimed. **20**, 2012–2021 (2018)
5. Wu, S., Ji, Q., Wang, S., Wong, H.S., Yu, Z., Xu, Y.: Semi-supervised image classification with self-paced cross-task networks. IEEE Trans. Multimed. **20**, 851–865 (2018)
6. Wang, F., et al.: Residual attention network for image classification. In: Proceedings of the IEEE Conference on Computer Vision and Pattern Recognition, pp. 3156–3164 (2017)
7. Huang, G., Liu, Z., Maaten, L.V.d., Weinberger, K.Q.: Densely connected convolutional networks. In: 2017 IEEE Conference on Computer Vision and Pattern Recognition (CVPR) (2017)
8. Krizhevsky, A., Sutskever, I., Hinton, G.E.: ImageNet classification with deep convolutional neural networks. In: Advances in Neural Information Processing Systems, pp. 1097–1105 (2012)
9. Zoph, B., Vasudevan, V., Shlens, J., Le, Q.V.: Learning transferable architectures for scalable image recognition. In: 2018 IEEE/CVF Conference on Computer Vision and Pattern Recognition (2018)
10. Simonyan, K., Zisserman, A.: Very deep convolutional networks for large-scale image recognition (2014)
11. Fu, K., Zhao, Q., Gu, I.Y.: Refinet: a deep segmentation assisted refinement network for salient object detection. IEEE Trans. Multimed. **21**, 457–469 (2019)
12. Chen, C., Ling, Q.: Adaptive convolution for object detection. IEEE Trans. Multimed. **21**, 3205–3217 (2019)
13. Tang, Y., Wu, X.: Scene text detection using superpixel-based stroke feature transform and deep learning based region classification. IEEE Trans. Multimed. **20**, 2276–2288 (2018)
14. Redmon, J., Farhadi, A.: YOLOv3: an incremental improvement. arXiv preprint arXiv:1804.02767 (2018)
15. He, K., Gkioxari, G., Dollár, P., Girshick, R.: Mask R-CNN. In: Proceedings of the IEEE International Conference on Computer Vision, pp. 2961–2969 (2017)
16. Girshick, R., Donahue, J., Darrell, T., Malik, J.: Rich feature hierarchies for accurate object detection and semantic segmentation. In: 2014 IEEE Conference on Computer Vision and Pattern Recognition (2014)
17. Chen, L., Wu, L., Hu, Z., Wang, M.: Quality-aware unpaired image-to-image translation. IEEE Trans. Multimed. **21**, 2664–2674 (2019)
18. Huang, X., Belongie, S.: Arbitrary style transfer in real-time with adaptive instance normalization. In: Proceedings of the IEEE International Conference on Computer Vision, pp. 1501–1510 (2017)
19. Zhu, J.Y., Park, T., Isola, P., Efros, A.A.: Unpaired image-to-image translation using cycle-consistent adversarial networks. In: Proceedings of the IEEE International Conference on Computer Vision, pp. 2223–2232 (2017)
20. Wang, T.C., Liu, M.Y., Zhu, J.Y., Tao, A., Kautz, J., Catanzaro, B.: High-resolution image synthesis and semantic manipulation with conditional GANs. In: Proceedings of the IEEE Conference on Computer Vision and Pattern Recognition, pp. 8798–8807 (2018)

21. Johnson, J., Alahi, A., Fei-Fei, L.: Perceptual losses for real-time style transfer and super-resolution. In: Leibe, B., Matas, J., Sebe, N., Welling, M. (eds.) ECCV 2016. LNCS, vol. 9906, pp. 694–711. Springer, Cham (2016). https://doi.org/10.1007/978-3-319-46475-6_43

22. Radford, A., Metz, L., Chintala, S.: Unsupervised representation learning with deep convolutional generative adversarial networks (2015)

23. Zhao, J., Mathieu, M., LeCun, Y.: Energy-based generative adversarial network (2016)

24. Arjovsky, M., Chintala, S., Bottou, L.: Wasserstein generative adversarial networks. In: International Conference on Machine Learning, pp. 214–223 (2017)

25. Berthelot, D., Schumm, T., Metz, L.: BEGAN: boundary equilibrium generative adversarial networks (2017)

26. Brock, A., Donahue, J., Simonyan, K.: Large scale GAN training for high fidelity natural image synthesis. arXiv preprint arXiv:1809.11096 (2018)

27. Guo, Y., Chen, Q., Chen, J., Wu, Q., Shi, Q., Tan, M.: Auto-embedding generative adversarial networks for high resolution image synthesis. IEEE Trans. Multimed. **21**, 2726–2737 (2019)

28. Xu, W., Keshmiri, S., Wang, G.R.: Adversarially approximated autoencoder for image generation and manipulation. IEEE Trans. Multimed. **21**, 2387–2396 (2019)

29. Karras, T., Laine, S., Aila, T.: A style-based generator architecture for generative adversarial networks (2018)

30. Johnson, J., Gupta, A., Fei-Fei, L.: Image generation from scene graphs. In: Proceedings of the IEEE Conference on Computer Vision and Pattern Recognition, pp. 1219–1228 (2018)

31. Hong, S., Yang, D., Choi, J., Lee, H.: Inferring semantic layout for hierarchical text-to-image synthesis. In: Proceedings of the IEEE Conference on Computer Vision and Pattern Recognition, pp. 7986–7994 (2018)

32. Tan, F., Feng, S., Ordonez, V.: Text2Scene: generating compositional scenes from textual descriptions. In: Proceedings of the IEEE Conference on Computer Vision and Pattern Recognition, pp. 6710–6719 (2019)

33. Zhao, S., Gao, Y., Jiang, X., Yao, H., Chua, T.S., Sun, X.: Exploring principles-of-art features for image emotion recognition. In: Proceedings of the 22nd ACM International Conference on Multimedia, pp. 47–56. ACM (2014)

34. Ng, H.W., Nguyen, V.D., Vonikakis, V., Winkler, S.: Deep learning for emotion recognition on small datasets using transfer learning. In: Proceedings of the 2015 ACM on International Conference on Multimodal Interaction, pp. 443–449. ACM (2015)

35. Yu, Z., Zhang, C.: Image based static facial expression recognition with multiple deep network learning. In: Proceedings of the 2015 ACM on International Conference on Multimodal Interaction, pp. 435–442. ACM (2015)

36. Wu, B., Jia, J., Yang, Y., Zhao, P., Tang, J., Tian, Q.: Inferring emotional tags from social images with user demographics. IEEE Trans. Multimed. **19**, 1670–1684 (2017)

37. Kim, H.R., Kim, Y.S., Kim, S.J., Lee, I.K.: Building emotional machines: recognizing image emotions through deep neural networks. IEEE Trans. Multimed. **20**, 2980–2992 (2018)

38. Zhou, Y., Shi, B.E.: Photorealistic facial expression synthesis by the conditional difference adversarial autoencoder. In: 2017 Seventh International Conference on Affective Computing and Intelligent Interaction (ACII), pp. 370–376. IEEE (2017)

39. Lu, Y., Tai, Y.W., Tang, C.K.: Attribute-guided face generation using conditional CycleGAN. In: Proceedings of the European Conference on Computer Vision (ECCV), pp. 282–297 (2018)
40. Song, L., Lu, Z., He, R., Sun, Z., Tan, T.: Geometry guided adversarial facial expression synthesis. In: 2018 ACM Multimedia Conference on Multimedia Conference, pp. 627–635. ACM (2018)
41. Ding, H., Sricharan, K., Chellappa, R.: ExprGAN: facial expression editing with controllable expression intensity. In: Thirty-Second AAAI Conference on Artificial Intelligence (2018)
42. Yeh, R., Liu, Z., Goldman, D.B., Agarwala, A.: Semantic facial expression editing using autoencoded flow (2016)
43. Lang, P.J.: Imagery in therapy: an information processing analysis of fear. Behav. Ther. **8**, 862–886 (1977)
44. Zhang, Q., Lee, M.: Emotion development system by interacting with human EEG and natural scene understanding. Cogn. Syst. Res. **14**, 37–49 (2012)
45. Bradley, M.M., Sabatinelli, D., Lang, P.: Emotion and Motivation in the Perceptual Processing of Natural Scenes. MIT Press, Cambridge (2014)
46. Simola, J., Le Fevre, K., Torniainen, J., Baccino, T.: Affective processing in natural scene viewing: valence and arousal interactions in eye-fixation-related potentials. NeuroImage **106**, 21–33 (2015)
47. Zhao, S., Ding, G., Huang, Q., Chua, T.S., Schuller, B.W., Keutzer, K.: Affective image content analysis: a comprehensive survey. IJCA **I**, 5534–5541 (2018)
48. Zhao, S., Yao, H., Gao, Y., Ding, G., Chua, T.S.: Predicting personalized image emotion perceptions in social networks. IEEE Trans. Affect. Comput. **9**, 526–540 (2016)
49. Karacan, L., Akata, Z., Erdem, A., Erdem, E.: Learning to generate images of outdoor scenes from attributes and semantic layouts (2016)
50. Isola, P., Zhu, J.Y., Zhou, T., Efros, A.A.: Image-to-image translation with conditional adversarial networks. In: Proceedings of the IEEE Conference on Computer Vision and Pattern Recognition, pp. 1125–1134 (2017)
51. Park, T., Liu, M.Y., Wang, T.C., Zhu, J.Y.: Semantic image synthesis with spatially-adaptive normalization. In: Proceedings of the IEEE Conference on Computer Vision and Pattern Recognition, pp. 2337–2346 (2019)
52. Osgood, C.E., Suci, G.J., Tannenbaum, P.H.: The Measurement of Meaning. Number 47. University of Illinois press, Champaign (1957)
53. Goodfellow, I., et al.: Generative adversarial nets. In: Advances in Neural Information Processing Systems, pp. 2672–2680 (2014)
54. Karras, T., Aila, T., Laine, S., Lehtinen, J.: Progressive growing of GANs for improved quality, stability, and variation. arXiv preprint arXiv:1710.10196 (2017)
55. Sak, H., Senior, A., Beaufays, F.: Long short-term memory recurrent neural network architectures for large scale acoustic modeling. In: Fifteenth Annual Conference of the International Speech Communication Association (2014)
56. Chung, J., Gulcehre, C., Cho, K., Bengio, Y.: Empirical evaluation of gated recurrent neural networks on sequence modeling (2014)
57. Salimans, T., Goodfellow, I., Zaremba, W., Cheung, V., Radford, A., Chen, X.: Improved techniques for training GANs (2016)
58. Gulrajani, I., Ahmed, F., Arjovsky, M., Dumoulin, V., Courville, A.C.: Improved training of Wasserstein GANs. In: Advances in Neural Information Processing Systems, pp. 5767–5777 (2017)
59. Geisler, W.S., Perry, J.S.: Statistics for optimal point prediction in natural images. J. Vis. **11**, 14 (2011)

60. Xiao, J., Hays, J., Ehinger, K.A., Oliva, A., Torralba, A.: SUN database: large-scale scene recognition from abbey to zoo. In: IEEE Computer Society Conference on Computer Vision and Pattern Recognition, pp. 3485–3492. IEEE (2010)

61. Zhou, B., Lapedriza, A., Khosla, A., Oliva, A., Torralba, A.: Places: a 10 million image database for scene recognition. IEEE Trans. Pattern Anal. Mach. Intell. **40**, 1452–1464 (2017)

62. Xu, B., Wang, N., Chen, T., Li, M.: Empirical evaluation of rectified activations in convolutional network. arXiv preprint arXiv:1505.00853 (2015)

63. Heusel, M., Ramsauer, H., Unterthiner, T., Nessler, B., Hochreiter, S.: GANs trained by a two time-scale update rule converge to a local nash equilibrium. In: Advances in Neural Information Processing Systems, pp. 6626–6637 (2017)

64. Buhrmester, M., Kwang, T., Gosling, S.D.: Amazon's mechanical turk: a new source of inexpensive, yet high-quality, data? Perspect. Psychol. Sci. **6**, 3–5 (2011)

65. David, A.M., Amores, J.: The emotional GAN : priming adversarial generation of art with emotion. In: NIPS 2017 Workshop (2017)

66. Kuperman, V., Estes, Z., Brysbaert, M., Warriner, A.B.: Emotion and language: valence and arousal affect word recognition. J. Exp. Psychol. Gen. **143**, 1065 (2014)

67. Kavalerov, I., Czaja, W., Chellappa, R.: cGANs with multi-hinge loss. arXiv preprint arXiv:1912.04216 (2019)

Feedback Recurrent Autoencoder for Video Compression

Adam Goliński[3], Reza Pourreza[1], Yang Yang[1(✉)], Guillaume Sautière[2], and Taco S. Cohen[2]

[1] Qualcomm AI Research, Qualcomm Technologies, Inc., San Diego, USA
{pourreza,yyangy}@qti.qualcomm.com
[2] Qualcomm AI Research, Qualcomm Technologies Netherlands B.V., Amsterdam, Netherlands
{gsautie,tacos}@qti.qualcomm.com
[3] Department of Engineering Science, University of Oxford, Oxford, England
adamg@robots.ox.ac.uk

Abstract. Recent advances in deep generative modeling have enabled efficient modeling of high dimensional data distributions and opened up a new horizon for solving data compression problems. Specifically, autoencoder based learned image or video compression solutions are emerging as strong competitors to traditional approaches. In this work, We propose a new network architecture, based on common and well studied components, for learned video compression operating in low latency mode. Our method yields competitive MS-SSIM/rate performance on the high-resolution UVG dataset, among both learned video compression approaches and classical video compression methods (H.265 and H.264) in the rate range of interest for streaming applications. Additionally, we provide an analysis of existing approaches through the lens of their underlying probabilistic graphical models. Finally, we point out issues with temporal consistency and color shift observed in empirical evaluation, and suggest directions forward to alleviate those.

1 Introduction

With over 60% of internet traffic consisting of video [1], lossy video compression is a critically important problem, promising reductions in bandwidth, storage, and generally increasing the scalability of the internet. Although the relation between probabilistic modelling and compression has been known since Shannon, video codecs in use today are only to a very small extent based on learning and

---

A. Goliński, R. Pourreza and Y. Yang—Equal Contribution.
Work completed during internship at Qualcomm Technologies Netherlands B.V. Qualcomm AI Research is an initiative of Qualcomm Technologies, Inc.

Electronic supplementary material The online version of this chapter (https://doi.org/10.1007/978-3-030-69538-5_36) contains supplementary material, which is available to authorized users.

© Springer Nature Switzerland AG 2021
H. Ishikawa et al. (Eds.): ACCV 2020, LNCS 12625, pp. 591–607, 2021.
https://doi.org/10.1007/978-3-030-69538-5_36

are not end-to-end optimized for rate-distortion performance on a large and representative video dataset.

The last few years have seen a surge in interest in novel codec designs based on deep learning [2–9], which are trained end-to-end to optimize rate-distortion performance on a large video dataset, and a large number of network designs with various novel, often domain-specific components have been proposed. In this paper we show that a relatively simple design based on standard, well understood and highly optimized components such as residual blocks [10], convolutional recurrent networks [11], optical flow warping and a PixelCNN [12] prior yields competitive rate-distortion performance among the learned methods.

We focus on the online compression setting, where video frames can be compressed and transmitted as soon as they are recorded (in contrast to approaches which require buffering several frames before encoding), which is necessary for applications such as video conferencing and cloud gaming. Additionally, in both applications, the ability to finetune the neural codec to its specific content holds promise to further significantly reduce the required bandwidth [6].

There are two key components to our approach beyond the residual block based encoder and decoder architecture. Firstly, to exploit long range temporal correlations, we follow the approach proposed in Feedback Recurrent AutoEncoder (FRAE) [13], which was shown to be effective for speech compression, by adding a convolutional GRU module in the decoder and feeding back the recurrent state to the encoder. Secondly, we apply a motion estimation network at the encoder side and enforce optical flow learning by using an explicit loss term during the initial stage of the training, which leads to better optical flow output at the decoder side and consequently much better rate-distortion performance. The proposed network architecture is compared with existing learned approaches through the lens of their underlying probabilistic models in Sect. 3.

We compare our method with the state-of-the-art traditional codecs and learned approaches on the UVG 1080p [14] and HEVC [15] video datasets by plotting rate-distortion curves. We show that our method performs competitively on the MS-SSIM [16] distortion metric in the low to high rate regime for the high-resolution data, and particularly in the 0.09-0.13 bits per-pixel (bpp) region, which is of practical interest for video streaming [17].

To summarize, our main contributions are as follows:

1. We develop a simple feedback recurrent video compression architecture based on widely used building blocks (Sect. 2).
2. We study the differences and connections of existing learned video compression methods by detailing the underlying sequential latent variable models (Sect. 3).
3. Our solution achieves competitive rate-distortion performance when compared with other learned video compression approaches as well as traditional codecs under equivalent settings (Sect. 4).

2 Methodology

2.1 Problem Setup

Let us denote the image frames of a video as $\mathbf{x} = \{\mathbf{x}_i\}_{i \in \mathbb{N}}$. Compression of the video is done by an autoencoder that maps $\mathbf{x}$, through an encoder f_{enc}, into compact discrete latent codes $\mathbf{z} = \{\mathbf{z}_i\}_{i \in \mathbb{N}}$. The codes are then used by a decoder f_{dec} to form reconstructions $\widehat{\mathbf{x}} = \{\widehat{\mathbf{x}}_i\}_{i \in \mathbb{N}}$.

We assume the use of an entropy coder together with a probabilistic model on $\mathbf{z}$, denoted as $\mathbb{P}_{\mathbf{Z}}(\cdot)$, to losslessly compress the discrete latents. The ideal codeword length can then be characterized as $R(\mathbf{z}) = -\log \mathbb{P}_{\mathbf{Z}}(\mathbf{z})$ which we refer to as the rate term[1].

Given a distortion metric $D : \mathbf{X} \times \mathbf{X} \to \mathbb{R}$, the lossy compression problem can be formulated as the optimization of the following Lagrangian functional

$$\min_{f_{\text{enc}}, f_{\text{dec}}, \mathbb{P}_{\mathbf{Z}}} \mathcal{L}_{\text{RD}} \triangleq \min_{f_{\text{enc}}, f_{\text{dec}}, \mathbb{P}_{\mathbf{Z}}} \sum_{\mathbf{x}} D(\mathbf{x}, \widehat{\mathbf{x}}) + \beta R(\mathbf{z}), \tag{1}$$

where β is the Lagrange multiplier that controls the balance of rate and distortion. It is known that this objective function is equivalent to the evidence lower bound in β-VAE [19] when the encoder distribution is deterministic or has a fixed entropy. Hence $\mathbb{P}_{\mathbf{Z}}$ is often called the *prior* distribution. We refer the reader to [6,8,20] for more detailed discussion. Throughout this work we use MS-SSIM [16] measured in RGB space as our distortion metric for both training and evaluation.

2.2 Overview of the Proposed Method

In our work, we focus on the problem of *online* compression of video using a *causal* autoencoder, i.e. one that outputs codes and a reconstruction for each frame on the fly without the need to access future context. In classic video codec terms, we are interested in the *low delay P (LDP)* setting where only I-frames[2] (Intra-coded; independent of other frames) and P-frames (Predictive inter-coded; using previously reconstructed past but not future frames) are used. We do not make use of B-frames (Bidirectionally interpolated frames).

The full video sequence is broken down into *groups of pictures* (GoP) $\mathbf{x} = \{\mathbf{x}_0, \mathbf{x}_1, \dots, \mathbf{x}_{N-1}\}$ that starts with an I-frame and is followed by $N-1$ P-frames. We use a separate encoder, decoder and prior for the I-frames and P-frames. The rate term is then decomposed as

$$R(\mathbf{z}) = -\log \mathbb{P}_{\mathbf{Z}}^{\text{I}}(\mathbf{z}_0) - \log \mathbb{P}_{\mathbf{Z}}^{\text{P}}(\mathbf{z}_1, \dots, \mathbf{z}_{N-1} | \mathbf{z}_0), \tag{2}$$

where a superscript is used to indicate frame type.

---

[1] For practical entropy coder, there is a constant overhead per block/stream, which is negligible with a large number of bits per stream and thus can be ignored. For example, for adaptive arithmetic coding (AAC), there is up to 2-bit inefficiency [18].

[2] We refer the reader to [21,22] and Sect. 2 of [4] for a good overview of frame structures in classic codecs.

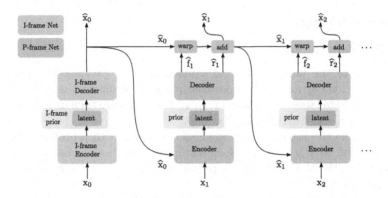

Fig. 1. Base architecture of our video compression network. I-frame $\mathbf{x}_0$ is compressed using a stand-alone image compression autoencoder. The subsequent P-frames are compressed with previous reconstructed frame as input and decoded with optical flow based motion compensation plus residual.

2.3   Network Architecture

I-frame compression is equivalent to image compression and there are already many schemes available [20,23–26]. Here we applied the encoder and decoder design of [25] for I-frame compression. Subsequently, we only focus on the design of the P-frame compression network and discuss how previously transmitted information can be best utilized to reduce the amount of information needed to reconstruct subsequent frames.

Baseline Architecture

One straightforward way to utilize history information is for the autoencoder to transmit only a motion vector (e.g., block based or a dense optical field) and a residual while using the previously decoded frame(s) as a reference. At the decoder side, decoded motion vector (in our case optical flow) is used to warp previously decoded frame(s) using bilinear interpolation [27] (referred to later as `warp` function), which is then refined by the decoded residual. This framework serves as the basic building block for many conventional codecs such as AVC and HEVC. One instantiation of such framework built with autoencoders is illustrated in Fig. 1. Here an autoencoder based image compression network, termed I-frame network, is used to compress and reconstruct the I-frame $\mathbf{x}_0$ independent of any other frames. Subsequent P-frames $\mathbf{x}_t$ are processed with a separate autoencoder, termed P-frame network, that takes both the current input frame and the previous reconstructed frame as encoder inputs and produces the optical flow tensor $\widehat{\mathbf{f}}_t$ and the residual $\widehat{\mathbf{r}}_t$ as decoder output. The architecture of our P-frame network's encoder and decoder is the same as the I-frame. Two separate prior models are used for the entropy coding of the discrete latents in I-frame and P-frame networks. The frame is eventually reconstructed as $\widehat{\mathbf{x}}_t \triangleq \mathtt{warp}(\widehat{\mathbf{f}}_t, \widehat{\mathbf{x}}_{t-1}) + \widehat{\mathbf{r}}_t$.

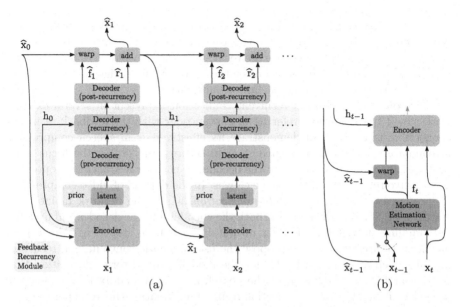

Fig. 2. (a) Video compression network with feedback recurrent module. Detailed network architecture for the encoder and decoder is described in Appendix A. (b) Encoder equipped with MENet, an explicit optical flow estimation module. The switch between $\widehat{x}_{t-1}$ and x_{t-1} is described at the end of Sect. 2.

For the P-frame network, the latent at each time t contains information about $(\widehat{f}_t, \widehat{r}_t)$. One source of inefficiency, then, is that the current time step's $(\widehat{f}_t, \widehat{r}_t)$ may still exhibit temporal correlation with the past values $(\widehat{f}_{<t}, \widehat{r}_{<t})$, which is not exploited. This issue remains even if we consider multiple frames as references.

To explicitly equip the network with the capability to utilize the redundancy w.r.t. $(\widehat{f}_{t-1}, \widehat{r}_{t-1})$, we would need to expose $(\widehat{f}_{t-1}, \widehat{r}_{t-1})$ as another input, besides x_{t-1}, to both the encoder and the decoder for the operation at time step t. In this case the latents would only need to carry information regarding the incremental difference between the flow field and residual between two consecutive steps, i.e. $(\widehat{f}_{t-1}, \widehat{r}_{t-1})$ and $(\widehat{f}_t, \widehat{r}_t)$, which would lead to a higher degree of compression. We could follow the same principle to utilize even higher order redundancies but it inevitably leads to a more complicated architecture design.

Feedback Recurrent Module

As we are trying to utilize higher order redundancy, we need to provide both the encoder and the decoder with a more suitable decoder history context. This observation motivates the use of a *recurrent* neural network that is meant to accumulate and summarize relevant information received previously by the decoder, and a decoder-to-encoder *feedback* connection that makes the recurrent state available at the encoder [13] – see Fig. 2(a). We refer to the added component as the *feedback recurrent module*.

This module can be viewed as a *non-linear predictive coding* scheme, where the decoder predicts the next frame based on the current latent as well as a summary of past latents. Because the recurrent state is available to both encoder and decoder, the encoder is aware of the state of knowledge of the decoder, enabling it to send only complementary information.

The concept of feedback recurrent connection is present in several existing works: In [13], the authors refer to an autoencoder with the feedback recurrent connection as FRAE and demonstrate its effectiveness in speech compression in comparison to different recurrent architectures. In [28,29], the focus is on progressive coding of images, and the decoder to encoder feedback is adopted for an iterative refinement of the image canvas. In the domain of video compression, [5] proposes the concept of *state-propagation*, where the network maintains a state tensor S_t that is available at both the encoder and the decoder and updated by summing it with the decoder output in each time step (Fig. 5 in [5]). In our network architecture, we propose the use of generic convolutional recurrent modules such as Conv-GRU [11] for the modeling of history information that is relevant for the prediction of the next frame. In Appendix E, we show the necessity of such feedback connection from an information theoretic perspective.

Latent Quantization and Prior Model

Given that the encoder needs to output discrete values, the quantization method applied needs to allow gradient based optimization. Two popular approaches are: (1) Define a learnable codebook, and use nearest neighbor quantization in the forward pass and a differentiable softmax in the backward pass [6,25], or (2) Add uniform noise to the continuous valued encoder output during training and use hard quantization at evaluation [8,23,24]. For the second approach, the prior distribution is often characterized by a learnable monotonic CDF function f, where the probability mass of a single latent value z is evaluated as $f(z + 1/2) - f(z - 1/2)$. In this work we adopt the first approach.

As illustrated in Fig. 2(a), a time-independent prior model is used. In other words, there is no conditioning of the prior model on the latents from previous time steps, and $\mathbb{P}_{\mathbf{Z}}^P(\mathbf{z}_1, \ldots, \mathbf{z}_{N-1}|\mathbf{z}_0)$ in Eq. (2) is factorized as $\prod_{i=1}^{N-1} \mathbb{P}_{\mathbf{Z}}^P(\mathbf{z}_i)$. In Sect. 3 we show that such factorization does not limit the capability of our model to capture any empirical data distribution.

A gated PixelCNN [12] is used to model $\mathbb{P}_{\mathbf{Z}}^P$, with the detailed structure of the model built based on the description in Fig. 10 of [6]. The prior model for the I-frame network $\mathbb{P}_{\mathbf{Z}}^I$ is a separate network with the same architecture.

Explicit Optical Flow Estimation Module

In the architecture shown in Fig. 2(a), the optical flow estimate tensor $\widehat{\mathbf{f}}_t$ is produced explicitly at the end of the decoder. When trained with the loss function $\mathcal{L}_{\mathrm{RD}}$ in Eq. (1), the learning of the optical flow estimation is only incentivized implicitly via how much that mechanism helps with the rate-effective reconstruction of the original frames. In this setting we empirically found the decoder was almost solely relying on the residuals $\widehat{\mathbf{r}}_t$ to form the frame reconstructions.

This observation is consistent with the observations of other works [2,5]. This problem is usually addressed by using pre-training or more explicit supervision for the optical flow estimation task. We encourage reliance on both optical flow and residuals and facilitate optical flow estimation by (i) equipping the encoder with a U-Net [30] sub-network called *Motion Estimation Network* (MENet), and (ii) introducing additional loss terms to explicitly encourage optical flow estimation.

MENet estimates the optical flow $\mathbf{f}_t$ between the current input frame $\mathbf{x}_t$ and the previously reconstructed frame $\widehat{\mathbf{x}}_{t-1}$. Without MENet, the encoder is provided with $\mathbf{x}_t$ and $\widehat{\mathbf{x}}_{t-1}$, and is supposed to estimate the optical flow and the residuals and encode them, all in a single network. However, when attached to the encoder, MENet provides the encoder directly with the estimated flow $\mathbf{f}_t$ and the previous reconstruction warped by the estimated flow $\texttt{warp}(\widehat{\mathbf{x}}_{t-1}, \mathbf{f}_t)$. In this scenario, all the encoder capacity is dedicated to the encoding task. A schematic view of this explicit architecture is shown in Fig. 2(b) and the implementation details are available in Appendix A.

When MENet is integrated with the architecture in Fig. 2(a), optical flow is originally estimated using MENet denoted as $\mathbf{f}_t$ and later reconstructed in the decoder denoted as $\widehat{\mathbf{f}}_t$. In order to alleviate the problem with optical flow learning using rate-distortion loss only, we incentivize the learning of $\mathbf{f}_t$ and $\widehat{\mathbf{f}}_t$ via two additional dedicated loss terms,

$$\mathcal{L}_{\text{fe}} = D(\texttt{warp}(\widehat{\mathbf{x}}_{t-1}, \mathbf{f}_t), \mathbf{x}_t), \mathcal{L}_{\text{fd}} = D(\texttt{warp}(\widehat{\mathbf{x}}_{t-1}, \widehat{\mathbf{f}}_t), \mathbf{x}_t).$$

Hence the total loss we start the training with is $\mathcal{L} = \mathcal{L}_{\text{RD}} + \mathcal{L}_{\text{fe}} + \mathcal{L}_{\text{fd}}$ where $\mathcal{L}_{\text{RD}}$ is the loss function as per Eq. (1). We found that it is sufficient if we apply the losses $\mathcal{L}_{\text{fe}}$ and $\mathcal{L}_{\text{fd}}$ only at the beginning of training, for the first few thousand iterations, and then we revert to using just $\mathcal{L} = \mathcal{L}_{\text{RD}}$ and let the estimated flow be adapted to the main task, which has been shown to improve the results across variety of tasks utilizing optical flow estimation [31].

The loss terms $\mathcal{L}_{\text{fe}}$ and $\mathcal{L}_{\text{fd}}$ are defined as the distortion between $\mathbf{x}_t$ and the warped version of $\widehat{\mathbf{x}}_{t-1}$. However, early in the training, $\widehat{\mathbf{x}}_{t-1}$ is inaccurate and as a result, such distortion is not a good choice of a learning signal for the MENet or the autoencoder. To alleviate this problem, early in the training we use $\mathbf{x}_{t-1}$ instead of $\widehat{\mathbf{x}}_{t-1}$ in both $\mathcal{L}_{\text{fe}}$ and $\mathcal{L}_{\text{fd}}$. This transition is depicted in Fig. 2(b) with a switch. It is worth to mention that the tensor fed into the encoder is always a warped previous reconstruction $\texttt{warp}(\widehat{\mathbf{x}}_{t-1}, \mathbf{f}_t)$, never a warped previous ground truth frame $\texttt{warp}(\mathbf{x}_{t-1}, \mathbf{f}_t)$.

3 Graphical Model Analysis

Recent success of autoencoder based learned image compression [9,20,23–26] (see [32] for an overview) has demonstrated neural networks' capability in modeling spatial correlations from data and the effectiveness of end-to-end joint rate-distortion training. It has motivated the use of autoencoder based solution to

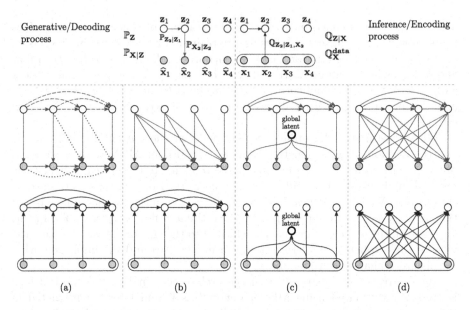

Fig. 3. Different combinations of sequential latent variable models and inference models proposed in the literature. (a) with the solid lines only is used in Lu *et al.* [2]. (a) with both solid and dashed lines is used in Liu *et al.* [7]. (a) with the solid and dotted lines is used in M-LVC (presented is a model for a buffer size of 2 past frames) [9]. (b) is used in both Rippel *et al.* [5] and our approach. (c) is used in Han *et al.* [8]. (d) is used in Habibian *et al.* [6]. The blue box around nodes $\mathbf{x}_{1:4}$ means that they all come from a single joint distribution $\mathbb{Q}_{\mathbf{X}}^{\text{data}}(\mathbf{x}_{1:4})$ and that we make no assumptions on the conditional structure of that distribution. See Appendix F for detailed reasoning about these graphical models. (Color figure online)

further capture the temporal correlation in the application of video compression and there has since been many designs for learned video compression algorithms [2,5–8,13]. These designs differ in many detailed aspects: the technique used for latent quantization; the specific instantiation of encoder and decoder architecture; the use of atypical, often domain-specific operations beyond convolution such as Generalized Divisive Normalization (GDN) [23,33] or Non-Local Attention Module (NLAM) [34]. Here we leave out the comparison of those aspects and focus on one key design element: the graphical model structure of the underlying sequential latent variable model [35].

As we have briefly discussed in Sect. 2.1, the rate-distortion training objective has strong connections to amortized variational inference. In the special case of $\beta = 1$, the optimization problem is equivalent to the minimization of $D_{\text{KL}}\left(\mathbb{Q}_{\mathbf{X}}^{\text{data}}\mathbb{Q}_{\mathbf{Z}|\mathbf{X}}||\mathbb{P}_{\mathbf{Z}}\mathbb{P}_{\mathbf{X}|\mathbf{Z}}\right)$ [36] where $\mathbb{P}_{\mathbf{Z}}\mathbb{P}_{\mathbf{X}|\mathbf{Z}}$ describes a sequential generative process and $\mathbb{Q}_{\mathbf{X}}^{\text{data}}\mathbb{Q}_{\mathbf{Z}|\mathbf{X}}$ can be viewed as a sequential inference process. $\mathbb{P}_{\mathbf{X}|\mathbf{Z}}$ denotes the decoder distribution induced by our distortion metric (see Sect. 4.2 of [6]), $\mathbb{Q}_{\mathbf{X}}^{\text{data}}$ denotes the empirical distribution of the training data, and $\mathbb{Q}_{\mathbf{Z}|\mathbf{X}}$ denotes the encoder distribution induced on the latents, in our case a Dirac-δ

distribution because of the deterministic mapping from the encoder inputs to the value of the latents.

To favor the minimization of the KL divergence, we want to design $\mathbb{P}_Z$, $\mathbb{P}_{X|Z}$, $\mathbb{Q}_{Z|X}$ to be flexible enough so that (i) the marginalized data distribution $\mathbb{P}_X \triangleq \sum_Z \mathbb{P}_Z \mathbb{P}_{X|Z}$ is able to capture complex temporal dependencies in the data, and (ii) the inference process $\mathbb{Q}_{Z|X}$ encodes all the dependencies embedded in $\mathbb{P}_Z \mathbb{P}_{X|Z}$ [37]. In Fig. 3 we highlight four combinations of sequential latent variable models and the inference models proposed in literature.

Figure 3(a) without the dashed line describes the scheme proposed in Lu *et al.* [2] (and the low latency mode of HEVC/AVC) where prior model is fully factorized over time and each decoded frame is a function of the previous decoded frame $\widehat{\mathbf{x}}_{t-1}$ and the current latent code $\mathbf{z}_t$. There are two major limitations of this approach: firstly, the marginalized sequential distribution $\mathbb{P}_X$ is confined to follow Markov property $\mathbb{P}_X(\mathbf{x}_{1:T}) = \mathbb{P}_{X_1}(\mathbf{x}_1) \prod_{t=2}^{T} \mathbb{P}_{X_t|X_{t-1}}(\mathbf{x}_t|\mathbf{x}_{t-1})$; secondly, it assumes that the differences in subsequent frames (e.g., optical flow and residual) are independent across time steps. To overcome these two limitations, Liu *et al.* [7] propose an auto-regressive prior model through the use of ConvLSTM over time, which corresponds to Fig. 3(a) including dashed lines. In this case, the marginal $\mathbb{P}_X(\mathbf{x}_{1:T})$ is fully flexible in the sense that it does not make any conditional independence assumptions between $\mathbf{x}_{1:T}$, see Appendix F for details. With a similar goal in mind, in a work concurrent to ours, Lin *et al.* [9] propose M-LVC which utilizes temporal correlations between consecutive frames' optical flows by explicitly predicting the flow of the currently coded frame using previous flows. In contrast our approach aims to extract the same optical flow (as well as higher order) redundancy implicitly via a learned recurrent state.

Figure 3(b) describes another way to construct a fully flexible marginalized sequential data distribution, by having the decoded frame depend on all previously transmitted latent codes. Both Rippel *et al.* [5] and our approach fall under this category by introducing a recurrent state in the decoder which summarizes information from the previously transmitted latent codes and processed features. Rippel *et al.* [5] use a multi-scale state with a complex state propagation mechanism, whereas we use a convolutional recurrency module (ConvGRU) [11]. In this case, $\mathbb{P}_X(\mathbf{x}_{1:T})$ is also fully flexible, details in Appendix F.

The latent variable models in Fig. 3(c) and (d) break the causality constraint, i.e. the encoding of a GoP can only start when all of its frames are available. In (c), a global latent is used to capture time-invariant features, which is adopted in Han *et al.* [8]. In (d), the graphical model is fully connected between each frame and latent across different time steps, which described the scheme applied in Habibian *et al.* [6].

One advantage of our approach (as well as Rippel *et al.* [5]), which corresponds to Fig. 3(b), is that the prior model can be fully factorized across time, $\mathbb{P}_Z(\mathbf{z}_{1:T}) = \prod_{t=1}^{T} \mathbb{P}_Z(\mathbf{z}_t)$, without compromising the flexibility of the marginal distribution $\mathbb{P}_X(\mathbf{x}_{1:T})$. Factorized prior allows *parallel* entropy decoding of the latent codes across time steps (but potentially still *sequential* across dimensions of $\mathbf{z}_t$ within each time step). On the inference side, in Appendix E we show that any connection from $x_{<t}$ to z_t, which could be modeled by adding a recurrent component on the encoder side, is not necessary.

4   Experiments

4.1   Training Setup

Here we provide the key information about the training setup, while the comprehensive description of the details of the architecture, training and datasets used (and how they were processed) are in Appendix A. Our training dataset was based on Kinetics400 [38], and we evaluate on UVG 1080p [14] and HEVC Classes BCDE [15]. The distortion metric used was $1-$MS-SSIM [16]. The GoP size of 8 was used during training.

4.2   Comparison with Other Methods

Comparison with Learning-Based Methods. In Fig. 4(a), we compare the performance of our solution with several learned approaches on UVG 1080p dataset in terms of MS-SSIM versus bitrate where MS-SSIM was first averaged per video and then averaged across different videos. The figures for the HEVC Classes BCDE datasets and comparison using PSNR metric are in Appendix H. When comparing using MS-SSIM metric, on UVG and HEVC-E, our method outperforms all the compared ones in MS-SSIM across the range of bitrates between around 0.05 bpp to around 0.13 bpp. For 1080p resolution this is the range of bitrates of interest for practitioners, e.g., Netflix uses the range of about $0.09-0.13$ bpp for their 1080p resolution video streaming [17]. On HEVC-BD, our method is outperformed by M-LVC and DVC, whereas on HEVC-C our method outperforms other methods for bitrate below <0.13 bpp. When comparing using PSNR metric, our method is outperformed by most other methods. This effect is expected since our method was not trained using MSE distortion metric, however we note that when compared on PSNR metric the performance drop of our method is larger than for the DVC(MSSSIM) model.

DVC [2,3], Liu *et al.* [7] and M-LVC [9] are all causal solutions, and they are trained and evaluated with GoP size of 12(UVG)/10(HEVC), 12, 16, respectively. Habibian *et al.* and Wu *et al.* are non-causal solutions and their results are reported based on GoP sizes of 8 and 12, respectively. Our results are evaluated at GoP of 8, same as in training.

We omit comparisons to Han *et al.* [8] because they provide results only for low resolution videos, and to Rippel *et al.* [5] because we lack the licensing rights to use all the Xiph dataset videos [39] they evaluate their method on.

Comparison with Traditional Video Codecs. We compared our method with the most popular standard codecs i.e. H.265 [22] and H.264 [40] on UVG 1080p dataset. The results are generated with three different sets of settings (more details are provided in Appendix C):

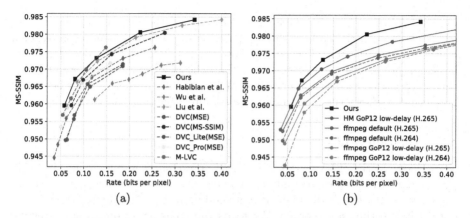

Fig. 4. Results on UVG dataset. (a) Comparison to the state-of-the-art learned methods. The DVC [3] results are presented for both models trained with MSE and MSSSIM distortion metrics. (b) Comparison with classic codecs.

- `ffmpeg` [41] implementation of H.264 and H.265 in low latency mode with GoP size of 12.
- `ffmpeg` [41] implementation of H.264 and H.265 in default mode.
- `HM` [42] implementation of H.265 in low latency mode with GoP size of 12.

The low latency mode was enforced to H.264 and H.265 to make the problem settings the same as our causal model. GoP size 12 on the other hand, although different from our GoP size 8, was consistent with the settings reported in other papers and provided H.264 and H.265 an advantage as they perform better with larger GoP sizes.

The comparisons are shown in Fig. 4(b) in terms of MS-SSIM versus bitrate where MS-SSIM was calculated in RGB domain. As can be seen from this figure, our model outperforms the `HM` implementation of H.265 and the `ffmpeg` implementation of H.265 and H.264 in both low latency and default settings, at bitrates above 0.09 bpp which, again, is the bpp range of interest for 1080p resolution videos. We note there are also computational aspects one should consider when comparing to these traditional codecs, see a discussion in Appendix I.

Qualitative Comparison. In Fig. 6 we compare the visual quality of our lowest rate model with `ffmpeg` implementation of H.265 at in low latency mode a similar rate. We can see that our result is free from the blocking artifact usually present in H.265 at low bitrate – see around the edge of fingers – and preserves more detailed texture – see structures of hand veins and strips on the coat. In Appendix D, we provide more examples with detailed error and bitrate maps.

As noted in Sect. 2.3, the dedicated optical flow enforcement loss terms were removed at a certain point and the training continued using $\mathcal{L}_{\mathrm{RD}}$ only. As a result, our network learned a form of optical flow that contributed maximally to $\mathcal{L}_{\mathrm{RD}}$ and did not necessarily follow the ground truth optical flow (if such were available). Figure 7 compares an instance of the optical flow learned in our network with the corresponding optical flow generated using a pre-trained FlowNet2 network [43]. The optical flow reconstructed by the decoder $\hat{f}$ has larger proportion of values set to zero than the flow estimated by FlowNet2 – this is consistent with the observations by Lu *et al.* [2] in their Fig. 7 where they argue that it allows the flow to be more compressible.

4.3 Ablation Study

To understand the effectiveness of different components in our design, in Fig. 5 we compare the performance after removing (a) decoder to encoder recurrent feedback, or (b) the feedback recurrent module in Fig. 2(a), or (c) the explicit optical flow estimation module. We focus the comparison on low rate regime where the difference is more noticeable.

Empirically we find the explicit optical flow estimation component to be quite essential – without it the optical flow output from the decoder has very small magnitude and is barely useful, resulting in consistent loss of at least 0.002 in MS-SSIM score for rate below 0.16 bpp. In comparison, the loss in performance after removing either the decoder to encoder feedback or the recurrent connection all together is minor and only show up at very low rate region below 0.1 bpp.

Similar comparisons have been done in existing literature. Rippel *et al.* [5] report large drop in performance when removing the learned state in their model (Fig. 9 of [5]; about 0.005 drop in MS-SSIM at bpp of 0.05), while Liu *et al.* [7], which utilizes recurrent prior to exploit longer range temporal redundancies, reports relatively smaller degradation after removing their recurrent module (about 0.002 drop in MS-SSIM in Fig. 9 of [7]).

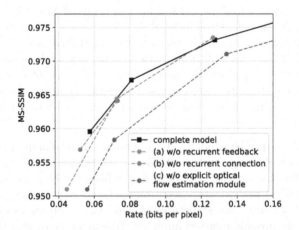

Fig. 5. Ablation study on UVG dataset. All models were evaluated at GoP of 8. Model (a) is obtained by removing the decoder to encoder feedback connection in Fig. 2(a). Model (b) removes the the feedback recurrent module. Model (c) removes the explicit optical flow estimation module in Fig. 2(b).

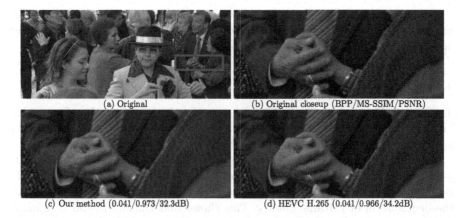

(a) Original

(b) Original closeup (BPP/MS-SSIM/PSNR)

(c) Our method (0.041/0.973/32.3dB)

(d) HEVC H.265 (0.041/0.966/34.2dB)

Fig. 6. An illustration of qualitative characteristics of our architecture versus H.265 (`ffmpeg`) at a comparable bitrate. (a) and (b) are the original frame and its closeup, (c) and (d) are the closeup on the reconstructed frames from our method and H.265. To make the comparison fair, we used HEVC with fixed GoP setting (`min-keyint=8:scenecut=0`) at a similar rate, so both methods are at equal bpp and show the 4th P-frame of a GoP of 8. Frame 229 of Tango video from Netflix Tango in Netflix El Fuente; see Appendix B for license information.

Fig. 7. An example of the estimated optical flow, left to right: two consecutive frames used for estimation, FlowNet2 results, our decoder output $\widehat{f}$. Note that the flow produced by our model is decoded from a compressed latent, and is trained to maximize total compression performance rather than warping accuracy. See Appendix B for license information.

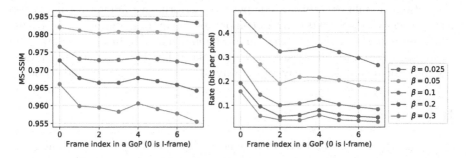

Fig. 8. Average MS-SSIM and rate as a function of frame-index in a GoP of 8.

We suspect that the lack of gain we observe from the feedback recurrent module is due to both insufficient recurrent module capacity and receptive field, and plan to investigate further as one of our future studies.

4.4   Empirical Observations

Temporal Consistency. We found, upon visual inspection, that for our low bitrate models, the decoded video displays a minor yet noticeable flickering artifact occurring at the GoP boundary, which we attribute to two factors.

Firstly, as shown in Fig. 8, there is a gradual degradation of P-frame quality as it moves further away from the I-frame. It is also apparent from Fig. 8 that the rate allocation tends to decline as P-frame network unrolls, which compounds the degradation of P-frame quality. This shows that the end-to-end training of frame-averaged rate-distortion loss does not favor temporal consistency of frame quality, which makes it difficult to apply the model with larger GoP sizes and motivates the use of temporal-consistency related losses [44,45]. For a figure investigating generalization of the model trained with GoP of 8 to evaluation with a GoP of 10, see Appendix J.

Second part of the problem is due to the nature of the MS-SSIM metric and hence is not reflected in Fig. 8. This aspect is described in the following section.

Color Shift. Another empirical observation is that the MS-SSIM metric seems to be partially invariant to uniform color shift in flat regions and due to that the low bitrate models we have trained are prone to exhibit slight color shift, similar to what has been reported in [46]. This color change is sometimes noticeable during I-frame to P-frame transitioning and contributes to the flickering artifact. One item for future study is to find suitable metrics or combination of metrics that captures both texture similarity and color fidelity. Details in Appendix G.

5   Conclusion

In this paper, we proposed a new autoencoder based learned lossy video compression solution featuring a feedback recurrent module and an explicit optical flow estimation module. It achieves competitive performance among learned video compression methods and delivers comparable or better rate-distortion results when compared with classic codecs in low latency mode. In future work, we plan to improve its temporal consistency, solve the color fidelity issue, and reduce computational complexity, paving the way to a practical learned video codec.

References

1. Sandvine: 2019 Global Internet Phenomena Report. https://www.ncta.com/whats-new/report-where-does-the-majority-of-internet-traffic-come (2019) Accessed 28 Feb 2020

2. Lu, G., Ouyang, W., Xu, D., Zhang, X., Cai, C., Gao, Z.: DVC: an end-to-end deep video compression framework. In: Proceedings of the IEEE Conference on Computer Vision and Pattern Recognition (2019)
3. Lu, G., Zhang, X., Ouyang, W., Chen, L., Gao, Z., Xu, D.: An end-to-end learning framework for video compression. IEEE Transactions on Pattern Analysis and Machine Intelligence (2020)
4. Wu, C.Y., Singhal, N., Krähenbühl, P.: Video compression through image interpolation. In: Proceedings of the European Conference on Computer Vision (2018)
5. Rippel, O., Nair, S., Lew, C., Branson, S., Anderson, A.G., Bourdev, L.: Learned video compression. In: Proceedings of the International Conference on Computer Vision (2019)
6. Habibian, A., van Rozendaal, T., Tomczak, J.M., Cohen, T.S.: Video compression with rate-distortion autoencoders. In: Proceedings of the International Conference on Computer Vision (2019)
7. Liu, H., shen, H., Huang, L., Lu, M., Chen, T., Ma, Z.: Learned video compression via joint spatial-temporal correlation exploration. In: Proceedings of the national conference on Artificial Intelligence (2020)
8. Han, J., Lombardo, S., Schroers, C., Mandt, S.: Deep probabilistic video compression. In: Advances in Neural Information Processing Systems (2019)
9. Lin, J., Liu, D., Li, H., Wu, F.: M-lvc: multiple frames prediction for learned video compression. In: Proceedings of the IEEE Conference on Computer Vision and Pattern Recognition (2020)
10. He, K., Zhang, X., Ren, S., Sun, J.: Deep residual learning for image recognition. In: Proceedings of the IEEE Conference on Computer Vision and Pattern Recognition (2016)
11. Shi, X., Chen, Z., Wang, H., Yeung, D., Wong, W., Woo, W.: Convolutional LSTM network: a machine learning approach for precipitation nowcasting. In: Advances in Neural Information Processing Systems (2015)
12. van den Oord, A., Kalchbrenner, N., Espeholt, L., Kavukcuoglu, K., Vinyals, O., Graves, A.: Conditional image generation with PixelCNN decoders. In: Advances in Neural Information Processing Systems (2016)
13. Yang, Y., Sautiére, G., Ryu, J.J., Cohen, T.S.: Feedback Recurrent AutoEncoder. In: IEEE International Conference on Acoustics, Speech and Signal Processing (2019)
14. Mercat, A., Viitanen, M., Vanne, J.: Uvg dataset: 50/120fps 4k sequences for video codec analysis and development. In: Proceedings of the 11th ACM Multimedia Systems Conference, MMSys 2020, New York, Association for Computing Machinery, pp. 297–302 (2020)
15. Bossen, F.: Common test conditions and software reference configurations. JCTVC-F900 (2011)
16. Wang, Z., Bovik, A.C., Sheikh, H.R., Simoncelli, E.P., et al.: Image quality assessment: from error visibility to structural similarity. IEEE Trans. Image Process. **13**, 600–612 (2004)
17. Summerson, C.: How much data does Netflix use? https://www.howtogeek.com/338983/how-much-data-does-netflix-use/ (2018) Accessed 28 Feb 2020
18. Pearlman, W.A., Said, A.: Digital Signal Compression: Principles and Practice. Cambridge University Press, Cambridge (2011)
19. Higgins, I., et al.: beta-VAE: learning basic visual concepts with a constrained variational framework. In: International Conference on Learning Representations (2017)

20. Theis, L., Shi, W., Cunningham, A., Huszár, F.: Lossy image compression with compressive autoencoders. In: International Conference on Learning Representations (2017)
21. Moreira, L.: Digital video introduction. https://github.com/leandromoreira/digital_video_introduction/blob/master/README.md#frame-types (2017) Accessed 02 Mar 2020
22. Sullivan, G.J., Ohm, J.R., Han, W.J., Wiegand, T.: Overview of the high efficiency video coding (HEVC) standard. IEEE Trans. Circuits Syst. Video Technol. **22**, 1649–1668 (2012)
23. Ballé, J., Laparra, V., Simoncelli, E.P.: End-to-end optimized image compression. In: International Conference on Learning Representations (2017)
24. Ballé, J., Minnen, D., Singh, S., Hwang, S.J., Johnston, N.: Variational image compression with a scale hyperprior. In: International Conference on Learning Representations (2018)
25. Mentzer, F., Agustsson, E., Tschannen, M., Timofte, R., Van Gool, L.: Conditional probability models for deep image compression. In: Proceedings of the IEEE Conference on Computer Vision and Pattern Recognition (2018)
26. Rippel, O., Bourdev, L.: Real-time adaptive image compression. In: Proceedings of the International Conference on Machine Learning (2017)
27. Jaderberg, M., Simonyan, K., Zisserman, A., Kavukcuoglu, K.: Spatial Transformer Networks. In: Advances in Neural Information Processing Systems (2015)
28. Gregor, K., Danihelka, I., Graves, A., Rezende, D.J., Wierstra, D.: DRAW: a recurrent neural network for image generation. In: Proceedings of the International Conference on Machine Learning (2015)
29. Gregor, K., Besse, F., Rezende, D.J., Danihelka, I., Wierstra, D.: Towards conceptual compression. In: Advances in Neural Information Processing Systems (2016)
30. Ronneberger, O., Fischer, P., Brox, T.: U-Net: convolutional networks for biomedical image segmentation. In: Medical Image Computing and Computer-Assisted Intervention (2015)
31. Xue, T., Chen, B., Wu, J., Wei, D., Freeman, W.T.: Video enhancement with task-oriented flow. Int. J. Comput. Vis. **127**, 1106–1125 (2019)
32. Hu, Y., Yang, W., Ma, Z., Liu, J.: Learning end-to-end lossy image compression: a benchmark. arXiv:2002.03711 (2020)
33. Ballé, J., Laparra, V., Simoncelli, E.P.: Density modeling of images using a generalized normalization transformation. In: International Conference on Learning Representations (2016)
34. Liu, H., et al.: Non-local Attention Optimized Deep Image Compression. arXiv:1904.09757 (2019)
35. Koller, D., Friedman, N.: Probabilistic Graphical Models: Principles and Techniques. MIT Press, Cambridge (2009)
36. Alemi, A.A., Poole, B., Fischer, I., Dillon, J.V., Saurous, R.A., Murphy, K.: Fixing a Broken ELBO. In: Proceedings of the International Conference on Machine Learning (2018)
37. Webb, S., et al.: Faithful Inversion of Generative Models for Effective Amortized Inference. In: Advances in Neural Information Processing Systems (2018)
38. Kay, W., et al.: The Kinetics Human Action Video Dataset. arxiv:1705.06950 (2017)
39. Xiph.org: Xiph.org video test media [derf's collection]. https://media.xiph.org/video/derf/ (2004) Accessed: 21 Feb 2020

40. Wiegand, T., Sullivan, G.J., Bjontegaard, G., Luthra, A.: Overview of the H.264/AVC video coding standard. IEEE Trans. Circuits Syst. Video Technol. **13**, 560–576 (2003)
41. Tomar, S.: Converting video formats with ffmpeg. Linux J. **2006**, 10 (2006)
42. HM developers: High Efficiency Video Coding (HEVC). https://hevc.hhi. fraunhofer.de/ (2012) Accessed 21 Feb 2020
43. Ilg, E., Mayer, N., Saikia, T., Keuper, M., Dosovitskiy, A., Brox, T.: FlowNet 2.0: evolution of optical flow estimation with deep networks. In: Proceedings of the IEEE Conference on Computer Vision and Pattern Recognition (2017)
44. Gao, C., Gu, D., Zhang, F., Yu, Y.: ReCoNet: real-time coherent video style transfer network. In: Proceedings of the Asian Conference on Computer Vision (2018)
45. Lai, W.S., Huang, J.B., Wang, O., Shechtman, E., Yumer, E., Yang, M.H.: Learning blind video temporal consistency. In: Proceedings of the European Conference on Computer Vision (2018)
46. Zhao, H., Gallo, O., Frosio, I., Kautz, J.: Loss functions for image restoration with neural networks. In: IEEE Transactions on Computational Imaging (2017)

MatchGAN: A Self-supervised Semi-supervised Conditional Generative Adversarial Network

Jiaze Sun[1(✉)], Binod Bhattarai[1], and Tae-Kyun Kim[1,2]

[1] Imperial College London, Exhibition Road, London SW7 2AZ, UK
{j.sun19,b.bhattarai,tk.kim}@imperial.ac.uk
[2] Korea Advanced Institute of Science and Technology, 291 Daehak-ro, Yuseong-gu, Daejeon 34141, Republic of Korea
https://labicvl.github.io/

Abstract. We present a novel self-supervised learning approach for conditional generative adversarial networks (GANs) under a semi-supervised setting. Unlike prior self-supervised approaches which often involve geometric augmentations on the image space such as predicting rotation angles, our pretext task leverages the label space. We perform augmentation by randomly sampling sensible labels from the label space of the few labelled examples available and assigning them as target labels to the abundant unlabelled examples from the same distribution as that of the labelled ones. The images are then translated and grouped into positive and negative pairs by their target labels, acting as training examples for our pretext task which involves optimising an auxiliary match loss on the discriminator's side. We tested our method on two challenging benchmarks, CelebA and RaFD, and evaluated the results using standard metrics including Fréchet Inception Distance, Inception Score, and Attribute Classification Rate. Extensive empirical evaluation demonstrates the effectiveness of our proposed method over competitive baselines and existing arts. In particular, our method surpasses the baseline with only 20% of the labelled examples used to train the baseline.

Keywords: Conditional generative adversarial network ·
Self-supervised learning · Semi-supervised learning · Face analysis

1 Introduction

Face attribute and expression editing [1–4] has attracted tremendous attention thanks to the ongoing advancements in GANs [5], in particular conditional GANs (cGANs) [1,6–9] which provide greater flexibility and control by incorporating labels in the generation process. However, deploying such cGANs in practice can be challenging as they rely heavily on large numbers of annotated examples. For instance, commonly used labelled datasets for training conditional GANs [1,7,10,11] such as CelebA and ImageNet contain examples in the order of 10^5 to 10^6, which might be expensive to obtain in many applications.

© Springer Nature Switzerland AG 2021
H. Ishikawa et al. (Eds.): ACCV 2020, LNCS 12625, pp. 608–623, 2021.
https://doi.org/10.1007/978-3-030-69538-5_37

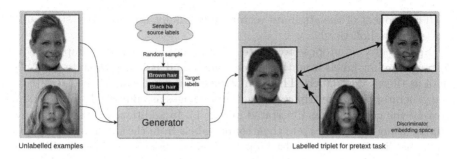

Fig. 1. The procedure of generating triplet examples for our pretext task.

To reduce the need of such huge labelled datasets in training cGANs, a promising approach is to utilise self-supervised methods which are successfully employed in a wide range of computer vision tasks including image classification [12,13], semantic segmentation [14], robotics [15], and many more. Recently, self-supervised learning is also gaining traction with GAN training [16–18], but prior work in this area [16,17] has mostly focused on the input image space when designing the pretext task. For instance, [17] proposed rotating images and minimising an auxiliary rotation loss similar to that of RotNet [12], which [16] also adopted but in a semi-supervised setting. In general, existing methods mostly incorporate geometric augmentations on the input *image space* as part of the pretext task. A main limitation of such approaches is their inability to generate new examples under each class label, for example rotating an image does not change its class label. In addition, our downstream task, attribute/expression editing, is more fine-grained in nature in comparison to tasks such as image classification on ImageNet. Therefore, we present a self-supervised method for training cGANs by making use of the *label space* from the target domain and, if available, source domain as well. Specifically, under a semi-supervised setting wherein only few labelled examples are available, we utilise the large number of unlabelled examples to automatically generate additional labelled examples for our pretext task. Hence, our approach is orthogonal to existing methods.

Our idea draws inspirations from [19], a self-supervised approach for reinforcement learning which trains a policy by randomly sampling imagined goals using a variational auto-encoder (VAE) [20]. In a similar fashion, we can task the generator in a cGAN with synthesising images conditioned on randomly sampled target labels as a means to automatically provide additional supervision to the network. Motivated by our end goal of attribute editing and classification, we require that given unlabelled examples from the same distribution as the labelled ones, irrespective of their true source attribute labels, the generator should map the source images to similar regions of the synthetic image manifold if assigned the same target label and different regions otherwise. We treat every augmented target label vector as a unique state that needs to be reached on the translated domain regardless of the source labels of input images. In other words, whilst standard cGANs such as StarGAN [1] and STGAN [10] consider each component of the attribute vectors individually, our pretext task considers these vectors holistically.

Specifically, we propose to create a large pool of labelled examples by uniformly sampling labels from the source domain and assigning them to unlabelled data as their target labels. These unlabelled real images are then translated by the generator to create triplets of synthetic images as additional training examples for the generator (as illustrated in Fig. 1). In addition, we also create such triplets using real images and their source labels from the small labelled pool to train the discriminator. Whilst triplets of real examples can help distill knowledge from the discriminator to the generator, both synthetic and real triplets are needed to maximise the benefits of our pretext task. The pretext task itself is trained using an auxiliary match loss optimised alongside existing losses of the baseline network [21]. This objective alleviates the overfitting problem for the discriminator in a semi-supervised setting as these triplets serve as additional supervision for the network. Unlike the standard triplet loss [22,23] which uses the Euclidean distance for comparison and fully shared weights between embeddings, we employ a learned convolutional head in the discriminator which takes *concatenated pairs* of embeddings for comparison in a manner akin to learning a custom metric. However, instead of learning a metric, we employ a cross-entropy loss to directly classify pairs with matched labels and those with mismatched ones. Compared to linear loss functions such as the hinge loss, the cross-entropy loss allows for more precise probability estimations and ultimately better performance. Unlike [17] which is purely geometric in nature, we view our approach as an image operation guided by augmented label codes performed on source images and is more in line with our end goal of attribute/expression editing.

We evaluated our method on two challenging benchmarks, CelebA and RaFD, which are popular benchmarks for facial attribute and expression translations. We take StarGAN [1] as our baseline cGAN, but our method is generic in nature. We compared the results both quantitatively and qualitatively. We used standard metrics Fréchet Inception Distance (FID) and Inception Score (IS) for quantitative comparisons.

2   Related Work

Image-to-Image (I2I) Translation with cGANs. cGANs [7] incorporate labels as additional inputs, allowing the network to handle multiple modalities and providing greater flexibility and control over generated examples. I2I translation and facial attribute editing frameworks such as Pix2pix [8] and IcGAN [24] have greatly benefited from employing cGANs, with IcGAN allowing for multi-attribute manipulation without needing to be retrained for different source-target combinations. StarGAN [1] and AttGAN [11] both improve upon IcGAN by using an end-to-end framework, an encoder-decoder architecture for the generator, and a cycle-consistency loss. STGAN [10] further improves upon these frameworks by using the difference between source and target labels as conditional input to the generator. All these methods rely heavily on source attribute labels which can be difficult to obtain in practical applications.

Self-Supervised Learning. Self-supervised methods have been successfully employed to fill the gap between unsupervised and supervised frameworks, particularly for image classification tasks. Well-known self-supervised approaches include predicting relative positioning of image patches [25], generating image content from surroundings [26], colouring greyscale images [27], counting visual primitives [28], and predicting rotation angles [12]. These pretext tasks all involve certain artificially designed geometric transformations on the input images. However, it might be challenging to choose the transformation most optimal for a specific task. Recently, a few approaches have been proposed which rely purely on the model's interaction with data, particularly in reinforcement learning. Grasp2Vec [15] learns object-centric visual embeddings purely through autonomous interaction between a robot and the environment. [19] uses a VAE to randomly sample imagined goals for the agent to perform. Both these frameworks serve as inspirations for MatchGAN.

Self- and Semi-Supervised Learning in GANs. Semi-supervised learning methods become relevant in situations where there are limited number of labelled examples and a large number of unlabelled ones. One of the popular approaches is to annotate unlabelled data with pseudo-labels [29]. Self-supervised approaches have also been explored in semi-supervised learning settings. For example, [13] employed the rotation loss [12] and outperformed fully-supervised methods with a fraction of examples labelled. As for GANs, [17] proposed to minimise the rotation loss [12] on the discriminator, mitigating the discriminator-forgetting problem and allowing more stable representations to be learned. In a semi-supervised setting, [16] proposed training an auxiliary classifier with the few labelled data which is then used to annotate the unlabelled data with pseudo-labels, and [30] differs from [16] by adding these pseudo-labels progressively and through consensus. These method, however, are reliant on the performance of the auxiliary classifier and add significant complexity to the training process.

3   Method

Our task is to perform I2I translation in a semi-supervised setting where the *majority* of training examples are unlabelled except for a *small* number. As training a large network in such a scenario could lead to overfitting, we aim to mitigate the problem by providing weak supervision using the large number of unlabelled examples available. In short, we propose to utilise the translated images and their associated target labels as extra training examples for a pretext task. The goal of the pretext task is to minimise an auxiliary match loss classifying positive and negative pairs of images in a manner akin to metric learning. Compared to optimising a cross-entropy loss across all possible target labels, this approach is more efficient and has been successfully adopted in one-shot learning [31] and face recognition [23]. We use StarGAN [1] as the baseline for our experiments, and as a result we will give a brief overview of its architecture and loss functions before introducing our method. However, we emphasise that our method is generic in nature and can be applied to any other cGAN.

3.1 Background on StarGAN

Overview. Here we provide a brief background on cGANs taking reference from StarGAN [1] but in a semi-supervised setting. Let X be the set of source images and Y the labels, where X is partitioned into labelled and unlabelled subsets, X^L and X^U, respectively. StarGAN aimed to tackle the problem of multi-domain I2I translation without having to train a new GAN for each domain pair. It accomplished this by encoding target domain information as binary or one-hot labels and feeding them along with source images to the generator. During training, the generator G is required to translate a source image $x \sim X$ conditioned on a target domain label $y \sim Y$. The discriminator D receives an image and produces an embedding $D_{emb}(x)$, which is then used to produce two outputs $D_{adv}(x)$ and $D_{cls}(x)$. The former, $D_{adv}(x)$, is used to optimise the Wasserstein GAN with gradient penalty [32] defined by

$$\mathcal{L}_{adv} = \mathop{\mathbb{E}}_{x \sim X; y \sim Y}[D_{adv}(G(x,y))] - \mathop{\mathbb{E}}_{x \sim X}[D_{adv}(x)] + \lambda_{gp} \mathop{\mathbb{E}}_{\hat{x} \in \hat{X}}[\|\nabla_{\hat{x}} D(\hat{x})\|_2 - 1]^2, \quad (1)$$

where $\hat{X}$ consists of points uniformly sampled from straight lines between X and the synthetic distribution $G(X,Y)$. The latter output $D_{cls}(x)$ consists of probabilities over attributes/expressions used for optimising a classification loss to help guide G towards generating images that more closely resemble the target domain. The classification loss for D and G are given by

$$\mathcal{L}_{cls}^D = \mathop{\mathbb{E}}_{x \sim X_y^L; y \sim Y}[-y \cdot \log(D_{cls}(x))], \quad (2)$$

$$\mathcal{L}_{cls}^G = \mathop{\mathbb{E}}_{x \sim (X^L \cup X^U); y \sim Y}[-y \cdot \log(D_{cls}(G(x,y)))] \quad (3)$$

respectively, where the subset $X_y^L \subset X^L$ consists of examples with label y. In addition, a cycle-consistency loss [33],

$$\mathcal{L}_{cyc} = \mathop{\mathbb{E}}_{x \sim X_y^L; y, y' \sim Y}[\|x - G(G(x, y'), y)\|_1], \quad (4)$$

is incorporated to ensure that G preserves content unrelated to the domain translation task. The overall objective for StarGAN is given by

$$\mathcal{L}_D = \mathcal{L}_{adv} + \lambda_{cls} \mathcal{L}_{cls}^D, \qquad \mathcal{L}_G = -\mathcal{L}_{adv} + \lambda_{cls} \mathcal{L}_{cls}^G + \lambda_{cyc} \mathcal{L}_{cyc}. \quad (5)$$

Achitectural Details. StarGAN is fully convolutional. Its generator consists of 3 downsampling convolutional layers, 6 bottleneck residual blocks, and 3 upsampling convolutional layers. Each downsampling or upsampling layer halves or doubles the spatial dimensions of the input. Instance normalisation and ReLU is used for all layers except the output layer. The discriminator consists of 6 downsampling convolutional layers with leaky ReLUs with a slope of 0.01 for negative values. The discriminator output $D_{emb}(x)$ has 2048 channels and is then fed through two separate convolutional heads to produce $D_{adv}(x)$ and $D_{cls}(x)$, with $D_{cls}(x)$ having passed through an additional Softmax layer if ground truths are one-hot or Sigmoid layer otherwise. With an input image size of 128×128, StarGAN has 53.22M learned parameters in total, comprising 8.43M from the generator and 44.79M from the discriminator.

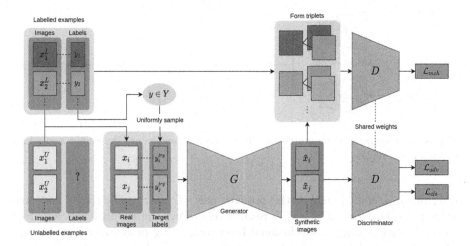

Fig. 2. Detailed pipeline of the proposed framework. Our contribution lies in augmenting the label space of the small-scale labelled pool followed by assigning them to the large-scale unlabelled pool as their target labels. We then generate triplets containing both matched and mismatched pairs based on the target labels in the synthetic domain and source labels in the real domain. Finally, we minimise a match loss as an auxiliary loss to the existing framework.

3.2 Triplet Matching Objective as Pretext Task

Pretext from Synthetic Data. Whilst existing self-supervised approaches mostly rely on geometric transformation of input images, we take the inspiration of utilising target domain information from reinforcement learning literature. [15] learned an embedding of object-centric images by comparing the difference prior to and after an object is grasped. However, this requires source information which can be scarce in semi-supervised learning settings. [19] utilised a variational autoencoder [20] to randomly generate a large amount of goals to train the agent in a self-supervised manner. Similar to [19], our self-supervised method involves translating unlabelled images to random target domains and using the resulting synthetic images to optimise a match loss (see Fig. 2).

Recently [17] proposed to minimize the rotation loss [12] on the discriminator to mitigate its forgetting problem due to the continuously changing generator distribution. Compared to this work which involves only four rotations, the number of possible goals in our setting grows exponentially with respect to the number of attributes (CelebA is multi-labelled) and this would be challenging to implement with a softmax in the same way. Imposing a triplet-like constraint also forces the generator to maintain consistency on translated attributes, ultimately allowing attributes to be retained better on synthetic images. Hence, we propose an auxiliary match loss based on label information as a pretext task for both G and D. A triplet consists of an anchor example x_a, a positive example x_p which shares the same label information as x_a, and a negative example x_n which has a different label. Unlike the standard triplet loss [22,23], we concatenate the

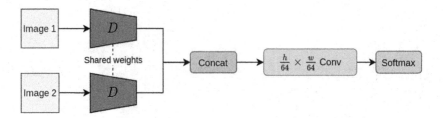

Fig. 3. Architecture of the match loss head, where h and w are the height and width of the input images.

discriminator embeddings of the positive pair $(D_{emb}(x_a), D_{emb}(x_p))$ and negative pair $(D_{emb}(x_a), D_{emb}(x_n))$ respectively along the channel axis and feed them through a single convolutional layer, producing probability distributions $D_{mch}(x_a, x_p)$ and $D_{mch}(x_a, x_n)$ respectively over whether each pair has matching labels. Specifically, we propose the following triplet matching objective

$$\mathcal{L}_{mch}^{D} = \mathop{\mathbb{E}}_{\substack{x_a, x_p \sim X_y^L ; x_n \sim X_{y'}^L \\ y \neq y' \sim Y}} -[\log(D_{mch}(x_a, x_p)) + \log(1 - D_{mch}(x_a, x_n))], \quad (6)$$

$$\mathcal{L}_{mch}^{G} = \mathop{\mathbb{E}}_{x_1, x_2, x_3 \sim (X^L \cup X^U); y \neq y' \sim Y} -[\log(D_{mch}(G(x_1, y), G(x_2, y)))$$
$$+ \log(1 - D_{mch}(G(x_1, y), G(x_3, y')))]. \quad (7)$$

Rather than using the standard triplet loss which sticks with the Euclidean distance as a single measurement, concatenation allows the network to continuously adapt itself to the pattern in the data and thus acquire more optimal ways of carrying out such comparisons, in a manner similar to learning a custom metric[1]. In addition, the cross-entropy loss allows the network to make more precise probability estimations compared to linear loss functions and ultimately learn more refined representations. Our overall loss function is given by

$$\mathcal{L}_D = \mathcal{L}_{adv} + \lambda_{cls}\mathcal{L}_{cls}^D + \lambda_{mch}\mathcal{L}_{mch}^D, \quad (8)$$
$$\mathcal{L}_G = -\mathcal{L}_{adv} + \lambda_{cls}\mathcal{L}_{cls}^G + \lambda_{cyc}\mathcal{L}_{cyc} + \lambda_{mch}\mathcal{L}_{mch}^G. \quad (9)$$

As some of the components in Eq. 8 and 9 require source labels, they cannot be directly implemented on unlabelled examples in a semi-supervised setting. As a result, we train the network with labelled and unlabelled examples in an alternating fashion as detailed in Algorithm 1.

Architectural Details. MatchGAN is built directly on top of StarGAN but includes an additional head for $\mathcal{L}_{mch}$ after the discriminator output $D_{emb}(x)$ (see Fig. 3). Specifically, a triplet of images (x_a, x_p, x_n) are passed through D

---

[1] However, concatenation does not enforce symmetry so it is not strictly a metric.

Algorithm 1. MatchGAN.

1: **Input:** Labelled set X^L with set of all possible class labels $Y = \{y_1, \ldots, y_K\}$ separated into disjoint sets $X^L = X_1^L \sqcup \cdots \sqcup X_K^L$ by label, and unlabelled set X^U.

2: **Initialise:** Generator G, Discriminator D, weights θ_G and θ_D, learning rates η_G and η_D, # of iterations N, batch size B, # of D updates per G update n_G.

3: **for** $i = 1, \ldots, N$ **do**

4:     **if** i is odd **then**

5:        Form a batch of B real images and labels $(R^{(i)}, Y_{src}^{(i)})$ chosen uniformly from k classes $\mathcal{K}_{src} \subset \{1, \ldots, K\}$, where $R^{(i)} = \bigsqcup_{j \in \mathcal{K}_{src}} R_j^{(i)}$ and each $R_j^{(i)} \subset X_j^L$.

6:        $\mathcal{L}_{cls}^D \leftarrow \frac{1}{B} \sum_{(r,y) \in (R^{(i)}, Y_{src}^{(i)})} -y \cdot \log(D_{cls}(r))$.

7:        Get $T_R^{(i)} = \{(x_a, x_p, x_n) : x_a, x_p \in R_{k_1}^{(i)}$ and $x_n \in R_{k_2}^{(i)}, k_1 \neq k_2 \in \mathcal{K}_{src}\}$, a set of triplets sampled from the mini-batch $R^{(i)}$.

8:        $\mathcal{L}_{mch}^D \leftarrow \frac{1}{|T_R^{(i)}|} \sum_{(x_a, x_p, x_n) \in T_R^{(i)}} -[\log(D_{mch}(x_a, x_p)) + \log(1 - D_{mch}(x_a, x_n))]$.

9:     **else**

10:        Sample mini-batch of B unlabelled real images $R^{(i)} \subset X^U$.

11:     **end if**

12:     Form a batch of B target labels $Y_{trg}^{(i)}$ chosen uniformly from k classes $\mathcal{K}_{trg} \subset \{1, \ldots, K\}$.

13:     Generate fake images $F^{(i)} = \{G(r, y) : (r, y) \in (R^{(i)}, Y_{trg}^{(i)})\}$.

14:     $\mathcal{L}_{adv}^D \leftarrow \frac{1}{B} \sum_{(r,f) \in (R^{(i)}, F^{(i)})} [D_{adv}(f) - D_{adv}(r) + \lambda_{gp}(\|\nabla_{\hat{x}} D_{adv}(\hat{x})\|_2 - 1)^2]$, where $\hat{x} = \alpha r + (1 - \alpha)f$ and $\alpha \sim U(0, 1)$ is random.

15:     $\theta_D \leftarrow Adam\left(\nabla_{\theta_D}(\mathcal{L}_{adv}^D + odd(i)(\lambda_{cls}\mathcal{L}_{cls}^D + \lambda_{mch}\mathcal{L}_{mch}^D)), \eta_D\right)$ using Adam [34], where $odd(i) = 1$ if i is odd or 0 otherwise.

16:     **if** i is a multiple of n_G **then**

17:        **if** i is odd **then**

18:           $\mathcal{L}_{cyc} \leftarrow \frac{1}{B} \sum_{(r,y,y') \in (R^{(i)}, Y_{src}^{(i)}, Y_{trg}^{(i)})} \|r - G(G(r, y'), y)\|_1$.

19:        **end if**

20:        $\mathcal{L}_{adv}^G \leftarrow \frac{1}{B} \sum_{f \in F^{(i)}} -D_{adv}(f)$.

21:        $\mathcal{L}_{cls}^G \leftarrow \frac{1}{B} \sum_{(f,y) \in (F^{(i)}, Y_{trg}^{(i)})} -y \cdot \log(D_{cls}(G(f, y)))$.

22:        Get $T_F^{(i)} = \{(x_a, x_p, x_n) : x_a, x_p \in F_{k_1}^{(i)}$ and $x_n \in F_{k_2}^{(i)}, k_1 \neq k_2 \in \mathcal{K}_{trg}\}$, a set of triplets sampled from the mini-batch $F^{(i)}$, where $F^{(i)} = \bigsqcup_{j \in \mathcal{K}_{trg}} F_j^{(i)}$ and each $F_j^{(i)}$ corresponds to target label y_j.

23:        $\mathcal{L}_{mch}^G \leftarrow \frac{1}{|T_F^{(i)}|} \sum_{(x_a, x_p, x_n) \in T_F^{(i)}} -[\log(D_{mch}(x_a, x_p)) + \log(1 - D_{mch}(x_a, x_n))]$.

24:        $\theta_G \leftarrow Adam\left(\nabla_{\theta_G}(\mathcal{L}_{adv} + \lambda_{cls}\mathcal{L}_{cls}^G + \lambda_{mch}\mathcal{L}_{mch}^G + odd(i)\lambda_{cyc}\mathcal{L}_{cyc}), \eta_G\right)$.

25:     **end if**

26: **end for**

27: **Output:** Optimal G.

---

to produce embeddings $(D_{emb}(x_a), D_{emb}(x_p), D_{emb}(x_n))$. The positive and negative pairs $(D_{emb}(x_a), D_{emb}(x_p))$ and $(D_{emb}(x_a), D_{emb}(x_n))$ are concatenated respectively along the channel dimension to produce 4096-channel embeddings.

These embeddings are then convolved and passed through a Softmax layer to produce probabilities of whether each image pair is matched. For input images of size 128×128, this head adds approximately 32.77K to the total number of learned parameters which is negligible compared to the 53.22M parameters in the StarGAN baseline, and thus has very little impact on training efficiency.

4   Experiments

4.1   Implementation Details

We used StarGAN [1] as a baseline for our experiments[2]. StarGAN unifies multi-domain image-to-image translation with a single generative network and is well suited to our label-based self-supervised approach. However, we would like to re-emphasise that our method is a general idea and can be extended to other cGANs. To avoid potential issues during training, we used the same hyper-parameters as the original StarGAN. Specifically, we trained the network for 200K discriminator iterations with 1 generator update after every 5 discriminator updates. We used the Adam optimiser [34] with $\beta_1 = 0.5$ and $\beta_2 = 0.999$, and the initial learning rates for both generator and discriminator were set to 10^{-4} for the first 100K iterations and decayed linearly to 0 for the next 100K. We trained the model using mini-batches of 16 examples (sampled from 4 random classes if from the labelled pool) and mapped to 4 random target classes. Training took approximately 10 h to complete on an NVIDIA RTX 2080Ti GPU.

4.2   Datasets

We evaluated our method on two challenging face attributes and expression manipulation datasets, The CelebFaces Attributes Dataset (CelebA) [35] and The Radboud Faces Database (RaFD) [36]. Both datasets were split into training and test sets, and we report results on the test set.

CelebA. CelebA contains 202,599 images of celebrities of size 178×218 with 40 attribute annotations. We selected 5 attributes including 3 hair colours (black, blond, and brown), gender, and age. The images were cropped to 178×178 then resized to 128×128. The experiments followed the official partition of 162,770 examples for training and 19,962 for testing. We created a semi-supervised scenario with limited labelled training examples by uniformly sub-sampling a percentage of training examples as labelled and setting the rest as unlabelled. The sub-sampling process was done to ensure that the examples were spread evenly between classes whenever possible to avoid potential class imbalance issues.

RaFD. RaFD is a much smaller dataset with 8,040 images of size 681×1024 of 67 identities of different genders, races, and ages displaying 8 emotional expressions. The images were cropped to 600×600 (centred on face) before being resized to 128×128. A total of 7 randomly selected identities, comprising 840 images, were

---

[2] Code and pretrained model at https://github.com/justin941208/MatchGAN.

chosen as the test set and the rest (60 identities comprising 7200 images) as the training set. Similar to CelebA, a semi-supervised setting was created by splitting the training set into labelled and unlabelled pools.

4.3 Baseline

Our baseline was established by setting λ_{mch} to 0 whilst leaving all other procedures unchanged. As for MatchGAN, the value of $\lambda_{mch} = 0.5$ was used for all experiments. To verify that our method is scalable to both small and large number of annotated data, we tested our approach with various percentages of training examples labelled. Specifically, we performed experiments setting 1%, 5%, 10%, and 20% of CelebA training data as labelled examples, and similarly for 10%, 20%, and 50% of RaFD training data as RaFD is a significantly smaller dataset. Finally, we also evaluated our method on the full datasets to verify the effectiveness of our method on benchmarks designed for supervised learning. We also tested the rotation loss [17] for comparison.

4.4 Evaluation Metrics

We employed the Fréchet Inception Distance (FID) [37] and Inception Score (IS) [38] for quantitative evaluations. FID measures the similarity between the distribution of real examples and that of the generated ones by comparing their respective embeddings from a pretrained Inception-v3 network [39]. IS also measures image quality but relies on the probability outputs of the same Inception-v3 network, taking into account the meaningfulness of individual images and the diversity of all images. If the generated images are of high quality, then FID should be small whereas IS should be large. We computed the FID by translating test images to each of the target attribute domains (5 for CelebA, 8 for RaFD) and comparing the distributions before and after translations. The IS was computed as an average obtained from a 10-fold split of the test set.

In addition to FID and IS, we also used GAN-train and GAN-test [40] to measure the attribute classification rate of translated images. In short, given a set of real images X with a train-test split $X = X_{train} \sqcup X_{test}$, GAN-train is the accuracy obtained from a classifier trained on synthetic images $G(X_{train})$ and tested on real images X_{test}, whereas for GAN-test the classifier is trained on real images X_{train} and tested on synthetic images $G(X_{test})$.

4.5 Ablation Studies

MatchGAN involves extracting triplets from labelled real examples and all synthetic examples - labelled and unlabelled. To show that the proposed method does not simply rely on the few labelled examples and that both unlabelled and synthetic examples are necessary to achieve good performance, the network was trained in several other scenarios in which various amounts of real and synthetic data used for updating the match loss $\mathcal{L}_{mch}$ were removed (shown in Table 1).

A few observations can be made from this table. First, including a large number of unlabelled data is essential for improving performance, which is clear from comparing A and B with the rest. Second, incorporating the match loss $\mathcal{L}_{mch}$ provides substantial improvement in performance, as observed from A vs B, and C vs D–G. This improvement was achieved despite the match loss not utilising all the available data, as seen from setups D–F. Third, match loss indeed benefits from training with synthetic examples which is evident from C vs D, and E vs F–G. Fourth, unlabelled synthetic examples can be used to achieve further performance improvement, as seen from F vs G. In addition, H was trained using the standard triplet loss [23] which G also outperforms. Therefore, G will be used as the default setup for MatchGAN in all following experiments.

Table 1. The results of the ablation studies – FID scores obtained using various amounts of training data. Setups A and C are baseline StarGAN [1], whereas the other setups update the match loss $\mathcal{L}_{mch}$ using different portions of the training data.

Setup		A	B	C	D	E	F	G	H [23]
Total number of training examples		2.5K	2.5K	162K	162K	162K	162K	162K	162K
Number of examples for $\mathcal{L}_{mch}$	Real (labelled)	0	2.5K	0	0	2.5K	2.5K	2.5K	2.5K
	Synthetic (labelled)	0	2.5K	0	2.5K	0	2.5K	2.5K	2.5K
	Synthetic (unlabelled)	0	0	0	160K	0	0	160K	160K
FID↓		24.20	17.26	16.11	13.78	13.66	10.88	**9.43**	14.86

4.6   Quantitative Evaluations

We evaluated the performance of our proposed method, the baseline, and rotation loss [17] using FID and IS and the results are shown in Table 2. In terms of FID, MatchGAN consistently outperformed the baseline in both CelebA and RaFD. For CelebA in particular, with just 20% of training examples labelled, our method was able to achieve better performance than the baseline with 100% of the training examples labelled. Our method also has a distinct lead over the baseline when there are very few labelled examples. In addition, our method was also on par with or even outperformed rotation loss in both datasets, again with a distinct advantage over rotation loss when labelled examples are limited.

In terms of IS, we still managed to outperform both the baseline and rotation loss in the majority of the setups. In other setups our method was either on par with the baseline or slightly underperforming within a margin of 0.02. We would like to emphasise that IS is less consistent than FID as it does not compare the synthetic distribution with an "ideal" one. In addition, IS is computed using the 1000-dimensional output of Inception-v3 pretrained on ImageNet which is arguably less suitable for human face datasets such as CelebA and RaFD. However, we included IS here as it is still one of the most widely used metrics for evaluating the performance of GANs.

In terms of GAN-train and GAN-test classification rates, our method outperformed the baseline in both CelebA and RaFD (shown in Table 3) under the

Table 2. Baseline vs Rotation vs MatchGAN in terms of FID and IS scores.

Dataset	Metric	Setup	Percentage of training data labelled					
			1%	5%	10%	20%	50%	100%
CelebA	FID↓	Baseline [1]	17.04	10.54	9.47	7.07	╱	6.65
		Rotation [17]	17.08	10.00	**8.04**	6.82	╱	5.91
		MatchGAN	**12.31**	**9.34**	8.81	**6.34**	╱	**5.58**
	IS↑	Baseline [1]	2.86	2.95	**3.00**	3.01	╱	3.01
		Rotation [17]	2.82	**2.99**	2.96	3.01	╱	3.06
		MatchGAN	**2.95**	2.95	2.99	**3.03**	╱	**3.07**
RaFD	FID↓	Baseline [1]	╱	╱	32.015	11.75	7.24	5.14
		Rotation [17]	╱	╱	28.88	10.96	**6.57**	**5.00**
		MatchGAN	╱	╱	**22.75**	**9.94**	6.65	5.06
	IS↑	Baseline [1]	╱	╱	**1.66**	1.60	1.58	1.56
		Rotation [17]	╱	╱	1.62	1.58	1.58	**1.60**
		MatchGAN	╱	╱	1.64	**1.61**	**1.59**	1.58

100% setup which has the best FID overall. MatchGAN again obtained a higher GAN-train accuracy than the baseline, indicating that the synthetic examples generated by MatchGAN can be more effectively used to augment small data for training classifiers. We report the results under the 100% setup as it has the lowest FID and that FID is considered one of the most robust metrics for evaluating the performance of GANs. We expect GAN-train and GAN-test in other setups to be proportional to their respective FIDs as well.

Table 3. Baseline vs MatchGAN in terms of GAN-train and GAN-test classification rate under the 100% setup. GAN-train for CelebA and GAN-test were obtained by averaging individual attribute accuracies, whereas top-1 accuracy was used when computing GAN-train for RaFD.

Dataset	Setup	GAN-train	GAN-test
CelebA	Baseline [1]	87.29%	81.11%
	MatchGAN	**87.43%**	**82.26%**
RaFD	Baseline [1]	95.00%	75.00%
	MatchGAN	**97.78%**	**75.95%**

4.7   Qualitative Evaluations

Figure 4 and 5 compare the visual quality of the images generated by Baseline and MatchGAN on CelebA and RaFD respectively. MatchGAN can be observed to produce images that are less noisy, less blurry, and more coherent. For instance, in the 1% setup in Fig. 4, the baseline can often be observed

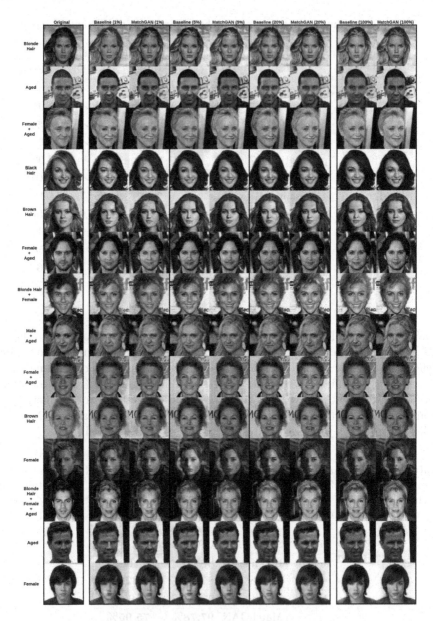

Fig. 4. Synthetic examples of MatchGAN vs Baseline on CelebA (zoom in for a better view). Each row corresponds to a single- or multi-attribute manipulation, with target attributes listed on the left side.

to produce artefacts, blurry patches, or incomplete translations (e.g. the brown patch in the hair in the fourth row) which are not present in the images generated by MatchGAN. Similarly on RaFD, MatchGAN generates more coherent

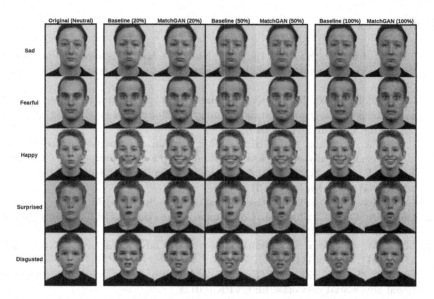

Fig. 5. Synthetic examples of MatchGAN vs Baseline on RaFD (zoom in for a better view). Each row corresponds to a single expression manipulation, with target expression listed on the left side.

expressions compared to the baseline (e.g. the "surprised mouth" in the fourth row in Fig. 5) and produces fewer artefacts. The image quality of our method also improves substantially with more labelled examples. In Fig. 4, the overall quality of the images generated by MatchGAN in the 20% setup is on par with or even outmatches that of the Baseline under the 100% setup in terms of clarity, colour tone, and coherence of target attributes, corroborating our quantitative results shown in Table 2.

5   Conclusion

In this paper we proposed MatchGAN, a novel self-supervised learning approach for training conditional GANs under a semi-supervised setting with very few labelled examples. MatchGAN utilises synthetic examples and their target labels as additional annotated examples and minimises a triplet matching objective as a pretext task. With 20% of the training data labelled, it is able to outperform the baseline trained with 100% of examples labelled and shows a distinct advantage over other self-supervised approaches such as [17] under both fully-supervised and semi-supervised settings.

Acknowledgements. This work is supported by the Huawei Consumer Business Group, Croucher Foundation, and EPSRC Programme Grant 'FACER2VM' (EP/N007743/1).

References

1. Choi, Y., Choi, M., Kim, M., Ha, J.W., Kim, S., Choo, J.: Stargan: unified generative adversarial networks for multi-domain image-to-image translation. In: CVPR (2018)
2. Chen, X., Duan, Y., Houthooft, R., Schulman, J., Sutskever, I., Abbeel, P.: Infogan: interpretable representation learning by information maximizing generative adversarial nets. In: NIPS (2016)
3. Pumarola, A., Agudo, A., Martinez, A.M., Sanfeliu, A., Moreno-Noguer, F.: Ganimation: anatomically-aware facial animation from a single image. In: ECCV (2018)
4. Karras, T., Laine, S., Aila, T.: A style-based generator architecture for generative adversarial networks. In: CVPR (2019)
5. Goodfellow, I., et al.: Generative adversarial nets. In: NeurIPS (2014)
6. Odena, A., Olah, C., Shlens, J.: Conditional image synthesis with auxiliary classifier gans. In: ICML (2017)
7. Mirza, M., Osindero, S.: Conditional generative adversarial nets. arXiv preprint arXiv:1411.1784 (2014)
8. Isola, P., Zhu, J.Y., Zhou, T., Efros, A.A.: Image-to-image translation with conditional adversarial networks. In: CVPR (2017)
9. Bhattarai, B., Kim, T.-K.: Inducing optimal attribute representations for conditional GANs. In: Vedaldi, A., Bischof, H., Brox, T., Frahm, J.-M. (eds.) ECCV 2020. LNCS, vol. 12352, pp. 69–85. Springer, Cham (2020). https://doi.org/10.1007/978-3-030-58571-6_5
10. Liu, M., et al.: Stgan: a unified selective transfer network for arbitrary image attribute editing. In: CVPR (2019)
11. He, Z., Zuo, W., Kan, M., Shan, S., Chen, X.: Attgan: facial attribute editing by only changing what you want. IEEE Trans. Image Process. 28(11), 5464–5478 (2019)
12. Gidaris, S., Singh, P., Komodakis, N.: Unsupervised representation learning by predicting image rotations. In: ICLR (2018)
13. Zhai, X., Oliver, A., Kolesnikov, A., Beyer, L.: S4l: self-supervised semi-supervised learning. In: ICCV (2019)
14. Zhan, X., Liu, Z., Luo, P., Tang, X., Loy, C.C.: Mix-and-match tuning for self-supervised semantic segmentation. In: AAAI (2018)
15. Jang, E., Devin, C., Vanhoucke, V., Levine, S.: Grasp2vec: learning object representations from self-supervised grasping. In: CRL (2018)
16. Lučić, M., Tschannen, M., Ritter, M., Zhai, X., Bachem, O., Gelly, S.: High-fidelity image generation with fewer labels. In: ICML (2019)
17. Chen, T., Zhai, X., Ritter, M., Lucic, M., Houlsby, N.: Self-supervised gans via auxiliary rotation loss. In: CVPR (2019)
18. Tran, N.T., Tran, V.H., Nguyen, B.N., Yang, L., et al.: Self-supervised gan: analysis and improvement with multi-class minimax game. In: NeurIPS (2019)
19. Nair, A.V., Pong, V., Dalal, M., Bahl, S., Lin, S., Levine, S.: Visual reinforcement learning with imagined goals. In: NIPS (2018)
20. Kingma, D.P., Welling, M.: Auto-encoding variational bayes. In: ICLR (2014)
21. Caruana, R.: Multitask learning. Mach. Learn. 28(1), 41–75 (1997)
22. Weinberger, K.Q., Blitzer, J., Saul, L.K.: Distance metric learning for large margin nearest neighbor classification. In: NIPS, MIT Press (2006)
23. Schroff, F., Kalenichenko, D., Philbin, J.: Facenet: a unified embedding for face recognition and clustering. In: CVPR (2015)

24. Perarnau, G., Van De Weijer, J., Raducanu, B., Álvarez, J.M.: Invertible conditional gans for image editing. In: NIPSW (2016)
25. Doersch, C., Gupta, A., Efros, A.A.: Unsupervised visual representation learning by context prediction. In: CVPR (2015)
26. Pathak, D., Krahenbuhl, P., Donahue, J., Darrell, T., Efros, A.A.: Context encoders: feature learning by inpainting. In: CVPR (2016)
27. Zhang, R., Isola, P., Efros, A.A.: Colorful image colorization. In: Leibe, B., Matas, J., Sebe, N., Welling, M. (eds.) ECCV 2016. LNCS, vol. 9907, pp. 649–666. Springer, Cham (2016). https://doi.org/10.1007/978-3-319-46487-9_40
28. Noroozi, M., Pirsiavash, H., Favaro, P.: Representation learning by learning to count. In: ICCV (2017)
29. Lee, D.H.: Pseudo-label : The simple and efficient semi-supervised learning method for deep neural networks. In: ICML (2013)
30. Wang, Y., Khan, S., Garcia, A.G., Weijer, J.v.d., Khan, F.S.: Semi-supervised learning for few-shot image-to-image translation. In: CVPR (2020)
31. Koch, G., Zemel, R., Salakhutdinov, R.: Siamese neural networks for one-shot image recognition. In: ICML 2015 Deep Learning Workshop (2015)
32. Gulrajani, I., Ahmed, F., Arjovsky, M., Dumoulin, V., Courville, A.: Improved training of wasserstein gans. In: NIPS (2017)
33. Zhu, J.Y., Park, T., Isola, P., Efros, A.A.: Unpaired image-to-image translation using cycle-consistent adversarial networks. In: ICCV (2017)
34. Kingma, D.P., Ba, J.: Adam: a method for stochastic optimization. In: ICLR (2015)
35. Liu, Z., Luo, P., Wang, X., Tang, X.: Deep learning face attributes in the wild. In: ICCV (2015)
36. Langner, O., Dotsch, R., Bijlstra, G., Wigboldus, D., Hawk, S., van Knippenberg, A.: Presentation and validation of the radboud faces database. Cogn. Emot. **24**(8), 1377–1388 (2010)
37. Heusel, M., Ramsauer, H., Unterthiner, T., Nessler, B., Hochreiter, S.: Gans trained by a two time-scale update rule converge to a local nash equilibrium. In: NeurIPS (2017)
38. Salimans, T., Goodfellow, I., Zaremba, W., Cheung, V., Radford, A., Chen, X.: Improved techniques for training gans. In: NIPS (2016)
39. Szegedy, C., Vanhoucke, V., Ioffe, S., Shlens, J., Wojna, Z.: Rethinking the inception architecture for computer vision. In: CVPR (2016)
40. Shmelkov, K., Schmid, C., Alahari, K.: How good is my gan? In: ECCV (2018)

DeepSEE: Deep Disentangled Semantic Explorative Extreme Super-Resolution

Marcel C. Bühler$^{(\boxtimes)}$ ⓘ, Andrés Romero$^{(\boxtimes)}$ ⓘ, and Radu Timofte$^{(\boxtimes)}$ ⓘ

Computer Vision Lab, ETH Zürich, Zurich, Switzerland
{buehlmar,roandres,timofter}@ethz.ch

Abstract. Super-resolution (SR) is by definition ill-posed. There are infinitely many plausible high-resolution variants for a given low-resolution natural image. Most of the current literature aims at a single deterministic solution of either high reconstruction fidelity or photo-realistic perceptual quality. In this work, we propose an explorative facial super-resolution framework, DeepSEE, for Deep disentangled Semantic Explorative Extreme super-resolution. To the best of our knowledge, DeepSEE is the first method to leverage semantic maps for explorative super-resolution. In particular, it provides control of the semantic regions, their disentangled appearance and it allows a broad range of image manipulations. We validate DeepSEE on faces, for up to 32× magnification and exploration of the space of super-resolution. Our code and models are available at: https://mcbuehler.github.io/DeepSEE/.

Keywords: Explorative super-resolution · Face hallucination · Stochastic super-resolution · Extreme super-resolution · Disentanglement · Perceptual super-resolution · Generative modeling

1 Introduction

In super-resolution (SR), we learn a mapping G_Θ from a low-resolution (LR) image x_{lr} to a higher-resolution (HR) image $\hat{x}_{hr}$:

$$\hat{x}_{hr} = G_\Theta(x_{lr}). \tag{1}$$

Simple methods, like bilinear, bicubic or nearest-neighbour, do not restore high-frequency content or details—their output looks unrealistic. Most modern super-resolution methods rely on neural networks to learn a more complex mapping. Typical upscaling factors are 4× to 8× [1–11]; generating 4^2, respectively 8^2 pixels for one input pixel. Very recent works upscale up to 16× [12–14] and 64× [15].

Electronic supplementary material The online version of this chapter (https://doi.org/10.1007/978-3-030-69538-5_38) contains supplementary material, which is available to authorized users.

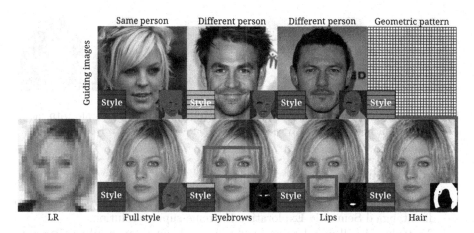

Fig. 1. Upscaling and manipulations with disentangled style injection. The bottom row shows the low-resolution input and four high-resolution variants; the top row displays the guiding images. Our model, *DeepSEE*, can apply the *full style* matrix from an image of the same person, and alter it with styles from guiding images. We learn 19 semantic regions, such as *eyebrows*, *lips*, *hair*, etc. *DeepSEE* also allows style extraction from *geometric patterns*, sampling in the solution space (Fig. 2), style interpolation (Fig. 6), semantic manipulations (Fig. 7), and upscaling to extreme magnification factors (Fig. 2 and Fig. 8).

The mapping between the low- and the high-resolution domain is not well defined. There exist multiple (similar) high-resolution images that would down-scale to the same low-resolution image. This is why super-resolution is an *ill-posed inverse problem*. Yet, most modern methods assume a ground truth; and learn to generate a single result for a given input [4,5,7–11,16,17].

To add more guidance, some methods leverage additional information to tackle the super-resolution problem. This can include image attributes [5,6,8,11], reference images [18,19] and/or a guidance by facial landmark [7,9,10]. Still, neither of those approaches allows to produce more than very few variants for a given input. Ideally, we could generate an infinite number of potentially valid solutions an pick the one that suits our purpose best.

Our proposed method, *DeepSEE*, is capable of generating a large number of high-resolution candidates for a low-resolution face image. The outputs differ in both appearance and shape, but they are overall consistent with the low-resolution input. Our method learns a one-to-many mapping from a low-frequency input to a disentangled manifold of potential solutions with the same low-frequencies, but diverse high-frequencies. For inference, a user can specifically tweak the shape and appearance of individual semantic regions to achieve the desired result. *DeepSEE* allows to sample randomly varied solutions (Fig. 2), interpolate between solution variants (Fig. 6), control high-frequency details via a guiding image (Fig. 1), and manipulate pre-defined semantic regions (Fig. 7). In addition, we go beyond common upscaling factors and magnify up to 32×.

Fig. 2. Multiple potential solutions for a single input. We upscale with factor 32× to different high-resolution variants. *Which one would be the correct solution?*

1.1 Contributions

i) We introduce *DeepSEE*, a novel face hallucination framework for **Deep** disentangled **S**emantic **E**xplorative **E**xtreme super-resolution.

ii) We tackle the ill-posed super-resolution problem in an **explorative** approach based on **semantic maps**. *DeepSEE* is able to sample and manipulate the solution space to produce an infinite number of high-resolution faces for a single low-resolution input.

iii) *DeepSEE* gives control over both shape and appearance. A user can tweak the **disentangled semantic** regions individually.

iv) We super-resolve to the **extreme**, with upscaling factors up to 32×.

2 Related Work

2.1 Fidelity vs. Perceptual Quality in Super-Resolution

Single image super-resolution assumes the availability of a low-resolution image carrying low-frequency information—basic colors and shapes—and aims to restore the high-frequencies—sharp contrasts and details. The output is a high-resolution image that is consistent with the low-frequency input image.

Traditional super-resolution methods focused on *fidelity*: low distortion to a high-resolution ground truth image. These methods based on edge [20,21] and image statistics [22,23] and relied on traditional supervised machine learning algorithms: support-vector regression [24], graphical models [25], Gaussian process regression [26], sparse coding [27] or piece-wise linear regression [28].

With the advent of deep learning, the focus shifted to *perceptual* quality: photo-realism as perceived by humans. Their results are less blurry and more realistic [2], defining more and more the current main stream research [1,3,14, 16,17,29–31].

Evaluation. Traditional evaluation metrics in super-resolution are *Peak Signal-to-Noise Ratio* (PSNR) or *Structural Similarity Index* [32] (SSIM). However, these *fidelity* metrics are simple functions that measure the distortion to reference images and correlate poorly with the human visual response of the output [2,4,16,17]. A high PSNR or SSIM does not guarantee a perceptually good looking output [33]. Alternative metrics evaluate perceptual quality, namely the

Learned Perceptual Image Patch Similarity (LPIPS) [34] and the *Fréchet Inception Distance* (FID) [35]. In this work, we emphasize our validation on high visual quality as in [4,16,17,36], exploration of the solution space [37] and extreme super-resolution [12–14].

2.2 Perceptual Super-Resolution

Super-resolution methods with focus on high fidelity tend to generate blurry images [2]. In contrast, perceptual super-resolution targets photo-realism. Training perceptual models typically includes perceptual losses [38,39], or Generative Adversarial Networks (GAN) [2,4,16,17,40].

Generative Adversarial Networks [41] (GAN) have become increasingly popular in image generation [42–46]. The underlying technique is to alternately train two neural networks—a generator and a discriminator—with contrary objectives, playing a MiniMax game. While the discriminator aims to correctly classify images as real or fake, the generator learns to produce photo-realistic images fooling the discriminator.

A seminal GAN-based work for perceptual super-resolution, SRGAN [16], employed a residual network [47] for the generator and relied on a discriminator [41] for realism. A combination of additional losses encourage reconstruction/fidelity and texture/content. ESRGAN [17] further improved upon SRGAN by tweaking its architecture and loss functions.

In this work, we propose a *GAN-based perceptual* super-resolution method.

2.3 Explorative Super-Resolution

One severe shortcoming of existing approaches is that they consider super-resolution as a *1:1* problem: A low-resolution image maps to a single high-resolution output [4,5,7–11,16,17]. In reality, however, an infinite number of consistent solutions would exist for a given low-frequency input. Super-resolution is by definition an *ill-posed inverse problem*. Downscaling many (similar) high-resolution variants would yield the same low-resolution image [3,15,48–52]. In our work, we regard super-resolution as a *1:n* problem: A low-resolution image maps to many consistent high-resolution variants.

In a concurrent work, Bahat *et al.* [37] suggest an editing tool with which a user can manually manipulate the super-resolution output. Their manipulations include adjusting the variance or periodicity for textures, reducing brightness, or brightening eyes in faces. Two recent works leverage normalizing flows [53,54] for non-deterministic super-resolution [51,55]. In our work, we allow to freely walk a latent style space and manipulate semantic masks to explore even more solutions.

To the best of our knowledge, [37] and ours are the first works targeting *semantically controllable* explorative super-resolution; and *DeepSEE* is the first method that achieves explorative super-resolution using semantically-guided style imposition.

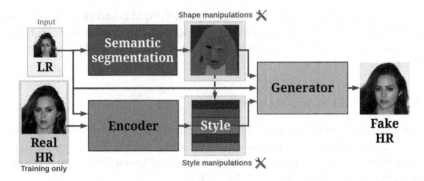

Fig. 3. Overview of components and information flow. *DeepSEE* guides the upscaling with a semantic map extracted from the low-resolution input, and a latent style matrix encoded from a high- or low-resolution image. During inference, a user can tweak the output by manipulating shapes and style codes.

2.4   Domain-Specific Super-Resolution

Typical domain-specific applications include super-resolution of faces [5,7–11], outdoor scenes [4] or depth maps [56–59]. Applying super-resolution in a constraint domain allows to leverage prior knowledge and additional guidance, like enforcing characteristics via attributes or identity annotations [5,6,8,11], facial landmarks [7,9,10], guiding images [18,19], or semantic maps [4,60].

In this work, we focus on super-resolution for faces, namely *face hallucination*. Despite the important roles of facial keypoints, attributes and identities, they are a high-level supervision that does not allow fine-grained manipulation of the output—oftentimes a desired property. In contrast to previous works, we use a predicted discrete semantic prior for each region of the face.

2.5   Extreme Super-Resolution

Recent extreme super-resolution train on the DIV8K dataset [61] and target 16× upscaling [12–14]. A concurrent work [15] searches the latent space of a pre-trained face generation model [42] to find high-resolution images that match a low-resolution image, when downscaled 64×.

3   DeepSEE

3.1   Problem Formulation

A low-resolution input $(x_{lr} \in \mathbb{R}^{H_{lr} \times W_{lr} \times 3})$ image acts as a starting point that carries the low-frequency information. A generator (G_Θ) upscales this image and hallucinates the high-frequencies yielding the high-resolution image $\hat{x}_{hr} \in \mathbb{R}^{H_{hr} \times W_{hr} \times 3}$. As a guidance, G_Θ leverages both a high resolution semantic map $(M \in \mathbb{R}^{H_{hr} \times W_{hr} \times N}$, where N is the number of the semantic regions) and independent styles per region ($S \in \mathbb{R}^{N \times d}$, where d is the style dimensionality). The upscaled image should thus retain the low-frequency information from the low-resolution image. In addition, it should be consistent in terms of the semantic regions and have specific, yet independent styles per region. We formally define our problem as

$$\hat{x}_{hr} = G_\Theta(x_{lr}, M, S). \tag{2}$$

Remarkably, thanks to the flexible semantic layout, a user is able to control the *appearance* and *shape* of each semantic region through the generation process. This allows to tweak an output until the desired solution has been found.

3.2   Architecture

Following the GAN framework [41], our method consists of a generator and a discriminator network. In addition, we employ a segmentation network and an encoder for style. Concretely, the segmentation network predicts the semantic mask from a low-resolution image and the encoder produces a disentangled style. Figure 3 illustrates our model at a high level and Fig. 4 provides a more detailed view. In the following, we describe each component in more detail.

Style Encoder. The style encoder E extracts N style vectors of size d from an input image and combines them to a style matrix $S \in \mathbb{R}^{N \times d}$. Remarkably, it can extract the style from either a low-resolution image x_{lr} or a high-resolution image x_{hr} and maps the encoded style to the same latent space S. The encoder disentangles the regional styles via the semantic layout M. The resulting style matrix serves as guidance for the generator. During inference, a user can sample from the latent style space S to produce diverse outputs. Please note that the encoder never combines high- and low-resolution inputs; the input is *either* a high-resolution image *or* a low-resolution image.

The style encoder consists of a convolutional neural network E_{lr} for the low-resolution and a similar convolutional neural network E_{hr} for the high resolution input. Their output is mapped to the same latent style space via a shared layer E_{Shared}. Figure 4 illustrates the flow from the inputs to the style matrix. The architecture for the high-resolution input E_{hr} consists of four convolution layers. The input is downsized twice in the intermediate two layers and upsampled again after a bottleneck. Similarly, the low-resolution encoder E_{lr} consists of four convolution layers. It upsamples the feature map once before the shared layer. The resulting feature map is then passed through the shared convolution layer E_{Shared} and mapped to the range $[-1, 1]$.

Inspired by Zhu *et al.* [62], as a final step, we collapse the output of the shared style encoder for each semantic mask using regional average pooling. This is an important step to disentangle style codes across semantic regions. We describe the regional average pooling in detail in the supplementary material.

Generator. Our generator learns a mapping $G_\Theta(x_{lr}|M, S)$, where the model conditions on both a semantic layout M and a style matrix S. This allows to influence the *appearance*, as well as the *size* and *shape* of each region in the semantic layout.

The semantic layout $M \in \{0, 1\}^{H_{hr} \times W_{hr} \times N}$ consists of one binary mask for each semantic region $\{M_0, \cdots, M_{N-1}\}$. For style, we assume a uniform distribution $S \in [-1, 1]^{N \times d}$, where each row in S represents a style vector of size d for one semantic region.

At a high level, the generator is a series of residual blocks with upsampling layers in between. Starting from the low-resolution image, it repeatedly doubles the resolution using nearest neighbor interpolation and processes the result in residual blocks. In the residual blocks, we inject semantic and style information through multiple normalization layers.

For the semantic layout, we use *spatially adaptive normalization* (SPADE) [44]. SPADE learns a spatial modulation of the feature maps from a semantic map. For the style, we utilize *semantic region adaptive normalization* in a similar fashion as [62]. *Semantic region adaptive normalization* is an extension to SPADE, which includes style. Like SPADE, it computes spatial modulation parameters, but also takes into consideration a style matrix computed from a reference image. In our case, we extract the style S from an input image through our style encoder as described in Sect. 3.2. For more details, please check the supplementary material.

Discriminator. We use an ensemble of two similar discriminator networks. One operates on the full image, and the another one on the half-scale of the generated image. Each network takes the concatenation of an image with its corresponding semantic layout and predicts the realism of overlapping image patches. The discriminator architecture follows [44]. Please refer to the supplementary material for a more detailed description.

Segmentation Network. Our training scheme assumes high-resolution segmentation maps, which in most cases are not available during inference. Therefore, we predict a segmentation map from the low-resolution input image x_{lr}. Particularly, we train a segmentation network to learn the mapping $M = Seg(x_{lr})$, where $M \in \{0, 1\}^{H_{hr} \times W_{hr} \times N}$ is a high-resolution semantic map.

3.3 *DeepSEE* Model Variants

We suggest two slightly different variants of our proposed method. The *guided* model learns to super-resolve an image with the help of a high-resolution (HR) reference image. The *independent* model does not require any additional guidance and infers a reference style from the low-resolution image.

The *guided* model is able to apply characteristics from a reference image. When fed a guiding image from the same person, it extracts the original characteristics (if visible). Alternatively, when feeding an image from a different

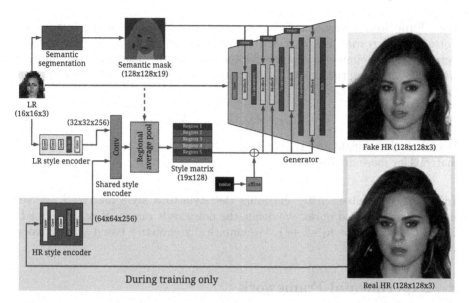

Fig. 4. *DeepSEE* architecture. Our Generator upscales a low-resolution image (LR) in a series of residual blocks. A predicted semantic mask guides the geometric layout and a style matrix controls the appearance of semantic regions. The noise added to the style matrix increases the robustness of the model. We describe the style encoding, generator and semantic segmentation in Sect. 3.2.

person, it integrates those aspects (as long as it is consistent with the low-resolution input). Figure 1 shows an example, where we first generate an image with the style from the same person and then alter particular regions with styles from other images. The second (*independent*) model applies to the case where no reference image is available.

The *independent* and the *guided* differ in the way the style matrix S is computed. For the *independent* model, we extract the style from the low-resolution input image: $S = E(x_{lr})$. In contrast, the *guided* model uses a high-resolution reference image x_{hr}^{ref} to compute the style $S = E(x_{hr}^{ref})$. It is worth to mention that for training, paired supervision is not necessary as we only require *one* high resolution picture of a person.

3.4 Training

The semantic segmentation network is trained independently from the other networks.

We train the generator, encoder and discriminator end-to-end in an adversarial setting, similar to [44,63]. As a difference, we inject noise at multiple stages of the generator. We list hyper-parameters and training details in the supplementary material. In the following, we describe the loss function and explain the noise injection.

Loss Function. Our loss function is identical to [44]. Our discriminator computes an adversarial loss $\mathcal{L}_{adv}$ with feature matching $\mathcal{L}_{feat}$: the L1 distance between the discriminator features for the real and the fake image. In addition, we employ a perceptual loss $\mathcal{L}_{vgg}$ from a VGG-19 network [39]. We define our full loss function in Eq. 3:

$$\mathcal{L} = \mathcal{L}_{adv} + \lambda_{feat}\mathcal{L}_{feat} + \lambda_{vgg}\mathcal{L}_{vgg} \tag{3}$$

We set the loss weights to $\lambda_{feat} = \lambda_{vgg} = 10$; please refer to the supplementary material for more details.

Injection of Noise. After encoding the style to a style matrix S, we add uniformly distributed noise. We define the noisy style matrix S' as $S' = S + U$, where $U_{ij} \sim Uniform(-\delta, +\delta)$. We empirically choose δ based on the model variant.

4   Experimental Framework

4.1   Datasets

We train and evaluate our method on face images from CelebAMask-HQ [64,65] and CelebA [11]. We use the official training splits for developing and training and test on the provided test splits. All low-resolution images (serving as inputs) are computed via bicubic downsampling. The supplementary material shows qualitative results on the Flickr-Faces-HQ Dataset [42] and on outdoor scenes from ADE20K [4,66].

4.2   Semantic Segmentation

We train a segmentation network [67,68] on images from CelebAMask-HQ [64, 65]. The network learns to predict a high-resolution segmentation map with 19 semantic regions from a low-resolution image. As a model, we choose DeepLab V3+ [67–69] with DRN [70,71] as the backbone.

4.3   Baseline and Evaluation Metrics

We establish a baseline via bicubic interpolation; we first downsample an image to a low-resolution and then upsample it back to the high resolution.

We compute the traditional super-resolution metrics *peak signal-to-noise ratio* (PSNR), *structural similarity index* (SSIM) [32] and the perceptual metrics *Fréchet Inception Distance* (FID) [35] and *Learned Perceptual Image Patch Similarity* (LPIPS) [34]. Our method focuses on generating results of high perceptual quality, measured by LPIPS and FID. PSNR and SSIM are frequently used, however, they are known not to correlate very well with perceptual quality [34]. However, we still list SSIM scores for completion and report PSNR in the supplementary material.

Table 1. We compare with related work for 8× upscaling on high-resolution images of size 128 × 128 (CelebA [11]) and 256 × 256 (CelebAMask-HQ [7,65]). We compute all metrics on the official test sets and list quantitative metrics for related work where checkpoints are available. Both our *DeepSEE* variants outperform the other methods on the perceptual metrics (LPIPS [34] and FID [35]). For qualitative results, please look at Fig. 5 and the supplementary material.

Method	a) 128 × 128			b) 256 × 256		
	SSIM ↑	LPIPS ↓	FID ↓	SSIM ↑	LPIPS ↓	FID ↓
Bicubic	0.5917	0.5625	159.60	0.6635	0.5443	125.15
FSRNet (MSE) [9]	0.5647	0.2885	54.48	–	–	–
FSRNet (GAN) [9]	0.5403	0.2304	55.62	–	–	–
Kim *et al.* [7]	**0.6634**	0.1175	11.41	–	–	–
GFRNet [18]	–	–	–	0.6726	0.3472	55.22
GWAInet [19]	–	–	–	0.6834	0.1832	28.79
Ours (indep.)	0.6631	**0.1063**	13.84	0.6770	0.1691	22.97
Ours (guided)	0.6628	0.1071	**11.25**	**0.6887**	**0.1519**	**22.02**

5 Discussion

We validate our method on two different setups. First, we compare with state-of-the-art methods in face hallucination and provide both quantitative and qualitative results. Second, we show results for extreme and explorative super-resolution by applying numerous manipulations for 32× upscaling.

5.1 Comparison to Face Hallucination Methods

To the best of our knowledge, our method is the first face hallucination model based on discrete semantic masks. We compare with *(i)* models that use reference images [18,19] and *(ii)* models guided by facial landmarks [7,9].

For *(i)*, we compare with GFRNet [18] and GWAInet [19], both of which leverage an image from the same person to guide the upscaling. Our method achieves the best scores for all metrics in Table 1 (b). For perceptual metrics, LPIPS [34] and FID [35], *DeepSEE* outperforms the other methods by a considerable margin. As we depict in Fig. 5, our proposed method also produces more convincing results, in particular for difficult regions, such as eyes, hair and teeth. We provide more examples in the supplementary material.

For models based on facial landmarks *(ii)*, Table 1 (a) compares *DeepSEE* with FSRNet [9] and Kim *et al.* [7].[1] *DeepSEE* achieves the highest scores for LPIPS and FID. The supplementary material contains a visual comparison.

---

[1] The models from [7,9] were trained to generate images of size 128 × 128, so we can evaluate in their setting on CelebA. [18,19] generate larger images (256×256, whereas CelebA images have size 218 × 178), hence we evaluate on CelebAMask-HQ [64,65].

GFRNet   GWAInet   Ours (indep.)   Ours (guided)   Ground truth

Fig. 5. Comparison to related work on 8× upscaling. We compare with our default solutions for the *independent* and *guided* model. The randomly sampled guiding images are on the top right of each image; the bottom right corner shows the predicted semantic mask (if applicable). Our results look less blurry than GFRNet [18]. Comparing to GWAInet [19], we observe differences in visual quality for difficult regions, like hair, eyes or teeth. With the additional semantic input, our method can produce more realistic textures. Please zoom in for better viewing.

Semantics   LR   Interpolation variants

Fig. 6. Interpolation in the style latent space. We linearly interpolate between two style matrices, smoothly increasing contrast. Please refer to the supplementary material for more examples.

It is important to note that given the same inputs (*e.g.* a low-resolution and a guiding image), all related face hallucination models output a single solution; despite the fact that there would exist multiple valid results. In contrast, our method can generate an infinite number of solutions, and provides the user with fine-grained control over the output. Figure 1 and Fig. 2 show several consistent solutions for a low-resolution image. *DeepSEE* can not only extract the overall appearance from a guiding image of the same person, but it can also inject aspects from other people; and even leverage completely different style images, for instance, geometric patterns (Fig. 1). We describe Fig. 1 in more detail in Sect. 5.2. In addition, our method allows to manipulate semantics, *i.e.* changing the shape, size or content of regions (Fig. 7), *e.g.* eyeglasses, eyebrows, noses, lips, hair, skin, etc. We provide various additional visualizations in the supplementary material.

Fig. 7. Manipulating semantics for $32\times$ **upscaling.** We continuously manipulate the semantic mask and change regional shapes, starting at the default solution (in the first column). In each subsequent column, we highlight the manipulated region and show the resulting image.

5.2 Manipulations

Our proposed approach is an explorative super-resolution model, which allows a user to tune two main *knobs*—the style matrix and the semantic layout—in order to manipulate the model output. Figure 3 shows these knobs in green boxes.

Style Manipulations. The first way to change the output image is to adapt the disentangled style matrix; for instance by adding random noise (supplementary material), by interpolating between style codes (Fig. 6), or by mixing multiple styles (Fig. 1). Going from one style code to another gradually changes the image output. For example, interpolating between style codes can make contrasts slowly disappear, or on the contrary, become more prominent (Fig. 6).

Semantic Manipulations. The second tuning knob is the semantic layout. The user can change the size and shape of semantic regions, which causes the generator to adapt the output representation accordingly. Figure 7 shows an example where we close the mouth and make the chin more pointy by manipulating the regions for lips and facial skin. Furthermore, we change the shape of eyebrows, reduce the nose and update the stroke of the eyebrows. It is also possible to create hair on a bold head or add/remove eyeglasses (please check the supplementary material). The manipulations should not be too strong, unrealistic or inconsistent with the low-resolution input. Our model is trained with a strong low-resolution prior and hence, only allows relatively subtle shape manipulations.

5.3 Extreme Super-Resolution

While most previous methods apply upscaling factors of $8\times$ [7,9,18,19] or $16\times$ [12–14], *DeepSEE* is capable of going beyond—with upscaling factors of

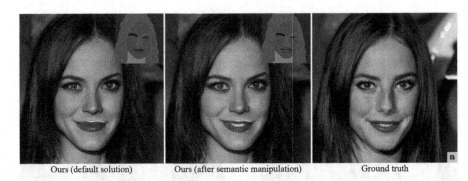

| Ours (default solution) | Ours (after semantic manipulation) | Ground truth |

Fig. 8. Extreme super-resolution. We show how manipulations can align the model output with an expected outcome. Our default solution shows a closed mouth, while given the ground truth, we would expect a smile. After manipulating the semantic mask, *DeepSEE* produces an image that very closely resembles the ground truth.

Table 2. Ablation study results. We explore the effect of style and semantics. Semantics have the strongest influence on both fidelity (PSNR, SSIM [32]) and visual quality (LPIPS [34], FID [35]), but the best results require both semantics and style. Finally, using a high-resolution guiding image (*guided*) from the same person provides an additional point of control to the user compared with the *independent* model.

Name	Semantics	LR-Style	HR-Style	SSIM ↑	LPIPS ↓	FID ↓
Prior-only	–	–	–	0.6168	0.1233	25.11
LR-style-only	–	✓	–	0.6485	0.1103	19.29
HR-style-only	–	–	✓	0.6507	0.1108	16.66
Semantics-only	✓	–	–	0.6543	0.1096	12.57
Independent	✓	✓	–	**0.6631**	**0.1063**	13.84
Guided	✓	✓	✓	0.6628	0.1071	**11.25**

up to 32×. Instead of reconstructing a single target, *DeepSEE* can generate multiple variants in a controlled way and hence, a user is more likely to find an expected outcome. Figure 8 shows an example where the default solution does not perfectly match the ground truth image. A user can now manipulate the semantic mask and create a second version, which is closer to the ground truth image. This shows the power of explorative super-resolution techniques for extreme upscaling factors.

6   Ablation Study

We investigate the influence of *DeepSEE*'s main components—semantics and style injection—in an ablation study. Section 6.1 describes the study setup and we discuss the outcome in Sect. 6.2.

6.1 Ablation Study Setup

We train four additional models, where we remove the components that inject semantics and/or style. For the first model (*prior-only*), we disable both semantics and style—the model's only conditioning is on the low-resolution input. For the *LR-style-only* and *HR-style-only* models, we do not use the semantic map, but we do condition on the style matrix computed from another low-/high-resolution image of the same person. Lastly, we train a *semantic-only* model that does not inject any style but conditions on semantics.

All models are trained for 7 epochs, which corresponds to 3 d on a single TITAN Xp GPU, with upscaling factor 8× and batch size 4. We use the CelebA [11] dataset. For details, please check the supplementary material.

6.2 Ablation Discussion

All performance scores improve when adding either semantics, style or both (Table 2). Comparing models with either semantics or style (*LR-style-only* and *HR-style-only* vs. *semantics-only*), the perceptual metrics (LPIPS [34] and FID [35]) show better scores when including semantics. Combining both semantic and style yields even better results for both the distortion measures (PSNR and SSIM [32]) and the visual metrics (LPIPS [34] and FID [35]). The performance between our two suggested model variants (the *independent* model and *guided* model) is very similar for fidelity metrics. In terms of perceptual quality, the *guided* image clearly beats the *independent* in FID. However, we empirically find that the *independent* model is more flexible towards random manipulations of the style matrix. Please refer to the supplementary material for visual examples.

7 Conclusion

The super-resolution problem is ill-posed because most high-frequency information is missing and needs to be hallucinated. In this paper, we tackle super-resolution in an explorative approach, *DeepSEE*, based on semantic regions and disentangled style codes. *DeepSEE* allows for fine-grained control of the output, disentangled into region-dependent appearance and shape. Our model goes beyond common upscaling factors and allows to magnify up to 32×. Our validation for faces demonstrate results of high perceptual quality.

Interesting directions for further research could be to identify meaningful directions in the latent style space (*e.g.* age, gender, illumination, contrast, *etc.*), or to apply *DeepSEE* to other domains.

Acknowledgments. We would like to thank the Hasler Foundation. This work was partly supported by the ETH Zürich Fund (OK), by Huawei, Amazon AWS and Nvidia grants.

References

1. Timofte, R., Agustsson, E., Van Gool, L., Yang, M.H., Zhang, L.: Ntire 2017 challenge on single image super-resolution: Methods and results. In: Proceedings of the IEEE Conference on Computer Vision and Pattern Recognition Workshops, pp. 114–125 (2017)
2. Blau, Y., Mechrez, R., Timofte, R., Michaeli, T., Zelnik-Manor, L.: The 2018 pirm challenge on perceptual image super-resolution. In: Proceedings of the European Conference on Computer Vision (ECCV) (2018)
3. Cai, J., Gu, S., Timofte, R., Zhang, L.: Ntire 2019 challenge on real image super-resolution: Methods and results. In: Proceedings of the IEEE Conference on Computer Vision and Pattern Recognition Workshops (2019)
4. Wang, X., Yu, K., Dong, C., Change Loy, C.: Recovering realistic texture in image super-resolution by deep spatial feature transform. In: Proceedings of the IEEE Conference on Computer Vision and Pattern Recognition, pp. 606–615 (2018)
5. Yu, X., Fernando, B., Hartley, R., Porikli, F.: Super-resolving very low-resolution face images with supplementary attributes. In: Proceedings of the IEEE Conference on Computer Vision and Pattern Recognition, pp. 908–917 (2018)
6. Li, M., Sun, Y., Zhang, Z., Xie, H., Yu, J.: Deep learning face hallucination via attributes transfer and enhancement. In: 2019 IEEE International Conference on Multimedia and Expo (ICME), pp. 604–609. IEEE (2019)
7. Kim, D., Kim, M., Kwon, G., Kim, D.S.: Progressive face super-resolution via attention to facial landmark. In: Proceedings of the 30th British Machine Vision Conference (BMVC) (2019)
8. Lee, C.H., Zhang, K., Lee, H.C., Cheng, C.W., Hsu, W.: Attribute augmented convolutional neural network for face hallucination. In: Proceedings of the IEEE Conference on Computer Vision and Pattern Recognition Workshops, pp. 721–729 (2018)
9. Chen, Y., Tai, Y., Liu, X., Shen, C., Yang, J.: Fsrnet: end-to-end learning face super-resolution with facial priors. In: Proceedings of the IEEE Conference on Computer Vision and Pattern Recognition, pp. 2492–2501 (2018)
10. Yu, X., Fernando, B., Ghanem, B., Porikli, F., Hartley, R.: Face super-resolution guided by facial component heatmaps. In: Proceedings of the European Conference on Computer Vision (ECCV), pp. 217–233 (2018)
11. Liu, Z., Luo, P., Wang, X., Tang, X.: Deep learning face attributes in the wild. In: Proceedings of International Conference on Computer Vision (ICCV) (2015)
12. Shang, T., Dai, Q., Zhu, S., Yang, T., Guo, Y.: Perceptual extreme super-resolution network with receptive field block. In: Proceedings of the IEEE/CVF Conference on Computer Vision and Pattern Recognition Workshops, pp. 440–441 (2020)
13. Gu, S., et al.: Aim 2019 challenge on image extreme super-resolution: Methods and results. In: 2019 IEEE/CVF International Conference on Computer Vision Workshop (ICCVW), pp. 3556–3564. IEEE (2019)
14. Zhang, K., Gu, S., Timofte, R.: Ntire 2020 challenge on perceptual extreme super-resolution: Methods and results. In: Proceedings of the IEEE/CVF Conference on Computer Vision and Pattern Recognition Workshops, pp. 492–493 (2020)
15. Menon, S., Damian, A., Hu, M., Ravi, N., Rudin, C.: Pulse: self-supervised photo upsampling via latent space exploration of generative models. In: The IEEE Conference on Computer Vision and Pattern Recognition (CVPR) (2020)
16. Ledig, C., et al.: Photo-realistic single image super-resolution using a generative adversarial network. In: Proceedings of the IEEE Conference on Computer Vision and Pattern Recognition, pp. 4681–4690 (2017)

17. Wang, X., et al.: Esrgan: Enhanced super-resolution generative adversarial networks. In: Proceedings of the European Conference on Computer Vision (ECCV) (2018)

18. Li, X., Liu, M., Ye, Y., Zuo, W., Lin, L., Yang, R.: Learning warped guidance for blind face restoration. In: Proceedings of the European Conference on Computer Vision (ECCV), pp. 272–289 (2018

19. Dogan, B., Gu, S., Timofte, R.: Exemplar guided face image super-resolution without facial landmarks. In: Proceedings of the IEEE Conference on Computer Vision and Pattern Recognition Workshops (2019)

20. Fattal, R.: Image upsampling via imposed edge statistics. In: ACM SIGGRAPH 2007 papers, pp. 95-es (2007)

21. Sun, J., Xu, Z., Shum, H.Y.: Image super-resolution using gradient profile prior. In: 2008 IEEE Conference on Computer Vision and Pattern Recognition, pp. 1–8. IEEE (2008)

22. Aly, H.A., Dubois, E.: Image up-sampling using total-variation regularization with a new observation model. IEEE Trans. Image Process. **14**, 1647–1659 (2005)

23. Zhang, H., Yang, J., Zhang, Y., Huang, T.S.: Non-local kernel regression for image and video restoration. In: Daniilidis, K., Maragos, P., Paragios, N. (eds.) ECCV 2010. LNCS, vol. 6313, pp. 566–579. Springer, Heidelberg (2010). https://doi.org/10.1007/978-3-642-15558-1_41

24. Ni, K.S., Nguyen, T.Q.: Image superresolution using support vector regression. IEEE Trans. Image Process. **16**, 1596–1610 (2007)

25. Wang, Q., Tang, X., Shum, H.: Patch based blind image super resolution. In: Tenth IEEE International Conference on Computer Vision (ICCV 2005), vol. 1, pp. 709–716. IEEE (2005)

26. He, H., Siu, W.C.: Single image super-resolution using gaussian process regression. In: CVPR 2011, pp. 449–456. IEEE (2011)

27. Yang, J., Wright, J., Huang, T.S., Ma, Y.: Image super-resolution via sparse representation. IEEE Trans. Image Process. **19**, 2861–2873 (2010)

28. Timofte, R., De Smet, V., Van Gool, L.: A+: adjusted anchored neighborhood regression for fast super-resolution. In: Cremers, D., Reid, I., Saito, H., Yang, M.-H. (eds.) ACCV 2014. LNCS, vol. 9006, pp. 111–126. Springer, Cham (2015). https://doi.org/10.1007/978-3-319-16817-3_8

29. Dong, C., Loy, C.C., He, K., Tang, X.: Image super-resolution using deep convolutional networks. IEEE Trans. Pattern Anal. Mach. Intell. **38**, 295–307 (2015)

30. Kim, J., Kwon Lee, J., Mu Lee, K.: Deeply-recursive convolutional network for image super-resolution. In: Proceedings of the IEEE Conference on Computer Vision and Pattern Recognition, pp. 1637–1645 (2016)

31. Timofte, R., Gu, S., Wu, J., Van Gool, L.: Ntire 2018 challenge on single image super-resolution: methods and results. In: Proceedings of the IEEE Conference on Computer Vision and Pattern Recognition Workshops, pp. 852–863 (2018)

32. Wang, Z., Bovik, A.C., Sheikh, H.R., Simoncelli, E.P.: Image quality assessment: from error visibility to structural similarity. IEEE Trans. Image Process. **13**, 600–612 (2004)

33. Blau, Y., Michaeli, T.: The perception-distortion tradeoff. In: Proceedings of the IEEE Conference on Computer Vision and Pattern Recognition, pp. 6228–6237 (2018)

34. Zhang, R., Isola, P., Efros, A.A., Shechtman, E., Wang, O.: The unreasonable effectiveness of deep features as a perceptual metric. In: CVPR (2018)

35. Heusel, M., Ramsauer, H., Unterthiner, T., Nessler, B., Hochreiter, S.: Gans trained by a two time-scale update rule converge to a local nash equilibrium. In: Advances in Neural Information Processing Systems, pp. 6626–6637 (2017)
36. Sajjadi, M.S., Scholkopf, B., Hirsch, M.: Enhancenet: single image super-resolution through automated texture synthesis. In: Proceedings of the IEEE International Conference on Computer Vision, pp. 4491–4500 (2017)
37. Bahat, Y., Michaeli, T.: Explorable super resolution. In: Proceedings of the IEEE/CVF Conference on Computer Vision and Pattern Recognition, pp. 2716–2725 (2020)
38. Johnson, J., Alahi, A., Fei-Fei, L.: Perceptual losses for real-time style transfer and super-resolution. In: Leibe, B., Matas, J., Sebe, N., Welling, M. (eds.) ECCV 2016. LNCS, vol. 9906, pp. 694–711. Springer, Cham (2016). https://doi.org/10.1007/978-3-319-46475-6_43
39. Simonyan, K., Zisserman, A.: Very deep convolutional networks for large-scale image recognition. In: International Conference on Learning Representations (ICLR) (2015)
40. Bulat, A., Tzimiropoulos, G.: Super-fan: integrated facial landmark localization and super-resolution of real-world low resolution faces in arbitrary poses with GANs. In: Proceedings of the IEEE Conference on Computer Vision and Pattern Recognition, pp. 109–117 (2018)
41. Goodfellow, I., et al.: Generative adversarial nets. In: Advances in Neural Information Processing Systems, pp. 2672–2680 (2014)
42. Karras, T., Laine, S., Aila, T.: A style-based generator architecture for generative adversarial networks. In: Proceedings of the IEEE Conference on Computer Vision and Pattern Recognition, pp. 4401–4410 (2019)
43. Karras, T., Laine, S., Aittala, M., Hellsten, J., Lehtinen, J., Aila, T.: Analyzing and improving the image quality of stylegan. In: Proceedings of the IEEE/CVF Conference on Computer Vision and Pattern Recognition, pp. 8110–8119 (2020)
44. Park, T., Liu, M.Y., Wang, T.C., Zhu, J.Y.: Semantic image synthesis with spatially-adaptive normalization. In: Proceedings of the IEEE Conference on Computer Vision and Pattern Recognition, pp. 2337–2346 (2019)
45. Choi, Y., Choi, M., Kim, M., Ha, J.W., Kim, S., Choo, J.: Stargan: unified generative adversarial networks for multi-domain image-to-image translation. In: Proceedings of the IEEE Conference on Computer Vision and Pattern Recognition, pp. 8789–8797 (2018)
46. Romero, A., Arbeláez, P., Van Gool, L., Timofte, R.: Smit: stochastic multi-label image-to-image translation. In: Proceedings of the IEEE International Conference on Computer Vision Workshops (2019)
47. He, K., Zhang, X., Ren, S., Sun, J.: Deep residual learning for image recognition. In: Proceedings of the IEEE Conference on Computer Vision and Pattern Recognition, pp. 770–778 (2016)
48. Ren, Z., He, C., Zhang, Q.: Fractional order total variation regularization for image super-resolution. Signal Process. **93**, 2408–2421 (2013)
49. Haris, M., Shakhnarovich, G., Ukita, N.: Deep back-projection networks for super-resolution. In: Proceedings of the IEEE Conference on Computer Vision and Pattern Recognition, pp. 1664–1673 (2018)
50. Li, Y., Dong, W., Xie, X., Shi, G., Jinjian, W., li, X.: Image super-resolution with parametric sparse model learning. IEEE Trans. Image Process **27**(9), 4638-4650 (2018)
51. Lugmayr, A., Danelljan, M., Van Gool, L., Timofte, R.: Srflow: learning the super-resolution space with normalizing flow. In: ECCV (2020)

52. Ravishankar, S., Reddy, C.N., Tripathi, S., Murthy, K.V.V.: Image super resolution using sparse image and singular values as priors. In: Real, P., Diaz-Pernil, D., Molina-Abril, H., Berciano, A., Kropatsch, W. (eds.) CAIP 2011. LNCS, vol. 6855, pp. 380–388. Springer, Heidelberg (2011). https://doi.org/10.1007/978-3-642-23678-5_45

53. Dinh, L., Sohl-Dickstein, J., Bengio, S.: Density estimation using real nvp. In: International Conference on Learning Representations (ICLR) (2017)

54. Kingma, D.P., Dhariwal, P.: Glow: generative flow with invertible 1x1 convolutions. In: Advances in Neural Information Processing Systems, pp. 10215–10224 (2018)

55. Xiao, M., et al.: Invertible image rescaling. In: ECCV (2020)

56. Wang, Z., Chen, J., Hoi, S.C.H.: Deep learning for image super-resolution: a survey. IEEE Trans. Pattern Anal. Mach. Intell., 1–23 (2020). https://doi.org/10.1109/TPAMI.2020.2982166

57. Riegler, G., Rüther, M., Bischof, H.: ATGV-net: accurate depth super-resolution. In: Leibe, B., Matas, J., Sebe, N., Welling, M. (eds.) ECCV 2016. LNCS, vol. 9907, pp. 268–284. Springer, Cham (2016). https://doi.org/10.1007/978-3-319-46487-9_17

58. Hui, T.-W., Loy, C.C., Tang, X.: Depth map super-resolution by deep multi-scale guidance. In: Leibe, B., Matas, J., Sebe, N., Welling, M. (eds.) ECCV 2016. LNCS, vol. 9907, pp. 353–369. Springer, Cham (2016). https://doi.org/10.1007/978-3-319-46487-9_22

59. Song, X., Dai, Y., Qin, X.: Deep depth super-resolution: learning depth super-resolution using deep convolutional neural network. In: Lai, S.-H., Lepetit, V., Nishino, K., Sato, Y. (eds.) ACCV 2016. LNCS, vol. 10114, pp. 360–376. Springer, Cham (2017). https://doi.org/10.1007/978-3-319-54190-7_22

60. Timofte, R., De Smet, V., Van Gool, L.: Semantic super-resolution: when and where is it useful? Comput. Vis. Image Underst. **142**, 1–12 (2016)

61. Gu, S., Lugmayr, A., Danelljan, M., Fritsche, M., Lamour, J., Timofte, R.: Div8k: Diverse 8k resolution image dataset. In: 2019 IEEE/CVF International Conference on Computer Vision Workshop (ICCVW), pp. 3512–3516. IEEE (2019)

62. Zhu, P., Abdal, R., Qin, Y., Wonka, P.: Sean: image synthesis with semantic region-adaptive normalization. In: Proceedings of the IEEE/CVF Conference on Computer Vision and Pattern Recognition, pp. 5104–5113 (2020)

63. Wang, T.C., Liu, M.Y., Zhu, J.Y., Tao, A., Kautz, J., Catanzaro, B.: High-resolution image synthesis and semantic manipulation with conditional GANs. In: Proceedings of the IEEE Conference on Computer Vision and Pattern Recognition, pp. 8798–8807 (2018)

64. Karras, T., Aila, T., Laine, S., Lehtinen, J.: Progressive growing of GANs for improved quality, stability, and variation. In: International Conference on Learning Representations (ICLR) (2018)

65. Lee, C.H., Liu, Z., Wu, L., Luo, P.: Maskgan: towards diverse and interactive facial image manipulation. In: Proceedings of the IEEE/CVF Conference on Computer Vision and Pattern Recognition, pp. 5549–5558 (2020)

66. Zhou, B., Zhao, H., Puig, X., Fidler, S., Barriuso, A., Torralba, A.: Scene parsing through ade20k dataset. In: Proceedings of the IEEE Conference on Computer Vision and Pattern Recognition (2017)

67. Chen, L.C., Papandreou, G., Kokkinos, I., Murphy, K., Yuille, A.L.: Deeplab: semantic image segmentation with deep convolutional nets, atrous convolution, and fully connected crfs. IEEE Trans. Pattern Anal. Mach. Intell. **40**, 834–848 (2017)

68. Chen, L.C., Papandreou, G., Kokkinos, I., Murphy, K., Yuille, A.L.: Rethinking atrous convolution for semantic image segmentation liang-chieh. IEEE Transactions on Pattern Analysis and Machine Intelligence (2018)
69. Chen, L.C., Zhu, Y., Papandreou, G., Schroff, F., Adam, H.: Encoder-decoder with atrous separable convolution for semantic image segmentation. In: Proceedings of the European conference on computer vision (ECCV), pp. 801–818 (2018)
70. Yu, F., Koltun, V.: Multi-scale context aggregation by dilated convolutions. In: International Conference on Learning Representations (ICLR) (2016)
71. Yu, F., Koltun, V., Funkhouser, T.: Dilated residual networks. In: Computer Vision and Pattern Recognition (CVPR) (2017)

*dp*VAEs: Fixing Sample Generation
for Regularized VAEs

Riddhish Bhalodia, Iain Lee, and Shireen Elhabian$^{(\boxtimes)}$

Scientific Computing and Imaging Institute, University of Utah,
Salt Lake City, UT, USA
{riddhishb,iclee,shireen}@sci.utah.edu

Abstract. Unsupervised representation learning via generative modeling is a staple to many computer vision applications in the absence of
labeled data. Variational Autoencoders (VAEs) are powerful generative
models that learn representations useful for data generation. However,
due to inherent challenges in the training objective, VAEs fail to learn
useful representations amenable for downstream tasks. Regularization-
based methods that attempt to improve the representation learning
aspect of VAEs come at a price: poor sample generation. In this paper, we
explore this representation-generation trade-off for regularized VAEs and
introduce a new family of priors, namely *decoupled priors*, or *dp*VAEs,
that decouple the representation space from the generation space. This
decoupling enables the use of VAE regularizers on the representation
space without impacting the distribution used for sample generation, and
thereby reaping the representation learning benefits of the regularizations
without sacrificing the sample generation. *dp*VAE leverages invertible
networks to learn a bijective mapping from an arbitrarily complex representation distribution to a simple, tractable, generative distribution.
Decoupled priors can be adapted to the state-of-the-art VAE regularizers without additional hyperparameter tuning. We showcase the use of
*dp*VAEs with different regularizers. Experiments on MNIST, SVHN, and
CelebA demonstrate, quantitatively and qualitatively, that *dp*VAE fixes
sample generation and improves representation for regularized VAEs.

1 Introduction

Is it possible to learn a *powerful generative model* that matches the true data
distribution with *useful data representations* amenable to downstream tasks in
an unsupervised way? —This question is the driving force behind most unsupervised representation learning via state-of-the-art (SOTA) generative modeling
methods (*e.g.,* [1–4]), with applications in artificial creativity [5,6], reinforcement
learning [7], few-shot learning [8], and semi-supervised learning [9]. A common

Electronic supplementary material The online version of this chapter (https://
doi.org/10.1007/978-3-030-69538-5_39) contains supplementary material, which is
available to authorized users.

© Springer Nature Switzerland AG 2021
H. Ishikawa et al. (Eds.): ACCV 2020, LNCS 12625, pp. 643–660, 2021.
https://doi.org/10.1007/978-3-030-69538-5_39

theme behind such works is learning the data generation process using *latent variable models* [10,11] that seek to learn representations useful for data generation; an approach known as *analysis-by-synthesis* [12,13].

Variational autoencoders (VAEs) [14,15] marry latent variable models and deep learning by having independent, network-parameterized *generative* and *inference* models that are trained jointly to maximize the marginal log-likelihood of the training data. VAE introduces a variational posterior distribution that approximates the true posterior to derive a tractable lower bound on the marginal log-likelihood, a.k.a. the evidence lower bound (ELBO). The ELBO is then maximized using stochastic gradient descent by virtue of the reparameterization trick [14,15]. Among the many successes of VAEs in representation learning tasks, VAE-based methods have demonstrated SOTA performance for semi-supervised image and text classification tasks [8,9,16–19].

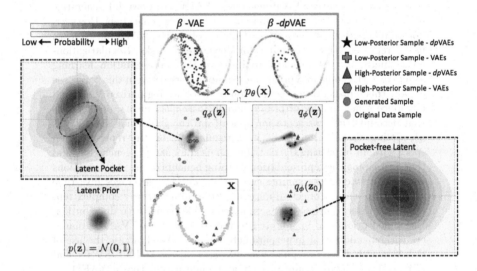

Fig. 1. *dp*VAE **fixes sample generation for a regularized VAE.** The green box shows β-VAE [2] (left column) and β-VAE with the proposed *decoupled prior* (right column), each trained on the two moons dataset. β-VAE: Top to bottom shows the generated samples (colors reflect probability of generation), the aggregate posterior $q_\phi(\mathbf{z})$ and the training samples. The low-posterior samples lie in the latent pockets of $q_\phi(\mathbf{z})$ (shown in enlarged section on the left) and correspond to off-manifold samples in the data space, and high-posterior samples correspond to latent leaks. The β-*dp*VAE decouples the representation $\mathbf{z}$ and generation $\mathbf{z}_0$ spaces. The generation space is pocket-free and very close to standard normal, resulting in generating samples on the data manifold. Furthermore, the representation learning is well established in the representation space (see Sect. 4.1 for more discussion). (Color figure online)

Representation learning via VAEs is ill-posed due to the disconnect between the ELBO and the downstream task [20]. Specifically, optimizing the marginal log-likelihood is not always sufficient for good representation learning due to the inherent challenges rooted in the ELBO that result in the tendency to *ignore latent variables* and *not encode information about the data in the latent space* [1, 11, 20–22]. To improve the representations learned by VAEs, a slew of regularizations have been proposed. Many of these regularizers act on the VAE latent space to promote specific characteristics in the learned representations, such as disentanglement [1–3, 6, 23, 24] and informative latent codes [25, 26]. However, better representation learning usually sacrifices sample generation, which is manifested by a distribution mismatch between the marginal (a.k.a. aggregate) latent posterior and the latent prior. This mismatch results in *latent pockets and leaks*; a *submanifold* structure in the latent space (a phenomena demonstrated in Fig. 1 and explored in more detail in Sect. 4.1). Latent pockets contain samples that are highly supported under the prior but not covered by the aggregate posterior (*i.e., low-posterior samples* [27]), while latent leaks contain samples supported under the aggregate posterior but less likely to be generated under the prior (*i.e., high-posterior samples*). This behavior has been reported for vanilla VAE [27, 28] but it is substantiated by augmenting the ELBO with regularizers (see Fig. 1).

To address this representation-generation trade-off for regularized VAEs, we introduce the idea of decoupling the latent space for representation (*representation space*) from the space that drives sample generation (*generation space*); presenting a general framework for VAE regularization. To this end, we propose a new family of latent priors for VAEs—*decoupled priors* or *dp*VAEs —that leverages the merits of invertible deep networks. In particular, *dp*VAE transforms a tractable, simple base prior distribution in the generation space to a more expressive prior in the representation space that reflects the submanifold structure dictated by the regularizer. This is done using an invertible mapping that is jointly trained with the VAE's inference and generative models. SOTA VAE regularizers can thus be directly plugged in to promote specific characteristics in the representation space without impacting the distribution used for sample generation. We showcase, quantitatively and qualitatively, that *dp*VAE with different SOTA regularizers improve sample generation, without sacrificing their representation learning benefits.

It is worth emphasizing that, being likelihood-based models, VAEs are trained to put probability mass on all training samples, forcing the model to *over-generalize* [29], and generating blurry samples (*i.e.,* off data manifold). This is in contrast to generative adversarial networks (GANs) [30] that generate outstanding image quality but could lack the full data support [31]. *dp*VAE is not expected to resolve the over-generalization problem in VAEs, but to mitigate poor sample quality resulting from regularization.

The contribution of this paper is fourfold:

- Analyze the latent submanifold structure induced by VAE regularizers.
- Introduce a decoupled prior family for VAEs as a general regularization framework that improves both sample generation and representation learning, without sacrificing the ELBO of the vanilla VAE.

- Derive the dpVAE ELBO of SOTA regularized VAEs; β-dpVAE, β-TC-dpVAE, Factor-dpVAE, and Info-dpVAE.
- Demonstrate empirically on three benchmark datasets the improved generation performance and the preservation of representation characteristics promoted via regularizers without additional hyperparameter tuning.

2 Related Work

To improve sample quality, a family of approaches exist that combine the inference capability of VAEs and the outstanding sample quality of GANs [30]. Leveraging the density ratio trick [30,32] that only requires samples, VAE-GAN hybrids in the latent (*e.g.,* [33,34]), data (*e.g.,* [27,29]), and joint (both latent and data *e.g.,* [35]) spaces avoid restrictions to explicit posterior and/or likelihood distribution families, paving the way for marginals matching [27]. However, such hybrids scale poorly with latent dimensions, lack accurate likelihood bound estimates, and do not provide better quality samples than GAN variants [27]. For instance, VAE variants, such as adversarial [36] and Wasserstein [37] autoencoders, introduce matching penalties (*e.g.,* adversarial or maximum mean discrepancy regularizers) to match distributions in the latent space. Nonetheless, such matching penalties, in contrast to dpVAE, modify the likelihood lower bound and use looser bounds for training, and hence introduce a trade off with sample reconstruction [38]. Expressive posterior distributions can lead to better sample quality [33,39] and are essential to prevent latent variables from being ignored in case of powerful generative models [21]. But results in [27] suggest that the posterior distribution is not the main learning roadblock for VAEs.

More recently, the key role of the prior distribution family in VAE training has been investigated [22,27,28]; poor latent representations are often attributed to restricting the latent prior to an overly simplistic distribution. Furthermore, Xu *et al.* presented a formal proof of the necessity and effectiveness of learning the latent prior and theoretically analyzed the failure of the aggregate posterior to match the unit Gaussian prior [28]. This motivates several works to enrich VAEs with more expressive priors. Bauer and Mnih addressed the distribution mismatch between the aggregate posterior and the latent prior by learning a sampling function, parameterized by a neural network, in the latent space [40]. However, this resampled prior requires the estimation of the normalization constant and dictates an inefficient iterative sampling, where a truncated sampling could be used at the price of a less expressive prior due to smoothing. Tomczak and Welling proposed the variational mixture of posteriors prior (VampPrior), which is a parameterized mixture distribution in the latent space given by a fixed number of learnable pseudo (*i.e.,* virtual) data points [41]. VampPrior sampling is non-iterative and is therefore fast. However, density evaluation is expensive due to the requirement of a large number of pseudo points, typically in the order of hundreds, to match the aggregate posterior [40]. A cheaper version is a mixture of Gaussian prior proposed in [42], which gives an inferior performance compared to VampPrior and is more challenging to optimize [40]. Autoregressive priors (*e.g.,* [43,44]) come with fast density evaluation but a slow, sequential sampling process. VQ-VAE [45,46] learns VAE prior using PixelCNN [47,48] to improve sample quality. Yet, unlike *dp*VAE, VQ-VAE is not trained end-to-end and modify the underlying assumption of latent Gaussian models.

The proposed decoupled prior is inspired by flow-based generative models [39,49–51], which have shown their efficacy in generating images (*e.g.,* GLOW [52]). Such methods hinge on architectural designs that make the model invertible. However, the strict invertibility of these architectures dictate very high-dimensional latent spaces, which are not condusive to representation learning and lead to computationally expensive and oftentimes prohibitively long training. In the context of VAEs, learning latent prior using invertible networks has been proposed by several works with the potential of generating high quality samples [38,53–55]. Nonetheless, the inherent trade-off between sample representation and generation has not been explored. Such a trade-off is substantiated with regularizers that promote predefined characteristics in the latent space, providing looser bounds for training. Here, we showcase the impact of these looser bounds on sample generation and how *dp*VAE fixes sample generation.

With differences between expressiveness and efficiency, none of these methods address the fundamental challenge of VAE training in concert with existing representation-driven regularization frameworks. The proposed decoupled family of priors addresses the mismatch between the latent prior and the aggregate posterior, which improves sample generation performance and is easy to integrate with existing VAE regularizers that endow representation learning properties to VAEs. Further, the decoupled prior by itself solves the fundamental problem of representation learning in VAEs without using ad-hoc regularizers (see Table 1).

3 Background

In this section, we briefly lay down the foundations and motivations essential for the proposed VAE formulation.

3.1 Variational Autoencoders

VAE seeks to match the learned model distribution $p_\theta(\mathbf{x})$ to the true data distribution $p(\mathbf{x})$, where $\mathbf{x} \in \mathbb{R}^D$ is the observed variable in the data space. The generative and inference models in VAEs are thus jointly trained to maximize a tractable lower bound $\mathcal{L}(\theta, \phi)$ on the marginal log-likelihood $\mathbb{E}_{p(\mathbf{x})}\left[\log p_\theta(\mathbf{x})\right]$ of the training data, where $\mathbf{z} \in \mathbb{R}^L$ is an unobserved latent variable in the latent space with a prior distribution $p(\mathbf{z})$, such as $p(\mathbf{z}) \sim \mathcal{N}(\mathbf{z}; \mathbf{0}, \mathbb{I})$.

$$\mathcal{L}(\theta, \phi) = \mathbb{E}_{p(\mathbf{x})}\left[\mathbb{E}_{q_\phi(\mathbf{z}|\mathbf{x})}\left[\log p_\theta(\mathbf{x}|\mathbf{z})\right] - \mathrm{KL}\left[q_\phi(\mathbf{z}|\mathbf{x})\|p(\mathbf{z})\right]\right] \qquad (1)$$

where θ denotes the generative model parameters, ϕ denotes the inference model parameters, and $q_\phi(\mathbf{z}|\mathbf{x}) \sim \mathcal{N}(\mathbf{z}; \boldsymbol{\mu}_\mathbf{z}(\mathbf{x}), \boldsymbol{\Sigma}_\mathbf{z}(\mathbf{x}))$ is the variational posterior distribution that approximates the true posterior $p(\mathbf{z}|\mathbf{x})$, where $\boldsymbol{\mu}_\mathbf{z}(\mathbf{x}) \in \mathbb{R}^L$, $\boldsymbol{\Sigma}_\mathbf{z}(\mathbf{x}) = \mathrm{diag}(\boldsymbol{\sigma}_\mathbf{z}(\mathbf{x}))$, and $\boldsymbol{\sigma}_\mathbf{z}(\mathbf{x}) \in \mathbb{R}_+^L$.

Since the ELBO seeks to match the marginal data distribution without penalizing the poor quality of latent representation, VAE can easily ignore latent variables if a sufficiently expressive generative model $p_\theta(\mathbf{x}|\mathbf{z})$ is used (*e.g.*, PixelCNN [47]) and still maximize the ELBO [11,21,56], a property known as *information preference* [1,21]. Furthermore, VAE has the tendency to not encode information about the observed data in the latent codes since maximizing the ELBO is inherently minimizing the mutual information between $\mathbf{z} \sim q_\phi(\mathbf{z}|\mathbf{x})$ and $\mathbf{x}$ [22]. Without further assumptions or inductive biases, these failure modes hinder learning useful representations for downstream tasks.

3.2 Invertible Deep Networks

The proposed decoupled prior family for VAEs leverages flow-based generative models that are formed by a sequence of *invertible* blocks (*i.e.*, transformations), parameterized by deep networks. Consider two random variables $\mathbf{z} \in \mathcal{Z} \subset \mathbb{R}^L$ and $\mathbf{z}_0 \in \mathcal{Z}_0 \subset \mathbb{R}^L$. There exist a bijective mapping between $\mathcal{Z}$ and $\mathcal{Z}_0$ defined by a function $g : \mathcal{Z} \rightarrow \mathcal{Z}_0$, where $g(\mathbf{z}) = \mathbf{z}_0$, and its inverse $g^{-1} : \mathcal{Z}_0 \rightarrow \mathcal{Z}$ such that $\mathbf{z} = g^{-1}(\mathbf{z}_0)$. Given the above condition, we can define the *change of variable formula* for mapping probability distribution on $\mathbf{z}$ to $\mathbf{z}_0$ as follows:

$$p(\mathbf{z}) = p(\mathbf{z}_0)\left|\frac{\partial \mathbf{z}_0}{\partial \mathbf{z}}\right| = p(g(\mathbf{z}))\left|\frac{\partial g(\mathbf{z})}{\partial \mathbf{z}}\right| \tag{2}$$

By maximizing the log-likelihood and parameterizing the invertible blocks with deep networks, flow-based methods learn to transform a simple, tractable base distribution (*e.g.*, standard normal) into a more expressive one. To model distributions with arbitrary dimensions, the $g-$bijection needs to be defined such that the Jacobian determinant can be computed in a closed form. Dinh *et al.* [50] proposed the *affine coupling layers* to build a flexible bijection function g by stacking a sequence of K simple bijection blocks $\mathbf{z}_{k-1} = g_\eta^{(k)}(\mathbf{z}_k)$ of the form,

$$g_\eta^{(k)}(\mathbf{z}_k) = \mathbf{b}_k \odot \mathbf{z}_k + (1 - \mathbf{b}_k) \odot [\mathbf{z}_k \odot \exp(s_k(\mathbf{b}_k \odot \mathbf{z}_k)) + t_k(\mathbf{b}_k \odot \mathbf{z}_k)] \tag{3}$$

$$g_\eta(\mathbf{z}) = \mathbf{z}_0 = g_\eta^{(1)} \circ \cdots \circ g_\eta^{(K-1)} \circ g_\eta^{(K)}(\mathbf{z}) \tag{4}$$

where $\mathbf{z} = \mathbf{z}_K$, $\odot$ is the Hadamard (element-wise) product, $\mathbf{b}_k \in \{0,1\}^L$ is a binary mask used for partitioning the k-th block input, and $\eta = \{s_1, ..., s_K, t_1, ..., t_K\}$ are the deep networks parameters of the scaling s_k and translation t_k functions of the K blocks (see the supplementary material for network architectures).

4   General Framework for VAE Regularization

In this section, we formally define and analyze how VAE regularizations affect the generative property of VAE. We also present the decoupled prior family for VAEs (see Fig. 2) and analyze its utility to solve the submanifold problem of SOTA regularization-based VAEs.

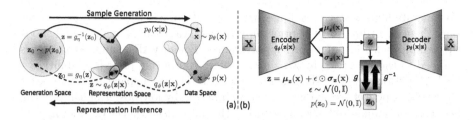

Fig. 2. *dp*VAE: (a) The latent space is decoupled into a *generation space* with a simple, tractable distribution (*e.g.*, standard normal) and a *representation space* whose distribution can be arbitrarily complex and is learned via a bijective mapping to the generation space. (b) VAE with the decoupled prior. The $g-$bijection is jointly trained with the VAE generative (*i.e.*, decoder) and inference (*i.e.*, encoder) models.

4.1 VAE Regularizers: Latent Pockets and Leaks

ELBO regularization is a conventional mechanism that enforces inductive biases (*e.g.*, disentanglement [1–3,6,23,24] and informative latent codes [25,26]) to improve the representation learning aspect of VAEs [20]. These methods have shown their efficacy in learning good representations but neglect the generative property. Empirically, these regularizations improve the learned latent representation but inherently cause a mismatch between the aggregate posterior $q_\phi(\mathbf{z}) = \mathbb{E}_{p(\mathbf{x})}\left[q_\phi(\mathbf{z}|\mathbf{x})\right]$ and the prior $p(\mathbf{z})$. This mismatch leads to *latent pockets and leaks*, or a *submanifold* in the aggregate posterior that results in poor generative capabilities. Specifically, if a sample $\mathbf{z} \sim p(\mathbf{z})$ (*i.e.*, likely to be generated under the prior) lies in a pocket, (*i.e.*, $q_\phi(\mathbf{z})$ is low), then its corresponding decoded sample $\mathbf{x} \sim p_\theta(\mathbf{x}|\mathbf{z})$ will not lie on the data manifold. This problem, caused by VAE regularizations, we call the *submanifold problem*.

To better understand this phenomena, we define two different types of samples in the VAE latent space that corresponds to two VAE failure modes.

Low-Posterior (LP) samples are highly likely to be generated under the prior (*i.e.*, $p(\mathbf{z})$ is high) but are not covered by the aggregate posterior (*i.e.*, $q_\phi(\mathbf{z})$ is low). The low-posterior samples are typically generated from the *latent pockets* dictated by the regularizer(s) used and are of poor quality since they lie off the data manifold. To generate low-posterior samples, we follow the logic of [27], where we sample $\mathbf{z} \sim p(\mathbf{z}) = \mathcal{N}(\mathbf{z};\mathbf{0},\mathbb{I})$, rank them according to their aggregate posterior support, *i.e.*, values of $q_\phi(\mathbf{z})$, and choose the samples with lowest aggregate posterior values. In the case of *dp*VAEs, samples are generated from $\mathbf{z}_0 \sim p(\mathbf{z}_0) = \mathcal{N}(\mathbf{z}_0;\mathbf{0},\mathbb{I})$, which is a standard normal, and then transformed by $\mathbf{z} = g_\eta^{-1}(\mathbf{z}_0)$ before plugging it into the aggregate posterior.

High-Posterior (HP) samples are samples supported under the aggregate posterior (*i.e.*, $q_\phi(\mathbf{z})$ is high) but are less likely to be generated under the prior (*i.e.*, $p(\mathbf{z})$ is low). Specifically, these are samples in the latent space that can produce good generated samples but are unlikely to be sampled due to the low support of the prior, and thereby they are samples that are in the *latent leaks*.

To generate high-posterior samples, we sample from $\mathbf{z} \sim q_\phi(\mathbf{z}) = \mathbb{E}_{p(\mathbf{x})}\left[q_\phi(\mathbf{z}|\mathbf{x})\right]$, rank them according to their prior support, *i.e.*, values of $\mathcal{N}(\mathbf{z}; \mathbf{0}, \mathbb{I})$, and choose the samples with lowest prior support values. For dpVAEs, sampled $\mathbf{z}$ are first mapped to the $\mathbf{z}_0$−space by $\mathbf{z}_0 = g_\eta(\mathbf{z})$ before computing prior probabilities.

VAE performs well in the generative sense if the latent space is free of pockets and leaks. A pocket-free latent space is manifested by low-posterior samples that lie on the data manifold when mapped to the data space via the decoder $p_\theta(\mathbf{x}|\mathbf{z})$. In a leak-free latent space, high-posterior samples are supported by the aggregate posterior, yet with a tiny probability under the prior, and thereby these samples fall off the data manifold. This submanifold problem is demonstrated using four SOTA VAE regularizers (see Fig. 1 and Fig. 3). With β-VAE [2], FactorVAE [3] and β-TCVAE [23], we can clearly see that the low-posterior samples lie in the latent pockets formed in the aggregate posterior (see Fig. 3b) and they lie outside the data manifold (see Fig. 3c), causing the sample generation to be very noisy (see Fig. 3a). In the case of InfoVAE, the low-posterior samples lie in regions with not much aggregate posterior support causing a slightly noisy sample generation (see Fig. 3a). More importantly, there are high-posterior samples that come from $q_\phi(\mathbf{z})$ but can very rarely be captured by a standard normal prior distribution. With the InfoVAE, for instance, the model fails to generate samples that lie on the tail-end of the top moon.

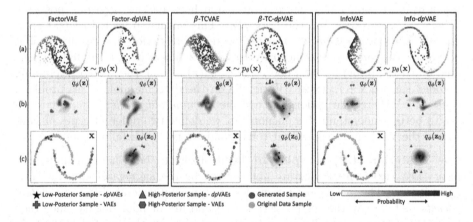

Fig. 3. Sample generation and latent spaces for regularized VAEs: Each block is a VAE trained with a different regularizer on the moons dataset, with and without the decoupled prior. In each block, (a) showcases the sample quality, (b) shows the aggregate posterior $q_\phi(\mathbf{z})$ with top five low- and high-posterior samples marked, and (c) shows the generation space for the decoupled prior and the training samples in the data space with corresponding low- and high-posterior samples are marked.

Although VAE regularizers improve latent representations, they sacrifice sample generation through the introduction of latent pockets and leaks. To fix sample generation, we propose a decoupling of the representation and generation spaces (see Fig. 2a for illustration). This is demonstrated for β-VAE with and without decoupled prior in Fig. 1, where the decoupled generation space $p(\mathbf{z}_0) \sim \mathcal{N}(\mathbf{z}_0; \mathbf{0}, \mathbb{I})$ is used for generation and all the low-posterior samples lie on the data manifold. We formulate this prior in detail in following section.

4.2 *dp*VAE: Decoupled Prior for VAE

Decoupled prior family, as the name suggests, decouples the latent space that performs the representation and the space that drives sample generation. For this decoupling to be meaningful, the representation and generation spaces should be related by a functional mapping. The decoupled prior effectively learns the latent space distribution $p(\mathbf{z})$ by simultaneously learning the functional mapping g_η together with the generative and inference models during optimization.

Specifically, the latent variables $\mathbf{z} \in \mathcal{Z} \subset \mathbb{R}^L$ and $\mathbf{z}_0 \in \mathcal{Z}_0 \subset \mathbb{R}^L$ are the random variables of the *representation* and *generation* spaces, respectively, where $p(\mathbf{z}_0) \sim \mathcal{N}(\mathbf{z}_0; \mathbf{0}, \mathbb{I})$. The bijective mapping between the representation space $\mathcal{Z}$ and the generation space $\mathcal{Z}_0$ is defined by an invertible function $g_\eta(\mathbf{z}) = \mathbf{z}_0$, parameterized by the network parameters η. VAE regularizers still act on the posteriors in the representation space, *i.e.*, $q_\phi(\mathbf{z}|\mathbf{x})$ and/or $q_\phi(\mathbf{z})$, without affecting the latent distribution of the generation space. Sample generation starts by sampling $\mathbf{z}_0 \sim p(\mathbf{z}_0)$, passing through the inverse mapping to obtain $\mathbf{z} = g_\eta^{-1}(\mathbf{z}_0)$, which is then decoded by the generative model $p_\theta(\mathbf{x}|\mathbf{z})$ (see Fig. 2a). These decoupled spaces can allow any modifications in the representation space dictated by the regularizer to infuse its submanifold structure in that space (see Fig. 3b) without significantly impacting the generation space (see Fig. 3c), and thereby improving sample generation for regularized VAEs (see Fig. 3a). Moreover, the decoupled prior $p(\mathbf{z})$ is an expressive prior that is learned jointly with the VAE, and thereby it can match an arbitrarily complex aggregate posterior $q_\phi(\mathbf{z})$, thanks to the flexibility of deep networks to model complex mappings. Additionally, due to the bijective mapping g_η, we have a one-to-one correspondence between samples in $p(\mathbf{z}_0) \sim \mathcal{N}(\mathbf{z}_0; \mathbf{0}, \mathbb{I})$ and those in $p(\mathbf{z})$.

To derive the ELBO for *dp*VAE, we replace the standard normal prior in (1) with the decoupled prior defined in (2). Using the change of variable formula, the KL divergence term in (1) can be simplified into[1]:

$$\mathrm{KL}\left[q_\phi(\mathbf{z}|\mathbf{x}) \| p(\mathbf{z})\right] = -\mathbb{E}_{q_\phi(\mathbf{z}|\mathbf{x})}\left[\sum_{k=1}^{K}\sum_{l=1}^{L} b_k^l s_k\left(b_k^l z_k^l\right)\right]$$
$$- \frac{1}{2}\log|\boldsymbol{\Sigma}_\mathbf{z}(\mathbf{x})| + \mathbb{E}_{q_\phi(\mathbf{z}|\mathbf{x})}\left[g_\eta(\mathbf{z})^T g_\eta(\mathbf{z})\right] \qquad (5)$$

where L is the latent dimension, K is number of invertible blocks that defines the decoupled prior in (4), s_k is the scaling network of the k−th block, $\boldsymbol{\Sigma}_\mathbf{z}(\mathbf{x})$ is the covariance matrix of the variational posterior $q_\phi(\mathbf{z}|\mathbf{x})$ (typically assumed to be diagonal), and b_k^l and z_k^l are the l−th element in $\mathbf{b}_k$ and $\mathbf{z}_k$ vectors, respectively.

---

[1] Complete derivation can be found in the supplementary material.

4.3   *dp*VAE in Concert with VAE Regularizers

The KL divergence in (5) can be directly used for any regularized ELBO. However, there are some regularized models such as β-TCVAE [23], and InfoVAE [1] that introduce additional terms other than KL $[q_\phi(\mathbf{z}|\mathbf{x})\|p(\mathbf{z})]$ with $p(\mathbf{z})$. These regularizers need to be modified when used with decoupled priors[2].

β-**dpVAE:** For β-VAE (both β-VAE-H [2] and β-VAE-B [57] versions), the only difference in the ELBO (1) is reweighting the KL-term and the addition of certain constraints without introducing any additional terms. Hence, β-*dp*VAE will retain the same reweighting and constraints, and only modify the KL divergence term according to (5).

Factor-dpVAE: FactorVAE   [3]   introduces   a   total   correlation   term KL $[q_\phi(\mathbf{z})\|q_\phi(\bar{\mathbf{z}})]$ to the ELBO in (1), where $q_\phi(\bar{\mathbf{z}}) = \prod_{l=1}^{L} q_\phi(z^l)$ and z^l is the l−th element of $\mathbf{z}$. This term promotes disentanglement of the latent dimensions of $\mathbf{z}$, impacting the representation learning aspect of VAE. Hence, in the case of the decoupled prior, the total correlation term should be applied to the *representation space*. In this sense, the decoupled prior only affects the KL divergence term as described in (5) for the Factor-*dp*VAE model.

β-**TC-dpVAE:** Regularization provided by β-TCVAE [23] factorizes the ELBO into the individual latent dimensions based on the decomposition given in [22]. The only term that includes $p(\mathbf{z})$ is the KL divergence between marginals, *i.e.,* KL $[q_\phi(\mathbf{z})\|p(\mathbf{z})]$. This term in β-TCVAE is assumed to be factorized and is evaluated via sampling, facilitating the direct incorporation of the decoupled prior. In particular, we can just sample from the base distribution $\mathbf{z}_0 \sim p(\mathbf{z}_0) = \mathcal{N}(\mathbf{z}_0; \mathbf{0}, \mathbb{I})$ and compute the corresponding sample $\mathbf{z} \sim p(\mathbf{z})$ using $\mathbf{z} = g_\eta^{-1}(\mathbf{z}_0)$.

Info-dpVAE: In InfoVAE [1], the additional term in the ELBO is again the divergence between aggregate posterior and the prior, *i.e.,* KL $[q_\phi(\mathbf{z})\|p(\mathbf{z})]$. This KL divergence term is replaced by different divergence families; adversarial training [34], Stein variational gradient [58], and maximum-mean discrepancy MMD [59–61]. However, adversarial-based divergences can have unstable training and Stein variational gradient scales poorly with high dimensions [1]. Motivated by the MMD-based results in [1], we focus here on the MMD divergence to evaluate this marginal divergence. For Info-*dp*VAE, we start with the ELBO of InfoVAE and modify the standard KL divergence term using (5). In addition, we compute the marginal KL divergence using MMD, which quantifies the divergence between two distributions by comparing their moments through sampling. Similar to β-TC-*dp*VAE, we can sample from $p(\mathbf{z}_0)$ and use the inverse mapping to compute samples in the $\mathbf{z}$−space.

---

[2] The ELBOs for these regularizers can be found in the supplementary material.

Table 1. Generative metrics (*lower* is better) for vanilla VAE and regularized VAEs using standard normal and decoupled priors. **FID** = Fréchet Inception Distance. **LP** = Low-Posterior FID score. **sKL** = symmetric KL divergence. **NLL** = Negative Log-Likelihood ($\times 10^3$)

Methods	MNIST				SVHN				CelebA			
	FID	LP	sKL	NLL	FID	LP	sKL	NLL	FID	LP	sKL	NLL
VAE [14,15]	137.4	165.0	1.26	3.56	78.9	83.8	53.67	0.386	81.4	79.0	59.3	9.26
*dp*VAE	**129.0**	**153.1**	**0.88**	**3.53**	**50.8**	**55.2**	13.02	**0.318**	**71.5**	**74.3**	**10.4**	**4.91**
β-VAE-H [2]	144.2	163.1	4.49	4.12	96.7	97.6	10.35	0.611	80.3	79.9	39.7	**6.93**
β-*dp*VAE-H	**127.1**	**127.4**	**1.07**	**2.98**	**65.2**	**67.7**	**4.05**	**0.592**	**67.2**	**72.5**	**33.5**	10.6
β-VAE-B [57]	130.8	163.6	2.74	3.11	61.7	68.5	2.62	0.606	75.7	79.6	25.8	12.5
β-*dp*VAE-B	**113.3**	**114.1**	**1.32**	**2.80**	**51.1**	**50.3**	**2.47**	**0.550**	**67.9**	**72.0**	**19.1**	**10.4**
β-TCVAE [23]	149.8	200.3	4.48	2.91	69.2	70.5	7.76	9.86	83.8	83.0	93.6	**9.33**
β-TC-*dp*VAE	**133.3**	**133.1**	**2.07**	**2.70**	**50.3**	**53.8**	**2.94**	**4.52**	**80.3**	**81.4**	**90.3**	10.0
FactorVAE [3]	130.5	191.2	1.04	3.50	97.2	108.5	1.91	**2.13**	82.6	86.8	71.3	**9.89**
Factor-*dp*VAE	**120.8**	**121.3**	**0.85**	3.60	**86.3**	**86.9**	1.57	2.36	**65.0**	**73.4**	**51.3**	12.2
InfoVAE [1]	128.7	133.2	2.89	2.88	81.3	83.2	4.91	**1.55**	76.5	79.1	30.6	**11.1**
Info-*dp*VAE	**110.1**	**110.5**	**1.70**	**2.81**	**62.9**	**67.7**	2.67	1.56	**68.9**	**72.9**	**20.3**	12.1

5   Experiments

We experiment with three benchmark image datasets, namely MNIST [62], SVHN [63], CelebA (cropped version) [64] to provide a fair comparison with SOTA regularized VAEs, which used the same datasets. We train these datasets with VAE [14,15] and five regularized VAEs, namely β-VAE-H [2], β-VAE-B [57], β-TCVAE) [23], FactorVAE [3] and InfoVAE [1]. We showcase, qualitatively and quantitatively, that *dp*VAEs improve sample generation while retaining the benefits of representation learning provided by the regularizers[3]

5.1   Generative Metrics

We use the following quantitative metrics to assess the generative performance of the regularized VAEs with and without the decoupled prior.

Fréchet Inception Distance (FID): The FID score is based on the statistics, assuming Gaussian distribution, computed in the feature space defined using the inception network features [65]. FID score quantifies both the sample diversity and quality. Lower FID means better sample generation.

Symmetric KL Divergence (sKL): To quantify the overlap between $p(\mathbf{z})$ and $q_\phi(\mathbf{z})$ in the representation space ($p(\mathbf{z})$ being the decoupled prior for *dp*VAEs or the standard normal), we compute sKL$= $ KL $[p(\mathbf{z})\|q_\phi(\mathbf{z})] + $ KL $[q_\phi(\mathbf{z})\|p(\mathbf{z})]$

---

[3] Architectures and hyperparameters are described in the supplementary material. Additionally, results showcasing that representation learning (specifically disentanglement) is not adversely affected by the introduction of decoupled priors are also presented in the supplementary material.

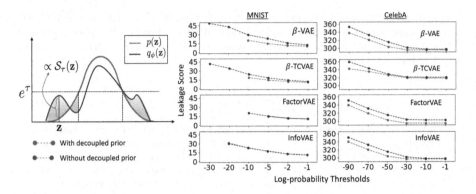

Fig. 4. *dp*VAEs have less latent leaks: Leakage scores for regularized VAEs on MNIST (a) and CelebA (b) data (missing values mean there are no samples with $\log(p(\mathbf{z})) < \tau$, implying zero leakage at that threshold). The illustration on the left represents the intuition behind the lekage score. For a probability threshold τ, the leakage score is proportional to the probaility difference at a sample in latent sapce, this area is marked in grey : $\mathbb{E}_{q_\phi(\mathbf{z})}[\mathcal{S}_\tau(\mathbf{z})]$.

through sampling (using 5,000 samples). sKL also captures the existence of pockets and leaks in $q_\phi(\mathbf{z})$. Lower sKL implies there is a better overlap between $p(\mathbf{z})$ and $q_\phi(\mathbf{z})$, indicating better generative capabilities.

Negative Log-likelihood: We estimate the likelihood of held-out samples under a trained model using importance sampling (with 21,000 samples) as in [15], where $\text{NLL} = \log \mathbb{E}_{q_\phi(\mathbf{z}|\mathbf{x})}[p_\theta(\mathbf{x}|\mathbf{z})p(\mathbf{z})/q_\phi(\mathbf{z}|\mathbf{x})]$. Lower NLL means better sample generation since the learned model supports unseen samples drawn from the data distribution.

Leakage Score: To assess the effect of decoupled priors on latent leaks (as manifested by high posterior samples), we devise a new metric based on log-probability differences. We sample from the aggregate posterior $\mathbf{z} \sim q_\phi(\mathbf{z})$. If $\log(p(\mathbf{z})) < \tau$, where $\tau \in \mathbb{R}$ is a chosen threshold value, then we consider the sample to lie in a "leakage region" defined by τ. This sample is considered a high-posterior sample at the $\tau-$level since the sample is better supported under the aggregate posterior than the prior (see Fig. 4). Based on the threshold value, these leakage regions are less likely to be sampled from. In order to not lose significant regions from the data manifold, we want the aggregate posterior corresponding to these samples to attain low values as well. To quantify latent leakage for a trained model, we propose a *leakage score* as $\text{LS}(\tau) = \mathbb{E}_{q_\phi(\mathbf{z})}[\mathcal{S}_\tau(\mathbf{z})]$, where for a given $\mathbf{z} \sim q_\phi(\mathbf{z})$ at a particular threshold τ, $\mathcal{S}_\tau(\mathbf{z})$ is defined in (6), where h is the identity function for VAEs and g_η for *dp*VAEs.

$$\mathcal{S}_\tau(\mathbf{z}) = \begin{cases} \log\left(\frac{q_\phi(\mathbf{z})}{p(h(\mathbf{z}))}\right) & \log(p(\mathbf{z})) < \tau \\ 0 & \log(p(\mathbf{z})) \geq \tau \end{cases} \tag{6}$$

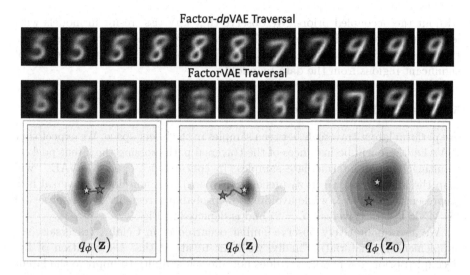

Fig. 5. Latent traversal for *dp*VAEs does not path through latent pockets: The top rows showcases latent traversal for FactorVAE and Factor-*dp*VAE on MNIST data. The orange box is the $q_\phi(\mathbf{z})$ for FactorVAE and the red line shows the traversal between starting and ending points (green and yellow stars, respectively). The green box shows the *same* traversal in $q_\phi(\mathbf{z}_0)$ that is mapped using g_η^{-1} to the representation space, demonstrated using $q_\phi(\mathbf{z})$. We see that the traversal path in $q_\phi(\mathbf{z})$ tries to avoid low probability regions, which correspond to better image quality. (Color figure online)

5.2 Generation Results and Analysis

In Table 1, we observe that *dp*VAEs perform better than their corresponding regularized VAEs without the decoupled prior. When comparing VAEs with and without decoupled priors (*e.g.,* InfoVAE and Info-*dp*VAE), we use the same hyperparameters and perform no additional tuning. This showcases the robustness of the decoupled prior wrt hyperparameters, facilitating its direct use with any regularized VAE. We report the FID scores on both the randomly generated samples from the prior and the low-posterior samples. As analyzed in Sect. 4.1, if the low-posterior samples lie on the data manifold, then the learned latent space is pocket-free. Results in Table 1 suggest that for all *dp*VAEs, the FID scores for the randomly generated samples and low-posterior ones are comparable, suggesting that all the pockets in the latent space are filled. Qualitative results of sample generation for CelebA and MNIST are shown in the supplementary material (due to space constraints). We show both the random prior and low-posterior sample generation with and without the decoupled prior for three different regularizers. Sample quality of *dp*VAEs is better or on par with those without the decoupled prior. But more importantly, one can observe a significant quality improvement in the low-posterior samples, which aligns with the quantitative results in Table 1. In Fig. 4, we report the leakage score $\mathrm{LS}(\tau)$ as a function of log-probability thresholds for different regularizers with and without the decoupled priors. We observe that dpVAEs result in models with lower latent leakage. This is especially true at lower thresholds, which suggests that even when $p(\mathbf{z})$ is small, the $q_\phi(\mathbf{z})$ is small as well, preventing the loss of significant regions from the data manifold.

5.3   Latent Traversals Results

We perform latent traversals between samples in the latent space. We expect that in VAEs, there will be instances of the traversal path crossing the latent pockets resulting in poor intermediate samples. In contrast, we expect dpVAEs will map the linear traversal in $\mathbf{z}_0$ (generation space) to a non-linear traversal in $\mathbf{z}$ (representation space), while avoiding low probability regions. This is observed for MNIST data traversal ($L = 2$) and is depicted in Fig. 5.

We also qualitatively observe similar occurrences in CelabA traversals (see supplementary material). Finally, we want to attest that the addition of the decoupled prior to a regularizer does not affect it's ability to improve the latent representation. We demonstrate this by observing latent factor traversals for CelebA trained on Factor-dpVAE, where we vary one dimension of the latent space while fixing the others. One can observe that Factor-dpVAE is able to isolate different attributes of variation in the data, as shown in Fig. 6.

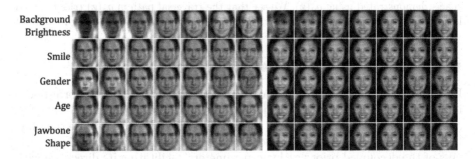

Fig. 6. Factor-dpVAE latent traversals across the top 5 latent dimensions: Traversals start with the reconstructed image of a given sample and move ±5 standard deviations along a latent dimension. Results from other dpVAEs similarly retain the latent space disentanglement.

6   Conclusion

In this paper, we define and analyze the submanifold problem for regularized VAEs, or the tendency of a regularizer to accentuate the creation of pockets and leaks in the latent space. This submanifold structure manifests the mismatch between the aggregate posterior and the latent prior which in turn causes degradation in generation quality. To overcome this trade-off between sample generation and latent representation, we propose the decoupled prior family as a general regularization framework for VAE and demonstrate its efficacy on SOTA VAE regularizers. *dp*VAE does not modify the ELBO of the vanilla VAE, rather it leverages learnable priors that are optimized jointly with the inference and generation models to match the aggregate posterior and the latent prior. We demonstrate that *dp*VAEs generate better quality samples as compared with their standard normal prior based counterparts, via qualitative and quantitative results. Additionally, we qualitatively observe that the representation learning (as improved by the regularizer) is not adversely affected by *dp*VAEs. Decoupled priors can act as a pathway to realizing the true potential of VAEs as both a representation learning and a generative modeling framework. Further work in this direction will include exploring more expressive inference and generative models (*e.g.,* PixelCNN [47]) in conjuction with decoupled priors. We also believe more sophisticated invertible architectures (*e.g.,*. RAD [66]) and base distributions will provide further improvements.

References

1. Zhao, S., Song, J., Ermon, S.: Infovae: balancing learning and inference in variational autoencoders. In: Proceedings of the AAAI Conference on Artificial Intelligence, vol. 33, pp. 5885–5892 (2019)
2. Higgins, I., et al.: beta-vae: learning basic visual concepts with a constrained variational framework. ICLR **2**, 6 (2017)
3. Kim, H., Mnih, A.: Disentangling by factorising. In: International Conference on Machine Learning, pp. 2654–2663 (2018)
4. Chen, X., Duan, Y., Houthooft, R., Schulman, J., Sutskever, I., Abbeel, P.: Infogan: interpretable representation learning by information maximizing generative adversarial nets. In: Advances in Neural Information Processing Systems, pp. 2172–2180 (2016)
5. Nguyen, A., Clune, J., Bengio, Y., Dosovitskiy, A., Yosinski, J.: Plug & play generative networks: conditional iterative generation of images in latent space. In: Proceedings of the IEEE Conference on Computer Vision and Pattern Recognition, pp. 4467–4477 (2017)
6. Mathieu, M.F., Zhao, J.J., Zhao, J., Ramesh, A., Sprechmann, P., LeCun, Y.: Disentangling factors of variation in deep representation using adversarial training. In: Advances in Neural Information Processing Systems, pp. 5040–5048 (2016)
7. Higgins, I., et al.: Darla: Improving zero-shot transfer in reinforcement learning. In: Proceedings of the 34th International Conference on Machine Learning-Volume 70, JMLR. org, pp. 1480–1490 (2017)
8. Rezende, D., Danihelka, I., Gregor, K., Wierstra, D., et al.: One-shot generalization in deep generative models. In: International Conference on Machine Learning, pp. 1521–1529 (2016)
9. Kingma, D.P., Mohamed, S., Rezende, D.J., Welling, M.: Semi-supervised learning with deep generative models. In: Advances in Neural Information Processing Systems, pp. 3581–3589 (2014)
10. Bengio, Y., Courville, A., Vincent, P.: Representation learning: a review and new perspectives. IEEE Trans. Pattern Anal. Mach. Intell. **35**, 1798–1828 (2013)
11. Alemi, A., Poole, B., Fischer, I., Dillon, J., Saurous, R.A., Murphy, K.: Fixing a broken elbo. In: International Conference on Machine Learning, pp. 159–168 (2018)

12. Yuille, A., Kersten, D.: Vision as Bayesian inference: analysis by synthesis? Trends Cogn. Sci. **10**, 301–308 (2006)
13. Nair, V., Susskind, J., Hinton, G.E.: Analysis-by-synthesis by learning to invert generative black boxes. In: Kůrková, V., Neruda, R., Koutník, J. (eds.) ICANN 2008. LNCS, vol. 5163, pp. 971–981. Springer, Heidelberg (2008). https://doi.org/10.1007/978-3-540-87536-9_99
14. Kingma, D.P., Welling, M.: Auto-encoding variational bayes. ICLR (2014)
15. Rezende, D.J., Mohamed, S., Wierstra, D.: Stochastic backpropagation and approximate inference in deep generative models. In: International Conference on Machine Learning, pp. 1278–1286 (2014)
16. Maaløe, L., Sønderby, C.K., Sønderby, S.K., Winther, O.: Auxiliary deep generative models. In: International Conference on Machine Learning, pp. 1445–1453 (2016)
17. Sønderby, C.K., Raiko, T., Maaløe, L., Sønderby, S.K., Winther, O.: How to train deep variational autoencoders and probabilistic ladder networks. In: 33rd International Conference on Machine Learning (ICML 2016) (2016)
18. Pu, Y., et al.: Variational autoencoder for deep learning of images, labels and captions. In: Advances in Neural Information Processing Systems, pp. 2352–2360 (2016)
19. Xu, W., Sun, H., Deng, C., Tan, Y.: Variational autoencoder for semi-supervised text classification. In: Thirty-First AAAI Conference on Artificial Intelligence (2017)
20. Tschannen, M., Bachem, O., Lucic, M.: Recent advances in autoencoder-based representation learning. In: Third workshop on Bayesian Deep Learning (NeurIPS 2018) (2018)
21. Chen, X., et al.: Variational lossy autoencoder. ICLR (2017)
22. Hoffman, M.D., Johnson, M.J.: Elbo surgery: yet another way to carve up the variational evidence lower bound. In: Workshop in Advances in Approximate Bayesian Inference, NIPS, vol. 1. (2016)
23. Chen, T.Q., Li, X., Grosse, R.B., Duvenaud, D.K.: Isolating sources of disentanglement in variational autoencoders. In: Advances in Neural Information Processing Systems, pp. 2610–2620 (2018)
24. Kumar, A., Sattigeri, P., Balakrishnan, A.: Variational inference of disentangled latent concepts from unlabeled observations. In: ICLR (2018)
25. Makhzani, A., Frey, B.J.: Pixelgan autoencoders. In: Advances in Neural Information Processing Systems, pp. 1975–1985 (2017)
26. Alemi, A.A., Fischer, I., Dillon, J.V., Murphy, K.: Deep variational information bottleneck. In: ICLR (2016)
27. Rosca, M., Lakshminarayanan, B., Mohamed, S.: Distribution matching in variational inference. arXiv preprint arXiv:1802.06847 (2018)
28. Xu, H., Chen, W., Lai, J., Li, Z., Zhao, Y., Pei, D.: On the necessity and effectiveness of learning the prior of variational auto-encoder. arXiv preprint arXiv:1905.13452 (2019)
29. Shmelkov, K., Lucas, T., Alahari, K., Schmid, C., Verbeek, J.: Coverage and quality driven training of generative image models. arXiv preprint arXiv:1901.01091 (2019)
30. Goodfellow, I., et al.: Generative adversarial nets. In: Advances in Neural Information Processing Systems, pp. 2672–2680 (2014)
31. Arjovsky, M., Chintala, S., Bottou, L.: Wasserstein generative adversarial networks. In: International conference on machine learning, pp. 214–223 (2017)
32. Sugiyama, M., Suzuki, T., Kanamori, T.: Density-ratio matching under the Bregman divergence: a unified framework of density-ratio estimation. Ann. Inst. Stat. Math. **64**, 1009–1044 (2012)

33. Mescheder, L., Nowozin, S., Geiger, A.: Adversarial variational bayes: Unifying variational autoencoders and generative adversarial networks. In: Proceedings of the 34th International Conference on Machine Learning-Volume 70, JMLR. org, pp. 2391–2400 (2017)
34. Makhzani, A., Shlens, J., Jaitly, N., Goodfellow, I., Frey, B.: Adversarial autoencoders. arXiv preprint arXiv:1511.05644 (2015)
35. Srivastava, A., Valkov, L., Russell, C., Gutmann, M.U., Sutton, C.: Veegan: Reducing mode collapse in gans using implicit variational learning. In: Advances in Neural Information Processing Systems, pp. 3308–3318 (2017)
36. Makhzani, A., Shlens, J., Jaitly, N., Goodfellow, I., Frey, B.: Adversarial autoencoders. In: International Conference on Learning Representations (2016)
37. Tolstikhin, I., Bousquet, O., Gelly, S., Schoelkopf, B.: Wasserstein auto-encoders. arXiv preprint arXiv:1711.01558 (2017)
38. Xiao, Z., Yan, Q., Amit, Y.: Generative latent flow. arXiv preprint arXiv:1905.10485 (2019)
39. Kingma, D.P., Salimans, T., Jozefowicz, R., Chen, X., Sutskever, I., Welling, M.: Improved variational inference with inverse autoregressive flow. In: Advances in neural information processing systems, pp. 4743–4751(2016)
40. Bauer, M., Mnih, A.: Resampled priors for variational autoencoders. In: The 22nd International Conference on Artificial Intelligence and Statistics, pp. 66–75 (2019)
41. Tomczak, J., Welling, M.: Vae with a vampprior. In: International Conference on Artificial Intelligence and Statistics, pp. 1214–1223 (2018)
42. Dilokthanakul, N., et al.: Deep unsupervised clustering with Gaussian mixture variational autoencoders. arXiv preprint arXiv:1611.02648 (2016)
43. Gregor, K., Danihelka, I., Graves, A., Rezende, D., Wierstra, D.: Draw: a recurrent neural network for image generation. In: International Conference on Machine Learning, pp. 1462–1471(2015)
44. Gulrajani, I., et al.: Pixelvae: a latent variable model for natural images. In: ICLR (2017)
45. Van Den Oord, A., Vinyals, O., et al.: Neural discrete representation learning. In: Advances in Neural Information Processing Systems, pp. 6306–6315 (2017)
46. Razavi, A., van den Oord, A., Vinyals, O.: Generating diverse high-fidelity images with vq-vae-2. In: Advances in Neural Information Processing Systems, pp. 14866–14876 (2019)
47. Van den Oord, A., Kalchbrenner, N., Espeholt, L., Vinyals, O., Graves, A., et al.: Conditional image generation with pixelcnn decoders. In: Advances in Neural Information Processing Systems, pp. 4790–4798 (2016)
48. Oord, A.v.d., Kalchbrenner, N., Kavukcuoglu, K.: Pixel recurrent neural networks. arXiv preprint arXiv:1601.06759 (2016)
49. Dinh, L., Krueger, D., Bengio, Y.: Nice: Non-linear independent components estimation (2014)
50. Dinh, L., Sohl-Dickstein, J., Bengio, S.: Density estimation using real nvp. In: ICLR (2017)
51. Rezende, D., Mohamed, S.: Variational inference with normalizing flows. In: Proceedings of the 32nd International Conference on Machine Learning. Volume 37 of Proceedings of Machine Learning Research., Lille, France, PMLR, pp. 1530–1538 (2015)
52. Kingma, D.P., Dhariwal, P.: Glow: Generative flow with invertible 1 x 1 convolutions. In: Bengio, S., Wallach, H., Larochelle, H., Grauman, K., Cesa-Bianchi, N., Garnett, R. (eds.) Advances in Neural Information Processing Systems 31, pp. 10215–10224. Curran Associates, Inc. (2018)

53. Huang, C.W., et al.: Learnable explicit density for continuous latent space and variational inference. arXiv preprint arXiv:1710.02248 (2017)
54. Das, H.P., Abbeel, P., Spanos, C.J.: Dimensionality reduction flows. arXiv preprint arXiv:1908.01686 (2019)
55. Gritsenko, A.A., Snoek, J., Salimans, T.: On the relationship between normalising flows and variational-and denoising autoencoders (2019)
56. Bowman, S.R., Vilnis, L., Vinyals, O., Dai, A., Jozefowicz, R., Bengio, S.: Generating sentences from a continuous space. In: Proceedings of The 20th SIGNLL Conference on Computational Natural Language Learning, pp. 10–21 (2016)
57. Burgess, C.P., et al.: Understanding disentangling in beta-vae. arXiv preprint arXiv:1804.03599 (2018)
58. Liu, Q., Wang, D.: Stein variational gradient descent: A general purpose Bayesian inference algorithm. In: Advances in Neural Information Processing Systems, pp. 2378–2386 (2016)
59. Gretton, A., Borgwardt, K., Rasch, M., Schölkopf, B., Smola, A.J.: A kernel method for the two-sample-problem. In: Advances in Neural Information Processing Systems, pp. 513–520 (2007)
60. Li, Y., Swersky, K., Zemel, R.: Generative moment matching networks. In: International Conference on Machine Learning, pp. 1718–1727 (2015)
61. Dziugaite, G.K., Roy, D.M., Ghahramani, Z.: Training generative neural networks via maximum mean discrepancy optimization. In: Proceedings of the Thirty-First Conference on Uncertainty in Artificial Intelligence, pp. 258–267. AUAI Press (2015)
62. LeCun, Y., Cortes, C.: MNIST handwritten digit database (2010)
63. Netzer, Y., Wang, T., Coates, A., Bissacco, A., Wu, B., Ng, A.Y.: Reading digits in natural images with unsupervised feature learning. In: NIPS Workshop on Deep Learning and Unsupervised Feature Learning (2011)
64. Liu, Z., Luo, P., Wang, X., Tang, X.: Deep learning face attributes in the wild. In: Proceedings of the IEEE International Conference on Computer Vision, pp. 3730–3738 (2015)
65. Szegedy, C., Vanhoucke, V., Ioffe, S., Shlens, J., Wojna, Z.: Rethinking the inception architecture for computer vision. In: Proceedings of IEEE Conference on Computer Vision and Pattern Recognition (2016)
66. Dinh, L., Sohl-Dickstein, J., Pascanu, R., Larochelle, H.: A RAD approach to deep mixture models. CoRR abs/1903.07714 (2019)

MagGAN: High-Resolution Face Attribute Editing with Mask-Guided Generative Adversarial Network

Yi Wei[1], Zhe Gan[2], Wenbo Li[3], Siwei Lyu[4], Ming-Ching Chang[1], Lei Zhang[2], Jianfeng Gao[2], and Pengchuan Zhang[2(✉)]

[1] University at Albany, State University of New York, Albany, USA
[2] Microsoft Corporation, Redmond, USA
penzhan@microsoft.com
[3] Samsung Research America AI Center, Mountain View, USA
[4] University at Buffalo, State University of New York, Buffalo, USA

Abstract. We present *Mask-guided Generative Adversarial Network* (MagGAN) for high-resolution face attribute editing, in which semantic facial masks from a pre-trained face parser are used to guide the fine-grained image editing process. With the introduction of a mask-guided reconstruction loss, MagGAN learns to only edit the facial parts that are relevant to the desired attribute changes, while preserving the attribute-irrelevant regions (*e.g.*, hat, scarf for modification 'To Bald'). Further, a novel mask-guided conditioning strategy is introduced to incorporate the influence region of each attribute change into the generator. In addition, a multi-level patch-wise discriminator structure is proposed to scale our model for high-resolution (1024×1024) face editing. Experiments on the CelebA benchmark show that the proposed method significantly outperforms prior state-of-the-art approaches in terms of both image quality and editing performance.

1 Introduction

The demand of face editing is booming in the era of selfies. Both the research community, *e.g.*, [4,6,9,15–17,20,24,28,31,35,36,39,43], and the industry, *e.g.*, Adobe and Meitu, have extensively explored to improve the automation of face editing by leveraging user's specification of various facial attributes, *e.g.*, hair color and eye size, as the conditional input. Generative Adversarial Networks (GANs) [7] have made tremendous progress for this task. Prominent examples in this direction include AttGAN [9], StarGAN [6], and STGAN [24], all of which use an encoder-decoder architecture, and take both source image and target attributes (or, attributes to be changed) as input to generate a new image with the characteristic of target attributes.

Electronic supplementary material The online version of this chapter (https://doi.org/10.1007/978-3-030-69538-5_40) contains supplementary material, which is available to authorized users.

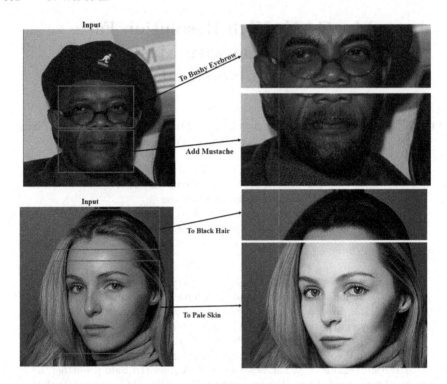

Fig. 1. Visual results of MagGAN on resolution 1024 × 1024. The specific sub-regions are cropped for better visualization

Although promising results have been achieved, state-of-the-art methods still suffer from inaccurately localized editing, where regions irrelevant to the desired attribute change are often edited. For instance, STGAN [24] can make undesired editing by painting the scarf to white for "Pale Skin" (left) and the hat to golden for "Blond Hair" (right) (see Fig. 2). Solution to this problem requires notions of relevant regions that are editable *w.r.t.* the facial attribute edit types, while keeping the non-editable regions intact. To illustrate this concept of region-localized attribute editing, we refer to the facial regions that are editable when a specific attribute changes as *attribute-relevant* regions (such as the hair region for "To Blonde"). Regions that should not be edited (such as the hat and other non-hair regions for attribute "To Bald") are referred to as *attribute-irrelevant*. Ideal attribute editing generator will only edit attribute-relevant regions while keeping attribute-irrelevant regions intact, to minimize artifacts. The second issue of most existing methods is that they only work with images of low resolutions (128 × 128). How to edit facial attributes of high-resolution (1024 × 1024) images is less explored.

In order to address these challenges, we present the **Mask-guided Generative Adversarial Network** (MagGAN) for high-resolution face attribute editing. The proposed approach is built upon STGAN [24], which uses a difference attribute vector as conditional input, and a selective transfer unit for attribute editing. Based on this, a soft segmentation mask of common face parts from a pre-trained face parser is used to achieve fine-grained face editing. On one hand, the facial mask provides useful geometric constraints, which helps generate realistic face images. On the other hand, the mask also identifies each facial component (e.g., eyes, mouth, and hair), which is necessary for accurately localized editing. With the introduction of a mask-guided reconstruction loss, MagGAN can effectively focus on regions that are most related to the edited attributes, and keep the attribute-irrelevant regions intact, thus generating photo-realistic outputs.

Another reason why existing methods cannot preserve the regions that should not be edited is about how the attribute change information is injected into the generator. Although most attribute changes lead to localized editing, the attribute change condition itself does not explicitly contain any spatial information. In order to better learn the alignment between attribute change and regions to edit, MagGAN further uses a novel mask-guided conditioning strategy that can adaptively learn *where to edit*.

To further scale our model for high-resolution (1024 × 1024) face editing (see Fig. 1 for visual results), we propose to use a series of multi-level patch-wise discriminators. The coarsest-level discriminator sees the full downsampled image, and is responsible for judging the global consistency of generated images, while a finer-level discriminator only sees patches of the generated high-resolution image, and tries to classify whether these patches are real or not. Empirically, this leads to more stable model training for high-resolution face editing.

Fig. 2. MagGAN (1st row) can effectively apply accurate attribute editing while keeping attribute-irrelevant regions (e.g., hat, scarf) intact. In comparison, the state-of-the-art STGAN [24] (2nd row) produces undesired modifications on these regions, e.g., whitening the scarf while manipulating "Pale Skin"

The main contributions of this paper are summarized as follows. (*i*) We propose MagGAN that can effectively leverage semantic facial mask information for fine-grained face attribute editing, via the introduction of a mask-guided reconstruction loss. (*ii*) A novel mask-guided conditioning strategy is further introduced to encourage the influenced region of each target attribute to be localized into the generator. (*iii*) A multi-level patch-wise discriminator structure scales up our model to deal with high-resolution face editing. (*iv*) State-of-the-art results are achieved on the CelebA benchmark, outperforming previous methods in terms of both visual quality and editing performance.

2   Related Work

The development of face editing techniques evolves along the automation of editing tools. In the early stage, researchers focused on developing attribute-dedicated methods for face editing [3, 21, 25, 32, 33, 42], *i.e.*, each model is dedicated to modifying a single attribute. However, such dedicated methods suffer from low automation level, *i.e.*, not being able to manipulate multiple attributes in one step. To this end, many works [6, 9, 15–17, 20, 24, 28, 31, 35, 36, 39, 43] started using attribute specifications, *i.e.*, semantically meaningful attribute vectors, as conditional input. Multiple attributes can be manipulated via changing the input attribute specifications. This work belongs to this category. Another line of works [5, 29, 34, 37, 45] improve the automation level of the face editing model by providing an exemplar image as the conditional input. Below, we briefly review recent attribute-specification based methods, and refer the readers to [44] for more details of methods that are not reviewed herein.

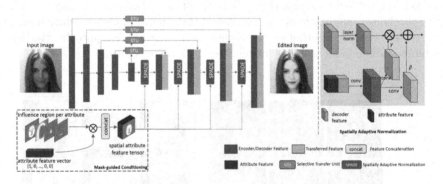

Fig. 3. Model architecture for the proposed Mask-guided GAN (MagGAN)

Many facial attributes are local properties (such as hair color, baldness, etc.), and facial attribute editing should only change relevant regions and preserve regions not to be edited. StarGAN [6] and CycleGAN [28] introduced the cycle-consistency loss to conditional GAN so as to preserve attribute-irrelevant details and to stabilize training. AttGAN [9] and STGAN [24] found that the reconstruction loss of images not to be edited is at least as good as the cycle-consistency loss for preserving attribute-irrelevant regions. STGAN [24] proposed the selective transfer units to adaptively select and modify encoder features for enhanced attribute editing, achieving state-of-the-art performance on editing success rate. However, in this paper, we show that neither the cycle-consistency loss nor the reconstruction loss is sufficient to well preserve regions not to be edited (see Fig. 2), and propose to utilize masks to solve this problem.

Semantic mask/segmentation provides geometry parsing information for image generation, see, *e.g.*, [12,22,30]. Semantic mask datasets and models are available for domains with important real applications, such as face editing [18,19] and fashion [23]. Recently, both [8] and [19] utilize mask information for facial image manipulation, where a *target/manipulated mask* is required in the manipulation process. In this paper, we focus on the setting of editing with attribute specifications, without requiring a target/manipulated mask. We only make use of a pre-trained face parser, instead of requiring users to provide the mask manually.

3   MagGAN

As illustrated in Fig. 3, face editing is performed in MagGAN via an encoder-decoder architecture [6,9]. The design of Selective Transfer Units (STUs) in STGAN [24] is adopted to selectively transform encoder features according to the desired attribute change. Inspired by StyleGAN [14,30], the adaptive layer normalization [2,11] is used to inject conditions through the de-normalization process, instead of directly concatenating the conditions with the feature map. Our full encoder-decoder generator is denoted as:

$$\hat{\mathbf{x}} = G(\mathbf{x}, \mathbf{att}_{\text{diff}}), \quad \mathbf{att}_{\text{diff}} = \mathbf{att}_t - \mathbf{att}_s, \tag{1}$$

where $\mathbf{x}$(or $\hat{\mathbf{x}}$) $\in \mathbb{R}^{3 \times H \times W}$ denote the input (or edited) image; $\mathbf{att}_s$(or $\mathbf{att}_t$) $\in \mathbb{R}^C$ are the source (or target) attributes. The generator takes the attribute difference $\mathbf{att}_{\text{diff}} \in \mathbb{R}^C$ as input, following [24].

3.1   Avoid Editing Attribute-Irrelevant Regions

Although notable results have been achieved, existing work still suffers from inaccurately localized editing, where irrelevant regions unrelated to the desired attribute change are often made. For example, in Fig. 2, STGAN [24] changes the scarf to white for "Pale Skin" (left), and changes the hat to golden for "Blond Hair" (right).

We leverage facial regions for effective facial attribute editing and modeling as a solution. We utilize a pre-trained face parser to provide soft facial region masks. Specifically, a modified BiseNet [38] trained on the CelebAMask-HQ dataset [19][1] is used to generates 19-class region masks, including various facial components and accessories. For each attribute a_i, we define its *influence regions* represented by two probability masks $M_i^+, M_i^- \in [0,1]^{H \times W}$. If attribute a_i is strengthened during editing, the region characterized by M_i^+ is likely to be changed; if a_i is weakened, the region characterized by M_i^- is likely to be changed. For example, for "Pale Skin", both M_i^+ and M_i^- characterize the "skin" region; for "Bald", M_i^+ characterizes the "hair" region while M_i^- characterizes the region consisting of "background, skin, ears" and "ear rings". In this setup, we propose the

---

[1] https://github.com/zllrunning/face-parsing.PyTorch.

following Mask-aware Reconstruction Error (MRE) to measure the *preserving quality* of the editing process (in preserving irrelevant regions that shall not be edited):

$$\text{MRE} = \frac{1}{HWC} \sum_{i=1}^{C} \left\| (1 - M_i^{\text{sgn}(\textbf{att}_{\text{diff},i})})(G(\textbf{x}, \textbf{att}_{\text{diff},i}\textbf{e}_i) - \textbf{x}) \right\|_1, \qquad (2)$$

where $\textbf{att}_{\text{diff},i}$ is the i'th entry of $\textbf{att}_{\text{diff}}$, and $\textbf{e}_i$ is the vector with i'th entry 1 and all others 0, $M_i^{\text{sgn}(\textbf{att}_{\text{diff},i})} \in \{M_i^+, M_i^-\}$. In the face editing experiments, since all attributes are binary and $\textbf{att}_s \in \{0,1\}^C$, we take the attribute change vector $\textbf{att}_{\text{diff}} := 1 - 2\textbf{att}_s$. In this case, the image preservation error is computed when *only one* attribute is flipped each time, and MRE is the total error.

In Sect. 4, we will report MRE for various previous methods and our models in Table 3. Existing approaches of both the cycle-consistency loss used in StarGAN [6] and the reconstruction loss in [9,24] are insufficient to preserve the regions that shall not be edited.

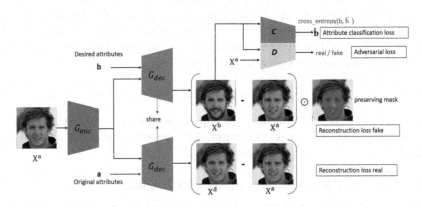

Fig. 4. MagGAN loss function design (Sect. 3.2). For better illustration, the preserving region is denoted by the non-grey region of human face

3.2   Loss Functions for Model Training

We aim to optimize MagGAN regarding the following four aspects: (*i*) preservation accuracy for regions that should be preserved; (*ii*) reconstruction error of the original image; (*iii*) attribute editing success; and (*iv*) synthesized image quality. Therefore, we design four respective types of loss functions for MagGAN training, as illustrated in Fig. 4.

Mask-Guided Reconstruction Loss. Continue from the design of MRE (2), we propose the following mask-guided reconstruction loss:

$$L_G^{\text{mre}} = \left\| M(\textbf{att}_{\text{diff}}, \textbf{x}) \cdot (\textbf{x} - G(\textbf{x}, \textbf{att}_{\text{diff}})) \right\|_1, \qquad (3)$$

where $M(\textbf{att}_{\text{diff}}, \textbf{x}) \in [0,1]^{H \times W}$ is a probability mask of the regions to be preserved.

The preserved mask $M(\mathbf{att}_{\mathrm{diff}}, \mathbf{x})$ is computed from both the attribute difference $\mathbf{att}_{\mathrm{diff}}$ and the probability facial mask $\mathbf{M}$ of image $\mathbf{x}$. We first feed image $\mathbf{x}$ into a face parser, and obtain a probability map $\mathbf{M} \in [0,1]^{19 \times H \times W}$ of the 19 facial parts, where $\sum_{i=1}^{19} \mathbf{M}_{i,h,w} = \mathbf{1}_{h,w}$. Since the semantic relationship between facial attributes and facial parts can be reasonably assumed to be constant, we explicitly define two binary relation matrices $\mathbf{AR}^+$ and $\mathbf{AR}^-$, the *attribute-part matrices* with dimension $C \times 19$, to characterize the relation between them. The i-th row of matrix $\mathbf{AR}^+$ or $\mathbf{AR}^-$ indicates which facial parts should be modified when the i-th attribute is strengthened, *i.e.*, $\mathbf{att}_{\mathrm{diff},i} > 0$, or weakened, *i.e.*, $\mathbf{att}_{\mathrm{diff},i} < 0$. Note that, if facial part has no explicit relationship with one attribute, the corresponding matrix entry of $\mathbf{AR}^+, \mathbf{AR}^-$ could be set to 0.

To obtain M, we first gather all parts $\mathbf{AR}^* \in [0,1]^{19}$ that are possibly influenced by attribute change $\mathbf{att}_{\mathrm{diff}}$, as,

$$\mathbf{AR}^* = \min\left\{1, \left(\mathbf{att}_{\mathrm{diff}}^{(+)}\right)^T \mathbf{AR}^+ + \left(\mathbf{att}_{\mathrm{diff}}^{(-)}\right)^T \mathbf{AR}^-\right\}, \qquad (4)$$

where $\mathbf{att}_{\mathrm{diff}}^{(+)} = (\mathbf{att}_{\mathrm{diff}} > 0)$ and $\mathbf{att}_{\mathrm{diff}}^{(-)} = (\mathbf{att}_{\mathrm{diff}} < 0)$. Finally,

$$M_{h,w}(\mathbf{att}_{\mathrm{diff}}, \mathbf{x}) = 1 - \sum_{i=1}^{C} \mathbf{M}_{i,h,w} * \mathbf{AR}_i^*. \qquad (5)$$

The influence regions M_i^+ and M_i^- in (2) can also be computed this way, with $\mathbf{att}_{\mathrm{diff}} = \mathbf{e}_i$ and $\mathbf{att}_{\mathrm{diff}} = -\mathbf{e}_i$.

Reconstruction Loss. Image reconstruction can be considered as a sub-task of image editing, because the generator should reconstruct the image when no edit is applied, $\mathbf{att}_{\mathrm{diff}} = \mathbf{0}$. Therefore, the reconstruction loss is defined as

$$\mathcal{L}_G^{\mathrm{rec}} = \|G(\mathbf{x}, \mathbf{0}) - x\|_1, \qquad (6)$$

where the ℓ_1 norm is adopted to preserve the sharpness of the reconstructed image.

GAN Loss for Enhancing Image Quality. The synthesized image quality is enhanced by the generative adversarial networks, where we use an unconditional image discriminator D_{adv} to differentiate real images from edited images. In particular, a Wasserstein GAN (WGAN) [1] is utilized:

$$\mathcal{L}_{D_{\mathrm{adv}}} = \mathbb{E}_{\widehat{\mathbf{x}}}[D_{\mathrm{adv}}(\widehat{\mathbf{x}})] - \mathbb{E}_{\mathbf{x}}[D_{\mathrm{adv}}(\mathbf{x})] + \lambda \mathbb{E}_{\mathbf{x}_{\mathrm{int}}}[(\|\nabla_{\mathbf{x}_{\mathrm{int}}} D_{\mathrm{adv}}(\mathbf{x}_{\mathrm{int}})\|_2 - 1)^2], \qquad (7)$$

where $\widehat{\mathbf{x}}$ is the generated image and $\mathbf{x}_{\mathrm{int}}$ is sampled along lines between the latent space of pairs of real and generated image.

The generator G, instead, tries to fool the discriminator by synthesizing more realistic images:

$$\mathcal{L}_G^{\mathrm{gan}} = -\mathbb{E}_{\mathbf{x}, \mathbf{att}_{\mathrm{diff}}}[D_{\mathrm{adv}}(G(\mathbf{x}, \mathbf{att}_{\mathrm{diff}}))]. \qquad (8)$$

Attribute Classification Loss. To ensure that the edited image indeed has the target attribute $\mathbf{att}_t$, an attribute classifier D_{att} is trained on the ground-truth image attribute pairs $(\mathbf{x}, \mathbf{att}_s)$ with the standard cross-entropy loss:

$$\mathcal{L}_{D_{\text{att}}} = \mathbb{E}_{\mathbf{x}}[KL(D_{\text{att}}(\mathbf{x}), \mathbf{att}_s)] . \tag{9}$$

The generator is trying to generate images that maximize its probability to be classified with the target attribute $\mathbf{att}_t$:

$$\mathcal{L}_G^{\text{cls}} = -\mathbb{E}_{\mathbf{x}, \mathbf{att}_{\text{diff}}}[KL(D_{\text{att}}(G(\mathbf{x}, \mathbf{att}_{\text{diff}})), \mathbf{att}_t)] . \tag{10}$$

In summary, the loss to train the MagGAN generator G is

$$\mathcal{L}_G = L_G^{\text{gan}} + \lambda_1 \mathcal{L}_G^{\text{rec}} + \lambda_2 \mathcal{L}_G^{\text{cls}} + \lambda_3 L_G^{\text{mre}}. \tag{11}$$

In experiments, we always take $\lambda_1 = 100$ and $\lambda_2 = 10$. We vary λ_3 to examine the effect of our proposed mask-guided reconstruction loss.

3.3   Mask-Guided Conditioning in the Generator

Another reason why the previous methods cannot preserve the regions that shall not be edited is about how the attribute change information is injected into the generator. Although most attribute changes should lead to localized editing, the attribute change condition $\mathbf{att}_{\text{diff}} \in \mathbb{R}^C$ does not explicitly contain any spatial information. In STGAN [24] (and other previous works for face attribute editing), this condition is replicated to have the same spatial size of some hidden feature tensor, and then concatenated to it in the generator. For example, in the SPADE block in Fig. 3 (Right), $\mathbf{att}_{\text{diff}}$ is replicated spatially to be $\mathbf{Att}_{\text{diff}} \in \mathbb{R}^{C \times H \times W}$ (the purple block)[2], and then concatenated to the decoder feature (the green block). It is hoped that the generator will learn by itself the localized property of attribute editing from this concatenated tensor. However, in practice, this is insufficient, even with the mask-guided reconstruction loss (3).

We propose to inject this inductive bias that the influence region of each attribute change is localized into the generator directly, by making use of masks. We view the i-th channel of $\mathbf{Att}_{\text{diff}}$, denoted as $\mathbf{Att}_{\text{diff}}^{(i)} \in \mathbb{R}^{H \times W}$, as the condition to edit attribute a_i. In previous work, $\mathbf{Att}_{\text{diff}}^{(i)} = \mathbf{att}_{\text{diff},i}\mathbf{1}$ that is uniform across the spatial dimension. Specifically, we propose:

$$\mathbf{Att}_{\text{diff}}^{(i)} = \mathbf{att}_{\text{diff},i} M_i^{\text{sgn}(\mathbf{att}_{\text{diff},i})}, \tag{12}$$

where M_i^+ and M_i^- are the influence regions of attribute a_i defined in (2). We illustrate this mask-guided conditioning process in Fig. 3 (bottom-left). Finally, we simply replace the original replicated tensor with the mask-guided attribute condition tensor, and obtain *a generator with mask-guided conditioning*. Note

---

[2] We use $\mathbf{att} \in \mathbb{R}^C$ to denote attributes without spatial dimension and $\mathbf{Att} \in \mathbb{R}^{C \times H \times W}$ for attributes with spatial dimensions.

that this mask-guided conditioning technique is generally applicable to both generators with and without SPADE.

The blending trick is another simple approach to preserve the attribute-irrelevant regions. More specifically, with the probability mask of attribute-irrelevant regions $M(\mathbf{att}_{\text{diff}}, \mathbf{x})$ defined in (3), we simply add a linear layer at the end of the generator:

$$\widehat{x} = M(\mathbf{att}_{\text{diff}}, \mathbf{x}) * x + (1 - M(\mathbf{att}_{\text{diff}}, \mathbf{x})) * G(\mathbf{x}, \mathbf{att}_{\text{diff}}). \qquad (13)$$

This blending trick improves our MagGAN performance in terms of MRE, but visually it introduces sharp transitions at the boundary of regions to be preserved. Therefore, we do not include this trick in our final MagGAN. More discussions are in Supplementary.

3.4 Multi-level Patch-Wise Discriminators for High-Resolution Face Editing

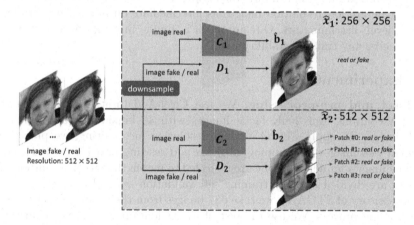

Fig. 5. Illustration of multi-level patch-wise discriminators

We describe our approach to scale up image editing in high resolutions. First of all, we empirically found that a single "shallow" discriminator cannot learn some global concepts, such as Male/Female, leading to low editing success. On the other hand, a single "deep" discriminator makes the adversarial training very unstable, leading to low image quality.

Inspired by PatchGAN [12] and several multi-level generation works [13,40, 41], we propose to use a series of multi-level patch-wise "shallow" discriminators, as illustrated in Fig. 5, for high-resolution face editing. The architecture of the discriminators are exactly the same without sharing weights. The coarsest-level discriminator (D_1) see the full downsampled image, and is responsible for global consistency in the image generation. The attribute classifier C_1 associated with it is effective in attribute classification, as in the low-resolution image editing case. The finer-level discriminators (D_2, etc.) see patches of the generated high-resolution image instead of the full one, and determine whether these patches are real or not. To maintain an unified architecture for discriminators across different levels, we still associate the finer-level discriminator with a classifier (C_2), which takes the average pooled feature as input for classification. The total loss for all PatchGAN discriminators are defined as:

$$\mathcal{L}_D = \frac{1}{P} \sum_{i=1}^{P} \left(\mathcal{L}_{D_{\text{att}}^i} + \mathcal{L}_{D_{\text{adv}}^i} \right), \tag{14}$$

where D_{att}^i, D_{adv}^i denote the attribute classifier and image discriminator of the ith PatchGAN discriminator, P is the number of total discriminators. In practice, we found these finer-level discriminators improve the editing performance.

Note that our generator only generates high-resolution images, which can be directly downsampled to lower resolutions and fed to coarse-level discriminators. On the contrary, generators in previous works [13,40,41] generate a high-resolution image in a multi-stage manner for the sake of training stability. They generate low-resolution images as intermediate outputs, which are fed to coarse-level discriminators. Our approach is simple in comparison, and we did not observe any training stability issue.

4   Experiments

Dataset and pre-processing. We use CelebA dataset [26] for evaluation. CelebA contains over 200K facial images with 40 binary attribute labels for each image. To apply CelebA to high-resolution face editing, we process the original web images by cropping, aligning and resizing into 1024×1024. When loading images for editing, they are re-scaled to match the target resolution. The images are divided into the training set, validation set and test set. Following the repository of STGAN[3], we take 637 images from the validation set to assess the training process. We use the rest of the validation set and the training set to train our model. The test set (nearly 20K) is used for evaluation. We consider 13 distinctive attributes including: *Bald, Bangs, Black Hair, Blond Hair, Brown Hair, Bushy Eyebrows, Eyeglasses, Male, Mouth Slightly Open, Mustache, No Beard, Pale Skin* and *Young*. Since most images in CelebA have lower resolution than 1024×1024, our "high-resolution" MagGAN models are not exactly trained with true high-resolution images. However, our results show the ability of MagGAN scale up to 1024×1024 resolution.

MagGAN exploits the information of facial masks, which are obtained using a pre-trained face parser with 19 classes (as mentioned in Sect. 3.1). Instead of taking a multi-label hard mask, we take the probability of each class as soft masks with smooth boundaries, which leads to improved generation quality. All the facial masks are stored in resolution 256×256. The two attribute-part

---

[3] STGAN: https://github.com/csmliu/STGAN.

relation matrices $AR^+, AR^- \in [0,1]^{13 \times 19}$ described in Sect. 3.2 characterize the relation between each edit attribute and corresponding facial component changes. Detailed definitions are in Supplementary.

Quantitative Evaluation. The performance of attribute editing are measured in three aspects, *i.e.*, (*i*) mask-aware reconstruction error (MRE), (*ii*) attribute editing accuracy and (*iii*) image quality.

Table 1 shows that MagGAN decreases the MRE significantly, indicating better preserving of regions that should be intact. This improvement is also obvious in the editing results in Fig. 8. Table 1 also reports the PSNR/SSIM score of the reconstructed image by keeping target attribute vector the same as the source one. MagGAN also improves PSNR/SSIM significantly.

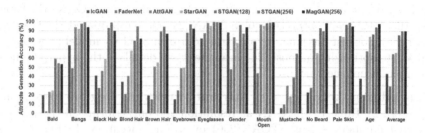

Fig. 6. Facial attribute editing accuracy of IcGAN [31], FaderNet [16], StarGAN [6], AttGAN [9], STGAN [24], STGAN(256) and our model MagGAN(256) (from left to right in rainbow colors in order). The last two models naming with "(256)" are the ones with image resolution 256 that are resized into 128 for evaluation

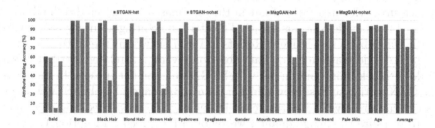

Fig. 7. Facial attribute editing accuracy of STGAN and MagGAN on hat samples and non hat samples of resolution 256 × 256

We also report the attribute editing accuracy by employing the pre-trained attribute classification model from [24]. We follow the evaluation protocol used in [9,24]. For each test image, reverse one of its 13 attributes at a time ($1 \rightarrow 0$ or $0 \rightarrow 1$), and generate an image after each reversion; so there are 13 edited images for each input image. The widely used evaluation metric is *attribute editing accuracy*, which measures the successful manipulation rate for the reversed

Table 1. Comparison of quantitative results with SOTA

Methods	MRE ↓	FID ↓	Avg Acc	PSNR	SSIM
AttGAN(128)	0.0713	10.23	64.9%	24.07	0.841
STGAN(128)	0.0627	7.75	85.8%	31.67	0.948
STGAN(256)	0.0530	1.21	90.4%	37.61	0.959
MagGAN(256)	0.0163	**1.10**	90.0%	40.25	0.984
MagGAN(512)	0.0141	1.20	89.1%	41.42	0.987
MagGAN(1024)	**0.0130**	1.31	**91.0%**	**42.94**	**0.994**

attribute each time, but ignores the attribute preservation error. Fig. 6 reports the facial attribute manipulation accuracy of previous works IcGAN [31], Fader-Net [16], AttGAN [9], StarGAN [6], STGAN [24] and our proposed MagGAN. To build the strongest baseline, we also train our own STGAN model at resolution 256×256, optimizing all possible parameters; see details of the hyperparameter tuning in Supplementary.

High Editing Accuracy *v.s.* Attribute-irrelevant Region Preserving. As shown in Table 1, MagGAN at resolution 256 outperforms all the previous reported numbers except STGAN(256) on average accuracy. In Fig. 6, compared with STGAN(256), MagGAN(256) is better in "Mustache", "No beard", "Gender", "Age" and worse in "Bald", "Bangs", "Black Hair", "Blonde Hair", "Brown Hair". We conjecture that STGAN(256) achieves this high accuracy by editing hat or scarf when they appear in the image; like coloring the hat to golden to get an editing success of "Blonde Hair". To verify this assumption, we separate the testing set into two groups – samples with hat, samples without hat by measuring the area ratio of hat in the face masks (we select threshold 0.1 to decide if the sample contains a hat). The attribute editing accuracy is evaluated on the two subsets respectively. Results in Fig. 7 show that the editing accuracy of MagGAN decreases a lot on hat subset on several hat-related attributes, *e.g.*, "Bald", "Black Hair", but on par with STGAN on non hat subsets. In this sense, MagGAN editing success is even higher than our strongest baseline STGAN(256) since it can preserve the attribute irrelevant regions, making editing more real.

To measure the image quality, we report FID (Fréchet Inception Distance) score [10]. The FID score measures the distance between the Inception-v3[4] activation distributions of original images and the edited images. Table 1 shows that the FID score improves significantly from resolution 128 to 256, but then get stalled and insensitive to image quality for 256 and higher resolutions. This is because the input size for Inception-v3 model is 299, and thus resolution increase from 128 to 256 is significant. However, all high resolution generations are first downsampled to evaluate the FID score. After all, MagGAN at all resolutions achieves the comparable result with the best FID score. Finally, due to smaller

---

[4] We pretrained an Inception-V3 model that achieves 92.69% average attribute classification accuracy on all 40 attributes of CelebA dataset.

batches in training for high resolutions, FID scores of MagGAN(512) and Mag-GAN(1024) are slightly lower than those of MagGAN(256).

Qualitative Evaluation. Apart from the quantitative evaluation, we visualize some facial attribute editing results at resolution 256×256 in Fig. 8, and compare our proposed model with the state-of-the-art method, *i.e.*, STGAN [24] (as it is the strongest baseline) and other variations.

Table 2. Results of user study for ranking methods on two subsets considering hat wearing

Winner method	w/ hat	w/o hat	Overall
MagGAN	**59.2%**	**52.1%**	**55.7%**
STGAN	37.7%	45.3%	41.5%
Tie	3.1 %	2.6%	2.8 %

User Study. We conduct user study on Amazon Turk to compare the generation quality of STGAN and MagGAN. To verify that MagGAN performs better on editing attribute relevant regions, we randomly choose 100 input samples from test set, 50 samples with hat or scarf and 50 samples without (since STGAN usually fails on person wearing hat). For each sample, 5 attribute editing tasks are performed by STGAN and MagGAN (500 comparison pairs in total). All 5 tasks are randomly chosen from 13 attributes, for subjects with hat, we increase the chance to select hair related attributes. The users are instructed to choose the best result which changes the attribute more successfully considering image quality and identity preservation. To avoid human bias, each sample pair is evaluated by 3 volunteers. The results are shown in Table 2, MagGAN outperforms STGAN on both hat samples and without hat samples.

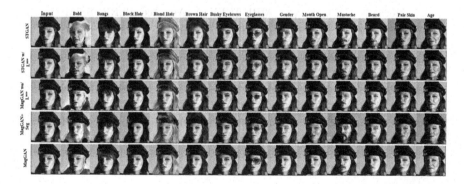

Fig. 8. Visual results of MagGAN variants on resolution 256 × 256. Each column represents edited images through one attribute reversing editing

5   Ablation Study

We conduct three groups of ablation comparisons in image resolution of 256×256, to verify the effectiveness of the proposed modules individually: (i) mask guided reconstruction loss, (ii) spatially modified attribute feature, and (iii) usage of SPADE normalization.

We consider seven variants, $i.e.$, (i) STGAN: STGAN at resolution 256×256, (ii) STGAN+cycle: STGAN with cycle-consistency loss instead of its original reconstruction loss, (iii) STGAN w/ L^{mre}: STGAN plus mask guided reconstruction loss, (iv) MagGAN w/o L^{mre}: MagGAN trained without mask guided reconstruction loss, (v) MagGAN w/o SP: MagGAN without using SPADE, (vi) MagGAN: our proposed model with the usage of mask-guided reconstruction loss and make-guided attribute conditioning. (vii) MagGAN+Seg: Instead of using a pre-trained face parser, build a face segmentation branch (adopting FCN[27] architecture) into generator as sub-task, making the whole model fully trainable.

Mask-guided Reconstruction Loss. We compare three reconstruction loss: (i) STGAN with only the reconstruction loss computed by reconstructed images, (ii) cycle-consistency loss which is applied in StarGAN [6], (iii) two parts of reconstruction loss (computed on reconstructed images and synthesized images respectively) proposed in Sect. 3.2. Row 1–3 of Table 3 report the quantitative results of STGAN applying each type of reconstruction loss respectively. We observe that adding mask guided reconstruction loss to generator training can effectively reduce Mask-aware Reconstruction Error (MRE). In Fig. 8, the synthesized image of STGAN w/ L^{mre} on attribute "Bald" and "Blonde Hair" also proves this assumption. But since the spatial information of mask is not directly injected into generator, STGAN w/ L^{mre} still cannot preserve the attribute-irrelevant regions well.

Table 3. Comparison of variants of MagGAN on 256×256

Methods	MRE ↓	FID ↓	Avg Acc	PSNR	SSIM
(i) STGAN	0.0530	1.21	90.4%	37.61	0.959
(ii) STGAN+cycle	0.0530	1.31	87.3%	36.14	0.970
(iii) STGAN w/ L^{mre}	0.0289	1.33	**95.6%**	38.48	**0.984**
(iv) MagGAN w/o L^{mre}	0.0397	1.22	89.6%	39.35	0.980
(v) MagGAN w/o SP	**0.0161**	1.23	89.9%	**40.40**	0.982
(vi) MagGAN	0.0163	**1.10**	90.0%	40.25	**0.984**
(vii) MagGAN+Seg	0.0612	2.39	90.3%	40.10	0.983

Mask-guided Attribute Conditioning. Utilizing mask-guided attribute conditioning instead of the spatially uniformed attribute conditioning provides generator with more spatial information of the interest regions. From Table 3, (i) $v.s.$

(iv), (iii) *v.s.* (vi) illustrate that the MRE score decreases obviously when mask-guided attribute conditioning is applied in generator. It implies that generator effectively takes the regions of interest and edits on these local regions. Taking advantage of both mask-guided reconstruction loss and attribute conditioning strategy, MagGAN achieves the best MRE and FID. And the visual results in Fig. 8 also show that MagGAN makes accurate editing on hair related attributes ('Bold', 'Blonde Hair', *etc* .), by preserving the region of hat while only remove or paint the hair. MagGAN w/o SP and MagGAN perform nearly the same as (v) *v.s.* (vi), which demonstrates the denormalization method does not affect much on performance. Finally, the quantitative results and visual results of (vii) MagGAN+Seg are bad, which indicates the incorporating mask segmentation branch as part of the generator is not a good choice. Since the mask-guided reconstruction loss and attribute conditioning requires accurate masks, training segmentation branch with generator from scratch makes the model hard to train and undermines the editing accuracy.

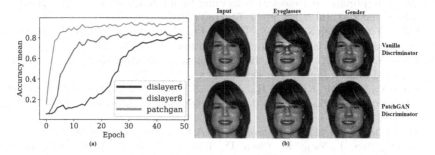

Fig. 9. Comparison of training with vanilla single discriminator and multi-level Patch-GAN discriminators on resolution 1024 × 1024: (a) attribute editing accuracy and (b) visual results

Multi-level PatchGAN Discriminator for High Resolution Editing. We apply PatchGAN discriminator to supervise training of high resolution image generation. We are able to scale the generated image resolution up to 1024×1024. In Fig. 9, we compare the 1024 version of training with a single discriminator and with our proposed multi-level PatchGAN discriminators. Under this setting, PatchGAN has 3 discriminators working on resolution 256 × 256, 512 × 512 and 1024, respectively. In Fig. 9 (a), when applying single vanilla discriminator, the generator converges slower than using PatchGAN discriminator and early stops at low editing accuracy. In Fig. 9 (b), editing effects on "Eyeglasses", "Gender" from PatchGAN are more obvious than original discriminator. We assume PatchGAN discriminators provide more supervise signal on global and local regions, thus helping generator learns more discriminative features for each attribute. See more visual results in supplementary.

6 Conclusion

In this paper, we propose MagGAN for high-resolution face image editing. The key novelty of our work lies in the use of facial masks for achieving more accurate local editing. Specifically, the mask information is used to construct a mask-guided reconstruction loss and mask-guided conditioning in the generator. Mag-GAN is further scaled up for high-resolution face editing with the help of Patch-GAN discriminators. To our knowledge, it is the first time face attribute editing is able to be applied on resolution 1024×1024.

References

1. Arjovsky, M., Chintala, S., Bottou, L.: Wasserstein gan. arXiv preprint arXiv: 1701.07875 (2017)
2. Ba, J.L., Kiros, J.R., Hinton, G.E.: Layer normalization. arXiv preprint arXiv: 1607.06450 (2016)
3. Chen, X., Duan, Y., Houthooft, R., Schulman, J., Sutskever, I., Abbeel, P.: Info-gan: Interpretable representation learning by information maximizing generative adversarial nets. In: NIPS, pp. 2172–2180 (2016)
4. Chen, Y.C., Shen, X., Lin, Z., Lu, X., Pao, I.M., Jia, J.: Semantic component decomposition for face attribute manipulation. In: CVPR (2019)
5. Chen, Y.C., Xu, X., Tian, Z., Jia, J.: Homomorphic latent space interpolation for unpaired image-to-image translation. In: CVPR (2019)
6. Choi, Y., Choi, M., Kim, M., Ha, J., Kim, S., Choo, J.: Stargan: unified generative adversarial networks for multi-domain image-to-image translation. In: CVPR, pp. 8789–8797 (2018)
7. Goodfellow, I., et al.: Generative adversarial nets. In: NeurIPS (2014)
8. Gu, S., Bao, J., Yang, H., Chen, D., Wen, F., Yuan, L.: Mask-guided portrait editing with conditional gans. In: CVPR (2019)
9. He, Z., Zuo, W., Kan, M., Shan, S., Chen, X.: Attgan: facial attribute editing by only changing what you want. IEEE Trans. Image Process. **28**(11), 5464–5478 (2019)
10. Heusel, M., Ramsauer, H., Unterthiner, T., Nessler, B., Hochreiter, S.: Gans trained by a two time-scale update rule converge to a local nash equilibrium. arXiv preprint arXiv:1706.08500 (2017)
11. Huang, X., Belongie, S.: Arbitrary style transfer in real-time with adaptive instance normalization. In: ICCV (2017)
12. Isola, P., Zhu, J.Y., Zhou, T., Efros, A.A.: Image-to-image translation with conditional adversarial networks. In: CVPR (2017)
13. Karras, T., Aila, T., Laine, S., Lehtinen, J.: Progressive growing of gans for improved quality, stability, and variation. In: ICLR (2018)
14. Karras, T., Laine, S., Aila, T.: A style-based generator architecture for generative adversarial networks. CoRR.abs/1812.04948 (2018)
15. Klys, J., Snell, J., Zemel, R.S.: Learning latent subspaces in variational autoencoders. In: NeurIPS, pp. 6445–6455 (2018)
16. Lample, G., Zeghidour, N., Usunier, N., Bordes, A., Denoyer, L., Ranzato, M.: Fader networks: manipulating images by sliding attributes. In: NIPS, pp. 5969–5978 (2017)
17. Larsen, A.B.L., Sønderby, S.K., Larochelle, H., Winther, O.: Autoencoding beyond pixels using a learned similarity metric. In: ICML, pp. 1558–1566 (2016)

18. Le, V., Brandt, J., Lin, Z., Bourdev, L., Huang, T.S.: Interactive facial feature localization. In: Fitzgibbon, A., Lazebnik, S., Perona, P., Sato, Y., Schmid, C. (eds.) ECCV 2012. LNCS, vol. 7574, pp. 679–692. Springer, Heidelberg (2012). https://doi.org/10.1007/978-3-642-33712-3_49

19. Lee, C.H., Liu, Z., Wu, L., Luo, P.: Maskgan: towards diverse and interactive facial image manipulation. arXiv preprint arXiv:1907.11922 (2019)

20. Li, H., Dong, W., Hu, B.: Facial image attributes transformation via conditional recycle generative adversarial networks. J. Comput. Sci. Technol. **33**(3), 511–521 (2018)

21. Li, M., Zuo, W., Zhang, D.: Deep identity-aware transfer of facial attributes. CoRR abs/1610.05586 (2016)

22. Li, W., et al.: Object-driven text-to-image synthesis via adversarial training. In: CVPR (2019)

23. Liang, X., et al.: Human parsing with contextualized convolutional neural network. In: ICCV (2015)

24. Liu, M., et al.: STGAN: a unified selective transfer network for arbitrary image attribute editing. In: CVPR, pp. 3673–3682 (2019)

25. Liu, M., Breuel, T., Kautz, J.: Unsupervised image-to-image translation networks. In: NIPS, pp. 700–708 (2017)

26. Liu, Z., Luo, P., Wang, X., Tang, X.: Deep learning face attributes in the wild. In: ICCV (2015)

27. Long, J., Shelhamer, E., Darrell, T.: Fully convolutional networks for semantic segmentation. In: Proceedings of the IEEE Conference on Computer Vision and Pattern Recognition, pp. 3431–3440 (2015)

28. Lu, Y., Tai, Y., Tang, C.: Attribute-guided face generation using conditional cyclegan. In: ECCV, pp. 293–308 (2018)

29. Ma, L., Jia, X., Georgoulis, S., Tuytelaars, T., Gool, L.V.: Exemplar guided unsupervised image-to-image translation. CoRR abs/1805.11145 (2018)

30. Park, T., Liu, M., Wang, T., Zhu, J.: Semantic image synthesis with spatially-adaptive normalization. In: CVPR (2019)

31. Perarnau, G., van de Weijer, J., Raducanu, B., Álvarez, J.M.: Invertible conditional gans for image editing. CoRR abs/1611.06355 (2016)

32. Shen, W., Liu, R.: Learning residual images for face attribute manipulation. In: CVPR, pp. 1225–1233 (2017)

33. Wang, Y., Wang, S., Qi, G., Tang, J., Li, B.: Weakly supervised facial attribute manipulation via deep adversarial network. In: WACV, pp. 112–121 (2018)

34. Xiao, T., Hong, J., Ma, J.: ELEGANT: exchanging latent encodings with GAN for transferring multiple face attributes. In: ECCV, pp. 172–187 (2018)

35. Xie, D., Yang, M., Deng, C., Liu, W., Tao, D.: Fully-featured attribute transfer. CoRR abs/1902.06258 (2019)

36. Yan, X., Yang, J., Sohn, K., Lee, H.: Attribute2Image: conditional image generation from visual attributes. In: Leibe, B., Matas, J., Sebe, N., Welling, M. (eds.) ECCV 2016. LNCS, vol. 9908, pp. 776–791. Springer, Cham (2016). https://doi.org/10.1007/978-3-319-46493-0_47

37. Yin, W., Liu, Z., Loy, C.C.: Instance-level facial attributes transfer with geometry-aware flow. CoRR abs/1811.12670 (2018)

38. Yu, C., Wang, J., Peng, C., Gao, C., Yu, G., Sang, N.: Bisenet: bilateral segmentation network for real-time semantic segmentation. In: ECCV (2018)

39. Zhang, G., Kan, M., Shan, S., Chen, X.: Generative adversarial network with spatial attention for face attribute editing. In: ECCV, pp. 422–437 (2018)

40. Zhang, H., et al.: Stackgan: text to photo-realistic image synthesis with stacked generative adversarial networks. In: ICCV (2017)
41. Zhang, H., et al.: Stackgan++: realistic image synthesis with stacked generative adversarial networks. IEEE Trans. Pattern Anal. Mach. Intell. **41**(8), 1947–1962 (2018)
42. Zhang, J., et al.: Sparsely grouped multi-task generative adversarial networks for facial attribute manipulation. In: ACM MM, pp. 392–401 (2018)
43. Zhang, Z., Song, Y., Qi, H.: Age progression/regression by conditional adversarial autoencoder. In: CVPR, pp. 4352–4360 (2017)
44. Zheng, X., Guo, Y., Huang, H., Li, Y., He, R.: A survey to deep facial attribute analysis. CoRR abs/1812.10265 (2018)
45. Zhou, S., Xiao, T., Yang, Y., Feng, D., He, Q., He, W.: Genegan: learning object transfiguration and object subspace from unpaired data. In: BMVC (2017)

EvolGAN: Evolutionary Generative Adversarial Networks

Baptiste Roziere[1]([✉]), Fabien Teytaud[2], Vlad Hosu[3], Hanhe Lin[3], Jeremy Rapin[1], Mariia Zameshina[4], and Olivier Teytaud[1]

[1] Facebook AI Research, Paris, France
{broz,jrapin,oteytaud}@fb.com
[2] Univ. Littoral Cote d'Opale, Dunkirk, France
teytaud@univ-littoral.fr
[3] University of Konstanz, Konstanz, Germany
{vlad.hosu,hanhe.lin}@uni-konstanz.de
[4] Univ. Grenoble Alpes, CNRS, Inria, Grenoble INP, LIG, Grenoble, France

Abstract. We propose to use a quality estimator and evolutionary methods to search the latent space of generative adversarial networks trained on small, difficult datasets, or both. The new method leads to the generation of significantly higher quality images while preserving the original generator's diversity. Human raters preferred an image from the new version with frequency 83.7% for Cats, 74% for FashionGen, 70.4% for Horses, and 69.2% for Artworks - minor improvements for the already excellent GANs for faces. This approach applies to any quality scorer and GAN generator.

1 Introduction

Generative adversarial networks (GAN) are the state-of-the-art generative models in many domains. However, they need quite a lot of training data to reach a decent performance. Using off-the-shelf image quality estimators, we propose a novel but simple evolutionary modification for making them more reliable for small, difficult, or multimodal datasets. Contrarily to previous approaches using evolutionary methods for image generation, we do not modify the training phase. We use a generator G mapping a latent vector z to an image $G(z)$ built as in a classical GAN. The difference lies in the method used for choosing a latent vector z. Instead of randomly generating a latent vector z, we perform an evolutionary optimization, with z as decision variables and the estimated quality of $G(z)$—based on a state-of-the-art quality estimation method—s an objective function. We show that:

- The quality of generated images is better, both for the proxy used for estimating the quality, i.e., the objective function, as well as for human raters. For example, the modified images are preferred by human raters more than

---

B. Roziere and F. Teytaud—Equal contribution.

H. Ishikawa et al. (Eds.): ACCV 2020, LNCS 12625, pp. 679–694, 2021.
https://doi.org/10.1007/978-3-030-69538-5_41

80% of the time for images of cats and around 70% of the time for horses and artworks.

- The diversity of the original GAN is preserved: the new images are preferred by humans and still similar.
- The computational overhead introduced by the evolutionary optimization is moderate, compared to the computational requirement for training the original GAN.

The approach is simple, generic, easy to implement, and fast. It can be used as a drop-in replacement for classical GAN provided that we have a quality estimator for the outputs of the GAN. Besides the training of the original GAN, many experiments were performed on a laptop without any GPU.

Fig. 1. For illustration, random images generated using StyleGAN2 (left) and Evol-GAN (right). Horses were typically harder than cats. The images generated by Evol-GAN are generally more realistic. The top-left example of a generated cat by Style-GAN2 has blood-like artifacts on its throat and the other is blurry. Three of the four StyleGAN2 horses are clearly unrealistic: on the bottom right of the StyleGan2 results, the human and the horse are mixed, the bottom left shows an incoherent mix of several horses, the top left looks like the ghost, and only the top right is realistic. Overall, both cats, and 3 of the 4 horses generated by EvolGAN look realistic. We show more examples of horses, as they are more difficult to model.

Figure 1 shows examples of generations of $EvolGAN_{StyleGAN2}$ compared to generations by StyleGAN2. Figure 2 presents our general approach, detailed in the Sect. 3.

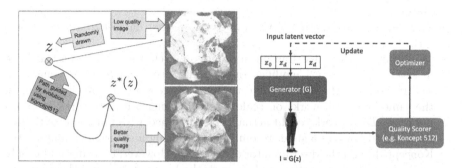

Fig. 2. General EvolGAN approach (left) and optimization loop (right). Our method improves upon a pre-trained generator model G, which maps a latent vector z to an image $G(z)$. In classical models, the images are generated by sampling a latent vector z randomly. We modify that randomly chosen z into a better $z^*(z_0)$ evolved to improve the quality of the image, typically estimated by Koncept512. For preserving diversity, we ensure that $z^*(z_0)$ is close to the original z_0. The original image is generated using PokeGan (Pokemon dataset) and the improved one is generated using EvolGAN (superposed on top of PokeGan): we see an elephant-style Pokemon, hardly visible in the top version.

2 Related Works

2.1 Generative Adversarial Networks

Generative Adversarial Networks [1] (GANs) are widely used in machine learning [2–9] for generative modeling. Generative Adversarial Networks are made up of two neural networks: a Generator G, mapping a latent vector z to an image $G(z)$ and a Discriminator D mapping an image I to a realism value $D(I)$. Given a dataset $\mathcal{D}$, GANs are trained using two training steps operating concurrently:

(i) Given a randomly generated z, the generator G tries to fool D into classifying its output $G(z)$ as a real image, e.g. by maximizing $\log D(G(z))$. For this part of the training, only the weights of G are modified.
(ii) Given a minibatch containing both random fake images $F = \{G(z_1), \ldots, G(z_k)\}$ and real images $R = \{I_1, \ldots, I_k\}$ randomly drawn in $\mathcal{D}$, the discriminator learns to distinguish R and F, e.g. by optimizing the cross-entropy.

The ability of GANs to synthesize faces [10] is particularly impressive and of wide interest. However, such results are possible only with huge datasets for each modality and/or after careful cropping, which restricts their applicability.

Here we consider the problem of improving GANs trained on small or difficult datasets. Classical tools for making GANs compatible with small datasets include:

- Data augmentation, by translation, rotation, symmetries, or other transformations.
- Transfer from an existing GAN trained on another dataset to a new dataset [11].
- Modification of the distribution in order to match a specific request as done in several papers. [12] modifies the training, using quality assessement as we do; however they modify the training whereas we modify inference. In the same vein, [13] works on scale disentanglement: it also works at training time. These works could actually be combined with ours. [14] optimizes the injected noise in a super resolution GAN using a criterion combining the Koncept512 and the discriminator of the GAN. However, their method is only applied to super resolution and their method cannot be applied directly to any generative model. [15] generates images conditionally to a classifier output or conditionally to a captioning network output. [16] and [17] condition the generation to a playability criterion (estimated by an agent using the GAN output) or some high-level constraints. [18] uses a variational autoencoder (VAE), so that constraints can be added to the generation: they can add an attribute (e.g. black hair) and still take into account a realism criterion extracted from the VAE: this uses labels from the dataset. [19] uses disentanglement of the latent space for semantic face editing: the user can modify a specific latent variable. [20] allows image editing and manipulation: it uses projections onto the output domain.
- Biasing the dataset. [21] augments the dataset by generating images with a distribution skewed towards the minority classes.
- Learning a specific probability distribution, rather than using a predefined, for example Gaussian, distribution. Such a method is advocated in [22].

The latter is the closest to the present work in the sense that we stay close to the goal of the original GAN, i.e. modeling some outputs without trying to bias the construction towards some subset. However, whereas [22] learn a probability distribution on the fly while training the GAN, our approach learns a classical GAN and modifies, a posteriori, the probability distribution by considering a subdomain of the space of the latent variables in which images have better quality. We could work on an arbitrary generative model based on latent variables, not only GANs. As opposed to all previously mentioned works, we improve the generation, without modifying the target distribution and without using any side-information or handcrafted criterion - our ingredient is a quality estimator. Other combinations of deep learning and evolutionary algorithms have been published around GANs. For instance, [23] evolves a population of generators, whereas our evolutionary algorithm evolves individuals in the latent space. [24] also evolves individuals in the latent space, but using human feedback rather than the quality estimators that we are using. [25] evolves individuals in the latent space, but either guided by human feedback or by using similarity to a target image.

2.2   Quality Estimators: Koncept512 and AVA

Quality estimation is a long-standing research topic [26,27] recently improved by deep learning [28]. In the present work, we focus on such quality estimation tools based on supervised convolutional networks. The KonIQ-10k dataset is a large publicly available image quality assessment dataset with 10,073 images rated by humans. Each image is annotated by 120 human raters. The Koncept512 image quality scorer [28] is based on an InceptionResNet-v2 architecture and trained on KonIQ-10k for predicting the mean opinion scores of the annotators. It takes as input an image I and outputs a quality estimate $K(I) \in \mathbb{R}$. Koncept512 is the state of the art in technical quality estimation [28], and is freely available. We use the release without any modification. [29] provides a tool similar to Koncept512, termed AVA, but dedicated to aesthetics rather than technical quality. It was easy to apply it as a drop-in replacement of Koncept512 in our experiments.

3   Methods

3.1   Our Algorithm: EvolGAN

We do not modify the training of the GAN. We use a generator G created by a GAN. G takes as input a random latent vector z, and outputs an image $G(z)$. While the latent vector is generally chosen randomly (e.g., $z \leftarrow \mathcal{N}(0, I_d)$), we treat it as a free parameter to be optimized according to a quality criterion Q. More formally, we obtain $z^*(z_0)$:

$$z^*(z_0) = \arg\max_z Q(G(z)) \text{ in the neighborhood of a random } z_0. \quad (1)$$

In this paper, Q is either Koncept512 or AVA. Our algorithm computes an approximate solution of problem 1 and outputs $G(z^*(z_0))$. Importantly, we do not want a global optimum of Eq. 1. We want a local optimum, in order to have essentially the same image – $z^*(z_0)$ must be close to z_0, which would not happen without this condition. The optimization algorithm used to obtain z^* in Eq. 1 is a simple $(1 + 1)$-Evolution Strategy with random mutation rates [30], adapted as detailed in Sect. 3.2 (see Alg. 1). We keep the budget of our algorithm low, and the mutation strength parameter α can be used to ensure that the image generated by EvolGAN is similar to the initial image. For instance, with $\alpha = 0$, the expected number of mutated variables is, by construction (see Sect. 3.1), bounded by b. We sometimes use the aesthetic quality estimator AVA rather than the technical quality estimator Koncept512 for quality estimation. We consider a coordinate-wise mutation rate: we mutate or do not mutate each coordinate, independently with some probability.

Algorithm 1: The $EvolGAN_{G,b,\alpha}$ algorithm

Parameters:
- A probability distribution $\mathcal{P}$ on $\mathbb{R}^d$.
- A quality estimator Q, providing an estimate $Q(I)$ of the quality of some $I \in E$. We use $Q = Koncept512$ or $Q = AVA$.
- A generator G, building $G(z) \in E$ for $z \in \mathbb{R}^d$.
- A budget b.
- A mutation strength $0 \leq \alpha \leq \infty$.
- A randomly generated $z \leftarrow random(\mathcal{P})$. $I = G(z)$ is the baseline image we are trying to improve.

```
1  for i ∈ {1,...,b} do
2  |    r := Clip(1/d, 1, α × uniform([0, 1]))
3  |    z' := z
4  |    for j ∈ {1,...,d} do
5  |    |    with probability r, z'_i ← random(P)_i (i^th marginal of P).
6  |    end
7  |    if Q(G(z)) < Q(G(z')) then
8  |    |    z ← z'
9  |    end
10 end
   Output    : Optimized image I' = G(z)
```

3.2 Optimization Algorithms

After a few preliminary trials we decided to use the $(1 + 1)$-Evolution Strategy with uniform mixing of mutation rates [30], with a modification as described in Algorithm 1. This modification is designed for tuning the compromise between quality and diversity as discussed in Table 1. We used $Clip(a, b, c) = \max(a, \min(b, c))$. Optionally, z_0 can be provided as an argument, leading to $EvolGAN_{G,b,\alpha,z_0}$. The difference with the standard uniform mixing of mutation rates is that $\alpha \neq 1$. With $\alpha = 0$, the resulting image I' is close to the original image I, whereas with $\alpha = \infty$ the outcome I' is not similar to I. Choosing $\alpha = 1$ (or $\alpha = \frac{1}{2}$, closely related to FastGA [31]) leads to faster convergence rates but also to less diversity (see Algorithm 1, line 2). We will show that overall, $\alpha = 0$ is the best choice for EvolGAN. We therefore get algorithms as presented in Table 1.

3.3 Open Source Codes

We use the GAN publicly available at https://github.com/moxiegushi/pokeGAN, which is an implementation of Wasserstein GAN [32], the StyleGAN2 [10] available at thispersondoesnotexist.com, and PGAN on FashionGen from Pytorch GAN zoo [33]. Koncept512 is available at https://github.com/subpic/koniq. Our combination of Koncept512 and PGAN is available at DOUBLE-BLIND. We use the evolutionary programming platform Nevergrad [34].

Table 1. Optimization algorithms used in the present paper. The last setting is new compared to [30]. We modified the maximum mutation rate α for doing a local or global search depending on α, so that the diversity of the outputs is maintained when α is small (Sect. 4.3). $||x||_0$ denotes the number of non-zero components of x.

$0 \leq \alpha \leq \infty$	behavior of $EvolGAN_{G,b,\alpha}$	$\mathbb{E}||z^*(z_0) - z||_0$ with budget b
$0 \leq \alpha \leq \frac{1}{d}$	standard $(1+1)$ evol. alg with mutation rate $r = \frac{1}{d}$	$\leq b$
$\alpha = 1$	uniform mixing of mutation rates [30] (also related to [31])	
$\alpha = \infty$	all variables mutated: equivalent to random search	
intermediate values α	intermediate behavior	$\leq \min(\max(\alpha, 1/d)bd, d)$

4 Experiments

We present applications of EvolGAN on three different GAN models: (i) Style-GAN2 for faces, cats, horses and artworks (ii) PokeGAN for mountains and Pokemons (iii) PGAN from Pytorch GAN zoo for FashionGen.

4.1 Quality Improvement on StyleGAN2

The experiments are based on open source codes [28,29,33–35]. We use the Style-GAN2 [10] trained on a horse dataset, a face dataset, an artwork dataset, and a cat dataset[1]. **Faces.** We conducted a human study to assess the quality of Evol-GAN compared to StyleGAN, by asking to 10 subject their preferred generations (pairwise comparisons, double-blind, random positioning). There were 11 human raters in total, including both experts with a strong photography background and beginners. 70% of the ratings came from experts. Results appear in Table 2. Faces are the most famous result of StyleGAN2. Although the results are positive as the images generated by EvolGAN are preferred significantly more than 50% of the time, the difference between StyleGAN2 and EvolGAN is quite small on this essentially solved problem compared to wild photos of cats or horses or small datasets.

Harder Settings. Animals and artworks are a much more difficult setting (Fig. 3) - StyleGAN2 sometimes fails to propose a high quality image. Figure 3 presents examples of generations of $StyleGAN2$ and $EvolGAN_{StyleGAN2,b,\alpha}$ in such cases. Here, $EvolGAN$ has more headroom for providing improvements than for faces: results are presented in Table 3. The case of horses or cats is particularly interesting: the failed generations often contain globally unrealistic

---

[1] https://www.thishorsedoesnotexist.com/,https://www.thispersondoesnotexist. com/,https://www.thisartworkdoesnotexist.com/,https://www.thiscatdoesnotexist. com/.

Table 2. Human study on faces dataset. $\alpha = \infty$, quality estimator $q = Koncept512$. Row X, col. Y: frequency at which human raters preferred $EvolGAN_{X,\infty}$ to $EvolGAN_{Y,\infty}$. By construction, for all α, $EvolGAN_{1,\alpha}$ is equal to the original GAN. The fifth row aggregates all results of the first four rows for more significance.

	$EvolGAN_{1,\infty} = G$	$EvolGAN_{10,\infty}$	$EvolGAN_{20,\infty}$	$EvolGAN_{40,\infty}$
$EvolGAN_{10,\infty}$	60.0			
$EvolGAN_{20,\infty}$	50.0	57.1		
$EvolGAN_{40,\infty}$	75.0	44.4	66.7	
$EvolGAN_{80,\infty}$	53.8	53.8	40.0	46.2
10-80 ag-gregated	60.4% ± 3.4% (208 ratings)			

Table 3. Difficult test beds. $\alpha = \infty$; same protocol as in Tables 2 i.e. we check with which probability human raters prefer an image generated by $EvolGAN_{G,b,\alpha}$ to an image generated by the original Gan G. By definition of EvolGAN, $\forall \alpha, G = EvolGAN_{G,1,\alpha}$. Number are above 50%: using EvolGAN for modifying the latent vector z improves the original StyleGAN2.

Dataset	Budget b	Quality estimator	score
Cats	300	Koncept512	83.71 ±1.75% (446 ratings)
Horses	300	Koncept512	70.43 ± 4.27% (115 ratings)
Artworks	300	Koncept512	69.19 ± 3.09% (224 ratings)

elements, such as random hair balls flying in the air or unusual positioning of limbs, which are removed by EvolGAN. For illustration purpose, in Fig. 3 we present a few examples of generations which go wrong for the original StyleGan2 and for $EvolGAN_{StyleGan2,b=100,\alpha=0}$; the bad examples in the case of the original StyleGan2 are much worse.

4.2 Small Difficult Datasets and $\alpha = 0$

In this section we focus on the use of EvolGAN for small datasets. We use the original pokemon dataset in PokeGAN [35] and an additional dataset created from copyright-free images of mountains. The previous section was quite successful, using $\alpha = \infty$ (i.e. random search). The drawback is that the obtained images are not necessarily related to the original ones, and we might lose diversity (though Sect. 4.3 shows that this is not always the case, see discussion later). We will see that $\alpha = \infty$ fails in the present case. In this section, we use α small, and check if the obtained images $EvolGAN_{G,b,\alpha,z}$ are better than $G(z_0)$ (see Table 5) and close to the original image $G(z_0)$ (see Fig.4). Figure 4 presents a Pokemon generated by the default GAN and its improved counterpart obtained by $EvolGAN$ with $\alpha = 0$. Table 5 presents our experimental setting and the results of our human study conducted on PokeGAN. We see a significant improvement when using Koncept512 *on real-world data* (as opposed to drawings such as Pokemons, for which Koncept512 fails), whereas we fail with AVA as in previous experiments (see Table 2). We succeed on drawings with

Table 4. LPIPS scores on FashionGen. As expected, $\alpha = 0$ mostly preserves the diversity of the generated images, while higher values of α can lead to less diversity for the output of EvolGAN. The LPIPS was computed on samples of $50,000$ images for each setting.

Context	LPIPS score
PGAN	0.306 ± 0.0003
$EvolGAN_{PGAN,b=40,\alpha=0}$	0.303 ± 0.0003
$EvolGAN_{PGAN,b=40,\alpha=1}$	0.286 ± 0.0003
$EvolGAN_{PGAN,b=40,\alpha=\infty}$	0.283 ± 0.0002

(a) Cherry-picked poor StyleGAN2 generation (b) Random EvolGAN generation (c) Cherry-picked poor EvolGAN generation (d) Cherry-picked poor StyleGAN2 generation

Fig. 3. For illustration, bad generations by StyleGAN2 and by EvolGAN. (a) Generation of a cat by StyleGAN2: we looked for a bad generation and found that one. Such bad cases completely disappear in the EvolGAN counterpart. (b) example of cat generation by EvolGAN: we failed to find a really bad EvolGAN generated image. (c) Example of bad horse generation by EvolGAN: the shape is unusual (looks like the muzzle of a pork) but we still recognize a horse. (d) Bad generation of a horse by StyleGAN2: some hair balls are randomly flying in the air.

Koncept512 only with $\alpha = 0$: on this dataset of drawings (poorly adapted to Koncept512), α large leads to a pure black image.

4.3 Quality Improvement

Pytorch Gan Zoo [33] is an implementation of progressive GANs (PGAN [36]), applied here with FashionGen [37] as a dataset. The dimension of the latent space is 256. In Table 6, we present the results of our human study comparing $EvolGAN_{PGAN,b,\alpha}$ to $EvolGAN_{PGAN,1,\alpha} = PGAN$. With $\alpha = 0$, humans prefer EvolGAN to the baseline in more than 73% of cases, even after only 40 iterations. $\alpha = 0$ also ensures that the images stay close to the original images when the budget is low enough (see Table 1). Figure 5 shows some examples of generations using EvolGAN and the original PGAN.

Table 5. Experimental results with $EvolGAN_{PokeGAN,b,\alpha=0}$. Reading guide: the last column shows the probability that an image $EvolGAN_{PokeGAN,b,\alpha=0,z} = G(z^*(z_0))$ was prefered to the starting point $PokeGAN(z_0)$. The dimension of the latent space is $d = 256$ except for mountains ($d = 100$). Koncept512 performs well on real world scenes but not on artificial scenes. For Pokemon with $\alpha = \infty$, the 0% (0 success out of 24 tests!) is interesting: the code starts to generate almost uniform images even with a budget $b = 20$, showing that Koncept512 fails on drawings. On mountains (the same GAN, but trained on real world images instead of Pokemons), and to a lesser extent on Pokemons for small α, the images generated using EvolGAN are preferred more than 50% of the time: using EvolGAN for modifying the latent vector z improves the original PokeGan network.

Type of images	Number of images	Number of training epochs	Budget b	Quality estimator	α	Frequency of image preferred to original
Real world scenes						
Mountains	84	4900	500	Koncept512	0	73.3% ± 4.5% (98 ratings)
Artificial scenes						
Pokemons	1840	4900	500	Koncept512	0	55%
Pokemons	1840	4900	2000	Koncept512	0	52%
Pokemons	1840	4900	6000	Koncept512	0	56.3 ± 5.2% (92 ratings)
Artificial scenes, higher mutation rates						
Pokemons	1840	4900	500	Koncept512	1/7	36.8%
Pokemons	1840	4900	20	Koncept512	∞	0%

Fig. 4. In both cases, a Pokemon generated by the default GAN (left) and after improvement by Koncept512 (right). For the left pair, after improvement, we see eyes and ears for a small elephant-style pokemon sitting on his back. A similar transformation appears for the more rabbit-style pokemon on the right hand side. These cherry-picked examples (cherry-picked, i.e. we selected specific cases for illustration purpose) are, however, less convincing than the randomly generated examples in Fig. 5 - Pokemons are the least successful applications, as Koncept512, with α large or big budgets, tends to push those artificial images towards dark almost uniform images.

$G(z_0)$ $G(z_{40}^*(z_0))$ $G(z_{320}^*(z_0))$ $G(z_0)$ $G(z_{40}^*(z_0))$ $G(z_{320}^*(z_0))$

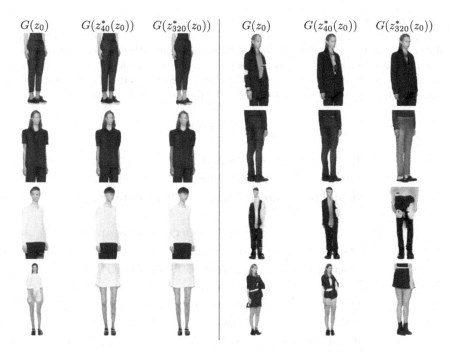

Fig. 5. Preservation of diversity, in particular with budget 40, when $\alpha = 0$. We present triplets $PGAN(z), PGAN(z_{40}^*(z)) = EvolGAN(PGAN, b = 40, \alpha = 0, z), PGAN(z_{320}^*(z)) = EvolGAN(PGAN, b = 320, \alpha = 0, z)$, i.e. in each case the output of PGAN and its optimized counterpart with budgets 40 and 320 respectively (images 1, 4, 7, 10, 13, 16, 19, 22 are the $G(z)$ and images 2, 5, 8, 11, 14, 17, 20, 23 are their counterparts $G(z_{40}^*(z))$ for budget 40; indices +1 for budget 320). With $\alpha = 1$ (unpresented) $PGAN(z)$ and $EvolGAN_{PGAN,b,\alpha,z}$ are quite different, so that we can not guarantee that diversity is preserved. With $\alpha = 0$ diversity is preserved with $b = 40$: for each of these 8 cases, the second image ($b = 40$) is quite close to the original image, just technically better—except the 8th one for which $G(z)$ is quite buggy and EvolGAN can rightly move farther from the original image. Diversity is less preserved with $b = 320$: e.g. on the top right we see that the dress becomes shorter at $b = 320$.

4.4 Consistency: Preservation of Diversity

Here we show that the generated image is close to the one before the optimization. More precisely, given $z \mapsto G(z)$, the following two methods provide related outputs: method 1 (classical GAN) outputs $G(z_0)$, and method 2 (EvolGAN) outputs $EvolGAN_{G,b,\alpha,z} = G(z^*(z_0))$, where $z^*(z_0)$ is obtained by our evolutionary algorithms starting at z with budget b and parameter α (Sect. 3.2). Fig. 5 shows some example generated images using PGAN and EvolGAN. For most examples, $G(z^*(z_0))$ is very similar to $G(z_0)$ so the diversity of the original GAN is preserved well. Following [38,39], we measure numerically the diversity of the generated images from the PGAN model, and from EvolGAN models based on it,

Table 6. Frequency (a.k.a score) at which various versions of $EvolGAN_{PGAN,b,\alpha,z} = PGAN(z^*(z_0))$ were preferred to their starting point $PGAN(z)$ on the FashionGen dataset. This experiment is performed with Koncept512 as a quality estimator. In most experiments we get the best results with $\alpha = 0$ and do not need more than a budget $b = 40$. The values are greater than 50%, meaning that EvolGAN improves the original PGAN network on FashionGen according to human preferences.

b	Frequency
	$\alpha = 0$
40	**73.33 $\pm$ 8.21% (30 ratings))**
320	**75.00 $\pm$ 8.33% (28 ratings))**
40 and 320 aggreg.	**74.13 $\pm$ 5.79% (58 ratings))**
	$\alpha = 1$
40	48.27 $\pm$ 9.44% (29 ratings)
320	67.74 $\pm$ 8.53% (31 ratings)
40 and 320 aggreg	58.33 $\pm$ 6.41% (60 ratings)
	$\alpha = \infty$
40	56.66 $\pm$ 9.20% (30 ratings)
320	66.66 $\pm$ 9.24% (27 ratings)
40 and 320 aggreg	61.40 $\pm$ 6.50% (57 ratings)
	All α aggregated
40	59.55 $\pm$ 5.23% (89 ratings)
320	69.76 $\pm$ 4.98% (86 ratings)
40 and 320 aggreg	64.57 $\pm$ 3.62% (175 ratings)

using the LPIPS score. The scores were computed on samples of $50,000$ images generated with each method. For each sample, we computed the LPIPS with another randomly-chosen generated image. The results are presented in Table 4. Higher values correspond to higher diversity of samples. EvolGAN preserves the diversity of the images generated when used with $\alpha = 0$.

4.5   Using AVA rather than Koncept512

In Table 7 we show that AVA is less suited than Koncept512 as a quality assessor in EvolGAN. The human annotators do not find the images generated using EvolGAN with AVA to be better than those generated without EvolGAN. We hypothesize that this is due to the subjectivity of what AVA estimates: aesthetic quality. While humans generally agree on the factors accounting for the technical quality of an image (sharp edges, absence of blur, right brightness), annotators often disagree on aesthetic quality. Another factor may be that aesthetics are inherently harder to evaluate than technical quality.

Table 7. Testing AVA rather than Koncept512 as a quality estimator. With AVA, EvolGAN fails to beat the baseline according to human annotators.

	$EvolGAN_{1,\infty} = G$	$EvolGAN_{10,\infty}$	$EvolGAN_{20,\infty}$	$EvolGAN_{40,\infty}$
$EvolGAN_{10,\infty}$	34.8			
$EvolGAN_{20,\infty}$	52.0	42.8		
$EvolGAN_{40,\infty}$	39.1	32.0	36.4	
$EvolGAN_{80,\infty}$	52.2	52.2	40.9	56.0%
$EvolGAN_{10-80,\infty}$ (aggregated)	44.5% ± 5.0%			
500	50.55 ± 3.05 %			

(a) Faces with StyleGAN2: reproducing Table 2 with AVA in lieu of Koncept512.

Dataset	Budget b	Quality estimator	score
Cats	300	AVA	47.05 ±7.05%
Artworks	300	AVA	55.71 ± 5.97 %

(b) Reproducing Table 3 with AVA in lieu of Koncept512.

Type of images	Number of images	Number of training epochs	Budget b	Quality estimator	α	Frequency of image preferred to original
Mountains	84	4900	500	AVA	0	42.5%
Pokemons	1840	4900	500	AVA	0	52.6%
Pokemons	1840	4900	500	AVA	1/13	52.6%

(c) Reproducing Table 5 with AVA rather than Koncept512.

5 Conclusion

We have shown that, given a generative model $z \mapsto G(z)$, optimizing z by an evolutionary algorithm using Koncept512 as a criterion and preferably with $\alpha = 0$ (i.e. the classical $(1 + 1)$-Evolution Strategy), leads to

- The generated images are preferred by humans as shown on Table 3 for Style-GAN2, Table 5 for PokeGan and Table 6 for PGAN on FashionGen
- The diversity is preserved, as shown on Fig. 5 and Table 4, when using a small value for α (see Sect. 3.2).

Choosing α. α small, i.e., the classical $(1+1)$-Evolution Strategy with mutation rate $1/d$, is usually the best choice: we preserve the diversity (with provably a small number of mutated variables, and experimentally a resulting image differing from the original one mainly in terms of quality), and the improvement compared to the original GAN is clearer as we can directly compare $EvolGAN_{G,b=d,\alpha=0,z}$ to $G(z)$—a budget $b \simeq d/5$ was usually enough. Importantly, evolutionary algorithms clearly outperformed random search and not only in terms of speed: we completely lose the diversity with random search, as well as the ability to improve a given point. Our application of evolution is a case in which we provably preserve diversity—with a mutation rate bounded by $\max(\alpha, 1/d)$, and a budget $b = d/5$, and a dimension d, we get an expected ratio of mutated variables at most $b \times \max(\alpha, 1/d)$. In our setting $b = 40, d = 256, \alpha = 0$ so the maximum expected ratio of mutated variables is at most $40/256$ in Fig. 5. A tighter, run-dependent bound, can be obtained by comparing z_0 and $z^*(z_0)$ and could be a stopping criterion.

Successes. We get an improved GAN without modifying the training. The results are positive in all cases in particular difficult real-world data (Table 3), though the gap is moderate when the original model is already excellent (faces, Table 2) or when data are not real-world (Pokemons, Table 5. EvolGAN with Koncept512 is particularly successful on several difficult cases with real-world data—Mountains with Pokegan, Cats, Horses and Artworks with StyleGAN2 and FashionGen with Pytorch Gan Zoo.

Remark on Quality Assessement. Koncept512 can be used on a wide range of applications. As far as our framework can tell, it outperforms AVA as a tool for EvolGAN (Table 7). However, it fails on artificial scenes such as Pokemons, unless, we use a small α for staying local.

Computational Cost. All the experiments with PokeGAN presented here could be run on a laptop without using any GPU. The experiments with StyleGAN2 and PGAN use at most 500 (and often just 40) calls to the original GAN, without any specific retraining: we just repeat the inference with various latent vectors z chosen by our evolutionary algorithm as detailed in Sect. 3.1.

Acknowledgments. Funded by the Deutsche Forschungsgemeinschaft (DFG, German Research Foundation), Project-ID 251654672, TRR 161 (Project A05).

References

1. Goodfellow, I., et al.: Generative adversarial nets. In: NeurIPS (2014)
2. Sbai, O., Elhoseiny, M., Bordes, A., LeCun, Y., Couprie, C.: DesIGN: design inspiration from generative networks. In: Leal-Taixé, L., Roth, S. (eds.) ECCV 2018. LNCS, vol. 11131, pp. 37–44. Springer, Cham (2019). https://doi.org/10.1007/978-3-030-11015-4_5
3. Zhu, S., Fidler, S., Urtasun, R., Lin, D., Loy, C.C.: Be your own prada: fashion synthesis with structural coherence. In: ICCV (2017)
4. Elgammal, A., Liu, B., Elhoseiny, M., Mazzone, M.: Creative adversarial networks. In: ICCC (2017)
5. Zhu, J.Y., Park, T., Isola, P., Efros, A.A.: Unpaired image-to-image translation using cycle-consistent adversarial networks. In: ICCV (2017)
6. Park, T., Liu, M., Wang, T., Zhu, J.: Semantic image synthesis with spatially-adaptive normalization. In: CVPR (2019)
7. Donahue, J., Krähenbühl, P., Darrell, T.: Adversarial feature learning. In: ICLR (2017)

8. Frid-Adar, M., Diamant, I., Klang, E., Amitai, M., Goldberger, J., Greenspan, H.: GAN-based synthetic medical image augmentation for increased CNN performance in liver lesion classification. Neurocomputing **321**, 321–331 (2018)

9. Nie, D., et al.: Medical image synthesis with context-aware generative adversarial networks. In: International Conference on Medical Image Computing and Computer-Assisted Intervention (2017)

10. Karras, T., Laine, S., Aittala, M., Hellsten, J., Lehtinen, J., Aila, T.: Analyzing and improving the image quality of stylegan (2019)

11. Noguchi, A., Harada, T.: Image generation from small datasets via batch statistics adaptation. CoRR abs/1904.01774 (2019)

12. Parimala, K., Channappayya, S.: Quality aware generative adversarial networks. In: Advances in Neural Information Processing Systems, pp. 2948–2958 (2019)

13. Yi, Z., Chen, Z., Cai, H., Mao, W., Gong, M., Zhang, H.: BSD-GAN: branched generative adversarial network for scale-disentangled representation learning and image synthesis. IEEE Trans. Image Process. (2020)

14. Roziere, B., et al.: Tarsier: evolving noise injection in super-resolution gans. arXiv preprint arXiv:2009.12177 (2020)

15. Nguyen, A., Clune, J., Bengio, Y., Dosovitskiy, A., Yosinski, J.: Plug & play generative networks: Conditional iterative generation of images in latent space (2016)

16. Volz, V., Schrum, J., Liu, J., Lucas, S.M., Smith, A., Risi, S.: Evolving mario levels in the latent space of a deep convolutional generative adversarial network. In: Proceedings of the Genetic and Evolutionary Computation Conference, GECCO 2018, pp. 221–228. Association for Computing Machinery, New York (2018)

17. Giacomello, E., Lanzi, P.L., Loiacono, D.: Searching the latent space of a generative adversarial network to generate doom levels. In: 2019 IEEE Conference on Games (CoG), pp. 1–8 (2019)

18. Engel, J.H., Hoffman, M., Roberts, A.: Latent constraints: Learning to generate conditionally from unconditional generative models. CoRR abs/1711.05772 (2017)

19. Shen, Y., Gu, J., Tang, X., Zhou, B.: Interpreting the latent space of gans for semantic face editing (2019)

20. Zhu, J.-Y., Krähenbühl, P., Shechtman, E., Efros, A.A.: Generative visual manipulation on the natural image manifold. In: Leibe, B., Matas, J., Sebe, N., Welling, M. (eds.) ECCV 2016. LNCS, vol. 9909, pp. 597–613. Springer, Cham (2016). https://doi.org/10.1007/978-3-319-46454-1_36

21. Mariani, G., Scheidegger, F., Istrate, R., Bekas, C., Malossi, C.: Bagan: data augmentation with balancing gan. arXiv preprint arXiv:1803.09655 (2018)

22. Gurumurthy, S., Sarvadevabhatla, R.K., Radhakrishnan, V.B.: Deligan: generative adversarial networks for diverse and limited data. CoRR abs/1706.02071 (2017)

23. Wang, C., Xu, C., Yao, X., Tao, D.: Evolutionary generative adversarial networks. CoRR abs/1803.00657 (2018)

24. Bontrager, P., Lin, W., Togelius, J., Risi, S.: Deep interactive evolution. In: Liapis, A., Romero Cardalda, J.J., Ekárt, A. (eds.) EvoMUSART 2018. LNCS, vol. 10783, pp. 267–282. Springer, Cham (2018). https://doi.org/10.1007/978-3-319-77583-8_18

25. Riviere, M., Teytaud, O., Rapin, J., LeCun, Y., Couprie, C.: Inspirational adversarial image generation. arXiv preprint 1906, 11661 (2019)

26. Wang, Z., Bovik, A.C., Sheikh, H.R., Simoncelli, E.P.: Image quality assessment: from error visibility to structural similarity. IEEE Trans. Image Process. **13**, 600–612 (2004)

27. Ye, P., Kumar, J., Kang, L., Doermann, D.: Unsupervised feature learning framework for no-reference image quality assessment. In: IEEE Conference on Computer Vision and Pattern Recognition (2012)
28. Hosu, V., Lin, H., Sziranyi, T., Saupe, D.: Koniq-10k: an ecologically valid database for deep learning of blind image quality assessment. IEEE Trans. Image Process. **29**, 1 (2020)
29. Hosu, V., Goldlucke, B., Saupe, D.: Effective aesthetics prediction with multi-level spatially pooled features. In: Proceedings of the IEEE Conference on Computer Vision and Pattern Recognition, pp. 9375–9383 (2019)
30. Dang, D.-C., Lehre, P.K.: Self-adaptation of mutation rates in non-elitist populations. In: Handl, J., Hart, E., Lewis, P.R., López-Ibáñez, M., Ochoa, G., Paechter, B. (eds.) PPSN 2016. LNCS, vol. 9921, pp. 803–813. Springer, Cham (2016). https://doi.org/10.1007/978-3-319-45823-6_75
31. Doerr, B., Le, H.P., Makhmara, R., Nguyen, T.D.: Fast genetic algorithms. In: Proceedings of the Genetic and Evolutionary Computation Conference, pp. 777–784 (2017)
32. Arjovsky, M., Chintala, S., Bottou, L.: Wasserstein generative adversarial networks. In: International Conference on Machine Learning, pp. 214–223(2017)
33. Riviere, M.: Pytorch GAN Zoo (2019). https://GitHub.com/FacebookResearch/pytorch_GAN_zoo
34. Rapin, J., Teytaud, O.: Nevergrad - A gradient-free optimization platform. https://GitHub.com/FacebookResearch/Nevergrad (2018)
35. Moxiegushi: Pokegan (2018). https://github.com/moxiegushi/pokeGAN
36. Karras, T., Aila, T., Laine, S., Lehtinen, J.: Progressive growing of GANs for improved quality, stability, and variation. In: ICLR (2018)
37. Rostamzadeh, N., Hosseini, S., Boquet, T., Stokowiec, W., Zhang, Y., Jauvin, C., Pal, C.: Fashion-Gen: The Generative Fashion Dataset and Challenge. Arxiv preprint 1806.08317 (2018)
38. Huang, X., Liu, M., Belongie, S.J., Kautz, J.: Multimodal unsupervised image-to-image translation. CoRR abs/1804.04732 (2018)
39. Zhu, J.Y., Zhang, R., Pathak, D., Darrell, T., Efros, A.A., Wang, O., Shechtman, E.: Toward multimodal image-to-image translation. In: Advances in Neural Information Processing Systems, pp. 465–476 (2017)

Sequential View Synthesis
with Transformer

Phong Nguyen-Ha[1]([✉]) [iD], Lam Huynh[1] [iD], Esa Rahtu[2] [iD], and Janne Heikkilä[1] [iD]

[1] Center for Machine Vision and Signal Analysis, University of Oulu, Oulu, Finland
{phong.nguyen,lam.huynh,janne.heikkila}@oulu.fi
[2] Computer Vision Group, Tampere University, Tampere, Finland
esa.rahtu@tuni.fi

Abstract. This paper addresses the problem of novel view synthesis by means of neural rendering, where we are interested in predicting the novel view at an arbitrary camera pose based on a given set of input images from other viewpoints. Using the known query pose and input poses, we create an ordered set of observations that leads to the target view. Thus, the problem of single novel view synthesis is reformulated as a sequential view prediction task. In this paper, the proposed Transformer-based Generative Query Network (T-GQN) extends the neural-rendering methods by adding two new concepts. First, we use multi-view attention learning between context images to obtain multiple implicit scene representations. Second, we introduce a sequential rendering decoder to predict an image sequence, including the target view, based on the learned representations. Finally, we evaluate our model on various challenging datasets and demonstrate that our model not only gives consistent predictions but also doesn't require any retraining for finetuning.

Keywords: Sequential view synthesis · Transformer · Multi-view attention

1 Introduction

View synthesis aims to create novel views of an object or a scene from a perspective of a virtual camera based on a set of reference images. It has been an active field of research already for several decades in computer vision and computer graphics due to its various application areas including free-viewpoint television, virtual and augmented reality, and telepresence [1–5].

Conventionally, the view synthesis problem has been addressed by using image-based or geometry-based approaches [1]. In pure image-based rendering, the novel view is warped from a densely sampled set of reference images or the light field without exploiting any geometric information, which obviously requires

Electronic supplementary material The online version of this chapter (https://doi.org/10.1007/978-3-030-69538-5_42) contains supplementary material, which is available to authorized users.

© Springer Nature Switzerland AG 2021
H. Ishikawa et al. (Eds.): ACCV 2020, LNCS 12625, pp. 695–711, 2021.
https://doi.org/10.1007/978-3-030-69538-5_42

a large amount of image data and limits the new viewpoints to a relatively small range. In geometry-based rendering, the novel view is generated using a 3D model that has been first created from the reference views using multi-view stereo or some other image-based modeling techniques. This allows for larger baselines between the views, but also sets high requirements to the quality of the 3D model. Between these two extremes, free viewpoint depth-image-based rendering (DIBR) uses depth maps associated to the reference views enabling 3D image warping to synthesize the novel view [3]. In practice, all these approaches tend to produce notable artifacts due to missing or inaccurate data, which reduced the quality of the rendered image.

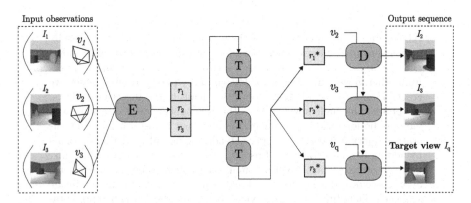

Fig. 1. Overview of our proposed Transformer-based Generative Query Network (T-GQN). Given a set of input images and camera poses $\{(I_n, v_n)\}$, where $n = 1, \ldots, N$, we obtain a set of N scene representations by passing them one-by-one through the encoder (E) network. We use a stack of transformer encoder (T) to perform the multi-view attention learning between these representation. Finally, we use each these attention representation r_n^* to sequentially render the output sequence using the decoder (D) network. The dashed arrow indicates that we initialize states of the decoder network using the computed states of the previous step.

Recently, researchers have adopted deep learning techniques to overcome the inherent limitation of the conventional approaches. This paper focuses on a family of neural rendering methods [6–10] that infer the underlying 3D scene structure and faithfully produces the target view even at a distant query pose. These methods use an aggregate function to represent the entire 3D scene as a single implicit representation. Although they manage to successfully render the target view, a large amount of data is required to train, which in turn, takes a long time to converge. We argue that because these methods focus on synthesizing only a single target image, they are inefficient when rendering target images for distant query poses that are subject to strong geometric transformations and occlusions with respect to the reference images.

In this paper, we introduce a Transformer-based Generative Query Network (T-GQN) to address the problem of novel view synthesis in a sequential manner.

We train an end-to-end model that sequentially renders a positionally ordered set of nearby-views and then predicts the target view at the final rendering step (as shown in Fig. 1). We claim that if the model is able to render the nearby-views accurately, it will be also capable of predicting the target view correctly. Since we do not have the nearby-views of the target pose, we train our model to render the input views. Moreover, instead of rendering the viewpoints using a single implicit scene representation, we use multi-view attention learning based on Transformer Encoder [11] to learn multiple scene representations. At each rendering step, we modify the decoder network of Generative Query Network (GQN) [6] to share its states through rendering steps. To summarize, our key contributions are as follows:

1. We reformulate the problem of single view synthesis into sequential view synthesis.
2. Our proposed T-GQN introduces two novel concepts: multi-view attention learning via the Transformer Encoder and a sequential rendering decoder. Our model extends the previously proposed GQN by sequentially rendering a pose-ordered set of novel views.
3. We demonstrate that our proposed framework achieves state-of-the-art performance on challenging view synthesis datasets. Moreover, our method reaches convergence faster and requires less computational resource to train.

The source code and the model are available at https://github.com/phongnhhn92/TransformerGQN .

2   Related Work

The literature related to view synthesis is extensive, and to limit the scope, we focus on a few deep learning based methods in this section that are most relevant to our method. We suggest a state-of-the-art report for an extensive review [12].

Many early solutions use regression to derive the pixel colors of the target view directly from the input images [13–17]. In [15], Tatarchenko et al. maps an image of a scene to an RGB-D image from an unknown viewpoint with an auto-encoder architecture and train their model using supervised learning. Instead of synthesizing pixels from scratch, other works explores using CNNs to predict appearance flow [16]. Later work by Sun et al. [17] presents a self-confidence aggregation mechanism to integrate both predicted appearance flow and pixel hallucination to achieve contractually consistent results. Although, those method manage to render plausible novel views, their results are limited to a scene with a single object or a slight change in viewpoints in the autonomous driving situation.

A great amount of effort has been dedicated to incorporate geometric information to the model. For example, [18–23] apply deep learning techniques to leverage geometry cues and learn to predict the novel view. The deep learning based-light field camera view interpolation [20,24] use a deep network to predict depth separately for every novel view. Another line of work [18,19,21] cleverly extract a Multiplane image representation of the scene. This representation offers regularization that allows for an impressive stereo baseline extrapolation. Recently, Choi et al. [22] use deep neural network to estimate a depth probability volume, rather than just a single depth value for each pixel of the novel view. Even though, they show promising results but they are limited to synthesizing a middle view among source images or a magnified view from a single input. In contrast, our proposed framework focuses on arbitrary target views and is able to learn from source images that vary in length.

Recent progresses in geometric deep learning proposes to represent a scene as a voxel-grid to enforce the 3D structure. These methods [25–27] use 3D convolution layers to learn 3D spatial transformations from the input views to the novel view and then apply GAN training [28] to enhance quality of the output image. Recently, Sitzman et al. [29] presents a continuous, 3D-structure-aware scene representation that encodes both geometry and appearance. Their work learns a mapping from world coordinates to feature representation of local scene properties. Another contribution of this paper is that authors empirically demonstrated that their method is able to show generalization across scenes for classes of single objects using an additional MLP network such as HyperNetwork [30]. In our paper, we evaluate our method on the novel view synthesis dataset which contains 2 millions scenes each (multiple combinations of objects types, colors, lightning positions). We argue that training their method to generalize to a large number of instances would be computationally expensive. In fact, this is an open research problem that has not yet been solved.

Recent **neural rendering** methods have introduced a generative model that understands the underlying 3D scene structure and faithfully produces the target view at the distant query pose [31–34]. Generative Query Network (GQN) [6] and its variant [7–9] are incorporating all input observation (images and poses) into a single implicit 3D scene representation to generate the target view. This aggregated representation contains all necessary information (e.g.. object identities, positions, colors, scene layout) to make accurate image predictions. Moreover, these methods corresponds to a special case of Neural Processes [35,36]. In this paper, we argue that generating the target view using such compact representation leads to poor predictions and slow training convergence.

3   Approach

In this section, we first provide the reader with a brief background of the Generative Query Network (GQN). Then we convert the problem of **single view synthesis** to the problem of **sequential view synthesis** by introducing our Transformer-based Generative Query Network (T-GQN) that extends the current GQN architecture with two novel building blocks: multi-view attention learning via Transformer Encoder and sequential rendering decoder.

3.1   Generative Query Network

Given the observations that include N images $I_n \in I$ and their corresponding camera poses $v_n \in V$, GQN [6] solves the **single view synthesis** problem by using a encoder-decoder neural network to predict the target image I_q at an arbitrary query pose v_q.

First, the encoder is a feed-forward neural network that takes N observations as input and produce a single implicit scene representation $R = \sum_{n=1}^{N} r_n$ by performing a element-wise sum of N encoded scene representation r_n. The decoder then takes R and v_q as an input and predicts the new view I_q' from that viewpoint. The decoder network is a conditional latent variable model DRAW [37,38] which includes M pairs of Generation and Inference convolutional LSTM networks. At each generation step, the hidden state of the Generation and Inference LSTM core is utilized to approximate the prior π and posterior distribution q. Since the target view I_q is fed into the Inference sub-network, minimizing the Kullback-Leibler (KL) distance between π and q would help the Generation sub-network to produce an accurate result. Both the encoder and decoder networks are trained jointly to minimize the ELBO loss $\mathcal{L}_{GQN}$ function:

$$\mathcal{L}_{GQN} = \left[-\ln \mathcal{N}(I_q | I_q') + \sum_{m=1}^{M} KL \left[\mathcal{N}(q_m) || \mathcal{N}(\pi_m) \right] \right] \tag{1}$$

In the next section, we will describe how we reformulate the problem of **single view synthesis** to the problem of **sequential view synthesis** to address this issue.

3.2   Sequential View Synthesis

As can be seen from Fig. 2 (a), GQN [6] predicts the target view I_q in a single rendering step. If the query pose v_q is distant from all input poses then the target view might look completely different than all input views. In this case, minimizing the above $\mathcal{L}_{GQN}$ loss does not guarantee to generate a plausible target view and it might take a long training time to reach the convergence.

We argue that if the model is able to predict an input view I_n' for $n > 1$ based on previous input data $\{(I_1, v_1), \dots, (I_{n-1}, v_{n-1})\}$ then it also renders the target view I_q at the query pose v_q provided that the camera poses $\{v_1, \dots, v_N, v_q\}$ have been organized as a sequence where the adjacent poses are the closest ones. To achieve such ability, we train our proposed T-GQN model using multiple rendering steps. Each rendering step of our model is identical with GQN except that we use different sets of input observations and query poses. In Fig. 2 (b) we illustrate these sets of input observations at each rendering step with boxes of different colors.

For example, in the first rendering step, we only allow the model to use the information inside the green box which includes the input view I_1 and its camera pose v_1. Then, our T-GQN model is trained to predict the next input view I_2' at the viewpoint v_2. Preventing the model to look at the input view I_2 would

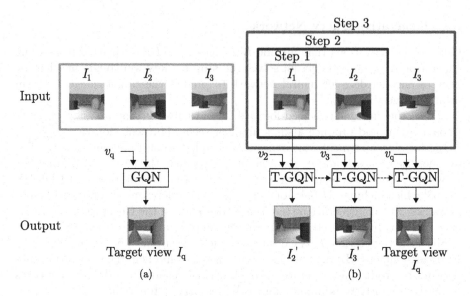

Fig. 2. An illustration of the single view synthesis (a) compared to our proposed sequential view synthesis (b). Previously proposed GQN [6] directly predicts the target view in a single rendering step, while our proposed T-GQN sequentially predicts novel views from an ordered set of N observations. The output set includes $N-1$ nearest views of the target view and the target view itself. Colored boxes indicate which input observations are encoded at each rendering step. (Color figure online)

encourage the model to reason about the given contexts and produce a global implicit scene representation that extrapolates beyond the given information. In the final rendering step, both GQN and our proposed T-GQN model are allowed to see all N input observations to render the target view but our model can leverage the past experiences from previous rendering steps to have a better approximation I_q' of the target image I_q. Furthermore, training our model in multiple rendering steps enforces our model to make consistent predictions of novel views at different viewpoints in a forward pass. This helps to stabilize the training process by making the network to produce deterministic results and also be able to reach the convergence faster than the former architecture. Note that our only use sequential view synthesis during training. In the testing time, we use randomly ordered sets of context views to have a fair comparison with other methods.

Therefore, the problem of single view synthesis can be redefined as the problem of sequential view synthesis by predicting a sequence of N novel views $S_{out} = \{I_2', ..., I_N', I_q'\}$ from a sequence of observations $S_{in} = \{(I_1, v_1), ..., (I_N, v_N)\}$. Since we are having N different target views then it would be beneficial to have N different scene representations. In order to have such multiple implicit scene representations, we use the Transformer Encoder [11] to learn the dependencies between input observations at each rendering step.

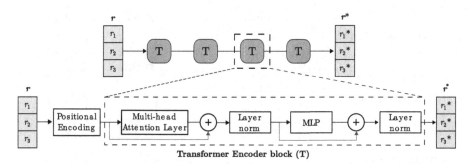

Fig. 3. Illustration of multi-view attention learning using a stack of Transformer Encoder (T) blocks. For the visualization purposes, we show how a single Transformer Encoder block is able to produce multiple implicit scene representations r^* using the input view representations r.

3.3 Multi-view Attention Learning via Transformer Encoder

Recent works in the Language Modeling task [11, 39–41] use the self attention-based Transformer Encoder to effectively learn dependencies between word embeddings in a sentence. Transformer Encoder takes a set of word embeddings as an input and produces another set of enhanced word embedding representations. Each of these representations reflects the long-range dependencies between input embeddings and they have been proven to be useful for training various language modeling tasks. Therefore, we can also take a set of scene representations r as an input and use the Transformer Encoder to produce another set of enhanced scene representations r^* that are trained to exploit the multi-view dependencies.

Figure 3 shows an example of how we use a stack of Transformer Encoder blocks to perform the multi-view attention learning and implicitly represent a scene using a set of multiple representations. Within a Transformer Encoder block, the most important component is the Multi-Head Attention layer using the self-attention mechanism [11]. The self-attention function produces an $N \times N$ matrix A of multi-view attention scores so that each row of the matrix A reflects the learned multi-view dependencies at each rendering step. In addition, we apply an attention mask m to the multi-view attention scores A. This attention mask allows us to control which part of the input representation sequence r we would like the model to ignore when computing the attention scores. We leave the implementation details of Transformer Encoder to the supplementary material. In practice, we found that applying this attention mask leads to better performance on datasets that have high similarities between viewpoints. When the input viewpoints are not overlapping, we found that better results are achieved without applying the attention mask.

If the movement of the camera is restricted then input viewpoints overlap with each other. Therefore, masking the attention scores would mean that the model is trained to predict the novel view using only a subset of the

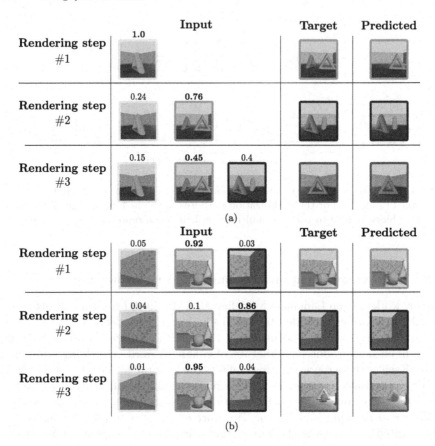

Fig. 4. Visualization of multi-view attention scores at each rendering step produced by our methods when (a) the camera movement is restricted and (b) the camera is free to move. Note that the order of the input sequence does not affect the learned multi-view attention scores. (Color figure online)

input sequence. Figure 4 (a) shows the multi-view attention scores of a camera-restricted example. In the 1st rendering step, we try to render the 2nd input view (green box) as the novel view. Since our model is only allowed to use the 1st view (yellow box) as the input, the predicted image only contains the cyan object. However, our model is able to render the missing orange object by putting higher scores on the 2nd input view in the next rendering step. Since the 1st input view does not have enough information to render the target view, our model learns to give it less attention and produce higher attention scores on another two input views.

When the camera movement is not restricted, the input sequence might contain views which do not necessary include information to render the target view. In this case, we allow the model to use all input observations by not applying the attention mask. In Fig. 4 (b), our model is able to give high attention scores to

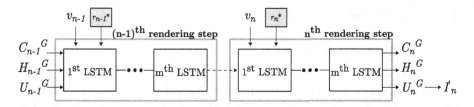

Fig. 5. Illustration of our proposed sequential rendering decoder. At each rendering step, we use the computed states from the previous rendering step as the initialization for the decoder network. The canvas state U_n^G is utilized to render the novel image I_n'.

input observations which are the ground-truth views in the first two rendering steps. Therefore, the first two predicted novel views are identical to the ground-truth because the model has already seen these novel views as inputs. However, our goal is to be able to predict the target view (red box) which has a distant query pose. Among three input observations, the 2nd input is the only view which contains information about objects on the scene. As can be seen in the last rendering steps, our model manages to pay most attention on the 2nd input view (green box) and gives low scores to the other two views and successfully predicts the target view despite the distant query pose.

3.4 Sequential Rendering Decoder

In this paper, we improve the decoder network of GQN [6] by applying a recurrent mechanism between rendering steps. In order to transfer the knowledge between rendering steps, computed LSTM states from previous steps are utilized as initialization for the current step as shown in the Fig. 5. Here, we simplify the notation by defining that C_n^G is the cell state of the mth Generation core at the nth rendering step. We apply this kind of notation to all cell states C, hidden states H and canvas states U of the decoder network. At the nth rendering step, the novel image I_n' is computed as follows:

$$I_n' = \text{decoder}(r_n^*, v_n, C_{n-1}^G, H_{n-1}^G, U_{n-1}^G, C_{n-1}^I, H_{n-1}^I) \qquad (2)$$

Since our model has multiple rendering steps, the prior and the posterior terms, π_n^m and q_n^m, are obtained from the mth LSTM core at the nth rendering step. We train our model using the modified ELBO loss function as follows:

$$\mathcal{L}_{TGQN} = \left[-\sum_{n=1}^{N} \ln \mathcal{N}(I_n|I_n') + \beta \sum_{n=1}^{N} \sum_{m=1}^{M} \text{KL}\left[\mathcal{N}(q_n^m) \| \mathcal{N}(\pi_n^m) \right] \right] \qquad (3)$$

By adding the β coefficient to the KL term, we emphasize discovering the disentangled latent factors [42]. This technique has proven to be effective to maximize the probability of generating the desired output and keeping the distance between the prior and posterior distribution small [43].

4 Experiments

4.1 Experimental Setup

As illustrated in the Fig. 2, to create a sequence of adjacent poses, we could, for example, use the overlap between the viewing frustums of the cameras to measure their adjacency. However, in our experiments we simply reordered all input observations based on the Euclidean distance between the translation vector of the query pose and the input poses that turned out to be sufficient to demonstrate the efficiency of our method. We choose to train our T-GQN model using three input observations to render a target view at an arbitrary query pose. Further details about our architecture are presented in the supplementary material.

4.2 Comparing with State-of-the-Art Methods

To evaluate our model, we compare against the GQN [6] and an improved variant of E-GQN [10]. We use two datasets: Rooms-Ring-Camera (RRC) and Rooms-Free-Camera (RFC), from [6] and one dataset: Rooms-Random-Objects (RRO) from [10]. The RRC dataset contains 2 millions rendered 3D square rooms that are composed of random objects of various shapes, colors and locations. Moreover, the scene textures, walls and lights are also randomly generated. In this dataset, the camera only moves on a fixed ring and always faces the center of the room. In case of the RFC dataset, the environment is the same with RRC except for the freely moving camera and objects rotated around their vertical axes. We also evaluate our method on the RRO dataset which includes complex 3D scenes with realistic 3D objects from the ShapeNet dataset [44].

Recent works [31,32] on view synthesis often require retraining for any testing scene. Although, they produce visually impressive novel views but they are not able to generalize to unseen data. Therefore, we decide to compare our method against Scene Representation Network (SRN) [29] which is the current top-performing technique for view synthesis which generalizes reasonably well on testing data. Due to computational constraints, we can not compare this method with the full RRC or RFC dataset. We instead use a small subset of 1000 scenes from the Shapard-Metzler-7-Parts (SM7) and 3500 scenes from the RRC dataset to train both our proposed model and SRN model. In this experiment, the ratio between the training set and testing set is 9:1.

4.3 Results

***Comparing against GQN*[6] *and E-GQN*[10]:** In our experiment, we have tested our model to sample several novel views given the same input views from the same scene. In the Table 1, we have reported the L1 and L2 distances between the rendered novel views and the ground-truth images across testing scenes. Since our testing models are probabilistic, we run our experiment several times and report the average and standard deviation based on the test runs. In each testing

Table 1. Quantitative comparison of results between our T-GQN model, original GQN [6] and E-GQN [10].

Model	# parameters (millions)	L1 (pixels)			L2 (pixels)		
		RRC	RFC	RRO	RRC	RFC	RRO
GQN (8 LSTM layers)	381	8.50 ± 7.01	14.23 ± 13.56	14.12 ± 8.19	18.62 ± 12.86	30.28 ± 25.69	21.79 ± 10.23
GQN (12 LSTM layers)	428	7.40 ± 6.22	12.44 ± 12.89	10.12 ± 5.15	14.62 ± 12.77	26.80 ± 21.35	19.63 ± 9.14
E-GQN	N/A	3.59 ± 2.10	12.05 ± 11.79	6.59 ± 3.23	6.80 ± 5.23	27.65 ± 20.72	12.08 ± 6.52
T-GQN without mask	382	3.30 ± 2.05	**9.25 ± 9.15**	6.31 ± 2.59	6.65 ± 4.29	**12.72 ± 10.56**	11.72 ± 5.23
T-GQN with mask	382	**2.31 ± 1.89**	11.65 ± 10.25	**5.28 ± 2.31**	**5.92 ± 2.69**	15.44 ± 13.37	**11.65 ± 5.13**

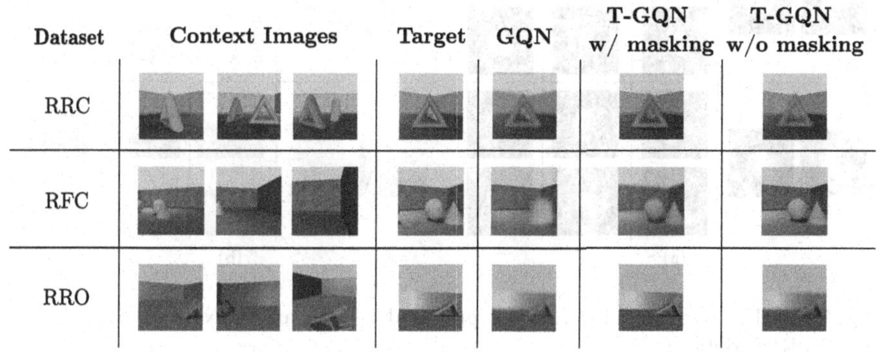

Fig. 6. Example of rendered novel views using our proposed T-GQN (with and without masking) and other methods. Overall, our proposed T-GQN model is able to produce better target view than previous methods. More examples can be found in the Appendix section. We urge the reader to zoom in for better visualization.

scene, we sample 10 independent viewpoints and use 3 of them as the input to our model to generate the rest of viewpoints as novel images.

Qualitative results shown in Fig. 6 demonstrate that the T-GQN model with or without the attention mask is able to render all novel images much sharper than the former architectures. Meanwhile, predicted target views from GQN [6] are often blurry and not able to get the correct object types, colors and positions. As explained in the Sect. 3.2, our model is able to predict nearby views of the novel view. Therefore, we include step-by-step renderings in the supplementary material.

As can be seen from Table 1, training our T-GQN model with the attention mask leads to a performance gain on the RRC and RRO datasets. In the case of the RFC dataset, our method without the attention mask performs significantly better than other methods including ours with the attention mask. In the free-camera case, the query poses are often far from the input poses so there may be not enough information from input views to generate the novel view. This explains the small gap of performance between our T-GQN model with masking on the RRC dataset and our T-GQN model without masking on the RFC dataset. In our paper, we apply a zero attention mask in testing the RFC dataset so that the model has access to all possible information. Our model then learns to attend to the relevant input views via our proposed multi-view attention learning described in Sect. 3.3. This highlights the strength of the Transformer architecture that learns to attend to the most relevant piece of information among input views.

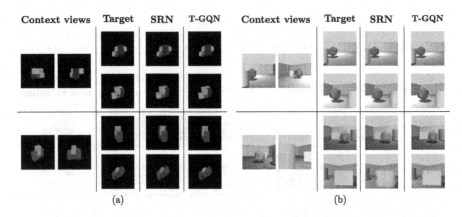

Fig. 7. Qualitative results between our proposed T-GQN and SRN on (a) SM7 dataset and (b) RRC dataset.

Table 2. Quantitative comparison of results between SRN, our proposed T-GQN model tested on the small subset of SM7 and RRC dataset.

Method	L1 (pixels)		L2 (pixels)	
	SM7	RRC	SM7	RRC
SRN	2.15	3.56	5.65	6.21
T-GQN	2.14 ± 0.21	1.92 ± 0.15	5.25 ± 0.34	2.96 ± 0.93

Comparing Against SRN [29]: We also benchmark novel view synthesis accuracy on few-shot reconstruction to compare our probabilistic T-GQN model with a deterministic view synthesis SRN [29]. As can be seen in Table 2 and Fig. 7, our proposed method manages to achieve similar results with SRN model on the SM7 dataset. In case of RRC dataset, our model performs significantly better than SRN. We argue that SM7 is an easy dataset which contains only a single rotating colored object. Therefore, learning to generalize between training and testing data of SM7 dataset is easier than with the RRC dataset.

As the number of training scenes increase, training a deterministic approach such as SRN to have good generalization across a large number of testing scenes is difficult and still an open challenge. Qualitative results in Fig. 7 (b) shows that our T-GQN model is not only able to render correct room layouts and object properties but also produce significantly sharper results than the previously proposed SRN method with the demanding RRC dataset. We discuss more about the capabilities of rendering novel views between our method and SRN in the supplementary material.

5   Ablation Study

To investigate the effectiveness of the proposed modules, we use our sequential rendering decoder to generate novel views using the aggregated scene representation R from [6] and denote this model as SeqGQN. Instead of using different multi-view attention representations at each rendering step, we use a single representation R as an input to all ConvLSTM layers in our proposed sequential rendering decoder network. The qualitative and quantitative results including the rendered novel views using SeqGQN are shown in Fig. 8 and Table 3. We observe that our full model significantly outperforms both SeqGQN and GQN. Although both GQN and SeqGQN are using the same aggregated scene representation R, SeqGQN is able to produce better and more accurate target views than the baseline. This result demonstrates that approaching the neural rendering in the sequential manner leads to more accurate view synthesis. We also find that each learned representation is fully capable of rending the novel view. Therefore, we can use a single scene representation r_n^* to render the novel view in the testing time. Further explanations are included in the supplementary material.

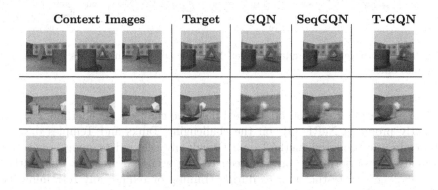

Fig. 8. Example of generated novel views compared between our proposed T-GQN and variants on the RRC dataset.

Since we are adding a large β coefficient into the KL loss term (Eq. 3), we are encouraging the model to approximate the posterior distribution q_n^m close to the prior distribution π_n^m as much as possible. If the query pose is far away from given input observations then it is hard to get a good estimate for q_n^m. In [6], the model is prone to mistakes because the target view is rendered in a single step. Using the sequential rendering decoder, we solve the problem by generating the nearby views of the target view before rendering the target view. As can be

Table 3. Quantitative results of T-GQN and its variants on the Rooms-Ring-Camera dataset.

Metric	GQN	SeqGQN	T-GQN ($\beta = 1$)	T-GQN ($\beta = 250$)
L1 (pixels)	7.40 ± 6.22	4.51 ± 2.35	3.7 ± 1.92	**2.31 ± 1.89**
L2 (pixels)	14.62 ± 12.77	8.2 ± 4.27	7.1 ± 2.47	**5.92 ± 2.69**
SSIM	0.85	0.882	0.905	**0.92**

seen from Table 3, training our T-GQN model with $\beta = 1$ leads to a drop of the overall performance. However, this model is still able to outperform both GQN and SeqGQN.

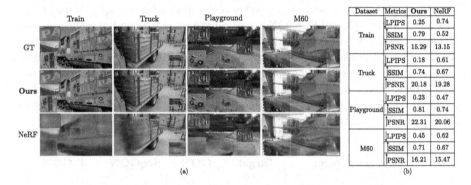

Fig. 9. Qualitative(a) and quantitative(b) results on 4 testing scenes of Tank and Temples dataset.

To evaluate our method on the real data, we compare our method with the recently proposed NeRF [31] on the challenging Tanks and Temples dataset. We train our proposed method on 10 randomly selected training scenes and evaluate the performance on 4 unseen testing scenes. Note that our method haven't seen any testing images during training or require any retraining like NeRF. However, as can be seen in Fig. 9, our method outperforms NeRF both qualitatively and quantitatively. This may be explained by the fact that NeRF makes an assumption of inward-facing scenes while our method does not have such limitations. On the flip side, our proposed method is not bounded to this condition and can generate plausible novel views in a wide variety of 3D scenes. This highlights the effectiveness of our method that generalize reasonably well on unseen data.

6   Conclusions

In this paper, we presented a method to synthesize novel views in a sequential manner. Instead of directly rendering the target view, we train our model to predict a sequence of novel views in multiple rendering steps. Using the Transformer Encoder, our proposed multi-view attention learning is able to learn different implicit scene representations for each rendering step. The experimental results demonstrate that our model is able to render more accurate novel views using less training time.

In the future works, we will explore different implicit neural scene representations to further improve the quality of synthesized images.

References

1. Chang, Y., Wang, G.P.: A review on image-based rendering. Virtual Reality Intell. Hardw. **1**, 39–54 (2019)
2. Tanimoto, M.: FTV: free-viewpoint television. Sig. Process. Image Commun. **27**, 555–570 (2012)
3. Smirnov, S., Battisti, F., Gotchev, A.P.: Layered approach for improving the quality of free-viewpoint depth-image-based rendering images. J. Electron. Imaging **28**, 1–17 (2019)
4. Joachimczak, M., Liu, J., Ando, H.: Real-time mixed-reality telepresence via 3D reconstruction with hololens and commodity depth sensors. In: Proceedings of the 19th ACM International Conference on Multimodal Interaction. ICMI 2017, pp. 514–515. Association for Computing Machinery, New York (2017)
5. Kolkmeier, J., Harmsen, E., Giesselink, S., Reidsma, D., Theune, M., Heylen, D.: With a little help from a holographic friend: the OpenIMPRESS mixed reality telepresence toolkit for remote collaboration systems. In: Proceedings of the 24th ACM Symposium on Virtual Reality Software and Technology. VRST 2018. Association for Computing Machinery, New York (2018)
6. Eslami, S.A., et al.: Neural scene representation and rendering. Science **360**, 1204–1210 (2018)
7. Rosenbaum, D., Besse, F., Viola, F., Rezende, D.J., Eslami, S.: Learning models for visual 3d localization with implicit mapping. arXiv preprint arXiv:1807.03149 (2018)
8. Kumar, A., et al.: Consistent generative query networks. arXiv preprint arXiv:1807.02033 (2018)
9. Nguyen-Ha, P., Huynh, L., Rahtu, E., Heikkilä, J.: Predicting novel views using generative adversarial query network. In: Felsberg, M., Forssén, P.-E., Sintorn, I.-M., Unger, J. (eds.) SCIA 2019. LNCS, vol. 11482, pp. 16–27. Springer, Cham (2019). https://doi.org/10.1007/978-3-030-20205-7_2
10. Tobin, J., Zaremba, W., Abbeel, P.: Geometry-aware neural rendering. In: Advances in Neural Information Processing Systems 32. Curran Associates, Inc. (2019)
11. Vaswani, A., et al.: Attention is all you need. In: Guyon, I., et al. (eds.) Advances in Neural Information Processing Systems 30, pp. 5998–6008. Curran Associates, Inc. (2017)
12. Tewari, A., et al.: State of the art on neural rendering. CoRR abs/2004.03805 (2020)

13. Olszewski, K., Tulyakov, S., Woodford, O., Li, H., Luo, L.: Transformable bottle-neck networks (2019)
14. Chen, X., Song, J., Hilliges, O.: Monocular neural image based rendering with continuous view control. In: Proceedings of the IEEE International Conference on Computer Vision, pp. 4090–4100 (2019)
15. Tatarchenko, M., Dosovitskiy, A., Brox, T.: Multi-view 3D models from single images with a convolutional network. In: Leibe, B., Matas, J., Sebe, N., Welling, M. (eds.) ECCV 2016. LNCS, vol. 9911, pp. 322–337. Springer, Cham (2016). https://doi.org/10.1007/978-3-319-46478-7_20
16. Zhou, T., Tulsiani, S., Sun, W., Malik, J., Efros, A.A.: View synthesis by appearance flow. CoRR abs/1605.03557 (2016)
17. Sun, S.-H., Huh, M., Liao, Y.-H., Zhang, N., Lim, J.J.: Multi-view to novel view: synthesizing novel views with self-learned confidence. In: Ferrari, V., Hebert, M., Sminchisescu, C., Weiss, Y. (eds.) ECCV 2018. LNCS, vol. 11207, pp. 162–178. Springer, Cham (2018). https://doi.org/10.1007/978-3-030-01219-9_10
18. Flynn, J., Neulander, I., Philbin, J., Snavely, N.: Deep stereo: learning to predict new views from the world's imagery. In: 2016 IEEE Conference on Computer Vision and Pattern Recognition (CVPR), pp. 5515–5524 (2016)
19. Zhou, T., Tucker, R., Flynn, J., Fyffe, G., Snavely, N.: Stereo magnification: learning view synthesis using multiplane images. In: SIGGRAPH (2018)
20. Kalantari, N.K., Wang, T.C., Ramamoorthi, R.: Learning-based view synthesis for light field cameras. ACM Trans. Graph. 35, 1–10 (2016)
21. Srinivasan, P.P., Tucker, R., Barron, J.T., Ramamoorthi, R., Ng, R., Snavely, N.: Pushing the boundaries of view extrapolation with multiplane images. In: IEEE Conference on Computer Vision and Pattern Recognition, CVPR 2019, Long Beach, CA, USA, 16–20 June 2019, pp. 175–184. Computer Vision Foundation/IEEE (2019)
22. Choi, I., Gallo, O., Troccoli, A., Kim, M.H., Kautz, J.: Extreme view synthesis. In: Proceedings of the IEEE International Conference on Computer Vision, pp. 7781–7790 (2019)
23. Tucker, R., Snavely, N.: Single-view view synthesis with multiplane images. In: The IEEE Conference on Computer Vision and Pattern Recognition (CVPR) (2020)
24. Mildenhall, B., et al.: Local light field fusion: practical view synthesis with prescriptive sampling guidelines. ACM Trans. Graph. 38, 1–14 (2019)
25. Nguyen-Phuoc, T., Li, C., Theis, L., Richardt, C., Yang, Y.L.: HoloGAN: unsupervised learning of 3D representations from natural images. In: The IEEE International Conference on Computer Vision (ICCV) (2019)
26. Sitzmann, V., Thies, J., Heide, F., Nießner, M., Wetzstein, G., Zollhöfer, M.: Deep-Voxels: learning persistent 3D feature embeddings. In: Proceedings of the Computer Vision and Pattern Recognition (CVPR). IEEE (2019)
27. Lombardi, S., Simon, T., Saragih, J., Schwartz, G., Lehrmann, A., Sheikh, Y.: Neural volumes: Learning dynamic renderable volumes from images. ACM Trans. Graph. 38 (2019)
28. Goodfellow, I., et al.: Generative adversarial nets. In: Ghahramani, Z., Welling, M., Cortes, C., Lawrence, N.D., Weinberger, K.Q. (eds.) Advances in Neural Information Processing Systems 27, pp. 2672–2680. Curran Associates, Inc. (2014)
29. Sitzmann, V., Zollhoefer, M., Wetzstein, G.: Scene representation networks: continuous 3D-structure-aware neural scene representations. In: Advances in Neural Information Processing Systems 32, pp. 1121–1132. Curran Associates, Inc. (2019)

30. Ha, D., Dai, A.M., Le, Q.V.: Hypernetworks. In: 5th International Conference on Learning Representations, ICLR 2017, Toulon, France, 24–26 April 2017, Conference Track Proceedings, OpenReview.net (2017)
31. Mildenhall, B., Srinivasan, P.P., Tancik, M., Barron, J.T., Ramamoorthi, R., Ng, R.: NeRF: representing scenes as neural radiance fields for view synthesis. In: Vedaldi, A., Bischof, H., Brox, T., Frahm, J.-M. (eds.) ECCV 2020. LNCS, vol. 12346, pp. 405–421. Springer, Cham (2020). https://doi.org/10.1007/978-3-030-58452-8_24
32. Li, Z., Xian, W., Davis, A., Snavely, N.: Crowdsampling the plenoptic function. In: Vedaldi, A., Bischof, H., Brox, T., Frahm, J.-M. (eds.) ECCV 2020. LNCS, vol. 12346, pp. 178–196. Springer, Cham (2020). https://doi.org/10.1007/978-3-030-58452-8_11
33. Dupont, E., et al.: Equivariant neural rendering (2020)
34. Niemeyer, M., Mescheder, L., Oechsle, M., Geiger, A.: Differentiable volumetric rendering: learning implicit 3D representations without 3D supervision (2019)
35. Garnelo, M., et al.: Conditional neural processes. In: Dy, J., Krause, A. (eds.) Proceedings of the 35th International Conference on Machine Learning. Volume 80 of Proceedings of Machine Learning Research, Stockholmsmässan, Stockholm Sweden, pp. 1704–1713 PMLR (2018)
36. Kim, H., et al.: Attentive neural processes. In: 7th International Conference on Learning Representations, ICLR 2019, New Orleans, LA, USA, 6–9 May 2019, OpenReview.net (2019)
37. Gregor, K., Danihelka, I., Graves, A., Rezende, D., Wierstra, D.: Draw: a recurrent neural network for image generation. In: Bach, F., Blei, D. (eds.) Proceedings of the 32nd International Conference on Machine Learning. Volume 37 of Proceedings of Machine Learning Research, Lille, France, pp. 1462–1471. PMLR (2015)
38. Gregor, K., Besse, F., Jimenez Rezende, D., Danihelka, I., Wierstra, D.: Towards conceptual compression. In: Lee, D.D., Sugiyama, M., Luxburg, U.V., Guyon, I., Garnett, R. (eds.) Advances in Neural Information Processing Systems 29, pp. 3549–3557. Curran Associates, Inc. (2016)
39. Devlin, J., Chang, M.W., Lee, K., Toutanova, K.: BERT: pre-training of deep bidirectional transformers for language understanding. In: Proceedings of the 2019 Conference of the North American Chapter of the Association for Computational Linguistics: Human Language Technologies, Volume 1 (Long and Short Papers), Minneapolis, Minnesota, pp. 4171–4186. Association for Computational Linguistics (2019)
40. Radford, A., Wu, J., Child, R., Luan, D., Amodei, D., Sutskever, I.: Language models are unsupervised multitask learners. OpenAI Blog **1**, 9 (2019)
41. Dai, Z., Yang, Z., Yang, Y., Carbonell, J., Le, Q., Salakhutdinov, R.: Transformer-XL: attentive language models beyond a fixed-length context. In: Proceedings of the 57th Annual Meeting of the Association for Computational Linguistics, Florence, Italy, pp. 2978–2988. Association for Computational Linguistics (2019)
42. Kingma, D.P., Welling, M.: An introduction to variational autoencoders. Found. Trends Mach. Learn. **12**, 307–392 (2019)
43. Higgins, I., et al.: beta-VAE: learning basic visual concepts with a constrained variational framework. In: ICLR (2017)
44. Chang, A.X., et al.: ShapeNet: an information-rich 3D model repository (2015)

Author Index

Printed in the United States
By Bookmasters